COMPANION TO CONTEMPORARY ECONOMIC THOUGHT

COMPANION TO CONTEMPORARY ECONOMIC THOUGHT

EDITED BY

David Greenaway
Michael Bleaney
and
Ian Stewart

LONDON AND NEW YORK

First published in 1991
by Routledge
11 New Fetter Lane, London EC4P 4EE

Simultaneously published in the USA and Canada
by Routledge
a division of Routledge, Chapman and Hall, Inc.
29 West 35th Street, New York, NY 10001

© 1991 Routledge

Phototypeset by Intype, London
Printed in England by Clays Ltd, St Ives plc

British Library Cataloguing in Publication Data
Greenaway, David
Companion to contemporary economic thought.
1. Economics. Theories
I. Title II. Bleaney, Michael III. Stewart, Ian
330.1

Library of Congress Cataloging-in-Publication Data
Companion to contemporary economic thought / edited by David
Greenaway, Michael Bleaney, and Ian Stewart.
p. cm.
Includes bibliographical references and index.
ISBN 0–415–02612–1
1. Economics. I. Greenaway, David. II. Bleaney, M. F.
III. Stewart, Ian.
HB34.C64 1991
330.1—dc20   91–23817
                                                    CIP

CONTENTS

v

II. ECONOMIC THEORY

CONTRIBUTORS

J. Richard Aronson is Professor of Economics at Lehigh University

V. N. Balasubramanyam is Professor of Economics at the University of Lancaster

Norman Barry is Professor of Politics at the University of Buckingham

William J. Baumol is Professor of Economics at Princeton University

Michael Bleaney is Lecturer in Economics at the University of Nottingham

Richard Blundell is Professor of Economics at University College London

Lawrence A. Boland is Professor of Economics at Simon Fraser University

Kenneth E. Boulding is Professor Emeritus at the Institute of Behavioral Sciences, University of Colorado, Boulder

Roger Bowles is Senior Lecturer in Social Sciences at the University of Bath

A. W. Coats is Professor of Economic History at Duke University

W. Max Corden is Professor of Economics at The Johns Hopkins University

Nicholas Crafts is Professor of Economic History at the University of Warwick

David Currie is Professor of Economics at the London Business School

Phyllis Deane is Professor Emeritus at the University of Cambridge

Clive Granger is Professor of Econometrics at the University of California at San Diego

David Greenaway is Professor of Economics at the University of Nottingham

Paul Hare is Professor of Economics at Heriot-Watt University

Kenneth Holden is Senior Lecturer in Economics at the University of Liverpool

John Hey is Professor of Economics and Statistics at the University of York

Paul Levine is Professor of Economics at the University of Leicester

Graham Loomes is Senior Lecturer in Economics at the University of York

Alasdair MacBean is Professor of Economics at the University of Lancaster

Ronald MacDonald is Professor of Economics at the University of Dundee

Ian McLean is Lecturer in Politics at University College, Oxford

Ross Milbourne is Senior Lecturer in Economics at the University of New
 South Wales
Chris Milner is Professor of Economics at the University of Loughborough
Grayham Mizon is Professor of Econometrics at the University of
 Southampton
Christian Montet is Professor of Economics at the University of Montpellier
Dennis C. Mueller is Professor of Economics at the University of Maryland
Denis O'Brien is Professor of Economics at the University of Durham
Attiat F. Ott is Professor of Economics at Clark University
Sir Alan Peacock is Emeritus Professor at Heriot-Watt University
David W. Pearce is Professor of Economics at the University College London
M. Hashem Pesaran is Professor of Economics at the University of
 Cambridge
Warren J. Samuels is Professor of Economics at Michigan State University
David Sapsford is Professor of Economics at the University of Lancaster
Malcolm Sawyer is Professor of Economics at the University of Leeds
Ronald Shone is Senior Lecturer in Economics at the University of Stirling
Robert M. Solow is Professor of Economics at Massachusetts Institute of
 Technology
Ian Stewart is former Lecturer in Economics at the University of Nottingham
Edward Tower is Professor of Economics at Duke University
W. Fred Van Raaij is Professor of Economics Psychology at Erasmus
 University
John Whalley is Professor of Economics at the University of Western Ontario

PREFACE

This book is designed to take stock of the current state of economics through the medium of a series of specially commissioned interpretative essays, written by leading commentators.

We asked the contributors to write in a manner that would be accessible to a non-specialist, a task that was not always easy to fulfil, but one that we feel they have accomplished extremely well. Indeed, the opportunity to write for a wider audience than the usual narrow circle of colleagues with similar interests has offered the authors a chance to take a step back and reflect on progress in their particular area of the subject – something for which the 'publish or perish' atmosphere of academic journals presents little scope. We have been rewarded by a very high standard of writing, characterized by unusual depth and perception.

The essays are organized into four sections, dealing with methodological perspectives, economic theory, applied economics and interfaces. Each section begins with an essay by one of the editors, so it is unnecessary to review the contents in any detail here. One of our contributors questioned whether so much space should be allocated to the first and last sections. Although we have not been able to cover particular areas of theory and application in quite as much depth as we might otherwise have done, we feel that this disadvantage is more than offset by the sense of perspective that is lent to the whole project by the extended discussion of methodology and of the relationship with other academic disciplines.

This has been a major undertaking for us, sometimes exhausting, sometimes frustrating, but always interesting. We were delighted with the responses we had to invitations to participate. We could not really have forecast such a positive response from distinguished scholars all over the world. We feel gratified by the quality of the papers we received. In our judgement all are of a very high quality. Some can accurately be described as quite outstanding and are sure to become recognized classics. We would like to record our appreciation to all contributors for their participation. We have learned a lot from commissioning and editing this book, and we hope that students and colleagues find it equally rewarding. It is our hope that there will be something in it for everyone interested in economics who has some background in the subject.

Finally, we would like to thank Jonathan Price of Routledge for his encouragement and support throughout. He was the instigator of the project, and was a constant source of good advice.

David Greenaway
Michael Bleaney
Ian Stewart

1

PREAMBLE

DAVID GREENAWAY

At the time of putting the finishing touches to this volume, the world appears to be a very turbulent place. The 'big' issues of the day include the unwinding of central planning in Eastern Europe and the transformation to market-based economies; market completion in Western Europe, and the potential for economic and monetary union; the possibility of a fourth oil shock; environmental degradation and the consequences of climatic change; the signing of some kind of agreement from the eighth round of the General Agreement on Tariffs and Trade (GATT) multilateral arrangements, which might yet shore up the multilateralist consensus which has served the world economy so well over the post-war period; and debt-driven stagnation in many developing countries. These are the issues which economists will be called to advise on. They promise to make the 1990s exciting, interesting and perhaps a little less comfortable than the 1980s.

How well placed is the economics profession to respond to such challenges? Have we reason to believe that recent advances in the body of knowledge and technical change put the present generation in a better position than the last generation of economists? Inevitably opinion within the profession is divided. Attitudinal surveys certainly reveal a perception that economics has gained in prestige over the post-war period (Grubel and Boland 1986; Greenaway 1990); and there has been a tremendous expansion in the number of economics programmes in schools and higher education. Definitional problems make it rather more difficult to identify the actual stock of 'economists' at a given point in time. Recent debate in the United Kingdom has addressed the question of whether the present stock is in some sense optimal, with as yet no resolution (Sloane 1990; Towse and Blaug 1990). Although we do not have enough hard evidence to resolve the question, we can say with some confidence that the stock has grown significantly over the post-war period. (For an interesting insight into the growth in the government economic service in the United Kingdom, see Cairncross and Watts 1989). Growing numbers, together with

1

changes in technology, have facilitated specialization by subdiscipline. With that specialization have come profound changes in the way we as economists approach our subject.

At the academic level, one of the most obvious symptoms of specialization is the number of specialist journals now available compared with twenty-five or thirty years ago. The growth has been really quite extraordinary. To illustrate the point, of the hundred and thirty or so economics journals listed in *Contents of Recent Economics Journals*, only about one-quarter go back beyond 1960. Those that do are the classic 'generalist' journals, such as the *Economic Journal, American Economic Review, Journal of Political Economy, Oxford Economic Papers, Quarterly Journal of Economics* and so on. Almost all the new entrants provide a service to a specialist audience. This development has had two effects. On the one hand, it has allowed specialization to take place. Young economists, armed with new techniques and the newest methods for testing their theories, have had a forum for communicating with other researchers interested in similar issues. This has reduced search costs for the specialist. Although it has resulted in some replication, and 'filling in', it has also facilitated progress in the sense of allowing a wider menu of models to be examined, a broader range of empirical results to be reported and therefore a more intensive investigation of particular issues. On the other hand, however, it has imposed much higher search costs on the 'generalist'. Moreover, it confronts any generalist keen to keep abreast of developments in all aspects of the subject with an almost impossible task.

This volume is an attempt to address both of the matters discussed so far; it aims to try and take stock of 'progress' in economics and it does so in a way that makes the content of each section and chapter accessible to the specialist who wishes to learn something about what other specialists do. Stocktaking and assessing progress are inevitably judgemental to a degree. The judgements which were made in framing this volume should be explained. We did *not* set out to have a volume of surveys; nor did we set out to be *wholly* comprehensive. Surveys have an important role to play. However, even the best surveys tend to be reference works for specialists (see for instance the excellent series of surveys published in the *Economic Journal* between 1987 and 1990). It is uncertain to what extent such surveys are read by non-specialists, i.e. there is a clear difference between a survey which attempts to be comprehensive in coverage and this book, which is more concerned to convey the flavour of specialists' work to non-specialists. Besides which, few if any fields can be surveyed thoroughly in the 7,000 words or so that we allowed to each of our contributors. Instead, we asked our authors to overview developments in a particular part of the discipline, showing where possible how this slotted into the wider firmament, as well as commenting on the contribution which the developments have made/are making.

This desire to contextualize also motivated the structure which we imposed on the volume – as well as having sections on economic theory and applied economics, we were anxious to include methodological perspectives and interfaces. The intention of these parts was to facilitate elaboration of the philosophical/methodological foundations, whilst at the same time tracing out the boundaries of the subject in relation to cognate disciplines.

With regard to the content of each part, again we had to exercise judgement. We did not set out to be completely comprehensive. The *New Palgrave Dictionary*, which runs to 4 million words, is without question the most comprehensive reference work in economics. Even this has been criticized by some reviewers for its omissions (Blaug 1988). Judged by this standard, there are bound to be perceived omissions in the present volume. We as editors are sensitive to this. Given the length constraint, however, to which we had to operate, we did what any other economists would have done and optimized. We hope that readers will find the coverage fairly comprehensive, balanced and up to date. Thus, we have tried to incorporate new issues like environmental economics and public choice theory, and new techniques like experimental economics and microeconometrics, alongside more long-standing issues such as growth theory and cost–benefit analysis. We feel that we have been as comprehensive as could reasonably have been expected in the context of a volume running to forty-one chapters.

Finally, to end where we began: the economics profession will be confronted with many challenges in commenting on the great issues of the day; is it well equipped to cope with those challenges? The work reviewed in this volume is testimony to the vitality of economics as a discipline. It also serves to illustrate the range of issues to which economic analysis can be applied, often with an input from cognate disciplines. This should certainly make the economics profession well positioned in offering informed comment on the great issues of the day.

REFERENCES

Blaug, M. (1988) *Economics Through the Looking Glass*, London: Institute of Economic Affairs, Occasional Paper 88.

Cairncross, A. and Watts, N. (1989) *The Economic Section*, London: Routledge.

Greenaway, D. (1990) 'On the efficient use of mathematics in economics: results of an attitude survey of British economists', *European Economic Review*, 34: 1339–52.

Grubel, H. and Boland, L. (1986) 'On the efficient use of mathematics in economics: some theory, facts and results of an opinion survey', *Kyklos* 39: 419–42.

Sloane, P. (1990) 'The demand for economists', *RES Newsletter* 70: 15–18.

Towse, R. and Blaug, M. (1990) 'The current state of the British economics profession', *Economic Journal* 100: 227–36.

I. METHODOLOGICAL PERSPECTIVES

2

THE ROLE OF THE METHODOLOGIST

IAN M. T. STEWART

2.1 INTRODUCTION

'Why begin the book by looking at methodology?'

We met this question more than once in the early stages of editing this volume. It emerged that different questioners meant different things by the enquiry. For some, the issue was: 'Why put methodological discussion at the beginning, before you have described what actually happens in current economics?' For others, the query really meant: 'When there are so many fascinating topics to explore in economic theory and application, why bother to have a section on methodology at all?'

After giving respectful consideration to these questions, we decided to keep to our original plan. We have thus included a substantial discussion of methodological issues, and have placed it in this first part of the volume.

In deciding to include rather than exclude chapters on methodology we were guided by the essential aim of the present volume. Our purpose, and that of our contributors, is not simply to describe the present state of the discipline; it is to place current economics *in perspective*. This giving of perspective, we believe, is one of the prime functions of methodology.

At base, the methodologist's task is to pose some simple, direct and possibly uncomfortable questions to economic theorists and practitioners. For example:

What are we doing?
Why are we doing it?
Are we doing it right? And what does 'right' mean, anyhow?
What use are our results to anyone?

It seemed to us that these were fine questions to address in a critique of the current discipline. Indeed, all the contributors to the volume do tackle these questions, with varying degrees of emphasis and explicitness. The task

7

in Part I is to explore the meaning of the questions themselves and to outline the criteria that may be employed in answering them.

This in turn helps to explain why we chose to place the methodological chapters at the beginning. We see the discussion of method as being a natural introduction to all that follows in the other three parts. Traditionally, the methodologist has considered the structure and validation of theory (covered here in Part II), its application to practical problems (Part III) and the relationship of economics to other fields of study (Part IV).

In the present chapter I shall first outline what I see as the main current themes of discourse in economic methodology. Next I shall review the striking expansion of methodological interest that has taken place in the past decade. Finally, I shall introduce each of the chapters that follow in Part I.

2.2 CURRENT THEMES IN ECONOMIC METHODOLOGY

Mercifully, methodologists these days have ceased agonizing over the question: 'What is economics?' It is by now accepted that economics is whatever the current academic and professional community define it to be. It is also recognized that different economists may have different definitions, none more correct than any other, and that in any case current economics covers so many diverse subdisciplines that a single definition would be otiose.

By contrast, there is another traditional question that is still a live issue in current methodology (see, for example, Eichner 1983; Rosenberg 1983): 'Is economics a science?' However, in the past decade or so there has been a notable shift in the way that economic methodologists approach this issue.

The traditional version of the question, somewhat simplified, runs thus: 'Somewhere out there in the world there is a procedure called "science". Philosophers know what it is, and it is typified by what physicists do. How closely does economic investigation resemble this procedure, and thus how far does economics merit being called a science?' Along with this traditional query have gone several associated questions, in particular: 'How far *should* economics try to emulate the procedure of "science"?'

As is by now popular knowledge, in recent years philosophers of natural science have abandoned the notion of a 'standard science'. In particular, physics – formerly viewed as the epitome of precise theory and hard data – has turned out instead to be a mysterious realm of approximations and chaos (see, for example, Zukav 1979; Capra 1983; Feyerabend 1987). Economic methodologists are still evaluating the implications of this shift for their own field of study. (See, for instance, O'Brien's discussion of chaos theory in Chapter 4 of this volume.) However, it has already brought with it a corresponding shift in the questions that methodologists pose about the nature of economic science. They now ask, for example: 'Are there different kinds of procedure, all of which fit a definition of "science" but do so in different ways? Could it be that the sciences formerly regarded as "hard" could learn something useful from the methods of the "soft" sciences? How far should economic method emulate each kind of science?'

Within this shifted frame of reference, the main threads of methodological discourse in current economics can all be traced back to venerable origins. The list which follows is my own suggested formulation of these main themes. It could be recast in many different ways, and clearly, whatever list is given, the listed areas of discourse must widely overlap and interact. All the themes are explored in detail in the coming chapters, and so I shall simply sketch them here with the aim of providing a set of signposts through these chapters. (To avoid duplication, I shall give only a bare minimum of bibliographical references in the remainder of this section.)

With these caveats, I suggest that the main themes are as follows:

1 What is the nature of theory in economics?
2 What can economists claim to know about reality?
3 How far can economists predict the future?
4 What insights can we gain by studying the historical development of economic thought?
5 How far do sociological concepts add to our understanding of developments within economic science?

Traditionally, and still today, discussion of these topics is frequently carried on under the banner of various 'schools' of economic thought. For example, the Austrians, the positivists and the institutionalists are each associated with their own distinctive cluster of methodological tenets (see Chapter 5, Chapter 6 and Chapter 7 respectively). Past controversies over method have sometimes resembled political disputes, with writers adopting the entire 'platform' of their favoured methodological school and attempting to demolish the position of another school *in toto*. Fortunately, today's methodologists are usually more eclectic in style.

Theory, testing and the 'assumptions controversy'

Headings 1 and 2 on the list are closely interrelated. This, of course, is because enquiries about the nature of economic theory often also entail considering how that theory can be tested against empirical observation. Under these combined headings comes a long-running methodological debate that has come to be known as the 'assumptions controversy'. This dispute dates back at least as far as nineteenth-century critiques of the notion of 'economic man'. The crux of the controversy, in essence, is the question: 'Should economic theory be judged by the realism of its assumptions or by the accuracy of its predictions?' Each methodological school in economics has suggested its own answer (or range of answers) to this query. Much of the voluminous literature on the 'assumptions controversy' has been couched in terms of attacks on, or defences of, the positivist school in economics. Boland reviews the present state of this debate in Chapter 6.

The word 'prediction' in this context, if interpreted in a strict sense, means simply 'a specific event that a theory suggests will be observed in reality', without necessarily implying a time dimension. However, in methodological disputes, as in everyday conversation, the word also often carries an associated shade of meaning, namely 'an event that is expected to take place in the future'. Thus the 'assumptions controversy' has also frequently involved discussion of heading 3 on the list above. Not surprisingly, those methodologists who have urged the primacy of 'testing by predictions' have also tended to express faith in the potential ability of economists to predict the future (if not in the present state of the art, then at some time soon when predictive technique has been refined). Conversely, those writers who favour judging theory by its assumptions have leant towards emphasizing the inherent and perhaps insoluble problems of quantitative prediction in the real world of economics.

Prediction and econometrics

Heading 3 on the list – how far can economists predict the future? – has also figured in another dispute, this time concerning the predictive value of econometric techniques. To be sure, as a few textbooks of econometrics do caution their readers, econometric 'predictions' should strictly be interpreted only in a non-time-specific sense; there is no epistemological basis for supposing that econometrics can foretell the future. In practice, however, the implied ability to look forward in time has proved irresistible as a motivation to most econometricians, and it is certainly accepted without question as the principal purpose of econometrics by policy-makers who look at the econometricians' results and by the grant-aiding bodies who provide funds for their activities.

A recurring theme in the coming chapters will be that of the 'crisis' that is widely agreed to have struck economics in the middle to late 1970s. Increasing disenchantment with the ability of econometrics to deliver the goods, in the shape of consistently accurate predictions, was arguably one of the mainsprings of this crisis. The question now at issue is: does econometric method have at least the potential to provide quantitative predictions to a worthwhile degree of accuracy, given more time for refinement in its techniques? Or does the nature of economic data mean that any attempt at systematic prediction is inherently futile, or at best so patchy in accuracy as to be a waste of effort?

Economic ignorance and the time dimension

Some economic methodologists, combining consideration of headings 2 and 3, have posed questions concerning what economists *can* know about the future. The issues under examination here go to more fundamental levels of epistemological discourse than mere questions of quantitative econometric prediction. One focus of critique for these writers has been the economic 'theory of decision-making under risk' (or 'under uncertainty'). All variants of this theory rest on assumptions about what the economic actor expects to happen in the future. For example, he can be assumed to choose his action on the basis of a set of possible outcomes, to each of which he attaches a particular probability. Methodological critics, notably Shackle (1988), have pointed out that such assumptions portray a degree of knowledge of the future that no real-world economic actor can ever possess, to the degree that they consider the theory worthless for any purpose other than as an abstract puzzle. (In Chapter 5, Barry discusses the rationale of Shackle's criticism.)

However, if future economic events cannot be predicted in probability terms, what can we say about their likelihood? Loasby (1976) and Hutchison (1977) have suggested that the term *ignorance* (rather than 'uncertainty') be used to signify a state of knowledge of the future in which outcomes, although not predictable in probability terms, are nevertheless not utterly unpredictable. However, at the date of writing this terminology has still not been widely accepted.

Hicks (1979) has contributed a suggestion that may help clarify the nature of ignorance. He proposes that in the field of economic observations the likelihood of various possible events can often be ranked ordinally, even though a cardinal measure of probability cannot be attached to them. Although Shackle (1988) has written a brief critique of Hicks's suggestion, current writers have still not fully explored the implications of this notion of ordinal likelihood.

History of economic thought

Heading 4 in the list of themes relates, of course, to the long-established field of study known as 'history of economic thought'. In Chapter 3, Deane discusses current developments in this discipline. She cites Schumpeter's definition of 'economic thought' as 'the opinions on economic matters that prevail at any given time or in any given society'. Thus the study of the history of economic thought falls squarely in the methodological field. It is not the same as the study of economic history, although the two disciplines overlap. (For a further discussion of the common ground between economics and history, see also Chapter 41 by Crafts.)

Sociological and ideological approaches

There are two main foci of current attention relating to the insights to be gained by using sociological or ideological analyses in economic methodology (heading 5 on the list of themes). The first such focus entails the application to economics of the well-known concept of 'scientific revolutions' originated by Kuhn (1970) and the alternative approach of Lakatos (1978), who speaks of the 'methodology of scientific research programmes'. The other principal focus relates not so much to the nature of economic science, but rather to sociological features of the economics profession itself. In Chapter 8, Coats discusses the latter topic in detail.

2.3 METHODOLOGY IN DECLINE AND REVIVAL

The past ten years or so have seen an extraordinary upsurge in the interest devoted to methodological questions in economics. This is all the more remarkable when we consider that during the previous three decades and more economic methodology had been in virtually total eclipse as far as most economists were concerned. In this section I shall briefly review these contrasting phases in methodological activity, as reflected in the literature, and offer some speculations about the causes of this fast-and-feast scenario. In examining the literature I shall focus principally on the books on methodology published in each period that were aimed at the general economic reader rather than the specialist, noting undergraduate texts in particular. My assumption is that the number of such books available provides a useful proxy for the general level of methodological interest among economists.

With hindsight, I believe, it can be seen that the periods of stagnation and expansion in methodological interest were separated by a brief watershed period in the late 1970s and 1980. During this time, various stimuli to methodological change – originating both from within economics and from the broad field of the philosophy of science – were converging to initiate the revival in methodological interest that became clearly apparent in the 1980s.

Methodology in decline: 1950 to the late 1970s

A landmark event of this long period was in 1953, when Friedman published his famous essay on 'The methodology of positive economics' (Friedman 1953). This paper had all the characteristics that are required to produce a long-running controversy in any academic literature. First, it was written by a charismatic authority in his field; second, it suggested ideas that seemed to many of its readers to be bold departures from current convention; last but not least, it was couched in vague and ambiguous language that could be interpreted by different people to mean different and indeed conflicting things.

In fact, what Friedman presented was simply his own perspective on the 'assumptions controversy' that had been in progress for a century and more before he wrote. To most readers of his essay, the methodological prescription he was conveying emerged as a stark and simple one: 'Judge economic theories solely by the accuracy of their predictions, and not at all by the realism of their assumptions.'

The battle of words over his essay was duly joined, and rumbled on in the journals for over a decade. Indeed, echoes of it can still be heard to this day. (For an overview of the controversy and a lead into its vast and tortuous literature see, for example, Stewart (1979) and Boland (1982), as well as Chapter 6 of the present volume.) However, all this went on purely within the province of methodological specialists; it remained out of sight of the general economist, who was more likely simply to find Friedman's paper (or ideas from it) reprinted in other sources as the received wisdom of economic methodology.

This process was reinforced by the appearance in 1963 of Lipsey's undergraduate textbook *An Introduction to Positive Economics* (Lipsey 1963). The book, which became a long-running bestseller, featured an assertive coverage of economic methodology that was based on some of Friedman's ideas plus Lipsey's own idiosyncratic interpretation of Karl Popper. (In Chapter 6 of the present volume, Boland analyses what successive editions of Lipsey's text had to contribute to the ideas of economic 'positivism'.)

Thus throughout the 1960s and into the 1970s, methodological specialists were devoting much of their energy to verbal wrangles about the possible interpretations of Friedman, while non-specialists – including successive cohorts of undergraduates reared on Lipsey – assumed that the last word on methodology had already been spoken. It is no wonder that this period, as Boland (1984) has aptly put it, was one of 'methodological paralysis'.

A further speculation is in order. It seems no coincidence that the years from the mid-1950s until the 1970s saw rapid expansion in the use of computers, and with it a parallel expansion in econometric method. With these new and exciting tools at their disposal, economists were eager to put into practice the Friedman–Lipsey dictum of 'prediction testing before all'. As I have already suggested, the notion of 'prediction' carried with it an enticing aura of scrying the future, both for economists and for those who employed them. With these developments afoot, it is not surprising that the profession in general had little taste for methodological caveats.

The book literature of the time reveals a few voices continuing to cry in the wilderness. Knight (1956) , Hutchison (1964) and Boulding (1970) presented accounts of economic science more spacious than the prevailing positivist doctrine. A symposium volume edited by Krupp (1966) helped show that

13

methodological critique was still alive. Shackle, in successive volumes, advanced his distinctive arguments on the opacity of the economic future and its implications for method (Shackle 1958, 1961, 1970). Devons (1961), writing from his experience as an applied economist, sounded notes of caution about what even modern methods could achieve in practice. From the Austrian camp, von Mises (1960, 1962) urged his aprioristic view of economic science, starkly opposed to the Friedman–Lipsey account. (Barry expands on the Austrian perspective in Chapter 5 of this volume.)

Methodology in transition: the late 1970s and 1980

Perhaps the first stirrings of coming change, as signalled by the book literature, can be traced back as far as the early 1970s, when Ward (1972) asked *What's Wrong with Economics?*. His question went unanswered by the positivist-econometric establishment of the time.

Meanwhile, momentous events had been taking place in the general philosophy of science. In 1962, Kuhn had presented his ideas on the structure of scientific revolutions, and a second edition of his book appeared eight years later (Kuhn 1970). In the journal literature, Imre Lakatos had been developing his alternative account of the 'methodology of scientific research programmes', and his collected papers later appeared in book form (Lakatos 1978). The ideas of Kuhn and Lakatos had stimulated the interest of methodologists in economics as in other academic fields; they eventually made their appearance in the book literature of economic methodology in a symposium volume edited by Latsis (1976). These new contributions helped to fuel the revival of methodological activity in economics – if for no other reason than that they diverted methodologists from further sterile discussion of Friedman and the 'assumptions controversy' (cf. Boland 1984).

There was another powerful stimulus for methodological change in this period, again originating from outside the field of economic methodology itself. This was the 'crisis' of confidence in economic theory and practice that developed from the early 1970s onwards. (See also Bleaney's discussion in Chapter 9.) As policy-makers and the public grew ever more dissatisfied with the ability of economics to deal with inflation and stagnation, so economists found it more and more urgent to reappraise their theories and techniques, and this process eventually extended all the way to a reassessment of the methodological principles on which these theories and techniques were founded.

It is interesting to reflect that if any one economic concept symbolizes this period of methodological self-satisfaction followed by reappraisal, it is the famous Phillips curve (Phillips 1958). Phillips wrote his paper at the time when Friedman's methodological prescriptions were first gaining ground. The curve itself was a copybook example of the results of following these prescriptions.[1] It was derived purely by empirical observation (of aggregate data), using a statistical line-fitting technique. It did not appeal to any theoretical 'assumptions', leaving matters of causality to be inferred by the reader. Its merits were judged in practice by its power to predict outcomes – the term 'predict' here, as usual, has the *de facto* sense of foretelling the future in quantitative terms.

In an almost uncanny way, the subsequent fate of the Phillips curve is paralleled by the fate of the methodology that gave rise to it. The demise of the curve, of course, was one of the unsolved puzzles in economics throughout the 1970s (and it remains unsolved to this day, many would add). With hindsight, we can now see that the predictive power of the Phillips curve was beginning to deteriorate from about 1970 onwards, but the departures from predicted values did not become a matter of serious concern until about 1972, i.e. at the same time as the first signs of dissatisfaction were emerging in the methodological field.

By three years or so later, it had become clear to economists that they had a problem on their hands. As the observed co-ordinates for wage inflation and unemployment moved further and further away from their predicted positions on the Phillips curve, economic theorists hurried to construct *explanatory* frameworks that might give some clue to where the curve was now, if indeed it was or ever had been anywhere. In the vanguard of these attempts was none other than Milton Friedman.

At the same time, applied economists and econometricians took worried looks at their quantitative predictions. If a relationship as stable as the Phillips curve could disintegrate in such spectacular fashion, what did this mean for empirical predictive techniques generally? Could it be, even, that people like Shackle and von Mises had been right all the time?

By the late 1970s, the revival in methodological debate was making its presence clearly felt in the book literature. Loasby (1976), Hutchison (1977) and, once again, Shackle (1979) each published books which examined the limitations on the ability of economic actors to foresee the future, and explored the implications of this for economic method generally. Hicks (1979) also offered new perspectives on the nature of economic prediction, as well as on the question of causality in economics. Fritz Machlup (1978) published a volume of his collected methodological papers. As further confirmation that a broadening in methodological interest was under way by the close of the decade, two books appeared that were aimed squarely at the undergraduate market: they were by Stewart (1979) and Blaug (1980).

Methodology in revival: the 1980s

Throughout the 1980s and until the present, heterodoxy and dispute have remained the order of the day in economics. Correspondingly, the upsurge of interest in methodological issues has been maintained. This has been reflected in the literature, with the publication of a steady stream of books on methodology aimed at the undergraduate and the non-specialist professional.

Katouzian (1980) presented a critique of positivism and of Kuhnian and Lakatosian ideas as they had been applied to economics. He also sounded the alarm about what he considered to be a 'self-perpetuating elite' within the economics profession (an allegation that is also examined by Coats in Chapter 8 of this volume).

The year 1982 saw the appearance of two books, both of which set out to consider alternatives to naïve positivism. Boland (1982) questioned economists' preoccupation with empirical evidence derived from induction, arguing that this must lead to conventionalism. Caldwell (1982) gave a historical overview and critique of various methodological approaches in economics, and issued a plea for 'methodological pluralism'. He subsequently edited a symposium volume of critical papers in methodology (Caldwell 1984). Boland went on, in two further books, to apply his methodological views to microeconomics (Boland 1986) and to the question of economic 'model-building' (Boland 1989). McCloskey (1986) advanced the startling suggestion that much of what we call 'theory' in economics is actually better regarded as rhetoric, i.e. as a dramatic means of persuading or impressing others. With this, he raised a methodological hare that is still being chased. Shackle – encouraged, one might hope, by the debacle of economic predictionism – published another volume of his collected papers, stressing yet again his central theme that 'Method in economic theory must start by considering time' (Shackle 1988). In the late 1980s two further undergraduate texts appeared, both of them integrating Kuhnian and Lakatosian ideas with the more traditional concerns of economic methodology: they were by Pheby (1988) and Glass and Johnson (1989).

To close this section, a word should be said about developments in the availability of journal literature on methodology. Even in the recent period of expansion that has just been described, methodological articles have remained a minority interest as far as most journal editors in general economics have been concerned. A notable exception has been the institutionalists' *Journal of Economic Issues*, long established as a welcoming haven for methodological work. Two important new outlets for methodological writing, however, were established during the 1980s. An annual, *Research in the History of Economic Thought and Methodology*, was founded in 1983. Its second volume contained a symposium of views on recent developments in economic methodology

(Samuels 1984). A further important milestone was the inauguration in 1985 of the journal *Economics and Philosophy*; it is devoted to discussion of issues on the interface between the two disciplines named in its title, including questions of methodology.

2.4 THE CHAPTERS IN PART I

Deane begins Chapter 3, on 'The role of history of economic thought', by sketching the nineteenth-century roots of the discipline. She reveals that economic writers of that period were already busy with the doctrinal and ideological squabbles that have marked economic discourse ever since. Indeed, if any subtitle could be attached to Deane's paper, it might well be 'Doctrine versus objectivity'. She argues that one potential benefit of studying the history of economic thought is that it can provide a perspective upon various warring doctrines, making it easier to develop an objective view of their relative faults and merits, differences and similarities, in so far as human frailty allows. Yet by the nature of the subject, this must always be done with hindsight. And the perspective gained must always be changing, as the ever changing present moves through time.

Several other pervasive features of the current economic scene, Deane points out, were also already in evidence by the late nineteenth and early twentieth centuries. One is the professionalization of economics (which Coats analyses in detail in Chapter 8). Another is the esteem that the academic community in economics has attached to 'high-powered theory' and the acquisition of specialized technical skills. These features in turn have had one consequence that has been familiar in the teaching of economics throughout most of this century, i.e. the tendency to relegate studies in the history of economic thought (and, indeed, all methodological studies) to the realm of non-mandatory courses.

Deane goes on to document the causes behind a resurgence of interest in the history of economic thought from the 1950s onwards. In some measure these causes were internal to the discipline, stemming from an upsurge in the availability of scholarly editions and translations of primary sources. However, Deane also points to external influences, i.e. those relating to the more general increase in interest in economic methodology that has already been mentioned in the present chapter. She draws attention in particular to the excitement generated by the sociologically oriented ideas of Kuhn and Lakatos.

Citing the work of Blaug, Deane suggests also that 'the failure of the economic orthodoxy of the 1950s and 1960s to resolve the analytical problems of the 1970s' was a further factor that helped revive interest in studies of the history of economic thought. In her closing section, she discusses in some detail two of the main analytical streams that have emerged in the course of her discipline's current expansion. The first of these entails new developments in the history of economic doctrine, and the second the use of historical method in studying the history of economics.

In Chapter 4, O'Brien discusses theory and empirical observation in economics. He begins by setting forth his central thesis. It is that, if any science is to make progress, it must engage in choices between theories, and that the principal role of data is to facilitate this process of theory choice. In his first main section, he explores the potentials and pitfalls that economists face in using data. Sounding a caution against claims for 'inductive logic' in economics, he points out that Karl Popper did not solve the problem of induction: he solved the problem of how knowledge can be gained from observation.

O'Brien next gives a critique of Friedman's famed proposition that the realism of assumptions is irrelevant to theory choice. Physicists, O'Brien points out, certainly do not ignore the truth of their initial assumptions. This is the more ironic in view of the scientistic bent of economic writers, such as Friedman, who have suggested that assumptions are irrelevant. O'Brien goes on to explore in some detail the implications of the fact that the replication of results is much more difficult in economics than in the physical sciences.

Discussing the question of measurement problems, O'Brien highlights the often ludicrous results of applying regression analysis to economic data. Regression technique, he reminds us, was originally developed for use in analysing the results of agronomic experiments, in which controls and repeated observations are the rule. In economics, by contrast, our data come most often from commonly available statistical series, of questionable validity and derived from one-off observations. O'Brien recommends some remedies that economists might begin putting in place to deal with these problems.

He next explores the currently popular suggestion that much of what economists write is actually rhetoric rather than testable theory. O'Brien's view is that a substantial part of economic literature does indeed take the form of rhetoric. In particular, the use of high-powered mathematics may often serve a rhetorical purpose. However, this is not the same as saying that rhetoric can somehow assist in theory choice or act as a substitute for it; in the end, the empirical data remain crucial.

Turning to consider the use of physics as a model for scientific endeavour in economics, O'Brien points up two questions for attention. First, is the methodology of physics, at least as it is understood by economists, a worthwhile ideal for economic method? Second, how closely does economists' understanding of physics reflect what modern physicists actually do? One possible way ahead, he suggests, may be to model economic method not on physics but on different areas of science, such as medicine. Alternatively, within physics, the still evolving study of chaos theory may present some challenging insights to economic method.

Exploring 'Austrian perspectives' in Chapter 5, Barry asserts the right of Austrian economics to be recognized as a distinct research programme. Its contributions to economic theory and method, he urges, need to be assessed independently of the penumbra of right-wing political diatribe that has come to be popularly associated with Austrian economics. Austrian theorizing emphasizes that economic events arise from human action, carried on in a world of ignorance and uncertainty.

Barry first reviews the origins of the Austrian approach, beginning with the work of Carl Menger. In the detailed reasoning of Menger's contribution, the trademarks of Austrian economics can already be detected. All economic phenomena are traced to the actions of individuals (the doctrine of methodological individualism). The causation of economic events is interpreted in terms of the individual actor's own subjective assessment and motivation. Thus generalizations concerning the 'essence of economic action' can be arrived at deductively, without reference to historical data. The prime purpose of economic analysis is to promote *Verstehen*, not to generate predictions or engage in empirical testing.

Contrary to common belief, Barry points out, Austrians from Menger onwards have not shunned the concept of equilibrium. However, they use it in a way that is distinctively different from that of other schools. The aim of Austrian economists is to describe and understand the *processes* by which economic systems may seek equilibrium. In contrast, the conventional neoclassicist is more interested in proving mathematically that an equilibrium can exist, and then analyzing the conditions that would allow it to exist.

Barry examines several of the central ideas of Austrian methodology. Looking first at the concept of subjectivism, he notes that to the Austrian thinker it implies that nothing in the economic universe can be regarded as objectively given. Even measures such as costs must continually be discovered by the actor in an ever changing world with an opaque future. And the economic actor does not simply react to whatever is discovered; rather, he is proactive, taking the initiative to do whatever seems most likely to bring about his subjectively desired state of affairs. Thus, to the Austrian school, any attempt to base economic analysis purely on 'objective observation' must miss out on the very heart of the economic process.

The Austrian view of entrepreneurship implies not just formal 'rationality', but rather a state of alertness to whatever opportunities may be revealed by market information. The concept seems to imply more than mere arbitrage; the entrepreneur is also proactive, not simply responding to price differentials but taking innovative leaps in the dark.

Barry looks finally at some aspects of the Austrian view of money and economic fluctuations, and at the implications of the Austrian approach for macroeconomic policy.

In Chapter 6, Boland examines 'Current views on economic positivism'. He begins by investigating the meaning (or, better, meanings) of the term 'positive economics'. Positive economics, points out Boland, is often delineated by contrasting it with something else. But with what? He reviews several such suggested contrasts from the literature – for example analytic versus synthetic, is versus ought, theoretical versus applied – and finds each one deficient as a clear description of what positive economics stands for. He suggests that the term 'positive' may in fact find its most important role as a rhetorical device. The unspoken implication is: 'Positive procedure is good'. Boland considers the possible sources of this presumption.

Boland goes on to distinguish four subschools of current economic positivism. They represent a continuum of views. At one extreme is the group of economists, still small in number, who advocate the use of experimental method in economics. (This development is reviewed in detail by Loomes in Chapter 29 of the present volume.) At the other end of the spectrum are the followers of Samuelson, who are willing to accept a methodological view in which theories only need to be testable in principle.

Between these two extremes are what Boland christens the 'Chicago' and 'LSE' schools of positive economics. The former, of course, includes the disciples of Milton Friedman, whose methodological stance Boland describes as 'simplistic instrumentalism'. It also reflects the more sophisticated accounts given by Becker and Stigler.

As regards 'LSE positivism', Boland notes that the gospel of this subschool for many years has been Lipsey's textbook *An Introduction to Positive Economics*. He uses a detailed analysis of the book's methodological prescriptions, as they have evolved through its several editions, to support his contention that modern economic positivism is 'profoundly confused'.

Why then, Boland continues, does current economic positivism still attract support? One of the answers, he suggests, lies in the function of positivism as rhetoric. A much emphasized claim of economic positivists is that their procedure is value free, and it is this aspect of their demeanour, far more than the philosophical niceties of their method, that endears them to policy-makers.

Entering into the positivist spirit, Boland goes on to build a model of the typical positivist journal article. Testing his model empirically, he reports a high degree of confirmation: in one prestigious journal, every article entailing investigation of real-world data conformed to his modelled article format.

As all model-builders must, Boland now looks behind his empirical results for some indication of causality. Why, he asks, is this standard article format so popular among positive economists? The answer he proposes is surprising, suggesting an agenda far removed from the declared philosophical aims of positivism.

In Chapter 7, Samuels sets forth the institutionalist perspective on economics. Institutionalists define their approach by reference to a central problem: 'the evolution of the organization and control of the economy as a whole'. Samuels stresses that, to the institutional economist, 'the economy encompasses more than the market', and this is a theme that recurs throughout his exposition. Rather than depending upon models of a conceptualized market, institutionalists are interested in the structures and processes that actually influence what happens in the wider economic world, of which the market itself is merely a part.

The institutional approach, says Samuels, has three facets: it is a body of knowledge, a means for solving problems and a protest movement. Institutional economists have protested at both the uncritical acceptance of existing economic institutions and the uncritical acceptance of economic theory that presupposes those institutions.

Institutionalists, explains Samuels, stress the importance of power in determining economic events. This does not mean simply power in the sense of the ability to dictate prices. Rather, it relates to the struggle between economic actors to gain various forms of rights and entitlement – in particular, the entitlement to control the available technology. In the institutionalist view, the concept of 'Pareto optimality' is seen as being specific to a particular configuration of the structure of entitlements. Since neoclassical economists ignore the significance of this power structure, they are viewed by institutionalists as legitimizing it, i.e. tacitly accepting the current socio-political status quo.

Samuels carries this theme through in his examination of institutionalist microeconomics. To the institutionalist, 'resource allocation is a function of power'. Indeed, all the familiar phenomena of conventional microeconomic theory turn out to be, to the institutionalist, merely superficial indicators of other and more important events. These events take the form of power plays, struggles for entitlement and jockeying for the ownership of rights. The government, far from being assumed extraneous to this economic process, is placed right in the centre of it, since control through government is seen as being simply one of the ways in which power struggles may be played out.

In the macroeconomic area also, questions of power and institutional structure are viewed as crucial. For example, institutionalists study the ways in which macroeconomic performance may be influenced by the distributions of income and wealth.

Samuels reviews a range of specific research areas currently being explored by institutional economists. The research agenda that he describes is well in the spirit of institutionalism. Its focus is not on building formalized models, but rather on seeking to discover and understand what causative forces – particularly those concerned with structures and power – are actually important in the widely defined economy.

Coats' central theme in Chapter 8 is a call for systematic research on

21

'the nature, historical evolution and significance' of the professionalization of economics. He points out that in recent decades there has been much talk of 'problems' and 'crises' in economics, but we have lacked firm data against which to assess the importance of these difficulties for economics as a profession.

Reviewing the possible reasons for the notable expansion in the demand for professionally trained economists in the past half-century, Coats suggests that this may partly have been a manifestation of the general tendency towards specialization of function that has frequently accompanied the process of industrialization. Of importance also has been the existence of a well-developed theoretical framework to which economists can point as helping establish their professional identity. The ideology of a value-free economic science has also been a potent factor in bringing about the formation within economics of a self-image of the professional economist.

At the same time, economists have not moved nearly as far as some other professions – medicine, for example – in setting up mechanisms that are designed as barriers to entry. Coats attributes this relatively *laissez-faire* attitude to another aspect of economists' own ideology, namely their distaste for introducing distortions into the operation of the market.

In any case, challenges Coats, what do economists know that other people do not? The possession of special expertise, after all, is a *sine qua non* for any profession. He argues that economists do have a distinctive contribution to make to the process of problem-solving, but that this contribution lies more in a basic economic 'way of thinking' than in the exercise of sophisticated mathematical or statistical techniques.

Reviewing the historical development of professionalization in economics, Coats suggests that the earliest emergence of a recognizable economics profession can be traced back to the Ricardians in the early nineteenth century. However, it was not until the later years of that century that separate academic courses in economics began to proliferate. Coats suggests that this development can be linked to the expansion in interest in economics that accompanied the marginalist revolution, which he calls the first major milestone in the process of professionalization. The second milestone was the Keynesian revolution, in which a shift in economists' theoretical paradigm was accompanied by a brisk expansion in the volume of official economic statistics.

In conclusion, Coats examines one frequently suggested shortcoming of the economics profession: the alleged existence within it of a closed self-perpetuating elite. While Coats agrees that such an elite may well exist, he poses the question: what would be the possible alternatives?

NOTE

1 I do not claim to know whether Phillips had read Friedman or had made a deliberate decision to follow Friedman's methodological directives.

REFERENCES

Blaug, M. (1980) *The Methodology of Economics*, Cambridge: Cambridge University Press.

Boland, L. (1982) *The Foundations of Economic Method*, London: George Allen & Unwin.

—— (1984) 'On the state of economic methodology', *Research in the History of Economic Thought and Methodology* 2: 173–7.

—— (1986) *Methodology for a New Microeconomics*, Boston, MA: Allen & Unwin.

—— (1989) *The Methodology of Economic Model Building: Methodology After Samuelson*, London: Routledge.

Boulding, K. (1970) *Economics as a Science*, New York: McGraw-Hill.

Caldwell, B. (1982) *Beyond Positivism: Economic Methodology in the Twentieth Century*, London: Allen & Unwin.

—— (1984) *Appraisal and Criticism in Economics*, Boston, MA: Allen & Unwin.

Capra, F. (1983) *The Tao of Physics*, 2nd edn, Boston, MA: New Science Library.

Devons, E. (1961) *Essays in Economics*, London: Allen & Unwin.

Eichner, A. (ed.) (1983) *Why Economics is not yet a Science*, Armonk, NY: M. E. Sharpe.

Feyerabend, P. (1987) *Farewell to Reason*, London: Verso.

Friedman, M. (1953) 'The methodology of positive economics', in M. Friedman, *Essays in Positive Economics*, Chicago, IL: University of Chicago Press.

Glass, J. and Johnson, W. (1989) *Economics: Progression, Stagnation or Degeneration?*, London: Harvester Wheatsheaf.

Hicks, J. (1979) *Causality in Economics*, Oxford: Basil Blackwell.

Hutchison, T. (1964) *'Positive' Economics and Policy Objectives*, London: Allen & Unwin.

—— (1977) *Knowledge and Ignorance in Economics*, Oxford: Basil Blackwell.

Katouzian, H. (1980) *Ideology and Method in Economics*, London: Macmillan.

Knight, F. (1956) *On the History and Method of Economics*, Chicago, IL: University of Chicago Press.

Krupp, S. (ed.) (1966) *The Structure of Economic Science*, Englewood Cliffs, NJ: Prentice-Hall.

Kuhn, T. (1970) *The Structure of Scientific Revolutions*, 2nd edn, Chicago, IL: University of Chicago Press.

Lakatos, I. (1978) *The Methodology of Scientific Research Programmes: Philosophical Papers*, vols 1 and 2, Cambridge: Cambridge University Press.

Latsis, S. (ed.) (1976) *Method and Appraisal in Economics*, Cambridge: Cambridge University Press.

Lipsey, R. (1963) *An Introduction to Positive Economics*, 1st edn, London: Macmillan.

Loasby, B. (1976) *Choice, Complexity and Ignorance*, Cambridge: Cambridge University Press.

Machlup, F. (1978) *Methodology of Economics and Other Social Sciences*, New York: Academic Press.

McCloskey, D. (1986) *The Rhetoric of Economics*, Brighton: Harvester Wheatsheaf.

von Mises, L. (1960) *Epistemological Problems of Economics*, Princeton, NJ: Van Nostrand.

—— (1962) *The Ultimate Foundation of Economic Science*, Princeton, NJ: Van Nostrand.

Pheby, J. (1988) *Methodology and Economics: A Critical Introduction*, London: Macmillan.

Phillips, A. (1958) 'The relationship between unemployment and the rate of change of money wage rates in the United Kingdom, 1861–1957', *Economica* 25: 283–99.

Rosenberg, A. (1983) 'If economics isn't science, what is it?', *Philosophical Forum*, 14: 296–314.

Samuels, W. (ed.) (1984) *Research in the History of Economic Thought and Methodology*, vol. 2, Greenwich, CT: JAI Press.

Shackle, G. (1958) *Time in Economics*, Amsterdam: North-Holland.

—— (1961) *Decision, Order and Time in Human Affairs*, Cambridge: Cambridge University Press.

—— (1970) *Expectation, Enterprise and Profit*, London: Allen & Unwin.

—— (1979) *Imagination and the Nature of Choice*, Edinburgh: Edinburgh University Press.

—— (1988) *Business, Time and Thought*, London: Macmillan.

Stewart, I. (1979) *Reasoning and Method in Economics*, London: McGraw-Hill.

Ward, B. (1972) *What's Wrong with Economics?*, London: Macmillan.

Zukav, G. (1979) *The Dancing Wu Li Masters*, Bungay, Suffolk: Flamingo.

3

THE ROLE OF HISTORY OF ECONOMIC THOUGHT

PHYLLIS DEANE

3.1 INTRODUCTION

The reasons why economists study (or teach) the history of economic thought are manifold, varying with the economic vision and immediate aims of the individual student (or expositor) as well as with the progress of the subject as a discipline. In the nineteenth century, for example, serious students of political economy began naturally enough by reading the writings of past masters and some went on to publish commentaries on what they had read. J. R. McCulloch, the first English historian of political economy, had written various articles on this theme (e.g. for the *Scotsman* newspaper and the *Encyclopaedia Britannica*) before he published his *Historical Sketch of the Rise of the Science of Political Economy* (1826), and in 1845 he produced the first annotated bibliography of economics (McCulloch 1938).

As one of the leading economists of his time McCulloch wrote with authority and from the perspective of the current Ricardian orthodoxy. The next author to write a history of political economy for the *Encyclopaedia Britannica* was an altogether different character. J. K. Ingram, an Irish academic of wide interests and little originality, had acquired his reputation as an authority on scientific economics by delivering a resounding presidential address at the 1878 meetings of Section F of the British Association for the Advancement of Science, where he pontificated on 'The present position and prospects of political economy' and announced the birth of a 'new economics'. His *History of Political Economy* (originally commissioned for the 1878 *Encyclopaedia*) was not so much a history of economic thought as a manifesto for the historicist critics of English classical economics. Such a vigorous onslaught on an orthodoxy already under heavy fire from several directions lent special interest to a subject which most students of economics found rather dry. When republished in book form – first in the United States at the instigation of Taussig, a distinguished professor at Harvard University, and subsequently in England in 1888 – it became the most successful nineteenth-century textbook in the history of economics.[1]

Since universities with honours schools in economics required their students to have at least second-hand knowledge of the writings which their current teachers reverently invoked in support of their own lectures, the professionaliz-ation of the discipline that gathered momentum in the late nineteenth and early twentieth centuries generated a rising demand for new textbooks on past economic thought. Most of them were either hack hagiographies or accounts that presented past theories as a 'monumental collection of errors' which could be confidently contrasted with the advanced state of the modern discipline.[2] A very few thoughtful lectures and texts helped to keep the subject alive for discriminating students. Samuelson, for example, in his 1961 presidential address to the American Economic Association cited Gide's and Rist's *History of Economics* and 'Alexander Gray's brief book, the busy student's friend' as being the two texts which students could rely upon for examination purposes in the 1930s (Samuelson 1962). Indeed, apart from Gide and Rist (1909), Gray (1931) and Roll's *History of Economic Thought* (1938), no general textbook of distinction was published in this area until Schumpeter's monumental *History of Economic Analysis* (1954b). The fact is that the rise of high-powered economic theory, which began to take shape in the late 1920s and 1930s, and the increasingly technical character of the skills required by a professional economist made it less and less common for a course in the history of economic thought to be regarded as a mandatory part of his basic training. As an undergraduate examination subject it was effectively crowded out by a prolifer-ation of specialist and technical options.

As a research subject it was to develop in depth and range if not so much in volume of output. Although a majority of undergraduates may have thought it irrelevant, there were leading thinkers who still gathered inspiration from it. In the twentieth century, as in the nineteenth, innovative theorists conscious of the deficiencies of current orthodoxy went back to the writings of past masters in search of unexploited or forgotten insights. Naturally they tended to interpret the classics in modern terms and in so doing generated stimulating debates among specialists in the areas concerned. As prestigious modern theorists assigned new roles to the history of economic thought they helped to glamorize it for ambitious research students seeking a viable dissertation topic. Contrasting examples of high theorists whose incidental incursions into the field can be said to have significantly advanced the history of economic thought (either directly or indirectly or by provoking scholarly criticism) would include Marshall, whose 'rehabilitation of Ricardo' drew a perceptive critique from W. J. Ashley in 1891, and Samuelson, whose dissection of Marxian models in 1957 and reconsideration of the Marxian notion of exploitation in 1971 provoked reactions that were both rigorous and vigorous. A more recent example whose impact on the history of thought has so far been slight is Morishima, who reinterpreted and extended the models he found in Walras's *Elements*, Marx's *Capital* and Ricardo's *Principles* by applying the specialist techniques of modern mathematical economic theory (Morishima 1973, 1977, 1990).[3]

More importantly, some leading mid-twentieth century theorists have pursued their researches into the history of economic thought so effectively that they have become recognized authorities in the area. Knight, Stigler and Hicks are among the most distinguished examples. So too was Schumpeter, who had a long-standing interest in the history of economics and spent the last nine years of his life revising and updating his early essay on the development of economic doctrine and method (originally published in German in 1914).[4] This was the project that expanded into the massive history of economic analysis which his wife edited for publication after his death. In effect, Schumpeter's *History* was a landmark in the history of economic thought. It provided a statement of aims and objectives which most later textbook writers drew upon heavily; a convenient starting point, by reason of its comprehensiveness, for almost all new research in the subject; and a mine of quotable passages and debatable issues for lecturers seeking to hold their audiences in non-mandatory courses.

3.2 FACTORS CONTRIBUTING TO A REVIVAL IN THE HISTORY OF ECONOMIC THOUGHT IN THE MID-TWENTIETH CENTURY

By the 1940s most economics graduates had been able to complete their basic training without needing to give any serious thought to theories not endorsed by the contemporary orthodoxy, while ambitious young teachers and researchers could find more promising ways of advancing their careers than by publishing articles on yesterday's economists. The 1950s, however, saw the beginnings of the modern era in the history of economics, an era in which the *general* interest and significance of original research in this field developed on an unprecedented scale. A new, less blinkered, generation of historians of economic thought was researching in what Stigler (1965) referred to as 'the last unsubsidized area in economics' – with a broader range of problems on their agenda and an expanding professional readership in their sights. Evidence of a widening of horizons in the English-speaking world, for example, showed up in the translation and publication of writings critical of current orthodoxy, such as Myrdal's *Political Element in the Development of Economic Theory* (Myrdal 1953), originally published in Swedish in 1929.[5] Also significant, although still of interest mainly to specialists in the history of Marxian economic thought, was the translation and publication in 1951[6] of selections from Marx's three-volume *Theories of Surplus Value*, first published posthumously in German in 1905–10.

The revival that slowly began to gather momentum in the 1950s was by no means a narrowly antiquarian research programme. Nor was it a reversion to what Coats once described as 'the proclivity to ancestor worship which was once an occupational disease among economists'.[7] It was a mounting stream of research output that, by the 1980s, had generated essential reading lists for students of advanced economic theory, a worthwhile set of clues to researchable projects for able Ph.D. candidates, a convenient analytical framework for doctrinal debates and a variety of intellectual problems to intrigue economic theorists, methodologists or historians of ideas. Before discussing some of the new approaches to the history of economic ideas that have characterized the period since about 1950, however, it is worth noticing certain related changes in the intellectual context which have affected the problem situation for this area.

Apart from the cumulative, and far from negligible, consequences of a steady trickle of high-quality research articles or monographs, there were two other factors – one internal and the other external to the discipline – that helped to arouse and sustain a more general interest in the history of economic thought. The first was the appearance of a significant stream of new definitive scholarly editions of world-famous economic classics and compilations of hitherto unpublished writings and correspondence relating to distinguished past economists. Amongst the most influential stimulants of new research and lively debate, for example, was the ten-volume edition of Ricardo's *Works and Correspondence* edited by Sraffa and Dobb (1951–73). After two decades of gestation the first two volumes emerged in 1951. Volume I contained the first variorum edition of Ricardo's *Principles*, plus a path-breaking introduction by the editors, and Volume II contained the text of Malthus's *Principles* embellished with Ricardo's own notes on it. This rich treasury of primary and secondary material was made accessible to all comers by the publication in 1966 of an index covering the ten volumes. The 29-volume edition of J. M. Keynes' *Collected Writings*, which began to come off the press in 1971 and was completed in 1989, has been even more effective in spawning controversies of immediate interest to economists generally. Other major enterprises of the same kind were the University of Toronto edition of J. S. Mill's *Collected Works*, which began to appear in the 1960s, and the University of Glasgow bicentenary edition of Adam Smith's complete writings, launched appropriately in 1976 with fine new editions of his *Wealth of Nations* and *Theory of Moral Sentiments* (Smith 1976a, b). But these are merely outstanding examples – impressive in scale as well as in quality and general interest. There were other new translations, annotated editions and compilations, too numerous to list in full, relating to such well-known economists as McCulloch, Walras, Jevons and

Marshall, as well as to certain individuals of more specialist interest, such as O'Brien's three-volume edition of the Overstone letters (O'Brien 1971).[8]

Publications such as these have made accessible to non-specialists a mass of primary material, often underpinned by editorial introductions, notes and commentaries that embody in-depth original research focused on key writers and their intellectual or historical connections. They could not fail to elicit interesting reviews and controversial reactions in learned journals with a broad professional readership. Indeed, by greatly reducing the research costs of entry into the debates, they encouraged a wide range of economists to intervene and to make useful contributions to the history of economic thought on a one-off or occasional basis.

The external factor which had a notable impact in the post-war decades on both the questions addressed by historians of economic thought and the interest for non-specialists of their answers was an upsurge of research and controversy on the history, sociology and philosophy of the sciences generally. Economists' general awareness of these new intellectual currents can be traced from the early 1960s when Kuhn's *Structure of Scientific Revolutions* became a best seller.[9] This book raised a variety of issues that seemed relevant to the social sciences in general and economics in particular. It was here that Kuhn – already well known as the author of a scholarly monograph on the Copernican Revolution – expounded his general theory on the way that scientific disciplines develop, progress and change through time. What gave his theory special significance, for both 'hard' and 'soft' scientists, was its rejection of the traditional assumption that progress in scientific knowledge is the result of a systematic cumulative objective process of research. The pivotal concept in Kuhn's theory was the notion of a paradigm, i.e. the idea of an articulated framework of assumptions, theories, analytical techniques and problems requiring solution which together constitute the common heritage of the practitioners of a given discipline. Although there was much semantic and philosophical debate about the precise meaning of the term, the idea was not in itself novel.[10] What was new and debatable was Kuhn's argument that only minor advances in scientific knowledge take place within the ruling paradigm of a science or discipline and that major advances are always the result of paradigm switches (for example, from a Copernican to a Newtonian to an Einsteinian world view) which are essentially irrational leaps in the dark.[11]

Kuhn's theory raised methodological and historiographical issues of at least as much interest to social scientists as to natural scientists. Scholars who believed in rational positive value-free canons of scientific progress were repelled by the implication that there were no *objective* criteria (separable from the changeable world views of practising scientists) on which to evaluate the advance of knowledge. Historians of economic analysis following in Schumpeter's footsteps, for example, preferred to adopt the alternative approach developed by Lakatos a few years later.[12] For Lakatos and his followers the history of science was envisaged as a history of competing or successive research programmes, each originally inspired by a major general theory which was sufficiently novel and impressive in its explanatory powers to stimulate a coherent and continuing set of enquiries designed to test, extend and articulate its implications or to eliminate its anomalies. In principle, the Lakatosian scenario provided the historian with rules to distinguish between research programmes that are either progressive (i.e. capable of predicting novel facts not deducible from rival research programmes) or degenerating (i.e. failing to grapple convincingly with problems that the current scientific community regards as important). On the other hand, historians of economic thought who are concerned to explain the evolving scientific beliefs and arguments of identifiable intellectual communities have been less outraged by Kuhn's invocation of sociological or ideological factors in the process of theory change, although they may well find his scenario too simplistic for their purposes.

There is of course more than one potentially fruitful approach to analysing the evolution of economic ideas, if only because different researchers have different questions in mind. What is interesting in the present context is not the methodological implications of Kuhnian, Lakatosian or other approaches. It is the fact that these debates on the history and philosophy of science inspired a stream of new research efforts designed to test hypotheses concerning the reasons for and nature of changes in the scientific structure of economic thought in past periods, and in particular to explore the character and ideological or historical context of the so-called revolutions or paradigm variations that are generally supposed to have taken place.[13] Nor were the debates on the philosophy of science the only external source of new questions for historians of economic thought to answer. Stigler, for example, was inspired by Merton's *Sociology of Science* (1973) to examine instances of multiple discoveries in economics in order to test the latter's intriguing hypothesis that 'all scientific discoveries are in principle multiples, including those that on the surface appear to be singletons'.[14]

3.3 NEW APPROACHES TO THE HISTORY OF ECONOMIC THOUGHT SINCE THE EARLY 1950s

It is convenient to begin a review of the new perspectives opened up in the post-war era by reference to Schumpeter's *History of Economic Analysis* (Schumpeter 1954b), for that more than any other single work gave professional economists a new view of the role of the history of economic thought in modern economics. Schumpeter himself presented his *magnum opus* as 'the history of the intellectual efforts that men have made in order to understand economic phenomena or, which comes to the same thing, the history of the analytic or scientific component of economic thought' (Schumpeter 1954b: 3). Written as it was by an original thinker with a brilliant international reputation, wide intellectual interests and a long, varied, academic and practical experience of economic affairs, it could hardly fail to attract the attention of the economics profession at large, despite its daunting size and encyclopaedic coverage.[15] What distinguished it from all previous histories of economic thought (apart from its comprehensive erudition) was first that it was a deliberate attempt to treat the history of economics as analogous to that of any hard science by focusing on economic analysis rather than on political economy or economic thought,[16] and second that the story was told with the uniquely Schumpeterian style, imagination and irreverently controversial evaluations of past heroes and their theoretical achievements and limitations.

Schumpeter's introduction summarized his personal vision of the role of the history of science (*any* science) by identifying four ways in which a modern scientist can gain by studying the history of his discipline.

1 Pedagogical benefits: for example, 'the state of any science at any given time implies its past history and cannot be satisfactorily conveyed without making this implicit history explicit' (Schumpeter 1954b: 4).
2 New ideas: for example, 'we learn to understand why we are as far as we actually are, and also why we are not further. And we learn *what succeeds and how and why*' (Schumpeter 1954b: 5, original emphasis).
3 Insights into patterns of reasoning: for example, 'even the most reticent scientists are bound to reveal their mental processes because scientific – unlike political – performance is self-revelatory by nature' (Schumpeter 1954b: 5).
4 An understanding of the evolution of scientific ideas.

It was this fourth source of gain, i.e. coming to grips with 'the process by which men's efforts to understand economic phenomena produce, improve, and pull down analytic structures in unending sequence' (Schumpeter 1954b: 6), which Schumpeter said was his main purpose to describe because of its particular importance for economic science. The special feature of economics that he stressed in this context was not simply that its subject matter is historically conditioned, but also that economists tend to be blinkered by deep doctrinal differences. The obvious remedy he saw for these blind spots was a systematic study of doctrinal history from which the economist who was pre-pared to open his mind to 'stimulating suggestions and useful if disconcerting ideas' could benefit from the work of predecessors working on the other side of the doctrinal barrier.

For the few specialist historians of economic thought who chose to teach and research in what was then (in the booming 1950s and 1960s) one of the least trendy areas of an expanding, increasingly technical and highly professionalized economic science, Schumpeter's *History* represented a timely advertisement and a conspicuous advance for a relatively neglected branch of economic knowledge.[17] It was not exactly the sort of text that could be recommended to the rank and file of undergraduates, but it inspired (and is still inspiring) a stream of worthwhile and enthusiastic followers who shared Schumpeter's belief in the pedagogical and methodological importance of teaching the history of economic analysis to students of modern economic theory. One of the earliest and deservedly most successful textbooks in the Schumpeterian succession was Blaug's *Economic Theory in Retrospect*, first published in 1962 and twice revised (Blaug 1978). It is a particularly interesting example, not only because it was widely read, but also because the revisions well reflect recent developments in the history of economic thought. As Blaug made clear in his original preface, the purpose of his history was to teach contemporary economic theory, to which he added, in the confident spirit of the early 1960s, that 'contemporary theory wears the scars of yesterday's problems now resolved, yesterday's blunders now corrected, and cannot be fully understood except as a legacy handed down from the past'.[18] However, by the time he embarked on his second revision the failure of the economic orthodoxy of the 1950s and 1960s to resolve the analytical problems of the 1970s had revived the interest of even mainstream economists in alternative economic doctrines, and also, predictably, their interest in the history of economic thought. In his third preface Blaug noted the 'signs of such a renaissance in the flood of articles and books that have appeared in the history of economics in the last few years, not to mention the reappearance of history-of-thought courses around the world' (Blaug 1978: xii).[19] The new research programmes that emerged in the history of economic analysis and the history of economic doctrine had by the 1970s induced him to rewrite drastically for the third edition those parts of his text dealing with Ricardian, Keynesian, Marxian and Austrian economics.

New developments in the history of doctrine

In some ways it was Marxian economics which contributed most conspicuously to the post-war research revival in the history of economic doctrine, for there was a remarkable increase in the volume of scholarly (as opposed to purely polemical) articles and monographs published in this area. The pre-war textbooks on the history of economics had treated Marx and his followers as irrelevant to their teleological account of the progress of scientific economics. Few mainstream economists looked long enough at Marx's text to write a formal critique of its economic analysis.[20] By the early 1950s a change in attitudes was apparent. It was symptomatic, for example, that Roll included (for the first time) an explicit assessment of Marx's economics in the 1953 edition of his widely read history of economic thought. Within the next two decades not one but a variety of research programmes and consequential debates were stimulating carefully considered evaluations of Marxian models and were generating a wider understanding of their significance for modern economists.[21] Since then a pervasive shift has occurred in mainstream economists' perception of Marx as an economic theorist and in their readiness to give credence to the research results of historians of ideas with a strong Marxist element in their teleological bias. The systematic exchange of ideas has of course been greatly facilitated by certain non-dogmatic Marxist specialists in the history of economic thought. Meek's *Studies in the Labour Theory of Value* (1956), for example, was designed to build a bridge between Marxian economists and their non-Marxist colleagues by explaining the Marxist rationale and demonstrating its applicability to actual socialist or capitalist economies.[22]

By the 1970s it was common for mainstream neoclassical economists to refer to Marx, whom the President of the American Economic Association had categorized dismissively in 1961 as 'a minor post-Ricardian', as 'a great classical economist' (see Samuelson 1962; Blaug 1978). This was a significant change of tune because the revival of interest in Marxian economics was closely associated with a contemporaneous revival of interest in Ricardian economics. The latter can be dated from the publication of Ricardo's *Works and Correspondence* edited by Sraffa and Dobb (1951–73) and especially from the questions raised there concerning the validity of certain generally received interpretations of Ricardo, authenticated by such prestigious authorities as Knight and Schumpeter. Blaug's *Ricardian Economics* (1958) was one of the earliest monographs to respond to the challenge. The link between Ricardian and Marxian doctrine, however, was most forcefully brought out in later writings by the editors themselves. Sraffa's *Production of Commodities by Means of Commodities: Prelude to a Critique of Economic Theory* (1960) was the surprising spark that ignited a hectic widely read set of doctrinal debates which spread through the learned journals of the discipline – surprising because Sraffa's slim volume was an uncompromisingly abstract piece of analysis focused on a theoretical problem that had dropped out of the economists' agenda for more than a century. In the event, Sraffa's solution to the problem that had baffled Ricardo – how to conceptualize a measure of value that is invariant to changes in either the wage rate or the profit rate – provided an analytical framework more consistent with a Marxian approach to the theory of value and distribution than with a neoclassical approach.

It was Dobb who brought out the implications for doctrinal history of Sraffa's 'prelude to a critique of [neoclassical] political economy'. Dobb's *Theories of Value and Distribution since Adam Smith* (1973) offered a new teleological direction for the evolution of scientific economics. The argument hinged on his discussion of 'two quite distinct and rival traditions in nineteenth-century economic thought as to the order and mode of determination of phenomena of exchange and distribution', tracing both back to Adam Smith (Dobb 1973: 112). One tradition, starting from Smith's cost of production theory of natural prices (an adding-up theory of value), goes through Senior, Mill, Jevons, Marshall and Walras to modern neoclassical general equilibrium theorists such as Samuelson, Arrow and Debreu; the other, starting from Smith's vision of the interdependence of the prices of final goods on the one hand and the class incomes which make up their cost of production on the other, goes through Ricardo, Marx and Sraffa to the neo-Marxists and neo-Ricardians of the mid-twentieth century. The idea of two traditions in economic thought was familiar enough in neoclassically oriented histories of economics, which of course spelt out the 'correct' vision as one in which the theory of distribution was a corollary to the theory of prices (of *all* goods and services) in long-term competitive equilibrium.[23] Dobb's monograph was the first to bring into sharp comparative focus the alternative vision of the economic system, illuminating the Ricardian–Marxist theory of value, which saw distribution as determined by class conflict and logically prior to pricing, value as dependent on the quantity of labour embodied in production and rises in real wages associated with a fall in real profits. According to Dobb, the crucial factor determining economists' choices between these two classical perspectives, each with its distinctive package of assumptions, concepts and theories, was ideology.[24]

The doctrinal debates unleashed by what is sometimes referred to as the 'Sraffa revolution' have ranged over a wide spectrum of issues of both detail and broad principle. Despite the ideological myopia that has muddied the message of many scholarly contributions to what is still an ongoing controversy, the various new interpretations of what Ricardo really meant, or how far he continued the Smithian tradition, or what was the nature of his legacy to modern economic theory, have appreciably extended the profession's critical grasp of alternative systems of political economy as well as of Ricardo's own system of ideas. It is not obvious that historians of economic thought have arrived at a greater degree of consensus on these questions, for the number of new fundamental questions raised by the debates has increased, as have the answers to some of the old questions. In the early 1950s, for example, the view that Ricardian economics represented a 'detour' from the orthodox tradition of economic theorizing was widely prevalent. Schumpeter insisted on it obsessively and repetitively in relation not only to Ricardo's distribution theory but also to his monetary theory.[25] The neo-Marxist and neo-Ricardian heirs of Sraffa generally agreed that Ricardo had stepped out of the line of the tradition running from Smith to twentieth-century classical orthodoxy, but they of course saw the marginal revolution taking the wrong turning.[26] However, against these diametrically opposed views of Ricardo's place in the lineage of today's mainstream economic analysis there was always a third perspective, which stressed the fundamental continuity of the evolution of economic ideas and downgraded both the idea of a Ricardian detour and that of a marginal revolution.

Hollander's series of monographs on the economics of the three leading English classical economists – Smith, Ricardo and Mill – documented the third view in formidable exegetical detail (Hollander 1973, 1979, 1986). In so doing he systematically disputed the currently received wisdom on what constituted the essence of the system of economic ideas proposed by each of his subjects. The thesis running through his three monographs, and repeated in a general text on classical economics (1987), was that each of these writers was concerned to a significant extent with the question of resource allocation that is central to neoclassical economics. The argument was that historians of economic thought have frequently obscured the fundamental continuity of classical and neoclassical ideas by focusing shortsightedly on relatively minor differences between Smith's and Ricardo's system of ideas on the one hand and Ricardo's and Mill's on the other.[27] In thus 'rehabilitating' Ricardo, Hollander explicitly endorsed 'the position adopted by Alfred Marshall who insisted that he himself wrote in the Ricardian tradition and objected to the strictures against Ricardo (and J. S. Mill) by Jevons and others' (Hollander 1986: 245). Much of the debate on these matters has revolved around ideologically inspired differences of emphasis, and the important feature of Hollander's weighty volumes is neither the detailed exegesis he employs to buttress his arguments, nor his rehabilitation of Ricardo as part of the classical–neoclassical lineage. Selective scriptural quotations cannot bridge points of view that are essentially ideological; nor is the popular sport of establishing pedigrees for today's rival schools of thought the most effective way of advancing scientific understanding of 'the process by which men's efforts to understand economic phenomena produce, improve, and pull down analytic structures in an unending sequence' (Schumpeter 1954b). What is significant about Hollander's wide-ranging attack on the received wisdom of the textbooks concerning the substance of nineteenth-century classical economics is the massive scholarship that he brings to bear on his analysis and the challenge that he poses for today's active researchers in the history of economics to test its conclusions systematically and in detail (see, for example, Peach (1984) for a response to this kind of challenge).

Nevertheless in many of the scholarly interventions in the doctrinal controversies that have certainly helped to encourage systematic research in the history of economic thought during the post-war decades, there has been a perceptible note of anxiety concerning the validity of deriving new interpretations of the classics by imposing on them a modern teleological grid. It surfaced, for example, when Collard (1973) complained of the 'stylized doctrinal history' that permeated much of the so-called 'two Cambridges debate' on capital theory. Or again, Peach (1986) deplored the excessive preoccuption of modern historians of economic thought with discovering rigorously consistent models in the writings of past theorists. In particular, for example, he criticized the 'new view' of Ricardo offered in a famous article by Hicks and Hollander (1977) for having 'constructively reinterpreted' their subject by setting up a Ricardian model 'which surpasses the earlier one in two ways, formal generality and misrepresentation'.[28] A similar concern was expressed more recently by Blaug (1985) in a paper written for a conference on the legacy of Ricardo: 'There is a real difference, I believe, between making out what Ricardo meant, or could have meant, and making out what he must have meant if he were truly rigorous, rigour being judged by the standards of modern economics.'

Historical approaches to the history of economics

Not surprisingly, perhaps, there has been a mounting reaction amongst specialist historians of economic thought against interpreting yesterday's economic analyses in terms of a modern analytical framework (with or without ideological overtones) on the grounds that it tends to detach the writings of past economists from their own operational context and to distort the message they intended to convey to their contemporaries – providing indeed a breeding ground for myths. True, mid-twentieth century writers usually insist that they propose to take full account of the historical and intellectual context in which past theories have been formulated before assessing their longer-term significance for the evolution of economic ideas.[29] However, there are many ways of painting in the background to a scenario which has already taken shape in the author's mind. There are also marked differences of approach to a research problem in the history of economics – differences that hinge on the point of view from which the investigator starts as well as on the point at which he expects to finish. A respect for historiographic criteria, for example, and a determination to arrive at a realistic account of the objectives and meaning of past economic analyses and their connections with external events or sociopolitical circumstances that affected or were affected by them do not ensure that the results will be empirically unambiguous.

The new horizons recently opened up by researchers whose methodology is informed by historiographic (rather than teleological, doctrinal or ideological) criteria have been the more varied because not all of them are themselves professional economists. Indeed, some proceed in directions which economists might find outlandish. Tribe (1977), for example, who set out to identify and analyse real historical unities of economic discourse in the seventeenth and eighteenth centuries, suggests that 'a thorough knowledge of contemporary economic theory is a great handicap to any prospective historian' of economic ideas. Reacting against the tradition that the history of economic analysis must be rewritten by each generation,[30] he insists that it is anachronistic to judge past economic texts on the basis of criteria formed by later discourses. His own *Land, Labour and Economic Discourse* (1978) is both a methodological critique of existing histories of economic thought and an enquiry into the intellectual conditions under which nineteenth-century political economy came into existence. He uses seventeenth-, eighteenth- and early nineteenth-century texts, for example, to document his argument that basic economic categories such as land and labour carry different meanings and have a different analytical function in pre-nineteenth-century writings, and also that eighteenth-century 'political oeconomy' (so called to distinguish it from nineteenth-century political economy) was focused on the household management of a polity rather than on an economy in the modern apolitical sense. The most heretical implication of this thesis is that the conventional 'canonization' of Adam Smith as the founder of modern economics is misconceived and that classical political economy (the first discourse to focus clearly on a capitalist economic system) did not come into existence before the second decade of the nineteenth century. In effect, Tribe's archaeological (rather than historical) approach,[31] focused on the evidence of the 'economic archive' rather than on the message of particular economic classics or individual theorists, challenges fundamentally the evolutionary role that economists have traditionally assigned to the history of their discipline and the heroic mould in which they have cast their past masters.

Such root and branch critiques of all existing histories of economic thought, however, are rather hard for the profession to swallow. There have been other better known, and hence more influential, attempts to restore respect for the original text and to check the drift towards myth so often associated with a retrospective approach to past economic ideas. At the other extreme from Tribe's austere deliberately depersonalized approach to his textual sources was Leijonhufvud's best-selling *Keynesian Economics and the Economics of Keynes* (1968). This dealt with history so recent as to be readily acceptable into an extended present by reinterpreting the message of a particular economic classic that was popularly credited (inside and outside the profession) with having launched the most recent and most radical revolution in economic theory. Moreover, it was published at a time when the new orthodoxy generated by the Keynesian revolution was being questioned by applied economists as well as by leading theorists and was losing its magic for politicians. In short, Leijonhufvud's critique of the current wisdom concerning what Keynes intended to convey in the *General Theory* (and what his successors subsequently made of it) brought the history of thought directly into the service of a modern theoretical debate.

The avowed primary objective of Leijonhufvud's study was 'to contribute towards a reappraisal of the conceptual framework which has crystallized out of the *General Theory*' (Leijonhufvud 1968: 6), and its explicit main thesis was 'that Keynes' theory is quite distinct from the "Keynesian" income-expenditure theory' (Leijonhufvud 1968: 8). He made it plain that his exegetical concern with 'what Keynes really said' was strictly secondary to his main purpose. However, two decades later, it is arguable that it was Leijonhufvud's demolition of certain widely accepted myths concerning what was actually there in the *General Theory*, and his carefully documented reinterpretation of what Keynes intended to convey, that represents the lasting legacy of his study – as well as the most memorable feature of its immediate impact on the profession in general. It gave a striking illustration of the extent to which an influential thinker's ideas can be not only diluted but positively falsified by dedicated disciples. For historians of economic thought, who are forever remarking that Ricardian or Marxian or Marshallian economics must not be confused with the economics of Ricardo or Marx or Marshall, this distortion came as no surprise. What *is* on the face of it surprising about the legends that grew up concerning what was in the *General Theory* is the rapidity with which they were accepted (or tacitly received) not only by the textbooks, but also by some of those who had lived through the Keynesian revolution and had good reason to feel that they had been part of it.

The myths[32] have now been exploded (or rehashed) and the textbooks largely amended. However, Leijonhufvud's interpretation of what Keynes meant to say was not so easily absorbed, either by the heirs of the Keynesian revolution or by its revisionists. It soon became obvious in the course of the ensuing debates that various alternative interpretations of Keynes's central message and of the sense in which it represented a revolution in economic theory were already current. Indeed, the number of new interpretations has continued to grow over the past two decades – partly in response to the challenge presented by Leijonhufvud, but much more because of the immensely increased volume of textual evidence that became accessible in the 29 volumes of Keynes's *Collected Writings* (1971–89).[33] The resulting proliferation of books, articles, conferences, seminars and graduate student courses devoted to reappraisals of the economics of Keynes (and of its relation to one or more of the kaleidoscopically shifting varieties of Keynesianism) would be hard to summarize at all concisely. However, since most are related to ongoing theoretical debates on current macroeconomic or monetary theory (rather than to a research programme in the history of economic thought), it is doubtful whether such a summary would have much relevance to this chapter. The lesson that does seem worth drawing here is that there is an unavoidably subjective, or ahistorical, element which vitiates interpretations of yesterday's economic analyses, undertaken with the object of contributing to an understanding of, or a solution to, today's theoretical problems.

There is an expanding area of research in the history of economic thought, however, where historiographical criteria do take precedence over doctrinal or ideological considerations and where the ultimate objective motivating the investigations is empirical rather than theoretical or pedagogical. The results of such enquiries tend to be relatively less controversial than most of those referred to above, but none the less important. Among the new trends characterizing research in the history of economic thought in the second half of the twentieth century, for example, has been a cumulatively substantial stream of projects which aim to bring into sharp focus the actual operational contexts within which specific economic theories, analyses and policy prescriptions have developed and with which they have interacted. Much of this work has been a by-product of broader investigations by specialists in the history of economic thought or by economic historians – both intellectual groups that have been traditionally concerned with processes of diffusion as well as of formalization or filiation of economic ideas. The essays collected, for example, in Eagly's *Events Ideology and Economic Theory* (1968), or the articles and extracts reprinted in Coats's *The Classical Economists and Economic Policy* (1971) illustrate the wide-ranging character and scope of some of the problems that have been considered under this kind of approach. What has given a general impetus and interest to such enquiries, however, has been the professionalization of the discipline and the unprecedented development – particularly after the Second World War – in the role of the academic economist as a policy adviser.[34]

Very many articles and a non-negligible number of monographs which examine – in varying degrees of generality and particularity – the role played by leading past economists who have offered advice to governments, the terms in which they have justified their prescriptions and the extent of their success in influencing policy-makers have now been published. These writings discuss *inter alia* the adequacy of economists' professional tools of analysis for addressing the problems they faced as advisers, the receptiveness of governments or social or political groups to their arguments, the nature and extent of consensus in the discipline on different questions and at different points of time, and the ways in which economists' theories and prescriptions have been influenced by (or have influenced) external currents of ideas and actual events. In 1964, for example, Stigler devoted his presidential address at the annual meeting of the American Economic Association to a discussion of the role of some of yesterday's leading economists who have advised on government policy, and warned his audience that the economist's influence 'has usually been small because he lacked special professional knowledge of the comparative competence of the state and of private enterprise' (Stigler 1983: 30). When he returned to the theme in the 1970s – at a time when professional economists were enjoying a less exalted repute – he insisted that 'The economist is truly and fundamentally important when he is increasing knowledge of the workings of the economic systems' but that, since his discoveries in this area are too specialized and technical to be readily intelligible outside the limited circle of his peers, 'the influence of an economist's work and the popular (non-professional) esteem in which he is held are most likely to be negatively correlated' (Stigler 1983: 67).[35]

One of the earliest and most widely read of the scholarly monographs on the general theme of 'the relationship of changes in the thinking and interests of economists to the methods and aims actually pursued by economic policy-makers' was Winch's *Economics and Policy* (1969). Dealing as it did with the first half of the twentieth century (and mainly with the period since 1920), it filled a gap in the history of economics and economic policies and events for the recent past and was thus of particular interest to undergraduates and non-specialists. It was followed by a variety of more specialized and detailed research monographs, such as the close study by Howson and Winch (1977) of the experience of the Economic Advisory Council in the 1930s, as well as by studies that reached further back into the past. For example, in *British Economic Thought and India*, Barber (1975) examined the effectiveness of the economic theory applied by writers who addressed the economic problems presented by India over the life span of the East India Company. Other historians of economic thought have considered the complex interactions between economic events, theories and policies with reference to shorter time spans and more narrowly defined topics. Berg (1980), for example, focused on the three decades or so following the Napoleonic Wars for her detailed examination of the theoretical and ideological implications of the 'machinery question'. She argued that this was the critical period when contemporaries first became fully aware of the technological changes implicit in the first Industrial Revolution and when classical political economy originated. Despite the apparently narrow problem she chose to investigate, however, her vision of what much of nineteenth-century debate was about and her 'analysis of the many different levels – political, social and intellectual – at which political economy was made and articulated' (Berg 1980: 8) had the effect of significantly broadening the perspectives opened up by her enquiry.

A widening of research horizons for scholars committed to a historiographical approach to the history of ideas has been a distinctive characteristic of much of the new work in the history of economic thought published over the past quarter of a century. To some extent it reflects the shift in the role of many professional economists towards more direct participation in the policy-making process that took place during and after the Second World War. More important, perhaps, than the global expansion in the number of economists employed as professionals in full-time government service has been the increase in the proportion of leading academic economists who have, at some time in their careers, assumed part-time or temporary responsibilities as economic advisers to leading politicians (in power or in opposition) as well as in the number of trained economists who now occupy political or administrative posts. Significantly, the term 'political economy', which had acquired anti-quarian or doctrinal overtones by the mid-twentieth century (being virtually ousted from orthodox textbooks in favour of ostensibly apolitical terms such as economic analysis or economic science or positive economics), began to come back into use in the 1970s – and not merely among writers seeking to distinguish their brand of discourse from the orthodox tradition. In effect, there have been pervasive changes in economists' perception of their pro-fessional role and of the scope and nature of their discipline.

In these circumstances, questions of the kind raised by Winch (1969), for example, concerning the relations between economic thought and policies were attracting the interest of professionals who had not previously paid much attention to the history of their discipline. When economists generally (and even non-professionals) were being stimulated by the debates on Leijonhufvud (1968) to read the *General Theory* for themselves, everyone could (and a great many did) quote Keynes's famous testimonial to the power of yesterday's economic thought:

> the ideas of economists and political philosophers, both when they are right, and when they are wrong, are more powerful than is commonly understood. Indeed, the world is ruled by little else. Practical men, who believe themselves to be quite exempt from any intellectual influences, are usually the slaves of some defunct economist. Madmen in authority, who hear voices in the air, are distilling their frenzy from some academic scribbler of a few years back.
>
> (Keynes 1936: 383)

When the debates between the monetarists and the Keynesians began to spill out of the learned journals into the financial pages of daily newspapers, every-one wanted to know what had happened to the so-called Keynesian revolution.

Meanwhile, the primary materials, as well as the incentives for fruitful research on twentieth-century experience of the connections between changes in socio-economic events and systems and in the objectives and perceptions of policy-makers on the one hand, and advances in economic knowledge (theoretical or empirical) on the other, have expanded enormously over the past two decades or so. Apart from the material contained in Keynes's *Collected Writings* (Keynes 1971–89) and in the numerous biographies, diaries and memoirs relating to what might be called the Keynesian era, a vast quantity of government records capable of shedding direct light on the interchange of ideas beween economists and policy-makers have become accessible to serious researchers since the mid-1960s.[36] Much of the recent historical research stimulated and facilitated by these developments has focused on such questions as whether or not Keynes was really revolutionary in his economic theory, or how far his economic prescriptions were sound responses to current events, and how and when the makers of economic policy responded to his theories and arguments. The results have been cumulatively impressive, often controversial and highly instructive, not only for historians but also for modern economists concerned with the ways in which economic concepts, theories and analyses have been used, or misused, by 'practical men' in or out of authority. They range, for example, from the monograph on *British Monetary Policy 1924–31* by Moggridge (1972), which dealt with the background to and the consequences of the 1925 return to gold, through a broad stream of articles and monographs debating the extent and timing of the Whitehall revolution in economic policy that might (or might not) be called Keynesian.[37] Nor of course has the historical research programme on economics and economic policies been limited to UK experience. Barber's *From New Era to New Deal* (1985), for example, deals with an American episode by discussing Herbert Hoover's theories of economic policy and the contemporary views of economists over the years 1921–33.

3.4 CONCLUSION

The revival of research in the history of economic thought that characterized the four decades since about 1950 has generated a broad stream of scholarly publications in this area – much of impressively high quality. Considerations of space ruled out even the sketchiest general survey of the range and quality of the results that have become available in English alone, and it is certainly not largely an English phenomenon. I have therefore limited myself to considering those sections of this very long research frontier where it seemed to me that the new perspectives opened up by contrasting approaches have been particularly interesting, not merely for academic specialists in some advanced areas of history or theory, but also for economists or historians generally. The above account aims to be illustrative rather than definitive and makes no attempt to bring into systematic critical review the most distinguished, or most progressive, research results so far achieved, or to identify trends and prospects for future research in the history of economic thought.[38] It represents the selective view of an observer travelling through a varied landscape with her back to a fast-moving engine.

NOTES

1 It ran through several English editions, including a posthumous one in 1915 edited by Richard Ely, with a supplementary chapter by W. A. Scott. According to Koot (1987), it was translated into German, Polish, Russian, Swedish, Czech, Serbian and Dutch.

2 See, for example, Boulding's account of the course he took as an undergraduate at the University of Edinburgh: 'The student first learned what was wrong with Adam Smith and all

the things in which he was wrong and confused, then he went on to learn what was the matter with Ricardo, then what was the matter with Marshall. Many students never learned anything that was right at all, and I think emerged from the course with the impression that economics was a monumental collection of errors' (Boulding 1971: 232).

3 It may be too soon to assess the impact of Morishima's recent incursions into the history of economic thought, but it is hard to believe that the ahistorical problems set by him (and other economists who rewrite the classics in a distinctively modern idiom) can substantively advance the subject. That indeed was not his objective.

4 The 1914 essay also appeared in English for the first time in 1954 (Schumpeter 1954a).

5 According to Hicks, who reviewed the English edition in the *Economic Journal* of December – and bracketed this 'important book' with Robbins's *Nature and Significance of Economic Science* (Robbins 1932) – Myrdal's thesis was widely influential in its German version (see Hicks 1983).

6 A complete and more authoritative translation in three volumes (also published by Lawrence and Wishart) began to appear in 1963 and it is the details for the 1969–72 reprint of that edition that are given in the References.

7 The passage in quotation marks is from Coats (1969: 11) in an article reviewing research priorities in the history of economic thought for the first issue of the *History of Political Economy* – the first specialist journal in the subject. Coats took a fairly gloomy view of the progress thus far achieved in published research. For example:

> in the past far too much effort has been devoted to *Dogmengeschichte*, to the writing of histories of economics for economists, and the task of identifying the sources and tracing the changing interpretations of individual concepts or theories. Moreover, this work has frequently been undertaken either by graduate students seeking a safe thesis topic, established economists in quest of a respectable lineage for their pet ideas, or senior members of the profession hoping to find some diversion in their leisure hours or their retirement.
>
> (Coats 1969: 12)

8 Some of these have already been mentioned (e.g. Marx 1969–72; Myrdal 1953). Others of special interest include the seven-volume edition of W. S. Jevons' *Papers and Correspondence* edited by Black and Konekamp (1971–80). Jaffe's translation of Walras's *Elements* (Walras 1954) and *Correspondence and Related Papers* (Jaffe 1965), and Whitaker's *Early Writings of Alfred Marshall* (Whitaker 1975). Samuel Jones Loyd, Lord Overstone, was an important figure in the nineteenth-century currency debates, and the papers and correspondence published by O'Brien (1971) arose out of a chance discovery made by the editor when he was researching his monograph on McCulloch (O'Brien 1970).

9 Kuhn (1970) was a revised second edition of the original essay and the ideas contained in it were further elaborated in Kuhn (1977), a collection of essays in which the author responded to his critics.

10 See, for example, Popper (1970: 51): 'A scientist engaged in a piece of research in, say physics, can attack his problem straight away. He can go at once to the heart of the matter: that is to the heart of an organized structure. For a structure of scientific doctrines is already in existence: and with it a generally accepted problems situation.'

11 See Kuhn (1970: 150): 'the proponents of different paradigms practice their trade in different worlds. One contains constrained bodies that fall slowly, the others pendulums that repeat their motions over and over again. In one solutions are compounds, in the other mixtures. One is embedded in a flat, the other in a curved matrix of space. Practising in different worlds the two groups of scientists see different things when they look from the same point in the same direction.'

12 See Lakatos and Musgrave (1970) which contains the paper in which Lakatos expounded his views on 'Falsification and the methodology of scientific research programmes'. It is reprinted with other papers on the theme in Lakatos (1978).

13 Much of the new research stimulated by the debates on the history and philosophy of science focused on methodological issues (considered elsewhere in this volume) but the new interpretations generated in the course of such enquiries had a significance beyond the methodological area. Amongst the most interesting work, for example, was that discussed in 1974 at the Napflion Colloquium on Research Programmes in Physics and Economics and

subsequently published in the volume containing papers presented at the economics sessions (Latsis 1976). Another widely read example is Hutchison (1978).

14 Stigler's paper (originally included in a Merton *Festschrift*) is reprinted in Stigler (1982) under the title 'Merton multiples denied and affirmed'. Patinkin (1982) also addressed Merton's multiple discoveries theory in relation to Keynes's *General Theory*.

15 Schumpeter had studied law and economics in Vienna under the leaders of the Austrian School of economists, held full professorships at the universities of Graz and Bonn before taking up the chair he held at Harvard from 1932 to 1950, was president of a Viennese private bank from the early 1920s until it crashed in 1926 and was Austrian Minister of Finance for several months in 1919. He was also in the front rank of economic theorists and economic historians.

16 Schumpeter defined the most general category – economic thought – as 'the opinions of economic matters that prevail at any given time or in any given society' (Schumpeter 1954b: 52).

17 Its timeliness was reinforced by the fact that Schumpeter's vision of the present state of economic science, to which his account of its past history was firmly related, was wholly in tune with that of the neoclassical general equilibrium theorists who were beginning to dominate the orthodox frontier of economic research in the 1950s. See, for example, Schumpeter (1954b: 242) where he attributed to Walras the discovery of the 'fundamental problem' of economic science and 'the Magna Carta of economic theory'. See also Samuelson (1962), who endorsed Schumpeter's conviction that Walras was the greatest of all economists in the following terms: 'Today there can be little doubt that most of the literary and mathematical economic theory appearing in our professional journals is more an offspring of Walras than of anyone else (and I stress the adjective *literary*).'

18 All three prefaces are reprinted in Blaug (1978): 'This book is a study of the logical coherence and explanatory value of what has come to be known as orthodox economic theory' (Blaug 1978: vii).

19 See also (p. xii) 'What has been revived, however, is not quite the good old history of economic thought that we knew fifteen or twenty years ago'.

20 One of the earliest was Robinson's *Essays on Marxian Economics* (1942).

21 The seven pages of 'notes on further reading' that Blaug appended to his new chapter on Marxian economics provides a useful overview of the character and range of this literature.

22 See also Meek's *The Economics of Physiocracy* (1962) and *Economics and Ideology* (1967), both again informed by a Marxist perspective.

23 See, for example, Knight (1956: 42): 'What is called "distribution theory" has to do with the pricing of productive services. These prices are significant in connection with the division of this product, but their prior and even more fundamental function is the dual one of apportioning productive capacity in the various forms among industries and among financial and productive units within industry.'

24 Note the subtitle to Dobb (1973), i.e. 'Ideology and economic theory'. See also Bronfenbrenner (1974: 482): 'Unlike Karl Marx, Dobb includes under "ideology" those positions which he likes as well as those which he does not, so the term has approximately the same meaning as Professor Myrdal's "political economy".'

25 See, for example, Schumpeter (1954b: 704, footnote) where he asserts as a *fact* 'that in matters of monetary as of general theory, Ricardian teaching is a detour and that it slowed up the advance of analysis'. Compare with Jevons's (1879) reference (in the preface to the second edition of his *Theory of Political Economy*) to 'that able but wrongheaded man David Ricardo [who] shunted the car of Economic science to a wrong line'.

26 In this they followed Marx, who saw Ricardo as 'the last of the scientific economists'.

27 See, for example, Hollander (1986: 167): 'The common notion that the Smithian form of Mill's *Principles* itself implies a breakaway from Ricardian theory is an error which has a counterpart in the belief that Smith, merely by dint of his broad concern for the application and social arrangement, falls *ipso facto* into a different analytical "school" from Ricardo. In both instances the misunderstanding flows from a neglect of the intended audience – the fact that unlike Smith and Mill, Ricardo was addressing professionals.'

28 Peach (1986: 124–5), in a paper on Ricardo's treatment of wages originally read to the 1985 Meeting of the British Association for the Advancement of Science. In the same paper Peach

points to 'the danger of a teleological "grid-reading" which conveniently "proves" a thesis by selective emphasis'.

29 See, for example, Hollander (1973: 17): 'It is our view that it is impossible to understand the underlying intention of the *Wealth of Nations* without ascertaining not only the nature of the British economy of Smith's day but equally or even more important, Smith's vision thereof'. See also the preface to Bowley's *Studies in the History of Economic Theory before 1870* (1973: viii) where, after stating that she was attempting 'to look at the treatment of various problems by a number of writings in their own analytical setting rather than from the point of view of modern economic theory', she commented frankly: 'The results of adopting this approach has surprised me and I am convinced that its neglect led me to misinterpret certain aspects of the theory of value and wages in my *Nassau Senior and Classical Economics.*'

30 Compare Blaug (1978: vii): 'There is a mutual interaction between past and present economic thinking for, whether we set it down in so many words or not, the history of economic thought is being re-written every generation.'

31 See, for example, Tribe (1978: 159): 'While this book deals with archaic discursive formations, it cannot be said that it is historical, for the chronological foundation and the teleological construction typical of the history of economics does not form the organizational basis of the text'.

32 For example, that Keynes rested his argument on the 'liquidity trap' or on the assumption that wages are inflexible in a downward direction or that saving and investment are both interest elastic.

33 Volume XXX, which appeared in 1989, contains the bibliography and index.

34 A special edition of the *History of Political Economy* (Coats 1981) was devoted to articles describing, for a sample of developed and underdeveloped countries, their experience of the increased role of economists in government since the Second World War, an event which Coats (1981: 342) identified as 'a watershed both in official economic and social policy and in the development of economics as an academic discipline and as a policy science'.

35 See also Jaffé (1975), where Léon Walras's lack of success as an economic adviser is discussed.

36 For example, until 1966 access to UK public records was denied to researchers until fifty years had elapsed from the date of the last paper in the file or bundle in which it was stored. The fifty year rule, first breached in 1966 to open up for scholars the official records covering the period of the First World War and its aftermath, was replaced in 1967 by a thirty year rule.

37 See, for example, Peden (1983), Booth (1986), Browning (1986), Corry (1986) and Rollings (1988) for a selection of the scholarly contributions to this ongoing research programme.

38 On recent past trends see, for example, the articles celebrating the first decade of the *History of Political Economy* which were published in that journal in 1983, especially those by Coats (1983) and de Marchi and Lodewyks (1983) in which developments in the journal literature in the period since 1968 are discussed.

REFERENCES

Ashley, W. J. (1891) 'The rehabilitation of Ricardo', *Economic Journal* 1 (1).

Barber, W. (1975) *British Economic Thought and India 1600–1858: A Study in the History of Development Economics*, Oxford: Oxford University Press.

—— (1985) *From New Era to New Deal: Herbert Hoover, the Economists and American Economic Policy 1921–33*, Cambridge: Cambridge University Press.

Berg, M. (1980) *The Machinery Question and the Making of Political Economy 1815–1848*, Cambridge: Cambridge University Press.

Black, R. D. C. and Konekamp, R. (eds) (1971–80) *Papers and Correspondence of William Stanley Jevons*, vols I–VII, London: Macmillan.

Blaug, M. (1958) *Ricardian Economics*, New Haven, CT: Yale University Press.

—— (1978) *Economic Theory in Retrospect*, 3rd edn, Cambridge: Cambridge University Press.

—— (1985) 'What Ricardo said and what Ricardo meant', in G. A. Caravale (ed.) *The Legacy of Ricardo*, Oxford: Basil Blackwell.

Bronfenbrenner, M. (1974) 'Review of Dobb's *Theories of Value and Distribution since Adam Smith*', *History of Political Economy* 6 (4): 481–6.

Boulding, K. E. (1971) 'After Samuelson who needs Adam Smith?', *Journal of the History of Political Economy* 3.

Booth, A. (1986) 'Simple Keynesianism and Whitehall 1936–47, *Economy and Society* 15 (1).

Bowley, M. (1937) *Nassau Senior and Classical Economics*, London: Allen & Unwin.

—— (1973) *Studies in the History of Economic Theory before 1970*, London: Macmillan.

Browning, P. (1986) *The Treasury and Economic Policy 1964–85*, London: Longmans.

Coats, A. W. (1969) 'Research priorities in the history of economics', *History of Political Economy* 1 (1).

—— (ed.) (1971) *The Classical Economists and Economic Policy*, London: Methuen.

—— (ed.) (1981) 'Economists in government', *History of Political Economy* 13 (3).

—— (1983) 'The first decade of *HOPE* (1968–79)', *History of Political Economy* 15 (3).

Collard, D. (1973) 'Léon Walras and the Cambridge caricature', *Economic Journal* 83.

Corry, B. (1986) 'Keynes's economics: a revolution in economic theory or economic policy?', in R. D. Collison Black (ed.) *Ideas in Economics*, London: Macmillan.

Dobb, M. H. (1973) *Theories of Value and Distribution since Adam Smith: Ideology and Economic Theory*, Cambridge: Cambridge University Press.

Eagly, R. V. (ed.) (1968) *Events, Ideology and Economic Theory*, Detroit, MI: Wayne University Press.

Gide, P. H. C. and Rist, C. (1909) *Histoire des doctrines économiques depuis les physiocrates jusqu'à nos jours*, Paris; *History of Economic Doctrines*, transl. R. Richards, London: Harrap.

Gray, A. (1931) *The Development of Economic Doctrine: an Introductory Survey*, London: Longmans, Green.

Hicks, J. R. (1983) *Classics and Moderns, Collected Essays*, vol. III, Oxford: Oxford University Press.

Hicks, J. and Hollander, S. (1977) 'Mr Ricardo and the moderns', *Quarterly Journal of Economics* 91 (2).

Hollander, S. (1973) *The Economics of Adam Smith*, London: Heinemann.

—— (1979) *The Economics of David Ricardo*, Toronto: Toronto University Press.

—— (1986) *The Economics of John Stuart Mill*, 2 vols, Toronto: Toronto University Press.

—— (1987) *Classical Economics*, Oxford: Basil Blackwell.

Howson, S. and Winch, D. (1977) *The Economic Advisory Council 1930–39: A Study of Economic Advice during Depression and Recovery*, Cambridge: Cambridge University Press.

Hutchison, T. W. (1978) *On Revolutions and Progress in Economic Knowledge*, Cambridge: Cambridge University Press.

Jaffé, W. (ed.) (1965) *Correspondence of Léon Walras and Related Papers*, vols I–III, Amsterdam: North-Holland.

—— (1975) 'Léon Walras: an economic adviser manqué', *Economic Journal* 85.

Jevons, W. S. (1879) *The Theory of Political Economy*, 2nd edn, London: Macmillan.

Keynes, J. M. (1936) *The General Theory of Employment, Interest and Money*, London: Macmillan.

—— (1971–89) *The Collected Writings of John Maynard Keynes*, eds D. Moggridge and E. Johnson, 30 vols, London: Macmillan.

Knight, F. H. (1956) *On the History and Method of Economics*, Chicago, IL: University of Chicago Press.

Koot, G. M. (1987) *English Historical Economics 1870–1926*, Cambridge: Cambridge University Press.

Kuhn, T. S. (1970) *The Structure of Scientific Revolutions*, Chicago, IL: Chicago University Press.

—— (1977) *The Essential Tension: Selected Studies in Scientific Tradition and Change*, Chicago, IL: University of Chicago Press.

Lakatos, I. (1978) *The Methodology of Scientific Research Programmes. Philosophical Papers*, vol. I, Cambridge: Cambridge University Press.

Lakatos, I. and Musgrave, A. (eds) (1970) *Criticism and the Growth of Knowledge*, Cambridge: Cambridge University Press.

Latsis, S. (ed.) (1976) *Method and Appraisal in Economics*, Cambridge: Cambridge University Press.

Leijonhufvud, A. (1968) *On Keynesian Economics and the Economics of Keynes*, New York: Oxford University Press.

McCulloch, J. R. (1845) *The Literature of Political Economy: A Classified Catalogue of Select Publications in the Different Departments of that Science with Historical Critical and Biographical Notices*, reprinted 1938, London: LSE Reprints Series.

de Marchi, N. and Lodewyks, J. (1983) 'HOPE and the journal literature in the history of economic thought', *History of Political Economy* 15 (3).

Marx, K. (1969–72) *Theories of Surplus Value*, 3 vols, London: Lawrence & Wishart.

Meek, R. L. (1956) *Studies in the Labour Theory of Value*, London: Lawrence & Wishart (2nd rev. edn 1973).

—— (1962) *The Economics of Physiocracy*, Cambridge, MA: Harvard University Press.

—— (1967) *Studies in Ideology and Other Essays*, London: Chapman and Hall.

Merton, R. K. (1973) *The Sociology of Science*, Chicago, IL: University of Chicago Press.

Mill, J. S. (1963) *The Collected Works of John Stuart Mill*, London: Toronto University Press and Routledge.

Moggridge, D. (1972) *British Monetary Policy, 1924–31: The Norman Conquest of $4.86*, Cambridge: Cambridge University Press.

Morishima, M. (1973) *Marx's Economics*, Cambridge: Cambridge University Press.

—— (1977) *Walras's Economics*, Cambridge: Cambridge University Press.

—— (1990) *Ricardo's Economics*, Cambridge: Cambridge University Press.

Myrdal, G. (1953) *The Political Element in the Development of Economic Theory*, trans. from German edn (1932) by Paul Streeten (original Swedish edn 1929), London: Routledge & Kegan Paul.

O'Brien, D. P. (1970) *J. R. McCulloch: A Study in Classical Economics*, London: Allen & Unwin.

—— (1971) *The Correspondence of Lord Overstone*, 3 vols, Cambridge: Cambridge University Press.

Patinkin, D. (1982) *Anticipations of the General Theory?*, Oxford: Basil Blackwell.

Peach, T. (1984) 'David Ricardo's early treatment of probability: a new interpretation', *Economic Journal* 94.

—— (1986) 'David Ricardo's treatment of wages', in R. D. Collison Black (ed.) *Ideas in Economics*, London: Macmillan.

Peden, G. C. (1983) 'Sir Richard Hopkins and the "Keynesian revolution" in employment policy, 1929–45', *Economic History Review* 36 (2).

Popper, K. (1970) 'Normal science and its dangers', in I. Lakatos and A. Musgrave (eds) *Criticism and the Growth of Knowledge*, Cambridge: Cambridge University Press.

Robbins, L. (1932) *An Essay on the Nature and Significance of Economic Science*, London: Macmillan.

Robinson, J. (1942) *An Essay on Marxian Economics*, London: Macmillan.

Roll, E. (1938) *A History of Economic Thought*, London: Faber & Faber (rev. edn 1953; new rev. edn 1973).

Rollings, N. (1988) 'British budgetary policy, 1945–54: a "Keynesian revolution"?', *Economic History Review* 41 (2).

Samuelson, P. (1957) 'Wages and interest: a modern dissection of Marxian economic models', *American Economic Review* 47.

—— (1962) 'Economists and the history of ideas', *American Economic Review* 52 (1).

—— (1971) 'Understanding the Marxian notion of exploitation: a summary of the so-called transformation problem between Marxian values and competitive prices', *Journal of Economic Literature* 9.

Schumpeter, J. A. (1954a) *Economic Dogma and Method: An Historical Sketch*, transl. by R. Aris from *Epochen der Dogmen- und Methodengeschichte* (1914), New York: Oxford University Press.

—— (1954b) *History of Economic Analysis*, edited from MS by E. B. Schumpeter, New York: Oxford University Press.

Smith, A. (1976a) *An Inquiry into the Nature and Causes of the Wealth of Nations (1776)*, eds R. H. Campbell, A. S. Skinner and W. A. Todd, Oxford: Oxford University Press.

—— (1976b) *The Theory of Moral Sentiments (1759)*, eds D. D. Raphael and A. L. Macfie, Oxford: Oxford University Press.

Sraffa, P. (1960) *Production of Commodities by Means of Commodities: Prelude to a Critique of Economic Theory*, Cambridge: Cambridge University Press.

Sraffa, P. and Dobb, M H. (1951–73) *The Works and Correspondence of David Ricardo*, 11 vols, Cambridge: Cambridge University Press.

Stigler, G. (1965) *Essays in the History of Economics*, Chicago, IL: University of Chicago Press.

—— (1982) *The Economist as Preacher*, Oxford: Basil Blackwell.

Tribe, K. (1977) 'The "histories" of economic discourse', *Economy and Society* 6 (3).

—— (1978) *Land, Labour and Economic Discourse*, London: Routledge.

Walras, L. (1954) *Elements of Pure Economics*, transl. by W. Jaffé, London: Allen & Unwin.

Whitaker, J. K. (1975) *The Early Economic Writings of Alfred Marshall 1867–1890*, 2 vols, London: Macmillan.

Winch, D. (1969) *Economics and Policy: A Historical Study*, London: Hodder & Stoughton.

4

THEORY AND EMPIRICAL OBSERVATION

DENIS P. O'BRIEN

4.1 INTRODUCTION

The interaction between theory and observation in economics is not a simple matter and it raises a number of complex issues. First, there is a persistent confusion between the 'is' and the 'ought' issues in methodology. The work of Kuhn (1970) and Lakatos (1978), which is of fundamental importance for the history and philosophy of science, has led to a persistent conflation of 'is' and 'ought' questions. The focus here will be on 'ought' questions. Second, there is in the literature of economic methodology what might be called an 'implied scientism'. Sometimes this can involve generalizations about what 'scientists' 'do' by people who themselves (unlike Kuhn and Lakatos) have neither scientific training nor much acquaintance with the literature on methodology written by scientists. But in any case the question of whether natural science, especially physics, is an appropriate model for economics is not one which should be left to emerge by implication, and the matter will be addressed explicitly below.

The focus of this discussion is upon empirical observation. To avoid misunderstanding, however, it is probably best to say at this early stage that theory *must* have primary importance. Data, as will become clear, are only of importance in the matter of *theory choice*. But theory choice is absolutely fundamental if a subject is to make progress rather than to exhibit the sort of self-contained record associated with the history of painting.

If the matter of theory choice does not arise, then the role of data will be much less pronounced. It is important to stress this because there are significant areas of economics, including such crowning achievements as the theory of international trade from Torrens (1815, 1833) and Ricardo (1817) to Meade (1952), which have very little empirical content. But they are not seriously challenged.

None the less, the role of empirical observation is, or should be, of fundamental importance in economics taken as a whole. It enters into theory formulation, theory application and theory choice.

4.2 THE POSSIBLE USES OF DATA

Induction?

There are standard philosophical grounds, dating from David Hume in the eighteenth century, for rejecting the idea that data can be used directly to provide us with reliable information. Simply accumulating facts and then looking vaguely for some pattern in them is not a direct source of information (although it can be a source of hypotheses). Although the observation of a particular conjunction of events may condition us *psychologically* to regard such a conjunction as stable, there is no *logical* basis for expecting the relationship to continue.

In any case, the data are not just 'there' to be modelled. We need the world of concepts and ideas in order to construct data at all. This should be apparent to any economist, for it clearly affects the form in which the official statistics, which are so often the raw material for regression analysis, are collected. Yet economists sometimes do not seem to be conscious of this. On the one hand there are those who believe that it is possible to model time series without recourse to theory at all, making reference to a 'data-generation process'; on the other, there are those who are prepared to use official figures, which have virtually no correspondence with the economic concepts, for testing hypotheses about income distribution based upon the theoretical concepts.

But Hume's general problem has particularly serious implications for economists. It is not just a philosophical fine point which may have dubious relevance in practice. Economics, far more than natural science, is vulnerable to 'parameter shift'. An observed pattern can change markedly in the course of a decade – as, for instance, recent monetary history shows.

Even more treacherous are what appear to be causal relationships apparently obtained by direct inspection of the data. While econometrics formally distinguishes between correlation and causation, econometric procedures subtly confuse the two (Black 1982).

Despite these points, there are amongst economists a number of writers who have resisted the idea that induction is impossible. This group contains writers of considerable standing including R. F. Harrod (1956). But, concluding that 'Harrod has not found the answer to Hume', A. J. Ayer wrote: 'I think that the moral to be drawn is that no theory of this logical type is going to be successful' (Ayer 1970: 37). That is the view of a philosopher; however, Hume's basic position, coupled with Popper's point that the probability of an occurrence and its information content are inversely related (Popper 1959:

270), has proved decisive for most economists – but not all. Nevertheless the reader should beware of references to 'inductive logic' which occur in the literature of economic methodology, for it is clear that there can be no such thing – at least, if induction is understood as it is here.

It is important to make this point because Popper's claim to have 'solved' the problem of induction has been widely misrepresented, particularly in the literature of economic methodology. The problem is that, if we cannot have induction, how can we have knowledge? Popper's solution is to solve not the problem of induction, which is insoluble, but the problem of knowledge by using another route – that of conjectures and refutations (Popper 1959: ch. 1). But if we proceed in this way the sources of the conjectures – our hypotheses – become vital.

The sources of hypotheses

To accept the logic of Hume's criticism of the possibility of induction as a source of knowledge is not necessarily to accept it as a criticism of data patterns as a source of hypotheses. If we take the position that virtually any source for the initial hypothesis is valid, it then follows that hunches formed by inspecting the data are a perfectly legitimate source of hypothesis.

Indeed, it is apparent that in the world of natural science 'pattern recognition' is of considerable importance. This is particularly ironic since it was also once considered important in economics, particularly in industrial economics; but, partly through a mistaken belief that Hume's criticism ruled it out, which arose in the 1960s, economists no longer consider it of any value.

In the formation of hypotheses, intuition also has a vital role. We certainly cannot rely entirely upon pattern recognition as a source of hypotheses. Imagination is of fundamental importance in the generation of hypotheses. But this role for the imagination does seem to be much more fruitful when it is associated with an intense curiosity about the real world and when it interacts with, and is constrained by, data from that world. As the great biologist François Jacob has emphasized, it is the constant interaction between imagination and experiment that produces scientific advance (Jacob 1988: 306).

But if we are to construct hypotheses we need to be able to make some assumptions concerning the world about which we are hypothesizing.

Assumptions

Since the publication of Friedman's influential essay in 1953, and particularly since the early 1960s, economists have tended to regard the realism and accuracy of assumptions as irrelevant. The basis for this is a part of Friedman's argument which has become known by Samuelson's name of the 'F-twist'

(Samuelson 1963). Essentially this amounts to the argument that because assumptions are unrealistic, but that what they neglect is of negligible importance, we can 'therefore' conclude not only that the unrealism of all assumptions is not a matter for concern but even that a theory is better the more unrealistic the assumptions.

As we shall see below, this series of *non sequiturs* derived from an initial confusion about what was meant by the unrealism of assumptions. However, it led to a form of instrumentalism – along the lines of 'we do not know why it works but it does'. While this approach seems to have a sort of engaging pragmatism, instrumentalism is, in the last resort, highly unsatisfactory if we are interested in truth. There is, as Popper has noted, a clear distinction between theories and computation rules, and the latter do not enable us to distinguish between true and false theories on their own (Popper 1974: 111–13). Moreover, we are left without resource when the computation rule breaks down. The position is thus essentially anti-rational. Indeed, to put the matter bluntly, a purely instrumentalist position would be unconcerned by the question of whether stock market prices were the results of individuals taking economic decisions or were produced by little green men from Mars, just as long as a computation rule, relating stock market prices to, for instance, changes in the rate of growth of the money supply, could be obtained.

It is perhaps ironic, since so much of this position is based upon what some economists, especially in the 1960s, believed to be the position in natural science, that the truth of the initial assumptions is not considered irrelevant in physics. Indeed, as one physicist has remarked: 'It is all too easy to derive endless strings of interesting-looking but untrue or irrelevant formulae instead of checking the validity of the initial premises' (Ziman 1978: 14).

Of course it is usual to object at this point that assumptions can never be completely accurate. But there are two points to be made here. First, assumptions are in the nature of a map which is accurate in outline while not reflecting every detail of the terrain described. While we clearly do not include every detail, we equally clearly do not want a map of Central London when we are in Northumberland. Second, it is – or should be, and is in natural science – the case that assumptions pre-package much previously learned information. The assumptions of a theory are necessarily based upon previous work by scientists which has stood up to both theoretical criticism and repeated replication. (Since the latter, as we shall see, is largely absent from economics, this may help to explain why economists have neglected this aspect of scientific procedure.)

Of course a degree of conventionalism is still required here; if we state what is in *ceteris paribus*, and regard the content of *ceteris paribus* as testable (Hutchison 1938), we get into a position of infinite regress (McCarthy 1978). But conventionalism – agreement between scientists about what it is reasonable to accept – has the basis, at least in natural science, that what it is agreed to accept has already been through a testing time of criticism and replication. Since this is so much less true in economics – a difference of kind and not merely of degree – it follows that the conventionalism used is likely to have a much shakier base than in physics and thus it is even more necessary to look at the assumptions which an economist is making.

Of course it is true even in natural science that scientists may *appear* to be neglecting assumptions. As one writer has noted, plant taxonomy is scorned by many modern biologists who prefer to concentrate on the molecular aspects. But 'their research is inevitably parasitic on a whole body of taxonomic knowledge' (Ziman 1978: 46).

Checking the assumptions is even more vital in economics for another reason: if we make statistical inferences from a body of data 'with large and uncontrollable variances' (Ziman 1978: 170), checking the assumptions does at least give us some idea of the possible sources of these variances.

It seems so obvious that the map-like accuracy of assumptions is *not* irrelevant that it is an interesting question how economists got themselves into their present position. The answer to this has been supplied, to some extent, by the philosopher Alan Musgrave (1981), in a dissection of Friedman's original essay. He shows that in the original Friedman paper, 'negligibility', 'domain' and 'heuristic' assumptions were confused. In the first group it is simply assumed that the disregarded factors are unimportant in their effect on the phenomenon under investigation. The assumptions in the second category limit the applicability of a theory to a particular set of circumstances. Those in the third category are made in order to develop a particular line of argument. Musgrave shows that Friedman failed to distinguish between these three categories of assumption and that, by focusing on the first category, he arrived at the F-twist.

In fact, however (as in the case of Central London and Northumberland), the realism of domain assumptions is critical. As Koopmans (1957: 139) pointed out at an early stage, it is necessary that we know to what a theory can be expected to apply.

But this, interestingly enough, leads us back to the concept of 'verification' which was a central concern of economic methodologists in the years before Friedman (Blaug 1980: ch. 3; cf. Robbins 1932), for domain assumptions are critical with regard to both applicability and falsifiablity. Thus we need to verify whether the assumptions which a theory makes are actually met in a case under consideration before we can conclude that the predictions of the theory can be expected to hold. But the problem goes deeper than this, for in order for economic knowledge to have any reliability we need to know the sensitivity of the model to falsity of its assumptions. Again, we necessarily conclude that the assumptions matter.

A standard reason for rejecting testing of a theory by its conclusions is the so-called Duhem–Quine thesis that we never test a single hypothesis but always a cluster of hypotheses and that when a theory fails a test we do not know which hypothesis has been faulted. But if we pay attention to the asumptions we are making we certainly have a better chance of knowing. Moreover, if we test two competing theories, with the same background knowledge for both, we do have some basis on which to make a choice. After all it is not very surprising that it is better not to throw away evidence voluntarily – and evidence about the truth or falsity of our assumptions is still evidence.

Testing

As noted in the previous section, economists nowadays tend to pay scant attention to assumptions. The bulk of their interest now centres upon the results of testing the conclusions of theories against the data. Although the immediate stimulus for this emphasis comes from Friedman, it can be traced back to the work of Popper (1959, 1963) who advanced the following propositions: first, a theory can never be proved but it can always be disproved; second, our scientific knowledge is always conditional and can never be absolute – all theories are permanently at risk of being falsified; third, the testing of hypotheses with the aim of falsification is both the correct way to proceed and, in practice, the way that science works. Popper's work is voluminous, subtle and enormously impressive. But a very simplified version of it, reflecting in part Friedman's absorption of Popper, became the ruling position in economics in the 1960s.

In fact, however, it did not take very long to discover that testing, on its own, was a limited programme. There are a number of standard difficulties, including multicollinearity in the data, the Duhem–Quine problem noted above, and the difficulty of discerning causality by purely statistical means when there is no control available (as is the case in economics), and these have all been rehearsed at length in the last ten years or so. In addition there are problems over what is to be judged to constitute falsification – precisely what degree of disconfirmation constitutes falsification? – and there is thus an important element of conventionalism in what we are prepared to count as evidence. Economists were at first neglectful of these points; indeed, much of the 1960s falsificationism was of an extremely crude kind which not only neglected the problems already mentioned but placed an extraordinary reliance upon published statistics (Coddington 1972: 9).

But the problems have to be recognized. Because of the Duhem–Quine problem there are in economics particular difficulties over *ceteris paribus* in testing theories, especially if investigators adopt the dogmatic position that the truth of assumptions is irrelevant. A particular problem with *ceteris paribus* is that it can be used to immunize a theory from testing, simply by claiming that a falsified theory must have failed because of some changes in initial conditions which were not allowed for – and which are themselves then not tested (McCarthy 1978: 13–14).

Economists should, but typically do not, deal with this problem by using tests in which there is a much greater prior knowledge about the auxiliary assumptions than about the hypothesis to be tested – this would constitute a 'well-constructed test' (McCarthy 1977: 8, citing Yoshida 1975).

Despite these difficulties, there is a strong case for persevering with testing, using well-constructed tests. In fact, although the difficulties are much less in natural science, physicists also face difficulties in testing hypotheses because the fit between theory and observation is far from perfect (Ziman 1978: 39). However, despite this, research workers 'Under the lash of scholarly competition . . . unconsciously act out the Popper principle of falsification, not only in relation to the theories but even against the objective "facts" claimed by their rivals' (Ziman 1978: 59). This is particularly important since it is replication of results outside the particular group which originally produced them which can be decisive in determining acceptance or rejection of a theory.

Reproducibility

In fact, the reproducibility of scientific results is a key issue to which economists have paid relatively little attention. The recent debate over cold nuclear fusion, aside from the entertainment value for non-scientists, has focused the attention of the wider non-scientific world upon this aspect as laboratories throughout the world have attempted to reproduce the results originally claimed by Pons and Fleischman (Garwin 1989).

But in the production of what Ziman has tellingly called 'reliable knowledge' it is reproducibility – testing – which is the key. Thus, when a research worker (Steele) claimed to have secured the inheritance of acquired characteristics in mice the reaction from his fellow biologists was that 'Clearly, the basic result must be repeated in other laboratories' (Taylor 1980; see also Mitchison 1980). Scientific activity involves the selection of those hypotheses that appear in the journals that will actually stand replication – perhaps as little as 10 per cent of the whole (Ziman 1978: 30–1, 40–1, 130, 143).

This issue of the reproducibility of results, second nature to the natural scientists, has been very largely ignored in social science. Perhaps the most dramatic illustration occurred in anthropology when a researcher (Freeman 1983), adopting an explicitly Popperian approach, treated Margaret Mead's account of Samoa as a series of hypotheses to be tested against the data rather than as received truth. To put it mildly, he found that Mead's results were not supported by the available data. But before economists enjoy the *schaden-*

freude too much, we should remember that assiduous avoidance of contact with data through fieldwork is the rule amongst economists – and what is at issue in the Samoa case relates to the results of fieldwork.

An example from the field of social psychology which springs readily to mind is the case of Sir Cyril Burt. Whether or not he fabricated his results on intelligence – and there is undoubtedly a strong body of opinion which believes that he did – it is indeed remarkable that it was not until after his death that a sustained attempt to check these results was made (Hearnshaw 1979).

Unfortunately every practising economist knows of areas where it is very difficult to reproduce the published results (see also Mayer 1980). There are, it is true, some bright spots in economics. The repeated investigations into the effects of mergers, and into the effects of exchange rate fluctuations on trade, have indeed involved replication of results in all sorts of different ways. But these are exceptional areas. Their exceptional nature derives from two main causes affecting most studies: technical econometric problems and data problems. (The possibility of moral hazard in the career structure – ease of publication of 'impressive' although non-reproducible results – will not be explored here.)

Measurement problems

Economists habitually employ regression as the first, and last, resort in dealing with data. Unfortunately the employment of regression techniques on time series data requires an enormous suspension of disbelief, and it now seems clear that this is not a fruitful suspension. We are employing a technique derived from agricultural experiments: in this, even the standard test of linearity requires a distribution of Y values for each X value, whereas in time series we have only one observation on Y for each value of X so that what passes as regression is in fact closer to the correlation analysis of the 1920s which enjoyed a transient vogue amongst economists. The lack of a distribution of Y for each X, and thus the absence of the possibility of repeated sampling, raises questions about significance levels which economists simply ignore. Randomization is a blatantly false assumption (Leamer 1983). The typical end-product of our suspension of disbelief is an estimated equation showing clear symptoms of multicollinearity in which the estimated parameters are, consequently, unstable. (This instability is a separate issue from instability in the basic economic relationships themselves which is also frequently ignored even though there are standard techniques, involving splitting the data, for testing for it.)

Partly because of the availability of standard computer packages, which are in themselves very desirable since they increase reproducibility, poor procedures are adopted, including routinely correcting for serial correlation without checking first for its existence.

In addition, it is well known that a reported regression equation in a published article, ostensibly significant at 5 per cent, may have been obtained after nineteen (unreported) insignificant equations. Indeed, it has been suggested that it would be desirable if all the regressions run could be reported (Mayer 1980). But, as it is, we have the computer, adept at tedious arithmetic, obligingly performing specification search (which of course invalidates the traditional theory of inference (Leamer 1983: 36)) and, worse, the possibility that economists are prone to adjust the theory to the equation which works (Blaug 1980: 257).

There seems to be even more reluctance to accept that data are frequently of poor quality (Wilber and Harrison 1978: 69; Mayer 1980: 169). We have already noted the problem over government statistics; and in fact access to the worksheets from which these statistics were compiled by no means always provides the research worker with confidence. This would be a problem even if it were true that government statistics correspond to economic concepts – which they rarely do.

A common set of 'dirty data' is then subject to different tests by economists. Natural science researchers do not have to trust other people's numbers; reproducing them is indeed critical for the acceptance of a new result. There is thus a fundamental difference between economics and physics or chemistry. Working from a common data set, we can only perform different statistical tests on the same data, and, as Coase is reported to have remarked, if you torture the data long enough they will confess. The answer to data problems is emphatically not just to use a different mathematical technique, which has, in one sense, become a substitute for more basic empirical work. As Mayer (1980: 176–7) has commented: 'The stress on using advanced mathematical tools allows us to have a good conscience while ignoring some very elementary rules of good research procedure'.

The answer, however, is assuredly *not* to give up hope. That way lies irrationalism. It might indeed be a very good idea to cool the love affair with one particular statistical technique – regression – and to be more modest in our demands upon data which, in truth, may only be suitable for tests which assume ordinal ranking. As has been argued by Mayer, improvements in data and (where not published) in its availability to other parties, and an increased emphasis upon the elementary requirement of replicability, would certainly be a start. In addition, economists should be prepared to construct their own data sets, and in a way which would allow their method of construction, as well as the resultant data, to be open for public inspection. Reid (1987) has suggested a series of rules which should be followed in the use of interviews and questionnaires, and acceptance of such rules would be an important first step.

4.3 THEORY CHOICE

Not all economists agree that we need to choose between theories. Rather, they favour 'methodological pluralism' (Caldwell 1982). If we are to treat economics as simply a self-contained art form, with no relevance to the real world, such a position may be defensible. However, if we are concerned with economic truth it is rather less easy to accept. Quite apart from the view (persuasive because it was formed while witnessing the rise of Nazism in Germany) that an 'anything goes' approach to methodology is likely to end up with mob rule or Stalin (Hutchison 1981: 218), there are persuasive scientific reasons for believing that we should have theory choice. Unless we have choice, we have no competition between theories. But if we have no competition between the theories, we can make no pretence of contributing to knowledge or of testing those theories to see whether there is anything of value in them. Moreover, economic policy, which affects the lives of ordinary people in a far more fundamental way than merely paying taxes for the upkeep of economists, is grounded in, and/or claims the support of, theory. Therefore the position will be taken here that we need to make theory choice.

One view is that conventionalism – the implied votes of the academic community – is the basis of theory choice (Tarascio and Caldwell 1979; Caldwell 1982). It is perhaps ironic that this (anti-Popperian) position has been arrived at by applying what is essentially a Popperian approach to the methodology of methodology. For those who end up at conventionalism have looked at the claims for what is supposed to be economic methodology, tested them against the practice of economists and decided that those claims have been falsified (Boland 1982; Caldwell 1982; McCloskey 1983, 1985, 1987). They thus fall back on the proposition that theory choice is governed by whatever economists agree to do. Yet this is ironic because it amounts to accepting that a confrontation between theory and evidence is a valid way of resolving disputes. In any case, we do not *have* to conclude that because economists do not follow their own rules there is no point in the rules and that we should accept what they do instead. Such a position is essentially circular; conventionalism amounts to saying that theory choice is explained by theory choice.

Clearly, we need to go further than this. One attempt to explain conventionalism is in terms of 'rhetoric'. This is such an important subject, however, that it will be considered below in a separate section.

Conventionalism involves fashion. But fashion on its own, without any attempt to decide what determines fashion, is a very bad guide to theory choice. It is also a bad guide to methodology itself. Philosophical positions which one could not possibly *not* believe ten years ago are now rejected as clearly false – so that we have had a succession of logical positivism, logical falsificationism and methodological anarchy. Those with slightly more knowledge of philosophy assure those with slightly less that 'real philosophers have given up positivism'. This argument is of course vulnerable to the charge that, if a once strongly held philosophical position is now considered outmoded, the new one may equally well be wrong.

In their drawings on the literature of the philosophy of science, economists of a conventionalist persuasion may have been misled because writers dealing with natural science *take for granted* that theory selection is on the basis of reliability. Because this is taken for granted it is not always brought out very clearly. But in fact 'scientific knowledge *evolves by critical selection*' (Ziman 1978: 131). Even a philosophy of science which appears to involve significant elements of conventionalism, such as that of Kuhn, has a requirement of reliable knowledge as its background. Despite all the material about paradigms and scientific revolutions, experience and experiment are essential for Kuhn.

This is not to deny the importance of intuition and its role in what has become known as 'methodological tenacity' – clinging to a theory which is in trouble – nor is it in any sense to deny the importance of logic which is vital for communication and consensus. But in natural science the empirical check on what can be accepted is always there.

This is very evident from the work of Lakatos. For Lakatos focuses upon competition between Scientific Research *Programmes* rather than between individual *theories* (an approach which has the advantage of getting away from the Duhem–Quine objection to testing individual theories), and in this competition between research programmes the testing of predictions about novel facts is absolutely central. In natural science, conventionalism arises because theories keep delivering results. It is productive of technology. In economics we cannot even produce the equivalent of turning on a light. Therefore conventionalism in economics needs careful examination as a justification of procedure.

Above all, testing is in natural science, and should be in economics, essential in cases of theory conflict. That a particular confrontation between theory and evidence may not be admitted as decisive by everyone is hardly surprising, given both human nature and methodological tenacity, but that such a refusal should be claimed to be destructive of the need for such confrontation is really very surprising. The precise form of confrontation with the data is a separate issue. All procedures, especially in economics where there is no scientific control, clearly face difficulties. But to claim that because it faces difficulties we give up on it seems to be a form of defeatism leading ultimately only to irrationalism. Of course it is true that one can cite all sorts of reasons why economists may believe that demand curves slope downwards, hardly any of which have reference to data (McCloskey 1987: 174), but this does not affect the basic point that, if there were economists who believed that demand curves slope upwards as a general rule, the empirical evidence would be vital.

Essentially, any subject with claims to truth needs empirical discipline. This is of course true in natural science; a striking example is Wegener's hypothesis of continental drift which was long resisted. It was a crucial piece of empirical evidence – rock magnetism – which resolved the controversy. Otherwise, without such discipline, we are left with a position reminiscent of Benjamin Franklin's characterization of theological disputes: 'one Divine says it is so, another Divine says it is not so'.

Rhetoric

It is the role of rhetoric in economics which has been the subject of McCloskey's highly entertaining writings (McCloskey 1983, 1985, 1987). McCloskey's position is that it is 'the aptness of economic metaphors, the relevance of historical precedents, the persuasiveness of introspections, the power of authority, the charm of symmetry, the claims of morality' (McCloskey 1983: 482) which persuade economists. He is notably entertaining about the role of mathematics as rhetoric, particularly in relation to Samuelson's *Foundations*. This is not an entirely new point; as Viner pointed out Swift, Defoe and Mandeville 'discovered early that a fool can be a bigger fool with the aid of mathematics than without' (Viner 1963: 16).[1] Mathematics as a form of rhetoric is related to the role of authority. The implication is that the mathematical expertise conveys a unique authority for the pronouncements, even where these extend to matters not covered by the mathematics.

It is of course perfectly true that rhetoric is not absent from physics. Since economists have typically borrowed most of their mathematics from natural science – possibly the wrong mathematics as we shall see later – it is perhaps worth observing that mathematics without an empirical check is also capable of leading natural scientists astray. The episode of continental drift has been referred to above. As already indicated, it was finally decided by empirical evidence. But, as Ziman has observed: 'The epistemological irony is that the geologists – supreme experts in the observation and interpretation of visual patterns – rejected first-rate evidence from fossils, rocks and landscapes because they thought it was in conflict with quantitative mathematical reasoning [on the strength of tides] which few of them really understood' (Ziman 1978: 94). However, the empirical evidence *did* ultimately prove decisive.

Without it, the danger is, as this physicist and others have pointed out, 'that enormous efforts can be made towards the displaced goal of solving more and more elaborate mathematical puzzles that have less and less relevance to any conceivable reality' (Ziman 1978: 173; Phelps Brown 1980: 6; Berry, in Wolpert and Richards 1988: 47). As Coddington has observed, without testing 'the development of economic theory may consist to an uncomfortable extent of formulating new questions to which the theories we have provide the answers, rather than creating theories which provide answers to the questions we originally wanted to ask and answer' (Coddington 1975: 541).

Coddington's paper is in fact a devastating dissection of the claims made for the policy relevance of general equilibrium analysis. In the course of his discussion he identifies another rhetorical device – one which has a history which certainly goes back to the Cambridge conflicts of the 1930s. This is the device of taking a theory which does not belong in a particular, e.g. general equilibrium, framework, fitting it into that framework, discarding everything that does not fit the framework and then pronouncing the theory invalid. Rhetorical devices such as these may, none the less, persuade. But ultimately they are deceptive. In the last resort they are of no help in deciding theory conflict – although they may fool people into thinking that they are – and empirical evidence must be crucial.

4.4 PHYSICS AS A MODEL

The influence of natural science, especially physics, upon economics is almost as old as economics. But this involves two problems. First, there is the question of whether physics – by which essentially economists mean nineteenth-century classical physics – is a proper model. Second, there is the question of whether physics, as a whole, is really as economists and methodologists think it is.

It is perfectly clear, for the reasons already indicated – the lack of replication where time series data are concerned and the lack of control – that physics is likely to be, at best, an imperfect model. In fact physicists themselves seem very doubtful about whether their subject provides a good model for economics. This is partly because the logic of empirical statements, as distinct from that of mathematical theory, falls into three categories: 'true', 'false' and 'undecided' (Ziman 1978: 26). The physicist's view here is that 'in the physical sciences, this objection, although a large nail in the coffin of doctrinaire positivism, is not of great practical significance. But when we go beyond biology to the behavioural and social sciences it is devastating' (Ziman 1978: 28).

But in any case the kind of physics which economists take as their model is essentially not modern physics but the physics of Newton. As a theoretical physicist has observed, economists 'have an outmoded paradigm of physics' (Berry, in Wolpert and Richards 1988: 44). This itself involves two issues. First, there is the problem that, since Heisenberg, it is accepted that we cannot simultaneously ascertain both the position and the velocity of a particle so that the objectivity and certainty of classical physics are disturbed. Second, it seems quite likely that the mathematics of smooth continuous twice-differentiable functions is not suitable for many economic problems. The issue of chaos will be examined in the next section, but there is also the question of catastrophe theory. Whether or not this proves, as its advocates claim, to provide an appropriate form of mathematical modelling for oligopoly (Woodcock and Davis 1978: 126–34), there is no doubt that in trying to model multiple outcomes and discontinuous changes it has recognized that economics is not well served by the mathematics of classical physics (see also Weisskopf 1979).

In matters of observation alone, there are very serious problems for economics compared with physics – the difference between disentangling 'noise' and 'signal' in physics and in economics is one of kind, not of degree (see also Ziman 1978: 67–70).

It is possible that economists might have done better to look at medicine as a model (Kornai 1983). While testing, and the pressures for success, are much stronger and more immediate in medicine, the role of observation in medicine has an important part to play in instructing economists. In the development of the cephalosporin group of antibiotics, hypothesis formation followed the development of a hunch which arose when looking at a sewage outfall into the sea (Florey 1955; Abraham 1962). The chance observation which was ultimately to result in penicillin is also well documented (Wilson 1976).

Moreover, medicine also indicates that a degree of instrumentalism does no harm as long as we do not stop there. The action of certain common substances, e.g. aspirin, is still not really understood; the structure of penicillin itself was only broken down some time after the development of the drug, while that of insulin was not discovered until as late as 1969 (Wolpert and Richards 1988: 69). But in all cases the researchers did not rest with instrumentalism.

Thus in the history of medicine there may well be lessons for economics. But it is physics – and classical physics at that – which has, both explicitly and implicitly, been taken as a model by economists. However, fairly recent mathematical developments indicate that this was probably not a very good choice.

Chaos

Chaos is an important mathematical development of which accounts for the non-specialist are gradually becoming available (Cvitanović' 1984; Bai-Lin 1984; Peitgen and Richter 1985; I. Stewart 1989). The basic nature of chaos can be stated as follows:

> The often repeated statement, that given the initial conditions we know what a deterministic system will do far into the future, is false. . . . Given infinitesimally different starting points, we often end up with wildly different outcomes. Even with the simplest conceivable equations of motion, almost any non-linear system will exhibit chaotic behaviour.
>
> (Cvitanović 1984: 3)

A simple deterministic equation of the form $X_{t+1} = F(X_t)$ 'can possess dynamical trajectories which look like some sort of random noise' (May 1976: 466). One of the critical things in chaos is that if the dynamic relation contains non-linear terms this produces fundamental consequences for the behaviour of the whole system. Recognition of the problem goes back to the nineteenth century with the formulation by P. F. Verhulst of a law of population growth containing a growth limitation. The algebraic form which he used for this has found much wider applications in the last twenty years because it turns out to describe certain aspects of turbulent flow.

Scientists themselves are aware of the widespread implications of this: 'Not only in research, but also in the everyday world of politics and economics we would be better off if more people realized that simple nonlinear systems do not necessarily possess simple dynamical properties' (May 1976: 467).

Variations in the non-linearity parameters produce changes in the paths followed by a dynamic system, and *bifurcations* – essentially, multiplication of the paths followed by the system – occur: 'The successive bifurcations take place in smaller and smaller regions of the phase space' (as the value of the non-linear parameters is changed) and ultimately 'practically all memory of the global structure of the original dynamical system is lost' (Cvitanović 1984: 18). As another source puts it: 'Every nonlinear rule leads to branch points, to forkings in the path at which the system may take one branch or another. Decisions are made whose consequences cannot be predicted because each decision has the character of an amplification' (Peitgen and Richter 1985: 61).

But equally important are the tiny differences in initial conditions. Lorenz has coined the term the 'butterfly effect' to indicate the smallness of change in initial conditions in a weather model, produced by the fluttering of a butterfly's wings, which could produce chaos as the system develops: 'A very small imprecision in the initial conditions can grow to an enormous effect in the later motion. Both the expert and the layman are confused to an equal degree by the complexity contained in what were thought to be simple equations' (Peitgen and Richter 1985: 62). Differences in initial conditions can also produce intermittent chaos – a condition which when shown graphically (Cvitanović 1984: 30) looks extraordinarily like the behaviour of some exchange rates. The implications even for classical mechanics are serious since this is no longer fully determinate (Bai-Lin 1984: 13). The implications for both meteorology and economics are absolutely devastating, especially as the problems increase markedly the higher the dimensions of the system.

Mathematicians, notably Mitchel Feigenbaum, have made considerable progress with chaos in recent years, but at low dimensions (Cvitanović 1984: 19, 30). For the moment the critical messages for economists are, it may be suggested, threefold. First, the sort of mathematics which economists have been inclined to think of as being well developed, simple and applicable to economics may well not be appropriate. Second, the fundamental conclusion of chaos theory that assumptions *do* matter is yet another reason for abandoning the pernicious doctrine that assumptions do *not* matter. Third, the implications for a purely falsificationist approach to economics are disastrous. If the bifurcations produce so many possible outcomes it is clearly impossible to rely solely upon falsification, above all in the area of macroeconomics.

4.5 ECONOMICS AS A SCIENCE?

Throughout the history of economics there has been a perpetual methodological tension between an axiomatic approach and an approach constrained by respect for the data. Simple contemplation of the contrast between Ricardo and Smith, or between Marshall and Edgeworth, is enough to illustrate this point. But none of these doubted that they were, at least in some sense, trying to do something scientific. If we are prepared to be modest in our aims, if we are prepared to respect the facts of a situation – as Smith indeed recognized facts as constraining imagination – if we are prepared to confront the results of our theorizing with data and to seek conscientiously to construct data sets, then there seems no reason why economics should not have a utilitarian, as distinct from a purely artistic, role. It seems virtually certain that economics will never become a 'hard science' (cf. Solow 1986), but it does not then follow that we simply give up on the data.

Economics has substantial achievements to its credit. While, as a physicist observed, if we want to learn about love we do not read a sociology handbook but, for instance, Jane Austen (Ziman 1978: 185), we do not turn to Jane Austen if we want to learn about inflation. If we want to learn about consumer choice we do not do so either (although we might have to concede that we would learn more from a book on marketing than from John Green's classic *Consumer Theory* (Green 1971). But we need to build upon this achievement and not to retreat into models which tell us nothing about the real world. One thing that we can certainly learn from physics is the idea that modelling which has no discernible reference to the real world is pure self-indulgence (Berry, in Wolpert and Richards 1988: 47).

Moreover, economists do have considerable influence and this influence should be exercised responsibly. It may well be true that they are prone to overrate their influence. But hubris is certainly not a monopoly of economists and its existence should not lead us to neglect the influence – for good *or ill* – which economists can have. They should thus be prepared to constrain the wilder flights of their imagination by reference not only to the facts which they assume but also, as far as possible, to the facts which they predict. They will never produce anything analogous to physics in this way, but they will at least avoid claiming the authority of their subject for both theories and prescriptions which have no basis whatever in the economic world.

NOTE

1 I am not of course suggesting that Professor Samuelson is a fool.

APPENDIX: SOME KEY REFERENCES

The literature of economic methodology dealing with the relationship of theory and observation is enormous and in recent years it appears to have grown particularly fast. Three classics are J.N. Keynes (1890), Robbins (1932) and Friedman (1953). By far the best modern books, in the opinion of the present writer, are those of I. M. T. Stewart (1979) and Blaug (1980), two complementary volumes which together provide an admirable basis for further reading. The McCloskey references (McCloskey 1983, 1985, 1987) and also Stigler (1977) should be read for enjoyment, and all of T. W. Hutchison's numerous methodological writings yield both enjoyment and illumination.

REFERENCES

Abraham, E. P. (1962) 'The cephalosporins', *Pharmacological Review* 14: 473–500.

Ayer, A. J. (1970) 'Has Harrod answered Hume?', in W. Eltis, M. Scott and J. Wolfe (eds) *Induction, Growth and Trade*, Oxford: Clarendon Press.

Bai-Lin, H. (1984) *Chaos*, Singapore: World Scientific Publishing.

Black, F. (1982) 'The trouble with econometric models', *Financial Analysts Journal* 38: 29–37.

Blaug, M. (1980) *The Methodology of Economics*, Cambridge: Cambridge University Press, reprinted 1982.

Boland, L. (1982) *The Foundations of Economic Knowledge*, London: Allen & Unwin.

Caldwell, B. (1982) *Beyond Positivism*, London: Allen & Unwin.

Coddington, A. (1972) 'Positive economics', *Canadian Journal of Economics* 5: 1–15.

—— (1975) 'The rationale of general equilibrium theory', *Economic Inquiry* 13: 539–58.

Cvitanović, P. (1984) *Universe in Chaos*, Bristol: Adam Hilger.

Florey, H. (1955) 'Antibiotic products of a versatile fungus', *Annals of Internal Medicine* 43: 480–90.

Freeman, D. (1983) *Margaret Mead and Samoa. The Making and Unmaking of an Anthropological Myth*, Cambridge, MA: Harvard University Press.

Friedman, M. (1953) *Essays in Positive Economics*, Chicago, IL: University of Chicago Press.

Garwin, R. L. (1989) 'Consensus on cold fusion is still elusive', *Nature* 338: 616–17.

Green, H. A. (1971) *Consumer Theory*, London: Penguin.

Harrod, R. F. (1956) *Foundations of Inductive Logic*, London: Macmillan.

Hearnshaw, L. S. (1979) *Cyril Burt, Psychologist*, London: Hodder & Stoughton.

Hutchison, T. W. (1938) *The Significance and Basic Postulates of Economic Theory*, New York: A. M. Kelley, reprinted 1965.

—— (1981) *The Politics and Philosophy of Economics*, Oxford: Basil Blackwell.

Jacob, F. (1988) *The Statue Within*, London: Unwin Hyman.

Keynes, J. N. (1890) *The Scope and Method of Political Economy*, London: Macmillan.

Koopmans, T. C. (1957) *Three Essays on the State of Economic Science*, New York: McGraw-Hill.

Kornai, J. (1983) 'The health of nations: reflections on the analogy between medical sciences and economics', *Kyklos* 36: 191–212.

Kuhn, T.S. (1970) *The Structure of Scientific Revolutions*, 2nd edn, Chicago, IL: University of Chicago Press.

Lakatos, I. (1978) *The Methodology of Scientific Research Programmes*, eds J. Worrall and G. Currie, Cambridge: Cambridge University Press.

Leamer, E. (1983) 'Let's take the con out of econometrics', *American Economic Review* 73: 31–43.

McCarthy, M. (1977) 'The status of the Leontief paradox', University of Kent Studies in Economics 21.

—— (1978) 'On *ceteris paribus*', University of Kent Studies in Economics 28.

McCloskey, D. (1983) 'The rhetoric of economics', *Journal of Economic Literature*, 21: 481–516.

—— (1985) *The Rhetoric of Economics*, Madison, WI: University of Wisconsin Press.

—— (1987) 'Rhetoric', in J. Eatwell, M. Milgate and P. Newman (eds) *The New Palgrave*, vol. 3, pp. 173–4, London: Macmillan.

May, R. M. (1976) 'Simple mathematical models with very complicated dynamics', *Nature* 261: 459–67.

Mayer, T. (1980) 'Economics as a hard science: realistic goal or wishful thinking?', *Economic Inquiry* 18: 165–78.

Meade, J. E. (1952) *A Geometry of International Trade*, London: Allen & Unwin.

Mitchison, N. A. (1980) 'Inheritance: the immunological challenge', *Nature* 288: 306.

Musgrave, A. (1981) ' "Unreal assumptions" in economic theory: the F-twist untwisted', *Kyklos* 34: 377–87.

Peitgen, H.-O. and Richter, P. H. (1985) *Schönheit im Chaos*, Bremen: University of Bremen.

Phelps Brown, H. (1980) 'The radical reflections of an applied economist', *Banca Nazionale del Lavoro Quarterly Review* no. 132: 3–14.

Popper, K. R. (1959) *The Logic of Scientific Discovery*, London: Hutchinson, reprinted 1974.

—— (1974) *Conjectures and Refutations*, 5th edn, London: Routledge & Kegan Paul (originally published 1963).

Reid, G. C. (1987) 'Applying field research techniques to the business enterprise', *International Journal of Social Economics* 14: 3–25.

Ricardo, D. (1817) *On the Principles of Political Economy and Taxation*, London: J. Murray.

Robbins, L. (1932) *An Essay on the Nature and Significance of Economic Science*, London: Macmillan; 2nd edn, 1935.

Samuelson, P. A. (1963) 'Discussion', *American Economic Review* (May Supplement) 53: 232.

Solow, R. (1986) 'Economics: is something missing', in W. Parker (ed.) *Economic History and the Modern Economist*, pp. 21–9, Oxford: Basil Blackwell.

Stewart, I. (1989) *Does God Play Dice?*, Oxford: Basil Blackwell.

Stewart, I. M. T. (1979) *Reasoning and Method in Economics*, London: McGraw-Hill.

Stigler, G. J. (1977) 'The conference handbook', *Journal of Political Economy* 85: 441–3.

Tarascio, V. and Caldwell, B. (1979) 'Theory choice in economics: philosophy and practice', *Journal of Economic Issues* 13: 983–1006.

Taylor, R. B. (1980) 'Lamarckist revival in immunology', *Nature* 286: 837–8.

Torrens, R. (1815) *An Essay on the External Corn Trade*, London: Hatchard.

—— (1833) *Letters on Commercial Policy*, London: Longman.

Viner, J. (1963) 'The economist in history', *American Economic Review* (Supplement) 53: 1–22.

Weisskopf, W. (1979) 'The method is the ideology: from a Newtonian to a Heisenbergian paradigm in economics', *Journal of Economic Issues* 13: 869–84.

Wilber, C. and Harrison, R. (1978) 'The methodological basis of institutional economics: pattern mode, storytelling, and holism', *Journal of Economic Issues* 12: 61–89.

Wilson, D. (1976) *Penicillin in Perspective*, London: Faber & Faber.

Wolpert, L. and Richards, A. (1988) *A Passion for Science*, Oxford: Oxford University Press.

Woodcock, A. and Davis, M. (1978) *Catastrophe Theory*, Harmondsworth: Penguin, reprinted 1985.

Yoshida, R. M. (1975) 'Five Duhemian theses', *Philosophy of Science* 42: 29–45.

Ziman, J. (1978) *Reliable Knowledge*, Cambridge: Cambridge University Press.

AUSTRIAN ECONOMICS: A DISSENT FROM ORTHODOXY

NORMAN P. BARRY

5.1 INTRODUCTION

The contemporary interest in Austrian economics is a remarkable phenomenon. From the period from the end of the last war until the mid-1970s all that was thought to be significant (for example, the account of the market, the subjectivist value theory and the theory of capital) had been incorporated into the mainstream of economic thought and its *distinctive* characteristics had been confined to the more arcane texts in the history of the discipline: a position validated by a prominent sceptic of its claim to originality, Milton Friedman, who once declared that 'there is no Austrian economics, there are only good economics and bad economics' (see Dolan 1976: 4).

In what follows I shall try to show that there are features in Austrian economics sufficiently distinctive to justify calling it an alternative 'paradigm', or at least a rival research programme, to what remains of the neoclassical orthodoxy. In so doing I do not wish to concentrate on the normative defence of capitalism, for which contemporary Austrian political economists are primarily known to the non-specialist, but on those elements of the Austrian system that have intrinsic value. Nevertheless, it cannot be denied that these elements are often best exemplified in certain policy areas in which the Austrian voice has been loud, notably in the problem of money, the explanation of the business cycle and the economic-philosophical critique of central planning. Overriding all these concerns is the important question of how the Austrians combine a rigorous *Wertfreiheit* (value freedom) in their explanation of economic phenomena, and indeed positivism with regard to value judgements in general, with a commitment to the welfare judgement that more or less unregulated markets maximize human well-being better than all known alternative economic sys-

This essay was written while the author was Visiting Scholar at The Social Philosophy and Policy Center, Bowling Green State University, Ohio, USA.

tems. However, it should be stressed that in many public policies, for example rent control, impediments to free international trade, price support schemes and so on, Austrian objections are obviously not unique but are found in economic philosophies that have markedly different foundations, especially the Chicago School.

Although the sources of Austrian economics[1] are to be found in the University of Vienna in the latter part of the last century, and during the intellectual heyday of the Hapsburg Empire, the phrase has now little geographical connotation. The architects of the Austrian version of the 'marginalist revolution', Carl Menger (1840–1921), Friedrich von Wieser (1851–1926) and Eugen von Böhm-Bawerk (1851–1914), were followed by writers, notably Ludwig von Mises (1882–1973) and Friedrich von Hayek (born 1899), whose reputations (especially so in the case of Hayek) were largely made in England and the United States. It was the sojourn of Mises in New York that spawned the 'American' generation of Austrian economists, Israel Kirzner and Murray Rothbard especially, who have continued to extend and refine the original paradigm. It is also the case that, perhaps regrettably and mistakenly, the 'exiling' of Austrian economics led to its being exclusively associated with a vigorous reassertion of *laissez-faire* as an economic doctrine rather than with the construction of genuine theory.

This was unfortunate because the economics of the 'second generation' of Austrians, mainly Mises and Hayek (although the German 'Austrian', Ludwig Lachmann should also be included), contained many theoretical components only hinted at by Menger and his immediate students. These included the extension of the idea of subjectivism to all aspects of the market process, the elaboration of the role of the entrepreneur in the market and a thorough examination of the methodology of economics in the light of contemporary developments in the philosophy of social science. In sum, all those enquiries represent a revulsion against the hitherto prevailing economic orthodoxy, with its belief in a body of 'objective' economic knowledge as precise and quantifiable as that found in the physical sciences, its stress on exact prediction as an overriding goal and its desire to formalize and to mathematize economic phenomena. In contrast, Austrian economists take the notion of *human* action in a world of ignorance and uncertainty as the focus of economic enquiry and adopt a concern of man whose subjective and unpredictable choices resist any incorporation into the framework of a *mechanistic* science. Yet, paradoxically, both modern formal neoclassical economics and Austrianism derive from a common source, the marginalist revolution of the 1870s.

5.2 CARL MENGER AND THE FOUNDATIONS OF AUSTRIAN ECONOMICS

The marginalist revolution of the 1870s is primarily known in the history of economic thought for its overthrow of the prevailing 'cost-of-production' (normally defined in terms of objective labour inputs) theory of value and its replacement by a theory that made price determination depend upon individual subjective choice at the margin. Through the work of Jevons, Walras and Menger, attention was turned away from the Classical emphasis on long-run historical factors, on the production side, that determine the course of economic development, towards the construction of a set of laws that determine how given resources are allocated towards the satisfaction of the wants of atomized and anonymous agents. *Demand* was now the key to price, and hence microeconomics constituted the field of enquiry for the economist.

In two major works (*The Foundations of Economics*, published in 1871, and *The Problems of Economics and Sociology*, published in 1883) Menger provided the Austrian contribution to marginalism and some important insights that were to differentiate this version from those of other marginalists, primarily Walras. In both these works (Menger 1950, 1963) he established the case for a science of economics, independent of history and inductive generalization, and an explanation for the emergence of familiar economic institutions, such as the equilibrating market and the phenomenon of money. Both enquiries involved the use of methodological individualism, the doctrine which holds that complex social phenomena can only be properly understood as logical constructions out of the actions, perceptions and attitudes of individuals, and subjectivism, understood in the neoclassical sense of price being dependent on demand in the context of scarcity.

It is thus that Menger understood a market economy in terms of 'exact' laws, generalizations about economic behaviour which held universally irrespective of time and circumstance, and the existence of which was denied by Menger's major antagonists, the German 'historicists', notably Gustav Schmoller. The kind of 'laws' Menger had in mind were diminishing marginal utility (hence the law of demand), Ricardo's law of rent and so on. However, these laws were not to be understood as predictive in a quantitative sense; the absence of perfect information on the part of individuals in a market and also the probability that not all of human action is governed by the pecuniary motive precluded precise forecasting of behaviour by an external observer. These laws captured the 'essence' of *economic* action, as opposed to other sorts of human endeavour, and specified, in an instructive phrase used later by Lionel Robbins, 'the necessities to which human action is subject'.[2] This ahistorical feature of Menger's thought and his insistence on there being nomothetic laws in the economic world, albeit subtly different from those used to explain physical phenomena, was an important legacy of Austrian economics.

However, what was perhaps of more significance was Menger's detailed consideration of those social phenomena that have emerged to fulfil human ends and purposes without being specifically designed: he calls these organic (the favoured word today is spontaneous) in contrast with those that are a product of deliberation or convention (though artifice might be a better word). In the *Problems of Economics and Sociology* he wrote that:

> Language, religion, even the state itself, and, to mention a few economic and social phenomena, the phenomena of markets, of competition, of money, and numerous other social structures are already met within epochs of history where we cannot properly speak of a purposeful activity of the community, as such, directed at establishing them.
>
> (Menger 1963: 146)

Of these spontaneously emerging phenomena the best example is money, for although in his monetary theory Menger was specifically concerned to show that the money good does not have to be provided by the state, and later Austrians have stressed the malign consequences that have resulted from the assertion of this monopoly by political authorities, the theoretical significance of the example is its illustration of the causal genetic method. This involves *abstraction* and hypothetical reconstruction, i.e. tracing in an imaginative manner the steps by which individual interaction produces the phenomenon in question. The causal genetic method contrasts nicely with the 'functional' method, used by the followers of Walras (1954), in the explanation of an equilibrating market: Menger and the Austrians understood this as a *process* by which dispersed knowledge is gradually integrated through the co-ordinating device of prices, while Walras attempted to represent an existing equilibrium in mathematical terms. Both approaches use the same 'exact' laws of microeconomics but for different purposes.

The immediate disciples of Menger, Böhm-Bawerk and von Wieser, were more concerned to extend the basic lessons of marginalism to all aspects of production and distribution in the theory of the allocative mechanism of the market rather than to develop his somewhat inchoate insights into the nature of the market process. However, Böhm-Bawerk (1959) is crucially important for his work on capital theory and for his economic rationale for interest in terms of the time element in the productive process, for his theory of the 'roundabout' methods of production (later taken up by Hayek in his theory of the business cycle) and for his incisive critique of Marxism (1975) and socialism in general.[3] Wieser (1893) was the first Austrian to articulate fully the theory of opportunity costs, which later became integral to the fully developed Austrian theory of subjective cost. However, not only were the works of these writers not that distant from the by then rapidly developing neoclassical paradigm, but also it would be an error to associate all Austrians with a combative defence of *unrestrained* capitalism; this is especially so in the case of Wieser, who espoused a moderately interventionist economic philosophy.

It was the second generation of Austrians, Mises, Hayek and their immediate disciples, who developed what is known today as the distinctive style of Austrian economics: an economics that is not just an orderly development of neoclassicism but a radical alternative. This alternative covers a number of key areas in the discipline: methodology, subjectivism, equilibrium and market process, entrepreneurship and the theory of money and economic dislocations.

5.3 METHODOLOGY

It would be quite wrong to suggest that there is a methodological doctrine to which all Austrian economists give an unqualified allegiance. Despite their well-known opposition to positivism, the rationale for this varies from thinker to thinker. At the most extreme, Mises displays a rigorous apriorism in which the familiar 'laws' of economics are deduced from certain indubitably true propositions about the human mind and are known prior to all experience.[4]

Thus from the proposition that man *acts* so as to achieve some future state of well-being, that he orders his preferences and that the world is characterized by scarcity, we can, for example, deduce the law of diminishing marginal utility, and hence the elements of price theory, without any reference to the satiety of wants or any other psychological state. Such laws are not capable of generating predictions and cannot be falsified by the 'facts': for example, if a person preferred more of a good at a higher price, we would not say that the law of demand had been falsified but only that he was not acting 'economically' in the traditional manner. Thus although the original economic law is 'inapplicable' in this case, the concept of action itself would not have been negated. The point of economic theory is not prediction but 'understanding' (*Verstehen*), making sense of what would otherwise be a mass of incoherent data by the use of certain ordering principles. Those data, because they are the product of unpredictable human actions, do not reveal 'regularities' (for example, there are no *constant* elasticities of demand) in the way that 'facts' in the physical world do. It follows from this that the nature of 'truth' in economic theory is established by valid reasoning from *true* premises. Whether or not such truths apply in a particular situation is a matter for historical investigation. This contrasts nicely with the positivism of the Chicago school which, in an instrumental sense, establishes true theories by empirical testing: whether the premises are true or not is not *directly* relevant; what matters is the testability of the purported theory.[5]

Most commentators regard extreme Misesian apriorism as unsatisfactory; according to Mark Blaug (1980: 93), it is 'cranky'. Indeed it is not a feature of all Austrian methodological thinking. However, much of Austrian theorizing does proceed by verbal deductive reasoning (especially the theory of money and the trade cycle) and is an attempt to make the world 'intelligible' through the use of explanatory concepts, such as subjectivism, the idea of *catallactics* (exchange) and the notion of entrepreneurship as a theoretically necessary co-ordinating device in a world of uncertainty.

Hayek (1948: ch. II) suggests, nevertheless, that there is at least one proposition in economics which is testable in the orthodox Popperian manner. As long ago as 1937 he argued that the market system, through the information conveyed by prices, does show a tendency towards an equilibrium; and he specifically distinguished the 'pure logic of choice' from the demonstration of empirical regularities in the real world.

However, the empirical content of economic theory is exceedingly small and it is indeed consistent with a whole range of economic phenomena. In his later work Hayek, while conceding that in principle economics was a predictive science, limited this to the prediction of patterns or classes of events, rather than discrete events.

> A theory will always define only a kind (or class) of patterns, and the particular manifestation of the pattern to be expected will depend on the particular circumstances (the initial and original conditions to which we shall refer as data).
>
> (Hayek 1967: 24)

It is the complexity of the data with which economics deals, the impossibility of specifying in a precise way the variables that impinge on human action, that prevents the construction of theories with a high empirical content. Vague though the idea of a pattern prediction is, for Hayek's purposes it is essential. For he does wish to show that there is some regularity in the economic world; not the least for the fact that his theory contains the implicit welfare judgement that a decentralized market system co-ordinates human action better than known alternative economic arrangements. However, that there is something beyond 'intelligibility' is not accepted by all subjectivist economists, two of whom, Ludwig Lachmann and G. L. S. Shackle (especially), deny that any such predictions can be made with confidence.

Irrespective of the arcane disputes that have emerged over the *ultimate* foundations of economics within the Austrian school, the commitment to subjectivism is common to all its adherents. But even this is highly contentious and requires special consideration.

5.4 SUBJECTIVISM

In conventional economic theory subjectivism refers only to the fact that value, the prices at which goods are exchanged one for another, depends ultimately on individual taste; there are no 'objective' values such as those proposed in pre-1870 Ricardian classical economics. However, this is as far as it goes for neoclassical orthodoxy, for once tastes are known and technological possibilities are given, then that allocation of productive resources required to generate the optimal array of wanted goods can be computed mathematically. Using the familiar neoclassical concept of rationality, economics becomes, in Robbins's famous words, the science that explains the allocation of scarce resources to competing ends: an exercise in the pure logic of choice.

However, in Austrian economics the notion of subjectivism pervades the whole of economic activity. It is a misdescription of economic life to say that anything (for example, production costs) is *given*, for in a world of uncertainty and change such 'facts' have to be found out by acting individuals, engaged in the unceasing quest for knowledge with which they can better themselves.[6] Rationality then is not the mere computation of means to ends but involves the selection of ends and the searching out, through a learning process, of the means necessary for their achievement. Furthermore, since all action takes place through time, and the future is largely (though not entirely) unknowable, the idea of there being a perfect allocation of resources is a fiction. For Mises especially, all human action is rational; in his terms, this means striving to remove some state of 'uneasiness' rather than merely reacting to some external data. It is this feature which is not captured in the neoclassical model and its absence, it is claimed, is responsible for the failure of orthodoxy to handle existing, and necessarily imperfect, market economies. That model, however, is remarkably good at representing in theoretical form hypothetical perfect markets.

What emerges from this consideration of subjectivism is a focus of attention on the *mental* aspects of economic behaviour, i.e. economic activity is ultimately about individuals evaluating states of affairs and choosing between alternative courses of action. An economic theory that neglected this in an exclusive preoccupation with what can be objectified in terms of quantifiable data, a prevailing attitude of positivism, will omit some of the basic features of economic life. Much of what is significant in economic phenomena is not directly observable.

A good example of this is in the treatment of costs. Of course, it is standard practice in microeconomics to treat the cost of anything as the value of the forgone alternative use of the same resource; thus, if I spend $100 on a television set, then its cost is the same money I could have spent on a washing machine. It is therefore tempting to regard costs as objectifiable in terms of monetary outlays, as indeed they can be *ex post*. But this would be to elide the true meaning of costs, which is that they are a subjective matter, residing in the necessarily private judgement of the decision-maker: costs are 'revealed' at the moment of decision and for that reason are incommunicable in an objective quantitative sense. As Kirzner (1986: 147) points out, the strict immeasurability of costs, and the impossibility of comparing them, is exactly analogous to the better known impossibility of making interpersonal comparisons of utility.

This might sound like nit-picking at the neoclassical model, except for the fact that theories of rational economic planning depend very much on there being an objective measure of cost in their comparisons of the values of competing economic projects. But if costs are only revealed in the unfolding of a market process through the actions of individual decision-makers, then what objective data do the planners have to work with (except, of course, their own subjective evaluations, which, presumably, is not what was intended by the original theory of economic planning)?

By similar reasoning, Austrian economists are sceptical about, if not actively opposed to, the meaning which is normally attributed to the concept of 'social' costs, the negative externalities imposed on the community by private agents. It is not denied that such phenomena occur in some sense or other, but it is claimed that we cannot speak meaningfully of sacrifices made by 'society', since society cannot literally be a decision-maker. How can a 'social' decision, for example, be made between a pollution-free environment with lower productivity and its opposite? Since the idea of an 'optimal pollution tax' must be conceptually incoherent, the consistent Austrian position implies that such problems have to be dealt with by individual negotiation within a specified property-rights structure (though it has been conceded that Austrians themselves have not made the innovative contributions in this area).

Yet however convincing the Austrian incorporation of subjectivism into the body of economics is, it could be maintained that it has a disabling effect. For if political economy involves the search for, and explanation of, the regularities that are to some extent apparent in economic life, does not the stress on uncertainty and unknowability preclude the existence of even Hayekian pattern predictions? Does not the exercise of making the world 'intelligible' commit us to a distressingly limited role for economic science? Furthermore, although Mises and Hayek repudiate the notion of an 'aggregate welfare function' for society as a whole as embodying a typical objectivist fallacy, their writings are replete with welfare judgements of a certain type.

The answers to these and other questions turn upon the concept of equilibrium, the interpretation of which is of paramount importance to a correct understanding of Austrian economics.

5.5 EQUILIBRIUM

Despite the familiar Austrian stress on disequilibria and the impossibility of perfect co-ordination of actions in a market society, and their claim that market processes should be the object of study for the economist, it would be false, as well as misleading, to suggest that the concept of equilibrium has been expunged from their vocabulary. Mises talks of an 'evenly rotating economy', a state of perfect equilibrium with goods constantly being reproduced under identical conditions, as a useful, though fictitious, theoretical benchmark against which we can illustrate the purpose of a genuine market process, i.e. its progress toward this nirvana, albeit subject to disruptions through changes in the data that confront individual transactors. In a subtly different fashion, Hayek talks of a 'dynamic equilibrium', in which individuals, through foresight, adjust their plans through time to achieve a perfectly co-ordinated (efficient) allocation of resources. Indeed, Hayek used just such a model in his *The Pure Theory of Capital* (1941), which is an extension of Böhm-Bawerk's theory of capital and interest and, as the title implies, is an exercise in abstract theorizing about economic circumstances unencumbered by ignorance, uncertainty and the potentially disequilibrating influence of money.

In all this, Hayek is not so very far from that general equilibrium theorizing that has been a feature of economics since Walras. But whereas the latter tradition is much more concerned with the (mathematical) proof of the existence of an equilibrium, the Austrians have devoted themselves to an enquiry into those causal factors that tend to bring about the tendency to equilibrium. This contrasts with a contemporary equilibrium theorist, Frank Hahn, who, while admitting that the prevailing neoclassical models do not reflect reality, still maintains that the method is sound: 'The student of general equilibrium believes that he has a starting point from which it is possible to advance towards a descriptive theory' (Hahn 1973: 324). The method of course is that of the functional representation of all the elements of an economic system in a mathematical form.

However, in Hayek's seminal (1937) paper 'Economics and knowledge' Hayek 1948: ch. II), he argues that the reason we are interested in equilibrium is because of the existence of an *empirical* phenomenon: a process towards equilibrium in a world of dispersed and incomplete information. This is in a sense an extension of the causal genetic method of Menger, the tracing out, hypothetically, of the steps by which individual actors generate an outcome (in this case, an equilibrating market) which is no part of any one agent's deliberate intention. It is also interesting to note that in the case of Mises this tendency is asserted in a typically aprioristic fashion. It follows, he says, from 'the activities of enterprising men, the promoters and speculators, eager to profit from the discrepancies in the price structure . . .' (Mises 1966: 355). Hayek, however, maintains that this supposed tendency is an empirical matter: 'It is only by the assertion that such a tendency exists that economics ceases to be an exercise in pure logic and becomes an empirical science' (Hayek 1948: 44) (see also Littlechild 1983). Nevertheless, he never indicates in any real sense how this may be falsified; in Austrian economics it is almost always claimed that failures in economic co-ordination are caused by some exogenous (government-inspired) impediment to the equilibrating process. This is by no means an unimportant point since a number of writers, broadly sympathetic to Austrian 'economic metaphysics', have had good reason to doubt this equilibrating tendency, and would banish the concept entirely from economic theory.

Irrespective of this complication, what is distinctive in the Mises–Hayek explanation of the equilibrating tendency is its stress on the competitive process (Hayek 1948). This is distinct from the idea of 'perfect competition' contained in general equilibrium theory since the latter presupposes a state of affairs in which competition has ceased; there are no possibilities of further improvements, prices exactly reflect marginal cost and each factor is paid its marginal product. Austrian theory, however, is about 'rivalrous competition' in which there are unexploited profitable opportunities. Hahn (1973: 322) conceded: 'general equilibrium is strong on equilibrium but very weak on how it comes about'.[7] Austrians maintain that it comes about (if, indeed, it comes about at all) through a continuous process of competition in which the entrepreneur plays a decisive role.

5.6 ENTREPRENEURSHIP

The mechanism by which this process occurs is entrepreneurship: a concept which has led a somewhat shadowy existence in the history of economic thought. The entrepreneur is often treated as a kind of 'manager', who is paid an income for a specific managerial role. Schumpeter (1939), however, made the first systematic analysis, focusing attention on the *disequilibrating* role of the entrepreneur: an agent with that kind of foresight and innovative ability which enables him to disrupt a pre-existing equilibrium leaving 'gales of creative destruction' in his wake. Despite the reference here to human creativity and innovative human action, there are significant differences between this conception of entrepreneurship and that developed by the Austrians.

In the work of Mises and Hayek entrepreneurship exemplifies that element of action that pertains to economizing, and is not captured by neoclassicism's formalistic notion of rationality. The entrepreneur is not paid an income as if he were a factor of production in a repetitive equilibrium system, for his role is specifically that of exploiting profitable opportunities (price differentials) that exist in disequilibrium states and it is by this action that the process of co-ordination is powered: profit is not a payment to a factor of production but a reward for superior foresight in exploitig these opportunities. In an important sense, then, entrepreneurship is a general category of human action that is exhibited by consumers, producers or any other agent in a market process. Hayek argued in a series of important post-war essays (Hayek 1948) that only through entrepreneurship (the activities of the much-derided 'middle-man' or market trader) can the necessarily dispersed knowledge that characterizes real-world economies be co-ordinated. Indeed, one of the major criticisms of a centrally planned economy is that, by replacing the entrepreneur with the salaried manager, fleeting and ephemeral economic knowledge, i.e. ever-changing information about tastes, production possibilities, costs and so on, will not be effectively utilized. It is a major claim of Austrian methodology that much of our knowledge of social affairs is 'tacit' rather than explicit. It is locked in the interstices of complex societies, possessed by the actors themselves, and incapable of precise articulation.

It is in the work of Israel Kirzner (1973, 1979, 1989) that the concept has been elaborated most succinctly, and in doing this he has created some controversy within the Austrian ranks. Kirzner uses the word 'alertness' to describe the phenomenon; the successful entrepreneur displays a purely mental skill in spotting some difference in factor price and product price (profit); furthermore, entrepreneurship is analytically distinct from ownership (though the roles may be combined in the same agent). Indeed, the entrepreneur (logically) requires no resources at all and his activities are, in a special way, 'costless': 'entrepreneurial profit is the discovery of something obtainable for nothing at all' (Kirzner 1973: 144). It is also the discovery of *error* in previous arrangements. But without all this a market process could not be 'nudged' towards an equilibrium state, although all the other features of a market make that in practice an unrealizable nirvana. It is this process of co-ordination that demarcates the Kirznerian entrepreneur from that of Schumpeter; it is the *discoordinating* role that is paramount in the latter.

A major criticism of Kirzner's theory of entrepreneurship is that, despite its being embedded in the Austrian theory of human action, it describes something almost 'mechanical' (see High 1982). That alertness to price discrepancies that drives the process inexorably towards equilibrium appears to be simple arbitrage and does not do justice to the creativity, imagination and judgement (i.e. of profitable opportunities) that is surely a feature of success in the market. Again, if entrepreneurship is a 'costless' mental activity, does this not imply, curiously, that there are no entrepreneurial losses (that there are was a point stressed by Mises)? These puzzles all seem to emanate from the fact that Kirzner pays insufficient attention to *uncertainty*. In his early work, *Competition and Entrepreneurship*, it hardly seems to be there at all.

In later work, Kirzner (1979, 1989) has emphasized the role of speculative creative activity in the market, and the way in which sheer acts of the imagination play a part in the unfolding of a market process. There is, then, a distinction between the envisaged future (which is in the mind of the transactor) and the actual future, and the recognition of this implies a concept of creative entrepreneurship that goes beyond arbitrage. However, Kirzner would still insist that all these phenomena are contained within the concept of alertness and that acts of innovation and discovery are steps in the whole process of equilibration. In other words there is some correspondence between the envisaged future and the future that occurs: it is not a matter of good fortune, but is explicable in terms of regularities in human action. But it is not at all clear that the phenomena of creative and imaginative acts in an economic process *and* the spotting of profitable opportunities through price differentials are both features of the same concept of alertness, for the latter activity is a response to existing discoordinated information in the economic world, while the former is the creation of that world itself. The Schumpeterian and Kirznerian entrepreneurs are not easily reconcilable.

In fact, Kirzner and other Austrians have good reason for rejecting the claim that a private enterprise market economy does not display regularities, that it is a chaotic world of flux and uncertainty which shows not even a tendency to equilibrium. For they want to say that it is the outcome of certain causal factors, notably the indication of relative scarcities by the price mechanism and the capacity of individuals to respond to profitable opportunities revealed by price differentials. Even though individual plans and expectations are disrupted by unforeseen changes in the data that confront individuals, information which is constantly fed back through the price system will lead to a co-ordination of human activities, although not, of course, an 'efficient' equilibrium end-state.

In contrast, extreme subjectivists doubt the reliability of even this modest process of the alignment of separate individual plans. Lachmann (1976) and Shackle (1972) maintain that the economic world is 'kaleidic', i.e. that there is a constant reshuffling of the elements in the economic system which produces ever-changing and temporary patterns rather than a long-run tendency towards equilibrium, a more or less smoothly co-ordinating process by which individuals adjust their actions to change. Co-ordination is a matter of serendipity rather than the outcome of the operation of causal laws.

The foundation of this view is the claim that much of economic life is about expectations. They are purely subjective phenomena, and there is no mechanism by which they can be co-ordinated,[8] at least in comparison with the way in which the price system indicates the relative scarcities of goods and services. The extreme subjectivist position seems to be that the economic world consists largely of private and essentially incommunicable perceptions about the future. It is an iconoclastic view because it implies that individual action, even when undisturbed by exogenous intervention, could produce patterns or economic arrangements which, although they fall short of even the minimal welfare criterion implicit in conventional Austrian economics, are unlikely to be improved by spontaneous action. This extension of Austrian economics bears an uncanny resemblance to Keynes's somewhat mysterious

Chapter 12 on subjectivism and expectations in *The General Theory of Employ-ment, Interest and Money* (1936).

Hayek's claim that the price system is a signalling device which conveys information to decentralized agents, and in effect guides their decisions, seems less than convincing when confronted by an economic world consisting essentially of thoughts and imagination. Ludwig Lachmann (1976, 1977), for example, makes much of the volatility of asset markets (in contrast with the relative tranquillity of ordinary product markets) and argues that the omnipresence of expectations there means that we do not observe a steady and co-ordinating process but only a series of shifting, day-to-day, equilibria with no Archimedean point. Under the influence of Weberian philosophy of social science, he maintains that economic theory's major intellectual role is to make this world intelligible.

Perhaps in a more spectacular fashion, Shackle (1972) argues that there is no necessary tendency to equilibrium in the economic world but that, since this world consists of nothing more than expectations and imagination, all we can hope for is temporary moments of co-ordination, ungoverned by any notion of an economic 'law' and detached from any overall destination. Co-ordination is indeed serendipitous, and chaos (or at least large-scale economic breakdown) cannot be excluded from a world in which each individual is a separate (and subjective) maker of the future. As he put it in a famous phrase: 'The future is unknowable but not unimaginable' (1972: 3).

The philosophical basis of Shackle's position consists of a stunning distinction that he makes between *reason* and *choice:*

> Rationalism, the belief that conduct can be understood as part of the determinate order and process of Nature, into which it is assimilated in virtue of the fact that men choose what is best for them in their circumstances, is a paradox. For it claims to confer upon man freedom to choose, yet to be able to predict what they will choose . . . for the sake of pre-reconciliation of choices, and also for its own unfathomable possibilities, the future must be assumed away.
>
> (Shackle 1972: 239)

What this means is that if we seek a rational scientific understanding of the economic world, an understanding which surely depends upon there being some order or regularity, then we are committed to the abandonment of the whole notion of choice, the meaning of which depends precisely upon unpredictability, and the exercise of choice lies in the imaginative acts.

Most economists are not prepared to accept the nihilism implicit in the Shackle position. There are surely some statements that can be made in economics which qualify as scientific, albeit in a less precise way than physics, and some regularities on which we can rely. Can it really be maintained that the constantly observed consequences of rent control in the housing market are merely disconnected temporary phenomena and not explicable in terms of the operation of an obvious nomothetic economic law? Surely not.

If what Shackle says is true, then it has serious implications for the welfare judgement, about the performance of markets, which is implicit in most of Austrian theory. It is likely that he has been influenced by the experience of large-scale breakdowns of market economies in the twentieth century. A serious question is whether such phenomena are caused by facts and circumstances endogenous to the market system itself or whether they are a product of exogenous factors, for example mismanagement of the money or the existence of government-created impediments to the co-ordinating processes of the market. A major claim of the Austrians is that the disturbances that we have witnessed are always caused by government, especially in its acquisition of the monopoly of money.

5.7 MONEY AND ECONOMIC FLUCTUATIONS

Although scholarly interest in Austrian economics is probably focused primarily on its contribution to microeconomics, it is the case that the informed public was attracted to the ideas of Mises and Hayek because of their perceived relevance to public policy – especially in the debate over inflation and unemployment that began in the early 1970s. This is in essence about macroeconomics, but the use of this term is likely to cause some confusion, largely because Austrian economists have historically been highly suspicious of macroeconomics, of either the Keynesian or monetarist variety. Their concept of human action, their extreme scepticism about the economic significance of large-scale magnitudes ('actionless aggregates') and their hostility to statistical measurement in general puts them firmly in the microeconomic camp. However, they have no objection to theories of the economy as a whole as long as these are logical constructions out of the actions of individuals. Their theories of money and the trade cycle involve just this type of theorizing.

For Austrians, the dislocations that occur in a market economy have a monetary origin: they are the result of exogenous factors rather than some flaw endemic to the exchange process itself.[9] However, the effects of money-generated disruptions are analysable with precisely the same conceptual framework that is used in microeconomics. Thus although an unexpected and *impermanent* increase in credit produces malign consequences, these arise out of typical features of human action: error, leading to mistaken investment decisions, followed by a process of readjustment through the correcting mechanisms of the price system. In a well-known phrase, although monetary factors *cause* the trade cycle, real factors *constitute* it (Hayek 1931: ch. 1). The main point is that the whole process is self-reversing and does not require positive government activity to hasten it.

In the 'classical' Austrian doctrine, a theory that seemed so inapposite when it was given a major hearing during the Depression of the 1930s, inflationary money does not affect the economy uniformly but produces a relative price effect: prices change disproportionately. The most important of these differential price changes is the market or money rate of interest (in equilibrium, the rate of interest exactly equates the demand and supply of loanable funds), thus making longer-term investments, those at the furthest stages of production, artificially more attractive. However, because these investments are not the product of an increase in genuine saving they are inherently unstable. Since the consumption–savings ratio remains the same as before the monetary injection, productive resources will have to be switched back to meet the consumer demand: this will leave production at the furthest stage starved of capital.[10] Thus, although these malinvestments emanate from a 'cluster of errors', the process is self-correcting, although at the cost of (temporary) unemployment in certain sectors of the economy.

This was not a theory that was likely to have much appeal in the 1930s, when there was high unemployment in all sectors of the economy. Not surprisingly, those circumstances led to theories that emphasized the lack of effective demand as the primary causal factor in depressions. Even Hayek was not immune to such thoughts, suggesting that a 'secondary depression' (indeed, a downward spiral) could occur as a result of the deflation that checked the original overexpansionary boom (Hayek 1975). However, the original message of the theory, that inflation has real effects on the structure of production rather than merely raising the general price level, remains today a major and distinctive feature of Austrian macroeconomics. As in the Chicago orthodoxy, 'money matters', and indeed the 'elementary' truth of the quantity theory of money has always been stressed by Hayek, but it matters in subtly different ways from those described by conventional monetarism: outside of equilibrium, money is never 'neutral'. It is for this reason, and others, that government should have no discretionary power over money (Hayek 1978; Barry 1981).

5.8 POLITICAL ECONOMY AND PUBLIC POLICY

I have suggested all along that, although Austrians can justifiably claim that their tracing out of those causal relationships that obtain in economic society is an exercise in value-free economics, there is an implicit welfare judgement in their economics, i.e. that an unhampered market economy is superior to known alternatives in exploiting resources for the benefit of the *anonymous* members of the public. This, of course, is a utilitarian judgement, but it is radically different from more familiar consequentialist welfare criteria that try to compare 'states of affairs' in terms of measurable utility. The prohibition against the comparing and adding of individual utilities, which is required for the comparison of end-states, is always enforced by Austrian economists.

The principle underlying the basic Austrian welfare judgement is an epistemological one – that no central body can have that knowledge which would be required to achieve a perfectly efficient outcome. The market is valued not because it is 'efficient' in the familiar technical sense but because it co-ordinates human actions with some predictability.

This can be illustrated nicely in the Austrian critique of socialism: a debate that took place originally in the late 1930s and was conducted within the terms of the neoclassical paradigm (Lavoie 1985). It was realized by market socialists that general equilibrium is quite an egalitarian form of economic organization: in it each factor of production is paid its marginal product, prices clear all markets, there is no excess or entrepreneurial profit, no monopolies or other market imperfections exist, and the array of goods and services that is produced exactly reflects the wants of consumers. However, existing capitalist markets are characterized by not merely inequality of resource ownership but a myriad of imperfections including monopoly 'rents', excess 'profits' and so on which seem to form a system of market power rather than free exchange.

The original objection of Mises (1935) to socialism (in his 1920 seminal essay) was that in the absence of a market it would be impossible to make the 'calculations' (i.e. solve the simultaneous equations) necessary to achieve an efficient allocation. In fact the 'market socialists', notably Lange, conceded the point that the market was an effective problem-solving device, and in their original model they retained a free market in consumption and in the choice of occupation while substituting state managers (to be paid an income) for entrepreneurs and centralized production rules for the private judgement of investors: there would be no capital market. In later versions of the model, high-speed computers would do the necessary calculations so that the state could 'mimic' the market's decision-making role but without its inefficiencies and unacceptable inequalities.

Hayek's objection to socialism has always been subtly different from that of Mises (Hayek 1948: chs VII, VIII and X). For him it is not merely a calculation problem, and he concedes that in a perfect world the state could mimic the market so as to produce an equilibrium; it is a problem about the *nature* of economic knowledge itself. If the exploitation of natural resources to make the most of opportunities requires an exercise in judgement and a capacity for discovery, then the subjective knowledge that is revealed in these activities is not capable of a translation into objective computable data (it would be so only if such data were infinitely repetitive, which in a human society they clearly are not). If entrepreneurs (who, of course, can be anybody) are the bearers of such tacit knowledge, then the 'excess' profits that accrue to them are simply the price we have to pay for their socially necessary activity. The problems of market socialism are most clearly visible in the issue of investment, for the absence of a capital market means that judgements about the viability of alternative projects must inevitably be the (subjective) judgements of political agents, who are not normally subject to the corrective mechanisms of decentralized markets.

If the market is a continuous process of self-correction, adjustment to circumstances and discovery of new opportunities, then it will always be characterized by features that look objectionable in the light of pure equilibrium theory. A non-socialist, for example, might still complain that the inefficiencies of monopoly could be corrected without in any further way socializing the private enterprise system. But even here Austrians would object to regulation on the same epistemological grounds. If a monopolist charges a price for his product that appears to be above the equilibrium price, so generating a welfare loss, how can the latter price be demonstrated? Indeed, the prospect of large profits may be the only way in which individuals can be induced to engage in risky activities (Littlechild 1981). Furthermore, as long as access remains open, then the monopolist remains under some constraint. These questions are not crude empirical ones, calculations of welfare loss and so on, but involve an understanding (*Verstehen*) of the way in which differing economic systems work.

5.9 AUSTRIAN ECONOMICS AND THE FUTURE

In contemporary public policy debates Austrian economists have been preoccupied, understandably, with questions of money and inflation. Indeed, they have produced some radical suggestions for the establishment of a sound currency (the *sine qua non* of a market system). However, in the realm of theory, further work is likely to be in the elaboration of the subjectivist method, the theory of entrepreneurship, particularly the theory of the firm and the role of the entrepreneur in it (see Ricketts 1987), and the construction of a viable methodological alternative to positivism. Perhaps the most important task is the formulation of a theory of property rights in the area of externalities; this is especially so in view of the fact that environmental questions are likely to provide new opportunities for the use of 'objectivist' solutions to economic problems. In fact, it is market economists not necessarily associated with the Austrian 'metaphysic' who have made the most fruitful advances in the fields of property rights and externalities.

Although the arguments against inflation, Keynesianism and state planning that have exercised the Austrians so much throughout the twentieth century may now seem a little *passé*, the Austrian research programme is prospering in other areas hitherto occupied exclusively by the neoclassical orthodoxy. Given the rivalry between competing alternative theories that is now such a feature of contemporary economic studies, no one approach is likely to secure a monopoly of knowledge.

NOTES

1 For good short introductions to Austrian economics, see Dolan (1976), Spadaro (1978), Reekie (1984), Shand (1984) and Littlechild (1986). See also Rothbards's (1962) comprehensive two-volume exposition of Austrian economics and methodology.
2 Robbins (1935) espouses an Austrian methodology of economics, although contemporary Austrians have been critical of his description of 'economizing action' as being too close to neoclassical orthodoxy. This is because, they allege, Robbins stresses too much the allocative function of the market and underplays creativity and entrepreneurship.
3 See his important essay 'Control or economic law' in Böhm-Bawerk (1962).
4 There are a number of important expositions of his uncompromising and often dogmatically expressed ideas. See especially Mises (1962) and the complete exposition of his philosophy, politics and economics in his *magnum opus, Human Action* (1966).
5 See Friedman's influential essay 'The methodology of positive economics' in Friedman (1953). Despite their methodological differences, Friedman and most of the Austrians share the same positivism about values.
6 It is this that leads Austrians to cast doubt on the attempts to formalize economic phenomena; see Mises (1966: chs 15 and 16) and Hayek (1948: ch. II).
7 For a critique of Hahn, see Barry (1988).
8 It does not at all follow that centralized control could improve upon the market in this respect. Both Lachmann and Shackle seem to be pointing out a general feature of the social condition, i.e. the unpredictability and uncertainty that accompanies specifically human action.
9 See Mises (1966: ch. 20) and Hayek (1931). For contemporary descriptions of the Austrian theory of money and the business cycle, see O'Driscoll (1977) and Barry (1979: ch. 8).
10 Paradoxically, in a depression the Austrian theory requires an increase in saving and a cut-back in consumption if recovery is to occur.

REFERENCES

Barry, N. P. (1979) *Hayek's Social and Economic Philsophy*, London: Macmillan.

—— (1981) 'Austrian economists on money and society', *National Westminster Bank Quarterly Review* 20–31.

—— (1988) *The Invisible Hand in Economics and Politics*, London: Institute of Economic Affairs.

Blaug, M. (1980) *The Methodology of Economics*, Cambridge: Cambridge University Press.

Böhm-Bawerk, E. (1959) *Capital and Interest*, transl. G. Muncke and H. Sennholz, South Holland, IL: Liberatarian Press (originally published in three volumes between 1909 and 1914).

—— (1962) 'Control or economic law', in *Shorter Classics of Eugen Böhm-Bawerk*, South Holland, IL: Libertarian Press.

—— (1975) *Karl Marx and the Close of His System*, ed. Paul Sweezey, London: Merlin Press (first published 1896).

Dolan, E. G. (ed.) (1976) *The Foundations of Austrian Economics*, Kansas City, KS: Sheed & Ward.

Friedman, M. (1953) *Essays in Positive Economics*, Chicago, IL: University of Chicago Press.

Hahn, F. H. (1973) 'The winter of our discontent', *Economica* 40: 322–30.

von Hayek, F. A. (1931) *Prices and Production*, London: Routledge.
—— (ed.) (1935) *Collectivist Economic Planning*, London: Routledge.
—— (1937) 'Economics and knowledge', *Economica* 4: 33–54. Reprinted in von Hayek, F. A. *Individualism and Economic Order*, London: Routledge, 1948.
—— (1941) *The Pure Theory of Capital*, London: Routledge.
—— (1948) *Individualism and Economic Order*, London: Routledge.
—— (1955) *The Counter-Revolution of Science*, Glencoe, IL: The Free Press.
—— (1967) *Studies in Philosophy, Politics and Economics*, London: Routledge.
—— (1975) *Full Employment at Any Price?*, London: Institute of Economic Affairs.
—— (1978) *The Denationalisation of Money*, London: Institute of Economic Affairs (1st edn 1976).
High, J. (1982) 'Alertness and judgement: comment on Kirzner', in I. Kirzner (ed.) *Method, Process and Austrian Economics*, pp. 161–8, Lexington, MA: D. C. Heath.
Keynes, J. M. (1936) *The General Theory of Employment, Interest, and Money*, London: Macmillan.
Kirzner, I. (1973) *Competition and Entrepreneurship*, Chicago, IL: University of Chicago Press.
—— (1979) *Perception, Opportunity and Profit*, Chicago, IL: University of Chicago Press.
—— (1986) 'Another look at the subjectivism of costs', in I. Kirzner (ed.) *Subjectivism, Intelligibility and Economic Understanding*, New York: New York University Press.
—— (1989) *Discovery, Capitalism and Distributive Justice*, Oxford: Basil Blackwell.
Lachmann, L. (1976) 'From Mises to Shackle: an essay on Austrian economics and the kaleidic society', *Journal of Economic Literature* 14: 54–62.
—— (1977) *Capital, Expectations and the Market Process*, Kansas City, KS: Sheed, Andrews & McMeel.
Lange, O. (1964) 'On the economic theory of socialism', in B. Lippincott (ed.) *The Economic Theory of Socialism*, pp. 57–142, New York: McGraw-Hill (first published 1938).
—— (1967) 'The computer and the market', in C. H. Feinstein (ed.) *Socialism, Capitalism and Economic Growth*, Cambridge: Cambridge University Press.
Lavoie, D. (1985) *Rivalry and Central Planning*, Cambridge: Cambridge University Press.
Littlechild, S. C. (1981) 'Misleading calculations of the social cost of monopoly power', *Economic Journal* 91: 348–63.
—— (1982) 'Equilibrium and the market process', in I. Kirzner (ed.) *Method, Process and Austrian Economics*, pp. 85–102, Lexington, MA: D. C. Heath.
—— (1986) *The Fallacy of the Mixed Economy*, 2nd edn, London: Institute of Economic Affairs (1st edn 1976).
Menger, C. (1950) *The Foundations of Economics*, transl. J. Dingwell and B. Hoselitz, Glencoe, IL: The Free Press (first published 1871).
—— (1963) *Problems of Economics and Sociology*, transl. F. J. Nock, Urbana, IL: University of Illinois Press (first published 1883).
von Mises, L. (1935) 'Economic calculation in the socialist commonwealth', in von Hayek, F. A. (ed.) *Collectivist Economic Planning*, pp. 87–130, London: Routledge.
—— (1962) *The Ultimate Foundation of Economic Science*, Princeton, NJ: Van Nostrand.
—— (1966) *Human Action*, 3rd edn, Chicago, IL: Henry Regnery (first published 1949).

Reekie, D. (1984) *Markets, Entrepreneurs and Liberty*, Brighton: Harvester Wheatsheaf.

Ricketts, M. (1987) *The Economics of Business Enterprise*, Brighton: Harvester Wheatsheaf.

Robbins, L. C. (1935) *The Nature and Significance of Economic Science*, 2nd edn, London: Macmillan (1st edn 1931).

Rothbard, M. N. (1962) *Man, Economy and State*, New York: Van Nostrand.

Schumpeter, J. S. (1939) *Business Cycles*, New York: Harrap.

Shackle, G. L. S. (1972) *Epistemics and Economics*, Cambridge: Cambridge University Press.

Shand, A. (1984) *The Capitalist Alternative: An Austrian View of Capitalism*, Brighton: Harvester Wheatsheaf.

Spadaro, L. M. (ed.) (1978) *New Directions in Austrian Economics*, Kansas City, KS: Sheed, Andrews & McMeel.

Walras, L. (1954) *Elements of Pure Economics*, transl. W. Jaffé, London: Allen & Unwin (first published 1874).

von Wieser, F. (1893) *Natural Value*, transl. C. A. Malloch, London: Macmillan (first published 1889).

6

CURRENT VIEWS ON
ECONOMIC POSITIVISM

LAWRENCE A. BOLAND

6.1 INTRODUCTION

Few economists today will be found waving the banner of 'economic positivism' or 'positive economics'. Does this mean that economic positivism is dead? Certainly not. Positive economics is now so pervasive that every competing view (except hard-core mathematical economics) has been virtually eclipsed. The absence of methodological flag-waving is thus easy to understand. There is no territory to dispute and thus no need to wave one's flag.

The dominance of economic positivism is abundantly evident in current textbooks. Almost every introductory textbook explains the difference between 'positive' and 'normative' economics and tries to make it clear that economists are interested in positive economics and capable of fulfilling the demands of economic positivism. Why should economists be interested in positive economics? Has economics fulfilled the demands of economic positivism? These two questions will be the focus of this chapter.

6.2 POSITIVE ECONOMICS VERSUS WHAT?

While every textbook clearly distinguishes 'positive' from 'normative' questions by characterizing the distinction with an 'is–ought' dichotomy, it is not clear that the history of the distinction supports such a dichotomy. John Neville Keynes is most often quoted to support the dichotomy despite the fact that, as Mark Blaug (1980: 141) points out, Neville Keynes actually provides a threefold distinction involving (a) the 'establishment of [existing empirical] uniformities', (b) the 'determination of ideals' or the 'criteria of what ought to be' and (c) the development of a practical 'art' to formulate 'maxims or precepts by obedience to which given ends may *best* be attained' (Keynes 1917: 32–5,

The author wishes to thank Irene Gordon, Zane Spindler and Stan Wong for reading and criticizing earlier drafts of this chapter.

emphasis added). Unfortunately, the widespread reliance on the 'is–ought' dichotomy has nullified Neville Keynes's best efforts to improve our understanding of positive economics.

While promoting 'positive methodology' in his famous 1953 essay, Milton Friedman tried to deny the 'is–ought' dichotomy by arguing that answers to 'ought' questions necessarily depend on a prior establishment of 'what is' (Friedman 1953). Nevertheless, most critics of Friedman's methodology think that he was arguing against normative economics and thus assume that he was only arguing in favour of positive economics (e.g. Koopmans 1957; Rotwein 1959; Samuelson 1963; Simon 1963). The presumption seems to be that one must always choose between 'is' and 'ought' questions as if they are inherently mutually exclusive.

To be fair, there is a good reason to presume that 'is' and 'ought' questions are mutually exclusive. David Hume had long ago argued that 'ought' statements cannot be deduced from 'is' statements and vice versa (Blaug 1980: 130). The mere mention of 'is' and 'ought' in the definition of positive economics thus seems to demand a sharp dichotomy such as the one between positive and normative economics as defined in the textbooks.

In addition to the is–ought distinction, there are other dichotomies that seem to support the separation between positive and normative economics. There is the philosopher's distinction between analytic and synthetic truths – the former do not depend on empirical questions while the latter do. There is the science versus art distinction which motivated early economic methodologists (such as Nassau Senior) – while 'science' was alleged to be about material truths, 'art' was considered to be about normative rules (Blaug 1980: 59). More recent dichotomies are the objective–subjective, descriptive–prescriptive and rational–irrational which are often considered direct correlates with the positive–normative distinction. And, of course, there is the more commonplace distinction between theoretical and applied economics that prevails in most economics departments today.

To this list I wish to add one more distinction – namely, the romantic–classical distinction often found in discussions of nineteenth-century British literature. Specifically, I think that one can recognize a distinction between 'romantic' and 'classical' postures concerning the realism of assumptions. While it might be considered romantic to assume that the world is the way one would like it to be, it would be classical to try dispassionately to make one's assumptions correspond to the way the world really is. For example, a romantic egalitarian might wish that wealth be evenly distributed; a classical realist would contend that one should not assume distributional uniformities unless there are good empirical reasons to do so.

So, given all these various dichotomies, how does one understand the nature of positive economics and why should one ever want to promote it? I think that the reason why there are so many different distinctions raised in the discussion of positive economics is that each of them represents something that positive economics is claimed *not* to be. That is, most people understand positive economics more by what it is argued not to be than by what it is argued to be in fact. Briefly stated, we have only a negative understanding of economic positivism!

6.3 POSITIVISM AS RHETORIC

There is a sense in which the distinction between positive and normative is completely confused. Positive policy advisers are in effect always recommending that their policy is the *best* way to achieve the given ends. This is evident even in John Neville Keynes's original discussion. It is difficult to conceive of a way one could ever avoid normative judgements. So, what is it that one is truly accomplishing when demanding that one's economic research or advice conform to the dictates of positivism?

The idea of 'positive' economics is mostly a matter of rhetoric (Boland 1989: epilogue). The rhetorical purpose is also evident in the use of some of the other dichotomies. We can find books entitled *System of Synthetic Philosophy* (Spencer 1896), *Positive Philosophy* (Comte 1974), *Scientific Management* (Drury 1968), *Objective Psychology of Music* (Lundin 1967), *Rational Economics* (Jackson 1988), *Descriptive Economics* (Harbury 1981) and so on. Whenever an author is extolling the virtues of a theory by claiming that it is a positive theory, he or she is usually asserting that it is not something of a scientifically unacceptable nature. What is acceptable in these matters is usually dictated by the prevailing view of 'scientific method'. However, it is not often clear why the term 'positive' must always indicate something acceptable or desirable.

Up to the time of Hume (late eighteenth century), most thinkers seemed to believe in the power of rational or logical thought and especially in its embodiment in science. By the term 'science' it was usually implied, following Francis Bacon's seventeenth-century view, that all science can be reduced to *positive evidence* from which in turn all systematic knowledge could be shown to follow by the logic of *induction*. This, I think, gives us a clue to why the accolade of 'positive' has for so long implied something good. Any theory which offers or is based on positive evidence – that is, on observations or hypotheses which make *positive contributions* towards an inductive proof of our systematic knowledge – is worthy of the title 'positive'. Given the common nineteenth-century belief in the viability of inductive science, 'positive' implied 'scientific', 'rational' and even 'objective'. The implication of objectivity follows from Bacon's promotion of inductivism as antidote to self-interested or prejudicial claims of knowledge (Agassi 1963). To be scientific, inductive proofs were to be based only on objective observations. Whether one's theory makes a positive contribution to scientific knowledge is solely a question of one's personal research skills. A true scientific researcher is objective, unprejudiced and unbiased to the point that any reported data will be beyond question. The remainder of science is simply a matter of objectively based inductive logic. As a corollary, if anyone errs in their scientific claims to knowledge, it could only be due to introduced biases, prejudice or injecting their subjective values.

In economics, the association between 'positive' and 'descriptive' seems to be a direct consequence of the reliance on Hume's view of the is–ought dichotomy. We describe 'what is' and prescribe 'what ought to be'. The association between 'positive' and 'applied' economics and between 'positive' and 'synthetic' statements is rather confusing. While it is easy to claim that one's theory is 'positive', it is more often thought that pure theory is not empirical (Hutchison 1938) and thus applied economics must be 'positive'. So, what did Böhm-Bawerk mean by the title of his book *Positive Theory of Capital* (Böhm-Bawerk 1889)? While it might be easy to see a connection between 'positive' and 'synthetic', their opposites do not seem connected. Hardly anyone would connect 'normative' with 'analytical' – except from the perspective that a normative conclusion is a logically contingent truth that depends on the acceptance of presumed values. But if analytical truths must be tautologies, then technically the connection is rather weak (Quine 1961: ch. 2).

The post-war influence of the logical positivists and the retrospective influence of Max Weber have combined to make the rhetoric of positivism even more confused. The logical positivists were those analytical philosophers who thought that verifiable scientific knowledge is distinguishable from unverifiable 'metaphysics'. The turn-of-the-century social scientist Max Weber is now credited as being a leader in developing the idea that scientific knowledge could be 'value free'. And to confuse things still more, Karl Popper presented a critique of logical positivism based on the logical grounds that a theory makes a positive contribution to scientific knowledge only if it is falsifiable (which most commentators seem to think means only that it is not a tautology). With all this confusion in mind, it may be difficult for us to determine even what 'positive' is not.

6.4 WHAT EVERYONE SEEMS TO THINK THAT 'POSITIVE' IS

Economic positivism as it is currently practised seems to be available in four different flavours. The first and most optimistic version is what I shall call *Harvard positivism*. It is represented by the recent attempts to develop 'experimental' economics and has its origins in the early teaching of Edward Chamberlin. At the other extreme is the weak minimalist version which I shall call

MIT positivism. Its weakness is due to the methodological view that says that to be of interest a theory need only be *potentially* refutable – there is no additional requirement that says it needs to be supported or tested by empirical evidence. In between these two extremes there are two more modest versions. One, which I shall call *LSE positivism*, does not require controlled experiments but does see economics as a scientific endeavour that emphasizes a necessary role for empirical quantitative data. The other one is *Chicago positivism* which includes both the simplistic instrumentalism of Friedman and the more complex confirmationism of Becker and Stigler.

Harvard positivism

Those positivists who advocate 'experimental economics' still comprise a very small segment of mainstream economics. The current movement seems to have its origin in the experiments that Chamberlin often inflicted on his students at Harvard University. The current leader of this group is Vernon Smith (1982).

The motivation for experimental economics is to overcome the obvious fact that most mainstream neoclassical models are self-professed abstractions which employ simplifying assumptions whose realism is always open to question. Given that any typical economic explanation is of the form 'if the world is of form X and people behave according to proposition Y, then we shall observe phenomena Z', the obvious questions facing any economist who claims to offer a positive explanation of economic phenomena Z are as follows. Is the world of form X? Do people in fact behave according to proposition Y? Do we observe phenomena Z?

Since it is usually difficult to determine whether people actually behave according to proposition Y, almost all empirical research is concerned with world X and phenomena Z. The usual approach is to build a model of the economy based on proposition Y and try to determine whether or not the model can be confirmed when confronted by the data *available* after the event. Unfortunately, the available data are seldom decisive in any direct way. Instead, many additional assumptions must be made and thus any conclusions reached are always conditional.

Harvard positivism offers a different approach. Rather than accept the limitation of available data (which are usually aggregative and thus open to many methodological questions), experimental economics proposes creating a real-world situation in which the assumptions of the typical neoclassical model are true with respect to the claimed form of world X. Specifically, the experimental economists attempt to construct a world which is in fact of form X and then determine whether the behaviour implied by proposition Y is logically consistent with the experimentally observed phenomena Z. The extent of the laboratory skill of the experimenter is always the sole determinant of whether the experiment represents a successful exercise in economic positivism.

MIT positivism

The followers of Paul Samuelson's methodology adopt a much less fundamentalist view of economic positivism. Following Samuelson, yet seeking to assure the optimistic promises of positivism, it is argued that the minimum condition for a positive contribution to economic understanding is that anyone's positive theory must be capable of yielding to refutations based on positive evidence. In short, all truly positive theories are empirically refutable *in principle*. All that can be assured by such a weak requirement is that the proposed positive theory is not a tautology, as Hutchison (1938) recognized in the late 1930s. It should be clear that this minimalist version of positivism is serving the interests of mathematical model-builders, who wish to avoid all the menial unpleasantness of dealing with complex real-world empirical data, more than the interests of those who are concerned with promoting truly positive economics. For the mathematical economists, the elegance of the model is always much more important than whether its assumptions are empirically realistic or whether its implications are useful with respect to economic policy.

Chicago positivism

Usefulness is the keystone of the positivism promoted by the followers of Chicago School economics. However, there are two aspects of usefulness. On the one hand, providing positive theories that can be used as instruments by policy-makers is one concern. On the other hand, being useful for promoting neoclassical economics in general, and confirming beliefs in the omnipotence of the market system in particular, is another concern of the Chicago School.

In his 1953 essay, Friedman gives a compelling argument for why anyone who is only interested in providing useful theories for policy-makers ought to eschew the typical philosophical prejudices associated with the group of analytical philosophers often called logical positivists and instead recognize that questions concerning the verifiability, falsifiability or even *a priori* realism of the behavioural assumptions of economic models are of much less concern than the usefulness of their results (Friedman 1953). It is easy to see that such an argument is really one favouring an instrumentalist methodology (Boland 1979). The interesting question is: why would Friedman or anyone else see his argument as one promoting some form of positivism?

Friedman's essay was not an argument against positivism but only one against the more sophisticated logical positivism. Positive evidence still matters for Friedman. His only restriction is to limit the evidence to that of results or predictions and thereby exclude *a priori* or logical analysis of models, assumptions and theories *as a determinant of the usefulness* of positive theories. Positive data obviously play an essential role in Friedman's methodology. But for Friedman the only relevant positive data will be successful predictions which assure the usefulness of a model or theory. There is nothing inherent in Friedman's methodological essay that would prevent his form of instrumentalism from being used by post-Keynesians or even Marxists.

When it comes to ideological questions, however, other members of the Chicago School are much more prominent. In 1977, George Stigler and Gary Becker offered a manifesto for those who believe in neoclassical economics. Their argument, simply stated, was that the Chicago School economists will offer models of the economy (i.e. of world X) which do not engage in analysis of the psychological (subjective) make-up of individual decision-makers but instead offer analyses of the objective (positive) cost situations facing the individual decision-makers and thereby explain any observable positive behavioural evidence in question (i.e. phenomena Z) – all observed changes in behaviour will be explained as consequences of observable and objective cost situations (Stigler and Becker 1977).

Each positive economic model which succeeds (they never seem to report any failures) is offered as yet more confirming evidence that any social or behavioural phenomena can be explained using an appropriately constructed neoclassical model (i.e. where proposition Y incorporates assumed maximization behaviour in a free-market system). For this branch of the Chicago School, the real purpose of neoclassical model-building is once again to confirm the truth of a market-based system of social co-ordination (Boland 1982).

LSE positivism

Stigler and Becker may be correct in promoting neoclassical economics as the only true explanation of social and individual behaviour, but if so, it ought to be tested in a more critical manner. At the end of the 1950s, a group of economists at the London School of Economics (LSE) proposed a more critical approach to economic model-building. While it is easy to find positive evidence to confirm anyone's favourite model, the 'scientific' issue is one of approaching the evidence in a less predisposed manner. Such an approach does not preclude *a priori* beliefs; it merely cautions one to let the positive evidence do the talking.

The LSE approach to positivism was the self-conscious product of a group of young economists led by Richard Lipsey who formed what was called the LSE Staff Seminar in Methodology, Measurement and Testing. The seminar was to some extent inspired by Popper's presence at LSE and his emphasis on criticism and empirical testing as the true basis for science (de Marchi

1988). The message of the seminar was captured in Lipsey's well-known 1960s textbook *Introduction to Positive Economics* (Lipsey 1963). The main thrust for Lipsey was the advocacy of developing an appreciation for real-world empirical data. His textbook became the major platform for all modern economic positivism.

The combination of testing and measurement is the hallmark of LSE positivism. It is thus not surprising to find that econometrics plays a prominent role. However, unlike the instrumentalist tendency found among American econometric model-builders (Boland 1986), LSE econometrics is supposed to be helping us to assess any economic proposition that might arise. The positive–normative distinction was to play a central role since it was thought that all normative statements are untestable and thus 'unscientific'.

6.5 MODERN ECONOMIC POSITIVISM IS PROFOUNDLY CONFUSED

As we have learned from historians of science (such as Thomas S. Kuhn and Joseph Agassi), most disciplines can be defined by their leading textbooks. The foundation of modern economic positivism continues to be Lipsey's textbook *Introduction to Positive Economics*. The evolution of this book closely reflects how the practice of positivism has developed over the last twenty-five years. However, if one examined the introductory 'Scope and method' part of the *first* edition of Lipsey's famous textbook (Lipsey 1963), it would be difficult to understand how this book has become the foundation for modern economic positivism. Lipsey proudly announces that his book is about *positive economic science*. The North American editions of his book play down the emphasis on 'science' (presumably because in North America such emphasis is considered pretentious) but then continue to share his emphasis on 'positive'. Yet a careful examination of the first edition shows that empirical evidence can be decisive *only in a negative way*. Specifically, Lipsey parrots that part of Popper's philosophy of science that claims that truly scientific theories can be refuted by empirical evidence but can never be verified by empirical evidence. In effect then, according to Lipsey *circa* 1963, his book is really about *negative* economic science!

This apparent inconsistency is abruptly corrected in the second edition where he says that he has 'abandoned the Popperian notion of refutation and [has] . . . gone over to a statistical view of testing that accepts that neither refutation nor confirmation can ever be final, and that all we can hope to do is discover on the basis of finite amounts of imperfect knowledge what is the balance of probabilities between competing hypotheses' (Lipsey 1966: xx). While this may accord better with common notions of science, it is not clear that there is anything positive (or negative!) left in the LSE version of positivism.

In the sixth edition we are told that only positive statements are testable. Normative statements are not testable because they depend on value judgements. Moreover, 'statements that could conceivably be refuted by evidence if they are wrong are a subclass of positive statements' (Lipsey 1983: 6). Therefore, practitioners of positive economics 'are concerned with developing propositions that fall into the positive, testable class' (Lipsey 1983: 7). But, looking closer, on page 5 it is asserted that a statement is called 'testable' if it can 'be proved wrong by empirical evidence', and then turning to page 13 we are told that it is 'impossible to refute any theory conclusively'! Unless Lipsey meant something different from what appears on page 5, it would seem that the class of positive economic statements is empty and thus positive economics is impossible. If there is any doubt about whether the advocates of LSE positivism are profoundly confused about methodology, the 1988 Canadian edition of Lipsey's book provides the proof: we are boldly told, 'There is no absolute certainty in any knowledge' (Lipsey *et al*. 1988: 24). How can one claim to know with absolute certainty that one cannot know with absolute certainty?

Their bold statement is self-contradictory and yet it appears to be the foundation of modern economic positivism. As is well known, anything can be proved with a foundation containing contradictions (for example, 2 equals 1, black is white etc.), and whenever it is possible to prove contradictory things the proofs are meaningless. Thus we would have to conclude that nothing can be accomplished with the modern positivist's methodology if that methodology is the one described in the various versions of Lipsey's famous book. I think that Lipsey should not have simply dropped Popper in order to avoid some 'problems that seem intractable to a believer in single-observation refutations' (Lipsey 1966: xx). While his move will please those philosophers of science who are all too eager to dismiss Popper's challenges to logical positivism, I think that Lipsey should have tried to examine those 'intractable' problems critically.

6.6 POSITIVE SCIENCE OR POSITIVE ENGINEERING?

Even though the philosophy of economic positivism has not been well thought out by its main proponents, it still captures all the satisfying notions that most mainstream economists seem to desire. On the one hand, it appears to support the commonly accepted view of explanatory science. On the other hand, it appears to support the appropriate cautions for a socially acceptable practice of social engineering. Specifically, both perspectives are served by the common view that positivism represents the avoidance of value judgements.

Explanatory science

Those economists today (including those from the Massachusetts Institute of Technology (MIT) or LSE) who see themselves as scientists offering explanations of economic phenomena will be pleased to find that adherence to positivism only requires assurances that the assumptions of one's model are falsifiable. Falsifiability of one's assumptions merely assures that the conclusions and explanations provided by the model will not be what economists call tautologies. To be careful here, it should be recognized that what economists mean by the term 'tautology' is not always what philosophers or logicians mean by that term. Economists think that, if it is impossible to conceive of how a given statement could be false, then that statement is a tautology. This includes both what philosophers call tautologies (statements that are true by virtue of the logical form alone) and quasi-tautological statements that are true by definition or depend on definition-like statements such as value judgements. It is the latter form of statements which is usually what economists mean by the term 'tautology'.

But why are economists so concerned with avoiding tautologies? The only methodological problem solved by avoiding tautologies is the one facing economists who wish to claim that their empirical tests of their models or theories represent positive contributions on the basis that their empirical evidence verifies or confirms their models (Boland 1977, 1989). The problem is that there are some statements which are of the form that economists call tautologies, yet that can also appear to be confirmed. The most obvious example is the 'quantity theory of money'. This 'theory' is represented by the equation $MV = PT$. On close examination it turns out that the two sides of this equation are merely what is obtained by reversing the order of summation between i and j for the double summation $\Sigma\Sigma p_{ij} q_{ij}$ (Agassi 1971). Confirming a statement which cannot conceivably be false cannot really contribute anything positive to economic science.

Social engineering

Those economists today who see themselves as providers of policy advice will be pleased to learn that adherence to positivism will assure them that their recommendations will not be easily dismissed. Policy-makers are seldom concerned with whether the consulting economists are dealing with tautological models or whether any theory is falsifiable. What is important is the assurance that the advice given is not just a reflection of the biases of the consulting economists.

So, what methodological problem is solved by expecting policy advisers to be practitioners of economic positivism? Given all the equivocation incorporated in the presentations of modern economic positivism (for example, Lipsey's text-book), there is no reason for a policy-maker to expect that the economist's advice will be firmly supported by empirical evidence. It all comes down to the economic researcher's making judgements about whether the available evidence should be sufficient reason to support or reject a given theory that was used to form the advice given. In most cases, it is the personal demeanour of the researcher that gives his or her research credibility. Note well, by stressing the importance of the personal demeanour of the researcher it is evident that positive economic engineering is merely a version of Bacon's inductivism.

If economists who provide policy advice could get away with wearing white laboratory coats, they would probably parade before television cameras so attired. But again, the demeanour of the practising economic positivist is more understood by what it is not. Nobody will believe an economist who claims to know the truth and refuses even to look at data. Nobody will believe an economist who is interested only in publicly promoting his or her personal value judgements. Nobody will believe the research done by someone who behaves like Goethe's young Werther. In other words, true believers, zealots and romantics need not apply for the job of economic adviser. And it seems firmly believed that adherence to economic positivism precludes such objectionable demeanour.

6.7 POSITIVE EVIDENCE ABOUT POSITIVE ECONOMICS

Having discussed the nature of the economic positivism explicitly discussed in positivist textbooks, the next consideration ought to be about how positivism is actually practised in positive economic analysis. The salient feature of all examples of 'positive' economic analyses is their conformity to just one format. Specifically, after the introductory section of a typical positive economics article there is a section entitled 'The model' or some variation of this. This is followed by a section entitled 'Empirical results' or something similar, and a final section summarizing the 'Conclusions'. The question that should be considered is: why do virtually all positivist papers conform to this one format? Is the dominance of this uniformity the *only* success of modern economic positivism?

A superficially true explanation of why a specific format is universally used is that it is a matter of rhetoric (McCloskey 1989). A trivial explanation would be that all journal editors require that format, but surely they are only responding to what they think the market demands. The concern here is not just why any particular individual might decide to organize a research paper according to the accepted format. Instead, the concern is why this particular format is so widely demanded.

I do not see any reason why the same principles of understanding embodied in the current practice of economic positivism – namely, model-building – should not also be applicable for the economic methodologist attempting to explain the empirical uniformity evident in the widespread practice of model-building itself. So, in order to explain or describe the practice of economic positivism, let me attempt to build a 'model' of the format of a typical article in the literature of positive neoclassical economics. Judging by what is often identified as a 'model' in positive economics, virtually every formal statement is considered a model. Nevertheless, there are some basic requirements.

In order to build my model of positive or empirical analysis, as with any model, the assumptions need to be explicitly stated. Let me begin by stating the obvious assumptions which form the visible core of the research programme of neoclassical economics. My first and most fundamental assumption is that every neoclassical model must have behavioural assumptions regarding maximization and market equilibrium. Furthermore, the results of the model must depend crucially on these assumptions.

The remaining assumptions are less fundamental to neoclassical economics but are required to provide the rhetoric of modern economic positivism. To provide the main necessary ingredient of the modern positivist approach, my second assumption is that every empirical model must yield at least one equation which can be 'tested' by statistically estimating its parametric coefficients.

My third assumption (which is required for the implementation of the second assumption) is that every empirical paper must presume specific criteria of 'truthlikeness' – so-called statistical testing conventions. For example, such statistical parameters as means and standard deviations, R^2 values, t statistics etc. must be considered. That is, every equation is a statement which is either true or false. However, when applying an equation to empirical data we supposedly know that the fit will not usually be perfect even if the statement (i.e. the equation) is true. So the question is: in what circumstances will the fitted equation be considered 'true'? The use of the testing conventions implies that the investigator is not attempting to determine the absolute truth of his or her model. Rather, the objective is to establish its acceptability or unacceptability according to standard testing conventions of one's chosen form of economic positivism.

My last assumption is that, in order to be published, every empirical paper must have contributed something to the advancement of 'scientific' knowledge. That is, it must establish some new 'facts' – namely, 'facts' which were previously unknown – by providing either new data or new analysis of old data.

In order to test this model of the methodology of neoclassical positive economics, the available data must be considered. First I must decide where to look for mainstream 'positive economics'. Obviously, one should expect to

99

find it in the pages of the leading economics journals. So, to test this model, I should be able to open any leading mainstream journal such as the *American Economic Review* or the *Economic Journal* and examine the contents of a few issues. To be relevant, the examination of the data should be restricted to those articles intended to be positive analysis. That is, those articles considered to be avant-garde theories or concerned with the more technical (mathematical) aspects of 'economic theory' should be avoided. Of course, topics such as 'history of thought' or 'methodology' should also be ignored if they can be found.

I performed this test for the *American Economic Review* for the year 1980 (Boland 1982: ch. 7). My examination of the articles selected as stated seemed to indicate that all of them conformed to the format specified by this model of positive neoclassical analysis. The only empirical question implied by this positive model is whether there are any exceptions to what I have claimed will be found in the mainstream journals. As expected I was able to report that there were none in the data considered. My model of positive analysis did fit the available data.

6.8 EXPLAINING THE USE OF THE STANDARD ARTICLE FORMAT

Despite the ease of confirming such a positive model of economic positivism, there is apparently no discussion of *why* papers *should* be written according to the observed format, apart from a recent discussion limited to the *rhetoric* of economic positivism (McCloskey 1989). Of course, there is no need to discuss the standard format if everyone agrees that it presents no problem and is doing its required job. My general theory is that the reason why the format is not discussed is that its purpose is simply taken for granted. Taking things for granted is a major source of methodological problems and inconsistencies in economics, although the problems are not always appreciated. This is the case with the widespread use of one common format for neoclassical empirical research papers. Perhaps there is no discussion because the job performed is merely one of an elementary filter, which presumes that only papers that can be expressed in the standard format could ever make a positive contribution to positive economics. This presumption is also not discussed anywhere. So, just what is the purpose of the standard format?

While there need not be anything inherent in positivism which would connect its practice with the development of neoclassical economics, the two are closely related. The purpose of the standard format for those articles which purport to provide positive neoclassical economic analysis is exactly the purpose for promoting positivism in the first place. The purpose is the facilitation of a long-run inductive verification of knowledge even though the format is promoted by people who would see themselves practising a more modest view of knowledge and method – a view which supposedly denies induction. At the root of this view is the conviction of manifest truth. More specifically, it is the conviction of neoclassical economists that neoclassical economics represents a true theory of society – that the real world is manifestly what neoclassical economists claim it is – and thus any model based *only* on facts generated in the real world will in the long run lead one to see the manifest truth which in this case is believed to be the veracity of neoclassical economics. Basing models only on facts generated in the real world is, of course, the claimed purpose of positivism.

To understand the relationship between the standard format and the research programme to verify neoclassical theory, we need to consider the following questions. What constitutes a successful positive analysis? What would be a failure? And, in order to determine what constitutes a success, it would seem that we ought to consider a more fundamental question: what is the objective of neoclassical model-building?

If the usual published positive neoclassical articles are actually considered contributions to 'scientific knowledge', then it can only be the case that the hidden objective of such positive economics is that of *Chicago positivism* – namely a long-term verification of neoclassical economics. Specifically, each paper which offers a confirmation of the applicability of neoclassical economics to 'real-world' problems must be viewed as one more positive contribution towards an ultimate inductive proof of the truth of neoclassical theory. My reason for concluding this is merely that logically all that can be accomplished by the typical application of neoclassical theory to 'real-world' phenomena is a proof that it is *possible* to fit at least one neoclassical model to the available data. Critics can always say that a model's fit may be successful in the reported case but it does not prove that it will be successful in every case (Boland 1989: chs 7, 8). I would argue that the agenda of positive neoclassical research programmes presumes that, if we can continue to contribute more confirming examples of the applicability of neoclassical economics, then eventually we shall prove that it is the only true theory of the economy.

6.9 POSITIVE SUCCESS OR POSITIVE FAILURE?

Clearly, an examination of the format of a typical positivist economic analysis reveals that, *as a form of rhetoric*, economic positivism has been very successful. But has it been successful at fulfilling the broader promises of positivism? This is a particularly important question for those of us who reject the possibility of an inductive proof for any theory such as neoclassical economics.

While many of the proponents of the market system of prices in general and of privatization in particular are also proponents of positive economic analysis to support their views, it is seldom recognized that advocacy of either view is inconsistent with a non-romantic practice of positivism. It is not difficult to imagine the positive economist's response to a simple observation that, while the positivist economists base their analysis of economic phenomena on the presumed existence of a perfectly functioning market system of prices, the world outside our windows is not such a perfectly functioning system.

For example, if the world were governed by a market system of prices without governmental interference or private collusion, then eventually society's resources would be optimally allocated according to the desires of all individual consumers. We are also told that the world outside our window is in a state of equilibrium and, specifically, all prices are equilibrium prices. For this reason, any subsequent introduction of governments into the model will usually be seen to result in suboptimal allocations of resources. Thus it is argued that privatization and the reliance on prices (as the only information appropriate for social co-ordination) is to be recommended.

To be fair, it should be recognized that the advocacy of privatization is a relatively recent phenomenon and not all advocates consider themselves to be positivists. Moreover, not all positivists advocate privatization despite what may seem to be the case today. During the 1950s and 1960s, most positivists were engaged in the advocacy of government interference in everyday economic affairs on the basis of what they called Keynesian economics. To these positivists it was enough to look outside our windows and see that the world is characterized by cyclical high unemployment and various levels of instability. Much of the academic effort in that period resulted in the development of the econometric approach to economic positivism which was intended to assist governments in the process of managing and 'fine-tuning' the economy.

It would seem that truly positive economists would shun such advocacy and simply and dispassionately explain the world the way it is. Namely, they should explain how phenomena are generated in a world where governments and collusion are commonplace. The obvious fact that many proponents of economic positivism are almost always engaged in the advocacy of simplistic engineering views such as either global privatization or governmental macroeconomic management should lead us to recognize that too often today economic positivism is mostly, and perhaps only, rhetoric.

REFERENCES

Agassi, J. (1963) *Towards an Historiography of Science, History and Theory*, Beiheft 2, The Hague: Mouton.
—— (1971) 'Tautology and testability in economics', *Philosophy of Social Science* 1: 49–63.
Blaug, M. (1980) *The Methodology of Economics*, Cambridge: Cambridge University Press.

Boland, L. (1977) 'Testability in economic science', *South African Journal of Economics* 45: 93–105.

—— (1979) 'A critique of Friedman's critics', *Journal of Economic Literature* 17: 503–22.

—— (1982) *The Foundations of Economic Method*, London: Allen & Unwin.

—— (1986) *Methodology for a New Microeconomics*, Boston, MA: Allen & Unwin.

—— (1989) *The Methodology of Economic Model Building: Methodology after Samuelson*, London: Routledge.

Böhm-Bawerk, E. (1889) *Positive Theory of Capital*, transl. W. Smart, New York: Stechert.

Comte, A. (1974) *Positive Philosophy*, New York: AMS Press (originally published 1855).

de Marchi, N. (1988) 'Popper and the LSE economists', in N. de Marchi (ed.) *The Popperian Legacy in Economics*, pp. 139–66, Cambridge: Cambridge University Press.

Drury, H. (1968) *Scientific Management*, 3rd edn, New York: AMS Press (originally published 1922).

Friedman, M. (1953) 'The methodology of positive economics', in *Essays in Positive Economics*, pp. 3–43, Chicago, IL: University of Chicago Press.

Harbury, C. (1981) *Descriptive Economics*, 6th edn, London: Pitman.

Hutchison, T. (1938) *The Significance and Basic Postulates of Economic Theory*, London: Macmillan.

Jackson, R. (1988) *Rational Economics*, New York: Philosophical Library.

Keynes, J. N. (1917) *The Scope and Method of Political Economy*, 4th edn, London: Macmillan.

Koopmans, T. (1957) *Three Essays on the State of Economic Science*, New York: McGraw-Hill.

Lipsey, R. (1963) *An Introduction to Positive Economics*, 1st edn, London: Weidenfeld & Nicolson.

—— (1966) *An Introduction to Positive Economics*, 2nd edn, London: Weidenfeld & Nicolson.

—— (1983) *An Introduction to Positive Economics*, 6th edn, London: Weidenfeld & Nicolson.

Lipsey, R., Purvis, D. and Steiner, P. (1988) *Economics*, 6th edn, New York: Harper & Row.

Lundin, R. (1967) *Objective Psychology of Music*, 2nd edn, New York: Wiley.

McCloskey, D. (1989) 'Why I am no longer a positivist', *Review of Social Economy* 47: 225–38.

Quine, W. (1961) *From a Logical Point of View*, revised edn, New York: Harper & Row (originally published 1953).

Rotwein, E. (1959) 'On "The methodology of positive economics" ', *Quarterly Journal of Economics* 73: 554–75.

Samuelson, P. (1963) 'Problems of methodology: discussion', *American Economic Review, Papers and Proceedings* 53: 231–6.

Simon, H. (1963) 'Problems of methodology: discussion', *American Economic Review, Papers and Proceedings* 53: 229–31.

Smith, V. L. (1982) 'Microeconomic systems as an experimental science', *American Economic Review* 72: 923–55.

Spencer, H. (1896) *System of Synthetic Philosophy*, New York: Appleton.
Stigler, G. and Becker, G. (1977) 'De gustibus non est disputandum', *American Economic Review* 67: 76–90.

7

INSTITUTIONAL ECONOMICS

WARREN J. SAMUELS

7.1 GENERAL POSITION IN HISTORICAL PERSPECTIVE

Institutional economics originated in the work of Thorstein Veblen, John R. Commons and Wesley C. Mitchell, as well as numerous others, including some, very eclectic, like John Maurice Clark, who worked within both institutional and neoclassical economics (Gruchy 1947; Mayhew 1987).[1] Institutional economics has at least three facets: it is a body of knowledge, an approach to problem-solving and a protest movement. Institutionalists both critique orthodox neoclassical and radical Marxist economics and affirmatively develop their own ideas. This has led to tensions within institutionalism: first, some institutionalists see their work as complementary to that of neoclassicism while others believe that the two are mutually contradictory; second, some emphasize criticism and others the creative development of a corpus of institutionalist theory; third, institutionalists themselves attempt to develop their ideas along different lines. The situation has left institutionalists exposed to the criticism that they have been essentially negative – a criticism whose incorrectness will be shown below. The three facets of institutionalism and the internal divisions within institutionalism will be considered in sequence.

Corpus of knowledge

Institutional economists understand their work to constitute a corpus of knowledge. The central problem by which institutional economists define their subject is the evolution of the organization and control of the economy as a whole, not solely the allocation of resources, distribution of income and determination of the aggregate levels of income, output, employment and prices within a given system. In so far as institutionalists are interested in the latter problems, they typically approach them with a wider range of variables, or a longer chain of reasoning, than do neoclassical economists. The critical

105

difference is that of the central organization and control problem, which leads them to study the wider range of variables. Institutionalists maintain both (a) that the economy encompasses more than the market and (b) that the operative allocative mechanism is not the pure conceptualized market *per se* but the institutions, or power structure, which form and operate through the actual market. Therefore they focus on the forces at work which govern the evolution of the organization and control of the economy, and perforce the institutional organization of the market, to the extent that there is a market. Compared with their orthodox and Marxian brethren, therefore, the institutionalists have quite different conceptions of the economy and of doing economics, but they also endeavour to produce a corpus of knowledge – their own body of theory.

Problem-solving

Institutional economists also believe that their work constitutes an approach to the ongoing solution of practical problems consisting of knowledge, insights and techniques of policy analysis to be brought to bear in problem-solving. In this respect, at least, institutional economists are not very different from other economists, who also motivate their work at least in part by its relevance to issues of policy, although the institutionalists' approach generally provides for a wider range of policy variables employed less mechanically.

Protest movement

Institutional economists also conduct protests against both the established market economy and the established body of orthodox theory which they see as too closely tied to existing institutional arrangements. They are not willing to accept the existing configuration of institutions as either necessarily or conclusively definitive of the Western economic system. For them, there is no reason to give existing institutional arrangements, especially their hierarchical structure, a privileged status solely because they exist.

Institutionalists have indeed been critical. They criticize the mechanistic positivism of neoclassical orthodoxy. They criticize its conception, or mode of modelling, of human nature. They criticize the exclusion of considerations of power from the neoclassical vision. They are critical of neoclassical practice which seeks determinate, equilibrium and optimal solutions, and have emphasized instead the study of the forces actually at work in the economy and the operation of adjustment processes, with neither pretence nor the appearance of conclusivity. They are particularly critical of theories and of the conduct of theorizing which give effect to existing institutional arrangements, or to those arrangements which are selectively assumed to exist, especially in the form of analysis which purports, on the basis of implicit normative premises, to reach

'optimal' solutions. They are also particularly critical of the mechanistic application of assumptions of rationality, competition, knowledge and, *inter alia*,
methodological individualism as being unrealistic and susceptible to ideologically driven use. They have been especially critical of the conventional treatment of the economic role of government in mainstream economics. The point
is, however, that institutionalists have done more than criticize. They have
developed alternative bodies of analysis, both theoretical and empirical, in each
of these respects and in almost all substantive areas of economics.

Neoclassicism has not been the only object of criticism by institutionalists,
nor the only major school to be contrasted with institutionalism. Marxian
economics is also manifestly relevant. Institutionalists agree with Marxians
that power is important, that systemic change needs to be considered within
economics, that methodological collectivism needs to be added to methodological individualism, that the economy (and the polity) are artefacts and subject
to reformation, and, *inter alia*, that the interests of the masses, for example
the working class, need to be given a place in economics otherwise excluded
or denigrated by implicit if not explicit emphasis on the hegemonic upper
classes.

But institutionalists are generally critical of Marxian economists for their
conception of economic class (tied to the notion of superstructure and foundation), for their teleological dialectical-materialist conception of economic
transformation (in contrast with the institutionalist conception of open-ended
Darwinian evolution), for their typical emphasis on revolution (in contrast with
either systemic reform or reform within the present system) and for their
narrow treatments of value theory and the economic role of government.

Institutionalists, however, have been to some extent divided among themselves. Some trace their origins to the work of Veblen and Clarence E. Ayres,
whereas others follow the lead of Commons. The differences are multiple and
complex but tend to focus on their respective approaches to the theory of
value. The Veblen–Ayres tradition sees technology and industrialization as
both the driving force and the source of value, the latter in the sense that
technology enables mankind to produce more and that whatever promotes
further production is valuable *per se* – a result, they find, inhibited by hierarchical institutions. In their view, institutions constitute a conservative force,
inhibiting the introduction of new technology and new organizational arrangements. This is at least somewhat ironic, in that these institutionalists denigrate
institutions, whereas institutionalists as a school of thought stress their importance; for them, the importance is negative (Neale 1987).

The Commons tradition, on the other hand, sees economic performance as
the product of a whole set of factors and forces, including technology and
institutions, with institutions viewed as a mode of choosing among technological alternatives. In their view, the important sphere of value is found in the

determination of the working rules of law and morals, which help structure and govern access to and use of power, i.e. determine whose interests are to count and when. In this respect, as in some others, the two strands of institutionalism approach a subject quite differently among themselves but even more differently from mainstream neoclassical economics, whose value theory focuses on the relative prices of economic goods. But, in other respects, all institutionalists have stressed the need to encompass within economics realistic and meaningful conceptions and theories of social change, social control, collective action, technology, the process of industrialization and the market as an institutional complex rather than an abstract mechanism.

7.2 METHODOLOGICAL ORIENTATION

As is often the case with heterodox schools of thought, institutional economists have devoted much attention to considerations of methodology (Samuels 1980; Mirowski 1987; Samuels and Tool 1989b).

1 Institutionalists have emphasized *Verstehen* (understanding) over prediction.
2 Institutionalists stress the limits (in the face of radical indeterminacy) of predicting the actual future *vis-à-vis* prediction in the context of a model.
3 Institutionalists perceive economic theory to be an inevitable blend of induction and deduction *vis-á-vis* aprioristic and formalistic deductivism.
4 Institutionalists approach the economy as an organic systemic evolutionary whole rather than a static machine.
5 Institutionalists stress instrumentalism and pragmatism, in part as a problem-solving basis of relevance *vis-à-vis* intellectual science fiction and puzzle-solving.
6 Institutionalists emphasize the inevitability of normative elements in economic theory, especially with regard to the applications of theory to questions of policy and the economic role of government, and particularly with respect to the status of the status quo. They stress the role of selective, often implicit, normative premises as to whose interests are to count.
7 Institutionalists affirm making values explicit and subject to open discussion and criticism rather than using values in an implicit or obfuscatory manner. They reject the practice of pretending to be positivists while practising an ostensibly limited but heavily selective normativism in the form of Pareto optimality and while otherwise avoiding serious and epistemologically sophisticated testing.
8 Institutionalists criticize the use of Newtonian physics as the archetype for economics.
9 Institutionalists call for pattern modelling rather than limited, if not dubious, causal explanation (Wilber and Harrison 1978).

10 Institutionalists emphasize methodological collectivism either *per se* or combined with an enriched and non-ideological methodological individualism,
but not the latter alone (Hodgson 1988).

With regard to the practice of economics, institutionalists hold, *inter alia*,
the following beliefs.

1 Institutionalists affirm cumulative and open rather than unilineal causation.
2 Institutionalists emphasize the limitations of rationality as fact or a limiting
assumption and/or ideology (Jensen 1987; Hodgson 1988).
3 Institutionalists stress the limits, especially with regard to coherence and
dispositiveness, of the neoclassical quest for determinate and presumptively
optimal equilibrium solutions.
4 Institutionalists affirm the study of adjustment processes, especially the
actual working out of things, including the factors and forces actually at
work and the processes of institutional adjustment and change (Bush 1987),
rather than the technical formal conditions of stability of equilibrium in the
context of some notion of *a priori*, pre-reconciled or predetermined order.

With regard to the study of the history of economic thought, institutionalists
have focused upon the following:

1 economic ideas as beliefs or a mode of discourse, as a system of meaning,
as well as in terms of truth;
2 the operation of power structure and ideology as filtration mechanisms at
work within the discipline in the development of ideas;
3 the fundamental tautologies and circularities at the basis of economic theory
and policy;
4 the practice of history of economic and methodological research in a fashion
which does not merely cast lustre on existing arrangements and the currently
dominant school of economic thought;
5 economics as knowledge, social control and psychic balm (by setting minds
at rest, through interpreting the status quo as coherent, orderly and har-
monious);
6 the sociological explanations of the development of twentieth-century economics;
7 the relation of language to meaning;
8 how general concepts require and/or enable further selective specification
in application.

7.3 POWER

For all institutionalists, technology is a principal force in systemic evolution and
economic performance. For those in the Veblen–Ayres tradition, technology is

more than a principal force, it is an imperative. For them it is the key progressive force in economic development, the source of value as well as the core of the process of industrialization (Tool 1977; Rutherford 1981; Lower 1987). For those in the Commons tradition, technology is less an imperative but no less a principal force. For them technology influences productive capacity, productivity, efficiency and organization, but it also constitutes a set of alternative ways of organizing and conducting production (Melman 1975). Therefore, while there are imperative aspects to technology, choice of technology is subject to power play as various economic actors attempt to utilize it for their own respective purposes (Klein 1974; Strassmann 1974; Samuels 1977).

All institutionalists comprehend the economy as a system of power (Samuels 1979; Samuels and Tool 1989a, c). Without denying the aspects of co-operation, harmony and the exhaustion of gains from trade. they stress elements and processes of conflict and power play. They emphasize, for example, that power structure (including legal rights) governs the determination of whose interests are to count: Pareto-optimal solutions, they affirm, are specific to the structure of entitlements or rights. Efforts to seek unique optimal solutions to problems, they therefore also affirm, inevitably give effect to presumptive antecedent assumptions as to whose interests are to count. Whereas the neoclassicist seeks to identify the optimizing properties of inter-action, the institutionalist, while not negating the former, also studies the processes within which optimization takes place and which channel the optimal results actually achieved.

For the institutionalist, as indicated above, the central economic problem is the organization and control of the economy, which is to say, the (re)formation of its power structure. Institutionalists have studied the economy as a whole, and such institutions as legal rights, property, contract and the corporation in terms of power. For them, power includes (Eichner 1987), but also substantially transcends, power as control by firms over price. Rather, it centres on power as participation in the economy, governing whose interest counts in resource allocation, in income distribution and in employment and real income determination. The economy, for the institutionalists, is a decision-making or discretionary process (Tool 1979), in which individual economic actors and subgroups thereof jockey for position and performance result, and not a neutral mechanism.

The economy is more than the market. The economy is the institutions which form the market and through which the market operates and which generates market results. The market is therefore subject to the forces which govern the organization and control of the economy, in large part through the (re)formation of institutions, in which the crux is power and power play. Power is inevitable and indeed essential to the economic system. Analyses in terms of imaginary pure conceptual markets must be distinguished, say the institutionalists, from analyses of how actually instituted markets operate. Institutions matter.

Institutionalism is therefore both a theory of social control and a theory of social change, including analyses of institutional adjustment and of the operation of institutions as modes of control and change. Not the least studied by institutionalists are private property, the corporation and the corporate system as well as government itself. In all these respects, the institutionalist argument that optimal solutions are power structure specific emphasizes an important but typically neglected aspect of neoclassical theory. The institutionalists also examine power, power structure and power play independent of the technical conditions of so-called optimality. Based on empirical evidence, for example, institutionalists avoid the trap of taking property and other rights as given and pre-eminent to man, and/or as either exogenous to the economy or determined by presumptive optimality (cost–benefit) reasoning itself.

In the institutionalist perspective, the denial of power by formal neoclassical theory effectively serves to legitimize the existing structure of exchange and exercise of power. It does so in part by accepting as optimal the marginal adjustments made by firms and other economic actors.

7.4 INSTITUTIONALIST MICROECONOMICS

The central microeconomic proposition of institutional economics is that the allocation of resources is a function not of the market but of the power structure which forms and operates through it. With this proposition all institutionalists are in complete agreement, however they may disagree otherwise. The institutionalist acknowledges that resource allocation can be examined in terms of market forces of demand and supply but argues that demand and supply are themselves in part a function of the structure of power (for example, rights) which is in turn a function of the use of government to protect one interest or another. This is itself a function of a contest over the control and use of government, in part for that very purpose. The allocation of resources is therefore not a matter of two curves or functions on a blackboard but of the forces which form and operate through them. In a word, resource allocation is a function of power.

So also is the distribution of income a function not of neutral 'natural' markets but of the exercise of power in the market and especially in the institutions which form and operate through the market. In this respect, it is true both that distribution is a function of power and that power is a function of distribution.

Institutional economists have thus argued for the study of, and to some extent have studied, the forces of socialization and individuation, such as advertising, custom and habit and, especially, status emulation, which govern the formulation of perceived individual self-interests and preferences. They study the forces involved in the production of the power structure which weights preferences across individuals, thereby governing whose interests count. In this they often tend to focus on culture, enculturation and cultural change, and thereby on the complex processes in which it is true both that values are derived from power and that power is derived from values (Hodgson 1988).

For the institutionalist, power is not a matter of price alone but of a host of structural factors. Similarly, valuation is understood to be more than a matter of price, more than a product of market forces: the economy as a whole, inclusive of but extending beyond the market, is comprehended as a valuational process. Values are expressed, as in neoclassical price theory, through choices made from within extant opportunity sets, but also through the dynamics of power structure and power play in the formation of opportunity-set structure. Allocation is thus a function of more than the market narrowly conceived – a matter of the entire system of organization and control of the economy. Moreover, the concept of values is expressed not only in terms of commodity and factor prices but also in terms of the values and the working rules of law and morals which govern participation and the exercise of discretion in the economy. The institutionalist concept of value thus extends beyond price to social values, which they affirm are inexorably present and influence the operation of the economy, in part channelling the formation of market prices (Tool 1986).

Institutionalists also have researched what they consider to have been the major transformation, during the last century, of the Western economic system – namely, the development of the corporate system and with it the emergence of centralized private, or private–public, sector planning. Prices in this system are administered and formed in part through mark-up, target return and/or profit-budgeted techniques, sometimes using highly sophisticated forms of optimal control theory. Firms, especially in the oligopoly core of the economy, which institutionalists see as coexisting along with the more or less competitive periphery, are price-makers rather than price-takers (Samuels and Tool 1989c).

Institutionalists thus emphasize the need to examine commodity and input markets in structural terms. This is true of both production and consumption (Hamilton 1987; Stevenson 1987) and both the oligopoly core and segmented or stratified labour markets. As for firms themselves, corporations are also structural phenomena. For example, while institutionalists are not enamoured of a simple-minded profit-maximization hypothesis, preferring something more complex (to include, for example, satisficing, market share, managerial lifetime earnings etc.), they emphasize that more important than profit-maximizing as a formal category is the process through which is formed the substance of what profit maximization means to corporate decision-makers.

7.5 INSTITUTIONALIST MACROECONOMICS

Institutionalist macroeconomics in part follows from its microeconomics, and as such resembles post-Keynesian macroeconomics: economic performance – here the levels of income, output, employment and prices – is a function of power. Institutionalists emphasize that the price mechanism does not work in a neo-Walrasian market-clearing manner. Institutionalists find it necessary to differentiate between the oligopoly core and the competitive periphery with regard to pricing and consequent macroeconomic performance. They affirm that the distributions of income and wealth influence macroeconomic perform-ance, and that the struggle over distribution generates both inflation and stagflation. They argue that the macroeconomic performance of labour markets reflects, first, their structural or segmentational features and, second, the circumstance that the demand for labour (and thus employment and unemploy-ment) is much more a function of final output (and effective demand for same) than of the relative price of labour, although they do not deny that labour can price itself out of the market or engender capital substitution. They find that government macroeconomic policy has been more concerned with stabilizing expectations for private sector corporate-system planning than full employment or, for that matter, price stability.

Following the tradition of Mitchell, institutionalists emphasize the pecuniary and especially the monetary nature of the economy (Dillard 1987). Following John Maynard Keynes, Gardiner C. Means, Alfred Eichner and John Kenneth Galbraith, among others, institutionalist macroeconomic theory stresses the dependence of macroeconomic performance on both behavioural variables and power structure (Peterson 1980, 1987). Many institutionalists, following Galbraith, perceive the existing system as willy-nilly one of microeconomic and macroeconomic planning and would substitute a more broad-based and self-conscious system of planning, whereas others, following Walter Adams and Willard Mueller, among others, more or less agree with the diagnosis but disagree with the prescription, calling instead for effective use of anti-trust policy to restore a truly market economy replacing the corporate system.

7.6 INSTITUTIONALIST RESEARCH IN SPECIALIZED FIELDS

Work by institutionalists in the various specialized substantive fields within economics not surprisingly reflects their general orientation, especially their emphasis on empirical research, albeit conducted within the institutionalist

113

paradigm, on how markets actually are organized and economic actors actually function, with due regard to structural and behavioural variables. Indeed, in these fields considerations of power are almost always supplemented with those of belief system (what is accepted as knowledge, for whatever reason) and psychology, which affect interests, preferences and life-styles.

In the field of labour economics, institutionalists, commencing with Commons and his student and successor at Wisconsin, Selig Perlman, have studied the formation of labour markets and the actions of participants therein to shape both market structure and performance to their desires, in part through influencing public opinion and government policy (protective labour market and labour relations legislation). Central to their studies have been the analyses of labour markets as arenas of mutual coercion, labour unions and collective bargaining. More recent work has continued to centre on labour–management relations and on dual, segmented or stratified labour markets. Here is a good example of the institutionalist distinction between choice from within opportunity sets and choice over the structure of opportunity sets: whereas human capital theory focuses on individual optimization of lifetime wealth, institutionalist labour economics focuses on the forces and factors (including corporate system and government policies) which govern who will have what opportunities to work within, a situation reminiscent of Perlman's distinction between opportunity-conscious management and job-conscious workers. Throughout, power is central (Woodbury 1987).

In the field of economic development, institutionalists focus on such factors as the inhibitive role of class structure and how it both directly and indirectly constrains modernization through, for example, upper-class control of government and other economic institutions and lower-class emulation of traditional upper-class-oriented customs. They have often stressed the channelling of peasant rationality brought about by religion, custom, fear and power structure (Street 1987, 1988; Fusfeld 1988; James 1988; Klein 1988).

In the field of international trade, institutionalists stress the impact of international power relations, including the role of alternative sets of rules governing internal and external transactions and of alternative international institutions, on trade relationships, comparative costs and capital flows. Institutionalists have also examined the conduct of political and economic imperialism as a historic component of international relations. They emphasize, among other things, that 'free markets', both domestically and internationally, are a function of the institutional arrangements which form and operate through them and which are a matter of 'instituted process' (Adams 1987).

In the field of industrial organization, institutionalists have stressed the importance of structural considerations. Some have concentrated on conventional notions of industrial concentration, while others have focused on the concept of a corporate system and on centralized private, or private–public, sector planning. Apparently all institutionalists concur on the identification of the modern Western economy as heavily concentrated and highly organized. As already noted, some prescribe stronger and more effective anti-trust legislation and enforcement in order to create a truly competitive market system, while others, taking the stituation as given, advocate responsible and accountable government planning in place of an already formed but irresponsible and uncontrolled private planning system (Dugger 1987; Munkirs and Knoedler 1987; see also Galbraith 1967).

7.7 ECONOMIC ROLE OF GOVERNMENT

In the institutionalist view, government is willy-nilly an important part of the economic system; indeed, the economic system would not be what it is without government. Both the basic economic institutions, which determine the nature of the economic system, and the structure of rights, which determines the power structure of the economy as well as the existential economic significance of natural resources (DeGregori 1987), are a function of government. Contrariwise, mainstream economics sees government principally as the source of innefficiency and distortion, and otherwise essentially ineffective. Institutionalists perceive that the mechanistic theorizing of neoclassical economists yields conclusions which exclude or denigrate government precisely because those theories have either ignored or taken as given the economic role of government.

Institutionalists perceive government to be inexorably a major means of collective action, and to be understood in terms of realistic and essentially non-ideological conceptions of social control and social change. Government is fundamentally involved, as both a dependent and independent variable, in the socio-economic power structure. The economy is an object of legal control and the government is a means of economic advantage. Government is an instrument available to whomever can control and use it. The rights of economic significance, for example property rights, which form the power structure generating and channelling the market, are fundamentally a matter of government policy. The economy is an artefact, in part produced by government and the uses to which government is put. Jockeying for power over government is a major social process. Part of that process is the selective manipulation of ideology. The critical practical issue is not government versus no government but the interests to which government will lend its support. Intervention is not a matter of government intruding into a situation in which it had hitherto been absent but of legal change of legal rights. Government is both a vehicle of the exercise of superior nominally private power and a check on that power in the interest of the otherwise relatively powerless. The corporate system has been formed through a symbiosis of the interests and beliefs of nominally private agents and of public officials. Both economy and polity arise, in the institutionalist view, in a common nexus (Samuels and Schmid 1981; Liebhavsky 1987, 1988; Dragun 1988; Dugger 1988; Gruchy 1988; Kanel 1988; Mitchell 1988; Randall 1988; Samuels 1988b).

7.8 CONCLUDING COMMENTS

Institutional economics focuses on power, institutions, technology, process and similar concepts. In doing so, institutional economics pursues a wider range of variables than does mainstream neoclassical economics but it also gives effect to a different conceptualization of the economic system and a different emphasis on, if not understanding of, the central economic problem. Institutionalists therefore seek to understand economic events and phenomena in terms not solely of resource allocation but also of structural organization-and-control causes and consequences. They eschew the quest for determinate optimal equilibrium solutions in favour of understanding what actually goes on in the economy, consistently denigrating conventional practices which both foreclose or otherwise finesse process and surreptitiously introduce implicit normative premises. In doing so, institutional economists maintain their traditions of (a) creating an alternative corpus of knowledge, thereby contributing to society's problem-solving capacities, and (b) critiquing both other schools of economic thought and the regnant economic order.

NOTE

1 The principal institutionalist publication is the *Journal of Economic Issues*, in its twenty-fifth year of publication in 1991. The volumes published by Transaction Books cited in the references below reprint materials from the *Journal*. See also Samuels (1988a), for which the sources of materials are wider.

REFERENCES

Adams, J. (1987) 'Trade and payments as instituted process: the institutional theory of the external sector', *Journal of Economic Issues* 21: 1839–60.

DeGregori, T. (1987) 'Resources are not, they become', *Journal of Economic Issues* 21: 1241–63.

Dillard, D. (1987) 'Money as an institution of capitalism', *Journal of Economic Issues* 21: 1623–47.

Dragun, A. (1988) in W. Samuels (ed.) *Institutional Economics*, vol. 3, part III, Aldershot: Edward Elgar.

Dugger, W. (1987) 'An institutionalist theory of economic planning', *Journal of Economic Issues* 21: 1649–75.

—— (1988) in W. Samuels (ed.) *Institutional Economics*, vol. 2, part II, Aldershot: Edward Elgar.

Eichner, A. (1987) 'Prices and pricing', *Journal of Economic Issues* 21: 1555–84.

Fusfeld, D. (1988) in W. Samuels (ed.) *Institutional Economics*, vol. 3, part II, Aldershot: Edward Elgar.

Galbraith, K. (1967) *The New Industrial State*, Boston, MA: Houghton Mifflin.

Gruchy, A. (1947) *Modern Economic Thought: The American Contribution*, New York: Prentice-Hall.

—— (1988) in W. Samuels (ed.) *Institutional Economics*, vol. 2, part II, Aldershot: Edward Elgar.

Hamilton, D. (1987) 'Institutional economics and consumption', *Journal of Economic Issues* 21: 1531–54.

Hodgson, G. (1988) *Economics and Institutions*, Philadelphia, PA: University of Philadelphia Press.

James, D. (1988) in W. Samuels (ed.) *Institutional Economics*, vol. 3, part II, Aldershot: Edward Elgar.

Jensen, H. (1987) 'The theory of human nature', *Journal of Economic Issues* 21: 1039–73.

Kanel, D. (1988) in W. Samuels (ed.) *Institutional Economics*, vol. 3, part III, Aldershot: Edward Elgar.

Klein, P. (1974) 'Economics: allocation or valuation?', *Journal of Economic Issues* 8: 785–811.

—— (1988) in W. Samuels (ed.) *Institutional Economics*, vol. 3, part II, Aldershot: Edward Elgar.

Liebhavsky, H. (1987) 'Law and economics from different perspectives', *Journal of Economic Issues* 21: 1809–35.

—— (1988) in W. Samuels (ed.) *Institutional Economics*, vol. 2, part II, Aldershot: Edward Elgar.

Lower, M. (1987) 'The concept of technology within the institutional perspective', *Journal of Economic Issues* 21: 1147–76.

Mayhew, A. (1987) 'The beginnings of institutionalism', *Journal of Economic Issues* 21: 971–98.

Melman, S. (1975) 'The impact of economics on technology', *Journal of Economic Issues* 9: 59–72.

Mitchell, W. (1988) in W. Samuels (ed.) *Institutional Economics*, vol. 2, part II, Aldershot: Edward Elgar.

Mirowski, P. (1987) 'The philosophical basis of institutional economics', *Journal of Economic Issues* 21: 1001–38.

Munkirs, J. and Knoedler, J. (1987) 'The existence and exercise of corporate power: an opaque fact', *Journal of Economic Issues* 21: 1679–706.

Neale, W. (1987) 'Institutions', *Journal of Economic Issues* 21: 1177–206.

Peterson, W. (1980) 'Power and economic performance', *Journal of Economic Issues* 14: 827–69.

—— (1987) 'Macroeconomic theory and policy in an institutionalist perspective', *Journal of Economic Issues* 21: 1587–621.

Randall, A. (1988) in W. Samuels (ed.) *Institutional Economics*, vol. 3, part III, Aldershot: Edward Elgar.

Rutherford, M. (1981) 'Clarence Ayres and the instrumental theory of value', *Journal of Economic Issues* 15: 567–73.

Samuels, W. (1977) 'Technology *vis-à-vis* institutions in the *JEI*: a suggested interpretation', *Journal of Economic Issues* 11: 871–95.

—— (ed.) (1979) *The Economy as a System of Power*, New Brunswick, NJ: Transaction Books.

—— (ed.) (1980) *The Methodology of Economic Thought*, New Brunswick, NJ: Transaction Books.

—— (1988a) *Institutional Economics*, 3 vols, Aldershot: Edward Elgar.

—— (1988b) in W. Samuels (ed.) *Institutional Economics*, vol. 2, part II, Aldershot: Edward Elgar.

Samuels, W. and Schmid, A. (1981) *Law and Economics: An Institutional Perspective*, Boston, MA: Martinus Nijhoff.

Samuels, W. and Tool, M. (eds) (1989a) *The Economy as a System of Power*, New Brunswick, NJ: Transaction Books.

—— and —— (eds) (1989b) *The Methodology of Economic Thought*, 2nd edn, New Brunswick, NJ: Transaction Books.

—— and —— (eds) (1989c) *State, Society and Corporate Power*, New Brunswick, NJ: Transaction Books.

Stevenson, R. (1987) 'The theory of production', *Journal of Economic Issues* 21: 1471–93.

Strassmann, P. (1974) 'Technology: a culture trait, a logical category, or virtue itself?', *Journal of Economic Issues* 8: 671–87.

Street, J. (1987) 'The institutionalist theory of economic development', *Journal of Economic Issues* 21: 1861–87.

—— (1988) in W. Samuels (ed.) *Institutional Economics*, vol. 3, part II, Aldershot: Edward Elgar.

Tool, M. (1977) 'A social value theory in neoinstitutional economics', *Journal of Economic Issues* 11: 823–46.

—— (1979) *The Discretionary Economy*, Santa Monica, CA: Goodyear.

—— (1986) *Essays in Social Value Theory*, Armonk, NY: M. E. Sharpe.

Wilber, C. and Harrison, R. (1978) 'The methodological basis of institutional economics: pattern model, storytelling, and holism', *Journal of Economic Issues* 12: 61–89.

Woodbury, S. (1987) 'Power in the labor market: institutionalist approaches to labor problems', *Journal of Economic Issues* 21: 1781–807.

8

ECONOMICS AS A PROFESSION

A. W. COATS

Every profession lives in a world of its own. The language spoken by its inhabitants, the landmarks familiar to them, their customs and conventions can only be learnt by those who reside there.

(Carr-Saunders and Wilson 1933: iii)

8.1 INTRODUCTION

Most economists see themselves, and wish to be seen by others, as professionals, although if pressed many would find it difficult to say precisely what that designation means. This is understandable, for the terms 'profession' and 'professionalization' have long been the subject of dispute among specialists, most of whom are sociologists and therefore not taken seriously by economists. Moreover, as noted later, there are specific reasons why the economics profession is difficult to define and identify. What is less understandable, indeed inexcusable, is the dearth of serious research on the nature, historical evolution and significance of the professionalization of economics, whether by economists or other scholars. Of course, there has been considerable discussion of the profession's problems, especially during and since the so-called 'crisis' of the late 1960s and early 1970s (e.g. Heller 1975; Coats 1977; Bell and Kristol 1981 among others), but most of this has been either occasional, personal partisan or mainly methodological. There is no full-scale published study of the growth of the economics profession in the United Kingdom or the United States, the two leading countries in the development of modern economics; and comparative work on the subject is still in its infancy[1] – although there has been some promising, but essentially preliminary, research on the role of economists in government that is referred to below. Consequently, given the current state of our knowledge, the following account must perforce be sketchy and impressionistic.

Some things, however, are indisputable. During the past half-century or so

119

the number of trained economists has increased remarkably by comparison with the rest of the period since Adam Smith published *The Wealth of Nations*, and this is attributable both to supply and demand forces. Prior to the late nineteenth century in the United Kingdom and the United States, and much later still in most other countries, there was little or no formal training in economics as we know it today. When the social sciences eventually emerged as a group of identifiable specialized disciplines, economics was in the vanguard, partly because it was a subject of obvious public interest and significance, but mainly because it was based on a well-developed and recognizable corpus of theoretical knowledge. The latter feature is nowadays seen as the *sine qua non* of a 'modern' science-based profession, as contrasted with such traditional professions as the church, the law and the military.

In the extraordinary global expansion of higher education after the Second World War economics was by no means the least of the disciplinary beneficiaries, and naturally enough this process called for a rapid growth in the numbers of academic teachers and researchers. However, this was but an extension of a much earlier and broader process of economic and social change – namely, the growth of specialization and division of labour in modern urban industrial communities. As one thoughtful sociologist has pithily observed; 'an industrializing society is a professionalizing society' (Goode 1960: 902). Another has claimed that:

> The development and strategic importance of the professions probably constitutes the most important change that has occurred in the occupational structure of modern societies. The growth of the professions has brought to prominence a set of occupations which never figured prominently in the ideological thinking that, after having crystallized in the late nineteenth century, has tended to dominate public discussion in the twentieth.
>
> (Parsons 1968: 536)

The weasel word 'ideological' is pertinent here in at least two distinct but interrelated senses. The first and more obvious of these is political. Thus radical, Marxist, institutionalist and other dissenting economists have argued that orthodox mainstream neoclassical doctrine explicitly or implicitly involves an acceptance of the socio-economic status quo. For example, marginal analysis focuses attention on small-scale incremental adjustments of present discontents, thereby discouraging more fundamental questioning of the existing order, and it is certainly true that when marginalism was gaining acceptance among academic economists around the turn of the century there was a concomitant narrowing of the discipline's scope (symbolized by the terminological shift from 'political economy' to 'economics'), a move that enabled economists to delegate to other social science specialists such troublesome issues as the distribution of income and wealth, the power structure and social justice. Such a contraction of scope is a familiar feature of the professionaliz-ation process. Of course, some critics strenuously resisted this constriction of their subject matter. However, the change was facilitated by the practice of distinguishing sharply between the 'science' (i.e. theory or analysis, sometimes referred to as economics 'proper') and the 'art' of political economy (i.e. the discussion of current economic problems and policies), so that the adept economist could both have her cake and eat it, i.e. she could participate as a detached impartial expert in public policy debates without thereby compromis-ing her scientific purity.[2] How far the laity acknowledged this differentiation of roles is another matter.

More recently, with the growth of non-academic employment opportunities in business, banking, local, regional and national government, and international agencies, an increasing number of economists have entered policy-making positions, and the consequent politicization of the subject has made the distinc-tion between the science and the art more and more difficult to sustain in practice. Especially during and since the Second World War – although the process was already well under way in some countries from the Great Depression of the early 1930s – professionally trained economists have occu-pied prominent positions as heads of state, cabinet ministers, principal official advisers to government, chief executives of large corporations and so on. They have been outspoken in public debates on contentious policy issues in many different forums at a variety of levels, and they played a major part in the construction and operation of the international economic organizations that have become so integral a part of the post-war world.

All this makes it difficult to maintain that economics is an essentially techno-cratic and apolitical subject. Indeed, one perceptive economist critic has per-suasively argued that there are not one but three distinct professional economic ideologies or world views – the conservative, liberal and radical versions – each with its own ideological assumptions, theories and policy preferences, and that by his definition the majority of academic economists are liberals (Ward 1979). This seems entirely appropriate, given the discipline's eighteenth-century liberal moral philosophical antecedents.

However, there is a second meaning of the word ideological that is particu-larly relevant here. This is the concept of professional ideology – the set of ideas, beliefs, values, standards and behaviour patterns that differentiates one category of professionals from others. As noted in the opening epigraph, a professional ideology is an integral part of the common culture shared by the workers in any reasonably well-defined field. It is circumscribed by the group's accepted aims, conventions and methodological rules; it is reinforced by the development of an esoteric language inaccessible to laymen; and it also usually embodies elements of 'tacit' knowledge which even experienced practitioners find difficult to articulate fully. In the economist's case a central tenet of this

121

ideology is the conception of the neutral objective scientific expert which underlies the above-mentioned distinction between 'science' and 'art', or between 'positive' and 'normative' economics, to use the current jargon (Hutchinson 1964). In the economics community the academic ideal, namely that of the pure research truth-seeker, the detached non-partisan expert, outweighs any more pragmatic conception of professionalism or public service; and when this ideal is transported into the non-academic realm it often takes the form of partisan advocacy of efficiency and market methods (Nelson 1987) which, according to some critics, are given unwarranted priority over considerations of equity – an emphasis facilitated by the efforts at the turn of the century to sever the links between political economy and ethics. These professional values are deep rooted, firmly stressed in the standard textbooks and inculcated, both tacitly and explicitly, in the initiation, training and socialization of new recruits to the field. And however remote from reality the conception of professional neutrality may seem, it has exercised a potent force in the creation and maintenance of the economists' collective professional identity.[3]

Of course, the subjective components of professional ideology count for little without the external dimension of public recognition of the occupation's cultural status, which takes the form of specialized appointments, above-average remuneration, the delegation of responsibility and authority, and social esteem. Command of esoteric knowledge and skills is usually certified by the award of degrees, diplomas and other qualifications, for which a lengthy period of training is required; and controls over entry, whether through the training process or direct regulation by a body issuing credentials, or both, serve to limit the supply of new recruits and thereby to maintain the profession's privileged status.

A profession is not a static phenomenon, identifiable simply by a fixed list of traits.[4] Professions grow and develop over time, and professionalization is a dynamic process that involves

> an attempt to translate one order of scarce resources – specialized knowledge and skills – into another – social and economic rewards. To maintain scarcity implies a tendency to monopoly: monopoly of expertise in the market, monopoly of status in the system of stratification.
>
> (Larson 1978: xvii)

Against the cynical view that the essence of professionalism is power – a species of conspiracy against the laity – there is the contrasting belief that the professional has a distinctive moral obligation to his or her clients, or to society at large – for instance in the obligation to use expertise responsibly in the service of others.[5] Whichever of these standpoints is preferred, it is clear that economists have not attained full professional status; indeed, they may not have seriously tried to do so. They have traditionally been ideologically opposed to monopoly, and this has led them to question the merits of professionalism more openly and persistently than other social scientists (Johnson 1972: 15).[6] How far they have sought detachment from the market-place, another characteristic associated with the professions, is a nice question (Herman 1982).

Although academic economists necessarily influence entry into the profession through their control of the degree process, they have consistently opposed any kind of formal professional accreditation. The leading British and American learned societies or professional organizations rely solely on the economic criterion, for they are open to anyone willing to pay the requisite membership fee, and economists have made no collective effort to prescribe standards of professional conduct, whether in universities or elsewhere. Even now, when the level of technical sophistication of PhD students from so-called elite graduate departments has reached heights that to older professionals seem dizzyingly abstract, there is often still no clear occupational discrimination in the non-academic world between (a) those with advanced rather than undergraduate degrees, (b) those with joint or mixed rather than single honours undergraduate degrees (Towse and Blaug 1988) and (c) those in higher management or civil service positions with no formal training whatsoever in economics. Sceptics may argue that it is not ideological distaste grounded in an inherited liberal moral philosophy that explains the reluctance to enforce strict controls over entry, a code of professional ethics or procedures for excommunicating those who fail to maintain acceptable standards of behaviour or performance. Rather, it is the wisdom of recognizing that that species of professionalism is simply unenforceable, perhaps even undefinable, in economics.[7]

Underlying this situation is a troublesome epistemological question: exactly what do economists 'know' (i.e. that other professionals do not)? Of course, trained economists can be expected to 'know' the corpus of economic analysis enshrined in innumerable conventional textbooks (which, incidentally, display a remarkable degree of uniformity). Presumably, they understand the nature and operations of the price mechanism far better than non-economists do; and also the functioning and interdependence of markets at home and abroad, the significance of scarcity and opportunity costs, the nature and functions of money, banking, finance etc., and so on. Yet many of the economist's fundamental ideas are elementary and very general, albeit with wide applicability. Do they suffice as a foundation for claims to expertise in non-academic settings?

Judging by half a century's experience of economists' employment in government the question can confidently be answered in the affirmative. After all, despite the well-publicized conflicts and disagreements within the profession, the demand for economists in the public service has been remarkably sustained, and although much less is known about their successes and failures in the private sector, no doubt the same answer applies there also. However, there are important reservations to be made which cannot be fully explained and justified here.

With respect to government employment, attention has usually been focused on the economists' role in the higher-level advisory or decision-making positions, whereas in demand terms activities within the bureaucratic machine are obviously more significant, albeit less glamorous. These activities vary enormously, and sweeping generalizations must therefore be suspect. Nevertheless, the nature, extent and effectiveness of the economists' work will obviously depend on such factors as the range and variety of the government's economic and social policies (*laissez-faire* is not good for the profession), the political climate (a degree of stability is essential), the character of the bureaucracy (corruption, politicization and inefficiency are obvious impediments) and the readiness to acknowledge the authority of the economist's expertise (which is dependent on the society's culture, the educational system and the degree of consensus within the economics community) (cf. Coats 1981, 1986; Pechman 1989). Economists can perform many different functions in many different contexts, but they are usually more effective in departments or agencies with a relatively clear economic purpose and responsibility. They may be temporary or permanent employees, working either in segregated specialist units (for example, as model-builders and forecasters) or as isolated free-floating individuals in close day-to-day contact with generalist administrators or with other specialists or professionals (and in such cases conflicts of professional values and ideologies may become significant). Much of the lower-level work consists of routine data collection, presentation and analysis, calling for little or no input of the economist's specialist knowledge and equipment. And as government work, like economics itself, has become more and more quantitative, partly in response to the almost insatiable demand for economic and social statistics, economists often find themselves working alongside other numerate specialists such as statisticians, mathematicians, operations researchers or accountants. It is in these situations that the economists' product can and must be differentiated, for in addition to their quantitative, technical and mathematical abilities they also possess a distinctive intellectual apparatus or 'way of thinking' that is unfamiliar to most (but not all) non-economists.[8] The value of this basic, seemingly elementary, mental equipment has repeatedly been stressed by senior professional practitioners reflecting on their experience in government. They have frequently been agreeably surprised by their ability to pose penetrating and effective questions that others were either unable or unwilling to ask. In this context, overemphasis on quantitative methods can be professionally as well as intellectually debilitating, for the solutions to complex policy problems can rarely be reduced to quantitative terms.

As is clear from comparative studies of national governments and international agencies, the tasks performed by a government economist will largely depend on the scale, structure and responsibilities of the organization in which he or she works. Many are employed within the several levels between the top official advisers and policy-makers and the humbler toilers in the bureaucratic vineyard, many of whom are mere number-crunchers. Policy proposals may originate anywhere within the government machine, or from outside, but much of the essential policy formulation and implementation occurs in the middle levels. Proposals are usually modified, refined and reshaped repeatedly – i.e. if they are not abandoned – while moving through the official channels; and once a firm decision has been made, implementation often necessitates its adaptation and interpretation to fit specific circumstances that were not envisaged by the original drafters and decision-makers. Economists contribute to all these activities.

Experienced government economists have learnt that if they are to be effective they must accept the facts of bureaucratic and political life. As Robert Nelson has observed in a valuable recent survey of a large literature, they cannot function simply as undeviating partisan advocates for efficiency. In practice they

> must also tailor their advocacy of market methods, efficient resource use, and other economic approaches to the political environment ... modify proposals to make them attractive in terms of equity, or to avoid infringing on real or perceived 'rights' ... recognize that they are members of an organization with which they must conform to some degree ... [and] develop and exercise skills in bureaucratic and political tactics, which are necessarily interwoven with their exercise of economic experience.
>
> (Nelson 1987: 50)

In official life personality, intuition, imagination, communication skills, speed and stamina may count for more than logic and technique, and the implications of these requirements for graduate training in economics will be considered later. What is clear at this point is that adherence to a strict form of professionalism, which tends to assume the omnipresence of rationality, may be positively harmful.[9] There are many complaints that much of the trained economist's hard-earned professional capital is useless or actively misleading in government work, while the academic emphasis on the value of originality is out of place in an organizational setting where teamwork is essential. Some prominent economists, like the late Harry G. Johnson, have claimed that good economists do not go into government, or, if they do, they do not stay good for long, since they rapidly suffer from professional obsolescence. Others believe that government work is necessarily corrupting, even if only mildly so, because of the unavoidable compromises involved.

8.2 PASSAGES IN THE HISTORICAL DEVELOPMENT OF THE ECONOMICS PROFESSION

Given the difficulties of definition, the history of the economics profession has no unambiguous starting point.[10] While the French Physiocrats may be seen as the first modern 'school' of economists in the intellectual rather than the sociological sense of that term, it is convenient to begin with the Ricardians, the first group of British economists to regard themselves, and to be recognized by important segments of the public, as experts in economic affairs. To a remarkable extent this status was attributable to the personal influence of David Ricardo himself, a retired stockbroker, the very epitome of the scientific intellectual, whose work drew upon and developed Adam Smith's ideas. Ricardo became widely acknowledged as the leading economic authority of the day because of the skill, lucidity and disinterestedness with which he analysed the hotly contested technical and policy problems of the currency, banking and international trade, both in his published writings and in his House of Commons speeches. At that time 'economist' was not yet a recognizable occupational category, and although scholars have suggested that either T. R. Malthus or J. R. McCulloch should be described as the first British professional economist, since each derived most of his income from economic teachings or writings, there was no clear demarcation between those who were qualified to write on economic subjects and those who were not. Despite Thomas Carlyle's familiar jibe about 'the gloomy professors of the dismal science', most of the leading economists spent a limited proportion, if indeed any, of their time in academic employment, and as academic instruction in political economy was woefully inadequate there was no reliable source of prospective new recruits. The Political Economy Club of London, founded in 1821, provided an organizational centre for the discussion and propagation of 'sound' doctrines, particularly free trade. However, it was but one of many such private clubs at home and abroad, and the other prerequisites of professionalization were lacking. The Ricardians' influence derived from their claim to scientific authority which they strenuously asserted in books, pamphlets, magazines, newspapers, official enquiries and parliamentary debates. For the present purpose, however, the most distinctive feature was their effort to distance themselves, as experts, from the amateurs, especially the despised 'practical' men. As Ricardo's ally, James Mill, confidently proclaimed: 'a reasoner must be hard pressed when he is driven to quote practical men in aid of his conclusions. There cannot be a worse authority, in any branch of political science, than that of mere practical men' (Mill 1824, cited by Coats 1964: 90). Mill insisted that: 'Among those who have so much knowledge on the subject as to entitle their opinion to any weight, there is wonderful agreement', despite some disputation 'on the minor questions involved' (Mill 1836, cited by Coats 1964: 90), while a few years later Robert Torrens, a fringe member of the Ricardian group, was confident enough to assert that an economist should be appointed to the Board of Trade because

> it partakes of the nature of a professional appointment, requiring a peculiar course of study, and knowledge of an almost technical nature. . . . Though the time may not have actually arrived, yet it is rapidly approaching, when it will be deemed as necessary to select the members of the Board of Trade from the Economists, as it is to take the Bishops from the Church, or the Law Officers from the Bar.
> (Torrens 1826, cited by O'Brien 1965: 32)

Needless to say, this forecast was wildly overoptimistic. Yet it illustrates the trend of opinion among the spokesmen for classical economics, which soon hardened into a rigid orthodoxy in the hands of popularizers and propagandists. Conceivably the intellectual groundwork for professionalization had been laid, but until the late nineteenth century the academic preconditions were insufficient to provide a significant supply of trained economists clearly differentiated from the many amateur practitioners, some of whom carried considerable weight with both the public and the professors.

The marginal revolution of the 1870s was a watershed in the development of the modern economics profession, a complex process that involved changes both within the discipline itself (for example, the shift from political economy to economics noted earlier) and in the higher educational system, which became the principal source of new recruits. In the late nineteenth and early twentieth centuries the essential institutional conditions for academic specialization were being established, such as degree courses, the shift of emphasis away from teaching towards research, the launching of new journals devoted exclusively to economics and the founding of new learned societies that eventually acquired quasi-professional status, even though they were open to all comers.[11] Among these organizations, the American Economic Association (1885) and the British Economic Association (1891, later the Royal Economic Society) were particularly significant (Coats 1960, 1968b). Both had a very heterogeneous membership, especially initially; both were effectively dominated by academics; and both served as models for similar bodies in other countries.

In an original and penetrating book, John Maloney (1985) has examined the influence of the Marshallian paradigm on the professionalization process in the United Kingdom. He distinguishes between a primary professional orthodoxy 'based on a theoretical paradigm capable of supporting a programme of research, uniting economists who have its partisanship, regular use and comparative mastery', and secondary professional orthodoxies that

> though dependent for their effect on the primary ones, feature a consensus on some policy question which, because it involves non-economic arguments, admits of a distinctively limited 'professional view'. This implies that the purely technical

questions of economic policy, because they impose the same strictly economic terms of discourse on everyone, have less power to create genuine professional orthodoxies.

(Maloney 1985: 230–1)

In the United States the primary professional orthodoxy was slower to emerge and to attain hegemonic status for a variety of reasons including the sheer size and diversity of the territory; the far greater number, heterogeneity and competitiveness of the higher educational institutions; the persistence of heterodox economic ideas, in part a legacy of the German historical school; and a culture far less deferential to intellectual and scientific authority than its British counterpart (Coats 1980). In both countries there was an influential secondary professional orthodoxy based on free-trade ideas, which serves as a reminder of the intimate interdependence of theory and practice in the development of professional economics.

This interdependence was strikingly revealed in the United Kingdom during the intense public controversy over tariff reform in the early years of this century. In 1903 fourteen leading economists signed a letter to *The Times* opposing Joseph Chamberlain's reform proposals and voicing their concern at 'the prevalence of certain erroneous opinions' in favour of protection, a doctrine which, they asserted, had been discredited 'partly for reasons of the same kind as those which, as now universally admitted, justified the adoption of free trade' (*The Times*, 15 August 1903, cited by Coats 1964: 100). Here is a prime example of orthodoxy at work: presumably the 'sound' doctrine propagated earlier by the Political Economy Club and subsequently 'universally admitted' should have been sufficient to counter the resurgence of protectionism, despite markedly changed historical conditions.

Unfortunately, the letter from the fourteen professors not only brought predictable howls of protest from Chamberlain's supporters, but also provoked a number of dissenting letters to *The Times* from reputable academic economists who either opposed or were not fully committed to free trade, whether as a scientific doctrine or as a policy. Some of them firmly objected to the attempt to bring the weight of scientific authority to bear on this controversial political issue (Coats 1964: 100–3).[12] Alfred Marshall, the most influential British economist of the day, soon bitterly regretted his participation, which breached his customary practice of cautious detachment from contentious public issues, and undoubtedly the public's reaction taught other economists the need to exercise individual and collective discretion, and to avoid exposing their deeper disagreements to the laity.

In the United States during this formative period the prevalence of serious threats to academic freedom provided an additional powerful incentive to self-restraint, and in due course, after considerable heart-searching, a kind of professional consensus emerged among the leading economists with respect to the proper forms and limits of professional participation in public affairs (Furner 1975). In neither country was there any concerted effort to devise a formal code of professional behaviour designed to protect the disciplinary practitioner. Yet in both cases, and especially in the United States, there was a growing sense of professional community born of the desire to combine the scientist's intellectual prestige and occupational security with the reforming urge to make a constructive impact on the discussion and solution of contemporary economic problems.

The Keynesian revolution of the late 1930s and 1940s was another major watershed in the professionalization of economics, as it was in the development of economic ideas and policy. Although both Keynes's ideas and his policy proposals proved to be deeply controversial, the conjunction of macroeconomic analysis and major advances in the supply of official statistics gave economists the wherewithal to demonstrate their potential value to society, and on this basis the expansion of the non-academic, especially government, economics profession gained substantial momentum. There had, of course, been many earlier examples of governments, public commissions, banks and businesses employing expert economic advisers, usually on an occasional or even personal basis, but sometimes more formally and permanently. Had the American participation in the First World War been more lasting, the number of economists in the federal service would surely have continued to grow apace, and the permanent complement of peacetime civil service economists might well have remained high. Indeed, it was in the early 1920s that American agricultural economists first became established in the federal administration, and it is no coincidence that their transatlantic counterparts became the first group of permanent economic specialists in British government, roughly a decade later (Coats 1976; McDean 1983). The Great Depression marked a new low in the profession's public esteem, for the economists' response to the urgent and widespread demand for explanations and solutions to the crisis proved to be confusing, often contradictory and therefore deeply disappointing to politicians and the general public alike. But the recovery and approach of war radically changed the climate of opinion.

During the 1940s the global centre of economics, both as a science and as a profession, shifted decisively and permanently from Europe, especially the United Kingdom, to the United States, and within that country in wartime Washington became the intellectual as well as the governmental centre of economists' ideas and activities (including, temporarily, the editorship of the leading professional journal, the *American Economic Review*). Keynes's theoretical ideas and policies dominated academic economics during the first two post-war decades, although never to the same degree in the United States as in the United Kingdom, and, indeed, the multi-centred distribution of academic resources in the United States and the challenge of dissenting orthodox and heterodox doctines combined to sustain the subject's intellectual vitality.

In retrospect it appears that America's post-war leadership was inevitable, in economics as in many other academic disciplines, given the country's overwhelming superiority in material and human resources – the latter's having been disproportionately strengthened by the influx of European emigrés, many of whom had crossed the Atlantic to escape Nazi persecution. The list of Presidents of the American Economic Association provides evidence of the recognition that some of these individuals evidently earned, and the presence of Paul Samuelson, Milton Friedman and George Stigler in the roster of Nobel Prizewinners testifies to the emergence of a cohort of distinguished Americans trained in their native universities during the 1930s who came to professional maturity in the ensuing decade.

This is not the place to examine post-1945 developments in economic doctrines. In the present context the most important consequence of the Americanization of economics (and, gradually, its internationalization also) has been that American methods of advanced training, theories and techniques, intellectual values and professional standards have become increasingly acknowledged and adopted throughout the world, obviously with varying time lags and degrees of resistance.[13] This process was enormously facilitated by a number of factors including the growth and acceleration of global communications; the movement of large numbers of foreign students who studied and obtained their professional credentials in the United States and, to a lesser extent, in the United Kingdom and Western Europe; the veritable army of American and British professors who have taught, studied and undertaken research or advisory work in foreign countries; the proliferation of international conferences, scholarly organizations and study groups; and, less conspicuously, the emergence of small but influential global networks of economic specialists (for example, in development economics, international trade and monetary affairs) and a cadre of economists employed by foreign governments, international agencies and other para-statal bodies. Another major force in the internationalization of economics, as in some other disciplines, has been the increasingly widespread and efficient distribution of research monographs, professional journals, official reports and, especially, relatively standardized elementary and advanced teaching texts and related materials. Of course, the flow of ideas, methods, techniques and various species of hardware and software has by no means been all one way, and there is some danger of overstating the extent of uniformity, especially if we focus on the conventional contents of the standard macroeconomics and microeconomics curriculum. However, as noted at the beginning of this chapter, in the present state of our knowledge we have embarrassingly little systematic data on the precise nature and differences of national 'styles' in training, research and publication (Johnson 1973).

8.3 RECENT DEVELOPMENTS AND CONCERNS

For a variety of historical and cultural reasons that cannot be explored adequately here, Americans have long been more fascinated (and worried) than their European counterparts by the nature, growth and influence of the professions. Consequently, matters of this kind have attracted more controversy and research in the United States than elsewhere.

Needless to say, much of the activity in this area stems from dissatisfaction with the status quo, and in the case of economics it is hardly surprising that the euphoria of the Keynesian era (c. 1945–65) was followed by a reaction both within and outside the economics community. The doctrinal challenges to Keynesian ideas from monetarists, post-Keynesians, Marxists, radicals, institutionalists and neo-Austrians were reinforced by the manifest inability of mainstream 'neoclassical' economists to cope with the problems associated with 'stagflation'. But the most distinctive feature of this particular 'crisis' was the extent to which it exposed the widespread and deep-seated loss of professional self-confidence. This was manifested in a veritable orgy of public self-flagellation led by some of the profession's most respected figures in a series of presidential addresses and invited public lectures (Heller 1975; Coats 1977). The critics focused on some of the familiar negative features of professionalism, such as rigidity, conformity, resistance to innovations (other than those of an approved species), the maintenance of tight disciplinary boundaries, the exclusion and/or denigration of dissenters, and excessively centralized control over access to resources, training and employment opportunities.

It is pertinent to note that professional standards, like methodological rules, have prescriptive and regulative as well as cognitive functions, and the quest for scientific truth or community service can easily be sacrificed to the interests of maintaining and advancing special privileges, securing higher remuneration, and protecting the field from encroachments by charlatans and those operating in closely related or overlapping disciplines or occupations.

These and many other features of the sociology of economics have been analysed and documented in a large, contentious, and often entertaining and insightful body of literature that is far too large to be cited extensively here. Not all of this outpouring can be dismissed, as some critics have been wont to do, as the work of cranks, dissidents and incompetents; some of it emanates from acknowledged leaders of the profession.[14] Some, indeed, regard these criticisms not as pathological, but rather as evidence of vigorous health (Heller 1975). Nevertheless, there is general recognition that too much well-publicized disagreement, especially with respect to fundamentals, may undermine the discipline's scientific status in the public's eyes.

Many of the most outspoken critics of the state of economics complain that the profession is too hierarchical and elitist, and that it is dominated by a

131

relatively small contingent of orthodox neoclassical economists centred in a few leading departments. As one President of the American Economic Association has declared, there is nowadays

> a new despotism. That consists in defining scientific excellence as whatever is closest in belief and method to the scholarly tendency of those who are already there. This is a pervasive and oppressive thing not the less dangerous for being, in the frequent case, both righteous and unconscious.
>
> (Galbraith 1973)

The professional establishment is said to control directly or indirectly the selection of officers of the American Economic Association, the editors and editorial boards of the Association's publications and other leading professional journals, the winners of the principal honours and awards, and the allocation of major research funds through the peer review system employed by the National Science Foundation and the principal private grant-giving agencies. Members of this elite also determine the basic requirements of core courses in the elite graduate schools, thereby controlling the means of certification, the entry of new recruits into the profession and their career prospects through both the informal communications network that influences most appointments and the publication process that so heavily shapes the individual's subsequent career. There are, of course, many specialist subgroups, invisible colleges, schools and networks, and occasionally an exceptional individual who has had the misfortune to be trained or appointed at one of the lesser institutions is spotted, like a star athlete, and recruited by a major league team. But for the most part the students of the leading graduate schools remain within the elite circuit, if they can, and in due course produce their own progeny who help to perpetuate the system.

Various useful studies have been undertaken to document this state of affairs. In particular, the journals network, which reveals both the core of the profession's reputational system and the processes whereby new ideas are generated and disseminated, has been extensively examined. Among the topics covered are the use of citation indexes to trace the institutional affiliations of authors of articles in the leading periodicals in an effort to determine how far there is a closed community of the elite; the prestige ratings of various journals; the earnings and career implications of publication in a leading journal; the mathematical and technical content of articles; the extent to which authors seriously endeavour to refute and/or empirically test their findings; the number of publications by 'star' economists; fashions, trends and cycles in the literature; and so on.[15]

Of course, every human organization, not least every academic discipline, necessarily has its leaders and followers, its superior performers and its mediocrities, and disputed scientific findings, evaluations and decisions cannot be settled by conventional democratic processes, even within the community of the competent. Moreover, it is natural for those in the establishment who have already achieved success to approve of the system in which they have attained their eminence, since their own virtues and abilities have been so fittingly recognized and rewarded. A telling example of this perspective is the complacent analysis of the process whereby private foundation grant allocations purportedly facilitate the concentration of research and talent in the already acknowledged 'best' university departments, thereby reinforcing their members' existing ability to attract able colleagues, hire research assistants, obtain any requisite equipment and produce more successful work, thus enhancing their department's visibility and prestige rating in the economics community (Stigler 1967).

Whether this system works well or badly depends on the alternative possibilities – a matter rarely considered, since it involves a massive counterfactual that not even the most ambitious exponent of the new cliometric history would undertake lightly. In practice professional inertia is likely to preclude any dramatic changes: most scientists are reformers, not radicals. Unfortunately both critics and defenders of the status quo too often base their assessments on personal experience and hearsay rather than reliable evidence, and there are underlying differences of professional values and standards, if not incommensurable paradigms.

Rather than elaborating on this subject by citing individual economists' views, which are hardly detached, it is more illuminating to turn to an impartial sociologist of science, Richard Whitley, who has reviewed modern economics from the standpoint of his ambitious comprehensive typology of the natural and social sciences. Whitley treats scientific fields as reputational systems of work organization and control in terms of specific key variables deriving from their individual histories and subject content. Against this background, Anglo-Saxon economics emerges as a unique case (Whitley 1984, 1986).[16]

As in physics, the theoretical core of economics dominates textbooks, training programmes, the communication system and academic posts and honours, but economics is distinct from other fields in that, unlike physics, there is a marked division between theoretical and empirical work. This is partly due to the lack of technical control over empirical work which limits the applied economist's dependence on the theorist (unlike the situation in physics), and also because of the existence of other audiences outside the theoretical establishment and the scientific or professional community. Competition by producers within the central core, although intense, is restricted to technical refinements and extensions of the analytical scheme to novel problems that can be tackled with existing techniques. The dominance of the established theoretical goals, and the degree of impersonality and formalization of co-ordination and control procedures, vary as between empirical specialisms

133

because the relatively intractable and unpredictable nature of empirical phenomena restricts the extent to which systematic comparison and validation of task outcomes can be accomplished through the formal communication system. The heterogeneity of applied fields is limited by 'rigid delimination' of the types of problems deemed legitimate and important; on the other hand, deviations on the periphery can be largely ignored by the intellectual elite who control the dominant communications media and training programmes.

This analysis is compatible with many of the familiar complaints from those dissatisfied with the state of the discipline, especially the excessive emphasis on a high level of abstraction, mathematization and formalization in advanced training programmes (cf. Bauer and Walters 1975; Hutchison 1977; Blatt 1983; Morishima 1984; Grubel and Boland 1986; Woo 1986) and the irrelevance of much of this work to contemporary problems and especially policy issues. The fact that one major school of economists based in Chicago has endeavoured to extend its 'imperialistic' sway (Stigler 1984) by applying a standardized analysis to a whole range of problems formerly thought to lie outside the economist's domain merely confirms the arguments of those who complain of the tendency towards uniformity in the discipline.

There are, of course, other contending approaches within mainstream economics that challenge the Chicagoans' approach. But this does not necessarily reflect a happy state of affairs, as suggested by the distinguished ex-Chicago economist who reported, sadly:

> What generates in me a great deal of scepticism about the state of our discipline is the high positive correlation between the policy views of a researcher (or, what is worse, his thesis director) and his empirical findings. I will begin to believe in economics as a science when out of Yale there comes an empirical thesis demonstrating the supremacy of monetary policy in some historical episode – and out of Chicago, one demonstrating the supremacy of fiscal policy.
>
> (Patinkin 1972: 142, cited by Hutchison 1977: 61)

Another recent critic, also with strong earlier Chicago associations, has outspokenly protested at the exaggeration of internal divisions within the discipline:

> The typical economist, alas, is harshly if unreflectively dogmatic, demanding that students or colleagues be members in good standing of this or that church. Sales people for university textbooks in the United States complain that an economics professor simply will not look at a text that does not come from the right church: he asks, shamefully, is the book monetarist or neo-classical or Marxist or Keynesian? . . . the extent of real disagreement among economists . . . is in fact exaggerated . . . [this] makes all the more puzzling the venom they bring to minor disputes.
>
> (McCloskey 1985: 184)

What this discloses about the character of textbooks, the extent of disagreements among economists, and their values – professional or other – cannot be further explored here.

Continuing concern about the state of economics as a discipline and a profession has led to recent official investigations sponsored by the Royal Economic Society and the American Economic Association – inspired in the latter instance by a disturbing study of graduate training in elite departments (Colander and Klamer 1987, 1989). The British study is complete, and can be considered more briefly because the major findings appeared in the March 1990 issue of *The Economic Journal*. It is broader in scope than its American counterpart for it focuses on the stock, supply, demand and patterns of employment of British economists, as well as some characteristics of economics departments in British universities and polytechnics (Dolton and Makepeace 1990; Towse and Blaug 1990). To a historian, the surprising thing is that no previous study of this kind has been undertaken (but cf. Booth and Coats 1978), whereas studies of the market for economists, their salaries and employment opportunities have quite frequently appeared in the United States, usually in reports initiated by or papers presented to the American Economic Association at the annual meetings. American labour economists have often taken an interest in these matters.

Among the findings of the Towse–Blaug study, the most striking are the limited size of the total flow demand for economists and the prediction that it will decline in the foreseeable future. Despite the loss of university posts (especially professorships) since the 1981 university cuts there is apparently still an excess supply of professional economists, so that reports of the 'dire straits' of economics departments have been exaggerated. The spectacularly high salaries attached to certain posts in the City of London are untypical, and there has been no mass exodus of academic economists to that centre. Unlike the United States, many non-academic economists in the United Kingdom have only an undergraduate degree, often of a non-specialized kind, although the reporters firmly insist that 'there is no warrant whatever for thinking that an undergraduate course in economics is a vocational preparation for a world of work in which the graduate will normally be called upon to use his economic expertise' (Towse and Blaug 1990: 98). On the other hand there are conclusions that would certainly strike a responsive chord across the Atlantic. For example, 'the constant complaint of virtually every employer of professional economists that new recruits lack familiarity with data sources, and have never been taught national income accounting' (Towse and Blaug 1990: 98), and the view widely held both inside and outside higher education that 'economics degrees are too theoretical, too impractical, too unrelated to the possible uses of economics in business and government ... [and that] teaching is indifferent to the actual pattern of employment of economics graduates' (Towse and Blaug 1990: 99).

Given the scale of the economics profession in the United States, the investigation conducted by the American Economic Association's Commission on Graduate Education in Economics is necessarily much larger than its British counterpart, although its terms of reference are narrower.[17] Of particular interest is the fact that the Commission has surveyed not only the six so-called elite departments but also other tiers of departments covering nine, fifteen, twenty and forty-two additional PhD programmes. No such systematic comparison has ever been undertaken previously.

Despite the loud and persistent chorus of complaints about the state of contemporary American economics, some of which have already been noted, and the general desire for changes in economics PhD programmes expressed by faculty, graduate students and recent PhDs in response to the survey, there was a large consensus in favour of the weights currently attached to various types of knowledge in the curriculum, according to which economic theory is given priority followed by econometrics, empirical economics, applications, institutions, history and literature. With respect to skills, it was generally acknowledged that the following were currently emphasized in PhD programmes, in descending order of importance: analytics, mathematics, critical judgement, applications, computation, creativity and communications. However, there was much less agreement that this was the way things should be. In agreement with many of the profession's public critics, it was felt that mathematics and computation were overrated and creativity was undervalued, and when recent PhDs were asked about the importance of various skills in their current jobs, whether in graduate economics programmes, business or government, they again ranked mathematics lower and communications skills and creativity higher than the weights assigned to them in current graduate teaching. Thus, as is probably the case in the United Kingdom, 'both faculty members and graduate students' sense that 'the mix of needed skills differs from the skills being developed in graduate training' (Hansen 1990). Departments offering PhD programmes tend to continue to appoint new recruits with much the same skills as already emphasized, rather than those more highly valued by prospective employers, but whether this is evidence of professional inertia or *faute de mieux* (the absence of suitable alternatives) is unclear. As Robert Solow argued in his comments, the results display more satisfaction with what is taught and the teacher's ability to teach it than what should be taught in a better, if not an ideal, world: 'If I knew how to teach creativity and critical judgment, I guess I would do it. I know how to recognize them [i.e. like pornography?], and can even offer examples, but that is very far from being able to teach them' (Hansen 1990: 448–50). On the whole, he felt, the survey results were 'predictably bland'.

Of course, by any standards the Commission's members constitute part of the profession's elite, so that radical proposals for change are hardly to be expected, especially given the strong practical sense that such ideas are hardly likely to be implemented. It is much too early to predict the outcome of this investigation, other than the Commission's recommendations, which will no doubt be vigorously discussed with a wide variety of reactions. The supplementary studies to appear later will undoubtedly add substantially to the accumulating, although uneven, body of data on the economics profession in the United States. And, in line with the opening paragraph of this chapter, we may conclude with the hope that other organizations and scholars will be encouraged to undertake serious research on the history, current condition and future prospects of the profession.

NOTES

1 In their classic volume Carr Saunders and Wilson (1933: 2) observe that: 'An adequate study of the rise of one of the great professions with its roots deep in the past would be the work of a lifetime'.

2 Furner (1975) provides a valuable analysis of this issue in which the economists figure prominently. Unfortunately there is no comparable study for a more recent period, or for the United Kingdom.

3 Professional ideology can, of course, be defined narrowly, as in Joseph Schumpeter's pertinent distinction between the ideology of the mathematical mind and that of the mind allergic to mathematics (Schumpeter 1949: 351). This particular ideological divide is nowadays much more significant in economics than it was forty years ago, for mathematical competence is now virtually a precondition of entry into the economics profession and an indispensable weapon in the early stages of a career. This is serious, notwithstanding jocular references to the 'spiralling "arms race" ' in econometrics and the intergenerational 'balance of terror' between established incumbents and their technically sophisticated young colleagues (Wiles 1984: 292). From a huge relevant literature the following citations must suffice: Bauer and Walters (1975) and Woo (1986). There are valuable remarks on the professionalization–mathematization link in other disciplines in Whitley (1977, 1984).

4 Many such listings have been proposed. One multivariate analysis identified six elements and twenty-one subelements (Jenkins 1970: 59).

5 Some analysts regard the service or fiduciary ideal as a middle-class rationale reflecting the professionals' self-deception, rather than any deliberate effort to deceive the lay public. Much of the literature vacillates between viewing professions as a broad educational and cultural stratum or as a distinctive species of occupational organization. Historically, the format is more applicable to the continental European so-called 'public' professions and the latter to the Anglo-American 'free' professions, although with the development of bureaucracy and the welfare state the distinction between them has become blurred.

6 The literature on professions and professionalism is vast, conflicting and sometimes even sensational. In a fascinating survey, a leading expert in the field, Walter Metzger, has coined the term 'professionism' to cover 'all systematic attempts to attribute historical trends – especially undesirable ones – to the rise of the professions or to the foibles of professionals' (Metzger 1987: 13). No doubt the economists too have suffered from the general decline of deference towards expertise.

7 There may indeed be some consolation in the Victorian dictum that a gentleman needs no code of ethics, whereas no such code will make a gentleman out of a crook!

8 Rhoads (1985) gives a perceptive political scientist's conception of the strengths and limitations of the professional economist's intellectual apparatus.

9 Commenting on the irrational elements in policy-making, a very experienced British ex-government economist remarked that 'the atmosphere of a large Government department is frequently almost indistinguishable from that of the loony bin. I use the term in no pejorative sense; it is simply one of the facts of official life' (Cairncross 1970). For fascinating and

illuminating stories of American economists' experiences in government service see Allen (1977).

10 According to one scholarly historian of economics the Sophists were the first 'professional instructors' in the subject (Gordon 1975: 2, 15).

11 Broadly speaking professional organization preceded doctrinal consolidation in American economics, whereas the opposite was true in the United Kingdom.

12 The editor of *The Times*, which supported Chamberlain's proposals, poked fun at 'the spectacle of these fourteen dervishes emerging from their caves and chanting their venerable incantations against the rising tide of inquiry . . . the day has gone by when the professors of political economy can impose opinions upon the country by the weight of authority. . . . A more scientific conception of their own science, which pretends to be, but never is, an experimental science, would save the professors from the painful discovery that they convince nobody who stands in need of conviction' (*The Times*, 18 August 1903, cited by Coats 1964: 101). Coats (1968a) gives a more extended account.

13 There is a perceptive, and at times amusing, analysis of the Americanness of American economics in a neglected article by Johnson (1977b).

14 The critics include J. K. Galbraith, N. Georgescu-Roegen, H. G. Johnson, T. Koopmans and W. Leontief in the United States, and P. Bauer, P. Deane, F. Hahn, T. W. Hutchison, E. H. Phelps Brown, G. D. Worswick and A. A. Walters in the United Kingdom. For examples of the sociologically oriented critical literature see Leontief (1971, 1982), Ward (1972), Leijonhufvud (1973), Johnson (1977a, b), Stanfield (1979), Katouzian (1980), Canterbery and Burkhardt (1983), Earl (1983, 1988), Wiles (1984), Coats (1985), Burkhardt and Canterbery (1986) and Tarascio (1986).

15 From a large output the following items must suffice: Bronfenbrenner (1966), Siegfried (1972), Lovell (1973), Eagly (1974), Stigler (1982a, b) and Liebowitz and Palmer (1984).

16 According to Whitley the key variables in any scientific field are the degrees of functional and strategic mutual dependence among scientists and the degrees of technical and strategic task uncertainty.

17 I am most grateful to my colleagues Anne Krueger, the Commission's Chairman, and Lee Hansen, its Executive Director, for making available the unpublished preliminary report, and also the additional comments by Commission members Alan S. Blinder, Claudia Goldin and T. Paul Schultz, and by Robert Solow. The final report is now available and is to be published in the *Journal of Economic Literature* (Hansen, forthcoming).

REFERENCES

Allen, W. R. (1977) 'Economics, economists, and economic policy: modern American experiences', *History of Political Economy* 9: 48–88.

Bauer, P. T. and Walters, A. (1975) 'The state of economics', *Journal of Law and Economics* 8: 1–23.

Bell, D. and Kristol, I. (eds) (1981) *The Crisis in Economic Theory*, New York: Basic Books.

Blatt, J. (1983) 'How economists misuse mathematics', in A. S. Eichner (ed.) *Why Economics is Not Yet a Science*, pp. 166–86, Armonk, NY: M. E. Sharpe.

Booth, A. and Coats, A. W. (1978) 'The market for economists in Britain (1945–1970)', *Economic Journal* 88: 436–54.

Bronfenbrenner, M. (1966) 'Trends, cycles, and fads in economic writing', *American Economic Review* 56: 538–52.

Burkhardt, J. and Canterbery, E. R. (1986) 'The orthodoxy and legitimacy: toward a critical sociology of economics', in W. J. Samuels (ed.) *Research in the History and Methodology of Economics* 4: 229–50.

Cairncross, A. K. (1970) 'Writing the history of recent economic policy', unpublished, quoted by permission.

Canterbery, E. R. and Burkhardt, J. (1983) 'What do we mean by asking whether economics is a science?', in A. S. Eichner (ed.) *Why Economics is Not Yet a Science*, pp. 15–40, Armonk, NY: M. E. Sharpe.

Carr Saunders, A. M. and Wilson, P. A. (1933) *The Professions*, Oxford: Clarendon Press.

Coats, A. W. (1960) 'The first two decades of the American Economic Association', *American Economic Review* 50: 555–74.

—— (1964) 'The role of authority in the development of British economics', *Journal of Law and Economics* 7: 85–106.

—— (1968a) 'Political economy and the tariff reform campaign of 1903', *Journal of Law and Economics* 11: 181–229.

—— (1968b) 'The origins and early development of the Royal Economic Society', *Economic Journal* 78: 349–71.

—— (1976) 'The development of the agricultural economics profession in England', *Journal of Agricultural Economics* 27: 1–11.

—— (1977) 'The current crisis in economics in historical perspective', *Nebraska Journal of Economics and Business* 16: 3–16.

—— (1980) 'The culture and the economists: American–British differences', *History of Political Economy* 10: 298–314.

—— (ed.) (1981) *Economists in Government: An International Comparative Study*, Durham, NC: Duke University Press.

—— (1985) 'The American Economic Association and the economics profession', *Journal of Economic Literature* 23: 1697–727.

—— (ed.) (1986) *Economists in International Agencies. An Exploratory Study*, New York: Praeger.

Colander, D. C. and Klamer, A. (1987) 'The making of an economist', *Journal of Economic Perspectives* 1: 95–111.

—— and —— (1989) *The Making of an Economist*, Boulder, CO: Westview Press.

Dolton, P. J. and Makepeace, G. H. (1990) 'The earnings of economics graduates', *Economic Journal* 100: 237–50.

Eagly, R. V. (1974) 'Contemporary profile of conventional economists', *History of Political Economy* 6: 76–91.

Earl, P. E. (1983) 'A behavioral theory of economists' behavior', in A. S. Eichner (ed.) *Why Economics is Not Yet a Science*, pp. 90–125, Armonk, NY: M. E. Sharpe.

—— (1988) 'On being a psychological economist and winning the games economists play', in P. E. Earl (ed.) *Psychological Economics. Development, Tensions Prospects*, pp. 227–42, Boston, MA: Kluwer.

Furner, M. O. (1975) *Advocacy and Objectivity: A Crisis in the Professionalization of American Social Science 1865–1905*, Lexington, KY: University of Kentucky Press.

Galbraith, J. K. (1973) 'Power and the useful economist', *American Economic Review* 63: 1–11.

Goode, W. (1960) 'Encroachment, charlatanism, and the emerging professions: psychology, sociology, medicine', *American Sociological Review* 25: 902–14.

Gordon, B. S. (1975) *Economic Analysis Before Adam Smith. Hesiod to Lessius*, London: Macmillan.

Grubel, H. G. and Boland, L. A. (1986) 'On the efficient role of mathematics in economics: some theory, facts and results of an opinion survey', *Kyklos* 39: 419–42.

Hansen, W. L. (1990) 'Educating and training new economics Ph.D.'s: how good a job are we doing?', Commission on Graduate Education in Economics, Preliminary Report, *American Economic Review, Papers and Proceedings* 80: 431–50.

—— (forthcoming) 'The education and training of economics doctorates: major findings of the American Economic Association's Commission on Graduate Education in Economics (report and tables), Madison, WI, January 1991', *Journal of Economic Literature*, to be published.

Heller, W. W. (1975) 'What's right with economics?', *American Economic Review* 65: 1–26.

Herman, E. S. (1982) 'The institutionalization of bias in economics', *Media, Culture and Society* 4: 275–91.

Hutchison, T. W. (1964) *Positive Economics and 'Policy' Objectives*, London: Allen & Unwin.

—— (1977) *Knowledge and Ignorance in Economics*, Oxford: Basil Blackwell.

Jenkins, H. G. (1970) 'Professional organizations', in J. A. Jackson (ed.) *Professions and Professionalization*, pp. 53–107, Cambridge: Cambridge University Press.

Johnson, H. G. (1973) 'National styles in economic research: the United States, the United Kingdom, Canada, and various European countries', *Daedalus* 102: 65–74. Reprinted in Johnson, H. G., *On Economics and Society*, Chicago, IL: University of Chicago Press, 1975.

—— (1977a) 'Methodologies of economics', in M. Perlman (ed.) *The Organization and Retrieval of Economic Knowledge*, pp. 496–509, Boulder, CO: Westview Press.

—— (1977b) 'The American tradition in economics', *Nebraska Journal of Economics and Business* 16: 17–26.

Johnson, T. J. (1972) *Professions and Power*, London: Macmillan.

Katouzian, H. (1980) *Ideology and Method in Economics*, London: Macmillan.

Larson, M. S. (1978) *The Rise of Professionalism: A Sociological Analysis*, Berkeley, CA: University of California Press.

Leijonhufvud, A. (1973) 'Life among the Econ', *Western Economic Journal* 11: 327–37.

Leontief, W. (1971) 'Theoretical assumptions and non-observed facts', *American Economic Review* 71: 1–17.

—— (1982) 'Academic economics', *Science* 217: 104–5. Reprinted in Eichner, A. S. (ed.) *Why Economics is Not Yet a Science*, pp. vi–xi, Armonk, NY: M. E. Sharpe, 1983.

Liebowitz, S. J. and Palmer, J. P. (1984) 'Assessing the relative impacts of economic journals', *Journal of Economic Literature* 22: 77–88.

Lovell, M. C. (1973) 'The production of economic literature: an interpretation', *Journal of Economic Literature* 11: 27–55.

McCloskey, D. (1985) *The Rhetoric of Economics*, Madison, WI: University of Wisconsin Press.

McDean, H. C. (1983) 'Professionalism, policy, and farm economists in the early Bureau of Agricultural Economics', *Agricultural History* 37: 64–82, 83–9.

Maloney, J. (1985) *Marshall, Orthodoxy and the Professionalization of Economics*, Cambridge: Cambridge University Press.

Metzger, W. P. (1987) 'A spectre is haunting American scholars: the spectre of "professionism" ', *Educational Researcher* 16: 10–19.

Mill, J. (1824) 'War expenditure', *Westminster Review* 2: 45.

Morishima, M. (1984) 'The good and bad uses of mathematics', in P. Wiles and G. Routh (eds) *Economics in Disarray*, pp. 51–77, Oxford: Basil Blackwell.

Nelson, R. H. (1987) 'The economics profession and the making of public policy', *Journal of Economic Literature* 25: 49–91.

O'Brien, D. (1965) 'The transition in Torrens' monetary thought', *Economica (N.S.)* 32: 269–301.

Parsons, T. (1968) 'Professions', in D. Sills (ed.) *The International Encyclopedia of the Social Sciences*, vol. 12, pp. 536–47, New York: Macmillan.

Patinkin, D. (1972) 'Keynesian monetary theory and the Cambridge School', *Banca Nationale del Lavoro Quarterly Review* 25: 138–58.

Pechman, J. A. (1989) *The Role of the Economist in Government: An International Perspective*, Washington, DC: Brookings Institution.

Rhoads, S. E. (1985) *The Economist's View of the World. Government, Markets, and Public Policy*, Cambridge: Cambridge University Press.

Schumpeter, J. (1949) 'Science and ideology', *American Economic Review* 39: 345–59.

Siegfried, J. J. (1972) 'The publishing of economic papers and its impact on graduate faculty ratings, 1960–1969', *Journal of Economic Literature* 10: 31–49.

Stanfield, R. J. (1979) 'The social structure of the economics community', in R. J. Stanfield, *Economic Thought and Social Change*, Carbondale, IL: Southern Illinois University Press.

Stigler, G. J. (1967) 'The Foundations and economics', in W. Weaver (ed.) *U. S. Philanthropic Foundations, Their History, Structure, Management and Record*, pp. 276–86, New York: Harper.

—— (1984) 'Economics: the imperial science?', *Scandinavian Journal of Economics* 86: 301–13.

Stigler, G. J. and Friedland, C. (1982a) 'The pattern of citation practices in economics', in G. J. Stigler (ed.) *The Economist as Preacher and Other Essays*, pp. 173–91, Chicago, IL: University of Chicago Press.

—— and —— (1982b) 'The citation practices of doctorates in economics', in G. J. Stigler (ed.) *The Economist as Preacher and Other Essays*, pp. 192–222, Chicago, IL: University of Chicago Press.

Tarascio, V. J. (1986) 'The crisis in economic theory: a sociological perspective', in W. J. Samuels (ed.) *Research in the History of Economic Thought and Methodology* 4: 283–95.

Torrens, R. (1826) Letter to Wilmot Horton, 7 November.

Towse, R. and Blaug, M. (1988) *The Current State of the British Economics Profession*, London: Royal Economic Society.

—— and —— (1990) 'The current state of the British economics profession', *Economic Journal* 100: 227–36.

Ward, B. (1972) *What's Wrong With Economics?*, London: Macmillan.

—— (1979) *The Ideal Worlds of Economics. Liberal, Radical, and Conservative Economic World Views*, New York: Basic Books.

Whitley, R. (1977) 'Changes in the social and intellectual organization of the sciences: professionalization and the arithmetic ideal', in E. Mendelsohn, P. Weingart and R. Whitley (eds) *The Social Production of Scientific Knowledge*, pp. 143–69, Dordrecht: Reidel.

141

—— (1984) *The Intellectual and Social Organization of the Sciences*, Oxford: Clarendon Press.

—— (1986) 'The structure and context of economics as a scientific field', in W. J. Samuels (ed.) *Research in the History of Economic Thought and Methodology* 4: 179–209.

Wiles, P. (1984) 'Epilogue: the role of theory', in P. Wiles and G. Routh (eds) *Economics in Disarray*, pp. 293–325, Oxford: Basil Blackwell.

Woo, H. K. H. (1986) *What's Wrong With Formalization – in Economics? – An Epistemological Critique*, Newark, CA: Victoria Press.

II. ECONOMIC THEORY

9

AN OVERVIEW OF EMERGING THEORY

MICHAEL BLEANEY

9.1 INTRODUCTION

One of the characteristics – perhaps in retrospect it will be viewed as the chief characteristic – of theoretical economics over the past decade has been the cooling of controversy and a gradual re-establishment of some form of consensus in the profession for the first time since the mid-1960s. This has undoubtedly been a tentative process, for which the Walrasian term *tâtonnement* springs to mind, but we have only to think back to the apparently irreconcilable gulf between different schools of macroeconomics in the 1970s to recognize how much movement there has been. In 1981 Daniel Bell and Irving Kristol edited a book of twelve essays entitled *The Crisis in Economic Theory* (Bell and Kristol 1981). Originally a special issue of the magazine *Public Interest*, this volume attracted some leading names of the economics profession as contributors, and Bell felt able to state in his Introduction that '[t]he twelve theorists represented here accept the fact that the consensus on economic theory has been broken' (Bell and Kristol 1981: xi). Kristol put it rather more strongly in his essay: 'It is widely conceded that something like a "crisis in economic theory" exists, but there is vehement disagreement about the extent and nature of this crisis' (Bell and Kristol 1981: 201).

A decade later, it is difficult to conceive of an editor of a book of essays about economics being in a position to write such comments. The atmosphere is more placid, more assured and more reminiscent of recovery from trauma than of trauma itself. A variety of explanations could be put forward to account for this. Theoretical progress may have left the old disputes behind and redefined them as alternative special cases of a more general theory. Alternatively, practical experience might have shown that one side was right and the other wrong. (This, however, would conflict with the well-known maxim that where you have two economists you have three opinions!) A further possibility is that the 'crisis' had more to do with the public perception of economics

145

than its actual content, and that with the return to some degree of normality in the macroeconomy the reputation of economists has recovered and with it their self-assurance. In this context we should also mention the spectacular decline of the Soviet model and the apparent wholesale acceptance of market reforms by economists throughout Eastern Europe and the Soviet Union, not to mention China, Vietnam and a growing number of developing countries.

In assessing the progress (if any) of economic theory over the past quarter of a century or so, we cannot avoid these issues. Economics interacts powerfully with social questions, it has (or is widely perceived to have) strong ideological overtones, and economic performance exerts a major influence on the electoral fate of governments. Economists themselves are also voters, consumers, parents. They are paid to get the economy right, and, if they fail to do so, find themselves at the receiving end of public indignation. Economic theory certainly does not exist in a vacuum.

9.2 A NEW SYNTHESIS?

The state of economics in the mid-1960s is often summarized by the term 'neoclassical synthesis'. Nowadays this expression has some pejorative overtones, implying an ill thought out combination of neoclassical microeconomics and Keynesian macroeconomics, and indeed it will be argued below that much of the recent progress in economic theory has been directly or indirectly concerned with achieving a much better integration of microeconomics and macroeconomics. Nevertheless it is important to recall how much of an advance this 'synthesis' represented compared with the state of theory in, say, 1930. The synthesis arose precisely because of the ineffectiveness of fifty years of neoclassical macroeconomics in establishing a simple coherent body of useful theory. We have only to look at the literature on the trade cycle to see this: far from moving towards a consensus view, the trade cycle theory of the 1920s (and this was the only area in which neoclassical theory systematically confronted macroeconomic issues) gave a strong impression of exploding into ever increasing variety. Keynesian theory cut through all this; it wrought profound changes not only in theory but also in political attitudes towards economic management. It provided the intellectual foundation for national income accounting and macroeconomic modelling, which was itself a major innovation made possible only by advanced computing power and new statistical information. The limitations of the 'neoclassical synthesis', however, were in part a product of its successes. Macroeconomics seemed to be increasingly driven by model-building, in the sense of obtaining a good statistical fit backed up by *ad hoc* theorizing, and the limitations of pure theory tended to be papered over by equation-searching. The Phillips curve was probably the most spectacular example of this: it was bolted into macroeconomic models as a robust replacement for the absent theory of the money wage level in the Keynesian system. Microeconomics, on the other hand, continued to assume that firms maximized profits and households maximized utility, but never took account of the quantity constraints that Keynes had suggested might be an important determinant of behaviour.

In the later 1960s the 'neoclassical synthesis' began to come apart at the seams, and it was the Phillips curve which proved the weakest point. The combination of inflation and unemployment could be, and often was, attributed to sociological factors underlying wage militancy, but to most economists such sociological influences seemed unpredictable and to a large degree inexplicable. Moreover, whatever their causes, such supply-side shocks found economics wanting in its policy prescriptions: there seemed to be no coherent theory of how to contain them. Keynesian economics was entirely oriented towards demand-side shocks, whilst the neoclassical tradition offered little except a faith in the resilience of markets in the face of a shock of any kind. As in the period 1929–33, a lacuna in economic theory that had previously lain hidden was brutally exposed by events. Theoretical weaknesses were dramatically brought home to economists and the public alike.

The 'crisis in economic theory' that emerged in the 1970s was the effect of these developments. Orthodoxy lost its self-assurance, and dissenting voices found more response. Both the radical right and the radical left in economics became more vociferous. With hindsight, however, this appears to have been a temporary phase (at least at the theoretical level). As supply-side shocks waned and a sustained disinflation began from 1982 onwards, publicly expressed dissatisfaction with economists' policy prescriptions became less frequent. On a theoretical plane, however, what was much more significant was that orthodox economics proved its fundamental resilience. By relaxing some of its more extreme assumptions, such as the availability of complete information, it was able to defend and enrich the basic tenets enshrined by the neoclassical tradition – that agents are motivated by self-interest – whilst Marxist and other radical schools, despite receiving a new lease of life, failed to display a similar level of adaptability and inventiveness (Marxist economics, in particular, was racked by doubts about fundamental principles). After a period of confusion and disorientation, considerable progress was made in remedying the weaknesses of existing theory, and particularly in bridging the chasm that seemed to have opened up between microeconomics and macroeconomics.

However, the most immediate effect of the crisis was a resurgence of neoclassical economics. Apparently killed off for good by wage-earners' demonstration of market power in the later 1960s, it was able to make a spectacular comeback by the introduction of price expectations into the model. Any nominal wage behaviour could be neatly explained as market clearing with appropriate assumptions about price expectations. Friedman (1968) was an early proponent of this view. However, Friedman did not explore the formation of expectations in any detail. But when Lucas (1972) revived the concept of rational expectations first introduced by Muth (1961), and Sargent and Wallace (1975) showed what powerful implications it could have in macroeconomic models, Keynesian economics found itself on the defensive. All the bright ideas seemed to be emerging from the new classical revivalist movement.

An outstanding feature of the Lucas–Sargent–Wallace approach was its drive for theoretical consistency. Its proponents sought to argue, or at least to imply, that this required the employment of flexprice models with atomistic markets in which no agents were quantity constrained. This argument failed to gain general acceptance, but the challenge to base macroeconomics in sound microeconomics was responded to with some rapidity. A well-known volume edited by Phelps (1971) was seminal in this regard. In that work it was taken as axiomatic that households were utility-maximizers and firms profit-maximizers, but the crucial step was that information was assumed to be costly to obtain. The resulting search model had some difficulty in accounting for the stylized facts of the labour market, and so different avenues were explored by later writers. The aim of this rapidly expanding body of research was to understand why it could be rational to adjust prices and wages only slowly, even in a market with many buyers and sellers. We can only briefly allude to the main ideas here. Baily (1974) and Azariadis (1975) came up with the notion of implicit contracts between employers and employees, in which firms were assumed to insure workers against income fluctuations. Others focused on the possibility that goodwill was important to maintaining productivity, or that monitoring of worker performance was costly (the so-called efficiency wage theory). Some argued that the search model was particularly applicable to the goods market, where the frequency of trades gives sellers a strong incentive to offer price guarantees to prevent customers from searching elsewhere for a better deal (Okun 1981). Limitations and asymmetries of information were also explored in credit markets (e.g. Stiglitz and Weiss 1981).

As already mentioned, much if not all of this work was motivated by the challenge to develop the microfoundations of Keynesian economics – to explain why, as Leijonhufvud (1968) expressed it, adjustment had to take place through quantity constraints in the short run because price adjustment was sluggish. If it could be shown that it was rational for agents to be circumspect about adjusting prices even when their motivation was assumed to be impeccably neoclassical, then Keynesian economics would have a much sounder theoretical basis. In combination with empirical work which has generally been unfavourable to the new classical models, this has formed the basis for a new theoretical consensus in which the microeconomic underpinning of Keynesian macroeconomics is much better understood, but the strictures about the previous neglect of expectations formation have also been taken to heart. What seems to be emerging is a 'neo-Keynesian synthesis', in which there is much greater cohesion between microeconomics and macroeconomics than at any time since the Keynesian revolution.

At the same time there have been considerable advances in many other aspects of economic theory. Anyone who had been put to sleep in 1970 and woken up in 1990 would have observed significant changes in the contents of the major economics journals. Game theory has come to be widely used in a variety of contexts, from oligopoly or monopoly with potential entrants to macroeconomic policy, as the chapters in this part show. Experimental economics has been born, and has given rise to a wealth of new theories about how people deal with uncertainty. This research links in neatly with the much greater emphasis that theorists now place on the information available to market participants. Econometrics has changed out of all recognition as improvements in computing power have turned forms of estimation that were previously impossible into routine operations. This has had its reflection in the theoretical work that has been done in econometrics, and it is reassuring that these developments have been accompanied by an increasing concern for quality control in applied work; the lively debate that has grown up about the 'right' way to do econometrics is an entirely new and extremely welcome phenomenon.

Returning to the questions posed at the beginning of this chapter, it seems fair to say that improvements in macroeconomic performance have removed some of the pressure that contemporary developments exerted on the economics profession during the 1970s. Economists may have contributed to this improvement in performance through sound policy advice, although this is perhaps questionable (theoretical analysis of the credibility of disinflationary policy, for example, clearly followed behind practice), and it may simply be that the public now has lower expectations of what economic science can achieve. The old theoretical argument was not really won by either side, but there have been some important theoretical innovations, such as rational expectations and developments in game theory, which have given economists the tools to grapple with issues that had previously seemed intractable. These innovations are illustrated in the remaining chapters of this section, to which we now turn.

9.3 THE CHAPTERS IN PART II

In Chapter 10, Pesaran summarizes recent work in the field of expectations. Expectations have been recognized to be important to economic behaviour for a long time, but explicit theorization of expectations formation is much more recent. When Keynes developed his theory of the demand for money in *The*

General Theory he assumed that the expected bond price was invariant to the current price, whereas when Tobin (1958) presented his alternative theory he chose to assume instead that the mean of the probability distribution of expected bond prices was always equal to the current price, yet neither felt called upon to justify his assumption about expectations.[1] Explicit modelling of expectations began in the mid-1950s with the development of the adaptive expectations hypothesis. Extensions of this were explored during the 1960s, but Muth's (1961) development of the concept of rational expectations was ignored until after 1970. Rational expectations assumes that the expectations of individuals coincide with the forecasts derived from the true model of the economy. Such expectations are optimal in the sense of being unbiased and having minimum mean square error, so that individuals have no incentive to depart from such an expectations-generating scheme, once it is adopted. Less clear is how they acquire the necessary information to adopt it in the first place. As Pesaran indicates, the learning process is problematic because of the influence of expectations on the system's behaviour; even if individuals are assumed to know the equational structure of the true model and to be uncertain only about the numerical values of the parameters, there may still not be convergence to rational expectations through learning. In the final section of the chapter Pesaran considers survey evidence on expectations. This evidence tends to refute the rational expectations hypothesis without, however, providing support for any alternative simple model. Pesaran concludes by suggesting that more research effort needs to be put into obtaining and improving direct measures of individuals' expectations of economic variables.

In Chapter 11 Sawyer provides an introduction to post-Keynesian macro-economics. This tradition stems from the work of Keynes and Kalecki, and probably its main unifying theme is a degree of scepticism about the usefulness of neoclassical economics. Sawyer organizes his discussion under the subheadings money and finance, prices, investment, labour and business cycles. In the field of money and finance the emphasis tends to be on the endogeneity of the money stock (at least in an economy with a developed financial sector), with inflation driving monetary growth rather than vice versa. Another area of investigation, particularly associated with the name of Minsky, is that of financial crises; here the policy of the central bank is recognized to be a significant factor in averting potential disaster. The post-Keynesian approach to price determination is not easily summarized since there exist clear differences of view between authors, but many post-Keynesians have followed Kalecki in postulating a largely cost-based theory of prices with demand factors playing at best a minor role except in the market for primary products. The interest rate tends to be downgraded as a determinant of investment. All this seems to add up to a view that 'money doesn't matter' since it can affect neither prices nor real effective demand. The labour market is interpreted in a manner consistent with this, and the stress is placed on factors that influence workers' behaviour in collective bargaining, such as the deviation of the real wage from trend, rather than the balance of demand and supply. In the field of consumption, post-Keynesian writers tend to favour a dual consumption function, with a higher propensity to save out of profits than out of wages. This formulation has more in common with Kalecki and Marx than with Keynes, but can be justified on the assumption that firms distribute only a limited fraction of profits to shareholders.

In Chapter 12 Mueller discusses public choice theory, an area which has seen enormous development over the past twenty years. As Mueller puts it, the subject matter of public choice theory is that of political science, but its methodology is that of economics; this chapter should be read in conjunction with Chapter 38 by McLean. The methodology is economic in the sense that individuals are assumed to be egotistical rational utility-maximizers. This principle is applied to politicians and bureaucrats as well as to voters.

In any democracy there is unlikely to be unanimity on most issues, although there may still be situations in which unanimity is desirable. Mueller considers recent research on direct democracy in some detail and carefully assesses the relative merits of unanimity and a simple-majority decision rule. A simple-majority rule can lead to cycles in the sense that pairwise voting between choices never produces a consistent ordering. Recent research has shown that in such situations control of the agenda can be an important determinant of the outcome – a conclusion with intuitive appeal to anyone with experience of committees! Mueller goes on to discuss some of the more recent work on the theory of representative democracy which has sought to enrich the original Downs model. He also considers the behaviour of bureaucrats and the objectives of lobbyists, particularly in the form of rent-seeking activities. Arrow's so-called 'impossibility theorem' attracted a great deal of attention when it first appeared. Mueller traces its implications in some detail and assesses further work in the area, in particular by Sen. The chapter concludes with a call for more research to be carried out on what actually determines voters' choices in representative democracy, given the increasingly large investments that political parties are making in trying to influence that choice.

In Chapter 13 Hey discusses the important issue of uncertainty in economics. The standard theory for dealing with uncertainty is subjective expected utility theory, the principle of which is as follows: a utility is ascribed to every possible outcome in a risky situation, and the individual seeks to maximize his or her expected utility, which is simply the mathematical expectation of the utility score given a subjective probability distribution over outcomes. Clearly there are many different types of gambles which can have the same subjective expected utility, and subjective expected utility theory rests on the assumption that these differences do not matter. As discussed by Hey, and also in more detail by Loomes in Chapter 29, experimental evidence suggests that these differences *do* matter in certain situations. Hey shows that subjective expected utility theory can be broken down into a set of axioms and explores the alternative theories that have been developed in the wake of these experimental results in terms of relaxing some or all of these axioms. This is an area which has undergone considerable advance in the 1980s, and Hey's chapter is an admirable introduction to the issues.

In Chapter 14 we turn to the theory of international trade policy. Corden discusses some recent models that suggest a justification for protectionist policy in an oligopolistic industry. The argument is not necessarily valid if the foreign government retaliates, but the underlying idea is that profits can be shifted from the foreign oligopolist to its domestic competitor through export subsidies or tariffs. Corden assesses these models in some detail and compares them with earlier work in which competitive markets were assumed. He argues that the new results are similar to those previously obtained in a competitive model with terms-of-trade effects (i.e. where the home country can gain by taxing exports because this shifts the terms of trade in its favour). Some of these new models have also brought in economies of scale, but Corden argues that the results do not differ significantly from those previously obtained with competitive industry models with economies of scale. A major point in his critique of these oligopoly-based models (dubbed by some 'the new international economics') is the restrictiveness of the Cournot assumption typically used in the analysis of the strategic game, according to which the opponent is assumed not to react to changes in one's own play (but see Montet's comments on this criticism of the Cournot assumption in Chapter 17, Section 17.2). Corden concludes by suggesting that the most important recent development in the theory of trade policy has come in the area of the political economy of government intervention, which investigates for the first time what is likely to determine the protectionist measures that governments take, rather than just assuming that they will be motivated by (hopefully good) economic theory. These issues are discussed by Milner in Chapter 34.

In Chapter 15 MacDonald and Milbourne survey recent developments in monetary theory. In a wide-ranging discussion, they demonstrate the present vitality of this area of the subject, in contrast with the 1960s and early 1970s when the main concern seemed to be with estimating demand-for-money functions. On the one hand, there has been renewed interest in the microfoundations of monetary theory. It is well known that Arrow–Debreu general equilibrium models have no role for money, since all possible future trades can be covered by contingent contracts. One line of investigation starts with a barter economy and shows how the requirement for a double coincidence of wants between traders creates an incentive to acquire frequently desired commodities, which thus become media of exchange. Other authors have introduced cash-in-advance requirements, in which goods must be bought with cash because for some reason or other sellers have no information about the creditworthiness of buyers. A slightly different discussion has considered whether non-interest-bearing money would in practice be replaced in transactions by interest-bearing bonds if the latter were available in sufficiently small denominations and provided that there were no legal obstacles. On the macroeconomic front a major new issue has been that of the credibility of monetary policy. This issue has arisen with the widespread adoption of pre-announced monetary targets as a significant component of disinflationary policy, and MacDonald and Milbourne provide an extended discussion of this area of research. Another area of debate, stimulated directly by the application of rational expectations to asset markets, has centred on the apparent volatility of asset prices, with empirical research focusing on whether this volatility merely reflects fluctuations in expected future returns or whether there is a strong 'speculative bubble' component. Finally, the authors discuss some new ideas on money demand, including the buffer stock theory, and some recent theories of the relationship between the money stock and real output involving credit rationing or costs of price adjustment.

In Chapter 16 the current state of environmental economics is elegantly surveyed by Pearce. Although important contributions were made in the nineteenth and early twentieth centuries, Pearce dates the evolution of environmental economics into a coherent subdiscipline somewhere in the 1960s. It was at this time that the notion of an extended equilibrium began to be formulated, with the neoclassical concept of general equilibrium being expanded to incorporate the natural environment. Pearce organizes his discussion under two major headings: the existence issue, which is concerned with whether such an extended equilibrium is theoretically possible and stable, and the valuation issue, which is concerned with how the natural environment would be shadow-priced in such an equilibrium. The existence issue is complicated by the second law of thermodynamics, which states that entropy always increases. This law rules out 100 per cent recyclability of resources, implying depletion over time. Later generations can be compensated for the depletion of natural capital if they are bequeathed sufficient man-made capital, but the issue of what, if any, discount factor to apply to the utility of future generations remains unresolved. Considerable research has been done on the valuation issue in the past twenty-five years, with a number of possible avenues being explored. One method uses travel cost as a proxy for admission price to popular beauty spots; another method uses property prices as a representation of the capitalized value of the services provided by the amenity. Finally there is the 'contingent valuation method' which uses questionnaires to elicit direct statements of willingness to pay from respondents. An interesting result is that people are willing to pay significant amounts just for the existence of certain aspects of the environment, without expecting to derive any utility from them. For example, the existence of whales is valued even by those who are unlikely ever to see any in the wild. Pearce concludes with an assessment of the role of economic instruments in solving the externality problems in this area.

In Chapter 17 Montet surveys recent advances in game theory and its applications in economics. Game theory entered economics with the publication of von Neumann and Morgenstern's *Theory of Games and Economic Behaviour* in 1944. However, little progress was made in the application of game theory to economic problems until relatively recently. This was partly because of a concentration on zero-sum games, which are of little interest to economics, and Montet regards the contributions of Schelling in the 1960s as a turning point in this respect: Schelling redefined strategic behaviour as an action designed to influence the choices of others through its effects on their expectations of one's own behaviour. In effect, strategic behaviour is a kind of signalling device designed to convey some message about what type of player the opponent faces, and this leads naturally into the issues of credibility and reputation with which we have now become familiar. Montet devotes the early part of his chapter to an admirably clear exposition of the basic concepts of modern game theory, and then goes on to consider its application in various areas of economics. His discussion of strategic behaviour amongst oligopolists should be read in conjunction with Chapter 24 by Baumol, whilst his treatment of macroeconomic policy games links in with the discussion of these issues in Chapter 15 by MacDonald and Milbourne, and in Chapter 23 by Currie and Levine.

In Chapter 18 we turn to development economics. Balasubramanyam and MacBean focus on international issues, beginning with a detailed examination of the structuralist case for protection. The structuralist case is based on the belief that openness to the international economy limits the possibilities of development in poor countries because of a combination of factors including a long-run downward trend in the relative price of primary commodities, discrimination in the rich countries against the manufactured exports of newly industrializing countries, and low elasticities of demand for primary products with respect to both price and income, which imply that a world-wide drive to expand exports of primaries would produce a marked depression of the price. These arguments form the intellectual basis for pursuing a course of import-substituting industrialization. The World Bank, in contrast, is an ardent exponent of structural adjustment, the main theme of which is a greater exposure to world prices and a reduction in market distortions, and the Bank has argued that more open and less distorted economies have performed better than those that have implicitly accepted the structuralist arguments. Balasubramanyam and MacBean carefully assess the evidence on these issues. They then turn to the question of foreign direct investment. They note that, despite frequent rhetorical attacks on multi-national firms, the governments of less developed countries have generally been keen to attract direct investment by them, at least in the manufacturing sector, as a means of importing technology. The same does not apply in the service sector, however, and Balasubramanyam and MacBean suggest that foreign direct investment might help to raise the efficiency level of certain parts of the service sector such as banking and insurance. They express some concern over the concessions which governments tend to make to attract foreign investment in manufacturing, since competition between governments in this area may raise the profitability of the investment without greatly increasing the aggregate flow.

In Chapter 19 Solow reviews recent work in growth theory. He starts by referring back to his own assessment in 1979 that without an injection of good new ideas there was little scope for new theoretical work in this area. He goes on to discuss a number of papers published within the last few years that do indeed seem to contain some interesting innovations. One theme, explored by Romer and Lucas, is to regard human capital as an additional factor of production which is subject to increasing returns on an economy-wide scale, although not at the firm level. In effect, investment in human capital directly increases the productivity of all workers by raising the average level of human capital in the economy. The underlying idea is that economies that have failed to invest in human capital cannot achieve the same growth rates as others, even though they have access to the same technology, because they do not have the knowledge to absorb it effectively. This is a neat modification of the standard neoclassical model, but it does possess the property that investment in human capital permanently raises the growth rate. Although this property might be considered rather implausible, it suggests a reason why the growth rates of developed economies today are considerably faster than was that of Great Britain during the industrial revolution. Solow also considers some recent applications of these ideas to international trade by Grossman and Helpman. The theme of their work is that countries may differ in their capacity for research and development (R & D), with the result that the structure of world demand may influence the total quantity of R & D that is carried out. Finally, Solow discusses the recent attempts to formalize Schumpeter which have been made by Krugman and by Aghion and Howitt; these theories are Schumpeterian in the sense that successful innovators earn temporary monopoly rents.

In Chapter 20 Shone reviews developments in open-economy macroeconomics. He points out that, in response to the relatively high levels of protection of the interwar period followed by the Bretton Woods arrangements set up in 1944, macroeconomics had tended to become a closed-economy subject, with extensions to the open economy focusing on the balance of trade in a world of fixed exchange rates. In response to increasing short-term capital flows the capital account began to be incorporated in the 1960s, with the differential between home and foreign interest rates entering as the crucial explanatory variable. The advent of floating exchange rates strongly reinforced this trend, with currencies coming to be regarded merely as alternative assets in a world dominated by 'hot money'; current account variables were now significant only as indicators of future changes in exchange rates, which would influence the expected rate of return on holdings of different currencies. Shone distinguishes carefully between models which assume price flexibility (continuous purchasing power parity) and those in which prices are sticky. He then introduces aggregate supply; the critical point here is that, because the price of imports can vary relative to that of home-produced goods, the product wage and consumption wage may not move together. Finally Shone considers the impact of wage indexation in such a model. The results clearly depend on the precise form of indexation in force. One interesting line of investigation concerns the optimal form of indexation in the presence of stochastic shocks of various kinds under different exchange rate regimes.

The economics of socialism is the subject matter of Chapter 21. This has recently become a topical issue – at least in the form of the dismantling of the economics of socialism! Hare outlines the basic principles of the Soviet model and the attempts at reform in the USSR and Eastern Europe. He then reviews theoretical treatments of the issues raised by the reformers, such as the question of the optimal degree of decentralization. This passes into a discussion of enterprise behaviour in a world of rationed inputs. Hare shows that even if enterprises are motivated to maximize profits (perhaps because profits are an important determinant of managerial bonuses), the responsiveness of output to market signals is reduced by the restrictions on the supply of inputs. Hare then turns to the theoretical analysis of shortage, a development particularly associated with the name of Kornai. He contrasts this with the empirically based approach of Portes and his co-workers, which is concerned with direct estimation of the importance of excess demand in consumer goods markets in planned economies. A different line of empirical work has been concerned with modelling the behaviour of planners in reaction to macroeconomic outcomes. For example, planners in Eastern Europe have tended to respond to unanticipated balance-of-payments surpluses by increasing investment. This research has some bearing on the ongoing controversy over the existence of investment cycles in planned economies. Overall, Hare's assessment is that there has been significant theoretical progress in this field in the last twenty years.

In Chapter 22 we turn our attention to the labour market, an aspect of economics which has witnessed intensive theoretical and empirical research in recent years. Sapsford focuses on the search aspect, which is based on the idea that sampling the wage rates offered by different firms is costly. If the probability distribution of wage offers is known, then it is rational to search until a certain wage (generally known as the 'reservation wage') is offered. If the probability distribution itself has to be discovered through searching, then it is more appropriate to decide on a particular size of sample. Sapsford summarizes the theoretical and empirical literature in this field.

Chapter 23 contains an elegant survey of the theory of international policy co-ordination by Currie and Levine. This has been a very active research topic in the last fifteen years, following the lead given by Hamada in a number of contributions which established the basic approach. Governments are viewed as minimizing a welfare loss function that includes such arguments as inflation and the deviation of output from some target value, and game theory is used to determine whether a co-operative solution yields a higher level of international welfare (defined as a weighted sum of the welfares of individual governments) than the Nash equilibrium that is likely to pertain in the absence of co-operation. Currie and Levine expound the basic results in terms of a simple natural rate model with floating exchange rates. In such a world, in the absence of international co-operation, monetary policy tends to be excessively tight and fiscal policy excessively lax because high real interest rates create favourable spill-over effects by pulling up the exchange rate. The authors then bring in the private sector by allowing for variation in the credibility of anti-inflation policies (this part of their chapter links in with the discussion of these issues by MacDonald and Milbourne in Chapter 15). It emerges that, if governments have credibility, international co-operation always improves welfare, but interestingly this is not necessarily the case if governments lack credibility. An altogether different question is whether the gains from international policy co-ordination are likely to be empirically significant. One aspect of this which has been much discussed recently is the impact of uncertainty and differences of view between governments about the workings of the macro-economy. Estimated welfare gains and losses from co-ordination vary considerably between studies, but Currie and Levine argue that the balance of results is quite strongly positive. The chapter ends with a consideration of some recent proposals for international policy co-ordination.

In Chapter 24 Baumol considers industry structure and the behaviour of firms. He compares and contrasts the different approaches offered by transactions theory, game theory and contestability theory. The transactions cost approach has given rise to no formal models; essentially it asks whether the internalization of interdependent activities within one firm is likely to involve fewer costs than having separate firms and using legal contracts to regulate their relationship. Baumol uses the example of vertical integration to illustrate these points. Game theory focuses on the strategic behaviour of firms in an oligopolistic market where they have a choice in the degree of aggressiveness towards rivals. The strategic element means that the structure of the industry is not determined simply by the shape of cost curves; in fact the number of firms may be either above or below the optimum (cost-minimizing) point. Contestability theory emphasizes the role of potential entrants to the industry, who may strongly influence the behaviour of incumbents even though no intention to enter is ever declared. Whereas in the game-theoretical analysis sunk costs represent a signal to rivals, according to contestability theory they should be regarded as an entry barrier. (It is also possible, however, for a monopolist to influence the perceived level of the entry barriers through its reaction to an attempted incursion; some recent work of this kind is discussed by Montet in Chapter 17.) If markets are perfectly contestable (without entry barriers), then in the long run entry and exit should force all firms to produce at the cost-minimizing point. The number of firms in the industry will then be determined by the level of demand in relation to this, although this itself will be influenced by pricing strategies. This proposition has stimulated empirical research designed to estimate industry cost curves. Contestability theory has also led to more precise formulation of concepts in this area; Baumol carefully explains what is meant by such concepts as the subadditivity of costs, which is related to but not precisely the same as what we generally know as economies of scale.

In Chapter 25 Aronson and Ott discuss the growth of the public sector. After presenting some statistics that indicate a long-run trend towards the growth of the public sector as a share of output, at least in the developed countries, they consider various hypotheses that have been put forward to explain this. One possibility is that the demand for services which tends to be provided by the public sector is income elastic but price inelastic; then if, as tends to be the case, productivity growth in this area is slower than in the economy as a whole, the output of these services tends to increase as a share of the total despite an increase in relative price. This is the case of unbalanced growth as first analysed by Baumol, and Aronson and Ott show that this theory has a fair amount of empirical support. Another set of hypotheses focuses on the fact that government activity tends to be financed by tax revenue rather than by user charges. The level of activity is then a political decision, and ideas from the public choice literature can be brought to bear on the issue. Not only is there scope for lobbying, which may produce an upward bias in public expenditure because the tax burden is diffused over the whole electorate, but models of voting can be used to analyse the issue of income redistribution through the tax system. The true cost of public expenditure is also rather opaque, and there may be elements of fiscal illusion involved. A final set of theories regards public expenditure as driven by what is regarded as an acceptable level of taxation – an idea that was originally suggested by the permanent increases in the share of the public sector in the gross domestic product (GDP) of the United Kingdom that seemed to accompany major wars. Having reviewed the theories, Aronson and Ott devote the final section of their chapter to a consideration of the empirical evidence.

9.4 CONCLUSIONS

Although the chapters in this part are eloquent testimony to the current vitality of economic theory, it is perhaps appropriate to conclude with a warning against complacency. There remain many phenomena which economists find difficult to explain. Two that might be cited are the historically unprecedented level of real interest rates and the persistence of unemployment in most West European countries in the 1980s. On both these issues many theories have been put forward, some of which have a certain degree of empirical support, but a convincing and widely accepted explanation still eludes us.

A second point is that theoretical models continue to be extremely pared-down, simplified representations of reality. They are likely to remain so in the interests of analytical tractability. This means that they can give us insights into the real world, but they cannot tell us how it works. These insights are powerful in the sense that they can change our whole way of thinking about issues, but they are also powerfully dangerous if we mistake the model for reality itself.

NOTE

1 However, in the last paragraph of his paper Tobin does include a brief discussion of the implications of alternative expectational assumptions.

REFERENCES

Azariadis, C. (1975) 'Implicit contracts and underemployment equilibria', *Journal of Political Economy* 83: 1183–202.

Baily, M. N. (1974) 'Wages and employment under uncertain demand', *Review of Economic Studies* 41: 37–50.

Bell, D. and Kristol, I. (1981) *The Crisis in Economic Theory*, New York: Basic Books.

Friedman, M. (1968) 'The role of monetary policy', *American Economic Review* 58: 1–17.

Leijonhufvud, A. (1968) *On Keynesian Economics and the Economics of Keynes*, Oxford: Oxford University Press.

Lucas, R. E. (1972) 'Expectations and the neutrality of money', *Journal of Economic Theory* 4: 103–24.

Muth, J. F. (1961) 'Rational expectations and the theory of price movements', *Econometrica* 29: 315–35.

Okun, A. M. (1981) *Prices and Quantities: A Macroeconomic Analysis*, Oxford: Basil Blackwell.

Phelps, E. S. (ed.) (1971) *Microeconomic Foundations of Employment and Inflation Theory*, London: Macmillan.

Sargent, T. J. and Wallace, N. (1975) ' "Rational" expectations, the optimal monetary instrument, and the optimal money supply rule', *Journal of Political Economy* 83: 241–53.

Stiglitz, J. E. and Weiss, A. (1981) 'Credit rationing in markets with imperfect competition', *American Economic Review* 71: 393–410.

Tobin, J. (1958) 'Liquidity preference as behaviour towards risk', *Review of Economic Studies* 25: 65–86.

10

EXPECTATIONS IN ECONOMICS

M. HASHEM PESARAN

10.1 INTRODUCTION

In comparison with some of the other important developments in our subject
the literature on expectations in economics is of recent origins and can be
traced back to the work of Knight (1921), Keynes (1936), Shackle (1949,
1955), Koyck (1954), Cagan (1956), Simon (1958) and Muth (1960, 1961).
Uncertainty and expectations hardly figure in the work of the classical economists, and even where expectations and their importance for decision-making
are discussed in Keynes's work, they are treated as a datum and hence do not
play a central role in the development of Keynesian macroeconomic theory.[1]
This is particularly striking considering that most decisions facing economic
agents are surrounded by uncertainty. In an uncertain environment, analysis
of economic behaviour inevitably involves expectations, and how expectations
are formed and the effect that they may have on current decisions become
issues of central importance for the development of dynamic economic theory
and time series econometrics. Under the influence of the pioneering work of
Muth (1961), the analysis of expectations formation and the explicit inclusion
of expectational variables in theoretical and empirical research have assumed
centre stage in many areas of economics. This is particularly true of intertemporal models of consumption, labour supply, asset prices, sales, investment
and inventory decisions as well as in theories of money, information processing,
search activity, labour contracts and insurance. The literature on expectations
in economics is vast and growing; a single essay on the subject can at best
provide only a partial account of some of the recent developments.[2] The
present chapter is not an exception. The focus will be on a discussion of
alternative models of expectations formation including adaptive, extrapolative
and rational expectations models. The learning problem is also briefly dis-

Partial support from the ESRC and the Isaac Newton Trust of Trinity College, Cambridge, is
gratefully acknowledged.

cussed and it is argued that, given the extreme information assumptions that underlie the rational expectations hypothesis (REH), a greater emphasis needs to be placed on the use of survey expectations in empirical economic analysis. This in turn requires larger and better surveys and the development of more appropriate techniques suited to the use of survey expectations in econometric models.

10.2 THE ADAPTIVE EXPECTATIONS HYPOTHESIS

The adaptive expectations hypothesis (AEH) in its simplest form was first utilized in economics by Koyck (1954) in an empirical analysis of investment, by Cagan (1956) in a study of the demand for money during hyperinflation, by Friedman (1957) in his analysis of the permanent income hypothesis and by Nerlove (1958) in a study of the agricultural supply function.

Let y^e_{t-i} be the expectations of y_{t-i} formed at time $t - i - 1$ with respect to the information set Ω_{t-i-1}. Then the first-order AEH can be written as

$$y^e_t - y^e_{t-1} = \theta(y_{t-1} - y^e_{t-1}) \qquad 0 < \theta < 1 \tag{10.1}$$

where θ is the adaptive coefficient and governs the magnitude of the revision in expectations. Under the AEH the change in expectations is assumed to be proportional to the size of the latest observed error of expectations. For this reason the simple AEH is also sometimes referred to as the first-order error-correction model.

Solving equation (10.1) yields the extrapolative expectations mechanism

$$y^e_t = \sum_{i=1}^{\infty} \omega_i y_{t-i} \tag{10.2}$$

with the geometrically declining weights

$$\omega_i = \theta(1 - \theta)^{i-1} \qquad i = 1, 2, \ldots \tag{10.3}$$

The AEH was put forward originally as a plausible updating formula, without any optimality property's being claimed for it. But, as shown by Muth (1960), the adaptive expectations formula (10.1) yields statistically optimal forecasts when the generating process underlying $\{y_t\}$ is an integrated first-order moving-average process. To see this suppose that

$$\Delta y_t = \varepsilon_t - (1 - \theta)\varepsilon_{t-1} \tag{10.4}$$

where the ε_t are identically and independently distributed random variables with zero means and a constant variance. Then the optimal forecast of y_t formed at time $t - 1$ is given by

$$E(y_t|\Omega_{t-1}) = y_{t-1} - (1 - \theta)\varepsilon_{t-1}$$

or upon using (10.4)

162

$$E(y_t|\Omega_{t-1}) = y_{t-1} - (1 - \theta)[1 - (1 - \theta)L]^{-1}\Delta y_{t-1} \qquad (10.5)$$

where L is the one-period lag operator (i.e. $Ly_t = y_{t-1}$). Applying $1 - (1 - \theta)L$ to both sides of (10.5) now yields

$$E(y_t|\Omega_{t-1}) - E(y_{t-1}|\Omega_{t-2}) = \theta[y_{t-1} - E(y_{t-1}|\Omega_{t-2})]$$

which has the same form as (10.1) and establishes the statistical optimality of the AEH under (10.4).

However, in general the AEH does not yield optimal forecasts. The optimality of the expectations formation process depends on the nature of the process generating $\{y_t\}$. In this respect two general approaches can be distinguished: the time series approach where expectations are formed optimally on the basis of a univariate time series model, and the REH where expectations are formed on the basis of a 'structural' model of the economy.

10.3 THE TIME SERIES AND THE EXTRAPOLATIVE APPROACHES TO MODELLING EXPECTATIONS

The time series approach represents a natural extension of the AEH and assumes that expectations are formed optimally on the basis of a univariate autoregressive integrated moving-average (ARIMA) model. Suppose that the process generating y_t can be approximated by the invertible ARIMA(p, d, q) model:

$$\phi(L)(1 - L)^d y_t = \theta(L)\,\varepsilon_t \qquad (10.6)$$

where $\phi(L)$ and $\theta(L)$ are polynomial lag operators of orders p and q respectively and all the roots of $\phi(z) = 0$ and $\theta(z) = 0$ fall outside the unit circle. The expectations of y_t are then given by

$$y_t^e = E(y_t|\Omega_{t-1}) = \sum_{i=0}^{\infty} \omega_i y_{t-i-1} = W(L)y_{t-1} \qquad (10.7)$$

where $W(L) = \sum_{i=0}^{\infty} \omega_i L^i$, and the weights ω_i are determined in terms of the parameter estimates of the ARIMA model (10.6).[3]

The time series approach is also closely related to the extrapolative method of expectations formation. Under the former $W(L)$ is estimated directly by first fitting the ARIMA model (10.6) to the data, while under the latter the choice of the $W(L)$ function is made on a priori grounds. Extrapolative expectations formation models include the 'return to normality' model

$$y_t^e = y_{t-1} - \lambda(y_{t-1} - y_{t-1}^*) \qquad \lambda > 0$$

where y_t^* represents the 'normal' or 'average' level of y_t. Different specifications of y_t^* can be entertained. For example, assuming

$$y_t^* = (1 - \omega)y_t + \omega y_t^e$$

163

yields the AEH, with $\theta = 1 - \lambda\omega$, while setting $y_t^* = (1 - \omega)y_t + \omega y_{t-1}$ gives the regressive expectations model[4]

$$y_t^e = y_{t-1} - \lambda\omega(y_{t-1} - y_{t-2})$$

More general extrapolative expectations formation models have also been discussed in the literature by Meiselman (1962), Mincer (1969) and Frenkel (1975). Meiselman (1962) proposed the error-learning model

$$_ty_{t+s}^e - _{t-1}y_{t+s}^e = \gamma_s(y_t - _{t-1}y_t^e) \tag{10.8}$$

where $_ty_{t+s}^e$ is the expectation of y_{t+s} formed at time t. The error-learning model states that the revision in expectations of y_{t+s} over the period $t - 1$ to t is proportional to the current error of expectations. Different expectations formation models can be obtained by assuming different patterns for the revision coefficients γ_s. Mincer (1969) shows that in general there is a one-to-one relationship between the error-learning model (10.8) and the general extrapolative specification (10.7). The revision coefficients are linked to the weights ω_i through the recursive relations

$$\gamma_s = \sum_{j=0}^{s-1} \omega_j\gamma_{s-1-j} \qquad s = 1, 2, \ldots \tag{10.9}$$

with $\gamma_0 \equiv 1$. For example, the simple AEH, which is an extrapolative model with exponentially declining weights, corresponds to the case where the revision coefficients are the same at all forecast horizons. Mincer (1969) also discusses the cases of falling and rising revision coefficients. He demonstrates that the revision coefficients will be falling (rising) when weights ω_i decline (rise) more than exponentially. The error-correction model and the general extrapolative model are algebraically equivalent, but the former gives a particularly convenient representation when observations are available on expectations formed at different dates in the past for the same date in the future.[5]

Despite the apparent generality of the extrapolative and error-learning models, they suffer from two major shortcomings. First, by focusing on the past history of y_t they ignore the possible effect on expectations of variables other than the past values of y_t.[6] Second, and more importantly, they assume that the weights ω_i are fixed and, in particular, remain invariant with respect to changes in the agent's decision environment such as changes in policy or technology. It is therefore important to consider other models of expectations formation that are not subject to these criticisms.

10.4 THE RATIONAL EXPECTATIONS HYPOTHESIS

While it is generally agreed that a satisfactory model of expectations formation should incorporate the effect of information on variables other than the past history of the variable in question, there is less agreement on the nature of the additional information to be incorporated in the expectations formation model and the manner in which this additional information is to be used by agents in forming their expectations. The REH put forward by Muth (1961) provides a possible answer to the problem at hand. It stands at the other extreme to the AEH and asserts that economic agents form their expectations optimally on the basis of the 'true' structural model of the economy and that subjective expectations held by individuals are the same as the objective expectations derived on the basis of the true model of the economy. It is this equality of the subjective and objective (conditional) expectations that lies at the heart of the REH. More specifically, let Ω_t be the information set known to the economic agent at time t and let $f(y_t|\Omega_{t-1})$ be the joint probability distribution of the random variables y_t entering the economic model. In its most general form the REH postulates that the individual's subjective conditional probability distribution of y_t coincides with the objective probability distribution $f(y_t|\Omega_{t-1})$. In most applications of the REH, particularly in the macroeconomic literature, attention has often been focused on the first and sometimes the second moments of the probability distribution, and expectations about other measures such as median, mode or higher-order moments have invariably been ignored.[7]

The REH is perhaps best explained in the context of a simple economic model. Consider the supply and demand model[8]

$$q_t^s = \beta_1 P_t^e + \alpha_1 x_{1t} + \varepsilon_{1t} \qquad \beta_1 > 0 \qquad (10.10)$$

$$q_t^d = \beta_2 P_t + \alpha_2 x_{2t} + \varepsilon_{2t} \qquad \beta_2 < 0 \qquad (10.11)$$

$$q_t = q_t^s = q_t^d \qquad (10.12)$$

where q_t^s is the total quantity of an agricultural product supplied in period t, q_t^d is the demand for the product, x_{1t} and x_{2t} are supply and demand shifters (the exogenous variables shifting the demand and supply curves), and P_t and P_t^e are the product price and its expectation formed by producers at time $t - 1$. Both the demand and supply functions are assumed to be subject to random shocks ε_{1t} and ε_{2t}. The market-clearing condition (10.12) also assumes that the product cannot be stored. Substituting for q_t^s and q_t^d in (10.12) and solving for P_t we obtain

$$P_t = \gamma P_t^e + z_t \qquad (10.13)$$

where $\gamma = \beta_1/\beta_2$ and

$$z_t = \beta_2^{-1}(\alpha_1 x_{1t} - \alpha_2 x_{2t} + \varepsilon_{1t} - \varepsilon_{2t}) \qquad (10.14)$$

Under the REH, the price expectations P_t^e are derived noting that $P_t^e =$

$E(P_t|\Omega_{t-1})$. Taking conditional expectations of both sides of (10.13) with respect to Ω_{t-1}, we have

$$P_t^e = E(P_t|\Omega_{t-1}) = (1 - \gamma)^{-1} E(z_t|\Omega_{t-1}) \qquad (10.15)$$

which translates the original problem of forming expectations of prices to that of forming expectations of the 'exogenous' or 'forcing' variables of the system. This is a general feature of the REH and is not confined to the present example. The solution of the rational expectations models requires a complete specification of the processes generating the forcing variables. Here we assume that the supply and demand shocks ε_{1t} and ε_{2t} are serially uncorrelated with zero means and that the exogenous variables x_{1t} and x_{2t} follow AR(1) processes

$$x_{1t} = \rho_1 x_{1,t-1} + v_{1t} \qquad (10.16)$$

$$x_{2t} = \rho_2 x_{1,t-1} + v_{2t} \qquad (10.17)$$

Now, using these results in (10.14) and taking conditional expectations we obtain

$$E(z_t|\Omega_{t-1}) = \beta_2^{-1}(\alpha_1\rho_1 x_{1,t-1} - \alpha_2\rho_2 x_{2,t-1})$$

which if substituted back in (10.15) yields the following expression for the price expectations:

$$P_t^e = (\beta_2 - \beta_1)^{-1} (\alpha_1\rho_1 x_{1,t-1} - \alpha_2\rho_2 x_{2,t-1}) \qquad (10.18)$$

A comparison of this expression with the extrapolative formula (10.7) discussed in the previous section now clearly reveals the main differences that exist between the REH and the extrapolative expectations hypothesis. Unlike the expectations formed on the basis of the extrapolative hypothesis, the rational expectations depend on the past history of variables other than past prices, and more importantly the weights attached to the past observations (namely $\alpha_1\rho_1/(\beta_2 - \beta_1)$ and $-\alpha_2\rho_2/(\beta_2 - \beta_1)$) are not invariant to changes in the processes generating the exogenous variables.[9] Under the REH a shift in the parameters of the x_{1t} and x_{2t} processes, brought about, for example, by changes in government policy, institutional arrangements or technical knowhow, will be fully and correctly perceived by producers who will then adjust their price expectations accordingly via (10.18).

Using (10.18) and (10.13) we now have the following price and output solutions:

$$P_t = \frac{\alpha_1}{\beta_2}\left(x_{1t} + \frac{\rho_1\beta_1}{\beta_2 - \beta_1} x_{1,t-1}\right)$$
$$- \frac{\alpha_2}{\beta_2}\left(x_{2t} + \frac{\rho_2\beta_1}{\beta_2 - \beta_1} x_{2,t-1}\right) + \beta_2^{-1}(\varepsilon_{1t} - \varepsilon_{2t}) \qquad (10.19)$$

$$q_t = \alpha_1 \left(x_{1t} + \frac{\rho_1 \beta_1}{\beta_2 - \beta_1} x_{1,t-1} \right) - \frac{\beta_1 \alpha_2 \rho_2}{\beta_2 - \beta_1} x_{2,t-1} + \varepsilon_{1t} \qquad (10.20)$$

On the assumption that the exogenous variables and the random shocks are independently distributed, the REH imposes a number of cross-equation parametric restrictions linking the parameters of the price and output equations given above to the parameters of the exogenous processes (10.16) and (10.17). The estimation of the equation system (10.16), (10.17), (10.19) and (10.20) gives nine parameter estimates with only seven unknowns (α_1, β_1, α_2, β_2, ρ_1, ρ_2), thus yielding two cross-equation parametric restrictions. The nature and number of cross-equation restrictions crucially depend on the processes generating the exogenous variables. For example, increasing the order of the autoregressive (AR) processes (10.16) and (10.17) from one to two increases the number of cross-equation parameter restrictions from two to seven.

These types of parametric restrictions that relate the reduced-form parameters of the rational expectations equations to the parameters of the processes generating the forcing variables play an important role in tests of the REH. It is important, however, to bear in mind that tests of cross-equation parametric restrictions are *joint* tests of the REH and the economic model that underlies it, and at best provide us with an *indirect* test of the REH. Rejection of cross-equation restrictions can always be interpreted as an indication of model mis-specification rather than as a rejection of the rationality hypothesis.

The dependence of rational expectations on the parameters of the exogenous (policy) variables also forms the basis of Lucas's critique of the mainstream macroeconometric policy evaluation (Lucas 1976). In models with rational expectations the parameters of the decision rules are usually a mixture of the parameters of the agents' objective functions and the stochastic processes generating the forcing variables. In consequence, there is no reason to believe that the parameters of the economic relations will remain unchanged under policy interventions. In the context of the above example the nature of the Lucas critique can be clearly seen in the coefficients of the variables $x_{1,t-1}$ and $x_{2,t-1}$ that enter the producer's output decision rule given by (10.20). These coefficients are mixtures of the parameters of the structural model (α_1, α_2, β_1, β_2) and the parameters of the exogenous (possibly policy) variables (ρ_1, ρ_2), and therefore cannot be assumed to be invariant to changes in ρ_1 and ρ_2.

10.5 OPTIMAL PROPERTIES OF THE RATIONAL EXPECTATIONS HYPOTHESIS

When expectations are formed rationally on the basis of the 'true' model, they possess a number of optimal properties, the most important of which is the orthogonality property

$$E(\xi_t|\Omega_{t-1}) = 0 \tag{10.21}$$

where $\xi_t = y_t - y_t^e$ is the error of expectations. In words this says that, under the REH, expectations errors are orthogonal to (or are uncorrelated with) the variables in the agent's information set. The proof of the orthogonality property is straightforward and follows almost immediately from the definition of the REH itself. Under the REH

$$\xi_t = y_t - E(y_t|\Omega_{t-1})$$

and

$$\begin{aligned}
E(\xi_t|\Omega_{t-1}) &= E(y_t|\Omega_{t-1}) - E[E(y_t|\Omega_{t-1})|\Omega_{t-1}] \\
&= E(y_t|\Omega_{t-1}) - E(y_t|\Omega_{t-1}) \\
&= 0
\end{aligned}$$

The orthogonality property is central to direct tests of the REH using survey data on expectations (this is discussed in more detail in Section 10.9) and to the tests of market efficiency. One important feature of the orthogonality property is that it holds with respect to any subset of Ω_{t-1}. For example, under the REH expectations errors will be uncorrelated with the past values of y_t (i.e. $E(\xi_t|y_{t-1}, y_{t-2}, \ldots) = 0$). This is usually referred to as the 'efficiency' property. The orthogonality property also implies the 'unbiasedness' and 'serially uncorrelated' properties

$$E(\xi_t) = 0$$

$$E(\xi_t\xi_{-i}) = 0 \qquad \text{for } i \neq 0$$

As an example consider the supply and demand model of the previous section. Using (10.18) and (10.19) we obtain the following expression for the error of price expectations:

$$\xi_t = P_t - P_t^e = \beta_2^{-1}(\alpha_1 v_{1t} - \alpha_2 v_{2t} + \varepsilon_{1t} - \varepsilon_{2t})$$

which is a linear function of serially uncorrelated random variables with zero means and clearly satisfies the unbiasedness, efficiency and orthogonality properties discussed above.

These properties need not hold, however, if expectations are formed on the basis of a mis-specified model or a model with correctly specified structure but incorrect parameter values. Once again consider the supply and demand example of the previous section but assume that the correct specification of the $\{x_{1t}\}$ process is given by the AR(2) process

$$x_{1t} = \rho_1^* x_{1,t-1} + \rho_2^* x_{1,t-2} + v_{1t}^* \tag{10.22}$$

and not by the AR(1) process given in (10.16). Under this form of mis-specification the error of price expectations will be[10]

$$\xi_t = \beta_2^{-1}\alpha_1 \; \rho_2^*\left(\frac{-\rho_1^*}{1 - \rho_2^*} \; x_{1,t-1} + x_{1,t-2}\right) + \beta_2^{-1}(\alpha_1 v_{1t}^* - \alpha_2 v_{2t} + \varepsilon_{1t} - \varepsilon_{2t})$$

which shows that in this mis-specified case the ξ_t still have zero means but are no longer serially uncorrelated and do not satisfy the orthogonality condition. In fact we have

$$E(\xi_t|\Omega_{t-1}) = \frac{\alpha_1 \rho_2^*}{\beta_2(1 - \rho_2^*)} \; [-\rho_1^* x_{1,t-1} + (1 - \rho_2^*)x_{1,t-2}]$$

which is non-zero, unless of course $\rho_2^* = 0$, in which case there are no mis-specifications and the order of the x_{1t} process is correctly perceived by the agent.

10.6 THE RATIONAL EXPECTATIONS HYPOTHESIS AND THE NEOCLASSICAL OPTIMIZATION APPROACH

Muth's account of the REH and our discussion of it implicitly assume a separation of the decision problem facing the economic agent into an 'optimization' part with given expectations and an expectations part with given decision rules. However, seen from the perspective of the expected utility maximization theory of decision-making, such a separation of the optimization problem from the expectations formation problem is unnecessary and will be a mathematically valid procedure only under the certainty equivalence assumption (see, for example, Lucas and Sargent 1981: ch. 1; Pesaran 1987: ch. 4). Under the expected utility maximization approach the problem of expectations formation arises only as part of the decision-making process. In this approach the expected utility of a single agent, usually regarded as a 'representative' household or firm, is maximized conditional on the information set available to the agent at the time that the decision is being made and subject to the constraints (such as budget or technological constraints) that the agent faces. The solution to this problem is obtained by the application of dynamic programming techniques and has been reviewed in the economic literature by, for example, Sargent (1987: ch. 1) and Stokey et al. (1989).[11] Here we give a taste of what this approach involves by applying it to the output decision problem of a monopolist producing a non-storable product subject to adjustment costs and demand uncertainties.

Suppose that the monopolist is risk neutral and faces the linear demand curve

$$p_t = \theta_0 - \theta_1 q_t + \varepsilon_t \qquad \theta_0, \theta_1 > 0 \qquad (10.23)$$

where q_t is the output, p_t is the market-clearing price and the ε_t are serially uncorrelated demand shocks with zero means. The profit function of the monopolist at time t is given by

$$\pi_t = p_t q_t - w_t l_t - \frac{\phi}{2} (l_t - l_{t-1})^2 \tag{10.24}$$

where w_t is the wage rate and l_t is the man-hours employed. The quadratic term in l_t in the profit function is intended to capture the adjustment costs arising from costs of hiring and firing workers. Initially we assume that the production function is given by the well-behaved function

$$q_t = f(l_t) \qquad f' > 0, f'' < 0, f(0) = 0 \tag{10.25}$$

The intertemporal optimization problem facing the firm can now be set up as

$$\max_{\{l_{t+\tau}\}_{\tau=0}^{\infty}} \mathrm{E}\left(\sum_{\tau=0}^{\infty} \beta^\tau \pi_{t+\tau} \middle| \Omega_t \right)$$

subject to the constraints (10.23) and (10.25) and for a given $\{w_t\}$ process. The information set Ω_t of the monopolist is assumed to include l_t and w_t and the past values of l_t, p_t, q_t and w_t. The parameter β is the discount factor assumed to lie in the range $0 < \beta < 1$. The first-order condition for this optimization, known also as the Euler equation, is given by[12]

$$\mathrm{E}\left(\frac{\partial \pi_{t+\tau}}{\partial l_{t+\tau}} + \beta \frac{\partial \pi_{t+\tau+1}}{\partial l_{t+\tau}} \middle| \Omega_t \right) = 0 \qquad \tau = 0, 1, 2, \ldots \tag{10.26}$$

Focusing on the current decision variable l_t and using relations (10.23)–(10.25) we have

$$\frac{\partial \pi_t}{\partial l_t} = [\theta_0 - 2\theta_1 f(l_t) + \varepsilon_t] f'(l_t) - \phi(l_t - l_{t-1}) - w_t$$

$$\frac{\partial \pi_{t+1}}{\partial l_t} = \phi(l_{t+1} - l_t)$$

and hence[13]

$$\phi(1 + \beta)l_t - [\theta_0 - 2\theta_1 f(l_t)]f'(l_t) = \phi l_{t-1} + \beta\phi\mathrm{E}(l_{t+1}|\Omega_t) - w_t \tag{10.27}$$

In general, this is a non-linear rational expectations equation and cannot be solved analytically. However, when $f(l_t)$ takes the linear form $f(l_t) = \alpha l_t$ we have

$$l_t = a + bl_{t-1} + c\mathrm{E}(l_{t+1}|\Omega_t) - dw_t \tag{10.28}$$

where

$$d^{-1} = \phi(1 + \beta) + 2\theta_1 a^2 > 0$$
$$a = da\theta_0 > 0$$
$$b = d\phi > 0$$
$$c = d\beta\phi > 0$$

This equation arises frequently in the rational expectations literature on adjustment costs and staggered wage contract models, and has been studied by Kennan (1979), Hansen and Sargent (1980) and Pesaran (1987: Section 5.3.4) for example. The solution of (10.28) depends on the roots of the auxiliary equation

$$1 = b\mu + c\mu^{-1}$$

and will be unique if one of the roots (say μ_1) falls inside the unit circle while the other (say μ_2) falls outside the unit circle. It is not difficult to show that in the case of the present example this condition is satisfied for all the *a priori* plausible parameter values of the structural parameters (i.e. for θ_0, θ_1, α, $\phi >$ 0 and $0 < \beta < 1$), and the unique solution of l_t will be given by

$$l_t = \frac{a}{c(\mu_2 - 1)} + \mu_1 l_{t-1} - \frac{d}{c\mu_2} \sum_{i=0}^{\infty} \mu_2^{-i} E(w_{t+i} | \Omega_t) \qquad (10.29)$$

which is a function of the monopolist's wage rate expectations. As an example suppose that the wage rate follows a first-order AR process with parameter ρ ($|\rho| < |\mu_2|$). Then (10.29) becomes[14]

$$l_t = \frac{a}{c} (\mu_2 - 1)^{-1} + \mu_1 l_{t-1} - \frac{d}{c} (\mu_2 - \rho)^{-1} w_t \qquad (10.30)$$

This solution clearly shows the dependence of the employment decision rule on the parameter of the wage process. Once again this is a common feature of the rational expectations approach and needs to be taken into account in the econometric analysis.

Formulation of the REH as a part of an expected utility maximization problem has an important advantage over Muth's version of the hypothesis. It explicitly integrates the expectations formation hypothesis within the neoclassical optimization framework and provides a closer link between economic theory and econometric analysis. However, in order to make this approach operational it is often essential that restrictive assumptions are made with respect to preferences, technology, endowments and information sets (see Pesaran 1988). Sometimes even apparently minor modifications to the specifications of technology and preferences can result in analytically intractable decision rules. For example, suppose that the linear production function underlying the decision rule (10.28) is assumed to be subject to random shocks and is given by

$$q_t = \alpha l_t \eta_t \qquad \eta_t > 0$$

171

where $\{\eta_t\}$ is a sequence of random variables distributed independently of l_t with mean 1. Further, assume that the realization of η_t is observed by the monopolist at time t (i.e. η_t is in Ω_t). Under this production technology we obtain

$$l_t = a_t + b_t l_{t-1} + c_t E(l_{t+1}|\Omega_t) - d_t w_t$$

where

$$d_t^{-1} = \phi(1 + \beta) + 2\theta_1 a^2 \eta_t^2 \qquad a_t = \alpha\theta_0\eta_t d_t$$

$$b_t = \phi d_t \qquad\qquad\qquad c_t = \phi\beta d_t$$

which is a linear rational expectations equation with random coefficients and does not seem to have an analytically tractable solution. Other examples of rational expectations models that do not lend themselves to closed-form solutions include the consumption-based intertemporal asset-pricing models discussed by Lucas (1978), Hansen and Singleton (1983) and Sargent (1987), and the stochastic optimal growth models discussed by Brock and Mirman (1972) and Danthine and Donaldson (1981) and reviewed by Stokey *et al.* (1989).

10.7 THE RATIONAL EXPECTATIONS HYPOTHESIS VIEWED AS A MODEL-CONSISTENT EXPECTATIONS HYPOTHESIS

In contrast with the version of the REH embodied in the expected utility maximization approach, Muth's own version of the hypothesis is best viewed as a 'model-consistent' method of expectations formation. It simply requires that 'expectations' and 'forecasts' generated by the 'model' should be consistent. The underlying economic model, or in Muth's own words 'The relevant economic theory', could have either Keynesian or monetarist features, and there is no requirement that all the behavioural relations in the model should be derived as solutions to a well-defined expected utility maximization problem.

In this approach the REH is viewed as one among several possible expectations formation hypotheses, with no presumption that the underlying model is necessarily correct. The choice among the rival expectations formation hypotheses is made on empirical grounds. As Muth himself puts it: 'The only real test [of the REH], however, is whether theories involving rationality explain the observed phenomenon any better than alternative theories' (Muth 1961: 330).

The model-consistent interpretation of the REH is relatively uncontroversial and has been adopted extensively in the econometric literature by the Keynesian and the neoclassical model-builders alike.[15] In these applications the REH is treated as a working hypothesis to be tested along with the other assumptions of the underlying model. This represents an 'instrumentalist' view of the REH and fits well with the mainstream econometric practice. Econometric implications of the REH in the areas of identification, estimation and hypothesis testing have been investigated in some detail in the literature and are reviewed by Pesaran (1987: chs 5–7). Most of the work carried out in these areas has so far been confined to linear rational expectations models under homogeneous information, but over the past few years important advances have also been made in estimation and numerical solution of non-linear rational expectations models (see, for example, Tauchen 1987; Hussey 1988; Duffie and Singleton 1989; Smith 1989). Some progress has also been made in the case of linear rational expectations models under heterogeneous information (Pesaran 1990a, b).

10.8 THE RATIONAL EXPECTATIONS HYPOTHESIS AND THE LEARNING PROBLEM

One of the fundamental assumptions underlying the REH is that agents know or are able to learn the 'true' model of the economy, at least in a probabilistic sense. While there can be no doubt that agents learn from their past mistakes, the issue of whether the learning process converges to the rational expectations equilibrium is an open one. Generally speaking, the learning problem has been studied in the literature using two types of framework: the rational (or Bayesian) learning model, and the boundedly rational learning model.

The rational learning model assumes that agents know the correct specification of the economic model but are uncertain about the values of some of its parameters. At first this appears to be the same as the estimation problem familiar in the econometric literature. However, on closer scrutiny it becomes clear that in a learning process where there are feedbacks from expectations to outcomes the estimation environment would not be time invariant and the usual proofs of the convergence of the parameter estimates to their true values would no longer be applicable. The main source of the difficulty lies in the fact that when learning is in process expectation errors do not satisfy the orthogonality property (10.21) and agents need to disentangle the systematic effect of expectation errors on outcomes from those of the other variables. Studies that consider the rational learning problem include Cyert and DeGroot (1974), Taylor (1975), Friedman (1979), Townsend (1978, 1983), Bray and Kreps (1987) and Feldman (1987a, b). Friedman and Taylor consider models with no feedbacks from expectations to outcomes and are therefore able to show convergence of the learning process to the rational expectations solution using standard results on the consistency of least squares estimates. The other studies deal with the more realistic case where there are feedbacks. Focusing on relatively simple examples, these authors are also able to show that the learning process converges to the rational expectations solution. In a more general setting, Bray and Kreps (1987) show that under rational learning subjective beliefs will (nearly) aways converge, although not necessarily to a rational expectations equilibrium. However, these convergence results are not as promising as they may appear at first. The rational learning framework assumes that except for a finite number of parameters the agents already know the 'true' model of the economy and that this is 'common knowledge'. This is almost informationally as demanding as the REH itself (cf. Bray and Kreps 1987).

An informationally less demanding learning framework is the 'boundedly rational model' studied by DeCanio (1979), Blume and Easley (1982), Frydman (1982), Bray (1983), Bowden (1984), Bray and Savin (1986), Fourgeaud et al. (1986) and Marcet and Sargent (1989a, b). In this framework the assumption that, except for some key parameters, agents know the 'true' structural model of the economy is avoided, but it is assumed instead that agents employ and remain committed to some 'plausible' learning rule. However, it is not explained what constitutes a 'plausible' learning rule, although in practice the learning rule is often derived assuming that agents know the reduced form of the economic model under consideration, which already attributes a significant degree of a priori common knowledge on their part. Another important criticism of the boundedly rational learning model lies in the fact that it does not allow for the possibility of revising the learning rule. Such an approach is justifiable if the chosen learning rule ensures convergence to the rational expectations equation. However, it is not satisfactory where the existence of non-convergent learning rules cannot, in general, be ruled out.

There are no general results on the convergence of boundedly rational learning models. Most results that are available refer to the learning problem in the context of simple models with a unique rational expectations equilibrium and are based on least squares learning.[16] Bray and Savin (1986) and Fourgeaud et al. (1986) consider the supply and demand model set out in Section 10.4. The pseudo-reduced-form equation of this model is given by

$$p_t = \gamma p_t^e + \alpha' x_t + \varepsilon_t$$

where $\gamma = \beta_1/\beta_2$ and

$$\varepsilon_t = \frac{\varepsilon_{1t} - \varepsilon_{2t}}{\beta_2} \qquad \alpha' x_t = \frac{\alpha_1' x_{1t} - \alpha_2' x_{2t}}{\beta_2}$$

Under the REH with complete learning, the expectations p_t^e are given by

$$p_t^e = \mathrm{E}(P_t|\Omega_{t-1}) = \frac{1}{1-\gamma} \alpha' x_t^e$$

but with incomplete learning P_t^e is based on an auxiliary model such as

$$p_t = \theta'z_t + u_t \tag{10.31}$$

where z_t is composed of variables in the agent's information set. At the beginning of period t, the available observations $p_1, p_2, \ldots, p_{t-1}; z_1, z_2, \ldots, z_{t-1}$ are used to obtain an estimate of θ (say $\hat{\theta}_t$), and price expectations are set as[17]

$$p_t^* = \hat{\theta}_t'z_t$$

and the equation for the evolution of prices over time is given by

$$p_t = \gamma(\hat{\theta}_t'z_t) + \alpha'x_t + \varepsilon_t$$

In view of the dependence of $\hat{\theta}_t$ on past prices, this equation represents a highly non-linear difference equation in P_t which in general will have a non-stationary solution even if $(x_t, z_t, \varepsilon_t)$ are drawn from a stationary distribution. The learning process is complicated because the agent needs to disentangle the effect of a change in the price which is due to a change in the exogenous variables from that which is due to incomplete learning. In the context of this model Bray and Savin (1986) show that the learning process converges when $\gamma < 1$, but to prove their result they make the rather restrictive assumption that the (x_t, ε_t) are identically and independently distributed. These authors also assume that $z_t = x_t$. Fourgeaud et al. (1986) derive the condition for the convergence of the learning process under less restrictive assumptions and also consider the case where z_t may differ from x_t. They show the important result that, when the auxiliary model (10.31) contains variables other than x_t, these extraneous variables also enter the price equation via expectations and will be a determinant of prices even in the rational expectations equation, which is a good example of self-fulfilling expectations.

The process of learning is further complicated by the presence of information costs. With costly information the expected benefit of acquiring the information needs to be weighed against the expected cost of its acquisition. It is no longer clear that complete learning is economically desirable even if it were possible in a world with no information costs. A good example of learning under costly information is the problem faced by a monopolist who wishes to learn about the parameters of the demand curve that he faces. Should the monopolist try to improve his estimates of the demand curve by varying output substantially over a number of periods, although he may be incurring a loss in the short run? Work on this and related areas is currently in process. This literature suggest that adherence to the principle of 'rationality' in itself may not be enough to generate expectations that are rational in the sense advanced by Muth.[18]

10.9 SURVEY EXPECTATIONS AND DIRECT TESTS OF THE RATIONAL EXPECTATIONS HYPOTHESIS

The tests of the cross-equation parametric restrictions that accompany the REH are based on the important presumption that expectations are intrinsically *unobservable*; this implies that the expectations formation processes can be analysed only indirectly via the economic model that embodies them.[19] This point of view in effect immunizes the REH against possible falsification. Although tests of cross-equation parametric restrictions are useful as tests of the consistency of the expectations formation process with the underlying behavioural model, they are of little help as tests of the theories of expectations formation. Such indirect tests can always be dismissed on the grounds that the model that embodies the REH is mis-specified.

The view that expectations do not lend themselves to direct measurements is rather extreme and is not shared by many researchers in the field. From early on economists such as Klein (1954), Modigliani and Sauerlender (1955), Haavelmo (1958: 356–7) and Katona (1958) fully recognized the importance of direct measures of expectations for analysis of the effect of expectations on economic behaviour and for study of the expectations formation process. Direct measures of expectations are currently available in most industrialized countries for a wide range of economic variables such as inflation, interest rates, exchange rates, sales, inventory levels, degree of capacity utilization and share prices. These measures are based on public and professional opinion survey data and are often in the form of qualitative responses – for example, whether a variable is expected to 'go up', 'stay the same' or 'go down'. It is felt that survey questions that require precise quantitative responses either will not be answered or will be answered with a wide margin of error. However, survey expectations are subject to a number of important shortcomings. The results of sample surveys can be sensitive to sampling errors and the phrasing of the questions. Respondents may not give a truthful expression of their opinion. Finally, the qualitative nature of the results of most surveys makes the task of their incorporation into empirical models difficult.[20] Despite these difficulties there has been a resurgence of interest in direct measures of expectations. For a brief discussion of some of the available expectations surveys, see Pesaran (1984, 1987: ch. 8) and Holden *et al.* (1985: 7–10). Detailed reviews of the literature on measurement of inflation expectations are given by Chan-Lee (1980), Visco (1984, 1986) and Lovell (1986). Wren-Lewis (1986) discusses the use of output expectations in the determination of employment in the UK manufacturing sector, Froot and Ito (1989) examine the relation between the short-term and long-term exchange rate expectations, and Dokko and Edelstein (1989) re-examine the statistical properties of Livingston stock price forecasts.

Survey expectations are used in the literature in a variety of contexts ranging from the microeconometric applications discussed by Nerlove (1983), Kawasaki *et al.* (1982, 1983) and McIntosh *et al.* (1989) to the more familiar macroeconometric applications alluded to above. In the former case ordinal responses on expectations and realizations are directly analysed, while in the latter case the qualitative responses are first converted to quantitative measures and the resultant measures are then used as data in econometric models. In both types of applications special attention needs to be paid to the problem of measurement errors in expectations. This problem can be particularly serious in the latter case where survey results are used after the conversion of ordinal responses into quantitative measures. The issue of measurement errors in inflation expectations and its econometric implications for testing the REH and the modelling of inflation expectations are discussed by Pesaran (1985, 1987).

When survey expectations are available, the REH can be tested directly by utilizing the observed expectations errors. A number of procedures have been suggested in the literature, and they are usually grouped under four broad headings: tests of unbiasedness, lack of serial correlation, efficiency and orthogonality. All these tests exploit the orthogonality property discussed earlier (see equation (10.21)). However, it is important to note that the first two tests are not valid when expectations are measured with systematic or random errors. The efficiency test is also a special case of the orthogonality test and is concerned only with the 'efficient' use of the information contained in the past values of the variable in question. For these reasons recent tests of the REH have tended to focus on the orthogonality test.

The empirical literature on the direct tests of the REH is vast and is still growing. The results of some of these studies are reviewed by Holden *et al.* (1985) and Lovell (1986). In general the studies do not support the REH. There is a clear need for the development of other models of expectations formation that allow for incomplete learning and are in better accord with the available data on survey expectations. We should also consider ways of improving the quality of survey expectations by paying closer attention to the problem of compilation and the processing of survey data. In particular we need to develop better methods of eliciting truthful expression of individuals' plans and intentions. It is only by recognizing the limitations of our subject that we can hope to progress.

10.10 CONCLUDING REMARKS

In this survey we have given a general overview of some of the issues that surround the analysis of expectations in economics. Given space limitations a number of important topics have not been addressed and some of the topics have been discussed very briefly. For example, problems of solution, identification, estimation and hypothesis testing in rational expectations models are only mentioned in passing. There is no discussion of the non-uniqueness problem that surrounds the solution of rational expectations models with future expectations. Empirical literature on the market efficiency hypothesis and on tests of the rational expectations – natural rate hypothesis are not discussed either. There are also important omissions in the area of the epistemological basis of the REH discussed, for example, by Boland (1982), Davidson (1982–3) and Bausor (1983).

NOTES

1 For a discussion of the role of uncertainty and expectations in Keynes's work see, for example, Lawson (1981), Begg (1982b), Coddington (1982), Patinkin (1984), Hodgson (1985) and Lawson and Pesaran (1985).
2 A large number of books and review articles that the interested reader may wish to consult have already appeared on the subject. These include Shiller (1978), Begg (1982a), Frydman and Phelps (1983), Sheffrin (1983), Shaw (1984) and Pesaran (1987). The edited volume by Lucas and Sargent (1981) is also noteworthy as it provides an excellent collection of some of the major contributions published during the 1970s.
3 The time series approach to modelling expectations has been discussed in the literature by, for example, Trivedi (1973), Feige and Pearce (1976) and Nerlove *et al.* (1979).
4 This model was first proposed by Goodwin (1947). See also Turnovsky (1970).
5 For examples of these types of data see Meiselman (1962) on the term structure of interest rates, and Froot and Ito (1989) and Pesaran (1989) on exchange rate expectations.
6 The same criticism is also applicable to the time series approach where the weights ω_i are derived optimally from the estimates of a univariate ARIMA representation of the y_t process.
7 This is justified when y_t has a multivariate normal distribution, but not generally.
8 This is a slightly generalized version of the model discussed by Muth (1961). He assumes that there are no demand shocks and sets $\alpha_1 = \alpha_2 = 0$.
9 As it happens, in the present simple example the rational expectations in (10.18) do not depend on past prices, but this is not necessarily the case in more complicated models where the decision-making process is subject to adjustment costs or habit persistence.
10 Notice that under (10.22) the pseudo-true value of ρ_1 in (10.16) is given by $\rho_1^*/(1 - \rho_2^*)$. This expression can be derived by taking the probability limit of the ordinary least squares estimator of ρ_1 in (10.16) under (10.22).
11 See also the two books on optimization by Whittle (1982, 1983).
12 This assumes that the solution to the Euler equation is an exterior one, namely one which results in strictly positive values for l_t.
13 Notice that since l_t is in Ω_t and the ε_t are serially uncorrelated, then

$$\mathrm{E}[\varepsilon_t f'(l_t)|\Omega_t] = f'(l_t)\,\mathrm{E}(\varepsilon_t|\Omega_t) = 0$$

Recall that p_t is not observed at the time the output decision is made and hence $\mathrm{E}(\varepsilon_t|\Omega_t) = \mathrm{E}(\varepsilon_t|\varepsilon_{t-1}, \varepsilon_{t-2}, \ldots) = 0$.
14 Recall that $|\mu_2| > 1$ and hence this solution will still be applicable even if the $\{w_t\}$ process has a unit root.
15 Arguments for the use of the REH in models with Keynesian features have been discussed by Wren-Lewis (1985).
16 See, however, Grandmont and Laroque (1990) where they consider a deterministic rational expectations model with multiple equilibria and show that if agents use 'unrestricted' least squares learning schemes the learning process diverges.
17 In the case of least squares learning, θ_t is given by $\theta_t = (\Sigma_{j=1}^{t-1} z_j z_j')^{-1} (\Sigma_{j=1}^{t-1} z_j p_j)$.
18 The monopolist problem is discussed by McLennan (1984) and more recently by Easley and Kiefer (1988). The general problem of the trade-off between current reward and information

acquisition has been discussed in the literature on the bandit problem. See Berry and Fristedt (1985) for a survey.

19 This view is particularly prelevant among the adherents of the REH (see, for example, Prescott 1977).

20 Methods for the conversion of qualitative responses to quantitative measures are proposed by Theil (1952), Knöbl (1974), Carlson and Parkin (1975) and Pesaran (1984).

REFERENCES

Bausor, R. (1983) 'The rational-expectations hypothesis and the epistemics of time', *Cambridge Journal of Economics* 7: 1–10.

Begg, D. K. H. (1982a) *The Rational Expectations Revolution in Macroeconomics*, Oxford: Philip Allan.

—— (1982b) 'Rational expectations, wage rigidity, and involuntary unemployment', *Oxford Economic Papers* 34: 21–47.

Berry, D. A. and Fristedt, B. (1985) *Bandit Problems: Sequential Allocation of Experiments*, London: Chapman and Hall.

Blume, L. E. and Easley, D. (1982) 'Learning to be rational', *Journal of Economic Theory* 26: 340–51.

Boland, L. A. (1982) *The Foundations of Economic Method*, London: Allen & Unwin.

Bowden, R. J. (1984) 'Convergence to "rational expectations" when the system parameters are initially unknown by the forecasters', unpublished manuscript, University of Western Australia.

Bray, M. M. (1983) 'Convergence to rational expectations equilibrium', in R. Frydman and E. S. Phelps (eds) *Individual Forecasting and Aggregate Outcomes*, Cambridge: Cambridge University Press.

Bray, M. M. and Kreps, D. M. (1987) 'Rational learning and rational expectations', in G. Feiwel (ed.) *Arrow and the Ascent of Modern Economic Theory*, London: Macmillan.

Bray, M. M. and Savin, N. E. (1986) 'Rational expectations equilibria, learning and model specifications', *Econometrica* 54: 1129–60.

Brock, W. A. and Mirman, L. J. (1972) 'Optimal economic growth and uncertainty: the discounted case', *Journal of Economic Theory* 4: 479–513.

Cagan, P. (1956) 'The monetary dynamics of hyperinflation', in M. Friedman (ed.) *Studies in the Quantity Theory of Money*, Chicago, IL: University of Chicago Press.

Carlson, J. A. and Parkin, M. (1975) 'Inflation expectations', *Econometrica* 42: 123–38.

Chan-Lee, J. H. (1980) 'A review of recent work in the area of inflationary expectations', *Welwirtschaftliches Archiv* 1: 45–85.

Coddington, A. (1982) 'Deficient foresight: a troublesome theme in Keynesian economics', *American Economic Review* 72: 480–7.

Cyert, R. M. and DeGroot, M. H. (1974) 'Rational expectations and Bayesian analysis', *Journal of Political Economy* 82: 521–36.

Danthine, J. and Donaldson, J. B. (1981) 'Stochastic properties of fast vs. slow growing economies', *Econometrica* 49: 1007–33.

Davidson, P. (1982–3) 'Rational expectations: a fallacious foundation for studying crucial decision-making processes', *Journal of Post-Keynesian Economics* 5: 182–98.

DeCanio, S. J. (1979) 'Rational expectations and learning from experience', *Quarterly Journal of Economics* 93: 47–57.

Dokko, Y. and Edelstein, R. H. (1989) 'How well do economists forecast stock market prices? A study of the Livingston Surveys', *American Economic Review* 79: 865–71.

Duffie, D. and Singleton, K. J. (1989) 'Simulated moments estimation of Markov models of asset prices', unpublished manuscript.

Easley, D. and Kiefer, N. M. (1988) 'Controlling a stochastic process with unknown parameters', *Econometrica* 56: 1045–64.

Feige, E. L. and Pearce, D. K. (1976) 'Economically rational expectations: are innovations in the rate of inflation independent of innovations in measures of monetary and fiscal policy?', *Journal of Political Economy* 84: 499–522.

Feldman, M. (1987a) 'An example of convergence to rational expectations with heterogeneous beliefs', *International Economic Review* 28: 635–50.

—— (1987b) 'Bayesian learning and convergence to rational expectations', *Journal of Mathematical Economics* 16: 297–313.

Fourgeaud, C., Gourieroux, C. and Pradel, J. (1986) 'Learning procedures and convergence to rationality', *Econometrica* 54: 845–68.

Frenkel, J. A. (1975) 'Inflation and the formation of expectations', *Journal of Monetary Economics* 1: 403–21.

Friedman, B. M. (1979) 'Optimal expectations and the extreme information assumptions of "rational expectations" macromodels', *Journal of Monetary Economics* 5: 23–41.

Friedman, M. (1957) *A Theory of the Consumption Function*, Princeton, NJ: Princeton University Press.

Froot, K. A. and Ito, T. (1989) 'On the consistency of short-run and long-run exchange rate expectations', *Journal of International Money and Finance* 8: 487–510.

Frydman, R. (1982) 'Towards an understanding of market processes, individual expectations: learning and convergence to rational expectations equilibrium', *American Economic Review* 72: 652–68.

Frydman, R. and Phelps, E. S. (eds) (1983) *Individual Forecasting and Aggregate Outcomes: 'Rational Expectations' Examined*, Cambridge: Cambridge University Press.

Goodwin, R. M. (1947) 'Dynamical coupling with especial reference to markets having production lags', *Econometrica* 15: 181–204.

Gordon, R. J. (1982) 'Price inertia and policy ineffectiveness in the United States, 1890–1980', *Journal of Political Economy* 90: 1087–117.

Grandmont, J.-M. and Laroque, G. (1990) 'Economic dynamics with learning: some instability examples', unpublished manuscript.

Haavelmo, T. (1958) 'The role of the econometrician in the advancement of economic theory', *Econometrica* 26: 351–7.

Hansen, L. P. and Sargent, T. J. (1980) 'Formulating and estimating dynamic linear rational expectations', *Journal of Economic Dynamic and Control* 2: 7–46.

Hansen, L. P. and Singleton, K. J. (1983) 'Stochastic consumption, risk aversion and the temporal behavior of asset returns', *Journal of Political Economy* 91: 249–65.

Hodgson, G. (1985) 'Persuasion, expectations and the limits to Keynes', in T. Lawson and H. Pesaran (eds) *Keynes' Economics: Methodological Issues*, London: Croom Helm.

Holden, K., Peel, D. A. and Thompson, J. L. (1985) *Expectations: Theory and Evidence*, London: Macmillan.

Hussey, R. (1988) 'Solving nonlinear rational expectations models with asymmetric adjustment costs', Working paper, Duke University.

Katona, G. (1958) 'Business expectations in the framework of psychological economics (toward a theory of expectations)', in M. J. Bowman (ed.) *Expectations, Uncertainty, and Business Behaviour*, New York: Social Science Research Council.

Kawasaki, S., McMillan, J. and Zimmermann, K. F. (1982) 'Disequilibrium dynamics: an empirical study', *American Economic Review* 72: 992–1004.

——, —— and —— (1983) 'Inventories and price inflexibility', *Econometrica* 51: 599–610.

Kennan, J. (1979) 'The estimation of partial adjustment models with rational expectations', *Econometrica* 47: 1441–55.

Keynes, J. M. (1936) *The General Theory of Employment, Interest and Money*, London: Macmillan.

Klein, L. R. (1954) 'Applications of survey methods and data to the analysis of economic fluctuations', in L. R. Klein (ed.) *Contributions of Survey Methods to Economic Fluctuations*, New York: Columbia University Press.

Knight, F. K. (1921) *Risk, Uncertainty and Profit*, London: Frank Cass.

Knöbl, A. (1974) 'Price expectations and actual price behaviour in Germany', *International Monetary Fund Staff Papers* 21: 83–100.

Koyck, L. M. (1954) *Distributed Lags and Investment Analysis*, Amsterdam: North-Holland.

Lawson, T. (1981) 'Keynesian model building and the rational expectations critique', *Cambridge Journal of Economics* 5: 311–26.

Lawson, T. and Pesaran, M. H. (eds) (1985) *Keynes' Economics: Methodological Issues*, London: Croom Helm.

Lovell, M. C. (1986) 'Tests of the rational expectations hypothesis', *American Economic Review* 76: 110–24.

Lucas, R. E. (1976) 'Econometric policy evaluation: a critique', in K. Brunner and A. H. Meltzer (eds) *The Phillips Curve and Labor Markets*, Amsterdam: North-Holland, Carnegie–Rochester Conference Series on Public Policy, vol. 1.

—— (1978) 'Asset prices in an exchange economy', *Econometrica* 46: 1429–45.

Lucas, R. E. and Sargent, T. J. (1981) *Rational Expectations and Econometrics Practice*, London: Allen & Unwin.

McIntosh, J., Schiantarelli, F. and Low, W. (1989) 'A qualitative response analysis of UK firms' employment and output decisions', *Journal of Applied Econometrics* 4: 251–64.

McLennan, A. (1984) 'Price dispersion and incomplete learning in the long run', *Journal of Economic Dynamics and Control* 7: 331–47.

Marcet, A. and Sargent, T. J. (1989a) 'Convergence of least squares learning mechanisms in self referential linear stochastic models', *Journal of Economic Theory* 48: 337–68.

—— and —— (1989b) 'Convergence of least squares learning in environments with hidden state variables and private information', *Journal of Political Economy* 97: 1306–22.

Meiselman, D. (1962) *The Term Structure of Interest Rates*, Englewood Cliffs, NJ: Prentice-Hall.

Mincer, J. (1969) 'Models of adaptive forecasting', in J. Mincer (ed.) *Economic Forecasts* and Expectations: Analysis of Forecasting Behaviour and Performance, New York: Columbia University Press for the National Bureau of Economic Research.

Modigliani, F. and Sauerlender, O. W. (1955) 'Economic expectations and plans of firms in relation to short-term forecasting, in short-term economic forecasting', NBER Studies in Income and Wealth, No. 17, Princeton, NJ: Princeton University Press.

Muth, J. F. (1960) 'Optimal properties of exponentially weighted forecasts', Journal of the American Statistical Association 55: 299–306.

—— (1961) 'Rational expectations and the theory of price movements', Econometrica 29: 315–35.

Nerlove, M. (1958) 'Adaptive expectations and cobweb phenomena', Quarterly Journal of Economics 72: 227–40.

—— (1983) 'Expectations plans and realizations in theory and practice', Econometrica 51: 1251–79.

Nerlove, M., Grether, D. M. and Carvalho, J. (1979) Analysis of Economic Time Series: A Synthesis, New York: Academic Press.

Patinkin, D. (1984) 'Keynes and economics today', American Economic Review, Papers and Proceedings 74: 97–102.

Pesaran, M. H. (1984) 'Expectations formations and macroeconometric modelling', in P. Malgrange and P.-A. Muet (eds) Contemporary Macroeconomic Modelling, Oxford: Basil Blackwell.

—— (1985) 'Formation of inflation expectations in British manufacturing industries', Economic Journal 95: 948–75.

—— (1987) The Limits to Rational Expectations, Oxford: Basil Blackwell. Reprinted with corrections 1989.

—— (1988) 'The role of theory in applied econometrics', Economic Record, Symposium on Econometric Methodology 336–9.

—— (1989) 'Consistency of short-term and long-term expectations', Journal of International Money and Finance 8: 511–16.

—— (1990a) 'Rational expectations in disaggregated models: an empirical analysis of OPEC's behaviour', Jacob Marschak Lecture delivered at the 9th Latin American Meeting of the Econometric Society, Santiago, Chile, UCLA Program in Applied Econometrics Discussion Paper 13.

—— (1990b) 'Solution of linear rational expectations models under asymmetric and heterogeneous information', unpublished manuscript, University of California at Los Angeles.

Prescott, E. (1977) 'Should control theory be used for economic stabilization?', Journal of Monetary Economics, Supplement 13–38.

Sargent, T. J. (1987) Dynamic Macroeconomic Theory, Cambridge, MA: Harvard University Press.

Shackle, G. L. S. (1949) Expectations in Economics, Cambridge: Cambridge University Press.

—— (1955) Uncertainty in Economics, Cambridge: Cambridge University Press.

Shaw, G. K. (1984) Rational Expectations: An Elementary Exposition, Brighton: Harvester Wheatsheaf.

Sheffrin, S. M. (1983) Rational Expectations, Cambridge: Cambridge University Press.

Shiller, R. J. (1978) 'Rational expectations and the dynamic structure of macroeconomic models: a critical review', *Journal of Monetary Economics* 4: 1–44.

Simon, H. A. (1958) 'The role of expectations in an adaptive or behavioristic model', in M. J. Bowman (ed.) *Expectations, Uncertainty, and Business Behavior*, New York: Social Science Research Council.

Smith, A. (1989) 'Solving nonlinear rational expectations models: a new approach', unpublished manuscript, Duke University.

Stokey, N. L., Lucas, R. E. and Prescott, E. C. (1989) *Recursive Methods in Economic Dynamics*, Cambridge, MA: Harvard University Press.

Tauchen, G. (1987) 'Quadrature-based methods for obtaining approximate solutions to nonlinear asset pricing models', unpublished manuscript.

Taylor, J. B. (1975) 'Monetary policy during a transition to rational expectations', *Journal of Political Economy* 83: 1009–21.

Theil, H. (1952) 'On the time shape of economic microvariables and the Munich business test', *Revue de l'Institut International de Statistique* 20: 105–20.

Townsend, R. M. (1978) 'Market anticipations, rational expectations and Bayesian analysis', *International Economic Review* 19: 481–94.

—— (1983) 'Forecasting the forecasts of others', *Journal of Political Economy* 91: 546–88.

Trivedi, P. K. (1973) 'Retail inventory investment behaviour', *Journal of Econometrics* 1: 61–80.

Turnovsky, S. J. (1970) 'Empirical evidence on the formation of price expectations', *Journal of the American Statistical Association* 65: 1441–54.

Visco, I. (1984) *Price Expectations in Rising Inflation*, Amsterdam: North-Holland.

—— (1986) 'The use of Italian data in the analysis of the formation of inflation expectations', unpublished manuscript, Banca d'Italia.

Whittle, P. (1982) *Optimization Over Time: Dynamic Programming and Stochastic Control*, vol. I, Chichester: Wiley.

—— (1983) *Optimization Over Time: Dynamic Programming and Stochastic Control*, vol. II, Chichester: Wiley.

Wren-Lewis, S. (1985) 'Expectations in Keynesian econometric models', in T. Lawson and M. H. Pesaran (eds) *Keynes' Economics: Methodological Issues*, London: Croom Helm.

—— (1986) 'An econometric model of UK manufacturing employment using survey data on expected output', *Journal of Applied Econometrics* 1: 297–316.

11

POST-KEYNESIAN
MACROECONOMICS

MALCOLM C. SAWYER

11.1 INTRODUCTION

Although many of the key ideas used by post-Keynesian macroeconomists can be traced back to at least the 1930s (particularly in the work of Kalecki and Keynes), it is only in the last fifteen to twenty years that a distinct school of thought under that title has emerged.[1,2] Post-Keynesian economics does not make the sharp distinction between microeconomics and macroeconomics which is made in the neoclassical–Keynesian synthesis, so that, although we focus on macroeconomics in this chapter, we must also consider a number of aspects which are generally considered microeconomic (e.g. pricing). In addition, the focus on macroeconomics means that there is an implicit use of a narrow definition of post-Keynesian economics.[3] The coverage of this chapter is also limited in (at least) one other respect: namely, we do not discuss development and growth. This is a serious omission since many post-Keynesian writers have stressed the dynamic nature of capitalist economies and the need for an analysis which overcomes the shortcomings of static equilibrium analysis. However, a proper consideration of growth would require much more space than is available.[4]

The work of Kalecki and Keynes, which provides the foundations for much of modern post-Keynesian macroeconomics, has two important common features.[5] The first is the relevance of aggregate demand for the determination of the level of economic activity, which involves the rejection of Say's law for a monetary economy. Further, both authors distinguished between investment expenditure and consumer expenditure, and saw the former as the active and fluctuating component of demand. The second common feature is the notion that the price level of output, decided upon by producers to maximize their profits (given the level of aggregate demand and money wages), serves to determine the level of real wages. A change in money wages, with a given level

I am grateful to Philip Arestis for comments on an earlier draft.

of real aggregate demand, would lead to a proportionate change in output price level in the case of a closed economy (for an open economy the change in output price level would reflect the relative importance of domestic labour and imported inputs). This can be summarized by saying that the real wages are set in the output markets rather than the labour markets.

In some respects, the interest in the work of Kalecki and Keynes in the past decade or so has highlighted a wide range of differences between them, which are reflected in differences between authors working within the post-Keynesian tradition (for further discussion of some of these differences see Sawyer (1985a: ch. 9)). The differences include the following.

1 The assumption of atomistic competitive markets (Keynes) or oligopolistic markets (Kalecki).
2 The related difference between the assumption of increasing marginal costs (Keynes) or (roughly) constant marginal costs (Kalecki).
3 The nature of money in a developed capitalist economy. In the *General Theory* (Keynes 1936) Keynes essentially assumed money to be created and controlled by the central bank, although in the *Treatise on Money* (Keynes 1930) he considered it to be created by private banks (see Moore (1984) for further discussion). Kalecki paid much less attention than Keynes to money, but made the working assumption that money was created by the private banking system (see Sawyer (1985a: ch. 5) for further discussion).
4 The use of equilibrium analysis. With some minor exceptions, Kalecki's analysis was cast in terms of cyclical movements and did not use equilibrium analysis, whereas Keynes made use of equilibrium analysis.
5 Expectations and the predictability of the future. These aspects of post-Keynesian economics are elaborated further below, but it suffices to say here that, whilst both saw expectations of the future as heavily influenced by past and current experiences, Keynes also emphasized the essential unknowability of the future.

This chapter is organized largely in terms of topics, namely money, prices, investment, labour sector and business cycles. In the discussion of these topics there is some indication of the assumptions made by Keynesians regarding the institutional arrangements of a capitalist economy.

11.2 MONEY AND FINANCE

A strong theme in post-Keynesian macroeconomics is that a monetary economy and a non-monetary economy operate in fundamentally different ways.[6] Since Walrasian general equilibrium analysis does not readily permit the introduction of money with any essential role, this leads to the rejection of any attempt to base a macroeconomics analysis of a monetary economy on Walrasian foundations. There would be no reason to hold money as a store of wealth 'for it is a recognized characteristic of money as a store of wealth that it is barren, whereas practically every other form of storing wealth yields some interest or profit. Why should anyone outside a lunatic asylum wish to use money as store of wealth?' (Keynes 1937). In his approach, individuals have a 'liquidity preference' to help insulate themselves against unforeseen events as 'our desire to hold Money as a store of wealth is a barometer of the degree of our distrust of our own calculations and conventions concerning the future'. But clearly in a static (or predictable) world such as that portrayed in Walrasian general equilibrium analysis, liquidity would be of no benefit.

The existence of financial assets permits the difference between *ex ante* savings and investment, for in the absence of financial assets any desire to postpone expenditure (i.e. to save) would still entail the acquisition of goods as a store of value (to provide future spending power). For ease of exposition we confine our attention to the case of a closed economy (since none of the essential insights in this section would be affected by the use of an open-economy approach).

The first question relates to the mechanism by which any difference between *ex ante* savings and investment is resolved. The pre-Keynesian answer was, of course, to see the rate of interest as the relevant price which adjusts to bring savings and investment into equality. Patinkin (1982) saw Keynes's original contribution as being a theory of effective demand which 'in more formal terms is concerned not only with the mathematical solution of the equilibrium equation $F(Y) = Y$, but with demonstrating the stability of this equilibrium as determined by the dynamic adjustment equation $dY/dt = \phi[F(Y) - Y]$ where $\phi > 0$'. In this quotation Y stands for output and $F(Y)$ is the aggregate demand function. Thus any difference between *ex ante* savings and investment (or equivalently between planned output and expenditure) leads to changes in the level of output and income.

The second question refers to the relationship between savings and invest-ment. The simple Keynesian model portrays savings as adjusting (through income changes) to the level of investment, with some forced savings in the short term. Chick (1986) argues that the relationship between savings and investment depends on the stage of development of the banking system. She postulates five stages through which banking systems have generally passed. In the first stage, a rudimentary banking system is only able to act as an intermediary between saver and investor, and then savings have to be made prior to investment. The banking system is then seen as (conceptually) evolving through the second, third and fourth stages until the fifth is reached, which is the one of contemporary interest. From the second stage onwards, 'invest-ment could precede saving; the matching saving in the first instance is the new bank deposit resulting from loan expansion. Subsequent banking developments have not changed that process; they have intensified it'. By the fifth stage, a sophisticated banking system has developed 'liability management' which entails 'at least from time to time actively seeking lending outlets rather than merely filling all reasonable loan requests', and when banks decide to lend much more than hitherto there will be a rapid increase in credit and the stock of money. However, the active nature of investment remains a feature of this fifth stage, where the sequence is seen to be plans for investment leading to application for loans, and then the granting of loans and creation of money, and finally the actual investment expenditure and the corresponding generation of savings.

This now leads into consideration of the nature of money. Debates over whether money should be treated as endogenous or exogenous (with respect to the actions of the private sector) can be traced back to at least the middle of the last century with the debates between the banking and currency schools. The Radcliffe Report (1959) discussed the difficulties of the definability and controllability of the money supply in ways which post-Keynesian economists would generally accept (for further discussion see Wulwick (1987)). Kaldor (1970) attacked the then emerging monetarist approach in part on the grounds that the stock of money was not subject to control by the government or central bank but rather adjusted to meet the 'needs of trade'. Kaldor and Trevithick (1981) argued that:

> Unlike commodity money, credit money comes into existence as a result of borrowing from the banks (by business, individuals or public agencies) and it is extinguished as a result of the repayment of bank debt (which happens automatically under a system where an excess of receipts over outlays is directly applied to a reduction of outstanding overdrafts). Hence in a credit money economy, unlike with commodity money, the outstanding 'money stock' can never be in excess of the amount which individuals wish to hold; and this alone rules out the possibility of there being an 'excess' supply of money which should be the *cause* (as distinct from the consequence) of a rise in spending.

Moore (1989) summarizes the post-Keynesian view of money in a developed economy thus:

> Credit money is both a financial asset and a liability of commercial banks. Since bank liabilities are only as good as the assets behind them, bank depositors ultimately are the creditors of bank borrowers. Whenever economic units choose to borrow from their banks, deposits and so bank money are created in the process. Whenever economic units choose to repay their bank loans, deposits are destroyed. . . . The terms on which credit money is issued, i.e. the interest rate charged on bank loans and paid on bank deposits, play a crucial role in governing the rate of growth of the money stock, and so of aggregate income.

Moore accepts that there is 'a reasonably stable relationship between changes in the base and changes in the broad money stock, and between changes in the broad money stock and changes in aggregate money income', but argues for the causation to run back from aggregate money income rather than forward from base money. The empirical evidence produced (e.g. Moore 1983, 1988, 1989) draws upon both regression analysis and Granger–Sims causality tests. He concludes that:

> The evidence appears overwhelmingly consistent with the proposition that the direction of causation runs from commercial bank loans to the money stock to the monetary base. This in turn clearly implies the much noted and documented empirical relationship between money and income reflects primarily 'reverse causation' running from income to money.
>
> (Moore 1989)

The theoretical argument is relatively straightforward. A planned increase in expenditure (whether arising from a planned real increase or in response to rising prices), in a monetary economy, has to be backed by money if the expenditure is to take place. Attention is often given to investment expenditure, but the argument is quite general for other forms of expenditure. In particular, the expansion of output (say in response to the prospect of a higher level of demand) requires the prior increase of inputs. Increased expenditure by a firm to purchase an increased level of material and labour inputs has to be financed, and may often require an increase in loans and thereby an increase in the money stock.

Four aspects of the significance of credit money in macroeconomic analysis are highlighted here. First, whilst there can be occasions on which an increase in the stock of money originates from changes in the behaviour of banks, the more usual situation is that the stock of money evolves in response to changes in demand. The creation of money occurs as a response to the demand for loans, and whether that money remains in existence or is destroyed (through loan repayment) rests on the desire to hold money.

Second, growth in the money stock is seen as a response to inflation, and not as a cause of inflation. For example, when costs rise, producers have to finance a higher nominal value of work in progress, and can do so through borrowing from the banks or through depletion of their holdings of money. The former route will then add to the stock of money, which expands as a consequence of cost rises rather than as an initiating cause.

Third, following Kalecki (1944), doubt is cast on the relevance of the Pigou real-balance effect in an economy where money is largely credit money (and not fully backed by gold). An important feature of credit money is that it does not constitute net worth for the private sector since such money represents an asset for the holder but a liability for the issuer (usually a bank). A fall in the price level then has no net effect on the real value of the stock of credit money, although it does redistribute real wealth from banks to others.

Fourth, the creation of credit money by private banks in response to loan demand from the private sector suggests that control by the government or central bank over the stock of money will be difficult. Banks, seeking to maximize profits, will often have incentives to frustrate controls over the size of the stock of money.

The creation and destruction of credit money will be relevant to cyclical movements in the macroeconomy. At a minimum, the stock of money has to evolve to permit fluctuations of economic activity. However, the operation of the financial system may be intimately involved with the business cycle. The response of the banking system to a demand for loans (for example, whether they are granted and at what interest rate) will impinge on the pattern of the cycle.

Minsky (1975, 1978, 1982) advances the 'financial instability hypothesis' which 'is designed to explain instability as a result of the normal functioning of a capitalist economy' (Minsky 1978). Limitations of space mean that there is room here to highlight only a few aspects of this hypothesis.

> Economic activity is seen as generating business cash flows. A part of these cash flows is applied to validate debt. Anticipated cash flows from business operations determine the demand for and supply of 'debts' to be used to finance positions in capital assets and the production of new capital assets (investment output). Money is mainly created as banks finance business and acquire other assets and money is destroyed as debts to banks are repaid or as banks sell assets.
>
> (Minsky 1978)

When the economy is relatively tranquil, then on the whole firms' expectations are fulfilled and their cash flows are able to meet their debt obligations. However, there are times when profits decline, leaving some firms unable to meet loan repayments. A full-blown financial crisis may develop from such an occurrence, depending to a large degree on the policy response of the central bank. The inability of firms to repay debt places banks in an exposed position as they have incurred financial obligations to other financial institutions.

11.3 PRICING

There are a number of distinct views of pricing within post-Keynesian macro-economic analysis.[7] Before discussing their differences, three elements of similarity can be noted. First, these theories of pricing suggest that prices will not be very responsive to demand, and indeed may react in a way often described as perverse, i.e. move in the opposite direction to demand. Second, prices are set by producers and not by some anonymous auctioneer or market. Thus prices will be set in the interests of the producers, and this usually entails prices set such that the firm plans to supply the demand forthcoming at those prices. In a sense, firms operate to equate planned supply with expected demand at the prices which they determine. Third, whilst prices have some allocative implications, they have other roles as well (which Gerrard (1989) labels as conductive, positional, strategic and financial). For example, in the approach of Eichner and others, prices are set so that the expected profits are sufficient to finance investment plans; in this sense prices could be said to have a financial role. Indeed, the linkage between price, profits and investment is generally seen as of considerable importance.

The pricing theory of Keynes (1936) has been much misunderstood and often associated with a crude price rigidity view.[8] However, as Chick (1983) notes: 'The assumption of fixed prices in Keynesian analysis is most strange, in view of the amount of space devoted in the *General Theory* to the consequences of expansion for prices. . . .' Indeed, a more accurate representation of Keynes would be that of rapid price adjustment (in marked contrast with the temporary equilibrium school) especially in the face of wage changes.[9] The equality between the real wage and the marginal product of labour is maintained through changes in price, so that a change in the nominal wage or in the level of economic activity (and thereby in the marginal product of labour) leads to a change in price.

Kalecki's approach, often described as the degree of monopoly, has also been much misunderstood and frequently dismissed as a tautology (for a discussion on the charge of tautology and other criticisms of the degree of monopoly theory see Sawyer (1985a: 28–36)). It should first be said that the degree-of-monopoly analysis is only intended to apply to part, albeit a particularly important part, of the economy. Kalecki made the distinction between cost-determined and demand-determined prices. The former type is associated with manufacturing and other industries where supply is elastic as a result of existing reserves of capacity. The latter type is associated with raw materials and primary foodstuffs. The cost-determined–demand-determined dichotomy has sometimes been likened to the fixed-price–flexprice dichotomy. There is a correspondence in the sense that in both cases the first-named type of price is viewed as unresponsive to demand. However, cost-determined prices are set within the model, i.e. they are endogenous, whereas fixed prices are determined exogenously.

Kalecki's analysis evolved over time (for a full discussion see Kriesler 1987 (see also Basile and Salvadori 1984–5; Lee 1986; Kriesler 1989)) but retained its central features, which can be summarized in the following manner. In the light of the history of the industry (for example, previous collusion or rivalry) and its structure (for example, level of concentration, barriers to entry), firms strive to maximize profits. The history and structure of the industry are the factors which combine to form the degree of monopoly. The higher the degree of monopoly, the higher will be the mark-up of price over (marginal) costs (for a formal model, which provides similar predictions, see Cowling (1982) based on Cowling and Waterson (1976)). The maximization of profits is not exactly achieved since 'in view of the uncertainties faced in the process or price fixing it will not be assumed that the firm attempts to maximize its profits in any precise sort of manner' (Kalecki 1971). Firms find it costly and difficult to measure marginal costs accurately, and approximate them by average direct costs (in fact, the approximate equality of marginal and average direct costs finds considerable empirical support). In this form, Kalecki's approach has links with the structure–conduct–performance paradigm in industrial economics.[10]

In some respects, Kalecki's particular contribution was to draw out the income distribution implications of pricing decisions. At the level of the firm, price p is seen as a mark-up m over average direct costs ADC, i.e.

$$p = (1 + m)\text{ADC} \tag{11.1}$$

If we write ADC as the sum of average labour costs wl and average material costs nf, where w is the money wage, n is the material input price and l and f are the labour and material inputs per unit of output respectively, this equation can be rearranged to give

$$\frac{\pi}{S} = \frac{m}{1 + m} \tag{11.2}$$

$$\frac{w}{p} = \frac{1}{1 + m} \left(l + \frac{nf}{w} \right)^{-1} \tag{11.3}$$

where π is profits, so that equation (11.2) links the ratio of profits to sales with the mark-up, and similarly equation (11.3) links the real wage with the mark-up. These relationships are derived for the firm level. It is argued that analogous relationships will hold at the economy level. It is not important that there is a precise aggregation from the firm to the economy, but rather the general idea of the influence of pricing decisions on income distribution and real wages is the important element.

Post-Keynesians have generally argued that there is a high propensity to save out of profits and that enterprises have a preference for internal finance over external finance. This view has underpinned Kaldor's theory of income distribution (Kaldor 1955). Steindl (1952) portrayed the steady state position for an industry as one where the profit margin is compatible with financing growth of capital equipment (where the algebraic expression of this is formally identical with equation (11.4) below). In our discussion of the approaches which focus on the links between price, profits and investment, for reasons of space we consider the contribution of one author only, namely Eichner, but note that there have been a number of authors who have also elaborated these links in different ways.[11]

191

In Eichner's approach, the large corporation ('megacorp' in his terminology) is mainly concerned with growth.

> The megacorp is an organization rather than an individual. . . . As an organization, the megacorp's goal is to expand at the highest possible rate. . . . It is expansion at the highest rate possible that creates the maximum opportunities for advancement within the organization, and thus personal rewards for those who are part of the firm's decision-making structure.
>
> (Eichner 1985)

This maximization of growth is subject to a number of constraints – among them the need to maintain a certain rate of growth of dividends.

> In pursuit of this goal, the megacorp can be expected to follow two behavioral rules. One of these is that it will attempt to maintain, if not actually to enlarge, its share of the market in the industries to which it already belongs while simultaneously undertaking whatever investment is necessary to lower its costs of production. The other behavioral rule is that it will attempt to expand into newer, more rapidly growing industries while simultaneously withdrawing from any older, relatively stagnant industries.
>
> (Eichner 1987)

Internal finance is generally preferred to external finance on the basis of lower cost and limitation of outside interference. Prices in mature oligopolistic industries are set by price leaders. Profits and growth are set by the interaction of the demand for and supply of finance (at the level of the firm). For a firm, a higher price generally means higher profits (it is assumed that firms face inelastic demand) and hence more finance for investment. However, a higher price reduces demand as well as the growth of demand and the need for investment. The firm then operates where its demand for investment funds is in balance with its ability to provide the finance from its profits.

For simplicity, take the case where the firm decides to rely on internal finance only. Then $gK = rP$, where g is growth rate, K is capital stock (so that the left-hand side is investment expenditure), r is retention ratio and P is profits (the right-hand side is finance available for investment). This can be rearranged to give

$$\frac{gv}{r} = \frac{P}{Y} \qquad (11.4)$$

where v is the capital-to-output ratio. These equations are intended to apply for the typical firm, and then by summation for the whole economy. The interpretation of (11.4) is that causation runs from left to right – growth expectations, capital-to-output ratio and retention ratio determine the profit share. Firms are then portrayed as adjusting prices to generate the required profit share with which investment is financed. This relationship has been derived from consideration of pricing, but can be seen more generally as resulting from the equality between savings and investment. The crucial aspect of equation (11.4) should be seen as the link between growth and the distribution of income (reflecting here by the profit share P/Y).

Although the approaches of Kalecki and Eichner suggest that prices will be relatively unresponsive to the level of and changes in demand, they still rest on maximization (even if that maximization is not precisely achieved). However, starting from Hall and Hitch (1939), there has been a stream of thought which rejects optimizing behaviour in favour of satisficing behaviour. Hall and Hitch argued that the results of their interviews with business people on price determination cast 'doubt on the general applicability of the conventional analysis of price and output pricing in terms of marginal cost and marginal revenue, and suggests a mode of entrepreneurial behaviour which current economic doctrine tends to ignore'. They argued that business pricing behaviour could be characterized as the addition of a mark-up to average direct costs, where average direct costs are relatively insensitive to the level of output. From the point of view of macroeconomic analysis, the approach derived from Hall and Hitch can be considered as rather similar to those of Kalecki and others, and empirical studies such as those of Godley and Nordhaus (1972) and Coutts *et al.* (1978) are in the cost-plus pricing tradition.

11.4 LABOUR SECTOR

The post-Keynesian analysis of the labour sector has two interrelated elements. The first is that the exchange of labour services and the determination of wages do not take place in a market as that term is usually understood (and for that reason this section is labelled 'labour sector' rather than 'labour market'). Wages are often set through collective bargaining, and relative wages have important status implications. Labour is a human input into production, and as such labour discipline, morale, commitment etc. are important influences on the level of productivity (for an introduction to the post-Keynesian approach to the labour sector see Appelbaum (1979)).

The second, and related, element is that bargaining between employer and employee (whether conducted individually or collectively, whether with a balance or imbalance of power) settles money wages but not real wages.

> There may be *no* method available to labour as a whole whereby it can bring the wage-goods equivalent of the general level of money-wages into conformity with the marginal disutility of the current volume of employment. There may exist no expedient by which labour as a whole can reduce its *real* wage to a given figure by making revised *money* wage bargains with the entrepreneurs. This will be our contention. We shall endeavour to show that primarily it is certain other forces which determine the general level of real wages.
>
> (Keynes 1936)

In its simplest formulation, the level of employment (and the level of economic activity generally) is determined by the level of aggregate demand and the real wage set by the equality between real wage and the marginal productivity of labour. Any variation in the money wage would be offset by a corresponding variation in the price level, leaving the real wage unchanged. In Keynes's formulation, prices move rapidly to ensure equality between the real wage and the marginal productivity of labour. In a Kaleckian approach, the real wage is set by the mark-up of prices over costs (including wages). The common feature is the idea that prices are determined after money wages are set, and that workers (individually or collectively) do not influence real wages.

The original formulation of the Phillips curve (Phillips 1958) was consistent with this view in that it sought to explain the evolution of money wages but not of real wages. In contrast, Friedman (1968) argued that the original Phillips curve was a mis-specification, and that real wages (rather than money wages) moved in response to the level of unemployment or excess supply of labour. However, the post-Keynesian position remains that real wages are strongly influenced by the product market (as illustrated by equation (11.2)) rather than set in the labour sector or market.

The post-Keynesian approach to money wage determination is that the labour sector cannot be usefully analysed in terms of a labour market (or markets) in which the supply and demand for labour interact in the manner envisaged by neoclassical economics. There are a variety of ways, however, in which the determination of money wages can be approached. The one which is followed here is based on the view that in industrialized economies wages are often settled or influenced through collective bargaining between trade unions and employers. But even when formal collective bargaining does not take place, the influences at work may be rather similar. For, as Routh (1980) argues, 'it is a mistake to imagine that there is a sharp division between unionized and un-unionized workers, for trade unions cannot do more than institutionalize and direct drives and aspirations that are already present in the individual worker'. Another approach, now often labelled neo-Keynesian, is to consider efficiency wages, implicit contracts etc. which reflect the variable productivity feature of labour (see, for example, Frank 1986).

In a simple formulation for a collective bargaining setting, the trade union is portrayed as taking the initiative in making a money wage claim (a more elaborate formulation might consider bargaining over employment, productivity levels etc.). The target money wage of unions in their bargaining is expressed as the product of current money wages, the ratio of expected prices to actual prices and an element which reflects movement towards target real wage:

$$w_t^* = w_{t-1} \frac{p_t^e}{p_{t-1}} \left(\frac{Tp_{t-1}}{w_{t-1}} \right)^c \tag{11.5}$$

where w is the money wage, p is the (appropriate) price level, p^e is the anticipated price level and T is the target real wage.

With allowance for the impact of unemployment on the achievement of this target, we can derive (for details see Sawyer 1982a, b) the following equation for money wage changes (for some empirical support see Henry *et al.* 1976; Arestis 1986):

$$\dot{w} = a + \dot{p}^e + bU_{t-1} + c\left[\ln T - \ln\left(\frac{w_{t-1}}{p_{t-1}}\right)\right] \qquad (11.6)$$

It can be seen that either $c = 0$ or a target real wage which always quickly adjusts to the actual real wage (i.e. $T = w_{-1}/p_{-1}$) would allow us to simplify equation (11.6) to an expectations-augmented Phillips curve (although without any implication that this equation represents the behaviour of an atomistic competitive labour market). A combination of $a = 0$ and no effect of unemployment on the wage bargaining outcome would generate a subsistence real wage view.

It is helpful to consider a steady state type of outcome in which (a) price expectations are fulfilled and (b) wages rise in line with prices (where for simplicity a no productivity growth case is considered). This yields

$$\ln\left(\frac{w}{p}\right) = c_0 + c_1 U + \ln T \qquad (11.7)$$

where $c_0 = c^{-1}a$ and $c_1 = c^{-1}b$.

Thus a steady state relationship between the real wage and the level of economic activity can be derived from this approach to money wage determination, and this is represented by the w curve in Figure 11.1. A second relationship between the real wage and the level of economic activity can be derived from the pricing side (for example, (11.3) when the mark-up m and labour productivity l depend on the level of output and economic activity). Such a relationship is illustrated by the p curve in Figure 11.1. The inequalities drawn in Figure 11.1 represent the anticipated price and wage changes. The upper inequality arises from price determination, whilst the lower one arises from wage determination. It can be seen that zone A would constitute a classic wage–price inflationary spiral, whilst zone D would be a deflationary spiral.[12] From zones B and C, price and wage determination would lead towards the real wage at point Z.

This view of inflation is essentially a conflict view (Rowthorn 1977; Sawyer 1983: ch. 1) in that zone A corresponds to the case where the claims on income shares made by enterprises and workers are in conflict. Point Z (at which the rate of inflation would be constant) represents some resolution of that conflict, although it may just mean that unemployment is sufficiently high

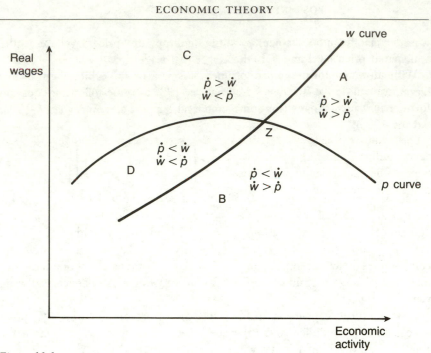

Figure 11.1

to restrain real wages. Point Z can also be viewed as a non-accelerating inflation rate of unemployment (NAIRU).

It can clearly be seen that point Z is determined without reference to the level of aggregate demand. There would appear to be no particular reason why point Z should be demand sustainable. By this we mean that there is no reason to think that the wages and profits implicit in point Z would generate a level of expenditure which would exactly match the output which firms intend to produce at point Z.

This poses the central question which has plagued Keynesian economics: what is the relationship between the demand and supply sides of the economy? The neoclassical–Keynesian synthesis pictures aggregate demand as crucial in the short-term determination of economic activity but with the supply side dominant in the long term. Adjustments in the price level, operating on the real value of the money stock, are seen as able to bring the level of demand into line with supply and full employment. In the post-Keynesian approach, such adjustments are ruled out on the grounds that money is credit money and, as indicated above, does not constitute net worth.

However, within the post-Keynesian approach there are numerous ways through which the supply side (as represented in Figure 11.1) can (partially) adjust to the demand side. Investment raises the capital stock and capacity, which would lead to shifts in the pricing equation. Workers' perceptions of the target real wage can change (say, under pressure from government) leading to a shift in the wage equation. The supply of labour can change through variations in age of entry into and exit from the workforce, movements between the workforce and the home and migration. The relationship between unemployment and capacity utilization changes as the size of workforce and capacity change.

The addition of aggregate demand considerations to a model such as that represented in Figure 11.1 would clearly lead to a problem of overdeterminacy. In effect, the Kaleckian approach has been to focus on the interaction between aggregate demand and the pricing equation. The NAIRU approach implicitly drops consideration of aggregate demand. The discussion of business cycles in Section 11.7 can be viewed in a similar light. Kaldor's model discussed there focuses only on aggregate demand without reference to the labour sector, whilst Goodwin's model does not provide for a role for aggregate demand (since it is assumed that all savings are invested).

11.5 INVESTMENT

Although investment expenditure has been given a central role in most post-Keynesian macroeconomic analysis, nevertheless there has been relatively little formal theorizing on the determinants of investment. This reflects a central problem which arises from the combination of the view that firms cannot easily undo investment decisions and that the forecasting of future events over the lifetime of much capital equipment is impossible. Thus, the use of formal models (such as that of Jorgenson (1963)) is rejected on the grounds that (at least at the economy level) investment decisions cannot be reversed and that firms cannot make precise profit-maximizing (or other) calculations based on well-based expectations of the future.

The approach of Keynes (1936) to investment decisions has often been identified with the notion that firms will adjust their capital stock up to the point where the marginal efficiency of capital is equated with the rate of interest. This is correct as far as it goes, but 'it was Keynes's view that "animal spirits" substantially dominated the investment decision' (Chick 1983). The equality between the marginal efficiency of capital and the rate of interest 'is merely that *part* of the decision which is amenable to economic analysis' (Chick 1983).

The marginal efficiency of capital rests on expectations about the future, and these expectations are viewed as insecurely based: 'The outstanding fact is the extreme precariousness of the basis of knowledge on which our estimates of prospective yield have to be made. Our knowledge of the factors which will govern the yield of an investment some years hence is usually very slight and often negligible' (Keynes 1936). Variations of the state of long-term expec-

197

tations were viewed as particularly significant 'since it seems likely that the fluctuations in the market estimation of the marginal efficiency of different types of capital . . . will be too great to be offset by any practicable change in the rate of interest' (Keynes 1936).

In Kalecki's approach, investment expenditure is inherently subject to cycles, and generates the business cycle. Kalecki begins his analysis with the distinction between investment decisions and actual fixed capital investment, where the lag between the two arises from the period of construction, delivery lags etc. Then current economic variables can be modelled as influencing investment decisions which in turn lead at some future date to actual investment expenditure.

Firms have a preference for internal funds, which arises in part from the view that internal funds are less costly in a variety of ways than external funds. The use of external funds involves various transactions costs of raising the loan or making new share issues. Since current profits largely determine the volume of internal funds available to a firm, they are an important determinant of investment through financial considerations. The use of external funds by a firm is limited eventually by the increasing costs of such funds as the amount of external funds required by a firm increases. Kalecki (1937b) introduced 'the principle of increasing risk'. In effect, the argument is that the greater the volume of borrowing which a firm wishes to undertake (relative to its profits and assets), the greater is the risk that it will be unable to repay the interest charges and the capital sum itself. Financial institutions take this increasing risk into account, and charge higher rates of interest for larger volumes of borrowing.

For firms collectively, investment expenditures are constrained by the available finance, which in turn is constrained by the available pool of savings and the willingness of banks to grant loans. Investment decisions are strongly influenced by the savings currently available, although these decisions will lead to levels of future investment expenditure and thereby to future savings levels. When a particular volume of investment expenditure has taken place, it will generate (in a closed private economy) the corresponding amount of savings. But those savings are available only after the investment has taken place and are not available to finance that investment. The finance would have to come from previous savings and the creation of credit by banks.

Firms increase their capital stock as finance becomes available as profits are made and savings undertaken. Thus some potential investment delayed in the past because of a lack of finance can now proceed as finance becomes available. Further, the incentive for a firm to own and operate capital equipment can be expected to depend on the prospective rate of profit on that capital equipment relative to the rate of interest at which the firm can borrow. The rate of profit would change either because profits change or because the capital stock changes. The latter would automatically change when non-zero net investment occurs. The former would arise from, *inter alia*, fluctuations in the level of output (and thereby profits) and in the degree of monopoly (influencing the ratio of profits to sales). Although the precise formulation has varied, the factors which Kalecki identified as influencing investment have generally been adhered to by post-Keynesians (and indeed incorporated into much econometric modelling of investment behaviour).

The perspective adopted on the modelling of expectations is particularly important in the context of fixed investment, since a decision on investment is seen as one which cannot easily be rectified. At the individual level, a firm would often find difficulty in selling second-hand capital equipment; at the aggregate level second-hand equipment can be thrown away (or sold overseas) but the decision cannot otherwise be undone.

> It is by reason of the existence of durable equipment that the economic future is linked to the present. It is, therefore, consonant with, and agreeable to, our broad principles of thought, that the expectation of the future should affect the present though the demand price for durable equipment.
>
> (Keynes 1936)

This consideration now leads us to some further discussion on the modelling of expectations.

11.6 EXPECTATIONS AND PREDICTABILITY

The post-Keynesian approach has always stressed the roles of expectations and perceptions in decision-making, with particular emphasis on their importance for investment decisions. Post-Keynesian macroeconomists have generally rejected any notion of 'rational expectations' as an appropriate approach to the modelling of individual expectation formation.[13] However, there has been a wide range of views on approaches to expectations and prediction of the future, ranging from a generalized adaptive expectations view through to the notion that the future is inherently unknowable.[14]

A frequently quoted starting point for this view is Keynes (1937), who argued that there are many future events for which 'there is no scientific basis on which to form any calculable probability whatever. We simply do not know.' This line of argument has been developed by Shackle (1972, 1989), in particular, who has focused on the 'human predicament' (of the impossibility of prediction because economic change is linked with changes in knowledge which we cannot know before they have occurred) and individual decision and action as a first cause but with no reference to any necessary relationships between economic variables. Further, the innovative ability of human beings can be stressed (particularly in connection with new ideas and technical progress).

This view has been accused of nihilism (Coddington 1983; but see Shackle 1983–4). However, if it is not possible to explain the level of investment expenditure, say, it may still be worthwhile exploring its consequences. Further, as Earl and Kay (1985) argue, people in uncertain complex situations unable to make detailed optimizing decisions may use 'rules of thumb', which can be analysed (for extensive discussion see Hodgson 1988, 1989).

One feature of the *General Theory* is that different decisions are treated differently. Consumer expenditure is a rather passive decision, heavily constrained by available income. Expenditure is influenced by 'social practices and institutions' and by 'habitual behaviour of individuals'. Investment expenditure, in contrast, is an active decision which is not tightly constrained by past income and which is strongly influenced by future prospects. A distinction is drawn between short-term expectations which are largely fulfilled[15] and long-term expectations relating to many years ahead which cannot be checked out and for which the necessary experience on which to base probabilistic estimates of the future cannot be acquired.

11.7 BUSINESS CYCLES

For post-Keynesian macroeconomists, the fluctuations in economic activity are an important feature of the world for which an explanation is sought. However, there are a number of different views on the causes of such fluctuations. Some of the monetary aspects of business cycles have been touched on above. Post-Keynesian approaches have focused on two other causes of cycles. The first arises from the fluctuating nature of investment and the impact of changes in the level of economic activity on the level of investment. The second arises from a conflict between workers and capitalists over income shares.

A particular difficulty which has plagued theories of the business cycle has been to find a mathematical formulation which would generate self-perpetuating cycles. The interaction of multiplier and accelerator (Samuelson 1939) led to a linear second-order difference equation, which would not be capable, in general, of generating a perpetual cycle. Formulations by Kalecki (for example, Kalecki 1935, 1937a) led to mixed difference–differential equations which may lead to self-perpetuating cycles (for further discussion of Kalecki's business cycles theories see Sawyer (1985a: 54–68)).

Kaldor (1940) realized that a non-linear formulation with multiple equilibria (for the equality between savings and investment) could lead to self-perpetuating cycles, and this was later formalized by Chang and Smyth (1971). The basis of this approach is that income changes in response to the difference between desired investment and savings (both of which are functions of income and the level of the capital stock). Changes in the capital stock depend on desired investment (which is assumed to be realized) minus the depreciation on existing capital stock. Chang and Smyth (1971) show that this pair of first-order differential equations generate a limit cycle (i.e. a self-perpetuating cycle towards which the relevant economic variable tends). This is a model of pure cycles with no long-term growth, so that cycles take place around stationary values of output and the capital stock.

The analysis by Goodwin (1967) draws upon the 'predator–prey' literature where the 'problem of the symbiosis of two populations – partly complementary, partly hostile' generates a pair of non-linear differential equations, the solution to which may involve a limit cycle. As such, it avoids having to invoke either ceiling and floors or random shocks to allow the continuation of cycles.

Goodwin's growth cycle, in contrast with Kaldor's approach, does not contain an independent investment function and hence assumes that savings determine the growth of the capital stock. It assumes a classical savings function (all wages spent, all profits saved), so that there is an equality between profits, savings and the increase in the capital stock (where all these variables are in real net terms). The growth rate of employment is equal to the growth of output minus the rate a of technical change. The labour force is assumed to grow at a constant rate b so that the rate of change e of the employment ratio (employment to labour force) is growth of output minus $a + b$. There is a struggle between workers and capitalists over real wages, where the power of workers is enhanced by high levels of employment. Goodwin (1967) shows that the resulting equations generate a limit cycle. Desai (1973) extends the analysis by introducing a money wage equation in a Phillips curve form and a price-adjustment equation based on mark-up pricing. Shah and Desai (1981) introduce induced technical change into the Goodwin model, with the effect that the system now converges back to the long-run equilibrium rather than cycling around it.

Skott (1989) combines two elements of the role of aggregate demand and the class struggle. The ratio of savings to income depends on profit share (reflecting differential savings behaviour) and the ratio of investment to income depends on output-to-capital ratio and profit share. The *ex post* equality of savings and investment is established through accommodating price adjustments. Output decisions are based on profit share and employment rate. The model is completed by two identities for the growth of the capital stock and of employment. A notable feature of this model is that prices and profit margins are flexible, but that labour market conditions have no impact on real wages or income shares.

These (and other) approaches to the business cycle illustrate (to varying degrees) a number of post-Keynesian themes, namely the cyclical nature of capitalist economics, the role of aggregate demand and the conflict over income distribution.

11.8 CONCLUDING REMARKS

In this chapter we have concentrated on the short-run macroeconomic analysis of the post-Keynesians. It is not possible in the space available to cover all aspects of post-Keynesian macroeconomics, and our focus here has been on the building blocks of macroeconomic analysis, with a neglect of complete post-Keynesian models. There has also been a neglect of the analysis of economic growth. Some of the different approaches within post-Keynesian analysis have been indicated (for example, pricing theories). Nevertheless, we hope to have shown that there are solid microeconomic foundations for post-Keynesian macroeconomic analysis, which provides a coherent view of the macroeconomics of developed industrialized economies.

NOTES

1 The term post-Keynesian was frequently used in the 1950s and 1960s to signify economic analyses based on extensions of the IS–LM interpretation of Keynes (1936). The post-Keynesian approach discussed in this chapter has little relationship with that interpretation.
2 Authors such as Kaldor, Robinson, Sraffa and others made many important contributions during the 1950s and 1960s which have strongly influenced post-Keynesian economists. However, the use of the term post-Keynesian to signify a range of approaches (of which short-run macroeconomics is discussed here) dates from the early 1970s.
3 Hamouda and Harcourt (1988) include Sraffian, Marxian etc. under the heading of post-Keynesian.
4 Amongst the important post-Keynesian writings in this area would be Robinson (1956), Kaldor (1957, 1961) and Pasinetti (1962, 1981).
5 For Kalecki's indication of these common features, see his review of Keynes (1936) which has been translated by Targetti and Kinda-Hass (1982).
6 A monetary economy is taken to be one not only with money (serving as a medium of exchange) but also with financial assets (including money) which are stores of wealth.
7 For the purposes of macroeconomic analysis, the view taken of pricing can be relatively simple. In general, the requirement is for a relationship between price and variables such as costs, demand etc. For other purposes, a more sophisticated view of the pricing process may be required.
8 In my view, the only author who could be described as post-Keynesian who comes close to such a view is Means (1936). However, there is a well-developed school of thought, beginning with Clower (1965) and Leijonhufvud (1968) (for example, Malinvaud 1977), which analyses the impact of non-instantaneous price and wage adjustment in the context of atomistic competition. The point here is that such an approach has little to do with the work of Keynes or post-Keynesians.
9 'In contrast, Keynes' treatment of the labor demand function implies that the market for current output is clearing. The *General Theory* seems perfectly consistent on this point. Keynes implies throughout that prices, as contrasted with wages, adjust instantaneously, to bring the quantity demanded into line with the quantity supplied, the latter being fixed in the short run. Thus Leijonhufvud would seem to have no basis for his contention that Keynes generally reversed the Marshallian ranking of relative price and quantity adjustment speeds' (Grossman 1972). See also Brothwell (1975) and Chick (1983).
10 Discussion of the structure–conduct–performance approach can be found in any industrial

economics text (for example, Clarke 1985; Sawyer 1985b). For a test of the relationship between industrial structure and profitability with reference to the Kaleckian degree-of-monopoly approach see Reynolds (1984).

11 Authors using this general approach include Wood (1975), Harcourt and Kenyon (1976), Ong (1981) and Shapiro (1981), as well as Eichner whose work is discussed in the text.

12 In this formulation, no essential distinction is made between price (wage) increases and price (wage) decreases. However, for many reasons, most post-Keynesians would anticipate a degree of downward price and wage inflexibility.

13 For a critical discussion of rational expectations see, for example, Colander and Guthrie (1980–1), Davidson (1982–3), Gomes (1982), Bausor (1983), Rutherford (1984) and Wible (1984–5).

14 Some models used by post-Keynesians could be said to have incorporated a 'rational expectations' view in one of two senses. The first is most apparent at the level of individual or firm behaviour when actual and expected values are conflated. For example, a distinction is generally not made between the expected demand curve facing a firm (on which a firm's decisions are based) and the actual demand curve facing a firm. The price–quantity decision of the firm is assumed to lie on the actual demand curve as well as on the expected demand curve. The second sense, which is reflected in the model of price–wage interaction presented in the text, is when some steady state is analysed in which expectations are fulfilled, which is algebraically equivalent to rational expectations.

15 'For the theory of effective demand is substantially the same if we assume that short-period expectations are always fulfilled' (Keynes 1973).

REFERENCES

Appelbaum, E. (1979) 'The labor market', in A. Eichner (ed.) *A Guide to Post-Keynesian Economics*, London: Macmillan.

Arestis, P. (1986) 'Wages and prices in the UK: the post-Keynesian view', *Journal of Post Keynesian Economics* 8: 339–58. Reprinted in Sawyer, M. (ed.) *Post-Keynesian Economics*, Aldershot: Edward Elgar, 1988.

Basile, L. and Salvadori, N. (1984–5) 'Kalecki's pricing theory', *Journal of Post Keynesian Economics* 7: 249–62.

Bausor, R. (1983) 'The rational expectations hypothesis and the epistemics of time', *Cambridge Journal of Economics* 7: 1–10.

Brothwell, J. F. (1975) 'A simple Keynesian response to Leijonhufvud', *Bulletin of Economic Research* 27: 3–21.

Chang, W. W. and Smyth, D. J. (1971) 'The existence and persistence of cycles in a non-linear model: Kaldor's 1940 model re-examined', *Review of Economic Studies* 38: 37–44.

Chick, V. (1983) *Macroeconomics after Keynes*, Oxford: Philip Allan.

—— (1986) 'The evolution of the banking system and the theory of saving, investment and interest', *Economies et Sociétés*, Cahiers de l'ISMEA Serie Monnaie et Production, no. 3: 111–26.

Clarke, R. (1985) *Industrial Economics*, Oxford: Basil Blackwell.

Clower, R. (1965) 'The Keynesian counter-revolution', in F. Hahn and F. Brechling (eds) *The Theory of Interest Rates*, London: Macmillan.

Coddington, A. (1983) *Keynesian Economics: The Search for First Principles*, London: Allen & Unwin.

Colander, D. C. and Guthrie, R. C. (1980–1) 'Great expectations: what the Dickens do "rational expectations" mean', *Journal of Post Keynesian Economics* 3: 219–34.

Coutts, K., Godley, W. and Nordhaus, W. (1978) *Industrial Pricing in the United Kingdom*, Cambridge: Cambridge University Press.

Cowling, K. (1982) *Monopoly Capitalism*, London: Macmillan.

Cowling, K. and Waterson, M. (1976) 'Price–cost margin and market structure', *Economica* 43: 267–74.

Davidson, P. (1982–3) 'Rational expectations: a fallacious foundation for studying crucial decision-making', *Journal of Post Keynesian Economics* 5: 182–98.

Desai, M. (1973) 'Growth cycles and inflation in a model of class struggle', *Journal of Economic Theory* 6: 527–45.

Earl, P. E. and Kay, N. (1985) 'How economists can accept Shackle's critique of economic doctrine without arguing themselves out of their jobs', *Journal of Economic Studies* 12: 34–48.

Eichner, A. S. (1985) *Towards a New Economics*, New York: M. E. Sharpe.

—— (1987) *The Macrodynamics of Advanced Market Economies*, New York: M. E. Sharpe.

Frank, J. F. (1986) *The New Keynesian Economics*, Brighton: Harvester Wheatsheaf.

Friedman, M. (1968) 'The role of monetary policy', *American Economic Review* 58: 2–17.

Gerrard, W. (1989) *Theory of the Capitalist Economy: Towards a Post-classical Synthesis*, Oxford: Basil Blackwell.

Godley, W. and Nordhaus, W. (1972) 'Pricing in the trade cycle', *Economic Journal* 82: 853–74. Reprinted in Sawyer, M. (ed.) *Post-Keynesian Economics*, Aldershot: Edward Elgar, 1988.

Gomes, G. M. (1982) 'The irrationality of rational expectations', *Journal of Post Keynesian Economics* 5: 51–65.

Goodwin, R. M. (1967) 'A growth cycle', in C. H. Feinstein (ed.) *Socialism, Capitalism and Growth*, Cambridge: Cambridge University Press.

Grossman, H. (1972) 'Was Keynes a Keynesian?', *Journal of Economic Literature* 10: 26–30.

Hall, R. and Hitch, C. (1939) 'Price theory and business behaviour', *Oxford Economic Papers* 2: 12–33. Reprinted in Sawyer, M. (ed.) *Post-Keynesian Economics*, Aldershot: Edward Elgar, 1988.

Hamouda, O. and Harcourt, G. (1988) 'Post Keynesianism: from criticism to coherence?', *Bulletin of Economic Research* 40: 1–33. Reprinted in Pheby, J. (ed.) *New Directions in Post-Keynesian Economics*, Aldershot: Edward Elgar, 1989.

Harcourt, G. C. and Keynon, P. (1976) 'Pricing and the investment decision', *Kyklos* 29: 449–77. Reprinted in Sawyer, M. (ed.) *Post-Keynesian Economics*, Aldershot: Edward Elgar, 1988.

Henry, S. G. B., Sawyer, M. and Smith, P. (1976) 'Models of inflation in the U.K.: an evaluation', *National Institute Economic Review* 76: 60–71.

Hodgson, G. (1988) *Economics and Institutions: A Manifesto for a Modern Institutional Economics*, Oxford: Polity Press.

—— (1989) 'Post-Keynesianism and institutionalism: the missing link', in J. Pheby (ed.) *New Directions in Post-Keynesian Economics*, Aldershot: Edward Elgar.

Jorgenson, D. (1967) 'The theory of investment', in R. Ferber (ed.) *Determinants of Investment Behaviour*, New York: National Bureau of Economic Research.

Kaldor, N. (1940) 'A model of the trade cycle', *Economic Journal* 50: 78–92.

—— (1955) 'Alternative theories of distribution', *Review of Economic Studies* 23: 83–100.

—— (1957) 'A model of economic growth', *Economy Journal* 67: 591–624.

—— (1961) 'Capital accumulation and economic growth', in F. Lutz (ed.) *The Theory of Capital*, London: Macmillan.

—— (1970) 'The new monetarism', *Lloyds Bank Review* 97: 1–18.

Kaldor, N. and Trevithick, J. (1981) 'A Keynesian perspective on money', *Lloyds Bank Review* 139: 1–19. Reprinted in Sawyer, M. (ed.) *Post-Keynesian Economics*, Aldershot: Edward Elgar, 1988.

Kalecki, M. (1935) 'A macrodynamic theory of business cycles', *Econometrica* 3: 327–44.

—— (1937a) 'A theory of the business cycle', *Review of Economic Studies* 4: 77–97.

—— (1937b) 'Principle of increasing risk', *Economica* 4: 440–7.

—— (1944) 'Professor Pigou on "The classical stationary state": a comment', *Economic Journal* 54: 131–2.

—— (1971) *Selected Essays on the Dynamics of the Capitalist Economy*, Cambridge: Cambridge University Press.

Keynes, J. M. (1930) *Treatise on Money*, London: Macmillan.

—— (1936) *The General Theory of Employment, Interest and Money*, London: Macmillan.

—— (1937) 'The general theory of employment', *Quarterly Journal of Economics* 51: 209–23.

—— (1973) *Collected Works*, vol. 14, *The General Theory and After: Part II, Defence and Development*, London: Macmillan.

Kriesler, P. (1987) *Kalecki's Microanalysis: The Development of Kalecki's Analysis of Pricing and Distribution*, Cambridge: Cambridge University Press.

—— (1989) 'Kalecki's pricing theory revisited', *Journal of Post Keynesian Economics* 11: 108–30.

Lee, F. S. (1986) 'Kalecki's pricing theory: two comments', *Journal of Post Keynesian Economics* 8: 145–8.

Leijonhufvud, A. (1968) *On Keynesian Economics and the Economics of Keynes*, Oxford: Oxford University Press.

Malinvaud, E. (1977) *The Theory of Unemployment Reconsidered*, Oxford: Basil Blackwell.

Means, G. C. (1936) 'Notes on inflexible prices', *American Economic Review* 26 (Supplement): 23–35.

Minsky, H. P. (1975) *John Maynard Keynes*, New York: Columbia University Press.

—— (1978) 'The financial instability hypothesis: a restatement', *Thames Papers in Political Economy*, Autumn.

—— (1982) *Can 'It' Happen Again*, New York: M. E. Sharpe.

Moore, B. (1983) 'Unpacking the post-Keynesian black box: bank lending and the money supply', *Journal of Post Keynesian Economics* 5: 537–56. Reprinted in Sawyer, M. (ed.) *Post-Keynesian Economics*, Aldershot: Edward Elgar, 1988.

—— (1984) 'Keynes and the endogeneity of the money stock', *Studi Economici* 22: 23–69.

—— (1988) *Horizontalist and Verticalists*, Cambridge: Cambridge University Press.

—— (1989) 'The endogeneity of credit money', *Review of Political Economy* 1: 65–93.

Ong, N.-P. (1981) 'Target pricing, competition and growth', *Journal of Post Keynesian Economics* 4: 101–16.

Pasinetti, L. (1962) 'Rate of profit and income distribution in relation to the rate of economic growth', *Review of Economic Studies* 29: 267–79. Reprinted in Sawyer, M. (ed.) *Post-Keynesian Economics*, Aldershot: Edward Elgar, 1988.

—— (1981) *Structural Change and Economic Growth*, Cambridge: Cambridge University Press.

Patinkin, D. (1982) *Anticipation of the General Theory? and Other Essays on Keynes*, Oxford: Basil Blackwell.

Phillips, A. W. (1958) 'The relation between unemployment and the rate of change of money wage rates in the United Kingdom, 1861–1957', *Economica* 25: 283–99.

Radcliffe Report (1959) *The Committee on the Workings of the Monetary System*, London: HMSO, Cmnd 827.

Reynolds, P. (1984) 'An empirical analysis of the degree of monopoly theory of distribution', *Bulletin of Economic Research* 36: 59–84.

Robinson, J. (1956) *The Accumulation of Capital*, London: Macmillan.

Routh, G. (1980) *Occupation and Pay in Great Britain, 1906–1979*, London: Macmillan.

Rowthorn, R. (1977) 'Conflict, inflation and money', *Cambridge Journal of Economics* 1: 215–39. Reprinted in Sawyer, M. (ed.) *Post-Keynesian Economics*, Aldershot: Edward Elgar, 1988.

Rutherford, M. (1984) 'Rational expectations and Keynesian uncertainty', *Journal of Post Keynesian Economics* 6: 377–87.

Samuelson, P. (1939) 'Interaction between the multiplier analysis and the principle of acceleration', *Review of Economics and Statistics* 21: 75–8.

Sawyer, M. (1982a) *Macro-economics in Question*, Brighton: Harvester Wheatsheaf.

—— (1982b) 'Collective bargaining, oligopoly and macroeconomics', *Oxford Economic Papers* 34: 428–48.

—— (1983) *Business Pricing and Inflation*, London: Macmillan.

—— (1985a) *Economics of Michal Kalecki*, London: Macmillan.

—— (1985b) *Economics of Industries and Firms*, London: Croom Helm.

Shackle, G. (1972) *Epistemics and Economics*, Cambridge: Cambridge University Press.

—— (1983–4) 'The romantic mountain and the classic lake: Alan Coddington's Keynesian economics', *Journal of Post Keynesian Economics* 6: 241–51.

—— (1989) 'What did the *General Theory* do?' in J. Pheby (ed.) *New Directions in Post-Keynesian Economics*, Aldershot: Edward Elgar.

Shah, A. and Desai, M. (1981) 'Growth cycles with induced technical change', *Economic Journal* 91: 1006–10.

Shapiro, N. (1981) 'Pricing and the growth of the firm', *Journal of Post Keynesian Economics* 4: 85–100.

Skott, P. (1989) 'Effective demand, class struggle and cyclical growth', *International Economic Review* 30: 231–47.

Steindl, J. (1952) *Maturity and Stagnation in American Capitalism*, Oxford: Basil Blackwell. Re-issued with new introduction by Monthly Review Press, 1976.

Targetti, F. and Kinda-Hass, B. (1982) 'Kalecki's review of Keynes' *General Theory*', *Australian Economic Papers* 21: 244–60.

Wible, J. R. (1984–5) 'An epistemic critique of rational expectations and the neoclassical macroeconomic research program', *Journal of Post Keynesian Economics* 7: 269–81.

Wood, A. (1975) *A Theory of Profits*, Cambridge: Cambridge University Press.

Wulwick, N. (1987) 'The Radcliffe central bankers', *Journal of Economic Studies* 14: 36–50.

12

PUBLIC CHOICE THEORY

DENNIS C. MUELLER

12.1 INTRODUCTION

Public choice can be defined as the economic study of non-market decision-making, or simply the application of economics to political science. Its subject matter is the same as that of political science: the theory of the state, voting rules, voter behaviour, party politics, the bureaucracy. Its methodology is that of economics, however. The basic behavioural postulate of public choice, as for economics, is that man, be he voter, politician or bureaucrat, is an egotistic rational, utility-maximizer.[1]

The first question that an economist might ask about politics is why government is needed at all? Why can the market not make all our collective choices for us? Modern economics' answer to this question is that markets fail. The external effects and indivisibilities associated with some goods lead to Pareto inferior allocations of resources when they are provided by the market. Government provision of these 'public goods' can be an efficient resolution of market failures. This explanation for government's existence is reviewed in Section 12.2.

If the state exists as analogue to the market for providing public goods, then it must accomplish the same preference revelation task for public goods as the market achieves for private goods. The public choice approach to non-market decision-making (a) makes the same behavioural assumptions as general economics (rational utilitarian man), (b) often depicts the preference revelation process as analogous to the market (voters engage in exchange, individuals reveal their demand schedules via voting, citizens exit and enter clubs) and (c) asks the same questions as traditional price theory. Do equilibria exist? Are they stable? Are they Pareto efficient? How are they obtained?

This paper borrows heavily from my *Public Choice II* (Mueller 1989). To save space, I have limited reference to who said what drastically. The reader should consult the book for more complete bibliographical references. My thanks go to Cambridge University Press for allowing me to reprint material from that book. Thanks also go to the Thyssen Foundation for financial support.

One part of public choice treats government as a black box or voting rule into which individual preferences (votes) are placed and out of which outcomes emerge. It is reviewed in Section 12.3. Another part sees government as composed of candidates, parties, representatives and bureaucrats, each with their own objectives, and constrained by electoral rules and ultimately voter preferences. This literature is reviewed in Section 12.4. Another large literature discusses what the properties of a political process ought to be. It is examined in Section 12.5. The chapter closes with a discussion of the distinction between allocation and redistribution and its fundamental importance for the selection of voting rules.

12.2 THE REASONS WHY GOVERNMENT EXISTS

Public goods and prisoners' dilemmas

Consider A and B living in anarchy. They can gather sufficient food to achieve utilities of 10 and 9 respectively. However, each can attain still higher utility by stealing from his neighbour (see Table 12.1). In anarchy, stealing is the dominant strategy with the outcome cell 3. From this 'natural' state, both individuals become better off by tacitly or formally agreeing not to steal. The movement from cell 3 to cell 1 is a Pareto move that lifts the individuals out of a Hobbesian state of nature (Bush 1972; Bush and Mayer 1974; Buchanan 1975a). An agreement to make such a move is a 'constitutional contract' establishing the property rights and behavioural constraints on each individual. Problems of collective choice arise with the departure from Hobbesian anarchy.

Table 12.1 Stealing as a prisoners' dilemma

		B	
		Does not steal	Steals
A	Does not steal	1 (10,9)	4 (7,11)
	Steals	2 (12,6)	3 (8,8)

Property rights and procedures to enforce them are Samuelsonian public goods in 'that each individual's consumption leads to no subtraction from any other individual's consumption of that good' (Samuelson 1954). Nearly all public goods can be depicted using a strategy box analogous to Table 12.1. It depicts the familiar prisoners' dilemma.[2] Despite the obvious superiority of the co-operative non-stealing outcome, the stealing strategies constitute an equilibrium pair, at least for a single play of the game. The co-operative solution may emerge, however, as the outcome of a 'supergame' of repeated prisoners' dilemma games. It emerges if each player links his choice of strategy to the other's choice, for example by playing the same strategy in the present game as the other player played in the previous game. If both players adopt this strategy *and* begin by co-operating, co-operation emerges in every play of the game (Axelrod 1984).

When numbers are large, however, a few players can cheat, and either not be detected, since the impact on the rest is small, or not be punished, since their punishment is too costly. Thus, voluntary compliance with behavioural sanctions or provision of public goods is more likely in small communities than in large (Coase 1960; Buchanan 1965b). Reliance on voluntary compliance in large communities or groups leads to free-riding and the underprovision or non-provision of the public good. Given incentives to free-ride, compliance requires the implementation of individualized rewards or sanctions (Olson 1965: 50–1, 132–67). Thus, democracy – formal voting procedures for making and enforcing collective choices – is an institution that is needed by communities of only a certain size and impersonality.

Externalities and the Coase theorem

An externality occurs when the consumption or production of one agent has an unintended impact on the utility or production function of another. Given the existence of externalities, a non-Pareto optimal allocation of resources is often assumed to result. Coase (1960) challenged this conventional wisdom. Pareto optimal resolutions of externalities could be and often were worked out between the affected parties without the help of government. His main result is commonly referred to as the Coase theorem: 'In the absence of transactions and bargaining costs, affected parties to an externality will agree on an allocation of resources which is both Pareto optimal and independent of any prior assignment of property rights'. Government intervention is not needed to resolve externality issues.

Resolution of a two-person externality through private bargaining and agreement is a plausible, if not inevitable, outcome. However, as the number of affected parties grows, the plausibility of obtaining private agreement diminishes. Imagine that all the residents along and users of a river like the Thames tried to negotiate with one another to reduce the discharge of pollutants into the river. As with public goods, government appears in the presence of externalities as a low transaction costs alternative to achieving Pareto efficiency when the number of individuals involved is large (Dahlman 1979).

Redistribution as a reason for government

It is easy to envisage government arising out of pristine anarchy to fulfil a collective need of the community. However, it is just as easy to envisage a distributional motivation behind the origin of the state. The best warrior becomes chief, and eventually extracts tribute from his fellow tribesmen. War and police activity begin as the primary activities of 'government', but gains from these activities are claimed by the authoritarian leader(s).

Thus, the state can be envisaged as coming into existence either to satisfy the collective needs of all members of the community or the wants of only part of it. The first explanation corresponds to the achievement of allocative efficiency, and the second to redistribution.

The distinction between allocative efficiency and redistribution is fundamental in economics and public choice. In the allocation of private goods, market exchange guides society 'as if by an invisible hand' from points inside the Pareto frontier to a point upon it. However, this point is chosen blindly. Since the distributional issue is resolved as a by-product of a process benefiting all parties, it need not become a bone of contention.

To obtain Pareto efficiency in the allocation of public goods, a collective choice process less anarchic than the market is required. A conscious choice of public good quantity must be made along with the means for paying for it. The distributional issue is more clearly visible in the allocation of public goods by a political process than it is in the allocation of private goods by the market. The possibility also arises that this and other distributional issues become dominant in the political process.

Although allocative efficiency and distributional issues are inevitably intertwined, it is useful analytically to separate them. Within public choice one can point to theories focusing almost exclusively on either the allocative efficiency–public good activities of government (Wicksell 1896), or its redistributional activities. In Aranson and Ordeshook's (1981) theory of the state, public goods emerge as a by-product of the primary government activity of redistributing wealth (see also Meltzer and Richard 1978, 1981, 1983; Peltzman 1980).

12.3 PUBLIC CHOICE IN A DIRECT DEMOCRACY

The unanimity rule

When government exists to provide public goods, the obvious voting rule is unanimous consent. Wicksell (1896) was the first to link the potential for all to benefit from collective action to the unanimity rule. Two main criticisms have been made against it. First, a groping search for a point on the contract curve might take considerable time (Black 1958: 146–7; Buchanan and Tullock 1962: ch. 6). The loss in time of community members seeking to discover Pareto optimal tax shares might outweigh the gains to those who are saved from paying a tax exceeding their public good benefits. An individual, uncertain over whether he would be so 'exploited' under a less than unanimity rule, might prefer such a rule rather than spend the time required to attain full unanimity. The second objection against a unanimity rule is that it encourages strategic behaviour (see Black 1958: 147; Buchanan and Tullock 1962: ch. 8; Barry 1965: 242–30; Samuelson 1969).

The 'bargaining problem' under the unanimity rule is the mirror image of the 'incentive problem' in the voluntary provision of a public good. However, recent experimental results obtained by Hoffman and Spitzer (1986) indicate that strategic bargaining may not be much of a problem. Their experiments essentially tested whether strategic bargaining under the unanimity rule over-turned Pareto optimal proposals in Coase-type externality situations. They found that 'if anything, efficiency improved with larger groups' (Hoffman and Spitzer 1986: 151), i.e. with groups as large as twenty on a side.

Unanimous agreement is also required on the final iteration under an auction mechanism to provide public goods proposed by Smith (1977). Experiments with small numbers of voters were characterized by fairly rapid convergence on the Lindahl equilibrium, and strategic misrepresentation of preferences was not observed (Smith 1977, 1979a,b, 1980).

The optimal majority

When a less than unanimous majority passes an issue, some individuals are made worse off via the committee's decision. A less than unanimity rule imposes costs on those made worse off that could be avoided through the expenditure of additional time to redefine the issue to benefit all. Buchanan and Tullock (1962: 63–91) refer to them as the 'external costs' of the decision rule (see also Breton 1974: 145–8). Against these costs must be set the loss of time reaching an agreement.

Thus, a trade-off exists between the external costs of having an issue that one opposes imposed, and the costs of time lost in decision-making. The various possibilities are shown in Figure 12.1 (Buchanan and Tullock 1962: 63–91). The costs of a particular collective decision are presented along the vertical axis, and the number of people 0 to N, i.e. the committee size, required to pass the issue are plotted along the horizontal axis. Curve C represents the expected loss of utility from the victory of a decision to which one is opposed. Curve D shows the decision time costs of achieving the required majority to

Figure 12.1 Choosing the optimal majority.

pass an issue. The optimal majority is the number of members which minimizes the sum of these two costs. This occurs at K, where the expected gain in utility from redefining a bill to gain one more supporter just equals the expected loss in time from doing so.

A simple majority as the optimal majority

Nothing so far indicates why $K/N = 1/2$ should be the dominant choice as the optimal majority, and yet it is. For any one rule to be the optimal majority for a wide class of decisions there must exist a kink in one of the cost functions at the point $N/2$ (Buchanan and Tullock 1962: 81). An explanation for a kink in D at $N/2$ can be obtained by considering further the internal dynamics of the committee. When less than half its membership is sufficient to pass an issue, the possibility exists that both an issue and its converse pass, greatly delaying the final choice of an issue. The simple majority rule has the smallest required majority which still avoids the possibility that self-contradictory issues will be passed (Reimer 1951). The potential for self-contradictory issues to pass raises the D curve to the left of $K/N = 0.5$. However, this change alters the optimum majority point only when the minimum of C + D would otherwise be on the left of the $K/N = 0.5$ point. Thus, the simple majority rule is optimal for a committee that places a relatively high weight on the opportunity costs of time.

212

Majority rule and redistribution

Once issues can pass with less than unanimous agreement, the distinction between allocative efficiency and redistribution blurs. Some are worse off under the chosen outcome than they would be if some other outcomes were selected, and a redistribution is effectively involved. The vertical and horizontal axes of Figure 12.2 depict the ordinal utilities of the rich and the poor. All members of each group have identical preferences. The point of initial endowment with only private good production is E. The provision of the public good can improve the utilities of both individuals, expanding the Pareto possibility frontier out to XYZW. Under the unanimity rule both groups of individuals must be better off with the public good for them to vote for it. So the outcome under the unanimity rule must be somewhere in the YZ segment along the Pareto possibility frontier.

However, there is no reason to expect the outcome to fall in this range under majority rule. A coalition can benefit by redefining the issue to increase its benefits at the expense of the non-coalition members. If the rich were in the majority they could be expected to couple the public good proposal with a sufficiently regressive tax package so that the outcome is in the XY segment. If the poor were in the majority, the taxes would be sufficiently progressive to produce an outcome in ZW. Given the opportunity to redefine the issue through the alteration of the public good quantity, the tax shares or both, we expect the outcome to fall outside the Pareto preferred segment YZ (Davis 1970).

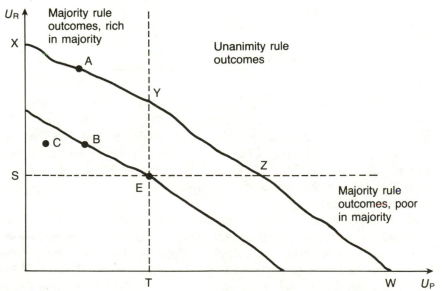

Figure 12.2

The process of transforming a proposal unanimously supported into one supported by only a simple majority resembles that described by Riker (1962) who takes the extreme position that politics involves *only* redistribution questions. Politics is a pure zero-sum game (Riker 1962: 29–31). Given that the game is to take from the losers, the winners can obviously be better off by increasing the size of the losing side, as long as it remains the losing side. Under majority rule this implies that the losing coalition be increased in size until the proposal passes by a 'bare' majority.

Cycling

The possibility that majority rule leads to cycles was recognized almost two hundred years ago by the Marquis de Condorcet (1785). Dodgson (1876) analysed the problem anew a hundred years later, and it has been a major focus of the modern public choice literature beginning with Black (1948b) and Arrow (1951). Consider three voters with preferences over three issues as in Table 12.2 (> implies preferred). X defeats Y, Y defeats Z and Z defeats X. Pairwise voting leads to an endless cycle. Majority rule can select no winner non-arbitrarily.

Table 12.2

Voter	Issue			
	X	Y	Z	X
1		>	>	<
2		>	<	>
3		<	>	>
Community		>	>	>

If X, Y and Z are sequentially higher expenditures on a public good, then the preferences of voters 1 and 3 are single-peaked in the public good–utility space (Figure 12.3). Voter 2's preferences are double-peaked, however, and herein is a cause of the cycle. Change 2's preferences so that they are single-peaked (e.g. she ranks Z > Y > X), and the cycle disappears. Y then defeats both X and Z, and the equilibrium lies at the preference peak of the median voter (Black 1948a).

If all issues were unidimensional, multipeaked preferences of the type depicted in Figure 12.3 might be sufficiently unlikely so that cycling would not be much of a problem. In a multidimensional world, however, preferences as in Table 12.2 seem quite plausible. For example, issues X, Y and Z might be votes on whether to use a piece of land for a swimming pool, tennis courts or a baseball diamond. Each voter could have single-peaked preferences on

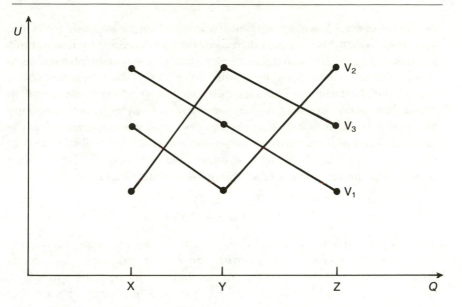

Figure 12.3 Voter preferences which induce a cycle.

the amount to be spent on each activity, and a cycle still appears over the issue of the land's use.

A great deal of effort has been devoted to defining conditions under which majority rule yields an equilibrium. Black's median voter theorem was general-ized by Plott (1967), who proved that a majority rule equilibrium exists if it is a maximum for one (and only one) individual and the remaining even number of individuals can be divided into pairs whose interests are diametrically opposed. Kramer (1973) later proved that when individuals have the usual convex indifference maps, and face a budget constraint, majority rule is certain to produce an equilibrium only when all individuals have identical indifference maps or, as Kramer puts it, when there is 'complete unanimity of individual preference orderings' (Kramer 1973: 295).

Thus, we return to a unanimity condition. If what we seek is to reveal preferences on public goods, the options appear to be as follows. A unanimity rule might be selected requiring a perhaps infinite number of redefinitions of the issue until one benefiting all citizens was reached. While each redefinition might, in turn, be defeated until a point on the Pareto possibility frontier had been reached, once attained no other proposal could command a unanimous vote against it, and the process would come to a halt. The number of times that an issue must be redefined before a passing majority is reached can be reduced by reducing the size of the majority required to pass an issue. While this 'speeds up' obtaining the *first* passing majority, it slows down, perhaps indefinitely, reaching the *last* passing majority, i.e. the one which beats all others, for under a less than unanimity rule, some voters are made worse off. This is equivalent to a redistribution from the opponents of a measure to its proponents. As with any redistribution measure, it is generally possible to redefine an issue transferring the benefits among a few individuals and obtain a new winning coalition. The Plott 'perfect balance' condition ensures an equilibrium under majority rule by imposing a form of severe symmetry assumption on the distribution of preferences which ensures that any redefinition of an issue always involves symmetric and offsetting redistributions of the benefits. The Kramer 'identical utility functions' condition removes all conflict, and thereby eliminates all questions of redistribution.

Agenda manipulation

McKelvey (1976) first established that, when individual preferences can produce a cycle with sincere voting under majority rule, an individual who controls the agenda can lead the committee to any outcome in the issue space. The theorem is developed in two parts. First, it is established that with a voting cycle it is possible to move the committee from any starting point S an arbitrarily large distance d from S. In Figure 12.4, let A, B and C be optima for three voters, and let S be the starting point. If each individual votes sincerely on each issue pair, the committee can be led from S to Z to Z' to Z'' in just three steps. The process can continue until one is any d one wishes

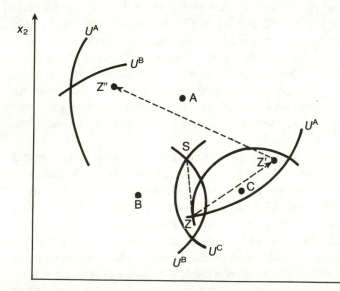

Figure 12.4 Agenda manipulation possibilities.

from S. If A were the agenda setter, she could force the committee under majority rule to choose her most preferred point A by choosing a d sufficiently large so that a majority prefers A to the point d distance from S. By not offering options that a majority prefers to A, she can keep it there.

There are two important implications of McKelvey's theorem. First, the power of the agenda setter may be substantial. If this power is vested in an individual or subcommittee, then precautions must be taken lest those with agenda-setting power secure a disproportionate share of the gains from collective action. Second, the existence of a voting cycle introduces a degree of unpredictability to the voting outcomes providing incentives for some to manipulate the process to their advantage.

May's theorem on majority rule

The cycling literature undermines the notion that majority rule is a quick way of resolving differences of opinion, and the agenda manipulation literature raises troubling normative questions. Yet, when asked to justify majority rule's popularity, students unfamiliar with public choice usually mention its justness, fairness or egalitarian properties. May (1952) provided a theoretical justification for this viewpoint by proving the equivalence between the majority rule group decision function applied to two issues (x, y) and four axioms. Stated informally the axioms are as follows.

1 Decisiveness: for a single set of preference orderings, the group decision function selects either x or y as the best element, or declares the committee indifferent between them.
2 Anonymity: a switch of one committee member's preferences from, say, $x P_i y$ to $y P_i x$, and the reverse switch of any other member (from $y P_j x$ to $x P_j y$) leaves the committee outcome unchanged.
3 Neutrality: if x defeats (ties) y for one set of individual preferences, and all individuals have the same ordinal rankings for z and w as for x and y (i.e. $x R_i y \rightarrow z R_i w$ etc.), then z defeats (ties) w.
4 Positive responsiveness: if the committee outcome is $x R y$, and one voter's preferences change from $y P_i x$ to $x R_i y$, or from $x I_i y$ to $x P_i y$, with all other voter preferences unchanged, then the committee outcome must be $x P y$.

The theorem is a most remarkable result. If we start from the set of all possible voting rules and impose conditions that we wish a voting rule to satisfy, we obviously reduce the number of viable candidates as more conditions are added. May's theorem tells us that once these four conditions are imposed the set of possible voting rules is reduced to just one, the simple majority rule.

The equivalence between majority rule and these four conditions implies that all the normative properties that majority rule possesses, whatever justness or egalitarian attributes it has, are captured somewhere in these four axioms, as are its negative attributes. The normative heart of the theorem lies in the anonymity and neutrality axioms.

Neutrality is an issue independence property (Sen 1970a: 72; Guha 1972). In deciding an issue pair, the ordinal preferences of each voter over only this pair are considered. Information concerning voter preferences on other issues is ruled out, and thereby one means for weighing intensities is eliminated. Neutrality requires that each issue pair is treated alike regardless of the nature of the issues involved. Thus, the issue of whether the lights on this year's community Christmas tree are red or blue is decided by the same kind of weighing of individual preference orderings as the issue of whether John Doe's property should be confiscated and redistributed among the rest of the community.

While the neutrality axiom guarantees that all *issues* are treated alike, anonymity requires that *voters* be treated alike. On many issues this is probably desirable. On the issue of the colour of the Christmas lights, a change of one voter's preferences from red to blue and of another's from blue to red probably should not affect the outcome. Implicit here is a judgement that the colour of the tree's lights is about as important to one voter as the next. This equal intensity assumption is introduced into the voting procedure by recording each voter's expression of preference, no matter how strong, as ± 1.

Now consider the issue of whether John Doe's property should be confiscated and distributed to the rest of the community. A voting procedure satisfying anonymity is blind as to whether it is John Doe or his worst enemy who is voting for the confiscation of John Doe's property. On such issues the implicit equal intensity assumption justifying anonymity is untenable.

The Rae–Taylor theorem on majority rule

Although on the surface they seem quite different, May's theorem on majority rule is quite similar to a theorem presented by Rae (1969) and Taylor (1969).

Rae sets up the problem as one of the choice of an optimal voting rule by an individual who is uncertain over his future position under this rule (Rae 1969: 43–4). Politics is viewed as a game of conflict. In choosing a voting rule, the individual seeks to avoid having issues he opposes imposed upon him, and to impose issues he favours on others. He presumes that the gains he will experience from the passage of a favourable issue will equal the loss from the passage of an unfavourable issue, i.e. that all voters experience equal intensities on each issue. Issues are impartially proposed so that each voter has the same probability of favouring or opposing any issue. Under these assumptions, the self-interested voter selects a rule which minimizes the probability of his supporting an issue that is defeated or opposing an issue that wins. Majority rule is the only rule satisfying this criterion.

The full flavour of the theorem can best be obtained by considering an example given by Barry (1965: 312). Five people occupy a railroad car which contains no sign either prohibiting or permitting smoking. A decision must be made as to whether occupants who wish to smoke are allowed to do so. The assumption that a non-smoker suffers as much from the smoking of others as they suffer from being stopped from smoking, i.e. the equal intensity assumption, seems defensible in this case. With this assumption, and uncertainty over whether one is a smoker or non-smoker, majority rule is the best decision rule. It maximizes the expected utility of a constitutional decision-maker.

This example illustrates both the explicit and implicit assumptions underlying the Rae–Taylor theorem. First, the situation is one of conflict. The smoker's gain comes at the non-smoker's expense, or vice versa. Second, the conflictual situation cannot be avoided. The solution to the problem provided by the exit of one category of passenger from the wagon is implicitly denied.[3] Nor does a possibility exist of redefining the issue to remove the conflict and obtain consensus. The issue must be voted up or down as is. Fourth, the issue has been randomly or impartially selected. In this particular example, randomness is effectively introduced through the chance assemblage of individuals in the car. The last assumption contained in the example is the equal intensity assumption. The importance of each of these assumptions to the argument for majority rule can best be seen by contrasting them with the assumptions that have typically been made in support of its antithesis – the unanimity rule.

Assumptions underlying the unanimity rule

As depicted by Wicksell (1896) and Buchanan and Tullock (1962), politics is a co-operative positive-sum game. The community is a voluntary association of individuals brought together to satisfy needs common to all. Since the association is voluntary, each member is guaranteed the right to preserve his own interests against those of the other members. This right is preserved by the power contained in the unanimity rule to veto any proposal that runs counter to an individual's interest, or through the option to exit the community.

Given that the purpose of collective action is the satisfaction of common wants, the natural way for issues to come before the assembly is from the members themselves. Each individual has the right to introduce issues which will benefit him and he thinks might benefit all. Should an initial proposal fail to command unanimous support, it is redefined until it does, or until it is removed from the agenda. Thus, the political process implicit in the argument for unanimity rule is one of discussion, compromise and amendment continuing until a formulation of the issue is reached benefiting all. The key assumptions underlying this view of politics are both that the game is co-operative and positive sum and that the process can be completed in a reasonable amount of time.

Table 12.3 summarizes the assumptions that have been made in support of the majority and unanimity decision rules. They are not intended to be necessary and sufficient conditions, but are more in the nature of the most favourable conditions under which each decision rule is expected to operate. It is immediately apparent from the table that the assumptions supporting one rule are totally opposed to the assumptions made in support of the other.

Majority rule or unanimity rule: redistribution or allocative efficiency

A follower of the debate over majority and unanimity rule could easily be forgiven for concluding that there is but one type of issue to be decided collectively and one best rule for making collective decisions. However, it should now be clear that the collective choice process is confronted with two fundamentally different types of collective decisions to resolve, corresponding to the distinction between allocation and redistribution decisions (Mueller 1977). The inherent differences between the underlying characteristics of these two types of decisions suggests both that they be treated separately conceptually, and as a practical matter that they be resolved by separate and different collective decision processes.

One of Wicksell's important insights was to recognize the distinction between allocation and redistribution decisions, and the need to treat them with separate collective decision processes. Indeed, in some ways he was ahead of his modern critics, for he not only recognized that distribution and allocation issues would have to be decided separately, but also suggested that unanimity would have to give way to majority rule to resolve the distribution issues (Wicksell 1896: 109, note m). However, Wicksell did not elaborate on how the majority rule would be used to settle distribution issues, and the entire normative underpinning for the use of the unanimity rule to decide allocation decisions is left to rest on an assumed just distribution having been determined prior to collective decision-making on allocation issues.

Unfortunately, none of the proponents of majority rule has elaborated on how the conditions required to achieve its desirable properties are established either. Somewhat ironically, perhaps, the normative case for using majority rule to settle property rights and distributional issues rests as much on decisions taken prior to its application as the normative case for using the unanimity rule for allocation decisions rests on a prior determined just income distribution. The Rae–Taylor theorem presupposes a process which is impartial, in that each voter has an equal chance of winning on any issue and an equal

Table 12.3 Assumptions favouring the majority and unanimity rules

Assumption	Majority rule	Unanimity rule
1 Nature of the game[a]	Conflict, zero sum	Co-operative, positive sum
2 Nature of issues	Redistributions, property rights (some benefit, some lose)[b] Mutually exclusive issues of a single dimension[b]	Allocative efficiency improvements (public goods, externality elimination) Issues with potentially several dimensions and from which all can benefit[c]
3 Intensity	Equal on all issues[d]	No assumption made
4 Method of forming committee	Involuntary: members are exogenously or randomly brought together[e]	Voluntary: individuals of common interests and like preferences join[f]
5 Conditions of exit	Blocked, expensive[g]	Free
6 Choice of issues	Exogenously or impartially proposed[h]	Proposed by committee members[i]
7 Amendment of issues	Excluded, or constrained to avoid cycles[j]	Endogenous to committee process[j]

Notes: [a] Buchanan and Tullock 1962: 253; Buchanan 1966: 32–3.
[b] Barry 1965: 312–14; Rae 1975: 1286–91.
[c] Wicksell 1896: 87–96; Buchanan and Tullock 1962: 80.
[d] Kendall 1941: 117; Buchanan and Tullock 1962: 128–30; Rae 1969: 41, n. 6.
[e] Rae 1975: 1277–8.
[f] Wicksell 1896, 87–96; Buchanan 1949. Of course, this assumption is common to all contractarian theories of the state.
[g] Rae 1975: 1293.
[h] This assumption is implicit in the impartiality assumed by Rae (1969) and Taylor (1969) in their proofs and in Barry's (1965) example (in particular on p. 313).
[i] Wicksell 1896; Kendall 1941: 109.
[j] Implicit.

expected gain (or loss) from a decision's outcome. Similar assumptions are needed to make a compelling normative case for May's neutrality and anonymity conditions. But what guarantees that these conditions will be met? To realize majority rule's potential for resolving property rights and redistribution issues some new form of parliamentary committee is needed that satisfies the conditions that majority rule's proponents have assumed in its defence. A constitutional decision is required.

But what rule is used to establish this new committee? If unanimity is used, those favoured by the status quo can potentially block the formation of this new committee, whose outcomes, although fair, would run counter to the interest of the status quo. But if the majority rule is employed, a minority may dispute both the outcomes of the distribution process and the procedure by which it was established. How does one defend the justness of a redistribution decision of a parliamentary committee to a minority which feels that the procedure by which the committee was established was unfair and voted against it at that time? This query seems as legitimate when raised against a majority rule decision, whose justification rests on the fairness of the issue proposal process, as it is when raised against a unanimity rule, which rests its justification on some distant unanimous agreement on property rights. At some point, the issue of how fairness is introduced into the decision process, and how it is agreed upon, must be faced.

We have run up against the infinite regress problem. The only satisfactory way out of this maze is to assume that at some point unanimous agreement on a set of rules was attained (see Buchanan and Tullock 1962: 6–8). We take up this question again in Section 12.5.

The demand-revealing process

In 1954, Samuelson cast a pall over the field of public economics by asserting that no procedure could be constructed to reveal the information on preferences required to determine the Pareto optimal quantities of public goods (Samuelson 1954: 182). So influential was this paper that for a generation economists merely repeated Samuelson's dictum and lamented the absence of a satisfactory procedure for revealing individual preferences. But then in the 1970s, all of a sudden, a revolution erupted. New procedures appeared, one after the other, which claimed to solve the preference-revelation problem.

To understand how the demand-revelation process[+] works, consider the choice between issues P and S. Assume a committee of three with preferences as in Table 12.4. A expects to be the equivalent of $30 better off from the victory of P, C expects to be $20 better off and B prefers the status quo S by the equivalent of $40. The procedure requires each voter to state in dollars his benefits from his preferred issue and then adds these figures, declaring

Table 12.4

Voter	Issue		Tax
	P	S	
A	30		20
B		40	0
C	20		10
Totals	50	40	30

the issue with the highest benefits the winner. In the present example this is P, since it promises gains of $50 to voters A and C, while S benefits B by only $40.

Voters are induced to declare their true preferences for the issues by charging them a tax dependent on the responses that they make and their impact on the final outcome. This tax is calculated in the following way. The dollar votes of all other voters are added and the outcome is determined. The dollar votes of the voter in question are now added in to see if the outcome is changed. If it is not, he pays no tax. If it is, he pays a tax equal to the net gains expected from the victory of the other issue in the absence of his vote. Thus, a voter pays a tax only when his vote is decisive in changing the outcome, and then pays not the amount he has declared but the amount needed to balance the declared benefits on the two issues. The last column of Table 12.4 presents the taxes of the three voters.

Under the tax each voter has an incentive to reveal his true preferences for the issues. Any amount of benefits from P that voter A declared equal to or great than 21 would leave the collective decision, and his tax, unchanged. If he declared net benefits of less than $20, S would win, and A's tax would fall from $20 to zero but his benefits of $30 would also disappear. A voter pays a tax only if his vote is decisive, and the tax that he pays is always equal to or less than the benefits he receives. Thus, there is no incentive to understate one's gains, for then one risks forgoing a chance to cast the deciding vote at a cost less than the benefits. Also, there is no incentive to overstate one's preferences, since this incurs the risk of becoming the decisive vote and receiving a tax above one's actual benefits, albeit less than one's declared benefits. The optimal strategy is honest revelation of preferences.

The procedure can reveal individual demand schedules, as its name implies. In this variant an equilibrium quantity is chosen satisfying the Bowen (1943) and Samuelson (1954) conditions for Pareto optimality. Groves and Ledyard (1977) have presented an important variant of the procedure that iterates the messages provided by each citizen and ensures an equilibrium choice of public good quantity at which incentive taxes are zero.

Point voting

The necessity to charge a tax to induce honest preference revelation makes the normative properties of the demand-revelation process dependent upon the initial income distribution. This disadvantage could be avoided by giving each voter a stock of vote money to use to reveal preferences for public goods, but without other value. The initial distribution of vote money could be made to satisfy any normative criterion one wished.

An iterative procedure is involved. An auctioneer first calls out a vector of public good quantities. Each individual's tax price is fixed and known. Each allocates her stock of vote points according to her intensity of preferences, indicating whether she desires an increase or decrease in a given public good quantity. The auctioneer then aggregates the vote points by a certain rule, and declares a new vector of quantities with higher quantities declared for those public goods whose aggregate vote points favoured an increase and lower quantities in the reverse case. Previous analyses of point voting have revealed a tendency to overload points on an individual's most intense issues, when the auctioneer merely adds the vote points as cast (Philpotts 1972; Nitzan *et al.* 1980; Nitzan 1985). However, Hylland and Zeckhauser (1979) showed that when the auctioneer adds the square root of each individual's vote points, the voter allocates points so that the procedure converges to a vector of Pareto optimal public goods quantities.

Voting by veto

The demand-revelation and point-voting procedures draw analogies with market mechanisms in that real money or vote money is used to express preferences and equilibrium is achieved through a *tâtonnement* process. The welfare properties of the procedures depend in part on the implicit interpersonal cardinal utility comparisons that arise from the aggregation of dollar or point votes. In contrast, voting by veto utilizes only ordinal utility information. Pareto optimality is achieved, as with the unanimity rule, through the rejection of Pareto inferior outcomes. The procedure also differs from the two previously discussed rules by allowing for the determination of both the quantity of a public good and the tax shares to finance it.

Voting by veto has two steps.[5] In the first, each individual proposes an outcome for the committee process. At the end of step 1 an $n + 1$ proposal set exists consisting of the proposals of the n committee members and a status quo issue s (what was done last year, zero levels of all public goods, ...). A random process is then used to determine an order of veto voting. The order of veto voting is announced to all members of the committee. The individual whom the random process placed first in the veto sequence begins by eliminating (vetoing) one proposal from the $(n + 1)$-element proposal set. The second veto voter eliminates one proposal from the remaining n proposals. Veto voting continues until all n members of the committee have vetoed one proposal. The one unvetoed proposal remaining in the issue set is declared the winner.

The veto-voting stage eliminates the lowest-ranked issues in each voter's preference ordering. Thus, viewed spatially, the procedure tends to pick a proposal at or near the centre of the distribution of most preferred outcomes for the committee. Knowledge of this property induces individuals to increase the probability of their proposal's winning by making proposals that are somewhere between their own most preferred outcome and the centre of the distribution of most preferred outcomes for the committee. The combined result of these two properties leads to the selection of a median/mean voter outcome in close analogy with majority rule.

A comparison of the three procedures

When Samuelson proclaimed that the task of revealing individual preferences for public goods was impossible, he was assuming that an individual's cost share would be tied to his stated preference for the public good (Samuelson 1954: 182). The demand-revealing and point-voting processes solve the preference-revelation problem by severing the link between stated preference and share of cost, as do other related processes like Smith's (1977) auction mechanism.

Although these processes do not make a voter's cost share directly related to his stated preferences for the public good, they do impose a cost upon the voter for moving the committee outcome. The demand-revealing and point-voting schemes require that the voter spend real or fungible vote money to change the committee outcome. Under voting by veto, vetos are not free goods, as with the unanimity rule. Each individual has just one proposal to make and one veto to cast.

In a Wicksellian tradition each procedure presumes that the key equity issues have been resolved prior to their application. The individual shares of the public good's costs are predetermined for both the demand-revealing and point-voting procedures. With demand revelation the outcomes are further dependent on the initial distribution of income, with point voting on the distribution of vote points. Voting by veto leaves aside the issue of initial income distribution.

The proposals differ as to how the gains from collective action are distributed. The demand-revelation process moves individuals out along their demand curves to maximize the sum of consumer surpluses across individuals. The gains from collective action are distributed to those with the lowest shares of the public good's costs and the highest initial incomes. With point voting the gains go to those with lowest initial tax shares and highest initial stocks of vote points. With voting by veto the analogy is with the cake-cutting exercise, as brought about by the random determination of an order of veto voting. The gains from collective action tend to be equal across individuals, and the process's normative characteristic is set by this egalitarian property.

Although each has its weak points, these three procedures give promise that the knotty problem of preference revelation in collective choice can be resolved as both a theoretical and a practical matter.

12.4 PUBLIC CHOICE IN A REPRESENTATIVE DEMOCRACY

Two-party competition – deterministic voting

With large numbers of voters and issues direct democracy is impossible, and representatives must be selected by some means. Public choice has focused on three aspects of representative democracy: the behaviour of representatives both during the campaign to be elected and while in office, the behaviour of voters in choosing representatives, and the characteristics of the outcomes under representative democracy. Representatives, like voters, are assumed to be rational economic men bent on maximizing their utilities. Downs (1957: 28) made 'the fundamental hypothesis of [his] model: parties formulate policies in order to win elections, rather than win elections in order to formulate policies', and the same assumption has generally been made in the literature.

Downs, following Hotelling (1929), depicted political opinion as lying along a single liberal–conservative (left–right) dimension. Each voter has a most preferred position along the spectrum for his candidate to take. The further the candidate is from this position, the less desirable his election is to the voter. Thus the Hotelling–Downs model assumes single-peaked preferences. If every voter votes for the candidate closest to his most preferred position, both candidates are driven towards the position favoured by the median voter. The result resembles Black's theorem for direct democracy demonstrating the victory of the issue favoured by the median voter, for in the Hotelling–Downs model there is only one issue to be decided: how far to the left or right will the winning candidate be?

If all voters vote, the median outcome holds regardless of the distribution of preferences. The result can be upset, however, if the distribution of voter preferences is either asymmetric or multimodal and voters abstain because of alienation. If the distribution is asymmetric but unimodal, the optimal position for each candidate is pulled towards the mode if voters become alienated as candidates move away from them (Comanor 1976). When the distribution of voter preferences is bimodal, the presence of alienation can lead the candidates away from the median towards the two modes (Downs 1957: 118–22). However, it need not. If weak, alienation can leave the median outcome unchanged, or produce no stable set of strategies at all, such is the strength of the pull towards the middle in a two-party winner-take-all system (Davis *et al*. 1970).

The results concerning the instability of majority rule equilibria in a multi-dimensional world carry over directly under representative democracy (Downs 1957: 54–62). The problem that a candidate faces in choosing a multi-dimensional platform which defeats all other platforms is the same, under majority rule, as finding an issue, in multidimensional space, which defeats all other issues. When all voters vote, no platform is likely to exist which can defeat all other platforms. To the extent that incumbents' actions in office commit them to the initial platform choice, challengers have the advantage of choosing the second winning platform. Cycling in a two-party system should appear as the continual defeat of incumbents.

Two-party competition – probabilistic voting

The cycling problem has haunted public choice since its inception. Cycling introduces indeterminacy and inconsistency into the outcomes of the political process that hamper the observer's ability to predict outcomes and cloud the normative properties of the outcomes achieved. The median voter theorem offers a way out of this morass of indeterminateness, a way out that numerous empirically minded researchers have seized. But the median voter equilibrium remains an 'artifact' of the implausible assumption that issue spaces are single dimensional (Hinich 1977).

Recently, however, several authors have modelled electoral politics under a 'probabilistic voting' assumption, and have proved that candidate competition leads to equilibrium outcomes with rather attractive normative properties (see, in particular, Coughlin and Nitzan 1981; Ledyard 1984). Probabilistic voting models seem plausible under the assumptions that candidates are uncertain about voter preferences, voters are uncertain about candidate platforms or extraneous factors (for example, ideology, errors) enter into a voter's choice. When used to analyse how a particular interest group with homogeneous preferences votes, say a group of farmers, probabilistic voting models, in contrast, assume that a candidate increases the fraction of the farm group's vote that he wins by increasing the benefits promised to it. Deterministic voting models assume that all votes of the group go to the candidate promising it the highest benefits.

Using a probabilistic voting model, Coughlin *et al*. (1990) show that competition for votes leads candidates to choose platforms which implicitly maximize an additive welfare function, albeit one which assigns different weights to different interest groups. However, this property raises important normative issues about the equilibria obtained in the competitive struggle for votes. When candidates are unsure of the votes of different groups, and these groups have different capabilities in approaching candidates, then an individual's benefits from political competition depend upon the interest group to which she belongs. The egalitarianism inherent in one man–one vote is distorted when interest groups act as intermediaries between candidates and citizens.

The quality of a vote

Probabilistic voting models give promise that democratic institutions can achieve normatively defensible outcomes. However, the probabilistic voting assumption is a two-edged sword. While it cuts cleanly through the forest of cycling results, it simultaneously undercuts the normative authority of the preferences aggregated, for it presumes uncertainty on the part of candidates about voter preferences, or on the part of voters of candidate positions or both. Indirectly, it raises the question of the quantity and quality of information available to candidates and voters.

One of Downs's most influential contributions to the science of politics was his development of the concept of 'rational ignorance'.[6] In a large electorate, each vote has a negligible probability of affecting the outcome. Realizing this, rational voters do not expend time and money gathering information about candidates. They remain 'rationally ignorant'. If this description of voter knowledge is accurate, as considerable survey evidence suggests that it is, then it is not clear precisely what the dimensions of the policy space over which candidates compete are.

Brennan and Buchanan (1984) have raised a related issue. They liken voter participation in the electoral process to a fan's 'participation' in a sporting match. By attending the match and cheering for one of the teams, the fan expresses a preference for that team. However, the fan is not deluded into thinking that his support contributes to the team's chances of success.

Voting, like cheering at a sporting game, is an expressive, not an instrumental, act. When an individual casts dollar votes for a Ford rather than a Toyota, this decision is instrumental in bringing about the final outcome. He drives a Ford. But a vote for candidate Ford over candidate Carter has no consequence upon the election's outcome. The inconsequential nature of a single vote frees the individual to allow random and extraneous considerations to intrude upon his choice of candidates. Even if political competition achieves a welfare maximum based upon the expressed preferences of voters, the question remains: what are these votes expressions of?

Rent-seeking

Traditional discussions of monopoly treat consumers' surplus on forgone output as the loss due to monopoly, and the profit (rent) rectangle as a pure redistribution of income from consumers to the monopolist. Suppose, however, that the monopoly exists because of the government. Say an airline is granted a monopoly over a route. If more than one airline could service the route, then the monopoly rent is a prize to be awarded to the airline which succeeds in inducing the government to grant it the monopoly. Airlines will invest to increase the probability of obtaining the monopoly. It was Tullock's (1967) initial insight that these investments constitute a social cost of monopoly in addition to the welfare triangle of lost consumers' surplus.

Buchanan (1980: 12–14) identified three types of rent-seeking expenditure:

1 efforts and expenditures of the potential recipients of the monopoly;
2 efforts of the government officials to obtain or react to the expenditures of the potential recipients;
3 third-party distortions induced by the monopoly itself or the government as a consequence of the rent-seeking activity.

Examples of each of these would be as follows.

1 The airlines employ lobbyists to bribe the government official who awards routes.
2 Since the income of this official is supplemented by bribes, lower-level officials invest time studying the airlines industry to improve their chances of obtaining this position.
3 The government's additional revenue from creating the monopoly leads to competition among other interest groups for subsidies.

Government regulation of price and output is one of the most conspicuous ways in which rent-seeking takes place. Posner (1975) estimated the social costs of rent-seeking regulation in six industries: physician's services, spectacles, milk, motor carriers, oil and airlines. On the assumption that the full rectangle of rents is dissipated through rent-seeking, the combined rent-seeking and consumers' surplus losses ranged from 10 to 60 per cent of industry sales under different demand elasticity assumptions.

Tariffs and quotas are another form of protection from competition that the government grants select industries. In her pioneering article, Krueger (1974: 55–7) studied rent-seeking in the issuance of import and other licences in India, and estimated a potential loss in 1964 of 7.3 per cent of national income. Figures for 1968 for import licences in Turkey imply a waste of resources equivalent to 15 per cent of GNP.

The supply of government output

In previous sections individual preferences of the citizen voter or interest group member determine outcomes in the public sector. Government, like the market, is viewed simply as an institution for aggregating individual demands for public policies. Candidates single-mindedly seek to be elected. Those in government are merely pawns of those outside in a competitive political system. Only in the rent-seeking literature do we glimpse another side to government. Politicians may also seek wealth and leisure. Their preferences may impinge on public sector outcomes.

Niskanen's pioneering book on bureaucracy lists the following possible goals of a bureaucrat: 'salary, perquisites of the office, public reputation, power, patronage, output of the bureau, ease of making changes, and the ease of managing the bureau' (Niskanen 1971: 38). All but the last two are assumed to be positively related to the size of the budget. Thus the bureaucrat is a budget-maximizer. Only the bureaucrats are assumed to know the production costs of their agency. This knowledge gives them power over their sponsors (parliament, ultimately the voters) and allows them to offer take it or leave it combinations of output and bureau budget in excess of those that the sponsors would most prefer, if they knew the bureau's true cost function. In the limit, the bureau can absorb all the consumers' surplus of the sponsors, with an accepted budget proposal twice the optimal size.

In Niskanen's model, the bureaucrats hold all the cards. They know their own cost function and the sponsor's demand function. The sponsors, ignorant of the true costs of supplying different outputs, react passively to the budget proposals of the bureau. But sponsors compete for votes on the basis of how well government programmes have served the interests of voters. Bureaucrats compete for promotions, and bureaus compete for funds on the basis of how well they are judged to have supplied the outputs that sponsors desire. The interests of the two main actors conflict, and the most general way to view the sponsor–bureau conflict over the bureau's budget is as a bargaining game between sponsor/demander and bureau/supplier (Breton and Wintrobe 1975, 1982; Miller 1977; Eavey and Miller 1984). The bureau has monopoly power to some degree and information (expertise) on its side. But the sponsor controls the purse strings. It can offer rewards and punishments, gather information to an extent and conceal its own hand. The most plausible outcome, as in most bargaining models, is a compromise. The bureau's budget falls short of the bureaucrat's target, but is greater than the sponsor would want. Slack and inefficiency are present to a degree.

Empirical tests of bureaucracy models

Power of the agenda setter

In Oregon each school district has a budget maximum determined by law. However, school boards can increase the budget size by proposing larger budgets at an annual referendum. If the newly proposed budget passes, it replaces the legally set limit. If it fails, the budget reverts to the level set by the law. This situation allows one to test hypotheses regarding school officials' motivation, assuming that the optimum level of expenditure would be that most preferred by the median voter. If the reversion level is below the most favoured budget size of the median voter, the school board can force her to choose a budget above her most favoured budget size by proposing a higher budget and promising her more utility than she receives from the reversion level.

Romer and Rosenthal (1978, 1979, 1982) found that, where the reversion levels were below the levels necessary to keep the school system viable, referenda were passed providing school budgets anywhere from 16.5 to 43.6 per cent higher than those estimated to be most preferred by the median voter. Further corroboration of the hypothesis was presented in the sixty-four districts that failed either to hold a referendum or to pass one (three districts). When the reversion budget exceeds the level favoured by the median voter, one expects that the school board does not call an election and simply assesses the full 100 per cent of its statutorily set base. The mean assessment for these sixty-four districts was over 99 per cent of their bases (see also Filimon 1982).

The Oregon system provides school officials with an unusually attractive opportunity to increase budget sizes by making take it or leave it referendum proposals. However, as noted above, most bureau budgets are the outcome of a bargaining process between the bureau and its sponsors. Eavey and Miller (1984) have shown, using classroom experiments, that merely granting the sponsor/demanders the right to confer and form coalitions increases their power *vis-à-vis* the agenda setter. The Eavey–Miller experiments produced outcomes falling between the review committee's and the agenda setter's most preferred choices.

Cost differences between publicly and privately provided services

The nature of a bureau's services may make it difficult to expand output beyond the level that the community demands. More children cannot be educated than are sent to school; more garbage cannot be collected than is put out. In this situation, a bureau's members still have an incentive to increase their budget by providing the output demanded at higher cost. The extra costs could reflect higher than competitive salaries, unnecessary personnel or general X-inefficiency. Numerous studies have compared the provision of similar services by public and private firms. In only two of some fifty studies surveyed by Borcherding *et al.* (1982), in which the quality of service was held constant, were public firms found to be more efficient than their private counterparts. In over forty, public firms were found to be significantly less efficient than private firms supplying the same service. The evidence that public provision of a service reduces the efficiency of its provision seems overwhelming.

Government as Leviathan

Brennan and Buchanan (1980) have modelled government as a monopolist. Political competition is thought to provide an ineffective constraint on government owing to the rational ignorance of voters, the uncertainties inherent in majority rule cycling and outright collusion among elected officials (Brennan and Buchanan 1980: 17–24). As in Niskanen's model, Brennan and Buchanan assume that the government's primary objective is revenue maximization.

With government viewed as a malevolent revenue-maximizer rather than a benevolent public-good-provider, many of the traditional propositions of the public finance tax literature are stood on their heads (Brennan and Buchanan 1980: 2). Traditional analysis assumes that the purpose of government is to raise a given amount of revenue subject to certain efficiency and equity constraints; Brennan and Buchanan assume that citizens seek to impose constraints on government bureaucracy limiting its revenues to a given amount. With the amount of revenue to be raised by taxation fixed, the optimal tax is the one which induces the minimum amount of distortion, i.e. the one which falls on the most inelastic sources of revenue. With the amount of revenue to be raised the maximand, citizens will limit government to more elastic tax bases, and shelter parts of their income and wealth from taxation entirely. Citizens, who expect bureaucrats to maximize their budgets, will constrain their ability to do so by constitutionally restricting the kinds of income and wealth that can be taxed.

The Leviathan model provides additional justification for Wicksell's (1986) prescription that expenditure proposals be tied to the taxes that would finance them. Wicksell made this proposal to ensure informed choices as to benefits and costs by citizens. It has the added advantage of ensuring budget balance and forcing the government to provide some public benefit to secure more revenue (Brennan and Buchanan 1980: 154–5).

While traditional analyses of debt and money creation assume that government's motivation is benign, in the hands of a Leviathan seeking ever new sources of revenue, both policy instruments become extremely dangerous.

Balanced budget constitutional amendments follow naturally, as do restrictions on the government's capacity to print money (Brennan and Buchanan 1980: 5, 6, 10).

12.5 NORMATIVE PUBLIC CHOICE

The Arrow impossibility theorem

The most influential effort in normative public choice has been Arrow's (1951) attempt to define a social welfare function in terms of a few basic ethical axioms that might indicate basic value judgements to be incorporated in the community's social contract or constitution.[7] The question posed is this. What ethical norms should constrain the social choice process, and what collective choice processes satisfy these norms? The answer is disappointing. Given but a few fairly weak and ethically uninspiring axioms, no process (voting, the market or otherwise) satisfies them.

Vickrey's (1960) statement of the axioms is as insightful as any.

1 Unanimity (the Pareto postulate): if an individual preference is unopposed by any contrary preference of any other individual, this preference is preserved in the social ordering.
2 Non-dictatorship: no individual enjoys a position such that whenever he expresses a preference between any two alternatives and all other individuals express the opposite preference, his preference is always preserved in the social ordering.
3 Transitivity: the social welfare function gives a consistent ordering of all feasible alternatives, i.e. $(a\,P\,b\,P\,c) \rightarrow (a\,P\,c)$ and $(a\,I\,b\,I\,c) \rightarrow (a\,I\,c)$.
4 Range (unrestricted domain): for every triple of alternatives x, y and u, each of the six possible strict orderings of u, x and y is contained in some admissible ranking of all alternatives for every individual.
5 Independence of irrelevant alternatives: the social choice between any two alternatives must depend only on the orderings of individuals over these two alternatives, and not on their orderings over other alternatives.

The intuition underlying the proof runs as follows. Unrestricted domain allows any possible constellation of ordinal preferences. When a unanimously preferred alternative does not emerge, some method for choosing among the Pareto preferred alternatives must be found. The independence assumption restricts attention to the ordinal preferences of individuals for any two issues, when deciding those issues. However, as we have seen in our discussions of majority rule, it is all too easy to construct rules which yield choices between two alternatives but produce a cycle when three successive pairwise choices are made. Transitivity forces a choice among the three, however. The social choice process is not to be left indecisive (Arrow 1963: 120). But with the information at hand – individual ordinal rankings of issue pairs – there is no method for making such a choice that is not imposed or dictatorial.

Relaxing the postulates

To avoid the impossibility result, the postulates must be relaxed. Consider first, however, the significance of the theorem as it stands, which stems precisely from the weakness of the postulates as now stated. Although, as we shall see, these axioms are somewhat stronger than they might first appear, they are weaker than one would wish to impose to satisfy reasonable notions of distributional equity. For example, there is nothing in the axioms to preclude one group, as long as it has more than one member, from tyrannizing the others if it stays on the Pareto frontier. Even allowing this and yet other violations of our ideas of equity we cannot find a process to choose from among the Pareto optimal set satisfying these axioms.

Relaxing unanimity and non-dictatorship seem hardly worth discussing, if the ideals of individualism and citizen sovereignty are to be maintained. However, the other three axioms require more detailed discussion.

Transitivity

One reason that Arrow gives for requiring transitivity is so 'that some social choice be made from any environment' (Arrow 1963: 120). However, to achieve this goal, the full force of transitivity is not needed. Possibility theorems have been proved replacing transitivity by quasi-transitivity (i.e. transitivity of only the strict preference relationship) or acyclicity ($x_1 P x_2 P \ldots x_{n-1} P x_n \rightarrow x_1 R x_n$) (Sen 1970a: 47–55). Unfortunately, quasi-transitivity vests an oligarchy with the power to impose its unanimous preference (Gibbard 1969); acyclicity gives veto power to every member of a particular subset of the committee (Brown 1975). Thus, as the consistency requirement is relaxed from transitivity to quasi-transitivity, and then to acyclicity, dictatorial power becomes spread and transformed, but does not disappear entirely. Requiring that the social decision process be decisive in some sense vests one individual or a subset of individuals with the power to decide or at least block any outcome.

The gain from relaxing transitivity is further reduced by considering the patterns of individual preference orderings required to ensure either quasi-transitivity or acyclicity. For majority rule, at least, the conditions that are necessary and sufficient for acyclicity are the same as those required for quasi-transitivity, and these in turn will also ensure transitivity when the number of individuals is odd (see Sen and Pattanaik 1969; Inada 1970; Sen 1977a).

Thus, if the property of having a choice made from every environment is to be maintained, little is lost by sticking to the full transitivity requirement.

Unrestricted domain

The justification for the unrestricted domain axiom is something akin to freedom of choice or expression. Each individual should be free to have any preference ordering. Although freedom of choice strikes a responsive chord, conflict can quickly arise when individuals have different preference orderings. Cycles are quite possible, and if we require transitivity, we are well on the way to an impossibility result.

There are two ways around this problem.

1 Replace the unrestricted domain with other axioms limiting the types of preference orderings entering the collective choice process, for example by placing constitutional constraints on the issues that can come up. The protection of certain property rights is one example of this type of constraint. Everyone can be a member of the community, but not every preference can be satisfied or necessarily even recorded in the collective choice process.
2 Restrict entry to those having preference orderings that make collective choices possible.

Single-peakedness can ensure that majority rule produces an equilibrium and, along with the other four axioms, a social welfare function. However, this way out requires strict restrictions on both the selection of issues to be decided and the voters to decide them (Slutsky 1977). Issues must all be one dimensional. Voters cannot simultaneously consider two issues: their preferences must be single-peaked in every dimension.

Single-peakedness implicitly assumes a degree of homogeneity of tastes – a consensus over how things are arranged (Sen 1970a: 71–5; Plott 1976: 569–75). Experimental work indicates that the probability of a cycle under majority rule decreases as voter preferences become more 'homogeneous' and increases with voter 'antagonism' (Plott 1976: 532). These results suggest restricting membership in the polity to those with homogeneous preferences. The theories of clubs and voting with the feet describe processes by which communities of homogeneous tastes might form (Tiebout 1956; Buchanan 1965a; Sandler and Tschirhart 1980). In the absence of externalities across clubs (local communities) and perfect mobility, free entry etc., such a process might avoid the Arrow problem. However, when spill-overs exist, some decisions have to be made by the aggregate population, and the impossibility problem appears here even when 'solved' in the smaller communities.

Independence of irrelevant alternatives

Of all the axioms, the independence of irrelevant alternatives has been subject to the most discussion and criticism. Restricting the choice between two alternatives to information on individual rankings of them excludes all information with which one might cardinalize and interpersonally compare utilities (Sen 1970a: 89–91). There are two justifications for excluding cardinal utility information from a collective choice process. First, the measurement of cardinal utilities is difficult and arbitrary, and any process combining interpersonally comparable cardinal utilities could be vulnerable to abuse by those making the cardinal utility measurements. This would appear to be Arrow's chief fear (Arrow 1963: 8–11). It rests on his view of the collective choice process as one in which public officials make choices *for* the collective (Arrow 1963: 106–8). Allowing these officials to engage in cardinal interpersonal utility comparisons vests them with a great deal of discretionary power.

Discretionary power does not arise, however, if the cardinal utility information is provided by the voters themselves, as, say, under point voting. However, procedures like point voting can be vulnerable to strategic manipulation. The independence axiom eliminates the incentive for strategic misrepresentation of preferences, but at the cost of also eliminating all non-dictatorial voting procedures (Gibbard 1973; Satterthwaite 1975).

Implications for public choice

The Arrow theorem states that no process can exist that satisfies the five defined axioms simultaneously. There are two promising avenues out of this paradox. One is to drop transitivity and abandon the search for *a best* alternative – *the* social preference. In its place could be substituted the requirement that the social choice process be fair or democratic or accord with some other generally held value. Alternatively, if a social ordering must be made, then either the independence axiom or unrestricted domain must be relaxed.

Relaxing unrestricted domain to allow only single-peaked preferences does not seem promising since so few issues are unidimensional. More realistically, we could allow for the revelation of preferences for public goods via voluntary association in private and local clubs. This solution solves the problem by imposing a form of unanimity condition, but leaves aside all distributional considerations and problems of resolving differences of opinion on globally public goods.

Where strategic behaviour is not present, one of the procedures that gathers information on the voters' preferences over the full set of alternatives, like point voting, can be used. However, the normative properties of these procedures depend heavily upon what issues are allowed into the decision set. Thus, relaxing either unrestricted domain or independence of irrelevant alternatives raises questions as to what issues are to be decided, who is to decide, and, of those who decide, which preferences shall be weighted and with what weights. Such choices directly or indirectly involve interpersonal utility comparisons, and must rest on some additional value postulates which if explicitly introduced would imply specific interpersonal utility comparisons. The latter cannot be avoided if a preferred social choice is to be proclaimed (Kemp and Asimakopulos 1952: Hildreth 1953; Bergson 1954; Sen 1970a: 123–5, 1974, 1977b).

The impossibility of a Paretian liberal

The theorem

Arrow's theorem states that it is impossible to satisfy four reasonable constraints on the social choice process without making one person a dictator over all social choices. Sen (1970a, b) sought to allow each person to be dictator over a single 'social' choice, for example the colour of paint in her bathroom, and arrived at yet another impossibility theorem. The key axiom he required was as follows.

> Acceptance of personal liberty: there are certain personal matters in which each person should be free to decide what should happen, and in choices over these things whatever he or she thinks is better must be taken to be better for the society as a whole, no matter what others think.
>
> (Sen 1976: 217)

He formalizes this condition by allowing each individual to be decisive for the social choice over one pair of alternatives, and shows that this condition, unrestricted domain and the Pareto principle produce a cyclic social decision function (1970a, b). The theorem is remarkable, as in the Arrow case, in that it achieves so much from so few constraints.

Sen illustrates his theorem with the following example. A copy of *Lady Chatterley's Lover* is available to be read and the following three social states are possible:

a A reads *Lady Chatterley's Lover*, and B does not;
b B reads *Lady Chatterley's Lover*, and A does not;
c neither reads it.

A, the prude, prefers that no one reads it, but would rather read it himself than have B read it. Lascivious B prefers most that prudish A read the book, but would rather read it himself than see it left unread. In symbols,

for A	$cPaPb$
for B	$aPbPc$

Invoking the liberal rule to allow B to choose whether he reads the book or not results in

bPc

Doing the same for A results in

cPa

However, both A and B prefer a to b; thus, by the Pareto principle

aPb

and we have a cycle.

Rights over Pareto

Sen's preferred solution to the paradox requires that the Pareto principle defer to liberal rights in certain situations (Sen 1976, 1982). Individuals, although meddlesome in nature, may have liberal values which they impose upon themselves so that parts of their preferences 'do not count' or receive 'different weight'. Liberal B might state that the only choice relevant for him is b or c and state

liberal B bPc

while liberal A states

liberal A cPa

The social ordering is now transitive with the liberally constrained outcome being the plausible one that B reads *Lady Chatterley's Lover* and A does not.

Sen's solution resolves the liberal paradox by assuming that individuals themselves behave so as to avoid what would otherwise be a paradox. However, if individuals are resolutely selfish and meddlesome, a conflict between liberal principles and Pareto optimality remains. The next solution relies entirely on the selfish meddlesome interests of individuals.

Pareto trades

In the original example, a certain degree of extra conflict is introduced by assuming that there is just one copy of the book to read. This difficulty is avoided by assuming that the book is available to both, and redefining liberalism so that each individual is decisive over an element pair (whether he reads *Lady Chatterley's Lover* or not) in all possible social states, i.e. independent of the other's choice. The decision options can now be illustrated by Table 12.5 in which the possibility d – both A and B read *Lady Chatterley's Lover* – has been

Table 12.5

| | B, the lascivious | |
	Does not read LCL	Reads LCL
A, the prude — Reads LCL	*a*	*d*
A, the prude — Does not read LCL	*c*	*b*

added. While Sen's condition grants A the choice of either row, given that B is constrained to the first column, the modified liberalism condition gives A the choice of row and B the choice of column.

Although this new liberalism principle will not solve the liberal's paradox, it does suggest a way out of it. Table 12.5 is the prisoners' dilemma. The Pareto inferior outcome *b* will come about if each individual exercises his liberal right without regard for the externality that this decision inflicts on the other (Fine 1975; Buchanan 1976). The way out of the dilemma, as in the case of other externalities, is to invoke another liberal axiom – all individuals are free to engage in mutually beneficial trades – and allow A and B to form a contract in which B agrees not to read the book in exchange for A's reading it (Coase 1960). The power to form such contracts requires that the liberalism axiom be redefined to allow an individual either to exercise his assigned right or to trade it away, i.e. to agree not to exercise it (Gibbard 1974; Buchanan 1976; Kelly 1976; Nath 1976; Breyer 1977; Barry 1986).[8]

Implications for public choice

The liberal paradox literature treats both liberal rights and the meddlesome preferences of individuals as exogenous. The desirability of enforcing liberal rights is taken for granted. The possibility of individuals with meddlesome preferences is assumed, and a paradox ensues. As such the theorems seem more relevant for ethics than for collective choice. If society wishes to avoid the paradox, individuals must (ought to) make their meddlesome tastes subservient to liberal values. A liberal society should count this set of preferences but not that set.

The theorems take on relevance for collective choice, when we think of liberalism not as a value to which I, the ethical observer, think society should conform, but as a value that members of society share and agree to uphold. Liberalism is then endogenous to the preferences or ethical beliefs of the individuals in society. If all individuals were like A and B, and all books like *Lady Chatterley's Lover*, it would be difficult to see how a liberal right to read what one wishes would ever emerge. In such a society, who reads what would be of concern to everyone and would be treated as other externality decisions.

If, however, most people are not like A and B and most books are not like *Lady Chatterley's Lover*, then having to reach a collective decision on who reads what for every book and person in society would involve tremendous decision-making costs. Rational self-interested individuals might agree to treat the choice of book that an individual reads as a purely personal matter. Society economizes on transactions costs, and thus is better off in the long run, if each individual is free to make this choice himself.

In the presence of such a long-run liberalism condition, books like *Lady Chatterley's Lover* and individuals like A and B may from time to time come along and lead to a conflict between liberalism and the Pareto principle. Individuals in society may agree, however, that their long-run interests are best served by also establishing the liberal right to waive or trade one's right to read what one chooses, when such trades are mutually beneficial. When such trades are possible and can be enforced, Pareto optimality is achieved in the short run. When the costs of making and enforcing such trades prevent them, the liberal right to read what one chooses can be seen as helping to block a situation that would be Pareto preferred if it were to come about. In this sense, liberalism can be seen as overriding the Pareto principle. However, if we assume that individuals act in their enlightened self-interest, and that liberal rights are collectively agreed upon by the individuals who will exercise them, then there cannot be a conflict between liberal rights and a long-run definition of the Pareto principle.

If liberal rights can produce Pareto inefficiencies in the short run and yet be Pareto efficient in the long run, how or by what criteria are these rights chosen? To establish a long-run rule allowing each individual to read what he chooses as being socially preferred, the set of all likely books to appear and all individual preference functions must somehow be envisaged and weighed. Interpersonal utility comparisons will be involved. The solution to Sen's paradox, as with Arrow's, rests ultimately on the use of cardinal interpersonally comparable utility information (Ng 1971).

Harsanyi's social welfare function

In both the preceding two sections it has been concluded that consistent collective choices require interpersonal utility comparisons. Harsanyi's (1955, 1977) social welfare function is predicated on the assumption that such comparisons can be made in an ethically defensible manner. Harsanyi distinguishes between an individual's personal preferences and his ethical preferences. The first are used to make day-to-day decisions; the second are used when moral or ethical choices are made. In making the latter, the individual weighs the consequences of a given decision on other individuals, and thus engages in interpersonal utility comparisons.

Harsanyi first derives a social welfare function, i.e. a weighted sum of the individuals' utilities, on the basis of the following three assumptions (Harsanyi 1955: 52).

1 Individual personal preferences satisfy the Von Neumann–Morgenstern–Marschak axioms of choice.
2 Individual moral preferences satisfy the same axioms.
3 If two prospects P and Q are indifferent from the standpoint of every individual, they are also indifferent from a social standpoint.

Next the weights on each individual's utility must be decided, and the utility indexes evaluated. It is here that Harsanyi derives the ethical foundation for his social welfare function. Each individual evaluates the social welfare function at each possible state of the world by placing himself in the position of every other individual and mentally adopting their preferences. To make the selection of a state of the world impartial, each individual assumes that he has an equal probability of being any other.

> This implies, however, without any additional ethical postulates that an individual's impersonal preferences, if they are rational, must satisfy Marschak's axioms and consequently must define a cardinal social welfare function equal to the arithmetic mean of the utilities of all individuals in the society.
>
> (Harsanyi 1955: 55)

Of course, practical problems of persuading people to evaluate states of the world using other individuals' subjective preferences remain (Harsanyi 1955: 55–9, 1977: 57–60). Nevertheless, Harsanyi holds that, with enough knowledge of other individuals, people could mentally adopt the preferences of other individuals, and the U_i terms in each individual's evaluation of social welfare would converge. Thus, the mental experiment of adopting other individuals' preferences combined with the equiprobability assumption produces the same kind of homogeneity of ethical preferences and unanimous choice of the best state of the world as Rawls (1971) achieves via the veil of ignorance in his analysis of just social contracts (Harsanyi 1955: 59).

The just constitution

Buchanan and Tullock (1962) develop a theory of constitutional government in which the constitution is written in a setting resembling that depicted by Harsanyi and Rawls. Individuals are uncertain over their future positions, and

241

thus select rules that weigh the positions of all other individuals. If we think of individuals at the constitutional stage as being utilitarians who implement the impartiality assumption by assuming that they have an equal probability of being any other individual, then the rules incorporated into the constitution maximize a Harsanyi-type social welfare function (Mueller 1973).

The Buchanan–Tullock theory is at once positive and normative – 'The uncertainty that is required in order for the individual to be led by his own interest to support constitutional provisions that are generally advantageous to all individuals and to all groups seems likely to be present at any constitutional stage of discussion' (Buchanan and Tullock 1962: 78) – and the tone of their book is strongly positivist in contrast with, say, the work of Rawls and Harsanyi. However, they also recognize the normative antecedents to their approach in the work of Kant and the contractarians (see, especially, Buchanan and Tullock 1962: Appendix 1). Indeed, they state that the normative content of their theory lies precisely in the unanimity achieved at the constitutional stage (Buchanan and Tullock 1962: 14).

One of Buchanan and Tullock's important contributions is to demonstrate the usefulness of the distinction between the constitutional and parliamentary stages of democratic decision-making. If unanimous agreement can be achieved behind the veil of uncertainty that shrouds the constitutional stage, then a set of rules can be written at this stage that allows individuals to pursue their self-interest at the parliamentary stage with full knowledge of their own tastes and positions. Redistribution takes place at the constitutional stage where uncertainty over future positions holds (Buchanan and Tullock 1962: ch. 13). Here, the similarity to Rawls is striking. Unlike Rawls, however, Buchanan and Tullock allow individuals not just more information about themselves at the parliamentary stage, but full information. With redistribution and similar property rights issues out of the way, the only decisions left to decide are allocational efficiency improvements of a prisoners' dilemma type. Unanimity out of pure self-interest is at least theoretically possible, and Wicksell's voluntary exchange theory of government can reign at this level of decision-making.

12.6 ALLOCATION, REDISTRIBUTION AND PUBLIC CHOICE

Rules for collective decision are needed, quite simply, because people live together. Their mere grouping into circumscribed geographic areas necessitates collective action. Some collective decisions can benefit all individuals; other decisions benefit only some. Even when everyone benefits, some do so more than others, raising an issue of how the 'gains from trade' are shared. Thus, collective choices can be grouped into two categories: those benefiting all community members, and those benefiting some and hurting others. These two categories correspond to the familiar distinction between moves from points off the Pareto frontier to points on it, and moves along the frontier – to allocation and redistribution.

Wicksell's (1896) fundamental contribution was to recognize the necessity of combining a discussion of the characteristics of the outcomes of government action – the allocation or redistribution decisions – with the inputs from the citizens via the voting process bringing these outcomes about. Although Wicksell distinguished between allocation and redistribution decisions, his focus was on the former. Redistribution decisions were assumed to have been justly decided at some prior time. Only allocative efficiency improvements were left to resolve – decisions of potential benefit to all. Here Wicksell's work takes on a distinctly contractarian and individualistic tone. Each citizen took part in the collective decision process to advance his own ends, and via the *quid pro quo* of collective decision-making outcomes were reached to the mutual benefit of all. Voting achieved the same outcome in the market for public goods as exchange achieved in markets for private goods. This contractarian *quid pro quo* approach to government has underlain much of public choice and the public expenditure theory of public finance, most visibly in the work of Buchanan and Musgrave.

Often this literature has a very optimistic tone. In *The Calculus of Consent*, Buchanan and Tullock describe government institutions which bear more than a passing resemblance to those of the United States, and which seem capable of satisfying a society's collective wants. Redistribution decisions are unanimously resolved at the constitutional stage. The day-to-day work of parliament is limited to deciding those issues in which unanimity is potentially possible. In the last twenty years several new and 'superior' voting procedures have been put forward. All have attractive properties that seem to circumvent most if not all of the paradoxes of collective choice. All are capable of achieving this magic only when limited to deciding allocative efficiency improvements.

The literature which focuses upon redistribution, or ignores the distinction between redistribution and allocation, thereby implicitly combining the two, has a discernibly more pessimistic tone. Equilibria do not exist. Their absence enables agenda setters to dictate outcomes. All voting procedures can be manipulated by strategic misrepresentation of preferences unless someone is a dictator. Outcomes may be Pareto inefficient. ... The mood of this new 'dismal' science is accurately captured by Riker (1982).

Much of the pessimism regarding the potential of democratic institutions stems from Arrow's theorem and its aftermath. Arrow sought a social welfare function that ranked alternatives by aggregating individual rankings. That none was found indicates that interpersonal utility comparisons must be made either directly via the decision rule, or indirectly through restrictions placed on the preference domain, or the types of issues that can be decided, or in some equivalent manner.

Several of the new voting procedures aggregate cardinal utility information supplied by the voters. If restricted to decisions which could potentially improve allocative efficiency, they contain the potential for achieving Pareto optimal allocations of resources. Experimental work and some limited applications indicate that they can work as theory predicts. Voting by veto relies only on ordinal utility information and provides another option for achieving a Pareto optimal allocation of resources in deciding public good–externality issues – an option that would avoid the implicit weighting of cardinal utilities inherent in the other procedures.

If political institutions can be designed to reveal preferences on allocative efficiency changes adequately, the question remains of how to resolve redistributional questions. The most important element in an answer to this question is the recognition that a separate set of procedures is required for these from that employed for allocative efficiency gains. Beyond this important insight, the public choice literature points in two distinct directions. First, the uncertainty inherent in the long-run nature of constitutional decisions can induce individuals to incorporate redistributional measures into the constitution. This potential could be enhanced by constituting the convention to maximize uncertainty over future positions (for example, have the constitution not go into effect until several years after ratification). Parliaments would then be freed to concentrate on allocative efficiency improvements.

When redistributional issues are of a binary nature, and equal intensities can be assumed for individuals on both sides, majority rule is attractive for settling distributional questions. The requirement that issues be binary immediately suggests a court of law, and the Supreme Court in the United States has used majority rule to resolve distributional questions (abortion, desegregation of schools). Other institutional arrangements can be envisaged.

The new voting procedures describe methods for aggregating individual preferences appropriate to a direct democracy. They could be used under a representative form of government, however, with the parliament functioning as a sort of representative town meeting. The other notion of representation extant in the literature sees citizens as choosing an agent to act for them but not necessarily as they would act if they were present. The citizens choose a government to govern for a prescribed length of time. This literature contains a more optimistic view of the results of voting than does the literature on committee voting in the Arrow tradition. When voting is limited to a pair of candidates or parties, who compete for the privilege of running (forming) the government, equilibrium platforms exist. Their properties (Pareto optimality, the maximization of a particular social welfare function) are not obviously inferior to those achieved by the market.

Competition between candidates increasingly takes the form of spending money to 'buy' votes. This money comes from interest groups, which seek to 'buy' legislation. The weights given to individual utilities in the social welfare function that political competition maximizes depend on the resources and organizational skills of the interest groups to which individuals belong. While the process of competition for votes may achieve a welfare maximum of sorts, it is not one in which all will be happy with the weights that their interests receive in the resulting equilibrium.

Moreover, the money candidates spend does not really buy votes. It buys television commercials, posters, placards and buttons, pollsters, canvassers and consultants. It buys all the instruments that modern marketing can devise to influence how an individual votes on election day. But in the end it is the decision the voter makes that determines the outcome of the election. The quality of these outcomes rests on the quality of this choice.

While the candidate competition models help to dispel concern over the existence of an equilibrium in policy space, they raise questions about the nature of the policy space over which competition takes place, and the weights given to individual preferences in the welfare function that this competition implicitly maximizes. More generally, they suggest the need for a shift in emphasis in public choice research from the outputs of the political process to its inputs – a shift from an emphasis upon the quality of the aggregate choices to the quality of the choices aggregated. Thus, important issues in public choice remain to be researched.

NOTES

1 Schumpter's (1950) use of this postulate influenced Downs's (1957: 3–20) seminal work. See also discussions by Buchanan and Tullock (1962: 17–39) and Riker and Ordeshook (1973: 8–37).
2 Other situations in which co-operation is required to achieve Pareto efficiency are discussed by Schelling (1966: ch. 2), Taylor and Ward (1982), Hirshleifer (1983, 1984) and Ward (1987).
3 Rae (1975) stresses this assumption in the implicit defence of majority rule contained in his critique of unanimity.
4 This procedure was first described by Vickrey (1961) with important subsequent advances offered by Clarke (1971, 1972) and Groves (1973). Tideman and Tullock (1976) offer a fine exposition of Clark's procedure.
5 This procedure was first discussed by Mueller (1978), with further development by Moulin (1979, 1981a, b, 1982) and Mueller (1984).
6 Although Downs derserves credit for making 'rational ignorance' part of the parlance of the science of politics, the idea is clearly present in Schumpeter's classic discussion of democracy (Schumpeter 1950: 256–64).
7 This interpretation was first put forward by Kemp and Asimakopulos (1952) and was subsequently endorsed by Arrow (1963: 104–5).
8 For Sen's response to this resolution of the paradox, see Sen (1986: 225–8).

REFERENCES

Aranson, P. H. and Ordeshook, P. C. (1981) 'Regulation, redistribution, and public choice', *Public Choice* 37: 69–100.

Arrow, K. J. (1951) *Social Choice and Individual Values*, New York: Wiley.

—— (1963) *Social Choice and Individual Values*, revised edn, New York: Wiley.

Axelrod, R. (1984) *The Evolution of Cooperation*, New York: Basic Books.

Barry, B. (1965) *Political Argument*, London: Routledge & Kegan Paul.

—— (1986) *'Lady Chatterley's Lover* and *Doctor Fischer's Bomb Party:* liberalism, Pareto optimality, and the problem of objectionable preferences', in J. Elster and A. Hylland (eds) *Foundations of Social Choice Theory*, pp. 11–43, Cambridge: Cambridge University Press.

Bergson, A. (1954) 'On the concept of social welfare', *Quarterly Journal of Economics* 68: 233–53.

Black, D. (1948a) 'On the rationale of group decision making', *Journal of Political Economy* 56: 23–34. Reprinted in Arrow, K. J. and Scitovsky, T. (eds) *Readings in Welfare Economics*, pp. 133–46, Homewood, IL: Richard D. Irwin, 1969.

—— (1948b) 'The decisions of a committee using a special majority', *Econometrica* 16: 245–61.

—— (1958) *The Theory of Committees and Elections*, Cambridge: Cambridge University Press.

Borcherding, T. E., Pommerehne, W. W. and Schneider, F. (1982) 'Comparing efficiency of private and public production: the evidence from five countries', *Zeitschrift für Nationalökonomie* 89: 127–56.

Bowen, H. R. (1943) 'The interpretation of voting in the allocation of economic resources', *Quarterly Journal of Economics* 58: 27–48. Reprinted in Arrow, K. J. and Scitovsky, T. (eds) *Readings in Welfare Economics*, pp. 115–32, Homewood, IL: Richard D. Irwin, 1969.

Brennan, G. and Buchanan, J. M. (1980) *The Power to Tax: Analytical Foundations of a Fiscal Constitution*, Cambridge: Cambridge University Press.

—— and —— (1984) 'Voter choice: evaluating political alternatives', *American Behavioral Scientist* 28: 185–201.

Breton, A. (1974) *The Economic Theory of Representative Government*, Chicago, IL: Aldine.

Breton, A. and Wintrobe, R. (1975) 'The equilibrium size of a budget maximizing bureau', *Journal of Political Economy* 83: 195–207.

—— and —— (1982) *The Logic of Bureaucratic Control*, Cambridge: Cambridge University Press.

Breyer, F. (1977) 'Sen's paradox with decisiveness over issues in case of liberal preferences', *Zeitschrift für Nationalökonomie* 37: 45–60.

Brown, D. J. (1975) 'Aggregation of preferences', *Quarterly Journal of Economics* 89: 456–69.

Buchanan, J. M. (1949) 'The pure theory of government finance: a suggested approach', *Journal of Political Economy* 57: 496–506.

—— (1965a) 'An economic theory of clubs', *Economica* 32: 1–14.

—— (1965b) 'Ethical rules, expected values, and large numbers', *Ethics* 76: 1–13.

—— (1966) 'An individualistic theory of political process', in D. Easton (ed.) *Varieties of Political Theory*, pp. 25–37, Englewood Cliffs, NJ: Prentice-Hall.

246

—— (1975) *The Limits of Liberty: Between Anarchy and Leviathan*, Chicago, IL: University of Chicago Press.

—— (1976) 'An ambiguity in Sen's alleged proof of the impossibility of a Pareto libertarian', Mimeo, Center for the Study of Public Choice, Blacksburg, VA.

—— (1980) 'Rent seeking and profit seeking', in J. M. Buchanan, D. Tollison and G. Tullock (eds) *Toward a Theory of the Rent-Seeking Society*, pp. 3–15, College Station, TX: Texas A&M Press.

Buchanan, J. M. and Tullock, G. (1962) *The Calculus of Consent*, Ann Arbor, MI: University of Michigan Press.

Bush, W. C. (1972) 'Individual welfare in anarchy', in G. Tullock (ed.) *Explorations in the Theory of Anarchy*, pp. 5–18, Blacksburg, VA: Center for the Study of Public Choice.

Bush, W. C. and Mayer, L. S. (1974) 'Some implications of anarchy for the distribution of property', *Journal of Economic Theory* 8: 401–12.

Clarke, E. H. (1971) 'Multipart pricing of public goods', *Public Choice* 11: 17–33.

—— (1972) 'Multipart pricing of public goods: an example', in S. Mushkin (ed.) *Public Prices for Public Products*, pp. 125–30, Washington, DC: Urban Institute.

Coase, R. H. (1960) 'The problem of social cost', *Journal of Law and Economics* 3: 1–44.

Comanor, W. S. (1976) 'The median voter rule and the theory of political choice', *Journal of Public Economy* 5: 169–77.

de Condorcet, M. J. A. N. (1785) *Essai sur l'Application de l'Analyse à la Probabilité des Decisions Rondues à la Pluralité des Voix*, Paris: Imprimerie Royale.

Coughlin, P. and Nitzan, S. (1981) 'Electoral outcomes with probabilistic voting and Nash social welfare maxima', *Journal of Public Economics* 15: 113–22.

Coughlin, P., Mueller, D. C. and Murrell, P. (1990) 'Electoral politics, interest groups, and the size of government', *Economic Inquiry* 28: 682–705.

Dahlman, C. J. (1979) 'The problem of externality', *Journal of Law and Economics* 22: 141–62.

Davis, J. R. (1970) 'On the incidence of income redistribution', *Public Choice* 8: 63–74.

Davis, O. A., Hinich, M. J. and Ordeshook, P. C. (1970) 'An expository development of a mathematical model of the electoral process', *American Political Science Review* 64: 426–48.

Dodgson, C. L. (1876) 'A method of taking votes on more than two issues'. Reprinted in Black, D., *The Theory of Committees and Elections*, pp. 224–34, Cambridge: Cambridge University Press, 1958.

Downs, A. (1957) *An Economic Theory of Democracy*, New York: Harper & Row.

Eavey, C. L. and Miller, G. J. (1984) 'Bureaucratic agenda control: imposition or bargaining?', *American Political Science Review* 78: 719–33.

Filimon, R. (1982) 'Asymmetric information and agenda control', *Journal of Public Economics* 17: 51–70.

Fine, B. J. (1975) 'Individual liberalism in a Paretian society', *Journal of Political Economy* 83: 1277–82.

Gibbard, A. (1969) 'Intransitive social indifference and the Arrow dilemma', Mimeo.

—— (1973) 'Manipulation of voting schemes: a general result', *Econometrica* 41: 587–602.

247

—— (1974) 'A Pareto-consistent libertarian claim', *Journal of Economic Theory* 7: 388–410.

Groves, T. (1973) 'Incentives in teams', *Econometrica* 41: 617–31.

Groves, T. and Ledyard, J. O. (1977) 'Optimal allocation of public goods: a solution to the "free rider" problem', *Econometrica* 45: 783–809.

Guha, A. S. (1972) 'Neutrality, monotonicity and the right of veto', *Econometrica* 40: 821–6.

Harsanyi, J. C. (1955) 'Cardinal welfare, individualistic ethics, and interpersonal comparisons of utility', *Journal of Political Economy* 63: 309–21. Reprinted in Arrow, K. J. and Scitovsky, T. (eds) *Readings in Welfare Economics*, pp. 46–60, Homewood, IL: Richard D. Irwin, 1969.

—— (1977) *Rational Behaviour and Bargaining Equilibrium in Games and Social Situations*, Cambridge: Cambridge University Press.

Hildreth, C. (1953) 'Alternative conditions for social orderings', *Econometrica* 21: 81–94.

Hinich, M. J. (1977) 'Equilibrium in spatial voting: the median voter result is an artifact', *Journal of Economic Theory* 16: 208–19.

Hirshleifer, J. (1983) 'From weakest-link to best-shot: the voluntary provision of public goods, *Public Choice* 41 (3): 371–86.

—— (1984) 'The voluntary provision of public goods – descending-weight social composition functions', Working paper 326, University of California at Los Angeles.

Hoffman, E. and Spitzer, M. L. (1986) 'Experimental tests of the Coase theorem with large bargaining groups, *Journal of Legal Studies* 15: 149–71.

Hotelling, H. (1929) 'Stability in competition', *Economic Journal* 39: 41–57.

Hylland, A. and Zeckhauser, R. (1979) 'A mechanism for selecting public goods when preferences must be elicited', KSG Discussion paper 70D, Harvard University, August.

Inada, K.-I. (1970) 'Majority rule and rationality', *Journal of Economic Theory* 2: 27–40.

Kelly, J. S. (1976) 'Rights exercising and a Pareto-consistent libertarian claim', *Journal of Economic Theory* 13: 138–53.

Kemp, M. C. and Asimakopulos, A. (1952) 'A note on "social welfare functions" and cardinal utility', *Canadian Journal of Economic and Political Science*, 18: 195–200.

Kendall, W. (1941) *John Locke and the Doctrine of Majority Rule*, Urbana, IL: University of Illinois Press.

Kramer, G. H. (1973) 'On a class of equilibrium conditions for majority rule', *Econometrica* 41: 285–97.

Krueger, A. O. (1974) 'The political economy of the rent-seeking society', *American Economic Review* 64: 291–303. Reprinted in Buchanan, J. M., Tollison, R. D. and Tullock, G. (eds) *Toward a Theory of the Rent-Seeking Society*, pp. 51–70, College Station, TX: Texas A&M Press, 1980.

Ledyard, J. O. (1984) 'The pure theory of large two-candidate elections', *Public Choice* 44: 7–41.

McKelvey, R. D. (1976) 'Intransitivities in multidimensional voting models and some implications for agenda control', *Journal of Economic Theory* 12: 472–82.

May, K. O. (1952) 'A set of independent, necessary and sufficient conditions for simple majority decision', *Econometrica* 20: 680–4.

Meltzer, A. H. and Richard, S. F. (1978) 'Why government grows (and grows) in a democracy', *Public Interest* 52: 111–18.

—— (1981) 'A rational theory of the size of government', *Journal of Political Economy* 89: 914–27.

—— (1983) 'Tests of a rational theory of the size of government', *Public Choice* 41: 403–18.

Miller, G. J. (1977) 'Bureaucratic compliance as a game on the unit square', *Public Choice* 19: 37–51.

Moulin, H. (1979) 'Dominance solvable voting schemes', *Econometrica* 47: 1337–51.

—— (1981a) 'The proportional veto principle', *Review of Economic Studies* 48: 407–16.

—— (1981b) 'Prudence versus sophistication in voting strategy', *Journal of Economic Theory* 24: 398–412.

—— (1982) 'Voting with proportional veto power', *Econometrica* 50: 145–62.

Mueller, D. C. (1973) 'Constitutional democracy and social welfare', *Quarterly Journal of Economics* 87: 60–80.

—— (1977) 'Allocation, redistribution and collective choice', *Public Finance* 32: 225–44.

—— (1978) 'Voting by veto', *Journal of Public Economy* 10: 57–75.

—— (1984) 'Voting by veto and majority rule', in H. Hanusch (ed.) *Public Finance and the Quest for Efficiency*, pp. 69–86, Detroit, MI: Wayne State University Press.

—— (1989) *Public Choice II*, Cambridge: Cambridge University Press.

Nath, S. K. (1976) 'Liberalism, Pareto principle and the core of a society', Mimeo, University of Warwick.

Ng, Y.-K. (1971) 'The possibility of a Paretian liberal: impossibility theorems and cardinal utility', *Journal of Political Economy* 79: 1397–1402.

Niskanen, W. A., Jr (1971) *Bureaucracy and Representative Government*, Chicago, IL: Aldine-Atherton.

Nitzan, S. (1985) 'The vulnerability of point-voting schemes to preference variation and strategic manipulation', *Public Choice* 47: 349–70.

Nitzan, S., Paroush, J. and Lampert, S. I. (1980) 'Preference expression and misrepresentation in point voting schemes', *Public Choice* 35: 421–36.

Olson, M., Jr (1965) *The Logic of Collective Action*, Cambridge, MA: Harvard University Press.

Peltzman, S. (1980) 'The growth of government', *Journal of Law and Economics* 23: 209–88.

Philpotts, G. (1972) 'Vote trading, welfare, and uncertainty', *Canadian Journal of Economics* 3: 358–72.

Plott, C. R. (1967) 'A notion of equilibrium and its possibility under majority rule', *American Economic Review* 57: 787–806.

—— (1976) 'Axiomatic social choice theory: an overview and interpretation', *American Journal of Political Science* 20: 511–96.

Posner, R. A. (1975) 'The social costs of monopoly and regulation', *Journal of Political Economy* 83: 807–27. Reprinted in Buchanan, J. M., Tollison, R. D. and Tullock, G. (eds) *Toward a Theory of the Rent-Seeking Society*, pp. 71–94, College Station, TX: Texas A&M Press, 1980.

Rae, D. W. (1969) 'Decision-rules and individual values in constitutional choice', *American Political Science Review* 63: 40–56.

—— (1975) 'The limits of consensual decision', *American Political Science Review* 69: 1270–94.

Rawls, J. A. (1971) *A Theory of Justice*, Cambridge, MA: Belknap Press.

Reimer, M. (1951) 'The case for bare majority rule', *Ethics* 62: 16–32.

Riker, W. H. (1962) *The Theory of Political Coalitions*, New Haven, CT: Yale University Press.

—— (1982) *Liberalism Against Populism*, San Francisco, CA: W. H. Freeman.

Riker, W. H. and Ordeshook, P. C. (1973) *Introduction to Positive Political Theory*, Englewood Cliffs, NJ: Prentice-Hall.

Romer, T. and Rosenthal, H. (1978) 'Political resource allocation, controlled agendas, and the status quo', *Public Choice* 33: 27–43.

—— and —— (1979) 'Bureaucrats versus voters: on the political economy of resource allocation by direct democracy', *Quarterly Journal of Economics* 93: 563–87.

—— and —— (1982) 'Median voters or budget maximizers: evidence from school expenditure referenda', *Economic Inquiry* 20: 556–78.

Samuelson, P. A. (1954) 'The pure theory of public expenditure', *Review of Economics and Statistics* 36: 386–9. Reprinted in Arrow, K. J. and Scitovsky, T. (eds) *Readings in Welfare Economics*, pp. 179–82, Homewood, IL: Richard D. Irwin, 1969.

—— (1969) 'Pure theory of public expenditure and taxation', in J. Margolis and H. Guitton (eds) *Public Economics*, pp. 98–123, New York: St Martin's Press.

Sandler, T. and Tschirhart, J. T. (1980) 'The economic theory of clubs: an evaluation survey', *Journal of Economic Literature* 18: 1481–521.

Satterthwaite, M. A. (1975) 'Strategy-proofness and Arrow's conditions: existence and correspondence theorems for voting procedures and social welfare functions', *Journal of Economic Theory* 10: 187–217.

Schelling, T. C. (1966) *Arms and Influence*, New Haven, CT: Yale University Press.

Schumpeter, J. A. (1950) *Capitalism, Socialism and Democracy*, 3rd edn, New York: Harper & Row.

Sen, A. K. (1970a) *Collective Choice and Social Welfare*, San Francisco, CA: Holden-Day.

—— (1970b) 'The impossibility of a Paretian liberal', *Journal of Political Economy* 78: 152–7.

—— (1974) 'Informational basis of alternative welfare approaches, aggregation and income distribution', *Journal of Public Economy* 3: 387–403.

—— (1976) 'Liberty, unanimity and rights', *Economica* 43: 217–45.

—— (1977a) 'Social choice theory: a re-examination', *Econometrica* 45: 53–89.

—— (1977b) 'On weight and measures: informational constraints in social welfare analysis', *Econometrica* 45: 1539–72.

—— (1982) *Choice, Welfare and Measurement*, Cambridge, MA: MIT Press.

—— (1986) 'Foundations of social choice theory: an epilogue', in J. Elster and A. Hylland (eds) *Foundations of Social Choice Theory*, pp. 213–48, Cambridge: Cambridge University Press.

Sen, A. K. and Patanaik, P. K. (1969) 'Necessary and sufficient conditions for rational choice under majority decision', *Journal of Economic Theory* 1: 178–202.

Slutsky, S. (1977) 'A voting model for the allocation of public goods: existence of an equilibrium', *Journal of Economic Theory* 14: 299–325.

Smith, V. (1977) 'The principal of unanimity and voluntary consent in social choice', *Journal of Political Economy* 85: 1125–39.

—— (1979a) 'An experimental comparison of three public good decision mechanisms', *Scandinavian Journal of Economics* 81: 198–215.

—— (1979b) 'Incentive compatible experimental processes for the provision of public goods', in V. L. Smith (ed.) *Research in Experimental Economics*, pp. 59–168, Greenwich, CT: JAI Press.

—— (1980) 'Experiments with a decentralized mechanism for public good decisions', *American Economic Review* 70: 584–99.

Taylor, M. J. (1969) 'Proof of a theorem on majority rule', *Behavioural Science* 14: 228–31.

Taylor, M. J. and Ward, H. (1982) 'Chickens, whales, and lumpy goods: alternative models of public-good provision', *Political Studies* 30: 350–70.

Tideman, T. N. and Tullock, G. (1976) 'A new and superior process for making social choices', *Journal of Political Economy* 84: 1145–59.

Tiebout, C. M. (1956) 'A pure theory of local expenditure', *Journal of Political Economy* 64: 416–24.

Tullock, G. (1967) 'The welfare costs of tariffs, monopolies and theft', *Western Economic Journal* 5: 224–32.

Vickrey, W. (1960) 'Utility, strategy, and social decision rules', *Quarterly Journal of Economics* 74: 507–35.

—— (1961) 'Counterspeculation, auctions, and competitive sealed tenders', *Journal of Finance* 16: 8–37.

Ward, H. (1987) 'The risks of a reputation for toughness: strategy in public goods provision problems modelled by chicken supergames', *British Journal of Political Science* 17: 23–52.

Wicksell, K. (1896) 'A new principle of just taxation', *Finanztheoretische Untersuchungen, Jena*. Reprinted in Musgrave, R. A. and Peacock, A. T. (eds) *Classics in the Theory of Public Finance*, New York: St Martin's Press, 1958.

13

UNCERTAINTY IN
ECONOMICS

JOHN D. HEY

13.1 INTRODUCTION

The title of this chapter was given to me by the editors of this volume. Whether they intended it or not, it is open to two interpretations: the treatment of uncertainty within economics, or the present uncertainty within the profession as to the appropriate treatment of uncertainty in economics. I shall interpret it in both ways. The schizophrenic nature of the title accurately reflects the present schizophrenic attitude towards the treatment of uncertainty by the profession: on the one hand, most economists applying uncertainty theory use subjective expected utility theory (SEUT) as their starting point (numerous examples can be found elsewhere in this volume); on the other hand, many economists studying uncertainty theory itself are increasingly turning away from SEUT as a valid starting point, largely because empirical evidence (usually of an experimental nature – see Chapter 29) casts doubt on the basic axioms of SEUT. I shall refer to SEUT as the 'conventional wisdom', and shall begin by discussing it, before moving on to the exciting new developments stimulated by the empirical evidence referred to above.

13.2 THE CONVENTIONAL WISDOM: SUBJECTIVE EXPECTED UTILITY THEORY

Descriptive subjective expected utility theory

Economists in all branches of economics – uncertainty included – like to assume that all economic agents are rational in some sense; until very recently, the economics of uncertainty took this in what now appears to be quite a strict sense, but one which at the time seemed very reasonable. I shall outline this below, after first defining the 'rules of the game'.

We are interested in describing (economic) behaviour under conditions of risk and uncertainty. For expositional reasons it will prove helpful to distinguish between static and dynamic decision problems: the former are one-off problems, where the economic agent takes a decision, 'nature' responds and then some outcome occurs – end of story; the latter are sequential problems in which the agent and 'nature' take turns at taking decisions and responding respectively, with the outcome finally determined when the entire sequence has been played out. It should be noted that I am excluding games (which are treated in Chapter 17) in which 'nature' and the agent compete strategically against each other; in this chapter, 'nature' responds randomly – unconnected with, and independently of, the agent's decision(s).

Let us begin with static problems and, to keep life simple, let us first consider a static problem under risk. We shall define such a problem as one in which probabilities can be attached to the various possible outcomes. Let us be more specific. The economic agent is trying to decide amongst several risky alternatives; let us denote a generic choice by C. Because it is a decision problem under risk, the final outcome of making such a choice is not known at the time of making the choice; however, we presume that the set of possible final outcomes is known. Let us denote this set $(A_1, \ldots, A_i, \ldots, A_N)$; without any harm we assume that this list is comprehensive in the sense that it contains all the possible outcomes of all the available choices. N could, of course, be very large (even infinite). If this is a decision problem under risk, then *ex definitione* probabilities can be attached (for each choice) to each of these final outcomes. Let us denote these for the generic choice C by $(p_1, \ldots, p_i, \ldots, p_N)$. So, given the choice C, the final outcome is A_1 with probability $p_1, \ldots,$ A_i with probability $p_i, \ldots$ and A_N with probability p_N. We shall assume that the economic agent has carefully listed these various final outcomes so that they are all mutually exclusive; as we have already assumed that the list is exhaustive it follows that each p_i is non-negative and that $\Sigma_{i=1}^{N} p_i = 1$.

Now we must build up the SEUT of rational choice amongst such risky alternatives. We do this in two stages: a descriptive stage and a prescriptive stage. The first stage effectively describes the economic agent's attitude to each of the final outcomes – in a risky choice context. Obviously this cannot be done in any absolute sense, but only in a relative sense; the most natural way of doing it is to describe the attitude of the agent to each final outcome relative to the best and worst outcomes. These must be meaningful terms, and so we first need to assume (in keeping with conventional certainty economics) that the agent has a preference ordering over the final outcomes (recall that these are all certain and known). This is the ordering axiom. For simplicity, let us suppose that the subscripts have been chosen so that A_1 is the most preferred ('the best') and A_N is the least preferred ('the worst'). Note that these may differ from agent to agent; that is of no consequence.

Now take some intermediate outcome A_i. By construction A_1 is at least as preferred as A_i while A_i is at least as preferred as A_N. We assume, without any loss of substance, that A_1 is strictly preferred to A_i (i.e. they are not equally desirable) and that A_i is strictly preferred to A_N. Now consider a risky choice involving the final outcomes A_1 and A_N with respective probabilities p and $1 - p$. Let us denote such a risky choice by $[A_1, A_N; p, 1 - p]$. If $p = 1$ then this risky choice $[A_1, A_N; p, 1 - p]$ is simply the certainty of A_1, which is strictly preferred to A_i; if $p = 0$ then this risky choice $[A_1, A_N; p, 1 - p]$ is simply the certainty of A_N which is strictly less preferred than A_i. Therefore for $p = 1$ we have $[A_1, A_N; p, 1 - p]$ preferred to A_i, while for $p = 0$ we have A_i preferred to $[A_1, A_N; p, 1 - p]$. We now assume continuity of preferences, so that as p decreases from unity to zero the risky choice $[A_1, A_N; p, 1 - p]$ becomes continuously less preferred. This is the continuity axiom. It implies that there is some value of p between unity and zero at which our economic agent is indifferent between A_i and $[A_1, A_N; p, 1 - p]$. For reasons which should become obvious, we shall denote this indifference point, which may well differ from agent to agent (since it reflects the agents' differing evaluations of A_i relative to A_1 and A_N and their differing attitudes to risk), by u_i. We shall call this the value the agent's utility of A_i (relative, of course, to A_1 and A_N) in the context of risky choice. It should be apparent that for each agent $u_1 = 1$ and $u_N = 0$, although intermediate u_i may differ from agent to agent.

An illustration should help. Suppose that A_1 receives £100, A_i receives £50 and A_N receives £0 (but note carefully that the outcomes need not be denominated in money – they can be anything). Now ask yourself: what must be the probability p for you to be indifferent between A_i (£50) with certainty and a gamble between £100 and £0 with respective probabilities p and $1 - p$? Clearly if $p = 1$ you would prefer the gamble; if $p = 0$ you would prefer the £50. If you did not care about the risk involved with the gamble (i.e. if you were risk neutral), then the indifference value would be $p = 0.5$; at this value the gamble would be a 50–50 gamble between £100 and £0 (with expected value £50). If, however, you did care about the risk and in fact disliked it (i.e. you were risk averse), then you would require a value of p greater than 0.5 for you to be indifferent. If, on the contrary, you actually liked risk (you were risk loving), then the indifference value of p would be something less than 0.5. For me, as I dislike risk, the relevant value would be around 0.7: I value £50 with certainty and a 70–30 gamble between £100 and £0 the same.

Prescriptive subjective expected utility theory

The continuity axiom just discussed requires that for each i there exists a u_i for which the individual is indifferent between receiving A_i with certainty and taking the gamble $[A_1, A_N; u_i, 1 - u_i]$. The independence axiom requires that this indifference holds irrespective of the context in which the choice problem occurs; therefore, at any stage, if the agent is about to receive A_i we can replace it by $[A_1, A_N; u_i, 1 - u_i]$ and he or she will be equally happy.

Armed with this new axiom let us now move on to the prescriptive stage. Consider the generic choice C described above and illustrated in Figure 13.1(a). We shall use the notation

$$[A_1, \ldots, A_i, \ldots, A_N; p_1, \ldots, p_i, \ldots, p_N]$$

to refer to this generic choice C, which yields A_1 with probability $p_1, \ldots, A_i$ with probability $p_i, \ldots$ and A_N with probability p_N.

Now the continuity axiom says that for each i there exists a u_i such that the agent is indifferent between A_i and the gamble $[A_1, A_N; u_i, 1 - u_i]$, while the independence axiom says that this indifference holds irrespective of the context. It therefore follows that we can amend the original choice C in Figure 13.1(a) to that in Figure 13.1(b) and the agent will be indifferent between the two formulations.

Now examine Figure 13.1(b); it is a two-stage gamble, and crucially the final outcome, whatever happens, is either A_1 or A_N. It is clear that, through the use of elementary probability rules, we can reduce it to the single-stage gamble shown in Figure 13.1(c). Technically, the two formulations (that in Figure 13.1(a) and that in Figure 13.1(b)) are the same, and so it would seem reasonable to assume that the agent is indifferent between the two formulations. This assumption is the reduction axiom.

Thus, under our various assumptions we have shown that the agent will be indifferent between the choice C as originally formulated in Figure 13.1(a) and the reformulation in Figure 13.1(c). Likewise, this can also be done for any other risky choice C′, as illustrated in Figure 13.2, where C′ is given by $[A_1, \ldots, A_i, \ldots, A_N; p'_1, \ldots, p'_i, \ldots, p'_N]$. Thus, the agent will be indifferent between the choice C′ as originally formulated in Figure 13.2(a) and the reformulation in Figure 13.2(b). Now let us ask which of C and C′ the agent will prefer. To answer this consider the reformulation of C and C′ as given in Figures 13.1(c) and 13.2(b) respectively. Both these reformulations are simply gambles involving the best and worst outcomes (A_1 and A_N respectively). Since A_1 is preferred to A_N, it seems reasonable to assume that the gamble in which the probability of receiving A_1 is the highest will be the most preferred. This is the monotonicity axiom. Thus the gamble in Figure 13.1(c) will be preferred by the agent to the gamble in Figure 13.2(b) if and only if

$$\sum_{i=1}^{N} p_i u_i \geq \sum_{i=1}^{N} p'_i u_i \tag{13.1}$$

How can we interpret this condition? Recall that we have termed u_i the utility of final outcome A_i. The left-hand side of equation (13.1) can then be interpreted as the expected utility of the outcome of choice C, since it is

Figure 13.1

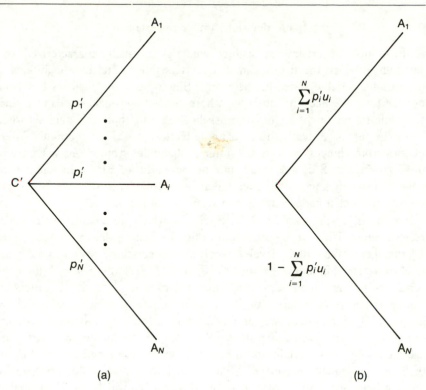

Figure 13.2

simply the weighted average of the various possible utilities, weighted by their respective probabilities: when choosing C the agent can expect utility u_1 with probability $p_1, \ldots$, utility u_i with probability $p_i, \ldots$ and utility u_N with probability p_N. Therefore we have shown that choice C will be preferred by the agent to choice C' if and only if the expected utility of choice C is at least as large as the expected utility of choice C'. Hence the name of the theory. (Note that the utilities are subjective, as they are agent specific.)

We can summarize the above as follows. The descriptive stage involves us finding the 'utilities' (the u_i) of each of the final outcomes by finding the value of u_i at which the agent is indifferent between A_i with certainty and the gamble $[A_1, A_N; u_i, 1 - u_i]$. The prescriptive stage allows us to predict the outcome of any choice problem: the agent simply makes that choice C for which the expected utility $\Sigma_{i=1}^{N} p_i u_i$ is the largest. This important result is used extensively in theories of economic decision-making under uncertainty.

So far, our discussion has been confined to simple static decision problems under risk. However, it is relatively straightforward to extend it to static decision problems under uncertainty and thence to dynamic decision problems under both risk and uncertainty. Let us first consider the former.

257

Static decisions under uncertainty

A situation of uncertainty as distinct from risk is usually characterized as a situation in which the decision-maker feels unable to attach probabilities to the various possible states of the world. Since the above analysis has been exclusively concerned with situations where the decision-maker *can* attach such probabilities, we might legitimately ask how we can apply this analysis when he or she cannot. Actually this is a simple matter: just as the economist infers utilities from choices, we can also infer probabilities from choices. Consider the following: let S denote some state of the world for which the agent feels unable to specify a probability; let $\bar{S}$ denote its complement. Thus, S is some state of the world happening; $\bar{S}$ is that event not happening.

Now consider the gamble $\{1, 0; S, \bar{S}\}$, by which we mean that the agent receives utility 1 if state S occurs and utility 0 if state S does not occur. Now ask the agent: 'What utility level u, received with certainty, gives you the same level of satisfaction as the gamble $\{1, 0; S, \bar{S}\}$?'. Clearly, if $u = 1$ then the certainty of u gives more satisfaction than the gamble $\{1, 0; S, \bar{S}\}$ (unless, of course, the agent considers state S certain to occur – in which case u and the gamble $\{1, 0; S, \bar{S}\}$ are equally preferred). Similarly, if $u = 0$ then the certainty of u gives less satisfaction than the gamble $\{1, 0; S, \bar{S}\}$ (unless, of course, the agent considers S as certain not to occur, in which case u and the gamble $\{1, 0; S, \bar{S}\}$ are equally preferred). Therefore, if continuity holds once again, there will be some value of u between 1 and 0 at which the individual is indifferent between u with certainty and the gamble $\{1, 0; S, \bar{S}\}$; for obvious reasons we call this value p. It can be interpreted as the subjective probability attached by the agent to the event S, since the indifference condition requires that the utility of u received with certainty equals the expected utility obtained from the gamble $\{1, 0; S, \bar{S}\}$. The latter is $1 \times P(S) + 0 \times P(\bar{S}) = P(S)$ where $P(S)$ denotes the probability of the state of the world S. Hence $p = P(S)$.

As with the derivation of the utilities, this derivation of the subjective probabilities requires some consistency conditions. Therefore, for example, if our agent is asked to specify the utility level at which he or she would be indifferent between that utility level and the gamble $\{a + b, b; S, \bar{S}\}$, then the answer must be $a \times p + b$. This seems innocuous. Moreover, it can be shown that the 'probabilities' so revealed satisfy the usual probability laws. For a start, it is obvious that these probabilities must lie between zero and unity with the extreme values taken only when a state is certain to occur or certain not to occur. In addition, these probabilities satisfy the addition law for mutually exclusive events: let S and S' be mutually exclusive and let p and p' be their respective subjective probabilities in the sense that the gamble $\{1, 0; S, \bar{S}\}$ has expected utility p and the gamble $\{1, 0; S', \bar{S}'\}$ has expected utility p';

then it is eminently reasonable that the gamble $\{1, 0; S \cup S', \overline{S \cup S'}\}$ will have expected utility $p + p'$.

Thus (subjective) probabilities can be inferred from choice just as (subjective) utilities can be inferred from choice. Therefore, in a situation of uncertainty as distinct from risk, the expected utility theorem still holds – the only difference is that the p_i should now be taken as subjective probabilities.

Dynamic decision problems

Now let us turn to dynamic problems. These are characterized as situations in which there is a sequence of decision points interspersed by gambles. On the surface such problems look distinctly different from one-off (static) choice problems of the type considered so far. However, they can be made to look the same by the simple device of reinterpreting the choice problem as being a choice over different strategies, with these being conditional choices. A simple illustration will make this clear. Consider Figure 13.3 which shows a simple dynamic choice problem: there are two decision (choice) nodes and two chance nodes. On the surface, it is not the same type of problem as that considered above. However, it can be transformed into a member of that class by redefining choice as choice over strategies; the members of this choice set consist of $(C_1; D_1, D_3)$, $(C_1; D_1, D_4)$, $(C_1; D_2, D_3)$, $(C_1; D_2, D_4)$ etc. (where $(C_1; D_1, D_3)$ for example denotes the choice of C_1 followed by D_1 or D_3 depending on the outcome of the chance node after C_1). Interpreted in this light, the problem appears as shown in Figure 13.4.

Now consider preference amongst strategies. According to our expected utility theorem, strategy $(C_1; D_1, D_3)$ is preferred to strategy $(C_1; D_2, D_3)$ if and only if

$$p_1 q_1 u(a_1) + p_1(1 - q_1)u(b_1) + (1 - p_1)q_3 u(a_3) + (1 - p_1)(1 - q_3)u(b_3)$$

$$> p_1 q_2 u(a_2) + p_1(1 - q_2)u(b_2) + (1 - p_1)q_3 u(a_3) + (1 - p_1)(1 - q_3)u(b_3)$$

This is so if and only if

$$q_2 u(a_1) + (1 - q_1)u(b_1) > q_2 u(a_2) + (1 - q_2)u(b_2)$$

But this is exactly the same condition as that implied by preference of choice D_1 over D_2 at the choice node (a) in Figure 13.3. We thus obtain the result that strategy $(C_1; D_1, D_3)$ is preferred to strategy $(C_1; D_2, D_3)$ (in Figure 13.4) if and only if choice D_1 is preferred to choice D_2 at node (a) in Figure 13.3. Generalizing, it follows that if D_1 is preferred to D_2 at (a) and D_3 is preferred to D_4 at (b), then of all the strategies in Figure 13.4 involving C_1, the most preferred must be $(C_1; D_1, D_3)$. Similarly, if D_5 is preferred to D_6 at (c) and D_7 to D_8 at (d), then $(C_2; D_5, D_7)$ is the most preferred of the strategies involving C_2. Finally, to decide whether $(C_1; D_1, D_3)$ is preferable to $(C_2; D_5, D_7)$ we compare

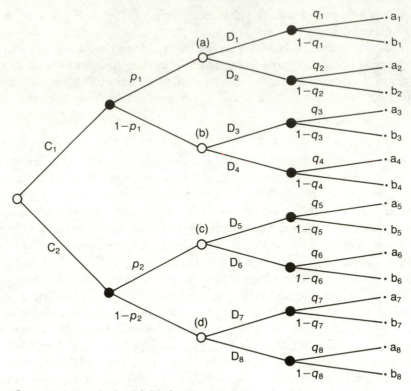

O   a choice node (and following upper-case letters indicate available choices)

●   a chance node (and following lower-case letters indicate (subjective) probabilities)

·   end points (and associated lower-case letters represent final consequences)

Figure 13.3

$$p_1 q_1 u(a_1) + p_1(1 - q_1)u(b_1) + (1 - p_1)q_3 u(a_3) + (1 - p_1)(1 - q_3)u(b_3)$$

with

$$p_2 q_5 u(a_5) + p_2(1 - q_5)u(b_5) + (1 - p_2)q_7 u(a_7) + (1 - p_2)(1 - q_7)u(b_7)$$

This is precisely as though we were imputing expected utility $q_1 u(a_1) + (1 - q_1)u(b_1)$ to node (a), expected utility $q_3 u(a_3) + (1 - q_3)u(b_3)$ to node (b) and so on.

The outcome of this line of reasoning is that we can use the expected utility theorem to solve the dynamic choice problem of Figure 13.3 by backward induction. We use the theorem to find the preferred choices, and the associated

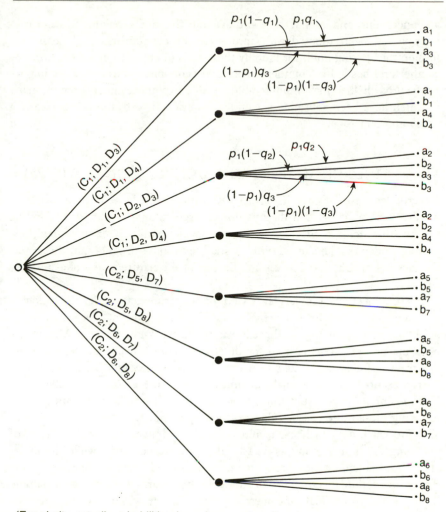

(For clarity not all probabilities have been entered)

Figure 13.4

expected utilities, at nodes (a), (b), (c) and (d). We then use these expected utilities in the theorem again to determine the preferred choice at the very first decision node. Moreover, this backward induction procedure is entirely equivalent to the solution based on the static version in Figure 13.4. In other words, we can apply the SEUT in dynamic problems through the use of backward induction.

This completes the brief account of the conventional wisdom. The reader will appreciate that it is both very simple and very profound: SEUT provides a simple comprehensive theory of economic decision-making under both risk and uncertainty and in both static and dynamic decision problems. Not surprisingly, it has been adopted with enthusiasm by economists in all fields, has formed the starting point for literally thousands of applications of one form or another and has led to countless articles in economics journals. More importantly, it has helped form innumerable testable hypotheses in economics, many of which have been substantiated under empirical investigation. It is clearly a very important theory.

13.3 EVIDENCE AGAINST THE CONVENTIONAL WISDOM

Nevertheless, SEUT has its critics. Recently, they have been growing in number – so much so that there is now a large volume of literature detailing various objections to SEUT and proposing alternative theories of decision-making under risk and uncertainty. I shall give some insights into these new theories below, but first I give some flavour of the nature of the objections to SEUT.

These objections are largely based on experimental evidence, which is described more fully in Chapter 29. To illustrate some of this evidence we shall find it helpful to use the expository device known as the Marschak–Machina triangle. This is used for illustrating choice over gambles involving just three possible final outcomes ($N = 3$ using our notation). Let A_1, A_2 and A_3 represent these three final outcomes, and let the associated probabilities be p_1, p_2 and p_3 respectively. Since $p_1 + p_2 + p_3 = 1$, it follows that any gamble involving these three can be fully specified by p_1 and p_3. Now consider Figure 13.5, in which a Marschak–Machina triangle is drawn. The probability p_1 of obtaining the best outcome is measured up the vertical axis, while the probability p_3 of obtaining the worst outcome is measured along the horizontal axis. Any point within the triangle, or along its boundaries, represents a gamble involving the three final outcomes: a point properly within the triangle represents a gamble with all three outcomes having a non-zero probability; a point on one of the boundaries (excluding the vertices) represents a gamble with one of the three probabilities zero; and each of the vertices represents a certainty (A_1 at V_1, A_2 at V_2 and A_3 at V_3).

In the usual fashion, we can represent an individual's preference ordering over the set of risky gambles involving these three outcomes by means of an indifference map in the triangle. If our individual acts in accordance with SEUT then his or her indifference curves are given by 'expected utility = constant', i.e.

$$p_1u(A_1) + p_1u(A_1) + p_3u(A_3) = k$$

where k is a constant. Since $p_1 + p_2 + p_3 = 1$, we can write this as

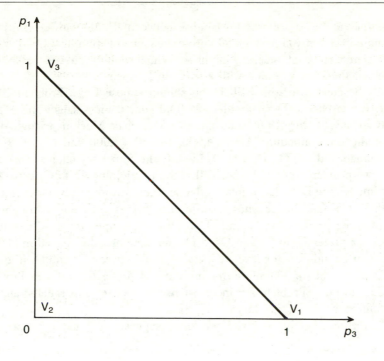

Figure 13.5

$$p_1 = \frac{p_3[u(A_2) - u(A_3)]}{u(A_3) - u(A_2)} + K \qquad (13.2)$$

where K is some other constant. This is clearly the equation of a straight line with slope $[u(A_2) - u(A_3)]/[u(A_1) - u(A_2)]$. Of course, this slope is constant within the triangle (where only the p are varying), and so the indifference map is a set of parallel straight lines. Furthermore, it can be shown that the more risk averse is the individual, the steeper will be these parallel straight-line indifference curves. Consider, for example, $A_1 = £100$, $A_2 = £50$ and $A_3 = £0$. Without loss of generality we can put $u(A_1) = 1$ and $u(A_3) = 0$. A risk-neutral person would have $u(A_2) = 0.5$ and hence indifference lines with slope 1, a moderately risk-averse person would have $u(A_2) = 0.6$, say, and hence indifference lines with slope $0.6/0.4 = 1.5$ and a very risk-averse person would have $u(A_2) = 0.9$, say, and hence indifference lines with slope $0.9/0.1 = 9$.

Now let us examine some of the empirical evidence which apparently conflicts with the predictions of SEUT. Consider the following two choice problems, in each of which a choice is to be made between the two options.

Problem 1 $C_1 = [£3,000; 1]$ $C_2 = [£4,000, £0; 0.8, 0.2]$
Problem 2 $D_1 = [£3,000, £0; 0.25, 0.75]$ $D_2 = [£4,000, £0; 0.2, 0.8]$

In Problem 1 you are asked to choose between £3,000 with certainty and a gamble in which you have an 80 per cent chance of winning £4,000 and a 20 per cent chance of receiving nothing. Which would you choose? Now ask yourself the same question with respect to Problem 2.

To be consistent with SEUT you should choose C_1 in Problem 1 if and only if you choose D_1 in Problem 2. (Did your choices satisfy this?) To see why consider Figure 13.6, which shows a Marschak–Machina triangle defined over the three amounts $(A_1=)$ £4,000, $(A_2 =)$ £3,000 and $(A_3 =)$ £0. The points labelled C_1, C_2, D_1 and D_2 identify the four risky choices specified in the two problems. It will be noted that the line joining C_1 to C_2 is parallel to the line joining D_1 to D_2. It follows that an agent whose behaviour is consistent with SEUT (and hence whose indifference curves are parallel straight lines) must either prefer C_1 to C_2 and D_1 to D_2 (for example, the solid indifference map), or prefer C_2 to C_1 and D_2 to D_1 (for example, the dashed indifference map), or be indifferent between C_1 and C_2 and between D_1 and D_2 (the dotted indifference map). Therefore, for instance, to prefer C_1 to C_2 in Problem 1 and D_2 to D_1 in Problem 2 is inconsistent with *any* set of parallel straight-line indifference curves, and hence with SEUT.

Unfortunately, the empirical evidence suggests that many people would

Figure 13.6

prefer C_1 to C_2 and D_2 to D_1, even after 'the error of their ways' is pointed out to them. In contrast, relatively few would prefer C_2 to C_1 and D_1 to D_2, while slightly fewer than 50 per cent would have preferences which are consistent with SEUT. This evidence suggests that some people's indifference curves are not parallel straight lines, but instead fan out across the triangle, being flatter at the bottom right and steeper at the upper left. This fanning-out hypothesis, articulated most eloquently by Machina (1987), obviously contradicts SEUT, which suggests that some alternative theory of decision-making under uncertainty should be sought by economists.

13.4 ALTERNATIVE THEORIES

An alternative theory would necessarily deny one or other of the axioms underlying SEUT. These were discussed above. The axiom which has come under most intense pressure – as being the one most relevant to the validity or otherwise of the fanning-out hypothesis – is the independence axiom. Let us reinterpret this axiom in the context of the triangle. First, however, we establish a very simple property of indifference lines in the triangle.

Consider Figure 13.7 and suppose that A and B are two points on the same indifference curve (so that our agent is indifferent between A and B). Let F be the gamble which yields A with probability q and B with probability

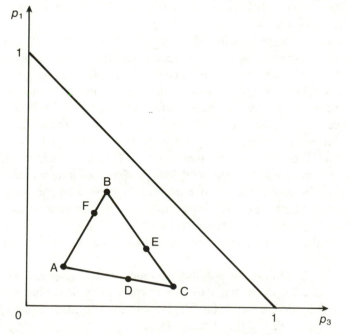

Figure 13.7

265

$1 - q$; geometrically F divides the line joining A to B in the ratio q to $1 - q$. Now, since (by construction) the individual is indifferent between A and B, then it seems trivial to argue that he or she must also be indifferent between F and A and B, since the choice of F leads to either A or B. This is the betweenness axiom. Thus the indifference curve through A and B must also pass through F. But q was chosen arbitrarily; it therefore follows that the indifference curve through A and B is the straight line joining A and B. The betweenness axiom therefore suffices to show that indifference curves in the triangle are straight lines. Let us now show how the independence axiom implies that these straight lines are parallel.

As before, consider Figure 13.7 and suppose that A and B are any two points on the same indifference curve. Let C be any other point within the triangle. Now suppose that D is defined as a gamble between A and C with respective probabilities p and $1 - p$, so that $D = [A, C; p, 1 - p]$. Geometrically, D divides the straight line joining A to C in the ratio p to $1 - p$. Similarly, define E as the gamble between B and C with respective probabilities p and $1 - p$, so that $E = [B, C; p, 1 - p]$. Again, geometrically, E divides the straight line joining B to C in the ratio p to $1 - p$. The independence axiom requires that, since A and B are indifferent, then D and E must also be indifferent. However, by elementary geometry, the line joining D to E is parallel to the line joining A to B. Hence the independence axiom implies that the straight-line indifference curves (implied by the betweenness axiom) are parallel straight lines.

It would seem reasonable to conclude that the fanning-out behaviour observed in experiments is not consistent with the independence axiom. This is what several researchers have concluded. In particular, Chew and MacCrimmon (see Chew 1983) have replace the (strong) independence axiom by the weak independence axiom which requires that, for A and B indifferent, there is for each q, a probability r for which $[A, C; q, 1 - q]$ and $[B, C; r, 1 - r]$ are indifferent. Note that strong independence requires that $r = q$. This leads to a modification (a generalization) of SEUT called weighted utility theory. Since the probability r in the weak independence condition is not dependent on C, it follows that the indifference curves implied by this weighted utility theory must be straight lines (again implied by the betweenness axiom) fanning out from a common point, as illustrated in Figure 13.8. This would be consistent with the empirical evidence cited above, and yet the theory would be empirically testable.

A further generalization is to drop any form of the independence axiom; this leads us back to straight-line indifference curves with no further restrictions, as illustrated in Figure 13.9. This is the indifference map implied by implicit expected utility theory (see Chew 1985).

We say 'no further restrictions' in the paragraph above, although this is not

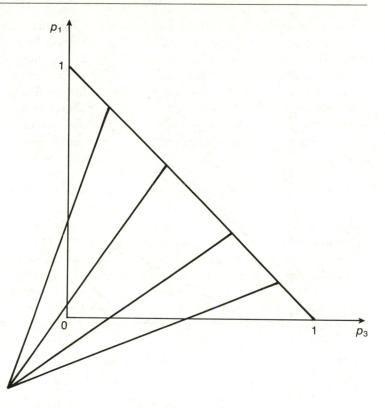

Figure 13.8

strictly the case: we assume that the indifference curves are upward sloping. However, this would seem to be minimally consistent with the requirement that A_1 is preferred to A_2 which is preferred to A_3.

Linearity of the indifference map is implied by the betweenness axiom. This seems harmless, and yet there are some who would deny it. Of particular interest is the theory discussed by Machina (1982) (generalized expected utility theory (GEUT), or 'SEUT without the independence axiom' to follow Machina himself). In contrast with the theories discussed above, Machina's approach is not axiomatic. Instead, he starts from the assumption that the individual has a well-defined preference ordering over the set of risky prospects. He then assumes that this preference order, which can be represented by a preference functional over this, is such that the functional is well behaved ('smooth') in a mathematical sense. Then, to make the theory testable, he imposes two hypotheses on the functional. The first, in essence, suggests that the implied indifference curves in the triangle are upward sloping; this appears harmless. The second, now immortalized in the literature as Machina's hypothesis two, implies the fanning-out hypothesis. Basically, the hypothesis is simply that the individual is more risk averse when faced with more attractive

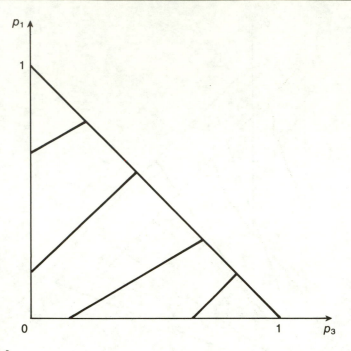

Figure 13.9

prospects; thus the indifference curves are steeper (display greater risk aversion) in the upper left-hand part of the triangle, and are flatter (display less risk aversion) in the bottom right-hand part of the triangle. Figure 13.10 illustrates thus.

Machina's GEUT, although it does not implicitly invoke the betweenness axiom, is an attractive theory: it is testable, and it explains a considerable part of the empirical evidence which appears to contradict SEUT. It explains the paradox discussed above, which is one of several variants of the Allais paradox. These variants are now generally referred to as either the common consequence effect or the common ratio effect. The paradox discussed above is an example of the latter; the original Allais paradox is an example of the former (for more details see Sugden 1986). However, one paradox that the Machina formulation cannot explain is the isolation effect.

Consider the example given by Kahneman and Tversky (1979). Two decision problems are presented.

Problem 3 In addition to whatever you own, you have been given 1,000. You are now asked to choose between $C_1 = [1,000, 0; 0.5, 0.5]$ and $C_2 = [500; 1]$
Problem 4 In addition to whatever you own, you have been given 2,000. You are now asked to choose between $D_1 = [-1,000, 0; 0.5, 0.5]$ and $D_2 = [-500; 1]$

In Kahneman and Tversky's experiments the majority of subjects chose C_2

268

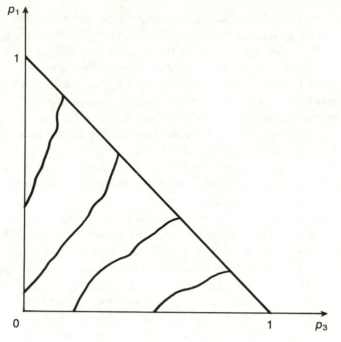

Figure 13.10

in Problem 3 and D_1 in Problem 4. However, note that in terms of final outcomes the two problems are identical. Specifically, $C_1 = [2,000, 1,000; 0.5, 0.5] = D_1$ and $C_2 = [1,500; 1] = D_2$. As Kahneman and Tversky remark, the majority behaviour is 'clearly inconsistent with utility theory'.

A similar problem arises with the preference reversal phenomenon. In this there are two risky prospects, conventionally called the P bet and the $ bet. The former has a high chance of winning a modest amount of money (and a small chance of losing an even more modest amount of money); the latter has a small chance of winning quite a large sum of money (and a high chance of losing a small sum of money). People are asked to say which they prefer. They are then asked to specify a certainty equivalent for each of the two bets: this is the smallest amount of money that they would be willing to pay to buy the bet. Let us denote these by C_P and $C_$$ respectively. The majority of people say that they prefer the P bet to the $ bet and yet they put C_P smaller than $C_$$. A very strange phenomenon! The main problem, of course, is that it implies lack of transitivity of the preference ordering over risky prospects, and hence denies the existence of a conventional indifference map in the triangle.

Two theories which claim to be able to explain both the preference reversal phenomenon and the isolation effect are prospect theory and regret theory. The first of these was one of the very earliest of the new alternative theories and was constructed in deliberate response to the experimental evidence discussed earlier (and presented in more detail in Chapter 29). In essence, it departs from SEUT in two respects: first, in asserting that probabilities are transformed before being used in the expected utility calculation (specifically with small probabilities being increased and large probabilities decreased); second, in postulating that the utility function is defined over changes in wealth from some given reference point (rather than over final wealth). This second characteristic enables the theory to account for the isolation effect; the first enables it to account for the preference reversal phenomenon.

In contrast, regret theory builds in (possible) intransitivities by deliberately being a theory of pairwise choice. Moreover, the theory builds upon the notion that, when one is choosing one of the two choices, one is also rejecting the other. This leaves open the possibility that the decision-maker may subsequently experience regret or rejoicing: the former if the actual decision led to a worse outcome than would have been the case if the other option had been chosen, and the latter if the actual decision led to a better outcome than would have been the case. According to Loomes and Sugden, the originators of regret theory, a rational decision-maker would take these potential emotions into account when taking the decision in the first case. Thus, instead of simply choosing the option that gave the highest expected utility, the decision-maker should maximize expected modified utility where the original utility is modified by these feelings of regret and rejoicing. Further details are given by Loomes and Sugden (1982, 1987).

All the above theories have taken the probabilities as given, and hence are implicitly theories of decision-making under risk. However, some of the theories – in particular those of the Machina (GEUT) and Kahneman and Tversky (prospect theory) – transform the probabilities before inserting them in some kind of expected utility function. This leads in turn to non-linear indifference curves in the Marschak–Machina triangle. (Note that the indifference curves in the triangle implied by regret theory with independent prospects are straight lines fanning out from a point outside the triangle, as with weighted utility theory.) In addition to these two theories (with non-linear indifference curves) there are a variety of other theories – under the general umbrella heading of expected utility theory with rank-dependent probability – in which the probabilities undergo some kind of transformation. One member of this class is my own economics of optimism and pessimism (Hey 1984), in which agents are presumed to increase the probabilities of favourable events and decrease the probabilities of unfavourable events if they are optimists and vice versa if they are pessimists. Other theories in this genre include Quiggin's anticipated utility theory and Yaari's dual expected utility. Segal (forthcoming) uses this type of theory to help explain the Ellsberg paradox (see p. 599).

One of the main difficulties involved with transforming the probabilities, and hence in working with preference functionals non-linear in the probabilities, is that one runs into difficulties with the reduction axiom. It will be recalled that this allows the theorist to collapse complicated multistage gambles into the (technically) equivalent single-stage gamble; more importantly, perhaps, it allows the generalization of SEUT to dynamic choice problems as discussed on p. 260. However, if preference is non-linearly related to the probabilities, then the theorist runs into severe difficulties with the reduction axiom, for preference now depends crucially on how the gambles are presented. This implicitly denies the reduction axiom (even though some theorists continue to operate with the reduction axiom despite dropping linearity, which seems to me to cause difficulties).

Realization that dropping the axioms underlying the SEUT is likely to cause difficulties with dynamic theories of choice under risk and uncertainty is slowly dawning on economists, and there are now a number of attempts to generalize the dynamic SEUT in similar ways to the various generalizations of static SEUT discussed above. Of particular concern is the modelling of any intrinsic desire for earlier or later resolution of uncertainty – SEUT essentially assumes that the decision-maker is indifferent about the timing of the resolution of uncertainty (except in so far as earlier resolution leads to greater opportunity for rescheduling plans). Ask yourself: do you like to know the outcome of some random event earlier (so as to get the uncertainty out of the way) or later (so that you can enjoy life before you know the outcome)? The question is not trivial. However, economists' attempts to model this are still not satisfactory.

Relatively untouched by research – at least in so far as progress is concerned – is the extension of the basic SEUT model to encompass genuine uncertainty as distinct from risk. Many economists are particularly unhappy about the reduction to risk of situations that they would regard as uncertain, but the consistency logic underlying the SEUT formulation requires this to be so. Some economists would like to think that some probability assessments are more uncertain than others, and there has been much talk of 'probabilities of probabilities'. However, under the SEUT axioms, these 'probabilities of probabilities' simply collapse to probabilities, especially with preference functionals linear in the probabilities.

The Ellsberg paradox neatly illustrates the source of such unease. In this, one ball is to be drawn at random from an urn containing ninety balls, of which thirty are known to be red (R) while sixty are some unknown combination of black (B) and yellow (Y). Now consider the two choice problems

Problem 5	C: win £100 if R drawn	D: win £100 if B drawn
Problem 6	C': win £100 if R or Y drawn	D': win £100 if B or Y drawn

The overwhelming empirical evidence shows that most people prefer C to D and D' to C'. This is a paradox (at least in the SEUT sense) in that the preference for C over D indicates that the agent has a subjective probability for R which is larger than that for B, while the preference for D' over C' indicates the contrary.

As noted above, Segal (forthcoming) has interpreted this as a problem connected with the reduction axiom. Others have connected it with the 'probabilities of probabilities' discussion above. There is less ambiguity related to the probability assessment of R and of (B ∪ Y), than to the probability assessment of B and of Y. In Problem 5 there is less ambiguity connected with the assessment of C than with D, while in Problem 6 there is less ambiguity connected with the assessment of D' than with C'. As yet, however, there is no consensus amongst economists about the appropriate modelling of such ambiguity.

13.5 CONCLUSIONS

As the preceding discussion shows, the economic theory of decision-making under risk and uncertainty is in a state of flux at present. While the practitioners continue to emphasize the conventional wisdom (SEUT) and to apply it to a whole host of economic problems (and there are few who would deny its normative appeal), the uncertainty theorists are actively reformulating the very foundations of the subject. At the moment, most attention is focused on the static theory of decision-making under risk, and most of the recent work has been connected with weakening the key axioms underlying SEUT, most crucially the independence axiom and the reduction axiom. A very useful paper for those readers wanting to learn more is that by Machina (1987) who builds on his earlier work (Machina 1982). Another useful survey along the same lines is that by Sugden (1986), while a deeper discussion along similar lines is given by Fishburn (1987). More detailed material, including further illustrations of indifference curves in the Marschak–Machina triangle, can be found in Camerer (1989) (who also presents a number of experimental tests of the various theories discussed above) and Weber and Camerer (1987). Material on dynamic decision-making is given by Chew and Epstein (1989), who rather belatedly take up the challenge laid down in earlier work by Kreps and Porteus (1978, 1979). The original Ellsberg paradox is presented in Ellsberg (1961), while a recent contribution to the ongoing debate on ambiguity is given by Hogarth and Kunreuther (1989). Both the latter paper and the paper by Camerer (1989) appeared in the new *Journal of Risk and Uncertainty*, which is entirely devoted to the discussion of the issues raised in this chapter. A closely related, but less economics-specific, journal is the new *Journal of Behavioral Decision Making*. This is an interdisciplinary journal, with contributions from political scientists, sociologists and psychologists as well as economists. Judging from the material reported on in this chapter, it may well be the case that economists need help from other disciplines in appropriately modelling uncertainty in economics.

REFERENCES

Camerer, C. F. (1989) 'An experimental test of several generalized utility theories', *Journal of Risk and Uncertainty* 2: 61–104.

Chew, S. H. (1983) 'A generalization of the quasilinear mean with applications to the measurement of income inequality and decision theory resolving the Allais paradox', *Econometrica* 51: 1065–92.

—— (1985) 'Implicit-weighted and semi-weighted utility theories, M-estimators and non-demand revelation of second-price auctions for an uncertain auctioned object', Working paper 155, Department of Economics, Johns Hopkins University.

Chew, S. H. and Epstein, L. G. (1989) 'The structure of preferences and attitudes towards the timing of the resolution of uncertainty', *International Economic Review* 30: 103–17.

Ellsberg, D. (1961) 'Risk, ambiguity and the Savage axioms', *Quarterly Journal of Economics* 75: 643–69.

Fishburn, P. C. (1987) 'Reconsiderations in the foundations of decision under uncertainty', *Economic Journal* 97: 825–41.

Hey, J. D. (1984) 'The economics of optimism and pessimism: a definition and some applications', *Kyklos* 37: 181–205.

Hogarth, R. M. and Kunreuther, H. (1989) 'Risk, ambiguity and insurance', *Journal of Risk and Uncertainty* 2: 5–36.

Kahneman, D. and Tversky, A. (1979) 'Prospect theory: an analysis of decision under risk', *Econometrica* 47: 263–91.

Kreps, D. M. and Porteus, E. L. (1978) 'Temporal resolution of uncertainty and dynamic choice theory', *Econometrica* 46: 185–200.

—— and —— (1979) 'Dynamic choice theory and dynamic programming', *Econometrica* 47: 91–100.

Loomes, G. C. and Sugden, R. (1982) 'Regret theory: an alternative theory of rational choice under uncertainty', *Economic Journal* 92: 805–24.

—— and —— (1987) 'Some implications of a more general form of regret theory', *Journal of Economic Theory* 41: 270–87.

Machina, M. J. (1982) ' "Expected utility" analysis without the independence axiom', *Econometrica* 50: 277–323.

—— (1987) 'Choice under uncertainty: problems solved and unsolved', *Journal of Economic Perspectives* 1: 121–54. Reprinted with alterations in Hey, J. D. (ed.) *Current Issues in Microeconomics*, London: Macmillan, 1989.

Segal, U. (forthcoming) 'The Ellsberg paradox and risk aversion: an anticipated utility approach', *International Economic Review*.

Sugden, R. (1986) 'New developments in the theory of choice under uncertainty', *Bulletin of Economic Research* 38: 1–24. Reprinted in Hey, J. D. and Lambert, P. J. (eds) *Surveys in the Economics of Uncertainty*, Oxford: Basil Blackwell, 1987.

Weber, M. and Camerer, C. F. (1987) 'Recent developments in modelling preferences under risk', *OR Spectrum* 9: 129–51.

14

STRATEGIC TRADE POLICY

W. MAX CORDEN

14.1 INTRODUCTION

In this chapter we review some recent developments in the theory of trade policy that are concerned with imperfect competition, strategic interactions as a result of oligopoly and economies of scale. All these developments have been described as 'the new international economics'. In the view of some they represent major breakthroughs. One purpose of this chapter is to examine how new some of this is and how it relates to the 'orthodox' theory. We shall focus on one major aspect of these developments, namely 'Brander–Spencer profit-shifting' and its policy implications. This is expounded in some detail in the next three sections. The conclusion is that it relates closely to the existing framework of the orthodox theory of trade policy.

The new developments are of two kinds. First, there are positive theories of international trade which take into account internal economies of scale and monopolistic competition and fit these into general equilibrium models. While one could not possibly suggest that economies of scale are new in international trade theory, since a huge literature list could be provided, the novelty has been in fitting economies of scale with monopolistic competition into a formal general equilibrium framework. A good reference which brings much of this material together is Helpman and Krugman (1985). We are not concerned with this topic here.

Second, there are theories which allow for oligopoly and strategic inter-actions among firms, and which introduce the idea that government policies, such as export subsidies or tariffs, may shift profits from a foreign firm to its domestic competitor, and that this may yield a national gain, at least provided that the foreign government does not retaliate. This 'profit-shifting' concept originated with a series of papers by Brander and Spencer (1981, 1983, 1984,

I am indebted to comments on an earlier draft from Isaiah Frank, Richard Pomfret, James Riedel and Richard Snape.

1985), and it has generated a large and highly sophisticated literature. This literature has led to an awareness of numerous qualifications of the theory and also to scepticism about its practical applicability. Apart from various articles to be referred to later, two comprehensive books on this subject are those of Krugman (1986) and Helpman and Krugman (1989).[1]

A genuinely new contribution to the theory of trade policy has been to allow for oligopoly and strategic interactions among private firms, as distinct from governments. A few earlier workers, notably Johnson (1953-4), have dealt with oligopolistic interactions among tariff-imposing governments in the theory of tariffs and retaliation. However, there has not been a hint of private sector oligopoly and strategic interactions in the formal 'pre-Brander-Spencer' trade theory literature.[2]

The motivation for the new developments has not, on the whole, been to advocate protection. As with so much earlier work in the field the aim has been, rather, to understand either what was actually happening or what some people were advocating. Here we should quote the pioneers.

> Finally, it should be emphasized that our arguments should not be taken as support for using tariffs. The highly tariff-ridden world economy that would result from each country maximising domestic welfare taking the policies of other countries as given would be a poor outcome. Our analysis is meant to contribute to an understanding of the motives that might underlie tariff policy, and provides support for the multilateral approach to trade liberalization.
>
> (Brander and Spencer 1984: 204)

While there have been plenty of occasions in the United States when protectionist policy proposals have been justified by what has been called 'strategic trade policy', these have not usually been based on the particular theories to be discussed here. Furthermore, the principal scholarly contributors in this new field have been quite clear about the limitations. The outstanding critique listing numerous objections, both theoretical and empirical, and above all on grounds of political economy, has come from Grossman (1986).

14.2 BRANDER–SPENCER PROFIT-SHIFTING THROUGH AN EXPORT SUBSIDY

A key model which originates with Brander and Spencer (1985) will now be expounded. This model, and a discussion of its qualifications, is also expounded by Helpman and Krugman (1989: ch. 5), and it is the central model in almost every survey of the subject. The principal qualifications were uncovered in a paper by Eaton and Grossman (1986), which is by now a minor classic. Here it will be shown, following a lead from Deardorff and Stern (1987), that this theory or model can be reinterpreted in terms of the orthodox theory of trade policy, and thus is one of the many special cases which orthodox theory illuminates.

Two firms, home-based and foreign-based, compete in a third market with a product not sold in either of their own markets. (Domestic consumption can be, and has been, introduced into the model, and it complicates the analysis but does not alter the main messages.) The number of firms is fixed, i.e. there is no entry in response to high profits. The model is set up so that all that matters for the national welfare of the two countries is the profits of the two firms net of subsidies or taxes. Wages are constant, as are (at the first stage of analysis) pre-tax profits elsewhere in the two economies. The aim of national policy is to shift profits away from the foreign firm towards the national firm, even though this may, incidentally, also shift income from the country's own taxpayers to the firms' owners. The market (i.e. the demand curve) for the combined output is fixed, and the consumers behave competitively. The government of the third country does not intervene. The greater the output of one firm, the less are the profits of the other.

A key assumption of the simplest version of the model is that the two firms 'play Cournot'. This crucial assumption has been varied, but we start with that case. It means that each firm determines its own output (equating perceived marginal revenue with marginal costs) on the assumption that the output of the other firm is fixed. Each firm faces a demand curve which is the total demand curve for the product in the third-country market minus the fixed output of the other firm. If the output of the other firm falls, its own output will rise (the marginal revenue curve shifts to the right) and its profits will increase. In Figure 14.1 marginal cost is assumed constant at OC (the simplest case), and the initial demand curve is DD and the marginal revenue curve is MR_0, so that the output of the home firm is initially XH_0. A decline in foreign output would shift the demand and marginal revenue curves to the right, hence moving the output equilibrium to the right (where the new marginal revenue curve crosses CC). Thus the home firm reacts to a change in the output of the foreign firm.

In this way the Cournot reaction curves of the two firms are derived in Figure 14.2, where FF is the foreign reaction curve (showing how XF varies as XH changes) and HH is the home reaction curve (showing how XH varies as XF changes). The Nash equilibrium is thus at N. The curve p_0 represents the profit level attained by the home firm at that point. Given foreign output XF_0 it maximizes profits at output XH_0.

Now suppose that the foreign reaction curve FF could indeed be taken as given, but that the aim is to maximize the profits of the home firm. In that case the home firm should choose output XH_1 (in Figure 14.2), which would bring the system to the Stackelberg equilibrium S where it reaches the highest profit level compatible with FF being given. This profit level is represented

Figure 14.1

Figure 14.2

by curve p_1. Immediately we ask: why does the firm not attain S? Why does the system reach N instead? The answer is that the home firm insists on 'playing Cournot'. In other words, the home firm conjectures that foreign output will not change when home output changes, i.e. the conjectural variation is zero, when actually it will change.

The next, and crucial, step in the argument is the suggestion that an export subsidy to the home firm will bring about the nationally optimal output S. In Figure 14.1 the subsidy lowers the cost curve to $C'C'$. This would increase home output even if foreign output stayed constant, but foreign output will actually decline (the demand curve shifts to the right), so that finally the output equilibrium in Figure 14.1 will be at J, yielding output XH_1. In Figure 14.2 the subsidy causes all the home country's equal profit curves to shift to the right, so that, given that the home firm continues to play Cournot, the home reaction curve moves to $H'H'$ and equilibrium is attained at the home country's optimum S.

We can immediately see the key assumption, and possibly the flaw, in this whole approach, and it is one which is familiar from the literature of game theory. Why is the home firm so unwise as to 'play Cournot', i.e. to assume that the foreign firm's output will not change when home output changes? In other words, why should there be a zero conjectural variation? The home firm must know that its own output will change whenever foreign output changes, so why should it ignore the same kind of reaction on the part of the foreign firm? If the government understands the model sufficiently to provide an appropriate export subsidy, why does the firm not understand it? This seems to be a very basic criticism but, for the moment, let us stick with this story and consider its significance in terms of orthodox trade theory.

Let us consider the orthodox terms-of-trade argument for protection, which can be interpreted as an argument for an export tax. This argument assumes a given foreign demand (or offer) curve, i.e. a foreign reaction curve taking general equilibrium effects into account, but also assumes that this demand curve does not shift strategically to deter an export tax at home. Thus it assumes absence of foreign retaliation. Let DD be this demand curve in Figure 14.1. The argument then goes very simply. Competitive producers will choose equilibrium E because each of them perceives its marginal revenue to be equal to price. However, the socially optimum equilibrium, which exploits the home country's monopoly power, is at A. Of course, if exporting were monopolized by a single firm it would naturally choose this point. But given competition, a tax equal to AG has to be imposed, and the price rises (the terms of trade improve) from E to G.

In the language of orthodox theory there is a trade distortion or divergence because the private and social marginal revenue curves diverge. This is called a '*trade* divergence' (Corden 1974: 31–2) to distinguish it from a 'domestic divergence' or distortion, which in this case would involve a divergence between the private and social marginal cost curves. Now what happens in the present model?

There is indeed also a 'trade divergence', but this time it causes exports to be too low rather than too high. This time there is a single producer at home so that the issue on which the orthodox terms-of-trade argument focuses disappears. This time the Cournot-playing home producer sees ('conjectures') an incorrect foreign demand curve, which fails to take into account the foreign output changes that its own changes in output provoke.

The correct demand curve is $D'D'$ (which is more elastic than DD), and the marginal revenue curve derived from it would determine equilibrium at H. The true optimal output is thus XH_1. If the firm perceived this demand curve, its conjectures would be 'consistent'. As Deardorff and Stern (1987: 50) have pointed out, 'there is in a sense a distortion here'. There is an imperfection of private information or in the private firm's understanding, and the government is assumed to know better.

It is worth stressing that the concept of a 'trade divergence' means only that the privately perceived marginal revenue curve diverges from the correct social curve, and not that intervention must be trade restricting and so improve the terms of trade. In this particular case the home country is made better off by a policy that increases exports and so worsens its terms of trade (from G to K in Figure 14.1). It is also worth noting that the idea that an argument for intervention can be based on a distortion that results from 'imperfection of private information' is very familiar.

I make no claim for originality, but draw attention to a section in Corden (1974: 252–3) which refers to the infant industry argument and is entitled 'Imperfection of private information'. It gives a detailed analysis of one basis for the popular infant industry argument and includes the following sentences which exactly apply to the present argument: 'But the case is not really very strong. First-best policy is for the state to spread more information. . . . Why should the private firm (or state enterprise) concerned have less information for the prospects for its own cost curves than a central state authority?' In the present case we would want to refer to 'prospects for demand' or 'behaviour of its foreign competitor' rather than cost curves.

In the orthodox terms-of-trade argument for a tariff or an export tax, optimal intervention has an adverse effect on the foreign country; hence it is 'exploitative'. This is also true in the present case with regard to the foreign competitor, although not with regard to the third – the consuming – country. The latter actually benefits when producing countries subsidize exports – a well-known proposition.[3]

The next step in the analysis worked out by Brander and Spencer is to allow the foreign government to subsidize exports also, taking as given not only the Cournot behaviour of the two firms but also the export subsidy of the home government. In other words, first the two governments and then the two firms play Cournot. The two governments know all about the behaviour of the two firms, but still, surprisingly, play the Cournot game with each other. Here it must be stressed that Brander and Spencer, together with the other principal contributors in this field, are aware of the difficulties and qualifications.

The general problems are much the same as in the theory of 'optimum tariffs and retaliation' as pioneered by Scitovsky (1941) and developed by Johnson (1953), and indeed, more generally, as developed in the theory of oligopoly. Ideas from dynamic game theory need to be used. An excellent review is given by Dixit (1987a).

Coming back to the simple case where the foreign government does not intervene, one point that was made by Eaton and Grossman (1986) and is given prominence by Helpman and Krugman (1989) is particularly important. If there is more than one domestic firm, a case for an export tax may be restored. The domestic firms compete with each other and generate external diseconomies for each other by lowering the price that all of them obtain on the third-country market. Hence there is a case for restraining them somewhat in their exporting. This is just the orthodox terms-of-trade argument for protection. The more domestic firms there are, the closer the model approaches the perfectly competitive form and the standard optimal tariff or export tax formula. As these authors point out, in a model with several home and foreign firms, all playing Cournot, there could, on balance, be a case for either an export tax or an export subsidy. However, this consideration does not, in itself, destroy the Brander–Spencer profit-shifting argument. Rather, it shows that there are several considerations affecting a net trade divergence, and hence possibly justifying intervention, of which their profit-shifting argument is a new one.

Everything clearly hinges on the 'conjectures' of the firms about each other's reactions. Cournot implies zero conjectures. 'Consistent conjectures', i.e. conjectures that turn out to be correct, by the home firm about the given foreign reaction curve would remove the case for intervention, other than the orthodox case for an export tax, with all its limitations. However, there are many possibilities about the conjectures, apart from zero and consistent conjectures. Thus the demand curve that the home firm perceives may take into account expected reactions of the foreign competitor, but not enough, or perhaps too much. If the government knows better, there is then, conceivably, a case for intervention, or at least for the education of the domestic producer by the government. However, since the producer might just as well overestimate the foreign reaction as underestimate it, there can be a case for an export tax even on these grounds.

Eaton and Grossman (1986) uncovered the following point which at first appeared rather devastating. Suppose that the firms 'played Bertrand' rather than Cournot. This means that each assumes that the other's price rather than quantity is given. They then show that optimal intervention will be an export tax and not a subsidy, with the intervention of each firm thus benefiting the other firm (intervention no longer being 'exploitative') although it will, of course, hurt consumers. In terms of our exposition it means that the 'true' demand curve D′D′ in Figure 14.1 is steeper rather than flatter than the perceived demand curve DD. Since Bertrand competition seems as plausible (or implausible) as Cournot competition, this insight introduces a major uncertainty not just about the magnitude but about the sign of the intervention that may be called for.

14.3 A SUBSIDY FOR CREDIBILITY: AN INFANT INDUSTRY ARGUMENT

Let us now discuss a different approach, which also originated with Brander and Spencer and which has a superficial similarity to the model just expounded – indeed the two appear to be confused in some papers. It is actually a more convincing approach, although it still has serious limitations. This time we assume that the two firms have as much knowledge as governments, and while they may be uncertain about each other's reaction they 'know the model'.

As before, each firm would gain from a decline in the other firm's output. In the extreme case, owing to economies of scale, there may be room for only one firm. The extreme case, usually given as the Boeing-Airbus story, is very special and it is better to stay within the existing model here. The position then is that each firm would like to fix its own output credibly and firmly and thus force the other firm to adapt its output to this. For example, in Figure 14.2, if the home firm fixed output XH_1 credibly, the foreign firm would choose point S on FF, and the home firm would then have maximized its profits given the predictable foreign reaction. Alternatively, the foreign firm might fix its output credibly, forcing the home firm to adapt and so reaching the foreign firm's Stackelberg point S′′ on HH. This is a true dynamic game theory situation – a true problem of strategy – analysed in the industrial organization literature.

The question then is: how can a firm achieve credibility in its output determination (making it clear that it will not change its output, whatever the other does) and so force the other to adapt to it? One answer is that it achieves a 'first-mover' situation, for example through installing capacity in advance of the other. However, there are always uncertainties in this game, and hence potential costs of competing in the effort to achieve this credibility. Finally both may lose, so that there is an incentive to collaborate in some form.

Where does trade policy come in? The basic idea is now that an export subsidy, or the promise of one, would give the home firm credibility in its output determination. I have not seen the next steps in the argument spelt out very carefully. Whatever the foreign output, the firm would have to be subsidized to cover its potential losses. The subsidy should be provided only on the condition that XH_1 is produced and might be scaled to the output of the foreign firm (disregarding practical aspects of this!), so that if the foreign firm actually chooses S, i.e. if credibility is successfully established and the foreign reaction has been correctly estimated, no subsidy would actually be paid. The enforcement by the government and the provision of the subsidy would have to be credible even if foreign output rose so that a large subsidy would have to be paid.

We have here a kind of infant industry argument that should be analysed in those terms. We might ask why a firm has to be underwritten by the government. Why can it not go on the capital market and borrow the necessary funds or obtain credit lines to underwrite possible losses? Presumably the more financial resources it has available, the more credible its threat or output decisions will be. This is an obvious and familiar point. And the US capital market, for which this theory is designed, is hardly imperfect – even though imperfection of the capital market is a familiar basis for an infant industry argument applying to developing countries.

The answer might be that strengthening the firm's financial resources would not give the firm complete credibility. It might be able to obtain the resources to sustain its output even if the foreign firm failed to respond by reducing *its* output, but it may not have the incentive to keep its output at the desired level (at S) at all costs. This is indeed correct. The argument is that, for some reason, the government has more credibility. It would hang on, even when a firm on its own would not. It would hang on even when it becomes probable that there would be a net loss for the country. The firm has the incentive because the subsidy would be conditional on sufficient output being maintained. In the extreme model, where only one of the two firms can survive, the subsidy would be conditional on the firm's staying in business.

The suggestion that a government has so much credibility is surely implausible. The suggestion is that, even when large subsidy payments are being made because the foreign firm has refused to give way, the government would continue to provide funds. In any case, the main conclusion is that this version of the argument – where the home and the foreign governments possibly compete in underwriting their firms' losses in the process of international competition – is a special case of the infant industry argument. The argument is logically sound and is an 'infant exporter argument'.[+]

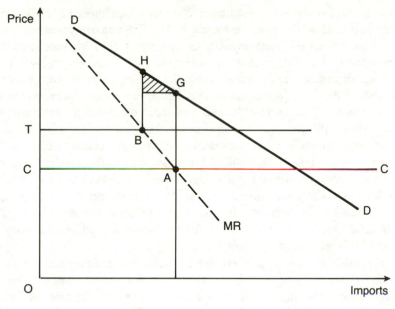

Figure 14.3

14.4 THE CASE FOR A TARIFF WITH MONOPOLY AND OLIGOPOLY

Brander and Spencer (1984) have also applied the profit-shifting approach to the case of a tariff. Can a country gain from a tariff when there is oligopoly, a foreign firm and a home firm competing in the home market (with two products that are imperfect substitutes), and when the foreign government is passive? As usual, Cournot competition or something similar is assumed. This is clearly a highly relevant issue since it represents a direct development of the massive literature of orthodox theory concerned with the gains and losses from tariffs in the absence of retaliation. We know that there can be a gain from intervention of some kind when there is either (or both) a trade divergence – an intervention possibly leading to an improvement in the terms of trade – or a domestic distortion such as an excess of price over marginal cost owing to monopoly. Is there more to it than that?

We might start by seeing what the implications are of having a simple monopoly either as foreign supplier or domestic producer. This means drawing on earlier literature. The following simple model is due to Katrak (1977) and Svedberg (1979). In Figure 14.3 DD is the home demand curve for a product supplied by a foreign monopolist, and MR is the marginal revenue curve. The monopolist's marginal cost curve is CC, which is assumed to be constant here. In the absence of intervention the output equilibrium is at A and the price is at G. A tariff of CT is then imposed. It raises the marginal cost of the monopolist and in the new equilibrium the output equilibrium is at B, output having fallen, while the price has risen to H. The country's terms of trade improve because of the tariff revenue per unit and decline because of the rise in price. With a linear demand curve as drawn, and as assumed by Katrak and Svedberg, there is an improvement. Brander and Spencer (1984) show that the slopes of the demand and marginal revenue curves are crucial, which can be seen from the diagram. Only if the demand curve is flatter than the marginal revenue curve will there be an improvement.

There must be the familiar consumption–cost of protection triangle, which is shaded in the diagram. The optimal tariff clearly must take this into account. However, if the conditions for a terms-of-trade improvement are fulfilled, there is bound to be a gain from a small tariff, i.e. the optimal tariff is positive.

In any case, we have here a familiar terms-of-trade argument for a tariff which would turn into an argument for an import subsidy if the marginal revenue curve were relatively flatter.

Now consider the situation where there is a single domestic producer, actual or potential, subject to economies of scale, but there are no potential terms-of-trade effects, the import price being given (small-country model). This is the model due to Corden (1967) and Snape (1977). In this model there can be a gain from a subsidy to domestic production because price initially exceeds marginal cost at home, reflecting the familiar domestic distortion of underconsumption of the product of a monopoly. While the subsidy leads to replacement of imports by dearer home output – which is the standard loss from protection – it also leads to increased consumption at home.

In Corden (1967) a tariff could not have a favourable effect because the domestic and the foreign product were assumed to be perfect substitutes, so that a tariff would actually reduce domestic consumption. However, in Snape (1977) the two products are differentiated, so that a tariff would lead to less consumption of the imported product and more of the home-produced one. The latter effect taken on its own represents a gain, given that (because there was monopoly) price must initially have exceeded marginal cost. Helpman and Krugman (1989) call this the 'production efficiency gain' of a tariff, and it refers to the reduction or elimination of one of the standard domestic distortions, namely that caused by having a domestic monopoly which tends to underproduce relative to the social optimum.

The earlier literature has thus provided two ingredients in an analysis of the effects of a tariff in the presence of oligopoly with product differentiation: first, that a tariff may squeeze the profits of the foreign firm and so improve the terms of trade; second, that it may lead to higher consumption of the domestic product, hence offsetting the domestic distortion of underconsumption caused by price exceeding marginal cost.

The profit-sharing effect proposed by Brander and Spencer (1984) rests essentially on the same kind of analysis as that expounded earlier with regard to the case for an export subsidy. They show that, when a tariff causes domestic production to replace imports, profits will shift towards the domestic firm and there will be a gain on that account. The interesting question is whether this effect is additional to the two effects just noted, or whether it is really an element in the terms-of-trade effect. On the basis of the analysis in Helpman and Krugman (1989: ch. 6) it seems that it must be reflected in the terms-of-trade gain, but, as they point out, it strengthens the possibility that there is such a gain. The point appears to be that the price that the foreign producer charges home consumers is likely to rise less when domestic production is increased as a result of the tariff (the true demand curve is more elastic in Figure 14.3) than when such import substitution does not take place.

14.5 TARIFFS FOR EXPORT PROMOTION

At this point we should note a widely cited paper by Krugman (1984) which also seems to make a case for a tariff in an oligopoly model but which introduces the additional consideration that a tariff may lead not just to replacement of imports by domestic production but also to fostering of exports.

Two firms compete in various markets, including the home market. Their method of competition is Cournot. They are subject to economies of scale. The home government then protects its own firm in the home market. This might be regarded as a kind of subsidization. Naturally, this shifts profits away from the foreign firm, just as it does in the Brander–Spencer model. The home firm's marginal costs fall, and the foreign firm reduces output and its marginal costs rise. This will cause the home firm to increase exports. Krugman thus shows that import protection acts as an export promotion device.

The question is whether this conclusion really depends on the assumption of Cournot oligopoly. Krugman writes: 'The idea that a protected domestic market gives firms a base for successful exporting is one of those heterodox arguments, common in discussions of international trade, which are incomprehensible in terms of standard models yet seem persuasive to practical men' (Krugman 1984: 191). In fact, the idea that a tariff can promote exports is familiar from the theory of dumping, which goes back to the 1920s. With regard to precise policy implications we might recall the work of Pursell and Snape (1973), who dealt with the same issue and also assumed economies of scale. Pursell and Snape assumed that there is a single domestic firm facing given world import and export prices, i.e. they used the small-country model. They found that a tariff may make discriminating monopoly possible for the first time, allowing prices at home to be raised and getting exports started.

Hence it is not necessary to assume oligopoly to obtain this result. Pursell and Snape (1973: 90) showed that a tariff will never be optimal in their case but 'there may be a case for a subsidy to enable the firm to set up (and export) . . .'. However, it appears from Helpman and Krugman (1989) that in the Cournot oligopoly case a tariff could be optimal from the point of view of the home country, assuming that the foreign government does not react. Actually, Pursell and Snape seem to be on stronger ground than Krugman (1984). In the small-country model, we need not allow for the reactions of either a foreign firm or a foreign government, whether Cournot or strategic. The model is actually not far from reality. In the Krugman model we have not only the familiar myopic Cournot behaviour of the two firms but also the passivity of the foreign government.[5]

14.6 CONCLUSION: IS THERE A NEW INTERNATIONAL ECONOMICS?

There has been a proliferation of models with oligopoly and profit-shifting, building on the pioneering work of Brander and Spencer, and contributors in this field are now beginning to go beyond static models of the Cournot type. It is not possible to expound all these models here. A fundamental problem is that each model seems to be a special case leading to particular results, depending on the size of various parameters and so on. There has been little search for general principles, and certainly no new paradigm has emerged so far. There is a new and highly sophisticated literature here, and also a significant new idea – namely the role of trade policy in 'profit-shifting' between oligopolistic firms – but since there is not a new paradigm there is certainly no 'new international economics'.

Recent developments, and many models, are surveyed by Dixit (1987a). The work is continuing. As Dixit says: 'It is premature to draw confident or firm policy implications from such an unfinished and ongoing body of research.' He also guesses that 'research on static models of oligopolistic trade and trade policy has more or less run its course. But dynamics remains a rich area for research' (Dixit 1987a: 354). A beginning has been made with empirical work, some of which is surveyed by Helpman and Krugman (1989: ch. 8) who also discuss the problems of quantification. However, Dixit (1987a: 359) concludes correctly that 'empirical work has lagged behind, and it needs to be improved greatly in both quality and quantity if we are to have a better idea of the scope and significance of these theoretical advances'. Actually, he has reported one of the most interesting pieces of empirical work in Dixit (1987b), where he applies the theory to the rivalry between US and Japanese firms in the automobile market, allowing for the use of both a tariff and a production subsidy. No doubt more empirical work is needed if this whole approach is not to be dropped completely (as possibly it should be).

Krugman (1987) has suggested that, in some sense, the new developments

replace existing trade theory or, at least, require a radical change in conclusions. These opinions are hedged, but the implication has been that existing
theory (pre-'new theory') rests on the assumption of perfect competition and
has led to the conclusion that, subject to minor qualifications, free trade is
best. In contrast, he has suggested that the new approach alters the structure
of the theory so fundamentally that the theoretical presumption in favour of
free trade disappears. It is suggested that the principal reason why free trade
is still not *passé* is based on political economy grounds. Therefore it is as well
to remind ourselves of the characteristics of the established theory of trade
policy as it has developed over a long period, possibly using Meade (1955) as
the starting point.

It does not argue that 'free trade is best'. If I may again quote myself:

> Theory does not 'say' – as is often asserted by the ill-informed or the badly
> taught – that 'free trade is best'. It says that, *given certain assumptions*, it is 'best'.
> Appreciation of the assumptions under which free trade or alternatively any
> particular system of protection or subsidization is best, or second-best, third-best,
> and so on, is perhaps the main thing that should come out of this book.
>
> (Corden 1974)

This comes from the introduction to Corden (1974), a book which then
goes on to analyse numerous arguments for trade intervention and for direct
subsidization of some kind, and to show under what circumstances various
interventions may be first best, second best and so on. At the end of the book
(Corden 1974: 412–14) I listed ten circumstances in which trade interventions
might (possibly, but not certainly) be first best. In the light of the new developments, a new edition of this book would no doubt have to list an eleventh
reason.

My conclusion is that the new developments represent elaborations that fit
into the existing framework, and will do so more once results from the new
developments become clearer. It will be possible to show that there are various
ways of dealing with oligopoly-induced distortions, which can be ranked
according to their welfare effects, and that in some cases trade policies or
direct subsidies or taxes could be first best, assuming no possible retaliation
by foreign governments and disregarding political economy and information
considerations. If retaliation is possible, i.e. if governments engage in strategic
interactions, the new developments will represent elaborations of the existing
body of 'tariffs and retaliation' theory.

Of course, political economy and the information problem cannot be disregarded and have actually persuaded most major contributors to the new literature, notably Grossman (1986), of the undesirability of basing interventionist
policies on these new theories. The information problems of engaging in
optimal intervention to offset the distorting effects of oligopoly appear to be

overwhelming.[6] However, political economy and information considerations also yield arguments against using the existing 'domestic distortion' theories to justify fine-tuning intervention policies, whether tariffs or subsidies. Indeed, the most important development in the theory of trade policy is concerned with the political economy of trade policy. It is no longer readily assumed that a regime in which interventions through trade policies or through more direct subsidies are customary or made easy will actually lead to policies that are nationally optimal. In a way it is surprising that so much of the sophisticated new work reviewed here should have been devoted to uncovering complex circumstances when intervention of some kind may be justified, ignoring information and political economy problems. After all, existing theory has already uncovered a mass of such circumstances, and is legitimately subject to the criticism of underplaying, if not ignoring, the information and political economy problems. For this reason the 'new' theories, while making some contribution, could be criticized as being really rather old-fashioned.

NOTES

1 Deardorff and Stern (1987) give an excellent survey of many of the issues, very much in the spirit of the present chapter. A comprehensive survey, with many references, which also discusses the broader issues, is that of Stegemann (1989). Other surveys of aspects of the subject, apart from those cited in the text, are Dixit (1984), Grossman and Richardson (1985), Greenaway and Milner (1986: ch. 12), Caves (1987) and Richardson (1989). With regard to policy implications, in particular, see Bhagwati (1989), who concludes 'I am strongly opposed to strategic trade policymaking: whether to shift profits to oneself or to retaliate against rivals allegedly doing this'.

2 It is the private oligopoly aspect (in practice, duopoly) which is new, not the absence of perfect competition. There have been many earlier contributions to the theory of trade policy that have allowed for private monopoly, whether domestic or foreign, and for internal economies of scale. See Bhagwati (1965) on the equivalence between tariffs and quotas and Corden (1974) which contains a whole chapter entitled 'Monopoly, market structure and economies of scale'. In the latter economies of scale also enter the discussion of the infant industry argument for protection, as they do in earlier literature. Some other relevant papers that allow for private monopoly are referred to later.

3 In the orthodox terms-of-trade argument a trade tax is Pareto inefficient from a world (although not a national) point of view, assuming perfect competition and absence of domestic distortions that have not been offset by appropriate subsidies or taxes. In this case, given private oligopoly, free trade is not necessarily Pareto efficient from a world point of view. It is just possible that a policy which benefits the home country and hurts its foreign competitor leads to a cosmopolitan Pareto improvement.

4 There are familiar problems when an industry is subsidized directly or indirectly on infant industry grounds. One consideration is that income is redistributed from taxpayers to the owners and probably also the employees of the industries concerned. Interventions that can possibly be justified on Pareto efficiency grounds have inevitable redistributive effects which may well be undesirable. Another familiar qualification is that the need to raise taxes to pay for subsidies creates inevitable distortions. In all the cases discussed here where a subsidy is actually paid (or the risk is run that one would have to be paid), these problems or objections arise. It is hard to believe that an income redistribution from taxpayers in general towards domestic oligopolies competing in international markets would be regarded either as neutral or favourable.

5 The latter assumption could perhaps be justified if the aim is to explain Japanese government intervention in the face of a passive US government.

6 Spencer (1986) provides a list of characteristics required for an industry to be considered for targeting, i.e. for its exports to be subsidized. It should also be recalled here that in other writings the originators of this body of theory, Brander and Spencer, did not really advocate protection on the basis of their analysis because of the possibility of retaliation and hence the ultimately adverse effects on all countries that a strategic trade policy regime would entail.

REFERENCES

Bhagwati, J. (1965) 'On the equivalence of tariffs and quotas', in R. Caves, H. Johnson, and P. Kenen (eds) *Trade, Growth, and the Balance of Payments*, Amsterdam: North-Holland.

—— (1989) 'Is free trade *passé* after all?', *Weltwirtschaftliches Archiv* 125: 17–44.

Brander, J. and Spencer, B. (1981) 'Tariffs and the extraction of foreign monopoly rents under potential entry', *Canadian Journal of Economics* 14: 371–89.

—— and —— (1983) 'International R&D rivalry and industrial strategy', *Review of Economic Studies* 50: 707–22.

—— and —— (1984) 'Tariff protection and imperfect competition', in H. Kierzkowski (ed.) *Monopolistic Competition and International Trade*, Oxford: Oxford University Press.

—— and —— (1985) 'Export subsidies and international market share rivalry', *Journal of International Economics* 18: 83–100.

Caves, R. E. (1987) 'Industrial policy and trade policy: the connections', in H. Kierzkowski (ed.) *Protection and Competition in International Trade*, Oxford: Basil Blackwell.

Corden, W. M. (1967) 'Monopoly, tariffs and subsidies', *Economica* 34: 50–8.

—— (1974) *Trade Policy and Economic Welfare*, Oxford: Oxford University Press.

Deardorff, A. and Stern, R. (1987) 'Current issues in trade policy: an overview', in R. Stern (ed.) *U. S. Trade Policies in a Changing World Economy*, Cambridge, MA: MIT Press.

Dixit, A. (1984) 'International trade policy for oligopolistic industries', *Economical Journal (Supplement)* 94: 1–16.

—— (1987a) 'Strategic aspects of trade policy', in T. Bewley (ed.) *Advances in Economic Theory – Fifth World Congress*, Cambridge: Cambridge University Press.

—— (1987b) 'Tariffs and subsidies under oligopoly: the case of the U. S. automobile industry', in H. Kierzkowski (ed.) *Protection and Competition in International Trade*, Oxford: Basil Blackwell.

Eaton, J. and Grossman, G. M. (1986) 'Optimal trade and industrial policy under oligopoly', *Quarterly Journal of Economics* 101: 383–406.

Greenaway, D. and Milner, C. (1986) *The Economics of Intra-industry Trade*, Oxford: Basil Blackwell.

Grossman, G. M. (1986) 'Strategic export promotion: a critique', in P. Krugman (ed.) *Strategic Trade Policy and the New International Economics*, Cambridge, MA: MIT Press.

Grossman, G. M. and Richardson, J. D. (1985) 'Strategic trade policy: a survey of issues and early analysis', *Special Papers in International Economics* No. 15.

Helpman, E. and Krugman, P. (1985) *Market Structure and Foreign Trade*, Cambridge, MA: MIT Press.

—— and —— (1989) *Trade Policy and Market Structure*, Cambridge, MA: MIT Press.

Johnson, H. G. (1953–4) 'Optimum tariffs and retaliation', *Review of Economic Studies* 21: 142–53.

Katrak, H. (1977) 'Multi-national monopolies and commercial policy', *Oxford Economic Papers* 29: 283–91.

Krugman, P. (1984) 'Import protection as export promotion: international competition in the presence of oligopoly and economies of scale', in H. Kierzkowski (ed.) *Monopolistic Competition and International Trade*, Oxford: Oxford University Press.

—— (ed.) (1986) *Strategic Trade Policy and the New International Economics*, Cambridge, MA: MIT Press.

—— (1987) 'Is free trade *passé*?', *Economic Perspectives* 1: 131–44.

Meade, J. E. (1955) *The Theory of International Economic Policy*, vol. 2, *Trade and Welfare*, London: Oxford University Press.

Pursell, G. and Snape, R. H. (1973) 'Economies of scale, price discrimination and exporting', *Journal of International Economics* 3: 85–92.

Richardson, J. D. (1989) 'Empirical research on trade liberalisation with imperfect competition: a survey', *OECD Economic Studies* 12: 7–50.

Snape, R. H. (1977) 'Trade policy in the presence of economies of scale and product variety', *Economic Record* 53: 525–34.

Spencer, B. (1986) 'What should trade policy target?', in P. Krugman (ed.) *Strategic Trade Policy and the New International Economics*, Cambridge, MA: MIT Press.

Stegemann, K. (1989) 'Policy rivalry among industrial states: what can we learn from models of strategic trade policy?', *International Organization* 43: 73–100.

Svedberg, P. (1979) 'Optimal tariff policy on imports from multinationals', *Economic Record* 55: 64–7.

15

RECENT DEVELOPMENTS IN MONETARY THEORY

RONALD MACDONALD AND ROSS MILBOURNE

15.1 INTRODUCTION

Monetary theory has undergone a remarkable change in the 1980s. The most important change has been in the method of analysis that is now used by the majority of economists investigating questions concerned with monetary theory. Generally speaking, in 1975 the monetary theory literature was of two types. A small literature beginning at the level of the individual agent (called the microfoundations literature) was concerned with why money was a useful commodity. However, most monetary theory, surveyed by Barro and Fischer (1976), effectively took it for granted that money was a useful commodity and proceeded to examine the optimal quantity of money holdings and the magnitude of income and interest rate elasticities. This analysis was in the context of aggregative models; any choice-theoretical models were generally partial equilibrium and were used to justify particular aggregative relationships.

The common theme of monetary theory in the 1980s has been the use of general equilibrium models which have as their foundation a representative agent solving a (generally intertemporal) optimization problem. One interpretation is that these models start from a general equilibrium Arrow–Debreu model (described later) and implant missing markets to generate a role for money. In this sense they are related to the microfoundations literature of the 1970s (also described later), but they are directed towards answering the questions of the aggregative macromodels. Not surprisingly, the answer, and the phenomenon explored, are different.

In this chapter we attempt to put the more important new themes into perspective; thus, we present a thematic survey rather than a literature survey (which is dealt with by Fischer's (1988) update of Barro and Fischer (1976)).

The authors would like to thank Mike Artis, David Backus, Jack Leach and the editors for comments. Research assistance for this paper was provided from a Special Research Grant from the University of New South Wales which is gratefully acknowledged.

We look at the common ground of choice-theoretical general equilibrium models, and explain their main ideas intuitively. Monetary theory naturally spills over into international finance and macroeconomics. Since these topics are dealt with elsewhere in this volume, we do not specifically concentrate on them except where they are directly relevant.

In the next section we discuss the structure of representative agent models. This includes a discussion of overlapping generations models which leads into a discussion of why money is held. We also discuss some related theory on asset prices. In Section 15.3 we deal with banking regulation and financial intermediation, and in Section 15.4 we discuss monetary policy credibility. Whilst we concentrate on these dominant new themes of the 1980s, some work has continued within the aggregative model approach, and we briefly mention these new developments and give concluding comments in Section 15.5.

15.2 REPRESENTATIVE AGENT MODELS

Most models of monetary economies of the 1980s, which attempt to explain aggregate phenomena, begin at the microeconomic level. A useful starting point is to consider an infinitely lived representative agent. If c_t denotes consumption during period t, $u(c_t)$ denotes the utility from that consumption and δ denotes the rate at which future consumption is discounted relative to present consumption, then the agent can be assumed to maximize, at time $t = 0$,

$$V = \mathrm{E}\left[\sum_{t=0}^{\infty} \delta^t u(c_t)\right] \tag{15.1}$$

where E represents the expected value. We consider the case where there is some uncertainty (to be discussed below) and assume that u satisfies the von Neumann–Morgenstern expected utility axioms. In this particular formulation, we assume that utility is time separable, so that utility derived from consumption today does not depend upon the last period's consumption. For simplicity, we have also omitted leisure since questions regarding labour supply are not considered here.

For expositional purposes, assume that income y_t is received at the start of each period, and that consumption is undertaken immediately. Savings will be $y_t - c_t$, upon which interest will be earned for the period. If r_t denotes the gross real interest rate, which is 1 plus the real interest rate, and a_t denotes the value of real assets, then a_t accumulates over time according to[1]

$$a_{t+1} = r_t(a_t + y_t - c_t) \tag{15.2}$$

The representative agent is assumed to maximize (15.1) subject to (15.2), and the resulting path of consumption and asset accumulation is assumed to represent the path of these variables for the aggregate economy. It is worthwhile deriving intuitively the agent's decision rule implied by (15.1) and (15.2). Suppose that, at period t, we consider a decrease in consumption by one unit. The loss in utility is $u'(c_t)$ where $u'(.)$ represents marginal utility. The decrease in consumption in period t allows an increase in consumption in, say, period $t + 1$. In that period we shall have r_t units of extra consumption (receiving interest on our additional saving of one unit) giving us a (discounted) increase in expected utility of $\delta E[r_t u'(c_{t+1})]$ where E represents the expectations operator. For the choices of c_t and c_{t+1} to be optimal, such a rearrangement cannot improve welfare. Thus one condition for welfare maximization is

$$u'(c_t) = \delta E[r_t u'(c_{t+1})] \tag{15.3}$$

In order to complete the model, and to make it a general equilibrium one, it is necessary to specify market-clearing conditions that at each point in time total consumption equals total output. It is also necessary to impose a transversality condition. If the planning period were finite, then we would want to give a value to any assets remaining at the end of the period. In the infinite case, we do not value assets outside the planning period, so that if we derive positive marginal utility from consumption we require

$$\lim_{t \to \infty} a_t \, \delta^t u'(c_t) = 0$$

This is like a lifetime resource constraint for infinite-horizon models, and it implicitly gives a finishing value for a_t in infinite time.

If all agents are identical, why would they trade money and other financial assets with each other? Unless the model can explain trade in financial assets, it could hardly serve as a basis for monetary theory. One way is to introduce heterogeneous agents; another way is to use the overlapping generations model introduced by Samuelson (1958). This model is used frequently to analyse different issues and is worth brief consideration.

Overlapping generations models

In overlapping generations models, exposition is simplified by assuming that each agent lives for two periods and receives income (generally) as an endowment of one unit whilst young and nothing whilst old.[2] This immediately generates a motive for saving (provided that consumption of zero is not an option which can be guaranteed by assuming that $u(0) = -\infty$). With agents saving whilst young, we require another group of agents to be dis-saving, because with no investment aggregate saving must be zero in equilibrium. This can be accomplished by having generations overlap. At each point in time there will be an old and a young generation alive, who are identical except for the phase of their life.

One method of generating a need for financial assets is to assume that goods are not storable. Then there will be a demand for financial assets as a means of transferring purchasing power from one period to the next. Without money (or some other asset), there would be no way that such a transfer could take place: the young could lend to the old, but the old would not be around to repay the debt when the current young became old. Samuelson suggested that money in the form of fiat currency (i.e. backed by law) would solve the problem. The young would then sell some of their output for fiat currency (i.e. purchase the fiat currency of the old who had acquired it in their first period). Because each agent has a finite life we do not need a transversality condition.

If the old held the stock M of money and the young at time t wanted to consume c_t^y and thus save $1 - c_t^y$, then the price p_t of one unit of consumption in terms of money satisfies $M = p_t(1 - c_t^y)$. Thus the young would receive M/p_t for each unit of output given up, and receive M/p_{t+1} units of consumption in the next period when they exchanged their money for goods (at price p_{t+1}). The gross rate of return on money is therefore $(M/p_{t+1})/(M/p_t)$ or $r_t = p_t/p_{t+1}$. For any given price path, actual consumption allocations are determined by (15.3), so that c_t is a function of p_t/p_{t+1}. It turns out, however, that the model can be satisfied by a number of price paths $(p_1, p_2, \ldots)$. This indeterminacy of the price path is a feature of this class of models which derives from the lack of a transversality condition and reappears in another context below.

In the model outlined above, money only has a role as a store of value, which could be filled by any asset. Any other asset such as land or physical capital which possesses positive marginal products would dominate money as a means of transferring consumption from one period to the next, so that the economy would quickly become non-monetary. As it stands, this model does not exploit the medium-of-exchange advantage that money possesses. Tobin (1980) has criticized Wallace (1980) for suggesting that these models, as they stand, are an explanation for the existence of money.

The simplest way that money can be reintroduced into the overlapping generations structure in the presence of other assets is to hypothesize directly on the ease with which transactions can be made with whatever we are defining as money relative to other assets. Some authors thus assume that real balances (denoted m_t) bring utility, and modify the utility function each period to be $u(c_t, m_t)$.[3] Examples of this are to be found in Fischer (1979), Weiss (1980) and Obstfeld (1983, 1984). Naturally, this gives a demand for money even though it is dominated in its rate of return by another asset.[4] One criticism of this type of model concerns whether money is yielding utility directly or indirectly through transactions costs. Thus, Clower (1967) has argued that inserting money in the utility function does not yield a theory where money plays a special role in transactions. Kareken and Wallace (1980) take exception to what they regard as the implicit theorizing of this approach since it does not allow the underlying model consistency to be checked. Since alternative approaches are linked to the microfoundations of money, it is worthwhile discussing this issue.

The microfoundations of money

The microfoundations literature seeks to answer the more fundamental question of whether and why money is in fact a useful commodity. Money is defined as something which satisfies the properties of medium of exchange, store of value and unit of account. In the intertemporal general equilibrium models of Arrow (1964) and Debreu (1959) money plays no role. Agents get together at the start of time and purchase or sell contingent contracts for each time period at equilibrium prices. At the occurrence of each event, contracts are swapped for goods and there is no need for a medium of exchange and thus no role for money.[5] This led Hahn (1973) to make the statement that 'the foundations of monetary theory have not yet been laid'. Note that overlapping generations models generate a need for money (or some financial asset) by ruling out trade between today's young and tomorrow's young. However, this does not explain the unique role of money as a means of exchange.

In order to explain the need for a medium of exchange (typically thought of as currency), transactions technologies have to be introduced. Starr (1972) shows that, with the double coincidence of wants requirement of barter, we might never reach equilibrium allocations, because if we are restricted to only completing trades involving goods that we want, we might not meet other traders in the correct sequence. Ostroy (1973) has demonstrated that, even with middlemen in each commodity, the informational requirements go beyond just a knowledge of equilibrium prices since excess supplies still have to be passed along in exactly the right sequence.

Jones (1976) shows how a medium of exchange will arise even in an economy which starts with barter. In the Jones model, agents note which commodity is the most frequently encountered (say potatoes). Some who are trading relatively rare commodities will reason that the probability of finding an exact match can be improved by an intermediate trade in potatoes and then another trade into the commodity of their choice. Once these people begin to trade in potatoes, this raises the probability of finding someone to accept potatoes in trade and more traders will be induced to use potatoes. If this process continues, then eventually the majority of trades will involve potatoes and so potatoes will become the medium of exchange.

It seems obvious, although it has not been modelled, that if potatoes are difficult to carry around there is an incentive for an agent to accept potatoes and issue paper claims against them which are easier to transport. (We could go back one stage and ask why a paper claim is easier to carry, but this does not seem to be fruitful; economic theory has to start with some basic assumptions.) Although gold was accepted as a medium of exchange, it was difficult to carry in large amounts. Thus there existed an incentive for banks to accept gold and issue bank notes against it – a role later taken over by central banks.

Does portability explain the existence of fiat currency? This issue is taken up by Kiyotaki and Wright (1989a), who make trading strategies endogenous (rather than random, as in Jones 1976). They allow different goods to have different storage costs and show that there may exist two types of Nash equilibria: a fundamental equilibrium in which the good with the lowest storage cost is chosen as the medium of exchange, and a speculative equilibrium in which agents rationally do not use the good with the lowest storage cost because they expect (correctly) that it will be less marketable. Kiyotaki and Wright make the important point that fiat currency will not be held unless people believe that it will be accepted by others. This is only a necessary condition for fiat currency to have value. Kiyotaki and Wright (1989b) point out that if fiat currency is dominated strongly enough by other assets or goods in rate of return or storability, other goods might be used as a medium of exchange even if everyone believes that everyone else will accept fiat currency. Conversely, the strength of belief in the acceptability[6] of fiat currency might be so great that it would still be used even if dominated by another good or asset in both rate of return and storability. Perhaps an example is a payments or credit card. This issue is also connected with price level determinacy in Section 15.3.

Other authors have picked up the theme that fiat currency may be valued when there is spatial separation of agents. Lucas (1980) and Townsend (1980) have shown that money is valuable when agents have to move through spatially separated points in their trading and, because they cannot establish credit relationships, must carry money to indicate purchasing power[7] (this is related to the cash-in-advance literature discussed below). Williamson (1987a) argues that if there were zero costs to setting up a bank then there would be one at every physical location which exchanges money for bonds. In this case payments could be made by an instantaneous transfer of bonds to money and then back to bonds so that no money would ever be held. Of course, this also relies on the instantaneous nature of the exchange, otherwise there would be time 'transfer costs' of the type implicit in the inventory-theoretical models proposed by Baumol and Tobin.

Cash-in-advance models

With the above ideas, one approach is to assume that money must be acquired before any transactions, and thus consumption, can be undertaken (see, for example, Lucas 1980). This is known as the Clower (1967) or cash-in-advance (CIA) requirement and can be written $c_t \leq m_t$. One justification for the CIA requirement is that the representative agent does not 'know' the seller of goods and the latter is unwilling to issue trade credit (or accept securities), as discussed above.

We can immediately notice one implication of the CIA assumption. Since money is dominated by other assets in its rate of return, agents will only acquire the real balances needed for consumption. If there is no uncertainty about consumption, then money holdings will be such that $m_t = c_t$ since there is an opportunity cost to holding additional real balances. Since $m_t = M_t/p_t$, where M_t refers to nominal balances at time t, $M_t = p_t c_t$. Thus the velocity of circulation is identically unity, and it cannot be affected by traditional arguments such as the rate of inflation and the rate of interest. Without further modification we obtain the strict quantity theory. One reason for this is because the time period is defined so that people cannot make variable trips to the bank as in the Baumol (1952) and Tobin (1956) formulations. Two exceptions within this framework are Lucas and Stokey (1983) and Svensson (1985). In the former, there are cash goods, which require money, and credit goods, which do not; relative price shifts between them give a variable velocity. In the latter, uncertainty about consumption means that, with real balances already decided, velocity will vary with consumption.

Lucas and Stokey (1987) use the CIA model with credit and cash goods to study how the behaviour of equilibrium quantities and prices, including the interest rate, depend on the stochastic processes generating the level of output and the growth of the money supply. In such a setting the authors offer a restatement of the famous Fisherian decomposition of the nominal interest rate into real and inflationary components. Thus it is demonstrated that shocks to real endowments affect real interest rates, via their effect on marginal rates of substitution, and monetary shocks affect inflation premiums. More generally, the analysis demonstrates the way in which different monetary policies induce different (real) resource allocations.

Although proponents of the CIA approach would argue that their procedure for introducing money into a general equilibrium setting is better than the money in the utility approach (see p. 294), Feenstra (1986) has demonstrated that the former model is a special case of the latter. In particular, Feenstra shows that the method of entering money directly into the utility function can be explicitly derived from an optimizing model with transactions costs or uncertainty.

Asset prices and speculative bubbles

One criticism of the intertemporal optimizing approach is that it seems inconsistent with the data in some important respects. One of these can be seen from equation (15.3). The stylized facts are that consumption is very smooth and does not show great variation, yet interest rates and asset prices (which influence rates of return) are extremely variable. These stylized facts seem inconsistent with (15.3). If c_t is roughly constant and r_t is not, then it requires $u'(.)$ to be very variable, which implies a very high concavity of the utility function or, equivalently, a very high degree of risk aversion for the representative agent.

Recent research on the term structure of interest rates, and more generally on asset prices such as stock prices and forward exchange rates, has utilized the first-order condition of the representative agent given by (15.3). One immediate implication of (15.3) is that the real rate of return r should be inversely related to the discount factor δ (and hence positively related to the rate of time preference). In order to tell more interesting stories about the behaviour of returns in the representative agent setting (and, in particular, to obtain a closed-form solution for asset prices), we have to impose some stochastic structure on the behaviour of consumption and specify the form of the utility function. Having thus restricted the basic model, we can explain the common findings of, say, a positive term premium on long-term bonds and a positive excess of common stock returns over a short-term riskless asset. For example, the former empirical finding (which Hicks (1938) originally suggested was due to liquidity preference) can be demonstrated to follow as long as consumption is a stationary process, and the latter effect can be decomposed into a component due to uncertainty with respect to the dividend payment (which is proportional to the coefficient of relative risk aversion) and a component which is proportional to the square of the coefficient of relative risk aversion (Campbell 1986).[8] However, on the latter point, Mehra and Prescott (1985) have argued that the historically observed equity premium in the United States is far too large to be consistent with a closed-form representative agent model with plausible parameter values. This conclusion has in turn generated a lively debate.

Motivated largely by the finding that actual asset prices tend to be excessively volatile relative to asset prices determined by fundamentals, a number of researchers have turned to non-fundamental factors (bubbles) to explain the determination of asset prices. In particular, bubble-blowing has become a popular pastime in the recent monetary literature. The bubble phenomenon can be explained in the following way. Suppose that the asset stock in (15.3) is a stock or equity share which sells for a real price (i.e. relative to the general price level) q_t in period t and returns a real dividend d_t during period t. The gross rate of return on this asset is $r_t = (d_t + q_{t+1}/q_t)$. If, for simplicity, we assume that agents are risk neutral (and therefore $u'(c_t) = u'(c_{t+1})$), (15.3) becomes

$$\delta E\left(\frac{d_t + q_{t+1}}{q_t}\right) = 1$$

or

$$q_t = \delta E(d_t + q_{t+1}) \tag{15.4}$$

The general solution to (15.4) is

$$q_t = \sum_{i=0}^{\infty} \delta^i E\left[d_{t+i} + A_t\left(\frac{1}{\delta}\right)^t\right] \tag{15.5}$$

where $E(A_{t+1}) = A_t$ and the expectation is taken at time t. It is easy to verify that (15.5) is the solution to (15.4) by substitution in (15.4).[9] The first term in (15.5) is called the dividend–share price formula, and states that the current price of a share is the discounted value of its future dividends. These dividends are the economic fundamentals which drive share prices. However, the second term, which is called a bubble, is not related to fundamentals and will be important if agents believe it to be so.

If A_t is a constant equal to A, the share price will grow at the rate $A(1/\delta)$ even with constant dividends. This is a pure capital gain unrelated to fundamentals. There are an infinite number of such paths, one for each value of A. If everyone believes that share prices will rise at some common rate, unrelated to fundamentals, then the price will go up by that amount; prices can rise through speculation, and moreover these expectations will be fulfilled. In this case it will be an expectations-consistent speculative bubble. Psychology will play a role in the determination of asset prices if this story is correct.

There is no natural transversality condition to tell us what A_t is. To rule out bubbles we have to impose a transversality condition that q_t is finite or that $A_t = 0$. This has no direct economic intuition, and appeal to super-rationality, that agents all assume that everyone else will assume the existence of no bubble so that q_t is always finite, is unconvincing. Diba and Grossman (1985) argue that, because asset prices cannot be negative, bubbles cannot develop in a negative direction. Consequently, they argue that they cannot develop in a positive direction either since the expected value of noise which starts the bubble must be zero.

There have been several apparent bubbles: for example, the South Sea bubble and the Tulipmania bubble (Garber 1989). In these cases, the bubble eventually burst and in any case the asset price did not rise at a rate consistent with a deterministic bubble. Blanchard (1979) models a collapsing bubble with the following structure:

$$A_{t+1} = \begin{array}{ll} A_t/\pi & \text{with probability } \pi \\ 0 & \text{with probability } 1 - \pi \end{array} \tag{15.6}$$

This structure satisfies $E(A_{t+1}) = A_t$ and thus represents a solution of (15.4). The bubble has a non-zero probability of collapse at any point in time, and once it collapses it is over since all future A_t are zero. However, with probability π it does not collapse and continues growing.

The existence of speculative bubbles has initiated debate which carries over into other areas such as exchange rates (see MacDonald and Taylor (1989) for a survey). The initial argument that speculation and psychological forces determine asset prices in the short run goes back to Keynes (1936), and the formulations above lend themselves to the view that rational bubbles can exist.[10] Not surprisingly, economists who believe in market forces and economic fundamentals as the driving force are keen to downplay the existence of speculative bubbles. Garber (1989) examines and reinterprets the Tulipmania events. Hamilton (1986) gives some examples of how an econometrician might incorrectly conclude that a speculative bubble exists when there is an expected regime change of which he is unaware. For example, suppose that, starting in ten periods from now, dividends were expected to increase to a new permanent level (or after-tax dividends via some permanent tax change). Then asset prices would begin to rise now by the increased discounted value of future dividends even if there was no bubble, and they would continue to rise until period 10. The econometrician would only observe a rising asset price with no change in current dividends (if his sample excluded the change in regime) and therefore might find the existence of a bubble when none exists (this is similar to the so-called 'peso' effect which is often used to explain the common finding of inefficiency in forward foreign exchange markets).[11]

15.3 BANKING AND FINANCIAL INTERMEDIATION

A long-held belief is that control of the money stock is necessary for price level control. It is easiest to see this by writing down a simple classical macro-model (with fixed capital stock) as follows:

$$n^d(w) = n^s(w) \equiv n \tag{15.7}$$

$$y = f(n) \tag{15.8}$$

$$y = c(y) + I(i - \pi^e) + g \tag{15.9}$$

$$\frac{M}{P} = L(i_m, i, y) \tag{15.10}$$

Equation (15.7) denotes equilibrium in the labour market in which the real wage w equates labour demand n^d and labour supply n^s. The equilibrium employment level is n. Output supply is given by (15.8). Equation (15.9) is the goods market equilibrium in which output equals aggregate demand which is a function of consumption c, investment I and government spending g. Consumption is a function of income, and investment is a function of the real interest rate written as the nominal rate minus the expected rate of inflation (which we take to be given). Equation (15.10) denotes equilibrium in financial markets and is written as real money demand L equals the real money supply. Real money demand is a function of the interest rate on money i_m, the interest rate on other assets taken together (bonds) and income.

The recursive nature of (15.7)–(15.10) means that w and n are determined in the labour market, y is determined by (15.8) and the real interest rate is determined by (15.9). With given π^e this determines i. Thus for P to be determined, the government must fix a nominal interest rate, the interest rate on money and the money stock. Recognition of this goes back at least to Patinkin (1965). Most governments do not pay interest on currency, and until recently prohibited the payment of interest on current deposits, thus setting $i_m = 0$.

In order to control the money stock, the central bank has to control credit created by the banking system. From the balance sheets of the commercial banks in aggregate, liabilities which consist of deposits D must equal assets which consist of reserves R plus bank loans to the public and private sectors, which are called domestic credit DC. From the balance sheets of the central bank, the monetary base H equals bank reserves plus currency C. The standard definition of the money stock is $M = C + D$. From the above balance-sheet identities it follows that $M = H + \text{DC}$. Thus, to control M, the central bank must control credit creation in addition to the monetary base.

To restrict credit, most central banks have imposed three sorts of regulations. First, minimum reserve requirements restrict the amount banks can lend. Second, interest rate ceilings have often been imposed: for example the prohibition of interest on current deposits and ceilings on mortgage rates. Third, portfolio restrictions and quantitative guidelines have been directly imposed. Some of these restrictions have also been imposed for prudential reasons.

Friedman (1960) has advocated intervention in credit markets to control M and assure price level stability. A new view questions the need for this intervention. This 'neo-Chicago' view claims that regulation and intervention in financial markets is welfare reducing, as it is for other markets, and argues for unrestricted financial intermediation. Leading proponents of this view are Black (1970) and Fama (1980, 1983). Fama argues that price-level control does not require restriction of financial intermediation; control of the monetary base or currency is sufficient. Fama notes that (15.10) could well apply to currency, since nothing is sacred about the standard definition of M provided that a well-defined demand for currency exists. With this scenario we do not need required reserves or portfolio restrictions which cause misallocations of resources.

This unregulated banking philosophy is in direct contrast with the quantity theory of money (unless the latter is defined as the monetary base), and this point was emphasized by Sargent and Wallace (1982). Sargent and Wallace interpret the restrictions applied to control the money stock as intervention to prevent some agents from trading securities by specifying a minimum denomination of bonds, and define an economy free from these restrictions as a *laissez-faire* economy or real-bills equilibrium, an interpretation which Laidler (1984a) rejects. It is not surprising that the *laissez-faire* or unrestricted intermediation equilibrium is Pareto optimal whereas the restricted interme- diation equilibrium is not, because the latter excludes some agents from taking part in the process of intermediation.

A theme related to the above points is the issue of why agents hold fiat currency. Wallace (1980) argues a legal restrictions theory of the demand for money: central banks artificially create a demand for money (fiat currency) by forcing commercial banks to hold reserves at the central bank in the form of currency, by failing to allow private money creation and by issuing bonds in large denominations. If interest-bearing government bonds were issued in any denomination and there was no requirement to hold reserves in currency, then no one would hold fiat currency. Thus a reserves requirement and the non- divisibility of bonds are both required to generate a demand for money.

One difficulty is the computation of interest accrual if small-denomination bonds are used as a medium of exchange. This also makes it difficult to see how private currency could also pay interest.[12] Makinen and Woodward (1986) and White (1987) provide historical examples where Wallace's assertion does not appear to hold: in the case considered by the former currency was preferred to a small-denomination interest-bearing bond, and in the case considered by the latter there were no required reserves or prohibition of private money, yet zero-interest banknotes circulated as money.

Harper (1988) points out that for the non-existence of currency in the absence of the Wallace restrictions there must be a type of electronic transfer accounting system. If agents each had accounts where transfers could be made instantaneously, then these deposits could earn interest which could be computed per second, say, and there would be no need for currency. If there was no currency, how would prices be determined? All prices could be quoted in some unit. Fama (1980) suggests beef or oil. Hall (1982) and Greenfield and Yeager (1983) suggest that something whose value is stable relative to most commodities is needed, so why not use a weighted average as is done now with the current price index. The point is that, if there is no demand for currency, we do not need a price of goods in terms of currency (or money). Of course, the points made by these authors are academic if there are reasons why a pure electronic transfer technology is more costly than the current institutional arrangement in which currency is demanded. If currency is demanded, then it must have a price relative to goods.

Another related issue concerns financial intermediation in general and why specialist agents (banks and others) exist. Why is not all borrowing and lending conducted directly between individuals? Not surprisingly, asymmetric or incomplete information plus economies of scale in collecting information and monitoring borrowers are the two reasons modelled. Williamson (1986, 1987b) uses spatial location as a reason why agents have sufficient information about each other to arrange direct loans; since monitoring is costly, specialists will emerge to take advantage of economies of scale in information collection. Townsend (1979), D. Diamond (1984) and Gale and Hellwig (1985) consider the types of contracts that would be signed between a financial intermediary and a borrower when the intermediary cannot directly observe the borrower's effort. Whenever the intermediary decides not to monitor the borrower, interest repayments must be the same, otherwise the borrower would have an incentive to lie about the true state. Stiglitz and Weiss (1981) show that banks might choose to quantity-ration rather than price-ration loans because a higher interest rate might induce more risky borrower behaviour which might adversely affect banks.

15.4 TIME CONSISTENCY AND POLICY CREDIBILITY

In this section we are concerned with the theory of monetary policy.[13] Although this area has a fairly long history in the macroeconomics literature, it has become particularly topical over the last ten years or so. This topicality has been induced, in part if not wholly, by the commitment of a number of OECD governments to implement pre-announced growth rules for various monetary aggregates.[14] Such commitment to what are essentially fixed-growth rules contrasts sharply with the discretionary monetary policies that were adopted by most governments for much of the post-war period.

The concept of time inconsistency can best be illustrated by the following example. Consider a government which announces monetary growth rates for a number of periods in the future. This allows private agents to form forecasts of inflation. At some later time, say leading up to an election, it is generally to the advantage of the government to depart from the pre-announced monetary growth rate (i.e. to act in a time-inconsistent fashion). The reason is that by (unexpectedly) raising the monetary growth rate, the usual Phillips curve[15] arguments suggest that the economy will experience higher output; higher inflation will come only later (hopefully after the election). If the public realizes that the government has an incentive to 'cheat' on the prior announced policy, it may not believe the policy to begin with. Thus the government may have a problem with credibility. The lack of credibility is a serious problem: it makes it difficult, for example, for the government to undertake an anti-inflationary policy (for if the announced monetary contraction is not believed, it may not lead to moderation in wage settlements). In general, lack of credibility will lead to Pareto inferior outcomes.

The strategic interdependences of the above make the analysis of time consistency suited to the game-theoretical framework,[16] and this is the approach adopted in the literature. The monetary authority is usually modelled as adopting a leadership role, which a representative agent follows. The literature attempts to address two basic issues: How serious is the time-consistency problem? How might the problem be resolved in the absence of precommitment?

We now turn to a simple example of the time consistency of monetary policy issue which should illustrate some of the issues raised above and some not hitherto addressed. As we have mentioned, two types of players are involved in a time-consistency game: a centralized policy-maker and the 'private sector' which is composed of rational forward-looking atomistic units who are individually unable to influence the actions of others and who take as given the actions of other agents and the centralized policy-maker. The literature uses versions of a model originally proposed by Kydland and Prescott (1977) where the central policy-maker is assumed to have a well-defined utility function given by

$$u_t = f(\Pi - \hat{\Pi}) + g(y_t - \hat{y}), \quad f'(.), g'(.) \lesseqgtr 0 \text{ as } (.) \gtreqless 0 \quad (15.11)$$

$$f''(.), g''(.) < 0$$

and output is assumed to be characterized by a surprise supply function given by

$$\begin{aligned} \hat{y} &= k y_n & k &> 1 \\ y_t &= y_n + \alpha(\Pi_t - \Pi_t^e) & \alpha &> 0 \end{aligned} \quad (15.12)$$

where Π_t is the actual inflation rate (assumed to be a choice variable of the monetary authority), Π_t^e is the expected inflation rate (formed by the private sector), y_t is the aggregate output, y_n is the natural rate of output (assumed to be exogenous) and a circumflex above a variable denotes that it is the policy-maker's desired value. The partial derivatives (denoted by primes) indicate that the inflation objectives of the policy-maker are characterized by rising costs when actual inflation deviates from its target value and that he obtains disutility when actual output deviates from its desired level. Crucially, the policy-maker regards the natural rate of output (unemployment) as being too low (high) because of various labour market distortions[17] and attempts to increase it by exploiting the supposed trade-off given in (15.12). Output may be above its natural rate to the extent that there is a positive element of unanticipated inflation. This is captured by the fact that $k > 1$ in the relationship between $\hat{y}$ and y_n.

Consider now monetary policy of the discretionary and fixed rules variety in the context of the above two-equation system. We assume that agents are fully rational (i.e. they condition their expectations on available information and they know the objectives and constraints facing others) and there is no uncertainty. First, if the policy-maker is precommitted to a particular monetary rule (and therefore inflation rate) rational agents will simply set $\Pi^e = \Pi$ and output will be at its natural level. Without precommitment the policy-maker has discretion to attempt to maximize (15.11) subject to the constraint (15.12): he will try to raise output above the natural rate by inducing an inflationary surprise. But because the private sector knows the objectives and constraints facing the authority, it will again set $\Pi^e = \Pi$ and output will equal its natural rate. Thus under the discretionary scenario we end up with a higher inflation rate but the same output level as we had with a fixed rule. This is an example of time consistency, because although $\Pi^e = \Pi$ is optimal *ex ante* it is not optimal *ex post* and therefore will not be credible if the policy-maker has discretion. Say, for example, that the policy-maker announces that he has a target for inflation of Π_1. This policy by itself cannot be credible, because once expectations have been formed the authority will have an incentive to renege on the policy and since the private sector understands this it will not believe the initial announcement.

A number of solutions to the time-inconsistency issue have been proffered in the literature. Perhaps the simplest remedy involves changing the legal framework within which the policy-maker operates so that his hands are tied and he cannot indulge in inflationary policies.[18] Although this may be fine in circumstances where the future is known with certainty, the existence of some form of uncertainty (see below) may make it desirable for the policy-maker to have some discretion in his use of monetary policy. An alternative way of circumscribing the power of the policy-maker in his monetary actions would be to force him to participate in an international monetary system which imposed monetary discipline, such as a fixed exchange rate regime (McKinnon 1984) or the gold standard (Mundell 1968). A third remedy may be found in ensuring that the monetary authority is politically independent and indeed has a penchant for conservative policies (Rogoff 1985), which we return to below when we come to discuss uncertainty. As a fourth solution it has been suggested that the government currently in office (assumed to be of the precommitted variety) puts in place incentive schemes for future governments to behave consistently. For example, Persson *et al.* (1987) argue that the future government should be placed in the situation where the marginal cost of deviating from the consistent plan at least equals its marginal benefit.

The ability of the private sector to force the government to produce time-consistent policies can be considered in a more realistic framework where reputation is important. The issue of reputation occurs as we move away from the type of monetary policy game discussed above, usually labelled a one-shot game (because the game is played only once and current behaviour is not affected by past or future encounters between the players), towards a repeated game where agents' actions depend upon past behaviour. In such a context, a government which had in the past always acted with commitment may decide to fool the public by engineering a monetary surprise. In the period of the monetary surprise the government produces an output gain (since $\Pi > \Pi^e$). However, its reputation suffers since in future periods the private sector will now be expecting the higher (discretionary) inflation rate (by assumption).[19] If the government discounts the future heavily, it is possible that this would be the optimal policy. But the point is that in a repeated game environment the policy-maker has to trade off the current gain from cheating against the future loss of reputation in terms of higher inflationary expectations. In such a set-up, equilibrium is achieved by reputational forces which operate through threat strategies which punish a rival for bad behaviour.

Reputational issues can be made more realistic and interesting by introducing uncertainty into the discussion. Perhaps one of the more interesting types of uncertainty is when the private sector is uncertain about the objectives of the policy-maker (referred to as endogenous or intrinsic uncertainty). Such uncertainty has been considered by Backus and Driffill (1985a, b) and restated by Barro (1986). These authors extend the model of Kreps and Wilson (1982) to the analysis of inflationary reputation. For example, Backus and Driffill (1985a) introduce two possible types of policy-maker into the above repeated game framework: the policy-maker can either be soft or hard on inflation. The hard policy-maker always goes for the low or zero inflation option, whilst the soft policy-maker has a preference for pushing output above the natural rate by producing unanticipated inflation. Private agents are aware of these alternative motives but are unaware of which type of policy-maker they face and have to infer this from the behaviour of inflation. If inflation is low the private sector may be tempted to conclude that the policy-maker is hard, but a soft policy-maker will also have an incentive (at least initially) to adopt a low inflation strategy and then induce an inflationary surprise once Π^e has been formed (clearly, if the soft policy-maker did not initially disguise his intentions he could not surprise the public). The point that the models illustrate, at the expense of simplistic assumptions, is that it may take some time for private agents to be convinced of the true motives of the government. If these insights hold up in more complicated scenarios, where there are more than two policy selections, it indicates that whether or not the government precommits itself to future policy may be less relevant, as regards the pattern of output and inflation, than whether or not precommitment is believed.

The uncertainty addressed in the above discussion is of the endogenous variety. A number of researchers have considered a variety of exogenous forms of uncertainty in the context of the time-consistency framework. The issue of political uncertainty, taken to mean uncertainty on the part of the private sector over the outcome of elections, has been considered by Alesina (1985), who generates a political business cycle in a model where two political parties which are not precommitted have different inflationary preferences. Perhaps a more important form of uncertainty is that emanating from the underlying stochastic structure of the economy. Thus, in our discussion hitherto, equations (15.12) was assumed to be deterministic. If, more realistically, it is assumed to be stochastic, then it is not clear that the optimal monetary policy is one in which the policy-maker adheres rigidly to a fixed rule. For example, Rogoff (1985) has demonstrated in this context that appointing a conservative central banker may result in gains for society, in terms of reduced expected and actual inflation, at the expense of the increased costs of his inability to respond flexibly to exogenous shocks. A further kind of uncertainty occurs when there are informational asymmetries and, in particular, when the policy-maker has superior information to the private sector. For example, Canzoneri (1985) considers a model in which the money demand function is stochastic and the policy-maker has information on the disturbance. The private sector then faces the problem of inferring whether a change in monetary growth, say, reflects the authorities' response to the shock (presuming that they deem it desirable to offset such shocks) or a discretionary monetary policy. Therefore a strict adherence to a monetary growth rule does not necessarily indicate commitment because the authority could be fooling the public with its superior information. Conversely, a monetary overshoot designed to compensate for a money demand shock may be misinterpreted by the public as a discretionary change, and therefore a policy which was initially successful in stabilizing inflation and output may result in $\Pi > \Pi^e$, with output above its natural rate. A reputation-based solution in this type of set-up might involve the private sector's setting up confidence bounds for the inflation rate: inflationary bouts within the bound reflect the authorities' response to money demand shocks whilst inflationary impulses outside the bounds are interpreted as opportunism (Green and Porter 1984). Canzoneri recognizes that confidence may break down at times, and this is seen as more plausible than other reputational equilibria (such as that of Barro and Gordon 1983) which are seen as being too stable.

Although much of the time-consistency literature is very elegant and instructive of the potential interactions between the government and private sector, and reinforces the adage that 'you can't fool all of the people all of the time', there are two fundamental issues underlying it that are rarely addressed. First, it is not entirely clear, at least for the majority of OECD countries, that their macroeconomic policy has suffered from an inherent inflationary bias in periods when there has been little or no precommitment. Compare, for example, the low inflation rates of the 1950–70 period, a time of (generally agreed) discretionary policy, with the relatively higher inflation of the 1975–85 period when most governments followed pre-announced monetary growth rates. It is also not clear that governments which have adopted precommitment have reaped the benefits suggested by the literature. More important, perhaps, is the failure of much of this literature to quantify the assumption that inflation is costly. It is not entirely clear what the costs of a few extra percentage points on the consumer price index actually are – the standard costs advanced, such as shoe-leather costs, the costs of administering prices and ensuring an inflation-neutral tax structure, seem infinitesimally small[20] compared with the output employment costs of a failed macroeconomic policy.

15.5 OTHER DEVELOPMENTS

In the preceding sections we have emphasized the themes of the new microeconomic approach to monetary theory. While these have been the dominant new themes, research has also continued in the context of the aggregative approach, and we conclude this chapter with a brief mention of the more notable investigations. One issue has been over the appropriate definition of monetary aggregates. Barnet (1980) has suggested an alternative to (simple sum) monetary aggregates. Barnett's aggregates weight each deposit component by its interest differential to the market rate as suggested by Divisia index theory. It was hoped that these aggregates would perform much better than the conventional aggregates in terms of the stability of the demand for money during the financial innovations and de-regulations of the period. However, this turned out not to be the case as the evidence was very mixed (Barnett *et al.* 1983). One potential reason is given by Milbourne (1986). Research in this area appears to have ceased.

Another theme which is devoted to explaining the instability of the demand for money is an approach called 'buffer stock theory', which argues for important disequilibrium effects in the money market. In particular, money demand is assumed not to adjust quickly to the money stock. Laidler (1984b) provides an exposition, although there are several different strands of this literature.[21] These models have been criticized especially on the grounds of their empirical testing and relevance.[22] Money demand instability has also been attributed to the phenomenon of currency substitution (see, *inter alia*, Vaubel 1980; Girton and Roper 1981; McKinnon 1982), i.e. the idea that under a system of floating exchange rates agents have an incentive, in terms of risk–return criteria, to hold a basket of currencies and substitute between them. Such substitution has been cited as a reason for the failure of monetary targeting in some OECD countries (Vaubel 1980) and the failure of national inflation rates to be determined by national money supply growth (McKinnon 1982). However, given that for most OECD countries the proportion of the total money supply held by foreign residents is small, it is unlikely that currency substitution has been important for this question.

The poor behaviour and unpredictability of monetary aggregates has focused on the question of whether monetary targeting is a useful policy tool. The debate on the criticisms of monetary targeting is surveyed by McCallum (1985). More generally, the poor response to monetary targeting has raised the question of whether any intermediate targeting (adjusting interest rates to fix an intermediate variable such as the money stock, which is then supposed to influence nominal income) is justified. Some opinion seems to run in favour of direct targeting (varying interest rates in direct response to nominal income) as discussed by Taylor (1985).

Finally, some researchers have attempted to model ways in which variations in the nominal money stock might cause variations in real output. These attempts are well surveyed by Blanchard (1987), and two explanations are worth brief mention. One is the literature on credit rationing (Stiglitz and Weiss 1981), which uses asymmetric information to explain why credit varies with little apparent change in corresponding interest rates. The macroeconomic implication is that changes in domestic credit might affect economic activity directly rather than via interest rates. A second strand is to argue that imperfect competition in goods markets causes a non-neutral response to changes in the money stock. In this argument, costs of adjusting prices (menu costs) may cause nominal rigidities (Mankiw 1985).

15.6 SUMMARY AND CONCLUSIONS

In this chapter we have discussed some prominent themes developed in monetary economics over the last ten years. Central to much of the recent monetary literature has been the use of microeconomic representative agent models to answer macroeconomic questions. In Section 15.2 we discussed the representative agent model in some detail and investigated why money should arise in such models. A standard way of introducing money into such models is to embed them into an overlapping generations framework and posit that money generates utility directly. This exogenously imposes money on the model, as does the cash-in-advance model. This is not important for some questions, but it does not address the fundamental question of why money exists.

Perhaps one of the more interesting recent developments is the shift in emphasis away from examining the effects of money on output to its effects on asset prices. One particularly interesting development has been the incorporation of non-fundamental factors into the determination of asset prices. Such bubble effects, and the underlying market psychology which drives them, are now regarded as being of crucial importance in explaining recent asset price behaviour. Essentially, this approach gives a nice theoretical underpinning to Keynes's beauty contest metaphor. The real issue is whether the current bubble models are satisfactory.

Theoretical developments which have had the most direct impact on economic policy relate to regulation and intervention in financial markets. The neo-Chicago view suggests that such intervention is welfare reducing and proposes unrestricted financial intermediation, a trend policy development in many countries. This follows as soon as we allow a divorce of administration of the medium of exchange (fiat currency) by banks from their role as an intermediary.

In Section 15.4 we examined in some detail the implications which the issue of time consistency has for the implementation of successful monetary disinflation. Various solutions to the time-inconsistency problem were discussed, and we concluded this section by sounding a reservation about its practical importance.

During the 1940s, 1950s and 1960s, innovations in monetary theory consisted largely of improvements and extensions to an existing and generally agreed framework. The 1970s witnessed some interest in the microfoundations of money, but are largely remembered for the incorporation of rational expectations and its consequences. At the macroeconomic level, the implication was that money was the driving force of business cycles and this overshadowed its microeconomic foundations. The 1980s witnessed a reversal of this: the microeconomic foundations of money became important, and the macroeconomic view of money and its control faded. As a result, a much larger set of phenomena and issues appeared than probably in any previous decade. For this we should be forever grateful.

NOTES

1 This implicitly assumes that there is an asset which will be held and is the subject of discussion below.
2 This follows Samuelson's (1958) original assumptions.
3 Money is usually introduced in this way into perfect foresight growth models, and a common finding in such models is that the stability and uniqueness of the perfect foresight equilibrium are sensitive to the cross-derivative between money and consumption.
4 See Poterba and Rotemberg (1987) for an empirical application.
5 Arrow (1964) has suggested that money may have a role in such models as a store of value. However, Hahn (1973) has argued that this form of money holdings is inessential because it does not affect the equilibrium allocation of goods.
6 As in the models proposed by Jones (1976) and P. Diamond (1984), acceptability speeds up

the exchange process via a higher probability of finding a compatible trader in the search process.

7 Lucas emphasizes that the messages which stores would have to send to each other regarding the creditworthiness of each customer would be very large and that fiat currency reduces such complicated bookkeeping.

8 For an application of this class of model to the term structure of interest rates, see Cox *et al.* (1981).

9 It might be thought that one way to solve (15.4) is to back-substitute by lagging (15.4) and substituting for q_{t-1} etc. However, this solution is invalid because it yields a solution for q_t of $\Sigma_{i=0}^{\infty}(1/\delta)^i d_{t-i}$. Because $\delta < 1$, this summation does not converge.

10 Tirole (1985) shows that any overlapping generations economy exhibiting a bubble must be Pareto inefficient since a higher value of A implies a higher capital gain. Since there is no upper bound on A there is no limit to the capital gain, and the allocation of any economy can be bettered by a larger bubble.

11 The peso effect was initially proposed by Krasker (1982).

12 Private money has been advocated by Hayek (1976) and King (1983).

13 Useful surveys of this topic are provided by Cukierman (1985), Honkapohja (1985), Fischer (1986), Rogoff (1987) and Blackburn and Christensen (1989).

14 Often targets are also set for elements of fiscal policy such as the ratio of government debt to GDP.

15 The Phillips curve monetary game considered in this section was introduced by Kydland and Prescott (1977), and extended by, *inter alia*, Barro and Gordon (1983), Backus and Driffill (1985a, b), Canzoneri (1985) and Rogoff (1985).

16 The time-consistency literature has borrowed a considerable amount from the game theory literature. As far as possible, and to keep the size of this section manageable, we try to minimize the use of this nomenclature. See Blackburn and Christensen (1989) for a discussion of such terminology.

17 Such as taxes, transfers, trade unions and minimum wage legislation.

18 This may not be such a Draconian solution as it sounds, since societies already have legislation for similar types of problem – the classic example usually given is that of patent rights which protect the incentive to innovate (see Taylor (1983) for a discussion).

19 This example is due to Fischer (1986). A further example is given by Barro and Gordon (1983).

20 There are also redistributional costs of inflation, but these can be dealt with through indexation.

21 For a survey see Milbourne (1988b).

22 See Milbourne (1988a) for a summary of the criticisms.

REFERENCES

Alesina, A. (1985) 'Rules, discretion and reputation in a two-party system', unpublished manuscript, Harvard University.

Arrow, K. (1964) 'The role of securities in the optimal allocation of risk bearing', *Review of Economic Studies* 31: 91–6.

Backus, D. and Driffill, J. (1985a) 'Inflation and reputation', *American Economic Review* 75 (3): 530–8.

—— and —— (1985b) 'Rational expectations and policy credibility following a change in regime', *Review of Economic Studies* 52 (2): 211–22.

Barnett, W. A. (1980) 'Economic monetary aggregates: an application of index number and aggregation theory', *Journal of Econometrics* 14: 11–48.

Barnett, W. A., Offenbacher, E. K. and Spindt, P. A. (1983) 'The new Divisia monetary aggregates', *Journal of Political Economy* 92: 1049–85.

Barro, R. J. (1986) 'Reputation in a model of monetary policy with incomplete information', *Journal of Monetary Economics* 17 (1): 3–20.

Barro, R. J. and Fischer, S. (1976) 'Recent developments in monetary theory', *Journal of Monetary Economics* 2: 133–67.

Barro, R. J. and Gordon, D. (1983) 'A positive theory of monetary policy in a natural rate model', *Journal of Political Economy* 91 (4): 589–610.

Baumol, W. (1952) 'The transaction demand for cash; an inventory theoretic approach', *Quarterly Journal of Economics* 66: 545–56.

Black, F. (1970) 'Banking and interest rates in a world without money: the effects of uncontrolled banking', *Journal of Bank Research* Autumn (1): 8–28.

Blackburn, K. and Christensen, M. (1989) 'Monetary policy and policy credibility', *Journal of Economic Literature* 27: 1–45.

Blanchard, O. J. (1979) 'Speculative bubbles, crashes and rational expectations', *Economics Letters* 3: 387–9.

—— (1987) 'Why does money affect output? A survey', Working paper 453, Massachusetts Institute of Technology.

Campbell, J. Y. (1986) 'Bond and stock returns in a simple exchange model', *Quarterly Journal of Economics* 101: 785–803.

Canzoneri, M. (1985) 'Monetary policy games and the role of private information', *American Economic Review* 75 (5): 1056–70.

Clower, R. (1967) 'A reconsideration of the microfoundations of monetary theory', *Western Economic Journal* 6: 1–8.

Cox, J. C., Ingersoll, J. E. and Ross, S. A. (1985) 'A theory of the term structure of interest rates', *Econometrica* 53: 385–408.

Cukierman, A. (1985) 'Central bank behavior and credibility – some recent developments', Mimeo, Federal Reserve Bank of St Louis.

Debreu, G. (1959) *The Theory of Value*, New Haven, CT: Cowles Foundation Monograph.

Diamond, D. (1984) 'Financial intermediation and delegated monitoring', *Review of Economic Studies* 51: 393–414.

Diamond, P. (1984) 'Money in search equilibrium', *Econometrica* 52: 1–20.

Diba, B. T. and Grossman, H. I. (1985) 'Rational bubbles in stock prices?', Working paper 1779, National Bureau of Economic Research.

Fama, E. F. (1980) 'Banking in the theory of finance', *Journal of Monetary Economics* 6: 39–57.

—— (1983) 'Financial intermediation and price level control', *Journal of Monetary Economics* 12: 7–28.

Feenstra, R. C. (1986) 'Functional equivalence between liquidity costs and the utility of money', *Journal of Monetary Economics* 17: 271–91.

Fischer, S. (1979) 'Capital accumulation on the transition path in a monetary optimizing model', *Econometrica* 47: 1433–9.

—— (1986) 'Time consistent monetary and fiscal policy: a survey', Mimeo, Massachusetts Institute of Technology.

—— (1988) 'Recent developments in macroeconomics', *Economic Journal* 98: 294–339.

Friedman, M. (1960) *A Program for Monetary Stability*, New York: Fordham University Press.

Gale, D. and Hellwig, M. (1985) 'Incentive-compatible debt contracts: the one period problem', *Reivew of Economic Studies* 52: 647–64.

Garber, P. (1989) 'Tulipmania', *Journal of Political Economy* 97: 535–60.

Girton, L. and Roper, D. (1981) 'Theory and implications of currency substitution', *Journal of Money, Credit and Banking* 13: 12–30.

Green, E. and Porter R. (1984) 'No cooperative collusion under imperfect price information', *Econometrica* 52 (1): 87–100.

Greenfield, R. L. and Yeager, L. B. (1983) 'A *laissez-faire* approach to monetary stability', *Journal of Money, Credit and Banking* 15: 302–15.

Hahn, F. (1973) 'On transaction costs, inessential sequence economics, and money', *Review of Economic Studies* 40: 449–62.

Hall, R. E. (1982) ' "Friedman and Schwartz" monetary trends: a neo-Chicagoan view', *Journal of Economic Literature* 20: 1552–6.

Hamilton, J. D. (1986) 'On testing for self-fulfilling speculative price bubbles', *International Economic Review* 27: 545–52.

Harper, I. (1988) 'Cashless payments systems and the legal restrictions theory of money', Discussion paper 211, University of Melbourne.

Hayek, F. (1976) *The Denationalisation of Money*, London: Institute for Economic Affairs.

Hicks, J. R. (1938) *Value and Capital*, Oxford: Clarendon Press.

Honkapohja, S. (1985) 'Expectations and the theory of macroeconomic policy: some recent developments', *European Journal of Political Economy* 1: 479–83.

Jones, R. A. (1976) 'The origin and development of media of exchange', *Journal of Political Economy* 84: 757–75.

Kareken, J. H. and Wallace, N. (eds) (1980) *Models of Monetary Economies*, Minneapolis, MN: Federal Reserve Bank of Minneapolis.

Keynes, J. M. (1936) *The General Theory of Employment, Interest and Money*, London: Macmillan.

King, R. G. (1983) 'On the economics of private money', *Journal of Monetary Economics* 12: 127–58.

Kiyotaki, N. and Wright, R. (1989a) 'On money as a medium of exchange', *Journal of Political Economy* 97: 927–54.

—— and —— (1989b) 'A contribution to the pure theory of money', Research Department Staff Report 123, Federal Reserve Bank of Minneapolis.

Krasker, W. (1980) 'The peso problem in testing the efficiency of forward exchange markets', *Journal of Monetary Economics* 6: 269–76.

Kreps, D. and Wilson, R. (1982) 'Reputation and imperfect information', *Journal of Economic Theory* 27 (2): 253–79.

Kydland, F. and Prescott, E. (1977) 'Rules rather than discretion: the inconsistency of optimal plans', *Journal of Political Economy* 85 (3): 473–91.

Laidler, D. (1984a) 'Misconceptions about the real-bills doctrine: a comment on Sargent and Wallace', *Journal of Political Economy* 92: 149–55.

—— (1984b) 'The buffer stock notion in economics', *Economic Journal (Supplement)* 94: 17–34.

Lucas, R. (1980) 'Equilibrium in a pure currency economy', *Economic Inquiry* 18: 203–30.

Lucas, R. and Stokey, N. (1983) 'Optimal fiscal and monetary policy in an economy without capital', *Journal of Monetary Economics* 12 (1): 55–93.

—— and —— (1987) 'Money and interest in a cash-in-advance economy', *Econometrica* 55: 491–514.

McCallum, B. T. (1985) 'On consequences and criticisms of monetary targetting', Discussion paper, Carnegie-Mellon University.

MacDonald, R. and Taylor, M. (1989) 'Economic analysis of foreign exchange markets: an expository survey', in R. MacDonald and M. P. Taylor (eds) *Exchange Rates and Open Economy Macroeconomics*, Oxford: Basil Blackwell.

McKinnon, R. (1982) 'Currency substitution and instability in the world dollar standard', *American Economic Review* 72: 329–33.

—— (1984) 'An international standard for monetary stabilisation', *Policy Analyses in International Economics*, vol. 8, Washington, DC: Institute of International Economics.

Makinen, C. E. and Woodward, G. T. (1986) 'Some anecdotal evidence relating to the legal restrictions theory of money', *Journal of Political Economy* 94: 260–5.

Mankiw, G. (1985) 'Small menu costs and large business cycles: a macroeconomic model of monopoly', *Quarterly Journal of Economics* 100: 529–39.

Mehra, R. and Prescott, E. (1985) 'The equity premium: a puzzle', *Journal of Monetary Economics* 15: 145–62.

Milbourne, R. D. (1986) 'Financial innovation and the demand for liquid assets', *Journal of Money, Credit and Banking* 18: 506–11.

—— (1988a) 'Re-examining the buffer-stock model of money', *Economic Journal (Supplement)* 97: 130–42.

—— (1988b) 'Disequilibrium buffer-stock models: a survey', *Journal of Economic Surveys* 2: 187–208.

Mundell, R. (1968) 'Towards a better international monetary system', unpublished manuscript, University of Chicago.

Obstfeld, M. (1983) 'The capital flows problem revisited', *Review of Economic Studies* 52: 605–24.

—— (1984) 'Multiple stable equilibria in an optimising perfect-foresight model', *Econometrica* 52: 223–8.

Ostroy, J. (1973) 'The informational efficiency of monetary exchange', *American Economic Review* 53: 597–610.

Patinkin, D. (1965) *Money, Interest, and Prices*, Evanston, IL: Harper & Row.

Persson, M., Persson, T. and Svensson, L. (1987) 'Time consistency of fiscal and monetary policy', *Econometrica* 55 (6): 1419–31.

Poterba, J. and Rotemberg, J. (1987) 'Money in the utility function: an empirical implementation', Paper presented at 1985 Austin Symposium on Economics.

Rogoff, K. (1985) 'The optimal degree of commitment to an intermediate monetary target', *Quarterly Journal of Economy* 100 (4): 1169–89.

—— (1987) 'Reputational constraints on monetary policy', in *Bubbles and Other Essays*, Amsterdam: North Holland, Carnegie-Rochester Conference Series on Public Policy, vol. 26, pp. 141–82.

Samuelson, P. (1958) 'An exact consumption-loan model of interest with or without the social contrivance of money', *Journal of Political Economy* 66: 467–82.

Sargent, T. J. and Wallace, N. (1982) 'The real-bills doctrine versus the quantity theory: a reconsideration', *Journal of Political Economy* 90: 1212–36.

Starr, R. (1972) 'Exchange in barter and monetary economies', *Quarterly Journal of Economics* 86: 290–302.

Stiglitz, J. and Weiss, A. (1981) 'Credit rationing in markets with imperfect information', *American Economic Review* 71: 393–410.

Svensson, L. E. O. (1985) 'Money and asset prices in a cash-in-advance economy', *Journal of Political Economy* 93: 919–44.

Taylor, J. B. (1983) 'Rules, discretion and reputation in a model of monetary policy: comment', *Journal of Monetary Economics* 12 (1): 123–5.

—— (1985) 'What would nominal GDP targetting do to the business cycle?', in K. Brunner and A. Meltzer (eds) *Understanding Monetary Regimes*, Amsterdam: North-Holland, Carnegie-Rochester Conference Series on Public Policy, vol. 22.

Tirole, J. (1985) 'Asset bubbles and overlapping generations', *Econometrica* 53: 1071–1100.

Tobin, J. (1956) 'The interest-elasticity of transactions demand for cash', *Review of Economics and Statistics* 38: 241–7.

—— (1980) 'Discussion of Wallace', in J. H. Kareken and N. Wallace (eds) *Models of Monetary Economics*, pp. 83–90, Minneapolis, MN: Federal Reserve Bank of Minneapolis.

Townsend, R. M. (1979) 'Optimal contracts and competitive markets with costly state verification', *Journal of Economic Theory* 21: 265–93.

—— (1980) 'Models of money with spatially separated agents', in J. H. Kareken and N. Wallace (eds) *Models of Monetary Economies*, Minneapolis, MN: Federal Reserve Bank of Minneapolis.

Vaubel, R. (1980) 'International shifts in the demand for money, their effects on exchange rates and price levels and their implications for the preannouncements of monetary expansion', *Weltwirtschaftliches Archiv* 116: 1–44.

Wallace, N. (1980) 'The overlapping generations model of fiat money', in J. H. Kareken and N. Wallace (eds) *Models of Monetary Economies*, pp. 49–82, Minneapolis, MN: Federal Reserve Bank of Minneapolis.

Weiss, L. (1980) 'The effects of money supply on economic welfare in the steady state', *Econometrica* 48: 565–78.

White, L. H. (1987) 'Accounting for non-interest-bearing currency: a critique of the legal restrictions theory of money, *Journal of Money, Credit and Banking* 19: 448–56.

Williamson, S. (1986) 'Costly monitoring, financial intermediation, and equilibrium credit rationing', *Journal of Monetary Economics* 18: 159–79.

—— (1987a) 'Transactions costs, inflation, and the variety of intermediation services', *Journal of Money, Credit and Banking*, 19: 484–98.

—— (1987b) 'Costly monitoring, loan contracts and equilibrium credit rationing', *Quarterly Journal of Economics* 102: 135–46.

16

ECONOMICS OF THE ENVIRONMENT

DAVID W. PEARCE

16.1 HISTORICAL BACKGROUND

The effective origins of environmental economics as a discipline lie in the 1960s at the time of the first environmental revolution. It seems wrong to date its emergence as a coherent body of thought any earlier because, by and large, modern environmental economics makes substantive use of neoclassical welfare economics, the principles of which were not fully codified until the work of Little (1950) and De Graaf (1957). None the less, there are significant precursors. The major contributions prior to the 1960s were in the following areas.

Ecological bounds on economic activity

The idea that natural environments set some absolute 'bound' or 'limit' on what it is feasible to achieve in an economy was already familiar from the work of Malthus (1798), while limits set by rising costs as lower-grade natural resources are exploited is fundamental to scarcity in the sense of Ricardo (1817). The 'limits' concept is also present in Mill's 'stationary state' (Mill 1857), in which the stock of people (i.e. the population level) and the stock of capital assets are constant. This 'constant stock' idea was popularized in Daly's 'steady state' (Daly 1973), creating unfortunate terminological confusion given that both stationary state and steady state had taken on other meanings in economics.[1] A belief in 'limits' is not a necessary feature of modern environmental economics, but the idea has prompted a considerable part of the thinking underlying modern theory. Neither is zero economic growth – the achievement of a 'steady state' in Daly's sense – an integral part of environmental economics. Indeed, it seems fair to say that few environmental economists embrace the 'steady state' philosophy. Again, however, the debate has been productive even for those who do not share 'anti-growth' sentiment since it has focused attention on the social costs of the way in which modern economies grow.

316

Pollution as externality

The impact of pollution on the Pareto efficiency of a freely functioning competitive system was formalized by Pigou (1920) in terms of the now classic divergence between private and social cost. Pollution gives rise to external costs, and the aim of social policy should be to achieve the socially optimal level of externality. This is unlikely to be zero unless the predicted damage from pollution is thought to be catastrophic in some sense (i.e. the marginal external cost curve is totally inelastic). The result that optimal externality is positive immediately divorced economists from many life scientists and environmentalists whose policy prescriptions have generally been phrased in terms of eliminating pollution. To some extent, this divergence of view is narrower than at first appears to be the case. Waste residuals disposed of to the environment are the source of pollution. No one argues for zero waste disposal, but environmentalists do argue for an upper limit of residuals disposal set by the capability of natural environments to absorb and harmlessly convert the wastes. This condition is formally equivalent to using a resource sustainably.

Exhaustible resource theory

The basics of the economics of depletable resources were formulated by Gray (1914). He developed what we would now call *user cost:* the sacrifice of future use caused by using up a unit of an exhaustible resource today. The cost of using an exhaustible resource was therefore made up of the sum of its extraction cost and this user cost element. Gray's analysis was elegantly formalized, and the link to discount rates clearly established, in the classic paper by Hotelling (1931), who showed that, under competitive conditions, the rent or royalty on a natural resource (the price net of extraction costs for the marginal unit) would increase over time at a percentage rate equal to the resource owner's discount rate. For a hypothetical resource with costless extraction, the 'Hotelling rule' states that the price of the resource rises at the discount rate.[2] This basic rule remains the cornerstone of the modern theory of optimal resource use.

Renewable resource use

The basic analytics of the optimal use of a renewable resource such as a fishery, forest or livestock were formulated by Gordon (1954) who showed how common property would lead to the exhaustion of rents, although not to the extinction of the resource, compared with the profit-maximizing behaviour of a single resource owner. The decisions about *how much* of the resource to harvest and *when* to harvest it are clearly interdependent since the resource biomass grows through time, thus increasing the potential offtake the longer is the delay in harvesting. The analysis of this problem in terms of forestry was brilliantly worked out by Faustman (1849). He showed that the optimal rotation period, i.e. the period between one harvest and the next, is determined by the balance of the gains from biomass growth by delaying felling and the costs in terms of forgone interest from investing the proceeds from timber felling now. The Faustman solution is still applicable to single-product forests, i.e. forests producing only timber, but has no validity if the forest is multifunctional.

By the 1960s, then, many of the building blocks necessary for the emergence of environmental economics were in place. It remained to fit them together and broaden the horizons. Although still not fully acknowledged by mainstream environmental economists, the critical contribution enabling a synthesis was Boulding's (1966) essay on 'spaceship earth', a magnificently unconstrained work of imagination and analysis.[3] Whereas the conventional textbook treatment depicted the economy as a linear system (resources flowing to production for consumption and investment), Boulding drew on the laws of thermodynamics to establish two propositions: (a) all resource extraction, production and consumption result in waste products ('residuals') equal in matter/energy terms to the resources flowing into these sectors, and (b) there is no possibility of the 100 per cent return (recycling) of these waste products to enter the resource flow again because of the second law of thermodynamics. The first law, the conservation of matter/energy, tells us that the economic system cannot destroy anything: whatever enters the economic system must reappear in the same or a transformed state elsewhere in it. The second law – the law of entropy – tells us that energy cannot be recycled at all, while many materials uses are so dissipative that we cannot recycle the transformed product (for example, lead in gasoline). All this adds up to the economy's being a circular system, not a linear one, with resources flowing through the economic system and then on to the environment as a sink for residuals and being partially recycled to become resources again. As the throughput of resources grows with economic growth, so the volume of residuals necessarily grows and comes up against the capacity of natural environments to absorb them and convert them to harmless products. The combination of the circular resource flow system and the limits set by the natural assimilative capacity of the environment explains why we cannot for long behave as if no such limits existed. In Boulding's terms, we must cease to behave as if we lived in a 'cowboy economy', with limitless new territory to be conquered, and learn to treat planet earth as a 'spaceship' – a circular system in which every effort has to be made to recycle materials, reduce wastes, conserve depletable energy sources and utilize the genuinely limitless energy sources such as solar power.

Boulding's synthesis was formalized in the materials balance models of Ayres and Kneese (1969) and Kneese *et al.* (1970). The additional critical finding of these contributions was that residuals are pervasive to the economic system and hence externality is pervasive. While it may have been preferable to say that externality is potentially pervasive, since actual externality depends on the residuals balance with assimilative capacity, the resulting picture contrasted starkly with the traditional (and, surprisingly, still propagated) image of externality as 'a minor resource misallocation' (Beckerman 1972: 327).

The materials balance principle established the extensive interdependence of economy and environment. Combined with the ecologist's observations about the complex interactions within natural environments, environmental economics thus became more 'holistic' in concept. Effectively, the general equilibrium view of an economy was being extended to a general equilibrium view of the economy-with-environment. Looked at from this standpoint, the two major issues to arise were as follows.

1 Whether there could be simultaneous equilibrium within the economy and between the economy and the environment, i.e. whether there exists a set of prices and quantities that would ensure the existence and stability of an extended equilibrium. We might call this the existence issue.
2 How the many economic functions of natural environments can be shadow-priced so as to determine what the optimal price–quantity configuration of an extended equilibrium would look like. This is the valuation issue.

Most of the concerns of environmental economists follow from these basic issues. The existence issue explains the concerns with physical laws as well as with economic behaviour, the environment versus economic growth debate, the questioning of neoclassical welfare economics models and the current debate on 'sustainability'. The valuation issue explains the search for techniques to place monetary measures on environmental functions which are generally unpriced, and, regardless of the ability to value ecosystem functions in monetary terms, to correct economic decisions which treat natural environments as if they are unpriced.

The history of environmental economics has still to be written.[4] In the meantime, a brief overview of the current 'state of the art' can be organized in terms of the existence, valuation and instruments classification employed above.

16.2 THE EXISTENCE OF ECONOMY–ECOLOGY EQUILIBRIUM

The existence issue can be stated as follows: does there exist some set of prices and quantities which secures general equilibrium within the economy and simultaneously gives rise to an equilibrium relationship with natural environments. The nature of an equilibrium with natural environments is difficult to formalize. One approach, pursued elegantly by Perrings (1987), is to say that economy equilibrium has to be consistent with physical laws. However, it is important to make the context dynamic, in contrast with the Ayres–Kneese (1969) model which is a static allocative model in the Walras–Cassel sense. An economy which treats natural resources as if they are free gifts is unsustainable and hence breaches the dynamic economy–environment equilibrium condition. Similarly, an economy which treats residuals as being subject to free disposal is also unsustainable. Economic models in which 'the environment is simultaneously a horn of plenty and a bottomless sink' (Perrings 1987: 5) are dynamically unstable. Conventional general equilibrium models either ignore environment altogether (the free gifts and free disposal axioms) or assume limitless substitution between resources. The former assumption is insupportable, while the latter at least offends the specificity of resources which limits substitution. The substitution of 'capital' for resources is in fact limited (a) because resources are embodied in capital, a point made repeatedly by Georgescu-Roegen (1979), so that the analysis of resource depletion is more akin to a Sraffian 'production of commodities' problem than a neoclassical production function one, and (b) because some resources serve life-support functions with no obvious substitutes.

Perrings' analysis concludes that any economic system based on prices will 'be driven from one disequilibrium state to the next by persistent external effects that result from the unobservability and uncontrollability of the processes of the environment through the price system' (Perrings 1987: 7). That is, any economic system that relies on prices as its means of allocating resources, both intratemporally and intertemporally, fails the test of environment–economy equilibrium. Essentially this is because changes in the economy have necessary implications for the environmental systems in terms of flows of energy and matter. In turn, these material/energy changes impact back on the economic system. The two-way process of interdependence is random, however, to a considerable extent. There is a high potential for uncertainty in the Shackle sense of novelty and surprise. While only the first law of thermodynamics and the 'quintessentially unknowable' nature of change in a technological dynamic system are needed to establish this result, the second law provides additional support by adding to the potential for surprise. As entropy increases so does our ignorance of how dissipated wastes behave in the whole set of interdependent ecosystems that make up the physical support for all economies. Perrings' emphasis on uncertainty might be illustrated by the sheer complexity and uncertainty of atmospheric and stratospheric diffusion processes in respect of gaseous emissions giving rise to ozone layer depletion and the greenhouse effect, or, just as effectively, by our understanding of the behaviour of micropollutants in hydrological ecosystems.

Perrings' book is perhaps the most rigorous exposition of the existence issue. Daly (1977, 1987) has persistently offered analogous concerns based on both thermodynamic laws, but far less formally and without Perrings' emphasis on uncertainty. Daly has done much to champion Georgescu-Roegen's (1971) concern with the second law, showing that it cannot be dismissed because its time-scale is alleged to be the 'heat death' of the universe (and hence beyond anyone's concern), or because it implies some energy theory of value in which normative product prices should reflect energy content. The former is irrelevant and the second was never embraced by Georgescu-Roegen (see Daly's (1986) response to Burness *et al.* (1980)). The relevance of entropy is that it is the measure of the qualitative difference between resources and their mass equivalent as residuals. The implications of this qualitative difference, in terms of non-recyclability and the pervasiveness of chemical transformations of residuals in ecosystems, is self-evidently important to policy within very human time-frames. Daly's prescription is for zero economic growth (ZEG), where growth is measured as positive changes in real gross domestic product (GDP), but positive 'development'. Growth is limited not only by the physical bounds (the 'biophysical limits') but by moral concerns for future generations, sentient non-humans and the impact of growth on moral standards. These 'ethico-social limits' are reinforced by the socially self-defeating nature of growth arising from the Easterlin paradox (Easterlin 1974) whereby growth results in no one feeling better off because of a phenomenon akin to the relative income hypothesis. The obvious problem with ZEG, however, is that, as far as biophysical limits are concerned, it has no unique status. The level of income corresponding to environment–economy equilibrium might be less than that existing at the time that ZEG is achieved, or more. If, however, Perrings is right and there is no extended equilibrium for economies reliant at least in part on price signals, ZEG again appears arbitrary as a prescription. Daly's response would be that ZEG is better than positive economic growth since it must be associated with a lower throughput of materials and energy, and hence a slower 'drawdown' of low-entropy resources. Moreover, people might be willing to adopt ZEG but not negative growth; real world policy should aim at the saleable as well as the optimal.

Others have investigated the objectives served by, and the requirements for, an extended equilibrium. Page (1977a, b, c) sets out conditions for what he calls 'permanent livability', a state of the economy which is sustainable through time and which serves a Rawlsian intergenerational fairness objective. A maximin principle applied in an intergenerational context would ensure that the maximum primary goods (goods which it would be irrational to prefer less of to more) are supplied to the least advantaged generation. Page argues that this entails 'equal access' to the resource base for each generation. The interpretation of at least some natural capital as a primary good is suggested by Pearce *et al.* (1989). The irrationality of preferring less to more of these types of natural capital arises from the life-support functions that they serve. In this way, Page's intergenerational fairness criterion is extended to be an existence issue – failure to behave 'fairly' breaches the condition for extended equilibrium.

Page suggests that in the Rawlsian 'original position' equal access will emerge as part of the rational process of decision-making. This would be the outcome of an understanding that resources are a collective good, of the need to formulate rules that do not require any one generation to plan over a time horizon encompassing all future generations, of the need to ensure that the first generation would not renege on the requirement because it is too burdensome and, of course, that the result is intergenerationally 'fair'. The general requirement is that the stock of *natural* capital be held constant through time, where constancy of stock has to be interpreted in terms of constant real prices or values (see also Pearce *et al.* 1989).

The focus on constancy of natural capital in Page's work contrasts with efforts to extend the neoclassical model in which capital is generally 'fungible'. Indeed, a fundamental distinguishing feature of the 'sustainability' school (Page, Pearce *et al.*, Perrings and, to some extent, Daly) is its concern about the limited substitutability of man-made capital K_m for natural capital K_n. An elegant statement of the conditions for intergenerational fairness in terms of constancy of total capital stock $K_m + K_n$ is given by Solow (1986). Solow's concern is with the standard ethical question of what rate of depletion of a non-renewable resource should be pursued if there is a concern with intergenerational equity. He points to the theorem of Hartwick (1977, 1978a, b), which states that to ensure a constant flow of consumption over time, i.e. intergenerational fairness in the sense of Rawls (Solow 1978), it is necessary to invest the entire economic rent from an exhaustible resource in reproducible capital. This rule has its practical counterpart in calls for the use of rents from North Sea oil reserves to build up manufacturing capacity in the United Kingdom or, in the context of developing economies such as Indonesia, calls for the diversification of the capital base of the economy to compensate for depletion of their oil and gas stocks and the stock of tropical forests. Solow shows that the Hartwick rule can be interpreted as one of holding a total stock of capital $K = K_m + K_n$ constant over time. As Solow puts it:

The neat interpretation of allowable consumption as the interest on an initial patrimony or resource endowment seems quite appropriate. It is a reminder of the old-fashioned obligation to 'maintain capital intact'.

(Solow 1986: 149)

The Hartwick–Solow rule holds for a constant labour supply and zero population growth. Once these conditions are relaxed the rule breaks down in several ways. In terms of the extended existence issue, the critical point is that technological progress must outpace population growth for there to be the *possibility* of constant per capita consumption (but the result is not guaranteed). Different beliefs about the extent to which GDP can be 'delinked' from resource and energy throughputs have traditionally defined the difference between optimists and pessimists in the environmental debate. Page (1977a) draws attention to the role which technology plays in adding to the risks faced by future generations, and hence to the possibility of reducing future productive capacity rather than increasing it.

It is also unclear what happens to the Hartwick–Solow result if K_n and K_m are not smoothly substitutable, since this appears to strike at the heart of Solow's assumption that 'recognition of the fact of substitutability or fungibility converts a matter of "simple justice" into a complicated question of resource allocation' (Solow 1986: 142). Maler (1986) adds a further important question about the uncertainty of the critical variables in the Solow model. If we do not know the elasticity of substitution of K_n and K_m, future population size, resource reserves and future technologies, how should we behave in terms of intertemporal resource allocation?

The role which discounting plays in intertemporal allocation decisions remains a deeply contested issue in environmental economics. Environmentalist concerns arise because discounting appears to shift social costs forward in time, thus offending the Rawls–Page–Solow concept of intergenerational fairness, a concern voiced historically by Pigou (1932). In terms of the extended equilibrium concept, discounting threatens long-run equilibrium by storing up combinations of problems for future generations: high discount rates tend to encourage earlier rather than later depletion of exhaustible resources; they can be consistent with renewable resource extinction (Clark 1976); they permit the adoption of unproven technologies which impose costs on future generations (nuclear waste disposal and station decommissioning, groundwater contamination, global warming, ozone depletion etc.).

The environmentalist critique has also centred on the very rationale for discounting which has typically been in terms of the factors giving rise to social time preference and to the positive marginal productivity of capital, or some weighted combination in second-best circumstances (Lind 1982). Consider the component parts of the standard formula for a consumption rate of interest, i.e.

$$s = uc + p$$

where s is the rate of discount, u is the elasticity of the marginal utility of consumption, c is the growth rate in real per capita consumption and p is the rate of 'pure' time preference. Critics have argued, echoing Ramsey (1929), that pure time preference is irrational, that the underlying value judgement that 'preferences should count' is inconsistent with moral obligation and duty, and that, even if wants are dominant, it is wants as they arise that matter, not today's assessment of tomorrow's wants (Goodin 1982).

The idea that positive discount rates are warranted because of uncertainty about the existence of a future generation, or the same individual in the future, is widely entertained (Sen 1961; Rawls 1972), and practical translations of life expectancy into positive discount rates have been made (Eckstein 1961; Kula 1984). However, if the effects of discounting are to leave future generations, who *may* exist, with high social cost burdens, then it seems odd to react to this uncertainty by imposing costs that may contribute to their non-existence. Goodin (1978) argues that this is effectively what some modern technological risks, for example from nuclear power, entail. That is, there is a different type of uncertainty involved, potentially catastrophic in nature, compared with that subsumed in the traditional expected utility rule. This concern is echoed by Page (1978) in respect of toxic chemicals where the probability of damage is low but the impact is potentially very large (the 'zero–infinity' dilemma). Expectations about future growth, i.e. assuming $c > 0$, also conflict with the environmentalist critique. For $c > 0$ we require environmental protection not destruction, yet it is the latter that is threatened by high discount rates. In short, using $c > 0$ as a justification for discounting is self-contradictory.

The alternative route to discounting, via observed positive marginal product on reproducible capital, has also been criticized. Parfit (1983) suggests that the opportunity cost argument relies on the ability to compensate future generations for damage done by setting up an initial endowment that grows at the opportunity cost rate to equal future damage or clean-up costs. If we are not able to do this, then future damage matters as much as current damage – its futurity cannot in itself be a reason for discounting. Parfit's objection here is really based on the more familiar criticism of hypothetical compensation, the Kaldor–Hicks–Scitovsky test, as the basis for deciding on potential Pareto improvement. This concern is echoed by some economists concerned with sustainability in terms of their focus on compensating investments for environmental losses arising from other projects (Klaassen and Botterweg 1976; Pearce *et al.* 1989; Spash and d'Arge 1989).

The main thrust of the environmentalist critique of discounting is that discount rates should be zero, implying indifference between generational effects. This contrasts with Page's (1977b) view that discounting is permissible, but only once the rules for permanent livability have been established. That is, the constancy of natural capital stock is first established as the means of ensuring intergenerational equal access, and then maximizing net present values (with positive discounting) would be permitted within the confines set by that rule. This idea is not dissimilar to the 'ecological bounds' in Pearce (1987) or even Daly's 'biophysical limits'. However, there is a more direct reason for rejecting zero discounting as a panacea for intergenerational fairness. While lower discounting increases the demand for preserved environments K_n, and for man-made capital K_m, the materials balance principle reminds us that resources are an input to capital. Depending on the relative elasticities of output to capital and of output to resource inputs and of materials and energy intensity, increased capital demand may have the effect of 'dragging through' the economy more materials/energy throughput, thus reducing environmental preservation (Krautkraemer 1985, 1988; Markandya and Pearce 1988). This possibility had already been foreseen in the seminal paper by Krutilla (1967).

A further reason for rejecting zero discounting as the basis for 'ecologically sensitive' planning decisions is given by Olson and Bailey (1981) who show that a consumer without pure time preference p (see p. 324) but facing positive interest rates r would 'cut consumption down to utterly abject levels in order to provide for the future' (Olson and Bailey 1981: 17). However, the Olson–Bailey result is problematic in begging the question, since the assumption of perpetual positive interest rates, i.e. positive marginal product of capital, is what is in question.

The environmental economics literature certainly supports the wider supposition that social discount rates lie below market rates (Lind 1982). Marglin's (1963) view that the welfare of future generations is a public good to the current generation – an efficiency, not an equity, rationale – implies lowering discount rates to leave more capital stock to future generations. Samuelson's concept of risk-pooling across projects (Samuelson 1964) and the Arrow–Lind view of risk-pooling across people (Arrow and Lind 1970) provide a rationale for using a riskless rate in the public sector compared with the higher risk-inclusive market rate. However, Fisher (1974) has pointed out that the Arrow–Lind theorem does not hold if the risks in question take on the attributes of a public 'bad', for example global warming, ozone depletion etc., suggesting that there is limited relevance to precisely the context under review, i.e. environmental damage.

The literature is still unable to offer much guidance to the selection of an appropriate discount rate in the context of environmental concern, and possibly in other contexts as well. It is for this reason that attempts have been made to modify project appraisal without seeking discount rate adjustments. Markandya and Pearce (1988) suggest the integration of a sustainability constraint, construed as some form of constant natural capital stock, into project appraisal. The implications are unclear but are perhaps likely to be more fruitfully explored than continuing with the lack of resolution so far achieved in the efforts to modify discount rates.

16.3 OPTIMAL RESOURCE DEPLETION AND USE

For an exhaustible resource, the Hotelling rule (Hotelling 1931) establishes that the royalty (or user cost), i.e. wellhead price net of extraction cost, should rise over time at the ruling rate of discount, i.e. the marginal product of capital. If extraction costs can be imagined to be zero, the more popular version of the rule emerges, namely that the wellhead price should rise over time at the rate of discount. These results hold for a competitive economy. As the price rises through time, substitution by other resources will be encouraged. Indeed, many modern models of optimal depletion assume a 'backstop' technology (Nordhaus 1973) which substitutes for the depleted resource once prices reach certain levels – examples might be desalinated seawater for depleted groundwater or surface water, tar sands for oil and (interestingly, fading from the real-world picture) fast-breeder reactor or even fusion electricity. In the absence of a backstop technology the limit to the Hotelling price rise process is the point of intersection of the demand curve with the price axis.

Much of the modern literature investigates the impact of relaxing the underlying Hotelling assumptions. Hotelling himself investigated the impact of monopoly, costs that rise as extraction increases (the Ricardian case), the influence of fixed investment costs and the effect of a severance tax (i.e. a tax on depletion), among other things.

Intuitively, we would expect monopoly to slow down the rate of depletion because of the gains to be made from restricting output. This intuition, supported by Hotelling, is what makes monopoly the 'friend' of the conservationist. Essentially, marginal revenue, not price, rises at the rate of discount in the costless extraction case. Hotelling seemed to think that this alone would retard depletion, but this is queried by Devarajan and Fisher (1981). Modern contributions focus on the relationship between the price elasticity of demand and quantity: if elasticity declines as quantity increases, then, generally, the monopolist depletes more slowly (Lewis 1963; Dasgupta and Heal 1979). The same result holds if the elasticity of demand increases over time, i.e. low elasticities now and higher ones later (Weinstein and Zeckhauser 1975; Stiglitz 1976). A separate literature analyses oligopolistic behaviour with respect to natural resources, mostly prompted by the OPEC experience (for surveys see Cremer and Weitzman 1976; Pearce 1981; Fisher 1987), and is generally unrelated to Hotelling's work.

The Hotelling rule is comparatively straightforward in the context of (barely imaginable) costless extraction or constant costs of extraction. However, costs are likely to vary positively with the rate of cumulative extraction, i.e. inversely with the remaining stock, because the best ores will be depleted first. In practice, this assumption is frequently confounded, but rigorous formulations of the impact of declining ore grades have been given in a number of papers (e.g. Solow and Wan 1976). There are also numerous demonstrations that the Hotelling price rule does not hold under these conditions. Instead, the royalty rises at the rate of discount less the percentage incremental cost caused by depleting the total stock (see, for example, Peterson and Fisher 1977). Where successive depletion of the stock adds to the 'above ground' stock of the resource (for example, diamonds), then the Hotelling rule may work in reverse, with the rising stock causing a fall in price over time (Levhari and Pindyck 1979).

Uncertainty about the size of reserves may result in slower depletion because of the costs of incurring a surprise if depletion does occur, a result that is hardly intuitively persuasive. Models in which uncertainty is treated by additional exploration to reduce it have more appeal (Arrow and Chang 1978; Hoel 1978; Devarajan and Fisher 1981). Uncertainty about future prices could deplete resources faster because of risk aversion (Weinstein and Zeckhauser 1975).

A number of recent contributions have analysed the effects on initial investment costs – 'set-up costs' – on the Hotelling path. The main finding is that the larger the resource reserve over which set-up costs can be distributed, the lower is the average investment cost and hence the more akin to increasing returns is the context in which the resource owner – the 'mine' – operates. As such it should occasion no surprise that the competitive price path yielded by the Hotelling analysis breaks down. There is effective market failure. Set-up costs may then lead to periods of constant extraction rates and constant prices (Campbell 1980).

Some authors have suggested that modern writers have added little of substance to the fundamental results secured by Hotelling. Others have contrasted real-world situations with the highly stylized abstractions even in the Hotelling models modified for monopoly, initial investment and stock-dependent costs. Bradley (1985) has urged more analysis of actual extractive industries in their institutional context, believing that the gains are 'substantially greater than the marginal gain from further refinements in optimizing models' (Bradley 1985: 328).

Empirically, natural resource prices do not appear to follow a Hotelling price path. Barnett and Morse (1963) and Barnett (1979) found a continuous declining trend since 1870 for US real unit costs of resources, with the possible exception of forestry. Barnett and Morse cite technological change as the main factor giving rise to 'reduced scarcity'. Brown and Field (1979) note that technological change can give the illusion of decreased scarcity, i.e. unit costs could decline up to the point of exhaustion of the resource, thus failing to signal future scarcity. Hall and Hall (1984) use real prices to replicate the Barnett and Morse finding of decreased scarcity up to the mid-1970s but show that real price rises thereafter, suggesting increased scarcity. Slade (1982) shows that price paths for minerals over time tend to fit a U-shaped pattern as technological change first outpaces declining ore grades and then fails to keep pace with the increased extraction costs because of declining grades.

All in all, the Hotelling analysis remains a powerful analytical tool in resource economics, but more caution than has been exercised is required to characterize its application to explain real-world resource depletion decisions. Similar strictures apply to its use as a normative guideline for a depletion policy.

16.4 THE VALUATION ISSUE

Independently of any view taken about the existence issue, environmental economists have been unanimous in seeking to extend the shadow-pricing of the environmental functions of ecosystems. This effort has resulted in a substantial literature which is conveniently reviewed in several sources (Freeman 1979; Bentkover et al. 1986; Johansson 1987; Pearce and Markandya 1989). The briefest of overviews is therefore offered here.

'Benefits assessment', i.e. the monetary evaluation of the environmental benefits of environmental policy, or its obverse, 'damage assessment', has had two main uses: first, to integrate better into cost–benefit analysis the unpriced functions of natural environments and, second, to illustrate the kinds of economic damage done to national economies by resource depletion and environmental pollution. Estimates of national environmental damage avoided through deliberate environmental protection policy, for example, have been produced by Freeman (1982) for the United States. His results suggest a 'saving' of some $26 billion in 1978, i.e. some 1.25 per cent of gross national product (GNP). Similar analyses by other authors, but of actual damage, amount to 0.5–0.9 per cent of Netherlands GNP and 6 per cent of German GNP (Pearce and Markandya 1989).

Various methodologies have been developed to place monetary estimates on environmental gain or loss. The dose–response functions approach concentrates on the physical 'response' to a 'dose' of pollution, measured by ambient pollution concentration or by exposure. In effect, economists have become 'macroepidemiologists', adopting statistical regression techniques to assess the effect of variables on damage such as mortality, morbidity, crop yields, materials deterioration, health of trees etc. Insights have been achieved because of the use of large data sets and because, in some cases, economic variables have been entered into the regressions in a more imaginative way than hitherto. Thus, simple regressions of air pollution on health as the dependent variable are unlikely to be revealing, but multivariate analysis involving age, socio-economic status, access to medical care and pollution variables is likely to be richer in information yielded. Classic works such as Ridker's (1967) study of air pollution were extended in sophisticated ways by Lave and Seskin (1977), which in turn launched a large literature (see, notably, Crocker *et al.* 1979; Ostro 1983, 1987). The 'mechanistic' nature of the dose–response valuation approach has been lessened by the introduction of household expenditure behaviour with respect to morbidity and mortality aversion, i.e. introducing 'health capital' (Grossman 1972). Examples of this development are Cropper (1981) and Gerking and Stanley (1986).

While the dose–response literature has the capability for monetization, for example, by applying a value-of-life figure to pollution-related mortality, monetization has been more directly approached through (a) travel cost models, (b) hedonic pricing and (c) contingent valuation. The travel cost model originates with an unpublished paper by Hotelling (1949) and an early formalization by Clawson and Knetsch (1966) building on earlier work by Clawson. The basic idea is simple: the distance travelled to a site is a proxy for price and the number of trips made is a proxy for quantity. Let the price for distance i be P_i and that for the shorter distance j be P_j, resulting in trips Q_i and Q_j. Then hypothesize that each group will respond to an admission charge in the same way as it does to an increase in travel costs. Then an increased fee from zero to $P_i - P_j$ will result in a decrease in demand from zone j of $Q_j - Q_i$, and so on. A demand curve can be traced out in this way. Just as the demand response to an admission fee can be estimated, so can the response to changes in environmental quality. All that is needed are the observations of the numbers of trips to areas of varying quality. The consumer surplus associated with improvements in quality can thus be estimated, as can the benefit of providing a new site, and so on. Effectively, the travel cost method estimates the demands for inputs to a household recreation production function in the sense of Becker (1965) (see Smith and Desvousges 1986). Individuals choose to visit sites in order to combine the site's services with other inputs to produce an activity such as fishing, swimming etc. The method has been extensively applied and offers a measure of the use value of a resource (see below). Developments of the analysis have included allowance for competing sites, congestion, different concepts of the value of time, and a variation of the approach that treats site characteristics rather than sites *per se* as the object of demand (see Deyak and Smith 1978; Morey 1981; Bockstael and McConnell 1983; Brown and Mendelsohn 1984).

A development of the hedonic price technique suggested by Griliches (1971) and Rosen (1974) relates property prices to site characteristics including pollution variables. Thus, a hedonic price function of the form

$$P_h = f(S_1, \ldots, S_n, D)$$

where P_h is the house price or rental, $S_1, \ldots, S_n$ are site characteristics and D is disamenity, yields an implicit price dP_h/dD. Function P_h is in fact a locus of equilibrium points on household willingness-to-pay functions, so that, technically, the implicit price is not the correct estimate of marginal willingness to pay. A procedure to derive an inverse demand function would be to take dP_h/dD and regress it in turn on income and pollution levels, making some assumption about the supply of properties with given characteristics. Most empirical studies estimate a form of the P_h function, and only a few go beyond to derive inverse demand curves (see Harrison and Rubinfeld 1978; Brookshire *et al.* 1981). Hedonic approaches have been extensively applied to air pollution (for surveys see Freeman 1979; Brookshire *et al.* 1982; Pearce and Markandya 1989) and to noise nuisance from traffic (Nelson 1982) and aircraft (Nelson 1980). Wilman (1984) and Feenberg and Mills (1980) report exercises for coastal beach pollution and water pollution respectively. All in all, the hedonic approach has advanced efforts to put money values on environmental damage and improvements. Controversy surrounds the accuracy of the results, notably in respect of the extent to which housing markets respond 'smoothly' to environmental variables and, unsurprisingly, with respect to the econometrics. The hedonic approach has also been applied to the 'value of human life'. Labour wages are regressed on labour supply characteristics and on workplace risk estimates. The coefficient linking wages to risk then gives a direct measure of the valuation of risk which, in turn, can be grossed up to produce a valuation of human life. While extensively applied in cost–benefit analyses of workplace safety, such values are also applicable to health hazards from pollutants, or can be 'borrowed' to apply to mortality estimates derived from macroepidemiological studies (see above). The approaches and empirical results are surveyed by Violette and Chestnut (1983) and Pearce and Markandya (1989). Theoretical objections to the idea of valuing life are given by Broome (1978), since willingness to pay to avoid certain death is constrained only by income and wealth, and willingness to accept compensation to suffer death is nonsensical. However, Ulph (1982) shows that it is the *ex ante* context that matters, i.e. values to avoid or accept finite risks, whereas Broome's strictures hold for an *ex post* interpretation of risk of death.

Probably the most fruitful approach to evaluation has been the 'contingent valuation method' (CVM). This is based on questionnaires designed to elicit direct willingness to pay from respondents. The methodology is exhaustively analysed and surveyed by Cummings *et al.* (1986). Since the context is one of hypothetical valuation, much of the literature is concerned with tests for response biases. Following Samuelson (1954), it is widely thought that valuations will not be 'accurate', because of strategic behaviour, i.e. the free-rider problem. Bohm (1972) was the first to construct an empirical experiment to test for strategic bias by sampling respondents according to different assumptions about how much they actually would pay for a benefit (a television programme in this case). Bohm found no evidence of strategic bias. Other studies have reached similar conclusions and the survey by Cummings *et al.* concludes that 'a basis does exist for diminishing the "priority" position in research that the strategic bias hypothesis has enjoyed for the past decade' (Cummings *et al.* 1986: 26).

Other forms of bias may also be present. Questionnaires may be designed in such a way as to give misleading results ('design bias'). For example, the questioner starts the bidding process with a starting bid which itself may 'set the scene' for the subsequent structure of bids. This might differ if a different starting point was adopted. Respondents also have to be informed of the way in which they will be expected to pay (hypothetically), i.e. the 'instrument' or 'vehicle' of payment (a local tax, direct charge, increase in a utility charge etc.) may affect the apparent willingness to pay. Respondents' valuations are also likely to vary with the amount and type of information they are given about the problem at hand. Lastly, the whole issue of hypothetical bias – the problem of knowing whether such values would be the same as in real markets – arises. The survey by Cummings *et al.* highlights the lack of familiarity that respondents have with trading off the goods under consideration in CVM studies (for example, a beautiful view or an endangered species) as a source of hypothetical bias. Efforts to reduce such bias by setting up 'pseudo-markets' in which actual money changes hands between questioner and respondent, i.e. a process whereby the hypothetical markets come to mimic better the familiarity, learning and experience attributes of real markets, do perhaps suggest that the hypothetical bias issue is not as serious as might be thought.

CVM techniques have been interesting not just because they add substantially to the economist's armoury of evaluation techniques, but also because they have been instrumental in uncovering other interesting features of preference revelation. Two can be highlighted. The first is that questions can be phrased to elicit a compensating variation or an equivalent variation or both. Where both willingness to pay (WTP) and willingness to accept (WTA) measures have been derived, the surprising finding is that WTA exceeds WTP by significant amounts, contrary to theoretical expectations that measures of consumer surplus should differ only marginally (Willig 1976). Broadly speaking, two schools of thought have emerged to explain the discrepancy. The first points to the generally non-repeated nature of CVM bids, i.e. bids are made only once in what is often an unfamiliar context. This contrasts with 'real' markets in which there is familiarity and repeated bids for a commodity. CVMs in which deliberate attempts to repeat the bidding process are made suggest a narrowing of the WTA–WTP gap (Brookshire and Coursey 1987; Coursey *et al.* 1987). The alternative view is that there is a genuine discontinuity in the valuation function, i.e. losses with reference to an existing position are valued quite differently from gains with respect to that position. This 'loss aversion' is detected both in CVMs and in other types of behaviour including real markets (Knetsch and Sinden 1984; Knetsch *et al.* 1987; Knetsch 1989). If the valuation function is in fact kinked around some initial endowment, there are potentially formidable implictions for consumer theory since consumers do not then appear to travel up and down indifference curves in a smooth manner (Knestch 1988). The issue remains unresolved in the literature, but the loss-aversion approach has strong support among psychologists where 'prospect theory' confirms it (Kahnemann and Tversky 1979).

The second interesting feature of the CVM has been the nature of the values uncovered. The idea that economic values are not all related to actual use or consumption of commodities had been suggested by Weisbrod (1964) and Krutilla (1967). Weisbrod noted the potential value associated with a concern to keep a good in being in order that an option to use is preserved. Krutilla had raised the idea of values unrelated to any use, direct or optional. CVM studies have in fact uncovered empirical estimates of these option values and existence values. As a general proposition, 'total' economic value can be said to comprise use values plus option values plus existence values. The literature has debated the nature of option value since the presupposition that it will be positive turns out to be a simplification. Option value can be seen as a form of insurance against uncertainty. If the uncertainty is about future supply (for example, an endangered species), then option value will typically be positive, but if the uncertainty relates to future demand (e.g. changes in tastes and income), then there is no determinate sign for option value (Bishop 1982). Existence values are positive, but raise controversial issues since it is unclear what their motivation is. Casual inspection of the membership of environmental groups suggests strongly that many people do have a positive WTP for preserving habitats and species that they will never visit or experience directly. This is confirmed by CVMs. However, such values might suggest 'counterpreferential' behaviour if they reflect some ethical commitment on the part of the valuer, possibly undermining the preference base for a theory of value. Some commentators have therefore preferred to explain existence value in terms of bequest motives – leaving the environmental asset to a future generation whose utility is thus part of the utility of the current generation – or sympathy. Alternative explanations which appear to be inconsistent with a preference-based value theory might be respect for the 'rights' of nature, or a notion of 'stewardship'. Not surprisingly, therefore, the very existence of existence value is disputed in the literature. Empirical estimates have produced some startling results, however, as with the finding that hypothetical visibility improvements to the Grand Canyon yield benefits, the overwhelming proportion of which derive from people who would not visit the area (Brookshire *et al.* 1985).

Advances in valuation procedures have thus been formidable in the last decade or so. To a considerable extent, they have focused on the perceptual benefits of natural environments. A greater challenge exists in respect of a better understanding of the economic value of ecosystems in general, for example the watershed protection functions of, say, a tropical forest, storm protection and water quality functions of wetlands, the role of natural genetic diversity in crop yields and in terms of potential scientific information, and so on. Some advances have been made in this respect, but because so many valuable ecosystems are either global in nature (oceans, atmospheres and stratospheres) or are located in developing countries (tropical forests, man-groves, many wetlands), the newer challenge is to develop valuation techniques in contexts where surrogate markets (labour and housing markets, for example) operate extremely imperfectly and CVMs are likely to be inoperable.

16.5 ECONOMIC INSTRUMENTS

The final issue relates to the mechanisms available for securing optimal levels of pollution and optimal rates of resource use and depletion, however that optimum is defined. The focus of the economics literature has been on (a) demonstrating that the 'command and control' approach to regulation is gener-ally inefficient, (b) exploring the virtues of the two main alternative contenders – charging systems and marketable pollution permits – and (c) testing the relevance of the idea that extended property rights will 'solve' externality problems.

Standard-setting characterizes most pollution regulation in practice. The economic objection to standard-setting is that it is likely to produce the optimal level of externality only by accident, although the informational demands for finding this optimum are as difficult for the design of optimal taxes as they are for standards. Additionally, the effectiveness of penalties for breaching standards is probabilistic – there has to be monitoring, detection and penalty. The debate over standard-setting in environmental economics is a special case of the 'prices versus quantities' debate in economics generally (Weitzman 1974). Uncertainty about the slopes of benefit and cost functions is liable to make standard-setting inefficient. In terms of dynamic efficiency, the polluter has no incentive to abate pollution up to the level of the standard, whereas a pollution charge is a charge on all outputs of pollutants.

The attraction of pollution charges or taxes is that they have the capacity to achieve optimal externality through automatic changes to polluters' behaviour. Once again, however, an optimal tax requires that the regulator knows the relevant cost and benefit functions, whereas information about private costs and benefits is 'asymmetric' – it is held by the polluter and has to be found out by the regulator. Tax solutions also raise problems of property rights. The idea of a tax is to generate optimal externality, but once the optimum is achieved the polluter is still paying tax on that optimal level. Such a charge suggests that the property rights to the environmental functions being used up by the polluter at the optimum belong to someone other than the polluter. Clearly, if property rights belong absolutely to the polluter, then all charges are wrong. The third alternative is that the polluter has the 'right' to emit optimal pollution, but no more than that. The nature of the charge and its general status are thus dependent on prior property rights allocations. Baumol and Oates (1971) demonstrated that taxes could provide a least-cost solution for the achievement of a pre-set standard that has no particular optimality properties.

A sizeable literature has emerged with respect to the idea of marketable pollution permits. Introduced in concept by Dales (1968), the permit idea is basically very simple. The regulatory authority decides on the acceptable level of pollution (the standard) and then issues certificates to pollute up to that level. These permits can then be traded in the market-place. Polluters with high costs of abatement will tend to purchase the permits and those with low costs will prefer to abate rather than buy the permits. In this way the distribution of abatement costs will be such that high-cost polluters will pollute up to the standard and low-cost polluters will abate pollution. Intuitively, then, the sum of abatement costs will be minimized for a given standard. Montgomery (1972) demonstrated that, if the permits are designed to relate to ambient impact rather than emissions, a competitive market in permits would achieve the cost-minimization features suggested by the intuitive approach just presented. The overwhelming attraction of such a system is that it does not fall foul of the problem of asymmetry of information faced by other regulatory mechanisms, i.e. the regulator need know nothing about the abatement costs of the polluters. Krupnick *et al.* (1980) criticize an ambient-based system on the grounds that, technically, each polluter will have to hold a portfolio of permits to reflect differing impacts at differing receptor points, imposing administrative and transactions costs on polluters. An emissions-based system will similarly be inefficient because it is damage done that matters rather than levels of emission, and emission–damage functions will vary from source to source. Krupnick *et al.* thus opt for a 'pollution offset' system in which permits are defined in terms of emissions, but the trade is constrained so that a given ambient standard is not violated, i.e. permits do not trade on a one-for-one basis but at some weighted price reflecting the variation in emission–damage functions. Marketable permits are highly attractive in concept. There is limited experience of their use, most of it in the context of US air pollution policy. An invaluable treatment of the issues is given by Tietenberg (1985).

Finally, the seminal work of Coase (1960) raises the possibility that a regulatory approach to pollution is not required at all. The Coase theorem suggests that optimal externality can be achieved independently of any initial allocation of property rights. It the polluter possesses the rights, then the sufferer can compensate the polluter up to the point of optimal externality. If the sufferer has the rights, then the polluter can engage in a similar compensation process. The elegance of the Coase theorem contrasts starkly with the real world of pollution problems, however. It is difficult to relate disaggregated damage to point sources of pollution, so that the potential for polluter and sufferer to 'come together' tends to be remote. Some sufferers, for example future generations, are not represented within the bargaining context. The Coase theorem also holds only under competitive conditions, although monopolistic competition also raises problems for the tax solution (Baumol and Oates 1988). The potential for inefficiency through securing returns to 'threats' also arises in the Coase context. Once the institutional framework is redefined to be one of local or central government representatives bargaining with polluters or their representatives, the attractions of market solutions fade further. Regulation of some form, ideally based on least-cost marketed permit systems, is likely to be less costly than the transactions costs involved in multi-party bargaining. Finally, the bargaining context breaks down further when the issue is global pollution (global warming, ozone depletion etc.), since the polluter and the sufferer coincide, or is indeterminate in the context of the wider economic values of tropical forests. These points underline the degree of 'desk-top' abstraction that has typified much of the pollution control economics literature, and the need to develop theory in a broader real-world context.

16.6 CONCLUSIONS

Environmental economics is now a firmly entrenched part of modern economics. While there is still a tendency to treat it as being outside the 'mainstream', its development has in fact contributed substantially to mainstream concerns, as with the findings over the apparent incompatibility of consumer surplus measures, possible challenges to the underlying assumptions of utility maximization and smooth substitution, and the idea of an extended equilibrium. It is a subject in flux, as might be expected given its relatively recent history. It has the potential to continue challenging some of the fundamental assumptions of twentieth-century theory. More importantly, it has the potential to contribute positively to environmental improvement and to improving directly the welfare of the population of the globe.

NOTES

1 Classical growth theory was essentially an analysis of the progression to an inevitable stationary state in which stocks are constant and economic growth, in the sense of positive growth in real consumption, was zero. This is Daly's 'steady state' as well. Steady states in this sense are also familiar in the life sciences, i.e. states in which total biomass is constant. The confusion arises because the term 'steady state growth' is used in modern neoclassical growth theory to refer to situations in which each stock (capital, labour force etc.) is growing at a constant rate such that the ratios between them are constant. Thus, if the labour force grows at l and capital at k, the ratio l/k is constant. (In 'balanced growth' $l = k$.) A steady state in this neoclassical sense was not what Daly intended to imply as a desirable social objective.

2 There are two prices to consider. The price 'in the ground' is the royalty and differs from the price 'above the ground', or 'at the wellhead', by the extraction cost. If extraction is hypothetically costless, the two prices are the same.

3 Remarkably, Boulding's essay is afforded virtually no attention in Martinez-Alier's survey of the history of 'ecological economics'. This partly reflects Martinez-Alier's unfortunate identification of ecological economics with the analysis of energy flows through economic systems (although even in this respect Boulding is a seminal writer), but may also reflect a personal distaste for Boulding's work – see the cryptic reference to Boulding in Martinez-Alier (1988: 2).

4 Martinez-Alier (1988) offers some interesting observations, but, as noted, his 'ecological economics' is really the analysis of energy flows though economic systems.

REFERENCES

Arrow, K. and Chang, S. (1978) 'Optimal pricing, use and exploration of uncertain natural resource stocks', Technical Report 31, Department of Economics, Harvard University.

Arrow, K. and Lind, R. (1970) 'Uncertainty and the evaluation of public investment decisions', *American Economic Review* 60: 364–78.

Ayres, R. and Kneese, A. (1969) 'Production, consumption and externalities', *American Economic Review* 59: 282–97.

Barnett, H. (1979) 'Scarcity and growth revisited', in V. K. Smith (ed.) *Scarcity and Growth Reconsidered*, Baltimore, MD: Johns Hopkins University Press.

Barnett, H. and Morse, C. (1963) *Scarcity and Growth: The Economics of Natural Resource Availability*, Baltimore, MD: Johns Hopkins University Press.

Baumol, W. and Oates, W. (1971) 'The use of standards and prices for protection of the environment', *Swedish Journal of Economics* 73: 42–54.

—— and —— (1988) *The Theory of Environmental Policy*, 2nd edn, Cambridge: Cambridge University Press.

Becker, G. (1965) 'A theory of the allocation of time', *Economic Journal* 75: 493–517.

Beckermann, W. (1972) 'Economists, scientists, and environmental catastrophe', *Oxford Economic Papers* 24: 237–44.

Bentkover, J. D., Covello, V. T. and Mumpower, J. (1986) *Benefits Assessment: The State of the Art*, Dordrecht: Reidel.

Bishop, R. (1982) 'Option value: an exposition and extension', *Land Economics* 58: 1–15.

Bockstael, N. and McConnell, K. (1983) 'Welfare measurement in the household production framework', *American Economic Review* 73: 806–14.

Bohm, P. (1972) 'Estimating demand for public goods: an experiment', *European Economic Review* 3: 111–30.

Boulding, K. (1966) 'The economics of the coming spaceship earth', in H. Jarrett (ed.) *Environmental Quality in a Growing Economy*, Baltimore, MD: Johns Hopkins University Press.

Bradley, P. (1985) 'Has the "economics of exhaustible resources" advanced the economics of mining?', in A. Scott (ed.) *Progress in Natural Resource Economics*, Oxford: Clarendon Press.

Brookshire, D. and Coursey, D. (1987) 'Measuring the value of a public good: an empirical comparison of elicitation procedures', *American Economic Review* 77: 554–66.

Brookshire, D., d'Arge, R., Schulze, W. and Thayer, M. (1981) 'Experiments in valuing public goods', in V. K. Smith (ed.) *Advances in Applied Microeconomics*, vol. 1, Greenwich, CT: JAI Press.

Brookshire, D., Schulze, W. and Thayer, M. (1985) 'Some unusual aspects of valuing a unique natural resource', Mimeo, University of Wyoming.

Brookshire, D., Thayer, M., Schulze, W. and d'Arge, R. (1982) 'Valuing public goods: a comparison of survey and hedonic approaches', *American Economic Review* 72: 165–77.

Broome, J. (1979) 'Trying to value a life', *Journal of Public Economics* 9: 91–100.

Brown, G. and Field, B. (1979) 'The adequacy of measures for signalling the scarcity of natural resources', in V. K. Smith (ed.) *Scarcity and Growth Reconsidered*, Baltimore, MD: Johns Hopkins University Press.

Brown, G. and Mendlesohn, R. (1984) 'The hedonic travel cost method', *Review of Economics and Statistics* 66: 427–33.

Burness, S., Cummings, R., Morris, G. and Paik, I. (1980) 'Thermodynamic and economic concepts as related to resource-use policies', *Land Economics* 56: 1–9.

Campbell, H. (1980) 'The effects of capital intensity on the optimal rate of extraction of a mineral deposit', *Canadian Journal of Economics* 13: 349–56.

Clark, C. (1976) *Mathematical Bioeconomics*, New York: Wiley.

Clawson, M. and Knetsch, J. (1966) *Economics of Outdoor Recreation*, Baltimore, MD: Johns Hopkins University Press.

Coase, R. (1960) 'The problem of social cost', *Journal of Law and Economics* 3: 1–44.

Coursey, D., Hovis, J. and Schulze, W. (1987) 'On the supposed disparity between willingness to accept and willingness to pay measures of value', *Quarterly Journal of Economics* 102: 679–90.

Cremer, J. and Weitzman, M. (1976) 'OPEC and the monopoly price of world oil', *European Economic Review* 8: 155–64.

Crocker, T., Schulze, W., Ben-David, S. and Kneese, A. (1979) *Methods Development for Assessing Air Pollution Control Benefits*, vol. 1, *Experiments in the Economics of Air Pollution Epidemiology*, Washington, DC: US Environmental Protection Agency.

Cropper, M. (1981) 'Measuring the benefits from reduced morbidity', *American Economic Review, Papers and Proceedings* 71: 235–40.

Cummings, R., Brookshire, D. and Schulze, W. (1986) *Valuing Environmental Goods: An Assessment of the Contingent Valuation Method*, Totowa, NJ: Rowman & Allanheld.

Dales, J. H. (1968) *Pollution, Property and Prices*, Toronto: University of Toronto Press.

Daly, H. (1973) *Steady State Economics*, San Francisco, CA: W. H. Freeman.

—— (1986) 'Thermodynamic and economic concepts as related to resource-use policies: a comment', *Land Economics* 62: 319–22.

—— (1987) 'The economic growth debate: what some economists have learned but many have not', *Journal of Environmental Economics and Management* 14: 323–36.

Dasgupta, P. and Heal, G. (1979) *Economic Theory and Exhaustible Resources*, Cambridge: Cambridge University Press.

De Graaf, J. V. (1957) *Theoretical Welfare Economics*, Cambridge: Cambridge University Press.

Devajaran, S. and Fisher, A. (1981) 'Hotelling's "Economics of Exhaustible Resources": fifty years later', *Journal of Economic Literature* 19: 65–73.

Deyak, T. and Smith, V. K. (1978) 'Congestion and participation in outdoor recreation: a household production approach', *Journal of Environmental Economics and Management* 5: 63–80.

Easterlin, R. A. (1974) 'Does economic growth improve the human lot?', in P. David and R. Weber (eds) *Nations and Households in Economic Growth*, New York: Academic Press.

Eckstein, O. (1961) 'A survey of the theory of public expenditure', in J. Buchanan (ed.) *Public Finances: Needs, Sources and Utilisation*, pp. 452–502, Princeton, NJ: Princeton University Press.

Faustmann, M. (1849) 'Berechnung des Wertes welchen Waldboden sowie noch nicht haubare Holzbestande fur die Waldwirtschaft besizten', *Allgemeine Forst und Jagd-Zeitung* 25: 441–55.

Feenberg, D. and Mills, E. (1980) *Measuring the Benefits of Water Pollution Abatement*, New York: Academic Press.

Fisher, A. C. (1974) 'Environmental externalities and the Arrow-Lind theorem', *American Economic Review* 63: 722–5.

Fisher, A. C. (1987) 'Whither oil prices: the evidence from theory', *Natural Resource Modeling* 2: 5–22.

Freeman, A. M. (1979) *The Benefits of Environmental Improvement*, Baltimore, MD: Johns Hopkins University Press.

—— (1982) *Air and Water Pollution Control*, New York: Wiley.

Georgescu-Roegen, N. (1971) *The Entropy Law and the Economic Process*, Cambridge, MA: Harvard University Press.

—— (1979) 'Comments on the papers by Daly and Stiglitz', in V. K. Smith (ed.) *Scarcity and Growth Reconsidered*, pp. 95–105, Baltimore, MD: Johns Hopkins University Press.

Gerking, S. and Stanley, L. (1986) 'An economic analysis of air pollution and health: the case of St. Louis', *Review of Economics and Statistics* 68: 115–21.

Goodin, R. (1978) 'Uncertainty as an excuse for cheating our children: the case of nuclear wastes', *Policy Sciences* 10: 25–43.

—— (1982) 'Discounting discounting', *Journal of Public Policy* 2: 53–72.

Gordon, H. S. (1954) 'Economic theory of a common-property resource: the fishery', *Journal of Political Economy* 62: 124–42.

Gray, L. (1914) 'Rent under the assumption of exhaustibility', *Quarterly Journal of Economics* 28: 466–89.

Griliches, Z. (ed.) (1971) *Price Indexes and Quality Change*, Cambridge, MA: Harvard University Press.

Grossman, M. (1972) 'On the concept of health capital and the demand for health', *Journal of Political Economy* 80: 223–55.

Hall, D. and Hall, J. (1984) 'Concepts and measures of natural resource scarcity with a summary of recent trends', *Journal of Environmental Economics and Management* 11: 363–79.

Harrison, D. and Rubinfeld, O. (1978) 'Hedonic housing prices and the demand for clean air', *Journal of Environmental Economics* 5: 81–102.

Hartwick, J. (1977) 'Intergenerational equity and the investing of rents from exhaustible resources', *American Economic Review* 66: 972–4.

—— (1978a) 'Substitution among exhaustible resources and intergenerational equity', *Review of Economic Studies* 45: 347–54.

—— (1978b) 'Investing returns from depleting renewable resource stocks and intergenerational equity', *Economic Letters* 1: 85–8.

Hoel, M. (1978) 'Resource extraction, uncertainty, and learning', *Bell Journal of Economics* 9: 642–5.

Hotelling, H. (1931) 'The economics of exhaustible resources', *Journal of Political Economy* 39: 137–75.

—— (1949) 'The economics of public recreation – an economic survey of the monetary evaluation of recreation in the national parks', Mimeo, US National Park Service, Washington, DC.

Johansson, P.-O. (1987) *The Economic Theory and Measurement of Environmental Benefits*, Cambridge, MA: Cambridge University Press.

Kahnemann, D. and Tversky, A. (1979) 'Prospect theory: an analysis of decisions under risk', *Econometrica* 42: 263–91.

Klaassen, L. and Botterweg, T. (1976) 'Project evaluation and intangible effects: a shadow project approach', in P. Nijkamp (ed.) *Environmental Economics*, vol. 1, Leiden: Nijhoff.

Kneese, A., Ayres, R. and d'Arge, R. (1970) *Economics and the Environment: a Materials Balance Approach*, Washington, DC: Resources for the Future,

Knetsch, J. (1988) 'The endowment effect and evidence of non-reversible indifference curves', Mimeo, Department of Economics, Simon Fraser University, Vancouver.

—— (1989) 'Environmental and economic impact assessments and the divergence between the willingness to pay and the compensation demanded measures of loss', Mimeo, Department of Economics, Simon Fraser University, Vancouver.

Knetsch, J. and Sinden, J. (1984) 'Willingness to pay and compensation demanded: experimental evidence of an unexpected disparity in measures of value', *Quarterly Journal of Economics* 99: 507–21.

Knetsch, J., Thaler, R. and Kahneman, D. (1987) 'Experimental tests of the endowment effect and the Coase theorem', Mimeo, Department of Psychology, University of California at Berkeley.

Krautkraemer, J. (1985) 'Optimal growth, resource amenities, and the preservation of natural environments', *Review of Economic Studies* 52: 153–70.

—— (1988) 'The rate of discount and the preservation of natural environments', *Natural Resource Modeling* 2: 421–39.

Krupnick, A., Oates, W. and Van De Verg, E. (1980) 'On marketable air pollution permits: the case for a system of pollution offsets', *Journal of Environmental Economics and Management* 10: 233–47.

Krutilla, J. (1967) 'Conservation reconsidered', *American Economic Review* 57: 777–86.

Kula, E. (1984) 'Derivation of social time preference rates for the United States and Canada', *Quarterly Journal of Economics* 99: 873–82.

Lave, L. and Seskin, E. (1977) *Air Pollution and Human Health*, Baltimore, MD: Johns Hopkins University Press.

Levhari, D. and Pindyck, R. (1979) 'The pricing of durable exhaustible resources', Working paper EL 79-053 WP, MIT Energy Laboratory.

Lewis, T. R. (1963) 'Monopoly exploitation of an exhaustible resource', *Journal of Environmental Economics and Management* 3: 198–201.

Lind, R. (1982) *Discounting for Time and Risk in Energy Policy*, Baltimore, MD: Johns Hopkins University Press.

Little, I. M. D. (1950) *A Critique of Welfare Economics*, Oxford: Oxford University Press, (2nd edn 1957).

Maler, K.-G. (1986) 'Comment on R. M. Solow "On the intergenerational allocation of natural resources" ', *Scandinavian Journal of Economics* 88: 151–2.

Malthus, T. (1798) *An Essay on the Principle of Population*, ed. A. Flew, London: Pelican.

Marglin, S. (1963) 'The social rate of discount and the optimal rate of investment', *Quarterly Journal of Economics* 77: 95–112.

Markandya, A. and Pearce, D. W. (1988) *Environmental Considerations and the Choice of Discount Rate in Developing Countries*, Washington, DC: Environment Department, World Bank.

Martinez-Alier, J. (1988) *Ecological Economics*, Oxford: Oxford University Press.

Mill, J. S. (1857) *Principles of Political Economy*, London: Parker.

Montgomery, W. (1972) 'Markets and licenses and efficient pollution control programs', *Journal of Economic Theory* 5: 395–418.

Morey, E. (1981) 'The demand for site-specific recreational activities: a characteristics approach', *Journal of Environmental Economics and Management* 8: 345–71.

Nelson, J. (1980) 'Airports and property values: a survey of recent evidence', *Journal of Transport Economics and Policy* 14: 37–52.

—— (1982) 'Highway noise and property values: a survey of recent evidence', *Journal of Transport Economics and Policy* 16: 117–30.

Nordhaus, W. (1973) 'The allocation of energy resources', *Brookings Papers on Economic Activity* 3: 529–70.

Olson, M. and Bailey, M. (1981) 'Positive time preference', *Journal of Political Economy* 89: 1–25.

Ostro, B. (1983) 'The effects of air pollution on work loss and morbidity', *Journal of Environmental Economics and Management* 10: 371–82.

—— (1987) 'Air pollution morbidity revisited: a specification test', *Journal of Environmental Economics and Management* 14: 87–98.

Page, T. (1977a) 'Equitable use of the resource base', *Environment and Planning, Ser. A* 9: 15–22.

—— (1977b) *Conservation and Economic Efficiency*, Baltimore, MD: Johns Hopkins University Press.

—— (1977c) 'Intertemporal and international aspects of virgin materials taxes', in D. W. Pearce and I. Walter (eds) *Resource Conservation: Social and Economic Dimensions of Recycling*, pp. 63–81, New York: New York University Press.

—— (1978) 'A generic view of toxic chemicals and similar risks', *Ecology Law Quarterly* 7: 207–44.

Parfit, D. (1983) 'Energy policy and the further future: the social discount rate', in D. MacLean and P. Brown (eds) *Energy and the Future*, Totowa, NJ: Rowman & Littlefield.

Pearce, D. W. (1981) 'World energy demand and crude oil prices to the year 2000', *Journal of Agricultural Economics* 34: 341–54.

—— (1987) 'Foundations of an ecological economics', *Ecological Modelling* 38: 9–18.

Pearce, D. W. and Markandya, A. (1989) *The Benefits of Environmental Policy: Monetary Valuation*, Paris: OECD.

Pearce, D. W. Barbier, E. and Markandya, A. (1989) *Sustainable Development: Economics and the Environment in the Third World*, Aldershot: Edward Elgar.

Perrings, C. (1987) *Economy and Environment*, Cambridge: Cambridge University Press.

Peterson, F. and Fisher, A. (1977) 'The exploitation of extractive resources: a survey', *Economic Journal* 87: 681–721.

Pigou, A. C. (1920) *The Economics of Welfare*, London: Macmillan (4th edn 1932).

Ramsey, F. P. (1929) 'A mathematical theory of saving', *Economic Journal* 38: 543–59.

Rawls, J. (1972) *A Theory of Justice*, Oxford: Oxford University Press.

Ricardo, D. (1817) *Principles of Political Economy and Taxation*, London: Everyman (reprinted 1926).

Ridker, R. (1967) *Economic Costs of Air Pollution*, New York: Praeger.

Rosen, S. (1974) 'Hedonic prices and implicit markets: product differentiation in pure competition', *Journal of Political Economy* 82: 34–55.

Samuelson, P. (1954) 'Pure theory of public expenditure', *Review of Economics and Statistics* 36: 387–9.

—— (1964) 'Discussion', *American Economic Review* 54: 93–6.

Sen, A. K. (1961) 'On optimising the rate of saving', *Economic Journal* 71: 470–98.

Slade, M. (1982) 'Trends in natural resource commodity prices: an analysis of the time domain', *Journal of Environmental Economics and Management* 9: 122–37.

Smith, V. K. and Desvousges, W. (1986) *Measuring Water Quality Benefits*, Boston, MA: Kluwer Nijhoff.

Solow, R. M. (1978) 'Intergenerational equity and exhaustible resources', *Review of Economic Studies* 41: 29–45.

—— (1986) 'On the intergenerational allocation of natural resources', *Scandinavian Journal of Economics* 88: 141–9.

Solow, R. and Wan, F. (1976) 'Extraction costs in the theory of exhaustible resources', *Bell Journal of Economics* 7: 359–70.

Spash, C. and d'Arge, R. (1989) 'The greenhouse effect and intergenerational transfers', *Energy Policy* April: 88–96.

Stiglitz, J. (1976) 'Monopoly and the rate of extraction of exhaustible resources', *American Economic Review* 66: 655–61.

Tietenberg, T. (1985) *Emissions Trading*, Baltimore, MD: Johns Hopkins University Press.

Ulph, A. (1982) 'The role of *ex ante* and *ex post* decisions in the value of life', *Journal of Public Economics* 18: 265–76.

Violette, D. and Chestnut, L. (1983) *Valuing Reductions in Risks*, Washington, DC: US Environmental Protection Agency.

Weinstein, M. and Zeckhauser, R. (1975) 'The optimal consumption of depletable natural resources', *Quarterly Journal of Economics* 89: 371–92.

Weisbrod, B. (1964) 'Collective consumption services of individual consumption goods', *Quarterly Journal of Economics* 78: 471–7.

Weitzman, M. (1974) 'Prices vs quantities', *Review of Economic Studies* 41: 477–91.

Willig, R. (1976) 'Consumer's surplus without apology', *American Economic Review* 66: 589–97.

Wilman, E. (1984) *External Costs of Coastal Beach Pollution: an Hedonic Approach*, Washington, DC: Resources for the Future.

17

GAME THEORY AND
STRATEGIC BEHAVIOUR

CHRISTIAN MONTET

17.1 INTRODUCTION

Game theory is concerned with the analysis of conscious interactions between agents. Each player behaves strategically in the sense that, in deciding which course of action to take, he takes into account the possible effects on the other players and the fact that the latter behave in the same way. Ecomonic life is replete with situations fitting the preceding description: oligopolistic markets, international trade policy, bargaining problems, international effects of macro-economic policies, the relation between governments and private agents etc. In fact, there is now a long history of the use of game-theoretical reasoning in economics.

As early as 1838, Cournot studied a situation of duopoly using an equilibrium concept which became a cornerstone of non-cooperative game theory after the work of Nash (1951). Edgeworth's 'contract curve', developed near the end of the nineteenth century, can easily be read in terms of 'the core', one of the equilibrium concepts of modern co-operative game theory.

However, the great moment in this history is the publication in 1944 of von Neumann and Morgenstern's *Theory of Games and Economic Behaviour*, which developed ideas put forward by von Neumann in 1928. This book announced a revolution in economic thinking by stating that: 'this theory of games of strategy is the proper instrument with which to develop a theory of economic behaviour' (von Neumann and Morgenstern 1944: 1–2).

Despite these promises, game theory was neglected to some extent for the next two decades. In the late 1960s, general disappointment about this new approach was widely diffused among economists, so much so that an author

I am grateful to Mike Bleaney, David Greenaway and Daniel Serra for helpful comments on an earlier draft of this chapter. I am also greatly indebted to my colleague Didier Laussel for common work and discussions on many issues discussed herein. Finally, I wish to thank my former student Jean-Stephane Michard who helped improve this text by his questions on the subject and his term paper.

could write in 1963: 'To date, there have been no serious attempts to apply the theory of games to market problems, or to economic problems in general' (Napoleoni 1963: 62). Such a statement sounds quite anachronistic in 1991, after years of rediscovery, development and now dominance of game theory in the economics literature.

Most of the recent advances in industrial organization, international trade theory, macroeconomic and monetary theory, and public economics have made use of game-theoretical analysis (to take just one illustration, *Advances in Economic Theory*, edited by Truman Bewley (1987) contains only three chapters out of eleven which have no direct relation to game theory).

It would be an interesting subject for future historians of thought to clarify the reasons why the marriage between game theory and economics did not succeed totally until the end of the 1970s.[1] We may make a few guesses. First, after the Second World War the perfect competition paradigm was still awaiting many extensions and developments; this prospect attracted the efforts of researchers in general equilibrium theory, international trade theory, growth theory and so on. Second, game theory has long suffered from misunderstandings of some of its basic concepts, like Cournot–Nash equilibrium,[2] and from a misplaced emphasis on issues of a purely technical nature, like zero-sum games, which are relatively uninteresting for economists. Third, the multiplicity of approaches and equilibrium concepts developed in the theory of games was unsatisfactory for economists used to the clear and unified modelling of perfect competition. Fourth, it was only after the recent development and diffusion of dynamic games techniques and the refinement and sharpening of equilibrium concepts, like the concept of subgame perfection, that many complex economic issues became tractable in terms of games.

In particular, the subtle concept of strategic moves, identified by Schelling (1960, 1965), is now applied to a variety of economic problems in the formal apparatus of dynamic game theory. Also, many issues involve imperfect information and it is only recently that the role of informational asymmetries in strategic behaviour have been fully acknowledged and tackled rigorously.

To summarize, we might say that a better and wider understanding of the Nash equilibrium concept, the stimulating insights of Schelling on strategic behaviour, recent developments of dynamic game theory, like the concept of perfect equilibrium due to Selten, and recent advances in the theory of games with incomplete or imperfect information explain the current flood of game-theoretical analysis in economics.

In this chapter we illustrate these ideas by focusing on the recent developments aimed at applying Schelling's insights in formal modelling. We shall try to present the main arguments with the help of a series of examples drawn from various areas of economic theory: industrial organization, international trade and trade policy, and monetary policy. The choice of different examples will give an idea of the multiplicity of applications of the new models and at the same time will illustrate the common structure of many of these applications.

Without denying the importance of co-operative game theory and bargaining theory, we shall concentrate on certain aspects of non-cooperative game theory only. In Section 17.2 we give a brief presentation of the major concepts and definitions. In Section 17.3 we discuss the strategic issues involved in the simple repetition of a one-period game (also called a stage game), and in Section 17.4 we are concerned with more subtle moves in various multi-stage games. In Section 17.5 we introduce imperfect information and its effects on equilibrium. In the final section we give a brief idea of the current problems and perspectives of this approach.

17.2 BASIC CONCEPTS AND DEFINITIONS

Most of the elements presented in the following section are becoming standard tools for economists (as happened in the case of calculus a few decades ago). Therefore we can expect that this kind of brief introduction to the basic concepts and methods of game theory will soon become unnecessary. However, for the moment such a detour is required in order for the reader to obtain a full understanding of the subsequent sections. Of course, a full exposition of the theory of games would require a whole book, and so the reader is referred to Bacharach (1976), Shubik (1982) and particularly Friedman (1986) for detailed presentations.

Before studying the economic examples it is necessary to clarify the concepts of game, strategy and strategic behaviour, the different types of games and the various equilibrium concepts most frequently used.

Description of a game

A game is a situation in which each agent seeks to maximize his pay-off by choosing the best plan of action, taking into account the interdependences with the other players.

A description of an agent's planned actions in all possible situations is called a strategy, and in a general and rather loose sense each agent is assumed to behave strategically. A particular game is then defined by a set of players, a set of strategies for each player from which the agent will choose the one he considers the best and a pay-off function for each agent. In an extensive form, the description of the game includes the move order (which player moves when) and the actions and information available at each move. The so-called normal form of the game condenses all these elements and provides pay-offs as functions of the players' strategies.

Formally, each agent i chooses a strategy a_i from the set A_i of available strategies. Agent i's pay-off function is $\pi^i(a_1, \ldots, a_i, \ldots, a_n)$, $i = 1, \ldots, n$, since it depends on every agent's strategies. In a (static) one-period game, a strategy is simply an action in given conditions. In a dynamic game, where time and history of the game matter, a strategy is a plan of action for each time period of the game.

The definition of strategies can be enlarged by allowing not only the choice of an action but also the choice of probability distributions over actions. In this case of randomization of strategies we speak of mixed strategies, as opposed to pure strategies in the other case. In this chapter, for both simplicity and intuitive appeal, we shall only give examples of pure strategies.[3]

Various classifications of games

Games can be classified according to various criteria: degree of harmony between the players, influence of time, and information conditions.

Harmony

Each player of a game is supposed to maximize his pay-off function. However, this general objective may include very different attitudes towards the other players. In certain cases, all the players have the same objective and thus are likely to co-operate. In other cases, there is a pure conflict: one agent wins what the other agents lose. The latter cases are called zero-sum games (or more generally constant-sum games). Despite the numerous examples of zero-sum games used in economics from von Neumann and Morgenstern's book to the traditional presentations of game theory in microeconomics textbooks, most economic problems involve elements of both conflict and co-operation, i.e. they are non-zero-sum games.[4] Non-zero-sum games may be co-operative or non-cooperative. They are co-operative when the agents can make binding agreements before acting, and are non-cooperative otherwise. For instance, two firms in duopoly may promise not to hurt each other, but there is no legal institution which could enforce this agreement; the game must be modelled as non-cooperative.

The equilibrium concepts used in co-operative and non-cooperative games are very different. We shall concentrate only on the latter since they are appropriate for studying Schellingian ideas on strategic behaviour.

Time

If the agents meet only once and make decisions for a single period of time, the game is static in nature. In a broad sense a game is dynamic when time matters, either because a single-stage play is repeated over many periods (repeated game) or because the game unfolds over time in multi-stage plays. In solving multi-period complex games time can be treated as either a discrete or a continuous variable; the latter approach is technically more demanding. When the number of periods is limited, dynamic games are solved by backward induction, a technique developed in dynamic programming (Bellman 1957).

For the most part, the situations dealt with in economics involve numerous meetings of the agents: firms operating in the same market know that they will have to meet again in many periods to come, and so do governments choosing their trade policies. Moreover, many economic variables, such as investment in capacity or advertising expenses, have clear effects on supply and demand conditions which will prevail in the future. All these features of economic life explain why dynamic games constitute the proper framework for studying strategic behaviour in economics.

Information

A crucial step in the description of a game is the specification of the structure of information for the different players. In most applications of game theory to economics it seems natural to assume that some information is private; for instance, each firm knows its own cost function but not the other players' costs. These informational asymmetries give rise to very rich possibilities of strategic behaviour such as bluffing or reputation-building.

It is now traditional to say that information is imperfect if the agents are ignorant of the previous actions of certain players and that information is incomplete if agents do not know their opponents pay-off functions (for instance, because they do not know an element required to compute the pay-off, such as the rival's costs in order to calculate its profits).

It is important to note that, even in asymmetric information games, a large part of information is assumed to be common knowledge among the players and that each agent's subjective probability distribution over the private infor-mation is also common knowledge (as is the assumption that each agent is rational).

Equilibrium concepts of non-cooperative games

Consider first a one-period model with perfect (and complete) information. A strong concept in non-cooperative equilibrium is the dominant strategy equilibrium, in which there is one optimal choice of strategy for each player no matter what the other players do. The prisoner's dilemma is the most famous example of a dominant strategy. Nice as this concept is, however, many games simply do not have a dominant equilibrium.[5] A less demanding concept, and in fact the one most widely used in non-cooperative game theory, is the

Nash equilibrium. In a rather loose way, we can say that at a Nash equilibrium each agent does the best he can given the other agents' actions. Formally, retaining the notation already used for strategies and pay-off functions, $a^N = (a_1^N, \ldots, a_n^N)$ is a Nash equilibrium if, for all $i = 1, \ldots, n$,

$$\pi^i(a_1^N, \ldots, a_{i-1}^N, a_i^N, a_{i+1}^N, \ldots, a_n^N)$$
$$\geq \pi^i(a_i^N, \ldots, a_{i-1}^N, a_i^N, a_{i+1}^N, \ldots, a_n^N)$$

for all $a_i \in A_i$.

At a Nash equilibrium the set of expectations concerning each agent's choice corresponds to the chosen actions and nobody wants to change his behaviour. A number of misunderstandings have long accompanied the static Nash equilibrium concept. Many commentators on the Cournot duopoly solution – the first and most famous example of a Nash equilibrium – criticized the supposedly myopic and rather irrational behaviour of firms. However, Cournot–Nash behaviour only appears irrational if one says that each firm chooses its best output given its rival's output and if, at the same time, one adds to the static model a kind of dynamic adjustment process (as is too often done in intermediate microeconomic textbooks). In fact it is quite consistent with rational behaviour. First, a true dynamic story implies a change in the nature of the game itself. Second, firms know their rival's best output response to each output of their own choice and they also know that their rival has the same information. If there is a unique pair of output levels for which the best choice of one agent matches the best choice of the other, it will be chosen by rational players (Johansen 1982). Of course, one major weakness of the Nash equilibrium concept lies in the risk of multiplicity of equilibria. Then there is no clear way of choosing among the possible candidates.

The concept of Nash equilibrium has a natural extension to dynamic games. At a dynamic Nash equilibrium each agent chooses the strategy (i.e. the plan of action for each time period of the game) that maximizes his pay-offs, given the other agents' strategies. The major problem with a dynamic Nash equilibrium is that it may involve irrational behaviour at a late stage of the game. A certain announced action may become irrational (non-utility-maximizing) at the moment when implementation was supposed to occur.

A stronger concept of equilibrium due to Selten (1975) permits us to get rid of these non-credible strategies. This concept, called perfect Nash equilibrium or subgame perfect equilibrium, requires that the strategies chosen by the players be a Nash equilibrium in every subgame (i.e. in every one-period game of the general game), whatever actions have gone before.[6]

When information is imperfect or incomplete, rational agents can be assumed to use subjective probabilities updated according to Bayes's rule. The corresponding equilibrium concept is called Bayesian equilibrium. It was introduced by Harsanyi (1967–8), who showed that a game with incomplete information can always be described as a Bayesian game. In fact, a game with incomplete information can be transformed into a game with imperfect information by introducing a new player, called 'nature', which selects the characteristics of each player. A Bayesian equilibrium is defined as a Nash equilibrium in which each player evaluates his pay-off as his expected utility conditional on his private information over the states of nature. However, this concept has the same problems as Nash equilibrium. The concept of perfect Bayesian equilibrium is an extension of the perfect Nash equilibrium to the case of games with imperfect (and incomplete) information. It combines the Bayesian equilibrium and the dynamic rationality of the perfect Nash equilibrium (in every subgame).[7]

Schelling's definition of strategic behaviour

In game theory the phrases 'strategy' or 'strategic behaviour' are generally used only to convey the idea of interdependence in decision-making. However, a recent reorientation of the theory, mainly due to Schelling (1960, 1965) has emphasized more subtle aspects of strategic behaviour.

Schelling defines a strategic move as: '(an action) . . . that influences the other person's choice, in a manner favourable to oneself, by affecting the other person's expectations of how oneself will behave' (Schelling 1960: 160). Commitments, threats and promises are basic means of influencing other people's choices in one's own interest. However, a commitment, a threat or a promise can affect the other player's expectations of one's own behaviour only if they are made credible. The difficulty of achieving credibility is in fact the major problem of strategic behaviour, since very often it is not in one's interest to enforce a commitment or implement a threat when the time comes to do so.

Generally, credibility is achieved more easily by a simultaneous use of several strategic moves. A promise can be rendered credible by the use of a credible threat (an example of this is given in Section 17.3). An irreversible commitment may enhance the credibility of further threats (see Section 17.4). In the case of perfect (and complete) information, credibility may be achieved by irreversible prior actions on tangible variables like capital, advertising expenses, product choice etc. When the information is partly private (and then asymmetric), it may be possible to influence other agents' expectations by 'investing in disinformation', i.e. signalling, bluffing etc.

It is clear from the above that the study of strategic behaviour in the sense proposed by Schelling implies that the game has a dynamic structure. The concept of subgame perfect equilibrium achieved by getting rid of plans of action which it is not in a player's interest to implement provides an interesting framework for studying strategic behaviour. Moreover, the richness of the analysis increases when information is asymmetric.

All these arguments explain why game theory has been applied to various areas of economics following recent developments in dynamic games and asymmetric information games.

17.3 THREATS AND PROMISES IN REPEATED GAMES

In this section we examine a simple combination of threats and promises which may yield a co-operative result in a non-cooperative game. Let us start by a standard application of the Nash equilibrium concept to a one-period game in economics; we shall then assume that this stage (or constituent) game is repeated over many periods. In order to avoid the frequently presented Cournot duopoly model and to show the versatility of the Nash concept we use the example of a tariff game.

The players are the governments of two large countries which produce and exchange two goods, good 1 and good 2. Each country's welfare can be increased by a tariff policy, optimally designed for improving the terms of trade.

To simplify matters, let us first suppose that the strategy set of each government is either free trade (FREE) or an optimal tariff (OPT). Table 17.1 gives the pay-off matrix of this simple one-shot game. Whatever the strategy chosen by the rival country, each government has an advantage in playing OPT. This game has a dominant strategy equilibrium (which of course is also a Nash equilibrium). The choice of free trade is more efficient for both countries, but it is not an equilibrium of the non-cooperative game. If a pre-play agreement were settled between the two players, each would be interested in reneging on it, and could do so in the absence of a supranational institution with coercive power.

Table 17.1

| | | Country 2 | |
		FREE	OPT
Country 1	FREE	(8, 8)	(2, 10)
	OPT	(10, 2)	(4, 4)

Of course, the choice of strategies need not be so limited as in this extreme example. We can consider an enlarged strategy set S for country 1 such as $S =]-1, \bar{t}]$, i.e. the tariff t takes any value between -1 (free imports) and $\bar{t}$ (prohibition of any import). Similarly, for country 2, $S^* =]-1, \bar{t}^*]$.

Let us further suppose that country 1 exports good 1 and imports good 2. The national prices of the two goods are related by

$$p_2^1 = p_2^2(1 + t) \qquad p_1^2 = p_1^1(1 + t^*)$$

where p_j^i is the price of good j in country i. The world relative price is $p = p_2^2/p_1^1$. Let $M_i(p, t)$, $i = 1, 2$, denote country i's import demand as a function of the terms of trade and the tariff level. Then the trade balance condition is

$$pM_1(p, t) = M_2(p, t^*) \qquad (17.1)$$

The pay-offs of the game are the values taken by the collective utility functions $U = U(p, t)$ and $U^* = U^*(p, t^*)$, which from (17.1) can be rewritten as functions of t and t^* only: $W(t, t^*)$ and $W^*(t, t^*)$.

In t–t^* space, functions W and W^* give welfare contours as illustrated in Figure 17.1. To be precise, somewhat restricted assumptions are needed to obtain the shapes of the welfare contours shown here (see McMillan (1986) and Dixit (1987) for a more detailed discussion). Readers more familiar with the economics of industrial organization will notice that the welfare contours are strictly analogous to the isoprofit curves in oligopoly analysis. Country 1's welfare increases as we move downwards and country 2's welfare increases as we move to the left. The locus of the maxima of these curves for country 1, i.e. the points corresponding to $\partial W/\partial t = 0$, is RR in Figure 17.1. It is known

Figure 17.1

351

as the home country's reaction function (as Dixit (1987) wrote, the term 'equilibrium locus' would be a better name since in a one-shot game there is not strictly such a thing as a reaction). The same locus for country 2 is R^*R^*. They are assumed to have negative slope and to cross only once (of course, these properties correspond to very precise assumptions). The intersection point N represents the Nash equilibrium of this game (in fact, autarky could be another Nash equilibrium (see Dixit 1987)).

As in the case of the prisoner's dilemma, the equilibrium is not Pareto efficient. Efficiency would require the same relative price in the two countries, i.e.

$$\frac{p_2^1}{p_1^1} = \frac{p_2^2}{p_1^2} \tag{17.2}$$

which requires

$$t + t^* + tt^* = 0$$

The locus of $t - t^*$ levels satisfying condition (17.2) is curve EE in Figure 17.1. The points between C and C^* are preferred to the Nash equilibrium by both countries, and in this case the free-trade solution lies on this segment. (This is not always true; see, for instance, Kennan and Reizmann (1988) for a different case.) The problem is that the countries cannot reach F or a point on CC^* without being constrained by an external force (like a powerful sort of General Agreement on Tariffs and Trade (GATT)).

However, the major weakness of the preceding reasoning is its static nature. We know from the economics of industrial organization that two firms confronting each other in numerous meetings in the same market may tacitly collude to reduce output and raise prices (Friedman 1971). Our two countries are certainly destined to have a long relationship; cannot they also 'collude' in reducing tariffs in order to maximize their welfare?

The repetition of the game over many periods allows strategic moves in the sense of Schelling. Each period's choices will depend on the history of the game and the memory of prior plays.

Consider first that the two governments expect an infinite repetition of the constituent game. The game consisting of all the repetitions is generally called a supergame. A strategy in the supergame is a plan of action for each period, and it is natural to plan different actions according to the rival's prior plays. Does this infinitely repeated game admit a perfect Nash equilibrium? There is an obvious solution: the repetition of the static Nash equilibrium. But there are other solutions, which are eventually more 'collusive'.

Let us revert again to the assumption that there are only two strategies in the stage game: free trade (F) and the static Nash equilibrium (N). A country may promise to be free-trader as long as the other country has not defected from the efficient solution, and threaten to revert permanently to the Nash tariff-ridden equilibrium otherwise.

The threat is credible since, after having observed a rival country's defection, a reversion to the static Nash point constitutes a subgame Nash equilibrium. If the losses induced by the collapse of the 'colluding' behaviour are sufficiently high compared with the gains from a unilateral defection, the promise to be friendly is also credible. The intertwined threats and promises would then generate self-enforcing co-operative behaviour.

Let us briefly state the conditions under which the promises are credible. Each country is supposed to maximize the sum of its discounted total welfare. Let W^F denote the total welfare for one period in the case of free trade, W^d the welfare that could be obtained by unilateral defection and W^N the welfare which can be reached in the static Nash equilibrium. Consider a country contemplating the choice of remaining in free trade or defecting in order to obtain transitory benefits.

If the two countries stay in free trade, the total welfare on the infinite horizon will be $W^F[1/(1 - \beta)]$ where β is a positive discount factor ($0 < \beta < 1$). If a country unilaterally defects it will obtain a welfare level $W^d > W^F$ during the first period, and thereafter the sum of the W^N until infinity. Therefore its total welfare will be $W^d + \beta W^N/(1 - \beta)$.

It is clear that this country will remain a free-trader if

$$\beta \geqslant \frac{W^d - W^F}{W^d - W^N} \tag{17.3}$$

or

$$W^d - W^F \leqslant \frac{W^F - W^N}{r} \tag{17.3'}$$

(where r is the rate of discount and $\beta = (1 + r)^{-1}$), i.e. if the discounted future losses more than offset the immediate gains.

Condition (17.3) will be met if the transitory gains from defection are bounded ($W^d < \infty$), if the reversion to the static Nash equilibrium constitutes a true punishment ($W^N < W^F$) and if β is high enough (close enough to unity).

The supergame analysis has many other interesting applications in economics. In particular, it may explain why a price-setting duopoly selling a homogeneous product is not stuck in marginal cost pricing as Bertrand (1883) found for a one-period confrontation of the two firms.

However, this modelling is not without its defects. First, the role played by history in this game is not fully satisfactory. History matters only because agents threaten to make it matter. More important aspects of history such as the possibility of learning from past actions require a different framework embodying asymmetric information between players (Kreps and Spence 1985).

A second and more important defect is the multiplicity of equilibria of the supergame. In our presentation above we restricted the choices at each period to two actions: the static Nash equilibrium or the Pareto efficient outcome (free trade). However, there may be many other tariff policies. A theorem of unknown origin, called the 'folk theorem', tells us that, for a discount factor sufficiently close to unity, any outcome between the static Nash point and free trade can be sustained as a perfect equilibrium of the supergame.[8]

A pre-play negotiation between the agents to find an agreement on the Pareto efficient outcome(s) does not solve the multiplicity problem since it conveys the idea that the agents could renegotiate after a defection in order to avoid the mutually costly punishments. This possibility of renegotiation crucially undermines the credibility of the threats supporting the collusive outcome. It is then interesting to refine the supergame analysis by finding the conditions of renegotiation-proof equilibria (see Shapiro (1989), reporting works by Farrell and Maskin (1987) and Pearce (1987)). But in any case this approach does not completely solve the problem of the multiplicity of equilibria.

Third, when the stage game is repeated only over a limited number of periods, it seems that the only perfect equilibrium is the simple repetition of the stage game Nash equilibrium. This result is easily deduced by checking each period equilibrium, starting with the last one and going back to the previous ones. In the last round there is no other credible action than the static Nash strategy. But a threat to punish defection at the penultimate round is then worthless and not credible. Therefore the static Nash equilibrium will also result at this stage, and so on back to the first round.

These criticisms of the supergame analysis raise the problem of the relationships between formal game theory and experimental studies of human behaviour. For instance, some experiments conducted by Axelrod (see Axelrod 1983) have shown that an efficient outcome may emerge from a non-cooperative finitely repeated game when agents adopt a tit-for-tat strategy. Each agent simply reproduces what its rival did at the previous stage: defect if it defected; co-operate if it co-operated. Axelrod underpins the interesting properties of tit-for-tat with regard to communication and human relations: it is a simple, clear and forgiving strategy. Unfortunately, formal game theory is still unable to integrate these characteristics.

The adoption of one equilibrium among the set of possible candidates is based on communication and behavioural rules such as simple rules of thumb between players or what Schelling calls 'focal points'. A great deal has still to be learnt from experimental economics in this area.

17.4 COMMITMENTS IN TWO-STAGE GAMES

Commitment is the more subtle of the strategic moves identified by Schelling and it lends itself to rich applications in economics: 'the essence of these tactics is some voluntary but irreversible sacrifice of freedom of choice. They rest on the paradox that the power to constrain an adversary may depend on the power to bind oneself...' (Schelling 1960: 22).

Everyone has experienced in real life the fact that a threat is more credible if there is no choice but to carry it into effect when the moment comes. Therefore it may often be worthwhile to suppress any way out of an announced plan of action. There are many applications of this argument in economics.

For instance, a firm enjoying a monopolistic position can credibly deter a potential entrant by building irreversible extra capacity which implies that a threat of flooding the market (and thus rendering entry unprofitable) would be carried into effect in the case of entry (Spence 1977; Dixit 1980; Fudenberg and Tirole 1984). A government may turn an international oligopolistic market outcome in favour of a domestic firm by announcing a subsidy policy in its favour. In this case the credibility of the threat, which it would not be rational in general to carry into effect, comes from the nature of the political decision process: ratification by votes in representative assembly and slowness for taking a novel decision (Krugman 1984; Brander and Spencer 1985).

The models built along these lines have the same basic structure. For simplicity and tractability the time structure is generally reduced to two periods.[9] In the first period the agents take 'strategic' decisions about variables whose influence lasts over the second period: capacity, research and development expenses, advertising expenditures and so on.

In the second stage the agents compete over 'tactical' issues, i.e. shorter-run decisions like price or quantity choices. The concept of subgame perfection is used so that the second-period equilibrium must be a Nash equilibrium whatever actions have been chosen before. The game is solved by backward induction: we first solve the second-period game for any value of the strategic variable and then solve for the first-period choice of the strategic variable level. We shall uncover some of the technicalities of this kind of game by the following example of strategic investment in a duopoly (using a framework presented by Dixit 1986).

Consider a duopoly producing two differentiated but similar products in quantities x_1 and x_2. The inverse demand functions are $p^i(x_1, x_2)$, $i = 1, 2$. We assume that they satisfy the usual properties expressed by the following inequalities: $p_i^i < 0$, $p_2^1 < 0$, $p_1^2 < 0$. Assuming that the utility function $U(x_1, x_2)$ is concave in (x_1, x_2) and that $p^i \equiv \partial U/\partial x_i$, we also have

$$p_2^1 = p_1^2 \qquad p_1^1 p_2^2 - p_2^1 p_1^2 \geq 0$$

355

Costs are functions of quantities and functions of a long-run strategic variable denoted K for capital: $C^i(x_i, K_i)$. Using subscripts to denote partial derivatives, we write the marginal costs as $C_i^i(x_i, K_i)$.

The firms compete in a two-stage game. In the first period they choose a level of capital expenditure K_i measured in period 1 money units. An increase in K leads to a marginal cost reduction, i.e. $C_{xK}^i < 0$.

In the second period, the firms choose the quantities to be produced (and sold). We shall model this second stage as a conjectural variation equilibrium. The concept of conjectural variations is often used for modelling the way that agents anticipate their rivals' reactions without having recourse to a fully dynamic framework. Many commentators have stressed the logical flaw in this model which remains static in nature. However, it constitutes a useful tool for cataloguing various kinds of equilibrium (for example, in oligopoly theory two nice values of the conjectural variation parameters give the Cournot–Nash equilibrium in quantities and the Bertrand–Nash equilibrium in prices respectively).

Each firm tries to maximize its total profit:

$$\Pi_i = \beta[p^i(x_1, x_2)x_i - C^i(x_i, K_i)] - K_i \qquad (17.4)$$

where β is again a positive discount factor. We are looking for the perfect Nash equilibrium of the game. First, we solve the second-stage subgame for given values of K_1 and K_2, and then, knowing how x_1 and x_2 depend on K_1 and K_2, we can solve the first-stage game.

Firms can only make credible threats concerning their planned levels of production. But they are also aware of the fact that irreversible investment in the first stage modifies the initial conditions of the game in the second stage. Therefore they take into account all the effects of the investments: reduction of costs and modification of the second-stage game. The sunk-cost nature of capital expenditures is of course a crucial condition of the strategic effect of K.

By choosing a certain level of K, each firm commits itself irreversibly to certain behaviour in the second stage.

The first-order conditions of the second-stage equilibrium are, as usual,

$$
\begin{aligned}
H^i(x_1, x_2, K_i) = P^i(x_1, x_2) + [P_i^i(x_1, x_2) \\
+ P_j^i(x_1, x_2)v_i]x_i - C_i^i(x_i, K_i) = 0
\end{aligned}
\qquad (17.5)
$$

where $v_i = (dx_j/dx_i)_c$ is the conjectural variation relation. Differentiating (17.5) gives in matrix form

$$
\begin{bmatrix} H_1^1 & H_2^1 \\ H_1^2 & H_2^2 \end{bmatrix}
\begin{bmatrix} dx_1 \\ dx_2 \end{bmatrix}
= -
\begin{bmatrix} H_K^1 & dK_1 \\ H_K^2 & dK_2 \end{bmatrix}
\qquad (17.6)
$$

A few additional assumptions are needed to obtain precise results:

$$H_1^1 < 0 \qquad H_2^2 < 0 \qquad (17.7a)$$

$$H_1^1 H_2^2 - H_2^1 H_1^2 > 0 \qquad (17.7b)$$

$$H_2^1 < 0 \qquad H_1^2 < 0 \qquad (17.7c)$$

Assumptions (17.7a) and (17.7b) are conditions of uniqueness and 'stability' of the static equilibrium (Dixit 1986). Assumption (17.7c) is a necessary and sufficient condition for having downward-sloping 'reaction curves' (or equilibrium loci of firms).

By setting the right-hand side in (17.6) equal to zero, we can obtain the following expressions for the slopes of the firms' reaction functions:

$$r_1 = -\frac{H_2^1}{H_1^1} \qquad r_2 = -\frac{H_1^2}{H_2^2} \qquad (17.8)$$

Now let us study the comparative statics effects of an increase in K_1, with K_2 kept constant.

Solving (17.6) for dx_1 and dx_2 gives

$$dx_1 = -\frac{H_2^2 H_K^1 dK_1}{\Delta}$$

where $\Delta > 0$ is the determinant of the matrix in (17.6) and

$$dx_2 = \frac{H_1^2 H_K^1 dK_1}{\Delta}$$

or, using (17.8),

$$dx_2 = -\frac{r_2 H_2^2 H_K^1 dK_1}{\Delta}$$

(in fact $dx_2 = r_2 dx_1$, which means that the equilibrium is shifted along firm 2's reaction function). The signs of r_2 and H_2^2 are determined by assumptions (17.7a) and (17.7c), but $H_K^1 dK$ may be positive or negative.

Consider the case where $H_K^1 > 0$, i.e. where the increase in K_1 leads to an increase in firm 1's marginal profit. Then dx_1 and dx_2 can be unambiguously signed: $dx_1 > 0$ and $dx_2 < 0$. More generally, in this case the output level of each firm is an increasing function of its capital stock and a decreasing function of the rival firm's capital stock. Now let us go back to the first stage of the game: each firm chooses its capital level, taking into account the direct effects on costs and indirect effects on the initial conditions of the second-period game. We are looking for a Nash equilibrium of this game.

The equilibrium conditions are

$$\beta[P^i(x_1, x_2) + P^i_i(x_1, x_2)x_i - C^i_i(x_i, K_i)]\frac{dx_i}{dK_i}$$

$$+ \beta P^i_j(x_1, x_2)x_1 \frac{dx_j}{dK_i} - (1 + \beta C^i_K) = 0$$

Using the second-stage equilibrium condition (17.5) and the expressions for the slopes of the reaction functions in (17.8), we obtain

$$\beta x_i p^i_j(x_1, x_2)(r_j - v_i)\frac{dx_i}{dK_i} - (1 + \beta C^i_K) = 0 \tag{17.10}$$
$$(<0) \qquad (?) \qquad (?)$$

The second term in (17.10) represents the direct effect of K and the first term is the indirect or strategic effect. The sign of the strategic effect depends on the sign of $r_j - v_i$ and the sign of dx_i/dK_i, which itself depends on the sign of H^1_K (given assumptions (17.7a) and (17.7b)). If, as we have assumed so far, $H^1_K > 0$, firm i will overinvest in the case where $r_j - v_i$ is negative, which encompasses the normal Cournot situation (with $r_j < 0$ and $v_i = 0$), and will underinvest in the case where $r_j - v_i$ is positive (which encompasses the normal Bertrand case).[10]

If $r_j = v_i$, a case known as 'consistent conjectures', the variable K has no strategic effect at all. In the case where $H^1_K < 0$, the results would simply be reversed.

This general framework can be applied to a variety of economic problems. The case put forward by Brander and Spencer (1985) for strategic trade policy is an example: the government subsidies act as a commitment like the variable K above. Since Brander and Spencer assume $H^1_K > 0$ and a Cournot second-stage game, they find that subsidies have a positive strategic effect (see Eaton and Grossman (1986) for a discussion of Brander and Spencer's argument in the general framework presented above).

This model is also well adapted to the study of the problem of an incumbent firm facing an entrant on a given market. The choice between a deterrent strategy and an accommodating strategy can be formally analysed (see, for instance, Fudenberg and Tirole 1984; Ware 1984). If entry cannot be deterred, the incumbent may adopt the different strategies summarized in Table 17.2 (using the zoological taxonomy suggested by Fudenberg and Tirole (1984)). Notice that we obtain the results of the third column if the game is Cournot in the second stage with downward-sloping reaction curves, a case of 'strategic substitutes' according to the phrases coined by Bulow et al. (1985). We would obtain the results of the fourth column if the game was Bertrand in prices with upward-sloping reaction curves (in the price space), a case of 'strategic complements'.

Table 17.2

		$r_j - v_i < 0$	$r_j - v_i > 0$
$H_K^1 > 0$	Investment makes the incumbent tough	Overinvestment: the incumbent wants to look like a 'top dog'	Underinvestment: the incumbent wants to look like a 'puppy dog'
$H_K^1 < 0$	Investment makes the incumbent soft	Underinvestment: the incumbent wants to have a 'lean and hungry look'	Overinvestment: the incumbent wants to look like a 'fat cat'

In the preceding example it was natural to assume that investment was 'making the incumbent tough', i.e. that an increase in K was likely to make the incumbent behave more competitively in the post-entry game. However, other types of investment, such as advertising, could make the incumbent soft ($H_K^1 < 0$), i.e. less likely to act competitively after entry. In such a case a commitment to low advertising expenditure may increase the credibility of a threat of fight after entry. If entry is inevitable and the second-stage game is a Bertrand price competition, i.e. $r_j - v_i > 0$, then the incumbent should overinvest to look like a 'fat cat' in order to avoid competition which is too rough in the second stage.

Many other models of strategic commitments in two-stage games could be developed (Fudenberg and Tirole 1986; Jacquemin 1987; Lyons 1987). Empirical studies of strategic moves of this kind have not yet been fully implemented. Actual examples of strategic deterrence are mentioned in Geroski and Jacquemin (1985) and reported from a questionnaire by Smiley (1988).

17.5 STRATEGIC USE OF INFORMATION

So far, we have assumed that all agents have perfect (and of course symmetric) information. Prior commitments aimed at improving the credibility of future threats had to bear on tangible variables, like real parameters of cost or demand functions. However, in the case of asymmetric information there is no need to act on tangible variables in order to modify the other players' expectations.

In a context of imperfect or incomplete information, agents may learn from history in the sense that they infer certain parameter values from the past actions of rival agents. For instance, a low price may signal low costs. There are then opportunities to use information to threaten a rival credibly. The analogy with the models discussed in Section 17.4 is obvious enough: trying to disinform a rival to one's own advantage is a costly activity similar to an investment.

A rich variety of strategic behaviour often observed in economic life can be analysed along these lines: predatory pricing or limit pricing in industrial organization (see Kreps and Spence 1985; Roberts 1987) or the building of

Figure 17.2

a reputation for anti-inflation toughness by a government (Blackburn 1987; Blackburn and Christensen 1989). Formal games of asymmetric information use the concept of perfect Bayesian equilibrium or one of its refinements – the concept of sequential equilibrium.

A simple example taken from Kreps and Wilson (1982a) will give an illustration of this kind of modelling and of the equilibrium concept generally used. In industrial organization it is frequently claimed that a firm might find it worthwhile to resist any entry into its market, even if this is costly, in order to build a reputation for toughness and thus discourage future potential entrants. Let us first put this story in terms of the famous 'chain-store paradox' (Selten 1978). Denote by I an incumbent firm operating on a given number of markets N. For each market there is a potential entrant E_i, $i = 1 , \ldots , N$. E_i has to decide whether to enter or not, and I must then respond either aggressively or non-aggressively. The pay-offs to E_i depend on firm I's reaction: $+1$ if I co-operates, -1 if it reacts negatively and zero in the case of non-entry. The corresponding pay-offs to I are $+1$, -1 and $+2$ respectively. The overall pay-off to I is the sum of the pay-offs obtained on each market. The entry decision is sequential, beginning with $i = 1$ and ending with $i = N$.

When information is perfect, the result of this game depends strongly on the number of markets. If there is only one market, the game can be described in extensive form as in Figure 17.2 where the pay-offs of E_1 and of I are given in parentheses. The outcome 'E_1 does not enter, I fights' is a Nash equilibrium of this game. But it is not subgame perfect, since the threat of fighting announced by I is not credible. Once E_1 has entered, it is in I's interest to accommodate. However, the story says that when there is a larger number of markets the incumbent has a strategic incentive to prey upon early entrants in order to deter future ones. This is typically true in the case of an infinite number of markets. It will resist any entrant, and since any potential entrant knows that the incumbent will have many further periods to recover its present expenses, the threat is credible and entry is actually deterred.

On the other hand, for any finite N there is a unique perfect equilibrium with accommodation at each stage. The argument is perfectly analogous to that used in Section 17.3 for finitely repeated games. At the final stage entry is inevitable, as in the one-period game shown in Figure 17.2. Therefore E_N will necessarily enter. E_{N-1} knows that I has no means of deterring E_N from entering, so that I has no incentive to fight in the penultimate round. E_{N-1} will then enter and so on back to E_1.

In the perfect information case, it is common knowledge that fighting is a dominated strategy for I at each stage. Therefore the story of predatory pricing to deter entry would seem to be without rational foundations. However, a major achievement of the new models of game theory with imperfect information is to show that predatory behaviour may be rational once there is some asymmetric information between the incumbent and the potential entrant. Firm I can credibly commit itself with some probability to prey upon each entrant (Milgrom and Roberts 1982), or fighting may be better for I than co-operating at certain stages (Kreps and Wilson 1982a). In any case, each potential entrant faces the risk of being confronted with a firm committed to fighting or loving to fight (even if this is irrational behaviour – 'a crazy type of firm'), and it will try to infer which type it is from past experiences.

The results of the Kreps–Wilson model can be stated as follows: 'for any given (small but positive) prior probability that cooperating is not the best response to entry in the stage game, there is an n^* such that if $N > n^*$ then both the normal and the crazy types of I prey on any entry into markets $n^*, \ldots,$ N' (Roberts 1987).

Let us give a simple illustration of this argument. Consider a case where N $= 2$. The incumbent firm may be a crazy firm I^C or a normal firm I^N. The prior probability on the crazy incumbent is π. The crazy firm will prey on any entrant (with a probability equal to unity); the normal incumbent is expected to prey on E_1 with a probability p.

Suppose that E_1 has entered. If I does not fight, E_2 can infer that it is a normal incumbent and it will enter. If I fights, his behaviour may reveal a crazy type of incumbent. Applying Bayes's rule, we find a posterior probability $\pi^* = \pi/[\pi + (1 - \pi)p]$ that I is of the crazy type and will again prey upon E_2. The expected pay-offs will thus depend on the value of π^*. It is obvious that a normal incumbent may find it worthwhile to prey even at a loss in the first stages in order to let the future potential entrants infer that they are confronted with a crazy firm.

The very simple two-stage example cited above may be misleading in conveying the idea that E_2 would be deterred after an observed entry of E_1. Rather, the reverse would happen. Since all the probabilities are common knowledge and since the game can be solved backwards, the first potential entrant will know the risk of being preyed on and will thus stay out. If entry occurs, it will be in the final stages of the game.

This game of reputation-building has many applications in economics. An especially interesting example is anti-inflation reputation-building by a weak government in order to exploit an inflationary boost (see Backus and Driffill 1985; Barro 1986; Blackburn and Christensen 1989).

Asymmetric information games still have many defects relating to the rationality assumptions, the common knowledge assumption or the multiplicity of equilibria (see Milgrom and Roberts (1987) for an insider critique). However, they certainly constitute a major advance in the analysis of strategic behaviour in economics.

17.6 CONCLUDING REMARKS

Recent years have witnessed a tremendous development of game-theoretical analysis in various areas of economics. In this chapter we have given just a few aspects of this large renewal of interest in the theory of games. Much more space would have been needed to cover all the advances made in great detail; one particularly important topic which has been omitted is bargaining theory (see Sutton 1986; Binmore and Dasgupta 1987; Rubinstein 1987).

Many aspects of strategic behaviour in industrial organization, international trade policy, macroeconomic policy and public choice, which had previously resisted analysis, are now being handled by formal models of games, including dynamic aspects and asymmetric information, and enriched by Schelling's ideas on strategic moves. The tools of game theory are now better understood and more judiciously chosen by economists. Thus, game theory is now generally perceived as more useful and interesting than was the case a few decades ago. At the same time, economics itself has gained in realism and relevance to real-world issues. This desirable process is not showing any sign of weakening and it is probable that the present enthusiasm for game theory will leave an irreversible taste for this approach in economics. In other words, we are not going to see another long period of disillusion as in the 1950s.

Of course many problems remain, especially the multiplicity of equilibria and the problem raised by the common knowledge assumption. However, further progress can be expected from experimental analysis and from the related fields of sociology and psychology. For example, recent advances in game-theoretical models in evolutionary biology (Maynard Smith 1982) seem to offer interesting prospects for economists (Dasgupta 1989).

NOTES

1 This is not to deny the good works published between 1944 and 1970, such as Shubik (1959), and especially the work on the 'shrinking of the core' when the number of agents increases, which is certainly one of the most exciting results in economics since the Second World War.
2 On this point, see the excellent comments by Johansen (1982).
3 However, we must acknowledge that mixed strategies may constitute very sophisticated forms of strategic behaviour. In certain types of games it may be in the interest of each player to render his choice partially uncertain (for example, in a two-player zero-sum game without a

saddlepoint, i.e. without maximin equilibrium, it pays each player to let his rival play first, thus delaying as long as possible his decision and keeping secret and uncertain the chosen strategy). When the players can communicate before the beginning of the game, they have other means for randomizing their decisions. They can devise a positive correlation between their random strategies. Such 'correlated strategies' allow the players to achieve higher expected values of gains than those they could obtain with simple mixed strategies (Aumann 1974, 1987).

4 However, we must not overlook the fact that zero-sum games help in the study of some problems of conflict inside more general games, including aspects of conflict and co-operation. In particular, if we allow the possibility of coalition formation, zero-sum games help in evaluating the relative strength of different coalitions.

5 The concept is very important from a normative point of view. Dominant strategies are of particular interest for the ideal decentralization of decision-making. This property explains why non-manipulable decision mechanisms, in which each agent's dominant strategy is the revelation of its true preferences, are so widely studied in public economics (see, for instance, Laffont and Maskin 1982).

6 For a more detailed study of recent refinements of the Nash equilibrium concept, see Van Damme (1983).

7 In general, there is a multiplicity of perfect Bayesian equilibria, depending on the *a posteriori* selection of probability distributions outside the equilibrium paths. Certain criteria have been devised in order to select reasonable equilibria in specific models. We can mention in this respect the 'sequential equilibrium' concept suggested by Kreps and Wilson (1982b) or the concept of 'stable equilibrium' discussed by Kohlberg and Mertens (1986).

8 In fact any individually rational outcome can be maintained as a Nash equilibrium of the supergame. An individually rational outcome is any outcome which gives each agent a pay-off no lower than the one it could obtain by its own actions (its maximin pay-off).

9 For a discussion of more general dynamic models see for instance Fudenberg and Tirole (1986) and Shapiro (1989) for applications to industrial organization and Blackburn (1987) for applications to macroeconomic policy.

10 The terms overinvest or underinvest are used to compare the situations with a case where the investment would have no strategic effect.

REFERENCES

Aumann, R. J. (1974) 'Subjectivity and correlation in randomized strategies', *Journal of Mathematical Economics* 1: 67–96.

—— (1987) 'Correlated equilibrium as an expression of Bayesian rationality', *Econometrica* 55: 1–18.

Axelrod, R. (1983) *The Evolution of Cooperation*, New York: Basic Books.

Bacharach, M. (1976) *Economics and the Theory of Games*, London: Macmillan.

Backus, D. and Driffill, E. J. (1985) 'Inflation and reputation', *American Economic Review* 75: 530–8.

Barro. R. J. (1986) 'Reputation in a model of monetary policy with incomplete information', *Journal of Monetary Economics* 12: 101–2.

Bellman, R. (1957) *Dynamic Programming*, Princeton, NJ: Princeton University Press.

Bertrand, J. (1983) 'Théorie des richesses', *Journal des Savants* 499–508.

Bewley, T. F. (ed.) (1987) *Advances in Economic Theory – Fifth World Congress*, Cambridge: Cambridge University Press.

Binmore, K. and Dasgupta, P. (eds) (1987) *The Economics of Bargaining*, Oxford: Basil Blackwell.

Blackburn, K. (1987) 'Macroeconomic policy evaluation and optimal control theory: a critical review of some developments', *Journal of Economic Surveys* 1 (2): 11–148.

Blackburn, K. and Christensen, M. (1989) 'Monetary policy and policy credibility: theories and evidence', *Journal of Economic Literature* 27: 1–45.

Brander, J. and Spencer, B. (1985) 'Export subsidies and international market share rivalry', *Journal of International Economics* 18: 83–100.

Bulow, J., Geneakoplos, J. and Klemperer, P. (1985) 'Multimarket oligopoly: strategic substitutes and complements', *Journal of Political Economy* 93: 488–511.

Cournot, A. A. (1838) *Recherches sur les Principes Mathématiques de la Théorie des Richesses*, Paris: Hachette. English translation, *Researches into the Mathematical Principles of the Theory of Wealth*, London: Hafner, 1960.

Dasgupta, P. (1989) 'Applying game theory: some theoretical considerations', *European Economic Review, Papers and Proceedings of the Third Annual Congress of the EEA* 33: 619–24.

Dixit, A. K. (1980) 'The role of investment in entry deterrence', *Economic Journal* 90: 95–106.

—— (1986) 'Comparative statics for oligopoly', *International Economic Review* 27: 107–22.

—— (1987) 'Strategic aspects of trade policy', in T. F. Bewley (ed.) *Advances in Economic Theory – Fifth World Congress*, Cambridge: Cambridge University Press.

Eaton, J. and Grossman, G. (1986) 'Optimal trade and industrial policy under oligopoly', *Quarterly Journal of Economics* 101: 383–406.

Farrell, J. and Maskin, E. (1987) 'Notes on renegotiation in repeated games', unpublished manuscript, Harvard University.

Friedman, J. W. (1971) 'A non-cooperative equilibrium for supergames', *Review of Economic Studies* 38: 1–12.

—— (1986) *Game Theory with Applications to Economics*, Oxford: Oxford University Press.

Fudenberg, D. and Tirole, J. (1984) 'The fat-cat effect, the puppy-dog ploy and the lean and hungry look', *American Economic Review, Papers and Proceedings* 74: 361–6.

—— and —— (1986) *Dynamic Models of Oligopoly*, New York: Harwood.

Geroski, P. and Jacquemin, A. (1985) 'Industrial change, barriers to mobility, and European industrial policy', *Economic Policy* 1: 170–218.

Harsanyi, J. (1967–8) 'Games with incomplete information played by Bayesian players, I–III', *Management Science* 14: 159–82, 320–34, 486–502.

Jacquemin, A. (1987) *The New Industrial Organization: Market Forces and Strategic Behavior*, Oxford: Clarendon Press.

Johansen, L. (1982) 'On the status of the Nash equilibrium in economic theory', *Scandinavian Journal of Economics* 84: 421–41.

Kennan, J. and Riezman, R. (1988) 'Do big countries win tariff wars?', *International Economic Review* 29: 81–5.

Kohlberg, E. and Mertens, J. F. (1986) 'On the strategic stability of equilibria', *Econometrica* 54: 1003–37.

Kreps, D. and Spence, A. M. (1985) 'Modelling the role of history in industrial organization and competition', in G. Feiwel (ed.) *Issues in Contemporary Microeconomics and Welfare*, London: Macmillan.

Kreps, D. and Wilson, R. (1982a) 'Reputation and imperfect information', *Journal of Economic Theory* 27: 253–79.

—— and —— (1982b) 'Sequential equilibria', *Econometrica* 50: 863–94.

Krugman, P. R. (1984) 'Import protection as export promotion: international competition in the presence of oligopoly and economies of scale', in H. Kierzkowski (ed.)

Monopolistic Competition and International Trade, New York: Oxford University Press.

Laffont, J. J. and Maskin, E. (1982) 'The theory of incentives: an overview', in W. Hildenbrand (ed.) *Advances in Economic Theory*, Cambridge: Cambridge University Press.

Lyons, B. (1987) 'Strategic behaviour by firms', in R. Clarke and T. McGuiness (eds) *The Economics of the Firm*, Oxford: Basil Blackwell.

McMillan, J. (1986) *Game Theory in International Economics*, London: Harwood.

Maynard Smith, J. (1982) *Evolution and the Theory of Games*, Cambridge: Cambridge University Press.

Milgrom, P. and Roberts, J. (1982) 'Predation, reputation and entry deterrence', *Journal of Economic Theory* 27: 280–312.

—— and —— (1987) 'Information asymmetries, strategic behaviour and industrial organization', *American Economic Review, Papers and Proceedings* 77: 184–93.

Napoleoni, C. (1963) *Economic Thought of the Twentieth Century*, English translation A. Cigno, London: Martin Robertson, 1972.

Nash, J. F. (1951) 'Non-cooperative games', *Annals of Mathematics* 54: 286–95.

von Neumann, J. and Morgenstern, O. (1944) *Theory of Games and Economic Behavior*, Princeton, NJ: Princeton University Press.

Pearce, D. (1987) 'Renegotiation-proof equilibria: collective rationality and intertemporal cooperation', unpublished manuscript, Yale University.

Roberts, J. (1987) 'Battles for market share: incomplete information, aggressive strategic pricing, and competitive dynamics', in T. F. Bewley (ed.) *Advances in Economic Theory – Fifth World Congress*, Cambridge: Cambridge, University Press.

Rubinstein, A. (1987) 'A sequential strategic theory of bargaining', in T. F. Bewley (ed.) *Advances in Economic Theory – Fifth World Congress*, Cambridge: Cambridge University Press.

Schelling, T. (1960) *The Strategy of Conflict*, Cambridge, MA: Harvard University Press.

—— (1965) *Arms and Influence*, New Haven, CT: Yale University Press.

Shapiro, C. (1989) 'Theories of oligopoly behavior', in R. Schmalensee and R. Willig (eds) *Handbook of Industrial Organization*, Amsterdam: North-Holland.

Selten, R. (1975) 'Reexamination of the perfectness concept for equilibrium points in extensive games', *International Journal of Game Theory* 4: 25–55.

—— (1978) 'The chain-store paradox', *Theory and Decision* 9: 127–59.

Shubik, M. (1959) *Strategy and Market Structure*, New York: Wiley.

—— (1982) *Game Theory in the Social Sciences*, Cambridge, MA: MIT Press.

Smiley, R. (1988) 'Empirical evidences on strategic entry deterrence', *International Journal of Industrial Organization* 6: 167–80.

Spence, M. (1977) 'Entry, capacity, investment and oligopolistic pricing', *Bell Journal of Economics* 8: 534–44.

Sutton, J. (1986) 'Non-cooperative bargaining theory: an introduction', *Review of Economic Studies* 53: 709–24.

Van Damme, E. (1983) *Refinements of the Nash Equilibrium Concept*, Berlin: Springer-Verlag.

Ware, R. (1984) 'Sunk cost and strategic commitment: a proposed three-stage equilibrium', *Economic Journal* 94: 370–8.

18

INTERNATIONAL
ASPECTS OF
DEVELOPMENT
ECONOMICS

V. N. BALASUBRAMANYAM AND A. I. MACBEAN

18.1 INTRODUCTION

Most issues in development economics arouse intense controversy, and none
more so than the international aspects. The early debates on the distribution
of gains from trade and investment between the less developed countries
(LDCs) and more developed countries (MDCs) are well known. The neo-
Marxist and dependency theories of underdevelopment, in fashion during the
1970s, revived and fuelled these controversies. The 1980s witnessed a
resurgence of the neoclassical orthodoxy with its advocacy of minimalist state
intervention in economic activity and outward-looking economic policies,
exemplified by the structural adjustment and stabilization policies of the World
Bank and the International Monetary Fund (IMF). The developments, however, have served to revive the old debate between the orthodox neoclassical, or
liberal, economists and the structuralists who have long emphasized structural
rigidities and market failure due to social, institutional and political factors
which act as bottlenecks to development. Their advocacy of state intervention
and regulation of foreign trade and investment as a way out of these bottlenecks
is well known. These debates between the orthodox neoclassical economists
and the structuralists might be relegated to the pages of history were it not
for the fact that the division continues to influence discussion on major policy
issues. These include the structural adjustment and stabilization policies of
the World Bank and the IMF, liberalization of trade in services, foreign direct
investment and the international debt problem.

In this chapter we review recent debates on some of these issues. In Section
18.2 we briefly discuss the structuralist case and provide the background for
the analysis of structural adjustment policies presented in Section 18.3. This

analysis suggests that increased flows of financial and technical resources from MDCs to LDCs are a necessary prerequisite for the success of stabilization programmes. Section 18.4 identifies foreign direct investment in both manufacturing and services as a major source and conduit of finance and technology and reviews the debate on foreign direct investment and liberalization of trade in services.

18.2 THE STRUCTURALIST CASE

The structuralist case can be summarized broadly as follows. Differences between the economic structures of LDCs (the periphery) and industrialized countries or MDCs (the centre) and their trading and financial links systematically inhibit the development of LDCs. First, LDCs have dual economies: a relatively advanced sector dominated by industries such as mining and plantation agriculture which export to the MDCs, and a backward sector dominated by subsistence farming and informal market activities. The backward sector is characterized by hidden unemployment. The problem of finding employment for a rapidly increasing population, especially labour migrating from the traditional sector, falls upon the modern sector. Its expansion depends on the rate of investment which in turn depends on savings and net inflow of foreign capital. Inflexible factor proportions and total dependence on imported capital goods are assumed. Difficulty in expanding the modern sector fast enough creates a structural tendency towards unemployment.

Second, as the modern sector is oriented towards foreign trade it has few linkages with the traditional sector. Its growth has weak spread effects on the rest of the economy.

Third, low income elasticities of demand and other product and factor market characteristics of LDCs' commodity exports, which differ from the maunfactures imported from the MDCs, cause persistent tendencies to payments disequilibrium and an adverse trend in their commodity (net barter) terms of trade (Prebisch 1950; Singer 1950, 1989; Nurkse 1959). The only escape routes from the adverse terms of trade and balance-of-payments constraints are to develop import substitutes, to diversify into manufactured exports or to depend for ever on economic aid. Of these, exporting is considered too difficult in the fact of MDC competition and also MDC protectionism (see Linder 1967). Import substitution would also be very difficult if the MDCs' powerful industries were allowed to compete on equal terms. Aid would help and is probably essential, but is necessarily limited in amount and duration. Hence the policy of import-substituting industrialization (ISI) with high protection as a shelter seems the only solution. The argument for ISI is reinforced by belief in the importance of beneficial externalities from manufacturing and a more general export pessimism based on the adverse trend in the terms of trade, by the risks caused by instability of commodity exports and by the danger of immiserizing growth if LDCs expanded their commodity exports in the face of inelastic world demand (Bhagwati 1958). This argument was later extended to exports of manufactures in terms of an alleged 'fallacy of composition' (Cline 1982). Cline's point was that what could be successful for a few economies like Korea, Taiwan, Hong Kong and Singapore could not be extended to the many LDCs. If they simultaneously expanded their exports, the MDCs would impose severe trade barriers.

Acceptance of the reasoning, and the empirical backing, behind the old and the new export pessimism would support those who decry markets and comparative advantage. It would suggest that in pursuit of growth and equity LDCs' governments should reduce their dependence on primary commodities and force the pace of industrialization. This would involve protection, justified on infant industry, terms-of-trade and balance-of-payments grounds. Within manufacturing, emphasis would be on ISI rather than exports.

Critics of the old and new export pessimism

Both the evidence for commodity exports pessimism and the policy conclusions derived have been questioned. Early studies were based on poor data which were not really appropriate (indices of relative prices of UK exports and imports for example). However, in the 1980s new time series were constructed which covered world trade from 1900 to the late 1980s. The upshot of recent studies is that there is some support for a declining trend in the price of commodity exports relative to manufactures, but the issue is complicated by structural shifts and cyclical movements (Spraos 1980; Sapsford 1985; Thirlwall and Bergevin 1985; Grilli and Yang 1988). The most recent study by Cuddington and Urzua (1989), using the World Bank data of Grilli and Yang (1988), concludes:

> Primary commodity prices (relative to manufactures) experienced an abrupt drop after 1920. Apart from this one-time structural shift, however, there is no evidence of an on-going, continual down-trend in the relative price of primary goods. That is, it is inappropriate to describe the movement of real primary commodity prices since the turn of the century as one of 'secular deterioration'.

However, even if it were true that relative prices of non-oil primary products in general were declining, would that constitute a conclusive case for shifting resources out of commodities and into manufactures? Changes in the character and quality of the products, especially of manufactures, make the index numbers very dubious. Moreover, the problem with such a general prescription is the diversity of LDCs and the differences in experience among commodities. Income elasticities for primary commodities tend to be within the range 0.3–0.5

(Bond 1987). Tastes change and fashions swing between natural and synthetic fibres. Some foods become fashionable, whilst the market for others stagnates. New uses are found for old raw materials. To forgo primary exports on the basis of a general trend could risk sacrificing higher returns than would be possible in import substitution. A nation's economic policy should be based on relatively detailed assessments of the specific opportunities which face its actual and potential activities – not on broad general trends. Assessment of future demand prospects should be an essential part of decisions on resource allocation, but so too should assessments of relative costs and productivities in different sectors and industries. Even where the prospects were for a substantial drop in real prices for the output of a project it could, over its lifetime, yield high private and social returns because costs fell faster or were so low that sufficient rents were earned in its initial years.

Flawed though it may be, structuralism has been influential. Central planning, detailed regulation, public ownership and control of economic activities have drawn support from structuralism. As a result, the economies of many LDCs have been cut off from international competition. Their domestic prices have lost touch with world prices just as in the centrally planned economies of the USSR and Eastern Europe. Their economies have become increasingly distorted. Exports and domestic food production have often been sacrificed to the promotion of inefficient industries.

Trade liberalization

Structuralism was, and remains, a powerful attack on the general position of conventional economics that countries (with specific and limited exceptions) will generally gain from trading freely with the rest of world. Over the last thirty years much empirical evidence has been assembled which appears to show that countries which pursued policies of import-substituting industrialization over an extended period generally have had less economic success than those which pursued more open-economy policies (Little *et al.* 1970; Bhagwati 1978; Krueger 1978; World Bank 1987, and references cited therein). A general revival of market-oriented analysis and policies, together with the failure of the centrally planned economies of Eastern Europe to deliver the goods, reinforced the critique of excessive government intervention in LDCs and of inward-looking policies for industrial development. These factors plus the growth of monetarism influenced the approach adopted by the IMF and the World Bank to the LDCs' balance-of-payments crises in the 1970s and 1980s. Both institutions strongly supported import liberalization as an important element of structural adjustment for recovery and growth.

IMF programmes are mainly concerned with the short run. The basic aim is an orderly adjustment between the country's aggregate expenditure (or absorption) and its aggregate output (or income) so as to reduce demand for imports and release resources for exports. The IMF is not indifferent to domestic objectives such as growth, employment and income distribution. Indeed, supply-side measures to improve efficiency and increase output are a normal part of its policy recommendations. However, its statutory need to recover loans quickly, a shortage of resources and its need to turn funds over rapidly mean that the IMF necessarily gives less attention to these objectives than to a rapid restoration of a viable balance-of-payments position (Khan and Knight 1986; Guitian 1987).

The crises of the 1970s led to recognition of the need for longer-term assistance than the IMF could provide, even with its Extended Fund Facilities (EFFs). To achieve this, World Bank Structural Adjustment Loans (SALs) were introduced in 1980. They are intended to:

> Support a program of specific policy changes and institutional reforms designed to reduce the current account deficit to sustainable levels; assist a country in meeting the transitional costs of structural changes in industry and agriculture by augmenting the supply of freely usable foreign exchange; act as a catalyst for the inflow of other external capital and help ease the balance-of-payments situation.
>
> (Stern 1983)

To this list (as subsequent statements by other Bank officials make clear) should be added: 'help recipient countries towards sustainable growth' (Cassen 1986; Michalopoulos 1987).

The difference between the World Bank SALs and the IMF adjustment programmes mainly lies in the time horizon and range of measures. The IMF's first concern is with financing and correcting balance-of-payments deficits in the short run, while the Bank's aim is a sustainable long-run balance-of-payments situation. Supply-side factors, such as the mobilization and reallocation of resources, figure more prominently in Bank advice.

However, the distinctions blur when the IMF has a series of programmes or uses its EFF. Generally, both organizations provide help to the same country and their activities are normally complementary. However, on occasion differences have arisen between them, for example in East Africa (Cassen 1986: 82–3). The main differences centre on depth of demand cuts. These can be due to differing judgements on economics or politics, but they are conditioned by the IMF's resource contraints. These make it less likely that the IMF can allow time for more sensitive supply-side approaches (Cassen 1986).

18.3 STRUCTURAL ADJUSTMENT POLICIES

The context of structural adjustment

Recognition of the need for structural adjustment invariably comes when a country runs into a severe payments crisis. Often the basic problems of resource misallocation, low efficiency, food deficits and falling exports are already visible. Offical and commercial loans in the 1970s postponed the crisis until many countries, saddled with large debts, encountered adverse movements in their terms of trade, soaring interest rates, and external and internal shocks. Accordingly, most countries adopt adjustment strategies when they have a liquidity crisis combined with macroeconomic imbalance and microeconomic distortions. Usually, much of their foreign exchange earnings is needed simply to service their debts, and commercial finance has ceased. Their macroeconomic imbalances are due to an excess of domestic expenditure over income. The distortions in the pattern of resource allocation are due to past misdirection of resources or an incentive pattern which has encouraged resources to move into unprofitable activities. Domestic prices do not reflect marginal opportunity costs, so that false signals are given to farmers and businessmen. The measures needed would be easier to apply if economic calm prevailed. Reducing trade barriers, for example, is easier when a nation has ample reserves and unemployment is low. However, crises seem necessary to generate the will to change (World Bank 1987; ch. 6). Only when countries have exhausted their reserves and credit do the IMF and the World Bank have much influence.

The content of structural adjustment programs

SAL programmes are broadly characterized by a package of demand-side, supply-side and international competitiveness measures. These measures overlap, but the categorization is based on primary objectives. Demand-side policies aim to reduce the rate of growth of demand. They include cuts in public expenditure, increased taxation, tight money and higher real interest rates.

Supply-side policies can be subdivided as follows: (a) policies designed to move resources from low-return activities to socially more profitable ones, thus encouraging efficient factor use and cutting waste; (b) policies designed to augment resources by giving incentives to domestic savings and investment, and to attract foreign investment and technology. The former measures include removing price controls, breaking up monopolies, reducing trade restrictions, adjusting taxes and subsidies, and de-regulating the financial sector. The two types of policies interact as greater efficiency in the use of existing resources raises output and so allows more saving, and increased productivity attracts investment.

A country's international competitiveness can be measured by the ratio of its costs of production of tradeable goods to the prices of the same goods in world markets. If its inflation rate is higher than that of its trading rivals or partners, or if its exchange rate appreciates, its competitiveness worsens. Either controlling inflation or devaluing lowers its real effective exchange rate, i.e. the inflation-adjusted rate of exchange weighted by the share of each of its main trading partners in its trade (see Khan and Knight 1986). In principle, the incentive effects of devaluation can be achieved by taxes on imports and subsidies to exports. There may be occasions when this is expedient, but it is expensive to administer and risks the imposition of countervailing duties in some markets.

Criticisms of structural adjustment programmes

Devaluing, freeing imports and removing export taxes should increase exports. For commodity exporters, increased exports may cause a fall in international prices as markets for commodities grow slowly and world demand is price inelastic. Should the fall be more than proportional to the increase in export volume, foreign exchange earnings would decline. When a country like Ghana adopts a set of structural adjustment policies which restore incentives to exporting cocoa, Ghana may enjoy success for a time. However, if Ghana's increased export volume depresses world cocoa prices, other exporters, and Ghana as well, may suffer.

Is it likely that structural adjustment policies would lead to immiserizing export growth? Much depends on how national decisions are made and on access to accurate information. Dominant suppliers should know if their commodity export revenue moves inversely to volume. If they devalued they could offset the adverse price effects by taxing the export. They need not sacrifice gains from liberalization simply because it would increase one export beyond its optimum. An export tax can prevent that.

The new export pessimists add a further risk that increased exports of manufactures by LDCs will trigger protection in MDCs. An important strand in this case is the 'fallacy of composition'. They argue that gains possible for a few newly industrializing countries (NICs) would prove impossible if many LDCs increased their exports (Cline 1982). A widely adopted switch from ISI to export-oriented policies would cause fears of job losses in industrial countries and provoke increased barriers against LDCs' exports. Cline's case is exaggerated (see Havrylyshyn 1987), but some concern about increased protectionism is justified (World Bank 1987; chs 8, 9).

It wold be optimal if adjustment could occur amidst buoyant demand. But even if few commodities at present enjoy such demand, this is no bar to profitable exporting. What countries need to know is the range of opportunities that face them. Exporting commodities may still offer many of the best returns. Opportunities for exporting manufactures continue to expand. Movement up the ladder of comparative advantage and growth in intra-industry trade offers further opportunities for manufactures.

Supply-side problems

Adjustment with growth requires that output be responsive to policy changes. Devaluation, reduced protection and a shift away from import restrictions are measures frequently adopted to shift resources from non-tradeable to tradeable goods and from import-substituting industries to exports. These policies free prices of outputs and inputs to signal the relative profitability of different activities. In many countries price controls and regulations have been endemic. They have shaped most economic activity. Removing controls to allow market forces to allocate both inputs and final goods has been a key aim of adjustment policies. But do they work? Will consumers and producers respond? Structuralists emphasize the difficulties. Neoclassical economists are more hopeful.

Conventional wisdom long held that LDC farmers respond poorly to price incentives. Reasons given included cultural factors, forms of land tenure, absentee landlords, share-cropping and so on. Recently emphasis has been placed on the risks to small farmers in effecting change, but limited access to inputs such as credit, irrigation, water, fertilizers, plant protection, transport and markets may also limit supply response.

Empirical research in India and elsewhere, however, has shown that farmers respond to prices. If the price of jute rises relative to that of rice, farmers in Bangladesh will substitute jute for rice. Elasticities are positive and sometimes greater than unity (World Bank 1986). For annual crops, at least, the evidence shows reasonable output responses within one or two seasons. LDC farmers on all continents seem willing to adopt new technologies provided that they are profitable. Small farmers may lag but the 'Green Revolution' technologies seem to be 'scale-neutral', and small farmers have soon followed large ones in adopting new seeds and technologies. Switches among crops, however, are easier than increasing total production. Many examples of response to prices are recorded in the literature cited in World Bank (1986). Strengthening institutions such as agricultural extension services, improving distribution of inputs and access to credits, and developing better land tenure systems are, nevertheless, important back-up policies in many countries (Lipton 1987).

Unfortunately, many of the LDCs' principal agricultural exports take years to progress from planting to harvest. Coffee, cocoa, tea, coconut, rubber and palm oil are good examples. To some extent, even in these cases, outputs can

373

be increased by extra gleaning of old berries, increased tapping of latex, increased use of fertilizers and plant protection. However, for most commodities short-run production elasticities are low. Mineral exports can also be subject to delay in responding to incentives. If mines are already operating near full capacity new shafts may have to be sunk, new seams opened and investment in exploration and development put into effect. Substantial delays may occur even with open-cast mines or dredging.

If such lags typify most traditional exports from LDCs, the implications for structural adjustment lending are serious. Most countries which undertake adjustment policies are already deeply in debt. If many years pass with little or no increase in exports while debt repayments continue, either growth will be negligible or more generous and longer-term aid will be needed. But even for countries specializing in tree crops and mining, export responses may be faster than the foregoing suggests. In crises, mines and plantations will often be working below capacity – partly because imports and other controls have caused shortages of equipment, spare parts and materials. Freeing the economy and obtaining aid may therefore lead to increased production and exports without new capacity.

With tree crops, as already noted, extra efforts to glean the fruits (sometimes from wild trees and shrubs) and rehabilitate plantations can provide a quick response to higher prices. In more sophisticated farming increased current inputs can raise production. But a further likely response to higher producer prices is a reduction in smuggling. While this may not increase actual exports, official foreign exchange receipts and tax revenues should rise. As smuggling is endemic in countries with severely distorted prices, restoring incentives can redirect smuggled exports to the official market (World Bank 1987).

The supply elasticity for exports of products which are also consumed at home will be much higher than that for production. Increased prices will tend to reduce domestic use and release more for export. Nevertheless, slow export response can be a real difficulty for structural adjustment.

Social costs of adjustment

Critics of SALs often focus on their distributional effects. The poor are expected to suffer more. SAL policies of reduced protection, privatization, expenditure cuts and high interest rates seem likely to reduce consumption and investment, thus slowing growth and cutting jobs. Unemployment and reduced incomes for urban workers seem inevitable. Removing price controls and devaluation will raise the domestic prices of food and other consumption goods. Moreover, expenditure cuts often fall heavily on health and education sectors upon which the poor and their children depend. Food subsidies may also be cut and export crops may displace some food crops. Caught between declining money incomes and rising costs, the poor seem likely to suffer disproportionately. But are these consequences inevitable? Are there any offsetting benefits to the poor? Are the hardships due to the SAL measures, world stagnation or preceding years of improvidence? Are the hardships only temporary?

A structural adjustment strategy aims to increase efficiency and growth. If it achieves these ends the standard of living of the poor could improve: more growth means more tax revenues and finance for social expenditures.

The majority of the poor in LDCs live in the countryside and depend on agriculture. As farmers they gain from policies which raise the prices of export crops and food. For landless labourers or tenants, the gains from such policies depend on how much demand for labour is increased, how wages are affected and how much of their income goes on food. Consumer goods may be cheaper and more readily available because of trade liberalization. In most developing countries exporting and food production are more labour-intensive activities than import-substituting industries. As most SAL measures stimulate exports and food production they should create more jobs.

Budget cuts reduce public sector jobs. These add to urban unemployment until renewed growth creates more jobs. But what alternatives exist? A country faced with a severe deficit and no credit has no option but to cut demand. If accepting SAL conditions gains IMF and World Bank assistance, the demand cuts may be less than under any alternative. Acceptance of IMF and World Bank conditions may open the way for renewed bilateral aid and commercial loans. This could allow scope to spread adjustment over a longer period with less need for drastic cuts in demand. But some social costs will result from SAL policies, particularly if they are underfunded. Years may pass before significant positive gains in growth and employment are achieved. Can SAL policies be designed so as to reduce the burden on the poor?

In brief, they can be, if adjustment can be early and orderly rather than belated and forced, i.e. like Korea in the early 1980s rather than Tanzania or Ghana in the mid-1980s. Social expenditures can be redirected to concentrate on the poor, for example primary schooling and preventive medicine. The poor can be compensated through targeted employment programmes, rural public works, food subsidies and nutrition programmes. Recently, the World Bank has shown that it can incorporate support for such measures to reduce the social costs of adjustment (see Huang and Nicholas (1987) for a description of the role of the World Bank).

Political risks of adjustment

Problems arise when the objectives of multilateral aid agencies and governments clash. The major objective of the governing party may be to retain power. Its priority would be to preserve instruments of control and party unity. Patronage accrues from the ability to allocate privileges such as import licences, permits and access to subsidized credit, government stores, subsidized food, education and health services. The controlling party will be reluctant to lose any of these levers. Governments, whether of the left or the right, are likely to be influenced in a mercantilist direction by the capacity to exert power through direct control over foreign exchange and other key resources.

Key elements of SALs entail liberalizing and dismantling rationing and licensing policies. SAL measures often involve efforts to increase the efficiency of public sector organizations or to privatize them. Both involve market tests of efficiency. Party hacks in sinecures have to be dismissed. Overmanned industries have to lose labour. Urban workers lose job security and minimum wage guarantees. At the same time removal of price controls and general subsidies to staple foods raises their cost of living. The disaffection of party members and the anger of labour unions may endanger the stability of the government.

Liberalization exposes import-competing industries to competition. Industrialists and workers in import-competing industries are losers from liberalization and become focal points for opposition. The tension between the long-run interest of the economy and the shorter-run interests of the ruling party in retaining power creates friction between governments and aid agencies, and may cause non-compliance with or abandonment of SAL policies before they can achieve their aims.

Why then do governments accept SALs? The starkest reason is that they see no alternative. If they do not agree to the conditions their economies may collapse and they would lose power anyway. By agreeing, they receive help from the IMF and the World Bank with a possibility of renewed access to commercial credit. At least if they buy time, with luck they may avoid implementing policies which most hurt their supporters. Sometimes a new government formed from the opposition may willingly embrace SAL policies at first, but if benefits are slow to come they too may be tempted by the levers and spoils of a more centrally controlled economy.

Recognition of the politics of adjustment can place multilateral organizations in a quandary. They believe that SAL measures will bring welfare gains, at least in the long run. But the politically powerful groups (public sector managers and workers, owners and workers in protected industries, urban dwellers generally, and politicians and civil servants) may lose income or influence. The probable gainers are those involved in exports, traditional and non-traditional, those in efficient import-competing industries and farmers. It would make sense to marshal the gainers as a counterweight to the opposition of the losers. Unfortunately, the gains are generally more diffuse and the losses more concentrated. Losing one's job may be more clearly associated with lost protection than a gain in farm incomes can be associated with devaluation. This, as opponents of protection have always found, is a serious obstacle to creating a lobby for reduction of trade barriers. Moreover, multilateral institutions are chary of interfering in national politics. Clearly, to aid and cajole governments into adopting and implementing liberalization measures is no easy task.

Evidence on structural adjustment lending

Recent empirical studies simply confirm the generalization that all LDCs, whether in receipt of SALs or not, have made efforts to adjust to debt and depression (Mosley 1991). Supply-side measures have shown great diversity, and no less so in those supported by SALs. Implementation has been partial, ranging from 25 to 90 per cent in the forthcoming study by Mosley, Harrigan and Toye of a sample of nine LDCs, to an average of 60 per cent in the World Bank's own evaluation (Mosley 1991). The effectiveness of the measures is hard to assess: some improvements in growth of gross domestic product (GDP), exports and balance of payments can be attributed to the SAL policies, but the anticipated increases in investment and foreign finances have not been achieved (Mosley 1991: Table 5).

Stablization and adjustment measures have undoubtedly caused hardship in many countries. Recognition of this has led to the adoption, for example in Ghana, of accompanying measures designed to alleviate hardship among the poorer sections of the community.

The successes of structural adjustment have been in the developing countries of Europe and East Asia in the 1970s. These were countries which were already more involved in manufacturing and had a relatively high proportion of skilled and educated workers. Their economies were more flexible than the predominantly commodity exporters characterizing sub-Saharan Africa and Latin American countries like Bolivia and Peru. There are special features, discussed earlier, which differentiate countries dependent on primary commodities from those with significant exports of manufacturers. Successful structural adjustment in the former group of countries requires additional resources and time.

However, adjustment is a necessary fact of life in the real world. Countries can postpone the need to do it for some time, but in the end it becomes inevitable. The alternative to a chaotic *ad hoc* process is the adoption of a coherent set of policies before that chaos arises. Adjustment is much easier if IMF programme loans and World Bank SALs can be obtained. If more resources could be made available, a longer time span could be permitted for the attainment of a sustainable balance of payments. That extra time could reduce hardships, but the outlook for increased aid resources is not hopeful. Alternative sources of resources such as foreign direct investment (FDI) may have to be sought. It is on this basis that we proceed to discuss issues relating to FDI.

18.4 FOREIGN DIRECT INVESTMENT

FDI flows from MDCs to LDCs have increased from an average of under $2 billion a year in the early 1970s to an average of around $10 billion a year during the 1980s (Table 18.1). A substantial proportion of such investment was accounted for by UK and US multinational enterprises (MNEs) in the manufacturing sectors of LDCs. By the mid-1980s the total stock of investment in LDCs amounted to around $200 billion, or 25 per cent of the world stock of FDI (United Nations 1988). Around 40 per cent of this stock is in a dozen countries, most of which are relatively large in terms of population and per capital income and are endowed with relatively cheap and efficient labour and/or natural resources (Table 18.2).

The increased flow of FDI and the visible presence of the MNEs in a select group of countries has spawned a vast literature on various aspects of the MNE and its operations in the LDCs. Within the constraints of this paper justice cannot be done to the vast range of issues and the literature which this has produced. We concentrate on three major themes: (a) the determinants of FDI in various LDCs; (b) empirical analysis of the costs and benefits of FDI to developing countries; (c) FDI and international trade in services.

Determinants of the magnitude of foreign direct investment

For all their public rhetoric concerning the pernicious effects of FDI on their economies, in practice most LDCs have ardently wooed foreign firms by

Table 18.1 Foreign direct investment in less developed countries

1 Year	2 Total world stock of FDI (US$million)	3 Stock of FDI in LDCs (US$million)	4 Stock in LDCs to total world (%)	5 Annual flows of FDI: world total (US$million)	6 Annual flows of FDI to LDCs (US$million)	7 Column 6 as percentage of 5 (%)
1971	146,136	32,242	22.1	12,000	1,942	16.2
1980	607,453	149,475	24.6	52,207	10,105	19.4
1981	664,270	164,490	24.8	56,817	15,015	26.4
1982	708,741	177,943	25.1	44,472	13,454	30.3
1983	752,835	188,209	25.0	44,094	10,265	23.3
1984	801,819	198,209	24.8	48,984	10,500	21.4
1985	851,130	210,184	24.7	49,312	11,475	23.3
1980–5[a]	731,041	181,502	24.8	49,314	11,802	22.9

Source: United Nations 1978, 1985
Note: [a]Average

Table 18.2 Stock of direct foreign investment in principal developing countries

	Total stock 1973 (US$billion)	Percentage of total stock (%)	Total stock 1983 (US$billion)	Percentage of total stock (%)
Argentina	2.5	5.3	5.8	4.1
Brazil	7.5	16.0	24.6	17.5
Mexico	3.1	6.6	13.6	9.6
Colombia	1.0	2.0	2.6	1.8
Chile	0.5	1.1	3.0	2.1
Peru	1.0	2.0	2.5	5.3
Venezuela	3.6	7.7	4.3	3.0
Singapore	0.6	1.3	7.9	5.6
Hong Kong	0.9	1.9	4.2	2.9
Malaysia	1.2	2.5	6.2	4.4
Indonesia	1.7	3.6	6.8	4.8
Philippines	0.9	1.9	2.7	1.9
Republic of Korea	0.7	1.5	1.8	1.2
Thailand	0.5	1.1	1.4	1.0
Nigeria	2.3	4.9	2.0	1.4
Egypt	0.1	0.2	2.1	1.5
Total	47.0		141.0	

Source: Estimates from data in International Monetary Fund 1985

offering them various incentives. These include tax concessions, tax holidays, generous depreciation allowances and various sorts of subsidies. To this list should be added incentives for investment provided by protection from competing imports through tariffs and quantitative restrictions. The pervasiveness of these incentives provides proof of the importance that LDCs attach to FDI and the technology and knowhow that accompanies it. In recent years the debt crisis has reinforced the role of FDI as a principal source of external finance to LDCs. While the lenders prefer FDI to other forms of investment, principally because it enables them to supervise and monitor projects, the borrowers for their part are able to share the risks of FDI projects with the lenders. For these reasons the determinants of FDI in LDCs rank high on the agenda of policy-makers and analysts.

The early literature on the issue focused on the effectiveness of various incentives offered by LDCs in attracting FDI. The consensus appears to be that, in general, such incentives have little impact on inflows of FDI and the host countries may have merely transferred income to MNEs by competing with each other. The significant determinants of FDI are not the incentives but the size of the market, growth potential, exchange stability, political stability, and attitudes to FDI and capitalism on the part of the host countries (Hughes and Seng 1969; Frank 1980; Lim 1983; Balasubramanyam 1986).

In a study sponsored by the World Bank, however, it was concluded that, in the case of two-thirds of the seventy-four projects surveyed, location decisions of foreign firms were made because of incentives offered by host countries (Guissinger 1986). But, as Guissinger notes, this indication of effectiveness of incentives was based on the assumption that competing countries would not alter their policies if a host country eliminated all its incentives. The broad conclusion to be drawn from these studies is that incentives *per se* may not be the principle determinants of FDI although, given other factors conducive to investment, they may tilt the balance in favour of countries offering incentives.

Guissinger also offers another piece of circumstantial evidence in support of the conclusion that incentives do matter. It is that the various types of factor-based incentives, such as cash grants, in effect translate into fairly high levels of effective protection. Guissinger estimates that in terms of present value a cash grant of 30 per cent amounts to an effective rate of protection of 18 per cent, and since it is the conventional wisdom that tariff protection attracts FDI, it is reasonable to conclude that factor-based incentives have similar effects.

The received wisdom that tariff protection attracts FDI is not universally accepted, however. For instance, Bhagwati (1978, 1985) has challenged the proposition that protection necessarily induces high levels of FDI. He argues that, with due adjustments for differences among countries for their economic size, political stability and attitudes towards FDI, in the long term the magnitude of FDI attracted by countries pursuing the export-promotion (EP) strategy will be higher than that attracted by those pursuing the import-substitution (IS) strategy. As is well known, the hallmark of the IS strategy is protection of domestic markets through a system of tariffs and non-tariff barriers to imports. The reasoning underlying Bhagwati's proposition is that incentives provided by the IS strategy are policy induced and they tend to be artificial and limited. As Bhagwati puts it: 'the IS strategy, on both domestic investments and FDI, has been cut from the same cloth; protect your market and attract home-based investments to serve the market' (Bhagwati 1985). In contrast, the EP strategy provides a distortion-free environment and FDI would be driven by market forces. The major incentive which the EP strategy provides is simply the conjunction of cheaper costs and the EP orientation. The magnitude of IS-oriented FDI, Bhagwati argues, will not ultimately be as large as EP-oriented FDI for the simple reason that it would be limited by the size of the host country market which induces it in the first place.

This hypothesis has far-reaching policy implications for LDCs, most of which are now seeking increased amounts of FDI, because of both the technology and knowhow it provides and its contribution to investible resources. However, an empirical verification of the hypothesis is beset with problems, mostly relating to the availability of the data required to quantify many of the determinants that Bhagwati identifies. The type of development strategies pursued by the various developing countries, which forms the crux of Bhagwati's hypothesis, is the most difficult variable to quantify. This is particularly true because of the precision with which Bhagwati defines EP and IS strategies.

The EP strategy equates the average effective exchange rate for imports (EERm) with the average effective exchange rate for exports (EERx). Effective exchange rate, in this context, is defined as the number of units of local currency actually received or paid for a dollar's worth of international transactions. If tariffs and quotas on imports are not matched by subsidies on exports, for instance, the EERm would be greater than the EERx. In this case, relatively more units of local currency would have to be paid for a dollar's worth of imports than can be obtained for a dollar's worth of exports, and the exchange rate system would bias production in favour of the domestic market and the country would be pursuing an IS strategy. In contrast, the EP strategy is one which equates the EERm with the EERx. The essential feature of the EP strategy, as defined by Bhagwati, is its neutrality; on balance, the policy-oriented incentives it provides favour neither production for the domestic market nor production for international markets. The market orientation of production is determined entirely by market forces, factor endowments, and the managerial and entrepreneurial skills of the country in question.

The data required to estimate EERx and EERm include tariff rates, import quotas, subsidies on exports and nominal exchange rates. Most of these data, apart from nominal exchange rates, are not readily available. In the absence of data to estimate EERx and EERm, empirical testing of Bhagwati's hypothesis has to rely on several proxies for identifying the type of development strategies that various countries are pursuing. One such attempt relying on various proxies for the identification of development strategies, including the World Bank distortion index, finds considerable support for Bhagwati's hypothesis (Balasubramanyam and Salisu 1991). However, more rigorous testing must await the availability of adequate data.

The hypothesis has implications for the sort of stablization and structural adjustment policies advocated by the IMF and the World Bank. It emphasizes the significance of a distortion-free investment climate and the limited usefulness of policy-induced incentives in attracting FDI. It is essential to note in this context that the hypothesis does not suggest that, in order to attract FDI, LDCs should embark on an EP strategy based on export subsidies. The EP strategy, as defined by Bhagwati, merely requires host countries to follow a neutral policy which does not bias production decisions in favour of either the domestic or the international market. In this scheme incentives do have a role: one which reinforces the inherent comparative advantage of the countries and does not artificially tilt investment decisions. In sum, the extant research on determinants of FDI suggests that, in general, LDCs desirous of increased inflows of FDI ought to provide a stable and distortion-free economic environment conducive to the operations of MNEs and not rely on policy-induced artificial incentives.

Costs and benefits of foreign direct investment

The second major theme in the literature relates to the costs and benefits of FDI to LDCs. Here the debate is replete with polemics, conjectures and casual empiricism, often liberally laced with ideological overtones. While the ardent advocates of the MNE regard it as a powerful agent of change endowed with an ability to transmit technology and knowhow to LDCs, its opponents regard it as no more than an instrument of neocolonialism. This colourful and thought-provoking debate has been ably reviewed in the literature (Streeten 1979; Jenkins 1987). We confine ourselves to a discussion of some of the available empirical evidence on the benefits and costs of FDI to LDCs.

Although there have been ambitious attempts at assessing the impact of FDI on host countries at the macroeconomic level (Bos *et al.* 1974), most researchers have attempted to assess the contribution of FDI to specific objectives of host countries: employment, balance of payments, output and exports. One of the earliest of such studies (Reuber *et al.* 1973), which was based on published information supplemented with survey data on eighty FDI projects in various LDCs, concluded that, in general, FDI had made a positive contribution to growth of income, employment, trade and technology transfer. The study also suggested that the costs of obtaining technology and knowhow as well as access to foreign markets through FDI may be no higher and possibly less than that entailed by alternative methods of obtaining these resources. The second of these findings is also supported by other studies on technology transfer (Balasubramanyam 1973; Vernon 1977). Subsequent studies, however, have been less sanguine than that of Reuber *et al.* on the contribution of FDI to balance of payments, employment and the social product of LDCs. One such study, which provoked considerable controversy and led to methodological innovations in the assessment of the costs and benefits of FDI, argued that in so far as the annual inflow of foreign private capital was lower than the outflows of dividends and profits on account of FDI, it had an adverse effect on the balance of payments of host countries (Streeten 1971). While evidence shows that on an annual basis outflows of foreign exchange do exceed inflows on account of FDI (Kidron 1965; United Nations 1973), it is open to question whether the mere fact that outflows exceed inflows implies a balance-of-payments problem. Streeten's suggestion was rebutted by several authors on the grounds that the balance of payments is a general equilibrium phenomenon, and the inflow–outflow comparison approach to it was much too narrow and limited in scope (Kindleberger 1969). The gist of the counter-argument is that, in so far as the balance of payments is a general equilibrium phenomenon, any investment which is productive and contributes to the national product is bound to improve it. Conversely, unproductive investments would have an adverse effect on the balance of payments.

Streeten's strictures on FDI and the balance of payments also inspired attempts at assessing the benefits and costs of FDI by utilizing the now famous technique of social cost–benefit analysis of investment projects pioneered by Little and Mirlees (1974). A feature of the Little–Mirlees (LM) technique is that it provides a method of estimating the benefits and costs of a project along with its balance-of-payments effects. In the LM approach to project evaluation the numeraire is the net foreign exchange savings that the project generates. In other words, all the costs of the project, including labour and material costs, and the output of the project are valued at border prices, i.e. import prices c.i.f. or export prices f.o.b. Therefore the resulting estimates of both costs and benefits are in terms of foreign exchange. The balance-of-payments effect of a project is simply the discounted present value of the value-added component of the project minus labour costs. This, in effect, is the savings generated by the project in terms of foreign exchange.

The LM technique, which has been described in greater detail elsewhere (MacBean and Balasubramanyam 1976), has been widely deployed to assess the benefits and costs of FDI projects in LDCs (Little and Tipping 1972; Lal 1975; Lall and Streeten 1977). Lal's analysis of a sample of four chemical projects in India, which were joint ventures between Indian and foreign firms, came to the conclusion that, while the private profitability of the projects was higher than the assumed social opportunity cost of capital at 6 per cent, the projects were socially unprofitable. Their private profitability was high only because of the high tariffs on competing imports that the government had imposed. In other words, the country would have been better off importing the products than producing them at home. Lall and Streeten's analysis of a sample of projects in India, Jamaica, Iran, Colombia and Malaysia comes to similar conclusions. They conclude disconcertingly that social income effects were negative for nearly 40 per cent of the total of 147 projects that they analysed. This implies, following our earlier discussion, that the balance-of-payments effects were also negative. But these effects were not related to the foreignness or transnationality of the projects. In assessing the contribution of FDI projects alone, however, the study found that the financial contribution of foreign capital was negligible: about a third of the foreign firms could be totally replaced by local ones and about half could be partly replaced, with the remainder being irreplacable. But Lall and Streeten admit that these conclusions should be treated with caution as most of them are based on impressionistic evidence, are subject to some of the well-known limitations of social cost–benefit analysis and perforce could not take into account many relevant factors including scale effects, managerial efficiency and so on. The cynics amongst us may say that this amounts to throwing the baby out with the bath water. Even so, Lall and Streeten's study was a pioneering effort at applying the technique of social cost–benefits analysis to the evaluation of FDI projects, and their conclusions urge policy-makers to investigate alternatives to FDI as methods of gaining access to the resources and products it provides.

It should be noted that, as Lall and Streeten acknowledge, the negative social effects of the projects were due to the high effective rates of protection afforded to most projects in the sample. Indeed, one of the frequent conclusions of several studies on the choice of techniques and factor proportions of foreign firms in LDCs is that indiscriminate protectionist policies are also responsible for the observed relatively high capital intensity of foreign-owned firms. Sheltered from international competition, most foreign firms had chosen to deploy techniques of production with which they were familiar rather than invest the time and money required to identify and adopt cost-saving labour-intensive technologies (White 1978; Balasubramanyam 1983).

There is some evidence in support of the proposition that in the presence of a competitive environment, free from excessive protection and factor and product market distortions, MNEs have made a positive contribution to the growth of employment, incomes and exports. Much of the evidence in favour of the proposition comes from the experience of LDCs such as Singapore, Hong Kong, South Korea and Taiwan, all of which have pursued the EP strategy of development (Hood and Young 1979; Hughes and Dorrance 1986). However, it should be added that, despite three decades of intensive research on various aspects of FDI in LDCs, there is no firm evidence on its costs and benefits. This is due partly to the non-availability of the required data and partly to the complex nature of the research problem, which requires an investigation of the benefits and costs of FDI relative to other methods of obtaining the resources it provides.

The one general conclusion that the literature permits, however, is that MNEs provide an efficient mechanism for the transfer of technology and knowhow, and FDI could be a potent force in the development process. But this conclusion is subject to the caveat that it could do so only in the presence of a favourable climate for investment. In the presence of high levels of effective rates of protection and factor and product market distortions of various sorts, the social rate of return from FDI could fall short of the private rate of return and could even be negative. While protection may attract FDI, it may also serve needlessly to transfer income to foreign firms. In any case, as discussed earlier, in the long term, protectionist policies may not even result in increased inflows of FDI. Admittedly, in the absence of protection, in the short run LDCs may fail to attract most of the capital-intensive import-substitution type of investments. But this may, in fact, be a blessing as projects which yield negative social rates of return are hardly worth attracting. In short, the contribution of FDI to LDCs may be as good or as bad as their trade and investment policies.

Foreign direct investment and services

Reviewing the debate on MNEs, Streeten (1979) wrote: 'In spite of the controversy, some of the steam has gone out of the debate. There is no longer the sharp distinction between those who think that what is good for General Motors is good for humanity and those who see in the multinational corporations the devil incorporated.' However, the launch of the Uruguay Round of trade negotiations under the aegis of the General Agreement on Tariffs and Trade (GATT) appears to have rekindled the debate on FDI. At the heart of this debate is the issue of liberalization of trade in services. The broad contours of the debate are by now well known. The enthusiasm of the MDCs, principally the United States, for a liberalized regime of international trade in services, the opposition of several LDCs to negotiations on services, let alone liberalization, and the ensuing compromise that negotiations will proceed on the so-called double-track mode are all now the stuff of history, ably reviewed in several studies (Bhagwati 1987; Feketekutty 1988; Hindley 1988; Nicolaides 1989).

The bone of contention between the MDCs and the LDCs on most of these issues is the pivotal role of MNEs and FDI in the production and delivery of services. Most services are, by their nature, intangible and non-storable, so that efficient transactions in services require the presence of the producers close to the consumers. Such proximity of producers to consumers often takes the form of FDI, although other modes of delivery such as trade, licensing and franchises do exist. For instance, the so-called long-distance services, such as music concerts, can be transmitted over the wires without the need for factor mobility across geographical borders. But the scope of these other modalities may be limited, and even in the case of long-distance services the proximity of the producer to the consumer may enhance efficiency and allow for a wider range of transactions. Indeed, available data suggest that FDI is a more important vehicle for delivering services across borders than trade. Thus, in 1982 US exports of private non-factor services amounted to $32 billion compared with $183 billion of sales by US service affiliates abroad. Similarly, US imports of services were $33 billion compared with $125 billion of sales by foreign firms in the US services sector (Sauvant and Zimny 1989).

As stated earlier, the reluctance of LDCs to negotiate on services arises in large part because of this pivotal role of FDI. Distrust of foreign firms, be they providers of services or manufacturing firms, is almost a way of life in most LDCs. However, there appears to be a curious divergence between their attitude towards FDI in manufacturing and their attitude towards FDI in services. Many LDCs harbour substantial amounts of FDI in their manufacturing sectors and are desirous of attracting increased amounts of such investment. Although FDI in the manufacturing sectors of most LDCs is subject to a variety of regulations and performance requirements of various sorts, it is also offered a number of incentives including protection against competing imports. In the case of services-oriented FDI, however, regulations abound while incentives are few and far between. More often than not foreign providers of services are hemmed in with a variety of non-tariff barriers (NTBs). These range from outright prohibitions on foreign suppliers to restrictions on their spheres of activity and the extent of their operations. Thus, in some LDCs foreign insurance companies are not allowed to engage in life insurance, banking firms are prohibited from accepting deposits and foreign companies are subjected to local contents requirements with regard to both equity and personnel. Another frequently observed regulation relates to repatriation of dividends, profits and royalties by foreign firms. All these regulations are in the nature of NTBs to the extent that they delimit the volume of operations of foreign service providers.

Why is the distrust and suspicion of foreign firms more acute in the case of services than manufacturing? One explanation, which belongs to sociology rather than economics, could be that services and providers of services in general are held in low esteem, and that their contribution to the development process is not accorded the recognition it deserves. Of interest in this context is the observation by Lal (1989) that in India the Brahminical tradition has long looked down upon merchants and is suspicious of the self-interested pursuit of profits which underlies their operations in the market. When the merchants also happen to be foreigners, nationalist sentiments are likely to reinforce such distrust and suspicion. The mounting evidence on the crucial role of services, such as banking and insurance, in the development process may serve to dislodge this traditional distrust of service providers. In recent years several studies have identified the substantial forward and backward linkages that exist between the manufacturing and service sectors. For instance, it is reported that in Canada a dollar's worth of exports contains on average about 25 cents worth of services (Harris and Cox 1988). A recent study on India, based on input–output tables and regression analysis, has estimated that if agricultural output increases by 1 rupee it will require 75 paise worth of banking and insurance services, and an increase of 1 rupee in manufacturing output generates 73 paise worth of demand for insurance and banking services (Saxena 1989).

Even so, it can be argued that services such as banking, insurance and telecommunications constitute the commanding heights of the economy, of which national ownership and control is essential. Indeed, most of the regulations relating to services current in many LDCs are designed to protect domestic producers and discriminate against foreign providers. Although the concern of the LDCs is understandable, three decades of experience with FDI in manufacturing should have served to allay their fears of foreign economic domination. The sovereignty at bay scenarios fashionable during the 1970s in the context of the growth and spread of MNEs in the manufacturing sector have failed to materialize. Most LDCs have proved to be adept at striking favourable bargains with the MNEs. In any case, most foreign providers of services may neither desire nor have the capabilities to dominate the domestic service sectors of LDCs. As Bhagwati (1987) puts it:

> one would have to be deranged to imagine the largest American banks taking over wholly from the largest five British banks in the United Kingdom if banking were fully liberalized. Yet such fears are routine in New Delhi and Dar-es-salaam. . . . Such scenarios do not make sense for New Delhi either, . . . it would be an act of insanity for a large American bank to open branches in India's vast hinterland, . . . its clientele and operations would most likely be in international transactions.

Yet another argument in support of the discriminatory regulations that most LDCs have imposed on foreign service providers is that they are designed to protect infant domestic providers of services. This is an old argument often rehearsed in the context of manufacturing industries. The pros and cons of the case for infant industry protection are well known. But in the context of services the argument is more complicated, because most though not all services are in the nature of inputs into manufacturing and other services. Protection of such services through subsidies for local firms and NTBs on foreign producers is likely to lower the effective rate of protection enjoyed by producers of final goods and services and thus prove inimical to their competitiveness. It is worth noting in this context that most LDCs which have attempted to protect their manufacturing industries levy a relatively low rate of tariffs on imported material inputs relative to that on final goods. They have done this in recognition of the fact that high levels of protection on inputs would lower the effective degree of protection enjoyed by final goods. It is inexplicable why they are reluctant to acknowledge this fact in the case of services which are also in the nature of inputs into the production process. Indeed, the one sphere of economic activity in which inefficiencies abound in many LDCs is banking, insurance and marketing. The London *Economist* may not be far off the mark when it suggests that: 'efficient services help oil the wheels of the economy; their absence can make development a painfully slow process. Might a deficit of trade in services, rather than a surplus, be a better way of promoting development?' (*Economist*, 3 July 1988). In sum, protection of domestic providers of services on infant industry grounds may serve to promote neither infant services nor the production and export of manufacturers. Protected infant services, much like infant producers of goods, may never mature, and producers of goods would be deprived of efficient and inexpensive service inputs.

Finally, what should be the negotiating stance of LDCs with regard to services? Much has been written on this issue (Bhagwati 1987; Hindley 1988; Balasubramanyam 1991; Nicolaides 1989). Suffice it to note here that the LDCs may have much to gain by negotiating from a position of strength with the MDCs as equal partners rather than as the weaker party to the negotiations. They can negotiate from a position of strength because, contrary to popular opinion, they do possess a comparative advantage in several lines of service activities. These include not only tourism and labour-intensive services such as construction, but also human-capital-intensive services such as the production of computer software (as in the case of India) and indeed in the export of skilled people. The exploitation of the comparative advantage that LDCs possess may require the temporary movement of labour abroad. The LDCs may be well advised to urge negotiations on a broad front, including the liberalization of trade in labour-intensive manufactures, temporary relocation of unskilled labour and exports of skilled labour. They should also recognize the fact that the distinction between goods and services may be somewhat blurred in so far as services are essential inputs into goods and vice versa. For this reason they should negotiate on liberalization of international transactions as a whole, rather than go for double-track negotiations which would inevitably include negotiations on FDI.

For the record it should be stated that some headway has been made in the negotiations on services, and, as the ministerial mid-term review of the negotiations held in Montreal in 1989 revealed, the MDCs recognize several of the concerns of the LDCs and are willing to make significant concessions in their favour. However, there is the danger that the larger the number of concessions the LDCs are able to wrest the harder will be the negotiating stance of the MDCs in spheres of activity of interest to LDCs, such as temporary migration of unskilled labour and exports of labour-intensive manufactures.

18.5 CONCLUSIONS

In this chapter we have briefly reviewed some of the major themes in development economics in recent years. We have by no means done justice to either the vast array of issues in open-economy development economics or the mammoth literature on these issues. Missing from the list of topics discussed here are foreign aid, the economics of the brain drain and the debt problem. These topics are excluded not because they are *passé* but because of exigencies of space. We have highlighted the major issues in the current debate on the structural adjustment and stabilization policies advocated by the World Bank and the IMF. Following a brief review of the case for a structuralist approach to development, we have analysed the benefits and costs associated with the structural adjustment and stabilization programmes which are to a large extent grounded in the liberal economic tradition. We have also identified the pre-conditions necessary for the success of these programmes, including the need for an increased flow of resources from the MDCs to the LDCs. FDI has been identified as one such major source of resources. On this basis we have reviewed the role of FDI in the development process, including the current debate on the role of FDI in services.

REFERENCES

Balasubramanyam, V. N. (1973) *International Transfer of Technology to India*, New York: Praeger.
—— (1983) 'Transnational corporations: choice of techniques and employment in LDCs', in H. Hughes and B. Weisbrod (eds) *Human Resources, Employment and Development*, London: Macmillan.
—— (1986) 'Incentives and disincentives for foreign direct investment in less developed countries', in B. Belassa and H. Giersch (eds) *Economic Incentives*, pp. 401–15, London: Macmillan.
—— (1991), 'International trade in services: the real issues', in D. Greenaway and T. O'Brian (eds) *Global Protectionism*, London: Macmillan.
Balasubramanyam, V. N. and Salisu, M. (1991) 'IS, EP and direct foreign investment in LDCs', in A. Koekkoek and C. B. Merries (eds) *International Trade and Global Development*, London: Routledge.
Bhagwati, J. N. (1958) 'Immiserizing growth: a geometrical note', *Review of Economic Studies* 25: 201–5.
—— (1978) *Anatomy and Consequences of Exchange Control Regimes*, New York: UN Bureau of Economic Research.
—— (1985) 'Investing abroad', Esmee Fairbairn Lecture, University of Lancaster.
—— (1987) 'Trade in services and the multilateral trade negotiations', *World Bank Economic Review* 1: 549–70.
Bond, M. E. (1987) 'An econometric study of primary product exports from developing country regimes to the world', *IMF Staff Papers* 34 (2): 191–227.
Bos, H. C., Saunders, M. and Secchi, C. (1974) *Private Foreign Investment in Developing Countries: A Quantitative Study on the Evaluation of the Macro Economic Effects*, Boston, MA: Reidel.
Cassen, R. H. (1986) *Does Aid Work?* Oxford: Clarendon Press.
Cline, W. (1982) 'Can the East Asian model of development be generalised?', *World Development* 10: 81–90.
Cuddington, J. T. and Urzúa, C. M. (1989) 'Trends and cycles in the net barter terms of trade', *Economic Journal* 99: 426–42.
Feketekutty, G. (1988) *International Trade in Services: An Overview and Blue Print for Negotiations*, Cambridge, MA: Ballinger.

Frank, I. (1980) *Foreign Enterprise in Developing Countries*, Baltimore, MD: Johns Hopkins University Press.

Grilli, E. R. and Yang, M. C. (1988) 'Primary commodity prices, manufactured goods prices, and the terms of trade of developing countries: what the long run shows', *World Bank Economic Review* 2: 1–49.

Guissinger, S. (1986) 'Do performance requirements and investment incentives work?', *World Economy* 9 (1): 79–96.

Guitian, M. (1987) 'The Fund's role in agriculture', *Finance and Development* June: 3–6.

Harris, R. and Cox, D. (1988) 'The service content of Canadian industries', Fraser Institute Service Sector Studies Project, Simon Fraser University, Vancouver.

Havrylyshyn, O. (1987) 'The fallacy of composition', unpublished background paper for *World Development Report*.

Hindley, B. (1988) 'Services sector protection: considerations for developing countries', *World Bank Economic Review* May: 205–24.

Hood, N. and Young, S. (1979) *The Economics of Multinational Enterprise*, London: Longman.

Huang, Y. and Nichols, P. (1987) 'The social costs of adjustment', *Finance and Development* 24 (2): 22–4.

Hughes, H. and Dorance, G. S. (1986) 'Economic policies and direct foreign investment with particular reference to the developing countries of East Asia', Paper prepared for the Commonwealth Secretariat.

Hughes, H. and Seng, Y. (1969) *Foreign Investment and Industrialisation in Singapore*, Canberra: Australian National University Press.

International Monetary Fund (1985) *Foreign Private Investment in Developing Countries*, Washington, DC: International Monetary Fund, January.

Jenkins, R. (1987) *Transnational Corporations and Uneven Development*, London: Methuen.

Khan, M. S. and Knight, M. D. (1986) 'Do fund-supported adjustment programs retard growth?', *Finance and Development* March: 30–2.

Kidron, M. (1965) *Foreign Investments in India*, Oxford: Oxford University Press.

Kindleberger, C. P. (1969) *American Business Abroad*, New Haven, CT: Yale University Press.

Krueger, A. O. (1978) *Foreign Trade Regimes and Economic Development: Liberalisation Attempts and Consequences*, Cambridge, MA: Ballinger.

Lal, D. (1975) *Appraising Foreign Investment in Developing Countries*, London: Heinemann.

—— (1989) *The Hindu Equilibrium: Cultural Stability and Economic Stagnation, India c. 1500 BC–AD 1980*, Oxford: Oxford University Press.

Lall, S. and Streeten, P. (1977) *Foreign Investment, Transnationals and Developing Countries*, London: Macmillan.

Lim, D. (1983) 'Fiscal incentives and direct foreign investment in less developed countries', *Journal of Development Studies* 19: 207–12.

Linder, S. B. (1967) *Trade and Trade Policy for Development*, New York: Praeger.

Lipton, M. (1987) 'Limits of price policy for agriculture: which way for the World Bank', *Development Policy Review* 5 (2): 197–215.

Little, I. M. D. and Mirlees, J. (1974) *Project Appraisal and Planning for Developing Countries*, London: Heinemann.

Little, I. M. D. and Tipping, D. G. (1972) *A Social Cost–Benefit Analysis of the Kulai Oil Palm Estate*, Paris: OECD.

Little, I. M. D., Scott, M. F. G. and Scitovisky, T. (1970) *Industry and Trade in Some Developing Countries: A Comparative Study*, Oxford: Oxford University Press.

MacBean, A. I. and Balasubramanyam, V. N. (1976) *Meeting the Third World Challenge*, London: Macmillan.

Michalopolous, C. (1987) 'World Bank programs for adjustment and growth', Paper prepared for the *Symposium on Growth Oriented Adjustment Programs*, sponsored by the World Bank and International Monetary Fund, Washington, DC.

Mosley, P. (1991) 'Structural adjustment: a general overview 1980–1989', in S. Lall and V. N. Balasubramanyam (eds) *Current Issues in Development Economics*, London: Macmillan.

Nicolaides, P. (1989) *Liberalising Trade in Services: Strategies For Success*, London: Royal Institute of International Affairs.

Nurkse, R. (1959) 'Patterns of trade and development', Wicksell Lectures, Stockholm.

Prebisch, R. (1950) *The Economic Development of Latin America and its Principal Problems*, New York: UN Economic Commission for Latin America.

Reuber, G. L., Crockell, H., Emerson, M. and Gallais-Hamonno, G. (1973) *Private Foreign Investment in Development*, Oxford: Clarendon Press.

Sapsford, D. (1985) 'The statistical debate on the net barter terms of trade between primary commodities and manufactures: a comment and some statistical evidence', *Economic Journal* 95: 781–8.

Sauvant, K. and Zimny, Z. (1989) 'Foreign direct investment in services: the neglected dimension in international service negotiations', in *Services and Development Potential: The Indian Context*, New York: United Nations.

Saxena, R. (1989) 'Role of producer services in the development process: A case study of India', in *Services and Development Potential: The Indian Context*, New York: United Nations.

Singer, H. W. (1950) 'The distribution of gains between borrowing and investing countries', *American Economic Review* May: 473–85.

—— (1989) 'Terms of trade and economic development', in J. Eatwell, M. Milgate and P. Newman (eds) *The New Palgrave: A Dictionary of Economics*, London: Macmillan.

Spraos, J. (1980) 'The statistical debate on the net barter terms of trade between primary commodities and manufactures: a comment and some additional evidence', *Economic Journal* 90: 107–28.

Stern, E. (1983) 'World Bank financing of structural adjustment', in J. Williamson (ed.) *IMF Conditionality*, Washington, DC: Institute for International Economics.

Streeten, P. (1971) 'Costs and benefits of multinational enterprises in developing countries', in J. H. Dunning (ed.) *The Multinational Enterprise*, pp. 240–58, London: Allen & Unwin.

—— (1979) 'Multinationals revisited', *Finance and Development* 16: 39–42.

Thirlwall, A. P. and Bergevin, J. (1985) 'Trends, cycles and asymmetries in the terms of trade of primary commodities from developed and less developed countries', *World Development* 13: 805–17.

United Nations (1973) *Multinational Corporations in World Development*, New York: United Nations.

—— (1978) *Transnational Corporations in World Development*, New York: United Nations.

—— (1985) *Transnational Corporations in World Development*, New York: United Nations.

—— (1988) *Transnational Corporations in World Development*, New York: United Nations.

Vernon, R. (1977) *Storm over Multinationals: The Real Issues*, London: Macmillan.

White, L. J. (1978) 'The evidence on appropriate factor proportions for manufacturing in less developed countries: a survey', *Economic Development and Cultural Change* 27: 27–59.

World Bank (1986) *World Development Report*, Washington, DC: World Bank.

—— (1987) *World Development Report*, Washington, DC: World Bank.

19

GROWTH THEORY

ROBERT M. SOLOW

19.1 INTRODUCTION

In 1980, to take a round number, the neoclassical growth model was already firmly established as the standard framework for long-run aggregative economics. Growth accounting, productivity and human capital studies, and other such empirical exercises could all be tucked neatly into a single theoretical package. Of course, there were alternative paradigms, but they remained minority tastes. The Kaldor–Kalecki–Robinson–Pasinetti line made life harder for itself by being part of a wholesale attack on mainstream economics. Anyway, it was not ever able to muster a body of serious applied work. Even the very interesting Nelson–Winter model of technological diffusion never caught on.

Apart from minor refinements and extensions, however, there did not seem to be any theoretical excitement brewing at the edges of growth theory. I will quote a remark of my own on this point, published in 1982 but written in 1979:

> I think there are definite signs that (growth theory) is just about played out, at least in its familiar form. Anyone working inside economic theory these days knows in his or her bones that growth theory is now an umpromising pond for an enterprising theorist to fish in. I do not mean to say confidently that this state of affairs will last. A good new idea can transform any subject; in fact, I have some thoughts about the kind of new idea that is needed in this case.
>
> (Solow 1982)

I am relieved to see those last two waffling sentences. The ink was barely dry on that paragraph when Paul Romer's 1983 Ph.D. thesis was deposited at the University of Chicago and set off at least a boomlet in growth theory, and neoclassical growth theory at that. Romer's ideas began to circulate in working paper form in 1985 and his first paper, 'Increasing returns and long-run growth', was published in 1986, to be followed by others. Robert Lucas's Marshall Lectures at Cambridge University in 1985 provided another variation on the same theme. Again, the text was circulated widely before being published as 'On the mechanics of economic development' in 1988. In both cases the broad theme was the endogenous determination of the long-run rate of growth through aggregate increasing returns to scale induced by human capital accumulation. The viability of perfect competition was preserved by making the stock of human capital into a 'social factor of production' not influenced perceptibly by any agent's decisions but influencing the productivity of all. Thus increasing returns to scale at the macroeconomic level are made compatible with constant returns at the microeconomic level. The analytical machinery of neoclassical growth theory can then be applied to achieve quite new results.

However, this was not the sort of 'new idea' I had been hoping for in 1982. I had in mind the integration of equilibrium growth theory with medium-run disequilibrium theory so that trends and fluctuations in employment and output could be handled in a unified way. That particular new idea has not yet made its appearance.

The next section of this survey is a very brief paraphrase of the one-sector neoclassical growth model, especially its characteristic assumptions and characteristic conclusions. It is there just to provide a common launching-pad for a discussion of more recent developments; it is terse because most economists are acquainted with the model and several excellent full-scale expositions are available.

In Section 19.3 the ideas of Romer, Lucas and others who have followed their trail are surveyed. This literature has turned up several different ways of achieving the endogenization of the growth rate, although they all have a family resemblance. Corresponding to these variations in the nature of the basic externality, there are some variations in the nature of the results achieved. My aim here is not a complete catalogue, but rather a few attractive examples to illustrate the power of the approach. In Section 19.4 I turn to a few papers that have carried the same set of ideas into the international trade context. Clearly, trade offers further scope for increasing returns to scale, with important consequences for the nature of gains from trade. In Section 19.5 a neat attempt to formalize Schumpeterian ideas within the 'new' framework is described. The last section is given over to a few reflections on the nature and uses of growth theory.

19.2 THE NEOCLASSICAL MODEL

There is a vast literature on the neoclassical model. The original papers are Solow (1956) and Swan (1956), with a distant ancestor in Ramsey (1928) and further important contributions by Cass (1965), Diamond (1965) and Koopmans (1965). A brief elementary exposition is given by Solow (1970), and a more advanced treatment is provided by Dixit (1976). Longer treatises, covering a wide variety of topics, are Burmeister and Dobell (1970) and Wan (1971). The early survey by Hahn and Matthews (1964) still makes interesting reading.

I shall, without fuss, limit myself to a completely aggregated model, with only one produced good Y that can be directly consumed C or accumulated as (non-depreciating) productive capital K. This sweeps a few problems and possibilities under the rug, but they are not particularly relevant to the recent theoretical developments that will be discussed later. The labour supply L is offered inelastically to the market; this also is a minor simplification. Labour supply (and employment) grow at a constant rate n: $L = L_0 \exp(nt)$.

Production is carried on in a number of identical firms using the common constant returns to scale technology $Y = F(K, L, t)$, where F is increasing, differentiable, concave and homogeneous of degree 1 in K and L, and t allows for exogenous 'disembodied' technological progress. Facing the same input prices, all firms will choose the same cost-minimizing ratio of capital to labour. The division of total output among firms is then indeterminate but unimportant (as long as competition is preserved). As usual, it is simplest to think in terms of a single price-taking firm. In aggregate terms,

$$Y = F[K, L_0 \exp(nt), t] \tag{19.1a}$$

$$dK/dt = Y - C \tag{19.1b}$$

The main thing to notice here is that the labour market is assumed to clear automatically. Employment is always equal (or proportional) to the given labour force.

As soon as consumption is determined, the model is complete. At this point there are two strands of thought to consider. They are not incompatible, but they call up different overtones or associations. The first strand, which might be called behaviourist, simply postulates a plausible or econometrically reasonable consumption function; for instance

$$C = (1 - s)Y \tag{19.1c}$$

where s might be constant or a function of any variables definable in terms of K, L and Y.

The alternative strand, which might be called optimizing, prefers to deduce consumption from utility maximization. Start at time zero with an initial stock of capital K_0. Any time path for consumption, extending from then into the infinite future, that satisfies (19.1a) and (19.1b) with non-negative $K(t)$ is said to be 'feasible'. Imagine the economy to be populated by immortal identical families whose preferences for consumption paths are fully described by the size of

$$V = \int_0^\infty U\left[\frac{C(t)}{L(t)}\right] \exp(-\beta t) \, dt$$

or (19.2)

$$V = \int_0^\infty U\left[\frac{C(t)}{L(t)}\right] L(t) \exp(-\beta t) \, dt$$

Then this strand of thought takes it as axiomatic that the economy follows the feasible consumption path that maximizes the appropriate V. In this formulation $U(.)$ is an increasing, strictly concave and differentiable instantaneous utility function and β is the utility time preference rate of every family.

In many cases the solution to this optimization problem can be expressed in 'closed-loop' form, i.e. there is a function of K, L and Y such that the optimal consumption at any time t is always $C[K(t), L(t), Y(t)]$. Even so, there is a subtle difference in interpretation between the behaviourist way and the optimizing way of looking at the problem. The optimization approach looks like a problem in intertemporal welfare economics, and was originally conceived as such by Ramsey and others. In that interpretation its solution does not represent the actual behaviour of even a highly idealized decentralized economy, but rather indicates the direction in which such an economy ought to be 'managed'. To interpret it descriptively is to imagine the economy to be completely transparent to the families that populate it. The firms merely carry out the wishes of the inhabitants. It is, so to speak, a planned economy, but planned by the representative family.

That does not make it wrong. There are informational and institutional circumstances under which the optimal path is the perfect foresight competitive equilibrium path. But it is certainly optimistic. The behaviourist version is only slightly less so. The labour market always clears (or at least the unemployment rate is always the same). If s is interpreted as the household saving rate, then the model assumes that firms will always invest at full employment exactly what households wish to save at full employment. Nevertheless the behaviourist version might be said to extend an invitation to think about ways in which the industrial sector and the household sector could fail to co-ordinate their actions. Things might then not be for the best in this best of all possible worlds.

Now suppose that the production function has two additional properties. First, it can be written in the special 'labour-augmenting' form $F[K, A(t)L]$ with $A(t) = \exp(at)$. The composite variable AL is usually called the input of labour in efficiency units, or sometimes just 'effective labour'. The second property is that, for each fixed input of effective labour, the marginal product of capital should be very large when the input of capital is very small and very small when the input of capital is very large. (This is usually called the 'Inada condition'.) Then there are some important general conclusions about the solution paths to the optimizing model; these are also true for the behaviourist model provided that the saving rate does not vary too much.

All solution paths tend to a steady state in which the ratio of capital to effective labour is constant. The value of this constant depends on the taste parameters – the utility function and rate of time preference in the optimizing version, and the saving function in the behaviourist version – and on the production function, but is independent of the initial conditions. Therefore, in (or near) the steady state K, Y and C are all growing at the same rate as $A(t)L$, namely $a + n$. Therefore the corresponding per capita quantities – capital per worker, output and income per worker, and consumption per worker – are all growing at rate a. It may be worth noting explicitly that the steady state ratio of savings and investment to total output is constant in both versions of the model. (Once exponential growth is achieved, dK/dt is proportional to K.) The two interpretations are essentially indistinguishable near steady states.

The main points are that the common asymptotic growth rate of income and consumption per head, and of the real wage if the labour market is competitive, is given by the rate of labour-augmenting technical progress. Differences in saving behaviour affect the steady state level of income per head, but not its long-run rate of growth. There may be transient variations in growth induced by changes in taste or in the saving–investment quota, but they disappear once the growth path settles down to a steady state. There are corresponding conclusions about the path of prices: rental on capital, real rate of interest and real wage. These follow from competitive markets and intertemporal arbitrage.

It is worth taking a moment to understand the requirement that technological change be labour augmenting, because the same point will recur in the next section. Suppose, for example, that technological change were both capital and labour augmenting at rates b and a. This is not general, of course, but it will suffice to make the point. If we are looking for an exponential steady state, then dK/dt will grow at the same rate as K itself. In any exponential steady state, then,

$$gK_0 \exp(gt) = sF\{K_0^{(g+b)t}, L_0 \exp[(a + n)t]\}$$

By constant returns to scale,

$$gK_0 \exp(gt) = sL_0 \exp[(a + n)t] \, F\left\{\frac{K_0}{L_0} \exp[(g + b - a - n)t], 1\right\} \tag{19.3}$$

There are now only two possibilities if this equation is to hold for all t. Either $b = 0$ and $g = a + n$, which is exactly the labour-augmenting case, or

$F\{(K_0/L_0) \exp[(g + b - a - n)t], 1\}$ must itself grow exponentially. This can happen only if $F(x, 1) = x^h$; thus g must equal $a + n + h(g + b - a - n)$ or $g = n + a + bh/(1 - h)$. Obviously this way out entails that $F(K, L)$ be Cobb–Douglas with elasticities h and $1 - h$ for K and L, and then $[\exp(bt) K]^h$ $[\exp(at) L]^{1-h}$ is identically the same as $K^h(\exp\{[a + bh/(1 - h)]t\} L)^{1-h}$. Therefore, even here, technological change can be said to be labour augmenting at a rate $a + bh/(1 - h)$. Pure labour augmentation is special, but it is exactly as special as the common fixation on exponential steady states. Nature is unlikely to favour either, but could come close to doing so.

19.3 INCREASING RETURNS AND EXTERNALITIES

The neoclassical model states that the long-run growth rate of output per worker is given by the rate of labour-augmenting technological progress, which it treats as exogenous. It would seem to follow that all national economies with access to the same changing technology should have converging productivity growth rates. There might be temporary or even prolonged differences in growth rates because countries that are still fairly close to their initial conditions, having started with lower ratios of capital to effective labour than they will eventually achieve in the steady state, will be growing faster than countries that are further along in that process. There will also be permanent differences in levels of productivity, either because some countries have faster population growth or lower savings rates than others (or equivalent differences in tastes) or perhaps because of deficiencies in climate or other factors not accounted for in the model. But it is the expected convergence of growth rates that really matters in the very long run. Something like convergence may be detectable in the recent record of the advanced industrial countries. However, it is almost impossible to see convergence in a comparison of those economies with the nations of Latin America, Africa and much of Asia. That is the observation that motivated Romer and Lucas to the theoretical extensions that underlie the 'new growth theory'. If there is not convergence, then the growth rate itself should somehow be endogenous (i.e. capable of differing from country to country).

Romer and Lucas take it as axiomatic that all economies have access to the same evolving technology. After all, textbooks are available everywhere and patents can be licensed. They conclude that the missing link is investment in human capital. National economies that appear not to share in the advance of technology have failed to make the prior human investments that make it possible to tap into the common pool of knowledge. The way to understand the determination of national productivity growth rates is to model the stock of human capital as a producible input. There are early examples of this approach in Arrow (1962) and Uzawa (1965).

There are other reasonable ways of proceeding. We might conclude from the record of persistent divergence in growth rates that all countries do not have access to the common technology in any effective sense. Political instability, for instance, might discourage or prevent the process of perpetual industrial modernization. Private and/or public corruption might be a similar obstacle. It is easy to think of tax systems, social institutions, religious beliefs and kinship structures, any of which would be more or less incompatible with the successful practice of changing high-technology industry. That path seems to lead back to exogeneity (at least economic exogeneity) and historical accident. The new growth theory could reply that all those apparently exogenous obstacles really reflect, at a deeper level, a deficient formation of human capital. Societies have to be taught, or teach themselves, the ways of industrial growth. Maybe so – but that only raises the question of whether, in such a society, the sort of activity normally modelled as human capital investment will have the kinds of effects postulated in a theory that draws its inspiration from countries which have already modernized. A school for commissars or ayatollahs will not produce engineers.

Nevertheless, the human capital explanation of divergence is more than plausible and, as Lucas and Romer have shown by example, it leads to some tractable and interesting economics. As a first step to see how the idea works, consider simple increasing returns to scale to conventional capital and labour. The neatest case occurs when the impact of increasing returns is 'labour-augmenting'. Suppose for instance that $Y = F[K, (AL)^\mu]$ where $F(x, y)$ is homogeneous of degree 1 in its two arguments and $\mu > 1$. There are increasing returns to scale in K and L: if both inputs are multiplied by $z > 1$,

$$F[zK, (AzL)^\mu] = F[zK, z^\mu(AL)^\mu] > F[zK, z(AL)^\mu] = zF[K, (AL)^\mu]$$

If, as in Section 19.2, $L = \exp(nt)$ and $A = \exp(at)$,

$$Y = F\{K, \exp[\mu(a + n)t]\}$$

and the rest of the argument goes just as it went before. The only amendment is that the asymptotic growth rate is now $\mu(a + n)$ and the per capita growth rate is $\mu a + (\mu - 1)n$. The only new parameter is the degree of increasing returns to scale.

The mere assumption of economies of scale changes very little. There is still no good account of permanent divergence of growth rates per capita other than differences in effective technology. Romer (1986) goes one step further and assumes that capital (human capital in his case) has increasing marginal productivity. That does make a large difference. In theory, it allows the growth rate to increase forever, although bounded above. That, by itself, is not very important. The possibility also arises of a low-level equilibrium trap, but that would also be the case in the basic neoclassical model. The most important consequence is more general. As with any divergent process, small shifts in initial conditions – small mid-course corrections – tend to magnify themselves into very large and even widening differences as time goes on. Now at last there is scope for historical happenstance or acts of policy to have large and enduring effects of the sort that we think we see in the data.

The operative mechanism in this story is the increasing marginal productivity of capital. It would work under constant returns also, but increasing returns is not unimportant either. In fact it is almost essential: with constant returns to scale, it is not possible to have $F(0, L) = 0$, positive marginal product of labour and increasing marginal product of capital simultaneously. Therefore increasing returns to scale make increasing returns to capital easier to come by.

It is now fairly straightforward to see how Romer (1986) proceeds. For brevity and clarity of exposition, he ignores pure time-dependent techological change and takes the supply of raw labour and physical capital as constant. The first two simplifying assumptions could easily be relaxed. To take physical capital seriously would introduce asset-choice complications that are important in their own right but would make the immediate problem slightly harder. Therefore the focus is on human capital. Since the idea is to make use of the neoclassical intertemporal competitive equilibrium model in its optimizing version, the main intellectual problem is to reconcile increasing marginal productivity of (human) capital with competition. This is resolved by introducing increasing returns through an external effect.

As usual in this context, the representative producing firm is just an agent of the representative household. The latter is interested in maximizing a discounted utility integral as in (19.2). The technology of the firm is represented by a production function $F(k, K, x)$, which now needs to be reinterpreted: x stands for fixed capital, raw labour and other inputs that are constant forever and can thus be dropped from the notation, k stands for the firm's current stock of human capital and K stands for the aggregate stock, which is equal to Sk if the economy contains S identical firms. K is what carries the externality. The single firm knows about K and its effects on its own production, but has no influence over it. F is homogeneous of degree 1 and concave in the firm's own decision variables k and x, so that the firm can act as a price-taking competitor. From the point of view of the economic observer, however, $F(k, Sk, x)$ exhibits increasing returns to scale in all its arguments together and is convex in k. That is, when account is taken of the externality generated by the aggregate stock of human capital, it has increasing marginal productivity.

It remains to specify how human capital is produced. The household firm (peasant family, in effect) can at any instant invest at a rate of I units of forgone consumption per unit time and generate new human capital at a rate of

$G(I, k)$ units per unit time if it already possesses k units of human capital. With the assumption that $G(I, k)$ is homogeneous of degree 1 in its arguments, this can be written $\dot{k}/k = g(I/k)$. For technical reasons it is assumed that $g(0) = 0$ and g is bounded above. The identity $I = Y - C$ completes the model.

Although the human capital vocabulary is used, it should be clear that k functions more like a stock of technological knowledge, and $G(I, k)$ describes how the expenditure of I units of output on research, when the firm's stock of knowledge is already k, adds new results to that stock. The main reason for reading the story in this way is that individual people are not immortal, and human capital *per se* tends to die with its bearer. Therefore the model is really about endogenous technological progress. As anyone who has done any research – even economic research – would know, it is a dreadfully mechanical model of the research process. If technological progress is to be endogenized, it ought to be in a way that allows not only for lumpiness and chance, but for the differential refractoriness of research problems. This specification suffers from another minor deficiency. If the firm captures any part of the externality it creates by its own investment in research, then it is subject to increasing returns to scale on its own. (Romer has made this observation himself.)

The main result of Romer's paper requires three semitechnical assumptions: first, $g(.)$ is bounded above by a constant α; second, $F(k, Sk, x)$, treated as a function of k, behaves more or less like k^ϕ for large k, where $\phi > 1$; finally, $\alpha\phi < \delta$ where δ is the utility discount rate. There is an absolute limit on the rate of growth of human capital; the externality-generated increasing returns to k cannot be more than polynomial in character; and the growth potential generated by this sort of technology cannot be too large relative to the discount rate. I call these requirements semitechnical because, although their function is just to ensure that postponing consumption forever cannot be the winning strategy, the restriction that they impose need not be trivial. Since $\phi > 1$, we must have $\delta > \alpha$, and there is no particular reason for that to happen. For an immortal consumer, δ might be fairly small.

Anyway, the end result is the existence of an equilibrium path on which C and k (and K) tend to infinity, provided that the initial stock of human capital is not too small. Since the supply of raw labour is constant in the background, C and k can be interpreted as quantities per capita. This competitive equilibrium is not efficient, of course. The externality sees to that: there is under-investment in human capital. The efficient path has the same qualitative appearance, however. The welfare economics is straightforward and does not need discussion here. The important point is that the human capital mechanism gives rise to an equilibrium in which consumption per capita grows without bound, even in the absence of exogenous technological progress. Without the human capital externality and the resulting increasing returns, the optimizing version of the neoclassical model without technological progress would lead to a finite-valued stationary state for consumption and output per head. The unboundedness at the upper end makes a significant difference. It allows the possibility for growth rates to increase over time, for larger economies to grow faster than small ones and for temporary glitches – episodes of bad public or private policy, for example – to have effects that magnify themselves over time instead of washing out.

The behaviourist version of the neoclassical model can sometimes do the same thing. Let the saving–investment rate be constant, for instance; then capital will accumulate forever and consumption per head will increase without bound if there is neither population growth nor technological progress. (Under diminishing returns, however, the rate of growth of output and consumption has to fall, although not necessarily to zero.) This observation points up both a weakness and a strength of the behaviourist interpretation. The weakness is that the constancy of the investment quota is essentially arbitrary – just assumed. The determination of saving and investment, and the mechanism by which they are brought into *ex post* equality, are too central to the whole story to be left essentially undiscussed. The strength is that, unlike the immortal isolated peasant family picture promoted by the optimizing version, it hints strongly that there is at least a possibility that the desire to save for generalized future consumption and the willingness to invest in specific items of productive capacity might not be adapted smoothly to one another by market interplay (speaking of temporary glitches).

Lucas (1988) extends and refines this analysis. The optimizing version of the neoclassical model remains, and is treated as a positive theory of a competitive economy with perfect foresight. The supply of raw labour is allowed to grow at a constant rate, and investment in physical capital is taken explicitly into account. The accumulation of human capital is introduced in a way that makes it a little more like the acquisition of skill and a little less like research, although here too it is assumed that human capital does not dissipate with the death of an individual person; it must be supposed that each generation automatically inherits the level of skill attained by its parents and has the option of adding to it. In Lucas's formulation, a worker is endowed with a unit of effort per unit time. Let u be the amount of effort devoted to production of the single good and $1 - u$ be the accumulation of human capital by a worker already embodying human capital at level h. Then

$$\dot{h}/h = \delta(1 - u) \tag{19.4}$$

The rate of growth of human capital is thus proportional to the time spent in training. The assumption that percentage increases in h are equally costly at any level of h is not innocuous; this is a point where independent evidence would be useful.

Human capital is incorporated in the productive technology for goods in the now established way – in part internally and in part externally. Lucas stays with Cobb–Douglas throughout. This is a user-friendly choice, and I believe that he is right to make it; in lesser hands, however, the Cobb–Douglas approach may be a little too user friendly. The production of goods is thus given by

$$Y = AK^\beta(uhN)^{1-\beta}H^\gamma \tag{19.5}$$

in which A is a constant, K now stands for the stock of physical capital, N is the (per firm) supply of raw labour and H is the economy-wide average level of human capital. If all workers are identical, $H = h$; the notational distinction is a reminder that the firm sees H as exogenous. Therefore the representative firm is subject to constant returns to scale in capital and effective labour, but the collectivity of firms exhibits increasing returns to scale with a scale of elasticity of $1 + \gamma$. The notation in (19.5) already embodies the assumption that the market for labour clears; uN is the supply of raw labour to goods-producing firms and uhN is the supply of labour in efficiency units. The household side of the model is just as before, except that Lucas once again works with the standard specific functional form $U'(C) = C^{-\sigma}$.

In this formulation there is no presumption of increasing marginal product of human capital. This would hold true if and only if $\beta < \gamma$. Lucas obtains rather similar results from a different source: the absence of diminishing returns in the creation of human capital. From (19.4), the steady state growth rate of h is $\delta(1 - u)$ and then it can be calculated that the growth rate of per capita output, consumption and capital investment is

$$\frac{1 - \beta + \gamma}{1 - \beta} \delta(1 - u)$$

in close analogy with the standard neoclassical model. Of course, u is endogenous and its steady state value has to be deduced from the equilibrium conditions. Let ρ be the utility discount rate and λ the population growth rate. Lucas shows that the equilibrium growth rate for per capita output (and its components) is

$$\frac{1 - \beta + \gamma}{1 - \beta} \frac{(1 - \beta)[\delta - (\rho - \lambda)]}{\sigma(1 - \beta + \gamma) - \gamma}$$

provided that the technical contition

$$\sigma \geqslant 1 - \frac{(1 - \beta)(\rho - \lambda)}{(1 - \beta + \gamma)\delta}$$

is satisfied. (This condition plays the same role as the corresponding one in Romer's model.)

What matters here is that the asymptotic per capita growth rate is not given simply by an exogenous rate of labour-augmenting technical progress. In the first place, there is no exogenous technical progress. In the second place, even if the human capital mechanism $\dot{h}/h = \delta(1 - u)$ is regarded as the moral equivalent of technological progress, the eventual per capita growth rate depends on all the parameters of the model – those describing the technology and those (σ and ϱ) describing tastes. Since the latter are the ultimate determinants of thrift in the optimizing model, Lucas can correctly say that he has found a connection between thrift and growth.

This model determines the paths of two stocks K and h, or hN, and not just one, and it has correspondingly two initial conditions. In the steady state, therefore, it determines two stock levels – the trend-adjusted values of K and h. The model provides one equation linking these trend-adjusted steady state levels of physical and human capital, i.e. it confines them to a curve. The curve has a positive slope; asymptotic K and h are higher or lower together. The model economy's destination along that curve is determined by its initial conditions: 'an economy beginning with low levels of human and physical capital will remain *permanently* below an initially better endowed economy' (Lucas 1988). Therefore the model has something to say about the large and persistent disparities that separate rich and poor countries. (It would be interesting to know what the model says about the paths followed by two countries, one of which starts with more physical but less human capital than the other.)

This exposition gives the flavour of the 'new view' of growth theory, but the evolution has not stopped there. I do not want to track down all the nooks and crannies, but I shall describe a few of the subsequent developments.

In an attempt to provide a more circumstantial model of endogenous technical change, Romer himself has tried to put some algebraic structure on Allyn Young's famous, if vague, notion of increasing returns through continuing specialization in production (Young 1928). The model is too complex to be described in detail. Its central feature is the combination of a powerful process for the generation of endogenous technical change with a powerful process for transferring technical change into the production of goods. The combination is perhaps too powerful. It is hardly surprising that it generates a powerful engine of growth.

In Romer (1987), the research activity produces new results exactly as in Lucas's equation (19.4). If effort and knowledge are treated as the two inputs into the production of knowledge, then the research process is homogeneous of degree 2. Doubling the input of previous knowledge and the input of current research effort will multiply the output of new results by four. This would perhaps not matter so much if it were offset by diminishing returns in the application of knowledge in the production of goods.

I will elide some detail in reporting Romer's characterization of the production of goods. Let R stand for the input of resources other than 'intermediate goods' in the production of output Y. Then

$$Y = R^{1-\mu} \int_0^A x(i)^\mu \, di \qquad (19.6)$$

where $x(i)$ is the utilization of an intermediate good of type i. There is in the background a complicated industrial structure in which research firms produce designs for new intermediate goods, another sector uses designs to produce intermediate goods and the final-goods sector uses them to produce final output. The sole function of research is to extend the range of known designs; hence A is chosen as the upper limit of the integral. (As the output of the research sector, A just replaces h in (19.4).)

Now suppose that $x(i) = x = A^{-1}$ for $0 < i < A$. That is, a unit quantity of intermediate goods is spread evenly over the available range; this is entirely natural given diminishing returns to each individual variety of intermediate goods. For convenience, set $R = 1$. Then $Y = A^{1-\mu}$. In other words, with a fixed input of 'other resources' and a fixed quantity of intermediate goods, aggregate output is unbounded as the range of intermediate goods goes to infinity. We can take this example a step further. Let the flow of research effort be constant at a. Then, by (19.4), A is proportional to $\exp(at)$ and $Y = \exp[a(1 - \mu)t]$. Unbounded exponential growth has been generated from constant input of primary resources. That is what I meant by saying that the combined mechanism for generating research and transferring it into goods is powerful. Our intuition has very little to hook onto here. I do not mean to suggest that the Romer mechanism is far-fetched. It is a clever way of solving a difficult modelling problem, and it may capture something real. But it is not ungenerous. In a way it is more generous than the assumption that technological progress is merely exogenously given; in this version, a step increase in the flow of research effort creates a permanent increase in the rate of growth. This central result is just cooked. That is not necessarily a bad thing, but neither does it carry instant conviction.

There is another major strand in this literature that emphasizes the joint endogenous determination of fertility and investment in human capital. Becker *et al.* (1988) hypothesize an increasing rate of return on human capital investment and generate a dichotomy between low-level Malthusian trap and a growth equilibrium driven by accumulation of human capital. Tamura (1989a, b) also produces a pair of locally stable steady states, one with high fertility and low stationary income per head and one with perpetual productivity growth. (There is an unstable equilibrium between these two.) In these papers no externality is associated with human capital. There is a form of 'embodiment' of human capital, however: human capital is not transferred across generations free of charge. I shall not go further into this line of thought. The detour into what Nerlove once called 'the new home economics' would be too lengthy. The papers already cited and Barro and Becker (1989) list many references.

I conclude this section by describing another ingenious model (Azariadis and Drazen 1988) that is both in the tradition and apart from it. The shared property is that the central mechanism is an aggregative externality induced by the cumulation of individually motivated investment in human capital or labour quality. The differences are, first, that Azariadis and Drazen choose to work within the two-year period overlapping generations model and not the immortal peasant family model. Their ancestor is Diamond rather than Ramsey. The second difference is the assumption that the externality kicks in at a series of thresholds; normal concavity holds in between.

A thread that runs through all these models is the assumption (intuition? induction?) that the individual yield on investment in human capital is higher when the economy-wide stock of human capital is larger. In the Azariadis–Drazen formulation this assumption, without any injection of strongly increasing returns to scale, is enough to generate the existence of two distinct equilibria: a low-level trap with no human capital investment, and a growth path leading to the usual sort of steady state. By itself this is not so remarkable. Other mechanisms can lead to the same sort of bifurcation in conventional neoclassical models.

A more interesting result follows from a special but not implausible extension. Suppose that the training technology has thresholds – levels of aggregate labour quality at which the pay-off to training rises sharply before giving way to a stretch of normal concavity until the next threshold is reached. (It is not hard to invent reasonable-sounding stories in which the achievement of widespread literacy or the spread of the Protestant ethic or the creation of an industrial labour force might represent such thresholds.) Then, as Azariadis and Drazen show, the model is capable of a multiplicity of equilibrium paths, each with positive human capital investment. These 'interior' equilibria can differ either in the level of output or in the rate of growth of output, depending on the exact nature of the human capital technology and the accompanying externality. This episodic structure is undoubtedly the most interesting by-product of the externality–increasing returns framework. As soon as there is more than one locally stable equilibrium path, initial conditions must necessarily play a central role in determining the long-run fate of the economy. History inevitably matters. For more on this important idea, see Dixit (1990) and Hahn (1990).

19.4 INTERNATIONAL TRADE

Under constant returns to scale and exogenous technological progress, national boundaries have no particular significance for growth theory. As soon as increasing returns enter the picture, international trade becomes a factor of double importance. In one direction, anything that enlarges the market can increase the level and rate of growth of output. Reciprocally, the allocation of comparative advantage can be dominated by the historical accident of who came first, either through pure scale effects or through learning by doing. An earlier paper by Ethier (1982) opened up this field before the current resurgence of growth theory, but I shall survey briefly only the recent explicitly growth-oriented literature.

Lucas saw the connection, of course, and worked out a particular model to illustrate the endogenous evolution of comparative advantage. He focused on a learning-by-doing case: commodities differ in the ease with which experience in production leads to lower costs. Lucas identified goods which are human capital intensive in this sense as 'high-technology' goods, and there is clearly something in that. There is also something missing: learning curves may be steep at first and then become flat, with the transition marking the point where a high-technology good becomes a routine commodity. Lucas shows how the allocation of comparative advantage depends on the initial distribution of human capital. His particular model suggests, although it does not quite imply, that the countries specializing in high technology will grow faster than the others and thus reinforce their comparative advantage. This is undoubtedly interesting. It could perhaps lead to a model in which some countries are able to switch from one high-technology good to a newer one, while others inherit the production of the now routinized commodity.

Krugman (1990) makes an important addition to these stories of endogenous innovation. He constructs a three-period model. In the first period entrepreneurs choose to 'invest' valuable resources in cost-reducing innovation. Those who succeed have a (temporary) monopoly on their new technology in the second period; they collect rents from their cost advantage over the marginal producer who still uses the old technology. In the third period the innovation becomes available to anyone as common property, and rents are dissipated. These sequences can be run together and overlapped to produce an ongoing history.

A few nice results follow from this simple set-up. The first is, once more, the possibility of many equilibria. The more innovative activity there is now, the higher the next period's real income will be. Successful innovators may then be able to collect higher rents. Therefore there is a force that makes investment in innovation profitable when a lot of such investment is taking place. (Obviously there may be a countervailing competitive force also.) The raw material is available for the existence of equilibria in which no one innovates because nobody else is innovating, as well as equilibria in which there is a lot of innovation.

The second result is a neat demonstration of the Schumpeterian notion that the monopoly conferred by successful innovation, although it creates a static efficiency loss, does more good than harm by promoting investment in innovative activity. The third result is the one relevant for the trade context. It costs about as much to invent a cost-reducing technology in a large economy as in a small economy. (This is why international comparisons of research expenditure per unit of gross national product (GNP) always seem a little irrelevant.) However, a given innovation is more valuable in a large economy than in a small one because there is a greater potential for rent. International integration may therefore encourage innovation and accelerate growth. This is a more powerful effect than any probable gain from static efficiency.

The series of papers by Grossman and Helpman (1988, 1989a, b) is probably the largest sustained effort in this field. In their main paper (Grossman and Helpman 1989a), they adopt the technological specification proposed by Romer (1988) and described in Section 19.3. There are two countries, each producing its own single final good and each having an intermediate-goods sector and a research sector. Research is funnelled to the country's own intermediate-goods sector, but there is trade in intermediate goods as well as in final output. Consumers buy only final products of both kinds; preferences are the same everywhere. The main distinction between the two countries turns on which of them has a comparative advantage in R&D relative to intermediate goods.

In view of Romer's work it is hardly surprising that this model generates an endogenous rate of growth for the two-country world. If neither country has a comparative advantage in R&D there is not much more to be said. Otherwise a whole new class of generalizations arises. For example, if there should be a shift in consumer preferences that strengthens the relative demand for the final good produced by the country with comparative advantage in R&D, the world growth rate falls in the new steady state. The reason is that the resources needed to satisfy the extra demand must come from the R&D and intermediate sectors. Since it is relatively less good at R&D the other country cannot fully offset this loss. Here is another example. A small tariff on imports of final goods or a small subsidy for exports of final goods reduces a country's share in the steady state production of intermediates and R&D. The world growth rate rises if and only if the country in question has a comparative disadvantage in R&D.

As a last example, this model produces some results that are inconsistent with some implications of the Krugman model. There, international integration always increased the world growth rate. In the Grossman–Helpman formulation, an isolated country with comparative advantage in R&D may slow its growth by integration with the rest of the world. Improved resource efficiency in countries with comparative disadvantage in R&D may slow the world economy as resources are reallocated among sectors world-wide. This inconsistency between models is not uncommon. In this particular case it suggests a narrow remark and a broad one. First, we may wonder whether 'comparative advantage in R&D' is a well-defined relation in world where IBM has laboratories in Zurich and New York. Second, there is real danger in overmodelling certain activities, like the generation of new technology, about which so little is known. The danger is that too much may hinge unsuspectedly on minor differences in formulation. The field is so wide open that it is hard to obtain any sort of grasp on robustness in the class of eligible models. Nevertheless, the sort of thinking described here is obviously of great importance for international trade. It offers the possibility of bringing the theory of comparative advantage out of the vineyards and flax fields into the world of high technology.

As a last illustration, I cite a paper by Kohn and Marion (1987). The technological assumptions are in the Romer–Lucas tradition, while the general framework is the Diamond overlapping generations set-up. The novelty is that the knowledge-based externality is intergenerational. Investment made in technology now will add to the cumulative stock of knowledge available to future generations, but the costs must be borne by the current generation. The question is whether it is unambiguously a good thing for a small country to integrate its capital market with the rest of the world at the world interest rate that happens to prevail.

There is space only to give the flavour of the results. A small country opening its capital market experiences a gains-from-trade effect that is perfectly conventional. However, there is a second effect that has to do with the knowledge externality. If the autarky interest rate is above the world rate, the lower local interest rate after integration will cause output to increase and generate a positive intertemporal externality with consequent benefit to future generations. Integration is then unambiguously a good thing. But suppose that the autarky interest rate happens to be below the world rate. After integration the domestic interest rate will be higher, and domestic output will fall. Less knowledge will be accumulated. Kohn and Marion (1987) show that those currently alive will be better off anyway, for standard gains-from-trade reasons, because they do not lose from the reduction in the accumulation of knowledge. But future generations will be worse off and this effect can swamp the gains from trade, especially if the difference in interest rates before and after is small, leading to a reduction in long-run welfare. There is an additional paradox in this case: the effective decision-makers, members of the current generation, are particularly tempted to vote the 'wrong' way.

19.5 FORMALIZING SCHUMPETER

Schumpeter has been a sort of patron saint of growth theory: many people worship at his shrine, but no miracles actually happen. That is presumably because the underlying ideas about the dynamics of entrepreneurship and innovation are vague, difficult or both. There have been a few attempts to embody Schumpeterian notions in a formal model. For some true believers this effort is just the first step in degrading the ideas. But without formalization there is no way of identifying the implications of those ideas sufficiently precisely to evaluate them. Nelson and Winter (1982) can be taken as a step in the Schumpeterian direction, and the paper by Krugman (1988) discussed in Section 19.4 is explicitly in that tradition. In this section I want to describe a recent analytically ambitious version of a Schumpeterian model of growth proposed by Aghion and Howitt (1989).

The model is built around the technological framework introduced into growth theory by Romer (1988), in which innovation takes the form of expanding the variety of intermediate goods available for production of final output (see equation (19.6)). It is thus, in a way, a marriage of Schumpeter and Allyn Young. Aghion and Howitt modify (19.6) to read

$$Y = R^{1-\mu} \int_0^1 \frac{x(i)^\mu}{c(i)} \, \mathrm{d}i \qquad (19.7)$$

The range of intermediate goods is now fixed, and so the Youngian side of the process is in suspense. Innovation takes the form of sporadic reductions in the cost parameters $c(i)$. To be precise, innovations occur as a Poisson process (depending on the resources devoted to research), and when one occurs it allows a uniform reduction in cost across all i in the unit interval. Innovations are not focused at a particular spot in the spectrum of intermediate goods; each innovation reduces all costs by a given factor $f < 1$. After j innovations have occurred, $c(i) = c_0 f^j$ for every i. This is, of course, highly special. It is the first of many such Santa Claus assumptions that are needed in order to capture this particular set of ideas in a tractable way. There is no other way of proceeding; one imagines that Monte Carlo simulation would be a productive device to explore alternatives if the model looks promising in its Santa Claus form.

'Creative destruction' occurs because each successful innovation renders the previous line of intermediate goods obsolete. Innovators collect rents only until the next innovation comes along, and this calculation is made by each potential innovator. There is, as there must be, a carefully designed industrial organization. Successful innovators in the research sector license their innovation to a continuum of monopolists in the intermediate-goods sector who, in turn, compete with one another in the sale of intermediate goods to the competitive final-output sector. Labour is used only in the research sector and in the production of intermediates; in (19.7) R refers to a fixed supply of 'land'.

The equilibrium concept involves perfect foresight in the sense that the endogenous variables (for example, wages, outputs, costs, profits) can all be predicted as a function of the cumulative number of innovations. But the identity of each successful innovator in the sequence and the calendar date at which each successive innovation occurs are both random. A steady state of the model is a situation in which the allocation of a (fixed) total of employment between research and the manufacture of intermediates is unchanging. Growth occurs if and only if some labour is allocated to research.

Aghion and Howitt (1989) show that every equilibrium path in this model converges to a steady state with positive growth, a steady state with zero growth, a two-cycle or a 'no-growth trap'. There is always a unique steady state. A two-cycle is an equilibrium in which research employment alternates between a high level and a low level; high manufacturing employment makes innovation so profitable that research employment expands in the next year, depressing manufacturing employment and reducing the reward to subsequent innovation. A no-growth trap looks a lot like a zero-growth steady state, but the mechanism is that the prospect of low manufacturing employment in even periods so depresses the incentive to research in odd periods that research stops altogether. A no-growth trap can occur even in an economy that possesses a positive-growth steady state.

The mean rate of growth (averaged over sequences of innovations) is endogenous in this model. It depends on the parameters of the research process, increasing with the ease of innovation and with the size of each innovation (the smaller is f). The average growth rate also increases with the size of the economy (as measured by total employment, say) and with the degree of monopoly power in the manufacture of intermediates. Generally speaking, the average growth rate and its variability rise and fall together. The most disconcerting of these generalizations is the positive association of size and growth. The world does not seem to work like that. However, any model will work like that if it features increasing returns to scale in production (as in (19.6)) and, in effect, increasing aggregative returns to research. The remedy would seem to be a little dose of diminishing returns somewhere. Where?

19.6 CONCLUSION

A serious evaluation of the 'new growth theory' will have to wait for a while. It is rather remarkable that just about all the work surveyed in this paper has been performed within the past five years. Much of it is still in working paper form. This burst of activity speaks well for the energy and cohesion of the small research community involved. But it leaves open the possibility that the second five years will see a further evolution of the theoretical model and the accompanying interpretation of the historical record, with the second period being at least as interesting as the first. Therefore only a few general remarks can be offered here.

To judge whether this theoretical enterprise has been a success we need a fairly clear idea of what could legitimately have been expected. If the goal of growth theory is the elaboration of a preferred complete model ready for formal econometric application to observed time series, as many economists seem to believe, then the new growth theory falls well short. One is struck by the proliferation of special assumptions about technology, about the nature of research activity, about the formation and use of human capital, about market structure, about family structure and about intertemporal preferences. Most of these particular assumptions have been chosen for convenience, because they make a difficult analytical problem more transparent. There is no reason to assume that they are descriptively valid, or that their implications have significant robustness against equally plausible variations in assumptions. The only sort of empirical control has come from the inspection of international cross-sections of levels and rates of growth of output and productivity, along with ancillary data. The question asked is whether the model as formulated is capable of reproducing the broad observed patterns. Yes is surely a much better answer than no. But the power of such tests must be very low against reasonable alternatives. Quite different families of models are probably capable of that sort of validation. (For example, Jones and Manuelli (1988) show that many of the desired results – endogenization of the growth rate and its susceptibility to permanent influence by government policy or accidental disturbance – can be achieved without increasing returns or externalities by relaxing one of the Inada conditions and assuming that the marginal product of capital is bounded away from zero as capital accumulates indefinitely.)

However, there is another respectable role for growth theory, or for theory more broadly, as a guide to intuition and therefore as a guide to observation and interpretation, not just as a basis for multiple regression equations. One of the advantages of this view is that it allows or even encourages trying out partial or incompletely specified models. From this more relaxed point of view the new growth theory seems to be much more successful. It does guide our intuition, and in obviously interesting directions that earlier versions of neoclassical theory tended to submerge. If only part of the ground has been explored, well, then, as Walt Whitman almost wrote, only part of the ground has been explored. There is room for more theoretical exploration and for piecemeal use of all available data to distinguish better from worse.

Finally, I want to return briefly to a point taken up earlier in this survey.

There is always a question in economic modelling about what should be taken as exogenous. The question may be harder in growth theory than elsewhere because the set of possible endogenous variables is that much wider. One of the main impulses motivating the new growth theory was precisely the wish to determine the growth rate itself, within the theory. That is certainly natural. The elimination of free parameters, or at least their replacement by 'more fundamental' ones, is one of the standing objectives of basic science, especially physics: 'Ultimately . . . one would hope to find a complete, consistent, unified theory that would include all these partial theories as approximations, and that did not need to be adjusted to fit the facts by picking the values of certain arbitrary numbers in the theory' (Hawking 1988: 155). After all, fundamental physics is said to be in hot pursuit of a Theory of Everything, and 'Everything' presumably includes GNP per capita.

However, there is another side to the story. Immediately before the sentence just quoted, Hawking writes:

> it would be very difficult to construct a complete unified theory of everything in the universe all at one go. So instead we have made progress by finding partial theories that describe a limited range of happenings and by neglecting other effects or approximating them by certain numbers. (Chemistry, for example, allows us to calculate the interactions of atoms, without knowing the internal structure of the atom's nucleus.)

The interests of economics might be served better if theorists aspired to the status of chemistry rather than fundamental physics.

All such analogies are for conversational purposes only. The right place to draw the line between exogenous and endogenous in economics is a matter of economics, not chemistry. That being so, I end with a caution. Just because growth theory deals with long runs of time and with comparisons between countries at different stages of development, it is vulnerable to the problem of institutional change and whatever that brings in the way of changing attitudes, incentives and behaviour. It seems dangerously provincial to take it for granted that social institutions are either optimally 'chosen' by some collective maximizer or else inevitably like those of idealized twentieth-century (or nineteenth-century) industrial capitalism.

REFERENCES

Aghion, P. and Howitt, P. (1989) 'A model of growth through creative destruction', Working paper, Massachusetts Institute of Technology.

Arrow, K. J. (1962) 'The economic implications of learning by doing', *Review of Economic Studies* 39: 155–73.

Azariadis, C. and Drazen, A. (1988) 'Threshold externalities in economic development', Working paper, University of Pennsylvania.

Barro, R. and Becker, G. (1989) 'Fertility choice in a model of economic growth', *Econometrics* 57: 481–501.

Becker, G., Murphy, K. and Tamura, R. (1988) 'Economic growth, human capital and population growth', Working paper, University of Iowa.

Burmeister, E. and Dobell, A. R. (1970) *Mathematical Theories of Economic Growth*, London: Macmillan.

Cass, D. (1965) 'Optimum growth in an aggregative model of capital accumulation', *Review of Economic Studies* 32: 233–40.

Diamond, P. A. (1965) 'National debt in a neo-classical growth model', *American Economic Review* 55: 1126–50.

Dixit, A. K. (1976) *The Theory of Equilibrium Growth*, Oxford: Oxford University Press.

—— (1990) 'Growth theory after thirty years', in P. Diamond (ed.) *Growth, Productivity, Unemployment*, pp. 3–22, Boston, MA: MIT Press.

Ethier, W. (1982) 'National and international returns to scale in the modern theory of international trade', *American Economic Review*, 72: 389–405.

Grossman, G. and Helpman, E. (1988) 'Product development and international trade', Working paper 2540, National Bureau of Economic Research.

—— and —— (1989a) 'Comparative advantage and long-run growth', Working paper 2809, National Bureau of Economic Research.

—— and —— (1989b) 'Endogenous product cycles', Working paper 2913, National Bureau of Economic Research.

Hahn, F. (1990) 'Solowian growth models', in P. Diamond (ed.) *Growth, Productivity, Unemployment*, pp. 23–40, Boston, MA: MIT Press.

Hahn, F. H. and Matthews, R. C. O. (1964) 'The theory of economic growth: a survey', *Economic Journal* 74: 779–902.

Hawking, S. W. (1988) *A Brief History of Time*, London: Bantam.

Jones, L. and Manuelli, R. (1988) 'A model of optimal equilibrium growth', Working paper, Northwestern University.

Kohn, M. and Marion, N. (1987) 'The implications of knowledge-based growth for the optimality of open capital markets', Working paper, Dartmouth College.

Koopmans, T. C. (1965) 'On the concept of optimal economical growth', in *The Econometric Approach to Economic Planning*, Amsterdam: North-Holland.

Krugman, P. (1990) 'Endogenous innovation, international trade, and growth', in *Rethinking International Trade*, ch. 11, pp. 165–82, Boston, MA: MIT Press.

Lucas, R. E., Jr (1988) 'On the mechanics of economic development', *Journal of Monetary Economics* 22: 3–42.

Nelson, R. and Winter, S. G. (1982) *An Evolutionary Approach to Economic Change*, Cambridge, MA: Harvard University Press.

Ramsey, F. P. (1928) 'A mathematical theory of saving', *Economic Journal* 38: 543–59.

Romer, P. M. (1986) 'Increasing returns and long-run growth', *Journal of Political Economy* 94: 1002–37.

—— (1987) 'Growth based on increasing returns due to specialization', *American Economic Review, Papers and Proceedings* 77: 56–62.

—— (1988) 'Endogenous technical change', Working paper.

Solow, R. M. (1956) 'A contribution to the theory of economic growth', *Quarterly Journal of Economics* 70: 65–94.

—— (1970) *Growth Theory: An Exposition*, Oxford: Oxford University Press, reprinted 1988.

—— (1982) 'Some lessons from growth theory', in W. F. Sharpe and C. M. Cootner (eds) *Financial Economics: Essays in Honor of Paul Cootner*, pp. 246–59, Englewood Cliffs, NJ: Prentice-Hall.

Swan, T. (1956) 'Economic growth and capital accumulation', *Economic Record* 32: 334–61.

Tamura, R. (1989a) 'Fertility, human capital and the wealth of nations', Working paper, University of Iowa.

—— (1989b) 'Convergence in an endogenous growth model: from heterogeneity to homogeneity', Working paper, University of Iowa.

Uzawa, H. (1965) 'Optimum technical change in an aggregative model of economic growth', *International Economic Review* 6: 18–31.

Wan, H. Y., Jr (1971) *Economic Growth*, New York: Harcourt Brace Jovanovich.

Young, A. A. (1928) 'Increasing returns and economic progress', *Economic Journal* 38: 527–42.

20

OPEN-ECONOMY MACROECONOMICS

RONALD SHONE

20.1 INTRODUCTION

Open-economy macroeconomics (OEM) only became a separate area of research in the late 1960s and early 1970s. Until that time, and some might argue even today, closed-economy macroeconomics (CEM) dominated. The rise of OEM has now reached the point where a number of textbooks are available outlining the subject area (for example, Dornbusch 1980; De Grauwe 1983; Rivera-Batiz and Rivera-Batiz 1985; Morley 1988; Shone 1989a), and there are many more in the area of international monetary economics and international finance (for example, Niehans 1984; Copeland 1989). This immediately raises the following questions. What is distinctive about OEM? Is OEM in some way different from CEM or does it simply use different techniques of investigation? Are the models used to analyse open economies different from those used to analyse closed economies? Are the policy conclusions of OEM different from those of CEM, or are the latter simply a special case of the former? Why is OEM a feature of the 1970s and 1980s and not the 1930s and 1940s? Finally, will macroeconomics in the future remain roughly in these two divisions: macroeconomics for closed economies and macroeconomics for open economies? These are just some of the questions that will be addressed in this chapter.

In order to give some perspective to developments, in Section 20.2 we distinguish three types of economies: a closed economy, an insular economy,[1] and an open economy. We also try to show that the present interest in OEM has in large part arisen from a more integrated world economy which requires to be understood. The insular economy is analysed in some detail in Section 20.3 because it has been fundamental to much of the international monetary economics taught, and the models employed became the basis of much policy

I am grateful to Thomas Moutos and Sheila Dow of the Division of Economics, University of Stirling, and to the editors for their helpful comments on an earlier draft.

416

advice until the advent of floating. With generalized floating in March 1973 the importance of OEM took on a major significance. In some respects, the world situation was ahead of theory. Macroeconomics had effectively treated economies as closed; at the very least, the exchange rate was assumed to be constant. This was a reasonable assumption under the Bretton Woods system which operated until 1971. However, with the advent of floating this assumption had to be replaced by the assumption of a floating exchange rate – free or managed. With the move to greater integration of both goods and asset markets, and the major shocks which confronted the world economy in the 1970s, much of macroeconomics was shown to be inadequate for analysing such events. The exchange rate had to be determined along with other macroeconomic variables. In Section 20.4 we look at the developments which have taken place to explain the determination of the exchange rate, which is the central variable in OEM. A number of surveys of macroeconomics, which are in fact surveys of CEM,[2] have highlighted two features which have dominated much of this work over the last ten years or more and will be the basis of much research in the future. These are rational expectations and a more detailed analysis of aggregate supply. Both these developments have important implications for the open economy, and we shall consider these in Section 20.5. In the final section we provide some comments on the developments in research in OEM which are likely to take place in the next few years.

20.2 WHAT IS OPEN-ECONOMY MACROECONOMICS AND WHY IS IT IMPORTANT?

In one sense, OEM is the bringing together of two areas of economics: macroeconomics (strictly CEM) and international economics (strictly international monetary economics). This view is shared by De Grauwe (1983) and Dornbusch (1980). The latter remarks in the opening sentence to his book, *Open Economy Macroeconomics*, that it 'reflects an attempt to integrate closed economy macroeconomics with the topics and problems arising in the economics of foreign trade and payments'. This would be worth doing only if economies were open.

Figure 20.1 indicates the openness of six economies for the period 1950–88, measuring openness as the sum of exports and imports as a percentage of GNP. What the diagram indicates is that many economies have become more open since 1950, and particularly since 1970 (although there is some evidence of a decline in the late 1980s). Of particular note is the increase in the openness of the US economy (which rose from 8 per cent in 1950 to 19 per cent in 1988).[3] The UK economy has always been an open economy, and CEM has been a very unsuitable means of analysing its problems.[4]

These measures of openness apply only to goods and services – and then

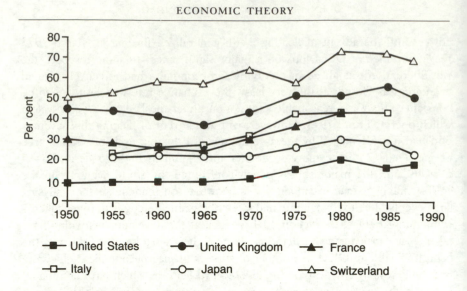

Figure 20.1 Economy openness (exports plus imports as a percentage of GNP).
Source: International Financial Statistics, *Yearbook*, 1988, 1989

only to goods and services actually imported and exported. There have been some attempts at measuring openness in terms of the share of tradeable goods, but this is more difficult to do. However, some theoretical analyses are based on openness measured in terms of tradeable goods and services (e.g. Aizenman 1985; Aizenman and Frenkel 1985).

It is quite clear that capital markets have become more integrated since 1950. This, even more than the current account, has meant that goods markets and asset markets must be analysed together. This, in turn, has required the development of a new set of models to analyse questions of the open economy. The closed economy need only be a single-good economy. An open economy, however, requires at least two goods: a domestically produced good and a foreign good. This results in a relative price (the 'terms of trade') which does not exist in closed-economy models. Furthermore, this relative price must involve the nominal exchange rate which translates the foreign good's price into the price in domestic currency. More significant from the point of view of modelling the open economy, the terms of trade enter both aggregate demand and aggregate supply. It follows, then, that such a relative price can influence resource allocation in the domestic economy and hence the level of employment. It also follows that any attempt on the part of the government in the home country to stabilize income can be thwarted by developments in the rest of the world. Furthermore, the effectiveness or otherwise of such policies may depend crucially on whether the exchange rate is fixed or floating. In other words, policy questions of major import cannot ignore the fact that the economy is open.

Before continuing, however, it is worth pointing out that (as in the discussion of de-industrialization) economists may be drawing incorrect inferences by concentrating on the post-war period (see Grassman 1980; Krugman 1989). There is little doubt that in this period the degree of openness has increased, leading to studies of implications (for example, Stewart 1983). However, the long-run analysis by Grassman (1980), although indicating a rise in openness for many countries for the period 1960–80, reveals a downward trend over the period 1875–1975. The rise in the 1970s and 1980s is really in comparison with the very low base of the protectionist interwar period. This implies that more detailed studies of openness are required, with comparisons of at least three historical periods: 1875–1914, 1918–39 and 1945–90. What Grassman's analysis *does* suggest is the unrealistic assumption of a closed-economy model for analysing most economies.[5]

20.3 THE INSULAR ECONOMY

In an attempt to deal with an open economy, analysts considered an economy which traded with the outside world and so was influenced by it. Since it was small itself, however, it had little (or no) impact on the world economy. Such an approach dealt with a small open economy. But this approach does not capture fully the type of models which grew up in the 1950s and 1960s. Although these dealt with small open economies, in the sense that trade was only a small percentage of GNP, they had additional characteristics which needed to be taken into account. In particular, it was necessary to take account of the controls which were still in place on capital movements. Second, it was necessary to allow for the insulation of the domestic monetary system from the foreign exchange market. We therefore refer to the insular economy: an economy which is small, involves controls on capital flows and insulates its monetary system from the foreign exchange market. We refer to the analysis of this type of economy as insular-economy macroeconomics (IEM) to distinguish it from CEM and (full) OEM.[6]

The insular economy has been fairly well documented by McKinnon (1981) and Kenen (1985), and here we shall be brief. It is necessary to discuss it, however, because it not only sets the models of the 1950s and 1960s into perspective, but also lays the foundation for the models developed to analyse the open economy of the 1970s and beyond.

Before discussing IEM, it is worth noting that such analysis cuts across the usual methodological debate between Keynesians and monetarists, which typified much of the work of the 1950s and 1960s. Both Keynesians and monetarists of this era (*c.* 1940–65) basically accepted the desirability of national autonomy, and as such implicitly (if not explicitly) accepted the insular economy model.

The insular economy was first analysed in a Marshallian framework. The balance of payments was the difference between the value of exports and the value of imports. Exports of goods[7] were equal to the difference between home production and home consumption, and the price of exports was set in terms of the home currency (hence the price abroad varied with variations in the exchange rate). In a two-country world, imports were equal to the difference between production in the foreign country and consumption in the foreign country. The price of imports was the ratio of the foreign (export) price to the exchange rate (quoted as the number of units of foreign currency per unit of domestic currency).[8] The exchange rate was assumed to be constant, in line with the Bretton Woods system which operated from 1944 to 1971. However, attention was directed to the consequence of a parity change in the exchange rate. This was an obvious line of research, since under a fixed exchange rate insular economies were charaterized by balance-of-payments crises, and any attempt to solve these was directed to policies for dealing with the current account of the balance of payments – including a devaluation.

Since, in a Marshallian framework, quantities were functions of relative prices and changes in relative prices resulted in changes in quantities which were dependent on elasticities of demand and supply, it was very soon established under what conditions a devaluation would improve the trade balance (in foreign currency). This was the Marshall–Lerner condition.[9] However, this 'elasticities approach', which was a partial equilibrium analysis, did not fit in very well with the Keynesian orthodoxy which developed soon after the publication of Keynes's *General Theory*.

Although in the *General Theory* Keynes assumed a closed economy, the model was soon extended by adding the trade sector and deriving open-economy multipliers. The first change was for small open economies which could ignore the impact that they had on the rest of the world; later changes dealt with two interrelated economies, where the imports of one country were the exports of the other. In these models, any exogenous domestic change would change income in the home country and, through the marginal propensity to import, change the exports of the foreign country, which would in turn alter the foreign level of income and the foreign level of imports. Under appropriate assumptions about the marginal propensities to import, the multiplier impacts of various shocks could be analysed. These typically Keynesian open-economy models had one similarity with the elasticities approach which had gone before: they assumed that the price level in each country was fixed. The implication of this assumption is that the real exchange rate and the nominal exchange rate move together. This follows immediately from the definition of the (logarithm) of the real exchange rate ρ, which is

$$\rho = s + p - p^* \tag{20.1}$$

where s is the nominal exchange rate in foreign currency per unit of domestic currency, p^* is the price level abroad and p is the price level at home, all in natural logarithms. Since prices in both countries are assumed to be fixed in local currency, then ρ and s move together.

More significant developments, at least from the point of view of Keynesian macromodelling, were the absorption approach developed by Alexander (1952, 1959), the analysis of internal and external balance developed by Meade (1951), Mundell (1962) and Swan (1963), and the Mundell–Fleming model outlined by Mundell (1963) and Fleming (1962). All these were an extension of Keynes's CEM model of income determination.

The importance of the absorption approach was to highlight the fact that a balance-of-payments deficit could arise only if domestic absorption was in excess of domestic income. Furthermore, it implied that, in a fully employed economy, a devaluation (an expenditure-switching policy) would only be successful in reducing a trade deficit if it were also accompanied by an expenditure-reducing policy. The significance of Alexander's analysis was in setting out the balance of payments in terms of national (open-economy) identities and then postulating some behavioural relationships (see Clement *et al.* 1967: ch. 7). In doing so it placed the analysis squarely within a Keynesian framework. It also had a direct policy significance. However, as with the elasticities approach, it had shortcomings. There were a number of attempts at a synthesis between the elasticities approach and the absorption approach, culminating in the paper by Tsiang (1961), which more than any other highlighted the implicit assumptions about monetary policy in both these approaches.

While macroeconomics was extending the Keynesian model and specifying more clearly the goods market and the money market by building on the work of Hicks (1937), OEM was taking a much more policy-oriented line of research. Meade (1951) had begun a major synthesis and had introduced the concepts of internal and external balance – internal balance was full employment with price stability, while external balance was a balance on the current and capital account of the balance of payments (Shone 1979). Tinbergen (1956) set out some of the economics of policy modelling, emphasizing instruments and targets. This early work led to the influential models of Swan (1963) and Mundell (1962), each giving a slightly different version of internal and external balance.[10] The internal/external balance was very much concerned with domestic monetary and fiscal policies which could offset foreign shocks while maintaining a balance of foreign payments.[11] Mundell, in particular, was concerned with the appropriate assignment of instruments for achieving the two targets of internal and external balance. This was a theme that Meade returned to in his Nobel Prize lecture (Meade 1978). One particular feature of Mundell's assignment was the recognition that the balance of payments had a significant capital account which could be influenced by monetary policy via the differential between domestic and foreign interest rates. In fact, in his analysis, monetary policy was assigned the role of achieving external balance, while fiscal policy was assigned the role of internal balance; the reverse assignment was unstable. Although internal/external balance analysis remains popular, it has a significant flaw when considering three policy objectives: full employment, balance-of-payments equilibrium and stable prices. In particular, the assignment question becomes decidedly imprecise (Shone 1989a: ch. 8.)

By the late 1960s the IS–LM CEM model and the IS–LM–BP OEM model had been fairly thoroughly worked out. Friedman (1953) had advocated flexible exchange rates, and this view was later endorsed by Meade (1955). Therefore the time was right to analyse monetary and fiscal policy under two exchange rate regimes: fixed and floating. This was done by Mundell (1963) and Fleming (1962), in particular, and their analysis has been referred to as the Mundell–Fleming model ever since. In international monetary economics, this model has taken on the same significance as the Heckscher–Ohlin model in pure trade theory. It is therefore worth describing briefly. Later developments will then be presented in relation to it.

The model consists of three equations: a goods market equilibrium (IS) curve

$$y = a_0 + a_1 y - a_2 r + g + [h_0 - h_1(s + p - p^*) - h_2 y] \quad (20.2)$$

a money market equilibrium (LM) curve

$$m - p = b_0 + b_1 y - b_2 r \quad (20.3)$$

and a balance-of-payments (BP) curve

$$h_0 - h_1(s + p - p^*) - h_2 y + h_3(r - r^*) = F \quad (20.4)$$

All variables except the domestic interest rate r, the foreign interest rate r^* and the balance of payments F are in natural logarithms. All parameters are positive, with the added restrictions that $0 < a_1 < 1$, $0 < b_1 < 1$ and $0 < h_2 < 1$. Equation (20.2) denotes equilibrium in the goods market (the IS curve), and shows income y equal to total expenditure. Equation (20.3) denotes equilibrium in the money market (the LM curve), which equates real money balances with the demand for real money balances. Equation (20.4) is the balance-of-payments equation, comprising the sum of the current account and the capital account. A balance-of-payments equilibrium requires $F = 0$.

The early formulation assumed perfect capital mobility ($h_3 = \infty$). Under a fixed exchange rate, s is fixed, and with the usual closed-economy assumptions of fixed price levels p and p^* are fixed. Thus, from equation (20.4), the perfect capital mobility assumption means that $r = r^*$. Given this, equation (20.2) determines the level of income. Equation (20.3) determines nominal money balances. With less than perfect capital mobility ($0 < h_3 < \infty$), and under the assumption of a fixed exchange rate, the three equations determine y, r and F. The model could also readily handle the situation of a floating exchange rate (s variable), which means $F = 0$. Under the assumption of perfect capital mobility, $r = r^*$, which means that income is determined from (20.3) and the (logarithm of the) exchange rate is determined from (20.2). If, however, there is less than perfect capital mobility, the three equations can solve for y, r and s simultaneously. The model could then readily compare the effectiveness of monetary and fiscal policy under alternative exchange rate regimes.[12] The central proposition derived by Mundell and Fleming is that under a freely floating exchange rate with perfect capital mobility and a fixed price level, fiscal policy is impotent in bringing about a change in income while monetary policy is effective. If the exchange rate is fixed, however, then the reverse is true. The model has spawned a voluminous literature in which the effectiveness of the policy under less rigid assumptions has been considered.

For example, there have been models making a distinction between the prices of domestic goods and the retail price index. Under this assumption the strict Mundell–Fleming results no longer hold because there is now a real balance effect occurring under a floating exchange rate system. Other models have introduced regressive expectations, resulting in both monetary and fiscal policies being effective even under the other extreme Mundell–Fleming assumptions. Finally, there have been models allowing for wage indexation, which we shall deal with in Section 20.5. For a a summary of these and other developments, see Frenkel and Razin (1987) and Shone (1989b), which basically indicate the limitations of the Mundell–Fleming model.

Although the absorption approach was introduced into the literature in the early 1950s and the monetary approach in the early 1960s, with a fixed exchange rate assumed in both, there have been recent attempts at a synthesis between these two techniques (for example, Frenkel 1980; Frenkel *et al.* 1980). It is argued that both approaches have limitations: the absorption approach concentrates on the IS relationship, while the monetary approach concentrates on the LM relationship. When looked at in this way, it is clear that neither approach can determine interest rates and equilibrium income. The synthesis is achieved by introducing a relationship which closes the system: namely, an aggregate supply relationship. However, this synthesis has not gone without its critics (see Taylor 1990).

20.4 EXCHANGE RATE DETERMINATION

The Mundell–Fleming model outlined in Section 20.3 was the basic frame-work for discussing most macroeconomic issues of the open economy. However, the increasing strain on the Bretton Woods system coincided with a rise in monetarism.[13] The main exponent of this, of course, was Milton Friedman.

However, Friedman had already advocated floating exchange rates in his famous 1953 article. The issue was later discussed by Meade (1955), Sohmen (1961) and Johnson (1970).[14] As we noted in the previous section, the Mundell–Fleming model could handle a floating exchange rate, but it was done in a very Keynesian framework. From the monetarist point of view it underplayed the role of money.

The monetary approach to the balance of payments[15] attempted to highlight the monetary nature of balance-of-payments deficits and surpluses under a fixed exchange rate regime. But at this time there was no clear monetarist view on exchange rate determination.

The monetary approach to exchange rate determination begins with the assumption that domestic and foreign bonds are perfect substitutes while bonds and money are not, on the grounds that money serves functions which other assets cannot serve so well. By Walras's law, one market can be ignored, and so monetarists ignored bonds and considered only the demand and supply of money. As with many approaches to exchange rate determination, there is no single monetary approach. A major distinction in the modelling occurs depending on the assumption about prices. Those models which assume that purchasing power parity holds continuously are flexible-price models, while other models, which are still fundamentally monetarist, assume short-run stickiness of prices but also assume that purchasing power parity holds in the long run.

The monetary approach to exchange rate determination, whether in the form of flexible prices or short-run sticky prices, takes purchasing power parity as its central concept along with the quantity theory of money. Since the exchange rate is the ratio of two price levels, it can be expressed (in logarithmic form) as

$$s = p^* - p \tag{20.5}$$

Relating money stocks to real income via the quantity equation in both countries, and assuming that the reciprocals of the income velocity of circulation of money are the same in each country, we have

$$s = (m^* - m) - (y^* - y) \tag{20.6}$$

However, this is considered to be a long-run result, and certainly does not take account of interest rates in the demand-for-money equation. Using equation (20.3) and assuming that the coefficients b_1 and b_2 are the same in both countries, we can express the short-run exchange rate as

$$s = (m^* - m) - b_1(y^* - y) + b_2(r^* - r) \tag{20.7}$$

What equation (20.7) shows is that the exchange rate depends on the demand and supply of domestic money and the demand and supply of foreign money. Hence, changes in the exchange rate arise because of changes in domestic and foreign variables. But, more importantly from a policy point of view, it suggests opposite responses of the exchange rate to changes in income than those predicted by the Keynesian OEM model. In the latter, a rise in income will result in a worsening of the trade balance which, under a floating exchange rate, will lead to a depreciation of the domestic currency. Under the monetary approach, equation (20.7) suggests that a rise in the domestic level of income will lead to an appreciation of the domestic currency.

Result (20.7) can be elaborated further by introducing interest rate parity, and so introducing exchange rate expectations into the framework.[16] Since the expected change in exchange rate equals the interest rate differential and, from purchasing power parity, also equals the expected inflation differential, the interest rate differential in equation (20.7) becomes the expected inflation differential. What this does is to direct attention to expectational considerations and, in particular, to how 'news' will affect these, and hence the exchange rate. Although 'news' is unanticipated, it must be part of the information set of the rational economic agent, and as such enter his behaviour. However, it is the testing of such hypotheses that has attracted the most attention (for a summary see MacDonald and Taylor 1989).

In the early monetary models of exchange rate determination it was assumed that purchasing power parity held continuously. Later models, especially those of Dornbusch (1976, 1980) and Buiter and Miller (1981, 1982), assume short-run stickiness of prices but allow purchasing power parity to hold in the long run. A feature of these models is that they lead to overshooting of the exchange rate. A corollary of the assumption of sticky prices is the assumption that asset markets are quick to clear. The result of this differential speed of adjustment is that, in the short run, adjustment falls on the exchange rate, which overshoots its target level. As prices in the goods market adjust, the exchange rate converges on its long-run solution. This model has gained considerable attention, not least because it attempts to explain exchange rate behaviour in the 1970s and 1980s.

The model takes the following form (which is slightly different from that originally given by Dornbusch):[17]

$$e = a_0 + a_1 y - a_2 r + g + [h_0 - h_1(s + p - p^*) - h_2 y] \quad (20.8)$$

$$m - p = b_0 + b_1 y - b_2 r \quad (20.9)$$

$$h_0 - h_1(s + p - p^*) + h_3(r - r^* + \dot{s}^e) = F \quad (20.10)$$

$$\dot{s}^e = \theta(\bar{s} - s) \qquad 0 < \theta < 1 \quad (20.11)$$

$$\dot{p} = \pi(e - y) \qquad \pi > 0 \quad (20.12)$$

The first three equations are the familiar goods market, money market and balance-of-payments equilibrium conditions respectively. The model differs from that given by Dornbusch in terms of equations (20.11) and (20.12). Equation (20.11) indicates that the exchange rate adjusts according to the gap between the equilibrium exchange rate (represented by $\bar{s}$, and assumed by Dornbusch to be the purchasing power parity rate) and the actual rate. Equation (20.12) indicates that prices adjust according to excess demand in the goods market. Dornbusch assumes perfect capital mobility so that equation (20.10) reduces to the condition that $r = r^* - \dot{s}^e$.

The money market is assumed to adjust instantaneously, and so the demand and supply of money are always equal. A crucial, but not very realistic, assumption for the model is that income is constant at its full employment level. Hence, in this model all adjustment falls on prices and the exchange rate (and hence on interest rates). Diagrammatically, the equilibrium exchange rate and price level are determined by the intersection of two phase lines in (p, s) space, one denoting equilibrium in the goods market (shown by the schedule $\dot{p}(.) = 0$) and the other denoting equilibrium in the asset market (shown by the

Figure 20.2 Overshooting as a result of monetary expansion.

schedule MM),[18] as illustrated in Figure 20.2. It is then possible to consider the effects of monetary and fiscal policy. Dornbusch (1976) considers, in particular, the effects of monetary expansion, which is illustrated in the figure. The initial situation is shown by point A where the two initial phase lines intersect. Note that point A lies on the 45° line ($d\bar{s} + d\bar{p} = 1$). A rise in the money supply shifts the MM schedule to the right (where $m_1 > m_0$). In the short run prices do not alter. With the added assumption that the money market must clear instantaneously, all adjustment in the short run falls on interest rates and the exchange rate. Thus the economy moves from point A to point B in the short run. In the long run, prices alter and so the goods market equilibrium shifts to $\dot{p}(m_1) = 0$ and the economy converges on its long-run equilibrium (point C). In the case of monetary expansion, therefore, the exchange rate overshoots its long-run equilibrium value in the short run.

The Dornbusch model is typical of the more dynamic approaches which are being taken to analyse exchange rate determination. It should be noted from equation (20.11) that expected changes in the exchange rate are being modelled, and take the form of regressive expectations. Alternative models of exchange rate determination along these lines assume rational expectations.[19] Furthermore, Dornbusch's overshooting model involves no supply-side effects of the exchange rate. Buiter and Miller (1981, 1982) not only consider supply-side effects but also allow for a non-zero interest rate expectation. A basic form of this model has also been employed by Buiter and Purvis (1983) to consider the effects of a domestic resource discovery on other sectors. It therefore attempts to explain the appreciation of sterling after the discovery of North Sea oil, and the consequential adverse effects on UK manufacturing.

However, no matter how much the monetary approach to exchange rate determination has been adapted, it appears that it does not hold up to empirical investigation. This is not surprising since it has a very simplistic view of open economies. However, it did direct attention towards the role of the asset market in exchange rate determination.

The monetary approach considers only two assets: money and bonds. Since domestic and foreign bonds are perfect substitutes, then there is no need to distinguish between them. The portfolio approach to exchange rate determination assumes three assets: money, domestic bonds and foreign bonds, where domestic and foreign bonds are not perfect substitutes. Wealth W is explicitly taken account of in this model. It consists of money M, domestic bonds B and foreign bonds F/S denominated in domestic currency (where S is the exchange rate); all other terms are in nominal values. Each of the three assets that make up wealth is a function of domestic and foreign interest rates. Thus, the simplest portfolio model, with static expectations, can be expressed as

$$W = M + B + F/S \qquad (20.13)$$

$$M = M(r, r^*)W \qquad M_r < 0, \quad M_{r^*} < 0 \qquad (20.14)$$

$$B = B(r, r^*)W \qquad B_r > 0, \quad B_{r^*} < 0 \qquad (20.15)$$

$$F/S = F(r, r^*)W \qquad F_r < 0, \quad F_{r^*} > 0 \qquad (20.16)$$

Determination of the exchange rate in this model arises from all markets interacting simultaneously. This is illustrated in Figure 20.3, where it should be noted that S is the level and not the logarithm of the exchange rate and is quoted in terms of foreign currency per unit of domestic currency. The schedule M denotes all combinations of S and r for which the demand and supply of money is equal, the schedule B denotes the (S, r) combinations for which the domestic bond market is in equilibrium and the schedule F denotes the (S, r) combinations for which the domestic demand for foreign bonds is equal to their supply. By Walras's law, one market can be dropped, and this is usually taken to be the money market. A stable equilibrium occurs if schedule B is steeper than schedule F. The initial equilibrium is at E_0 where all schedules intersect.

Unlike the monetary model, in the portfolio balance model the effect of fiscal policy is ambiguous because of the possible substitution between domestic and foreign bonds. In the case of an increase in domestic bond sales (a shift to the right in the schedule B from B_0 to B_1), for instance, the exchange rate will appreciate if domestic and foreign assets are close substitutes (the schedule F shifts to the right by only a small amount, as shown by schedule F_1 in Figure 20.3), but will depreciate if they are not close substitutes (the schedule F shifts to the right by a large amount, as shown by schedule F_2 in Figure 20.3).

Various versions of the model have been analysed,[20] but they tend to be complex and unwieldy. Certainly the model, in its various forms, has not stood up to empirical testing.

However, this is not the only form of model that is employed to consider exchange rate determination. The equilibrium models and the new classical economics literature, with their emphasis on rational expectations, market clearing and proper microfoundations for macroeconomic behavioural equations, have also attempted to deal with the determination of the exchange rate.[21] In the case of equilibrium models, consistency in modelling requires that all markets clear continuously: labour markets, commodity markets and foreign exchange markets. On the other hand, the new classical approach pays particular attention to the underlying microeconomic foundations, where behavioural equations are derived from maximizing considerations. However, the models still require assumptions to be made about how markets function. Either they assume that markets clear continuously (and so are similar to the equilibrium models) or they assume short-run stickiness of wages and prices

Figure 20.3 Increase in *B*, where domestic and foreign assets have different degrees of substitutability.

(very much like the Dornbusch model discussed above), in which case they differ from the equilibrium models.

All this modelling of exchange rate determination reveals a general inadequacy, especially when tested against the facts. Some of the models are reasonable when exchange rate movements are small, but when they are large, which they have been in the 1970s and 1980s, they give very poor explanations indeed. However, the problem of testing is difficult. An endogenous exchange rate must be tested within a whole model, and it is the whole model which is under test and not just the part which attempts to specify the exchange rate.

20.5 SUPPLY-SIDE ECONOMICS AND THE OPEN ECONOMY

The opening up of Keynes's closed-economy model indicated more explicitly how the balance of payments and the exchange rate entered the aggregate demand relationship: in particular, how competitiveness (the real exchange rate) entered import and export equations. Even the later developments in terms of the IS–LM–BP model, and the Mundell-Fleming model, concentrated on opening the economy only from the point of view of aggregate demand. But, of course, goods and services in an open economy have to be produced. Furthermore, inputs into the production process are often imported and are themselves subject to change as exchange rates change. Even where goods are produced and consumed at home and require no imported inputs, they can still be influenced indirectly by exchange rates to the extent that wage claims will be based on maintaining a real wage – where the price deflator involves the prices of domestically produced goods and imported goods. Therefore the more recent modelling of the open economy has directed attention very much to specifying aggregate supply in more precise terms. These developments are occurring in tandem with a much closer analysis of aggregate supply even for those researchers interested only in the closed economy.[22] Of course, this research will also have implications for open-economy models.

The aggregate supply relation is derived from the demand and supply of labour along with the aggregate production function. In these models capital stock is usually assumed to be constant, the demand for labour is derived by equating the marginal physical product of labour with the real wage and the supply of labour is derived from the income–leisure choice. To establish the level of employment an assumption must be made about how the labour market functions: in particular, whether it is continuously in equilibrium or whether there is some degree of wage stickiness and a disequilibrium labour market is assumed. However, once the level of employment is determined, then this determines the level of real income via the aggregate production function.

What has been outlined so far would be applicable to a closed-economy model. Of some significance in these models is the introduction of price expectations. The supply of labour, in particular, is assumed to be related to the expected real wage. It is then necessary to model price expectations explicitly, which would influence the aggregate supply curve. But when considering an open economy model, it is essential to distinguish not only these features but also the various types of prices. An open economy has two types of goods: domestically produced goods and imported goods. The general price index p_c (in logarithms) is a weighted average of home-produced goods prices p_h and imported goods denominated in domestic currency ($p_I = p_h^* - s$), i.e.

$$\begin{aligned} p_c &= \lambda p_h + (1 - \lambda)p_m \qquad 0 < \lambda < 1 \\ &= \lambda p_h + (1 - \lambda)(p_h^* - s) \end{aligned} \qquad (20.17)$$

On the demand side for labour the marginal physical product is equated with the real wage, where the price deflator is for home-produced goods. Assuming a simple Cobb–Douglas production function, we can express the demand for labour in logarithmic form as follows (see Gray 1976; Flood and Marion 1982; Marston 1982; Turnovsky 1983):

$$\ln v_1 + v_0 + (v_1 - 1)l^d = w - p_h \qquad 0 < v_1 < 1 \qquad (20.18)$$

On the supply of labour, however, the relevant real wage is the nominal wage deflated by the expected consumer price index. The supply curve can therefore be expressed in logarithms as

$$l^s = \gamma_0 + \gamma_1(w - p_c^e) \qquad \gamma_1 > 0 \qquad (20.19)$$

where the expected consumer price p_c^e is defined in a similar manner to equation (20.17).

Additional complications arise, however, if labour has contracted wages adjusted by an indexation factor. If the (logarithm) of the nominal wage w is assumed to be equal to the contracted wage $\bar{w}$ adjusted by an indexation factor f, i.e.

$$w = \bar{w} + f \qquad (20.20)$$

then it is possible to establish a variety of indexation models depending on assumptions about the labour market and about the different possible indexations.[23] For instance, if

$$f = k_1(p_h - p_h^e) + k_2[(p_h^* - s) - (p_h^* - s)^e] \qquad k_1, k_2 \geqslant 0 \quad (20.21)$$

and we assume that the contracted wage is set such as to equate the expected demand and supply of labour, then we obtain the following contracted wage:

$$\bar{w} = \frac{v_0 + \ln v_1 - \gamma_0(1 - v_1) + p_h^e + \gamma_1(1 - v_1)p^e}{1 + \gamma_1(1 - v_1)} \qquad (20.22)$$

Actual employment is then assumed to be determined by the demand for labour. Once this is determined, it can be substituted into the production function to determine the short-run aggregate supply curve, which is given by the following expression:[24]

$$y = d_0 + d_1 p_h + d_2 p_h^e + d_3(p_h^* - s)^e + d_4(p_h^* - s) \quad (20.23)$$

where $d_0 > 0$, $d_1 > 0$ and $d_4 < 0$, while d_2 and d_3 cannot readily be signed. However, on reasonable assumptions for the parameters in equations (20.17)–(20.21), d_2 is negative and d_3 is positive (see Shone 1989b). What it does show is that the short-run aggregate supply curve is positively sloped in (y, p_h) space. What about the long-run aggregate supply curve? In the long run, when price expectations are fully anticipated (so that $p_h^e = p_h$), the aggregate supply curve relating real income and home-produced goods prices p_h is also positively sloped. A rise in home goods prices will lead to a rise in the consumer price index, and this will shift the short-run aggregate supply curve upwards. However, the rise will not be as great as the increase in the home goods price because λ lies between zero and unity. Hence, the long-run supply curve must be positively sloped.[25]

Equation (20.23) also indicates that, if the price of imported goods increases, then this too will shift the short-run aggregate supply to the left (upwards). This in turn will raise the consumer price level, and hence will lead to an increase in wage claims as workers attempt to offset the decline in their real wage. The impact of this will depend on at least three things:

1 the degree of openness of the economy;
2 the type of wage indexation process in operation;
3 the assumption made regarding labour market clearing.

However, having made a distinction in the labour market between home-produced prices and the consumer price index, it is also important to be clear on the price deflator in the demand-for-money equation, since this will have an important bearing on macroeconomic adjustments in an open economy. In particular, the demand-for-money equation now takes the form

$$m - p_c = b_0 + b_1(y + p_h - p_c) - b_2 r \qquad (20.24)$$

indicating that the real money balance $m - p_c$ is a function of the nominal value of output $y + p_h$, deflated by the consumer price index p_c, and the nominal rate of interest r.

The implication that follows from this analysis is that changes in the exchange rate will influence aggregate supply because of the impact on the price of imported goods in home currency and hence on the consumer price index. The money market will also be affected by the differential impact on changes in home goods prices and the consumer price index. This is indicative of a series of difficulties which disappear in closed-economy models, but which must be taken into account in analysing the typical open economies which characterize the real world.

The model just developed is quite elaborate in terms of the workings of the labour market, but it does illustrate the recent research taking place in this area. It also illustrates how much more complex an open economy can be. Because of this, a number of authors have attempted to set out a simpler version of the model by simply stipulating that the (short-run) aggregate supply curve is a positive function of the terms of trade, which in logarithms is $(p_h - p_h^* + s)$ (see Moutos 1989). However, this approach leaves much of the adjustment mechanism in the labour market unexplained.

Although the model we have presented here is deterministic, it must be pointed out that almost all indexation models are presented in stochastic terms. In a closed-economy context the optimal degree of wage indexation depends on the characteristics of the stochastic disturbances. However, the models for open economies fall into three categories, which are illustrated in Figure 20.4.

In the first category, the exchange rate regime is treated as exogenous and consideration is directed to the optimal wage indexation, e.g. Flood and Marion

Figure 20.4

(1982) and Aizenman (1985). For instance, Flood and Marion showed that a small open economy with a fixed exchange rate should adopt a policy of complete wage indexation; however, an economy with flexible exchange rates should employ a policy of partial wage indexation. Aizenman, on the other hand, showed that under flexible exchange rates the optimal degree of wage indexation rises with the degree of openness (defined in terms of the relative size of the traded goods sector). In the second category it is the actual wage indexation which is treated as exogenous and consideration is then given to the optimal exchange rate regime (fixed or floating) (e.g. Sachs 1980; Bhandari 1982; Marston 1982). The third category attempts to consider optimal exchange rate intervention and the optimal wage indexation as a simultaneous process (e.g. Turnovsky 1983; Aizenman and Frenkel 1985).

What we see in this literature is a marriage of closed-economy sticky-price models with the literature on foreign exchange rate intervention. More recently, attention has also turned to the information content of real wages. Aizenman (1986) considers two types of labour market: one in which the labour market clears, and one which involves labour contracts. He then considers two shocks: a monetary shock which is not observed by firms and a firm-specific shock which is observed by firms. He concludes that, in a Walrasian auction labour market, the real wage gives information on the non-observable aggregate productivity shock. In the case of labour contracts, the information content of the real wage is insufficient for assessing the aggregate productivity shock. Aizenman therefore argues that nominal contracts inflict two types of costs: (a) a reduction in information to the decision-maker; (b) a reduction in the flexibility of wage adjustment to unanticipated shocks.

As long as there is no general agreement on whether to have flexible-price models or sticky-price models (or both), there will be two parallel streams of research since each can be considered in the context of an open economy.

20.6 FUTURE RESEARCH IN OPEN-ECONOMY MACROECONOMICS

A considerable amount of research is taking place in the area of OEM. Models attempting to explain the determination of the exchange rate are still inadequate, and much more will take place on this front. Although the emphasis will be on explaining the short-run exchange rate, since this has the greatest variation, there is still no agreement on its long-run determination. Some recent notions that the real exchange rate can be explained by microeconomic factors of resource allocation will reinforce the research efforts of those attempting to establish the microfoundations of macroeconomic relationships.

A major development in pure trade theory is the analysis of trade under increasing returns, which are considered a major independent source of trade. However, a world characterized by increasing returns is also characterized by imperfect competition. This has led to an integration between trade theory and industrial organization. This work is summarized by Helpman and Krugman (1985, 1989). There is also evidence of a desire to introduce imperfect competition into OEM models. Typical of such modelling is the work of Dixit (1984) and Helpman (1988), while Svensson and van Wijnbergen (1989) explicitly assume monopolistic competition in their sticky-price model which deals with the international transmission of monetary policy. This rejection of the Walrasion auctioneer and market clearing is also followed by van de Klundert and Peters (1988) who deal with the consequences of monopolistic competition and costly price adjustment in a dynamic macroeconomic model. They admit that their approach, along with many others, involves an *ad hoc* modelling of the labour market.

There have already been a number of attempts at a more thorough analysis of shocks. In attempting to compare different exchange rate regimes, or the possible impacts on the economy of exchange rate intervention, the nature of shocks in different markets is paramount. However, the source of shocks cannot be considered independently of other considerations, such as the form and extent of wage indexation. The analysis of shocks, and the related problem of stabilization, will (I am sure) give rise to a consideration of consistency between monetary rules, fiscal rules and exchange rate rules – an issue of policy co-ordination which will be discussed in Chapter 23.

Most of the early models dealing with exchange rate dynamics were largely for small open economies. Turnovsky (1986), however, considers the effects of monetary and fiscal policies in a symmetric two-country macroeconomic model. The model is basically the indexation model we presented in Section 20.5, but written out for two economies, with a clear link occurring in terms of the retail price index. The dynamics is specified in terms of a simple price-adjustment equation, i.e. a simple Phillips curve for each economy. Using a technique introduced by Aoki (1981), Turnovsky breaks down the dynamics of systems into averages and differences. Basically the averages describe aggregate IS and LM curves for the world economy. This rather new analytical technique could very well spawn a new literature in the area of OEM. Although symmetry is vital in Turnovsky's model, future models will need to relax this assumption, and when they do some new insights will no doubt occur.

To the extent that OEM is conducted within the context of rather elaborate models (usually more elaborate than CEM models), the difficulty of testing is raising particular problems for econometricians. The question which is paramount here is whether small manageable models are sufficient to analyse and test economic hypotheses or whether large simulation models are the inevitable way forward.

Although some economists have always believed that 'institutions matter', macroeconomists are only now beginning to take this more seriously, particularly in the area of labour economics and in attempts to endogenize government behaviour.

NOTES

1 The concept of the insular economy was used by McKinnon (1981) and later by Kenen (1985).
2 The most obvious are Barro and Fischer (1976) and Fischer (1988). They classify research into seven topics – none of which are concerned with the open economy. In particular, Fischer's (1988) survey has no mention of the exchange rate!
3 Macroeconomics has been, and still is, dominated by American academics. It was only when the US economy began to become more open, and the advice supplied by macroeconomists (which was based on CEM) became inadequate, that OEM was significantly studied.
4 It is therefore very surprising that Keynes, in his *General Theory*, chose to deal with a closed economy. The Keynesian open economy developed in the 1950s was a very crude form of open economy.
5 Although Blanchard and Fischer (1989: 537) admit that 'it is not possible to ignore international trade in goods and assets when analyzing the actual behavior of any economy', their *Lectures in Macroeconomics* deals almost exclusively with a closed economy!
6 The term 'open-economy macroeconomics' usually refers to both the IEM and the (full) OEM which typifies present-day analysis. 'Small open economies' was another popular representation of the type of economies under review (e.g. Prachowny 1975).
7 Although services were recognized as part of the current account balance, attention centred on the trade account – exports less imports of goods.
8 The models therefore assumed that each country specialized in the production of just one traded good.
9 The Marshall–Lerner condition is dealt with in most international monetary economics textbooks; but see Kenen (1985) and Rivera-Batiz and Rivera-Batiz (1985).
10 It is interesting to note that Mundell was Canadian and was very concerned with the Canadian open economy, and Swan was Australian and was equally concerned with the open-economy questions of Australia. Mundell considered the situation in terms of interest rate and govern-

ment spending as instruments, while Swan considered internal and external balance in terms of competitiveness (the real exchange rate) and expenditure. It was the introduction of capital mobility that made Mundell's analysis the more interesting.

11 Although internal balance was considered to be full employment with stable prices, domestic prices were usually assumed to be constant. The internal/external balance literature is much less applicable in a world of inflation (see Shone 1989a: Appendix 8.2).

12 The literature on this is quite extensive. For a review of the basics see Frenkel and Mussa (1985) and Kenen (1985); its overall significance today is reviewed by Frenkel and Razin (1987) and Shone (1989b).

13 However, there had been an early international application by Polak (1957).

14 Although it is often claimed that floating was discussed in the 1960s before the advent of generalized floating in 1973, it was not extensively discussed in the literature. There were, of course, some major advocates of floating, but the usual four citations (Friedman 1953; Meade 1955; Sohmen 1961; Johnson 1970) can hardly be classified as a major swing on the part of the economics profession. The decision to float was a political decision based on necessity and not on reasoned arguments in its favour.

15 The literature on the monetary approach to the balance of payments is quite voluminous. But for a recent discussion which places this in a historical perspective see Taylor (1990) and the reference cited therein.

16 See MacDonald (1988) and MacDonald and Taylor (1989) for a review of this literature.

17 We have written it slightly differently (a) to show how it compares with the Mundell–Fleming model and (b) to make clear what assumptions are being made.

18 The slope of the goods market phase line is given by $-[h_1 + (a_2/h_2)]/h_1$, while the slope of the asset market phase line is $1/h_2\theta$.

19 These models tend to be extensions of either the Dornbusch (1976) model or the Buiter and Miller (1981) model.

20 For a summary of the various portfolio models see MacDonald (1988).

21 A brief discussion of these models is given by Dornbusch (1989).

22 For some of these see Sapsford and Tzannatos (1990).

23 This particular indexation factor is taken from Turnovsky (1983). A slightly simpler one is used by Aizenman and Frenkel (1985).

24 Although the coefficients are not given in detail, they can be derived from all previous equations.

25 The only condition where this would not be true is if domestic goods prices and imported goods prices in home currency increased by the same percentage.

REFERENCES

Aizenman, J. (1985) 'Wage flexibility and openness', *Quarterly Journal of Economics* 400 (2): 539–50.

—— (1986) 'Stabilization policies and the information content of real wages', *Economica* 53 (210): 181–90.

Aizenman, J. and Frenkel, J. A. (1985) 'Optimal wage indexation, foreign exchange intervention, and monetary policy', *American Economic Review* 75: 402–23.

Alexander, S. S. (1952) 'Effects of a devaluation on a trade balance', *IMF Staff Papers* 2: 263–78.

—— (1959) 'Effects of a devaluation: a simplified synthesis of elasticities and absorption approaches', *American Economic Review* 49: 22–42.

Aoki, M. (1981) *Dynamic Analysis of Open Economies*, New York: Academic Press.

Barro, R. J. and Fischer, S. (1976) 'Recent developments in monetary theory', *Journal of Monetary Economics* 2 (2): 133–67.

Bhandari, J. S. (1982) *Exchange Rate Determination and Adjustment*, New York: Praeger.

Blanchard, O. J. and Fischer, S. (1989) *Lectures in Macroeconomics*, Cambridge, MA: MIT Press.

Buiter, W. H. and Miller, M. (1981) 'Monetary policy and international competitiveness: the problems of adjustment', *Oxford Economic Papers* 33: 143–75.

—— and —— (1982) 'Real exchange rate overshooting and the output cost of bringing down inflation', *European Economic Review* 18: 85–123.

Buiter, W. H. and Purvis, D. D. (1983) 'Oil disinflation and export competitiveness: a model of the "Dutch Disease" ', in J. Bhandari and B. H. Putnam (eds) *Economic Interdependence and Flexible Exchange Rates*, pp. 221–47, Cambridge: Cambridge University Press.

Clement, M. O., Pfister, R. L. and Rothwell, K. J. (1967) *Theoretical Issues in International Economics*, London: Constable.

Copeland, L. S. (1989) *Exchange Rates and International Finance*, Reading, MA: Addison-Wesley.

De Grauwe, P. (1983) *Macroeconomic Theory for the Open Economy*, London: Gower.

Dixit, A. (1984) 'International trade policy for oligopolistic industries', *Economic Journal (Supplement)* 94: 1–16.

Dornbusch, R. (1976) 'Expectations and exchange rate dynamics', *Journal of Political Economy* 84: 1161–76.

—— (1980) *Open Economy Macroeconomics*, New York: Basic Books.

—— (1989) 'Real exchange rates and macroeconomics: a selective survey', *Scandinavian Journal of Economics* 91 (2): 401–32.

Fischer, S. (1988) 'Recent developments in macroeconomics', *Economic Journal* 98 (391): 294–339.

Fleming, J. M. (1962) 'Domestic financial policies under fixed and under floating exchange rates', *IMF Staff Papers* (3): 369–80.

Flood, R. P. and Marion, N. P. (1982) 'The transmission of disturbances under alternative exchange-rate regimes with optimal indexing', *Quarterly Journal of Economics* 97: 43–66.

Frenkel, J. A. (1980) 'Exchange rates, prices and money, lessons from the 1920s', *American Economic Review, Papers and Proceedings* 70: 235–42.

Frenkel, J. A. and Mussa, M. L. (1985) 'Asset markets, exchange rates, and the balance of payments', in R. W. Jones and P. B. Kenen (eds) *Handbook of International Economics*, vol. 2, Amsterdam: North-Holland.

Frenkel, J. A. and Razin, A. (1987) 'The Mundell–Fleming model a quarter century later', *IMF Staff Papers* 34 (4): 567–620.

Frenkel, J. A., Gylfason, T. and Helliwell, J. F. (1980) 'A synthesis of monetary and Keynesian approaches to short run balance of payments theory', *Economic Journal* 90 (359): 582–92.

Friedman, M. (1953) 'The case for flexible exchange rates', in *Essays in Positive Economics*, pp. 157–203, Chicago, IL: University of Chicago Press.

Grassman, S. (1980) 'Long-term trends in openness of national economies', *Oxford Economic Papers* 32 (1): 123–33.

Gray, J. A. (1976) 'Wage indexation: a macroeconomic approach', *Journal of Monetary Economics* 2: 221–35.

Helpman, E. (1988) 'Macroeconomic effects of price controls: the role of market structure', *Economic Journal* 98 (391): 340–54.

Helpman, E. and Krugman, P. R. (1985) *Market Structure and Foreign Trade*, Cambridge, MA: MIT Press.

—— and —— (1989) *Trade Policy and Market Structure*, Cambridge, MA: MIT Press.

Hicks, J. R. (1937) 'Mr Keynes and the "Classics": a suggested interpretation', *Econometrica* 5: 147–59.

Johnson, H. G. (1970) 'The case for flexible exchange rates, 1969', *Federal Reserve Bank of St Louis Quarterly Review* 52: 12–24.

Kenen, P. B. (1985) 'Macroeconomic theory and policy: how the closed economy was opened', in R. W. Jones and P. B. Kenen (eds) *Handbook of International Economics*, vol. 2, Amsterdam: North-Holland.

van de Klundert, Th. and Peters, P. (1988) 'Price inertia in a macroeconomic model of monopolistic competition', *Economica* 55 (218): 203–17.

Krugman, P. (1989) *Exchange Rate Instability*, Cambridge, MA: MIT Press.

MacDonald, R. (1988) *Floating Exchange Rates. Theories and Evidence*, London: Unwin Hyman.

MacDonald, R. and Taylor, M. P. (eds) (1989) *Exchange Rates and Open Economy Macroeconomics*, Oxford: Basil Blackwell.

Marston, R. C. (1982) 'Wages, relative prices and the choice between fixed and flexible exchange rates', *Canadian Journal of Economics* 15 (1): 87–118.

McKinnon, R. I. (1981) 'The exchange rate and macroeconomic policy: changing postwar perceptions', *Journal of Economic Literature* 19 (2): 531–57.

Meade, J. E. (1951) *The Balance of Payments*, vol. 1, Oxford: Oxford University Press.

—— (1955) 'The case for variable exchange rates', *Three Bank Review* 27: 3–28.

—— (1978) 'The meaning of "internal" balance', *Economic Journal* 88: 423–35.

Morley, R. (1988) *The Macroeconomics of Open Economies*, London: Edward Elgar.

Moutos, T. (1989) 'Real wage rigidity, capital immobility and stabilisation policies', *Economic Notes* 3: 335–42.

Mundell, R. A. (1962) 'The appropriate use of monetary and fiscal policy for internal and external stability', *IMF Staff Papers* 9: 70–9.

—— (1963) 'Capital mobility and stabilization policy under fixed and flexible exchange rates', *Canadian Journal of Economics* 29: 475–85.

Niehans, J. (1984) *International Monetary Economics*, Oxford: Philip Allan.

Polak, J. J. (1957) 'Monetary analysis of income formulation and payments problems', *IMF Staff Papers* 6: 1–50.

Prachowny, M. F. J. (1975) *Small Open Economies*, Lexington, MA: Lexington Books.

Rivera-Batiz, F. L. and Rivera-Batiz, L. (1985) *International Finance and Open Economy Macroeconomics*, London: Macmillan.

Sachs, J. D. (1980) 'Wages, flexible exchange rates, and macroeconomic policy', *Quarterly Journal of Economics* 94: 731–47.

Sapsford, D. and Tzannatos, Z. (eds) (1990) *Current Issues in Labour Economics*, London: Macmillan.

Shone, R. (1979) 'Internal and external balance – problems of interpretation', *Journal of Economic Studies* 6 (2): 216–26.

—— (1989a) *Open Economy Macroeconomics*, Brighton: Harvester Wheatsheaf.

—— (1989b) 'Is there anything left of the Mundell-Fleming model?', Discussion paper 89/14, University of Stirling.

Sohmen, E. (1961) *Flexible Exchange Rates*, Chicago, IL: University of Chicago Press.

Stewart, M. (1983) *Controlling the Economic Future*, Brighton: Harvester Wheatsheaf.

Svensson, L. E. O. and van Wijnbergen, S. (1989) 'Excess capacity, monopolistic competition and international transmission of monetary disturbances', *Economic Journal* 99 (397): 785–805.

Swan, T. W. (1963) 'Longer run problems of the balance of payments', in H. W. Arndt and W. M. Corden (eds) *The Australian Economy*, Melbourne: F. W. Cheshire.

Taylor, M. P. (1990) *The Balance of Payments*, London: Edward Elgar.

Tinbergen, J. (1956) *Economic Policy: Principles and Design*, Amsterdam: North-Holland.

Tsiang, S. C. (1961) 'The role of money in trade-balance stability: synthesis of the elasticity and absorption approaches', *American Economic Review* 51: 912–36.

Turnovsky, S. J. (1983) 'Wage indexation and exchange market intervention in a small open economy', *Canadian Journal of Economics* 16 (4): 574–92.

—— (1986) 'Monetary and fiscal policy under perfect foresight: a symmetric two-country analysis', *Economica* 53 (210): 139–57.

21

ECONOMICS OF SOCIALISM

PAUL G. HARE

21.1 INTRODUCTION

The socialist economies that have operated for much of the post-war period – the USSR, the six Eastern European members of the Council for Mutual Economic Assistance (CMEA) together with Yugoslavia and Albania, China and a number of smaller developing countries – had very different political, institutional and economic management systems from those that characterize developed Western economies. Perhaps the most significant differences were indicated by the dominant position of the communist party in socialist political systems, by the prevalence of state ownership of most productive assets and by the use of plan targets rather than the market mechanism to determine what is produced, by whom it is produced and to whom it should be allocated. Of course there were differences between the socialist countries in the details of these arrangements, but the basic features were common to all. In this chapter I shall be dealing, for the most part, with what might be considered the typical socialist economy as it was before the collapse of communism in Eastern Europe in 1989 (Hawkes 1990; Rollo 1990), without worrying greatly about these individual differences.

Even before 1989, many of the socialist economies had undergone a process of evolution. In their early years, most experienced a period of extremely centralized and very detailed planning of almost all aspects of economic life. This version of the socialist economic model is commonly referred to as the traditional socialist economy, or the traditional model, and its main elements and characteristics are described in Section 21.2. After a time, the traditional model turned out to have some serious shortcomings, which gave rise to pressures for economic reform. In some countries these pressures led to efforts to improve the centralized management system, while elsewhere there were calls for decentralization and market-oriented reforms. More recently, the

I am grateful to the editors for helpful comments on the original version of this chapter.

communist governments in Eastern Europe have collapsed in the face of increasing economic difficulties and pressure for political liberalization; in some countries, this is already leading to the re-emergence of market-type economies (Hare 1990; Kaser 1990). These various stages and forms of reform are reviewed in Section 21.3.

Not surprisingly, the socialist economy has attracted the attention of more theoretically minded economists – from both East and West – seeking to explain and hence understand the system's *modus operandi*. Accordingly, against the background information provided in Sections 21.2 and 21.3, in Section 21.4 – the core of the chapter – some of the more interesting and illuminating theoretical approaches that have been devised for modelling the socialist economy are set out. Because of space limitations I have chosen to concentrate on just four topics: modelling the notion of decentralization, enterprise behaviour with rationed inputs, shortage and priorities, and planners' behaviour. These are sufficient to illustrate the types of analysis that have proved to be the most useful. Finally, the chapter ends with a short assessment of our present level of understanding of the functioning of a socialist economy.

21.2 THE TRADITIONAL SOCIALIST ECONOMY

The centrally planned socialist economy is typically managed as if it were a single large corporation with the crucial difference (compared with Western models of the large corporation) that the system is not operating in a competitive environment. In addition, most transactions between enterprises are not effected through markets. In the state-owned sector of the economy (which accounts for the overwhelming bulk of production in most cases), the organizational structure takes the form of an administrative hierarchy, as shown in Figure 21.1. The figure shows four levels in the structure. This is a convenient simplification for the present discussion, although in practice there are sometimes more levels (for example, trusts or associations intermediate between enterprises and ministries). The communist party has not been shown, although it thoroughly interpenetrates the economic apparatus and is dominant at the highest levels. For fuller accounts of the traditional planning system, with some analysis of its problems and alternative approaches to planning, see Nove (1977), Cave and Hare (1981), Smith (1983), Dyker (1985) and Ellman (1989).

The Council of Ministers formally approves plans and the associated measures to secure their implementation, although the functional bodies do most of the work of monitoring the economy, as well as elaborating plans for current production, investment and foreign trade. Although plans are formulated for five-year and one-year periods (and occasionally, in outline, for longer periods), it is the latter which forms the operational plan that guides economic activity

Figure 21.1 Organizational structure of a centrally planned economy.

in any given period. Once an annual plan has been agreed, it is developed into branch plans which are sent to the branch ministries (the third level in Figure 21.1), which in turn break them down further into plans for each individual enterprise.

Typically, enterprise plans are very detailed. They are likely to cover such items as output (by value, sometimes broken down to narrower product groups to give the so-called assortment plan), material inputs, working capital, investment, wages fund, deliveries to major customers (sometimes including export deliveries, especially under contracts with other socialist countries) and so on. Consequently, the principal responsibility of enterprise managers is the organization of production within the enterprise. They are further constrained by the central fixing of prices (usually according to some formula based on average cost, but with extremely long intervals between revisions) and by a financial regime under which above-plan profits are mostly transferred to the state budget, with only modest retentions to provide for bonuses and other enterprise-level discretionary spending. Bonuses themselves are typically contingent on plan fulfilment. However, since plans are so detailed, it has proved impossible to insist that every element be fulfilled prior to the award of bonuses to managers and workers. Instead, two or three of the plan indicators (usually gross output, increasing profits or sales) have come to be used as bonus-forming indicators, with understandable consequences in terms of distortions (avoidable inefficiencies) in enterprise activities.

Plans themselves are formulated through an iterative process involving information flows up and down the planning hierarchy. Based on preliminary reports on the economy for one year, the central planning office (in consultation with other functional bodies) prepares guideline figures for the next year (the plan year). These figures cover overall growth rates of output and the main components of demand, and may also identify some of the most important investment projects to be initiated during the year. After securing Council of Ministers approval – and it is here that political pressures can most easily be brought to bear on planning – the planning office works out a more detailed draft plan which is then broken down to ministry and then enterprise levels. At this point, enterprises have the chance of either proposing revised output targets – usually easier ones to improve the chances of plan fulfilment – or requesting a change in the inputs provisionally allocated to them – again, usually an increase, for the same reason. The resulting proposals are passed up the hierarchy and aggregated at each stage.

The planning office then elaborates a set of material balances for the economy, based on its original draft proposals and on the revised proposals from enterprises. Each material balance consists of a list of sources of supply for some item (for example, steel), including imports, set against a corresponding list of uses, including exports. Essentially, therefore, the balances can be regarded as the planned economy equivalent of the supply–demand equations that appear in Walrasian models of a market-type economy, with the difference that prices play at most a very minor role in the set of relevant arguments. If the original balances were consistent, it is virtually certain that the revised ones will not be: enterprises as a whole will typically be seeking to produce less output with more input. Consequently, adjustments are required to restore balance.

Occasionally, adjustment might be brought about by further consultation with enterprises, or by changing some prices. More usually, time constraints on the planning process and the normal ineffectiveness of price signals combine to locate the adjustment within the planning office and the other central agencies. It can take several forms: a reduction of input norms, with enterprises effectively being required to manage with fewer inputs; a reduction in low-priority uses of a product; an adjustment of imports or exports; or, in the case of small discrepancies, doing nothing and relying on the economy's inherent flexibility. The final plan sent down to enterprises will be based on these adjusted material balances. Since all the calculations are carried out at a fairly high level of aggregation, the resulting plan will inevitably contain numerous discrepancies and inconsistencies – mainly minor – by the time it reaches the enterprises. Hence in the process of implementation there has to be a good deal of accommodation and further adjustment to make the plan work. This, of course, is one reason why it would be impossible to use all the plan targets as bonus-forming indicators.[1]

In this approach to planning, foreign trade tends to be treated as a residual in the sense that the socialist economies import what they cannot or do not produce, and export what they must in order to maintain overall payments balance. Relatively little attention has been paid to comparative advantage, nor to effective international economic co-operation with the socialist bloc.[2] Since the currencies of socialist countries are not freely convertible, these countries operate two distinct trade balances with different trading practices. Trade with Western countries is conducted multilaterally and a single 'hard currency' trade balance is formed. Trade with the socialist bloc is mainly bilateral and, although settled in the so-called transferable rouble, a surplus with one country cannot usually be used to effect purchases in another; thus financial surpluses do not guarantee access to markets. Moreover, this is also true within an individual centrally planned economy; thus an enterprise with a surplus cannot purchase what it wants in domestic markets without authorization from a superior body. To this extent the economy is far from being wholly monetized. Not surprisingly, this situation is reflected in banking practices, whereby enterprises can secure access to credit or other funds only on the basis of the approved plan or with high-level authorization. Monetary policy merely shadows and supports the plan.

The only areas of the traditional socialist economy in which markets do have some significance are those which concern households, namely the labour market and the markets for consumer goods. Since the 1950s there has been little or no direction of labour in the socialist countries (except in China), and relatively little formal rationing of consumer goods. However, with centrally fixed wages and consumer prices, and plan-determined demand for labour and supply of consumer goods, households have certainly faced some constraints on their choices: hence there is queuing for some goods, excess supply of others and persistent imbalances in the labour market. Plans are gradually adjusted in the light of perceived disequilibria, but the process is quite slow and supply can lag continually behind demand.

21.3 REFORMING THE SOCIALIST ECONOMY

The economic system outlined in the previous section turned out to be an effective mechanism for mobilizing resources and promoting growth. In the 1950s and 1960s in particular, investment ratios in excess of 20 per cent of national income were maintained, large numbers of unproductive workers moved out of agriculture into industry where their productivity was far higher and growth rates of national product were commonly in the range of 5–10 per cent per annum. Consumption (and hence living standards) grew more slowly and erratically, and trade performance, especially in hard currency markets, was not very strong, but in the first post-war decades these shortcomings were not so evident.

Several factors combined to create pressure for economic reform in most of the socialist countries (in differing proportions in different countries) including the following:

gradual decline in the achieved growth rates;
inability to maintain high growth rates of factor inputs (both capital, and also labour moving out of agriculture);
poor and worsening trade performance, especially in hard currency markets;
persistent microeconomic inefficiencies, including pervasive shortage;
poor quality of production and poor innovative performance.

Taken together, these points constitute a comprehensive indictment of the traditional model, although they apply in very different degrees in different countries. Thus, it is important to realize that East Germany appeared to function tolerably well under the old system, while Hungary was already moving towards a comprehensive political reform before the dramatic events of 1989 in Eastern Europe. In between these extremes could be found the other socialist countries. In all cases, economic performance compared unfavourably with average OECD performance, and in the most serious instances (such as Poland) economic crisis reflected a fundamental failure of central planning.

Since the available literature on economic reforms in the socialist countries is extensive (Kornai 1986; Marer 1986; Hare 1987; Richet 1989), the present discussion can be brief. The most important distinction to emphasize concerns the types of reform pursued by various countries. Thus reforms can usually be classified as follows:

1 improving the centralized system;
2 market-oriented reforms, subdivided into goods and factor markets, international trade and institutional reforms;
3 political reforms.

Category 3 reforms were only being seriously considered in Poland and Hungary before 1989, but are now proceeding rapidly even in the USSR; a detailed analysis of this most recent tendency is beyond the scope of this chapter. Category 1 reforms are based on the view that the centralized model is essentially 'correct', but that it can be improved by a variety of minor reforms. Such reforms have included simplifying plans by reducing the number of compulsory plan indicators, price reform, the combination of enterprises into larger units (so that the planners have fewer units to deal with) and the computerization of certain plan calculations. The change from output to profit-based bonuses can be seen in the same light, since it involves no real change in the way the economy operates.

The countries which took a more radical approach, and introduced market-oriented reforms, clearly accepted that the centralized model was no longer adequate. However, although there is a well-established literature on such reforms by East European economists in particular (Kornai 1959; Brus 1972; Sik 1972), some of the theorizing about markets under socialism has been notably naive in two important respects. First, it has sometimes been completely uncritical in its general support for markets; second, it has frequently seriously underestimated the impediments to their effective operation stemming from elements of the traditional model not yet subject to reform.

In the product markets (including the markets for intermediate goods), radical reform involves abandoning the traditional annual plan imposed from on high (albeit based on some consultation with enterprises) and allowing enterprises both to determine their own outputs and to make their own arrangements to secure deliveries of the required inputs. When Hungary introduced such a reform in 1968 it was certainly considered astonishingly radical, especially as it was combined with price reform, a relaxation of central controls over prices and credit, the introduction of a proper system of profits taxation and various other measures. While these reforms certainly had important positive effects, they were not as dramatic or as sustained as the proponents of change had envisaged. This was basically because the maintenance of domestic monopoly positions in a wide range of markets prevented competition from working properly, and continuing restrictions on most imports protected domestic firms. Moreover, the lack of institutional change meant that in many respects the economy functioned in a similar way to before, with detailed financial controls of various kinds merely replacing the earlier plan instructions. Also, continuing shortage implied that goods still had to be rationed; instead of being done by the central authorities, however, the task was largely taken on by enterprises themselves, subject only to those central directives required to enforce national priorities (for example, to ensure that contracts to deliver exports to CMEA partners were fulfilled).

This mixed experience by Hungary eventually resulted in calls to take the reforms a stage further. This gradually began to happen in the 1980s. Thus the 1980s reforms included the small-scale introduction of a capital market to facilitate intersectoral transfers of capital: bonds could be purchased by both enterprises and the general public, and an increasing number of enterprises issued shares for sale to other enterprises. Similarly, the old rules making it almost impossible for workers to be hired or fired without central permission were relaxed to bring about a more efficient allocation of the workforce. These factor market reforms are undeniably important, but they proceeded quite slowly and cautiously until the end of the decade.

At the same time, a good deal of organizational change was going on. Thus the unified state bank was decomposed into a bank of issue and a network of commercial banks, industrial ministries were combined into a single ministry for industry and some larger enterprises were broken up into smaller units. In addition, constraints on the formation of new small firms (private, co-operative or state-owned) were relaxed (this is now the most dynamic sector in Hungary), and the larger firms are now, in theory, subject to the disciplines of a recently introduced bankruptcy law. These changes represented an enormous shift away from the traditional centralized model; however, although radical, such reforms may still be insufficient to improve economic performance significantly. Let us briefly consider why.

First, the central apparatus of tight political control over the economy, together with the higher levels of the bureaucracy, remained in place and was bound to fight for its survival. Among other things, such political factors substantially undermined the possible effectiveness of the bankruptcy provision, because most large enterprises knew perfectly well that they would not be allowed to fail. Second, continuing weaknesses in production reinforced the centre's tendency to restrict imports to protect domestic firms; the result was a vicious circle from which it was not easy to escape. Third, the liberalization of the economy was most marked for smaller economic units; once they grew beyond a quite modest size, they were subject to all the controls which restricted the larger production units. Moreover, the entry of new units remained just as problematic as it ever was where large-scale operations were concerned. One particularly serious effect of the protected position of domestic firms, especially when allied with shortage conditions in certain markets, was firms' lack of interest in innovation, especially product innovation. Even when firms did innovate, this was often motivated by saving particular inputs where there were shortages, which may not correspond at all to cost minimization with markets functioning normally. Overall, therefore, competition scarcely had a chance to be effective among the larger firms which produced the bulk of output. Increasingly, it came to be accepted that what was required was a series of political changes which would remove most microlevel economic decisions from the political sphere where they traditionally resided.

In Eastern Europe, at least, such change began to look very likely in 1989. Starting with the election of the region's first non-communist government in Poland (led by Solidarity) and agreements about multi-party elections in Hungary (following the renaming of, and subsequent split in, the communist party), it became clear that political change was suddenly a real possibility. The USSR under Gorbachev was no longer prepared to use force to suppress dissent in CMEA partner countries, and the domestic political elites themselves were less inclined to resort to force than previously (although by the end of 1989, its use was considered in East Germany and Czechoslovakia, and serious violence marked the fall of Ceaucescu in Romania). By mid-1990, elections to form new governments had been held in all of Eastern Europe (except Albania) and several countries were strongly committed to liberalization and marketization. This applied most obviously to Poland and Hungary, but Czechoslovakia was not far behind and East Germany was committed to reunification with West Germany.

For several countries, the result has been a complete change in the economic agenda. From seeking to improve planning in various ways, the agendas are increasingly dominated by such issues as privatization and property rights, tax reform and market liberalization, and macroeconomic policy.

21.4 MODELLING THE SOCIALIST ECONOMY

In this section we move on from the provision of general information about the functioning and transformation of socialist economies to examine some of the models that have been developed to describe and explain their behaviour. Four areas of analysis are reviewed here, starting with the question of decentralization.

Decentralization

The basic idea of decentralization is very simple. To illustrate it, consider an extremely simple economy where production is constrained by the function

$$F(x) = 0 \tag{21.1}$$

where $x = (x_1, \ldots, x_n)$ is a vector of inputs and outputs, and the economy seeks to maximize a social welfare function $U(x)$. There are two ways of achieving the optimum. The centralized method involves direct solution of the problem

$$\max U(x) \text{ subject to } F(x) = 0 \text{ and } x \in X \tag{21.2}$$

where the set X introduced in (21.2) merely constrains some or all of the relevant economic variables to satisfy certain reasonable conditions (for example, non-negativity, although the details are unimportant for present purposes). This, in effect, is what central planners are seeking to do when formulating a plan.

The decentralized method requires a price vector p to be fixed. Then if prices are set correctly, firms can be instructed to maximize profits, i.e. choose $x \in X$ to solve

$$\text{max } px \text{ subject to } F(x) = 0 \qquad (21.3)$$

Let the maximum profit be π^* and consider the problem

$$\text{max } U(x) \text{ subject to } px = \pi^* \qquad (21.4)$$

If the prices are chosen correctly (and a number of technical conditions, mainly to do with convexity, are also satisfied), then the solutions to (21.3) and (21.4) will be identical; moreover, both will be identical with the solution to (21.2). Properly chosen prices therefore achieve the decentralization of the plan; this is shown in Figure 21.2 for the two-sector case.

Why is this result of interest? Probably the main reason is that in practice the centralized problem (21.2) is too complex to solve directly. For this reason, central plans always contain errors, inconsistencies and so on even if they are formulated as carefully as possible. Hayek's critique of central planning drew attention to this problem, referring both to the usual dispersion of economically relevant information and to the high costs of collecting and processing it to construct a central plan. Hence, so the argument goes, decentralizing using prices might enable central objectives for the economy to be achieved more effectively. It is worth observing here that the formal result about decentraliz-

Figure 21.2 Decentralizing a plan using prices. E is the optimum plan (solution to (21.2)). The slope of AB (the tangent to $U(.)$ and $F(.)$ at E) defines the relative prices which achieve decentralization. At prices p, E is the solution to (21.3) and (21.4).

ation obtained above is really just a restatement of the familiar second fundamental theorem of welfare economics (Koopmans 1957; Lavoie 1985).

The first decentralized planning procedure – a sequence of information exchanges between centre and lower level units leading to the construction of a plan for the economy – was developed by Lange (1938). The centre proposed a price vector, firms were to respond by announcing their profit-maximizing production vectors and the centre would then adjust prices in the light of the estimated excess demands and supplies. After a number of iterations, this procedure was expected to converge to an equilibrium price vector which would achieve the desired decentralization.

Subsequent writers have developed other procedures based on different information flows (including, sometimes, horizontal flows). Malinvaud (1967) proposed a set of criteria for desirable procedures. These included the requirement that intermediate plan proposals should be feasible and that successive proposals should increase social welfare. However, some of the more interesting procedures, which correspond to the institutional practices of real socialist economies, do not satisfy these conditions (for example, Kornai and Lipták 1965).

Hurwicz (1973, 1986) has tried to formalize the whole approach of this literature into a general model of information flows between agents and an associated notion of informational decentralization. Unfortunately, this has not commanded general acceptance for a number of reasons. First, other aspects of decentralization such as the decentralization of authority have been considered important by some authors (for example, Heal 1973). Second, Hurwicz's approach is restrictive in that it does not allow various degrees of decentralization and seems to be inapplicable to complex organizational structures. (Kornai and Martos (1981) put forward an alternative formulation which recognizes several types of decentralized structure and so avoids this difficulty.) Third, real planning procedures only have time for two or three iterations, so that what is of interest is not the allocation to which the procedure ultimately converges, but its behaviour in the early stages. Only Marschak (1972) has analysed this aspect at all well; most writers have simply ignored the issue. Fourth, Montias (1976) in particular has noted that incomplete decentralization (for example, disaggregating certain controls in the presence of inappropriate prices) can lead to an allocation of resources inferior to the centralized allocation, and this raises a lot of questions about the whole package of measures that should be regarded as a decentralization. Finally, there is the ever present problem of incentives, especially at enterprise level. This is sufficiently important to merit a fuller discussion.

In the planning procedures that we have been reviewing it is generally assumed that all agents, including enterprises, will follow the rules of the game, including the requirement to supply correct information at each iteration.

However, there is no compelling reason for enterprises to do this, and every reason for them to submit information which, in their judgement, will eventually result in a plan more favourable to themselves. In this sense, planning procedures are not typically incentive compatible, and many agents can be expected to engage in strategic behaviour in the process of plan formulation. These game-theoretical aspects of planning are beyond the scope of the present chapter (but see Chapter 17 for an account of the relevant game theory). Clearly, they cast considerable doubt on the analysis of decentralization in planned economies as traditionally carried out.

Enterprise behaviour with rationed inputs

The socialist enterprise transforms inputs into outputs just like firms anywhere else. But its behaviour is likely to be different from that of its capitalist counterpart because the prevailing incentive system may lead to it to maximize some objective other than profits, because it faces rather different constraints and because the markets in which it trades do not operate in line with the familiar supply–demand model of elementary microeconomics. Since these differences can be formulated and combined in many different ways, it is apparent that many models of the socialist enterprise can be constructed. Accordingly, and simply to convey an idea of the type of model that has proved interesting to study, I restrict attention in this subsection to just one model, based on a formulation originally developed by Portes (1969).

The firm produces a single output y, using a vector of inputs $z = (z_1, z_2, \ldots, z_m)$, with the production function (which, as usual, is assumed to be well behaved)

$$y = f(z) \tag{21.5}$$

The firm receives a plan (y^P, z^P) as a result of exchanges of information with higher-level bodies. The output target y^P is a requirement to supply at least this quantity to specified customers, and any amount of output can be sold at the fixed official price p. The planned input allocation z^P means that the firm is permitted to purchase up to z_i^P of input i ($i = 1, 2, \ldots, m$) at the official price q_i. If the firm requires additional inputs, it can only obtain them at a cost exceeding the relevant q_i, reflecting the need to engage in unofficial, informal and possibly illegal transactions, and the costs of doing so. The average price paid for planned and above-plan inputs $q_i(z_i)$, $i = 1, 2, \ldots, m$, where $x_i = \max(0, z_i - z_i^P)$, is assumed to be an increasing function of the amount purchased, as shown in Figure 21.3. Of course, if it is physically impossible to obtain a particular input, $q_i(x_i)$ for that input is vertical; conversely, if there is no effective rationing, it is horizontal.

Suppose now that the firm seeks to maximize its profits as measured in

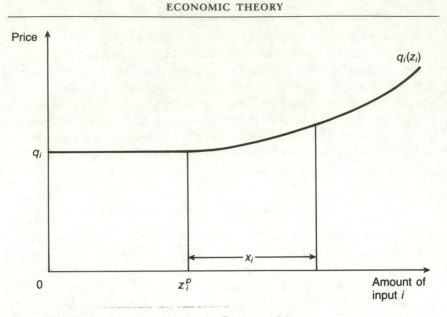

Figure 21.3 Enterprise input costs in the Portes model.

terms of the prices which it faces, perhaps because managerial bonuses are based on profits. Then the firm will maximize profits

$$\Pi = py - q(z)z \qquad (21.6)$$

subject to the production function (21.5). In general terms, it is perfectly possible to characterize the solution to this problem in the usual form of a set of marginal (first-order) conditions, and then to differentiate these to investigate comparative statics effects of variations in p, q and z^P. (As formulated, the output target y^P has no effect, although it would be easy to amend the model to allow for some impact on the solution.)

Rather than proceeding in this way, we focus on the special case of two inputs, so that the familiar isoquant map can be used. As Figure 21.4 shows, while isoquants are as usual, isocost lines are now curved and have discontinuous slopes at the boundaries of the four indicated quadrants, where the rationing regime shifts. Clearly, the effect of parameter changes depends on the location of the initial solution to (21.5) and (21.6). Thus if planning is slack and the optimal initial position lies in quadrant 1, then the analysis is the standard textbook one since the firm faces no additional constraints. However, if the initial solution is at E in quadrant 4, with the firm producing above plan ($y^* > y^P$) but using a different mix of inputs from the planned allocation, then it will respond to changes in p, q_1, q_2 and z_2^P but not in z_1^P. The responses are easy to calculate. As we would expect, in the presence of rationing, output and input responses are usually smaller than they would be

452

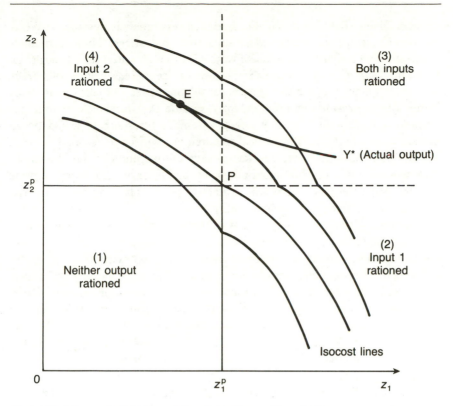

Figure 21.4 Input choices in a planned economy with rationing.

without it; the firm becomes less responsive to market signals when it faces restrictions on input supplies.

Shortage and priorities

From the early 1950s in Eastern Europe, and from much earlier in the USSR, shortage conditions have been both widespread and persistent. Shortage has occurred in the markets for intermediate goods as well as in the consumer goods market. It has also been evident in the markets for labour, capital (excess demand for investment resources) and foreign exchange. Such a phenomenon clearly demands some explanation, but until the present decade this was mainly couched in terms of overambitious planners, planners' errors or exogenous shocks. While the first of these had some validity for a time, the last two are not very convincing since they fail to explain why shortage should always arise.

Kornai (1980) located the analysis of shortage within a model of enterprise behaviour under socialism, in which soft budget constraints and enterprise quantity drives combined to reproduce shortage conditions throughout the economy. Household behaviour was modelled very much as in standard Western models, with hard budget constraints and fixed prices. Thus households respond to price signals in the usual way, even though enterprises typically do not. The result of both responses implies that price increases do not generally succeed in eliminating the shortage, because enterprises will take up any slack in the system provided by the adjustments made by households. Within this framework of analysis, the only effective remedy for shortage would be an economic reform sufficiently radical to force enterprises to respond to price signals. As indicated earlier, this was already the intention of the Hungarian reforms some years ago, but it had not succeeded prior to the political reforms of 1989–90; enterprises were still protected by the planning hierarchy and bankruptcy had not yet become a reality.

Somewhat different in emphasis was the approach of Portes and others developed around the same time. This alternative approach sought to model the shortage phenomena in socialist countries as the repressed inflation regime of a quantity-constrained macroeconomic model. Since the mid-1970s, models of this kind were developed by various macroeconomists (for example, Barro and Grossman 1976; Malinvaud 1977; Muellbauer and Portes 1978) and, at least in their aggregated forms, they admitted a small number of equilibrium states. These included the familiar Keynesian equilibrium as well as the repressed inflation equilibrium just referred to. The latter was characterized by the simultaneous occurrence of excess demand in both the goods market and the labour market. Moreover, in a socialist economy with centralized wage and price fixing, it was not unreasonable to suppose that inflation would indeed be suppressed and shortage would persist.

For its supporters, the Portes approach had the advantage that it did not postulate shortage as a maintained hypothesis, but was able to test for its presence. In addition, it had the interesting policy implication that shortage could be eliminated by suitable changes in the price structure; radical reform was not required. On the other hand, critics like Kornai argued with some force that the approach failed to reflect the special institutional features of socialist countries which made shortage endemic, notably the paternalism of the state which protected producers (although, interestingly, consumers were not protected to the same extent) and so allowed them to raise output even when making losses. The issue will not be resolved easily. (For a thorough survey of alternative approaches, see Davis and Charemza (1989).)

Whatever approach to the analysis of shortage is adopted, an aspect which has received little attention so far is the effect of the priority system. As Davis (1989) has emphasized, all socialist countries operate priority systems whereby some branches (or even individual enterprises) have higher priority than others in the allocation of resources. This can be for reasons connected with defence, export commitments to CMEA partners or general industrial policy. In some ways we can see the priority system, or preference system as it is called in Hungary, as a substitute for price signals in guiding resource allocation. When superimposed on general shortage, the system implies that certain branches will be relatively privileged and will not experience much if any shortage, while for others the extent of shortage will be much greater. Overall, the result of priorities is a degree of shortage that varies considerably across the economy.

In the long term, the most damaging effect of shortage is that firms need to pay little or no attention to marketing existing products, or to improving and developing their available range. Hence innovation, even when officially encouraged, is relatively sluggish and not always concentrated in areas which lead to real product and process improvements. Instead, much attention is devoted to ameliorating whatever the most serious current shortages happen to be, with little regard to costs.

Planners' behaviour and macroeconomic policy

For much of the post-war period, most macroeconomic analysis of Western economies treated policy formation in a very crude and simple way. In effect, policy-makers were supposed to choose instruments – to do with fiscal and monetary policy in the main – and the rest of the economy was expected to respond as if the chosen policies would continue forever. Expressed in these terms, it is apparent that this procedure assumes that economic agents, whether firms, households, financial institutions or whatever, are fairly unintelligent. However, since agents often have access to almost the same information about the economy as the government, and can, in principle, construct models of the economy in a very similar way, it should be possible for them to anticipate how government policy will change and to respond accordingly. Likewise, the government should be able to foresee such reactions and allow for them in its policy-making. This is one of the main lessons from the rational expectations literature in macroeconomics. As is by now well known, it sometimes implies that government policy is likely to be ineffective (see Chapter 10).

In a centrally planned economy we might expect there to be little or no role for macroeconomics, given the established framework of annual and five year plans. However, although the main instrument is basically a set of plan revisions rather than the Western market-type instruments of credit policy, tax rates and structure, exchange rate and government expenditure, macroeconomic policy does have an important part to play. The planners do respond to various macroeconomic indicators in reasonably predictable and systematic ways and, at least to a limited extent, enterprises and households can anticipate these reactions. Consequently, some of the lessons of the rational expectations approach also apply to the socialist economies.

Empirical work (Gács and Lackó 1973; Wolf 1985a, b) has shown how

455

planners were likely to react to unexpectedly favourable or unfavourable outcomes, whether these resulted from errors in the original plan formulation or
from random shocks of various kinds. For instance, in the smaller Eastern
European countries it was quite usual for a better than expected hard currency
trade balance in one year to be translated into higher investment levels in the
subsequent year or two, not least because the planners judge that the economy
can afford higher imports of machinery from hard currency countries.

Also, many of the planned economies experienced fairly regular investment
cycles (Bajt 1971; Bauer 1978). Of course, these were not generated by the
sorts of mechanism analysed in Western business cycle theory. Indeed, there
is considerable controversy as to the precise mechanism(s) that could be
involved (to the extent that, originally, the very existence or possibility of such
cycles under socialism was vigorously denied). Probably the most promising
approach is to relate these cycles to our earlier discussion of shortage. The
same state paternalism and enterprise quantity drive that contributed to the
generation and reproduction of shortage also allowed enterprises to promote
investment with scant regard for costs and without fear of bankruptcy in the
event of failure. Consequently, ministries faced constant pressure to approve
new investment projects, but at the same time the top levels of the system
lacked the information that would allow them to judge immediately whether
investment commitments were adequate or excessive. In practice, the most
effective signal that investment is excessive was a rapid extension of project
completion times and an accumulation of uncompleted investment well beyond
what the planners regarded as normal. At such times, the brakes were applied
sharply (mainly by stopping new projects for a while) and resources were
concentrated on completing some of the projects experiencing serious delays.
In several of the smaller East European countries (although not the USSR),
the result of this process was a cycle in overall investment spending, associated
with alternately faster and slower rates of increase in productive capacity;
interestingly, however, and in contrast with Western cycles, these socialist
phenomena were never accompanied by unemployment or by noticeable fluctuations in current production. Presumably, in a shortage economy, the per-
iodic cut-backs in investment merely resulted in fluctuations in the system's
overall degree of shortage about its normal state (to employ Kornai's useful
terminology). Alternatively, consumption goods production might adjust to
accommodate investment fluctuations in order to maintain an approximately
constant degree of shortage in the system. This could occur either as a result
of good planning or, as Kornai would probably argue, as a result of autonomous
behaviour by enterprises and households.

21.5 ASSESSMENT

What have we learnt from this overview of the economics of socialism? As far as practice is concerned, it is clear that the initial hopes and expectations (and ideologies) about the inherent economic superiority of socialism over capitalism have not proved to be justified. After some years of rapid growth (which in many cases can be explained as a period of post-war recovery and 'catching up'), centrally planned economies experienced economic slowdown domestically, poor results in world markets and persistent shortage in many domestic markets. As we saw, various types of economic reform were introduced, and at times these achieved temporary successes (as in Hungary after 1968). However, we can now see that the system of central planning, and the functioning of the socialist economy, cannot be transformed into a dynamic, technically and socially progressive system on the basis of the economic reforms that were introduced prior to 1990, not even the most radical ones. Too much of the old system remained intact, and the established political structures still facilitated the reassertion of traditional relationships.

On the analytical side, we have reviewed a number of models that have been or could be applied to the traditionally managed socialist countries. All of them, it seems, are of some interest and have contributed to our understanding of these economies. However, only the analysis of shortage comes at all close to capturing the really fundamental economic problem facing the socialist countries, and even this analysis has relatively little to say about remedies. Consequently, most of the available analysis does not take us far towards the elaboration of new economic solutions for these countries.

At this point, especially in view of the events of 1989 referred to above, it would be all too easy to conclude on a rather negative (and, from the standpoint of the market-type economies, excessively self-satisfied) note, by suggesting that the only proper course for the socialist economies would be an immediate return to capitalism. Leaving aside the immense political difficulties – both internal and external – of such a decision, this begs a number of questions.

1 If, for the moment, we interpret capitalism to refer to the use of markets and the development of a market orientation in the planned economies, what practical steps could existing planned economies take to achieve this transition?

2 How should property relations in the socialist economies be changed?

3 If, ultimately, a transition (back) to capitalism is envisaged, as is clearly the case in some countries, what sort of capitalism should it be? What mix of private and state activity would be appropriate? What sorts of social objectives can be achieved? What would a suitable regulatory framework look like?

4 How would the proposed economic transition interact with the political structure, and how could supportive political change come about? In the

case of the smaller socialist countries, what role could the USSR be expected to play?

5 How should international economic relations, such as collaboration and trade within the CMEA countries, the role of multinationals, the exchange rate and tariff/quota policy, be developed?

6 How should the new structures accommodate the less pleasant aspects of market economies such as unemployment, bankruptcy and major structural change?

As readers will appreciate, these are difficult and important questions which require a great deal of analysis. Most are already being discussed by economists in Eastern Europe, who are well aware of the high stakes being played for in their economies. Increasingly, we would also expect more of the work on socialist economies going on in the West to be devoted to such questions and issues (for some analysis of the transition in Eastern Europe, see *European Economy*, March 1990). At present, however, we still have a long way to go.

NOTES

1 Hayek long ago recognized the impossibility of constructing a perfect plan, both for computational and informational reasons, a situation which has not markedly changed despite impressive advances in our computing techniques. However, Hayek's arguments, and subsequent developments in the same spirit, have little to say against the necessarily imperfect central planning that we are discussing.

2 The Council for Mutual Economic Assistance (CMEA, or Comecon) has not proved an effective vehicle for promoting investment collaboration and most Eastern trade took place on the basis of bilateral deals between pairs of governments. From January 1991, CMEA was abandoned and Eastern European trade is now all conducted in hard currencies at world prices.

REFERENCES

Bajt, A. (1971) 'Investment cycles in European socialist economies', *Journal of Economic Literature* 9 (1): 53–63.

Barro, R. and Grossman, H. (1976) *Money, Employment and Inflation*, Cambridge: Cambridge University Press.

Bauer, T. (1978) *Tervgazdaság, Beruházás, Ciklusok (Planned Economy, Investment, Cycles)* Budapest: Közgazdasági és Jogi Könyvkiadó.

Brus, W. (1972) *The Market in a Socialist Economy*, London: Routledge & Kegan Paul.

Cave, M. and Hare, P. G. (1981) *Alternative Approaches to Economic Planning*, London: Macmillan.

Davis, C. (1989) 'Priority and the shortage model: the medical system in the socialist economy', in C. Davis and W. Charemza (eds) *Models of Disequilibrium and Shortage in Centrally Planned Economies*, London: Chapman and Hall.

Davis, C. and Charemza, W. (eds) (1989) *Models of Disequilibrium and Shortage in Centrally Planned Economies*, London: Chapman and Hall.

Dyker, D. A. (1985) *The Future of the Soviet Economic Planning System*, Beckenham: Croom Helm.

Ellman, M. (1989) *Socialist Planning*, 2nd edn, Cambridge: Cambridge University Press.

Gács, J. and Lackó, M. (1973) 'A study of planning behaviour on the national economic level', *Economics of Planning* 13 (1–2): 91–119.

Hare, P. G. (1987) 'Economic reform in Eastern Europe', *Journal of Economic Surveys* 1 (1): 25–58.

—— (1990) 'From central planning to market economy: some microeconomic issues', *Economic Journal* 100: 581–95.

Hawkes, N. (ed.) (1990) *Tearing Down the Curtain*, London: Hodder & Stoughton.

Heal, G. (1973) *The Theory of Economic Planning*, Amsterdam: North-Holland.

Hurwicz, L. (1973) 'The design of resource allocation mechanisms', *American Economic Review* 48: 1–30.

—— (1986) 'Incentive aspects of decentralization', in K. J. Arrow and M. D. Intriligator (eds) *Handbook of Mathematical Economics*, vol. 3, Amsterdam: North-Holland.

Kaser, M. (1990) 'The technology of decontrol: some macroeconomic issues', *Economic Journal* 100: 596–615.

Koopmans, T. C. (1957) *Three Essays on the State of Economic Science*, New York: McGraw-Hill.

Kornai, J. (1959) *Overcentralisation in Economic Administration*, Oxford: Oxford University Press.

—— (1980) *Economics of Shortage*, Amsterdam: North-Holland.

—— (1986) 'The Hungarian reform process', *Journal of Economic Literature* 24 (4): 1687–737.

Kornai, J. and Lipták, T. (1965) 'Two-level planning', *Econometrica* 33: 141–69.

Kornai, J. and Martos, B. (eds) (1981) *Non-price Control*, Budapest: Akadémiai Kiadó.

Lange, O. (1938) 'On the economic theory of socialism', in B. Lippincott (ed.) *On the Economic Theory of Socialism*, Minneapolis, MN: University of Minnesota Press.

Lavoie, D. (1985) *Rivalry and Central Planning*, Cambridge: Cambridge University Press.

Malinvaud, E. (1967) 'Decentralised procedures for planning', in E. Malinvaud and M. Bacharach (eds) *Activity Analysis in the Theory of Growth and Planning*, London: Macmillan.

—— (1977) *The Theory of Unemployment Reconsidered*, Oxford: Basil Blackwell.

Marer, P. (1986) 'Economic reform in Hungary: from central planning to regulated market', in *East European Economies: Slow Growth in the 1980s*, vol. 3, Washington, DC: US Government Printing Office.

Marschak, T. (1972) 'Computation in organisations: the comparison of price mechanisms and other adjustment processes', in C. B. McGuire and R. Radner (eds) *Decision and Organization*, Amsterdam: North-Holland.

Montias, J. (1976) *The Structure of Economic Systems*, New Haven, CT: Yale University Press.

Muellbauer, J. and Portes, R. (1978) 'Macroeconomic models with quantity rationing', *Economic Journal* 88: 788–821.

Nove, A. (1977) *The Soviet Economic System*, London: Allen & Unwin.

Portes, R. (1969) 'The enterprise under central planning', *Review of Economic Studies* 36: 197–212.

Richet, X. (1989) *The Hungarian Model: Markets and Planning in a Socialist Economy*, Cambridge: Cambridge University Press.

Rollo, J. M. C. (1990) *The New Eastern Europe: Western Responses*, London: RIIA/Pinter.

Sik, O. (1972) *The Bureaucratic Economy*, New York: IASP.

Smith, A. H. (1983) *The Planned Economies of Eastern Europe*, Beckenham: Croom Helm.

Wolf, T. A. (1985a) 'Economic stabilization in planned economies', *IMF Staff Papers* 32 (1): 78–131.

—— (1985b) 'Exchange rate systems and adjustment in planned economies', *IMF Staff Papers* 32 (2): 211–47.

22

THE LABOUR MARKET: UNEMPLOYMENT AND SEARCH THEORY

DAVID SAPSFORD

22.1 INTRODUCTION

Unemployment and search are two areas of economics which have each spawned a large, and still rapidly growing, literature. Inevitably, therefore, in this chapter we can do little more than introduce the reader to a selection of the major issues involved and advances in knowledge achieved in each of these important areas. We begin with a discussion of the nature and causes of unemployment, and in Section 22.3 we provide a brief discussion of the historical origins of the economics of search and present some simple models of labour market search. In Section 22.4 we explore the consequences of relaxing some of the restrictive assumptions on which the simple models of the previous section are based. In Section 22.5 the analysis of the preceding sections is used to investigate the contributions which search theory has made to improving our understanding of certain aspects of the unemployment problem, and a brief review of the relevant empirical evidence is provided. In the final section we offer some concluding remarks.

22.2 UNEMPLOYMENT

An unemployed worker is one who is unable to find employment under prevailing economic conditions. Although any factor of production can be unemployed, economists have devoted particular attention to the unemployment of labour, primarily because of the mental, and sometimes also physical, sufferings and hardships experienced by the unemployed and their dependants.

Unemployment is a topic which abounds with alternative definitions and classifications. For example, in one survey Hughes and Perlman (1984: 26) cite the existence in the literature of no fewer than seventy different types of unemployment! However, for the purpose of this chapter we shall focus our

461

attention, at least initially, on one of the most widely discussed classifications of unemployment to be found in the literature. This approach identifies the following four types of unemployment: frictional, seasonal, structural and cyclical (or demand deficient).

According to this classification a worker is said to be *frictionally unemployed* if he or she is temporarily unemployed between jobs. Frictional unemployment is that which results from workers moving between jobs; as long as people change jobs, and as long as it takes a non-zero time to move from one job to another, some positive amount of frictional unemployment will exist. Frictional unemployment may therefore be seen as a consequence of the short-run changes which constantly occur in a dynamic economy in response to changes in the patterns of the demand for and the supply of goods and services. In short, frictional unemployment arises because the supply of labour does not adjust instantaneously to changes in the pattern of labour demand, with the consequence that unemployed workers and unfilled vacancies exist side by side. *Structural unemployment* arises when workers find that their skills are not employable either because they have become technologically outdated or perhaps because there is no demand for them in the particular locality in which they live. The essential characteristic of structural unemployment is the existence of a mismatch between the skills (or locations) possessed by the unemployed on the one hand and those required by existing job vacancies on the other. *Seasonal unemployment* is that which arises as a consequence either of the lower levels of economic activity which occur in certain sectors of the economy at particular times of the year (for example, in the agricultural, building and tourist industries during the winter months) or of certain institutional characteristics of the labour market, most notably the existence of a particular school-leaving date or dates. Last in this fourfold classification is *cyclical* or demand-deficient unemployment which is seen as a consequence of the lack of aggregate demand which occurs during certain phases of the business cycle.

One attractive feature of the foregoing classification is that it directs attention quite clearly to the fact that different policy responses are required to 'cure' different sorts of unemployment. For example, while policies which bring about an increase in the level of aggregate demand may be prescribed as a cure for unemployment of the cyclical/demand-deficient variety (the so-called Keynesian cure), these will make little impact on either frictional or structural unemployment. Since the essential feature of structural unemployment is the existence of a mismatch between the attributes of workers (the supply side of the labour market) and the requirements of firms (the demand side), its cure lies in the implementation of various educational and retraining policies designed to match the skills of workers with the requirements of prospective employers. As we have seen, frictional unemployment (or as it is sometimes alternatively called, search unemployment) arises because the process of matching unfilled vacancies with unemployed workers is non-instantaneous. In consequence, it is often argued that the 'cure' for frictional unemployment (or more correctly the means of minimizing its extent) lies in the implementation of policies which succeed in improving the information flows which occur between the frictionally unemployed and employers with unfilled vacancies, provided that such policies do not bring about an offsetting increase in the number of workers leaving their existing jobs in search of new ones. As we shall see in the following sections, models of job search have shed considerable light on a whole range of issues, including the factors which determine the time that it takes a frictionally unemployed worker to find an acceptable job offer and, by the same token, the factors which determine the time that it takes employers to find suitable workers to fill their vacancies.

22.3 MODELLING SEARCH BEHAVIOUR

During the post-war period economists have devoted considerable attention to the analysis of markets characterized by imperfect information regarding trading opportunities. It has been argued that under such circumstances it is rational for the individual market participant to undertake an amount of market search, the objective of which is to obtain an improvement in the extent of his/her information or knowledge regarding the various alternatives which are available. For example, in the labour market context, individual workers will, in general, possess less than perfect information regarding available job opportunities, while individual employers will likewise be imperfectly informed regarding labour availability. Search theorists argue that, when confronted with such imperfect information, it is rational for both the worker and the employer to engage in some form of information gathering or search exercise. Clearly, both costs and benefits are involved in such search activity and, as we shall see, search theory considers the ways in which the rational individual searcher balances one against the other in the design of an optimal search strategy. Although in our own discussion of search we shall concentrate exclusively upon labour market search, it is important to realize that the principles involved apply equally and analogously to the case of consumer search for goods in the market when confronted with uncertainty regarding both price and quality.

It has long been recognized by economists that the problem of the selection by the individual agent of the optimal amount of search is essentially an aspect of the theory of investment (Pissarides 1985). However, formal models of the search process did not begin to appear until developments in both the theory of human capital and the theory of choice under uncertainty had progressed sufficiently far. Naturally, interest in search processes increased in the early 1960s with the emergence of the economics of information (Stigler 1961,

1962). The literature on search theory is extremely large (and still growing), and in order to provide insight into its main results we focus our attention in this section on a highly simplified model, the assumptions of which are gradually relaxed in Section 22.4.[1] To set the scene for what follows we begin our discussion with a consideration of the various costs and benefits involved in the search process.

Basic concepts

Consider the case of a worker who is looking for a job but has less than perfect information regarding the set of available job opportunities. For simplicity, we assume that all workers in the labour market in question are homogeneous and that the worker faces not a single market wage offer (as would be the case in simple models of the labour market which invariably unrealistically assume complete knowledge on the part of labour buyers and sellers)[2] but a variety of wage offers summarized by some known frequency distribution. More precisely, the wage offer is assumed to be a random drawing from some distribution of wage offers which has a known probability density function denoted by $f(.)$ and a cumulative distribution function $F(.)$. If we denote the wage offer by w it follows immediately that

$$\frac{\mathrm{d}F(w)}{\mathrm{d}w} = f(w)$$

For simplicity, we assume that all the characteristics of the jobs other than the wages are known and are identical across different jobs. Under this set-up uncertainty arises because, although the worker knows both the form and parameters of $F(.)$, he/she does not know which particular employer is offering which particular wage. Confronted with this situation the individual can begin to discover which firms are offering which wages by canvassing various firms – a phenomenon which is referred to as search (Stigler 1961: 213). In practice, a wide variety of alternative methods of searching out information regarding job offers exists (including visits to employment agencies, both state and private, browsing through newspapers and trade publications, enquiries through personal contacts and so forth), each of which can be used either individually or in combination with other methods. However, for the purposes of the current discussion we assume that the search process takes a form where the worker selects a firm at random and submits a job application.[3] Quite literally, we can think of a worker as selecting a firm at random (from the telephone directory perhaps) and then enquiring as to the magnitude of its wage offer via its personnel office.

If search were a costless activity we would expect the worker to carry on searching across different firms until he/she discovers the maximum wage on offer, regardless of the time it takes. In such a case, high-wage firms would be inundated with applications while low-wage firms would have none, and a 'law of one price' mechanism would operate, with high-wage firms lowering their offers and low-wage firms raising theirs until eventually all firms offer the same wage. Under such circumstances the wage offer distribution becomes degenerate, with the consequence that the problem of uncertainty regarding wage offers disappears, as does the problem of how best to search. Crucial to the theory of search is the assumption that each time a worker canvasses a potential employer he/she incurs a cost. The costs of search include not only such direct costs as the travel expenses incurred in visiting firms (to attend for interview perhaps) but also various opportunity costs (including leisure or earnings foregone during the time spent writing letters, filling in application forms, visiting firms and so on). For the purposes of the current discussion we make the usual assumption that search costs are known and fixed and take the form of some constant lump-sum expense, denoted by c, which is incurred each time an offer is sampled from the distribution (i.e. each time an approach is made to a firm) regardless of whether the offer is rejected or accepted.

Turning now to the benefits of search, it is clear that the more search that the worker undertakes the more likely it is that he/she will discover a high-wage firm. However, each additional unit of search undertaken imposes an additional cost c upon the worker, and it therefore follows that a rational worker will only continue searching as long as the marginal benefit of search exceeds its marginal cost. In order to derive the optimal amount of search it is simply necessary for the worker to continue searching up to the point where the marginal benefit of search equals its marginal cost. Given that information is imperfect, the worker is assumed to evaluate the expected benefit from search as the mean (or expected value) of the wage distribution $f(w)$:

$$E(w) = \int_0^\infty wf(w) \, dw \qquad (22.1)$$

Having sketched out the nature of the costs and benefits encountered in the search process, we now ask the question: according to what principles might the individual worker conduct his/her search? Two of the most commonly offered answers to this question are that before setting out on his/her search the individual worker decides on either (a) the number of firms to approach before calling off the search or (b) some minimum acceptable wage offer (the reservation wage) which is such that an offer will be accepted if it is greater than or equal to the reservation wage but rejected in favour of continued search if it falls short of the reservation wage. According to view (a) the individual worker follows the following search rule: canvass a sample of firms of a predetermined size, say n^*, and accept the largest wage offer from the n^* received if this constitutes an improvement over his/her present situation. However, according to view (b) the individual follows a sequential rule according to which he/she embarks on a search with a predetermined reservation wage in mind and continues searching until a wage offer greater than or equal to this is received.

Case (a), which was first considered by Stigler (1962), is referred to in the literature as the fixed (or optimal) sample size rule, while case (b) is termed the sequential decision rule.

Fixed sample size rule

Equation (22.1) gives the expected value of the benefit from search which can be thought of as representing the highest wage offer likely to be encountered after visiting one firm (i.e. undertaking one unit of search). It can be rewritten as

$$E(w) = E(\max w | x = 1) \qquad (22.2)$$

given that, with a sample of size 1, the only wage in the sample is the maximum. When deciding on the optimal number of firms to visit, the searcher must compare the expected benefits for samples of different sizes. Thus, for instance, setting $n = 2$ and assuming sampling with replacement, there are various pairs of wage offers which the searcher may expect to encounter. The probability associated with each of these offers, given the assumption of replacement, is simply the product of their respective individual probabilities. Taking the product of the larger of the two wages in each sample and the probability of that sample and integrating across all such samples, the searcher arrives at the expected maximum wage offer from samples of size 2, which is denoted by $E(\max w | x = 2)$.[4] Proceeding in the same manner for samples of size 3, 4 and so on[5] the individual is able to chart the maximum expected wage from all possible sample sizes. Clearly, as n increases, $E(\max w | n)$ approaches the highest wage available. The shape usually assumed for the $E(\max w | n)$ function against sample size n is plotted in Figure 22.1, which reveals that, although the expected benefits from search increase with the number of firms sampled, the additional expected return to increasing the number of sampled firms decreases with n, with the consequence that there are diminishing marginal returns to search.

In order to determine the optimal sample size, the individual worker equates the marginal expected benefit of search with its marginal cost. Since we have assumed that the unit costs of search are constant (at c per firm sampled), the cost associated with sampling n firms is simply cn, as indicated by the straight line of slope c passing through the origin in Figure 22.1. Since the marginal cost of search is c, while the expected marginal benefit is the gradient of the $E(\max w | n)$ function, we see that the optimum size of sample is n^* firms,

Figure 22.1 Fixed sample size rule.

which is simply the point at which the gradient of E(max $w|n$) equals c. Clearly, the optimal value of sample size maximizes the distance between the expected return and cost curves.

The preceding analysis therefore gives rise to the fixed sample size rule (or Stigler rule) for the conduct of search. According to this rule, prior to commencing job search the individual determines the optimal number n^* of firms to approach such that the expected marginal benefit of search is equal to its marginal cost. Having canvassed or applied to each of these n^* firms, the worker accepts the largest wage offer from the n^* received, provided that this exceeds the wage currently being earned (say $\bar{w}$). Notice that if the individual is already employed and engaging in 'on the job' search, then $\bar{w}$ is the wage in his/her existing employment, whereas in the case of an unemployed worker $\bar{w}$ can be taken to represent the level of unemployment and related benefits after due allowance for the non-monetary disbenefits and benefits associated with unemployment.

Despite its extreme simplicity, the fixed-size model of search has been found to yield a number of entirely reasonable predictions regarding individual search behaviour. In particular, the model predicts that, all other things being equal, an increase in the gradient of the total cost curve in Figure 22.1 results in a decrease in the optimal size of the sample of firms to be approached. In other words, the model predicts quite reasonably that as search costs rise (fall), the amount of search undertaken will fall (rise). Another possibility concerns a deterioration in wage offers. Such a deterioration will lead to a decrease in the value of E(max $w|n$) for each value of n and will therefore give rise to a downward shift in the E(max $w|n$) curve in Figure 22.1 which, all other things being equal, will result in a decrease in the optimal amount of search.

Despite the plausibility of this model's predictions and their robustness to variations in the assumptions, the plausibility of the underlying behaviour assumed in the model has been widely questioned. Specifically, while it is perhaps reasonable to argue that searchers set out with some notion of the maximum number of firms which it would be worthwhile to approach, it is probably true that in practice most of us would stop short of submitting this number of job applications if we came across a sufficiently high wage offer in our searches. This view is widely accepted in the literature, and it is to models of this complexion that we now turn.

Reservation wages and sequential search models

The basic idea of sequential decision rule, or reservation wage, models of job search is that the individual does not decide prior to commencing search on the number of searches to be undertaken, but instead decides upon some minimum acceptable wage offer termed the reservation wage. Accordingly, in such models the individual is assumed to evaluate the optimal value of the reservation wage prior to embarking on his/her search. If this exceeds the value of the wage $\bar{w}$ associated with that individual's current situation, search is undertaken and continues, no matter how long it takes, until a wage offer greater than or equal to the reservation wage is received. Once such an offer is received it is immediately accepted. In simple versions of such models it is frequently assumed that, having accepted this offer, the individual remains in employment for ever, in which case it is convenient to interpret the wage offer as the discounted present value of the lifetime earnings from the job in question.

Clearly, such models can be characterized in terms of the following stopping rule, where w denotes the current wage offer and w^* the individual's reservation wage:

$$\begin{aligned} &\text{if } w < w^* \text{ reject } w \text{ and keep on searching} \\ &\text{if } w \geq w^* \text{ accept wage offer } w \end{aligned} \tag{22.3}$$

Any search strategy taking this form is said to possess the reservation wage property.

Consider now the determination of the optimal value of the reservation wage. Assume, as in the preceding subsection, that the individual knows the distribution $f(w)$ of wage offers and that unit search costs are constant at c. Assume also that the individual searcher is risk neutral and seeks to maximize the expected net benefit of search. On the basis of these assumptions it can be shown that the optimal policy for the job searcher is to follow a stopping rule of form (22.3) and that the value of the reservation wage itself can be derived by setting the marginal cost of obtaining an additional job offer equal to the expected marginal return to one more offer.

To illustrate the simplest version of the sequential search model, we assume that the individual job-seeker ventures out each and every day in search of work. We also assume that each day he/she generates exactly one wage offer which he/she accepts or rejects according to rule (22.3); recall that days when he/she receives no offer are treated as cases where the sampled firm offers a zero wage. On the assumption that the searcher retains the highest job offer[6] the return from ceasing search after the nth day is given by

$$Y_n = \max(w_1, w_2, \ldots, w_n) - nc \qquad (22.4)$$

where w_t denotes the wage offer received on day $t (= 1, \ldots, n)$. The searcher's objective is to evaluate the reservation wage which maximizes the value of $E(Y_n)$. By (22.3), the first wage offer w_1 will only be accepted if $w_1 \geq w^*$. The expected return from the optimal policy is simply $E \max(w_1, w^*) - c$. Given that w^*, by definition, is the expected return from pursuing the optimal stopping rule we see that the optimal expected return from the optimal stopping rule satisfies

$$w^* = E \max(w_1, w^*) - c \qquad (22.5)$$

If we write $E \max(w_1, w^*)$ as

$$E \max(w_1, w^*) = w^* \int_0^{w^*} dF(w) + \int_{w^*}^{\infty} w \, dF(w)$$

$$= w^* \int_0^{w^*} dF(w) + w^* \int_{w^*}^{\infty} dF(w) + \int_{w^*}^{\infty} w \, dF(w)$$

$$- w^* \int_{w^*}^{\infty} dF(w)$$

$$= w^* + \int_{w^*}^{\infty} (w - w^*) \, dF(w)$$

it follows from (22.5) that

$$c = \int_{w^*}^{\infty} (w - w^*) \, dF(w) = H(w^*) \qquad (22.6)$$

where

$$H(\tilde{w}) \int_{w^*}^{\infty} (w - \tilde{w}) \, dF(w)$$

Expression (22.6) is an important result. By plotting the $H(\tilde{w})$ function, which is convex, non-negative and strictly decreasing, on a graph of search costs against wage offers we are able to read off the optimal value of the

Figure 22.2 The optimal reservation wage.

reservation wage (denoted by w^*) associated with a given level of unit search costs c.[7] It is immediately seen from Figure 22.2 that the lower the costs of search the higher is the optimal value of the reservation wage, and hence (see below) the longer is the duration of search. The economic interpretation of condition (22.6) is quite straightforward: namely the critical value w^* associated with the optimal stopping rule is selected so as to equate the marginal cost c of obtaining one more job offer with the expected marginal return $H(w^*)$ from one further observation. Notice also that in order to evaluate the optimal reservation wage w^* it is only necessary for the job searcher to behave in a myopic fashion, in the sense that he/she need only compare the return from accepting employment with the expected return from exactly one further unit of search.

Further insight into this simple sequential search model can be obtained by recognizing that the number of offers needed until w^* is exceeded is a random variable which has a geometric distribution. If we denote this random variable by N and the probability of receiving a wage offer greater than the reservation wage w^* by $p = 1 - F(w^*)$, it follows immediately that $\mathrm{pr}(N = k) = p(1 - p)^{k-1}$ for $k = 1, 2, \ldots$ and that the expected search duration is given by

$$E(N) = \frac{1}{p} = \frac{1}{1 - F(w^*)} \tag{22.7}$$

which indicates that the greater w^* is, the greater is the expected time spent searching.

Using this result we can write the expected gain from following the policy embodied in rule (22.3) as

$$V = \frac{-c}{1 - F(w^*)} + \int_{w^*}^{\infty} \frac{w \, dF(w)}{1 - F(w^*)} \qquad (22.8)$$

Given that the expected duration of search is $1/[1 - F(w^*)]$, the first term in expression (22.8) is simply the costs incurred in searching out an offer of at least w^*, while the second term is the conditional expected value of an offer given that it is at least w^*. Rearrangement of (22.8) gives

$$c = \int_{w^*}^{\infty} (w - v) \, dF(w)$$

which on comparison with expression (22.6) gives $v = w^*$, i.e. the total expected gain (net of search costs) from following the optimal strategy is precisely equal to the reservation wage w^*.

22.4 SOME EXTENSIONS

The two models described in Section 22.3 form the basis of the wide range of alternative and more advanced approaches to be found in the literature. To give the reader some insights into the range of alternatives we now explore the consequences of relaxing some of the restrictive assumptions on which these simple models were based.

Discounting

One obvious extension to the sequential search model arises if we introduce discounting. Although, as already mentioned, it is common in the literature to find the wage offer interpreted as some discounted present value of future wages, the model is easily extended to include discounting explicitly. In the simplest of expositions it is assumed that search costs are incurred and wage offers are received at the end of the period in question, so that the present value of some wage offer w is simply βw (where $\beta \equiv 1/(1 + r)$ denotes the discount factor and r is the 'appropriate' rate of discount) and the discounted cost of the first period's search is likewise βc. Writing $\beta[\text{E max}(w_1, w^*) - c]$ as the analogue of (22.4) and repeating the analysis we obtain

$$c = H(w^*) - rw^* \qquad (22.9)$$

as the analogous condition to (22.5) in the case with no discounting. Condition (22.9) shows that the reservation wage w^* is negatively related to the rate of discount r. Thus we now have the additional and entirely plausible prediction that the higher the discount rate is, the lower is the reservation wage and, using (22.7), the shorter is the duration of search.

471

Random job offers

So far we have assumed that the individual receives exactly one job offer in each period. This assumption can be relaxed in a variety of ways, and two specific versions of the case where the number of job offers received per period is a random variable are considered by Lippman and McCall (1976).

In the first case it is assumed that at most one offer is received each period. Letting q denote the probability of receiving no offer in a given period, we obtain, on the assumption that the search cost is incurred at the beginning of the period in question, the following analogue of (22.4) in the simple case already considered:

$$w^* = - \text{E}\left(\sum_{k=0}^{\tau} c\beta^{k-1} \right) + \text{E}(\beta^{\tau})[\text{E} \max(w_1, w^*)] \qquad (22.10)$$

Recognizing τ as a geometrically distributed random variable with parameter q and using $\text{E}(\beta^{\tau}) = q/(q + r)$, after some rearrangement we obtain the following expression which represents the generalization of (22.6):

$$c = \frac{q}{1 + r} H(w^*) - \frac{r}{1 + r} w^* \qquad (22.11)$$

Given the properties of the function $H(.)$ it follows from expression (22.11) that the reservation wage declines as the probability q of receiving a job offer decreases, i.e. when the chances of being offered a job decrease, the individual becomes less choosy.

In the second case considered by Lippman and McCall it is assumed that the number of offers received in a given period is a non-negative random variable with an expected value equal to unity. Although the proof is not presented here it is interesting to note that, in this case, it can be shown that the reservation wage will be lower than in the situation where exactly one offer is received in each period.

Non-constant reservation wages

The various versions of the sequential search model discussed so far have been based on the assumptions that the distribution of wage offers $f(w)$ is known with certainty and that the individual possesses an infinite time horizon. In each case the reservation wage was found to be invariant over time. Consequently, in such models, if an offer is refused once it will continue to be refused for all time. Accordingly, it is immaterial whether or not the job searcher is allowed the possibility of recalling previously received offers. However, the body of empirical evidence seems to suggest quite clearly that individuals' reservation wages do *not* remain constant with respect to the duration of unemployment as predicted by the models considered so far (e.g. Kiefer and Neumann 1979). Two main reasons for fluctuating reservation wages can be found in the literature. These are, first, the existence of a finite time horizon and, second, informational changes regarding the wage offer distribution. It is to these issues that we now turn, but it is clear that once we move away from the constant reservation wage idea the question of recall becomes of considerable importance.

Finite-horizon models

Consider now the case where the individual possesses a finite time horizon and assume, as before, a known distribution of wage offers. Assume also that recall is not permitted, so that any offer must be accepted immediately, otherwise it is lost. Let $V_n(w)$ be the maximum benefit (earnings) net of search costs which is attainable as viewed from a position n periods before the horizon date, which can conveniently be thought of as retirement. If discounting is ignored, it follows that

$$V_n(w) = \max\left[w, -c + \int_0^\infty V_{n-1}(x) f(x) \, dx\right] \qquad (22.12)$$

where the x denote future wage offers. The corresponding expression in the case of sampling with recall is

$$V_n(w) = \max\left[w, -c + \int_w^\infty V_{n-1}(x) f(x) \, dx\right] \qquad (22.12a)$$

The reservation wage in the no-recall case when n periods remain, which is denoted by w_n^*, is the value of w which equates the two terms on the right-hand side of expression (22.12), i.e.

$$w_n^* = -c + \int_0^\infty V_{n-1}(x) f(x) \, dx \qquad (22.13)$$

The individual's optimal search strategy, given that n periods remain, is therefore of the usual sort, namely to continue searching if $w < w_n^*$ and to stop searching and accept w if $w > w_n^*$. Expression (22.13) holds for $n \geqslant 1$. In the final period it pays the individual to accept any positive offer so that $w_0^* = 0$. Therefore given that $V_0(w) = w$ it follows that

$$w_1^* = -c \int_0^\infty x f(x) \, dx \geqslant w_0^*$$

and a straightforward induction argument (Hey 1979: 110) reveals that

$$w_n^* \geqslant w_{n-1}^* \qquad \text{for all } n \qquad (22.14)$$

Expression (22.14) reveals the important result that in this finite-horizon no-recall model the reservation wage is *not* constant. Instead, it is seen to decline (or more correctly not to increase) as the number of periods left before the horizon falls. In other words, we see that the introduction of a finite time horizon into the model results in the additional prediction that the individual's reservation wage falls as time passes and retirement approaches.

However, the analysis becomes considerably more complicated if we allow for the possibility of recall. Although this case is not discussed here, it is interesting to note that with recall it is not clear whether or not the reservation wage declines over time. Indeed, in some formulations the very existence of a reservation wage is thrown into doubt (for further discussion, see Lippman and McCall (1976: 168–71)).

Adaptive search

The second situation generating the reservation wage as a function of time, namely the case where the individual possesses imperfect knowledge regarding the distribution of wage offers $f(.)$, gives rise to what is termed adaptive search. The basic idea in such models is that each wage offer which the searcher receives provides some information with which he/she can update his/her assessment of the wage distribution and thereby recalculate the reservation wage. In such models, each wage offer not only represents an employment opportunity but also constitutes a piece of information which can be used to update the prior distribution of offers. In all the models so far considered the distribution of wage offers has been assumed to be known, and in consequence the reservation wage was found either to be constant or to decline through time. The incorporation of adaptive or learning mechanisms into search models is by no means a straightforward matter, although it is easy to see that such mechanisms give rise to the possibility that reservation wages may increase as search proceeds if, for instance, the searcher learns that his/her skills are more highly prized than he/she originally estimated. Although various schemes for updating the prior distribution are considered in the literature, the general flavour of these models can be illustrated by considering the simple case in which the searcher is assumed to update his prior distribution in Bayesian fashion, recalculate the reservation wage and then, in the light of this, decide whether to accept the wage or to continue searching. In this model there is assumed to be no recall and it is further assumed that, while the form of the wage offer distribution is known, one or more of its parameters are only known up to a prior probability distribution.

Assume that the searcher has only imperfect knowledge regarding the k

parameters $\gamma = (\gamma_1, \ldots, \gamma_k)$ of the wage offer distribution $\phi(w)$ and that he/she has a prior distribution $h(\gamma|\theta)$ over the unknown parameters summarizing all the information that he/she has about the moments of the wage distribution, where θ is a vector of parameters of the prior. As offers are received θ is revised in a Bayesian manner and a new value is computed as, say, $\theta' = T(\theta, w_1, w_2, \ldots, w_n)$. After each observation the prior distribution $h(\gamma|\theta)$ is revised, and then a decision is made regarding whether to accept the offer or to continue searching. Let $V_n(w, \theta)$ denote the maximum expected return when an offer of w has just been received, where θ incorporates the information contained in the offer w and a total of n further offers will be forthcoming. Now $V_0(w, \theta) = w$ and

$$V_n(w, \theta) = \max \left\{ w, -c + \int_0^\infty \int_0^\infty V_{n-1}[x, T(\theta, x)] \, \phi(x|\gamma) \, h(\gamma|\theta) \, \mathrm{d}x \, \mathrm{d}\gamma \right\}$$

(22.15)

If we let $Z_{n-1}(\theta)$ denote the second term on the right-hand side of this expression, we again see that the optimal search policy possesses the reservation wage property since it is of the following form: accept employment if $w \geqslant Z_{n-1}(\theta)$, but continue searching if $w < Z_{n-1}(\theta)$. Clearly, the precise pattern taken by reservation wages over time in this model depends on the way in which the various components of $Z_{n-1}(\theta)$ in (22.15) vary across time.

Employer search

Although our discussion has so far focused on job search by workers, it is of interest to notice that the same basic ideas have also been employed to model situations where employers search for workers to fill their vacancies. To illustrate the flavour of this branch of the literature we consider briefly what is perhaps the simplest model of sequential employer search. This model is exactly analogous to the simple case of worker sequential search considered in Section 22.3, except that while workers face a distribution of wage offers, employers searching for new employees face a distribution of marginal products. In the employer search literature it is generally recognized that, unlike wage rates which form a fairly clear signal to the job searcher, the productivities of job searchers are less easy for the searching employer to assess. Hence it is argued that the employer has an incentive to seek out information about the characteristics of job searchers which may be positively correlated with their productivity in the job in question, most obviously via their performance in aptitude tests, their previous educational achievements and so forth. The costs of such screening, including the opportunity cost of time, constitute employer search costs, and the following simple model of employer search corresponds to the simple job search model of Section 22.3, but with marginal products replacing wages.

For a given wage offer, let the employer's search cost be k (assumed constant) and the marginal product and the distribution of marginal products be m and $\phi(.)$ respectively. Repeating the analysis embodied in equations (22.4)–(22.6), we find that the optimal search strategy for the employer is one involving a reservation level of productivity:

accept applicant if $m \geqslant \eta^*$
reject if $m < \eta^*$

where the minimum acceptable or reservation productivity η^* is obtained as the solution of

$$k = \int_{\eta^*}^{\infty} (m - \eta^*) \, d\phi(m) = G(\eta^*)$$

which is analogous to expression (22.6) for the case of the employee.

22.5 EMPIRICAL EVIDENCE

Before proceeding to look at the empirical evidence it is useful to summarize the predictions of the basic model and the various extensions considered above. In the case of the model with fixed sample size we saw that prior to commencing search the individual decides on the optimal number of firms to approach such that the expected marginal benefit of search is equated to its marginal cost. Having applied to each of these firms, the searcher accepts the largest of the offers received. In contrast, the central feature of sequential models of job search is the reservation wage property. In the basic version of the sequential search model we saw that the optimal value of the individual's reservation wage, and the expected duration of his search, are inversely related to the magnitude of search costs. Thus the model predicts that, all other things being equal, the lower the cost of the search, the higher is the reservation wage and the longer is the expected duration of search. We also saw that in such models the reservation wage is negatively related to the discount rate and positively related to the probability of receiving a job offer in a given period. Finally, we saw how the incorporation of both finite horizons on the part of workers and imperfect information regarding the distribution of wage offers can result in reservation wages which vary as time passes.[8]

Search theory is exceedingly rich in theoretical predictions and in consequence has generated a large empirical literature concerned with testing such predictions. Within the confines of the present chapter we consider only the empirical literature relating to search and unemployment.[9] The marked increase in the levels of unemployment experienced in the United Kingdom, the United States and other industrialized countries during the 1970s and 1980s relative to the early 1960s had led many economists to explore the extent to which such increases can be explained in terms of job search behaviour.

The pool of unemployment workers is a *stock*, the size of which at any moment is determined by two factors: the rate of *flow* into unemployment and the *duration* of the unemployment spells experienced by individual workers. Subdivision of the United Kingdom's unemployment stock into its flow and duration components (Sapsford 1981; Metcalf and Richardson 1986) reveals that the rate of inflow into unemployment has remained remarkably stable (at almost 4 million per year) since the late 1960s, indicating that the increase in unemployment through the 1970s and 1980s is largely attributable to increases in the duration of unemployment spells. Naturally enough, economists faced with this increase in the duration of unemployment spells turned their attention to the theory of job search for an explanation. As we saw in (22.7), job search theory predicts that the expected duration of a period of search unemployment is simply

$$E(N) = \frac{1}{1 - F(w^*)}$$

which indicates that the greater is the value of the reservation wage w^*, the longer is the expected duration of search. Therefore expression (22.7) suggests that an explanation of why UK unemployment rose requires an understanding of the behaviour of reservation wages over the period in question.

Consider the case of an unemployed worker searching for a job and assume that the probability $q(n, h)$ that the individual searcher will receive n offers during a period of duration h has a Poisson distribution such that

$$q(n, h) = \exp(-\lambda h) \frac{(\lambda h)^n}{n!}$$

Then, given a constant reservation wage w^*, the probabilistic rate at which a worker escapes unemployment is given by

$$\phi = \lambda[1 - F(w^*)] \qquad (22.16)$$

which is simply the rate λ at which job offers arrive multiplied by the probability that a random offer is acceptable.[10] Alternatively we might adopt a probabilistic approach. If we allow the escape rate ϕ, the reservation wage and the probability $p(t)$ that a job offer is received at time t each to vary with time, we obtain

$$\phi(t) = p(t)[1 - F(w_t^*)] \qquad (22.17)$$

which implies that the probability of escaping unemployment at time t is the product of the probability of receiving a job offer and the probability that this offer is acceptable.

Expressions (22.17) forms the backbone of empirical work on the duration of spells of search unemployment. It illustrates that the probability of escaping unemployment is influenced by two sets of factors: first, those which affect the value of the reservation wage; second, those which affect the probability $p(t)$ of locating a vacancy. We have already explored the determinants of the reservation wage, and we now turn to those of $p(t)$. It is often argued (e.g. Bean *et al.* 1987) that the value of $p(t)$ will be determined primarily by demand conditions since it seems reasonable to argue that the probability of locating a vacancy will rise with the number of vacancies in existence. However, $p(t)$ will also depend on the intensity of search, since the more firms that the worker samples in any time period, the more likely it is that he/she will locate a vacancy. One particular issue which has attracted considerable attention in the empirical literature concerns the influence of unemployment (and related) benefits upon the extent of unemployment. Higher unemployment benefits are seen as reducing the cost of search, in terms of forgone earnings, and therefore (from Figure 22.2) as giving rise to an increase in the reservation wage which according to (22.17) and all other things being equal, results in a decline in the rate of escape from unemployment. The extent to which the rising unemployment levels observed during the 1970s and 1980s can be accounted for by the levels of state unemployment benefits or insurance is a question which has generated a large and sometimes highly charged debate. For example, Maki and Spindler (1975) and Minford (1983) concluded that the level of unemployment benefit exerted a large and significant effect on UK unemployment over the post-war period, while Benjamin and Kochin (1979) concluded that the increase in UK unemployment in the inter-war years was largely induced by the operation of the benefit system prevailing at the time. However, it is apparent that the results of such studies are highly sensitive to the particular assumptions adopted regarding both the form and magnitude of benefits actually received (Nickell 1984), and in a whole range of further studies (Cubbin and Foley 1977; Lancaster 1979; Nickell 1979a, b; Sawyer 1979; Junankar 1981) the effect of benefits on unemployment, although generally still significant, was found to be much less marked than in the studies previously cited. Such studies typically take the replacement ratio (i.e. the ratio of benefits received when unemployed to income earned when employed) as a measure of the extent of subsidy offered to search. In one of the most authoritative studies to date, Nickell (1979a) concluded that the duration of unemployment is significantly affected by the replacement ratio, with an estimated elasticity, defined in household terms, of between 0.6 and 1.0. Between 1964 and 1973 actual unemployment in the United Kingdom rose by 92 per cent, and Nickell's analysis suggested that only about one-seventh of this could be attributed to benefits. Atkinson *et al.* (1984) also found a weak positive association between benefits and unemployment and reported estimated elasticities for different subsamples which range from around 0.1 to less than 1.0. One further interesting feature of the latter studies is that the long-term unemployed (defined as those out of work for 26 weeks or more) seem to be much less sensitive to variations in the replacement ratio than those only recently unemployed. Disaggregation by age (Narendranathan *et al.* 1985) further suggests that the average duration of unemployment spells for young men is much more sensitive to their replacement ratio than is the case for older workers.[11]

22.6 CONCLUDING REMARKS

In this chapter we have been concerned with the theory of job search, a basic feature of which is that time spent searching for an acceptable job offer is seen as a productive activity – a form of investment on the part of the searching worker in improved future wages.

Indeed, it has been argued that, rather than adopting policies (such as cutting the real value of unemployment benefits) designed to reduce search unemployment, governments might do better to recognize that longer search can bring an externality gain from an improved match of people to jobs. As Sinclair (1987: 187) argues, if every worker accepts the first job offered, allocation in the labour market is likely to be less efficient than if workers and employers are more selective about accepting and making offers.

Although the material covered in this chapter has inevitably been limited, we have seen how the individual worker (or indeed employer), faced with imperfect information regarding the set of opportunities available to him/her, can formulate optimal search strategies in both the fixed-sample-size and sequential search cases. In the latter context, we explored the derivation of the optimal reservation wage and examined a variety of influences upon it. Search theory offers the economist a rich array of predictions, and a number of the most important of these have been discussed in this chapter.

NOTES

1 More detailed surveys of search theory are given by Lippman and McCall (1976), McKenna (1986, 1987) and Mortensen (1986) for example.

2 Stigler (1962), for example, cites as 'a tolerably pure estimator of the dispersion of wage offers to homogeneous labour' data relating to job offers received by Chicago business graduates which revealed a coefficient of variation of 7.9 per cent, which he notes is approximately equal to the coefficients revealed in national surveys of wage offers received by graduates.

3 The case where no offer is received can be treated as a zero-wage offer.

4 See McKenna (1989) for some illustrated calculations.

5 With obvious notation we can write

$$E(\max w|n = 2) = E[\max(w_i, w_j)|n = 2]$$

$$= \int_0^\infty \int_0^\infty \max(w_i, w_j) f(w_i) f(w_j) \, dw_i \, dw_j$$

where max (w_i, w_j) denotes whichever is the larger of the two wage offers w_i and w_j. Similarly
$$E(\max w|n = 3) = E[\max(w_i, w_j, w_k)|n = 3]$$

$$= \int_0^\infty \int_0^\infty \int_0^\infty \max(w_i, w_j, w_k) f(w_i) f(w_j) f(w_k) \, dw_i \, dw_j \, dw_k$$

and so on for larger values of n.

6 Given (22.3) it is clearly immaterial in the present context whether retention of the highest previous offer or retention of only the most recent one is assumed, since search continues until the reservation wage is exceeded. In more complex models, however, these assumptions do give alternative results (Lippman and McCall 1976).

7 In the context of the general expression $H(.)$, w and $\tilde{w}$ can be thought of as denoting the value of the wage offer and reservation wage respectively, recalling that the *optimal* value of $\tilde{w}$ is denoted by w^*.

8 An alternative explanation of a reservation wage which declines with the period of search arises if we allow the job searcher to be liquidity constrained, for example by his inability to borrow in the official credit market (Mortensen 1986; 859–61).

9 However, those interested in such further issues as the determination of quits, the extent of on-the-job search and the like can find useful surveys in both Mortensen (1986) and McKenna (1987).

10 In the case where the reservation wage varies with the duration of search, perhaps through the existence of a finite horizon, the distribution of completed spells of search is given by

$$\Omega(t) = 1 - \exp\left[-\int_0^t \phi(\tau) \, d\tau\right]$$

where $\phi(t) = \lambda[1 - F(w_t^*)]$. In the case where the reservation wage declines with search duration $\phi'(t) > 0$ and the escape rate is said to display positive time dependence.

11 Although we have considered only the influence of unemployment benefits, via search, on unemployment it is interesting to note that some recent evidence for the various member countries of the OECD (Bean *et al.* 1987) seems to suggest, at least as far as the United Kingdom is concerned, that the rise in unemployment observed through the 1970s and 1980s was in large part attributable to the influence of demand upon $p(t)$ in expression (22.17) rather than to the influence of the reservation wage via the term $1 - F(w_t^*)$.

REFERENCES

Atkinson, A., Gomulka, J., Micklewright, J. and Rau, N. (1984) 'Unemployment benefit, duration and incentives in Britain: how robust is the evidence?', *Journal of Public Economics* 23 (1): 3–26.

Bean, C., Layard, R. and Nickell, S. (1987) 'The rise in unemployment: a multi-country study', in C. Bean, R. Layard and S. Nickell (eds) *The Rise in Unemployment*, pp. 1–22, Oxford: Basil Blackwell. Also published in *Economica (Supplement)* 53 (1986): S1–S22.

Benjamin, D. and Kochin, L. (1979) 'Searching for an explanation of unemployment in inter-war Britain', *Journal of Political Economy* 89 (3): 441–78.

Cubbin, J. and Foley, K. (1977) 'The extent of benefit induced unemployment in Great Britain; some new evidence', *Oxford Economic Papers* 29 (1): 128–40.

Hey, J. (1979) *Uncertainty in Microeconomics*, Oxford: Martin Robertson.

Hughes, J. and Perlman, R. (1984) *The Economics of Unemployment*, Brighton: Harvester Wheatsheaf.

Junankar, P. (1981) 'An econometric analysis of unemployment in Great Britain, 1952–75', *Oxford Economic Papers* 33 (3): 387–400.

Kiefer, N. and Neumann, G. (1979) 'An empirical job search model with a test of the constant reservation wage hypothesis', *Journal of Political Economy* 87 (1): 69–82.

Lancaster, T. (1979) 'Econometric methods for the duration of unemployment', *Econometrica* 47 (4): 939–56.

Lippman, S. and McCall, J. (1976) 'The economics of job search: a survey, Parts I and II', *Economic Inquiry* 14 (2): 155–89; 14 (3): 347–68.

McKenna, C. (1986) 'Theories of individual search behaviour', *Bulletin of Economic Research* 38 (3): 189–207.

—— (1987) 'Models of search market equilibrium', in J. Hey and P. Lambert (eds) *Surveys in the Economics of Uncertainty*, pp. 110–23, Oxford: Basil Blackwell.

—— (1989) 'The theory of search in labour markets', in D. Sapsford and Z. Tzannatos (eds) *Current Issues in Labour Economics*, pp. 33–62, London: Macmillan.

Maki, D. and Spindler, Z. A. (1975) 'The effect of unemployment compensation on the rate of unemployment in Great Britain', *Oxford Economic Papers* 27 (3): 440–54.

Metcalf, D. and Richardson, R. (1986) 'Labour', in M. J. Artis (ed.) *The UK Economy: A Manual of Applied Economics*, 11th edn, pp. 266–332, London: Weidenfeld & Nicolson.

Minford, P. (1983) *Unemployment: Cause and Cure*, Oxford: Martin Robertson.

Mortensen, D. (1986) 'Job search and labor market analysis', in O. Ashenfelter and R. Layard (eds) *Handbook of Labor Economics*, vol. 2, pp. 849–919, Amsterdam: North-Holland.

Narendranathan, W., Nickell, S. and Stern, J. (1985) 'Unemployment benefit revisited', *Economic Journal* 95 (378): 307–29.

Nickell, S. (1979a) 'The effect of unemployment and related benefits on the duration of unemployment', *Economic Journal* 89 (353): 34–49.

—— (1979b) 'Estimating the probability of leaving unemployment', *Econometrica* 47 (5): 1249–66.

—— (1984) 'A review of *Unemployment: Cause and Cure* by P. Minford', *Economic Journal* 94 (376): 946–53.

Pissarides, C. (1985) 'Job search and the functioning of labour markets', in D. Carline, C. Pissarides, W. Siebert and P. Sloane (eds) *Labour Economics*, pp. 159–85, London: Longman.

Sapsford, D. (1981) *Labour Market Economics*, London: Allen & Unwin.

Sawyer, M. (1979) 'The effects of unemployment compensation on the rate of unemployment in Great Britain: a comment', *Oxford Economic Papers* 31 (1): 135–46.

Sinclair, P. (1987) *Unemployment: Economic Theory and Evidence*, Oxford: Basil Blackwell.

Stigler, G. (1961) 'The economics of information', *Journal of Political Economy* 69 (3): 213–25.

—— (1962) 'Information in the labor market', *Journal of Political Economy* 70 (5): 94–105.

23

THE INTERNATIONAL CO-ORDINATION OF MACROECONOMIC POLICY

DAVID CURRIE AND PAUL LEVINE

23.1 WHAT IS INTERNATIONAL POLICY CO-ORDINATION?

The aim of this chapter is to survey the state of knowledge on the question of international macroeconomic policy co-ordination, and to consider the direction in which current arrangements for such co-ordination are likely to develop. Academic interest in this area has grown dramatically over the past ten to fifteen years for a number of reasons. First and foremost, there is the recognition of the growing interdependence between the economies of nations arising from increased flows of trade, the internationalization of the financial sector and the growth of transnational production. Second, macroeconomists have developed a keener interest in a more systematic approach to policy issues *per se*. Finally, the introduction of game-theroretical concepts into open-economy macroeconomics has provided the profession with the necessary tools to pursue issues to do with international policy co-ordination. In this chapter we are concerned with the extensive and rapidly growing research literature on this subject, and also with questions of policy co-ordination in practice.

What is meant by international policy co-ordination? The report by the Group of Thirty (1988) on this issue defined it helpfully as the process whereby 'countries modify their economic policies in what is intended to be a mutually beneficial manner, taking account of international economic linkages'. In our context, what is at issue is the way in which governments may adjust their monetary, fiscal and exchange rates in view of the reciprocal impact of these policies on other countries. The definition refers to intention, not outcome; there is no presumption that co-ordination will be mutually beneficial, merely that it is intended to be so (otherwise governments would have no interest in co-ordination). The scope of the definition is broad, covering a range of forms of co-ordination from the ambitious to the limited. At the ambitious end is

This research was carried out under Economic and Social Research Council grant WB01250034.

the Bonn Summit of 1978, where the Group of Seven (G7) countries agreed to a comprehensive package deal (see Putnam and Bayne 1987; Holtham 1989).[1] At the more limited end, there is the multilateral surveillance process carried out by the International Monetary Fund (IMF) under the Bretton Woods fixed exchange rate system, and that more recently established by the G7 countries since the Plaza Accord of 1985. Surveillance of this kind may act to co-ordinate policies between countries, albeit in a partial and limited way. Third, the definition allows for forms of agreement that extend beyond issues of macroeconomic policy; it includes co-ordination agreements where macroecomonic policy adjustments are traded for adjustments in other spheres of policy. The Bonn Summit provides an example of this: Germany agreed to a policy of macroeconomic reflation in exchange for US agreement to raise oil taxes with a view to reducing US energy consumption and thereby G7 dependence on OPEC, while Japan agreed to measures to liberalize trade and open up its internal market (see Putnam and Bayne 1987).[2] At the current time, there is scope for macroeconomic policy adjustments to be linked to environmental or defence policies.

Following the Bonn Summit, the first half of the 1980s saw a period when governments were primarily concerned to 'put their own house in order', combating inflation by means of tight monetary policy. In this period, which saw a large and sustained appreciation of the dollar, international policy co-ordination was out of favour. But by 1985, concern over the substantial misalignment of the dollar led to renewed interest in macroeconomic co-ordination, particularly on the part of the United States. The Plaza Accord of September 1985 was to co-ordinate monetary policy actions to manage the steady decline of the dollar from its February 1988 peak. A series of G7 summits since then have reaffirmed co-operation over monetary policy. The most significant of these was the Louvre Accord, which agreed to 'cooperate closely to foster stability of exchange rates around current levels'. (For a review of this period, see Funabashi (1988).) This set in place a loose arrangement of unannounced exchange rate zones that has influenced policy since then, particularly amongst the G3 countries (the United States, Germany and Japan), despite particular episodes when these informal zones have been threatened by foreign exchange market pressure. This period of co-ordination may provide the basis for a move towards a more formalized system of monetary co-ordination based on exchange rate targeting (see Group of Thirty 1988), although many obstacles may impede that development (Currie et al. 1989).

These developments have given rise to a number of questions concerning macroeconomic policy co-ordination. Is co-ordination desirable in principle? Can co-operative agreements be sustained or are they vulnerable to reneging by one or more of the countries participating in the arrangement? How large are the co-ordination gains in practice? Does model uncertainty undermine the case for co-ordination? What is the scope for limited forms of co-operation such as agreements focusing on the exchange rate or on simple rules which assign monetary and fiscal policy to stabilizing specified target macroeconomic variables?

In the following, we survey the existing literature on macroeconomic policy co-ordination, and consider what answers can be provided to these questions. In Section 23.2, we set out the basic theoretical framework, derived from Hamada, for analysing the potential inefficiency of uncoordinated policy-making, using an illustrative model that we also draw on in later sections. In Section 23.3, we extend the analysis using the model to take account of issues of reputation and sustainability; the recent literature has demonstrated that in an interdependent world the benefits of reputation and co-ordination are interlinked. In Section 23.4 we review the empirical literature on measuring the gains from policy co-ordination. Then, in Section 23.5, we consider the distinction between discretionary and rule-based forms of co-ordination. We conclude in Section 23.6 by considering specific proposals for co-ordination in the G3 or G7 context.

One area that we neglect completely is the developing literature on north–south interactions and policy co-ordination (see Currie and Vines 1988). This is an important area, but one in which the emerging literature has yet to reach even tentative conclusions.

The field we have covered is a fast-moving one, where many issues remain the subject of active research. Inevitably, therefore, this survey is a snapshot. Reflecting this, we seek in the conclusion to point to research issues that would merit greater attention in future work.

23.2 THE INEFFICIENCY OF NON-COOPERATIVE POLICIES

We start by surveying the analytical literature dealing with international macroeconomic policy issues. In general terms the case for policy co-ordination arises because of policy spill-overs between countries, i.e. the fact that policy changes in one country have an impact on other countries. In the absence of spill-overs, there would be no need for co-ordination: each country can set its own policy without consideration for policy in the rest of the world. In the presence of spill-overs, uncoordinated decision-making by governments may well result in an inefficient outcome. A better outcome for all countires may well result if governments agree between themselves a mutually acceptable co-ordinated policy, taking account of the interdependences between them. However, as we note later, co-ordination need not necessarily lead to a better outcome: if policy-makers lack credibility, co-ordination may make matters worse, not better.

In practice, police spill-overs are pervasive, particularly as increased integration makes countries more open to influences from the rest of the world. Both monetary and fiscal policy in one country will influence other countries through trade flows, goods, prices, asset prices (including the exchange rate) and capital flows. These interdependences are appreciable in closely integrated economies such as the European Community, and they are significant, although smaller, even for the larger economies such as the G3 countries (see Bryant *et al.* 1989).

It is also important to note that co-ordination does not require any coincidence of objectives. Governments may have conflicting objectives, but still find it advantageous to co-ordinate. This it true more generally of co-operation in social life. Differences of objectives do not undermine the scope for co-operation; if they did, co-operation would be much less pervasive than it is in practice.

These points can be illustrated, together with the gains from co-ordination, by using an analysis based on Hamada's seminal articles on the gains from full co-operation and from partial co-operation in the form of internationally agreed 'rules of the game' (Hamada 1974, 1976, 1979, 1985). In this section, we examine Hamada's contribution using a simple two-country model which will also serve to demonstrate the more recent contributions to the literature discussed in the following sections.

Hamada adopts a stylized game-theoretical framework which others have subsequently followed. Each country or bloc is regarded as one entity of 'player' in an international macroeconomic policy game and each has a number of macroeconomic policy objectives such as targets for GDP, inflation and the current account balance. To achieve these objectives the government of each country has a small number of instruments, say one fiscal instrument and one monetary instrument. In order to assess policies each policy-maker adopts a welfare measure (or welfare loss function) which penalizes deviations of target variables and instruments from desired values.

In a two-country world, Hamada then examines how successful the countries would be if they co-operated in pursuit of their objectives. This requires countries to agree to co-ordinate their policies in an appropriate manner to minimize a joint welfare loss function. This joint welfare function is a weighted average of the two individual welfare functions, with the weight determined by relative bargaining power. (It should be noted that this does not require countries to share common objectives; indeed there is nothing to prevent the individual objectives of countries being totally at odds with one another.)

We use this framework in analysing our two-country model. The model is a symmetrical natural rate model. On the demand side the model is given by

$$y_t = a_1 e_t - a_2 r_t + a_3 y_t^* + a_4 g_t \tag{23.1}$$

$$y_t^* = -a_1 e_t - a_2 r_t^* + a_3 y_t + a_4 g_t^* \tag{23.2}$$

485

where y_t denotes output at time t, g_t is government expenditure, e_t is the real exchange rate measured so that a rise represents a depreciation for the first country and r_t is the expected real interest rate. Demand in country 1 is raised by a depreciation of its real exchange rate, a fall in the real interest rate, an increase in government expenditure and a rise in demand in country 2. Starred variables denote country 2. All variables except the interest rate are in logarithms and all are measured in deviation form about an equilibrium in which output is at its natural rate.

To complete the demand side of the model, we include money demand functions of the form

$$m_t = p_t + c_1 y_t - c_2(r_t + \pi_t^e) \tag{23.3}$$

$$m_t^* = p_t^* + c_1 y_t^* - c_2(r_t^* + \pi_t^{*e}) \tag{23.4}$$

where m is the logarithm of the nominal money supply, p is the logarithm of the price level and π_t^e denotes expectations of inflation π_t based on information available at the beginning of period t. Thus the real demand for money is assumed to depend on real income and the nominal rate of interest.

The supply side of the model is given by

$$y_t = -b_1 e_t - b_2 r_t + b_3(\pi_t - \pi_t^e) \tag{23.5}$$

$$y_t^* = b_1 e_t - b_2 r_t^* + b_3(\pi_t^* - \pi_t^{*e}) \tag{23.6}$$

Equations (23.5) and (23.6) are Lucas supply curves augmented with real exchange rate and real interest rate effects. The former arises in an open economy because an appreciation in real exchange rate drives a wedge between the producer and consumer real wage (see, for example, Artis and Currie 1981). An increase in the expected real interest rate reduces output because it depresses the desired level of capital stock, and hence reduces the equilibrium capital stock and equilibrium supply.

The model is completed by the uncovered interest rate parity condition which, in terms of real exchange rate and the expected real interest rate, implies that

$$e_t = r_t^* - r_t + e_{t+1,t}^e \tag{23.7}$$

where $e_{t+1,t}^e$ denotes expectations of e_{t+1} formed at time t.

For the first policy-maker we assume an intertemporal welfare loss function, defined in terms of deviations of output and inflation from their desired levels, at time t of the form

$$W_t = \frac{1}{2} \sum_{i=0}^{1} \lambda^i [(y_{t+i} - \hat{y})^2 + a\pi_{t+i}^2] \qquad 0 < \lambda \leqslant 1 \tag{23.8}$$

with a similar expression with starred variables for country 2. λ is a discount factor which is assumed to be the same for both countries. The quadratic function penalizes non-zero inflation and output deviations around a target y.

In this model, policy effects may come from changes in the money supply or fiscal policy. In analysing the model, it is a useful simplification to focus on the rate of inflation as the main indicator of the thrust of monetary policy, since this permits us to ignore the money demand relationships (23.3) and (23.4). Since a given rate of inflation π is associated with a particular path for the monetary supply, this is not misleading. Moreover, the empirical stability of money demand relationships, especially in the United States and the United Kingdom, suggests that this may well be a more helpful way to think of the conduct of policy.

For reasons of exposition we start by considering the model under adaptive inflation expectations, so that each country exhibits a short-run inflation–output trade-off. Expansionary monetary policy may therefore reduce the real rate of interest and move the economy temporarily to a higher level of output, but with higher associated inflation. The lower real interest rate will lead to a fall in the real exchange rate because of capital outflows. This in turn will add to the wedge between producer and consumer prices, and will reduce the short-run output gains. Thus, because of the effects on the exchange rate, monetary expansion has a smaller output benefit domestically and a larger inflationary consequence.

Now consider the spill-over effects of policy from one country to another. Monetary expansion in country 2 expands output, and therefore raises demand for that output of country 1. In addition, the exchange rate of country 2 falls, so that country 1 enjoys an improvement in the terms of trade. This increase in the real exchange rate of country 1 improves its inflation–output trade-off by the converse of the mechanism that worsens that of country 2. Country 1 can therefore enjoy a non-inflationary increase in output. Therefore the spill-over from policy changes in one country onto the other is positive.

These results are shown schematically in terms of the Hamada diagram in Figure 23.1. This illustrates the two-country case assumed in our model, but the argument generalizes in a straightforward way to many countries. We represent the policy instrument of country 1, in this case taken to be π, on the vertical axis and the policy instrument π^* of country 2 on the horizontal axis. The objective function of country 1 defines a set of indifference curves, connecting points of equal welfare, as perceived by country 1. In the absence of spill-overs, these indifference curves would be vertical lines, with the welfare level defined uniquely by the instrument setting π of country 1. However, with spill-overs, the instrument setting π^* of country 2 influences the welfare of country 1. As a consequence, the indifference curves become ellipses around the bliss point B_1 (or point of highest welfare) of country 1. Similar elliptical

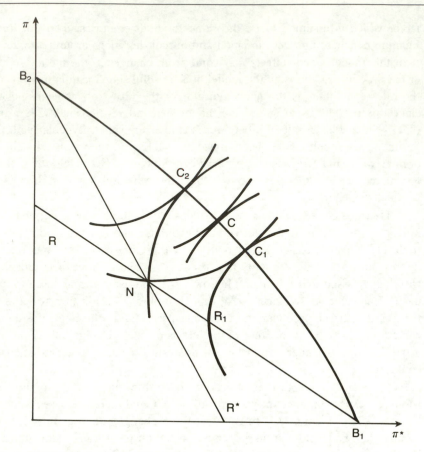

Figure 23.1 Hamada diagram for monetary policy.

indifference curves map out points of equal welfare around the bliss point B_2 of country 2.

Efficient policies are those for which the indifference maps of the two countries are tangential. These are represented by the contract curve joining B_1 and B_2. These policies are Pareto efficient, in the sense that one country's welfare can rise only if the other country's welfare falls.

Unco-ordinated decision-making is not likely to lead to policies on the efficient contract curve. This can be seen as follows from Figure 23.1. In the absence of co-ordination, country 1 will treat country 2's policy as given when deciding upon its own policy. For any setting π^* it will therefore choose R_1 to maximize its welfare. Thus it chooses π to give the point of tangency between the indifference curve and the vertical line corresponding to π^*. Varying π^* then traces out the reaction function R of country 1 connecting the horizontal points on its indifference curves.

The reaction function R* of country 2 can be defined similarly by depicting the optimal choice of π^* for given π. R* connects the points where the indifference curves of country 1 are vertical.

The outcome of uncoordinated decision-making is the Nash point N given by the intersection of the two reaction functions. At this Nash outcome, both countries are doing the best they can given the policies of the other country. However, the outcome is inefficient. The Nash point is Pareto inferior to at least a subset C_1C_2 of co-ordinated policies lying on the contract curve.

This Hamada diagram illustrates neatly the potential inefficiency of uncoordinated decision-making. By treating the other country's (or countries') policy actions as given, governments carry out policies that, in the aggregate, are undesirable. A more efficient outcome can be obtained by agreeing jointly on a policy in a co-operative manner.

In our model, this inefficiency arises from the incentive for each government to adopt a tighter monetary policy than is optimal. This is because a tighter policy appears to give the benefit of a higher real exchange rate, and a better inflation–output trade-off. In fact the benefit is not realized, since both countries adopt an overtight monetary stance, and the effect on the exchange rate cancels. However, a country that unilaterally relaxes monetary policy will suffer a fall in the real exchange rate, so that in the absence of co-ordination there is no incentive to relax monetary policy.

So far, we have focused on the conduct of monetary policy. However, a similar policy game arises for fiscal policy. A fiscal expansion in country 1 will expand demand, and hence output, at the same time as it drives up real interest rates. From (23.5) the rise in real interest rates will damage the supply side of the economy by discouraging capital accumulation. However, it will also cause an exchange rate appreciation, with offsetting favourable supply-side effects. The supply-side effects on country 2, by contrast, will be reinforcing and negative: country 2 will experience both a fall in its real exchange rate and a rise in real interest rates, both of which will reduce supply. For fiscal policy, therefore, the spill-over effects from one country to the other will be negative. Thus countries will have an incentive to run overexpansionary fiscal policies, and in the absence of co-ordination real interest rates will be higher than optimal, with consequent damage to the supply side. This case is illustrated in Figure 23.2: the different slope of the fiscal policy reaction functions relative to Figure 23.1 reflects the negative spill-over effects.

Combining the monetary and fiscal policy games leads to the conclusion that uncoordinated policy-making may have a bias towards overexpansionary fiscal policy and tight monetary policy, resulting in unduly high real interest rates.

The Hamada diagram illustrates the point that the case for co-ordination depends on policy spill-overs. In the absence of spill-overs, the bliss point for

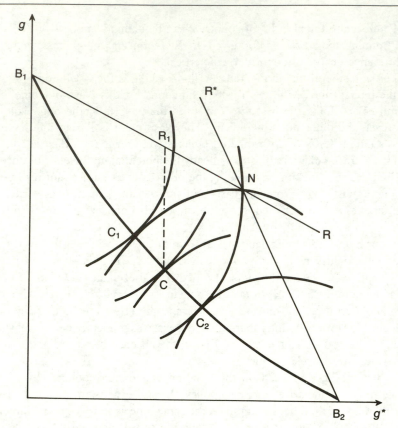

Figure 23.2 Hamada diagram for fiscal policy.

each country becomes a line (vertical for country 1 and horizontal for country 2), so that the optimal policy setting for one country is independent of that for the other. In this case, both countries can obtain their optimal welfare setting, and uncoordinated policy-making is not inefficient. However, this is a special and rather unlikely case, since policy spill-overs are prevalent. In particular, in our model, the key spill-over arises on the supply side from the impact of the real exchange rate on the inflation–output trade-off.

The Hamada diagram also shows that co-ordination of policy does not require agreement over objectives by governments. The objectives of governments can be quite different, and yet co-ordination of policy can be desirable. The bliss points of the two countries differ, so that there is an intrinsic policy conflict. None the less, this conflict is best dealt with by co-operation, so that policies put the economy on the efficient contract curve C_1C_2. The precise point on C_1C_2 that is chosen will depend on the process of bargaining that arrives at the agreed co-ordinated policy.

490

23.3 PRIVATE SECTOR EXPECTATIONS AND THE SUSTAINABILITY OF CO-ORDINATION

It is important to note that the co-ordinated outcome suffers from the problem of free-riding or reneging. In terms of Figure 23.2, if country 1 thinks that country 2 will continue with the agreed policy at C, say, then it pays country 1 to renege to point R_1 on its reaction function R. This will be all the easier if it is difficult to monitor policy actions, so that country 1 can argue with some plausibility that it is adhering to the agreed policy bargain while it is simultaneously reneging. Moreover, the incentive to renege may be stronger for co-ordinated policies between many countries, since the non-reneging countries may well have some incentive to continue with the agreed policy amongst themselves even though one of their number has reneged. Against this, appropriate forms of credible retaliation or threat can help to avoid reneging. Thus, for example, in the case of two countries, if each country states that it will revert to the Nash uncoordinated policy if the other country reneges, this may well be sufficient to sustain the co-ordinated policy.

This last point focuses attention on the issue of the sustainability of co-ordinated policies. However, the question of sustainability of policies has wider ramifications that touch on the issues of time inconsistency and reputation in policy. These issues arise because of the presence of an intelligent forward-looking private sector, so that, to be sustainable, policies must carry credibility with this sector. So far, we have ignored expectations in our model. We now examine their effects.

We start by noting that forward-looking behaviour by the private sector may enlarge the range of policies available to the government. To see this, consider the example of a government that wishes to reduce inflation by tightening monetary policy (by raising short-term interest rates, for example). In the absence of forward-looking expectations, such a tightening will only begin to reduce inflation when the policy is enacted (whether through its effect on aggregate demand or, in the context of an open economy, by inducing an appreciation of the exchange rate). But with forward-looking expectations, the announcement of a future tightening of monetary policy is sufficient to reduce inflation if the announcement is believed (although the reduction may be smaller in magnitude). The expectation of a tighter monetary policy in the future will immediately raise longer-term real interest rates, thereby dampening aggregate demand. The interest rate increase will lead to an appreciation of the exchange rate, with consequences for the behaviour of domestic prices and wages. Thus the announcement of tight money in the future, if it is believed, will act to reduce inflationary pressures now. One example of such announcement effects is provided in the UK medium-term financial strategy (MTFS). In announcing a gradual phased reduction of monetary growth over a five-year horizon, the MTFS combined announcement of future tightening of monetary policy with an immediate change in policy.

The literature has directed considerable attention to whether such announcements of future policy action are generally credible. The standard answer has been in the negative. It is argued that there will be an incentive for governments to renege on the announcement when the time comes to carry it out. Thus the policies are said to time inconsistent (Kydland and Prescott 1977). In the above example, if the announcement of tight monetary policy in the future does indeed bring down the rate of inflation, then the incentive to tighten monetary policy in the future will no longer exist. The private sector, if it is sufficiently astute, can pursue this line of reasoning for itself and consequently the initial announcement will not be believed. Thus, it is argued, time-inconsistent policies which seek to exploit the power of policy announcements are not credible. Credible policies are those which are time consistent, i.e. those which incorporate no future incentive to renege. However, the costs of imposing time consistency can be rather high, when measured in terms of the performance of stabilization policy. The non-credibility of announcements is therefore costly.

It may be that governments can precommit their policy action, so sustaining that time-inconsistent policy. But in general there are other plausible circumstances in which announcements of future policy changes are generally credible. It is essential to view the policy problem as a repeated policy game, responding to continuing stochastic shocks to the economy, in contrast with the one-shot policy game implicitly assumed in the above argument. The presence of continuing stochastic disturbances affects governments' incentives to adhere to policy announcements. The temptation to renege on policy announcements made in response to past disturbances is tempered by the fear that credibility will be lost and that policy will be less able to cope with future disturbances (Currie and Levine 1987). If the rate of discount is not too high, this repeated nature of the policy problem may well eliminate any incentive to renege, rendering policy announcements both credible and sustainable. In terms of the above example, the government will not renege if it expects the economy to be subjected to continuing inflationary disturbances, to which policy must react. This argument will be strengthened if a government's reputation extends across a range of its activities, so that reneging in the sphere of macroeconomic policy has implications for its credibility in microeconomic policy, for example.

If reputational policies are sustainable in some circumstances, then it becomes relevant to analyse regimes of co-ordination both with and without reputation. This multiplies the possible cases to be considered. This is all the more true since there is no reason to suppose that all governments have similar reputations. (Indeed it is possible to analyse the operations of the European

Monetary System (EMS) in terms of just such an asymmetry between Germany and the other countries.) However, with co-operation, the co-operating governments must jointly either enjoy reputation or not. Thus, in the two-country case, there are two asymmetrical and four symmetrical non-cooperation regimes. The symmetrical regimes are shown in Table 23.1.

Table 23.1 Four symmetric regimes

Relations between governments and private sector	Relations between governments	
	Co-operation (C)	Non-cooperation (NC)
Reputation (R)	CR	NCR
Non-reputational (NR)	CNR	NCNR

Of the four regimes described in Table 23.1, the co-operative reputational regime (CR) is the fully optional policy, and therefore the best regime if it is sustainable. The other regimes involve suboptimality, essentially because they involve some form of non-cooperation between the three players (the two governments and the private sector in the game). (Thus CNR involves co-operation between governments, but not between them and the private sector, and NCR involves a form of co-operation between each government and the private sector, but not between the two governments.)

We now return to our model to examine some of the consequences of forward-looking expectations. The formal solution of this model is set out in full by Currie and Levine (1990); here we sketch the main properties of the solution. In its single-country properties, the model is akin to that of Barro and Gordon (1983). The model is a natural rate one, with equilibrium output in country 1 being determined as the equilibrium between supply and demand from equations (23.1) and (23.5). However, inflation surprises caused by unexpected changes in monetary policy or other variables can lead to temporary one-period deviations from equilibrium output. This is illustrated in Figure 23.3. The horizontal axis measures deviations $\hat{y}$ of output from equilibrium, so that equilibrium is along the vertical axis with output at its natural rate. Equilibrium is possible at any rate of inflation. Government policy preferences are depicted by the indifference curves U_1, U_2, U_3 (in order of declining utility), with the highest level of utility at the infeasible bliss point of $\hat{y}$, so that output is at its desired level. PC_1 and PC_2 denote two of a family of one-period inflation–output trade-offs corresponding to different expected inflation rates: by springing a monetary surprise on the private sector, the government can move the economy along PC_1 to obtain a higher level of output (for one period only, however) at the expense of somewhat higher inflation.

The policy problem for the single country is relatively straightforward, as considered by Barro and Gordon (1983). A government that can precommit

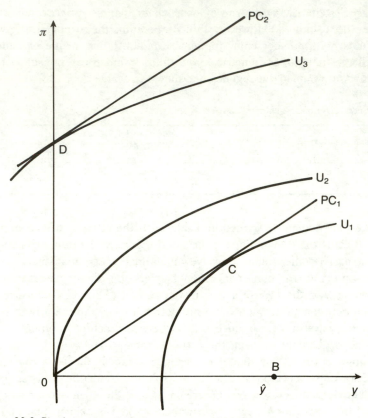

Figure 23.3 Single country inflation–output trade-off.

or has reputation (for reasons that we return to later) will opt for 0, where inflation is zero and output is at its equilibrium level. However, if it is short-sighted and lacks reputation, it may be tempted to spring a monetary surprise on the private sector in order to achieve a one-period output gain, moving along the one-period inflation–output trade-off PC_1 to C which yields higher government utility in the short run. But if the private sector anticipates this, it will raise its expectations of inflation, so that the one-period inflation–output trade-off moves to PC_2. In this case, equilibrium for a government without reputation will be at D, where there is no incentive for it to spring an inflation (or disinflation) surprise.

Now consider the four regimes shown in Table 23.1. The best regime is necessarily CR: in this, governments jointly set monetary policy so as to spring no monetary surprises. The consequence is zero inflation in both countries. Fiscal policy is set jointly, taking full account of the adverse supply-side effects of overexpansionary fiscal policy.

In CNR matters are rather different. The absence of reputation means that the private sector expects an overexpansionary monetary policy: the consequence is that the inflation equilibrium is at point D in Figure 23.3. Inflation performance is therefore substantially worse than the optimum. Fiscal policy is also overexpansionary: governments ignore the ongoing consequences of high government spending on long-term real interest rates, and hence the supply side.

We now consider the non-cooperative cases. NCNR also results in higher inflation, as in the CNR regime. Interestingly, however, inflation in the NCNR case is somewhat lower than in the CNR case. This is because, if governments do not act together, they face a more adverse inflation–output trade-off when they spring a monetary surprise, since the exchange rate falls against them. Thus the PC curves in Figure 23.3 are steeper than for the CNR case, and the resulting non-cooperative inflation equilibrium is at a lower inflation rate. This is an illustration of the Rogoff (1985) result that co-operation need not pay. In the absence of reputation, so that co-operation with the private sector is absent, co-operation between governments may not be helpful.

However, in terms of fiscal policy, co-operation without reputation will be helpful in our model. This is because, in the absence of co-operation, governments have an incentive to expand fiscal policy to obtain the beneficial effects of an appreciated exchange rate at the expense of the other country. This 'beggar thy neighbour' effect results in a more expansionary fiscal policy in the absence of co-operation and hence higher real interest rates and a more adverse supply-side performance. This illustrates the point that the Rogoff result need not hold, and co-operation may be helpful even without reputation.

Finally, there is the case of non-cooperation with reputation. The presence of reputation means that monetary policy will ensure zero inflation in both countries; co-operation is not necessary for anti-inflationary purposes. Thus, in terms of inflation performance, the NCR regime is as good as the CR regime. But in terms of fiscal policy, the NCR regime is inferior to all the others. Because of non-cooperation, the beggar thy neighbour effect results in an overexpansionary fiscal policy, as in the NCNR regime. But the presence of reputation reinforces this effect: a government without reputation carries credibility only for the current period, whereas a government with reputation can commit to an expansionary fiscal policy over a run of years. This will have larger effects on anticipated real interest rates and hence on the current exchange rate. Reputation therefore allows a government to operate its beggar thy neighbour fiscal policy with greater effect. The consequence is still more adverse effects on real interest rates and supply-side performance.

This case illustrates the point due to Currie and Levine (Currie *et al.* 1987; Levine and Currie 1987) that, in the absence of co-ordination, reputation may not pay. This can be regarded as a counterpoint to the Rogoff (1985) result that, in the absence of reputation, co-operation may not pay.

To sum up, then, of the four regimes depicted in Table 23.1, CR is the optimal regime, but the ranking of the remaining three regimes is ambiguous. The ranking in terms of inflation performance will be NCR, followed by NCNR, with CNR delivering the worst performance. But in terms of real interest rates and supply-side performance, this ranking is completely reversed, with CNR delivering the best performance and NCR the worst. When these effects are combined, the overall relative ranking will clearly depend on empirical magnitudes and policy preferences over inflation and output.

To conclude this section, we return to the question of whether the CR regime can be sustained by the threat of reversion to one of the other regimes: the equivalent of sustaining the co-operative equilibrium by means of the threat of reversion to the Nash point. This has two aspects. Governments can credibly sustain the co-operation between them required for the CR regime by threatening to revert to a non-cooperative regime (e.g. NCR), and if this performs sufficiently poorly, that threat may be sufficient to sustain co-operation. Reputational policies can be sustained by the mechanisms discussed above, i.e. by the threat of a loss of credibility and the reversion to a non-reputational regime (e.g. NCNR). Research using both theoretical and empirical multilateral models shows generally optimistic results on the question of whether the CR regime is sustainable in both these senses and therefore is a viable regime (see Levine and Currie 1987; Levine et al. 1989).

23.4 THE EMPIRICAL GAINS FROM CO-ORDINATION

We have set out in the previous section the general case for policy co-ordination. But what does the empirical evidence on the matter suggest?

At the outset, we should note the general pervasiveness of policy interdependences between economies on the presence of which the general case for co-ordination rests. Thus governments may be reluctant to expand unilaterally, or to offset a deflationary tendency, because of the resulting balance-of-payments deficits and downward pressure on the exchange rate. The consequence may be a deflationary bias in the world economy. Governments may tend to tackle inflationary pressures by a combination of tight money and an appreciated exchange rate, coupled with expansionary fiscal policy to offset the output consequences of the resulting loss of competitiveness; the consequences at the world level may be unduly high real interest rates and an inappropriate monetary–fiscal policy mix. (We have noted this tendency in the formal model analysed in the previous two sections.) Governments may reasonably treat commodity prices as determined in world markets, and neglect any effects of their own expansionary policy actions on commodity prices. However, if generalized, such demand expansion may prove overinflationary because of the consequences for the commodity terms of trade. Governments may have inconsistent objectives concerning their desired current account position, and uncoordinated policy intiatives to try to secure these may well prove disruptive to the international economy.

These and other policy interdependences have been an important aspect of the experience of floating exchange rates over the past decade and a half. As the discussion suggests, certain of the spill-overs are likely to exert opposite biases to the stance of macropolicy overall. But the different dynamics by which these effects will be governed are likely to be rather different, so that in a changing world the biases will not be offsetting in any helpful manner. The existence of these spill-overs therefore suggests a *prima facie* case that the international co-ordination of macropolicy might well lead to appreciable benefits in terms of a more stable, better functioning economy.

Despite this, much of the literature on international policy co-ordination gives a somewhat negative view of the benefits to be expected (for a recent survey, see Currie *et al.* 1989). The pioneering study by Oudiz and Sachs (1984) suggests rather minor gains, equivalent to less than 0.5 per cent of GDP, from complete and perfect co-ordination of monetary and fiscal policy among the G3 countries (the United States, Japan and Germany) for the period 1984–6. Such calculations give an upper bound for the realizable gains from the actual process of policy co-ordination, with its imperfections and delays, and so these results give little support to the advocates of co-ordination. Some later work gives still less encouragement. Rogoff (1985) points out that international policy co-ordination may actually be welfare decreasing if the co-ordination process eases the constraints on governments to engage in inflationary monetary expansions. In his example, governments without reputation are deterred in part by the prospect of a depreciating exchange rate from springing monetary surprises on their private sectors with a view to raising output. Co-ordination to peg the exchange rate results in a greater incentive to spring monetary surprises, so that the equilibrium inflation rate rises, with an overall fall in output. Although the example is specific, it is a general point that co-ordination without reputation may be counterproductive (see Currie *et al.* 1987; Levine and Currie 1987). Frankel and Rockett (1988) investigate the consequences of the plausible assumption that governments differ about their view of the world. Using six of the international models participating in the recent Brookings model comparison exercise (Bryant *et al.* 1989) as representing possible views of the world, they examine all the 216 possible combinations of the two governments (the United States and the rest of the world can subscribe to any of the six models, and the true state of the world can in turn be any of the six models). Co-ordination gives benefits in just over 60 per cent of the combinations; in more than a third of the combinations, co-ordination makes matters worse for at least one of the countries.

However, this rather pessimistic view of the benefits to be expected from international policy co-ordination has been questioned by more recent work. The Frankel–Rockett result that model uncertainty greatly reduces the benefits to be derived from international co-ordination depends crucially on the assumption that policy-makers stubbornly take no account of the presence of differences of views of the world in formulating their policies. Frankel (1987) shows that the use of a compromise model in the case of disagreement about the true structure of the world increases appreciably the probability of benefits from co-ordination. Holtham and Hughes Hallet (1987) show that ruling out 'weak' bargains, in which one party or the other expects the other party to be made worse off by the bargain, greatly improves the success rate of co-ordination when it occurs. They argue that governments would wish to rule out such bargains because they are likely to be reneged on and will jeopardize future co-ordination attempts. Ghosh and Masson (1988) show that the presence of model uncertainty may appreciably raise the benefits of co-ordination, provided that governments design co-ordination policies with explicit regard to the presence of model uncertainty. It may be objected that policy-makers are indeed stubborn in recognizing only one view of the world, but this is hardly consistent with the significant exchange of views in such matters in international forums; moreover, this would point to the need to educate policy-makers on the dangers of this approach rather than to avoid international co-ordination.

Recent work has also placed in context the Rogoff (1985) result that, in the absence of reputation, co-ordination may be undesirable. Levine and Currie (1987) and Currie et al. (1987) show a related result that, in the absence of co-ordination, reputational policies may be undesirable. This is because the co-ordination failures, especially those with respect to the exchange rate, that arise with uncoordinated policies are increased when governments have reputation, so that they can more readily ifluence market expectations. Currie et al. (1987), using a two-bloc reduced version of the OECD Interlink model, find that the uncoordinated reputational policy is very prone to instability, because governments are tempted to engage in self-defeating competitive appreciations of their exchange rates to combat inflation, coupled with fiscal expansion to avoid undue consequences of output. (We noted this in our theoretical model in Section 23.3.) The resulting interest rate spiral can easily prove unstable. The non-reputational policies, by contrast, are prone to excessive inflation for reasons analogous to those of the Barro and Gordon (1983) model.

An implication of these findings is that the gains from reputation and the gains from co-ordination can be secured only jointly, at least in the international policy-making context. Currie et al. (1987) use the reduced version of the OECD Interlink model to measure these gains empirically. The benefits of co-ordinaton with reputation are found to be rather small in the face of purely temporary disturbances to supply or demand. However, the benefits are estimated to rise steeply as the persistence of the disturbance increases. Moreover, these benefits rise through time: uncoordinated non-reputational policies are more likely to push undesirable adjustments into the discounted future, so that the long-run consequences of these policies are dismal. In the long run, the gains from co-operation in the face of permanent supply or demand shocks are very considerable indeed, amounting to some 15 per cent of GDP for 1 per cent disturbances. This provides an upper bound for the benefits of co-ordination, since in any historical episode disturbances are likely to be a combination of shocks of different persistence. Holtham and Hughes Hallett (1987) use seven alternative models of the international economy drawn from the Brookings model comparison exercise to obtain estimates of the gains from co-operation of the order of 4–6 per cent of GDP. Interestingly, they find greater benefits from models with rational expectations, suggesting that the potential benefits from international policy co-ordination with reputation may be considerable, particularly if co-ordination focuses on how policy should adjust to persistent or permanent disturbances to the international economy.

A further reason why the gains as estimated from the empirical models may not be large is that the models tend to emphasize demand-side spill-overs, largely because they have an inadequate specification of the supply side. Yet supply-side spill-overs may be more important. An important spill-over in the 1980s has been through high real interest rates induced by a mismatch of US monetary and fiscal policy. High real interest rates have an important effect on capital accumulation in the rest of the world, and hence on supply-side performance. However, our empirical models are rather weak in supply-side modelling, and so these effects are probably poorly captured.

23.5 WHAT FORM OF CO-ORDINATION?

We have argued in the previous section that there may well be potential gains from the co-ordination of macroeconomics policy among the main G7, or more particularly G3, economies. In this section, we consider the form that this co-ordination might take.

At the outset, it is helpful to distinguish between the rule-based forms of co-ordination and *ad hoc* or discretionary forms of co-ordination. Rule-based forms of co-ordination are exemplified by regimes such as the Gold Standard, the Bretton Woods system and the EMS. In such regimes, co-ordination may take an implicit, rather than an explicit, form, with the requirement that rules be observed replacing the need for overt consultation and agreement on the co-ordination of policy. By contrast, *ad hoc* forms of co-ordination take the form of one-off bargains negotiated explicitly between the parties to the agreement. The experience of co-ordination amongst the G3 countries since the breakdown of the Bretton Woods system has been of this type. with a series of summits, notably Bonn in 1978 and the later Plaza and Louvre Accords.

Although this distinction appears straightforward in practice, the recent theoretical literature might appear to have dissolved it. It is true that the pioneering paper by Kydland and Prescott (1977) on time inconsistency drew the same sharp distinction between rules and discretion. However, the more recent literature emphasizes that the time-consistent discretionary policy can be expressed as a time-invariant feedback rule (see, for example, Currie and Levine 1987). Thus it suggests that the relevant distinction is not between rules and discretion, but rather between those rules with, and those without, reputation. However, this argument rests on very specific assumptions. In particular, it assumes that policy-makers have stable preferences, that these preferences are quadratic and that the policy-makers have a model of the world which is stable and linear in structure. Without these assumptions, the distinction between discretionary co-ordination and rule-based forms becomes very real. A rule book for the conduct of international macroeconomic policy may well act to limit the shifts in policy that might otherwise arise from changes in the preferences or views of the world of policy-makers, unless these changes are large enough to lead to the rule book's being torn up.

What other advantages may accrue from a rule-based approach to co-ordination? First, explicit well-designed rules may provide the best means of harnessing the benefits of reputation in policy-making, which, as we argued in Section 23.4, may be essential if international policy co-ordination is to be beneficial (see Currie *et al.* 1987; Levine and Currie 1987). This may be so even if the rules are rather simple and rigid in form, such as an exchange rate commitment to an adjustable peg arrangement, which, as Giavazzi and Pagano (1988) demonstrate, may be advantageous in establishing a reputation for resisting inflationary pressures.

Second, there is the point that the adoption of a rule-based system may encourage the parties to the agreement to consider the repeated aspects of the policy game. In the presence of continuing stochastic disturbances to the system, the scope for advantageous co-operative bargains becomes much greater, so that co-ordination is more likely (cf. the 'folk theorem' of game theory). This is because countries in different circumstances may find it hard to formulate co-ordinated policies because of the difference in initial conditions. But such differences in initial conditions become less important in the presence of ongoing stochastic disturbances, because such disturbances create the prospect that at some future date positions will be reversed; this increases the willingness of both sides to agree to a set of rules that involve a sharing of the adjustment process. *Ad hoc* summitry that does not generate guidelines or rules for policy may well limit the scope for advantageous bargains too much.

Finally, there is the argument that in internationally agreed set of rules may helpfully act as an external discipline on the conduct of governments. This was clearly true of Bretton Woods, and is also true of the EMS (cf. the Mitterrand experiment of 1982 and its aftermath, where the incoming Socialist administration first embarked on expansionary fiscal policies and then reversed them in order to observe the constraints imposed by EMS membership). This constraint may act in at least two ways, which may be in large part observationally equivalent. It may constrain erratic shifts in the stance of government, arising from shifting preferences, from affecting macroeconomic policy, thereby ensuring greater predictability of policy. It may also allow governments to carry out policies more readily by pointing to the obligations of pre-existing international agreements which reduce the necessity of arguing the domestic case for such policies.

Against this, a rule-based system has a number of potential drawbacks. A rule book must in large part be symmetrical in the obligations that it imposes on the parties that agree to it. This does not exclude the possibility that the rule book may operate asymmetrically in its effects (as with the EMS as we discuss below), or that it includes certain asymmetries with respect to one key party (as with the US role with Bretton Woods). But it seems implausible that a rule book could incorporate wholly different rules for the different parties. In contrast, one-off summit agreements may readily incorporate asymmetries and indeed almost certainly will, since the chance of symmetrical obligations arising from a one-off bargain are rather remote.

A related point is that a rule-based approach also makes it much harder to strike bargains over a range of policy areas. An example of such a bargain is provided by the 1978 Bonn Summit. This involved the United States agreeing to a change of energy policy and Japan agreeing to trade liberalization, while Germany engaged in macroeconomic expansion. The macroeconomic aspects of the Bonn Summit have since been criticized, perhaps unfairly (see Holtham 1989), but the other aspects of the bargain were undoubtedly beneficial. It is hard to see how such a deal could have been struck within a rule-based approach.

23.6 ALTERNATIVE PROPOSALS FOR GROUP OF SEVEN CO-OPERATION

What more specific guidance does the academic literature give as to the form that international co-operation may take? There are a variety of proposals on offer, ranging from Tobin's proposal for a tax on international financial transactions to proposals for a return to the Gold Standard.

However, the most detailed and developed proposal for international macro-policy co-ordination is the target zone proposal of Williamson (1985). In its early form, this was simply a proposal that policy should be directed to limiting the variation of real exchange rates to lie within a certain, rather wide, band around the equilibrium (full employment exchange rate (FEER)) level, calculated so as to give medium- to longer-run current account equilibrium. This was open to the objection that it provided no anchor for domestic inflation, since a given real exchange rate is consistent, in principle, with any evolution of nominal variables. While the original proposal could be defended as an attempt to internalize a key policy externality (namely the ability of some countries to engage in Reaganomics at the expense of others), rather than as a fully comprehensive set of rules for the conduct of international macropolicy, it was certainly vulnerable to the objection that it did little to encourage policy-makers to focus on the links between exchange rate targets and adjustments to underlying fiscal and monetary policies. It is therefore helpful that the most recent statement by Williamson and Miller (1987) of the extended target zone proposal sets out a comprehensive set of rules for the conduct of monetary and fiscal policy in pursuit of real exchange rate targets and domestic nominal income targets (of a flexible type).

Thus Williamson and Miller propose the following elements to their scheme. First, interest differentials between countries should be varied to keep exchange rates within a given band around the agreed equilibrium level for the real exchange rate, chosen so as to give medium- to longer-run current account equilibrium. Second, domestic fiscal policy should be varied to take account of domestic targets for nominal demand growth; with the targets being chosen to take account of the need to reduce inflation towards zero, to expand demand in the face of low-capacity utilization and to adjust the current account towards equilibrium.

Stated in this way, the proposals put at least as much weight on the adjustment of monetary and fiscal policy in a way consistent with the achievements of exchange rate and other targets as on the achievement of the exchange rate targets themselves. Thus they bridge the gap between the academic literature on policy co-ordination which was reviewed briefly in Section 23.5, and the practice of policy co-ordination over the last few years since the Plaza Accord. It is also of interest that model-based appraisals of the proposals also place the emphasis on the rules for monetary and fiscal policy, rather than on the exchange rate zone element (see, for example, Edison *et al.* (1987) and Currie and Wren-Lewis (1989, 1990); for a theoretical appraisal, see Alogoskoufis (1989)). These appraisals suggest that the extended target zone proposal has merit, and would have been likely to have improved on historical performance had it been in force over the past decade. Currie and Wren-Lewis (1989) also find advantages in the implied assignment of monetary policy to the external objective and fiscal policy to the internal objective, relative to the alternative suggested by Boughton (1989) and implicit in much IMF discussion (IMF

1987) that fiscal policy should be assigned to external balance and monetary policy to the domestic objective.

We do not attempt here to assess the technical merits of the extended target zone proposal. We merely note that certain modifications of the Williamson–Miller rules might well yield benefit; for example, Currie and Wren-Lewis (1990) suggest that the rules may be over-restrictive in precluding a real exchange rate appreciation in response to higher inflation relative to the rest of the world. We also note that there is a need for further assessment of the scheme, particularly to see how far the rules can be made robust in performance with respect to differences in model structure.

Here we merely conclude by noting certain features of the proposal that are helpful in consideration of how the process of policy co-ordination can be taken further. These features are not specific to the Williamson–Miller proposal and might be incorporated in other rules for the co-ordination of policy.

First, the rules can be thought of as a concrete means of making sense of the 'indicators' debate initiated by G7 summit meetings. By incorporating a variety of relevant variables into the two key targets for the real exchange rate and the growth of domestic demand, and by proposing simple rules linking these targets to policy instruments, the proposal imposes a simple and helpful structure on an otherwise thoroughly muddled discussion. If the 'indicators' debate is to go forward, this surely represents the line of advance.

Second, the proposals in their latest form have the considerable merit of emphasizing the necessity of adjustments of fiscal and monetary policy if exchange rate targets are to be pursued. This is a helpful antidote to the wishful thinking of recent policy initiatives (for further discussion on this point, see Currie *et al.* 1989).

Third, the proposals have sufficient flexibility to be consistent with the gradual evolution, described above, of the policy process from a one-off bargain towards a more complete rule book for the conduct of policy. This flexibility has several forms. The proposed permissible zones of variation for the exchange rate are wide, and therefore off considerable flexibility. We can well imagine wide limits being set initially as part of a more general one-off package, and these limits then becoming more stringent over time. Also, there is scope within the proposals for countries to set their domestic nominal demand objectives in individual ways, giving greater or lesser weight to the inflation objective relative to capacity utilization. Thus the proposals do not seek to impose on countries how they should manage their domestic economies, but rather merely seek to limit undesirable spill-overs onto the rest of the world.

Fourth, the proposals offer flexibility in the degree of emphasis placed on the underlying rules for the conduct of monetary and fiscal policy relative to the stabilization of real exchange rates. Of course, a central aim of the rules is to limit exchange rate variation, but there is a choice as to whether to lead with the exchange rate objective or with the underlying policy adjustments. Recent experience can be taken to suggest that leading with the exchange rate objective will push fiscal and monetary policy into the background, with possibly unfortunate consequences for the viability of the co-ordination proposal. Against that, co-operation amongst the G7 central banks represents the practical basis for co-ordination on which to build (see Group of Thirty 1988). An increased emphasis on the rules for the conduct of monetary and fiscal policy within current arrangements for exchange rate management may well offer the most practical way forward in the evolution towards a new rule book for the conduct of international macroeconomic policy.

NOTES

1 The G7 countries comprise the seven leading OECD countries, namely the United States, Japan, Germany, France, the United Kingdom, Italy and Canada. The first three of these comprise the Group of Three (G3) countries.
2 The US and Japanese policy adjustments had an undoubtedly beneficial effect, but the German reflation was inappropriately timed, coming as it did just before the second OPEC oil price hike and thereby adding to subsequent German inflationary pressures (but see Holtham 1989). German reluctance to be drawn into co-ordinated policy initiatives in the 1980s was based, in part, on this experience.

REFERENCES

Alogoskoufis, G. (1989) 'Stabilization policy, fixed exchange rates and target zones', in M. Miller, B. Eichengreen and R. Portes (eds) *Blueprints for Exchange Rate Management*, New York: Academic Press.

Artis, M. and Currie, D. A. (1981) 'Monetary targets and the exchange rate: a case for conditional targets', *Oxford Economic Papers, (Supplement)* 33: 176–200.

Barro, R. J. and Gordon, D. A, (1983) 'Rules, discretion and reputation in a model of monetary policy', *Journal of Monetary Economics* 17: 101–22.

Boughton, J. (1989) 'Policy assignment strategies with somewhat flexible exchange rates', in M. Miller, B. Eichengreen and R. Portes (eds) *Blueprints for Exchange Rate Management*, New York: Academic Press.

Bryant, R. C., Currie, D. A., Frenkel, J. A., Masson, P. R. and Portes, R. (eds) (1989) *Macroeconomic Polices in an Interdependent World*, Washington, DC: International Monetary Fund.

Currie, D. A. and Levine, P. (1987) 'Credibility and time consistency in a stochastic world', *Journal of Economics* 47 (3): 225–52.

—— and —— (1990) 'The international coordination of monetary policy: a survey', in C. Green and D. Llewellyn (eds) *Surveys in Monetary Economics*, vol. I, Oxford: Basil Blackwell.

Currie, D. A. and Vines, D. (1988) *Macroeconomic Interactions between North and South*, Cambridge: Cambridge University Press.

Currie, D. A. and Wren-Lewis, S. (1989) 'Evaluating blueprints for the conduct of international macropolicy', *American Economic Review, Papers and Proceedings* 79 (2): 264–9.

—— and —— (1990) 'Evaluating the extended target zone proposal for the G3', *Economic Journal* 100: 105–23.

Currie, D. A., Holtham, G. and Hughes Hallet, A. (1989) 'The theory and practice of international policy coordination: does coordination pay?', in R. Bryant, D. A. Currie, J. A. Frenkel, P. Masson and R. Portes (eds) *Macroeconomic Policies in an Interdependent World*, Washington, DC: International Monetary Fund.

Currie, D. A., Levine, P. and Vidalis, N. (1987) 'Cooperative and noncooperative rules for monetary and fiscal policy in an empirical two-bloc model', in R. Bryant and R. Portes (eds) *Global Macroeconomics: Policy Conflict and Cooperation*, London: Macmillan.

Edison, H. J., Miller, M. H. and Williamson, J. (1987) 'On evaluating and extending the target zone proposal', *Journal of Policy Modelling* 9 (1): 199–224.

Frankel, J. A. (1987) 'Obstacles to international macroeconomic policy coordination', Working paper 87/28, International Monetary Fund.

Frankel, J. A. and Rockett, K. E. (1988) 'International macroeconomic policy coordination when policy makers do not agree on the true model', *American Economic Review* 78: 318–40.

Funabashi, Y. (1988) *Managing the Dollar: From the Plaza to the Louvre*, Washington, DC: Institute for International Economics.

Ghosh, A. and Masson, P. (1988) 'Model uncertainty, learning and gains from policy coordination', Working paper 88/114, International Monetary Fund.

Giavazzi, F. and Pagano, M. (1988) 'The advantage of tying one's hands: EMS discipline and central bank credibility', *European Economic Review* 32: 1055–82.

Group of Thirty (1988) *International Macroeconomic Policy Coordination*, London: Group of Thirty.

Hamada, K. (1974) 'Alternative exchange rate systems and the interdependence of monetary policies', in R. Z. Aliber (ed.) *National Monetary Policies and the International Financial System*, Chicago, IL: University of Chicago Press.

—— (1976) 'A strategic analysis of monetary interdependence', *Journal of Political Economy* 84: 677–700.

—— (1979) 'Macroeconomic strategy and coordination under alternative exchange rates', in R. Dornbusch and J. A. Frenkel (eds) *International Economic Policy*, Baltimore, MD: Johns Hopkins University Press.

—— (1985) *The Political Economy of International Monetary Interdependence*, Cambridge, MA: MIT Press.

Holtham, G. (1989) 'German macroeconomic policy and the 1978 Bonn Summit', in R. Bryant and E. Hodgkinson (eds) *Can Nations Agree?*, Washington, DC: Brookings Institution.

Holtham, G. and Hughes Hallett, A. (1987) 'International policy cooperation and model uncertainty', in R. Bryant and R. Portes (eds) *Global Macroeconomics: Policy Conflict and Cooperation*, London: Macmillan. (An extended version is available in Discussion paper 190, Centre for Economic Policy Research, London.)

IMF (International Monetary Fund) (1987) *World Economic Outlook*, April, October.

Kydland, F. E. and Prescott, E. C. (1977) 'Rules rather than discretion: the inconsistency of optimal plans', *Journal of Political Economy* 85: 473–92.

Levine, P. and Currie, D. A. (1987) 'Does international policy coordination pay and is it sustainable? A two country analysis', *Oxford Economic Papers* 39: 38–74.

Levine, P., Currie, D. A. and Gaines, J. (1989) 'The use of simple rules for international policy agreements', in M. Miller, B. Eichengreen and R. Portes (eds) *Blueprints for Exchange Rate Management*, New York: Academic Press.

Oudiz, G. and Sachs, J. (1984) 'Macroeconomic policy coordination among the industrial economies', *Brookings Papers on Economic Activity* 1: 1–64.

Putnam, R. and Bayne, N. (1987) *Hanging Together: Cooperation and Conflict in the Seven-Power Summits*, 2nd edn, London: Sage.

Rogoff, K. (1985) 'Can international monetary policy coordination be counter-productive?', *Journal of International Economics* 18: 199–217.

Williamson, J. (1985) *The Exchange Rate System*, 2nd edn, Wasington, DC: Institute for International Economics.

Williamson, J. and Miller, M. H. (1987) *Targets and Indicators: A Blueprint for the International Coordination of Economic Policy*, Washington, DC: Institute for International Economics.

24

DETERMINANTS OF
INDUSTRY STRUCTURE
AND CONTESTABLE
MARKET THEORY

WILLIAM J. BAUMOL

24.1 INTRODUCTION

The structure of an industry is generally acknowledged to affect profoundly the behaviour of prices and outputs in the theory of the market, and it acts as a critical determinant of the performance of the individual enterprise in the theory of the firm. It substantially affects our evaluation of an equilibrium in welfare economics and plays a key role in analyses of the appropriate role of government intervention in the operations of firms and industries. Industry structure is not, of course, determined by chance, and is presumably profoundly affected by economic influences. Yet, until fairly recently, the main body of economic theory proceeded as though it were exogenously determined – as it were, imposed upon the economy by forces or entities unknown.

At least three lines of inquiry have recently begun to change this. The oldest of these is the game-theoretical literature which provides a variety of models offering insights on the determination of the structure of oligopolistic markets in different circumstances (see Chapter 17). The second is found in the writings that interpret firms as devices for the containment of transactions costs, an approach with which Williamson (1985) is most closely associated. The analyses under this heading probably also concern themselves mostly with the case of oligopoly, although they do undoubtedly pertain to a wider variety of circumstances. The third strand of relevant analysis emerges from contestable markets theory. While that discussion applies equally (and equally narrowly) to perfect competition, oligopoly, monopoly and other market forms, its generality is nowhere near as great as this may appear to suggest, since the analysis

The author is extremely grateful to the C. V. Starr Center for Applied Economics at New York University for its support of the work underlying this paper.

507

holds rigorously only for the case of *perfect* contestability, a theoretical concept whose counterparts in reality may be as rare as those of perfect competition.

Despite such limitations, it seems clear that these three developments represent considerable progress in an important arena that was almost totally unexplored before, and the fact that much work still remains to be done here should only serve to stimulate the interest of economists in what has already been accomplished.

24.2 WHAT IS INDUSTRY STRUCTURE?

The term 'industry structure' encompasses a variety of elements far richer than the elementary textbooks usually report. It is true that 'perfect competition', 'monopolistic competition', 'oligopoly' and 'pure monopoly' all refer to different structural forms. However, other significant elements enter a full description of the structure of a particular industry. For example, one industry will be integrated vertically to a greater degree than another, with the former relying on central planning and direct controls to achieve the degree of co-ordination that the latter will carry out with the aid of contracts, or by simple recourse to the market and the guidance of the price mechanism. In addition, the industry's structure encompasses the breadth of its product line, i.e. the choice between narrow specialization and substantial diversification, and issues such as the degree to which research and development (R&D) and innovation are institutionalized as a routine part of the operations of the firm or are left to chance. The strategic measures, if any, that are built into the normal operations of the industry as deliberately designed bulwarks against entry can also be taken as a significant structural attribute of the industry, both for the analysis of its performance and for the design of appropriate policy.

This broadening of the term is not a semantic exercise but a substantive issue, for what is intended is a listing of all the types of organizational attributes that, in one variety or another, are common to many if not most industries – organizational attributes that materially affect behaviour and that should not be overlooked in policy design. The emphasis upon the wide variety of attributes that make up the structure of an industry is also significant for the discussion here because it facilitates an explanation of the roles of the three lines of analysis of the determination of industry structure that will be described.

24.3 ON THE PERTINENT DOMAINS OF THE THREE TYPES OF ANALYSIS

It is a mistake to consider transactions theory, game theory and contestability theory to be rival bodies of analysis. On the contrary, they are complementary endeavours, each undertaking to shed light in areas to which the others do not apply. These differences help to explain their particular contributions to the understanding of the determinants of industry structure. The territory covered by transactions and game analysis, and from which contestability theory is excluded, is composed of those industries whose production process requires the suppliers to incur *substantial sunk investments*, that are necessarily of a specialized character. It is only in the presence of such sunk costs that entry can conceivably be hazardous and costly. For, by definition, in the absence of sunk costs an entrant that finds its incursion to have yielded disappointing results can withdraw without impediment, taking all its (unsunken) investment outlays along with it. Thus, costless exit is tantamount to costless entry. It is only the presence of impediments to entry that permits firms to conspire and to form coalitions in order to profit at the expense of rivals or consumers, that makes a producer dependent on the performance of circumscribed numbers of input suppliers and that renders interdependent economic agents vulnerable to poor performance by those upon whom they must depend. This, in turn, leads to the adoption of costly mechanisms that can be used to monitor and control the behaviour of those other parties.

In contrast, complete absence of sunk costs, and the consequent non-existence of entry barriers, is the hallmark of perfect contestability. In such an area the market mechanism works (almost) perfectly, at least in theory, eliciting, where two or more suppliers are present, the pricing and output decisions that are necessary for maximization of economic welfare. For example, excessive prices, excessive profits or inefficiencies in production all constitute profit opportunities for entrants who are less grasping or more efficient than the misbehaving incumbents in the market. The latter will then be vulnerable to loss of their customers to the newcomers unless those suppliers modify their undesirable behaviour. There is no point in engaging in predatory profit sacrifices or other similar strategic moves in order to drive out the entrants, since with sunk costs entirely absent the latter can leave without cost to themselves, only to re-enter should the incumbents relapse into their old behaviour patterns.

To return to the domain of sunk costs, it is clear that two general possibilities present themselves. Suppliers in a market with substantial sunk costs can engage in combat with rivals or can combine with some potential rival to threaten or actually engage in combat with others. Alternatively, potential combatants or players who are suspicious of one another's intentions or prospective behaviour can undertake to institute measures which to some degree ensure that each party will behave in a manner acceptable to the other. The first of these two types of development entailing active rivalry is, of course, the field studied by game theorists. The latter course of events, in which institutional arrangements are deliberately designed to provide some co-ordination of behaviour and protection of the interests of the parties involved, is the terrain of transactions analysis. The discussion of recent contributions to the analysis of the determination of industry structure will begin with this last approach.

24.4 TRANSACTIONS ANALYSIS: STRUCTURE AS A MEANS TO REDUCE CO-ORDINATION COSTS

Although transactions analysis offers rich insights into business behaviour and throws new light on policy issues, it has so far provided no formally coherent analytical structure. Consequently, there is no way in which its general model can be described and its implications for industry structure shown. Rather, it is necessary to proceed, as this literature has done, via particular topics and individual examples. Using this approach it will be shown here how the need for specialized sunk investment can influence the degree of vertical integration.

Consider a product whose most efficient mode of production uses an input which itself can best be produced with the aid of a very expensive machine that is at the same time so specialized that to others it has little more than scrap value. The interests of the producer of the final product will therefore be harmed if the input supplier fails to acquire that machine. However, such an investment entails a considerable risk for the input supplier, for if the final-product manufacturer turns to another input supplier in the near future, or adopts another manufacturing process, or goes out of business altogether, most of the funds sunk in the specialized machine will be lost. The danger of all this to the final-product manufacturer is that it will dissuade the input supplier from acquiring the machine, with the detrimental consequences falling in good part upon the former.

To avoid this damaging course of affairs the final-product supplier must find some way to commit himself – to curtail his own freedom of action – thereby persuading the input supplier that it is reasonably safe to acquire the machine. This, incidentally, illustrates the point that rules which preclude such a commitment entail loss of a valuable asset to the individual whose freedom is protected in this way, just as mediaeval monarchs found themselves paying higher interest rates than their subjects because there was no way in which a king could commit himself to be forced to repay. Our final-product manufacturer is not normally so circumscribed and has two general types of option. First, he can enter into a long-term contract with the input supplier, promising to purchase at least some specified amount of the input per year for a fixed number of years. The alternative is merger with the input supplier, i.e. vertical integration.

Contracts may well be satisfactory in such circumstances, but they also entail some difficulties. It is difficult to write explicit provisions covering every pertinent issue. For example, suppose that quality control by the input supplier deteriorates. At what point does this release the input buyer from his contractual purchase obligations? How does one monitor compliance? What recourse is either party offered when it doubts the other party's compliance with the contract terms? What if the buyer goes bankrupt? Should funds be held in escrow to compensate the seller in such an event? All these matters are costly to spell out and to implement. Add to this the fact that it is impossible to design a contract that covers completely *every* element of performance and specifies what is to be done in every contingency, and it becomes clear that the contract is inevitably a very imperfect solution to the problem under discussion.

However, the alternative course, vertical integration, runs into comparable problems. In an integrated firm the decisions of the input supply subsidiary can be controlled only at a cost. In a large enterprise rigid controls from the top will entail bureaucratic inefficiencies, close monitoring of performance of the subsidiary and the like. Incentive problems abound. Decentralized decisions within the firm are not easy to co-ordinate etc.

There is no need to continue. The point is that both options are costly and imperfect, and rational choice between contract and integration – a choice determining this element of firm and industry structure – will entail a balancing of the transactions costs of the two courses of action. It is also clear how this choice is forced upon the affected parties when a large sunk investment is required for efficiency, for if neither contract nor integration is undertaken it may be too risky for the input supplier to undertake the investment, and this may prove the worst of the three available outcomes.

This example shows how transactions analysis throws light on the determination of elements of industry structure that other approaches are forced to miss. Yet it seems to tell us little about what is apt to be considered the most urgent question in this arena: what determines which of the major market forms – oligopoly, monopoly etc. – that the industry adopts or finds forced upon itself?

24.5 GAME-THEORETICAL LIGHT ON INDUSTRY STRUCTURE

From its inception, game theory provided material pertinent to the determination of industry structure. The analysis in the volume by von Neumann and Morgenstern (1944), the fountainhead of the literature, contains extensive discussions of the concept of coalitions, their formation and their survival. Clearly, the number and size of the coalitions into which a market is divided is a decisive influence upon its structure. More recent work, some of which will be described below, goes more directly into the issue. Still, it is not being suggested here that the literature offers a generalized discussion of the determinants of structure. This is all but precluded by the profusion and diversity of the models that game theory provides, which is presumably a reflection of the rich variety of possibilities that may arise in circumstances where the interdependence of the decisions of the constituent firms is obvious to the participants and where strategic considerations pervade the decision processes. Consequently, it is only possible to offer illustrations of relevant game-theoretical analyses, abandoning any attempt at generalization. In any case, a more comprehensive account of strategic behaviour is given in Chapter 17.

Here we shall deal with some recent papers in which the strategic elements entering into merger decisions and affecting the magnitude of the merged entity have been considered. As a reference point we shall assume that there exists some magnitude of the merged entity that is optimal (efficient) when strategic elements are left out of consideration. The magnitude of that optimal merged entity is presumably determined by the availability of economies of scale and scope, which in turn determine the magnitude of that entity consistent with minimization of the resources cost of producing the industry's output vector. However, as we shall see next, strategic considerations may dictate that the merged entity that actually emerges is either smaller or larger than the optimum.[1]

The two-period intertemporal models of oligopoly undertake to analyse strategic behaviour using a simple scenario. An incumbent firm (or set of firms), call it firm 1 (set of firms 1), undertakes a commitment, such as an investment or a merger, during the initial period. We can represent the magnitude of the commitment, whose measurement and definition will obviously depend on the nature of the commitment, as the variable K. The size of K is assumed not to affect any rival directly, but it does affect some element of firm 1's behaviour in the second period; say, it affects the magnitude of that firm's decision variable x_1. The size of that decision variable, in turn, affects its rival(s), firm(s) 2, which responds by altering the magnitude of its own decision variable x_2. Let us calibrate these two variables so that an increase in x_1 is damaging to the interest of firm 2 and vice versa. Then the strategic object of firm 1 is to select a value of K which, via its effect on x_1, induces firm 2 to reduce the magnitude of x_2. That is, in selecting the profit-maximizing value of K, firm 1 will consider not only K's benefits to itself, but also its benefits achieved indirectly through depression of the value of x_2.

Let us use K^* to represent the value of K that maximizes the direct benefits of the commitment to firm 1, and K^s to represent the profit-maximizing value of K taking both direct and strategic benefits into account. Then, depending on the signs of dx_1/dK and dx_2/dx_1, we may obtain either $K^s > K^*$ or the reverse. In particular if $dx_1/dK < 0$, then we shall clearly have $K^s > K^*$ if

$dx_2/dx_1 > 0$, because then the excess K will depress x_1 whose lower value will, in turn, depress x_2. This is the pattern that Fudenberg and Tirole (1984) refer to as a 'fat-cat strategy', in which firm 1 makes an overcommitment that leads it to contain its aggressiveness, eliciting a similar response from firm 2. This behaviour is reversed when dx_2/dx_1 is negative, and the result is $K^5 < K^*$. This is Fudenberg and Tirole's 'lean-and-hungry strategy', in which firm 1's undercommitment enhances its aggressiveness and this intimidates 2 into more accommodating behaviour.

All this applies to merger analysis in the following way. Let K, or rather M, represent the magnitude of a merger, as evaluated, say, by the number of participating firms. Consider two alternative scenarios. In the first, firms compete in terms of size of output q (Cournot competition), while in the second, price p is the instrument of competition (Bertrand competition). Then x_i in the preceding discussion should be replaced by q_i in the output competition case, and by p_i in the price competition case. But, normally, we expect that a rise in p_1 is apt to lead to a rise in p_2 by cutting the sales losses to firm 2 that follow from an increase in price. That is, we expect $dp_2/dp_1 > 0$. However, where quantity is the instrument of competition the inequality is reversed, since an increase in 1's output works to saturate the market.

Salant et al. (1983) and Davidson and Deneckere (1985) use these observations to argue that, because mergers tend to make its participants less aggressive ($dx_1/dM < 0$), this means that in the presence of output quantity competition one will tend to have $M^s < M^*$, and that the reverse will tend to be true under price competition, for precisely the reasons summarized in the preceding paragraphs.

This, then, is a clear illustration of the way in which game-theoretical analysis sheds light on the considerations that affect industry structure in the presence of oligopoly with sunk commitments.

24.6 DETERMINATION OF STRUCTURE IN PERFECTLY CONTESTABLE MARKETS

Contestability theory, the third current avenue of analysis of the determination of industry structure, deals with a case which is analytically very different from those to which transactions theory and game theory apply. It is the case in which market forces are almost as powerful, and firms almost as powerless, as those under perfect competition. Under perfect contestability the market need not derive its strength from large numbers of actual incumbents, because of the presence of potential entrants who can enter without incurring unrecoverable costs and in numbers sufficient to discipline the firms already extant. This, incidentally, facilitates formal analysis by rendering prices parametric, i.e. by taking them out of the firm's control, just as they are under pure competition. But for our purpose, what is most distinctive about perfect contestability is that, unlike perfect competitive analysis or game theory, it does not pertain exclusively or even primarily to one particular market form. Any industry, regardless of its market form, can (in theory) be perfectly contestable, provided that it requires no sunk costs of any of its enterprises. This feature, permitting an industry to be perfectly contestable and yet to assume any of the market forms, is what adapts contestability theory to the study of industry structure.

The procedure that it uses for the purpose is disturbingly simple. It rests on the theorem that under perfect contestability any output vector must, in the long run, be produced at minimum cost, since otherwise there will be a profit opportunity for an efficient entrant or group of entrants, who will be in a position to take over the market as a result of their superior efficiency and the reduced prices that it permits them to charge. But production at minimum cost requires adoption of the cost-minimizing industry structure. Suppose, for example, that the output bundle of an industry can be produced most cheaply by a hundred firms, but that it is currently being done by only two. In the absence of entry costs this will invite incursions by smaller and presumably more efficient enterprises, which the incumbents will be powerless to prevent. The process of entry will come to a halt only with the establishment of the hundredth enterprise, because then and only then will all opportunities for profitable entry have been exhausted. In this way, the market forces in a regime of contestability will decree that this industry cannot adopt a duopoly structure, and that it must end up with a structure that is perhaps closer to pure competition than to oligopoly.

This bit of reasoning, then, is disquietingly elementary, and it only attains sophistication and complexity when it turns to the next step – the calculation of the cost-minimizing number of enterprises, the distribution of their sizes, the extent of the product line of each cost-minimizing firm etc. Obviously, the answers depend on the character of the pertinent multi-product cost functions of the firms. Concepts such as scale economies, complementarity in production of the various industry products and efficient scale of production for each possible set of output proportions must be formalized and recast into analytically tractable forms, and their roles in the process must be laid out. The theory has, indeed, provided such an analysis, which can be considered a first step in the required direction. These methods will be described briefly in the next section (for an extensive discussion, see Baumol *et al.* (1988: chs 5, 6)).

The analysis brings out another complication. As we know, the previous literature shows that the output levels and prices that emerge in a market depend on the market form that happens to prevail there. For example, it is generally agreed that prices will be higher and outputs smaller, *ceteris paribus*, under monopoly than under perfect competition. However, contestability theory shows that the reverse is also true – that industry structure is, in turn, affected by prices and outputs. For example, imagine a single-product industry whose firms have U-shaped average cost curves. Suppose, for example, that the point of minimum average cost is an output of 1 million units per year. Then, if the market's effective demand leads to the purchase of 1 million units, the industry's cost-minimizing industry structure will obviously be a monopoly. However, if quantity demanded doubles, the most efficient structure becomes a duopoly. It follows from all this that it is illegitimate to proceed seriatim, first seeking to explain the structure assumed by an industry and then undertaking to analyse the prices and outputs that emerge from that structure along with cost and demand conditions. Rather, at least in theory, it is necessary to take the mutual interdependence of structure and output sizes into account and to analyse them simultaneously. Contestability theory has attempted to do this also.

Indeed, in a formal sense, it seems to have succeeded, and none of the critics of contestability analysis seem to have raised any doubts on that score. The major failure of the analysis is that its explanation of structure determination is known to work only in the theoretical and abstract world of perfect contestability. Beyond that, there are conjectures that a similar body of reasoning applies approximately, but unfortunately there is no hard evidence so far. This is a shortcoming, indeed, for application to the real world, where neither competition nor contestability can ever be perfect. Still, the analysis has proved to have some connection with the world of reality; for example, it has inspired a small flood of econometric industry studies, some of which explore the cost-minimizing structure of particular real industries and attempt to make comparisons between that efficient structure and the one that prevails in reality (see Baumol *et al.* 1988: ch. 17, Section E).

24.7 CONTESTABILITY-THEORETICAL METHODS OF ANALYSIS OF INDUSTRY STRUCTURE

Among such novelties as have been provided by contestability theory, those that have perhaps attracted the most attention among academic economists are the ones offering new or modified analytical methods. Accordingly, in this section we undertake to describe the character of the methods that the theory employs to analyse the determination of industry structure. In the discussion some of the basic concepts used for the purpose will be described, among them *cost subadditivity* both as the definition of natural monopoly (when it holds for the industry) and as a universal requirement for optimality of firm size and product line; *declining ray average cost* as the indicator of local scale economies; *trans-ray convexity* as the criterion of product complementarity in production; and finally the *efficient-scale locus* for the outputs of firms with varying output proportions. The key role of subadditivity in the structure of an industry will be described, and the difficulty of testing for its presence either empirically or in a theoretical model will then be described and explained. Finally, two theorems that are at the heart of the analysis will be reported.

At one point, common wisdom seemed to hold that the presence of economies of scale is the necessary and sufficient condition for an industry to be a natural monopoly. It seems difficult to dispute that both in common parlance and among economists the term 'natural monopoly' connotes a case where the output of an industry can be produced more cheaply by a single firm than by any set of several enterprises, and, as will be shown presently, that is not the same as scale economies. Indeed, the definition of natural monopoly that has just been offered is precisely what is meant by the term 'subadditivity of costs'.

Formally, *subadditivity* is defined as follows. Let $C(Y)$ represent the total cost of producing output vector Y, and let Y^i be the output vector produced by firm i. Now, if we select any set of values of Y^i such that

$$\sum Y^i = Y$$

i.e. such that the output Y is totally divided up among the firms in question, then the cost function $C(Y)$ is strictly subadditive at vector Y if and only if

$$\sum C(Y^i) > C(Y)$$

In other words, the (aggregate) cost function is strictly subadditive at Y if there exists no set of firms and no subdivision of Y among those firms that permits Y to be produced at least as cheaply as can be done by a single enterprise.

It should be clear that this definition constitutes the formal translation of the commonly used natural monopoly concept. However, it is more than that, for a moment's thought should confirm that any cost-minimizing industry structure, whether it encompasses two firms or a thousand, must satisfy the following requirement. If in the efficient industry structure firm i is assigned the output vector Y^i, then the cost function of firm i must be (non-strictly) subadditive at Y^i. Moreover, if the efficient solution is to be unique, then cost must be strictly subadditive at that point. That this must be so is clear, since if the function were not subadditive there, then costs could be reduced by reassigning Y^i from firm i and subdividing it among some two or more enterprises, thus contradicting the stipulation that the initial assignment minimizes total cost. Thus, while the concept of subaddivity is crucial for the analysis of natural monopoly, it is, at least latently, of comparable importance for the case of 'natural oligopoly', i.e. that in which oligopoly is the cost-minimizing structure, or the case of 'naturally perfect competition' etc., for in each such case it is necessary that every firm in the cost-minimizing solution be assigned an output vector at which its cost is subadditive.

Now, while subadditivity is a concept that easily lends itself to intuitive comprehension, it is unfortunately not easy to deal with directly in a formal or a statistical analysis. For example, while it is indeed related to scale economies, in a multi-product firm scale economies are neither necessary nor sufficient for subadditivity. That they are not necessary is easily proved by a counter-example provided by Faulhaber (1975). Consider a single-product industry in which three units of output are to be supplied. If each unit is produced by a different firm, it will cost $14 to produce. A single firm can produce two units for $18 and three units for $30. Clearly, the cheapest way to produce the three units is via a single firm, and so the function is strictly subadditive at output $Y = 3$. Yet between $Y = 2$ and $Y = 3$ average cost obviously increases from $9 to $10, and marginal cost rises throughout. Therefore economies of scale do not prevail everywhere, despite the presence of strict subadditivity.

While it can be shown that scale economies are sufficient (although not necessary, as was just demonstrated) for subadditivity in a single-product firm, the reason that sufficiency fails in the multi-product case is instructive and easy to grasp. It is true that, where scale economies prevail, costs cannot be saved by replacing the firm with several scaled-down miniversions of itself, i.e. by dividing all its output quantities proportionately among a set of smaller enterprises. However, scale economies do not preclude the possibility of enhancement of efficiency by dividing the output vector of, say, a sixteen-product firm among sixteen smaller enterprises each specializing in the production of a single good. If that should be possible, the initial arrangement would clearly not satisfy the subaddivitity requirement. In other words, scale economies, without the simultaneous presence of complementarity in the production of the firm's various products, cannot guarantee the unavailability of a production arrangement involving more and smaller firms, meaning the failure of subadditivity. Thus subadditivity, that fundamental concept, has no analytically simple equivalent in the concept of scale economies, and it possesses no other known proxy that lends itself to direct analysis.

It follows straightforwardly from this that it is also very difficult to carry out an econometric test to determine whether subadditivity is present or absent. For, to prove subadditivity, it is necessary to show that there exists *no* combination of smaller enterprises, whether two or ten thousand, that can produce the output vector of the firm in question at a cost below the latter's. However, to investigate this involves not only the substantial combinatorial problem entailed in studying all the possible subdivisions of that output vector but also obtaining data about the costs that would be entailed by any and all possible firms offering smaller output vectors. That is, statistical estimates are required of the costs of even firms far smaller than any that are currently in operation or which have been in operation in the reasonably recent past. Unfortunately, as we know, data of this sort may simply be unavailable because no firm anywhere near that scale of operation may have existed in the recent past. Put

517

another way, we may be able to estimate the shape of the cost function statistically only in the neighbourhood of the current output vector of the firm in question. Yet to test for subadditivity directly it is necessary, at least in principle, to have an estimate of the shape and position of the cost surface for every output vector below that of our firm. The econometric difficulties that this entails should be clear.

Add to this the fact that there is no known analytical test of subadditivity, i.e. no operational rule analogous to the maximization requirements that the first derivative of a one-variable maximand be zero and that its second derivative be negative, and it becomes clear that the subadditivity concept, despite its intuitive simplicity, is not a concept that makes the analyst's life easier.

Since no one knows how to mount a direct assault on the matter, it has proved necessary to proceed indirectly. Analysts have dealt with the problem by formulating a set of conditions sufficient to guarantee subadditivity – conditions that are amenable both to formal analysis and to econometric estimation. Although, as is true of any sufficient conditions, failure of those conditions does not *dis*prove subadditivity, it has been helpful to have a set of conditions which, if satisfied, assure us that subadditivity does hold.

To describe the sufficient conditions which seem to have proved most useful we must first define two other concepts, declining ray average costs and trans-ray convexity, which are related respectively to scale economies and complementarity in production of several products. Intuitive reasons have already been given indicating why both of these are critical for subadditivity.

Declining ray average costs refer to the behaviour of costs along a ray in output space, i.e. to what happens to average costs when every output in the bundle of outputs of the firm (industry) is increased by the same proportion. Thus, for any output vector Y, any other output on the same ray as Y is given by kY, where k is a scalar parameter, and the ray average cost is $C(kY)/kY$. If we arbitrarily take Y as the unit vector on that ray, then the declining ray average cost at point kY on the ray through Y is defined to hold if and only if

$$\frac{\mathrm{d}[C(kY)/kY]}{\mathrm{d}kY} = \frac{\mathrm{d}[C(kY)/k]}{\mathrm{d}k} < 0$$

This can also be taken to be the definition of local economies of scale at point kY. In any event, the concept is surely familiar and requires no further discussion.

In contrast, our indicator of complementarity in production of several products, trans-ray convexity, has appeared only in the contestability literature and requires some explanation. For simplicity, we shall deal with a firm or industry that produces exactly two outputs, X and Y, and let (x, y) be any point in output space and $(x^*, 0)$ and $(0, y^*)$ be any two points on the output space axes such that the line segment connecting them contains (x, y). Then the cost function is said to be *trans-ray convex* at (x, y) if there exists any line segment such as that just described where the cross-section of the cost function above line segment $(x^*, 0)(0, y^*)$ is convex, i.e. U-shaped. Roughly speaking, this means that given any two points of relative specialization along that line, of which one, point R, involves predominantly the production of X, and the other, point S, involves predominantly the production of Y, then any intermediate, and consequently less specialized, point T will entail a cost lower than an average of the cost of R and the cost of S. Clearly, this is merely a formalized way of expressing the attribute that on the cost surface in question specialized production is more costly than production involving intermediate quantities of all of the products in question. Thus, it is clearly a form of complementarity assumption. (It is called 'trans-ray convexity' because the U-shaped cross-section is convex, and because the line segment $(x^*, 0)(0, y^*)$ must cross every ray in the non-negative quadrant of the output space graph.)

While the proof will not be given here, it is not difficult to demonstrate the following basic proposition: a sufficient set of conditions to guarantee that a cost function is strictly subadditive at some output vector Y is that the cost function has strictly declining ray average costs at all $Y^* < Y$ and that it be (non-strictly) trans-ray convex at Y.

The intuitive explanation of this result is simple. Where this pair of conditions is satisfied it will never be economical to subdivide the outputs of a single-firm producer of Y, because declining ray average costs ensure that scaled-down versions of the firm will incur disproportionately higher costs and trans-ray convexity ensures that the same will be true of smaller specialized firms. Thus, either approach to subdivision of output vector Y among a number of smaller enterprises must increase costs, meaning that the cost function is subadditive at Y.[2]

The importance of this proposition is that it provides an indirect method that can be used to test for subadditivity. Even if we cannot check for subadditivity directly, either analytically or econometrically, if we can verify that the two parts of the sufficient condition of the theorem are satisfied, then it follows that subadditivity must hold. Since both declining ray average cost and trans-ray convexity are relatively tractable conditions, this is the course that has been followed in much of the theoretical literature, and even more in the empirical literature.

One more theorem – the one that is central to the actual process of determining industry structure – will be reported. This is a proposition that sets bounds upon the number of firms in a cost-minimizing industry structure in a multi-product industry, given some limited information on the industry cost structure. From this number of enterprises we can then infer whether in contestable market equilibrium the industry will be a monopoly, an oligopoly or some other standard market form. The special difficulties with which this theorem grapples arise out of the multi-product character of the industry, which means that firms may differ in the sets of products they turn out, as well as in the magnitudes of the outputs of each of those products. Thus we cannot simply take each of those firms in the n-enterprise case to be responsible for an nth of the output vector of the industry.

A description of this theorem requires us to define one last concept – the locus of efficient scales. For each different output proportion, i.e. for each different ray in output space, we expect that there will be some level of output k^*Y at which the ray average cost for the ray's output bundles attains its minimum value. That value of k^*Y can be referred to as the efficient scale of output for the ray through point Y, and we shall assume here that for each ray in output space k^* is unique. Then we define the *efficient-scale locus* (the M locus) as the set of all points k^*Y for every ray in the non-negative orthant (quadrant) of output space.

Now, let us surround this locus with two (hyper)planes. The first of these, the lower linear bound L, lies everywhere on or below the locus, but as far away from the origin as possible.[3] Similarly, the upper linear bound U is the hyperplane that lies everywhere on or above the locus, but is as close to the origin as possible. Let Y^1 be the industry output vector, and let l and u be two scalar constants such that lY^1 lies on L and uY^1 lies on U, and where, naturally, $l \leq u$. Then we have the following proposition:[4] if n is the number of firms in a cost-minimizing industry structure, then

$$1/2u \leq n \leq 1/2l$$

Roughly speaking, this proposition is the multi-product counterpart of the intuitively obvious result for the single-product case that if Y is industry output, m is the efficient scale and Y/m is an integer, then the cost-minimizing number of firms must be Y/m. The variety of product lines available to the firms in the multi-product case is what accounts for the range that must surround the cost-minimizing number of firms there.

This discussion has gone on at sufficient length to indicate the spirit of the analysis of industry structure determination to be found in the contestability literature, so the exposition will be carried no further.

24.8 FINAL REMARKS

It is clear that there has been considerable progress toward analysis of the endogenous influences which affect and, perhaps, largely determine industry structure in practice. The variety of approaches that have been employed undoubtedly enhances the prospects for further advances in this important field. Its importance for theory, whose objective is understanding of the workings of economic phenomena, seems self-evident. Its importance for the design of policy is equally clear, since we cannot hope to make enduring changes in the structure of an industry, where that is deemed desirable, unless we understand what influences make that structure what it is.

One conclusion that follows from the preceding discussion merits re-emphasis. While it may be legitimate as an analytical simplification to deal separately with the determination of prices and outputs on the one hand and with the determination of industry structure on the other, it is now clear that such a disjunction is, in principle, incorrect. As is indicated by the reiterated dependence of the industry structure solutions and the pertaining constructs upon the industry output vector Y^I throughout the preceding section, industry structure clearly is dependent on industry output which, in turn, is dependent upon prices. However, it is a commonplace of received economic theory that prices and outputs are themselves dependent upon the structure assumed by the industry in question. In short, this is yet another case in which fully legitimate analysis cannot escape explicit recognition of the simultaneity of the underlying relationships.

NOTES

1 The following discussion draws heavily on the excellent survey by Shapiro (1987) of the game-theoretical literature on oligopoly behaviour (see especially pp. 60–77).
2 For a proof, see Baumol (1977).
3 Here we measure distance from the origin along the ray through the industry output vector Y^1.
4 The statement of the proposition is only approximately correct, but it is sufficiently close for present purposes. For a rigorous statement and a derivation, see Baumol et al. (1988: ch. 5, Section F, and ch. 5, Appendix III).

REFERENCES

Baumol, W. J. (1977) 'On the proper cost tests for natural monopoly in a multiproduct industry', *American Economic Review* 67: 809–22.

Baumol, W. J., Panzar, J. C. and Willig, R. D. (1988) *Contestable Markets and the Theory of Industry Structure*, revised edn, San Diego, CA: Harcourt Brace Jovanovich.

Davidson, C. and Deneckere, R. (1985) 'Incentives to form coalitions with Bertrand competition', *Rand Journal of Economics* 17: 404–15.

Faulhaber, G. R. (1975) 'Cross-subsidization: pricing in public enterprises', *American Economic Review* 65: 966–77.

Fudenberg, D. and Tirole, J. (1984) 'The fat-cat effect, the puppy-dog ploy and the lean and hungry look', *American Economic Review, Papers and Proceedings* 74: 361–6.

von Neumann, J. and Morgenstern, O. (1944) *Theory of Games and Economic Behavior*, Princeton, NJ: Princeton University Press.

Salant, S., Switzer, S. and Reynolds, R. (1983) 'Losses from horizontal merger: the effects of an exogenous change in industry structure on Cournot–Nash equilibrium', *Quarterly Journal of Economics* 98: 185–99.

Shapiro, C. (1987) 'Theories of oligopoly behavior', Discussion paper 126, Woodrow Wilson School, Princeton University.

Williamson, O. E. (1985) *The Economic Institutions of Capitalism*, New York: Free Press.

25

THE GROWTH OF THE PUBLIC SECTOR

J. RICHARD ARONSON AND ATTIAT F. OTT

25.1 INTRODUCTION

What distinguishes the public from the private sectors of the economy? Activities in the private sector may be for profit or not for profit, but are carried out voluntarily by individuals and groups in the market-place. Public sector activities may or may not use the market-place but are decided upon through a political process. In this case, the group is called government and our participation is not voluntary in the same sense that it is in the private sector. The two sectors interact. The private sector creates the wealth that is tapped by the public sector. However, the public sector has an essential role to play in creating the environment in which private economic agents can prosper.

Private sector growth is essential for a nation's economic well-being. Measured through gross national product (GNP), production, sales etc., increased values are interpreted as signs of economic health. Although it is generally accepted that public sector activity is also essential for economic welfare, growth of the public sector is not always greeted happily. One point of view suggests that a large and growing public sector is detrimental to efficiency and the health of the economy. It has even become fashionable to describe the growth of the public sector in the demonic terms of Leviathan,[1] the point here being that public sector meddling and control can reduce people's freedom and economic incentive. At the other extreme, however, there are those who assign to the government a critical role in the process of economic development. According to this view, a large government size promotes economic growth by reducing dependence on external forces, especially in the less developed world.

We divide this chapter into four parts. In Section 25.2, we define the public sector and provide some general data to show its tendency to grow over time. Our discussion includes an analysis of some of the problems of measuring the growth and size of the public sector. Some of these problems are interesting, but it is not surprising to learn that the public sector has grown in most countries. A more interesting question is why it has grown.

In Section 25.3, we describe several theories of public sector growth, no one of which offers a complete explanation. The wide variety of hypotheses on this subject suggests that the issue is complex but at the same time provides many insights in helping us understand the size of government. The normative aspects of public sector activity must also be confronted. To some, the public sector is needed to offset the failure of the market-place. Students of the subject, such as Richard Musgrave, have explained the concept of market failure in both the allocation and distribution of resources and looked to government as the institution best suited for correcting such defects (Musgrave 1951; Musgrave and Musgrave 1989). To others, the public sector is a Leviathan that produces instability and saps the strength of the economic agents that create value. Scholars such as Milton Friedman and James Buchanan fear that a government growing too fast and regulating too much reduces people's economic freedom, induces perverse economic behaviour and dulls the incentives that create wealth.[2] The current empirical research in this area is described and analysed in Section 25.4. Some concluding remarks are offered in the final section.

25.2 PUBLIC SECTOR GROWTH

Public sector defined

Public sector activity is the activity of governmental units. This means that we are interested in the affairs of national governments and of state and local authorities as well. Currently, there are over 80,000 such units in the United States. What do all these governments do? Functions that in the opinion of most are best handled by government include national defence, domestic law, order and safety, and providing capital infrastructure and social overhead capital. There is less uniformity of thought when government is involved in running business enterprises. Certain utilities have often been run or controlled by the public sector (for example, electricity, gas, water, sewers etc.) without much controversy. However, some governments also run steel companies, airlines, railroads and liquor stores. The swings from 'nationalizing' industries to 'privatizing' them suggest that there are strong differences in people's views on how best to provide some essential public services.

Governments become involved in altering the distribution of income. Social security transfers income from those working to those retired; health programmes transfer resources from those who are healthy to those who are not; and through the use of debt, income can be redistributed between the general taxpayer and the bond holder. In the United States, the amount spent on redistribution far exceeds the amount spent on the purchase of goods and services.

The size of the public sector will obviously vary from country to country. Some will assign more functions to government than others will, and some will have a stronger taste for public services than others will. Moreover, the allocation of responsibilities between different levels of government will also vary, with some countries relying more on the central government than others. The differences exist because groups have different political systems, because the demographic forces at work differ, because countries differ in income and wealth and because people differ in their preferences for publicly supplied goods and services.

Measuring the public sector

By conventional budget and income measures, the public sector's share of national income has increased in all countries of Western Europe and North America over the last century. However, measuring the size of the government by the ratio of government expenditures to income or GNP is not altogether satisfactory. The regulatory activities of government also have an important impact on private sector decisions. However, these indirect effects are not easily quantifiable and the conventional narrower measure of the scope of government activity is commonly used.

We must proceed with some care even with this 'narrow' measure of the size of the public sector, especially when international comparisons are being attempted regarding the size and growth of the public sector. We must take account of the fact that countries can change in size (in both area and population) and that prices of publicly supplied goods may change at a different rate from the overall price level.

Table 25.1 presents summary data for the growth of the US public sector for the period 1929–87. During this period, the total expenditures of federal, state and local governments in current dollars increased from $10.3 billion to $1,574.4 billion. This amounts to a healthy average annual rate of increase of 9 per cent. We also separate the expenditures of state and local governments from those of the central government and find that, since the Great Depression, the federal government has grown faster than the state and local sector. Do these very raw figures offer conclusive evidence about the growth of the US public sector? The answer is, no. First, we should note that during this time period the country has grown in both size and wealth. States have been added, population has grown and per capita income has increased.

We can obtain a better idea of the increasing size of the public sector by comparing the rate of growth in government spending with the rate of growth in prices, income and population. Between 1929 and 1987, prices in the

Table 25.1 Growth of public sector, selected years

Year	Public sector spending			GNP	Popu-lation (million)	Price index (1982 = 100)	As a percentage of GNP		Per capita total spending in constant dollars
	Total	Federal	State and local ($billion)				Total (%)	Federal (%)	
1929	10.3	2.7	7.8	103.9	121.8	14.6	9.9	2.6	585
1939	17.6	9.0	9.6	91.3	130.9	12.7	19.3	9.9	1,059
1949	60.0	42.0	20.2	260.4	149.2	23.5	23.0	16.1	1,711
1959	131.9	91.7	47.0	495.8	177.8	30.4	26.6	18.5	2,440
1969	290.2	191.3	119.0	963.9	202.7	39.8	30.1	19.8	3,599
1979	768.3	521.1	327.7	2,508.2	225.1	78.6	30.6	20.8	4,343
1987	1,574.4	1,074.2	602.8	4,526.7	243.9	117.7	34.8	23.7	5,475
Average annual growth rates									
1929–87	9.0	10.8	7.7	6.7	1.2	3.7			3.9
1929–39	5.5	12.7	2.1	−1.3					6.1
1939–49	13.0	16.6	7.7	7.1					4.9
1949–59	8.2	8.1	8.8	6.7					3.6
1959–69	8.2	7.6	9.8	6.9					3.9
1969–79	10.2	10.5	10.6	10.0					1.9
1979–87	9.3	9.4	7.9	7.6					2.9

Sources: Economic Report of the President, 1989, p. 401; ACIR, *Significant Features of Fiscal Federalism*, 1988 edn, volume I, pp. 2–3

United States increased by roughly 3.7 per cent per annum. This rate of inflation is measured by the GNP deflator. Thus, if we correct the current dollar figures for the rate of inflation, we still see a growing public sector. Roughly speaking, the public sector in the United States seems to have grown at an average annual rate of 5.3 per cent.

Between 1929 and 1987, the population of the United States grew at an annual rate of 1.2 per cent per annum. Thus, even after correcting our public expenditure figures for changes in prices and population, we see substantial growth. Public expenditures per person, in 1982 dollars, increased at an annual rate of approximately 4 per cent between 1929 and 1987.

Another way of estimating the size of government is to express the size of the public sector in relation to the overall size of the economy. Between 1929 and 1987 the annual rate of increase in GNP (6.7 per cent per annum) was lower than the annual rate of increase in government spending (9 per cent). Table 25.1 shows total US public sector spending relative to GNP. The level, which was 10 per cent in 1929, rose to 35 per cent in 1987. Once again the conclusion can be drawn that the public sector has grown.

Public sector growth has been neither continuous nor constant over time. There have been stretches of time in which the growth of the government sector has kept up with the growth of GNP (for example, during the 1969–79 decade) and times in which government growth has surpassed that of GNP (for example, 1929–39 and 1939–49). Moreover, it is not always true that the central government growth has been consistently above that of the state and local governments. As the data reported in the lower part of Table 25.1 indicate, the growth rates of the state and local sector exceeded those of the federal government in the 1950s and 1960s. The different growth patterns exhibited by the two sectors over the last fifty years are noteworthy. Whereas the state–local sector has grown steadily and gradually, the federal sector growth path was characterized by growth peaks (the 1930s and 1940s) followed by lower growth rates in subsequent decades. Despite these peaks and valleys, the overall growth of the public sector, particularly relative to GNP, lends credence to the view that government is a growth industry.[3]

Table 25.2 provides some data describing the public sectors of countries other than the United States. From the table we can see that in relative terms the US public sector is not particularly large. This international comparison concentrates solely on the activities of central governments and reports central government expenditures as a percentage of gross domestic product (GDP). In many other countries, especially the industrialized ones, government expenditures as a percentage of GDP are higher than in the United States. Notice also that, although the table covers only a short period of time (1977–87), there is definitely a drift upward in public expenditures as a percentage of GDP across nations.

Table 25.2 International comparisons (central government expenditures as percentage of gross domestic product)

	USA	UK	Sweden	West Germany	India	Canada	Australia	Brazil
1977	22.2	36.7	41.1	29.6	17.2	21.3	28.2	23.5
1978	22.2	38.4	44.8	29.5	18.7	21.5	24.0	23.8
1979	21.0	38.1	45.7	29.1	19.6	20.6	27.6	22.2
1980	27.8	40.6	46.5	30.6	18.7	21.3	26.8	23.5
1981	24.5	41.5	48.3	31.6	18.0	22.3	26.9	26.0
1982	25.4	43.7	49.0	32.0	18.9	24.8	27.2	28.8
1983	25.2	42.5	49.9	31.5	18.9	24.6	29.5	30.4
1984	24.6	41.5	47.9	31.7	20.8	25.2	30.4	28.3
1985	25.7	41.3	48.3	31.3	22.5	24.6	30.9	38.2
1986	25.0	39.9	49.0	30.5	23.9	23.2	30.4	34.4
1987	24.1	n.a.	43.4	30.5	22.5	n.a.	29.7	n.a.

Source: Government Finance Statistics Yearbook, vol. XII, 1988, pp. 94, 95
Note: n.a., not available.

Before moving on to a discussion of the theories of growth, we must stress the fact that budget expenditures offer a very imperfect technique of measuring the size and impact of government. First, a significant component of public spending is in the form of inputs rather than outputs, which makes it difficult to interpret their growth as improvement in well-being. Moreover, expenditures are not the only variable that can be used to measure public sector activity. Another variable which might be considered is the total level of employment. In addition, it is also important to recognize that the power and size of government is often felt through its role in harmonizing conflicts between private and social interests. Quantifying these types of activities is a task yet to be handled in a satisfactory manner.

25.3 THEORIES OF PUBLIC SECTOR GROWTH

There are many theories and hypotheses to explain the size and growth of government. None by itself offers a complete explanation, but together they offer important insights that improve our understanding of the problem. We begin our analysis by providing an overview of Wagner's law, the notion that government expenditures have a tendency to rise as a percentage of national income. We then describe the various theories of government growth under the following headings: internal economic theories, internal political theories and external theories.

Wagner's law

Adolph Wagner, a German economist, is generally credited with first discovering the tendency for growth in government spending relative to national income. As a result, this tendency is usually referred to as Wagner's law. Writing in the mid-nineteenth century, Wagner explained the increase as a result of the natural path of civilization. That government expenditures should rise with increased national income is not surprising. There is little reason to doubt that the goods and services supplied by government are 'normal'. But why should the public sector increase relative to the private economy?

Wagner neither believed that it was possible to determine theoretically an optimal relationship between the fiscal requirement of the state and national income, nor that the public sector would eventually engulf all economic activity. However, he did suggest that since the state's fiscal needs represent only one element in a person's household budget, there exists a proportion of public expenditure to national income that may not be overstepped.

For Wagner, the long-run growth of the public sector is a product of economic development which carries with it larger populations and denser living arrangements, both of which may call for increased governmental activity. Economic growth also means a greater division of labour, the rise of large business organizations and a more complex set of economic relationships among people, all of which may understandably lead to greater governmental activity (Musgrave and Peacock 1967: 1–15).

Further insight into the growth of the public sector comes from another nineteenth-century German scholar, Ernst Engel. Engel's interest was in consumption patterns. He showed that the poorer the family, the greater is the proportion of its total expenditure devoted to food. It was from such thinking that we obtain Engel's laws, the fourth of which holds that, as income increases, the percentage of outlays for sundries becomes greater.[4] Are public goods then to be thought of as luxury goods? Certainly it is too simplistic to think of all public goods as being of the same type. Defence expenditures might be thought of as necessities and have been shrinking in relation to national income as Engel's law would predict. And if one wants to think of welfare payments as luxuries, more confirmation of Engel's approach to understanding the public sector can be found.[5]

The work of Wagner and Engel provides a description rather than an explanation of public sector growth. In what follows we discuss a number of economic and political theories that add to our understanding of the problem.

Internal theories – economic

What we call internal economic theories treat the level of public spending as the outcome of a market for publicly provided goods and services. That is, demand and cost conditions and the size of the community determine public expenditures. The problem then reduces to one of understanding price and income elasticities for public goods and the tax-sharing effect.

To see how the tax-sharing effect might work consider the concept of a 'public good'. Public goods are defined technically as those goods which we all enjoy in common (i.e. they are offered in joint supply) and which it is very difficult or expensive to exclude anybody from enjoying.[6] For our purposes, the joint consumption characteristic is more important. It implies that each person consumes (but may not enjoy) the same amount of the good and that one person's consumption does not subtract from the consumption of anyone else (i.e. there are neither crowding nor congestion costs). Under such conditions and assuming constant costs of public goods provision, what are the implications of adding one more person to the group? As the group becomes larger, the tax price per citizen falls (because of tax sharing), and this may result in an increased demand for public goods. A growing government sector can therefore be attributed to a larger community's taking advantage of what appears to be a reduction in the relative price of public goods.

Aside from the tax-sharing effect, which is crucial in the case of population growth or decline, the public may actually underestimate the relative price of public goods. Stubblebine (1963), Buchanan (1967) and Goetz (1977) argue that, since tax systems are usually complicated, citizen taxpayers hardly know what taxes they are actually paying. In the case of debt finance, people underestimate the future tax payments needed to service the bonds. The consequences of this cost underestimation are that the demand for public goods and the budget size will be larger than it would have been if prices were correctly perceived.

Income growth as well as population growth increases demand. A faster growth of government expenditures than national income implies an income elasticity greater than unity for public goods and services. But how much of the growth in government expenditures can be explained by the growth of population, price and income? An often quoted figure cited by Borcherding (1977a: ch. 2; 1985) suggests that the answer is about 38 per cent. When spending is related to GNP, these three growth factors explain why US public budgets absorbed 18 per cent of GNP in 1978, with the actual share being 35 per cent (Borcherding 1985: 368), so that a good part of the increase in expenditures in absolute terms and in relation to GNP can be chalked up to citizen preferences, be they of the President, the Congress or perhaps the median voter. Yet there remains much to explain.

One of the most interesting insights into the growth of the public sector is found in Baumol's theory of unbalanced growth (Baumol 1967). The basic premise of this theory is that economic activities can be classified as either stagnant (with low or zero technical progress) or technologically progressive. Some economic enterprises or sectors will be more productive than others, where productivity is defined as output per worker-hour. The way that this seemingly innocent notion leads to an explanation of the growth of the public sector is through the importance of labour in the production of goods and services. Baumol points out that, although labour may simply be a factor input, there are times when labour itself is an output, and it is where labour is an output as well as an input (services) that productivity growth will be less.

Consider the implication of this proposition for an economy consisting of two sectors: one progressive and one non-progressive. Over time, productivity (i.e. output per worker-hour) increases in the progressive sector whereas the non-progressive sector exhibits no growth. In a competitive economy, labour receives the value of its marginal product. Thus, the real wage in the progressive sector will grow at the rate of technological progress. Increased productivity in the progressive sector can support wage increases without increasing unit costs. However, unless labour markets are sealed off from each other, competitive pressure will transmit those wage increases to the non-progressive sector. This means that, with the passage of time, the unit cost of a consistently non-progressive or stagnant enterprise will rise monotonically and without limit relative to the cost in the productive sector.

The demand for the output of the non-progressive sector depends on the relative price of these goods and on income. The rise in the relative price will, of course, reduce the demand, while the rise in income will increase it.[7] If the price effect is dominant, then the continuously rising relative costs in the less productive sector might result in these goods being driven off the market.

However, if the demand for goods provided by this sector is very inelastic, for either market or political reasons, an ever rising portion of the labour force will be shifted to the non-productive sector. Moreover, the level of spending on the goods and services provided by this sector will rise relative to expenditures on the goods produced in the productive sector.

Assuming that the public sector is one with low or zero productivity growth, Baumol's model predicts that public expenditure growth will be faster in activities with the highest income elasticities of demand and the lowest price elasticities of demand. This prediction about the growth of government is difficult to test empirically.[8] Confirmation of the theory when applied to government activity hinges on our ability to define the output of government.[9] In our introductory section we have already made mention of this problem. The government expenditures that we track are essentially input values; very little progress has been made in trying to measure the output of the public sector.

Despite this problem, there is great strength in the central thrust of the Baumol theory. The public sector is labour intensive, and government output is usually in the form of services rather than goods. If the price elasticity of demand for public sector services is low, if productivity growth only occurs in the private sector and if labour market pressures lead to uniform wage increases throughout the economy, then there is reason to believe that in terms of dollars spent per year the public sector will grow relative to the private sector.

Internal theories – political

What we call internal political theories explain the level of public spending as the result of a political process. The study of public choice offers many insights into understanding the growth of the public sector (see Chapter 12). Public choice analysis begins with the presumption that self-interest is the motivating force behind people's actions in the public as well as the private sector. Public sector agents no less than private sector agents are considered rent-seekers. To think of public sector decisions being made solely in the 'public interest' is not so much wrong as naïve. Elected officials are seen as individuals trying to maximize their incomes and/or power by increasing spending on programmes that would enhance their chances of being re-elected. Bureaucrats (public choice scholars prefer this term to 'civil servant') are also power-brokers, but in this case the objective is to promote growth of their function or, in simpler terms, to maximize their agency's control of budget resources.[10]

Public choice analysts worry about the problems arising because of the asymmetry of expenditures and taxes and because of fiscal illusions that may be pondered from the use of debt finance. For example, politicians have learned that voters react positively to expenditure programmes but negatively to tax increases. Most expenditure programmes make friends. Since programme

531

beneficiaries may be concentrated within one or a few groups, for example social security recipients, these people are likely to lend support to the politician promoting them. But what about the tax side of the budget? Taxes to finance specific programmes are generally spread over a much larger group than those receiving benefits. Hence tax increases to finance benefits may not be correctly perceived and opposition to programme growth may not be voiced. In other instances, taxpayers may find no connection between benefits and costs of public expenditures and as a result may approve of the expenditures but oppose tax increases. It is not surprising, therefore, that where fiscal constraints are loose and borrowing is easy there will be a tendency for deficits to occur and for the public sector to grow.

Also, financing government programmes with debt may create a fiscal illusion. A substitution of debt finance for tax finance may cause people to underestimate the price of public goods and thereby increase their demand for more spending. However, not everyone accepts the idea that debt will fool people. Informed individuals realize that the servicing of debt requires future tax payments, the present value of which is equivalent, under certain conditions, to the value of an immediate tax payment. This is the Ricardian 'equivalence theorem', and to the extent that it is true, people's demand for public services should not be influenced by the financing technique employed by government.[11]

How seriously should we take this theorem? It is doubtful that voters will permanently misperceive their tax burden; at the same time, the Ricardian equivalence theorem may be asking too much of voters. It is not likely that people accurately see or believe that the higher future taxes associated with the debt have reduced their net worth to exactly the same amount as if the project were financed with immediate taxation. In effect, citizen voters may be more inclined to approve expenditures financed with debt rather than taxation even when the real cost of the two options is equivalent.

There is a group of public choice theorists who reject the view that voters suffer from fiscal illusion or that they are myopic (Peltzman 1980; Meltzer and Richard 1981). According to this group, voters know that the government must extract resources to pay for public services. Government grows not because of any fiscal illusion but because of the ability of interest groups to dominate policy decisions in their favour and to use the government for redistributive purposes. The logic behind such models is simple. Assuming that the amount of spending is determined solely by majority voting and that voters are fully informed, Peltzman shows that incentives to redistribute wealth politically are the key determinants of the relative size and growth of the public sector (Peltzman 1980: 221). This conclusion is arrived at by a two-stage process. First, Peltzman uncovers a politically 'dominant' strategy for redistribution of wealth which yields the greatest benefits for the greatest number.

Next, he demonstrates that, once found, competition among politicians for votes will lead them to choose that policy and implement it upon election. The basic premise that underlies the choice of this dominant strategy is that political preferences are motivated by self-interest. With the assumption of full information, this means that the politically dominant redistribution policy is one that maximizes the difference between the number of people who perceive the policy as the best deal (gainers or beneficiaries) and the number of people who view it as the worst deal (losers or taxpayers).

Because taxpayers and transfer recipients interact in the economy, there is a limit beyond which redistribution will not be pushed. To illustrate, suppose that A and B are alternative schemes for the redistribution of income. Scheme A involves increasing the pension benefits of retirees with financing through higher taxes on wage-earners. Scheme A redistributes income from workers to the retired population. Scheme B is a plan to change the tax structure by reducing rates on personal income while increasing rates on income from capital (i.e. raising the corporate tax rate). Which of these two schemes is likely to emerge as the dominant strategy? Under A, the number of gainers – pensioners – is smaller than the number of losers – wage-earners. On the other hand, scheme B reduces the tax bite on most people while raising it on a 'few' taxpayers – owners of capital. Since income from capital tends to be concentrated at the higher level of the income distribution, and because taxes on income from capital such as the corporate income tax are not well understood or accurately perceived, scheme B emerges as the dominant redistribution strategy because it promises to deliver more gainers than losers.

Meltzer and Richard's (1981) framework, although differing somewhat from that of Peltzman, leads to similar conclusions. Starting with the assumptions of full information, majority rule and self-interest, they come to the conclusion that the size of the government depends on the relationship between mean income (average income of the population) and the income of the decisive or median voter. If there are changes in relative income – income of the decisive voter relative to mean income – the size of government changes. Meltzer and Richard consider the extension of voting rights to be significant for the size of government. They state: 'Extensions of the franchise that increase the number of voters who benefit from income redistribution increase votes for redistribution' (Peltzman 1980: 221). The effect on the level of the tax rate (for redistribution purposes) will depend on the relative position of the decisive voter. If that position shifts down, the distribution of income, tax rates and spending rise; if it shifts up, the level of spending and the size of government decrease. If the relative position of the decisive voter remains unchanged, the size of the public sector will stabilize.

External theories – the displacement effect

Another view of the growth of the public sector holds that the increase in the size of the public sector arises from external shocks to the system. In the analysis by Peacock and Wiseman (1961, 1979), the public sector is explained in terms of displacement, inspection and concentration effects. During settled times, people can be expected to develop notions of acceptable effective rates of taxation. With real economic growth, the more or less fixed tax rate structure will produce increasing amounts of revenue and public spending. This means that there is an obvious connection between growth in national income tax receipts and growth in public spending. However, this does not explain the rise in the ratio of public expenditures to national income.

Large-scale social disturbances, such as wars and depression, change people's ideas about the limits of taxation and the desirable level of public spending. The result, called a displacement effect, shifts expenditures and revenues to new higher leels. The 'higher' level of public spending does not revert to the lower levels after the disturbance has passed; rather, it creates a newly accepted level of public activities. According to Peacock and Wiseman, there are two reasons why public expenditures will be maintained at the new higher level even after the crisis has passed. First, the public sector is now in a position to finance projects that it always wanted but which it formerly thought beyond its ability to afford. Second, the social upheaval unveils new obligations which must be taken on by government. Peacock and Wiseman call this the inspection effect.

Growth in national income or occurrence of a national crisis such as a war also gives rise, they suggest, to a concentration effect. That is, a tendency may exist for the central government to grow relative to local authorities. Economic development brings with it improvements in transportation, communication and mobility that promote the desire for uniformity in government services. The central government is said to be better equipped to provide uniformity, and perhaps reap greater economies of scale in the provision of public services. Moreover, the concentration of power limits the restraints on taxes brought about by competition among local authorities. Brennan and Buchanan (1980) draw an analogy between a centralized government and a private sector monopolist seeking to maximize profits. A monolithic government seeks to exploit its citizens through the maximization of tax revenues. Accordingly, they argue that the most powerful constraint on the size of government is fiscal decentralization. Concentration/centralization may thereby in itself help to explain a portion of public sector growth.

However, evidence in support of the displacement–concentration effects is not altogether conclusive, at least since the end of the Second World War. When only non-defence expenditures of industrialized countries are considered, it may even be true that there is a trend towards lower values in the ratio of central to total government expenditures (Oates 1972: 230; Aronson 1985: 115–16).

Up to now, we have presented several theories explaining why governments grow. But which ones offer the best explanations? A great deal of empirical research has been carried out in hopes of answering such a question. We now review several of these attempts.

25.4 EMPIRICAL ANALYSIS: AN OVERVIEW

This section of the chapter is organized in much the same way as the theoretical part. The empirical tests are discussed under four headings: testing for Wagner's law; tests of the Baumol model; empirical studies based on the public choice model; empirical tests of the Leviathan hypothesis and the displacement effect.

Testing for Wagner's law: causality between government expenditures and national income

Until recently, empirical tests of Wagner's law consisted of regressing aggregate (or per capita) public sector expenditures on per capita income and a few other variables. A typical representation is an equation (in logarithmic form) like the following:

$$E = A + bY + CP + dN$$

where E is the real per capita government expenditure, Y is the real per capita income, N is the population, P is the relative price of a unit of public good and A represents all other factors.

For Wagner's law to hold, the income elasticity of demand b for public sector goods must be greater than unity. If $b > 1$ then increases in income or economic development give rise to an expanding public sector relative to the economy. However, if $b < 1$, then increases in income will cause the ratio of public sector activity to national income to fall. When $b = 1$, the relative size of the public sector remains constant over time. Borcherding's (1977b) survey of the empirical literature suggests that $b = 0.75$, although Peltzman (1980) found the elasticity of 'permanent income' (calculated as a moving-average income) to be equal to unity. Therefore it appears that the simplified notion of Wagner's law does not hold empirically.

A basic shortcoming of this type of statistical test is that the direction of causality between government expenditures and national income is not necessarily clear. The Keynesian school of thought tends to treat government expenditures as an exogenous policy variable, not influenced by the level of national income. In effect, discretionary changes in government spending have a direct impact on the level of economic activity. However, we also know that at least a portion, and a sizeable one at that, of public sector expenditure is tied to the aggregate level of economic activity. Transfer payments, employment compensation etc. do vary in response to changes in national income. Because of this dependence, we can make the observation that 'causality' may run both ways – from national income to expenditures and the other way round as well.

In recent years, empirical tests of Wagner's law have relied on a more sophisticated econometric model than the simple regression equation given above. These tests make use of a concept of causality developed by Granger (1969) and elaborated upon by Sims (1972). Simply stated, a variable X (national income) causes changes in another variable Y (government spending), if the present (or future) value of Y can be better predicted by using past values of X than by not doing so. Testing Granger causality is carried out by means of an equation like

$$\log E_t = b_0 + b_1 t + b_2 \log Y_t + u_t$$

where E_t is the per capita public sector expenditures in time period t; Y_t is the per capita national income in time period t; b_0, b_1, b_2 are parameters and u_t is the error term. According to the Granger causality test, Wagner's law holds if $b_2 > 1$. Under this condition increases in national income will result in the ratio of government activity to income rising. If $b_2 < 1$, increases in national income will cause the ratio to fall, and if $b_2 = 1$, changes in national income will not change the ratio of government expenditures to income.

Using this method, Wagner and Weber (1977) empirically evaluated Wagner's law for a sample of thirty-four countries. The data used covered the period 1950–72. Real government expenditure per capita (alternatively real government consumption per capita) was used as the measure of government activity. Real GNP per capita (or real national income per capita) was used as the measure of income. Wagner and Weber rejected Wagner's law because of the high percentage of cases where it did not hold according to the causality test ($b_2 < 1$). Their empirical findings led them to conclude that 'Wagner's Law can hardly be considered a "law" at all' (Wagner and Weber 1977: 65).

Wagner and Weber's finding is not universally endorsed. Other studies such as those of Sahni and Singh (1984), Singh and Sahni (1984) and Singh et al. (1986) found the causality between government expenditures and gross national income to be bidirectional for the United States, India and Canada. Delorme et al. (1988), using quarterly data, found a unidirectional causality from income to government spending for the Federal Republic of Germany, no significant causal relationship for the United Kingdom and a two-way causality between GNP and government expenditures for the United States. Using annual data for the United States, the causality was one way – from

GNP to expenditure. The latter finding is consistent with those of Ram (1986), who also uncovered a unidirectional causality for the United States.

Variations on the above causality test have been reported. Replacing the national income variable by government revenues (on the assumption that the revenue base is elastic with respect to national income), we can test for the direction of causation between government spending and government revenues. This variation on the 'main' theme of causality evaluates whether projected revenue or planned expenditure should be viewed as the more fundamental determinant of the size of the public sector.

Using annual data for the US federal sector covering the period 1929–82, Manage and Marlow (1986) investigated the causal relationship between budget outlays and receipts using three alternative measures. They carried out their tests with data measured in nominal, real and net of interest payments terms and found the causality flows to be mainly bidirectional (58 per cent of the cases); the remaining cases (42 per cent) indicate a unidirectional link from revenues to outlays. The latter result is supported by the findings of Holtz-Eakin *et al.* (1987) for local governments in the United States. However, Anderson *et al.* (1986) found causality to run the other way, from federal expenditures to revenues, and Von Furstenberg *et al.* (1986), working with quarterly data for the federal government over the period 1954–82, reinforced the finding that the causal flow is between government spending and revenue – 'spend now and tax later'. When the data set was broadened to include several countries the pattern of causality was less clear. Ram (1988a) investigated the direction of causation between revenues and expenditures across federal and state and local governments using annual data covering the period 1929–83 and quarterly data for the post-war era (1947–83). He uncovered important differences between causality patterns for the federal sector and the state and local government sector. In the post-war period, Ram found causality to be from revenue to expenditure in the federal data, and from expenditure to revenue in the state–local sector. The results with annual data show the same pattern except that some bidirectional flows were observed for the federal sector.

Ram (1988b), using a Granger causality test applied to a sample of twenty-two countries, investigated the pattern of causal flows between government revenues and government expenditures in a multi-country setting. In most cases he found no statistically significant flow of causality in either direction. Moreover, when the test results were significant, he found as many cases where causality runs from revenue to expenditures as when the causal flow is in the opposite direction. For the US federal government, however, the direction of causality was from revenue to expenditure, supporting the contention that GNP causes government expenditures and not vice versa.

537

Tests of the Baumol model

How important are rising costs in the 'non-progressive' sector in explaining the growth of public spending? Bradford *et al.* (1969) investigated the applicability of the Baumol model to local government spending in the United States. Keeping in mind the inherent difficulties associated with measuring public sector output, the findings are of some interest. By comparing the rate of growth of various measures of unit costs of local government output with the rate of growth in the wholesale price index (an index relatively low in service component), Bradford *et al.* offer a direct test of Baumol's contention that the technology of the public sector is stagnant. The empirical evidence supports this contention. Over the period 1947–67, the costs per pupil per day in public elementary and secondary schools have increased at a rate of 6.7 per cent per annum compared with a rise in the money cost of producing farm and industrial output (WPI) of only 1.4 per cent per year. In terms of opportunity costs, we can say that, over this period, the number of units of a WPI bundle of goods which must be given up for a pupil-day of public school education rose by about 4–5 per cent per annum (Bradford *et al.* 1969: 190). The same finding holds for other categories of public services – health and hospitals, police and fire protection, and public welfare. It is worth noting, however, that the magnitude of the cost disease tends to vary with the type of local government. Cost pressures are much more intense on the governments of the large central cities than on those of smaller suburban municipal units (Bradford *et al.* 1969: 202). Lower rates of productivity growth in the public sector are only one of many possible explanations of the growth of public spending.

Spann (1977) offers another test of Baumol's unbalanced-growth model by comparing the model's predictions of public sector growth with actual patterns of government expenditure growth. Specifically, Spann tests the empirical validity of two predictions: first, a growth in the government's real per capita expenditure and, second, faster growth in public activities with the highest income elasticities of demand and the lowest price elasticities of demand.

Spann divides the economy into a private progressive sector and a public non-progressive sector. Output in the former is produced using labour and technology as inputs, while in the latter only labour is used. The demand for public sector output depends on relative prices (public versus private), income and population. Per capita demand then depends on the rate of technological progress in the private economy (income growth) and income and price elasticities. To avoid the problem of output measurement in the public sector, Spann concentrates on the price variables rather than the amount of real output. Public expenditures measure the output of the public sector evaluated by the price of public sector output. The rate of growth of real public sector expenditures is given by the sum of two terms: the rate of growth in the price of public sector output relative to the price of private sector output, and the rate of growth of public sector output. Since labour is the only factor of production, the public sector share of GNP is simply the labour used to produce the public sector share divided by the total labour force. This simplification allows Spann to express the growth rate of government's share of GNP as the sum of the income and price elasticities multiplied by the rate of technical progress.

Using US data on the rate of growth of productivity in the private sector and real per capita government expenditures (nominal expenditures deflated by the consumer price index), and relying on estimates reported in the literature of price and income elasticities of the demand for public sector output, Spann calculates Baumol's 'predicted growth rates'. For the period 1950–60, he finds the predicted growth rates for government expenditures per capita to be in the range 2.7–2.9 per cent. The actual growth rate for this period was 3.6 per cent. With respect to the government's increasing share of GNP the estimates were in the range 0.64–0.84 per cent compared with an actual growth rate of 2 per cent. Because elasticity estimates are not available for the federal sector, Spann relies on reported estimates for the state–local sector services to test Baumol's second proposition. The annual rate of expenditure growth turned out to be positively related to the sum of the elasticities. The lowest growth rates were found for those activities for which the sum of the price and income elasticities were negative (sanitation, health and hospitals); highest growth rates were found for those activities for which the sums were positive (education).

Tests of public choice theories

The empirical evidence regarding the growth of government indicates the rising importance of transfer payments. Who are the main beneficiaries of transfers and why has this device become more popular? Stigler (1970, 1973) claims that public expenditures are designed to benefit primarily the middle class. He also notes that, during the nineteenth century, benefits of public spending were not tailored to a specific group and taxes were not tied to personal income. In the twentieth century, however, both taxing and spending activities of the public sector became tied to personal income. With a majority voting system, those individuals in the majority can vote themselves a tax-share break through a host of redistributive programmes.

The redistributive theme of Peltzman (1980) and of Meltzer and Richard (1981) discussed earlier offers a 'modern' restatement of Stigler's thesis. The empirical literature on the link between interest groups and redistribution is quite convincing. Peltzman finds much redistribution going both ways – from rich to poor and from poor to rich. He constructs two indices, one to measure interest groups' ability to influence the political outcome (ability) and the second to measure inequality in the distribution of income. Peltzman's exhaustive statistical analysis of a large sample of developed and developing nations documents a 'strong' link between the growth of the 'middle class' and the growth of governments. The levelling effect – the reduction in income inequality according to Peltzman – created the necessary conditions for growth of government: a broadening of the political base that 'stood to gain from redistribution . . . the growth of "ability" seemed to catalyze politically the spreading of economic interest in redistribution' (Peltzman 1980: 285). Demsetz (1982) is in agreement with this basic finding. He offers evidence linking the growth in government redistribution for the period 1950–72 to the levelling of income effect.

The search for Leviathan and the displacement effect

Writing in a popular business magazine in 1972, Milton Friedman remarked: 'Can we halt Leviathan?' Citing statistics on government spending in the United States, Friedman reported total government spending to have risen from less than 15 per cent of national income in 1930 to about 40 per cent (in fact, 37.9 per cent) in 1972. On the basis of this empirical observation, he noted that neither legislated ceilings nor any other administrative device will halt Leviathan (Friedman 1972). Friedman's casual empiricism was soon to be followed by rigorous tests that took the empirical research in more than one direction. The traditional search relied on the historical mode of analysis. Beck (1976, 1979), Dubin (1977), Nutter (1978), Peltzman (1980) and Ott (1980, 1983) established a growth trend for government spending in Western democracies. This avenue of research gives rise to mixed results. Evidence on the growth of government was sensitive to measurements, definitions and the level of disaggregation of governmental units The one empirical finding on which studies seem to agree is that, when growth is measured in current prices, governments in the West have been growing rapidly. The highest growth rates were evident in both government consumption expenditures and transfer payments.

Another example of the historical analysis can be found in the study of the growth of UK government by Peacock and Wiseman (1961). Their empirical search focused on the displacement–concentration hypothesis. As outlined earlier, under this hypothesis we would expect the ratio of government spending to national income to be fairly constant over time until disturbed by an exogenous shock. The UK data confirmed the Peacock–Wiseman proposition. Peltzman (1980) reports historical growth trends for both the United States and the United Kingdom. From the data we find the ratio of spending to GDP in the United Kingdom to have remained fairly constant at around 10 per cent from 1860 until the First World War, when the ratio rose to 50 per cent. From 1920 to the Second World War, the ratio stabilized at around 20–25 per cent until displaced upwards once again to over 50 per cent. It then declined to levels between 30 and 50 per cent.

The upward displacement pattern of federal spending is also evident from US historical trends. The most obvious influence on the pattern has been war. The ratio of federal government spending to GNP rose from 5 per cent in 1869 (and a low of 2 per cent in 1912–13) to 25 per cent during the First World War and 45 per cent during the Second World War. After the Second World War, the percentage fell back somewhat but has remained near 20–24 per cent since 1976.

The 'specific event' associated with the upward displacement effect can also be found in Niskanen's (1971) model of bureaucracy. Niskanen treats concentration of bureaucratic power as an 'exogenous' event like 'war' or 'national crisis'. The underlying assumption here is the centralization of government functions into fewer bureaucratic agencies. The empirical evidence one seeks is an association between concentration of government functions and a growing government sector. Some support for the Niskanen model can be found from US historical trends. According to Peltzman, 'the concentration ratio is much higher today than in 1800 (about 0.60 versus 0.35)' (Peltzman 1980: 215). However, Peltzman also points out that the growth in the ratio of US government spending to GNP since 1950 has been accompanied by a decline of about 0.10 in the centralization ratio. Comparing the ratio of government spending to GDP with the concentration ratios for sixteen developed countries over the period 1953–73, Peltzman finds that a 'temporal stability' in the concentration ratio goes hand in hand with the world-wide expansion of public sectors.

The relationship between the degree of 'decentralization' and the growth of public sector activities has also been explored by Oates (1972, 1985). In his study *Fiscal Federalism* (Oates 1972) he used a sample of fifty-seven US county governments to search for a positive association between the degree of fiscal centralization and the size of government. In a more recent study (Oates 1985), he has sought to provide an empirical assessment of Leviathan, as suggested by Brennan and Buchanan (1977), with the aid of an international sample of forty-three countries and a sample consisting of the forty-eight contiguous states of the United States. Specifically, he tested the following two alternatives to the Leviathan hypothesis: (a) there is no systematic relationship between fiscal decentralization and the size of government; (b) greater decentralization is positively associated with public sector size. (The presumption here is that loss of economies of scale would increase cost, and hence the level of expenditures. Alternatively, citizens in smaller communities may empower their 'local' governments with more functions and responsibilities.) Oates's findings, reported in both studies, failed to uncover evidence linking fiscal decentralization to the size of the public sector.

Several other economists have undertaken the search for the Brennan–Buchanan Leviathan with mixed results. Studies that focused on local governments seem to find some support for the centralization hypothesis. With the exception of the study by Forbes and Zampelli (1989), a positive association between the centralization ratio and the size of the government has been ascertained from analysis of the data (Eberts and Cronberg 1988; Marlow 1988; Wallis and Oates 1988; Zax 1989). At higher levels of government, state or national, the evidence is not supportive or is less clear cut.

25.5 CONCLUSIONS

In our survey we have described a wide range of microeconomic and public choice theories to help explain why government has grown and grown relative to national income. All these theories are interesting and provide important insights. Growth may come from external shocks causing a displacement effect, or from the inner workings of the market-place or political system. The notion that the root cause of government growth is that government is inherently less productive than the private sector is particularly interesting. The insights provided by public choice theory are also crucial to our understanding of the problem. The implications of budget asymmetry, fiscal illusion and voting strategies have deepened our understanding of people's behaviour and are worthy of continuous study.

Empirical evidence to date is far from conclusive about the source of growth of the public sector. Future research may shed more light on this question, although it is not likely that it will be able to sort out completely how each theory contributes to public sector growth. However, empirical analysis has given us estimates of price and income elasticities and therefore enabled us to conclude that Wagner's law in its simplest form is not particularly enlightening. We now understand that growth in government is more complicated than a mere response to growth in income. Moreover, empirical research reminds us that even the direction of causality is complicated. Does income growth lead to government growth or vice versa? None the less, we have confidence that the theories discussed above are more than logical constructs. They contribute significantly to our economic knowledge.

NOTES

1 *Leviathan* is the title of a famous treatise by Thomas Hobbes. Using the name of this symbol of evil to describe government can be credited to James Buchanan (see Musgrave 1981: 78).
2 For an excellent review of the Leviathan hypothesis see Higgs (1987: 3–76).
3 One individual who has cast some doubt on this otherwise generally accepted notion is Morris

Beck, who develops special price deflators for government expenditures which show that in real terms the public sector may not have grown as fast as many believe (Beck 1981).
4 For some discussion of Engel's laws see Stigler (1954).
5 For more on government spending as a luxury good see Musgrave (1978).
6 For the classic treatment and development of the concept of public goods, see Samuelson (1954, 1955).
7 Baumol's original paper (Baumol 1967) ignored the income effect of productivity growth on the demand for public goods. This criticism was made by Lynch and Redman (1968) and Keren (1972).
8 There are a number of empirical tests for the private economy which lend support to Baumol's predictions concerning the rise of unit cost in stagnant activities. For details see Baumol *et al.* (1985: 806–17).
9 In the empirical research (Bradford *et al.* 1969; Spann 1977), the output of the public sector is defined as public sector expenditures divided by the price of public sector output.
10 For a discussion of bureaucratic growth see Parkinson (1955), Niskanen (1971) and Vickers and Yarrow (1988).
11 See Shoup (1960), Barro (1974) and Rizzo and Peacock (1987).

REFERENCES

Anderson, W., Wallace, M. S. and Warner, J. T. (1986) 'Government spending and taxation: what causes what?', *Southern Economic Journal* 52 (3): 630–9.

Aronson, J. (1985) *Public Finance*, New York: McGraw-Hill.

Barro, R. (1974) 'Are government bonds net worth?', *Journal of Political Economy* 82: 1095–118.

Baumol, W. J. (1967) 'Macroeconomics of unbalanced growth', *American Economic Review* 57: 415–26.

Baumol, W. J., Batey-Blackman, S. and Wolff, E. (1985) 'Unbalanced growth revisited: asymptotic stagnancy and new evidence', *American Economic Review* 75: 806–17.

Beck, M. (1976) 'The expanding public sector: some contrary evidence', *National Tax Journal* 29: 15–21.

—— (1979) 'Public sector growth: a real perspective', *Public Finance* 34 (3): 313–56.

—— (1981) *Government Spending, Trends and Issues*, New York: Praeger.

Borcherding, T. E. (1977a) *Budgets and Bureaucrats: The Sources of Government Growth*, Durham, NC: Duke University Press.

—— (1977b) 'One hundred years of public expenditures, 1902–1970', in T. E. Borcherding (ed.) *Budgets and Bureaucrats: The Sources of Government Growth*, Durham, NC: Duke University Press.

—— (1985) 'The causes of government growth: a survey of the U.S. evidence', *Journal of Pubic Economics* 28: 359–82.

Bradford, D. F., Malt, R. A. and Oates, W. E. (1969) 'The rising cost of local public services: some evidence and reflections', *National Tax Journal* 22: 185–202.

Brennan, G. and Buchanan, J. M. (1977) 'Towards a tax constitution for Leviathan', *Journal of Public Economics* 2: 255–74.

Buchanan, J. (1967) *Fiscal Institutions and Individual Choice*, Chapel Hill, NC: University of North Carolina Press.

Delorme, C. D., Cartwright, P. A. and Kespohl, E. (1988) 'The effect of temporal aggregation on the test of Wagner law', *Public Finance* 43: 373–87.

Demsetz, H. (1982) 'The growth of government', in *Economic, Legal and Political Dimensions of Competition*, Amsterdam: North Holland, de Vries Lectures No. 4.

543

Dubin, E. (1977) 'The expanding public sector: some contrary evidence – a comment', *National Tax Journal* 30 (1): 95.

Eberts, R. W. and Cronberg, T. J. (1988) 'Can competition among local governments constrain government spending?', *Economic Review, Federal Reserve Bank of Cleveland* 1: 2–9.

Forbes, K. F. and Zampelli, E. (1989) 'Is Leviathan a mythical beast?', *American Economic Review* 3: 68–77.

Friedman, M. (1972) 'Can we halt Leviathan?', *Newsweek* 6 November: 98.

Goetz, C. (1977) 'Fiscal illusion in state and local finance', in T. E. Borcherding (ed.) *Budgets and Bureaucrats: The Sources of Government Growth*, Durham, NC: Duke University Press.

Granger, C. W. J. (1969) 'Investigating causal relations by econometric models and cross-spectral methods', *Econometrica* 37: 409–68.

Higgs, R. (1987) *Crisis and Leviathan*, Oxford: Oxford University Press.

Holtz-Eakin, D., Newey, W. and Rosen, H. (1987) 'The revenue–expenditure nexus: evidence from local government data', Working paper, National Bureau of Economic Research.

Keren, M. (1972) 'Macroeconomics of unbalanced growth: comment', *American Economic Review* 62: 149.

Lynch, L. and Redman, E. L. (1968) 'Macroeconomics of unbalanced growth: comment', *American Economic Review* 58: 884–6.

Manage N. and Marlow, M. L. (1986) 'The causal relation between federal expenditures–receipts', *Southern Economic Journal* 3: 617–29.

Marlow, M. L. (1988) 'Fiscal decentralization and government size', *Public Choice* 56: 259–86.

Meltzer, A. H. and Richard, S. F. (1981) 'Tests of a rational theory of the size of government', *Journal of Political Economy* 89: 914–27.

Musgrave, R. A. (1951) *The Theory of Public Finance*, New York: McGraw-Hill.

—— (1978) *The Future of Fiscal Policy: A Reassessment*, Leuven: Leuven University Press.

—— (1981) 'Leviathan cometh – or does he?', in *Tax and Expenditure Limitations*, Washington, DC: Urban Press.

Musgrave, R. A. and Musgrave, P. B. (1989) *Public Finance in Theory and Practice*, New York: McGraw-Hill.

Musgrave, R. A. and Peacock, A. T. (1967) *Classics in the Theory of Public Finance*, London: Macmillan.

Niskanen, W. A., Jr (1971) *Bureaucracy and Representative Government*, Chicago, IL: Aldine.

Nutter, G. W. (1978) *Growth of Government in the West*, Washington, DC: American Enterprise Institute.

Oates, W. E. (1972) *Fiscal Federalism*, New York: Harcourt Brace Jovanovich.

—— (1985) 'Searching for Leviathan: an empirical study', *American Economic Review* 77: 748–57.

Ott, A. F. (1980) 'Has the growth of government in the West been halted?', in W. J. Samuels and L. L. Wade (eds) *Taxing and Spending Policy*, Lexington, MA: D. C. Heath.

—— (1983) 'Controlling government spending', in C. Stubblebine and T. Willets (eds) *Reaganomics*, pp. 79–108, Washington, DC: Institute for Contemporary Studies.

Parkinson, C. (1955) 'Parkinson's law', *Economist* 19 November.

Peacock, A. T. and Wiseman, J. (1961) *The Growth of Expenditures in the United Kingdom*, New York: National Bureau of Economic Research.

—— and —— (1979) 'Approaches to the analysis of government expenditure growth', *Public Finance Quarterly* 7: 3–23.

Peltzman, S. (1980) 'The growth of government', *Journal of Law and Economics* 23: 209–87.

Ram, R. (1986) 'Government size and economic growth: a new framework and some evidence from cross-section and time series data', *American Economic Review* 79: 183–204.

—— (1988a) 'Additional evidence on causality between government revenue and government expenditures', *Southern Economic Journal* 3: 763–9.

—— (1988b) 'A multi country perspective on causality beween government revenue and government expenditure', *Public Finance* 2: 261–9.

Rizzo, I. and Peacock, A. (1987) 'Debt and growth in public spending', *Public Finance* 42: 283–96.

Sahni, B. S. and Singh, B. (1984) 'On the causal directions between national income and government expenditure in Canada', *Public Finance* 39: 359–93.

Samuelson, P. A. (1954) 'The pure theory of public expenditure', *Review of Economics and Statistics* 36: 387–9.

—— (1955) 'Diagrammatic exposition of a theory of public expenditure', *Review of Economics and Statistics* 37: 350–6.

Shoup, K. (1960) *Ricardo on Taxation*, New York: Columbia University Press.

Sims, C. A. (1972) 'Money, income and causality', *American Economic Review* 62: 540–52.

Singh, B. and Sahni, B. S. (1984) 'Causality between public expenditure and national income', *Review of Economics and Statistics* 66: 630–44.

—— and —— (1986) 'Patterns and directions of causality between government expenditures and national income in the United States', *Journal of Quantitative Economics* 2: 291–308.

Spann, R. M. (1977) 'The macroeconomics of unbalanced growth and the expanding public sector: some simple tests of a model of government growth', *Journal of Public Economics* 2: 397–404.

Stigler, G. J. (1954) 'The early history of empirical studies of consumer behaviour', *Journal of Political Economy* 62: 95–113.

—— (1970) 'Director's law of public income distribution', *Journal of Law and Economics* 13: 1–10.

—— (1973) 'General economic conditions and national elections', *American Economic Review* 63: 160–7.

Stubblebine, C. (1963) 'The social imbalance hypothesis', Ph.D. Thesis, University of Virginia.

Vickers, J. and Yarrow, G. (1988) *Privatization*, Cambridge, MA: MIT Press.

Von Furstenberg, G. H., Green, R. J. and Jin-Ho Jeong (1986) 'Tax and spend, or spend and tax?', *Review of Economics and Statistics* 2: 179–88.

Wagner, R. E. and Weber, W. E. (1977) 'Wagner's law, fiscal institutions, and the growth of government', *National Tax Journal* 30: 59–68.

Wallis, J. J. and Oates, W. E. (1988) 'Does economic sclerosis set in with age? An empirical study of the Olson hypothesis', *Kyklos* 3: 397–417.

Zax, J. S. (1989) 'Is there a Leviathan in your neighborhood?', *American Economic Review* 3: 560–7.

III. APPLIED ECONOMICS

26

THE ROLE OF APPLIED ECONOMICS

DAVID GREENAWAY

26.1 INTRODUCTION

In any science, 'application' involves confronting testable hypotheses with real-world situations and real-world data. This is equally true of economics. Theorizing generates testable propositions; exposing those propositions to data using empirical methods, which range from the casual to the sophisticated, generates results. In turn these results may provide support for a specific hypothesis, or may give cause for rethinking the theoretical basis to the problem. In some ways the basic process is more complicated in economics than in other disciplines, largely because the process of data generation is rather different, certainly than is the case in the natural sciences. Subject to some qualifications to be made later, economists are generally not in a position to generate their own data set, nor are they well placed to engage in replication. Nevertheless the basic proposition that methodologically there are similarities between applied economics and applications in other sciences still holds.

Part III of this volume is concerned with evaluating the role of applied economics, and indeed the role of the applied economist. The chapters which follow focus on the tools of applied economics and the constraints which face economists in the process of giving policy advice. In this chapter we seek to do several things in introducing the subject matter: in the next section we set the scene by reviewing developments in applied economics over the last quarter of a century; in Section 26.3 we then discuss the contribution which applied economics makes to the resolution of controversy/conflict in the discipline; and in Section 26.4 we review the chapters which follow in the rest of Part III.

26.2 DEVELOPMENTS IN APPLIED ECONOMICS

If we think of applied economics in the sense defined above, i.e. as confronting propositions generated by economic analysis with real-world data, there is certainly a lot more applied economics around now than there was at the end of the Second World War! This assertion can be justified by reference to the amount of processed information of an applied nature which is reported in all parts of the spectrum – from the popular media to specialist academic journals.[1] Judged by the number of specialist magazines and journals which are now available, as well as the proportion of space in more general media which is devoted to issues in applied economics, the output of applied economists broadly defined has increased significantly. Why is this? Well, there appear to be a number of factors which tie in with the 'production function' in question. Applied economics tests propositions, using real-world data, to satisfy not only professional curiosity but a demand for economic advice. Over the post-war period, the 'number' of testable propositions has increased with developments in theory; the data base which economists can rely upon has become richer; the technology with which they work has improved; and on the demand side, more information is required. In addition to this, there are pressures tied into the incentive structure under which academic economists operate which have probably also contributed to the growth. A few comments on each of these is in order.

Michael Bleaney has already considered, in Chapter 9, the role of economic theory, and the essays in Part II of this volume give some idea of the enormous growth in the literature on economic theory over the last few decades. The range of problems in which economists are interested is significantly wider and the theoretical foundations of applied economics are arguably more secure as a consequence. Theory is only one input to the process, however; the other is raw data. Here too major developments have occurred in both the quantity and quality of information available. More data series are available from national governments, research centres and international organizations.[2] Moreover, as the technology of data collection improves and becomes more intensive in its use of human and physical capital the scope for human error diminishes, with obvious implications for the quality of data. There remain of course significant, and at times embarrassing, gaps in our knowledge (as for instance in the case of information on elasticities); nevertheless the fact remains that applied economists have a much richer data set to work with, and one which continues to expand.

Increasing information places increased demands on analysts. A key development in allowing analysts to meet these challenges has been technical change in the methods used. This has been dramatic in two respects: first the techniques of data processing, and second the mechanics of data processing. With respect to the former, developments in econometric and statistical theory have sharpened the scientific basis of the discipline. The range of tools which is now available is far greater – something which one can see just by comparing a modern text on econometrics with one written in 1960 (e.g. Johnston 1963; Maddala 1990). Improvments in software have brought many of these developments to the aid of the 'average' applied economist in the form of user-friendly econometric packages like PC-GIVE, DATAFIT, SHAZAM and RATS. Tied in with this is the ready availability of computer hardware which is up to the task of running this software. Here developments over the last decade in particular have been quite remarkable. Desk-top work stations now have the power and the memory to process large-scale data sets using programmes which could formerly only be run on a mainframe computer, at substantial cost both in time and resources.

So applied economists are now in a position, with a relatively small investment, to equip themselves with the means to expose economic propositions to large-scale data sets, using fairly sophisticated econometric techniques. What about their output? Where is the demand which sustains all this activity? It is partly driven by the incentive structure under which academic economists operate: pressures to publish generate an increased demand for journals to take this material (Grubel and Boland 1986; Greenaway 1990), and academic journals can in fact survive on relatively low circulation lists. However, there is much more to it than that. There has certainly been a significant increase in demand for economic advice and economic information over the post-war period. We see this in government for example: prior to the Second World War the Economic Section of the Cabinet had a handful of economists (see Cairncross and Watts 1989); by the late 1980s, the Government Economic Service comprised some 400 specialist economists. We see it also in the private sector with the growth of economic sections within companies and the growth of private sector consultancies. Finally we see it also in major multinational organizations like the World Bank, the International Monetary Fund, the Organization for Economic Co-operation and Development and the European Community. The reasons for this are not hard to find. The two most distinctive features of post-war economic growth have been increased specialization and increased openness. Both drive increased demands for information on, and analysis of, economic trends.

To sum up, over the post-war period the demand for the output of the 'applied economist' has increased, and the ease with which that output can be produced has increased. But what about the 'value' of the output – has it resulted in improvements in the way in which the economy performs? Has it reduced the legendary propensity for economists to disagree?

551

26.3 APPLIED ECONOMICS, CONFLICT RESOLUTION AND POLICY ADVICE

Jokes about disagreements between economists are legion (some are also very funny!). As with all caricatures there is also some truth behind them (even if on occasions this is no more than a grain). Economists do disagree on many issues, and they do so for entirely legitimate reasons. Economics is not an 'exact' science but a behavioural science. As such, potential for disagreement deriving from differences in perceptions about human behaviour exist. In addition, however, there is scope for genuine professional disagreement between analysts on purely technical matters, for instance on the specification of a given relationship. Moreover, this can be compounded by the problem of 'observational equivalence', i.e. two theories could generate the same data. Obviously when this occurs there are real problems of discriminating between hypotheses – both parties can legitimately claim to be right! It must be said that this is not just true of economics; it also applies to allegedly more 'exact sciences' (biology, medicine, the earth sciences and so on). The difference between economics and others is that economists are obliged to act out their controversies or air their uncertainties more publicly and more frequently than other professional groups. This is partly because there is a wider interest in matters of economic analysis, and partly because many more lay persons have an opinion to offer, compared with other matters. The contrast between discussion about whether interest rates will rise at a given time and the benefits of a particular form of cancer therapy is an interesting case in point – there are many more self-proclaimed experts around on the former!

The data series which economists work with also create potential for controversy. Although improvements in data collection and data processing were mentioned above, problems with the data-generation process remain. Normally data are generated as a by-product of other activities; providers may have little direct interest in their accuracy, or in some cases may even have an interest in biasing them. One side-effect of this is the frequent revision of data series. Thus, in the case of national income data, this can continue for up to five years, which obviously makes discriminating between alternative macroeconomic hypotheses more difficult. Again, it is worth noting that this is not peculiar to economics. Self-selection bias is frequently identified as a source of measurement error in medical trials for instance.

The point is that disagreements among economists may be exaggerated. There is more convergence than the lay person is aware of and, as Michael Bleaney argued earlier, that degree of convergence has increased over the last quarter of a century. That this has occurred is partly a result of the output of applied economics. On many issues the accumulation of empirical evidence on specific issues has served to break through the veil of ignorance in places and to persuade the majority of economists to one particular point of view rather than another. For example, initial thinking on the role of expectations in the late 1960s generated furious controversy, but a growing body of literature has persuaded the vast majority of economists that expectations are important; in the 1950s and 1960s the role of import protection in economic development was fiercely debated, but empirical evidence has persuaded most economists that import protection can have significant costs, and that some forms of protection tend to be far more costly than others; 'monetarism' is a term which generated the strongest of emotions fifteen years ago, yet most analysts now agree that 'money matters'.[3]

These are just a few examples to illustrate a point. In the same way that we have to be careful not to exaggerate the extent of disagreement, we must be equally careful not to exaggerate the degree of convergence, nor to exaggerate the role of applied economics in this respect. Controversy still reigns on a great many issues and this is at least in part due to the fact that, sophisticated as our tools are, impressive as some of our data bases are, we still do not have the means of discriminating convincingly between alternative hypotheses. This often seriously constrains the contribuiton which the applied economist can make. Moreover, policy advice is often as much about 'what ought to be' as about 'what is', a factor which often places the economist cum technical advisor in an invidious position. The role of judgement in the process of giving economic advice is crucial in these circumstances.

Applied economists, therefore, cannot be expected to deliver unequivocal judgements on every issue they confront, nor can they be expected to dip into their tool kit, boot up the appropriate software, and resolve every controversy. This is simply asking too much. There are fundamental methodological problems which Ian Stewart addressed in Chapter 2; there are data problems, data-processing problems, and the unwelcome face of 'value judgements' is never far from the scene. These are inherent features of the exercise. Indeed some would argue that such systemic constraints are so deep-rooted that we are kidding ourselves if we believe that applied economics can resolve anything. This is unnecessarily nihilistic. Carefully executed and appropriately qualified, applied economics should be, and can be, enlightening. I would argue that over the post-war period it has been enlightening, and that economic analysis has made progress as a consequence.

26.4 AN OVERVIEW OF PART III

The chapters in Part III aim to place some of these issues in perspective. Clive Granger has been one of the great pioneers of time series analysis in the last twenty years. Time series are one of the most fertile fields for applied economists. Much of the raw material we rely upon is in the form of time series data and, as time has progressed, the stock of raw material with which we can work has expanded. Really major developments have occurred here, not only in the techniques of analysing time series, but also in the evaluation procedures used in discriminating between competing models. Granger provides a skilful and insightful analysis of these developments. His essay is not a history of thought, but it does neatly set the issues in historical perspective, beginning with an appraisal of multivariate analysis and ending with some comments on empirical explorations of chaotic series. In between, in the core of the chapter he explains developments in cointegration, forecasting and the estimation of time-varying parameters. Cointegration in particular is changing the way in which applied economists approach the study of time series. Many analysts claim that the technique offers a foundation for a common starting point for all time series analysis, encompassing as it does less general approaches such as error-correction type models.

Of course time series analysis, as well as cross-sectional and longitudinal data analysis, are attempts to blend theory and measurement. Exposing economic theory to observed facts essentially defines the domain of econometric analysis. In Chapter 28 Grayham Mizon evaluates a part of this domain which is crucially important yet frequently neglected: namely the role of measurement and testing. As Mizon emphasizes, given the enormous increase in the quantity of data available, and the increase in computing power for handling that data, issues of measurement are becoming more rather than less important. In discussing aspects of the quality of data he comments on alternative sources, measurement problems and alternative uses of data. This leads naturally to an appraisal of the role of testing. As he notes, 'In order for economic analysis to be influential . . . the credentials of the underlying economic model need to be established.' Central to this is the process of satisfying the conditions for model congruence. As Mizon notes, considerable progress has been made in this respect in recent years. One particularly interesting ingredient of this discussion is the role of the work of the 1989 Nobel Laureate, Haavelmo. This was seen as a controversial award by many. As Mizon emphasizes, his seminal work in the 1940s laid the foundations to recent advances in model evaluation.

One of the striking contrasts between the social sciences and the natural sciences is the limited opportunities for generating experimental data in the former. Graham Loomes is one of the pioneers of 'experimental economics', a rapidly growing body of work which is making attempts to right this situation to some degree. The scope for genuinely experimental work in economics is severely constrained. Nevertheless, a burgeoning literature reports the results of a range of experimental work which focuses largely, although not exclusively, on choice under uncertainty. In Chapter 29 Loomes examines the origins of experimental work, and guides us through the host of methodological objections which have been levelled against this way of doing things. He also provides an account of the more important results which have arisen from experiments conducted both at the level of the individual and across a range of agents aggregated into a market. The subject matter of experimental economics causes discomfort to some economists. In some cases this is borne out of genuine anxieties about the technology of this approach – the 'environments' within which experiments are conducted are necessarily synthetic. In other cases it is probably fashioned more by the fact that many of the results challenge 'received wisdom' in consumer theory in particular. In so doing they also challenge vested interests! Fortunately 'vested interests' are now beginning to build up behind the experimental bandwagon, such that the approach can be given a run for its money. Moreover, as Van Raaij argues in Chapter 40, economists are beginning to learn from the experience of psychologists.

Of all the tools which the applied economist has at his or her disposal, shadow pricing and its application in the context of cost–benefit appraisal is one of the most widely used. The concept of a shadow price is not a new one in economics; it is in fact as old as the concept of external effects. Systematic estimation of shadow prices, however, is a more recent phenomenon, and has been closely tied into the development of work on cost–benefit analysis and project appraisal. In Chapter 30 Edward Tower explains the concept of a shadow price, examines the role of shadow prices in a fully determined system and discusses their use in the context of effective protection and domestic resource cost analysis. The latter is a particularly good example to work with since policy appraisal in developing countries in recent years has relied heavily upon it. Moreover, it is also an indicator which has generated no small measure of controversy. In the 1960s the technique stopped being widely used in industrialized countries largely because of disillusionment with making distributional judgements. As Tower argues, however, the limitations of the measure generally have more to do with too much being asked of it. Appropriately qualified it can be of real assistance in policy appraisal.

One of the major problems with early work on cost–benefit analysis and domestic resource cost analysis was that the framework was fundamentally partial equilibrium, yet most of the policy changes being investigated had general equilibrium consequences. Recently this particular constraint has been alleviated by the development of large-scale computable general equilibrium models (CGEMs). One of the pioneers of this new technology is John Whalley. In Chapter 31, Whalley skilfully introduces us to the origins of CGEMs, their usefulness and their limitations. The great strength of this technology is that it provides a framework for modelling the Walrasian system of general equilibrium. The development of this line of analysis provides an interesting example of the role of technical change in applied economics. As a consequence of increased computing power, humble two-sector models have evolved into sophisticated models of the complete economic system – models which are capable of providing answers to a rich menu of questions. Despite the impressive developments which have occurred, however, there are serious limitations – the output of a given CGEM has been shown to be sensitive to, *inter alia*, model structure, basic functional forms and solution methods. As with other techniques, therefore, the judgement of the applied economist is a key ingredient in the exercise. As Pope said, 'a little knowledge is a dangerous thing'. Technical change has done a lot to make the hardware and software for computable general equilibrium modelling more widely accessible; it has not had the same effect on 'judgement'. Results have to be carefully qualified, and carefully interpreted.

Another new development which has been driven partly by technical change and partly by data availability is the growing area of microeconometrics. A major constraint on cross-section work is the influence of history dependence or state dependence, i.e. the results of a particular exercise are sample specific. The growing availability of panel data means that this is something which the applied economist need be less and less concerned with. Richard Blundell synthesizes and reviews development in this important field in his essay. His discussion is motivated by reference to three different types of data available in microeconometric research: discrete choice models; limited dependent variable models; and panel data models. The first refers to models which investigate 'zero–one' decisions, the second to situations where a specific data set is truncated or censored and the third to cross-section data which have been pooled over a relatively long period of time. Analysis along these lines has provided very real opportunities to applied economists to study microeconomic behaviour more systematically and more fully than one would have imagined possible fifteen years ago. The data points available are simply enormous, and very real progress is being made in modelling and investigating individual or household responses to various economic stimuli.

Whereas microeconometrics is one of the newest of preoccupations of applied economists, macroeconometric forecasting is one of the oldest. This is partly a reflection of the more modest data requirements of macroeconometric forecasting and partly a consequence of the interest of applied economists in the early post-war years, but it is also due to the demands of central government and private agents for forecasts of economic activity at the aggregate level. Firms and industries have for long generated their own market-based forecasts, since the benefits of this can be largely internalized. This is less true of macro forecasts. In Chapter 33, Kenneth Holden evaluates the methods of macro forecasting, as well as the practice thereof. The stages involved in generating a forecast are carefully specified, and the role of methodological starting point is highlighted. Recent developments in the identification of stationarity, accuracy analysis and the combining of forecasts are all analysed. As with other developments covered in Part III, Holden reports on the very real progress that has been made in recent years; like·others he, too, correctly emphasizes the art of judgement in the use of forecasts; in addition he points to growing convergence of practice.

Applied economics is both a means to an end and an end in itself. It is an end in itself in so far as it is the meat and drink of academic enquiry. It is a means to an end in so far as it informs policy advice. Policy-makers, appraised by policy advisors, formulate policy. Advisors in turn presumably come to a judgement by reference to the relevant economic analysis and evidence. Policy formulation, however, is not simply a case of well-informed benign 'guardians' maximizing a social welfare function, the principal argument of which is national income. As we saw in Chapter 12 by Mueller in Part II, interest group activity is central to the process. In Chapter 34 Chris Milner extends this theme. To motivate the analysis he focuses on trade policy. This is a useful foundation for the analysis since income redistribution is generally a key element in the process. The way in which interest group behaviour can fashion not only the decision to intervene but also the choice of instrument is examined. Empirical evidence on the 'political economy of protection' is assessed, and is not found wanting – there is a growing literature which supports the view that interest groups have an important influence on the making of economic policy. The lesson to be drawn from this for applied economics is that we need to take an interest not only in the economic market-place but also in the political market-place, a theme which is taken further by McLean in Part IV.

The role of the economist in giving advice against this backcloth is explored in the final essay in Part III by Sir Alan Peacock. Peacock is admirably well qualified for this task – not only is he an applied economist of great standing, but he has also spent time advising government from the inside and the outside. Peacock begins by recognizing the dangers which economists face once they become integrated into the policy advice business – in particular the danger that they become 'hired guns'. The possibility of being thrust into this position is, of course, fashioned partly by the constraints under which economists in government operate, but also by the fact that economists have to exercise judgement. The nature of economic science is such that, as we have seen throughout this review of Part III, the economist constantly has to make judgements. Unlike in the natural sciences, we do not have the luxury of making unequivocal pronouncements on the outcome of particular experiments. Rather, we have carefully to weigh up evidence which is often subject to sample-specific bias. The qualifications which the professional advisor feels that he or she must offer can be erroneously equated with equivocation by political masters – a trait which is not regarded as an endearing one!

557

NOTES

1 Quite a number of specialist journals which deal specifically with applied economics have emerged in recent years including, *inter alia*, *Journal of Policy Modelling*, *Economic Modelling*, *Applied Economics* and *Journal of Applied Econometrics*.
2 This is a very definite long-run trend, although there are fluctuations around that trend. Thus, for example, the Conservative governments of the 1980s administered substantial cuts in Central Statistical Office manpower.
3 Cobham (1984) provides an interesting discussion of some of these issues in the context of macroeconomic policy.

REFERENCES

Caincross, A. and Watts, N. (1989) *The Economic Section*, London: Routledge.
Cobham, D. (1984) 'Convergence, divergence and realignment in British macro-economics', *Banca Nazionale del Lavoro Quarterly Review* 146: 159–76.
Greenaway, D. (1990) 'On the efficient use of mathematics in economics: results of an attitude survey of British economists', *European Economic Review* 34: 1339–51.
Grubel, H. G. and Boland, L. (1986) 'On the efficient use of mathematics in economics: some theory, facts and results of an opinion survey', *Kyklos* 39: 419–42.
Johnston, J. (1963) *Econometric Methods*, New York: McGraw-Hill.
Maddala, G. (1990) *Introduction to Econometrics*, New York: Macmillan.

27

TIME SERIES
ECONOMETRICS

CLIVE W. J. GRANGER

27.1 INTRODUCTION

A great deal of the data found in the areas of macroeconomics, finance and trade comes in the form of time series, as does much of the data in industrial organization and parts of microeconomics. A time series is a sequence of observations on an economic variable at essentially equal intervals of time; for example, industrial production is measured or estimated monthly, GNP quarterly and population annually. A rather different type of data consists of the prices of a stock of all transactions on an exchange during a day; observations are then not taken at constant intervals, although similar techniques of analysis are generally used.

As these series are observed it can be argued that there must be a generating mechanism that produces the group of stochastic processes known as 'the economy'. The main objective of time series analysis is to produce models that in some way approximate the central generating mechanism. Naturally, the models produced can only use observed data, and the correct specifications may not be available so that only approximations are possible. In practice, the models produced may also be limited by the quality of data available and the ability of the models to handle many series simultaneously. Once the model is achieved, the second set of objectives such as forecasts, policy decisions and tests of economic hypothesis, is usually easily obtained. Unfortunately, the modelling process is usually not an easy one, requiring decisions about the functional form of the model, what variables to use and what lags to include. For instance, several analysts using the same data may well reach rather different approximations, although their models may well produce similar forecasts. It is clearly important not only to produce a presentable model but also to support this model with a battery of evaluation procedures to convince

This paper is dedicated to Andre Gabor and Brian Tew, my teachers, colleagues and friends at Nottingham.

a potential user, such as a policy-maker, that it can be used with confidence. A discussion of the relevance of producers and consumers of models, the process of modelling and the process of evaluation can be found in Granger (1989).

Historically, the models considered were univariate, linear, homoscedastic (constant variance residuals) and largely designed for stationary series. The workhorse model was the autoregressive moving-average (ARMA)(p, q) in which the current variable x_t of the series is explained by p lags of itself and has a moving-average component of order q, or in symbols

$$x_t = \sum_{j=1}^{p} a_j x_{t-j} + \varepsilon_t + \sum_{j=1}^{q} b_j \varepsilon_{t-j} \qquad (27.1)$$

The basic building block of these models is the white noise series ε_t, with zero mean, so that covariance $(\varepsilon_t, \varepsilon_s) = 0$, $s \neq t$. These models are explained in detail in the classic book by Box and Jenkins (1976) and in more recent texts, such as Granger and Newbold (1987). In time series terminology, analysis of these models involves three stages. The first stage is that of identification, i.e. the choice of model to be fitted, which here means the choice of the parameters p, q; the second stage is that of estimation, which consists of estimating the other parameters of the model, i.e. the as and the bs plus the variance of ε_t (assumed to be constant); the third stage consists of evaluating the quality of the achieved estimated model. As models and techniques have evolved these three stages remain important components of an empirical analysis. However, there is now much more interest in multivariate non-linear heteroscedastic models appropriate for use with non-stationary but non-explosive series. This expanded area of interest has produced time series models closer to the more traditional econometric simultaneous equation models that are discussed at length in most econometric texts, although there still remain important differences between the two approaches. The central differences concern the extent to which some economic theory is used in the model specification and how simultaneity is handled. Traditional time series models largely ignored any underlying theory, and were viewed as 'atheoretical' or 'agnostic', and whilst this is still often true there is now frequently an attempt to produce time series models which have useful economic implications that can immediately be checked with economic theories.

The usual first step in the analysis of one or a group of series is to perform a pre-analysis to search for the presence of dominant components in the series, such as strong seasonals, deterministic trends in mean, changes in level or outliers. It is general practice to remove such components before further analysis is attempted. Both simplistic and sophisticated methods are available, and their use often produces undesirable side-effects on the subsequent analy-

560

sis. However, as these topics are carefully covered in various statistics and econometrics texts they are not discussed in any detail here. In what follows it will usually be assumed that the series to be analysed contain no outliers, missing variables, strong seasonal components or obvious deterministic trends in mean or variance.

One group of dominant components that may still be present are integrated processes, which are sometimes known as 'stochastic trends' although they need not have the properties often associated with a trend. These components are discussed further in Section 27.3. A survey of the more traditional links between time series and econometrics is given by Granger and Watson (1986).

27.2 MULTIVARIATE MODELS

One natural extension of the univariate ARMA model is the multiple-input single-output model or ARMAX, which is such that the current value y_t of the series of interest is explained by lagged values of itself, lagged (and possibly also current) values of a vector x_t of explanatory variables and a moving-average residual. For such a model to be useful for forecasting or policy guidance several steps ahead, forecasts are also needed for future x_t values and so models for the xs have to be constructed. A more direct procedure is to stack the y_t and the x_t together, giving a vector y_t to be jointly modelled either as a vector ARMA (VARMA) model or, more simply, as a vector autoregressive (VAR) model. These are examples of multiple-input multiple-output models. In a VAR model, each component of y_t is explained by lagged values of itself and also of all other components and can be denoted VAR(p) if all lags of up to order p are considered. The residuals should be a vector white noise process and any simultaneity in the system can be modelled through contemporaneous correlations between the components of this white noise process. If y_t has N components, one difficulty is seen to be the potentially large number of parameters to be estimated (N^2p). It is thus desirable to choose p to be as small as possible whilst producing a model that will approximate the true dynamics of the process. One way of reducing the number of parameters to be estimated is to assume the existence of constraints linking them or to introduce Bayesian priors. For example, if we believe that the individual series are all approximately random walks, then the coefficient of the first lag of itself could be given a normally distributed prior with mean unity and variance σ^2, say, and all other lags could be given a prior with mean zero and variances σ^2/k, where k is the lag. A wide variety of such priors on lags are considered by Doan *et al.* (1984). Like any Bayesian procedure, if the priors selected include the truth with a reasonably high probability, a well-estimated model can result, as the priors effectively increase the amount of information upon which the estimates are based. However, if inappropriate priors are selected, a worthwhile approximation to the truth may not be achieved. An alternative way of reducing the number of parameters may occur if VARMA(p', q') models are used, provided that $p' + q' < p$, as is often found in practice. A fairly simple procedure for identifying and estimating these models has been suggested by Hannan and Rissanen (1982). In the first step of this procedure, VAR(p) models are estimated for a variety of p values and the 'best' of these are selected using Akaike's information criterion (AIC)

$$\text{AIC}_k = \log D_k + \frac{2n^2k}{N}$$

where N is the sample size, n is the dimension of vector y_t, k is the order of the VAR model considered and D_k is the determinant of the covariance of the residuals. This criterion is known to 'overfit' in the sense that if the true value of p is p_0 (finite), then the AIC criterion is inclined to choose a value of p that is somewhat greater than p_0. For the present purposes this is not a disadvantage. The vector of residuals from this first VAR model can be denoted $\hat{e}_t$ and is used as approximations of the residuals from the eventual ARMA(p', q') model. A group of models of the form

$$y_t = p' \text{ lags of } y_t + q' \text{ lags of } e_t + \varepsilon_t$$

is now fitted for a variety of values of p' and q'. Note that each model essentially involves just a regression on the observable lagged y_t and $\hat{e}_t$, although a maximum likelihood procedure will often be used. The 'best' model is now chosen using the Bhansali information criterion (BIC)

$$\text{BIC}(p, q) = \log D_{p, q} + (p + q)n^2 \frac{\text{lag } N}{N}$$

with the same notation used above for the AIC. Again the residuals should be approximately a white noise process but may be contemporaneously correlated.

Once a VAR or VARMA model has been constructed it can immediately be used to provide forecasts of the vector y_t. The h-step forecast of y_{t+h} made at time t is obtained by assuming that the model is correct, writing down how y_{t+h} will be generated according to the model and replacing all elements with either their known values or their forecasts. The formation of forecasts is thus iterative, as the forecast of y_{t+h} will involve those of y_{t+j}, $j = 1, \ldots, h - 1$. More details and the justification for the procedure can be found in Granger and Newbold (1987: ch. 8). Causality tests can also be performed directly using the model. As causality testing is far from a new topic, it will not be discussed here. A number of papers discussing recent innovations in this area can be found in the special issue on causality of the *Journal of Econometrics*, vol. 39, 1988. The main decision that has to be made in this type of modelling is the contents of the vector y_t, which determines the information set upon which the forecasts and tests are based.

A use for VAR or VARMA models suggested by Sims (1980) is to trace the effects on the various components of y_t of specific shocks on innovations to the system, such as technology shocks, policy shocks (money supply, government expenditure), demand or supply shocks, trade shocks and so forth. It is of course necessary for the appropriate variables to be included in the vector y_t for such an analysis to be possible. A problem that immediately arises is how to identify these shocks, given that they are not directly observed and because of the contemporaneous correlation between the components of the residuals ε_t of the model. One way of achieving identification is to triangularize the simultaneous components of the ys. Thus the variable whose shock is of interest, say money supply, is in the first equation of the model and this equation contains no contemporaneous values of other ys. The equation for the second component of y_t will now involve current money supply plus all the usual lags and possibly also moving-average terms. The equation for the third component of y_t will now contain current values of the first two components and so forth. With this reformulated model a simulation can now be performed by pretending to shock the first variable by one positive standard deviation at time t and then by simple accounting estimating the effects on all the variables at time $t + 1$, $t + 2$ etc. The effect may be transitory, so that the values of a variable are influenced up to a peak and then decline to zero, or may be permanent, so that the shock has some effect on a variable into the indefinite future. These permanent shocks are related to the unit root properties of the model, as discussed in Section 27.3. The results are potentially interesting for understanding the economic system, but there are some problems with interpretation. The triangularization is arbitrary, and a different ordering of variables can affect the outcome; it is also inclined to overemphasize the size of the impacts of shocks on other variables. The results will often also be strongly affected by the size and contents of the vector y_t, and adding or deleting some variable may produce rather different interpretations. Various difficulties are discussed by Runkle (1987). McNees (1986) has compared the quality of forecasts produced by Bayesian VAR models with forecasts from econometric models. For some variables at least the VAR forecasts are superior for both short and long horizons.

27.3 UNIT ROOT MODELS AND COINTEGRATION

Most traditional econometric analysis and much of current economic theory assumes, or appears to assume, that the series involved are stationary, possibly after the removal of deterministic trends. However, a second important class of variables known as integrated variables, where integrated here means a sum, was introduced into econometrics as a result of the work of Box and Jenkins. If x_t is a stationary series and y_t is the sum of all past xs from time zero then

y_t is integrated, and is denoted $y_t \sim \mathrm{I}(1)$. A more general notation is $\mathrm{I}(d)$, where d denotes the number of times a series needs to be differenced to achieve stationarity. In this notation a stationary series is thus $\mathrm{I}(0)$. An example is wealth being accumulated net savings, so that if savings is $\mathrm{I}(0)$, then wealth would be $\mathrm{I}(1)$. A second example is if x_t is production minus sales of a firm; then the level of inventory is the accumulation of x_t over the history of the firm. Using the lag operator B, so that $B^k x_t = x_{t-k}$, an $\mathrm{I}(1)$ integrated process y_t will be generated by

$$(1 - B)a(B)y_t = b(B)\varepsilon_t$$

where $a(1) \neq 0$, $b(1) \neq 0$, ε_t is white noise and the unit root is $1 - B$. As the inverse of $1 - B$ is the summation operator, the relationship between this generating mechanism and the previous introduction to this section should be clear.

Integrated processes are of importance because of their unusual properties and because they seem to occur frequently in economics. Most important macroeconomic series seem to be (at least) $\mathrm{I}(1)$, including production and GNP (both per capita), price indices, imports and exports, exchange rates, prices of speculative commodities and stock prices. Particular examples are given by Nelson and Plosser (1982).

An extensive survey of the properties of unit root processes has recently been provided by Diebold and Nerlove (1989). Their emphasis is on testing for the presence of unit roots, and several alternative tests are discussed. A simple and popular test, in which the change of a series is regressed on its lagged level and possibly also on several lagged changes, was proposed by Dickey and Fuller (1981). The null hypothesis that the series is $\mathrm{I}(1)$ uses the t statistic of the coefficient b in the equation

change of variable $= b$(lagged level of variable) $+$ lagged changes
$+$ white noise residual

as the test statisic. Special tables have to be used to obtain critical values as this stastic does not have a t distribution under the null. Many other tests are available, some of which allow for the presence of linear trends in the process. The tests have reasonable power for series of 200 terms or more, but naturally have difficulty in distinguishing between an exact unit root and roots that are less than, but near to, unity. Further, the tests are quite easily disrupted by the presence of a strong seasonal in the series or a subtle change in level or in trend. In these cases, the test may suggest the existence of a unit root when it does not exist, largely because an insufficiently wide set of alternative generating mechanisms is not being considered.

There has been a great deal of discussion about whether macroeconomic series can be considered as having a stationary component plus a deterministic (linear) trend or have a generating mechanism containing a unit root. Both mechanisms can produce fairly smooth series containing long swings, as observed in actual economic data. It is fairly difficult to distinguish between these two types of models using in-sample tests, but post-sample or forecasting tests should be able to distinguish them. At present, the post-sample evidence suggests that unit roots are the better explanation. This may be because unit root models are naturally adaptive, so that if there is a change of structure they will follow the change and continue to produce adequate forecasts. Stable models, such as a specific stationary ARMA process plus a linear trend, cannot adapt. In may also be preferable to consider unit root models plus a non-linear deterministic trend as the actual generating mechanism.

It is also interesting to ask why I(1) processes occur. In some cases economic theory can provide an explanation. The efficient market theory of speculative prices suggests that stock market prices, bond prices, commodity prices and interest rates should be (near) random walks, and Hall's life-cycle theory gives consumption also as a near random walk. In some models a unit root process is introduced by making technology, or accumulated level of knowledge, be generated with a unit root. Further discussion by economic theorists is surely required.

It is generally true that the linear combination of I(0) variables is I(0) and similarly generally a linear combination of I(1) variables is I(1). However, it is possible for both x_t and y_t to be I(1) but for there to exist a unique coefficient A such that $z_t = x_t - Ay_t$ is I(0). When this occurs x_t and y_t are said to be cointegrated. Such an occurrence is somewhat unlikely, and so when it does happen special properties can be expected. Cointegration will occur when the series involved can be decomposed as

$$x_t = Aw_t + \tilde{x}_t$$
$$y_t = w_t + \tilde{y}_t$$

where $\tilde{x}_t, \tilde{y}_t$ are both I(0) and w_t is I(1). As I(1)ness is a dominant property, x_t and y_t will both be I(1) but $z_t = x_t - Ay_t$ becomes a linear combination of I(0) series and so will itself be I(0). It can be shown that if a pair of series are cointegrated they must have an I(1) common factor, and all other components must be I(0). It is also possible to give an equilibrium-type interpretation to cointegration. If the pair of series (x_t, y_t) are plotted as points in an (x, y) plane, so that each pair represents a single point at each time, then the line $x = Ay$ can be thought of as an 'attractor' in that the points (x_t, y_t) will be inclined to lie around it rather than drift away, as z_t is I(0) with zero mean and is proportional to the distance of (x_t, y_t) from the line. If the process were to become deterministic at time t_0, it would quickly move towards the line and eventually lie exactly on it. This property corresponds to the 'centre of gravity' type of equilibrium that is encountered in classic macroeconomic theory. A closely related generating mechanism is known as the 'error-correction model'. Here the change in x_t is given by

$$\text{change in } x_t = a_1 z_{t-1} + \text{lagged changes } x_t, y_t + \text{residual}$$

plus a similar equation for the change in y_t, with at least one of a_1, a_2 being non-zero. If x_t, y_t are I(1) and z_t is I(0), then all components of the error-correction model are I(0), with the residuals being white noise, and so the equations are balanced in that all variables have similar temporal properties. It can be shown that if x_t, y_t are cointegrated then they must be generated by a bivariate error-correction model and vice versa; if x_t, y_t are generated by an error-correction model then they must be cointegrated. The error-correction model can be thought of as the disequilibrium mechanism that leads to the equilibrium or attractor introduced above, as the next changes in x_t and y_t are affected by the current size of the disequilibrium error z_t. These concepts are discussed at greater length by Granger (1986) and in more generality in various papers in the special issues of the *Oxford Bulletin of Economics and Statistics*, vol. 68, August 1986, and *Journal of Economic Dynamics and Control*, vol. 12, June–September 1988, and in *Advances in Econometrics*, 1989.

One simple way of testing for cointegration is introduced by Engle and Granger (1987). The first step is to perform an ordinary least squares regression $x_t = \hat{A}y_t + z_t$, take the residual z_t and test if z_t is I(0) using the Dickey–Fuller test discussed on p. 564. However, as z_t is estimated rather than being directly observed, slightly different critical values have to be used. It should be noted that the ordinary least squares (OLS) estimate $\hat{A}$ of A converges to A at a much faster rate than do usual OLS estimates. An alternative test procedure introduced by Johansen (1988) uses a maximum likelihood estimator of the error-correction model. It can be also used with multivariate generalizations of cointegration. In multivariate situations there may be several cointegrating combinations. Pairs or groups of economic series have been considered in a number of papers, and cointegration appears to have been found between aggregate disposable income and non-durable consumption, and between interest rates of various terms, for example.

A variety of generalizations of the simple form of cointegration are being investigated, including time-varying parameter cointegration, non-linear attractors, error-correction models in which the z_{t-1} terms are replaced by non-linear functions of z_{t-1}, cointegration of seasonal components and deeper levels of cointegration, including dynamic and multi-cointegration. In the latter, if x_t, y_t are I(1) and cointegrated, so that $z_t = x_t - Ay_t$ is I(0), then the accumulated zs,

$$Sz_t = \sum z_{t-j} \qquad j = 0, \ldots, t$$

will be I(1). x_t, y_t are said to be multi-cointegrated if x_t and Sz_t are cointegrated.

An example is when x_t is the production of some industry, y_t is the sales of that industry, $x_t - y_t$ is the change of inventory and Sz_t is the level of inventory (apart from the initial inventory, which is a constant). It is found that inventory and sales are often cointegrated. Engle and Granger (1991) have edited a book of readings mentioning some of these developments. One direct implication of cointegration is that long-run forecasts of x_t, y_t, derived from the error-correction model, will jointly lie on the line $x = Ay$ and so will 'hang together' in more sensible ways then might be forecast from ARIMA or VAR models.

A further implication involves 'causality' between the variables. In the last twenty years many papers have appeared testing for a form of causality in which one variable helps improve the forecastability of another. Discussions of the concept can be found in Granger and Newbold (1987: ch. 7) or entries in the *New Palgrave Dictionary*. If x_t, y_t are cointegrated it follows directly from the error-correction model that at least one variable must cause the other. This suggests that pairs of prices from a fully efficient speculative market cannot be cointegrated, for example.

27.4 FORECASTING AND ARCH

If a least squares forecasting criterion is used, the optimum forecast of x_{n+h} given the information set I_n available at the time n at which the forecast is made is well known to be the conditional mean

$$f_{n,h} = \mathrm{E}(x_{n+h}|I_n)$$

Given any of the various models discussed above, it is easy to form such forecasts, under the assumption that the model is correct. In practice, various competing forecasts, using different information sets and different modelling strategies, will be available. These can be compared by their relative forecasting abilities, i.e. by comparing sums of squares of forecast errors. An alternative procedure, which will often also produce superior forecasts, is to combine the various forecasts. This can easily be achieved by regressing the actual value of the series onto the various forecasts, a constant and a lagged value of the actual series. Any forecast that does not enter this regression significantly can be dropped, as it is dominated by the others. Further discussion of the combination of forecasts can be found in the special issue of the *Journal of Forecasting*, 1989.

A point forecast is of little value for decision-making without some indication of uncertainty. For more conventional economic forecasts, 95 per cent confidence intervals around the point forecast are embarrassingly wide and so 50 per cent intervals or interquartile ranges are sometimes recommended. A further problem is that the variances of forecast errors may vary through time, as suggested by the considerable interest shown by econometricians in heteroscedasticity. Just as the conditional mean $f_{n,h}$ will be a function of the information set I_n used, so may be the conditional variance

$$h_n^2 = \text{E}[(x_{n+h} - f_{n,h})^2 \mid I_n]$$

Methods for modelling h_n^2 are less advanced than those for $f_{n,h}$. It should be noted that the forecast errors $e_{n,1} = x_{n+1} - f_{n,1}$ will usually be white noise but the squared error may not be, suggesting that conditional variances may be forecastable.

Denoting the one-step forecast errors by $\varepsilon_t = x_t - f_{t-1}$, Engle (1982) has considered the specification

$$h_t^2 = \sum_{j=1}^{q} \gamma_j \varepsilon_{t-j}^2$$

and called the resulting process autoregressive conditional heteroscedastic. If the variance is changing through time in a predictable way, then the obvious advantage in modelling the variance is that, by allowing for heteroscedasticity, better estimates of the parameters in f_t are achieved and better estimates of the confidence intervals around the mean forecasts should be also be obtained. Engle (1982) considers various forms for h_t, discusses their properties and estimation techniques, and uses a Lagrange multipler procedure to test for autoregressive conditional heteroscedasticity (ARCH). He applied the technique to inflation data from the United Kingdom and found clear evidence of predictable variances: 'the standard deviation of inflation increased from 0.6 percent to 1.5 percent over a few years, as the economy moved from the rather predictable sixties into the chaotic seventies'.

The representation of h_t given above can obviously be generalized to include observed driving variables. As an example, Granger et al. (1985) investigated the relationship between retail and wholesale prices, where the variances for each equation were as given above supplemented by squared lagged own and other prices and squared other forecast errors. Enriching the ARCH specification resulted in better models as measured by likelihood ratios and also gave a more interesting model interpretation. Wholesale prices were found to cause consumer prices in both mean and variance. Squared consumer prices did not cause the variance in wholesale prices. If models were constructed ignoring ARCH, consumer prices appeared to cause wholesale prices, but when ARCH was used, this causation became rather weak.

Because, in practice, variances do change through time in predictable ways, the use of ARCH models can be recommended, particularly when greater attention is paid to providing confidence intervals to forecasts than is currently the case. Further areas of clear importance for this development are those parts of economics, such as finance, that use variance as a measure of risk.

If h_t enters an equation linearly, for a price, say, representing an estimate of the current level of risk, the model is called 'ARCH in mean'. The models can be generalized so that the variance is itself long memory, and this seems to be particularly relevant for financial data.

27.5 STATE SPACE MODELS: TIME-VARYING PARAMETERS

A class of models that provides a convenient theoretical structure and which have the potential for providing important future developments and applications are based on a state space representation (fundamental references are Harvey (1981) and Aoki (1987)). The state variables connected to a specific information set I_t are a vector x_t which contains all the information in I_t at time t. x_t may not be completely observed but estimates for the value at time t can be obtained. Because of its basic property, x_t must be a Markov process, so that in its linear form x_t must be a linear function of just x_{t-1} plus an innovation – a white noise input that represents the new information about the system accumulated in the time period $t - 1$ to t. This gives the state variable an updating equation

$$x_t = Tx_{t-1} + u_t \qquad (27.2)$$

The actual observed variables in the system y_t can then be thought of as being generated by the measurement equation

$$y_t = \beta x_t + v_t \qquad (27.3)$$

The number of conponents of the vector x_t will usually be much larger than that of y_t to pick up the possibly complicated dynamics of the y series, but the form of the pair of equations (27.1) and (27.2) is basically very simple. Any ARIMA model can quite easily be put into a state variable form, but not uniquely. In some cases it is possible to interpret the state variables as particular unobserved components, such as 'trends' or seasonals, but such interpretations are not always available. The state space representation is particularly convenient because estimation of parameters and updates of estimates of x_t can be obtained from the Kalman filter algorithm, as discussed by Anderson and Moore (1979).

A potentially very important use of these techniques is with models having time-varying parameters.

Consider a simple relationship between a pair of observed series x_t, y_t of the form

$$y_t = \beta_t x_t + v_t \qquad (27.4)$$

where the coefficient β_t is allowed to change through time. Throughout economics, changes in relationships can be expected as tastes, behaviour, rules and technologies change. For example, y_t could be residential demand for electricity per household in some region and x_t could be temperature. Over a period of several years appliance efficiencies and house insulation qualities would change, and behaviour could change. Thus, the relationship between demand and temperature would probably evolve. On some occasions, the reasons for changing parameters will be known and are due to changes in measurable quantities, but often the causes of the change are not observable, as the efficiency and insulation levels in the above example illustrate. If we believe that parameter changes are quite slow, then a possible strategy for modelling these changes is to assume an AR(1) model with a coefficient near unity, so that

$$\dot{\beta}_t = \alpha \dot{\beta}_{t-1} + u_t \qquad \dot{\beta}_t = \beta_t - \bar{\beta} \qquad (27.5)$$

with α near unity, for example. Here β_t is not strictly observable, although it can be estimated from the observed series.

These two equations are similar in form to (27.3) and (27.4) but with x_t replaced by β_t and β in (27.3) replaced by the observed time-varying x_t. It follows that similar estimation and updating techniques can be found. It is usually recommended that a test for time-varying parameters is applied before such a model is estimated. There is some evidence that better fitting and better forecasting models can be achieved by using time-varying parameters, although a great deal more experience is needed. It is probably preferable to see whether the parameter variation can be explained from economic facts.

27.6 CHAOS AND NON-LINEAR MODELS

There has been some development of non-linear univariate time series models but little has been attempted at similar multivariate generalizations. Obvious models are non-linear autoregressive series such as

$$x_t = g(x_{t-1}) + \varepsilon_t \qquad (27.6)$$

which is known to produce a stationary series provided that $|g(x)| < |x|$ for all x, and bilinear series, such as

$$x_t = \alpha x_{t-1} \varepsilon_{t-2} + \varepsilon_t$$

A basic reference is Priestley (1988). There is some evidence that bilinear models often out-forecast linear models using economic data, but their specification and estimation is fairly difficult.

Some non-linear relationships between series have been investigated using non-parametric techniques. For example, Engle $et\ al.$ (1986) considered the effect of temperature on electricity demand on a region where electricity was used for both heating and cooling houses. This is an area of research where much development can be expected in the future.

An active field of research which has been successful in the natural sciences but is probably less relevant for economics is that concerning deterministic chaos. If an equation such as (27.6), but without the stochastic innovations, is used to generate a sequence x_t, it is possible for a particular class of functions $g(.)$ to obtain a series that appears to be white noise when linear tests are applied, so that all estimated autocorrelations are asymptotically zero. The theory of such processes involves some particularly elegant mathematics and leads to processes having what are called 'strange attractors'. In theory, such processes are long memory, as they can be forecast perfectly throughout the future, but in practice, if any x_t is observed with any error, future forecasts quickly diverge from true values and the process is short memory. Brock *et al.* (1987) have developed a test for non-linearity using these ideas, but, although it is very general, it seems to require larger samples than are usually available in economics and also seems to be rather fragile about assumptions required for its use. Many other tests for non-linearity are available. Some recent ones based on neural networks (White 1989) appear to be promising both for univariate series and for detecting non-linear relationships between series.

27.7 OTHER TOPICS

The main links between the time series approaches to econometric modelling and the more classical approaches have been developed within discussions of model-building methodology. The process by which a satisfactory specification of a model is achieved and how the model is then evaluated remains controversial. Different authors propose quite different procedures, with alternative amounts of emphasis on the use of economic theory and pre-testing, for example. Some workers, such as Pagan and Hendry, recommended starting from large models and then simplifying them to obtain a parsimonious model that is data coherent, whereas the earlier strategies proposed by Box and Jenkins start with univariate models and then grow to bivariate etc. VARMA models, or possibly ARMAX (single dependent variable, multiple explanatory variable) models. Some authors (such as Zellner and Leamer) suggest strong emphasis on Bayesian techniques, whereas most model constructions make little formal use of these ideas. A book of readings on the methodology of time series modelling is Granger (1989).

An area in which theory seems to have useful practical implications concerns temporal and cross-sectional aggregation of time series. It is known, for example, that temporal aggregation can produce much simpler models – ARIMA(p, d, q) becomes ARIMA (o, d, d) or ARIMA (o, d, $d - 1$) for stock and flow variables if aggregation is over sufficiently long periods – and this has been observed with actual data. Cointegration is preserved with temporal aggregation. Cross-sectional aggregation can produce either more complicated or simpler models, depending on the presence or otherwise of common factors in the components. When there are no common factors, models at the micro-level which are non-linear, have time-varying parameters and are heteroscedastic can become linear, constant parameter and homoscedastic. A number of papers concerning these questions appear in Barker and Pesaran (1989).

Amongst other topics that used to be given a lot of attention and are now rather quiet, although still showing some action and remaining potentially important, are seasonal adjustment and spectral or frequency analysis. Most seasonal adjustment techniques used by government agencies are univariate and use two-sided, possibly non-linear, filters. These procedures can destroy interesting aspects of the data. Most empirical workers would prefer to have available non-seasonally adjusted data and then analyse the seasonal component using causal models. However, such data are not easily available in all countries.

REFERENCES

Anderson, B. P. O. and Moore, J. B. (1979) *Optimal Filtering*, Englewood Cliffs, NJ: Prentice-Hall.

Aoki, M. (1987) *State Space Modelling of Time Series*, New York: Springer-Verlag.

Barker, T. and Pesaran, H. (1990) *Disaggregation in Economic Modelling*, Cambridge: Cambridge University Press.

Box, G. E. P. and Jenkins, G. M. (1976) *Time Series Forecasting and Control*, revised edn, San Francisco, CA: Holden-Day.

Brock, W., Dechart, W. F. and Scheinkman, J. (1987) 'A test for independence based on the correlation dimension', Working paper, Department of Economics, University of Wisconsin.

Dickey, D. A. and Fuller, W. A. (1981) 'Likelihood ratio tests for autoregressive time series with a unit root', *Econometrica* 49: 1057–72.

Diebold, F. X. and Nerlove, M. (1989) 'Unit roots in economic times series: a selective survey', in T. B. Fomby and G. F. Rodes (eds) *Advances in Econometrics*, New Haven, CT: JAI Press.

Doan, T., Litterman, R. B. and Sims, C. A. (1984) 'Forecasting and conditional projection using realistic prior distributions', *Econometric Reviews* 3: 1–10.

Engle, R. F. (1982) 'Autoregressive conditional heteroscedasticity with estimates of the variance of UK inflation', *Econometrica* 50: 987–1008.

Engle, R. F., Granger, C. W. J., Ric, J. and Weiss, A. (1986) 'Semi-parametric estimates of the relation between weather and electricity sales', *Journal of the American Statistical Association* 81: 310–20.

Engle, R. F. and Granger, C. W. J. (1987) 'Cointegration and error-correction: representation, estimation and testing', *Econometrica* 55: 251–76.

—— and —— (1991) *Readings in Cointegration*, in preparation.

Granger, C. W. J. (1986) 'Developments in the study of cointegrated economic variables', *Oxford Bulletin of Economics and Statistics* 48: 213–28.

—— (1989) *Modelling Economic Series: Readings in Econometric Methodology*, Oxford: Oxford University Press.

Granger, C. W. J. and Newbold, P. (1987) *Forecasting Economic Series*, 2nd edn, San Francisco, CA: Academic Press.

Granger, C. W. J. and Watson, M. W. (1986) 'Time series and spectral methods in econometrics', in Z. Grilliches and M. D. Intriligator (eds) *Handbook of Econometrics*, vol. II, Amsterdam: Elsevier.

Granger, C. W. J., Robins and Engle, R. F. (1985) 'Wholesale and retail prices', in E. Kuh and T. Belsley (eds) *Model Reliability*, Cambridge, MA: MIT Press.

Hannen, E. J. and Rissanen, J. (1982) 'Recursive estimation of mixed autoregressive-moving average order', *Biometrika* 69: 81–94.

Harvey, A. C. (1981) *Time Series Models*, New York: Wiley.

Johansen, S. (1988) 'Statistical analysis of cointegration vectors', *Journal of Economic Dynamics and Control* 12: 231–54.

McNees, S. M. (1986) 'Forecasting accuracy of alternative techniques: a comparison of U. S. macreoeconomic forecasts', *Journal of Business and Economic Statistics* 4: 5–15.

Nelson, C. R. and Plosser, C. I. (1982) 'Trends and random walks in macroeconomic time series', *Journal of Monetary Economics* 10: 139–62.

Priestley, M. B. (1988) *Nonlinear and Non-Stationary Time Series Analysis*, New York: Academic Press.

Runkle, D. E. (1987) 'Vector autoregressions and reality', *Journal of Business and Economic Statistics* 5: 437–56.

Sims, C. A. (1980) 'Macroeconomics and reality', *Econometrica* 48: 1–48.

White, H. (1989) 'An additional hidden unit test for neglected nonlinearity in multilayer feedforward networks', Working paper, Department of Economics, University of California at San Diego.

573

28

THE ROLE OF
MEASUREMENT AND
TESTING IN ECONOMICS

GRAYHAM E. MIZON

28.1 INTRODUCTION

Economic theory and econometric analysis are two of the essential ingredients of economics. However, the fact that developments in each of these areas have occurred at different times and rates has sometimes been interpreted mistakenly as yielding information about their relative importance, or at least about the economics profession's perception of their relative importance. Hence it is not surprising that the relative merits, and respective roles, of economic theory and econometrics have long been issues that have exercised the minds of economists. Recent illustrative examples of economists commenting on economic theory and empirical evidence being out of joint are provided by the following:

> Although these conclusions ran counter to much of the conventional wisdom in the field of industrial organization and left a disconcerting number of mistakes and misperceptions to explain, the logic leading to them seemed compelling. And because *no mere fact was ever a match in economics for a consistent theory*, these ideas began to represent the basis of a new consensus.
>
> (Milgrom and Roberts 1987: 185, emphasis added)

> In economics the tendency of theory to lag behind observation seems to be endemic, and, as theorists, few of us consider this to be a 'terrible state'. But as noted by Lakatos (1978: 6), 'where theory lags behind the facts, we are dealing with miserable degenerating research programmes'.
>
> (Smith 1989: 168)

In these examples the advantages of achieving congruence between theory and observation (and the drawbacks of not doing so) are illustrated: Milgrom and

The financial support for this research from the Economic and Social Research Council (ESRC) Macroeconomic Research Consortium programme grant 'Appraising model evaluation techniques' (ESRC grant B01250024) is gratefully acknowledged.

574

Roberts were drawing attention to the fact that inconsistencies between theory and observation can lead to the development of richer theories (as opposed to *ad hoc* adjustments merely employed to accommodate errant facts) which are coherent with observation; Smith was highlighting the desirability of the simultaneous development of the theoretical and empirical wings of economics. A primary purpose of this chapter is to review the roles of economic theory and empirical analysis in economics. It will be argued not only that each has a distinct role, but that both are essential if economics is to be scientific. Particular emphasis will be placed on the role of measurement in economics, thus echoing the sentiments expressed by Malinvaud in his Presidential Address to the European Economic Association in 1988:

> Scientific knowledge comes from observation. In a mature science, most of past observations have been so much processed within theories that one often loses sight of the many origins in the real world from which a particular result has been derived. But from time to time scientists of a discipline find it necessary to reflect on the role of observation in their field and on the way in which it is dealt with.
>
> (Malinvaud 1989: 205)

The observations generated in the process of measurement can be the focus of data analysis which aims to summarize and describe them, or they can be used as the lifeblood of inference drawn from econometric modelling, which constitutes a major part of the body corporate of scientific economics. Each of these activities, data analysis and econometric modelling, will be described and their roles assessed below. Indeed, the fact that there has been an enormous increase in the types, quality and quantity of data available, and that major advances have been made in the development of methods for building and evaluating econometric models, as well as great increases in computing power, has made an assessment of the roles of measurement and testing in economics all the more relevant and important. In the next section the roles of measurement and *a priori* theory are discussed, and in the following section the importance of rigorous model evaluation and testing, when theory and measurement are combined in economics, is emphasized. The final section of the chapter contains concluding remarks.

28.2 MEASUREMENT AND THEORY

That theory and measurement are essential in a science is rarely doubted, but their respective roles have been, and will no doubt continue to be, questioned. The ebb and flow of their relative fortunes within economics is well illustrated by the changes in the motto adopted by the Cowles Commission (later Cowles Foundation) for Research in Economics, which for many years was Lord Kelvin's dictum 'Science is measurement' but was later changed to 'Theory and measurement' (see Malinvaud (1988: 188–9) for more discussion of the contributions of the Cowles Foundation researchers to economics). Something which has been doubted many times, however, is the scientific nature of economics. The *Shorter Oxford English Dictionary* defines science as 'a branch of study which is concerned either with a connected body of demonstrated truths, or with observed facts systematically classified and more or less colligated by being brought under general laws, and which includes trustworthy methods for the discovery of new truth within its own domain'. How does economics stand up to these requirements? Whilst there are few, if any, '*demonstrated* truths' in economics – incontrovertible and controlled experiments are rare – there is no shortage of 'observed facts'. In addition, a major role of economic theory is to provide a systematic classification of such observed facts and, via its fundamental laws, to colligate these facts. Determining whether economic theory does indeed provide an adequate characterization of the observed facts is one of the roles of econometric analysis. Hence, noting that economic theory and econometrics together purport to embrace 'trustworthy methods for the discovery of new truth', it appears that economics in conjunction with econometrics has the potential to be scientific. If this conjunction is successful, it will yield theories, and models to implement them, that will 'survive the process of testing and transformation, so that they remain in use, and hence alive, long after the disappearance of the problem which first gave rise to them' (Ravetz 1971: 209).

In practice there is one aspect of economics, as perceived by many people, that is non-scientific, and that is its failure to discriminate between alternative competing theories for the same phenomenon. This is evidenced at one level by the jokes, at the expense of the economics profession, in which the number of explanations proffered for any economic phenomenon of interest will be no less than the number of economists consulted, and at another level by judgements such as the following:

> In many areas of economics, different econometric studies reach conflicting conclusions and, given the available data, there are frequently no effective methods for deciding which conclusion is correct. In consequence, contradictory hypotheses continue to co-exist sometimes for decades or more.
>
> (Blaug 1980: 261)

In any discipline it is healthy that alternative theories be available to account for the same phenomena in order that it maintain its vitality and avoid stagnation. Such rival explanations may be developed simultaneously or sequentially in time, but in both cases it is essential that the credentials of all theories are evaluated and compared. A profession which allows alternative theories for the same phenomena (especially those with different policy implications) to coexist for substantial periods of time without serious attempts to discriminate between them is likely to lose its credibility, and is indeed non-scientific.

Model discrimination requires the credentials of each model to be established and compared. This involves checking the congruence of each model with *a priori* theory and sample data, and testing the encompassing ability of those models that achieve this congruence (see Mizon (1984) and the next section). Concentrating for the moment on each model's congruence with *a priori* theory and sample information, it should be noted that congruence with both is required. Hence, the relevance, elegance, simplicity and internal consistency of a model, even when accompanied by the knowledge that its progenitor has an impeccable pedigree, are not sufficient to establish a model's credentials. A model must also be coherent with observation – hence the important role of measurement in economics.

Alternative measurements: sources of data

The most obvious form of measurement for establishing 'scientific facts' is that associated with controlled laboratory experiments. However, until relatively recently, controlled experimental data have been rare in economics, and this has been a feature of economics (and other social sciences) which has lessened its claim to be scientific. Whilst the physicist or chemist can go to the laboratory and set up a more or less 'controlled' experiment to assess the explanatory power of a new hypothesis, and to determine its ability to accomodate and at least match the explanatory power of rival theories, the economist typically has to rely on the measurements contained in non-experimental data, especially those collected by governments and other public agencies. However, economists now have access to the results of quasi-controlled experiments such as those concerned with negative income taxes, electricity time-of-day pricing, housing allowance subsidies and medical expenses reimbursement. Although these experiments, which have mainly been performed in the United States, have yielded valuable information, they have not been unqualified successes. Hausman (1982), in reviewing the contribution to economics of this type of experiment, concludes that, because the experiments have to be conducted over substantial periods of time so that economic agents can adjust their behaviour to the incentive structure of the experiment, the results are contaminated by attrition and duration effects. However, some economists have managed to persuade individuals to participate in laboratory experiments of relatively short duration which are more akin to classical experiments. Precisely because these experiments are conducted in the rarified atmosphere of the 'controlled' experiment, they have been criticized for being artificial and, by implication, less relevant. Smith (1989) assesses, and defends, the value of such experiments in economics. Manifestly, there is much to be learned from, and about appropriate ways to conduct, such experiments in economics.

The major sources of economic data are government agencies, which collect data on a continuous basis on prices, quantities and indicators of aggregate economic performance, as well as international bodies such as the Organizaton for Economic Co-operation and Development (OECD), the International Monetary Fund (IMF) and the International Labour Organization (ILO), which tend to concentrate on the collection of data to enable international comparisons. The economics profession is largely a passive consumer of such data, although from time to time it does influence the nature of the data collected. Also, the relative merits of alternative indices, and alternative methods of collection (for example, surveys and censuses), have traditionally been the concern of economic and social statisticians, and have rarely been of public interest. However, as statistical evidence of varying qualities is more frequently used in political and public debate, so there has been an increase in the public awareness of these issues. For example, the numerous changes in the definition of aggregate unemployment in the United Kingdom since 1979 have served to heighten the public's awareness of the importance of these issues, as well as making empirical analysis of the behaviour of unemployment and other related variables difficult because of the absence of consistent time series data. Atkinson *et al.* (1989) contains an example in which the recent refinements in the collection of data on the distribution of wealth in the United Kingdom meant that the authors had to construct estimates in order to have a longer time series measured on a consistent basis, rather than use the most recent official figures. Decisions on the types, definitions, frequency and sampling schemes for the collection of non-experimental data are ones on which the economics profession should have some influence, and increasingly has had in many countries.

There are three broad categories of non-experimental data: time series, cross-sectional and longitudinal (sometimes panel) data. Whilst time series data are particularly suited to analysing the evolution of economic and social relationships between variables through time, the fact that the composition of the variable being measured might itself change with time means that time series data cannot provide a complete picture. For example, a time series econometric model of aggregate unemployment behaviour can yield valuable information about its temporal evolution, but none about the changing mix of skills in the unemployment pool or about changes in unemployment duration. Cross-sectional data are better suited to the analysis of any homogeneity that exists in the behaviour of economic and social agents or units, but studies using such data are limited by inherent heterogeneities in behaviour and by the absence of information on temporal changes in behaviour and relationships. It is therefore important to note that the last ten years has seen a dramatic increase in the quantity of longitudinal data collected, and a corresponding increase in the development of techniques and models for analysing such data.

Hsiao (1986) and Heckman and Singer (1987) are examples of contributions in this area.

Although census data provide comprehensive information on the phenomena being measured, they are extremely expensive to collect and so are less common than survey data. Indeed, the collection of survey data in recent years has proved to be a rich source of information, both for the provision of time series on national and international aggregates and especially in the generation of cross-sectional and longitudinal microdata on social and economic behaviour. For example, in the United Kingdom the Family Expenditure Survey and the General Household Survey have facilitated much research on household expenditure and labour supply decisions, as well as detailed assessments of the likely effects of alternative fiscal policies. The activities of the Office of Population Censuses and Surveys in the collection and analysis of such data have also had a much higher profile recently in the United Kingdom. In addition, the Economic and Social Research Council (ESRC) has encouraged research in this area by the creation of, initially, the ESRC Survey Archive, and, more recently, the ESRC Research Centre on Micro-social Change in Britain at the University of Essex. These activities and developments are not confined to the United Kingdom, but are to be found in other countries (individually and in groupings like the European Economic Community) and international organizations. However, the riches that are to be collected from these sources come with costs and responsibilities. Surveys require careful design if their potential for providing valuable information is to be realized. Hence the statistical theory for the design of surveys, and statisticians well versed in the application of this theory, have crucial roles to play. However, the responsibilities do not end with survey design. As a result of careful design, in order to ensure that the relevant strata of the population are adequately represented in the survey, the collected observations are far from being identically and independently sampled. It is therefore imperative that the methods of analysis used take account of the complex designs employed in the collection of survey data. In particular, routine application of standard linear regression methods will rarely be appropriate. The fact that there will be 'non-response' from some of the carefully selected members of the sample and 'attrition' from membership of panels further adds to the difficulties associated with the collection and analysis of survey data. In the last twenty years important contributions have been made to this topic by both statisticians and econometricians. Skinner *et al.* (1989) provide recent examples.

Measurement problems

In attempting to develop models which are consonant with economic theory and empirical evidence, economists face the further problem that many economic theory variables are latent, or conceptual, variables which can never be observed. The most obvious example is the concept of equilibrium which is employed in most areas of economic theory. Friedman's permanent income and permanent consumption are other examples of theory concepts which are unobservable. The investigator who uses economic theory involving latent variables must specify an appropriate mapping between observed and latent variables. No matter how carefully chosen such a mapping is, its very existence implies a gap between the theoretical and empirical models. Spanos (1982) provides a valuable discussion of the problems associated with latent variables, and analyses some of the available solutions in the context of dynamic econometric models.

Since the observed variables used in place of latent variables are at best approximations to the latent variables, the result of their use is the introduction of measurement errors into the analysis. Hence there is a close link between the problems of modelling using latent variables and modelling in the presence of measurement errors. However, measurement errors arise for many reasons in addition to the presence of latent variables. There is in fact a long history of questioning the accuracy of economic measurements, of which the contribution of Morgenstern (1950) is one of the most frequently cited. There is also a large literature on the analysis of errors-in-variables models. Indeed, in the early days of econometrics, errors in variables were thought to be at least as important as, if not more important than, errors in equations (see Morgan (1990) for a historical review). A further measurement problem lies in the fact that not only can data contain measurement errors, but they can also contain missing observations. There is now an extensive literature which addresses the problems of inference when models are to be analysed using data which have missing observations. A technique that has proved valuable in this context is the use of the Kalman filter (see Harvey and Pierse (1984) for an exposition). A particular example of missing observations results from the time aggregation of data. Data may have been collected on a monthly basis but only made available quarterly. Equally, data may be available on both a monthly and a quarterly basis, so that it is possible to generate quarterly predictions either from a quarterly model or from an aggregation of the forecasts from a monthly model. In addition to temporal aggregation and disaggregation, there can be cross-sectional aggregation/disaggregation. Pesaran et al. (1989) give a recent analysis of this aggregation issue, in which conditions for 'perfect aggregation' are discussed and an illustration is provided for UK employment demand functions using time series data on forty industries and their aggregation into twenty-three industries.

Hence, although the detailed study of the definitions (including changes in them), sources (including the effects of any implied sample selection biases), accuracy and the general nature and quality of data is not one of the high-prestige areas of activity within the economics profession, it is none the less critically important. It was therefore pleasing to see one chapter of *The Handbook of Econometrics* (Griliches 1986) provide a comprehensive review of these issues and an assessment of the developments since Morgenstern (1950).

Measurement problems, and in particular the latent variable problem, have sometimes been put forward as reasons for discounting empirical evidence that is unfavourable to economic theories. This has the effect of a 'hard core' theory's being afforded a 'protective belt' because inappropriate measurement renders the empirical evidence irrelevant. Similarly, hard core theory can be immunized from the onslaught of adverse empirical evidence with the help of modification designed to accommodate the errant observations. Neither the argument of inappropriate measurement, nor the manipulation of hypotheses to enable them to accomodate any facts, is an impressive approach to adopt in defence of a theory. Malinvaud (1989: 220–1) gives a clear discussion of this point, as illustrated by his statement that:

> the history of science has never been such as the permanent juxtaposition of research programmes among which one would choose on the basis of prior beliefs or tastes; it is on the contrary seen as a succession of programmes constantly superseding each other with theories of ever-increasing empirical content. According to Lakatos, correctly read, a programme is 'degenerating' when it is characterised by the endless addition of ad hoc adjustments that merely accommodate whatever new facts become available.
>
> (Malinvaud 1989: 220)

The use of data: description, modelling and calibration

The uses made of data are multifarious, and not just as a result of the existence of many types, sources and qualities of data. There are alternative approaches to the use of data which reflect distinct views on the relative importance of economic theory, statistical modelling, and data analysis in economics. An enduring concern of economists has been, and remains, the search for an explanation of business cycles, and this topic illustrates well some of the contrasting approaches to the use of data. Three alternative approaches to the analysis of business cycles are now briefly considered: the first relies on descriptive data analysis, the second employs structural econometric models of the 'probability approach' and the third uses general equilibrium theory.

Prior to the 1940s the major contributions to the analysis of business cycles were largely descriptive and addressed the issues of appropriate measurement, choice of indices and graphical representation of the key variables. Indeed, the business cycle analysis associated with the National Bureau of Economic Research (NBER) in general, and Burns and Mitchell (1946) in particular, relied on data analysis and descriptive statistics, and did not have a stochastic

581

specification for the models. An alternative approach, which explicitly introduced a stochastic framework for the analysis, was adopted by the researchers at the Cowles Commission during the 1940s. The importance of having a probability model was emphasized by Koopmans (1937), and the 'probability approach', in which inference from sample data must be based on, and evaluated relative to, a prespecified statistical model, was developed from the seminal work of Haavelmo (1944). The importance of Haavelmo's contributions to econometrics, and especially the foundations that he provided for a theory of econometric modelling, is described by Spanos (1989) and was recognized by the award of the Nobel Prize for Economics in 1989. That this prize was awarded in 1989 for work published in 1944 in part reflects the fact that the focus of the Cowles researchers was on statistical issues associated with the probability approach and that Haavelmo's additional contribution of laying the foundation for econometric modelling methodology has taken much longer to achieve widespread recognition. Working within the framework of the probability approach to econometrics, the gifted researchers at the Cowles Commission achieved important advances such as the laying of the statistical foundations for likelihood inference in simultaneous equations models (Hood and Koopmans 1953), the incorporation of *a priori* theory of economic structure into limited and full information statistical analysis of econometric models and the development of the appropriate statistical theory for the analysis of dynamic simultaneous equations models (Mann and Wald 1943; Koopmans 1950). The work of the Cowles Commission came to dominate econometrics, and despite the considerable computational burden of the maximum likelihood procedures that they developed, applied work which adopted the probability approach was carried out (e.g. Klein 1950). Epstein (1987) and Morgan (1987, 1990) provide valuable historical perspectives on these developments.

The contrast between the data analytical approach of the NBER and the probability approach of the Cowles Commission was highlighted in the review of Burns and Mitchell (1946) by Koopmans (1947). Koopmans criticized the purely empirical approach of the NBER researchers and supported the structural equations approach within the framework of what has now become known as the Haavelmo distribution (Spanos 1989). However, in addition to arguing strongly for a more rigorous use of the methods of statistical inference, Koopmans criticized the practice of 'measurement without theory', and emphasized the importance of using economic theory in econometric analysis. In fact, for a variety of reasons (Epstein 1987; Morgan 1990), the emphasis of research at the Cowles Commission from the end of the 1940s switched from statistical analysis to economic theory. This emphasis on economic theory, sometimes to the exclusion of any assessment of the empirical veracity of models, is reflected today in much of the literature on 'real business cycle analysis', which is the third approach to the explanation of business cycles. The seminal paper by Kydland and Prescott (1982) provided a stimulus for the development of general equilibrium theory models designed to represent the stylized facts of the business cycle. Rather than use empirical observations to estimate the parameters of, and test hypotheses about, these models, the 'stylized facts' are used to 'calibrate' them. This approach assigns economic theory (which is empirically untested) the dominant role in developing models for economic analysis. Even though researchers who use this approach can argue that their models have the advantage of being based on the logically consistent and economically appealing general equilibrium theory, it is difficult to see how they can be taken seriously in the longer term unless they have been shown to be coherent with the observed data rather than simply being calibrated relative to the stylized facts. Plosser (1989) provides a review of the literature on real business cycle analysis, and argues in favour of paying more attention to the empirical evaluation of real business cycle models.

The recent published debates on econometric methodology (see Pagan (1987) for an overview and Granger (1990) for a collection of some of the more important papers in this area) have also provided different perspectives on the roles of economic theory and empirical analysis. For example, Sims (1980) has argued that in the analysis of simultaneous equations models too much reliance has been placed on economic theory, in that many of the *a priori* restrictions used to identify the parameters of such models are incredible. For modelling the dynamic relationships between economic variables Sims proposed that vector autoregressive (VAR) models be used, since they are capable of providing a good characterization of such relationships without having to resort to the use of incredible identifying restrictions. An important part of Sims's argument is that in econometric modelling it is important to use a class of model that can provide a good statistical description of the data. The alternative – choosing the class of model on the grounds of conformity with economic theory – does not ensure that such models will be statistically well specified, and hence inferences drawn from analysis of them are invalid. An intermediate position between these alternative modelling strategies would be one in which each economic-theory-based model is subjected to rigorous statistical evaluation after it is estimated and is modified in the light of revealed inadequacies. Indeed, this position may well be the best description of what many careful investigators attempt to do today. However, such a strategy was criticized by Haavelmo (1958) as concentrating on 'repair work', rather than boldly adopting a statistically well-specified framework within which it is possible to assess the usefulness of fundamental economic theories. Hence the strategy of patching up inadequate models (or specific-to-general modelling) is seriously flawed, despite the fact that the motivation for using it might be the desire to find models which accord with both economic theory and the empirical evidence. Further, the argument that all models should be rigorously evaluated is consonant with Leamer's emphasis on the need to assess the adequacy of each model's specification – Leamer (1978) provides a comprehensive and persuasive analysis of the role of specification searching in econometric modelling. Whilst many of the contributors to the debate on econometric methodology agree that model evaluation is needed, not all of them realize, or accept, the importance of having a statistically well-specified model in which to embed the models of primary interest and hence provide a statistically valid benchmark against which to test them. This point concerns the validity of the act of evaluating a model. If the alternative hypothesis against which a model is being evaluated is itself mis-specified, then each of the tests used in such evaluation is invalid in general! Model development, on the other hand, is concerned with the process by which adequate models are found, and as such does not determine the validity of a model (Hendry and Mizon 1990a). There is therefore an important distinction between *model evaluation* and *model development*. In the next section we elaborate on this point by considering in more detail the issues of model design, evaluation and comparison.

28.3 EVALUATION AND TESTING

There is now a wealth of empirical evidence available for economists to use in the creation, development and evaluation of their theories. As indicated in Section 28.2, the vast quantity and variety of data which are now collected and made accessible not only makes the assessment of the empirical relevance of economic theory possible, but places a responsibility on the economics profession to adopt a scientific approach to the evaluation of its theories. This task has been made easier by the major advances which have taken place in computer technology, including the enormous increase in the power of computers, especially microcomputers, and the development of powerful and sophisticated econometric software to run on personal computers (for example, PC GIVE (Hendry 1989) and Data FIT (Pesaran and Pesaran 1987)). Packages like GAUSS provide more flexibility for the sophisticated user of statistical and econometric techniques. Reassuringly, there has been a corresponding growth in the volume and sophistication of empirical research in economics. There has also been an increased awareness of the importance of evaluating and testing economic models, and this is the focus of attention in this section.

In order for economic analysis to be influential and durable, the credentials of the underlying economic model need to be established. Of particular relevance for economists is the desirability of making full use of the available information. It is therefore important that economists demonstrate that their models are congruent with *all* the available information. Emphasis is placed on *all* information, since it is tempting to believe that all that is required in order to establish the credentials of a theory is that the model chosen to implement it provide a good explanation of the data and that the estimated parameters have the expected magnitudes and signs. However, this approach, which is closely akin to the average economic regression approach discussed by Gilbert (1986), has the drawback that it cannot even be guaranteed to achieve its stated objective. If the model is statistically mis-specified the usual methods of inference are invalid, and so the use of point estimates, standard errors and test statistics to assess the veracity of the theory's predictions cannot be relied on. The dangers of using economic analysis which is confined to a particular class of model prescribed by economic theory, without regard to the statistical properties of that class, and then seeking to use empirical evidence to confirm a particular theory have been described and illustrated by Mizon (1989). Confirmationism, or the use of empirical evidence to confirm theories, has a number of fundamental weaknesses. First, it is possible for two or more alternative models of the same phenomenon to be confirmed by the data. Examples of this are easy to generate, particularly when the models are characterized by simple, rather than partial, regression coefficients. Let y_t be the variable to be explained, with model 1 (M_1) positing a set of regressors x_{1t} as the explanation and model 2 (M_2) positing the regressor set x_{2t}, so that

$$M_1: y_t = x'_{1t}\beta_1 + u_{1t} \qquad \text{with } \beta_1 > 0$$

$$M_2: y_t = x'_{2t}\beta_2 + u_{2t} \qquad \text{with } \beta_2 < 0$$

Then it is perfectly possible for the least squares estimates of β_1 and β_2 to confirm M_1 and M_2 respectively by having the 'correct' signs. However, there are many assertions implicit in the specification of M_1 and M_2 which have not been tested. For example, if the implicit assertion that the errors u_{it} for $i = 1, 2$ have zero means, constant variances and are serially uncorrelated were incorrect, the inferences about the signs of β_1 and β_2 based on the least squares point estimates and standard errors would be invalidated. Hence it is important to determine that the statistical properties of the estimated models are such that they do not invalidate the methods of inference used in interpreting the results. Mizon (1989) and Driffill *et al.* (1990) give illustrations of the dangers of uncritically using empirical evidence to confirm the hypothesis that there is a significant positive association between aggregate inflation and a measure of relative price variability. The second fundamental weakness of confirmationism lies in the fact that, although both M_1 and M_2 can be statistically well specified with respect to their own information sets $\{y_t, x_{1t}, t = 1, 2, \ldots, T\}$ and $\{y_t, x_{2t}, t = 1, 2, \ldots, T\}$ respectively, they are both likely to be found inadequate when evaluated in the context of the larger information set $\{y_t, x_{1t}, x_{2t}, t = 1, 2, \ldots, T\}$. This will happen when each of M_1 and M_2 contains part of the explanation of y_t, but neither provides a complete explanation. It is then critical for an investigator to decide what is the relevant information set for the

585

phenomenon being analysed. Note, however, that, if the relevant information sets are said to be the first two mentioned above, then M_1 and M_2 are not alternative models of the same phenomenon. Mizon (1989) gives a numerical example of the joint confirmation of alternative models implying the invalidity of both, using simple versions of a monetarist theory and a Keynesian theory for the explanation of the generation of aggregate inflation.

The weaknesses of confirmationism arise from restricting attention to part of the available information, namely a particular economic theory and data directly associated with it, rather than evaluating a model relative to all the available information. The concept of model congruence (Hendry 1985; Hendry and Mizon 1990a) provides the means of avoiding these weaknesses. Congruence requires that a model be coherent with sample information, with the properties of the measurement system and with *a priori* theory, and that it can encompass rival models. The importance of each of these requirements for model congruence will be discussed below.

A potential alternative source of evidence for establishing the credentials of a model is its pedigree. It has been argued that the origin of a model, and the route by which it was developed, are important characteristics to consider in its evaluation. However, the evaluation of a model, and the act of its discovery or development, are distinct activities with different purposes. Whether a particular model is the result of a data mining search or is the creation of a Nobel Laureate in economics does not *per se* determine its quality or its validity. The validity and usefulness of a model can only be assessed by evaluating its performance, and this can be done most effectively by checking its congruence. The origin and route by which a model is developed are important determinants of the efficiency of search for a congruent model, but it is congruence, not pedigree, that is at issue in assessing the validity of a model. In fact, much of the discussion of econometric methodology has been concerned with model development, as is evidenced by the constructive proposals for modelling made by Sims (1980) and Leamer (1982). In view of the perceived failure of econometrics to live up to the unrealistically high expectations formed of it in the 1960s and 1970s, it is not surprising that analyses of the 'failure' should have resulted in the proposal of constructive remedies. However, there are no sufficient conditions for the development of good models, although some strategies for their development are likely to be more efficient than others (see Hendry and Mizon (1990a) for more details).

In the absence of sufficient conditions for model adequacy, congruence provides a set of necessary conditions, and as such provides a minimum set of conditions for a model to satisfy in order to be an adequate characterization of the data and to be economically interpretable and relevant, as well as performing at least as well as rival models of the same phenomenon. A detailed description of the concept and requirements of model congruence can be

Table 28.1 Congruence

Information source	Model characteristic under scrutiny
1 Sample information	
(a) Past	Dynamic specification
	Granger causality
(b) Present	Weak exogeneity
	Innovation errors
	Homoscedasticity
	Functional form
	Skewness and kurtosis
(c) Future	Parameter constancy
	Predictive accuracy
2 Measurement system	
(a) Domain of variation	Boundedness
	Functional form
(b) Time series properties	Serial correlation
	Stationarity
	Integratedness
	Cointegration
	Deterministic non-stationarity
	(e.g. trend, regime shifts)
(c) Cross-sectional properties	Skewness and kurtosis
	Multimodality
	Heterogeneity
	Sample selection
3 *A priori* theory	
(a) Economic theory	Theory consistency
	Economic interpretability
	Information set
	Structural hypotheses
	Parameters of interest
	Functional form
4 Rival models	
(a) Sample	Variance dominance
	Parametric encompassing
	Forecast encompassing
	Parsimonious encompassing
(b) *A priori* theory	Information set
	Structural hypotheses
	Parameters of interest
	Functional form

found in Hendry (1985, 1987) and Hendry and Mizon (1990a), and so will not be repeated here. However, Table 28.1 provides a listing of the sources of information against which a model can be tested for congruence, and the features of a model under scrutiny corresponding to each source of information.

Inspection of Table 28.1 reveals that, for a model to be congruent with past, present and future sample information, it must pass a wide range of diagnostic checks for model adequacy, many of which are now standard features of computer programmes such as PC GIVE and Data FIT. However, congruence requires more than that a model have no indication of mis-specification as judged by the standard diagnostic test statistics. Congruence with the measurement system covers the requirement that the chosen form of model should not be capable of producing fitted, or predicted, values of endogenous variables that are outside the known domain of measurement for those variables. It also covers the requirement that, if the variables being modelled are stationary, the explanatory variables must also be stationary collectively even though they might be non-stationary in isolation. In particular, the recent literature on integrated variables, and cointegrated combinations of them, has established that there are restrictions on the class of models that can be used to model the behaviour of non-stationary variables (see Granger (1986) and Hylleberg and Mizon (1989) for more details). Hence it is important to determine the time series properties (such as the degree of integratedness, the number of cointegrating vectors and the form of any deterministic non-stationarities) of the variables contained in the modelling information set. Similarly, inspection of the frequency distribution of variables can yield valuable information on skewness, kurtosis and multimodality, which then has implications for the choice of functional form and class of model to be used if the chosen model is to be congruent with these features of the data.

The next major source of information listed in Table 28.1 is *a priori* theory, and it is the requirement that a model be congruent with this source of information that ensures that the model has an economic interpretation and is economically relevant, and facilitates discussion of its properties and implications. In discussing the congruence of a model with *a priori* theory it is relevant to return to the issue of the role of economic theory in econometric modelling by discussing an apparent difference between the perspective of an economist and that of an econometrician in the testing of an economic theory. In this caricature the economist sees the role of economic theory as dominating that of empirical evidence, and so confines attention to the class of models that conforms to the economic theory. This might be achieved either by using data simply to provide numerical estimates of parameters which are restricted to take values that conform to economic theory, or by only considering further those estimated models which do conform to economic theory when the parameters of a model are estimated freely. In the latter approach economic theory is being used as a model selection criterion, in that only those models that are in agreement with a particular economic theory are deemed to be acceptable. The approach to modelling labelled confirmationism consists in requiring a model to be congruent with *a priori* theory only, and eschews testing its congruence with sample information, the measurement system or with the information contained in rival models. The caricature econometrician, in contrast, will require a model to be congruent with sample information and the properties of the measurement system in order to ensure that rival economic theories can be tested, and compared validly, within a statistically well-specified class of model.

In discussing the testing of a model's congruence with economic theory mention has been made of testing economic theories. However, whilst it is possible sensibly to test a particular model (strictly hypothesis) against a statistically well-specified alternative, and to regard the model as falsified if the test results in a rejection, the falsification of a theory requires more than this. Even though a particular model used to represent a theory may be at variance with the empirical evidence, so that the model is inadequate, the theory will only be regarded as falsified if there is an alternative model available that is consistent with the empirical evidence. This observation helps to motivate the next requirement of a congruent model, namely that it be congruent with the information contained in rival models and so encompass its rivals (see Mizon (1984), Mizon and Richards (1986) and Hendry and Richard (1990b) for more details of the concept of encompassing). Requiring a model to encompass its rivals first ensures that they are all defined on the same probability space and hence have a common information set, and second ensures that the rival models are inferentially redundant in that the encompassing model is capable of generating all inferences derivable from its rivals. An advantage of this is that an investigator is forced to consider what the parameters of interest are, and correspondingly what the appropriate information set is. Once the relevant information set has been determined, the validity of subsequent inference requires that a statistically well-specified model (i.e. one which is congruent with the sample information and the measurement system for that information set) be found, and this will constitute the Haavelmo distribution. The rival models are then testable as restricted versions, or reductions, of the Haavelmo distribution. Hendry and Richard (1990b) have shown that, for any model to encompass its rivals within this framework, it must be a valid reduction of the Haavelmo distribution, and that such a model will be unique unless there are observationally equivalent encompassing models. These results indicate that the Haavelmo distribution provides an appropriate framework within which to evaluate any particular model, and suggest that a strategy of seeking non-rejectable reductions of the Haavelmo distribution is likely to be an efficient approach to the discovery of a congruent model. This framework has been used by Hendry and Mizon (1990b) to propose that structural econometric models be evaluated via testing their ability to encompass the VAR model for all the variables in the information set. This proposal implies that VAR models and structural econometric models have complementary roles in modelling, rather than representing alternative approaches to the modelling of economic time series. An unrestricted VAR (provided that it is congruent with the sample information and the measurement system) constitutes the Haavelmo distribution, and structural econometric models form an important class of parsimonious and economically relevant models to be tested as reductions of the VAR. In this approach to modelling, economic theory and data evidence have complementary, rather than competing, roles, and the testing of hypotheses associated with dynamic specification and economic structure is valid.

28.4 CONCLUSIONS

It has been argued that the assessment and demonstration of the coherence of economic models with empirical observation is essential in economic science. Hence both measurement and testing have important roles in economics. Measurement of economic phenomena, although fraught with conceptual and practical difficulties, is a vital source of information for the formulation and testing of economic models. Economic theories, if not implemented in economic models and subjected to the hazard of empirical falsification, lack credibility. The evaluation of economic models by checking their congruence with sample information, the measurement system and the information contained in rival models is a demanding, although impressive, way to establish their credentials. However, it is important that this evaluation be made within a statistically well-specified framework, which has been termed the Haavelmo distribution. It is then possible for the complementary roles of economic theory and empirical evidence to be exploited in the development of models which have an economically interpretable structure and no evidence of statistical misspecification.

REFERENCES

Atkinson, A. B., Gordon, J. P. F. and Harrison, A. (1989) 'Trends in the shares of top wealth-holders in Britain, 1923–81', *Oxford Bulletin of Economics and Statistics* 51: 315–32.

Blaug, M. (1980) *The Methodology of Economics: Or How Economists Explain*, Cambridge: Cambridge University Press.

Burns, A. F. and Mitchell, W. C. (1946) *Measuring Business Cycles*, New York: National Bureau of Economic Research.

Driffill, E. J., Mizon, G. E. and Ulph, A. M. (1990) 'The costs of inflation', in B. Friedman and F. H. Hahn (eds) *The Handbook of Monetary Economics*, vol. II, ch. 19, Amsterdam: Elsevier.

Epstein, R. J. (1987) *A History of Econometrics*, Amsterdam: North-Holland.

Gilbert, C. L. (1986) 'Professor Hendry's econometric methodology', *Oxford Bulletin of Economics and Statistics* 48: 283–307.

Granger, C. W. J. (1986) 'Developments in the study of cointegrated economic variables', *Oxford Bulletin of Economics and Statistics* 48: 213–28.

—— (ed.) (1990) *Modelling Economic Series: Readings in Econometric Methodology*, Oxford: Oxford University Press.

Griliches, Z. (1986) 'Economic data issues', in Z. Griliches and M. D. Intriligator (eds) *Handbook of Econometrics*, vol. III, ch. 1, Amsterdam: Elsevier.

Haavelmo, T. (1944) 'The probability approach in econometrics', *Econometrica (Supplement)* 12.

—— (1958) 'The role of the econometrician in the advancement of economic theory', *Econometrica* 26: 351–7.

Harvey, A. C. and Pierse, R. G. (1984) 'Estimating missing observations in economic time series', *Journal of the American Statistical Association* 79: 125–31.

Hausman, J. A. (1982) 'The effects of time in economic experiments', in W. Hildenbrand (ed.) *Advances in Econometrics*, Cambridge: Cambridge University Press.

Heckman, J. J. and Singer, B. S. (eds) (1987) *Longitudinal Analysis of Labor Market Data*, Cambridge: Cambridge University Press.

Hendry, D. F. (1985) 'Monetary economic myth and econometric reality', *Oxford Review of Economic Policy* 1: 72–84.

—— (1987) 'Econometric methodology: a personal perspective', in T. F. Bewley (ed.) *Advances in Econometrics*, vol. 2, ch. 10, pp. 29–48, Cambridge: Cambridge University Press.

—— (1989) *PC-GIVE User's Manual*, version 6.0/6.01, Oxford: Oxford Institute of Economics and Statistics.

Hendry, D. F. and Mizon, G. E. (1990a) 'Procrustean econometrics: or stretching and squeezing data', in C. W. J. Granger (ed.) *Modelling Economic Series: Readings in Econometric Methodology*, Oxford: Oxford University Press.

—— and —— (1990b) 'Evaluation of dynamic econometric models by encompassing the VAR', in P. C. B. Phillips and V. B. Hall (eds) *Models, Methods and Applications of Econometrics, Essays in Honor of Rex Bergstrom*, London: Centre for Economic Policy Research.

Hendry, D. F. and Richard, J. F. (1990) 'Recent developments in the theory of encompassing', in B. Cornet and H. Tulkens (eds) *Contributions to Operations Research and Econometrics: XXth Anniversary of CORE*, Cambridge, MA: MIT Press.

Hood. W. C. and Koopmans, T. C. (1953) *Studies in Econometric Method*, New York: Wiley, Cowles Commission Monograph 14.

Hsiao, C. (1986) *Analysis of Panel Data*, Cambridge: Cambridge University Press.

Hylleberg, S. and Mizon, G. E. (1989) 'Cointegration and error correction mechanisms', *Economic Journal (Conference Supplement)* 99: 113–25.

Klein, L. R. (1950) *Economic Fluctuations in the United States 1921–1941*, New York: Wiley, Cowles Commission Monograph 11.

Koopmans, T. C. (1937) *Linear Regression Analysis of Economic Time Series*, Haarlem: Netherlands Economic Institute, Publication 20.

—— (1947) 'Measurement without theory', *Review of Economics and Statistics* 29: 161–72.

—— (1950) *Statistical Inference in Dynamic Economic Models*, New York: Wiley, Cowles Commission Monograph 10.

Kydland, F. E. and Prescott, E. C. (1982) 'Time to build and aggregate fluctuations', *Econometrica* 50: 1345–70.

Lakatos, I. (1978) *Philosophical Papers*, Cambridge: Cambridge University Press.

Leamer, E. E. (1978) *Specification Searches: Ad Hoc Inference With Nonexperimental Data*, New York: Wiley.

—— (1982) 'Let's take the con out of econometrics', *American Economic Review* 73: 31–44.

Malinvaud, E. (1988) 'Econometric methodology at the Cowles Commission: rise and maturity', *Econometric Theory* 4: 187–209.

—— (1989) 'Observation in macroeconomic theory building', *European Economic Review* 33 (2/3): 205–23.

Mann, H. B. and Wald, A. (1943) 'On the statistical treatment of linear stochastic difference equations', *Econometrica* 11: 173–220.

Milgrom, P. and Roberts, J. (1987) 'Information asymmetries, strategic behavior, and industrial organisation', *American Economic Review, Papers and Proceedings* 77: 184–93.

Mizon, G. E. (1984) 'The encompassing approach in econometrics', in D. F. Hendry and K. F. Wallis (eds) *Econometrics and Quantitative Economics*, ch. 6, Oxford: Basil Blackwell.

—— (1989) 'The role of econometric modelling in economic analysis', *Revista Española de Economia* 6: 165–91.

Mizon, G. E. and Richard, J.-F. (1986) 'The encompassing principle and its application to nonnested hypotheses', *Econometrica* 54: 657–78.

Morgan, M. S. (1987) 'Statistics without probability and Haavelmo's revolution in econometrics', in L. Kruger, G. Gigerenzer and M. S. Morgan (eds) *The Probabilistic Revolution*, vol. 2, *Ideas in the Sciences*, ch. 8, pp. 171–200, Cambridge, MA: MIT Press.

—— (1990) *The History of Econometric Ideas*, Cambridge: Cambridge University Press.

Morgenstern, O. (1950) *On the Accuracy of Economic Observations*, Princeton, NJ: Princeton University Press.

Pagan, A. R. (1987) 'Three econometric methodologies: a critical appraisal', *Journal of Economic Surveys* 1: 3–24.

Pesaran, M. H. and Pesaran, B. (1987) *Data-FIT: An Interactive Econometric Software Package*, Oxford: Oxford University Press.

Pesaran, M. H., Pierse, R. G. and Kumar, M. S. (1989) 'Econometric analysis of aggregation in the context of linear prediction models', *Econometrica* 57: 861–88.

Plosser, C. I. (1989) 'Understanding real business cycles', *Journal of Economic Perspectives* 3: 51–77.

Ravetz, J. R. (1971) *Scientific Knowledge and its Social Problems*, Oxford: Oxford University Press.

Sims, C. A. (1980) 'Macroeconomics and reality', *Econometrica* 48: 1–48.

Skinner, C. J., Holt, D. and Smith, T. M. F. (eds) (1989) *Analysis of Complex Surveys*, Chichester: Wiley.

Smith, V. L. (1989) 'Theory, experiment and economics', *Journal of Economic Perspectives* 3: 151–69.

Spanos, A. (1982) 'Latent variables in dynamic econometric models', Ph.D. Thesis, University of London.

—— (1989) 'On re-reading Haavelmo: a retrospective view of econometric modeling', *Econometric Theory* 5: 405–29.

29

EXPERIMENTAL METHODS IN ECONOMICS

GRAHAM LOOMES

29.1 INTRODUCTION

It is scarcely eighteen months since I finished writing a chapter about experimental economics for a collection of papers designed to familiarize undergraduates with various developments at the frontiers of microeconomics. Rereading that chapter as part of the preparation for writing this one, I became conscious of just how much more experimental material has appeared during the last year and a half, and how rapidly the quantity and quality of this literature continues to grow. But I also became conscious of another reaction: the feeling that now that experimental methods have demonstrated their potential by producing a range of articles which have earned places in all the major economics journals, we may in future need to pay increasing attention to some of the problems and limitations which have come to light.

In a short chapter such as this, it is simply not feasible to provide a comprehensive survey of experimental economics research to date; nor will it be possible to discuss in detail the various 'problems and limitations' referred to above. Nevertheless I shall try to give a flavour of both, together with sufficient references to other surveys and collections to enable those who wish to do so to pursue their particular interests further.

In discussions about the use of experimental methods in economics, certain questions frequently recur. What are the areas of economics for which experiments are most suitable? What can you learn from experiments that you cannot discover by other means? How sensitive are experimental results to the design of the experiment, or the nature of the people that take part in them? Can you *really* take the observed behaviour of groups of volunteers spending short

I should like to acknowledge funding from Economic and Social Research Council Awards B00232163 and R000231194 for some of the experiments reported in this paper. I should also like to thank the Nuffield Foundation for support in the form of a Social Science Research Fellowship during the period when this chapter was being written.

periods of time in carefully controlled environments and draw any meaningful conclusions about the way things work in 'the outside world'? In short, what is the case for allocating scarce time and money to this form of research instead of spending it in more conventional ways?

In the course of this chapter I shall try to discuss the important issues raised by all these questions. I shall not necessarily address them one by one in the order above, but the first provides a convenient place to start.

29.2 HOW EXPERIMENTS HAVE CHALLENGED CONVENTIONAL WISDOM

In his very readable survey article, Roth (1988) discusses several of the areas in which a good deal of experimental work has been done. One of these areas is concerned with individual decision-making in the face of risk and uncertainty. As John Hey indicates in Chapter 13 of this book, economists' treatments of problems involving risk and uncertainty generally rely heavily upon the expected utility approach pioneered by von Neumann and Morgenstern (1947) and Savage (1954). This approach is built upon a small number of axioms/postulates which, separately and collectively, appear to provide a compelling basis for rational decision-making. Indeed, from its earliest days, the elegance, versatility and normative appeal of this approach seemed so obvious to most economists that it was rapidly adopted and widely applied, and quickly established itself as the 'conventional wisdom'.

However, right from its inception there were dissenting voices, some of them economists, but more of them working in fields such as cognitive psychology and management science. As part of their critique of expected utility theory, they began to devise experimental tests.

Now expected utility theory is in many ways an ideal subject for experimental investigation. It makes a number of clear predictions about patterns of individuals' decisions which can easily be tested by presenting a reasonably large sample with the appropriate decision problems and observing whether their responses are consistent with, or violate the patterns of behaviour entailed by the theory. Moreover, in so far as violations occur, it is possible to see whether they can be attributed to random errors, or whether they indicate some significant and systematic alternative pattern(s) of behaviour – in which case, theorists may be stimulated to modify expected utility theory in some way or to devise new decision models to account for these results. If these new models also produce distinctive and potentially refutable predictions, they too can be subjected to fresh experimental tests.

This is precisely what has happened during the last forty years, and particularly during the past two decades. In Chapter 13, John Hey indicates some of the tests that have been run. These have stimulated the development of alternative models which, in their turn, are being subjected to further experimental tests. The references at the end of that chapter include several papers which provide good introductions to this literature, but another four come to mind which may also be of interest: a book edited by Kahneman *et al.* (1982) which contains a number of papers drawing attention to various areas of decision-making under uncertainty which psychologists consider to be particularly vulnerable to bias and inconsistency; a chapter by Thaler (1987) discussing, as its title suggests, the psychology of choice and its implications for conventional assumptions in economics; a book by Fishburn (1988) which deftly describes a whole host of alternative models and their relationships with each other and with the experimental evidence; finally, a survey by Butler and Hey (1987) which refers to a number of experiments which go beyond tests of one or other axiom and instead look at models based on expected utility such as search theory and the theory of optimal consumption under uncertainty.

The case for experimental research in the area of individual decision-making rests not only upon the fact that it is possible to design and run simple yet telling experiments, but also on the fact that it is difficult, if not impossible, to test these models and discriminate between competing hypotheses using any other method of research. Under non-experimental conditions there are so many uncontrolled and potentially confounding factors that it is often difficult to reach any conclusions with confidence. Experimental investigations have the great advantage that they can control for many of these factors and focus attention on the impact of particular variables or the robustness of particular assumptions. Critics may suggest that this 'lack of reality' is precisely what strips experimental work of its 'relevance'. I shall return to this issue later, but for now I shall just make the point that many theoretical models are likewise highly simplified abstractions from the complexities of the real world, but in so far as they are used to make predictions about behaviour or to underpin prescriptions about policy, we are entitled (if not obliged) to test them, and as long as an experiment is a fair and appropriate test of such a model, its results should have no less status than the model which is being tested. Indeed, we might argue that simplicity is actually a great virtue: if a model such as expected utility theory fails substantially and systematically to account for decisions involving even the simplest kinds of risky alternatives, how likely is it to provide an adequate account of the rather more complicated problems that face decision-makers in the non-experimental world? But this is another question to which I shall return after mentioning some of the other areas of economics which have attracted the attention of experimenters.

In his survey article, Roth (1988) focuses on several such areas: bargaining behaviour, a field in which he and various co-authors have conducted a range of experiments to test existing theory and provide insights for further theoretical developments; other aspects of game theory, such as the prisoner's dilemma and the free-rider problem in the provision of public goods; and various patterns of behaviour in auctions. As with individual decision theory, all these topics lend themselves to experimental investigation because it is possible for researchers to design experimental environments which contain all the essential features of the problems being studied, and which enable them to vary particular parameters while holding others constant and to observe the impact (or lack of impact) of such changes on the patterns of participants' responses. Moreover, as with individual decision theory, these are all areas in which it is difficult to reach many very clear conclusions on the basis of non-experimental evidence alone. Roth's (1988) discussion of the 'winner's curse' is a good case study of the potential for productive interaction between field data and experimental studies.

As with individual decision theory, the effect of experimental work in these areas has been to challenge certain key assumptions which had previously been widely and almost unquestioningly accepted and to draw attention to considerations which had previously been somewhat neglected. A good example of this can be found in Thaler (1988), where he describes a series of experiments involving various forms of the ultimatum game. In its simplest single-stage form, the game can be described as follows. You are paired with someone else whose identity is unknown to you, and with whom you cannot communicate directly. You are told that there is a sum of money – say £10 – to be divided between the two of you, with x going to the other person and £10 − x coming to you. Your task it to nominate a value of x. Once you have made your decision, this information is transmitted to the other person who, like you, knows the rules of the game and the total to be divided. His task is either to accept your offer of x (in which case he actually receives x and you receive £10 − x) or else to reject your offer, in which case you both receive nothing. What value of x should you offer?

The conventional wisdom in this case runs as follows. Assuming that the other person is a rational economic agent who, like yourself, prefers more to less, you should offer him a penny. He will accept, because a penny is better than nothing (which is the consequence of rejecting your offer) and you will have received £9.99 and done as well as you can. If you offer him nothing, there is no reason for him not to reject, in which case you receive nothing also. If you offer any sum greater than a penny, you are giving yourself less rather than more for no purpose, since a penny should be enough to induce him to accept.

Yet while this response may be in line with the standard game-theoretical approach, it runs counter to many people's intuitions – and also to a good deal of experimental evidence of the sort discussed by both Roth (1988) and Thaler (1988) in relation to this and other more complex bargaining games.

Both reach a broadly similar conclusion, to the effect that considerations of justice and fairness appear to have a significant impact on people's behaviour.

Such an impact may arise from at least two sources. It may be that, even if you believe that the other person is likely to accept an offer of a penny, such an unequal division may offend your own sense of fairness which you value sufficiently to encourage you to make a more equitable offer. Or it may be that, even if you yourself place no value on fairness in this context, you acknowledge that the other person may take a different view, and that he may feel so resentful about being offered a penny while you allocate yourself £9.99 that he prefers to receive nothing and make sure that you receive nothing also.

Experimental evidence suggests that both types of response may be at work to some extent (just as both 'fear' and 'greed' may contribute to the free-rider problem (see Rapoport 1987)). Moreover, both Roth and Thaler draw attention to the point that the non-monetary considerations that enter into bargaining behaviour may be sensitive to the conditions of the experiment and the amount of information that each player has about the other. For example, it may matter whether bargaining is face to face or conducted via a computer; it may matter whether or not bargainers start with some initial endowment, whether those endowments are equal or unequal and whether they were allocated at random or were earned; in addition, the particular way in which the instructions are worded may matter, as indicated in a paper by Hoffman and Spitzer (1985).

Two sorts of conclusion might be drawn from all this evidence. The conclusions that Roth and Thaler draw are (a) that bargaining is a complex social process involving non-monetary motives that require further experimental study, and (b) that in its present form standard game theory performs poorly on both descriptive and prescriptive grounds. Those who are persuaded of these conclusions may find the idea of a programme of further experiments, perhaps linked to the kind of re-evaluation of game theory suggested by Binmore (1987, 1988), an attractive and worthwhile line of future research.

29.3 THE SCEPTIC'S REACTION

However, a quite different, rather more hostile, conclusion might be drawn. A sceptic might agree that subjects' behaviour appears to be sensitive to various features of the experimental design, but might interpret this as a sign that the results are largely an artefact of the experiment, of little value or relevance outside the artificial environment in which they were produced.

Let us put this view forcefully in the (fictitious) words of a (not so fictitious) participant in a research workshop or faculty seminar who has sat impatiently waiting for the presenter to finish describing the results of an experiment which appear to strike at the heart of expected utility theory or game theory

597

or some other cornerstone of conventional economic wisdom. At the first opportunity, he mounts an aggressively dismissive assault:

'Well, what do you expect? You take a group of people – whatever people come most readily to hand – and thrust them into an artificial and unfamiliar situation. You then describe the experiment, perhaps getting them to read through several pages of instructions, followed by some test questions and/or a few minutes "practice time". Then you set them going, with no real opportunity to acclimatize to the situation or think things through, still less to take advice and plan some course(s) of action. Instead, they have to go straight into action.

'They know that you're running an experiment, and so they know you're looking for something. Despite your protestations, they may believe there is *a* right answer which will be rewarded. Or they may want to please you, or create a favourable impression of themselves. Or they may simply feel pressure to do *something*, and so they look for cues, and seize upon whatever the experimental design (consciously or unconsciously) suggests to them. At best, their behaviour is a first approximation, vulnerable to all kinds of biases from extraneous sources and from the way the experiment is set up and the way the decision problems are framed. Small wonder your results are so sensitive to the experimental design, and diverge substantially from the equilibrium solutions associated with informed clear-thinking rational behaviour.

'But the real world differs from your experimental environment in certain important ways. If I'm going to enter into negotiations about something that matters to me, I'll think out my strategy and tactics carefully in advance. If I'm searching for a job, a house, a car or some other major item of expenditure, I'll engage in a rather more varied and sophisticated search procedure than your experiments allow. If I'm deciding how much insurance to buy, or thinking about whether to move from a job wth a low variance income to a job with a bigger variance but higher expected income, I'll lay out the alternatives carefully, think about the possible consequences, take advice if necessary, and weigh up the pros and cons until I reach a considered balanced judgement.

'And if we're talking not just about individuals or households, but about private companies, public corporations, political and industrial interest groups and government departments, I'll go further. We're talking then about agencies run by highly experienced specialists who can, if need be, buy in additional consultancy from the relevant experts. These are not five-minute first-guessers: millions of pounds may be at stake, and your entire research budget is but a fraction of what they are prepared to spend to work out their optimal strategy.

'That's what the real world is like, and what economists are – or should be – interested in is what actually happens out there. Our models may be abstractions, but if they give us reasonable accounts of actual behaviour which stand up well enough to sophisticated econometric tests, are we really supposed to call those models into question simply on the basis of a few little experiments involving a motley collection of novices spending an hour or two earning paltry sums of pocket-money? How can that begin to compare with the evidence of what experienced agents actually do in situations where their decisions really matter?'

Now although such views are rarely expressed so directly (at least, not in face-to-face discussions), they do represent widely held concerns and misgivings. For those involved in experimental work, it is tempting to react defensively in a number of ways: for example, by attacking the poverty of much of the non-experimental data and the breath-taking leaps of faith which underpin some econometric exercises; or by referring to Simon's (1979) Nobel Lecture where he points to significant discrepancies between economic models and the corresponding 'real-world' data; or by citing some of the cases discussed by Akerlof and Dickens (1982) in their paper about the economic consequences of cognitive dissonance, a pervasive real-world phenomenon which sits uneasily with standard economic ideas of what constitutes rational behaviour.

All these points, and others, could justifiably be made. But this should not deflect attention from the serious concerns and doubts about experimental work expressed in the preceding few paragraphs. If experimental research is worth its place, and hopes to thrive, it must address those points. There are signs that a number of researchers have begun to do so, as indicated below. But as will also become apparent, the questions are still far from being completely resolved.

Some of these issues are addressed by Plott (1987), who discusses certain aspects of 'parallelism', i.e. the question of how far laboratory observations can inform our understanding of the larger and more complicated non-experimental world and feed into practical policy-making. In this chapter I shall focus on a slightly different problem which is of concern not only to critics but also to exponents of experimental methods, and which bears not only upon the generalizability of laboratory results to other contexts but also raises questions about the validity of those results even at the laboratory level. I shall consider in more detail the question of bounded rationality, limited information-processing capacity and the scope for learning and adjustment.

29.4 SOME LESSONS FROM INDIVIDUAL DECISION EXPERIMENTS

Let us begin by considering some experimental evidence which has attracted great interest and provoked a good deal of controversy during the past two decades: the preference reversal phenomenon. This phenomenon is mentioned by John Hey in Chapter 13, and Roth (1988) gives a good account of it. However, it is an example of what I referred to at the beginning of this chapter – the rate at which the literature has moved on even within the last year or so – and it also illustrates some points about learning, and about the interaction between experimental testing and the selection and development of theory; hence what follows can be seen as supplementing Hey and Roth.

In the form originally reported by the psychologists Lichtenstein and Slovic (1971), the preference reversal phenomenon worked as follows. Subjects were given a lottery ticket offering a relatively small probability of a reasonably good monetary gain and a corresponding large probability of a small loss. This was called the '$-bet', and subjects were asked to state the smallest certain amount of money for which they would be prepared to sell that bet. They were also presented with another lottery ticket offering a rather larger probability of a more modest gain, with the other outcome being a small loss. This was called the 'P-bet' and subjects were also asked to state a minimum selling price for this bet. Finally, they were offered the two bets side by side, and asked which one they would choose. Conventional theory predicts that an individual should choose whichever bet he placed the higher value on. But Lichtenstein and Slovic found that a substantial proportion of their sample not only violated this prediction, but did so in a systematic way: the great majority of those who committed a 'violation' placed a higher value on the $-bet, but picked the P-bet in a straight choice between the two. The opposite form of violation – placing a higher value on the P-bet but opting for the $-bet in a straight choice – was much less frequently observed.

This result stimulated a series of follow-up experiments, together with a number of possible explanations. Many of these are reviewed by Roth (1988), and I shall not rehearse them in detail here. The main point emerging from the numerous replications and modifications of the basic experimental design is that the phenomenon stubbornly refused to go away. Providing monetary incentives to encourage careful choice and elicit accurate and truthful valuations, controlling for possible wealth effects and making the prizes really quite large – none of these modifications caused the phenomenon to disappear, nor even to be much reduced. Since the phenomenon appeared to be so robust, effort and attention began to focus on providing an explanation.

Three broad types of explanation have been advanced.

1 A number of subjects have non-transitive preferences of a kind that conform with skew symmetric bilinear utility theory (Fishburn 1985) or regret theory (Loomes and Sugden 1983, 1987).

2 A number of subjects have transitive preferences, but violate some other axiom of expected utility theory. This violation interacts with the mechanisms used in the experimental design and results in announced prices which deviate systematically from individuals' true certainty equivalents in such a way as to produce the preference reversal pattern. Explanations along these lines have been suggested by Holt (1986), Karni and Safra (1987) and Segal (1988).

Notice that both these types of explanations have something in common with each other and with expected utility theory: they all assume that individuals have clear well-specified preferences which they apply to any decision problem (whether in the form of making a choice or giving a valuation), and that they make the decision which is optimal for them in the light of their preferences. In other words, learning does not come into it: however their preferences have been formed, they simply apply these preferences to any decision problem presented to them by the experimenter, and any deviation from their optimal response will be ascribed to random error. However much experience and feedback they acquire, however many different ways the problem is framed, their actual responses, if not identical, will be randomly distributed around their optimal response. However, the third type of explanation is different.

3 Many individuals do *not* have instantaneous access to a full set of precise ready-made preferences. They may have basic underlying preferences, but when presented with a fresh and specific decision problem, they have to 'solve' that problem using limited information-processing capabilities in conjunction with somewhat imprecise basic preferences. Unable to provide an instant optimal solution, they may adopt some rule of thumb, or heuristic, the nature of which may vary depending on the kind of problem to be solved and the way it is presented.

So, in contrast with 1 and 2, the implication of 3 is that the pattern of responses elicited is *not* independent of the procedure used to elicit them. There is the possibility of what Tversky *et al.* (1990) refer to as failures of procedure invariance. In the context of preference reversals, this means that people are liable to treat valuation problems systematically differently from choice problems. In a valuation task, they may for example use an 'anchoring and adjustment' heuristic: because they are asked to supply a response in the form of a value, they may begin to solve the problem by anchoring on to the amount they might win and then adjust downwards to take account of the fact that they might not win. If, as has been suggested, 'adjustments are typically insufficient' (Tversky and Kahneman 1982: 15), this heuristic will tend to favour the $-bet in the valuation task since it offers a much higher anchor. In contrast, in a straight choice, people may pay more attention to the probability of winning, in which case they will tend to favour the P-bet to a greater extent in the choice task. Putting the two together produces the systematic pattern of preference reversals so regularly observed.

Three questions follow on from all this. First, can we discriminate between 1, 2 and 3? The obvious way to try to do so is by conducting appropriately designed experiments, and several such attempts have been reported during the past couple of years. These include those of Loomes *et al.* (1989, 1991), Schkade and Johnson (1989) and Tversky *et al.* (1990). The details of these and other experiments, and a fuller discussion of various possible interpretations, are given by Loomes (1990). The essential points can be summarized as follows. A good deal of evidence – some direct evidence from these recent experiments, together with circumstantial evidence from earlier experiments –

runs counter to explanation 2 and suggests that the answer lies with 1 and/or 3. Loomes *et al.* (1989, 1991) reported a number of experiments which eliminated the valuation task and involved only pairwise choices. If the preference reversal phenomenon were due entirely to failures of invariance, the systematic violations of conventional theory should have disappeared. But in fact an asymmetric pattern of non-transitive choices analogous to the preference reversal phenomenon was observed. The frequency of violations, not surprisingly, was lower than in the standard preference reversal design, but at around 15–20 per cent it was quite substantial, and the asymmetry was clearly statistically significant. This is consistent with explanation 1. However, Tversky *et al.* (1990) asked for two valuations *and* three pairwise choices and concluded that, although some asymmetric non-transitivity was present, the main source of preference reversals was a failure of invariance in the form of the relative overpricing of the $-bet. Loomes (1990) used a series of preliminary choices to iterate towards valuations of the $- and P-bets, as well as asking subjects to make a direct choice between the two. On the basis of the choice data, higher rates of non-transitive cycles were observed; however, there were also many cases where the P-bet was chosen but the valuation of the $-bet was so high that it could not be explained by non-transitive preferences alone. This suggested that there must also be systematic failures of invariance, and these appeared to become more frequent and more pronounced as the highest pay-off of the $-bet increased relative to the highest pay-off of the P-bet. Finally, Schkade and Johnson (1989) used computerized displays and 'mouse' technology to trace the way in which subjects accessed information about the bets in the process of reaching their final responses. They concluded that the evidence supported the idea that valuations and choices were treated differently, and that valuations were sensitive to the anchors used – although there is also evidence which can be interpreted as consistent with a model such as regret theory.

The overall conclusion appears to be that, although explanation 2 can be rejected, failures of transitivity and failures of invariance both seem to be in evidence. These are not mutually exclusive, and their relative contributions to the preference reversal phenomenon has not yet been established beyond doubt (and, indeed, may never be precisely quantified, since the relative contributions may themselves vary with factors such as the parameters of the lotteries or the particular format in which the problems are presented).

Following on from this, the second question is: given that failures of invariance do occur, are there other manifestations besides preference reversals? It appears that there are a number of other phenomena which might be attributed to failures of invariance: Hershey and Schoemaker (1985) and Johnson and Schkade (1989) discuss discrepancies between certainty equivalences and probability equivalences; Goldstein and Einhorn (1987) report reversals involving 'attractiveness ratings' and MacCrimmon and Smith (1986) report reversals when probability equivalences are used; Knetsch and Sinden (1984, 1987) and many others have observed a disparity between willingness to pay and willingness to accept which is much greater than conventional theory would suggest; Tversky *et al.* (1988) have provided evidence of substantial choice versus matching discrepancies; finally, Tversky *et al.* (1990) showed evidence of high rates of time-preference reversals. Although it may be possible to account for some of these phenomena without relying on some failure of invariance, no single unified account of that kind currently exists.

So we come to the third question: if human beings are vulnerable to so many failures of invariance, what are their true preferences and how can we elicit them? Unless all these discrepancies actually reflect some (as yet undiscovered) coherent model of non-expected utility preferences, people would presumably wish to remove any contradictions and inconsistencies in their responses if they were made aware of them and given time to reconsider. In other words, one possible implication of attributing violations of expected utility theory to failures of invariance is that if people were not simply presented with unfamiliar decision problems and asked to give quick responses, but were instead given experience, feedback and the opportunity to learn and adapt, these violations would tend to wither away.

Various attempts to test this proposition have been made by some experimental economists whose primary field of activity has not yet received much attention in this chapter, although it is a major area of work, and arguably the area which is most distinctively 'economic'. I am referring to the body of experiments which investigate market behaviour.

29.5 SOME LESSONS FROM MARKET EXPERIMENTS

Whereas experiments about individual decision-making have tended to produce many serious challenges to the conventional wisdom, market experiments have often appeared to provide good support for standard economic propositions. As Smith (1989: 162) points out: 'Concepts of noncooperative equilibrium have performed well in a large number of experimental markets – better than they have had a right to perform given that they were never intended to be tested . . .'. He notes what he calls the gap between the psychology of choice and agents' economic behaviour in experimental exchange markets and suggests a possible reconciliation, which I shall paraphrase as follows. In the first round or two of many market experiments, a good deal of disequilibrium trading typically occurs, but as participants gain experience and acquire feedback, prices and quantities tend to converge towards the relevant equilibrium. Perhaps the responses to questionnaires or individual decision experiments are like the first round of a market experiment, i.e. first approximations which are liable to be influenced by all manner of beliefs, framing effects and so on. However, if these initial decisions 'are not sustainable in a market clearing or noncooperative equilibrium, subjects adapt their expectations and behaviour until they attain such an equilibrium' (Smith 1989: 166).

Roth (1988: 1018–20) reviews some of the experiments which sought to use market experience to eliminate either the preference reversal phenomenon or the disparity between willingness to pay and willingness to accept. The overall impression gained from these experiments and others (see, for example, Knetsch *et al.* 1988) is that the experience of repeated market trading may somewhat reduce the disparities, but by no means eliminates them. Thus if failures of invariance are the primary source of such phenomena, the implication is that even the rapid low-cost reasonably well-focused feedback provided by many simple experimental markets is not enough to induce sufficient learning to eliminate them. Of course, another conclusion is also plausible: namely, that the violations of conventional theory are not eliminated because to some extent they have a genuine basis in some non-conventional decision model(s).

Evidence which appears to support the latter conclusion can be found in some of the more recent bargaining experiments. For example, Ochs and Roth (1989) conducted an experiment in which each subject took part in ten rounds of bargaining under the same general circumstances but with a different person in each round. To allow for possible learning effects, they based most of their tests on tenth-round data, although they noted that 'while experience makes some difference . . . , at the aggregate level round 10 is not very different from other rounds' (Ochs and Roth 1989: 362). They concluded 'that the subgame-perfect equilibrium predictions that come from assuming that players' monetary payoffs are a good proxy for their utility payoffs are not at all descriptive of the results we observed. This is true not merely of the point predictions . . . but also of the qualitative predictions . . .' (Ochs and Roth 1989: 378). Thus it appears that repetition and experience do not necessarily cause people to adapt their behaviour in the direction that current theory implies.

Although this behaviour is rather troublesome as far as conventional game-theoretical assumptions are concerned, much of it is rationalizable if we allow that bargainers take valued notions of fairness into account. There are other cases, however, where it is not so easy to find a rationale for observed behaviour which departs substantially from what are conventionally regarded as optimal, or even dominant, strategies – and in these cases might we not expect experience and learning to have a greater impact? To examine this question, let us consider some evidence arising from second-price sealed-bid auction experiments.

A second-price sealed-bid auction operates much as its name suggests: each would-be buyer enters a sealed bid and the object for sale is sold to whoever has entered the highest bid, but they are only charged a price equal to the second-highest bid. When this form of auction is first described to people, they often find it a little strange. Most people are more familiar with two other types of auction: the first-price sealed-bid auction where the highest bid wins and the winner pays the full amount he has submitted; or the English auction, where the bidding is open and buyers can revise their bids upwards in response to one another until the object is sold to the buyer whose latest bid is not superseded by anyone else.

The relationship between all these forms of auction (and also another type, the Dutch auction) is the subject of an experiment by Coppinger *et al.* (1980). Their basic procedure was to give each subject a private redemption value for winning the object of a particular auction (i.e. each subject was told exactly how much the experiment would pay him/her for winning a particular auction), and then buyers were put into different auction environments and their behaviour in each was observed and various comparisons were made.

You, the reader, might like to put yourself in the position of a subject and consider what you would do in a second-price auction. Suppose that I have told you that if you win the auction I will pay you £12.50. I have also told all the other subjects what each of them will be paid, should they win. This information is totally private to each of you – no subject knows anyone else's redemption value. Now you have to submit a bid on the basis that if you put in the highest bid you will win and I will pay you £12.50, from which I will subtract the price that you must pay to the auctioneer, namely the second-highest bid that was submitted. Your net payment for winning will therefore be £12.50 − x, where x is the second-highest bid. Of course, if you do not put in the highest bid and therefore do not win the auction, you receive nothing. Now, what bid would you submit?

According to conventional theory, this decision should present no problem: there is a simple strategy which is not merely optimal, it is dominant, i.e. it is always at least as good as any other strategy you might adopt and sometimes better. The dominant strategy is to bid your full redemption value, no more and no less. If you bid more than your redemption value, you could win the auction but end up worse off than if you had lost it. For example, suppose that you bid £13.00 and win, with the second-highest bid being £12.75. You have won and so you are entitled to your redemption value, which is £12.50, but you are obliged to pay the auctioneer a price equal to the second-highest bid, namely £12.75. Therefore you end up losing 25 pence, whereas if you had simply bid your redemption value you would have failed to win the auction but you would not have lost any money. Alternatively, suppose that you bid less than your redemption value: for example, suppose that you bid £12.00. It then turns out that the highest bid submitted by any of the others is £12.20. That person wins the auction and you receive nothing, whereas if you had bid your full redemption value, *you* would have won – and after deducting the

£12.20 from your £12.50, you would have made a profit of 30 pence. Therefore entering a bid which is exactly equal to your redemption value can never be worse, and tends to be better, then entering any other bid above or below that value: in short, entering your redemption value is the dominant strategy.

However, this dominance is not immediately obvious to many subjects. Coppinger et al. (1980: Table 8) show that, in the first second-price sealed-bid auction in which they took part, twenty-one out of thirty-one subjects entered bids below their redemption values, i.e. two-thirds of the sample violated dominance in this context. However, after taking part in a succession of these auctions, there appeared to be signs of learning: in the last trial in which they took part, only ten of the thirty-one subjects entered bids below their redemption values.

Two cautionary notes should be added, however. First, even after there had been some opportunity to learn, about a third of the sample were still not using the dominant strategy (including two who had apparently done the right thing in their first trial). Second, the subjects in Coppinger et al.'s experiments were not permitted to enter bids above their redemption values. In a later experiment by Kagel et al. (1987), subjects were not prevented from bidding above their redemption values, and many were observed to do so. Moreover, Kagel et al. (1987: 1298) report that 'no obvious tendency for prices to converge to the dominant bid price over time was observed'. One possible implication of this is that Coppinger et al.'s results (which are not particularly encouraging anyway) may give an overoptimistic view: a number of subjects who appeared to have discovered the dominant strategy may in fact have been wanting to bid more than their redemption value but were prevented from doing so by the experimental design. A second point that emerges is one made by Kagel et al. in their discussion of the reasons why overbidding did not disappear over time even though it is a dominated strategy liable to lead to losses. They report that, in their experiment,

> the probability of losing money conditional on winning the auction averages .36, with the overall probability of losing money averaging .06. These punishment probabilities are weak, given that bidders start with the illusion that bids in excess of (the redemption value) increase the probability of winning without materially affecting the price paid, and the majority of the time the auction outcomes support this supposition.
>
> (Kagel et al. 1987: 1299–1300)

In other words, the structure of a second-price sealed-bid auction is such that it is possible to deviate from the dominant strategy without necessarily being punished; indeed, deviant behaviour may even appear to succeed and thereby be reinforced. Contrast this with an English auction, where the (same) dominant strategy is much more transparent – so much so that subjects hardly have to think about it. To see this, imagine, as before, that your redemption value is £12.50. So far, perhaps, you have sat back while other subjects have been bidding against each other. The bidding has now reached £12.20 and the competition seems to have abated. Will you continue to sit back and let the auction be won by someone else, or will you bid £12.25? And if the other person raises his bid in response, it requires little thought to see that it will be worth your while to stay in the bidding up to, but not beyond, your redemption value. Thus, if your redemption value happens to be higher than anyone else's you would expect to win the auction at a price approximately equal to the point at which your closest competitor drops out, i.e. at a price equal to the second-highest redemption value. This is the efficient outcome which conventional theory would predict for English and second-price sealed-bid auctions alike, but as the experimental evidence shows, this outcome is actually rather less likely to occur in the case where the dominant strategy is not transparently obvious. In short, the fact that a strategy is dominant is, by itself, no guarantee that it will be generally adopted or quickly learnt, even in conditions where subjects have repeated experience of the market, unless the structure of the market makes the dominance property obvious or else provides powerful and direct feedback in the form of rapid and unambiguous punishments and/or rewards.

It might seem that this is an unduly pessimistic suggestion. Should it not be set against the observation by Smith, quoted earlier, suggesting that concepts such as non-cooperative equilibrium have repeatedly been shown to perform better than they had a right to do? Does it not do less than justice to much of the evidence reviewed by Plott (1987, 1988) in the most comprehensive surveys to date of experimental work in the area of industrial organization – evidence which testifies to the remarkable equilibrating power of 'double-auction' markets where 'the overwhelming result is that these markets converge to the competitive equilibrium even with very few traders' (Plott 1988: 14)?

My response is that this kind of evidence does not necessarily contradict the allegedly pessimistic suggestion made above, but may actually tend to support it. A number of those earlier experiments had certain basic features in common. For example, buyers were given well-specified redemption value schedules and sellers were given precise information about their marginal costs. Moreover, production was instantaneous and sellers only 'produced' units once a sale had been agreed. So although agents did not know the contents of each other's schedules, this did not matter greatly, for they each had available to them a simple rule, and as long as they followed it they could not go seriously wrong. For a buyer, the rule was not to pay more for a unit than it could be traded in for, and for a seller the rule was not to sell a unit for less than it cost to produce.

With all bids and offers, successful and unsuccessful, being made in the public arena, subjects acquire a great deal of information at very low cost. Moreover, with aggregate value and cost schedules stable (for a number of rounds at least) and with each side armed with simple decision rules whose joint effect is to encourage buyers to buy as long as redemption values exceed price, while sellers are encouraged to sell up to the point where marginal cost is just below price, it seems that conditions could hardly be more conducive to a rapid convergence to competitive equilibrium.

In a recent paper, Mestelman and Welland (1988) modified the basic design by introducing advance production: sellers now had to decide before trading began how many units to produce, in the knowledge that if any units remained unsold at the end of that round's trading they would become worthless. The authors reported with approval how well the double-auction market continued to perform. But perhaps this is not surprising since all the conditions favourable to learning continued to exist. Of course, it was now possible for sellers to make mistakes and produce more than buyers were prepared to purchase at a price which covered marginal costs, but such mistakes were instantly and surely punished, with the result that any early aberrations were quickly eliminated.

However, suppose that the design is modified further, and in a way which cushions sellers against instant retribution of the kind described above. That is, suppose that we require advance production but allow any unsold units to be carried forward into the next round. This was the basic idea behind an experiment reported by Loomes (1989). Instead of scrapping unsold units at the end of each round, subjects were told that the experiment would last for ten rounds and only those units still unsold after close of trading in the tenth round would become worthless. Buyers could also hold inventories if they wished, although they too were told that any units unredeemed at the end of the experiment would be lost.

Details of the experimental design were circulated in advance, including sample value and cost schedules. Aggregate value and cost schedules remained constant throughout – including during the three preliminary practice rounds, at the end of which subjects were taken through the motions of scrapping any unsold/unredeemed units. Thus as far as possible conditions were intended to allow subjects to plan ahead and behave purposefully. The only real difference from the structure of many earlier experiments was that the direct link between mistake and instant punishment was attenuated.

Twelve sessions were run, and the results provided a considerable contrast to those reported by Mestelman and Welland and those observed in many earlier double-auction markets. There was no tendency to converge towards the competitive equilibrium, nor any other equilibrium, and efficiency levels were markedly lower than is usual in double-auction markets. To the extent that there was any general pattern, it was for prices in early rounds to exceed the competitive equilibrium level and for both buyers and sellers to build up inventories, followed by falling prices and reduced production as sellers tried to shed excess stock while buyers who already had units in hand were under no great pressure to buy. By the last two periods prices had generally fallen substantially below competitive equilibrium levels.

In another recent experiment Smith *et al.* (1988) also allowed inventories in a double-auction market for dividend-bearing assets, and they also observed a good deal of volatility in the data, including a number of 'bubbles' and 'crashes'. They experimented with a range of treatment variables, including the experience of the subjects. They concluded that, given sufficient time and with experience, there is a tendency for most of their experimental markets to converge to 'near' the rational expectations price just prior to the last trading period. At one point they claim: 'It appears that *replication with essentially the same subjects* eventually will create a "professional" market with common expectations in which bubble tendencies are extinguished and replaced by intrinsic value pricing' (Smith *et al.* 1988: 1135, original emphasis). It is worth noting, however, that they also report indications that general experience in asset trading is not sufficient to guard against bubble–crash behaviour, and that other small changes to the environment can 'interfere' with learning.

It has been suggested to me that if my experiment had run for, say, twenty-five rounds with unsold/unredeemed units being scrapped every five rounds, I might have observed better convergence. Subjects may have failed to reach an equilibrium in the first or second set of five rounds, but by the third or fourth set they would have learned their lessons so that something 'near' to equilibrium would be achieved during the last five or ten rounds. However, if this is what it takes to achieve an equilibrium, it illustrates the rather demanding conditions that may have to be met if strong rational expectations predictions are to succeed. In almost every respect the conditions facing subjects in market experiments are already much more favourable than one would normally find in the non-experimental world: value and cost schedules are usually known with certainty, or at least up to a well-specified probability distribution; there is a large amount of information about all agents' trading behaviour available at very low cost; there is great stability in the general environment, with usually no more than one or two exogenous disturbances; and so on. Yet even with all this, the experiments cited above suggest that conventional equilibrium concepts may have poor predictive power unless the experimental design provides frequent repetition of the same situation buttressed by a fairly high level of well-focused reinforcement. This contrasts with the non-experimental world where buyers are uncertain about their own preferences (see Heiner (1985) for more on this), sellers have limited knowledge even about their own marginal costs, there is great uncertainty about the behaviour of others and feedback is generally sluggish, diffuse and difficult to interpret.

Notice that this argument is pulling in the opposite direction to the attack mounted by the hostile seminar participant 'quoted' earlier. His claim was that the higher stakes and greater motivation and expertise in the non-experimental world would punish poor performances and encourage conformity with models rooted in economic rationality, whereas inexperienced subjects confronted with unfamiliar environments with little opportunity for reflection or learning are liable to be vulnerable to all kinds of errors and biases. In contrast, I am suggesting that the kind of rational behaviour assumed by many economic models makes heavy demands upon the quantity and quality of information and feedback, and upon the ability of economic agents to learn the right lessons and make the adjustments necessary to develop anything like theoretically optimal strategies. In a world of continual flux and change, characterized better by disequilibrium than by equilibrium, the demands of conventional theory may simply be too heavy to be met.

However, this does not lead to the conclusion that we should abandon modelling or give up experimental work. Rather, the suggestion is that we should shift the focus away from comparative statics analysis based on assumptions that some equilibrium exists and that (somehow) movements in the direction of that equilibrium will occur, and look instead at the process of reaction and adjustment in a world that can never really be expected to attain equilibrium. Moreover, it is suggested that less emphasis should be given to optimal strategies which, as experiments show, are difficult enough for agents to generate even under highly favourable conditions, and that more attention should be given to the heuristics, rules of thumb and approximations which agents fall back on to deal with the environment and the problems presented to them. This is a daunting task, but experiments may be able to contribute by creating more limited environments where the complexity is to some extent controlled and where the role of particular variables can more readily be observed. If we can succeed in identifying and modelling various rules and heuristics, we can examine their descriptive and normative implications, and take due account of them in our forecasts and policy proposals. Hey (1982, 1987) and Sterman (1989) provide examples of how experiments can be used in this way, and we may expect to see much more research along these lines in future.

29.6 CONCLUDING REMARKS

In the short run the results of experimental research in economics may be discomforting, in that they may challenge many cherished assumptions and intellectual vested interests, and raise a host of doubts and difficult questions about conventional models. But the demonstrable ability to generate fresh sources of data, suggest new insights and provide a powerful stimulus to theoretical developments and practical applications gives experimental methods an important role in economic research, and one which we can expect to see consolidated and expanded to the long-term benefit of the discipline.

REFERENCES

Akerlof, G. and Dickens, W. (1982) 'The economic consequences of cognitive dissonance', *American Economic Review* 72: 307–19.

Binmore, K. (1987) 'Modeling rational players: part I', *Economics and Philosophy* 3: 179–214.

—— (1988) 'Modeling rational players: part II', *Economics and Philosophy* 4: 9–55.

Butler, D. and Hey, J. (1987) 'Experimental economics: an introduction', *Empirica* 14: 157–86.

Coppinger, V., Smith, V. and Titus, J. (1980) 'Incentives and behavior in English, Dutch and sealed-bid auctions', *Economic Inquiry* 18: 1–22.

Fishburn, P. C. (1985) 'Nontransitive preference theory and the preference reversal phenomenon', *International Review of Economics and Business* 32: 39–50.

—— (1988) *Nonlinear Preference and Utility Theory*, Brighton: Harvester Wheatsheaf.

Goldstein, W. M. and Einhorn, H. J. (1987) 'Expression theory and the preference reversal phenomenon', *Psychological Review* 94: 236–54.

Heiner, R. A. (1985) 'Experimental economics: comment', *American Economic Review* 75: 260–3.

Hershey, J. C. and Schoemaker, P. J. H. (1985) 'Probability vs. certainty equivalence methods in utility measurement: are they equivalent?', *Management Science* 31: 1213–31.

Hey, J. D. (1982) 'Search for rules for search', *Journal of Economic Behavior and Organization* 3: 65–81.

—— (1987) 'Still searching', *Journal of Economic Behavior and Organization* 8: 137–44.

Hoffman, E. and Spitzer, M. (1985) 'Entitlements, rights and fairness: an experimental examination of subjects' concepts of distributive justice', *Journal of Legal Studies* 14: 259–97.

Holt, C. A. (1986) 'Preference reversals and the independence axiom', *American Economic Review* 76: 508–15.

Johnson, E. J. and Schkade, D. A. (1989) 'Bias in utility assessments: further evidence and explanations', *Management Science* 35: 406–24.

Kagel, J., Harstad, R. and Levin, D. (1987) 'Information impact and allocation rules in auctions with affiliated private values: a laboratory study', *Econometrica* 55: 1275–1304.

Kahneman, D., Slovic, P. and Tversky, A. (eds) (1982) *Judgement Under Uncertainty: Heuristics and Biases*, Cambridge: Cambridge University Press.

Karni, E. and Safra, Z. (1987) ' "Preference reversal" and the observability of preferences by experimental methods', *Econometrica* 55: 675–85.

Knetsch, J. and Sinden, J. (1984) 'Willingness to pay and compensation demanded: experimental evidence of an unexpected disparity in measures of value', *Quarterly Journal of Economics* 99: 507–21.

—— and —— (1987) 'The persistence of evaluation disparities', *Quarterly Journal of Economics* 102: 691–5.

Knetsch, J., Thaler, R. and Kahneman, D. (1988) 'Experimental tests of the endowment effect and the Coase theorem', Mimeo.

Lichtenstein, S. and Slovic, P. (1971) 'Reversals of preferences between bids and choices in gambling decisions', *Journal of Experimental Psychology* 89: 46–55.

Loomes, G. (1989) 'The impact of inventories in an experimental double auction market', Mimeo.

—— (1990) 'Preference reversal: explanations, evidence and implications', in W. V., Gehrlein (ed.) *Intransitive Preference*, Basel: Baltzer.

Loomes, G. and Sugden, R. (1983) 'A rationale for preference reversal', *American Economic Review* 73: 428–32.

—— and —— (1987) 'Some implications of a more general form of regret theory', *Journal of Economic Theory* 41: 270–87.

Loomes, G., Starmer, C. and Sugden, R. (1989) 'Preference reversal: information processing effect or rational nontransitive choice?', *Economic Journal (Conference Supplement)* 99: 140–51.

——, and —— and —— (1991) 'Observing violations of transitivity by experimental methods', *Econometrica* 59: 425–39.

MacCrimmon, K. R. and Smith, M. (1986) 'Imprecise equivalences: preference reversals in money and probability', Working paper 1211, University of British Columbia.

Mestelman, S. and Welland, D. (1988) 'Advance production in experimental markets', *Review of Economic Studies* 55: 641–54.

von Neumann, J. and Morgenstern, O. (1947) *Theory of Games and Economic Behavior*, 2nd edn, Princeton, NJ: Princeton University Press.

Ochs, J. and Roth, A. E. (1989) 'An experimental study of sequential bargaining', *American Economic Review* 79: 355–84.

Plott, C. R. (1987) 'Dimensions of parallelism: some policy applications of experimental methods', in A. E. Roth (ed.) *Laboratory Experimentation in Economics: Six Points of View*, New York: Cambridge University Press.

—— (1988) 'An updated review of industrial organizational applications of experimental methods', Mimeo.

Rapoport, A. (1987) 'Research paradigms and expected utility models for the provision of step-level public goods', *Psychological Review* 94: 74–83.

Roth, A. E. (1988) 'Laboratory experimentation in economics: a methodological overview', *Economic Journal* 98: 974–1031.

Savage, L. J. (1954) *The Foundations of Statistics*, New York: Wiley.

Schkade, D. A. and Johnson, E. J. (1989) 'Cognitive processes in preference reversals', *Organizational Behavior and Human Decision Processes* 44: 203–31.

Segal, U. (1988) 'Does the preference reversal phenomenon necessarily contradict the independence axiom?', *American Economic Review* 78: 233–6.

Simon, H. A. (1979) 'Rational decision making in business organizations', *American Economic Review* 69: 493–513.

Smith, V. L. (1989) 'Theory, experiment and economics', *Journal of Economic Perspectives* 3: 151–69.

Smith, V. L., Suchanek, G. and Williams, A. (1988) 'Bubbles, crashes and endogenous expectations in experimental spot asset markets', *Econometrica* 56: 1119–52.

Sterman, J. D. (1989) 'Modeling managerial behavior: misperceptions of feedback in a dynamic decision making experiment', *Management Science* 35: 321–39.

Thaler, R. (1987) 'The psychology of choice and the assumptions of economics', in A. E. Roth (ed.) *Laboratory Experimentation in Economics: Six Points of View*, New York: Cambridge University Press.

—— (1988) 'Anomalies: the ultimatum game', *Journal of Economic Perspectives* 2: 195–206.

Tversky, A. and Kahneman, D. (1982) 'Judgment under uncertainty', in D. Kahneman, P. Slovic and A. Tversky (eds) *Judgment Under Uncertainty: Heuristics and Biases*, Cambridge: Cambridge University Press.

Tversky, A., Sattath, S. and Slovic, P. (1988) 'Contingent weighting in judgment and choice', *Psychological Review* 95: 371–84.

Tversky, A., Slovic, P. and Kahneman, D. (1990) 'The causes of preference reversal', *American Economic Review* 80: 204–17.

30

COST–BENEFIT ANALYSIS AND PROJECT APPRAISAL

EDWARD TOWER

30.1 INTRODUCTION

In this chapter we explain the essential concepts needed to perform logically consistent and useful applied cost–benefit analyses and suggest how to implement them. We present the concepts of a shadow price and marginal social value, explain how to use them and discuss their calculation in fully determined and partially determined systems using linearized and non-linearized models. We review several important issues in shadow pricing: the choice of numeraire, shadow prices as border prices, the shadow price of foreign exchange, negative shadow prices, relationships between shadow prices, why competitive firms break even at shadow prices and when shadow prices equal producer prices. We then analyse the role of two simple cost–benefit indicators – the effective rate of protection and domestic resource cost – which have been used as cost–benefit measures by policy advisors in evaluating projects and policies, particularly in less developed countries. A major theme of the chapter is that shadow prices are sensitive to the adjustment mechanism assumed, so that any shadow-pricing exercise is worthless without a specification of the mechanisms at work in the economic model underlying the calculation.

Much of the treatment of shadow prices in the literature is not useful or is difficult to use. The practical manuals (for example, Squire and Van der Tak 1975; Ray 1984) are not very useful, and are hard to understand because they focus on formulae for shadow price calculation almost to the exclusion of the basic logic of shadow prices. The important and superbly crafted work of Dreze and Stern (1987) is inaccessible to many because it is necessarily mathematical and skimps on intuition. This leaves a niche for this chapter, because the most important theorems in shadow-pricing are intuitively derivable, and so the investment in mathematics is not essential, and to derive

The author is grateful to the Walker Foundation of the Pittsburgh National Bank for support for the study.

shadow prices one need only solve a computable general equilibrium model, which for simple and useful modelling requires limited mathematical sophistication.

This chapter is designed to be an introduction to the issue of shadow-pricing which is accessible to the informed economist who has not read in this particular area. We adopt the vocabulary and some of the structure used by Dreze and Stern (1987).

30.2 THE CONCEPT OF SHADOW PRICE AND ITS USE

An economy can be described as a model consisting of a set of equations which describe how a set of endogenous variables (such as utilities, employment, prices, wages and outputs) depend on a set of exogenous variables (such as world prices, tariffs, quotas and quantities of goods and factor services supplied net by the government). We define an objective function to be a function of the variables that the policy-maker cares about. The standard form is a Bergson–Samuelson welfare function, i.e. welfare is a function of the utilities of the citizenry. The objective function may include other arguments, such as the balance of trade in oil and the price of bread. Henceforth, we shall refer to this objective as 'social welfare'. We define a 'project' as a perturbation of the governmental excess supplies of goods and factor services. Thus a project might be the hiring of 2 person-years of labour to grow and sell three bags of potatoes. We define a 'policy' as a reaction function which relates variables under the control of the government, i.e. 'control variables', directly and indirectly to the governmental excess supplies. Thus, a policy might consist of an income tax structure, import quotas which depend on domestic prices and a structure of excise tax rates which depend on the budget deficit. A 'fully determined' policy is a set of equations which uniquely relate the values of these control variables to the other (endogenous and exogenous) variables. A 'feasible' policy solves the model. For example, an infeasible policy would be one which fails to solve an accounting identity such as government purchases unmatched by taxation or the issuance of money or debt, or one which fails to obey a binding political or economic constraint. When more than one feasible policy exists, the government is assumed to choose the one which maximizes social welfare.

The shadow value of a project is the contribution it makes to social welfare, assuming that the best feasible policy is selected. In order to enable us to use the calculus, we shall confine our attention mostly to 'small' projects. This shadow value is a general equilibrium concept, in that after the project the economy is assumed to have achieved equilibrium in all markets. Obviously, the shadow value of the project will depend on the policy. For example, the desirability of the project may depend on whether lump-sum taxes are available to finance it, or whether it must depend for its inputs on a sole domestic supplier who is protected with an import quota. Thus, all shadow values are conditional on the specification of the set of feasible policies. If the project is small, its contribution to the objective is the sum of the contributions made by the incremental changes in its excess supplies. In the example above this is the contribution made by −2 person-years of labour plus the contribution made by +3 bags of potatoes. The contribution made by a unit of each item is defined as its 'shadow price'. Thus, the contribution of a small project is the sum of its excess supplies evaluated at shadow prices. If the project is large, its shadow value is the finite change in social welfare generated by the non-infinitesimal perturbation of the economy and the shadow value is no longer the sum of the governmental excess supplies multiplied by corresponding shadow prices. Similarly, the social value of a non-incremental tax reform is the finite change in social welfare that it generates, and this change is no longer the sum of the parameter changes multiplied by marginal social values. The role of shadow prices is now apparent: they enable the policy advisor to evaluate the contribution to social welfare of any hypothetical small project.

Closely related to the shadow price is the 'marginal social value (MSV) of parameters'. The MSV of an exogenous parameter like the world price, a foreign tariff, foreign aid, the intercept of a foreign excess demand curve or a domestic tax rate (frozen by political considerations) is the contribution to social welfare of a unit increase in the parameter. Thus, the MSV bears the same relationship to its parameter that a shadow price bears to a good or factor service. The MSV is useful for judging incremental tax reform. It is also useful for judging the impact of hypothetical economic disturbances, such as changed world prices, and in formulating bargaining strategies for payments for military bases and international economic negotiations.

For the reformer of taxes, one sort of MSV is particularly useful. This is the MSV of an increase in a particular tax which is sufficient to raise one additional unit of real revenue, assuming that the revenue is then redistributed in a neutral way such as a lump-sum tax (LST). This is, of course, simply the marginal welfare cost of tax collection.

For the reformer of foreign trade regimes, one particularly useful calculation is the MSV of a tariff increase or quota reduction sufficient to create one more job in the sector in question. This is the marginal welfare cost of using a trade barrier to create additional sectoral employment.

30.3 CALCULATING SHADOW PRICES IN A FULLY DETERMINED SYSTEM

Calculating shadow prices in a fully determined system is a straightforward exercise that can be carried out using any spreadsheet program, such as Lotus,

Quatro, or Excel, that permits the user to invert a matrix. We provide some examples below. A non-linear model with governmental excess supplies and tax rates exogenous is specified. The model is linearized, with most variables expressed as proportional changes. The incremental changes in governmental excess supplies are expressed in value terms at initial prices, tax and tariff changes are expressed as changes in *ad valorem* rates, and welfare changes are normalized so that the marginal social value of income to some standard household is unity. The model is then expressed in matrix form. The left-hand side consists of a matrix of coefficients post-multiplied by a column vector of proportional changes in the endogenous variables. The right-hand side consists of a matrix of coefficients multiplied by the proportional changes in the exogenous variables. The left-hand matrix is inverted and post-multiplied by the right-hand matrix. the (i, j)th term of the resulting reduced form matrix is the multiplier which shows the percentage change in the ith endogenous variable caused by a 1 per cent change in the jth exogenous variable. The row of this matrix which shows the change in social welfare is the set of shadow prices and marginal social values.

The other rows of the matrix (for example, the real-revenue row and the row for employment in import-competing industry) can be used along with the social welfare row to calculate useful cost—benefit ratios when these other variables concern some constituencies, as in the examples of tax and trade policy reform considered above.

The matrix can also be used to calculate shadow prices and marginal social values under alternative policies. For example, the shadow value of a project can be calculated first assuming LST collection. The real-revenue row can be used to calculate the impact of the project on the government budget. If it is hypothesized that a particular excise tax might be used to finance the project, the shadow value of the project can be recalculated as the LST shadow value plus the product of the change in required real revenue to leave the government's budget balanced and the social welfare multiplier for the tax in question divided by the real revenue multiplier of the tax in question. Thus, shadow prices which account for distorting taxes are typically larger than LST shadow prices. Alternatively, of course, we could calculate the shadow prices by holding real revenue exogenous and allowing the chosen tax rate to be endogenous. This discussion emphasizes the dependence of shadow prices on the policy (for example, the tax closure) assumed. The numbers generated measure the importance of using efficient taxes to absorb revenue losses associated with projects.

My colleagues and I have carried out several such projects. They are fairly simple exercises, whose logical structure is easy to follow. Gan and Tower (1987) examine trade policy in Malaysia, both in the short run where the capital stock's sectoral allocation is frozen and in the long run where international capital mobility is assumed to drive the Malaysian rate of return on capital down to the world rate. This study emphasizes how import and export taxes combine to make trade liberalization particularly desirable, and investment in the export sector far more attractive than investment in import-competing sectors. The differences between the long- and short-run analyses remind us that applied shadow-pricing exercises are typically comparative statics exercises that depend on the time horizon considered. Thus, such exercises frequently are little more than reminders to policy-makers of the distortions that exist in their economies and rough guesses of how large their impacts are.

Su (1990) finds for a price-taking Taiwan that some relatively low tariffs have negative marginal social values meaning that they should not be reduced without simultaneously reducing other tariffs. Tower and Christiansen (1988) estimate the opportunity cost of the fertilizer subsidy in Malawi, emphasizing that the distorting effects of the taxes needed to finance it will reduce economic efficiency, and that if the industrial sector is taxed to finance the subsidy the primary effect on income distribution is to redistribute real income from those in the industrial sector to landowners. Han and Tower (1988) explore the effects of highly distorting trade and agricultural policy in Sudan, arguing that some taxes exceed their maximum revenue levels and the regime as a whole discriminates against agriculture. The study also finds that, with such highly distorting taxes in place, shadow prices are extremely sensitive to the assumptions made about tax financing.

Loo and Tower (1989) explore the effects on less developed contries (LDCs) of increased world-wide agricultural prices generated by agricultural liberalization in the developed world. The study argues that indirect effects will multiply the terms-of-trade effects on the welfare of those countries considerably. The particular story told is that resources in LDCs are typically over-allocated to industry because of import protection and export taxes. Consequently, an increase in agricultural prices moves resources in LDCs in the correct direction – towards agriculture. In addition, more taxes are earned from increased collections of export taxes and increased collections of import tariffs. The government is then assumed to balance its budget by lowering distorting taxes. Thus, the marginal social value of increased world-wide agricultural prices to the LDCs may be quite high. Clearly, the MSV here depends on the parameters assumed and the precise story told.

Two points are worth noting. So long as economists disagree, they may be able to agree on the appropriate framework for calculating shadow prices and MSVs in a general sense, but their specific calculations will differ. Also, any comparative statics or dynamic calculation with welfare changes determined is a shadow price or MSV calculation, even if not referred to as such. For further discussion of the role of modelling in policy reform see Tower and Loo (1989).

30.4 CALCULATING SHADOW PRICES IN AN INCOMPLETELY DETERMINED SYSTEM

Before the advent of personal computers, it was desirable to construct policy models that required no matrix inversion. Hence, one resorted to partial equilibrium models or general equilibrium models with particularly simple structures, for example the presence of only one mobile primary factor of production, fixed proportions for intermediate inputs, the absence of non-traded goods and the avoidance of income effects. The availability of personal computers and software to invert matrices has shrunk the premium placed on models with simple structures, but until recently it has been necessary for convenience to resort to linearized completely determined systems.

Moreover, some compelling simple analytical models of shadow prices illustrate the issues involved and develop the intuition of the shadow-pricer. Some useful examples are Srinivasan and Bhagwati (1978), Bhagwati and Srinivasan (1981), Maneschi (1985), Tower and Pursell (1987) and Tower *et al.* (1987). The computable general equilibrium model of Jenkins and Kuo (1985) is also useful.

In 1988, a useful user-friendly software package with a relatively inexpensive student edition became available (Brooke *et al.* 1988). This package maximizes an objective function subject to a set of simultaneous non-linear equations and constraints. Consequently, it can be used to evaluate large projects when policy is fully determined and to calculate shadow prices and MSVs when multiple policies are feasible. For example, optimum tax structures can be calculated using this software. An example of such a calculation is that of Loo and Tower (1990). In their paper, the structure of optimum agricultural export taxes and excise taxes is calculated for a government which wishes to maximize a social welfare function that includes utility of the representative citizen and the level of nutrition, where nutrition is treated as a merit want. Many useful calculations along these lines can be carried out.

Convergence is not a problem. The simulator first replicates the benchmark equilibrium. Then he permits those policy instruments which the fiscal authorities are permitted to optimize to change by a small amount in each simulation from the levels found in the previous simulation, permitting them to move in directions which increase social welfare. The process stops when a local maximum is found. For syllabuses and other materials used in teaching applied general equilibrium modelling see the contributions by P. Dixon, B. Parmenter and A. Powell, D. Fullerton, T. Hertel, D. Kendrick and S. Robinson in Tower (1990).

619

30.5 COMPENSATED AND UNCOMPENSATED SHADOW PRICES AND THE CHOICE OF NUMERAIRE

So far we have defined shadow prices and MSVs as the total derivatives of social welfare with respect to the exogenous quantities and parameters. There are two degrees of freedom in specifying utility functions. Consequently, there are two degrees of freedom in specifying social welfare. Thus, only relative shadow prices are unique. The conventional choice is to measure shadow prices and MSVs in one of two numeraires.

As discussed in the next section, under weak assumptions goods which are traded internationally at fixed world prices have shadow prices which are proportional to world prices. Therefore a natural numeraire is foreign exchange. With this numeraire all such goods are shadow-priced at their world prices. This is referred to as the Little–Mirrlees numeraire after Little and Mirrlees (1974).

We interpret this shadow price as an answer to the following question. Suppose that the government were to purchase one unit of an item from the private sector, adjusting its (tax, exchange rate, trade and other) policy optimally (subject to whatever constraints exist). How much foreign exchange must the government release for use by the private sector to leave social welfare unchanged? That is, how much foreign exchange released from the hands of the government compensates the private sector for loss of a unit of the item in question? Following Sieper (1981), we label this a 'compensated shadow price'. While we could conceptually select any good or factor or change of exogenous parameter as the compensatory item, and hence the numeraire, foreign exchange is the standard numeraire. Moreover, to avoid undue focus on any particular foreign currency, standard procedure is to define a unit of foreign currency as that amount which trades at the market exchange rate for one unit of domestic currency (call it the peso), and to measure these units of foreign currencies as 'border pesos'.

When all consumers can be treated as one representative consumer, a natural choice for numeraire is to measure shadow prices as equivalent variations in income. Using this numeraire, the shadow price of an item is the increase in expenditure at constant prices which would generate the same increase in utility that release of one unit of the item from government inventories generates after all general equilibrium effects have worked themselves out. This is equivalent to measuring shadow prices as utility increases, where the marginal utility of income is normalized at unity.

When there are multiple consumers, and the objective is a Bergson–Samuelson welfare function, we normalize the social welfare function by normalizing the marginal utility of income for all agents at unity and normalizing the utility weight in the welfare function for one particular group at unity. The approach outlined in these two paragraphs is known as measuring shadow prices in the 'UNIDO numeraire' after UNIDO (1972). We follow Sieper in referring to these as uncompensated shadow prices. For expositional convenience, we use the term 'shadow price' to refer to an uncompensated shadow price.

30.6 SHADOW PRICES AS WORLD PRICES

Under what circumstances are shadow prices of goods proportional to world prices? It is important to remember that in a distortionless economy (for example, with LSTs only, fixed world prices and no externalities) where the government is unconcerned about income distribution, shadow prices are proportional to market prices. This is a useful check when debugging models. Obviously, in this circumstance, shadow prices are proportional to world prices.

Now, consider an economy rife with distortions, but free of quantitative restrictions on international trade which pertain to particular classes of good. Define a unit of a good with a fixed world price as that amount which sells for one unit of currency on world markets. Suppose that the government purchases one unit of the good from an agent at market price, and simultaneously sells to the agent, again at market price, one unit of foreign currency. The agent will have augmented his domestic currency holdings by t units, where t is the import tariff or export subsidy on the good expressed as a proportion of the world price. If he now imports one more unit of the good, paying the import tariff (or exports one less, thereby forgoing the export subsidy), his holdings of domestic currency, foreign currency and inventories are all unchanged, and the initial equilibrium is replicated. If equilibrium is unique, the economy's equilibrium will be unchanged. This leaves social welfare unchanged. Since the change in social welfare equals the net governmental sales of items valued at shadow prices, the shadow value of the good purchased must equal the shadow value of the foreign exchange sold, and our proposition is proved.

The proposition will hold as long as we let social welfare depend on the utilities of the country's residents, domestic prices to buyers and sellers, quantities of goods produced and consumed by the private sector, and factors supplied by households, but not (directly) on quantities of factors absorbed by the public sector, quantities of goods produced by the public sector or quantities of goods traded internationally. This result is useful both for debugging the computable general equilibrium models which generate shadow prices, and for enabling policy-makers to think clearly about the potential importance of international trade.

One special case of this analysis is presented by Bell and Devarajan (1983) for the case of adjustment in an import tariff, while another is presented by Dinwiddy and Teal (1987) for the case of adjustment in an excise tax. Special cases in which the proposition is violated are the import quota of Bhagwati and Srinivasan (1981), and rationing the consumption of some good to be equal to some function of its output in the public sector (Blitzer *et al.* 1981). For further discussion, see the pioneering papers by Warr (1977) and Dreze and Stern (1987: 961).

30.7 THE SHADOW PRICE OF FOREIGN EXCHANGE

Some confusion has centred around the concept of 'the shadow price of foreign exchange'. As discussed by Tower and Pursell (1987), Balassa (1974) argues that the shadow exchange rate should be used both to convert domestic real income (producer and consumer surplus) into foreign exchange and to shadow-price domestic non-traded goods and factors of production, where foreign exchange is the numeraire. These are two different concepts, and in general they will have different numerical values.

Warr (1980) clarified the issue by referring to the former concept as 'the shadow price of foreign exchange in utility numeraire'. It is the answer to the following conceptual experiment. Suppose that the government sold one unit of foreign currency. After all general equilibrium effects worked themselves out, what is the increase in utility of the representative citizen, where marginal utility of income is normalized to equal unity? In other words, what is the increase in real income of the representative citizen? More generally, the shadow price of foreign exchange is the contribution that a unit governmental sale of foreign exchange makes to social welfare. Like all shadow prices, its numerical value will depend on the adjustment mechanism (policy) postulated. Sieper (1981) has argued that the concept is unnecessary, because one can work solely with uncompensated shadow prices. However, suppose that we wish to know how much impact increased foreign aid consisting of a gift of foreign exchange to the government of a LDC will have on the LDC's economic welfare. Then, we must multiply the size of the gift by the shadow price of foreign exchange. Alternatively, suppose that we wish to make the point that foreign exchange will be more useful under free trade, or with relatively uniform tariffs, than with highly differential tariffs and quantitative restrictions. The difference in usefulness is the difference between the shadow price of foreign exchange in utility numeraire under the alternative policy environments. Finally, to convert shadow prices in foreign exchange numeraire to utility numeraire, we need only multiply by the shadow price of foreign exchange in utility numeraire.

The shadow price of foreign exchange in units of non-traded goods or factors of production is the ratio of the shadow price of foreign exchange to the shadow price of the other item in question. Some formulae are presented in Dreze and Stern (1987) and Tower and Pursell (1987), but for practical purposes it is most sensible to calculate these from a computable general equilibrium model, and the concept can be fully understood without command of the analytic formulae.

30.8 THE POSSIBILITY OF NEGATIVE SHADOW PRICES

A number of workers have drawn attention to the possibility of negative shadow prices. The existence of negative shadow prices seems paradoxical. However, such paradoxes can occur in distorted economies. Growth in the supply of a factor with a negative shadow price is by definition immiserizing economic growth, i.e. growth which diminishes utility. The simplest example of this is the notion that increased availability of a factor used intensively in export production can so expand exports that world prices fall markedly enough to reduce foreign exchange earnings and economic welfare. Lucas *et al.* (1987) have discussed whether shadow prices can be negative. They note that if the government is able to dispose freely of goods and services, then they can continue to buy goods with negative shadow prices, thereby increasing economic welfare, until the shadow price for incremental units rises to zero. No difficulty with the budget constraint emerges, because shadow prices take into account the method of taxation used to finance the government purchase. Thus the existence of negative shadow prices hinges on the assumption of costly disposal, or that the government is constrained to vary its excess supplies only incrementally.

The issue of what constraints face a government is reflected in the distinction between first- and second-best shadow prices. First-best shadow prices are those which obtain after incentives have been optimized. In the absence of externalities and distorting taxation, first-best shadow prices would be market prices and first-best marginal social values of policy parameters would be zero. Thus there are multiple sets of shadow prices which depend on the nature and severity of constraints assumed, i.e. the policy postulated.

If it is assumed that policy-makers have optimized and have full information about how the economy operates, then marginal social values of all policy parameters are zero and no shadow prices are negative. However, if the modeller believes that he has a better understanding than policy-makers of how the economy works, and he wishes to educate policy-makers about the costs of following ill-informed policies, it is worthwhile calculating the costs and benefits of departures from the status quo, treating all policy parameters and governmental excess supplies as exogenous. Such calculations are also worthwhile if the modeller believes that the current balance of policies and projects are the result of a pluralistic political regime, and the balance of political power will be altered by the cost—benefit analysis provided.

One problem with using any arbitrary good, factor or policy parameter as numeraire is that its shadow price in utility numeraire may be negative, and if this is the case, it would be a confusing numeraire to use. The shadow price of foreign exchange in real-income numeraire is likely to be positive, which makes it a more suitable numeraire than most items. However, Bhagwati *et al.* (1984), Postlewaite and Webb (1984) and Yano (1983) have all discovered cases where receipt of a transfer can immiserize a country. This amounts to concluding that the decumulation of foreign exchange may reduce a country's real income, i.e. the shadow price of foreign exchange may be negative. Their arguments hinge on more than two countries and variable world prices. An additional way of obtaining a negative shadow price of foreign exchange would be to assume that the transfer was effected by adjusting a distorting tax in the country in question. Thus, a negative shadow price of foreign exchange is certainly a possibility, if not a plausibility.

30.9 RELATIONSHIPS BETWEEN SHADOW PRICES AND MARGINAL SOCIAL VALUES: PARTIAL EQUILIBRIUM ANALYSIS IN A GENERAL EQUILIBRIUM FRAMEWORK

The feasibility of fully specifying the economic system as an explicit computable general equilibrium model and solving for shadow prices has reduced the importance of analytical relationships between shadow prices, such as those stressed by Tower and Pursell (1986) and Dreze and Stern (1987), which can be used to calculate shadow prices. Are they irrelevant?

All computable general equilibrium models are highly aggregated, even those with hundreds of sectors. Consequently, the shadow prices that flow from them refer to highly aggregated factor and commodity groups. Typically, a project evaluation exercise requires detailed analysis of a particular subsector. If we can use an analysis of only one part of the economy to evaluate shadow prices for narrowly defined goods and factors in terms of shadow prices for aggregates, already calculated from a computable general equilbrium model, then specialization has occurred and resources have been saved. Analytical formulae which relate shadow prices and permit such savings are derived by Tower and Pursell (1986) and Dreze and Stern (1987).

Such formulae are also important because they help debug computable general equilibrium models. One such formula is the proportionality between shadow prices and world prices, which we discussed on pp. 621–3. We now turn to several more such formulae and their rationale. We can only provide some of the easiest to master. For further work see Tower and Pursell (1986) and Dreze and Stern (1987).

30.10 WHY COMPETITIVE FIRMS BREAK EVEN AT SHADOW PRICES

Diamond and Mirrlees (1976) have shown the following. If, for a product which is produced with constant returns to scale and under competitive conditions, the government takes over some of the private sector's production by withdrawing inputs and producing output in the same proportions that the private sector had been previously using, no levels of outputs or inputs or prices will alter. This will leave welfare unchanged. Therefore, the shadow price of the output must equal the shadow price of the resources needed to perform the activity. That is, competitive firms break even at shadow prices.

Using similar logic in a competitive economy, as discussed by Tower and Pursell (1986), if the government adjusts its excess supplies of goods and factors in such a way that no prices change, social welfare is unchanged and so the shadow price of the package of incremental excess supplies must equal zero. Thus, in a two-sector model with two perfectly mobile factors of production, for example, we could hypothetically change the government's excess supply of one of the factors, say labour, and record the change in the government's excess supplies for the two goods which freezes prices. Since no prices of goods or factors have altered, welfare is unchanged. Therefore the shadow value of the incremental labour excess supply plus the shadow value of the incremental excess supplies of the two goods equals zero. If we know the goods' shadow prices via the logic discussed on pp. 621–2 or from simulating a computable general equilibrium model, we can calculate the shadow price of labour from the above relationship. For a more general and mathematical (but less intuitive) treatment of these and other ideas to be discussed in the following sections, see Dreze and Stern (1987).

30.11 MARGINAL SOCIAL VALUES AND SHADOW PRICES

A similar logic relates to the calculation of MSVs of policy and other parameters. The MSV of an incremental increase in an excise tax can be calculated in terms of shadow prices by visualizing the following experiment. Increase the excise tax on widgets incrementally. Hold the producer price of widgets and the prices of all other goods constant by adjusting government excess supplies. Note the social welfare change. If social welfare is a Bergson–Samuelson social welfare function, this is the sum of the incremental changes in utilities (measured as equivalent income variations) for the various agents weighted by the Bergson–Samuelson weights attached to them, where the Bergson–Samuelson weight for individual h is the social utility of individual h's income (see Dreze and Stern 1987: 930). By the definition of MSVs and shadow prices, this welfare change equals the MSV of the incremental tax increase plus the shadow value of the government's incremental excess supplies. A partial computable general equilibrium model or a simple analytical calculation can be used to determine the welfare change and the shadow value of the incremental excess supply basket. The MSV is then calculated from the resulting equation. A similar approach can be used to find MSVs for other policy parameters like other taxes, tariffs, exchange rates and quotas and non-policy parameters like technical change and world prices.

30.12 THE MARGINAL SOCIAL VALUE OF A LUMP-SUM TRANSFER

To find the MSV of a lump-sum transfer to an individual h, we imagine that the government makes an incremental transfer to the individual and then supplies incremental amounts of commodities and labour to the economy so that no prices change. If we assume a Bergson–Samuelson social welfare function, the social welfare change is the Bergson–Samuelson welfare weight for individual h multiplied by the utility change. The social welfare change equals the MSV for the lump-sum transfer times the transfer plus the shadow value of the incremental excess supply basket. Knowing the first and third of these elements enables us to find the transfer's MSV (see Dreze and Stern 1987: 929).

For example, as Scott (1974) notes and Tower and Pursell (1987) prove, the shadow value of a unit of foreign exchange in utility numeraire when preferences can be aggregated, all goods are traded and world prices are fixed is calculated as follows. Imagine a 1 peso transfer to the representative consumer. With the marginal social welfare of income normalized to equal unity, social welfare rises by one unit. This is the sum of the marginal propensities to consume multiplied by consumer prices. The cost in foreign exchange of this unit rise in social welfare is the sum of the marginal propensities to consume weighted by world prices. The shadow price of foreign exchange is the social welfare generated by a unit of foreign exchange. Thus, the shadow price of the amount of foreign exchange which exchanges for 1 peso is calculated as the reciprocal of this cost. If there are no tariffs, this shadow price is unity.

30.13 WHEN SHADOW PRICES EQUAL PRODUCER PRICES

Dreze and Stern (1987: 937–40) note that when the government is able to control the output and allocation of profits of a private firm fully through quantitative constraints or unrestricted commodity taxation plus profits taxation, the private firm is in effect part of the government. Optimality dictates that the aggregate of government firms be on its production possibility frontier.

Therefore the government must equate the marginal rates of transformation of the net outputs of all its fully controlled firms. If all production frontiers of fully controlled firms are assumed to be convex, efficiency is attained by maximizing output for all fully controlled firms at shadow prices. Thus, at the optimal solution, producer prices for fully controlled firms will be proportional to shadow prices.

30.14 THE EFFECTIVE RATE OF PROTECTION AS A GUIDE TO PROJECT EVALUATION AND TAX REFORM

The ideal tool for policy and project analysis is cost–benefit analysis using computable general equilibrium models as discussed above. Before computable general equilibrium models were developed, analysts used the effective rate of protection (ERP) as one of their standard tools. A consensus seems to have developed that the ERP is a partial equilibrium concept, and that computable general equilibrium models have made the use of the concept archaic. Is the concept still useful?

Tower (1984, 1991) notes that many different definitions of the concept have been used. The Corden ERP calculation involves integrating tradeable goods sectors with the non-tradeables sectors which feed into them. I believe that this formulation is more useful than the Balassa formulation, because it answers an important question which I do not believe the Balassa formulation does. The standard calculation of the ERP is

$$\text{ERP} = \frac{\text{value added at producer prices}}{\text{value added at world prices}} - 1$$

We can think of a sector as producing a basket of goods: final goods in positive quantities and intermediate inputs in negative quantities. The ERP is the proportional difference between the price of this basket at producer prices (which by an accounting identity equals payments to primary factors of production) and at world prices. Thus it is the implicit subsidy to the production of this basket.

Using this calculation, assuming fixed proportions in using intermediate inputs in production and treating non-traded goods in the Corden fashion, an important equivalence proposition emerges: if the existing system of tariffs, taxes and quotas is replaced with value-added subsidies equal to the ERPs and consumption taxes equal to the initial tariffs plus consumption taxes, then the equilibrium will be unchanged. Thus the ERP for sector j is an implicit value-added subsidy, i.e. an implicit subsidy to the activity of converting primary factor services into net output in sector j.

From this idea, a normative proposition emerges: if the primary factors are supplied inelastically, world prices are fixed and consumption is in fixed proportions, economic efficiency is achieved by equalizing ERPs across sectors. Despite this, as Bhagwati and Srinivasan (1981) note, reducing the highest ERP in a system does not necessarily increase efficiency because the pattern of induced resource movement may be perverse. But since the ERP is an implicit subsidy, it still follows that at the margin the ERP measures the inefficiency of a sector in using domestic resources (primary factors of production) to earn or save foreign currency, and so these calculations can demonstrate the costs to policy-makers of differentiated tax structures. We now draw on Tower and Loo (1989) to clarify this idea.

In the incremental cost–benefit ratio approach to the ERP, the Corden ERP coefficient (the ERP + 1) is thought of as the ratio of the value of primary factors at domestic market prices attracted into a sector at the margin divided by the change in foreign exchange earned or saved owing to increased production in the sector (the value of the basket of incremental net production at world prices), assuming that inputs and outputs in all other tradeable goods sectors, the consumption bundle and world prices are frozen. Thus the jth ERP can be calculated as the product of a simulation which assumes that the government releases one unit of a primary factor of production from a project into the economy, where the output of each tradeable goods sector except the jth is held constant by, say, an immobile labour force or direct controls, and consumption is frozen by excise tax adjustments or the combination of a fixed-proportions consumption function and LST variation which leaves real expenditure unchanged.

The ERP coefficient for the jth sector is then given by the ratio of the value of the primary factor absorbed by the jth sector and the non-tradeables that feed into it to the change in the economy's balance of trade (net earnings of foreign currency) evaluated at the market exchange rate. As Gan and Tower (1987) argue, such a simulation is the easiest way to calculate ERPs when a CGE model has been built and some intermediate inputs are non-traded.

This interpretation of the ERP is a measure of the efficiency of the sector in converting primary factor services into foreign exchange at the margin. Moreover, it is the product of a well-defined simulation, and so it is a general equilibrium calculation in the sense that we know conceptually how policy instruments are being manipulated in our thought experiment and we have left nothing out. Thus, I feel that it is best to describe the ERP as a simple general equilibrium concept, reserving the term partial equilibrium for those analyses where the analyst has not figured out what things are being held constant or where he has recognized that he is only approximating the truth.

The implication of this incremental cost–benefit approach is that shifting a dollar's worth of primary factors from sector M to sector X will result in increased net foreign exchange earnings equal to

$$\frac{1}{1 + ERP_X} - \frac{1}{1 + ERP_M} = \frac{ERP_M - ERP_X}{(1 + ERP_X)(1 + ERP_M)}$$

Thus, any policies which drive factors from a highly protected sector M into a less protected sector X will be beneficial. For example, if sector M is an importable with an ERP of 422 per cent and X is an exportable with an ERP of −5 per cent (to use Han and Tower's (1988) figures for industry and agricultural exports in Sudan), cutting protection to M while devaluing the currency to maintain aggregate competitiveness would be desirable, in that for every Sudanese pound's worth of labour and capital shifted net foreign exchange earnings would rise by 0.86 Sudanese pounds, which could then be allocated to expenditure on other needed goods. Similarly, projects that draw resources from export- into import-competing sectors will be inefficient, with the inefficiency measured by the expression above. To conclude, the ERP can be useful in discussions of the potential benefits from policy reform, and it is a perfectly rigorous concept, but it is supported by a strong and somewhat unrealistic set of assumptions.

Finally, no one is impressed by results from computable general equilibrium models which cannot be explained, because such exercises do not tickle the intuition. In explaining the results of a computable general equilibrium simulation, I find that it is often helpful to draw on sector-by-sector estimates of ERPs in combination with the factor flows that result from perturbations of the model (see, for example, Gan and Tower 1987; Han and Tower 1988; Loo and Tower 1989, 1990).

30.15 DOMESTIC RESOURCE COST

A variant of the effective rate of protection that has been used to evaluate projects and policies in LDCs is the domestic resource cost (DRC) coefficient (see, for example, Krueger 1966, 1972; Balassa and Schydlowsky 1968, 1972; Bruno 1972; Bhagwati and Srinivasan 1981). The ERP coefficient is defined as 1 + ERP. It is the value of a sector's factor services at producer prices divided by its net output at world prices. Thus, if there are constant returns to scale it represents the value of incremental resources needed to acquire a unit of increased output at world prices. The DRC is the same ratio, except that resources are valued at shadow prices in foreign exchange numaraire. The standard use of the DRC is to argue that the DRC is a cost–benefit ratio, so that sectors with DRCs greater than unity should be discouraged by tax, trade and industrial policy, while those with DRCs less than unity should be encouraged.

Bliss (1987), Corden (1984) and Krueger (1984) have argued that if the only distortions in the economy are trade barriers then the ERP coefficient and the DRC are identical. However, there is a conflict. Bhagwati and Sriniva-san have noted that, following the Diamond–Mirrlees argument cited above, if a sector produces with constant returns to scale under competition, then the shadow value of its factors equals the shadow value of its net output. If all protection consists of tariffs, shadow prices are world prices. Consequently, in this case the DRCs for all sectors equal unity. The ERP and the DRC are certainly not identical. If, however, the protection takes the form of quotas on international trade, and there are no other distortions, then shadow prices equal market prices and the DRC does equal the ERP coefficient.

What useful information does the DRC for a proposed project give? If the government is contemplating a project which uses primary factors of production to produce a set of net outputs which it buys or sells on world markets, so that any quotas only apply to private transactions, then shadow prices for the net outputs are world prices and the DRC for the proposed project gives the correct cost–benefit ratio.

Another use would be a particular form of liberalization. Suppose that quotas on imports and exports are relaxed. The benefits from liberalizing a set of binding quotas on net imports are the sum of the quota changes multiplied by the shadow prices. The costs are the quota changes at world prices. The ratio of the former to the latter is a DRC of sorts, and the welfare gain from the liberalization is this DRC times the increased value of net imports at world prices. However, this definition and use of the DRC is far from that conventionally used. In general, the DRC as conventionally defined will not be useful in assessing the welfare impact of changed taxes and trade barriers. For that we must calculate the MSVs of the fiscal parameter changes explicitly from general equilibrium models.

To conclude, the DRC was developed while the idea of a shadow price was simultaneously evolving. The DRC is a cost–benefit ratio of limited applica-bility. Since it depends on shadow prices, and since shadow prices are the products of particular specifications of adjustment mechanisms, different mod-ellers will calculate different DRCs from the same data, while ERPs are not modeller specific as long as all modellers have agreed on what constitutes primary factors and on use of the Corden method or an alternative method of calculation. To calculate DRCs correctly, unlike ERPs, requires simulating a general equilibrium model. Thus, there is no saving by calculating a DRC rather than performing correct cost–benefit analysis. For these reasons, I see no practical role for DRCs.

30.16 SUMMARY

The shadow price is the effect on social welfare of a unit increase in the quantity of a good or factor supplied by the public sector. The marginal social value of a parameter is the effect on social welfare of a unit increase in that parameter. Using these we can calculate the effect of any hypothetical small project or policy change. Non-linear models can be used to calculate the effects of hypothetical large projects and policy changes. However, all calculations depend on the objective function, the adjustment mechanisms and the constraints on the fiscal authority. Thus a shadow price is worthless unless it is accompanied by a precise statement of how the model describes the economy. Disagreements about how to model will persist. Consequently, there will always be at least some disagreement on numerical values for shadow prices. The appropriate calculation of shadow prices depends on the arts of the econometrician, theorist, political economist and model-builder. The exercise of calculating MSVs and shadow prices is useful both for the numbers it generates to help guide particular economic policies and for the principles it illustrates to help formulate general economic strategy. Recent advances in the formulation and calculation of applied general equilibrium models have made it possible to calculate shadow prices quickly and cheaply, so that they and the models which generate them have become useful tools for policy analysis.

REFERENCES

Balassa, B. (1974) 'Estimating the shadow price of foreign exchange in project appraisal', *Oxford Economic Papers* 26: 147–68.

Balassa, B. and Schydlowsky, D. M. (1968) 'Effective tariffs, Domestic cost of foreign exchange and the equilibrium exchange rate', *Journal of Political Economy* 76: 348–60.

—— and —— (1972) 'Domestic resource costs and effective protection once again', *Journal of Political Economy* 80: 63–9.

Bell, C. and Devarajan, S. (1983) 'Shadow prices and project evaluation under alternative macroeconomic specifications', *Quarterly Journal of Economics* 97: 457–77.

Bhagwati, J. N., Brecher, R. and Hatta, T. (1984) 'The paradoxes of immiserizing growth and donor-enriching (recipient-immiserizing) transfers: a tale of two literatures', *Weltwirtschaftliches Archiv* 120: 228–43.

Bahgwati, J. N. and Srinivasan, T. N. (1981) 'The evaluation of projects at world prices under trade distortions: quantitative restrictions, monopoly power in trade and nontraded goods', *International Economic Review* 22: 385–99.

Bliss, C. (1987) 'Taxation, cost–benefit analysis, and effective protection', in D. Newbery and N. Stern (eds) *The Theory of Taxation for Developing Countries*, ch. 6, New York: Oxford University Press for the World Bank.

Blitzer, C., Dasgupta, P. and Stiglitz, J. (1981) 'Project appraisal and foreign exchange constraints', *Economic Journal* 91: 58–74.

Brooke, A., Kendrick, D. and Meeraus, A. (1988) *GAMS: A Users' guide*, Redwood City, CA: Scientific Press.

Bruno, M. (1972) 'Domestic resource costs and effective protection: clarification and synethesis', *Journal of Political Economy* 80: 16–33.

Corden, W. M. (1984) 'The normative theory of international trade', in R. W. Jones and P. B. Kenen (eds) *Handbook of International Economics*, vol. I, ch. 2, Amsterdam: North-Holland.

Diamond, P. A. and Mirrlees, J. A. (1976) 'Private constant returns and public shadow prices', *Review of Economic Studies* 43: 41–8.

Dinwiddy, C. and Teal, F. (1987) 'Project appraisal and foreign exchange constraints: a comment', *Economic Journal* 97: 479–86.

Dreze, J. and Stern, N. (1987) 'The theory of cost–benefit analysis', in A. Auerbach and M. Feldstein (eds) *Handbook of Public Economics*, vol. II, ch. 14, pp. 909–90, Amsterdam: North-Holland.

Gan, K. P. and Tower, E. (1987) 'A general equilibrium cost–benefit approach to policy reform and project evaluation in Malaysia', *Singapore Economic Review* 32: 46–61.

Han, K. and Tower, E. (1988) 'Trade, tax and agricultural policy in a highly distorted economy: the case of Sudan', Political economy working paper, Duke University, Durham, NC.

Jenkins, G. P. and Kuo, C.-Y. (1985) 'On measuring the social opportunity cost of foreign exchange', *Canadian Journal of Economics* 18: 400–15.

Krueger, A. O. (1966) 'Some economic costs of exchange control: the Turkish case', *Journal of Political Economy* 74: 466–80.

—— (1972) 'Evaluating protectionist trade regimes: theory and measurement', *Journal of Political Economy* 80: 48–62.

—— (1984) 'Trade policies in developing countries', in R. W. Jones and P. B. Kenen (eds) *Handbook of International Economics*, vol. I, ch. 11, Amsterdam: North-Holland.

Little, I. M. D. and Mirrlees, J. A. (1974) *Project Appraisal and Planning for Developing Countries*, New York: Basic Books.

Loo, T. and Tower, E. (1989) 'Agricultural protectionism and the less developed countries: the relationship between agricultural prices, debt servicing capacities and the need for development aid', in A. B. Stoeckel, D. Vincent and S. Cuthbertson (eds) *Macroeconomic Consequences of Farm Support Policies*, pp. 64–93, Durham, NC : Duke University Press.

—— and —— (1990) 'Agricultural liberalization, welfare, revenue and nutrition in LDCs', in I. Golden and O. Knudsen (eds) *The Impact of Agricultural Liberalization on Developing Countries*, pp. 307–42, Paris: OECD and World Bank.

Lucas, R. E. B., Pursell, G. and Tower, E. (1987) 'Resolution: *ex ante* versus *ex post* DRC's and the possibility of negative shadow prices', *Journal of Development Economics* 26: 173–4.

Maneschi, A. (1985) 'The shadow pricing of factors in a multicommodity specific factors model', *Canadian Journal of Economics* 18: 843–53.

Postlewaite, A. and Webb, M. (1984) 'The effect of international commodity transfers: the possibility of transferor-benefiting, transferee-harming transfers', *Journal of International Economics* 16: 357–64.

Ray, A. (1984) *Issues in Cost Benefit Analysis: Issues and Methodologies*, Baltimore, MD: Johns Hopkins University Press.

Scott, M. F. G. (1974) 'How to use and estimate shadow exchange rates', *Oxford Economic Papers* 26: 169–84.

Sieper, E. (1981) 'The structure of general equilibrium shadow pricing rules for a tax distorted economy', Mimeo, Australian National University and Monash University.

Squire, L. and Van der Tak, H. G. (1975) *Economic Analysis of Projects*, Baltimore, MD: Johns Hopkins University Press.

Srinivasan, T. N. and Bhagwati, J. N. (1978) 'Shadow prices for project selection in the presence of distortions: effective rates of protection and domestic resource costs', *Journal of Political Economy* 86. Reprinted in Bhagwati, J.N. *International Trade: Selected Readings*, ch. 17, Cambridge, MA: MIT Press, 1981.

Su M.-J. (1990) 'The Taiwanese tariff: a linearized CGE approach', Ph.D. Thesis, Duke University, Durham, NC.

Tower, E. (1984) 'Effective protection, domestic resource cost and shadow prices: a general equilibrium perspective', Staff working paper 664, World Bank, Washington, DC.

Tower, E. (compiler) (1990) *Economics Reading Lists, Course Outlines, Exams, Puzzles and Problems*, Durham, NC: Eno River Press.

—— (1991) 'On the symmetry between effective tariffs and value added subsidies', in V. Canto and J.K. Dietrich (eds) *Industrial Policy and International Trade*, Greenwich, CT: JAI Press, Contemporary Studies in Economic and Financial Analysis, vol. 62.

Tower, E. and Christiansen, R. (1988) 'A model of the effect of a fertilizer subsidy on income distribution and efficiency in Malawi', *Eastern Africa Economic Review* 2: 49–58.

Tower, E. and Loo, T. (1989) 'On using computable general equilibrium models to facilitate tax, tariff, and other policy reforms in less developed countries', in M. Gillis (ed.) *Tax Reform in Developing Countries*, pp. 391–416, Durham, NC: Duke University Press.

Tower, E. and Pursell, G. G. (1986) 'On shadow pricing', Staff working paper 792, World Bank, Washington, DC.

—— and —— (1987) 'On shadow pricing labor and foreign exchange', *Oxford Economic Papers* 39: 318–32.

Tower, E. Pursell, G. G. and Han K. (1987) 'Shadow pricing in a specific factors model: comment', *Canadian Journal of Economics* 20: 399–402.

UNIDO (United Nations Industrial Development Organization) (1972) *Guidelines for Project Evaluation*, New York: United Nations.

Warr, P. (1977) 'On the shadow pricing of traded commodities', *Journal of Political Economy* 85: 865–72.

—— (1980) 'Properties of optimal shadow prices for a tax-distorted open economy', *Australian Economic Papers* 19: 31–45.

Yano, M. (1983) 'Welfare aspects of the transfer problem', *Journal of International Economics* 15: 277–90.

31

APPLIED GENERAL EQUILIBRIUM MODELLING

JOHN WHALLEY

31.1 INTRODUCTION

In the last few years, economists have begun to use computers with large data sets to explore just how useful Walrasian general equilibrium analysis can be made for policy analysis. These developments provide the basis for this chapter. Joseph Schumpeter once characterized the Walrasian system of general equilibrium as the 'Magna Carta' of economics (Blaug 1968: 576) – the broad integrating framework which captured the interplay between economic forces on a system-wide basis. However, others have instead questioned whether the Walrasian system could ever be more than a broad organizational framework for thinking through the implications of interdependence between markets and economic actors.

Despite these debates, making the Walrasian system of general equilibrium operational has been a preoccupation of economists for several decades. In the 1930s, active debates took place on the feasibility of calculating a Pareto optimal allocation of resources in a socialist economy which planners could then use (see von Mises 1920; Robbins 1934; Lange 1936; Hayek 1940). The subsequent development by Leontief (1936, 1941) and others of input–output analysis was a conscious attempt to take Walras onto an empirical and ultimately policy-relevant plane. The linear and non-linear programming planning models developed in the 1950s and 1960s, based on the work of Kantorovitch (1939), Koopmans (1947) and others, were viewed at the time very much as an improvement on input–output techniques through the introduction of optimization and choice into Leontief's first attempt at usable general equilibrium analysis.

Today, with the use of applied general equilibrium models for policy evaluation, the same idea of operationalizing Walras is driving a new generation of economists forward. Developments in the tax area have moved on from the

634

early two-sector models of Harberger (1962) and Shoven and Whalley (1972) to much larger-scale modelling efforts such as those of Piggott and Whalley (1977, 1985) for the United Kingdom and Ballard *et al.* (1985) and Goulder and Summers (forthcoming) for the United States. Other tax-modelling efforts such as those of Summers (1981), Auerbach *et al.* (1983) and others focused on overlapping generations models have also begun to grow in both importance and use.

In the trade area, global general equilibrium models developed by Deardorff and Stern (1986) and Whalley (1985) have been used to evaluate policy options in General Agreement on Tariffs and Trade (GATT) negotiating rounds. In Australia, a large-scale modelling effort by Dixon *et al.* (1982) has been used by government agencies to look at that country's trade options. A series of country models constructed at the World Bank (see Dervis *et al.* 1982) have been used to provide inputs into country lending decisions as far as trade liberalization options for various developing countries are concerned. In addition, issue-specific models in areas such as agriculture (Golden and Knudsen 1990) and textiles (Trela and Whalley 1990) are being ever more widely used.

The same is true in other applied areas of economics – there is a growing application of applied general equilibrium techniques. In traditional environmental analysis (Bergman 1989), newer global environmental issues (Manne and Richels 1990), development economics (Robinson 1989) and real business cycle analysis in the macro area (Greenwood and Huffman 1989), increasing use of these techniques is evident. The issues for those outside this field are: What are these techniques? Can they be used for other issues? How easy is it to apply them?

31.2 APPLIED GENERAL EQUILIBRIUM TECHNIQUES

Before describing in more detail some of the efforts of recent applied general equilibrium modellers, it is perhaps worthwhile presenting in clearer form an example of the analytical framework they use.[1] A traditional general equilibrium model identifies a number of consumers, each with an initial endowment of commodities and a set of preferences. The latter yield household demand functions for each commodity, with market demands given by the sum of individual consumer's demands. Commodity market demands depend on all prices, are continuous, non-negative and homogeneous of degree zero (i.e. no money illusion) and satisfy Walras's law (i.e. at any set of prices the total value of consumer expenditure equals consumer income). On the production side, technology is described by either constant returns to scale activities or non-increasing returns to scale production functions, with producers maximizing profits.

The zero homogeneity of demand functions and the linear homogeneity of profits in prices (i.e. doubling all prices doubles money profits) implies that only relative prices are of any significance; the absolute price level has no impact on the equilibrium outcome. Thus, equilibrium is characterized by a set of relative prices and levels of production by each industry such that market demand equals supply for all commodities (including disposals if any commodity is a free good). Since producers are assumed to maximize profits, this implies that in the constant returns to scale case no activity (or cost-minimizing techniques if production functions are used) does any better than break even at the equilibrium prices.

A simple numerical example

A numerical example is a good way of illustrating this approach, although in representing actual economies much more specificity is required than in the general form of the model. Here, a simple numerical example presented by Shoven and Whalley (1984) is outlined. In this example, there are two final goods (manufacturing and non-manufacturing), two factors of production (capital and labour) and two classes of consumer (a 'rich' consumer group which owns all the capital and a 'poor' group which owns all the labour). There are no consumer demands for factors (i.e. no labour–leisure choice). Each consumer group generates demands by maximizing a constant elasticity of substitution (CES) utility function subject to its budget constraint. The CES utility functions are

$$U^c = \left[\sum_{i=1}^{2} (a_i^c X_i^c)^{(\sigma_c - 1)/\sigma_c} \right]^{\sigma_c/(\sigma_c - 1)} \tag{31.1}$$

where X_i^c is the quantity demanded of good i by the cth consumer, the a_i are share parameters and σ_c is the substitution elasticity in consumer c's CES utility function. The consumer's budget constraint is $P_1 X_1^c + P_2 X_2^c \leqslant P_L W_L^c + P_K W_K^c = I^c$, where P_1 and P_2 are the consumer prices for the two goods, W_L^c and W_K^c are consumer c's endowment of labour and capital and I^c is the income of consumer c. Maximizing this utility function subject to the budget constraint yields the following demands:

$$X_i^c = \frac{(a_i^c)^{\sigma_c} I^c}{P_i^{\sigma_c} \Sigma_{j=1}^{2} (a_j^c)^{\sigma_c} P_j^{1-\sigma_c})} \qquad i = 1, 2, c = 1, 2 \tag{31.2}$$

CES production functions are assumed. These functions are

$$Q_i = \phi_i [\delta_i L_i^{(\sigma_i - 1)/\sigma_i} + (1 - \sigma_i) K_i^{(\sigma_i - 1)/\sigma_i}]^{\sigma_i/(\sigma_i - 1)} \qquad i = 1, 2 \tag{31.3}$$

where Q_i denotes output of the ith industry, ϕ_i is a scale or units parameter,

δ_i is a distribution parameter, K_i and L_i are capital and labour factor inputs, and σ_i is the elasticity of factor substitution.

In this example there are six production function parameters (i.e. ϕ_i, δ_i and σ_i for $i = 1, 2$), six utility function parameters (i.e. a_1^1, a_1^2, a_1^2, a_2^2, σ_1 and σ_2) and four exogenous variables (the endowments W_L and W_K of labour and capital for each of the two consumers).

An equilibrium solution to the model is given by the four prices P_1, P_2, P_L, P_K, and the eight quantities X_1^1, X_1^2, X_2^1, X_2^2 and K_1, K_2, L_1, L_2 which meet the equilibrium conditions that market demand equals market supply for all inputs and outputs, and that zero profits apply in each industry. Once the parameters are specified and the factor endowments are known, a complete general equilibrium model is available. Tax and other policy variables can then be added as desired.

Table 31.1 presents the values for all the parameters and the exogenous variables in the numerical example used by Shoven and Whalley. The equilibrium solution is reported in Table 31.2. Only relative prices are relevant in this model and, somewhat arbitrarily, labour has been chosen as the numeraire. At the equilibrium prices, total demand for each output equals production, and producer revenues equal costs. Labour and capital endowments are fully employed, and consumer factor incomes plus transfers equal consumer expenditure. Because of the assumption of constant returns to scale, the per unit costs in each industry equal the selling price, meaning that economic profits are zero. Expenditure by each household exhausts its income.

Shoven and Whalley also introduce taxes into this model in *ad valorem* form (see also Shoven and Whalley 1973; Shoven 1974) as producer taxes on inputs and consumer taxes on income or expenditure. Revenues are redistributed to consumers. They show how this example can be used to evaluate the effects of introducing a 50 per cent tax on the use of capital in the manufacturing

Table 31.1 Production and demand parameters and endowments used by Shoven and Whalley for their two-sector general equilibrium numerical example

Production parameters			
	ϕ_i	δ_i	σ_i
Manufacturing sector	1.5	0.6	2.0
Non-manufacturing sector	2.0	0.7	0.5

Demand parameters						
	Rich consumers			Poor consumers		
	a_1^1	a_2^1	σ^1	a_1^2	a_2^2	σ^2
	0.5	0.5	1.5	0.3	0.7	0.75

Endowments		
	K	L
Rich households	25	0
Poor households	0	60

637

Table 31.2 Equilibrium solution for Shoven and Whalley's general equilibrium model (parameter values specified in Table 31.1)

Equilibrium prices

Manufacturing output	1.399
Non-manufacturing output	1.093
Capital	1.373
Labour	1.000

Production

	Quantity	Revenue	Capital	Capital cost
Manufacturing	24.942	34.898	6.212	8.532
Non-manufacturing	54.378	59.439	18.788	25.805
Total		94.337	25.000	34.337

	Labour	Labour cost	Total cost	Cost per unit output
Manufacturing	26.366	26.366	34.898	1.399
Non-manufacturing	33.634	33.634	59.439	1.093
Total	60.000	60.000	94.337	

Demands

	Manufacturing	Non-manufacturing	Expenditure
Rich households	11.514	16.674	34.337
Poor households	13.428	37.704	60.000
Total	24.942	54.378	94.337

	Labour income	Capital income	Total income
Rich households	0	34.337	34.447
Poor households	60.000	0	60.000
Total	60.000	34.337	94.337

industry. Once introduced in this way, the equilibrium behaviour of the model can be investigated as taxes change, and on that basis evaluations of tax reform and other policy initiatives can be made. Thus the effects of all the taxes which characterize modern tax systems (personal, corporate, sales, excise, property, social security, resource and other taxes) can be analysed using these techniques.

31.3 DESIGNING LARGER-SCALE REALISTIC MODELS

The main differences between the models used to analyse actual policy proposals and the numerical example above lie in their dimensionality (i.e. the number of sectors and consumer types modelled), their parameter specification procedures and use of data, and their inclusion of more complex policy regimes than a simple tax on one factor in one sector.[2]

A wide range of issues are encountered in designing larger-scale applied general equilibrium models to be used in actual policy environments. Should the model be of the traditional fixed-factor static form, or should it be dynamic?

How are substitution possibilities in production and demand to be incorporated? How are parameter values to be chosen? Are literature estimates to be used, or is some other approach to be followed? Are some of the parameters, for instance, to be estimated? How are trade, investment, government expenditures or other features to be treated? How much difference do various alternative treatments make? How is the model to be solved – using a fixed-point solution method guaranteed to work, or a potentially quicker linearization, or some other procedure? How are computed equilibria to be compared? Which summary statistics are to be used in evaluating policy changes?

Model structure

Although the appropriate general equilibrium model for any particular policy analysis varies with the issue, most current applied models are variants of static two-factor models that have long been employed in public finance and international trade. Most involve more than two goods, even though factors of production are classified in the two broad categories of capital and labour services. In some models these are further disaggregated into subgroups (labour, for instance, may be identified as skilled or unskilled). Intermediate transactions are usually incorporated through either fixed or flexible input–output coefficients.

The rationale for proceeding in this way is that a range of policy issues are frequently analysed theoretically, using similar theoretical frameworks, and it is natural to retain the same basic structure for applied work. This is particularly the case if the major contribution of numerical work is to advance from qualitative to quantitative analysis. Also, most data on which the numerical specifications are based come in a form consistent with the two-sector approach. For instance, national accounts data identify wages and salaries and operating surplus as major cost components. Input–output data provide intermediate transaction data, with value added broken down in a similar way. This all suggests a model in which capital and labour are identified as factor inputs.

The partition between goods and factors in two-sector type models can also be used in these models to simplify computation and thus sharply reduce execution costs. By using factor prices to generate cost-covering goods prices, consumer demands can be calculated and the derived demands for factors which meet consumer demands can be evaluated. Thus, even a model with a large number of goods can be solved by working only with the implicit system of excess factor demands.

There is also a range of more specific model design issues which are usually encountered, including the treatment of investment, foreign trade and government expenditures. Where there are no international capital flows, the level of investment in the model reflects household savings decisions (broadly defined to include corporate retentions). These are based on constant savings propensities in static models, but on explicit intertemporal utility maximization in dynamic models. Government expenditures usually reflect transfers and real expenditures, with the latter frequently determined from assumed utility-maximizing behaviour for the government. In this approach the government is treated as a separate consumption-side agent that buys public goods and services. In a few cases (such as Piggott and Whalley 1984), models have been used with public goods explicitly appearing in household utility functions, although this complicates the basic approach.

As regards the treatment of time, some of the static equilibrium models have been sequenced through time to reflect changes in the economy's capital stock due to net saving. Models such as those of Summers (1981), Auerbach *et al.* (1983) and Fullerton *et al.* (1983) have been used to analyse intertemporal issues in tax policy, such as whether a move from an income tax to a consumption tax (under which saving is less heavily taxed) is desirable. This approach links a series of single-period equilibria through savings decisions that change the capital stock of the economy through time. Saving, in turn, is based on maximization of a utility function defined over current and expected future consumption. Myopic expectations (i.e. expected future rates of return on assets equal current rates of return) are often assumed to simplify computations. Saving in the period augments the capital stock in all future periods. The general equilibrium computed for each period is such that all markets clear, including that for newly produced capital goods. The economy thus passes through a sequence of single-period equilibria in which the capital stock grows. Tax changes that encourage higher saving typically cause lowered consumption in initial years, and eventually higher consumption due to the larger capital stock.

In treating external sector transactions, a common approach in many models is to specify a set of export demand and import supply functions which the economy being analysed is assumed to face (see the discussion in Whalley and Yeung 1984). These functions reflect the assumed behaviour of foreigners to changes in domestic prices induced by tax policy changes. These excess demand functions must also satisfy external sector balance for any set of prices (Walras's law for the foreign country). The external sector specification can be important in these models. The effects of policy changes on an economy which is a taker of prices on world markets, for instance, will be significantly different from those for a closed economy. Similarly, international capital mobility considerations can also be important. Although these are usually ignored, Goulder *et al.* (1983) have shown how their incorporation can change the analysis of policy options compared with a model with immobile capital.

Choosing functional forms

In addition to selecting the general model structure when building an applied general equilibrium model to represent an actual economy, it is also necessary to choose particular functional forms. The major constraints on the choice of demand and production functions are typically that they be consistent with the theoretical approach and are analytically tractable. The first consideration involves choosing functions that satisfy the usual demand- and production-side restrictions assumed in general equilibrium models such as Walras's law. The second consideration requires that excess demand responses be easy to evaluate for any price vector considered as a candidate equilibrium solution for the model.

The choice of a specific functional form by the modeller usually depends on how elasticities are to be used in the model. The general approach is one of selecting the functional form that best allows key parameter values (for example, income and price elasticities) to be incorporated, while retaining tractability. This largely explains why the functional forms used are so often drawn from the family of 'convenient' forms (Cobb–Douglas, CES, linear expenditure system (LES), translog, generalized Leontief or other flexible functional forms).

Demands from Cobb–Douglas utility functions are easy to work with, but have unitary income and uncompensated own-price elasticities and zero cross-price elasticities. These restrictions are typically implausible. For CES functions, if all expenditure shares are small, compensated own-price elasticities equal the elasticity of substitution in preferences. It may thus be unacceptable to model all commodities as having essentially the same compensated own-price elasticities. One alternative is to use hierarchical or nested CES functions, adding further complexity in structure. Another is to use translog expenditure functions, although here the issues which arise are the global properties of these more flexible functional forms, such as concavity. Unitary income elasticities implied by Cobb–Douglas or CES functions can also be relaxed by using LES functions with a displaced origin, but the origin displacements need to be specified.

On the production side, where only two primary factors enter the model, CES value-added functions are usually assumed. If more than two factors are used, hierarchical CES functions or translog cost functions are again used. Intermediate requirements functions can be modelled as fixed coefficients, or intermediate substitutability can be introduced.

Choice of parameter values

Parameter values for the functions in the models are also crucial for the results of simulations using these models. The procedure most commonly used has come to be labelled 'calibration' (Mansur and Whalley 1984). In this approach, the economy under consideration is assumed to be in equilibrium in the presence of existing tax policies, i.e. at a so-called 'benchmark' equilibrium. Parameters for the model are then calculated such that the model can reproduce the equilibrium data as a model solution.

The main feature of this calibration procedure that has both attracted interest and raised concerns is that there is no statistical test of the resulting model specification implied by calibration. The procedure for calculating parameter values from a constructed equilibrium observation is deterministic. This typically involves the key assumption that the benchmark data represent an equilibrium for the economy under investigation, and required parameter values are then calculated using the model equilibrium conditions. If the equilibrium conditions are not sufficient to identify the model, additional parameter values (typically elasticities) are exogenously specified until the model is identified. These are usually based on a literature search or, less frequently, on separate estimation. In contrast with econometric work that often simplifies the structure of economic models to allow for substantial richness in statistical specification, in these models the procedure is quite the opposite. The richness of the economic structure only allows for a crude statistical model which, in the case of calibration to a single year's data, becomes deterministic.

Because the widespread use of deterministic calibration in these models is clearly troubling, it is perhaps worthwhile outlining some of the reasons why the calibration approach is so widely used. First, in some of the applied models several thousand parameters may be involved, and to estimate all the model parameters simultaneously using time series methods requires either unrealistically large numbers of observations or overly severe identifying restrictions. Partitioning models into submodels (such as a demand and production system) may reduce or overcome this problem, but partitioning does not fully incorporate the equilibrium restrictions that are emphasized in calibration. Also, benchmark data sets are usually constructed in value terms, and their separation into price and quantity observations make it difficult to sequence equilibrium observations with consistent units through time as would be required for time series estimation. Finally, the dimensions used in these models make the construction of benchmark equilibrium data sets a non-trivial exercise. Some of the large-scale data sets have required upwards of eighteen months' work, so that if time series are to be constructed the required workload may not be sustainable.[3]

Calibration usually involves the data for a year, or a single observation represented by an average over a number of years, and it is only in the Cobb–Douglas case that the benchmark data uniquely identify a set of parameter values. In other cases, the required values for the relevant elasticities needed to identify the other parameters in the model are usually based on other sources. Typically, heavy reliance is placed on literature surveys of elasticities and, as many other modellers have observed, it is surprising how sparse (and sometimes contradictory) the literature is on some elasticity values (see Mansur and Whalley 1984). Also, although this procedure might sound straightforward, it is often difficult because of differences among studies.

Elasticity values in these models are most conveniently thought of as pre-specifying the curvature of isoquants and indifference surfaces, with their position given by the benchmark equilibrium data. Because the curvature of CES indifference curves and isoquants cannot be inferred from the benchmark data, extraneous values of substitution elasticities are required. Similarly, for LES demand functions, income elasticities are needed upon which to base the origin co-ordinates for utility measurement.

In practice, data representing benchmark equilibria for use in calibration are constructed from national accounts and other government data sources. In these data, the available information does not satisfy microconsistency conditions (for example, payments to labour from firms will not equal labour income received by households), and a number of adjustments are needed to ensure that the equilibrium conditions of the models hold. In these adjustments, some data are taken as correct and others are adjusted to reflect consistency.

Because these benchmark data are usually produced in value terms, in using the data in a general equilibrium model units must be chosen for goods and factors such that separate price and quantity observations are obtained. A widely employed convention, originally followed by Harberger (1962), is to assume units for both goods and factors such that they have a price of unity in the benchmark equilibrium.

Solving general equilibrium models

Many of the early general equilibrium models typically used Scarf's algorithm (Scarf 1967, 1973) for solution. Some of the more recent models continue to rely on Scarf-type methods, but use faster variants of his original algorithm due to Merrill (1971), Eaves (1974), Kuhn and MacKinnon (1975) and van der Laan and Talman (1979). Merrill's refinement seems to be the most widely used. Newton-type methods or other local linearization techniques can also be used. These often work as quickly, if not more quickly, than the methods listed above, although convergence is not guaranteed.

Another approach, implicit in Harberger's original work, is to use a linearized equilibrium system to solve for an approximation to an equilibrium, in some cases refining an initial estimate using a multi-step procedure so that approximation errors are eliminated. This approach was also adopted by Johansen (1969), and has been further refined by Dervis *et al.* (1982), Dixon *et al.* (1982) and others.

Execution costs for existing models at present seem manageable. Standard off-the-shelf computer routines have not yet emerged for the complete sequence of data adjustment, calibration and equilibrium computation, but for equilibrium solution the MPS.GE package due to Rutherford (1982) is now in widespread use. What currently seems to be the case is that it is no longer the solution methods that constrain model applications but the availability of data and the ability of modellers to specify key parameters and capture the essence of the issues under debate.

Evaluating impacts of policy changes

Theoretical literature on welfare economics is usually followed in making comparisons between equilibria in order to arrive at policy evaluations stemming from the use of these applied models. For welfare impacts, Hicksian compensation variations (CVs) and equivalent variations (EVs) are commonly used as summary measures of welfare impact by agent. Economy-wide welfare measures are often computed by aggregating CVs or EVs over consumer groups. While this is consistent with practice in cost–benefit literature, the theoretical shortcomings in using the sum of CVs or EVs as an aggregate welfare criterion are well known.

Current applied models also provide a detailed evaluation of who gains, who loses and by how much as a result of a policy change. No single summary measure need be chosen if the policy analyst is interested only in the detailed impacts of any policy change. In addition to welfare impacts, other impacts of policy changes can be investigated, such as income distribution effects using Lorenz curves or Gini coefficients. Alternative income concepts (for example, gross of tax or net of tax) can also be used in such calculations. Changes in relative prices can be evaluated, as can changes in the use of factors of production across industries, or changes in the product composition of consumer demands.

Uniqueness of equilibrium

One final point to keep in mind is that the applied general equilibrium approach to policy analysis may not be particularly instructive if the equilibrium solution to any of these models is not unique for any given policy specification. Uniqueness, or the lack of it, has been a long-standing interest of general equilibrium theorists (Kehoe 1980). There is no theoretical argument, however, that guarantees uniqueness in the models currently in use. Researchers have conducted *ad hoc* numerical experimentation (approaching equilibria from different directions and at different speeds) with some of the models, but have yet to find a case of non-uniqueness. In the case of the US tax model due to Ballard *et al.* (1985), uniqueness has been numerically demonstrated by Kehoe and Whalley (1985). The current working hypothesis adopted by most modellers seems to be that uniqueness can be presumed in the models discussed here until a clear case of non-uniqueness is found.

31.4 CONCLUSIONS AND RECENT DEVELOPMENTS IN TRADE MODELLING

Developments in the applied general equilibrium modelling area over the last ten to fifteen years have suggested that the Walrasian equilibrium model stressing economy-wide interacting effects between markets can indeed be applied to contemporary policy issues. A wide variety of larger general-purpose to smaller issue-specific models have been built in recent years, and their use is spreading in both academic research and government and international agencies. Problems remain, not the least of which are poor data, weak model parameter estimates and choice of functional forms, but this promises to be a rich field of economic research in the years ahead.

Understanding how this field of applied equilibrium analysis is evolving in all the various areas of application is difficult, but it may be helpful to readers to concentrate on developments in one area – trade policy modelling – as an example of how the field is developing in more detail.

General equilibrium numerical modelling entered the trade literature in the early 1970s driven, in part, by the challenge posed by Scarf (1973) and others to implement the then emerging general equilibrium computational techniques in an operationally meaningful manner, and in a way which would ultimately be useful for policy analysis. Trade was one of the first and most natural areas of application for those computational techniques, given the extensive use of general equilibrium analysis in theoretical trade (Heckscher–Ohlin type) literature from the 1950s and earlier (Samuelson 1948).

The period prior to 1984 saw a substantial volume of computational trade modelling. There were global trade models which analysed the effects of the then current GATT Tokyo Round (Deardorff and Stern 1979, 1986; Whalley and Brown 1980; Whalley 1985), there were early analyses of customs unions, such as Miller and Spencer (1977), and there were single-country trade policy analyses, such as Boadway and Treddenick's (1978) analysis of Canadian protection and a series of related models constructed at the World Bank

(Dervis *et al.* 1982). The early 1980s also subsequently saw the emergence of work attempting to integrate some of the then new theoretical literature on scale economies and market structure into the still relatively new numerical general equilibrium work (Harris 1984a, b). Numerical general equilibrium trade modelling seemed to be a novel and exciting field with many potential policy applications.

There is now newer work under way in the research community, however, which represents a continuing forward momentum in the area. These developments cover work on short-run dynamics and interactions between current and capital account (Goulder and Eichengreen 1989), focused sectoral models (de Melo and Tarr 1988; Trela and Whalley 1988; Wigle and Whalley 1988; Tarr 1989) and analyses of strategic trade policy issues in particular sectors (Baldwin and Krugman 1986; Smith and Venables 1988). The emerging trend thus seems to be towards smaller issue-focused trade modelling, in contrast with the larger multi-purpose models of the late 1970s.

While many weaknesses of general equilibrium trade modelling remain, what was claimed to be a potentially important policy evaluation tool ten or more years ago seems in practice to be proving to be so. Given both the limited alternatives available to policy-makers wishing to analyse trade policy options and the relative inconclusiveness emerging from other branches of applied economics, the best guess seems to be that the relative attractiveness of this type of work will probably continue to grow over time.

NOTES

1 The discussion in this section draws on Shoven and Whalley (1984).
2 This section draws on the discussion in Whalley (1987).
3 See Piggott and Whalley (1985) and St-Hilaire and Whalley (1983, 1987) for more discussion of how these larger-scale data sets are constructed.

REFERENCES

Auerbach, A. J., Kotlikoff, L. J. and Skinner, J. (1983) 'The efficiency gains from dynamic tax reform', *International Economic Review* 24: 81–100.

Baldwin, J. R. and Krugman, P. R. (1986) 'Market access and international competition: a simulation study of 16K random access memories', Working paper 1936, National Bureau of Economic Research.

Ballard, C., Fullerton, D., Shoven, J. B. and Whalley, J. (1985) *A General Equilibrium Model for Tax Policy Evaluation*, Chicago, IL: University of Chicago Press.

Bergman (1989) 'Acid rain and environmental issues', Paper presented at a *Conference on Applied General Equilibrium, San Diego, CA, 7–9 September.*

Blaug, M. (1968) *Economic Theory in Retrospect*, 2nd edn, London: Heinemann Educational.

Boadway, R. and Treddenick, J. (1978) 'A general equilibrium computation of the effects of the Canadian tariff structure', *Canadian Journal of Economics* 11(3): 424–46.

Deardorff, A. V. and Stern, R. M. (1979) *An Economic Analysis of the Effects of the Tokyo Round of Multilateral Trade Negotiations on the United States and the Other Major Industrialized Countries*, Washington, DC: US Government Printing Office, MTN Studies 5.

—— and —— (1986) *The Michigan Model of World Production and Trade: Theory and Applications*, Cambridge, MA: MIT Press.

Dervis, K., de Melo, J. and Robinson, S. (1982) *General Equilibrium Models for Development Policy*, New York: Cambridge University Press.

Dixon, P., Parmenter, B., Sutton, J. and Vincent, D. (1982) *ORANI: A Multi-Sectoral Model of the Australian Economy*, Amsterdam: North-Holland.

Eaves, B. C. (1974) 'Properly labelled simplexes', in G. B. Dantzig and B. C. Eaves (eds) *Studies in Optimization*, pp. 71–93, Menasha, WI: Mathematical Association of America, MAA Studies in Mathematics 10.

Fullerton, D., Shoven, J. B. and Whalley, J. (1983) 'Replacing the U.S. income tax with a progressive consumption tax: a sequenced general equilibrium approach', *Journal of Public Economics* 20: 1–21.

Golden, I. and Knudsen, O. (eds) (1990) *Modelling the Effects of Agricultural Trade Liberalization on Developing Countries*, Washington, DC: World Bank/OECD.

Goulder, L. and Eichengreen, B. (1989) 'Trade liberalization in general equilibrium: inter-temporal and inter-industry effects', Working paper 1695, National Bureau of Economic Research.

Goulder, L. H. and Summers, L. H. (forthcoming) 'Tax policy, asset prices, and growth: a general equilibrium analysis', *Journal of Public Economics*.

Goulder, L. H., Shoven, J. B. and Whalley, J. (1983) 'Domestic tax policy and the foreign sector: the importance of alternative foreign sector formulations to results from a general equilibrium tax analysis model', in M. Feldstein (ed.) *Behavioural Simulation Methods in Tax Policy Analysis*, pp. 333–64, Chicago, IL: University of Chicago Press.

Greenwood, J. and Huffman, G. (1989) 'Tax analysis in a real business cycle model: on measuring Harberger triangles and Okun gaps', Paper presented at a *Conference on Applied General Equilibrium, San Diego, CA, 7–9 September*.

Harberger, A. C. (1959) 'The corporation income tax: an empirical appraisal', in Tax Revision Compendium, House Committee on Ways and Means, 86 Congress, I Session, pp. 231–40.

—— (1962) 'The incidence of the corporation income tax', *Journal of Political Economy* 70: 215–40.

Harris, R. (with Cox, D.) (1984a) *Trade, Industrial Policy and Canadian Manufacturing*, Ottawa: Ontario Economic Council.

Harris, R. (1984b) 'Applied general equilibrium analysis of small open economies with scale economies and imperfect competition', *American Economic Review* 74: 1016–32.

Hayek, F. A. (1940) 'Socialist calculation: the competitive solution', *Economica* 7: 125–49.

Johansen, L. (1969) *A Multi-Sectoral Study of Economic Growth*, Amsterdam: North-Holland.

647

Kantorovitch, L. V. (1939) *Mathematical Methods in the Organization and Planning of Production*, Leningrad: Publication House of the Leningrad State University.

Kehoe, T. (1980) 'An index theorem for general equilibrium models with production', *Econometrica* 48: 1211–32.

Kehoe, T. and Whalley, J. (1985) 'Uniqueness of equilibrium in a large scale numerical general equilibrium model', *Journal of Public Economics* 27: 247–54.

Koopmans, T. C. (1947) 'Optimum utilization of the transportation system', *Proceedings of the International Statistical Conferences*, New York: Wiley.

Kuhn, H.W. and MacKinnon, J. G. (1975) 'The sandwich method for finding fixed points', Technical Report, Department of Economics and Mathematics, Princeton University.

van der Laan, G. and Talman, A. J. (1979) 'A restart algorithm without an artificial level for computing fixed points on unbounded regions', in H. O. Petigen and W. Heidelberg (eds) *Functional Differential Equations and Approximations of Fixed Points*, Berlin: Springer-Verlag.

Lange, O. (1936) 'On the economic theory of socialism', *Review of Economic Studies* 4: 53–71, 123–42.

Leontief, W. W. (1936) 'Quantitative input and output relations in the economic system of the United States', *Review of Economic Statistics* 18: 105–25.

—— (1941) *The Structure of the American Economy 1919–1929*, Cambridge, MA: Harvard University Press.

Manne, A. S. and Richels, R. G. (1990) 'Global CO_2 emission reductions – the impacts of rising energy costs', *Energy Journal* 12: 87–107.

Mansur, A. and Whalley, J. (1984) 'Numerical specification of applied general equilibrium models: estimation, calibration and data', in H. Scarf and J. B. Shoven (eds) *Applied General Equilibrium Analysis*, New York: Cambridge University Press.

de Melo, J. and Tarr, D. (1988) 'Welfare costs of U.S. quotas in textiles, steel and autos', Mimeo, World Bank, Washington, DC.

Merrill, O. H. (1971) 'Applications and extensions of an algorithm that computer fixed points of certain non-empty convex upper semi-continuous points to set mappings', Technical Report 71–7, Department of Industrial Engineering, University of Michigan.

Miller, M. H. and Spencer, J. E. (1977) 'The static economic effects of the U.K. joining the E.E.C.: a general equilibrium approach', *Review of Economic Studies* 44: 71–93.

von Mises, L. (1920) 'Die Wirtschaftsrechnung in Sozialistischen Gemeinwesen', *Archiv für Socialwissenschaften* 47. English translation in *Collectivist Economic Planning*, ed. F. A. Hayek, London, 1935.

Piggott, J. and Whalley, J. (1977) 'General equilibrium investigation of U.K. tax subsidy policy: a progress report', in M. J. Artis and A. R. Nobay (eds) *Studies in Modern Economic Analysis*, pp. 259–99, Oxford: Basil Blackwell.

—— and —— (1984) 'Net fiscal incidence calculation: average versus marginal effects', Mimeo.

—— and —— (1985) *U.K. Tax Policy and Applied General Equilibrium Analysis*, Cambridge: Cambridge University Press.

Robbins, L. C. (1934) *The Great Depression*, London: Macmillan.

Robinson, S. (1989) 'Computable general equilibrium models of developing countries:

stretching the neoclassical paradigm', Working paper 513, Department of Agriculture and Resource Economics, University of California.

Rutherford (1982) 'Computing general equilibria in a complementary format. NORGE: a general equilibrium model of the Norwegian economy', Engineer's Degree Thesis, Department of Operations Research, Stanford University.

Samuelson, P. A. (1948) 'International trade and the equalization of factor prices', *Economic Journal* 58: 181–97.

Scarf, H. E. (1967) 'On the computation of equilibrium prices', in W. J. Fellner (ed.) *Ten Economic Studies in the Tradition of Irving Fisher*, New York: Wiley.

Scarf, H. E. (with Hansen, T.) (1973) *The Computation of Economic Equilibria*, New Haven, CT: Yale University Press.

Shoven, J. B. (1974) 'A proof of the existence of a general equilibrium with *ad valorem* commodity taxes', *Journal of Economic Theory* 8: 1–25.

Shoven, J. B. and Whalley, J. (1972) A general equilibrium calculation of the effects of differential taxation of income from capital in the U.S.,' *Journal of Public Economics* 1: 281–331.

—— and —— (1973) 'General equilibrium with taxes: a computational procedure and an existence proof', *Review of Economic Studies* 60: 475–90.

—— and —— (1984) 'Applied general equilibrium models of taxation and international trade', *Journal of Economic Literature* 22: 1007–51.

Smith, A. and Venables, A. J. (1988) 'Completing the internal market in the European Community: some industry simulations', *European Economic Review* 32: 1501–25.

St-Hilaire, F. and Whalley, J. (1983) 'A microconsistent equilibrium data set for Canada for use in tax policy analysis', *Review of Income and Wealth* 29: 175–204.

—— and —— (1987) 'A microconsistent data set for Canada for use in regional general equilibrium policy analysis', *Review of Income and Wealth* 33: 327–44.

Summers, L. H. (1981) 'Capital taxation and accumulation in a life cycle growth model', *American Economic Review* 71: 533–44.

Tarr, D. G. (1989) *A General Equilibrium Analysis of the Welfare and Employment Effects of U.S. Quotas in Textiles, Autos and Steel*, Washington, DC: US Federal Trade Commission.

Trela, I. and Whalley, J. (1990) 'Global effects of developed country trade restrictions on textiles and apparel', *Economic Journal* 100: 1190–205.

Whalley, J. (1985) *Trade Liberalization Among Major World Trading Areas*, Cambridge, MA: MIT Press.

—— (1987) 'Operationalizing Walras: experience with recent applied general equilibrium tax models', in T. Bewley (ed.) *Advances in Econometrics, Fifth World Congress*, vol. 2, Cambridge: Cambridge University Press.

Whalley, J. and Brown, F. (1980) 'General equilibrium evaluations of tariff cutting proposals in the Tokyo Round and comparisons with more extensive liberalization of world trade', *Economic Journal*.

Whalley, J. and Yeung, B. (1984) 'External sector closing rules in applied general equilibrium models', *Journal of International Economics* 16: 123–38.

Wigle, R. and Whalley, J. (1988) 'Endogenous participation in agricultural support programs and *ad valorem* equivalent modelling', Working paper 2583, National Bureau of Economic Research.

32

MICROECONOMETRICS

RICHARD BLUNDELL

32.1 INTRODUCTION

The need for familiarity with microeconometric techniques in applied economics has arisen as a result of the increasing use of individual-level data sources in the analysis of economic behaviour. This not only reflects the growing availability of such data but also our increasing ability, as applied economists, to utilize microlevel data sources effectively on microcomputers. Whether it be the study of household behaviour or the study of firms' behaviour, analysis based at the 'individual' level is persuasive. It avoids the problem of aggregation bias as well as identifying the factors that lead to a different distribution and usage of resources across households and firms. However, in microeconometrics distinct issues relating to endogenous selection, censoring and individual heterogeneity have to be faced. Indeed, it may often be difficult to draw useful inferences from cross-section data, especially where history dependence or state dependence is important. Longitudinal data or panel data which follow individual economic agents through time can be utilized so as to avoid some of these drawbacks, and in addition panel data combine the attractive features of time series analysis with individual-level behaviour. Our purpose in this chapter is to provide the applied economist with sufficient background on modern microeconometrics to choose appropriate estimators so as to exploit both the data source and the economic model.

It is as important to be aware of the limitations of some microeconometric techniques as it is to acknowledge their usefulness. Microeconometric estimators are typically not robust to changes in what may be termed 'incidental' assumptions. For example, normality of preference and measurement errors

This chapter has benefited enormously from courses taught jointly with Manuel Arellano and Mark Stewart. My colleagues Costas Meghir and Richard Smith also deserve special thanks, although none of the above can be held responsible for errors herein. Finance from the Economics and Social Research Council under projects B0023 2150 and B0023 2307, under which many of these ideas were developed, is gratefully acknowledged.

may not be central to the economic hypothesis under investigation but may well be critical for consistent estimation of its parameters using commonly available econometric techniques. In general, since many microeconometric models are rendered necessarily non-linear through selectivity or censoring, stochastic assumptions become critically important. As a result many recent developments have focused on weakening the reliance on parametric distributions and have sought to utilize semiparametric or non-parametric estimators (see, for example, Manski 1975, 1989, 1990; Heckman 1990; Newey *et al.* 1990). These developments are important but have not yet become common practice in applied econometrics, and as there is still a strong reliance in applied microeconometrics on estimators whose properties rest on parametric assumptions, this is the area on which we shall focus in this chapter. Moreover, there does now exist a well-developed battery of easily implementable diagnostic tests which will provide some indication of model reliability.

Our discussion of microeconometrics will be split three ways. To some extent this will reflect the different areas of development in microeconometrics but, perhaps more accurately, it identifies the different types of data available in microeconometric research. The first area of analysis will be on discrete choice models. These models usually reflect the discreteness of decisions made at the individual level but may also reflect discreteness in data collection. For example, whether or not a company issues shares and whether or not an adult decides to enter the labour market reflect discrete decisions. Quite naturally, the microeconometric approach to modelling these data would begin by associating probabilities with each outcome and looking to economics to suggest factors which may influence the parameters of the distribution underlying these probabilities. Together with an assumption on the sampling method used to generate the data source, it is natural to move directly to the specification of a sample likelihood or joint distribution for the discrete outcomes. As a result, likelihood methods are more common in this area of microeconometrics, and the usefulness of distribution theory and of sampling techniques is more apparent.

Some of the issues that distinguish economic models from general statistical models are often pushed to the background in the discussion of microeconometrics. Two such aspects of behaviour, which are rather central to applied economics, are simultaneity and state dependence. In standard discrete microeconometric models these are generally ignored and yet they are common features of most structural economic models. Introducing them is relatively complex and has only relatively recently become the focus of serious attention in econometrics. In dealing with these issues it is natural to consider models that mix discrete and continuous decisions. Indeed, such models will form the second area of microeconometrics which we shall analyse. As many microeconomic decisions, for example expenditure, hours of work, unemployment dur-

651

ation and earnings, involve both continuous and discrete outcomes, this second set of models lies at the heart of day-to-day microeconometric analysis. The continuity of part of the decision provides the analyst with considerably more information and is usually the subject of a more refined economic model. However, as the discrete decision is often inextricably tied to the continuous decision, these models are inherently non-linear and display possibly the most fragile features of microeconometrics.

Making discrete or mixed continuous-discrete models dynamic is quite challenging, and as a result truly dynamic microeconometric models, i.e. those using panel data, have typically not incorporated discrete or censored decisions. In so far as they quite clearly should move towards the incorporation of these non-linearities there is evidence in the recent microeconometrics literature of a coming together of all these areas. However, in this chapter we have decided to treat dynamic models and panel data analysis separately in Section 32.4.

There are many textbooks and references that cover parts of the material in this chapter. By far the most useful references are the books by Madalla (1983), Hsiao (1986), Gourieroux (1989) and Pudney (1989). The first three cover available techniques, while Pudney presents a unique mixture of economic application and econometric technique, although discussion of panel data models is excluded. In addition to these references the chapters on microeconometric techniques in Chow (1983), as well as the many journal papers referred to in the discussion that follows, will prove useful.

32.2 DISCRETE CHOICE MODELS

Discrete choice models have a long history in applied economics. Their introduction into econometrics is most closely associated with the path-breaking work of McFadden (1973) in his development of the logit and multinomial logit models.[1] Initial work in this area, dating back to that of Tobin (1958), was hampered by the underlying non-linearity which is a distinguishing feature of much of what is usually labelled microeconometrics. Traditionally, econometrics had dealt with models that were attempting to explain the mean behaviour of continuous variables. At the microlevel, however, there was a growing need to model discrete behaviour effectively. For example, the empirical analysis of consumer behaviour was increasingly considering discrete decisions, like the ownership of durables and the choice of transport modes, rather than simply the aggregate demand for consumer goods. Similarly, at the firm level interest was focused on discrete hiring and firing decisions as well as on plant location and product choice which were naturally qualitative or discrete variables.

When the outcome of interest is discrete, knowledge of the mean of the underlying distribution alone is often of limited interest. The object of interest is more usually the probability of an outcome, given particular values for certain explanatory factors. Often such a model is set up so that it is the mean that varies exclusively with these explanatory factors. However, in relating discrete behaviour to such factors we are usually required not only to specify the mean (or median) function but also to make a complete statement of the probability distribution itself. This is necessary in order to associate a unique probability with any particular value taken by the mean function. Such distribution functions are non-linear and are generally written as integrals for which there is no explicit solution. The normal distribution which underlies the probit model would be such a case. One of the attractions of the logit model is that the distribution function can be solved explicitly. The log odds ratio in the logit case is, in fact, linear in the mean function.

Single discrete outcomes – binary models – are only occasionally the appropriate modelling framework. More often than not the outcomes can take on multiple discrete values. This may be because there are genuinely distinct discrete goods on offer, as in the case of transport mode or occupational choice. Alternatively, it may reflect some discrete packaging of the same good such as is the case for part-time versus full-time work. In the former situation a multinomial model is required, whereas in the latter an ordered model with the same underlying univariate distribution may be more appropriate. In the case of the multinomial model the extension of the logit is straightforward. In the multinomial logit model all log odds ratios remain linear in the explanatory factors relating to each pair of decisions. Other models, such as the probit model, only extend easily under independence. However, it is well known that the multinomial logit also makes strong assumptions on the independence across outcomes. This is often known as the assumption of independence from irrelevant alternativews (IIA). Yet, until the important recent work of McFadden (1989), discrete choice models that extend the option space with unrestricted dependence over more than three or four choices have been all but intractable.

Ordered discrete choice models often reflect the 'grouped' way in which the data are collected. For example, earnings data may be given in ranges. The main distinction across types of models in this case is whether the boundaries of the groups are given or not. Sometimes such boundaries would be meaningless, such as where the data referred to a ranking by individuals over some set of products. Where they are provided, the model becomes closer and closer to the standard regression model as the groups become smaller. Seeing the standard model as a limiting case of the grouped model will often prove helpful in what follows. Often the grouping occurs over a range of the variable of interest. For example, earnings data may be exactly available for those above the tax threshold, where accurate figures are required by the tax collection agency, but only available in grouped intervals below the threshold.

Such data would be termed censored data and the appropriate modelling framework is that which goes under the general title of limited dependent variable models to be dealt with more fully in the next section.

Binary choice models

In binary choice models the dependent variable y_i is a binary variable which takes the value unity if a certain option is chosen by individual i or a certain event occurs (and takes the value zero if not). The probability of the event is usually assumed to be a function of explanatory variables as follows:

$$P_i = \text{pr}(y_i = 1) = F(x_i'\beta) \qquad i = 1, \ldots, N \qquad (32.1)$$

where x_i is a k-vector of exogenous explanatory variables relating to the ith individual in the sample. The conditional expectation of y_i given x_i is simply equal to $F(x_i'\beta)$ in this case since the probability weighted sum of outcomes for y_i equals the probability P_i itself. For the present x_i will be assumed exogenous for the estimation of β, and as a result the parameters underlying the determination of x_i can be ignored in the estimation of β. Since F is required to lie in the interval $(0,1)$ and be increasing in $x_i'\beta$, natural choices for F will be cumulative distribution functions. For example, the cumulative normal distribution will be used for the probit model whereas the logistic distribution is chosen for the logit model. Despite these obvious choices the dominance of linear least squares methods in applied economics and the ease of computation for such methods has resulted in a substantial use of the linear probability model to which we first turn our attention.

The linear probability model

In the linear probability model the function F is taken to be the identity function resulting in the following probability rule:

$$\text{pr}(y_i = 1) = x_i'\beta \qquad (32.2)$$

which, as noted above, we shall often refer to as P_i. Since $E(y_i) = \text{pr}(y_i = 1)$, the model implies

$$y_i = x_i'\beta + e_i \qquad (32.3)$$

where $e_i = y_i - E(y_i)$ is a random variable with zero mean. This approach has an obvious appeal as it results in the familiar linear regression equation. However, estimation using least squares gives rise to a number of problems.

The distribution of e_i given x_i is not normal. Given x_i, e_i will have a discrete probability distribution such that e_i can take the values $1 - x_i'\beta$ and $-x_i\beta$ with probabilities P_i and $1 - P_i$ respectively. As a result the conventional standard errors, t statistics and R^2 will be biased. Moreover, $P_i = x_i'\beta$ can take values less than zero or greater than unity which renders the model rather unappealing on grounds of interpretation. Similarly, the predicted probability $P_i = x_i'\beta$, can lie outside the unit interval. Note that even if these could be constrained (by a modified estimation technique to lie inside the unit interval), values of x from outside the sample range could still generate predictions greater than unity or less than zero. In addition, the disturbances will be heteroscedastic. Indeed, from the distribution of e_i given above, the variance is simply

$$
\begin{aligned}
E(e_i^2|x_i) &= (1 - x_i'\beta)^2 P_i + (-x_i'\beta)^2(1 - P_i) \\
&= (1 - x_i'\beta)x_i\beta \\
&= P_i(1 - P_i)
\end{aligned}
\tag{32.4}
$$

Hence the variance is not constant across i and, in addition to biased standard errors, the ordinary least squares (OLS) estimates are not efficient.

The logit and probit models

Taking F in (32.1) to be the standard normal distribution function results in the probit model, while taking F to be the logistic distribution function results in the logit model. Thus, for the probit model,

$$
\operatorname{pr}(y_i = 1) = \left(\frac{1}{2\pi}\right)^{1/2} \int_{-\infty}^{x_i'\beta} \exp \frac{-\theta^2}{2} \, d\theta
\tag{32.5}
$$

whilst for the logit model we have

$$
\operatorname{pr}(y_i = 1) = [1 + \exp(-x_i'\beta)]^{-1}
\tag{32.6}
$$

While the logit (and probit) model can be justified as a smooth monotonic transformation of the real line $(-\infty, +\infty)$ into the unit interval $(0,1)$, there are also appealing theoretical arguments for its use. In particular, the logit model can result from utility maximization with stochastic utility function (McFadden 1973). Nevertheless, the strength of an apparently incidental assumption on the distribution cannot be ignored. Estimates should always be compared with results from less restrictive models (see, for example, Manski's (1975) maximum score estimator now available in LIMDEP). The advantage of the probit or logit model assumptions, if acceptable, is their complete parametric description of the whole probability distribution.

Estimation of logit and probit models using individual-level data

Having described the probability distribution for y_i it is natural to consider a maximum likelihood approach to estimation since this can be thought of as maximizing the joint distribution of the y_i conditional on x seen as a function of the unknown β parameters. Notice that, although we have had to specify the complete distribution function for each y_i, it is only a function of the β parameters. This is because both logistic and normal distributions are completely described by their mean and variance and, as we have seen, the variance can be arbitrarily scaled to unity. However, both distributions are symmetric about their mean, and if this were to be relaxed parameters reflecting higher-order moments of the distribution would be required. As it is, the probability distribution for any y_i is fully described by β alone, and as a result so is the joint distribution for any random sample represented simply by the product of these probabilities. Provided that the sample is not endogenously stratified (or selected) in some way, this result remains and the sample likelihood is given by

$$L = \prod_{i=1}^{N} (P_i)^{y_i} (1 - P_i)^{y_i} \tag{32.7}$$

where $P_i = F(x_i'\beta)$ and N is the sample size. The corresponding log likelihood is given by

$$\log L = \sum_i \{y_i \log[F(x_i'\beta)] + (1 - y_i) \log[1 - F(x_i'\beta)]\} \tag{32.8}$$

and the maximum likelihood estimator of β is the value that maximizes this expression. The β derivative of $\log L$ can be written as

$$\frac{\partial \log L}{\partial \beta} = \sum_i \left\{ \left[\frac{y_i}{F(x_i'\beta)} - \frac{1 - y_i}{1 - F(x_i'\beta)} \right] f(x_i'\beta)x_i \right\}$$

$$= \sum_i \frac{y_i - F(x_i'\beta)}{F(x_i'\beta)[1 - F(x_i'\beta)]} f(x_i'\beta)x_i \tag{32.9}$$

where f is the derivative of F and hence is the corresponding density function. The maximum likelihood estimator of β will be the solution of the implicit 'normal' equations: $\partial \log L/\partial \beta = 0$. Although, in general, such a solution will be unique, iterative methods are required to obtain the maximum likelihood estimator. These usually require special programs, although many are now available for microcomputers and maniframes (LIMDEP, TSP etc.)

In these models

$$E \frac{\partial^2 \log L}{\partial \beta \, \partial \beta'} = -\sum_{i=1}^{N} \frac{[f(x_i'\beta)]^2}{F(x_i'\beta)[1 - F(x_i'\beta)]} x_i x_i' \tag{32.10}$$

The negative of the inverse of this expression evaluated at the maximum likelihood estimator provides an estimate of the asymptotic variance–covariance matrix. This can be used to perform hypothesis tests on the structure of the discrete model and will be referred to further below.

The most obvious method of predicting y_i is to associate the most likely outcome with each data point. This can be achieved by adopting the rule

$$y_i = \begin{cases} 1 & \text{if } \hat{F}_i \geq \frac{1}{2} \\ 0 & \text{if } \hat{F}_i < \frac{1}{2} \end{cases} \qquad (32.11)$$

and counting the number of correct predictions for $y_i = 1$ and $y_i = 0$. Although this is common practice, these models are not designed to make individual predictions and are much better used to examine the expected outcome for any specific set of x. Since $\hat{F}_i$ is the estimated expected value of y_i given x_i, averaging the predicted values across relevant subsets of the data to check the actual and estimated proportions is much more informative. If, for example, only 20 per cent of the sample takes the value zero then, unless the model fits extremely well to each observation, the chances of finding more than a few predicted zeros would be low, despite the model's predicting well the average numbers of zeros for individuals in certain cells. Indeed, for the logit model the average prediction across the whole sample equals the true sample proportion.

In order to interpret these models it is useful to observe that

$$\frac{\partial p_i}{\partial x_j} = \beta_j f_i = \begin{cases} \beta_j P_i(1 - P_i) & \text{for the logit model} \\ \beta_j f[F^{-1}(P_i)] & \text{for the probit model} \end{cases}$$

In both cases the effect is largest at $P_i = \frac{1}{2}$ and tends to zero as P_i approaches zero or unity.

Multiple choice models and the independence of irrelevant alternatives assumption

In this section we shall focus attention on extensions to the logit mode. Bivariate and higher-order extensions to the probit model will be dealt with in the discussion of limited dependent variable models that follows. Consider the case of three alternatives, indexed 0,1,2 (the extension to more alternatives is straightforward). Then the probabilities are given by

$$P(y_i = j) = \frac{\exp(x'_{ji}\beta_j)}{1 + \exp(x'_{1i}\beta_1 + \exp(x'_{2i}\beta_2)} \qquad (32.12)$$

for $j = 1$ and $j = 2$ and $j = 3$ defined by

$$\sum_{j=0}^{2} P(y_i = j) = 1 \qquad \text{for each } i$$

Moreover,

$$\log \frac{P(y_i = j)}{P(y_i = 0)} = x'_{ji}\beta_j \qquad j = 1, 2 \qquad (32.13)$$

Examination of the theoretical underpinnings of this model reveals one important desirable feature and one important weakness.

Consider a stochastic utility function comprising the following systematic and random components

$$U_{ji} = S_{ji} + \varepsilon_{ji} \qquad j = 0, 1, 2 \tag{32.14}$$

where ε_{ji} represents the unobservable and random component of utility for choice j by individual i. It can be shown that this results in the multinomial logit model if and only if the ε_{ji} are independent and have extreme value (type 1) distributions.

The extreme value distribution has an important property: the maximum of a group of extreme value variates itself has an extreme value distribution. Models derived from utility theory using other distributions are in general far more complex and difficult to handle than the multinomial logit. However, the important weakness of the model is that it requires the assumption that the ε_{ji} are independent. As a result the model ignores any similarities among the alternatives. This is evident from expression (32.13) above.

Ordered-response models

In some situations the categories are ordered in some logical way. The latent variable model can be usefuly extended to this case where

$$y_i^* = x_i'\beta + \varepsilon_i \tag{32.15}$$

in which y_i^* is not observed but we know which of m categories it belongs to. These categories are intervals of the range of the continuous variable y^*. Suppose that these exhaust the real line and define

$$\lambda_0 < \lambda_1 < \lambda_2 \ldots < \lambda_m \tag{32.16}$$

with

$$\lambda_0 = -\infty \qquad \text{and} \qquad \lambda_m = +\infty$$

Then the observed variable is defined by

$$y_i = j \qquad \text{if } \lambda_{j-1} < y_i^* < \lambda_j \tag{32.17}$$

We can consider two distinct models within this framework. The first is the ordinal-level probit model. In this case y_i^* is an artificial variable. The λ_j ($j = 1, \ldots, m - 1$) are parameters of the model. If we assume $\varepsilon_i \sim N(0, \sigma^2)$, the scale of y_i^* and hence of the λ_j is arbitrary. Hence we can normalize by taking $\sigma^2 = 1$. This is appropriate since y^* has no 'real' units of measurement as we have

$$P(y_i = j) = P(\lambda_{j-1} < y_i^* < \lambda_j)$$
$$= P(\lambda_{j-1} - x_i'\beta < \varepsilon_i < \lambda_j - x_i'\beta) \qquad (32.18)$$
$$= F(\lambda_{j-1} - x_i'\beta) - F(\lambda_j - x_i'\beta)$$

Thus the log likelihood is given by

$$\log L = \sum_{i=1}^{n} \sum_{j=1}^{m} j_{ji} \log [(\lambda_j - x_i'\beta) - F(\lambda_{j-1} - x_i'\beta)] \quad (32.19)$$

in which j_{ji} is a binary indicator for the jth group.

The second class of models are those with a grouped dependent variable. This is the case considered in the useful paper by Stewart (1983) in which y_i^* is a real continuous variable, but the data set does not give the actual value of the variable, only which of a number of groups (or ranges) it falls in. The key differences from the ordered probit model is that the λ_j are now given constants (the ends of the ranges) rather than parameters of the model and σ^2 is identified. If we let $e_i \sim N(0, \sigma^2)$, then

$$p(y_i = j) = P(\lambda_{j-1} < y_i^* < \lambda_j)$$
$$= F\left(\frac{\lambda_j - x_i'\beta}{\sigma}\right) - F\left(\frac{\lambda_{j-1} - x_i'\beta}{\sigma}\right) \qquad (32.20)$$

and the log likelihood is given by

$$\log L = \sum_{i=1}^{n} \sum_{j=1}^{m} j_{ji} \log \left[F\left(\frac{\lambda_j - x_i'\beta}{\sigma}\right) - F\left(\frac{\lambda_{j-1} - x_i'\beta}{\sigma}\right) \right]$$

This is then maximized with respect to (β, σ).

32.3 LIMITED DEPENDENT VARIABLES AND ISSUES OF SAMPLE SELECTION

Censored or truncated observations for variables of particular interest to applied microeconomists are a common occurrence in cross-section data. Income variables, hours of work, hourly wage rates and commodity expenditures by households, as well as share issues and the buying of investment goods by firms, all generally display such features. In this section we shall explore practical techniques for estimating and interpreting econometric models where the dependent variable is censored or truncated. Illustrations will be drawn from some of the many recent applications, particularly those using UK microdata. Extensions of the standard 'Tobit' and 'truncated' models that have proved useful in applied research will be developed along with a discussion of some simple diagnostic tests of critical assumptions underlying the standard and more general models.

659

The Tobit model and estimation using censored data

Censored data occur frequently in applied economics. Hours of work for a sample including non-workers, expenditures on infrequently purchased durables and the share issues of firms are all examples. The common feature of such models is that a non-negligible proportion of any (random) sample will include censored observations. In all these examples the censoring point is zero and corresponds to non-workers, non-purchase and no share issues respectively for each case. Although the censoring is common to all these examples, it is by no means clear that a common model structure is applicable to all. Indeed, in what follows emphasis will be placed on the range of possible models available and the importance of choosing the appropriate model for the economic application at hand.

Each model for any censored data source begins by specifying a latent regression model. Typically, this will describe the model specification in the absence of censoring. For example, we can follow the standard linear regression framework and describe the latent dependent variable y_i^* according to

$$y_i^* = x_i'\beta + u_i \qquad u_i \sim N(0, \sigma^2) \tag{32.21}$$

where x_i is a k-vector of exogenous explanatory factors and β is the corresponding parameter vector for each individual $i = 1, \ldots, N$. As in the probit model a normality assumption is made on the latent error structure. As also is the case in the probit model this assumption is critical to the asymptotic properties of the estimators described below. Indeed, the constant variance assumption underlying (32.21) will also turn out to be necessary to generate the usual properties.

The different types of censoring models are distinguished by the observability of rule on y_i. The simplest of these, and by far the most popular, is the Tobit model for which the censoring rule has the form

$$y_i = \begin{cases} y_i^* & \text{if } y_i^* > 0 \\ 0 & \text{if } y_i^* \leq 0 \end{cases} \tag{32.22}$$

In this case y_i^* is observed when $x_i'\beta + u_i$ exceeds zero. For example, if this is a model of desired consumption, the individual i is observed to buy when desired consumption of the good is positive. In microeconomic terms the Tobit model describes behaviour at a corner solution. Many examples of censored data do not correspond to a corner solution – the infrequency model of purchasing durables and the fixed-cost model of labour supply are two good examples. However, the Tobit model provides the ideal framework for considering the econometric issues which arise in this censored data framework.

Estimation of β must account for the censoring in the data. An OLS regression of y_i on x_i would produce a biased estimate of β. Indeed, the bias would be towards zero for the slope parameters. As a result OLS estimates can be shown to underestimate the impact of response coefficients. This is easy to recognize since the presence of a bunching of values for y_i at zero can be seen to 'pull' the regression line towards the horizontal axis. Eliminating the zero values for y, and estimating on the remaining *truncated* data set is no better. In this case the regression line is also biased toward the horizontal axis. Observations with low values for x, but high positive realizations for u_i remain in the sample, while individuals with similar x characteristics but negative realizations for u_i are eliminated since their corresponding y_i^* is negative and, as a result, y_i is zero. The mean of u_i, given y_i positive, is therefore also positive and positively correlated with $x_i\beta$.

If we order the observations such that the first N_1 refer to individuals with y_i positive, then the OLS estimator over the truncated sample is simply

$$\hat{\beta} = \beta + \left(\sum_{i=1}^{N_1} x_i x_i' \right)^{-1} \sum_{i=1}^{N_1} x_i u_i \tag{32.23}$$

The bias is therefore given by

$$E(\hat{\beta}) = \beta + \left(\sum_{i=1}^{N_1} x_i x_i' \right)^{-1} \sum_{i=1}^{N_1} x_i E(u_i \mid y_i > 0) \tag{32.24}$$

under the assumed exogeneity of x_i. The extent of the OLS bias therefore rests on the size of the term $E(u_i \mid y_i > 0)$. This is easily evaluated using $y_i = x_i\beta + u_i$ to write

$$E(u_i \mid y_i > 0) = E(u_i \mid u_i > -x_i'\beta)$$

$$= \sigma E\left(\varepsilon_i \mid \varepsilon_i > -\frac{x_i'\beta}{\sigma} \right) \quad \text{where } \varepsilon_i = \frac{u_i}{\sigma}$$

$$= \sigma \frac{\phi(z_i)}{1 - \Phi(z_i)} \tag{32.25}$$

where $z_i = -x_i'\beta/\sigma$ and ϕ and Φ are the standard normal density and distribution functions, respectively. The ratio term following σ in the above expression is simply the mean of a standard normal distribution function truncated from below at z_i. It can be found in most statistics textbooks. It is often termed the hazard ratio or inverse Mill's ratio since it measures the conditional expectation of individual i with characteristics x_i remaining in the sample after truncation. We shall summarize the above result by writing

$$E(u_i \mid y_i > 0) = \sigma \lambda_i \tag{32.26}$$

where λ_i represents the normal hazard ratio as in (32.25). The OLS bias from a truncated regression now depends on the extent to which λ_i differs from zero. This clearly happens when $x_i'\beta$ tends to infinity, i.e. when the chance of truncation is low.

In order to avoid these biases the direct use of OLS has to be dropped. However, we shall show that least squares algorithms can be derived to achieve consistent and efficient estimates. To derive the sample likelihood for the Tobit model it will be useful to define a dummy variable reflecting the incidence of the censoring. Thus we define

$$D_i = \begin{cases} 1 & \text{if } y_i^* > 0 \\ 0 & \text{otherwise} \end{cases} \tag{32.27}$$

The probability that y_i^* is positive is simply the probability that $D_i = 1$ and is given by $\Phi(x_i'\beta/\sigma)$. However, for positive observations and in contrast with the probit model, y_i^* is observed. As a result the actual normal density function, which we label f_i, enters as the contribution to the likelihood by observation i. For observations below the censoring point y_i^* is not observed and the probability $\text{pr}(D_i = 0)$ enters instead. The sample likelihood from a random sampling scheme therefore has the form

$$L = \prod_{i=1}^{N} (f_i)^{D_i} \left[1 - \Phi\left(\frac{x_i'\beta}{\sigma}\right) \right]^{1-D_i} \tag{32.28}$$

where $\Phi(\ )$ is the standard normal cumulative distribution as before. The likelihood function of the Tobit model is a mixture of density and distribution functions.

The additional information on the positive observations used in the Tobit model in comparison with the probit model can be seen to bring rewards. The parameter σ is now indentified since the units of y_i now bear some economic meaning and are not invariant to scale. Moreover the interpretation of the model parameters requires more care. The probability of an uncensored observation is given by

$$\text{pr}(y_i > 0) = \Phi\left(\frac{x_i'\beta}{\sigma}\right) \tag{32.29}$$

and

$$\frac{\partial \Phi_i}{\partial x_{ij}} = \phi\left(\frac{x_i'\beta}{\sigma}\right) \frac{\beta_j}{\sigma} \tag{32.30}$$

Further, the conditional expectation is given by

$$E(y_i | y_i > 0) = x_i'\beta + \sigma\lambda_i \tag{32.31}$$

The derivative of the conditional expectation is therefore

$$\frac{\partial E(y_i | y_i > 0)}{\partial x_{ij}} = \beta_j - \beta_j \lambda_i \frac{x_i' \beta}{\sigma} + \lambda_i \qquad (32.32)$$

and not simply β_i. The unconditional expectation may be decomposed as

$$E(y_i) = E(y_i | y_i > 0) \, P(y_i > 0)$$

or, taking logarithms, by

$$\log[E(y_i)] = \log[E(y_i | y_i > 0)] + \log\left[\Phi\left(\frac{x_i' \beta}{\sigma}\right)\right] \qquad (32.33)$$

so that a total elasticity of a change in an x_{ij} has the following useful decomposition property:

$$e_{ij} = e_{ij}^c + e_{ij}^P \qquad (32.34)$$

A simple least squares iterative procedure is available (Fair 1977) and is closely related to the EM algorithm (Chow 1983). For example, the first-order conditions for maximizing (32.28) can be written

$$\sigma^2 = \frac{1}{N_1} \sum_{i=1}^{N} D_i(y_i - x_i' \beta) y_i \qquad (32.35)$$

and

$$\sum_{i=1}^{N} D_i \, x_i x_i' \beta = \sum_{i=1}^{N} D_i x_i y_i + \sigma \sum_{i=0}^{N} (1 - D_i) x_i \tilde{\lambda}_i \qquad (32.36)$$

where $\tilde{\lambda}_i$ is simply the hazard corresponding to those censored observations and is given by

$$\tilde{\lambda}_i = - \frac{\phi(z_i)}{\Phi(z_i)} \qquad (32.37)$$

The first-order conditions for β can be conveniently rewritten as

$$\beta = \left(\sum_{i=1}^{N} x_i x_i' \right)^{-1} \sum_{i=1}^{N} x_i \tilde{y}_i \qquad (32.38)$$

with

$$\tilde{y}_i = \begin{cases} y_i & \text{for } D_i = 1 \\ x_i' \beta + \tilde{\lambda}_i & \text{otherwise} \end{cases}$$

Together (32.37) and (32.38) specify a two-step least squares iterative technique.

663

It is also easy to derive an expression for the bias in the least squares estimator $\hat{\beta}$. We can write

$$E(\hat{\beta}) = \left(\sum x_i x_i'\right)^{-1} \sum x_i \, E(y_i) \tag{32.39}$$

but also note that

$$E(y_i) = \Phi\left(\frac{x_i'\beta}{\sigma}\right) x_i'\beta + \sigma\phi\left(\frac{x_i'\beta}{\sigma}\right) \neq x_i'\beta \tag{32.40}$$

from (32.29) and (32.31). Under certain normality assumptions Goldberger (1981) and Green (1981) derive the useful result

$$\text{plim}(\hat{\beta}) = \Phi\left(\frac{\beta_0}{\sigma_y}\right)\beta \tag{32.41}$$

Since the ratio of non-limit to total observations provides a consistent estimator for Φ, the inverse of this ratio provides a suitable (asymptotic) adjustment for the least squares slope parameters.

The selectivity model, the double-hurdle model and other extensions to the Tobit model

Before describing in detail the many useful extensions to the Tobit model that have been developed in recent years for dealing with more general forms of censoring, it is worth briefly considering the truncated regression model. In this model the censored observations are missing so that a selection rule of the following form operates:

$$y_i = \begin{cases} y_i^* & \text{if } y_i^* > 0 \\ \text{not observed} & \text{if } y_i^* \leq 0 \end{cases} \tag{32.42}$$

Clearly it is not necessary that the truncations point be at zero.

When the notation developed for the Tobit model is used, the likelihood function for a truncated sample is simply the product of conditional densities

$$L = \prod_{i=1}^{N_1} \frac{f(y_i)}{1 - \Phi(z_i)} \tag{32.43}$$

and similar iterative techniques to those adopted for the Tobit model are available. In the Blundell and Walker (1982) model y_i is a vector of household decision variables for households with working wives. In this case (32.43) is preserved with $f(y_i)$ replaced by a joint density and the probability of 'truncation' Φ_i remains the same. The model is closely related to the switching regression model to be described below. The interpretation of estimated coefficients in the truncated model is clearly related to the derivative of the conditional expectation in (32.32).

Our first extension of the Tobit model is the popular selectivity model introduced formally into the econometrics literature by Heckman (1979). To describe this model we introduce a bivariate model in which

$$y_{1i}^* = x_{i1}'\beta_1 + u_{1i} \tag{32.44}$$

$$y_{2i}^* = x_{21}'\beta_2 + u_{2i} \tag{32.45}$$

In this model y_{1i}^* is observed if $y_{2i}^* > 0$. In this sense the model corresponds closely to the truncated model since the sample of observations on y_{1i} is a truncated example. In Heckman's example the first equation represented a wage equation while the variable y_{2i}^* defined a binary dependent variable describing the participation decision, i.e. the observability rule for y_1 is given by

$$y_{1i} = \begin{cases} 1 & \text{if } y_{2i}^* > 0 \\ 0 & \text{if } y_{2i}^* \le 0 \end{cases} \tag{32.46}$$

In principle y_{2i} replaces the D_i dummy of the Tobit model.

OLS estimation of the parameters determining y_1 from the truncated sample is, in general, biased in the same way as for the truncated model described earlier. Indeed, following our earlier discussion of least squares bias we can consider the conditional expectation

$$E(u_{1i} | y_{2i}^* \ge 0) = E\left(u_{1i} | u_{2i} \ge - \frac{x_{2i}'\beta_i}{\sigma_2} \right) \tag{32.47}$$

$$= \frac{\sigma_{12}}{\sigma_2} \lambda_{2i}$$

in which λ_{2i} has the same form as λ_i in the earlier expression. This is the common definition of selectivity bias.

The novelty of Heckman's (1979) paper is in the 'two-step' estimator he proposed. First ϕ_{2i} and Φ_{2i} are estimated by probit on (32.45) to form λ_{2i}, and then the 'selectivity-corrected' regression

$$y_{1i} = x_{i1}'\beta_1 + \frac{\sigma_{12}}{\sigma_2} \lambda_{2i} + \varepsilon_{2i} \tag{32.48}$$

is estimated on the selected sample by least squares. A t-test for $\sigma_{12}/\sigma_2 = 0$ is an asymptotically optimal test of selectivity bias as shown by Melino (1982)

Although attractive, the selectivity model takes a large step from the Tobit model since it acts as if y_{1i}^* has no impact on its own selection except indirectly through a correlation with y_{2i}^* through the σ_{12} term in (32.48). This would seem to be appropriate for many cases where either y_1 is not well defined outside the selected sample or its lower limit is unknown – such as the general fixed costs of work model introduced by Cogan (1981). Its importance in microeconometric models of labour supply has been shown conclusively by Mroz (1987).

In certain cases, durable expenditures for example, y_{2i} may well be better used to describe an additional 'hurdle' omitted in the Tobit model, possibly reflecting credit availability in our durable good example. However, it may be unnecessary to drop the Tobit observability rule altogether. This is the case of the double-hurdle model introduced by Cragg (1971).

In this model the observability rule for the selectivity model is replaced by y_{1i}^* observed if y_{1i}^* and y_{2i}^* are both positive. Two 'hurdles' determine observability and we once more define a dummy variable $D_i = 1$ when y_1^* is observed. The probability of $D_i = 1$ is now the probability of the joint event describing the observability rule. If we define Φ_{1i} to represent the cumulative standard normal evaluated at $x'_{1i}\beta/\sigma_1$ and Φ_{2i} to represent the corresponding distribution function describing the conditional distribution of u_{2i} conditional on u_{1i}, the sample likelihood has the form

$$L = \prod_{i=1}^{N} (f_i\Phi_{2i})^{D_i} (1 - \Phi_{1i}\Phi_{2i})^{(1-D_i)} \qquad (32.49)$$

It is interesting to note that this approaches the Tobit model as $\Phi_{2i} \to 1$. The double-hurdle model therefore serves as a useful extension to the Tobit model, removing the assumption of 'reservation price or wage' behind many of the applications of that model. A useful restriction in estimation is the independence of u_{2i} and u_{1i}. However, in most applications this would seem unlikely and should at least be tested.

A further extension to the standard model is the switching regressions model. In this model the observability rule is given by

$$\begin{array}{lll} y_{1i}^* & \text{observed if} & D_i = 1 \\ y_{2i}^* & \text{observed if} & D_i = 0 \end{array} \qquad (32.50)$$

where D_i in this case is some binary dependent variable determined by an underlying normal latent regression model

$$D_i^* = x'_{3i}\beta_3 + u_{3i} \qquad \text{with } u_{3i} \sim N(0,1) \qquad (32.51)$$

There exist two-step estimation methods which are similar to Heckman's two-step method in the selectivity model. The parameters of (32.51) are estimated by probit and a selectivity adjustment is constructed so that the least squares technique can be used on the selected samples observed by the selection rule (32.50). For example, (32.44) can be rewritten as

$$y_{1i} = x'_{1i}\beta_1 + \frac{\sigma_{13}}{\sigma_3} \lambda_{3i} + \varepsilon_{3i} \qquad \text{for } D^*_{3i} > 0 \qquad (35.52)$$

Given an estimate λ_{3i} from the probit model for (32.51), least squares will provide consistent estimates of β_i and σ_{13}/σ_3 in (32.52).

On the other hand, the sample likelihood is given by

$$L = \prod_{i=1}^{N} \left(\int_{-x'_3\beta_3}^{\infty} g(y_{1i}, \xi_i) \, d\xi_i \right)^{D_i} \left(\int_{\infty}^{-x'_{3i}\beta_3} g(y_{2i}, \xi_i) \, d\xi_i \right)^{1-D_i} \qquad (32.53)$$

where g is the bivariate normal density. This expression is considerably simplified by writing g as the product of conditional and marginal distribution so that

$$\int_{-x'_{3i}\beta_3}^{\infty} g(y_{1i}, \xi_i) \, d\xi_i = f(y_{1i}) \int_{-x'_{3i}\beta}^{\infty} f(\xi_i | y_{1i}) \, d\xi_i \qquad (32.54)$$

as in the discussion of the double-hurdle likelihood. Where there are restrictions across parameters in β_1, β_2 and γ, as in King (1980), maximum likelihood would seem most appropriate. This model is also closely related to 'disequilibrium' models which permit endogenous choice of regime.

Diagnostic tests

A common characteristic of the models discussed above is the importance of the complete specification of the underlying probability distribution. This is a result of the censoring and selection rules underpinning the model specifications, and is in direct contrast with the general linear model in which the asymptotic properties of the estimators are generally invariant to the exact error distribution. Consistency in the Tobit model and its generalizations depends critically on the correctness of the assumed normal/constant variance assumption. Models that work with more general distributional assumptions are, in general, difficult to estimate and as a result *diagnostic tests* against misspecification have been developed. These should be used alongside the recent move to non-parametric and semi-parametric estimation of such models (see, for example, the important work of Powell (1989), Heckman (1990), Manski (1990) and Newey *et al.* (1990). Since estimation under the alternative is difficult, diagnostic tests have been developed within the class of score or Lagrange multiplier (LM) tests which are as efficient (asymptotically) as the more usual likelihood ratio or Wald tests but do not require estimation under the alternative hypothesis.

Score tests developed for the standard linear model (for example, Breusch and Pagan 1980; Chow 1983: ch. 9) can be simply extended for the models considered here. All tests can be based on residual analysis and for limited or discrete dependent variable models these are simply replaced by generalized residuals (see Jaque and Bera 1982; Chesher and Irish 1987; Gourieroux *et al.* 1987). See also the attractive χ^2 tests of Andrews (1988a,b).

Residual techniques have also proved useful for the analysis of simultaneity and exogeneity in Tobit models and the like. For the simple recursive model, Blundell and Smith (1986) have developed a test asymptotically equivalent to the LM test. If an element of x_i (say x_{ji}) is considered possibly endogenous with reduced form

$$x_{ji} = \Pi_j' z_{ji} + v_{ji} \qquad (32.55)$$

then entering the least squares residuals from (32.55) in the Tobit model (or similar models such as selectivity, probit, truncated etc.) as an additional regressor provides consistent estimates of the parameters under simultaneity, and a t-test on the coefficient of the residual provides an asymptotically optimal test of simultaneity or exogeneity of x_{ji}.

32.4 PANEL DATA

Panel data are cross-section data that have been pooled over time where the *same* individual agents are followed through time. Company or firm data are a good illustration of this, and a common feature of such data sets is that, whereas the number N of agents (firms or households) is large, the number T of time periods is relatively small. For example, we may have in excess of 400 firms in each company cross-section but only twelve or thirteen annual observations on each.

A number of attractive features of such data immediately suggest themselves. Time series or temporal analysis can be explored without suffering the aggregation bias common in 'macroeconometric' studies. Moreover, the consistency of the estimated parameters can often be proved for fixed T provided that the cross-section dimension is 'large'. Features common to individual firms across time but which differ across firms in any time period can be relatively easily eliminated, thus removing much of the importance of modelling unobservables which makes analysis on single cross-sections so difficult. This is particularly true where firm- or individual-specific unobservables are correlated with included regressors. Most importantly perhaps, panel data allow the analyst to exploit the large variation in circumstance of different individuals in any cross-section while still recovering temporal effects in behaviour.

As an illustration of this we can imagine investigating the relationship between taxation and investment behaviour. Clearly, this process is dynamic and there are many features of adjustment costs etc. that are specific to individual firms or companies. To examine the nature of these effects we need to follow individual firms through time. Equally, however, firms face very different tax positions (tax exhaustion for example) and very different product market structures. Across-firm variation is therefore necessary to pin down accurately the separate impact of capital taxation, for example, from other influences on investment expenditures.

As in nearly all applied econometrics, information improvements in the data set, for example moving from single cross-sections to panel data sets, bring with them some disadvantages. Although these in no way outweigh the usefulness of panel data they do raise some important statistical issues. The primary concerns for our purposes are attrition and non-randomness of the sample. These two problems, are, of course, related. Attrition occurs when individual firms leave the panel. Where this happens randomly, there is only a loss of information and efficiency. Where it happens non-randomly or endogenously, serious econometric difficulties may occur (Hausman and Wise 1979) and clearly call for the use of selection correction estimators of the type introduced in Section 32.3. Whichever way attrition occurs and even if there is no attrition, a changing structure of the population of individuals or firms over time may result in the panel data's losing their representativeness and becoming non-random as time proceeds.

Models for panel data

One important aspect of panel data analysis is the decision of whether or not to pool the data across individuals or firms. To consider this we begin with the simplest of linear models

$$y_{it} = \alpha_i + \beta_i x_{it} + u_{it} \qquad \text{for } i = 1, \ldots, N, \, t = 1, \ldots, T \qquad (32.56)$$

Where N is the number of firms in each cross-section and T is the number of time periods. In practice, T may differ across individuals or firms, i.e. reflecting births and deaths of firms. Such a sample is called an unbalanced sample. for the purposes of our discussion we shall retain the balanced panel assumption.

Notice that in (32.56) both intercept and slope parameters are allowed to differ across firms, and to begin we shall consider a test of parameter constancy across firms. This is often referred to as a pooling test, although we may wish to pool in order to exploit parameter constancy across a subset of the parameters. To begin with we shall assume that each u_{it} is normally distributed and derive an F test of parameter constancy. If we define the within-group sums of squares as

$$W_{xxi} = \sum_t (x_{it} - \bar{x}_i)^2 \tag{32.57}$$

$$W_{xyi} = \sum_t (x_{it} - \bar{x}_i)(y_{it} - \bar{y}_i) \tag{32.58}$$

$$W_{yyi} = \sum_t (y_{it} - \bar{y}_i)^2 \tag{32.59}$$

where $\bar{x}_i$ and $\bar{y}_i$ are the firm i specific means of x_{it} and y_{it} respectively, then the estimates of α_i and β_i are given by

$$a_i = \bar{y}_i - b_i \bar{x}_i \tag{32.60}$$

$$b_i = (W_{xxi})^{-1} W_{xyi} \tag{32.61}$$

The regression residual sum of squares in this single-regressor case is again simply

$$\text{RSS}_i = W_{yyi} - (W_{xxi})^{-1}(W_{xyi})^2 \tag{32.62}$$

If we define $\bar{x}$ and $\bar{y}$ to be the means on the total pooled sample and correspondingly define

$$T_{xx} = \sum_i \sum_t (x_{it} - \bar{x})^2 \tag{32.63}$$

$$T_{xy} = \sum_i \sum_t (x_{it} - \bar{x})(y_{it} - \bar{y}) \tag{32.64}$$

$$T_{yy} = \sum_i \sum_t (y_{it} - \bar{y})^2 \tag{32.65}$$

then the estimates under the pooling restriction are given by

$$a = \bar{y} - b\bar{x} \tag{32.66}$$

and

$$b = (T_{xx})^{-1} T_{xy} \tag{32.67}$$

In this case the residual sum of squares can be expressed as

$$\text{RSS} = T_{yy} - (T_{xx})^{-1}(T_{xy})^2 \tag{32.68}$$

which we might wish to compare with the residual sum of squares from the unrestricted regressions

$$\text{RSS}_u = \sum_i \text{RSS}_i \tag{32.69}$$

Since RSS_u has $TN - 2N$ degrees of freedom and RSS has $TN - 2$ degrees of freedom the appropriate F ratio statistic for constancy of all α_i and β_i across firms is

$$F = \frac{(\text{RSS} - \text{RSS}_u)/(2N - 2)}{\text{RSS}_u/(TN - 2N)} \tag{32.70}$$

As we shall see, of rather more interest may be a test of constancy of each β_i since allowing α_i to vary across firms is not difficult to handle and will be shown to be equivalent to the popular fixed-effect model. In this case the regression model under the null hypothesis is simply

$$y_{it} = \alpha_i + \beta x_{it} + u_{it} \tag{32.71}$$

in which case estimates of each α_i are given by

$$\alpha_i^* = \bar{y}_i - \beta^* \bar{x}_i \tag{32.72}$$

and

$$\beta^* = (W_{xx})^{-1} W_{xy} \tag{32.73}$$

where

$$W_{xy} = \sum_i \sum_t x_{it} (y_{it} - \bar{y}_i) \tag{32.74}$$

and

$$W_{xx} = \sum_i \sum_t x_{it} (x_{it} - \bar{x}_i) \tag{32.75}$$

This is commonly known as the dummy variable regression model (or fixed-effect model). In production function studies, for example, where y is output and x is input, α_i may represent the managerial input that is specific to the ith firm. β^* is then an estimate of the production function parameters free from managerial input bias. The test of this model is simply an F test as before where RSS is replaced by the appropriate RSS for model (32.71) given by

$$\text{RSS}^* = W_{yy} - (W_{xx})(W_{xy}) \tag{32.76}$$

and where the numerator degrees of freedom are replaced by $N - 1$.

Historically, the most popular model for panel data has been the variance components model. The most usual form for this type of model is where the individual effect α_i in (32.56) is written as $\alpha_i = \tau_i + \alpha^0$ and τ_i is assumed to be random across individuals and distributed independently of x_i. More specifically we write

$$y_{it} = \alpha_0 + \beta x_{it} + \tau_i + u_{it} \tag{32.77}$$

where

$$E(\tau_i) = E(u_{it}) = 0$$

$$\text{cov}(\tau_i \tau_i) \quad = \sigma_\tau^2 \qquad \text{for } i = j$$

$$\quad = 0 \qquad \text{otherwise}$$

$$\text{cov}(u_{it}, u_{js}) \quad = \sigma_u^2 \qquad \text{for } i = j, t = s$$

$$\quad = 0 \qquad \text{otherwise}$$

$$\text{cov}(\tau_i, u_{js}) \quad = 0 \qquad \text{all } i, j \text{ and } s$$

This produces correlation between residuals across time since

$$\text{cov}(\varepsilon_{it}, \varepsilon_{is}) = \begin{array}{ll} \sigma_u^2 + \sigma_\tau^2 & \text{for } t = s \\ \sigma_\tau^2 & \text{otherwise} \end{array}$$

Clearly, such a model requires generalized least squares (GLS) estimation but this can be achieved in a very simple manner by writing

$$\beta^+ = \frac{W_{xy} + \theta B_{xy}}{W_{xx} + \theta B_{xx}} \tag{32.78}$$

where

$$\theta = \frac{\sigma_u^2}{\sigma_u^2 + T\sigma_\tau^2}$$

and W refers to within-group moments as described above and B refers to the between-group moments

$$B_{xx} = T_{xx} - W_{xx}$$
$$B_{xy} = T_{xy} - W_{xy}$$
$$B_{yy} = T_{yy} - W_{yy}$$

Interestingly, the estimator reduces to the OLS estimator

$$b = (T_{xx})^{-1}T_{xy}$$

when $\theta = 1$ and the fixed-effect or dummy variable model estimator

$$\beta^* = (W_{xx})^{-1}W_{xy}$$

when $\theta = 0$. For obvious reasons β^* is also known as the within-groups (WGG) estimator. Clearly β^+ throws away much less cross-section variation than β^*, especially when B_{xx}, B_{xy} and B_{yy} are large relative to W_{xx}, W_{xy} and W_{yy}, and is as a result generally more efficient. However, β^+ requires each τ_i to be independent of x_i. Such correlated fixed effects can be expected to be quite common in applied economics and thus this presents a severe drawback for the GLS estimator.

Random versus fixed effects and specification tests

Model (32.71) is a popular model for panel data and displays some of the distinct advantages of using even two or three 'waves' of panel data over a single cross-section. To see this imagine that the objective is to estimate (32.71) from a single cross-section. In this case we can write the model as

$$y_{it} = \alpha_0 + \beta x_{it} + \tau_i + u_{it} \qquad (32.79)$$

Since we have no time series data we may as well combine τ_i and u_{it} as our disturbance term ε_{it} and estimate the model

$$y_i = \alpha_0 + \beta x_i + \varepsilon_i \qquad (32.80)$$

for the $i = 1, \ldots, N$ cross-section observations recorded in period t.

Now ε_i and not u_i, which we have assumed above was distributed independently of x_i, represents the 'true' disturbance term. It also contains the individual specific effect τ_i which, although constant over time for firm i, could be distributed in a generally unrestricted way, i.e. in (32.80) all individual specific effects which are unobservable (u_{it} and τ_i) must be distributed independently of (or at least uncorrelated with) x_i. Moreover, in order to use F tests for hypotheses on β we need to assume normality of both u_{it} and τ_i.

With at least two repeated observations on each individual, τ_i can be taken into an individual-specific intercept and the model can be estimated using the dummy variable or WG estimator without the need to specify the exact distribution of α_i across firms. Indeed, although the number of α_i parameters increases with N, β^* will still be unbiased and large-N consistent.

A common practice is to estimate the first-differenced form of (32.79) given by

$$y_{it} - y_{it-1} = \beta(x_{it} - x_{it-1}) + v_{it} \qquad (32.81)$$

where $v_{it} = u_{it} - u_{it-1}$ which would be MA(1) with unit root if u_{it} was white noise. We shall return to the estimation of models of this form later, but for now it is sufficient to point that (32.81) removes the fixed effect by first-differencing, whereas the WG estimator (32.73) removes the fixed effect by subtracting group means as in (32.74) and (32.75).

To see the real loss from estimating the fixed-effect model we only need to introduce a set of important but non-time-varying regressors – for example, education, parental income etc. in earnings equations, and location, length of time in existence before first time period etc. in investment equations. To consider a specific model of this type we can write

$$y_{it} = \alpha_0 + \beta x_{it} + \delta z_i + \tau_i + u_{it} \qquad (32.82)$$

where the z_i vary across individuals alone. If we are unwilling to state anything about the distribution of τ_i, then eliminating the within-group mean will eliminate all that we can say about δ. The variance components model, on the other hand, assumes $E(\tau_i | x_{it}, z_i) = 0$ for all i and t. As suggested above, in many cases this is certainly a worrying assumption that should be tested. However, it does allow estimation of δ. As we noted above, whatever the correlation between α_i and z_i or x_{it}, the WG estimator β^* will be unbiased and large-N consistent.

673

A comparison between these two estimators provides an ideal test for the assumptions on τ_i necessary to make the GLS estimator β^* not only unbiased and consistent but also efficient. If we write

$$q = \beta^* - \beta^+ \tag{32.83}$$

then we can see that under the null that $E(\tau_i | x_{it}, z_i) = 0$, plim $q = 0$, whereas under the alternative this plim differs from zero since β^a is inconsistent. However, since

$$\text{var } q = \text{var } \beta^* - \text{var } \beta^+ \tag{32.84}$$

it is quite straightforward to derive a Hausman type test for this hypothesis.

An example of just this test and a comparison of the estimators involved is given in Table 32.1. This is reproduced from the study of earnings determination by Hausman and Taylor (1981). In this study the dependent variable is the log wage and $N = 750$. Only two years, four years apart, are used. It is clear from the $\chi^2(3)$ test that the assumptions underlying the GLS estimator are rejected, and by comparing columns GLS and WG there is evidence that experience and the individual effect τ_i are correlated. However, it is also clear that the move from GLS to WG eliminates our ability to identify the time-invariant effects of race, union and schooling.

Table 32.1 Wages and experience

	OLS	GLS	WG
Experience (it)	0.0132	0.0133	0.0241
	(0.0011)	(0.0017)	(0.0042)
Bad health (it)	−0.0843	−0.0300	−0.0388
	(0.0412)	(0.0363)	(0.0460)
Unemployed last year (it)	−0.0015	−0.0402	−0.0560
	(0.0267)	(0.0207)	(0.0295)
Race (i)	−0.0853	−0.0878	−
	(0.0328)	(0.0518)	
Union (i)	0.0450	0.0374	−
	(0.0191)	(0.0296)	
Years of schooling (i)	0.0669	0.0676	−
	(0.0033)	(0.0050)	

Specification test, $\chi^2(3) = 20.2$

Source: Hausman and Taylor 1981

Dynamic panel data models

A major advantage of having repeated observations over time is the ability to model dynamic response from microdata. The simplest model of this type could be written

$$y_{it} = \gamma y_{i(t-1)} + \tau_i + u_{it} \qquad i = 1, \ldots, N, \, t = 1, \ldots, T \tag{32.85}$$

The WG estimator of γ is OLS on the transformed equation

$$y_{it} - \bar{y}_i = \gamma(y_{it-1} - \bar{y}_{i,-1}) + u_{it} - \bar{u}_i$$

where the grouped means are constructed according to

$$\bar{u}_i = \frac{1}{T}(u_{i1} + \ldots + u_{iT})$$

as before. However, since in dynamic models of this type $y_{it-1} - \bar{y}_{i,-1}$ and $u_{it} - u_i$ are correlated, $\hat{\gamma}_{\text{WG}}$ will be biased even for large N when T is small.

The size of the asyptotic bias of the WG estimator is given by Nickell (1981) and takes the form

$$\plim_{N \to \infty} (\hat{\gamma}_{\text{WG}} - \gamma) = -\frac{(1 + \gamma)h(\gamma, T)}{T - 1}\left[1 - \frac{2\gamma h(\gamma, T)}{(T - 1)(1 - \gamma)}\right]^{-1}$$

where

$$h(\gamma, T) = 1 - \frac{1}{T}\left(\frac{1 - \gamma^T}{1 - \gamma}\right)$$

These are evaluated in Table 32.2 and display a strong downward bias for commonly found values of T.

Table 32.2 Asymptotic biases of the within-group estimator in an autoregresive model

T	$\gamma=0.05$	$\gamma=0.05$	$\gamma=0.95$
2	−0.52	−0.75	−0.97
3	−0.35	−0.54	−0.73
10	−0.11	−0.16	−0.26
15	−0.07	−0.11	−0.17

Source: Nickell 1981

Alternatively, the unobservable effect τ_i can be eliminated by taking first differences

$$y_{it} - y_{i(t-1)} = \gamma(y_{i(t-1)} - y_{i(t-2)}) + (u_{it} - u_{i(t-1)}) \qquad (32.86)$$

The OLS estimator $\tilde{\gamma}$ in this equation will also be biased, but the bias in this case will not tend to zero as $T \to \infty$ since

$$\plim_{N \to \infty} (\tilde{\gamma} - \gamma) = -\frac{1 + \gamma}{2}$$

A consistent estimator of γ, in the absence of serial correlation in u_{it}, is given by

$$\tilde{\gamma}_{IV} = \frac{\displaystyle\sum_{t=1}^{T}\sum_{i=1}^{N} (y_{i(t-2)} - y_{i(t-3)})(y_{it} - y_{i(t-1)})}{\displaystyle\sum_{t=1}^{T}\sum_{i=1}^{N} (y_{i(t-2)} - y_{i(t-3)})(y_{i(t-1)} - y_{i(t-1)})} \qquad (32.87)$$

which is equivalent to an instrumental variable regression on the first-differenced model that uses Δy_{-2} as the instrument for Δy_{-1}. This estimator was proposed by Anderson and Hsiao (1982). With serial correlation of a moving-average type, suitable lags of Δy can be chosen as instruments. When u_{it} it autoregressive the model should first be transformed so as to induce a moving-average error structure and then the instrumental variable estimator is appropriate.

The introduction of further explanatory factors in (32.85) does not change the essential arguments raised above. However, if these factors are strictly exogenous (i.e. future and past values are independent at u_{it}), then they can used as instruments in the WG or GLS model. When they are only weakly exogenous they must be treated like $y_{i(t-1)}$ and a first-differenced instrumental variable technique should be adopted.

There are, of course, many additional estimators that can be utilized in dynamic panel data models but these generally derive from those discussed above (Arellano and Bond 1988a, b). The important point to note is that the unobservable fixed effects (the τ_i) act like an autoregressive error term and, as a result, invalidate the use of standard least squares techniques on dynamic panel data models. The asymptotic bias shown in Table 32.2 gives some indication of how serious and misleading the use of inappropriate estimators can be. Moreover, it shows that in cross-section models where the history of the process matters (i.e. lagged dependent variables or state dependence), particular care should be paid when individual specific effects are likely to be present.

32.5 CONCLUSIONS

To provide anything but a glimpse into features that set microeconometrics apart from 'standard' econometrics in such a short space would be asking too much. However, it is important that applied economists are aware of available techniques in microeconometrics and are able to choose between them. These two criteria formed the motivation for this chapter. All the techniques covered in this discussion have been deliberately chosekn so that they are both simple and currently available for use on microcomputers. However, some of the important new developments in non-parametric and semiparametric estimation have been indicated. These are likely to become a central theme in microeconometrics over the coming years as the sensitivity of models to apparently innocent parametric assumptions becomes more widely acknowledged and understood.

NOTE

1 A useful historical background to the use of these models in psychometrics, biometrics and sociometrics is provided by McFadden (1982).

REFERENCES

Anderson, T. W. and Hsaio, C. (1981) 'Formulation and estimation of dynamic models using panel data', *Journal of Econometrics* 18: 570–606.

Andrews, D (1988a) 'Chi-Square diagnostic tests for econometric models: introduction and applications', *Journal of Applied Econometrics* 37: 135–56.

—— (1988b) 'Chi-square diagnostic tests for econometric models: theory', *Econometrica* 56 (6): 1419–53.

Arellano, M. and Bond, S. R. (1988a) 'Some tests of specification for panel data: Monte Carlo evidence and an application to employment equations', *Review of Economic Studies*, forthcoming.

—— and —— (1988b) 'Dynamic panel data estimation using DPD – a guide for users', Working paper 88/15, Institute for Fiscal Studies.

Blundell, R. W. and Smith, R. J. (1986) 'An exogeneity test for the simultaneous equation Tobit model', *Econometrica* 54: 679–85.

—— and Walker, I. (1982) 'Modelling the joint determination of household labour supplies and commodity demands', *Economic Journal* 351–64.

Breusch, T. S. and Pagan, A. R. (1980) 'The Lagrange multiplier test and its applications to model specification in econometrics', *Review of Economic Studies* 239–53.

Chesher, A. D. and Irish, M. (1987) 'Residuals and diagnostics for probit, tobit and related models', *Journal of Econometrics* 34: 33–61.

Chow, G. C. (1983) *Econometrics*, New York: McGraw-Hill.

Cogan, J. F. (1981) 'Fixed costs and labor supply', *Econometrica* 49: 945–64.

Cragg, J. G. (1971) 'Some statistical models for limited dependent variables with applications to the demand for durable goods', *Econometrica* 289–344.

Fair, R. C. (1977) 'A note on the computation of the Tobit estimator', *Econometrica* 1723–8.

Goldberger, A. S. (1981) 'Linear regression after selection', *Journal of Econometrics* 919–38.

Gourieroux, C. (1989) *Econometric des Variables Qualitative*, 2nd edn, Paris: Economica.

Gourieroux, C., Monfort, A., Renault, E. and Trognon, A. (1987) 'Generalised residuals', *Journal of Econometrics* 34: 5–32.

Green, W. H. (1981) 'On the asymptotic bias of the ordinary least squares estimator of the Tobit model', *Econometrica* 505–9.

Hausman, J. and Taylor, W. E. (1981) 'Panel data and unobservable individual effects', *Econometrica* 49: 1377–98.

Hausman, J. A. and Wise, D. A. (1979) 'Social experimentation, truncated distributions and efficient estimation', *Econometrica* 919–38.

677

Heckman, J. J. (1979) 'Sample selection bias as a specification error', *Econometrica* 153–61.
—— (1990) 'Varieties of selection bias', *American Economic Review* 80 (2): 313–18.
Hsiao, C. (1986) *Panel Data*, Cambridge: Cambridge University Press.
Jarque, C. M. and Bera, A. K. (1982) 'Efficient specification tests for limited dependent variable models', *Economic Letters* 153–60.
King, M. A. (1980) 'An econometric model of tenure choice and demand for housing as a joint decision', *Journal of Public Economics* 14 (2): 137–60.
McFadden, D. (1973) 'Conditional Logit analysis of qualitative choice behaviour', in P. Zarembka (ed.) *Frontiers in Econometrics*, New York: Academic Press.
—— (1982) 'Qualitative response models', in W. Hildenbrand (ed.) *Econometrics*, Econometric Society Monograph.
—— (1989) 'A method of simulated moments in estimation of multinomial probits without numerical integration', *Econometrica* 57: 995–1026.
Maddala, G. S. (1983) *Econometrics*, chs 9. 7–9. 10, New York: McGraw-Hill.
Manski, C. F. (1975) 'Maximum score estimation of the stochastic utility model of choice', *Journal of Econometrics* 3: 205–28.
—— (1989) 'Anatomy of the selection problem', *Journal of Human Resources* 24: 343–60.
—— (1990) 'Nonparametric rounds on treatment effects', *American Economic Review* 80 (2): 319–23.
Melino, A. (1982) 'Testing for sample selection bias', *Review of Economic Studies* 151–3.
Mroz, T. A. (1987) 'The sensitivity of an empirical model of married women's hours of work to economic and statistical assumptions', *Econometrica* 55: 765–800.
Newey, W. K., Powell, J. L. and Walker, J. R. (1990) 'Semiparametric estimation of selection models: some empirical results', *American Economic Review* 80 (2): 324–8.
Nickell, S. (1981) 'Bases in dynamic fixed effect models', *Econometrica* 1417–26.
Powell, J. (1989) 'Semiparametric estimation of censored selection models', unpublished manuscript, University of Wisconsin-Madison.
Pudney, S. (1989) *Modelling Individual Choice: The Econometrics of Corners, Kinks and Holes*, Oxford: Basil Blackwell.
Stewart, M. B. (1983) 'On least squares estimation when the dependent variable is grouped', *Review of Economic Studies* 50: 737–54.
Tobin, J. (1958) 'Estimation of relationships for limited dependent variables', *Econometrica* 24–36.

33

MACROECONOMETRIC FORECASTING

KENNETH HOLDEN

33.1 INTRODUCTION

In this chapter the development of the methods used in econometric forecasting are reviewed. First, the traditional approach is explained and some of the problems it poses are discussed. In Section 33.3 the various statistical methods of forecasting are reviewed and their links with economic modelling are considered. The different ways in which the accuracy of forecasts can be assessed are presented in Section 33.4, while the benefits from combining forecasts are the subject of Section 33.5. Conclusions are given in Section 33.6. Since Fildes (1988) gives a comprehensive summary of the organizations producing economic forecasts and conducting business surveys we do not consider these further here.

33.2 TRADITIONAL ECONOMETRIC MODELLING

The history of econometric forecasting goes back to the work of Tinbergen (1939) who is usually credited with constructing the earliest econometric models.[1] After the Second World War, the work of Klein and his various associates (for example, Klein and Goldberger 1955) led to the estimation of econometric models for the United States and most other industrialized countries. These models were used for *ex ante* forecasting and also for policy analysis.

The approach adopted in constructing these models has been referred to as 'traditional' econometric modelling and can be stylized as consisting of the following stages.

Many of the ideas discussed in this chapter are presented in more detail in Holden *et al.* (1990). The support of the Economic and Social Research Council under grant B01350033 is acknowledged, and thanks are due to K. C. Cleaver for comments on an earlier draft. The usual disclaimer applies.

1 Use the appropriate economic theory to decide which variables are of interest in explaining macroeconomic behaviour. These variables are then classified as those to be explained by the model (endogenous) and those to be taken as outside the model (exogenous).
2 Formulate the theory as a series of equations linking the variables together. This requires the choice of a unit time interval, decisions about the precise timing of the variables (so that leads and lags are chosen) and the use of some method of forming the expectational variables.
3 Obtain data on each of the variables. This involves relating the theoretical concepts to the available series.
4 Apply appropriate econometric techniques to the equations and the data to obtain numerical estimates of the parameters.
5 Examine the results to see whether they are satisfactory. If this is not the case, the earlier stages are repeated with appropriate changes until the results become satisfactory.
6 Given the estimated values of the parameters and projections of the future values of the exogenous variables, the future values of the endogenous variables can be forecast.

This statement of the traditional approach to econometric modelling helps to indicate some of the problems that occur when it is applied in particular circumstances. First, considering stage 1, there is no agreement amongst economists as to what the appropriate theory is in macroeconomics. There are many theoretical controversies which are unresolved, and even where there is general agreement on the framework (such as that income affects consumption) there is room for disagreement on the details (say, on how to define income and consumption). The choices of which variables are endogenous and which are exogenous are partly determined by the forecasting objectives, but again there is scope for disagreement between economists of different persuasions.

In stage 2, when economic relationships are formulated as equations, the linear (in parameters) form is usually chosen for convenience. To some extent this can be justified by reference to Taylor's theorem by which a non-linear function can be expanded as a power series with the first two terms giving the linear relationship and the higher-order terms, which make the relationship non-linear, being ignored. A disturbance term is included to reflect omitted (and, by implication, assumed to be unimportant) factors and/or to indicate the stochastic nature of the relationship so that it is typical, rather than individual, behaviour which is described. The choice of unit time period (usually a year, a quarter or a month) is generally affected by the availability of data, rather than by a consideration of what is the natural decision-making period for agents.[2] This also has implications for leads and lags since with annual data there is more scope for adjustment within the unit period than there is with quarterly or monthly data. The choice of lengths of leads and lags tends to be an empirical matter since economic theory has little specific to say on this. However, this is not so with the treatment of expectational variables where among the alternative theoretical approaches are the adaptive and rational methods for determining expectations, each of which has some basis in economic theory. As an alternative, it is sometimes possible to use survey data as direct measures of expectations.[3] Also, the role of policy variables should be considered at this point, bearing in mind the Lucas (1976) critique.

The data stage, stage 3, involves moving from theoretical concepts to observable values. Generally economists do not have the resources to collect data according to their own definitions and so have to rely on the data series compiled by official statisticians. Here there are problems in defining how theoretical concepts, like income, capital stock and consumption, relate to data collected for accounting or administrative purposes. There are doubts concerning the accuracy of data from sample surveys, the assumptions used in the compilation of index numbers, the impact of the hidden or 'underground' economy and the implications of aggregation. In some cases, published data are initially in a preliminary form and are then revised, possibly several times, before settling on a particular value which is presumably closer to the true value than the earlier estimates. Of course, series which are not revised are not necessarily accurate. These problems of data errors or 'errors in variables' should not be ignored and need to be treated explicitly.[4]

The estimation stage, stage 4, requires the use of suitable methods for obtaining numerical estimates of the unknown population parameters. Since econometric models involve systems of simultaneous equations, ordinary least squares (OLS) is not generally an appropriate estimation method. Instead, a single-equation method (such as two-stage least squares or instrumental variables estimation) or a systems method (such as three-stage least squares or full information maximum likelihood estimation) should be used. The problems here are that when there is uncertainty about the full specification of the model, so that several alternative formulations are consistent with the economic theory, the use of these methods can become time consuming, and the properties of the resulting estimators are not known for the relatively small sample sizes which are used.

In stage 5, the results of estimation are assessed to see whether they are acceptable. There are two aspects to this: the economic and the statistical. When economic theory is written in the form of equations a number of restrictions are imposed on the coefficients. These are mainly exclusion restrictions, by which other variables are given zero coefficients, and so included variables are expected to have non-zero coefficients. In some cases there will be an indication from the theory that the estimated coefficients should have particular signs, and in other cases there will be some idea of the numerical value of the coefficients. If the observed coefficients do not agree with the prior expectations, there is a major problem. Either the theory is wrong, and needs to be revised, or there are peculiarities in the data which have given perverse results, and these need to be corrected or overcome by using alternative data. With regard to the statistical aspect of the assessment, the coefficients on the included variables should all be significant, the overall explanatory power of the model should be acceptable and the assumptions underlying the estimation method (for example, an absence of autocorrelation and heteroscedasticity) should be valid. Some of the statistical tests, such as those for omitted variables, can indicate specification errors. Finally, the properties of the model as a whole can be examined by simulation methods. These can show the sensitivity of the model to small changes in the coefficients and also the short-run and long-run impact of changes in policy variables.

The conclusion that a model is inadequate usually leads to a reconsideration of the earlier stages in the procedure. A review of the economic theory can suggest alternative formulations involving different variables. Problems with the data can lead to the utilization of new information. The presence of autocorrelation or other violations of the assumptions can imply that different specifications or estimation methods should be used. Eventually this process of repeating stages 1–5 will result in a model which satisfies the main criteria of being consistent with the theory and accepted by the data.

In stage 6 – forecasting the future values of the endogenous variables – projections of the future values of the exogenous and poicy variables are needed. For the exogenous variables, some simple extrapolation method such as a univariate Box-Jenkins model (Box and Jenkins 1970) might be used. For policy variables, the forecaster needs to exercise judgement in choosing likely values. In the absence of alternatives a no-change assumption could be used.

It is at the point of producing forecasts that one of the most controversial adjustments takes place, since the forecaster generally does not accept the crude forecasts from the model but decides to use judgement to change them. This is known as applying 'tender loving care' (Howrey *et al*. 1974) and involves the forecaster's taking account of the many factors, such as the effects of strikes and policy announcements, which are not covered by the model. Also, any forecast for the recent past will differ from the observed outcome and a 'residual adjustment' may be made to put the model back on track.

Perhaps the most important objection to the methods of econometric forecasting is the Lucas (1976) critique, which essentially says that the parameters of a model are derived under certain assumptions about the policy behaviour. If these assumptions change, so will the parameters, and hence any forecasts (or simulations) will be misleading.

Hendry and his co-workers have criticized the traditional approach to economic modelling in a series of papers (for example, Hendry 1974; Davidson *et al.* 1978). They characterize it as being 'specific to general' in that economic theory is claimed to lead to a specific equation which, if it is found to be unsatisfactory, is then expanded to take account of particular empirical problems. Thus, for example, a static equation in which first-order autocorrelation occurs can be generalized by adding lagged variables. The result is that a more complex model, which is consistent with the data, is found. Henry points out that such an approach cannot test whether the theory is correct, since the final model must be accepted by the data. While recognizing that this procedure could end up with the correct model, this is unlikely. Other critics, including Leamer (1983), call the whole process 'data mining' or 'fishing' for the required results.

As an alternative procedure, Hendry[5] proposes starting with a general model which incorporates all the relevant variables from economic theory and which has unrestricted dynamics. This model must be accepted by the data (and so have white noise residuals) and will have a large number of parameters. It would not be a sensible final model. The general model is rearranged to reduce multi-collinearity and to include patterns of variables which relate to equilibrium conditions, such as the error-correction formulation discussed in equation (33.14) in Section 33.3. The model is estimated and, by testing the significance of the coefficients, is reduced to the smallest size which is compatible with the data. The accepted model is evaluated extensively by an analysis of residuals, structural stability and predictive performance, before finally being used for forecasting. This extensive testing of the model has had a major impact on the way models are reported in the United Kingdom and, by implication, on their properties and forecasting performance.

The 'general to specific' approach relies on (a) the use of economic theory to indicate which variables are to be included in the general model, (b) the data set being extensive enough to discriminate between the alternative formulations of the model and (c) the existence of a unique order in which the possible restrictions on the general model are tested. Of these, perhaps the third is the least likely to be correct.

Another methodology is proposed by Leamer (1983) who adopts a Bayesian approach in which a general family of models is specified and the tentative prior distributions are formed using economic theory. Next, the posterior distributions are found by using the data, and the sensitivity of inferences to the choice of priors (which is called extreme bounds analysis) is examined. If this sensitivity is high, inferences are said to be 'fragile', and the prior is revised to see whether this fragility can be reduced. Details are discussed by Pagan (1987), but as the method has not been commonly used in economic forecasting we shall not consider it further here.

33.3 STATISTICAL ALTERNATIVES

Within the statistics literature there is a long tradition of time series forecasting using extrapolation techniques. These include random walk models, simple moving averages, various forms of exponential smoothing and filtering methods.[6] The main characteristics of the methods are their reliance on the statistical properties of the data series and the absence of any contribution (in the form of prior restrictions) from economic theory. However, in some special cases, a time series model can have an economic interpretation. For example, a variable which follows an autoregressive integrated moving-average (ARIMA) process of order (0,1,1) can arise from an adaptive expectations mechanism (see, for example, Holden *et al.* 1985: Section 2.9). Also, some simple structural econometric models have reduced forms which can be written as univariate time series models.

More generally, a class of models known as vector autoregressive (VAR) models have become a popular method of econometric forecasting. There are three approaches which lead to VAR models. First, following Zellner and Palm (1974), a dynamic simultaneous econometric model can be written:

$$AY + BX = CE \qquad (33.1)$$

where A, B and C are matrices of polynomials in the lag operator, Y and X are vectors of endogenous and exogenous variabes respectively and E is a vector of white noise residuals. Now, if the path of the exogenous variables can be represented by an autoregressive moving-average (ARMA) process[7] so that

$$DX = GE \qquad (33.2)$$

where D and G are matrices of lag polynomials and D is invertible, then

$$X = D^{-1}GE \qquad (33.3)$$

and, substituting into (33.1) and rearranging, we obtain

$$AY = (C - BD^{-1}G)E$$

$$= HE \qquad (33.4)$$

Assuming that H is invertible, we can write this as

$$H^{-1}AY = E$$

or

$$JY = E \qquad (33.5)$$

where J is a matrix of lag polynomials. This is a VAR model in which the restrictions implicit in the structural model (33.1) have been ignored but could, in principle, be imposed.

The second approach leading to a VAR model starts with the univariate ARMA model for a variable Y:

$$\Phi(L)Y_t = \theta(L)\varepsilon_t \tag{33.5}$$

where Φ and θ are polynomials in the lag operator L and ε is a white noise error term. If each of the lag polynomials is invertible the Y has both a moving-average (MA) representation, as in

$$Y_t = \Phi(L)^{-1}\theta(L)\varepsilon_t \tag{33.7}$$

and an autoregressive (AR) representation, as in

$$\theta(L)^{-1}\Phi(L)Y_t = \varepsilon_t \tag{33.8}$$

The obvious multivariate generalization, in the case of two variables Y_{1t} and Y_{2t}, is the vector ARMA (VARMA) model

$$\Phi_{11}(L)Y_{1t} + \Phi_{12}(L)Y_{2t} = \theta_{11}(L)\varepsilon_{1t} + \theta_{12}(L)\varepsilon_{2t} \tag{33.9}$$

$$\Phi_{21}(L)Y_{1t} + \Phi_{22}(L)Y_{2t} = \theta_{21}(L)\varepsilon_{1t} + \theta_{22}(L)\varepsilon_{2t} \tag{33.10}$$

and this can be written in matrix form as

$$\Phi(L)Y_t = \theta(L)\varepsilon_t \tag{33.11}$$

If the VARMA model is completely unrestricted there will be problems in determining the orders of the AR and MA processes. Also, Judge *et al.* (1985) show that a VARMA representation of a model will not be unique since two different VARMA processes can represent the same autocovariance structure of the variables. This can be seen from (33.11) where, if $\Phi(L)$ is invertible,

$$Y_t = \Phi(L)^{-1}\theta(L)\varepsilon_t$$

which is an MA model and is indistinguishable from the special case of (33.11) where $\Phi(L)$ is the unit matrix. Similarly, if $\theta(L)$ is invertible, Y has a VAR representation.

Despite these problems of non-uniqueness, however, Baillie *et al.* (1983), Canarella and Pollard (1988) and Baillie (1989) give examples where, by postulating a formal underlying structure, there are explicit non-linear cross-equation restrictions on the parameters of the general VARMA model.

The third approach leading to VAR models follows from the work of Sims (1980) in which, after reviewing the traditional procedures in economic modelling, he states that the restrictions arising from economic theory which are imposed on structural models are incredible and cannot be taken seriously. These restrictions are needed in order to achieve identification. First, Sims objects to the arbitrary normalizations which occur when an equation is claimed to 'explain' one of the several endogenous variables it includes. Next, he criticizes the 'one equation at a time' specification procedure for macro-economic models where restrictions which are appropriate for partial equilib-rium models are imposed, frequently resulting in undesirable systems proper-ties. When equations are dynamic the identification situation is more complex. Hatanaka (1975) points out that, when lagged dependent variables and serially correlated errors are present, the usual identification rules do not apply unless the exact lengths of lags and orders of serial correlation are known *a priori*. Similarly, policy variables are frequently assumed to be exogenous when in fact they are at least partly endogenous. Sims infers that only strictly exogenous variables can help with identification, and therefore many apparently identified models are not in fact identified. The third area of concern is the treatment of expectations variables. Behaviour depends on the expected future values of variables and these can be affected by any information currently available. Thus any variable entering an equation in a system can affect expectations, and there are clearly problems over identification.

To deal with these criticisms of the traditional modelling approach, Sims proposes estimating unrestricted reduced forms in which each current endogenous variable is a function of lagged values of all the variables in the system. There are no restrictions based on prior knowledge. Thus for the k endogenous variables $y_{1t}, y_{2t}, \ldots, y_{kt}$, the jth equation in the system is

$$y_{jt} = f(y_{1t-1}, y_{1t-2}, \ldots, y_{1t-L}, y_{2t-1}, \ldots, y_{2t-L}, \ldots, y_{kt-L}) \quad (33.12)$$

where L is the common lag on each of the endogenous variables. Here, the variables on the right-hand side are the same in every equation and do not include any current values. This results in the useful property that OLS is a valid method of estimation. In (33.12) there are kL parameters per equation, plus a constant and any other deterministic variables, giving at least k^2L parameters in the system.

Sims does not discuss how the list of variables is selected, but presumably a knowledge of macroeconomics would imply that national income, consumption, prices and unemployment are suitable variables. Beyond this, the inclusion of extra variables such as money and credit might be regarded as being contro-versial since there is disagreement as to their importance. Since the variables are all required to be endogenous, a Granger (1969) causality test can be used to check this. For two variables y_{1t} and y_{2t}, the test requires the regression of each of the variables on past values of both variables:

$$y_{1t} = \sum \alpha_i y_{1t-i} + \sum \beta_i y_{2t-i} + \varepsilon_{1t}$$

$$y_{2t} = \sum \tau_i y_{1t-i} + \sum \delta_i y_{2t-i} + \varepsilon_{2t}$$

where the summations start at $i = 1$ and are for some lag length k which makes the ε white noise. A standard F test of zero restrictions is conducted. If the β_i are zero then past values of y_2 do not help to predict y_1 and so y_2 does not Granger cause y_1. Hence y_1 is exogenous with respect to y_2. Variables which are not found to be exogenous will be included in the VAR model. The choice of the common lag length L in (33.12) is also arbitrary, but Sims suggests a likelihood ratio test for deciding whether the value of L can be reduced.[8]

As has been seen, one problem with the unrestricted VAR modelling procedure is the large number of parameters included in the model. Litterman (1986a,b) reports that very good in-sample fits are obtained but the out-of-sample forecasts are poor. This is because of the lack of precision in the coefficient estimates owing to multicollinearity. One solution is to use economic theory to decide which parameters to set to zero, but this is against the spirit of VAR modelling. Webb (1988) has suggested using a grid search over a range of lag patterns and selecting the one which minimizes some selection criterion. Doan *et al.* (1984) have adopted a Bayesian framework in which the forecaster has prior ideas about the values of the parameters and the data are used to revise these ideas. This gives the Bayesian VAR (or BVAR) model. Initially, each variable is modelled by a random walk with drift so that

$$y_t = y_{t-1} + c + \varepsilon_t \tag{33.13}$$

where c is a constant ε is a white noise disturbance. The coefficients on all the other lagged variables are set at a mean value of zero but have a non-zero variance which is assumed to decline as the length of the lag increases. This results in a specification with a small number of parameters and the possibility of the data changing a zero coefficient to non-zero if there is a sufficiently strong influence. Another aspect of the BVAR approach is that the parameters are re-estimated each period using the Kalman filter.[9]

The time series methods of forecasting discussed so far assume that the variables (or their differences) are covariance stationary. This requires the variable to have a constant mean, a constant and finite variance, and constant covariances. Variables which are stationary are said to be integrated of order zero. If a variable can be transformed to be stationary by first-differencing it is said to be integrated of order one.

The recent development of interest in non-stationary times series is having an impact on forecasting methods. Philips (1987) demonstrates that the standard t tests in regression are not valid when the variables are non-stationary. More generally, Engle and Granger (1987) consider the properties of two or more related variables, each of which is integrated of order one but has a resulting combination which is stationary (or integrated or order zero). Such variables are said to be cointegrated. The implications of cointegration for economic modelling and forecasting are far-reaching. First, if the variables in an equation are not cointegrated then, because the error term is non-stationary, the relationship is likely to be mis-specified and, at a minimum, reliable estimation of the parameters will be difficult. Second, Engle and Granger have proved that if x and y are both integrated of order one, have constant means and are cointegrated, then an error-correcting data-generating mechanism or error-correction model exists and takes the form

$$\Delta y_t = -\alpha_1 u_{t-1} + \text{lagged}(\Delta y, \Delta x) + d(L)\varepsilon_{1t}$$
$$\Delta x_t = -\alpha_2 u_{t-1} + \text{lagged}(\Delta y, \Delta x) + d(L)\varepsilon_{2t}$$

(33.14)

where

$$u_t = y_t - \beta x_t \qquad (33.15)$$

and Δ is the first-difference operator. Here $d(L)$ is a finite polynomial in the lag operator L, ε_i is a white noise error process and

$$|\alpha_1| + |\alpha_2| \neq 0 \qquad (33.16)$$

The interpretation of (33.14) is helped by considering the equilibrium situation when the differenced terms in (33.14) are zero and it collapses to (33.15) with u_t equal to zero, i.e. in equilibrium y is proportional to x. Hence, from (33.15), u measures the deviation from the equilibrium value and, since u is stationary with a mean of zero, deviations from equilibrium in period $t - 1$ are partly corrected in period t. Thus the error-correction mechanism, which has an economic interpretation, provides a link between structural models and time series models. For forecasting, the error-correction mechanism is important because it implies that a model that only includes first differences of variables will be mis-specified if the levels of the variables are cointegrated. This could happen if, for example, a VAR model is fitted to first-differenced data.

So far, the models considered here have been linear in the parameters of the model. There is, of course, no theoretical reason why the underlying data-generation process should be linear, and several forms of non-linear statistical model have been proposed. For example, Granger and Anderson (1978) discuss bilinear models, Tong (1983) presents threshold AR models and Priestley (1980) considers state-dependent models. These are not commonly used in economic modelling. However, a special form of non-linearity in which a deterministic process appears to be random, known as deterministic chaos, has application in economics (Van der Poeg 1986) and forecasting (Brock and Sayers 1988; Frank and Stengos 1988).

33.4 ACCURACY ANALYSIS

While it may seem obvious that an accurate forecast is one that is correct, a simple classification of forecasts as being right or wrong is not helpful. Instead, there are basically four ways of analysing the accuracy of forecasts which are used in the literature. These are (a) checking for unbiasedness and efficiency, (b) calculating measures such as the root mean square error and inequality coefficients, (c) examining forecasts for a particular epoch and (d) decomposing the forecast error into its components.

The first of these is concerned with the use of information and is related to the concept of rational expectations. An optimal forecast can be defined as one which is the best that can be made in the particular circumstances. It is the prediction from economic theory using all the relevant information that is available at the time that the forecast is made, and is referred to as the rational expectation of the variable. Strictly, the concept of optimality should be defined with reference to the cost function of the user of the forecasts, and the optimal forecast equates the marginal costs and benefits from forecasting. Feige and Pearce (1976) call such forecasts the 'economically' rational expectations. If a quadratic cost function is assumed, the rational expectation will be unbiased and efficient. Unbiasedness requires an expected forecast error of zero. Efficiency means that the available information has been fully exploited and so the forecast errors are uncorrelated with this information.

The standard test of whether a series of forecasts is unbiased is based on estimating

$$A_t = \alpha + \beta F_t + u_t \qquad (33.17)$$

where A and F are the actuals and the forecasts respectively, and testing whether α is zero and β is unity. Holden and Peel (1990) show that strictly this is a test for inefficiency, and they suggest using a simple t test on the mean forecast error as a test for unbiasedness. They find evidence from estimating (33.17) which shows that there is non-rationality, giving scope for improving the forecasts.[10]

The method of testing for efficiency is to define the 'relevant' information set and then see whether the forecast errors are correlated with it. Holden and Peel (1985) chose the information set to be the four most recently observed actual values of the variables, while McNees (1978) used the latest known forecast errors. Again, the evidence in these studies implies that a better use of the relevant information would have resulted in more accurate forecasts.

The second method of assessing forecast accuracy involves calculating a numerical measure of the accuracy. The simple measures, such as the mean error and mean absoulte error, are generally not used since a quadratic cost function is assumed which gives a higher weight to larger errors. Instead, the mean square error (MSE) and its square root, the root mean square error (RMSE), are preferred, where

$$MSE = \frac{\Sigma(A_t - F_t)^2}{n} \qquad (33.18)$$

and n is the number of forecasts. The MSE can be expanded to be the sum of the variance of the forecast error plus the square of the mean error, and so increases as either of these increase. Ashley *et al.* (1980) have proposed a test for comparing two MSEs.

One problem with the RMSE is that it has the same units as the forecasts so that comparisons between series are difficult. Theil (1966) has suggested dividing the MSE by the mean squares of the actuals, so that

$$U^2 = \frac{MSE}{\Sigma A_t^2/n} \qquad (33.19)$$

The inequality coefficient U takes the value zero for perfect forecasts and unity if all the forecasts are zero (which is a no-change forecast if A and F are rates of change variables), and is greater than unity if the forecasts are worse than the no-change forecasts. For most levels variables forecasts of zero are unlikely to be sensible and so this interpretation of U is not used. Granger and Newbold (1973) propose decomposing the MSE into the proportions due to bias, the proportion due to β in (33.17) differing from unity and the disturbance or residual proportion. Good forecasts would have low values for the first two of these and a high disturbance proportion.

The third way of analysing forecast accuracy is to examine in detail how accurate the forecasts were during a particular period. Examples of this for the United Kingdom are given by Artis (1982), who examines forecasts published late in 1981, Barker (1985), who considers the forecasts made in 1979 and 1980 for the period when the Thatcher Government first took office, and Wallis (1989), who looks at forecasts for the recessions of 1974–5 and 1979–81. Such studies allow a detailed examination of the timing of turning points, the depth of a recession and the way in which forecasts are revised as new information becomes available. They tend to consider periods when the economy is changing rapidly so that forecasting is difficult.

The final way of examining forecast accuracy is to recognize that the observed forecast error can be allocated to particular types of error, i.e. the forecast errors from a model can be split into components corresponding to (a) the error due to the model, (b) the error due to the incorrect projection of the exogenous and policy variables and (c) the errors resulting from judgemental and residual adjustments. In order to be able to examine these sources of error in detail the analyst requires co-operation from the modelling organization since access is needed to the econometric model and the data set used to make the forecasts. Artis (1982) reports such a study for UK forecasts made in 1981. As the outcomes were not known at the time that the study was made, the emphasis was on the differences between the forecasts. Three sets of forecasts were considered: the main forecasts as published by each forecaster, forecasts with 'common assumptions' about the paths of the exogenous variables and a 'constant residuals' set of forecasts in which the effects of judgemental adjustments are removed. Artis found that the most important differences occurred because of the judgemental adjustments.

Wallis *et al.* (1986) conducted a similar study but had the outcome series so that forecast errors could be examined. Again, the residual adjustments were found to be important and these tended to compensate for errors in the models and errors in the exogenous assumptions.

33.5 COMBINING FORECASTS

It is well know that when forecasts from a number of economic models are compared they are generally found to be different. Also, there is empirical evidence (see, for example, Holden and Peel (1983), or compare McNees (1979) and McNees (1988)) that the best forecaster for a particular variable over a particular period is likely to be dominated by another forecaster in a different period. The question then is: should forecasts from one particular forecaster be selected or should some form of average of those available be taken? If the agent is convinced that one particular model is correct, then it will be appropriate to ignore the other forecasts. However, in the absence of such a conviction it is sensible to take account of forecasts from other models.

Bates and Granger (1969) demonstrate that two unbiased forecasts can, in general, be combined to give a new forecast which will have a smaller error variance than either of its components. They consider several ways in which the weights for combining the forecasts can be chosen, and also determine the optimal combination. Granger and Ramanathan (1984) put this result in the regression framework by considering the equation

$$A_t = \beta_1 F_{1t} + \beta_2 F_{2t} + u_t \qquad (33.20)$$

where A is the outcome series, F_1 and F_2 are unbiased forecasts of A and u is a disturbance with a mean of zero. It is clear that taking expectations of (33.20) gives

$$\beta_1 + \beta_2 = 1 \qquad (33.21)$$

and so the optimal least squares forecast of A is obtained by estimating (33.20) subject to (33.21). Given a series of outcomes and two sets of forecasts, the parameters (weights) in (33.20) can be estimated and it can then be used for forecasting outside the estimation period. For biased forecasts, Granger and Ramanathan propose including a constant term in (33.20). The restriction (33.21) should still be imposed. The method generalizes for any number of forecasts.

These results imply that if there are several forecasts available then it is sensible to include them all in a combination. However, it is clear that the multi-collinearity of two identical series of forecasts will cause computational problems and so in this case one should be dropped. More generally, since the weights are related to the variances and covariances of the forecasts, the gains from combining forecasts will be greatest when the forecasts are 'different' in the sense of utilizing independent information. This implies taking forecasts from different models (say Keynesian, monetarist, input-output) and techniques (say econometric, time series, surveys).

One assumption that is important in using the regression method for combining forecasts is that the variances and covariances between the forecasts are constant. If this is not the case the weights will vary over time and while *ex post* a combined forecast gives a better fit in the estimation period it will not give good *ex ante* forecasts. The weights may be unstable. In these circumstances a better combined forecast might be obtained by taking the mean of the available forecasts. This has some attractions since the forecasters might be expected to know their own track record and so should be able to correct for any past biases. Thus, *ex ante*, any forecast from an economic modelling organization should be unbiased and can therefore be written as the true value plus a random error (which has a mean of zero).[11] The average of a number of such forecasts will also have a mean equal to the true value.

There is an extensive literature on combining forecasts, including a special issue of the *Journal of Forecasting* in June 1989, and a survey by Clemen (1989). The picture that emerges is that the theoretical benefits from combining forecasts do not always occur in practice. However, some general guidelines can be stated. First, the forecasts should be from different forecasting methods, and their past performance should be analysed to see whether the variances and covariances appear to be constant. If they are not, the best combined forecast might be the simple average. Next it is necessary to decide whether all the forecasts should be used. A forecast with large errors in the past might be discarded. If a particular forecast has autocorrelated errors this implies that it can be improved by taking account of the autocorrelation. Finally, some method of combination should be chosen. The optimal combination is from regressing the outcomes on the forecasts, including an intercept term, and constraining the weights to sum to unity.

33.6 CONCLUSIONS

Since the 1960s, when the earliest econometric models were first used regularly for forecasting, both the methods of econometrics and the structures of the industrialized economies have undergone considerable change. Forecasting the future state of the economy remains a challenge. While current econometric models are radically different from their predecessors, their forecasting ability has not improved dramatically. However, forecasts are still needed, and at present the best way of obtaining them is from econometric models.

NOTES

1 For recent histories of econometric modelling see Christ (1985), Epstein (1987) and Morgan (1989). The particular contributions of Tinbergen and Theil are discussed by Hughes Hallett (1989).
2 Corrado and Greene (1988) show how monthly data and forecasts can be used in a quarterly model to improve forecast accuracy. Wallis (1986) considers the more general problem of incomplete current information.
3 See Holden *et al.* (1985), for example, for a discussion of expectations formation and measurement.
4 See Johnston (1984) for a discussion of errors in variables problems and Trivellato and Retorre (1986) for a direct application to forecasting. Judge *et al.* (1985) also review the general problem of unobservable variables. Malinvaud (1980) and Lee *et al.* (1990) consider aggregation problems.
5 Gilbert (1986) sets out the methodology. See also Pagan (1987) who compares this approach with traditional modelling and Leamer's (1983) extreme bounds analysis discussed below. Leamer (1989) provides a more general critique.
6 A review of extrapolation methods is provided by Fildes (1979) and Makridakis *et al.* (1982, 1984). For a unified treatment see Harvey (1984).
7 The types of variables which cannot be represented by an ARMA process are those that are non-stationary, zero-one dummy variables and time trends. The first of these can generally be transformed (by differencing) while the others, being deterministic, can easily be forecast.
8 See Sims (1980: footnote 18). Gordon and King (1982) criticize this test.
9 The RATS package is used to estimate BVAR models (Doan and Litterman 1988).
10 See McNees (1978) and Holden and Peel (1985) for further examples. Holden *et al.* (1985) review the empirical evidence and Baillie (1989) surveys the tests.
11 Incomplete current information and/or a forecast horizon of more than one period will result in the errors following a moving-average process of order $L + H - 1$, where L is the length of the information lag and H is the length of the forecast horizon (Brown and Maital 1981).

REFERENCES

Artis, M. J. (1982) *Why do forecasts differ?*, London: Bank of England, Papers presented to the Panel of Academic Consultants, no. 17.
Ashley, R., Granger, C. W. J. and Schmalensee, R. (1980) 'Advertising and aggregate consumption: an analysis of causality', *Econometrica* 48: 1149–68.
Baillie, R. T. (1989) 'Econometric tests of rationality and market efficiency', *Econometric Reviews* 8: 151–86.
Baillie, R. T., Lippens, R. E. and McMahon, P. C. (1983) 'Testing rational expectations and efficiency in the foreign exchange market', *Econometrica* 51: 553–74.

Barker, T. (1985) 'Forecasting the economic recession in the UK 1979–82: a comparison of model-based *ex ante* forecasts', *Journal of Forecasting* 4: 133–51.

Bates, J. M. and Granger, C. W. J. (1969) 'The combination of forecasts', *Operational Research Quarterly* 20: 451–68.

Box, G. E. P. and Jenkins, G. M. (1970) *Time-Series Analysis: Forecasting and Control*, San Francisco, CA: Holden-Day.

Brock, W. A. and Sayers, C. L. (1988) 'Is the business cycle characterised by deterministic chaos?', *Journal of Monetary Economics* 22: 71–9.

Brown, B. W. and Maital, S. (1981) 'What do economists know? An empirical study of experts' expectations', *Econometrica* 49: 491–504.

Canarella, G. and Pollard, S. K. (1988) 'Efficiency in foreign exchange markets: a vector autoregressive approach', *Journal of International Money and Finance* 7: 331–46.

Christ, C. F. (1985) 'Early progress in estimating quantitative economic relationships in America', *American Economic Review* 44: 32–61.

Clemen, R. T. (1989) 'Combining forecasts: a review and annotated bibliography', *International Journal of Forecasting* 5: 559–88.

Corrado, C. and Greene, M. (1988) 'Reducing uncertainty in short-term projections: linkage of monthly and quarterly models', *Journal of Forecasting* 7: 77–102.

Davidson, J. E. H., Hendry, D. F., Srba, F. and Yeo, S. (1978) 'Econometric modelling of the aggregate time series relationship between consumers' expenditure and income in the United Kingdom', *Economic Journal* 88: 661–92.

Doan, T. A. and Litterman, R. B. (1988) *User's Manual for RATS*, Evanston, IL: VAR Econometrics.

Doan, T., Litterman, R. and Sims, C. (1984) 'Forecasting and conditional projection using realistic prior distributions', *Econometric Reviews* 3: 1–100.

Engle, R. F. and Granger, C. W. J. (1987) 'Cointegration and error correction: representation, estimation and testing', *Econometrica* 55: 251–76.

Epstein, R. J. (1987) *A History of Econometrics*, Amsterdam: North-Holland.

Feige, E. L. and Pearce, D. K. (1976) 'Economically rational expectations: are the innovations in the rate of inflation independent of innovations in measures of monetary and fiscal policy?', *Journal of Political Economy* 84: 499–522.

Fildes, R. F. (1979) 'Quantitative forecasting – the state of the art: extrapolative models', *Journal of the Operational Research Society* 30: 691–710.

—— (1988) *World Index of Economic Forecasts*, Aldershot: Gower.

Frank, M. and Stengos, T. (1988) 'Chaotic dynamics in economic time series', *Journal of Economic Surveys* 2: 103–33.

Gilbert, C. L. (1986) 'Professor Hendry's econometric methodology', *Oxford Bulletin of Economics and Statistics*, 48: 283–307.

Gordon, R. J. and King, S. R. (1982) 'The output cost of disinflation in traditional and vector autoregressive models', *Brookings Papers on Economic Activity* 205–44.

Granger, C. W. J. (1969) 'Investigating causal relations by econometric models and cross-spectral methods', *Econometrica* 37: 24–36.

Granger, C. W. J. and Anderson, A. P. (1978) *An Introduction to Bilinear Time Series Models*, Göttingen: Vandenhoeck & Ruprecht.

Granger, C. W. J. and Newbold, P. (1973) 'Some comments on the evaluation of forecasts', *Applied Economics* 5: 35–47.

Granger, C. W. J. and Ramanathan, R. (1984) 'Improved methods of combining forecasts', *Journal of Forecasting* 3: 197–204.

Harvey, A. C. (1984) 'A unified view of statistical forecasting procedures', *Journal of Forecasting* 3: 245–75.

Hatanaka, M. (1975) 'On the global identification of the dynamic simultaneous equation model with stationary disturbances', *International Economic Review* 16: 545–54.

Hendry, D. F. (1974) 'Stochastic specification in an aggregate demand model of the United Kingdom', *Econometrica* 42: 559–78.

Holden, K. and Peel, D. A. (1983) 'Forecasts and expectations: some evidence for the UK', *Journal of Forecasting* 2: 51–8.

—— and —— (1985) 'An evaluation of quarterly National Institute forecasts', *Journal of Forecasting* 4: 227–34.

—— and —— (1990) 'On testing for unbiasedness and efficiency of forecasts', *The Manchester School* 58: 120–7.

Holden, K., Peel, D. A. and Thompson, J. L. (1985) *Expectations: Theory and Evidence*, Basingstoke: Macmillan.

——, —— and —— (1990) *Economic Forecasting: An Introduction*, Cambridge: Cambridge University Press.

Howrey, E. P., Klein, L. R. and McCarthy, M. D. (1974) 'Notes on testing the predictive performance of econometric models', *International Economic Review* 15: 366–83.

Hughes Hallett, A. (1989) 'Econometrics and the theory of economic policy: the Tinbergen–Theil contributions 40 years on', *Oxford Economic Papers* 41: 189–214.

Johnston, J. (1984) *Econometric Methods*, 3rd edn, New York: McGraw-Hill.

Judge, G. G.., Carter-Hill, R., Griffiths, W. E., Lutkepohl, H. and Tsoung-Choo Lee (1985) *The Theory and Practice of Econometrics*, 2nd edn, New York: Wiley.

Klein, L. R. and Goldberger, A. S. (1955) *An Econometric Model of the United States 1929–1952*, Amsterdam: North-Holland.

Leamer, E. E. (1983) 'Let's take the con out of econometrics', *American Economic Review* 73: 31–43.

—— (1989) 'Planning, criticism and revision', *Journal of Applied Econometrics (Supplement)* 4: S5–S27.

Lee, K. C., Pesaran, M. H. and Pierse, R. G. (1990) 'Testing for aggregation bias in linear models', *Economic Journal (Supplement)* 100: 137–50.

Litterman, R. B. (1986a) 'A statistical approach to economic forecasting', *Journal of Business and Economic Statistics* 4: 1–4.

—— (1986b) 'Forecasting with Bayesian vector autoregressions – five years experience', *Journal of Business and Economic Statistics* 4: 25–38.

Lucas, R. E. (1976) 'Econometric policy evaluation: a critique', *Journal of Monetary Economics, Supplement* 19–46.

McNees, S. K. (1978) 'The rationality of economic forecasts', *American Economic Review* 68: 301–5.

—— (1979) 'The forecasting record for the 1970s', *New England Economic Review* September/October: 33–53.

—— (1988) 'How accurate are macroeconomic forecasts?', *New England Economic Review* July/August: 15–36.

Makridakis, S., Andersen, A., Carbone, R., Fildes, R., Hibon, M., Lewandowski, R.,

Newton, S., Parzan, E. and Winkler, R. (1982) 'The accuracy of extrapolation (time series) methods: results of a forecasting competition', *Journal of Forecasting* 1: 111–53.

——, ——, ——, ——, ——, ——, —— and —— (1984) *The Forecasting Accuracy of Major Time Series Methods*, Chichester: Wiley.

Malinvaud, E. (1980) *Statistical Methods of Econometrics*, 3rd edn, Amsterdam: North-Holland.

Morgan, M. S. (1989) *The History of Econometric Ideas*, Cambridge: Cambridge University Press.

Pagan, A. (1987) 'Three econometric methodologies: a critical appraisal', *Journal of Economic Surveys* 1: 3–24.

Philips, P. C. B. (1987) 'Time series regression with unit roots', *Econometrica* 55: 277–302.

Priestley, M. B. (1980) 'State dependent models: a general approach to non-linear time series analysis', *Journal of Time Series Analysis* 1: 47–71.

Sims, C. A. (1980) 'Macroeconomics and reality', *Econometrica* 48: 1–48.

Theil, H. (1966) *Applied Economic Forecasting*, Amsterdam: North-Holland.

Tinbergen, J. (1939) *Statistical Testing of Business Cycle Theories*, Geneva: League of Nations.

Tong, H. (1983) *Threshold Models in Non-linear Time Series Analysis*, Berlin: Springer Verlag, Lecture Notes in Statistics 21.

Trivellato, U. and Rettore, E. (1986) 'Preliminary data errors and their impact on the forecast error of simultaneous-equations models', *Journal of Business and Economic Statistics* 4: 445–53.

Van der Ploeg, F. (1986) 'Rational expectations, risk and chaos in financial markets', *Economic Journal (Supplement)* 96: 151–62.

Wallis, K. F. (1986) 'Forecasting with an econometric model: the "ragged edge" problem', *Journal of Forecasting* 5: 1–14.

—— (1989) 'Macroeconomic forecasting – a survey', *Economic Journal* 99: 28–61.

Wallis, K. F., Andrews, M. J., Fisher, P. G., Longbottom, J. A. and Whitley, J. D. (1986) *Models of the UK Economy: A Third Review*, Oxford: Oxford University Press.

Webb, R. H. (1988) 'Commodity prices as predictors of aggregate price change', *Economic Review of the Federal Reserve Bank of Richmond* 74 (6): 3–11.

Zellner, A. and Palm, F. (1974) 'Time series analysis and simultaneous equation econometric models', *Journal of Econometrics* 2: 17–54.

34

INTEREST GROUPS AND POLICY FORMULATION

CHRIS MILNER

34.1 INTRODUCTION

One indication of the growing interest among economists in issues of public choice has been the greater attention given in the last two decades to the political economy of protectionism. If we hypothesize that producers and particular income groups are the demanders of protection and elected representatives are the suppliers of protection, then the form and content of trade policy can be viewed as the outcome of the political market-place. If, in turn, voters and their elected representatives pursue their own self-interest, this public choice model predicts that Pareto efficient policies will be implemented under majority rule, *when conditions such as perfect information, zero voting costs and costless income redistribution apply.* In a vote between a trade policy that restricts aggregate consumption opportunities and one that enlarges those possibilities, the majority should vote for unrestricted trade since it is possible to make a majority of voters (or even all voters) better off.

The fact that protectionism is widespread among industrial democracies and that levels and forms of protection vary between industries suggests that the basic public choice model (as outlined above) is inappropriate or incomplete. There are imperfections in political markets that encourage, for instance, the formation of lobbies or interest groups and allow such groups, individually or in coalitions, to influence the determination or conduct of trade policy. Therefore in this chapter we shall seek to examine why interest groups seek protection (and/or rents), and how they influence the level and form of protection. By restricting the subject matter to trade policy rather than policy formulation in general, the aim is to provide a richer illustration of the recent efforts by applied economists to 'endogenize' the modelling of economic policy than would be possible if a wider range of economic policies were considered. (Besides which, applications to other areas of policy are considered in Chapter 12.)

The remainder of this chapter is organized as follows. In Section 34.2 the public choice theory of trade policy determination is extended and reviewed. In Section 34.3 interest group models of protection and rent-seeking are considered. Section 34.4 provides a brief review of some empirical studies on the interest group model of protection. Finally, some summary conclusions are offered in Section 34.5.

34.2 EXTENDING THE PUBLIC CHOICE APPROACH

The view that majority rule will induce Pareto efficient policies is clearly not consistent with empirical evidence in the case of trade policy. The longevity of agricultural protectionism and of protection by industrial countries against clothing and textile imports from developing countries, and the growth of new forms of protectionism in the last two decades, are evidence of this. The application of public choice theory to trade policy might more realistically require that

1 the possibility for redistribution along the utility–possibility frontier is restricted;
2 information costs are recognized;
3 representatives, rather than direct, democracy is allowed for;
4 the free-rider problem associated with changes in trade policy is incorporated into the analysis.

Let us consider each of these additional factors in turn.

The classic work on income distribution and trade is that of Stolper and Samuelson (1941). They demonstrate, in a standard two-good two-factor (capital and labour) Heckscher–Ohlin model, that the factor used more intensively in the import-competing sector will gain in real income terms from protection, whereas the other factor will lose. In the case of a capital-abundant industrialized economy this will mean that protection will raise real wages.[1] Therefore we might explain the emergence of protectionism in this case by a predominance, in voting terms, of workers (only) over the owners of capital. But this is insufficient since that same majority could do better by voting for free trade combined with the redistribution of income in its favour through lump-sum taxes. Limitation on redistribution possibilities is therefore one factor that may explain protectionist pressures. Most countries have some form of compensation to owners of factors adversely affected by import growth, but they usually do not compensate in full for the loss incurred by these individuals.

Even if full redistribution of income in the context of free trade is possible, majority voting may still not produce Pareto efficient policies if there is incomplete information about the effects of trade policies on the availability and prices of imported goods and competing domestic goods. Indeed, if the protection-induced increases in prices for particular products are small relative to total incomes, it may be rational for consumers to avoid the search costs required to identify the cause and extent of the price rises. The existence of positive search costs and uncertain, possibly small, welfare loss avoidance for any one of a large number of individuals, when confronted with the prospect of increased protection in a particular industry or product range, may well account for limited collective consumer resistance to producer pressures for protection.

Again, it may be possible for voters to give a complete and accurate or unconstrained expression of preferences through the voting process, but the wishes of the electorate may not be fully reflected in the actions of their elected representatives. If political markets operate perfectly, the actions of elected representatives will reflect the wishes of voters under the threat of being replaced by new candidates promising to reflect the wishes of the electorate. But incumbent representatives have special advantages which may allow them to act independently. They may, for instance, be more willing to support particular policies on ideological grounds because they do not wish further re-election or because their well-established incumbent status imposes high entry costs on new candidates or parties.[2]

But, in any case, the opinions of the electorate on specific policy issues are rarely sought through the ballot box. Individual representatives are subject not only to electoral pressures on their voting behaviour, but also often to pressures arising from ownership of the party 'ticket', from ideologically motivated groups within the party and from organized pressure groups outside the party apparatus. Lobbying is a way in which the views of the electorate on individual policy issues can be made known to their representatives without the need for continuous balloting. But the scale and effectiveness of lobbying activity is invariably not uniform across interests. Therefore the free-rider and externality problems associated with organizing pressure groups are often used to explain why protectionism exists even though consumers represent a majority of voters and why some industries are more protected than others. Consumers are too numerous and widely dispersed to form effective anti-protection pressure groups. Consequently, the costs of forming and sustaining the consumer lobby are likely to be very large, and since it is impossible to exclude free-riders from the benefits of reduced protection the required funding for such pressure group formation is unlikely to be forthcoming. Producers, by contrast, are likely to be able to form pressure groups more easily, especially if the producer group is small and geographically concentrated. As a result, the costs of co-ordinating and monitoring the group are lower and free-riders are more easily identifiable.[3]

Thus, if lobbying from pressure groups has a significant influence on trade policy decisions, we would expect that producer interests will tend to be represented better than consumer interests and that some industries will be more effective than others in pressing for protection. However, the extent to which industries press for protection will not depend only on the costs of forming and maintaining a lobby. The extent and distribution of the benefits from protection are also important. Export industries, for instance, do not benefit from tariff protection on their export sales, and any gains from higher prices for products sold on the home market may be offset by reduced export sales following retaliatory tariff measures abroad. Even in the case of non-export industries, where there is no direct threat from retaliation, the investment decision in lobbying activities by individual producers will be fashioned by the producer's judgement of others' supply response as well as his own. The producer benefits from protection mainly take the form of temporary rents, and the extent and duration of these rents will depend on the speed and extent of the total supply response of *all* existing producers and new entrants. Thus the existence of some net benefits from lobbying for protection is not a guarantee that rent-seeking will actually take place. Indeed, we would expect that supply responses to protection will vary between industries, being smaller and therefore less of a discouragement to protectionist efforts in the case of depressed industries subject to intensifying foreign competition, since new investment (from existing or new entrant producers) is less likely in those sectors with below average long-term rates of return. This interpretation is certainly consistent with the observed concentration, over a long period of time, of protectionist measures on declining industries.

Therefore, by extending the public choice model in the ways described above, we can see how a demand for protection can be created, and why it might be provided by the political market-place as an outcome of democratic procedures. However, it has been assumed thus far that individuals are welfare-maximizers whose welfare depends only on their own consumption, and that the protection is supplied only by the legislative branch of government. Both these assumptions merit further consideration.

Considerations of equity and social justice may have significant influences on policy formulation. Corden (1974) employs a 'conservative social welfare function' to explain why trade policy intervention may be used to avoid significant reductions in the real income of specific sections of society, for example low-income workers in specific industries or regions. In itself, though, this does not explain why trade protection rather than other policy instruments that redistribute income is used to satisfy equity considerations. It may be that the more selective and flexible means of hidden income redistribution permitted by trade policy interventions compared with explicit redistribution from direct income tax arrangements is an appealing means of pursuing self-interest. The insurance policy principle has been referred to by some commentators on commercial policy (see, for example, Cassing 1980). An individual may support tariff or other trade restrictions in another industry if he/she thinks that it increases the probability of protection should his/her industry need it in the future. Thus there may be coalitions of interest through both space (i.e. between threatened industries at one point in time) and time (i.e. between industries currently subject to increased foreign competition and those with expectations of increased competition from abroad in the future). Whether it is enlightened self-interest, genuine altruism or collective interest, the important thing to note in the current context is that we would expect interest group behaviour to be more effective in achieving its objective to the extent that the group self-interest is consistent with the wider interests of non-members of the group. Thus, interest groups that can appeal to 'self-sufficiency', 'way of life' or 'military necessity' arguments[4] may be more successful in lobbying for protection.

Success in inducing a supply of protection has been defined thus far in terms of inducing political decisions motivated by electoral consequences and constrained by ideological goals. Even a party committed ideologically to free trade may, if uncertain of re-election, concede the demands made by pressure groups for protection if the pressure groups can deliver votes in marginal constituencies and/or contribute to the financing of the election campaign. However, interest groups do not only lobby vote-motivated politicians; they also seek to influence the bureaucracy. The legislative and executive branches of government do place constraints on the actions of the public sector bureaucracy, but a 'rational' model, i.e. a constrained utility-maximizing model, of the behaviour of public bureaucrats is likely to offer some additional insights into the success of interest groups in influencing policy. If the main elements in the bureaucrats' utility function are prestige and power within the administration and within their area of influence or responsibility, then they may very well see it as important to support the interests of that area. Where responsibilities are allocated on a distinct sectoral basis, for example an agriculture industry or a division focused on specific manufacturing industries, the bureaucrats' vested interest and the industry/pressure group interest in protection coincide. Alternatively, it might be the case that interest groups seek to 'capture' the relevant area in the bureaucracy. Corruption of officials is one means of capture, but clearly more subtle means are also available. Public bureaucrats, for reasons of self-interest, may wish to influence legislation, which they may be able to do through the advice they give or by virtue of their greater access to information or as a result of their involvement in the drafting of the detail of legislation. But bureaucrats often also have considerable discretionary power vested in them by legislation. Given their greater control over measures of 'administrative protection', they have an incentive to promote the use of this form of protection rather than legislative reform; the possibility of their 'capture' is less evident to the other branches of government and the dependence

701

of the industry pressure groups on the administration is increased.[5] Again, therefore, we would need to modify the simple public choice theory of trade policy to allow for the conduct of government on the effectiveness of interest groups in lobbying for trade interventions; the more that administrative responsibilities are organized on lines that coincide with economic sectors and interest groups, and the more that the administration has discretionary control over policy instruments, the greater the probability, *ceteris paribus*, of successful lobbying by interest groups.

34.3 MODELLING PROTECTION AND RENT-SEEKING

What emerges from the foregoing discussion is that the degree of protection and the form of protection are endogenously determined in the political market-place rather than set by a benevolent government seeking to maximize some social welfare function of the Bergson–Samuelson type. Protection is therefore thought of in a conflict resolution setting. The market for protection is political, with both a demand side and a supply side; the interest group model represents the demand side.

If capitalists and workers in a particular industry lose or expect to lose in real income terms as a result of unrestricted international trade, and if they can organize themselves voluntarily into an interest group, they will 'demand' or seek protection or some form of assistance from policy-makers. Thus the demand for protection can be modelled as a function of the perceived benefits from protection minus the costs of obtaining that protection:[6]

$$R = B - (F + V) \qquad (34.1)$$

where R is the net real income benefit obtainable from protection, B is the gross benefit from protection, F is the fixed cost of obtaining protection and V is the variable cost of obtaining protection. B can be thought of as the increment to producers' surplus resulting from a given level of protection, where the marginal benefits of increased protection are positive up to the prohibitive tariff t_p, but total benefit increases at a decreasing rate. F can be thought of as sunk costs associated with lobbying for protection. These may result from fixed costs of interest group formation. At their simplest they can be thought of as a fixed commission paid to a professional lobbyist to retain his or her services. V then varies according to how much actual lobbying is undertaken, i.e. the marginal cost of obtaining protection is positive. This is likely to increase at an increasing rate because higher and higher levels of protection are increasingly costly to obtain, as other industry groups and consumer groups become increasingly resistant as protection levels increase. Clearly, there will be an 'optimal' level of protection from the interest group's standpoint; it will maximize its net gains from lobbying efforts by collecting and spending funds up to the point where the additional cost of protection-seeking activities equals the additional income benefits from further protection. We might refer to this as the target rate of protection t^*. It can be anywhere between $t^* = 0$, when F is sufficiently large, and $t^* = t_p$. If the supply of protection is given, the exact value of t^* will be determined by the configuration of the B and V functions over the relevant range. Figures 34.1 and 34.2 present the essential features of the interest group model. If $F = 0$, t^* lies between zero and t_p. If $F > 0$, t^* lies between $t_j > 0$ and t_p. Thus, for instance, if $F = F_2$ (i.e. there are positive set-up costs), $t_2 < t^* < t_p$. B and V will, of course, vary across industries. For instance, in Figure 34.2, V_2 lies wholly below V_1. As a result, with a given benefit function, the target tariff for industry 2 exceeds that for industry 1. For many industries, the benefit function may be entirely below the V function so that no protection will be sought. We can expect inter-industry variations in the B and V functions to be fashioned by inter-industry variations in international competitiveness and industrial structure. (We return to some of these factors again in the consideration of empirical evidence in Section 34.4.)

It is possible to extend the analysis in a number of ways to allow for imperfections and political markets and differences in the way in which administrative and institutional structures and constraints influence the supply of protection to alternate industries. Indeed, such extensions appear to be necessary if we are to be able to offer 'endogenous' explanations for rent-seeking by means of alternative instruments of protection. Otherwise, why is it that some industries are helped by the imposition of import quotas (some overt and some hidden), others by the maintenance of higher tariffs and yet others by direct forms of subsidization of various kinds?[7]

Obviously, a general determinant of the type of assistance sought by an industry is its balance of trade. An import-competing industry will seek protection against imports in such forms as tariffs, while an export-oriented industry will press for export subsidization. (Of course, the existence of substantial amounts of two-way or intra-industry trade complicates such predictions.) However, predominantly import-competing industries can be expected to prefer quotas over tariffs on the grounds that their effects are more predictable. A tariff may be offset by lower foreign prices as foreign suppliers accept lower profits or continue to lower their unit costs. Government officials also may prefer quantitative restrictions since, with orderly marketing agreements and 'voluntary' export restraints, the government can apply protection selectively and thus avoid complaints or possible retaliation. Existing foreign firms may also favour source-specific quotas over tariffs since they reap some of the rents. However, the protected domestic industry often actually finds that quantity controls do not have the expected restrictive effect owing to quality upgrading and increased imports from unrestricted countries. As a result of these

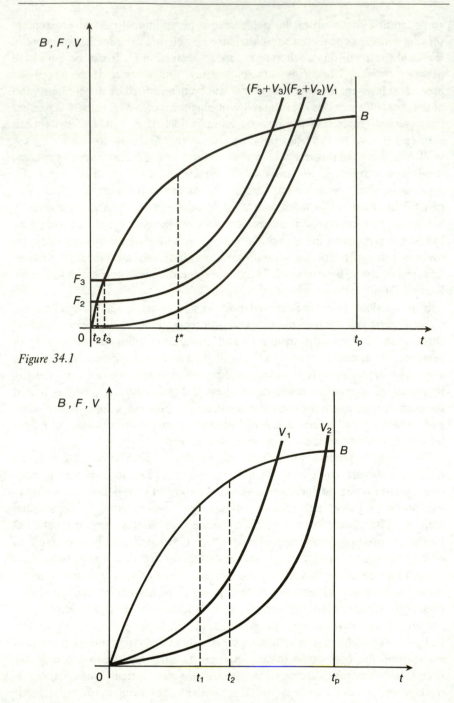

Figure 34.1

Figure 34.2

responses, industries often follow a pattern of protection-seeking that involves progressively more restrictive means, for example more and more bilateral quota agreements, as in the case of textiles and apparel. In recent years US import-competing industries have increasingly sought protection under the laws dealing with alleged 'unfair' trade practices. The anti-dumping and countervailing duty laws tend to have weaker injury requirements than other routes for securing protection. It is also easier to rally public support for protection on grounds of unfair actions by foreign suppliers than on the basis of injury that might be caused by inefficient management of the domestic industry.

Government subsidies directed only at an industry's exports are more difficult to obtain than import protection, owing to the explicit ban on export subsidies imposed by the General Agreement on Tariffs and Trade (GATT). However, subsidized export credits are permitted, provided that the government is a signatory to an international undertaking on official export credits. Special tax breaks for exporting firms are also allowed under certain conditions. Consequently, lobbying by export-oriented firms in the developed countries is usually aimed at both these forms of export subsidization.

An alleged drawback of most forms of subsidization is that they are revenue-depleting from the government's standpoint, whereas tariff protection, for example, is actually a revenue-producing activity. But this drawback does not appear to have been very effective in restraining the extensive subsidization that some countries undertake. When an export-oriented industry suffers injury due to loss of foreign markets, it may be just as difficult in terms of electoral pressure to refuse adjustment assistance in the form of subsidies as to deny tariff assistance to an injured import-competing industry.

The analysis thus far has focused on the process by which increased import competition facing an industry may lead it to lobbying for import protection. Some economists (for example, Krueger 1974; Bhagwati 1980; Bhagwati and Srinivasan 1980) have also modelled the manner in which import protection leads to lobbying for the rents or revenue arising from protection. In a pioneering paper on rent-seeking, Krueger (1974) showed that, when there is a system of binding quantitative restrictions in which the right to import depends on the possession of an import licence, competition is likely to arise among importers for the rents associated with the ownership of import licences. This rent-seeking activity involves the use of resources; Bhagwati (1982) coined the phrase 'directly unproductive profit-seeking' (DUP) activities to describe this feature of protectionist regimes. It can range from investment in excess capacity in order to obtain a large share of import licences to lobbying or actually bribing government officials who make the allocative decisions.

Bhagwati and Srinivasan (1980) also introduced the term 'revenue-seeking' to describe the situation in which economic agents lobby for a slice of the tariff revenue resulting from the adoption of protective tariffs. When quantitative restrictions are applied to all imports or just to imports of a single sector, competition for these rights to import will arise among importers in order to capture the rents therefrom. In contrast, with tariffs, imports are allocated by the price system, and the tariff revenue usually goes into the public treasury in the same way as any tax revenue. Generally, neither customs officials nor any other government officials associated with the import process have the authority to allocate the tariff proceeds among particular groups. The distribution of government revenues customarily involves legislative and executive processes that are only loosely related to their revenue-raising decisions. Consequently, the many different groups lobbying for government expenditures favourable to their own interests usually do so without regard to particular financing or tax source. One revenue situation that may increase lobbying activity is a substantial rise in tax revenues that is unrelated to increased government-spending plans. This could occur, for example, when there is an appreciable revenue-enhancing rise in tariffs on most imports. Various interest groups may then lobby government officials for a share of these extra revenues. However, when the tariff for only a specific industry is increased, any increase in tax revenue is likely to be too small to trigger a general increase in lobbying activity.

That some rent-seeking activities are wasteful of economic resources does not mean, however, that we should view all interest group behaviour as welfare lowering. Interest group pressures to earmark tariff revenues generated by temporarily protective tariffs may, for instance, encourage industries to adjust to changing comparative advantage more quickly than they would if tariff proceeds became part of general tax revenues.[8] Informational expenditures associated with rent-seeking activity *may* also be socially desirable, even though the private interest of those lobbying for protection is to present the information in a way that maximizes the chances of receiving protection. But considerations of optimality still have relevance in the context of a political economy analysis of trade policy. The particular set of industries actually assisted or protected as a result of lobbying by interest groups may not be (indeed, is unlikely to be) that set of industries that would maximize the welfare of the voting majority (for a given level of informational expenditure). The ability to organize into effective lobbies varies between industries, and as a result inter-industry differences in the levels of 'endogenous' protection are also unlikely to be 'optimal' in resource allocation terms (even under the second-best conditions of political processes that do not yield free trade coupled with income compensation for the losers). However, the regulatory scheme or arrangements which induced that particular pattern of protection may be efficient. Becker (1983) argues that any regulatory scheme represents an equilibrium for the purpose of distributing rents among interested parties; regulatory regimes emerge because they are efficient means of satisfying the conflicting demands placed upon the regulatory authorities.

34.4 EMPIRICAL EVIDENCE ON INTEREST GROUPS AND TRADE POLICY

Empirical research on the political economy of trade policy falls broadly into two camps. There are those studies that try to explain industry differences in the levels and form of protection. Alternatively, there are a number of studies that focus on the characteristics of voters and their political representatives as possible determinants of legislative decisions relating to trade policy or of administrative decisions relating to the application or operation of trade policy legislation. The first set of studies is more concerned with the demand side (i.e. the characteristics of interest groups) and the second set with the supply side (i.e. the characteristics of political processes) of the political market-place. Clearly, in the present context we are more concerned with the first set of studies. It would be unrealistic to anticipate, however, that we will be able to explain endogenous/cross-industry variation in levels and forms of protection by reference to 'demand' factors alone. Indeed, we may anticipate simultaneous equation bias in any single-equation regressions which include only determinants of the demand for protection on the right-hand side, and thereby omit the 'supply' response of voters, elected representatives and administrators. Of necessity, in what follows we shall concentrate mainly on the first set of studies.[9]

In addition to the above problem, cross-sectional analysis faces other substantial problems. First, there are measurement and proxying problems: measuring, for instance, the extent of protection where multiple and often non-overt measures of assistance are employed, or proxying the political and economic industry characteristics or determinants of the effectiveness of lobbying activity. Second, there may be industry-specific factors or idiosyncracies that influence the nature and effectiveness of lobbying activity but which are difficult to capture in cross-sectional analysis. Third, it is difficult to formulate tests and incorporate proxies for explanatory variables that enable one to discriminate between alternative hypotheses about inter-industry differences in protection. Finally, it must be recognized that the actual and expected pay-off to interest groups does not necessarily vary directly with the level of protection obtained by *different* industries. As Figures 34.1 and 34.2 show, the optimal or target level of (tariff) protection t^* may be lower for a powerful lobby than for a less powerful one. Given these difficulties, therefore, it is not surprising that unequivocal empirical support for an 'interest group' explanation of protection is not identifiable. Nonetheless, there are some consistent inter-industry characteristics of the empirical results in this area that merit mention.

These characteristics can be considered under two headings:

1 those that relate to the industry's ability and willingness to finance and resource lobbying activity;
2 those that relate to the scale of the benefits or rents accruing from protection.

The first set of factors relate to the cost function V in Figure 34.1. In this context, it has been argued that the *ability* to form interest groups is directly related to the total income of the potential members of the lobby and the degree of industry concentration and indirectly related to the number and geographical spread of the firms in an industry. In general, the industrial concentration and income size variables do not turn out to be significant in most regression analyses.[10] The number of firms variable tends to perform better and in the expected manner. It might by hypothesized that the *willingness* of those in an industry subject to greater import competition will be affected by the extent of the decline in producer incomes resulting from greater import competition and the degree of resource flexibility in the industry. Many of the proxies (for example, average wage and average age of workers) used for resource flexibility in empirical studies have performed well.[11] These results are consistent with the interest group hypothesis, but it is difficult to argue that the results establish that where capital and labour are less able to move into alternative production lines they are more willing to contribute to lobbying activities. The results may also be consistent with a 'comparative advantage' or narrow economic explanation of protection: low-wage labour-intensive industries in relatively capital-abundant economies tend to be activities of comparative disadvantage that are more likely to be 'supplied' with protection on fairness or electoral grounds.

Of course, expectations of the lobby about the willingness of voters, legislators and administrators to grant assistance-protection will influence the expected shape of the costs of lobbying schedule V in Figures 34.1 and 34.2, in which case it is possible to incorporate supply-side factors from the political market-place into the interest group model. Thus a particular industry may expect it to be less costly to lobby for protection if the authorities are under pressure to supply protection to only a few other industries and/or there is little threat of retaliation against other export-oriented industries. But cross-sectional single-equation regressions cannot be used to distinguish between the relative importance of demand factors and 'expected' (and actual) supply response factors in determining inter-industry differences in protection. Thus the size of an industry (in sales or employment terms) might influence the (expected) variable costs of lobbying for various reasons. On the one hand, the potential members of the lobby for a large industry are likely to recognize their electoral importance and therefore the lower probability of resistance from elected officials to their demands. On the other hand, industry size may, but only *may*, increase the problems of co-ordination, reduce the likelihood of product specialization and homogeneity of interest, and increase the significance of protected (higher-priced) items affecting the real income of the members of the lobby. Pincus (1975) and Greenaway and Milner (1989) find some support for the hypothesis that tariff protection is positively related to the importance of the industry to the economy. But it cannot be established from this evidence which of the above interest group influences is operative. Indeed, even if the electoral influence of industry size applies, it is difficult to establish the extent to which protection is 'supplied' in response to actual lobbying by interest groups or to a recognition by elected officials of their own interests.

As the preceding discussion indicates, proxying and simultaneity problems make it difficult to test the interest group model in a way that differentiates it from competing hypotheses concerning the reason(s) for inter-industry differences in protection. For instance, there is much empirical evidence to show that labour-intensive industries and those that use relatively little human capital tend to have higher rates of protection.[12] Should this be interpreted as support for the argument that low-wage industries with low adjustment flexibility are more likely to overcome the free-rider constraint on lobbying activity, or for the argument that other voters are more sympathetic towards low-income workers? Such questions are difficult to resolve by reference to the available empirical evidence. The interaction of low wages and high levels of, or increases in, import penetration may induce altruistic attitudes on the part of voters towards an industry, and thereby reduce the perceived costs of lobbying. This is consistent with the interest group explanation of trade policy formation. However, a positive association between measures of comparative disadvantage and protection is capable of alternative explanation. Lavergne (1983) finds that the most significant variable explaining US tariff protection even after the Tokyo Round is the pattern of tariff protection embodied in the Smoot–Hawley tariff of 1930. The fact that the relative tariff protection[13] afforded to different industries in the United States has not changed substantially in the last sixty years *could* be interpreted as evidence that trade policy can be analysed in terms of the conservative social welfare hypothesis rather than the interest group hypothesis. Alternatively, interest groups operating sixty years ago may have set the tariff structure, and a similar pattern of interest group power may have prevailed over this period!

34.5 SOME CONCLUDING THOUGHTS

What can we conclude from this review of the empirical evidence? First, the pattern of protection across industries is not random: despite measurement problems, both political and economic factors seem to influence the observed pattern of protection in a systematic manner. Second, although it is difficult to distinguish between competing hypotheses, some of the evidence is consistent with an interest group hypothesis of endogenous trade policy formation. Finally, the fact that the empirical evidence is consistent with several models or hypotheses about the determinants of trade policy may mean that we should view the pressure or interest group model as a complementary rather than a complete model of protection. The interest group model identifies the characteristics of industries that have the greatest probability of forming effective lobbies to obtain rents or relief from foreign competition. The actual or revealed structure of protection is an equilibrium outcome in the market for protection of a wider range of factors. The interest group model is one component only of the rich theoretical insights provided by the political economy approach to the study of policy formulation. There is a tendency in the analysis of trade policy, as in many areas of economic policy, to argue that economic factors and/or the characteristics of interested parties explain the form and content of policy, and that there is little need to dwell on purely political considerations. Measurement errors would make it difficult in any event to search for evidence of purely economic or purely political influences, but such a search does not make sense in the context of 'endogenous' policy formulation. The study of economic policy needs to treat economic and political factors as simultaneous and interacting forces that jointly determine equilibrium conditions in the political market-place.

NOTES

1 The Stolper–Samuelson model is of course long run in nature, and in the shorter run the income distributional effects may be rather different if we allow for sector-specific capital. Mussa (1974), for instance, shows that a tariff raises (lowers) the real return on specific capital in the import-competing (export) sector and that real wages in both sectors may rise or fall.

2 Brock and Magee (1980) use a game-theoretical framework to analyse the manner in which political parties, in a two-party setting, select trade policy. For a broader perspective on the political economy of protectionism, see Baldwin (1982).

3 The rationale for and influence of pressure groups has been emphasized by writers such as Olson (1965) and Pincus (1975).

4 These broader goals for protection are those discussed by Johnson (1960) in his analysis of the 'scientific tariff'.

5 Messerlin (1981) argues that individual bureaucracies strive more strongly than government politicians to protect their economic sector. Finger et al. (1982) provide an empirical analysis of the extent of administered protection in the United States.

6 This type of model of lobby-determined protection has been employed by Feenstra and Bhagwati (1982), Findlay and Wellisz (1982), Baldwin (1984) and Frey (1984).

7 It is the case that some 'sensitive' industries in industrialized countries are protected by a number of instruments. But the use of different instruments, whether for the same industry or for alternative industries, as well as the level of protection requires explanation within a political economy framework.

8 Earmarking tariff revenues in this way has been proposed by Hufbauer and Rosen (1983).

9 Excellent reviews of this literature are given by Baldwin (1985) and Ray (1989).

10 For example, see Saunders (1980) and Helleiner (1977). Greenaway and Milner (1989) have

found some support for industrial concentration variables in a study of nominal and effective protection in the United Kingdom. Caves (1976) also found in the case of Canada that geographically concentrated production and relatively large firm size were positively related to tariff protection.

11 This has been shown by Caves (1976) and Helleiner (1977) for Canada, and by Anderson (1980) for Australia.

12 See, for example, Stern (1963), Cheh (1976) and Ray (1981) for the United States, Caves (1976) and Helleiner (1977) for Canada, and Anderson (1980) for Australia.

13 Lavergne (1983) also shows that non-tariff protection (NTBs) has been used to supplement high-tariff protection. Marvel and Ray (1983) also confirm that NTBs have provided complementary protection to US industries that had lost least tariff protection during the Kennedy Round of GATT negotiations.

REFERENCES

Anderson, K. (1980) 'The political market for government assistance to Australian manufacturing industries', *Economic Record*, 56: 132–44.

Baldwin, R. E. (1982) 'The political economy of protectionism', in J. N. Bhagwati (ed.) *Import Competition and Response*, Chicago, IL: University of Chicago Press.

—— (1984) 'Rent-seeking and trade policy: an industry approach', *Weltwirtschaftliches Archiv* 120: 662–76.

—— (1985) *The Political Economy of US Import Policy*, Cambridge, MA: MIT Press.

Becker, G. (1983) 'A theory of competition among pressure groups for political influence', *Quarterly Journal of Economics* 98: 317–400.

Bhagwati, J. N. (1980) 'Lobbying and welfare', *Journal of Public Economics* 14: 355–63.

—— (1982) 'Directly-unproductive, profit-seeking (DUP) activities', *Journal of Political Economy* 90: 988–1002.

Bhagwati, J. N. and Srinivasan, T. N. (1980) 'Revenue-seeking: a generalization of the theory of tariffs', *Journal of Political Economy* 88: 1069–87.

Brock, W. A. and Magee, S. P. (1980) 'Tariff formation in a democracy', in J. Black and B. Hindley (eds) *Current Issues in Commercial Policy and Diplomacy*, London: Macmillan.

Cassing, J. H. (1980) 'Alternatives to protectionism', in J. Leveson and J. W. Wheeler (eds) *Western Economies in Transition*, Boulder, CO: Westview Press.

Caves, R. E. (1976) 'Economic models of political choice: Canada's tariff structure', *Canadian Journal of Economics* 9: 278–300.

Cheh, J. H. (1976) 'A note on tariffs, non-tariff barriers and labour protection in United States manufacturing industries', *Journal of Political Economy* 84: 289–94.

Corden, W. M. (1974) *Trade Policy and Economic Welfare*, Oxford: Clarendon Press.

Feenstra, R. C. and Bhagwati, J. N. (1982) 'Tariff-seeking and the efficient tariff', in J. N. Bhagwati (ed.) *Import Competition and Response*, Chicago, IL: University of Chicago Press.

Findlay, R. C. and Wellisz, S. (1982) 'Endogenous tariffs, the political economy of trade restrictions and welfare', in J. N. Bhagwati (ed.) *Import Competition and Response*, Chicago, IL: University of Chicago Press.

Finger, J. M., Hall, H. K. and Nelson, D. R. (1982) 'The political economy of administered protection', *American Economic Review* 72: 452–66

Frey, B. (1984) *International Political Economics*, Oxford: Martin Robertson.

711

Greenaway, D. and Milner, C. R. (1989) 'What determines the structure of protection in the UK: comparative costs or interest group behaviour', Mimeo.

Helleiner, G. K. 1977) 'The political economy of Canada's tariff structure: an alternative model', *Canadian Journal of Economics* 10: 318–26.

Hufbauer, G. C. and Rosen, H. (1983) 'Managing comparative advantage', Mimeo.

Johnson, H. G. (1960) 'The cost of protection and the scientific tariff', *Journal of Political Economy* 68: 327–45.

Krueger, A. O. (1974) 'The political economy of the rent-seeking society', *American Economic Review* 64: 291–303.

Lavergne, R. (1983) *The Political Economy of US Tariffs. An Empirical Analysis*, New York: Academic Press.

Marvel, H. P. and Ray, E. J. (1983) 'The Kennedy Round: evidence on the regulation of international trade in the United States', *American Economic Review* 73: 190–7.

Messerlin, P. A. (1981) 'The political economy of protectionism: the bureaucratic case', *Weltwirtschaftliches Archiv* 117: 496.

Mussa, M. 1974) 'Tariffs and the distribution of income: the importance of factor specificity, substitutability and intensity in the short and long run', *Journal of Political Economy* 82: 1191–2043.

Olson, M. (1965) *The Logic of Collective Action: Public Goods and the Theory of Groups*, Cambridge, MA: Harvard University Press.

Pincus, J. (1975) 'Pressure groups and the pattern of tariffs', *Journal of Political Economy* 83: 757–78.

Ray, E. J. (1981) 'Tariff and non-tariff barriers in the United States and abroad', *Review of Economics and Statistics* 63: 161–8.

—— (1989) 'Empirical research on the political economy of trade', Paper presented to the International Agricultural Trade Research Consortium Symposium, Auberge Mont Gabriel, Canada.

Saunders, R. S. (1980) 'The political economy of effective protection in Canada's manufacturing sector', *Canadian Journal of Economics* 13: 340–8.

Stern, R. M. (1963), 'The US tariff and the efficiency of the US economy', *American Economic Review, Papers and Proceedings* 54: 459–70.

Stolper, W. F. and Samuelson, P. A. (1941) 'Protection and real wages', *Review of Economic Studies* 9: 58–73.

35

ECONOMIC ADVICE AND ECONOMIC POLICY

ALAN PEACOCK

35.1 INTRODUCTION

Although economists have been active as government advisers since the time of the Cameralists,[1] it is within living memory that they have formed a recognizable cadre within the public service. Thus, while in the late 1920s Winston Churchill could jest about the Treasury's tame economist, R. G. Hawtrey, being 'released from the dungeon in which we were said to have immured him, have his chains struck off and the straw brushed from his hair and clothes to be admitted to the light and warmth of the Treasury Boardroom' (Roseveare 1969), sixty years later government economic advisers have become public figures with the popular attribution of great influence if not power. Nor is this an exclusively British phenomenon (for evidence, see Coats 1981).

The study of the economist's role in government is the natural concomitant to this growth in employment opportunities. First, there are the many accounts written by those who have served in senior positions in government which provide valuable raw material on the variety of tasks that they have been asked to undertake and on their 'successes' and 'failures'.[2] Second, there are studies which ponder over the vexed question as to how economic advice should be organized. Should economists be members of government departments in which they become fully integrated with the political process, or can they operate more effectively as members of some independent advice-giving body?[3] Third, how far do the value judgements of economists on policy matters determine the thrust of their advice (see Coughlin 1989)? How far do such judgements affect the government's choice of advisers and the position of permanently employed advisers who disagree with the government whom they serve (see Peacock 1979)?

An economist entering government service or called upon to advise a government will no doubt find it useful to consult the works of those who have

This contribution draws heavily on two earlier articles by the author (Peacock 1987, 1988).

713

considered these matters. However, he/she must begin with the realization that the economist is part of his/her own subject matter. If the economist firmly believes in the robustness of utility theory, then presumably he/she accepts that utility maximization is as much a characteristic of an economist as of other human beings. Why should economists analyse the behaviour of 'bureaucrats', often concluding that they are 'rent-seekers' rather than dispassionate guardians of the public interest, without recognizing that the pot may be calling the kettle black?

While it is tempting to build a model of the economists' utility function which is capable of testing, it is sufficient for the purpose of this contribution to offer a few *obiter dicta* which I am sure most economists would consider plausible if not beyond question, and I claim that these *obiter* are at least based on close personal observation. Economists certainly attach importance to long-term income prospects and to prestige and power, but those with any self-respect at all trade these off against reputation with their peer group and the associated 'desire for excellence' which Alfred Marshall regarded as characteristic of professional people.

The implication of this view of the economist as a utility-maximizer is that he has sufficient incentive to resist becoming solely a lackey of the government whose service he enters. This has been disputed by two economists whose views I greatly respect. James Buchanan and Harry Johnson repeatedly warned economists about the corrupting influence of government, and the strong possibility that they would soon acquire the attributes of those self-seeking bureaucrats who stalk the pages of their works on public choice analysis. However, even if I assert that the economist's own motivation would offer sufficient safeguard against the hazards of advising governments, it may be helpful to offer a few words of advice to anyone attracted by the excitements described by those who have chronicled their careers in government. If all of us maximize, subject to constraints, it is as well to be warned about the nature of those constraints. This is what I have attempted to do in the following homily.

35.2 PROPOSITION 1: 'BEWARE THE OPTIMIZATION PARADIGM'

The following assumptions are made in a typical policy model employed by economists in attempting to justify their own role.

1 Governments have objectives in which trade-offs are clear and which can be translated into some quantitative form, i.e. appear as terms in a set of equations.

2 Governments maximize these objectives subject to constraints, which are

known and accepted. Problems arise in defining the extent of constraints, including admission of 'feedback' (see, for example, Alt and Chrystal 1983).
3 Governments have an interest in choosing instruments which minimize the 'cost' of implementing policies, including feedback effects.

If the economic and political system were subject to conditions which would exercise skills similar to those of a control engineer, then the role of advisers would be clear. They would have a clearly scientific role designed to improve the predictive capacity of economic and political models so that the precise relations between the dependent variables, (the policy aims) and the independent variables (the instruments) would be known as far as possible. Research effort would undergo constant adaptation as the government welfare function changed, or as new instruments needed to be devised as old ones 'wore out'. Politicians would choose policies, and economic and political advisers – heavily influenced by research input – would choose the instruments. Some economists, notably Ragnar Frisch, the Nobel Laureate in Economics, have claimed that in fulfilling their professional role in government as advisers backed by first-class research effort, the economists would create a political consensus in respect of economic policies (see Bergh 1981).

In a general sort of way the type of macroeconomic policy models used by those responsible for economic planning perform the kinds of co-ordinating function suggested by our paradigm. Such models force policy-makers to specify targets which can be translated into dependent variables for which values can be found, for example numbers unemployed or inflation measured by a consumers' price index. It allows economic advisers to specify the quantifiable links between movements in these target variables and to point the 'mix' of policy instruments (taxes, borrowing and expenditure variables) in the 'right' direction. It gives direction to the research effort necessary to establish these links in a fully articulated macroeconomic model and to the properties of the computation system which has to be able to offer sensible and speedy simulations of policy scenarios.

At the same time, it must be realized that such models can only embody a strictly limited range of objectives, primarily short term, which can be given quantitative expression. Their usefulness depends not only on econometric skill but also on the judgement which enters into the choice of the values of certain important independent variables, notably concerning the anticipated behaviour of trading partners which has to be reflected in forecasts of the volume of world trade. Furthermore, their influence on policy depends on their credibility with politicians in power who are not necessarily impressed by the technical skill of the model-builders. In short, the macroeconomic policy models convey a very restricted view of the skills required in advising governments on economic question as well as a false impression of the kind of situation in which the economic adviser may find himself.

It is paradoxical that it has been certain branches of economic research which have led some economists to question the relevance of the paradigm. In itself, this would be a convenient myth to perpetrate if one wanted to create the most congenial conditions for advisers and their research staffs. Let me elaborate this point. The development of public choice theory and the associated economic theory of bureaucracy has led professional economists to look closely at the motivation of politicians and bureaucrats, to build models of their behaviour and to devise testable predictions of the consequences of their attempts to maximize utility. This is not the place to evaluate this contribution to our understanding of government of the economics of politics. Both Chapter 12 and Chapter 38 are directed at this. I would only remark that its value in this context lies in the attention drawn to certain facets of political and administrative behaviour which are relevant to understanding the forces governing the 'supply' of policy advice to government and the 'demand' for such advice.

If, following Downs, it is broadly true that political parties in power endeavour to maximize their length of life in office, then it may not be in the interests of a government to specify too exactly its economic and social targets for fear of political 'backlash'. If targets such as the rate of unemployment and inflation matter, there may be a temptation to operate a 'political business cycle' in order to win elections. Individual politicians as members of a government may trade off political ambitions within their party against the need for collective responsibility for decision-making. They will differ in their degrees of commitment to government objectives and also to the choice of instruments which, as department heads, they have under their immediate control. The monitoring of the actions of public officials, we are told, is difficult because they have discretionary power, which enables them to promote policies of their own as well as to pursue their personal ambitions, material and otherwise. As the objectives of all these various parts of government and those whose actions they seek to control – industry and consumers – conflict, and as each group has weapons at its disposal to influence if not to deny the 'supply' of services upon which the other depends, then the 'control system paradigm' is inapplicable and needs to be replaced by one which highlights the importance of multi-sector bargaining (Peacock 1979).

This account of the incompleteness of the optimization paradigm is designed to offer a warning to the economist entering government offices that his niche cannot be precisely defined. He/she will not find themselves adjusting their activities and behaviour within the limits set by clearly discernible constraints. The signals that might guide them are often difficult to read, often because those who demand their services may not themselves be sure why they want economic advice at all. These homiletic effusions can be illustrated from

716

personal experience by two examples. A Minister of State once summoned me urgently to give my 'professional judgement', as he called it, on whether it was more important to 'beat inflation than to cure unemployment'. He was clearly surprised when I suggested that when he had made his own mind up on the question I might conceivably be able to tell him what the consequences of his position would be, but that my own value judgements were not relevant. My second example comes from advising an international agency in which my main task was to comment on the policy research papers of its members. My role seemed as precisely defined as it could be. After two weeks, I was politely admonished for working through the papers too quickly. The quality of my comments was not in dispute: I was merely working too fast and was told that 'I should let the incoming papers mature longer in my in-tray'!

35.3 PROPOSITION 2: 'THERE IS NO "WELCOME" MAT SPREAD BEFORE YOU'

You are an economist with a good training and a good research and publication record behind you and you are asked to join a department of government concerned with economic affairs. You are excited at the prospect and are bubbling over with ideas for immediate execution. Hold yourself in check. As a wise predecessor of mine in government advised me: 'Do not announce your arrival except to those who pay you. Do not look for work. Let everyone else find out for themselves that you exist – even ministers. Only respond, do not initiate. This gives you six months to find out what is going on, and who will take you seriously and who will not.' Why did he say this? Let me explain.

Take first of all your value systems. You may be tempted to say that your values are irrelevant and that you are there to demonstrate the virtues of economics as a positive science. The first thing that will happen is that you will find an administrator with a training in philosophy who proves that your Paretian or your neo-utilitarian axioms which 'demonstrate' the desirability of certain policies in preference to others are nothing more than political nostrums in disguise. If you adopt the other tack and say that you are content to accept the value judgements of others and to examine their implications for the design of policy measures, incredulity will be written over the faces of your audience, and at least one unkind member of it will say that you would be willing to do a cost–benefit study of the design of torture chambers. In this 'catch-22' situation, particularly if you are young or youngish, it is better to admit some political bias. To say that you have Social Democratic leanings will probably make you sound respectable and relatively harmless!

Second, your professional competence will be subject to ordeal by scepticism. Practically every senior administrator believes that he is at least as good an economist as you are and that only the doctrine of comparative advantage prevents him from seeking the abolition of your post. You will be put to the test through the obvious device of showing that the government macroeconomic model performs worse than those of outsiders and that all such models contain margins of error which are greater than the changes in gross domestic product (GDP) which you wish to see brought about by policy instruments. You have to admit this, and a possible reply is to claim that such models perform at least marginally better than 'back of the envelope' calculations. If you are brave, ask your questioner to give particular reasons why he thinks that the model performs badly so that you can help to rectify it. Nine times out of ten you can point out to him, tactfully of course, that his 'model' embodies much stronger assumptions than that of the economists. There will usually be one senior administrator who positively welcomes your presence. Avoid him or her if you can. Unsullied by an economics education, he has probably been working away for years on an economic theory of his own designed to transform the economy. He will want to spend hours with you, his kindred spirit, and if you tell him that he is a crank you may have made an enemy for life. The general line to take with your colleagues can be summed up in a paraphrase of the wise words of Alice Rivlin, the economist and ex-director of the US Congressional Budget Office: 'The main problem with economists is that we make decisions harder for you, but you can't do without us' (see Rivlin (1983) for the original statement).

It must follow that any 'original' views that you may have about the use of policy instruments are not likely to be greeted with cries of approval. For example, all forms of tax reform, you will discover, have been proposed before. Of those, as in the Gospel of St Matthew, Chapter 22, verse 14, 'many are called but few are chosen'. Those that succeed are probably the legacy of some quite catastrophic event, such as the survival of the income tax in the United Kingdom after the Napoleonic Wars and the system of pay-as-you-earn taxation, its great-grandson, after the Second World War. From time to time, intelligent but inexperienced ministers who consult outside advisers may insist on the 'working-up' of schemes which have some passing intellectual attraction strong enough to require administrators to respond. I went through an elaborate exercise in which I had to produce at very short notice a scheme for preventing wage inflation in which employers were to be taxed if they allowed wage claims which exceeded some policy 'norm'. Various 'placebos' were built into the variants of the scheme, including the compulsory investment of the tax in shares in the offending company which would ultimately become the property of employees. Senior administrators watched with amused tolerance as the scheme went through the various hurdles which they had erected to prevent it reaching the status of a Cabinet paper. They slept easily in their beds for they knew that even having reached that stage it would be rejected, as indeed it was, without discussion. You begin to realize that Maurice Laure, the inventor of the value-added tax, must have been a genius in salesmanship as well as an accomplished French expert on fiscal matters.

In short your 'triumphs', as perceived by senior administrators, will not be measured simply by your ability to promote new ideas that imply changes in administrative procedures alongside changes in the direction of economic policy. While upwardly mobile young administrators may sympathize with your attempts to differentiate your product, for they themselves draw attention to their capabilities by doing much the same, the sceptical, hardened and long-serving campaigners will think otherwise. Often as not, you will be asked to produce new ideas or fresh arguments, not to promote change but to impede it.

35.4 PROPOSITION 3: 'THE PART IS GREATER THAN THE WHOLE'

A few years ago two of my young colleagues at York were invited to write a report on some aspects of the economics of income taxation in a South American country. They were very shocked at their reception, and possibly even more shocked when I told them that I was not surprised at their experience. As they stepped off the plane, they were met by a charming young official from the Ministry of Economic Planning who gave them a list of the conclusions which his ministry expected them to reach about tax reform. This attack on their professional virtue was renewed by the Revenue Service, which informed them through an equally charming official that full co-operation was assured, provided that they would feel able to reach the conclusion that no changes in the structure of the income tax were necessary! One cannot blame my colleagues for not having been brought face to face with my proposition 3: 'The part is greater than the whole'.

In the early days of this century the Cambridge don F. M. Cornford wrote a splendid tract, *Microcosmographia Academica*, designed as a guide to the young academic who sought to understand and to participate in the politics of academe. It is a book packed with wit and wisdom, and is still in print after eighty years. Cornford spent some time in government and noted with regret that academic life was one genus of a larger species. 'College feeling', he came to realize, was a kind of parochial loyalty exactly corresponding to 'departmental feeling' in government, which 'like other species of patriotism, consists in the sincere belief that the institution to which you belong is better than the institution to which other people belong' (Cornford 1908). It is certainly my experience that departmental loyalties are extremely important in government and are reinforced in the United Kingdom by the placing of cabinet ministers in administrative change of a department. This offers them the strong temptation to employ the policy instruments that they control in order to dramatize

719

their policy role, subject to the overall constraint of having to accept some collective political strategy at cabinet level if only in the interests of preserving political credibility with the electorate. Just as nations or indeed football teams have 'anthems' which prescribe the nature and bounds of this patriotic feeling, departments have crude symbols of their aims. Therefore, the purpose of the Inland Revenue in the United Kingdom is summed up in the phrase 'protect the revenue at all costs', whereas the Treasury is there to 'protect the expenditure estimates'. Ministries of Agriculture and Industry are somewhat cynically regarded as 'captives' of farmers and industrialists respectively, whereas in the United Kingdom, at least, the famous Board of Trade (now incorporated in the Department of Trade and Industry (DTI)) has long been in the business of trying to stop ministers from erecting tariff barriers.

It is easy to see that as governments took on more and more direction of the economy, economic co-ordination, blissfully assumed to be the policy paradigm of economists, became more and more essential – and more and more difficult to achieve. Even if there is lip-service to such co-ordination, there will be strong competition between departments, spurred on by the natural ambitions of ministers and senior officials, to be 'in the lead' in economic policy matters. At the very least – and this is where the adviser has an important role – such ambitions cannot be realized without the minister and his senior officials being manifestly well informed on economic matters, and, if possible, better informed than 'rival' ministries.

Let me quote an example from experience. The perceived task of the DTI in the United Kingdom is to protect the interests of industry (if not of industrialists) whether or not these interests coincide with the interests of other groups 'sponsored' by other departments. In 1974, in the shadow of the famous oil crisis, a long-drawn-out battle took place against the Treasury and the Inland Revenue in order to obtain relief for industry from profits taxation through a change in the method of valuing their stocks, which would have offended against the doctrine of 'protect the revenue at all costs'. One of the main factors in achieving 'victory' (as the DTI saw it) was the fact that the department controlled the main sources of financial information and the speed of their general release within government. Officials were thoroughly primed in the ways in which this information could be used to support their case.

It might appear from these observations that an economist who placed any value on professional integrity, reputation with his peer group and pride in the job would find such a situation intolerable. Offering advice that is designed purely to promote the interests of the 'home team' would quickly gain one the reputation of being a hired gun – and such news travels fast through the ranks of fellow professionals. If his economic analysis and associated policy recommendations are non-negotiable, how is an economist going to conduct himself in the company of those whom he advises and may control his own promotion prospects if he stays in government? I am convinced from personal experience that sticking to one's professional guns is not only a morally unassailable position but is also one which does not necessarily produce this dilemma of choice. For one thing, the 'departmental line' may not be clearly drawn, in which case an uncompromising professional line may win one not only respect but even allies. If any decision involves interdepartmental negotiation on economic policies, then it may be possible to form a coalition of economists across departments, who could form a formidable pressure group in support of the 'correct' policy action to take.

However, if a senior economist, as he must be, is forced to stand alone in his professional judgement and derives utility from fighting for his corner, then he has to be prepared to 'market' his views. This requires that the economist pay particular attention to the clarity of his argument and to the putting of his advice within a context which the minister can understand. 'Working one's passage' with the minister is a test not only of expository skill but frequently of patience and tact. It is for this reason that senior administrators may prefer the economists to filter their advice through them rather than risk what may be a potentially explosive confrontation!

Let me give you an example which illustrates this. In the mid-1970s I was faced with preparing a cost-benefit analysis for the building of additional Concorde aircraft. A very careful study was made by my staff, which included an experienced economist who was also trained as an engineer. The economist's task was to work out whether the benefits exceeded the costs, having regard to the time pattern of both benefits and costs. To enable a comparison to be made with the alternative use of the resources necessary to produce Concordes, some appropriate rate of discount had to be chosen in order to evaluate costs and benefits which occur at different points in future time. Defining the benefits as increases in real output and accepting the then agreed 'test rate of discount', as it is called in the trade, the calculation showed that the net present value of additional Concordes would be negative.

It would have been naive and counterproductive to have offered the minister the conclusion that he should not finance the building of more Concordes and, in any case, any firm policy recommendation would have to come from or be approved by the administrative head of the department. I was therefore careful to point out that (a) any calculations of this kind were subject to inevitable uncertainty about future revenues and were sensitive to the rate of discount which was chosen, and (b) the definition of benefit was confined to increases in net output and therefore ignored both distributional effects and any perceived non-economic benefits.

The strength of the economic approach, I argued, lay in demonstrating to the minister that, if he accepted the project, he would have to convince his Cabinet colleagues that they placed a minimum value on the non-economic benefits at least equal to the differences between the discounted costs and benefits or to the negative present value which had been calculated. In this way, I was able to avoid making a political judgement which would have annoyed the minister.

The outcome may be of interest. The minister could quite easily have sought to justify acceptance of the project by arguing that the non-economic benefits, such as international prestige and employment effects, were paramount. However, there was a particular reason why the minister was not anxious to emphasize the non-economic benefits. Concordes were being built in his own constituency and his majority was not secure! To have emphasized the social benefits would have laid him open to the charge of political bribery. He therefore rejected the calculations mainly on the grounds that the 'test rate of discount' was too high, an argument which was readily supplied by one of his party's own economic advisers! This was defeat, I hope, with honour untarnished!

35.5 PROPOSITION 4: 'PUT NOT THY TRUST IN PRINCES'

I have concentrated so far on advisers on economic questions who are employed by government, but I have not considered the position of advisers who may be brought in to make recommendations *ad hoc*, as with specially appointed commissions or committees on matters of national importance. Although I have these kinds of adviser in mind, this is not to say that my views are not necessarily applicable to 'internal' advice-giving situations.

No homily on advice-giving would be complete without a reference to Machiavelli, and it is all set out for us in his *Discourses* (see Machiavelli 1950: Book III). In Chapter XXXVV, ominously entitled 'Of the danger of being prominent in counselling any enterprise, and how that danger increases with the importance of such enterprise', Machiavelli asks the question: what is the fate of the advice-giver if his advice is taken/not taken and if it is accepted/not accepted? We can construct a 'pay-off' matrix representing the marginal utility to the advice-giver of alternative outcomes (Table 35.1). Our Italian philosopher is quite explicit about the signs in the elements! If your advice is taken by the prince or republic and is wrong, then your enemies destroy you. If it is taken and is right, then 'glory is not assured', particularly if your advice contravenes that of others. If your advice is not taken and is wrong you will

Table 35.1

	Advice right	Advice wrong
Advice taken	+ (?)	− (?)
Advice not taken	+ (?)	0 (?)

be ignored, and if it is not taken and you are right, then you may be in credit and be listened to more carefully in future. You would have thought that Machiavelli would have advised his readers to keep out of the advice game, but, thinking of prominent people, he claims that for them to withhold counsel would be to risk the charge of disloyalty. (For them, unfortunately, it is the only game in town!) He concludes that if you are forced willy-nilly into the position of giving advice, then do not advocate any enterprise 'with too much zeal' but 'give one's advice calmly and modestly'. Amen to that!

As with many creative minds, what interests us in their speculation is the methodology rather than the results, and this example from Machiavelli is no exception. I would make two points about it of relevance to advice-giving. The first is that, whereas Machiavelli's game-players are forced to play and for high stakes, we consider a situation where no one is forced either to give or to take advice and where the consequences of being wrong or right are fortunately nothing like as severe. In consequence, we find that the supply of advice is very inelastic with respect to money price and the position of the supply curve is such that a very large quantity of it will be supplied free. Economists are falling over themselves to tell governments what to do about economic policy, and the main ingredient of positive utility is more likely to be the prospect of a respectable professional audience in a refereed journal than of being taken seriously by government. (I have known economists say that the moment when governments like their ideas is the moment to reconsider them very carefully!) It is an added bonus if one is paid by anyone for expounding one's views on what government economic policy ought to be. In practice, one finds that a large segment of government demand for economic advice consists of requests to internal economic advisers to provide a running commentary on the relevance of the countless proposals emanating from a whole range of sources. Only occasionally will this commentary lead to the stage where it will be followed up, perhaps by hiring the originator of the idea as a consultant.

The second point concerns the position of the *ad hoc* adviser who presumably has taken on the job of heading a commission or a committee or joining one of these bodies because he/she will derive positive utility from giving right advice and having it taken, otherwise he/she would not be in the game. Anyone in this position should think very carefully about assigning probabilities to the outcomes. As my previous exposition indicates, it is far from certain that there will be agreement within government as to what would constitute good advice, given the shifting power structure and conflicts of interests within government. Even if you satisfy the 'prince' (i.e. the minister) who has hired you, the politics of government may force him to make bargains with colleagues who have different interests and the cost to him may be the sacrifice of your proposals. Therefore when I quote the Psalms – 'put not your trust in princes' – I am not saying that princes are untrustworthy but that they may not be able to deliver.

Let me give an example. In late 1983 the Conservative government decided to review the state pension scheme. Index linked and earnings related, and with a growing proportion of pensioners per head of population, the scheme, as with many others in Western Europe, threatens to become a formidable fiscal burden. I was taken on, along with two others, as adviser to the Government Inquiry into Retirement Provision. Although the chairman was the Secretary of State for Health and Social Security, he was surrounded by ministers representing employment, trade, tax and budgetary matters, all being briefed by departmental officials. My own proposal was to scrap the earnings-related element in the state scheme, although to retain some fiscal advantages for voluntary saving for retirement and to raise the basic flat-rate pension to protect the poor. The net result in budgetary terms would have been a rise in pensions expenditure in the short run compensated by a much greater fall in such expenditure in the longer run. The Treasury strongly opposed *any* immediate increase in expenditure as contrary to their 'rule' (See section 35.4), implying that any future savings should be subject to an infinite rate of discount. The 'protection of the revenue' meant implacable opposition to anything smelling of a tax concession to savers, even though this might increase the rate of private saving as an offset to a fall in public saving. Neither the Treasury nor the Inland Revenue would allow the discussion to be extended to the case which could be made for cutting other kinds of spending or raising other taxes elsewhere in order both to meet their rigid rules and to implement the pension scheme, even though they had no *locus standi* in political decisions which are a Cabinet matter. The final proposals embodied a series of compromises. I had to be satisfied with the fact that my proposals had a 'run for their money'!

35.6 CONCLUSION

The distillation of my views on the constraints that a utility-maximizing economist may encounter in advising governments may leave the impression that I am both critical of how government business is conducted and offering positive discouragement to those who would enter its service. This is not the case, and appeal to simple economic analysis will demonstrate how I could not come to such a conclusion.

First, the present thrust of economics training puts considerable emphasis on the backing of any generalization by empirical evidence, particularly if the proposition in question is to be the basis for personal action. The evidence that I have provided is partial, impressionistic and qualitative. In particular, I have concentrated only on the more dramatic situations in which an economist in government might find him/herself. The degree of exposure to the constraints that I have outlined varies as between governments and between departments within government. At most, I have provided a point of departure for further enquiries that would-be advisers would wish to make by, for example, sampling the literature which I have already listed.

Second, it is easy to fall into the common trap of comparing an actual situation in which an economist might pursue a career, with all the hazards that may entail, with some idealized alternatives. The problems of adjustment of professional economists can be said to arise from the propensity to construct economic models of organizational behaviour that oversimplify the work situations in which they are likely to find themselves. This is certainly true of economic models of government, but it can be equally true of industrial and financial undertakings and of non-profit-making organizations, all of whom employ economists. A parallel 'early warning system' about employment in these alternative institutions would contain similar elements. It is doubtful if the familiar office notice, 'you don't have to be mad to work here – but it helps', is sold exclusively to particular sectors of the economy.

Finally, a utility-maximizing economist with a good training and a continuing interest in professional matters will know that it is rational to keep alternative employment opportunities under review and will accumulate a stock of information on job specifications. Additionally, risk-loving economists may be tempted to try their hand at setting up on their own as economic consultants. It is a sign of the coming to maturity of economics that economists can contemplate an optimal career structure which permits mobility between government, international organizations and the private sector to an extent which would not have seemed possible when I first entered the profession. Whatever the course of action, a spell in government is a useful discipline, in that one has been placed in the position of thinking on one's feet and of having to meet impossible deadlines.

NOTES

1 For a useful short account of the activities of the Cameralists, see Recktenwald (1987).
2 Amongst many examples, see Cairncross (1971), Roberts (1984), Roll (1985), Henderson (1986) and MacDougall (1987). For an international cross-section of views, see Pechman (1989).
3 This has been a major preoccupation in the United States (Tobin 1966; Salant 1973; Nelson 1987; Rivlin 1987). For German experience, see Wallich (1984).

REFERENCES

Alt, J. E. and Chrystal, K. A. (1983) *Political Economics*, Part III, Brighton: Harvester Wheatsheaf.
Bergh, T. (1981) 'Norway: the powerful servants', in A. W. Coats (ed.) *Economists in Government: An International Survey*, Durham, NC: Duke University Press.

725

Cairncross, A. K. (1971) *Essays in Economic Management*, Nos 10 and 11, London: Allen & Unwin.

Coats, A. W. (ed.) (1981) *Economists in Government: An International Survey*, Durham, NC: Duke University Press.

Cornford, F. M. (1908) *Microcosmographia Academica*, Cambridge: Bowes & Bowes.

Coughlin, P. J. (1989) 'Economic advice and political preferences', *Public Choice* 61 (3).

Henderson, P. D. (1986) *Innocence and Design: Influence of Economic Ideas on Policy*, Oxford: Basil Blackwell.

MacDougall, D. (1987) *Don and Mandarin*, London: John Murray.

Machiavelli, N. (1950) *The Prince and the Discourses*, New York: Modern Library Edition.

Nelson, R. H. (1987) 'The economics profession and the making of public policy', *Journal of Economic Literature* 25 (1).

Peacock, A. (1979) *The Economic Analysis of Government and Related Themes*, ch. I, Part IV, Oxford: Martin Robertson.

—— (1987) 'Some gratuitous advice to fiscal advisers', in *The Relevance of Public Finance for Policy-Making*, Detroit, MI: Wayne State University Press.

—— (1988) 'An economic anlysis of economic advice giving', *Atlantic Economic Journal* 16 (3).

Pechman, J. A. (ed.) (1989) *The Role of the Economist in Government: An International Perspective*, London: Harvester Wheatsheaf.

Recktenwald, H. C. (1987) 'Cameralism', in J. Eatwell, M. Milgate and P. Newman (eds) *The New Palgrave Dictionary of Economics*, vol. I, London: Macmillan.

Rivlin, A. (1983) 'An intelligent politician's guide to dealing with experts', in *The Rand Graduate Institute: Commencement Address 1974–83*, Santa Monica, CA: Rand Graduate Institute.

—— (1987) 'Economics and the political process', *American Economic Review* 75 (1).

Roberts, P. C. (1984) *The Supply Side Revolution*, Cambridge, MA: Harvard University Press.

Roll, E. 1985) *Crowded Hours*, London: Faber.

Roseveare, H. (1969) *The Treasury*, Harmondsworth: Penguin.

Salant, W. S. (1973) 'Some intellectual contributions of the Truman Council of Economic Advisers to policy-making', *History of Political Economy* 5 (1).

Tobin, J. (1966) *The Intellectual Revolution in U.S. Economic Policy-Making*, London: Longmans Green.

Wallich, H. C. (1984) 'The German Council of Economic Advisers in an American perspective', *Journal of Institutional and Theoretical Economics* 140 (2).

IV. INTERFACES

36

ECONOMICS AND RELATED DISCIPLINES

MICHAEL BLEANEY AND IAN STEWART

36.1 THE NATURE OF ECONOMICS

The interface between economics and other disciplines is not something which attracts sustained attention amongst economists. It is the sort of subject about which they might muse in the coffee bar, but they would be unlikely to commit their thoughts to paper. Many people, if asked to produce a prospectus for an overview volume of the present kind, would probably not have included a section on 'interfaces'. We have chosen to devote a significant proportion of this volume to the subject precisely because it appears to us to be an important but underexplored area.

One compelling reason why economists do not bother themselves too much about the relationship between economics and other disciplines is that they have enough trouble keeping up with what is going on in economics itself. The volume of academic literature produced grows annually, as the university systems of the world expand and more academic economists are employed. Until about 1930 it would probably have been reasonable to expect everyone to be well informed about the latest ideas in virtually any area of the subject, but the accelerating rate of output has necessitated increasingly narrow specialization, and this process has been facilitated by the growing number of specialist journals. Nowadays, breadth of knowledge tends to be the exception rather than the rule. In an effort to keep the rest of the profession abreast of the latest research, survey articles have proliferated and at least two journals which are entirely devoted to this kind of article have recently been established.

Nevertheless, this is clearly not the whole explanation. Indeed, economics is almost certainly a more unified discipline than most. The fundamental body of theory is common ground, and as a practising economist one can be fairly certain that economists in other specialisms are applying techniques that one can understand and would probably apply oneself in the same circumstances. There is neither a vast body of theory that is specific to one specialism, as in

729

mathematics, nor a tremendous investment in specific factual knowledge, as in history. Finally, despite the existence of minority schools of thought such as the post-Keynesians, there is not the wide divergence of approach that currently affects literary and artistic studies. In fact, it is probably precisely the feeling that economists *need* to be aware of what is going on elsewhere in the discipline that has created the demand for survey articles.

What is it, then, that unifies economics? This is a difficult question to answer, but the key must surely lie in the existence of certain axioms that are implicitly accepted by all economists. These axioms can be summarized in the maxim that people and institutions are in rational pursuit of goals that are defined by a set of preferences that can be taken as stable. It was the marginalist school of the later nineteenth century that established this definition of economics and made the exploration of its implications the foundation of its research programme, although this is not to say that much that had been written previously was actually inconsistent with this approach. The rational pursuit of goals is usually taken to mean the maximization of some objective function, although it does not necessarily exclude other formulations, such as 'satisficing' behaviour, provided that they can be justified as a rational response to uncertainty and lack of information. The assumption that tastes and preferences are stable has the effect of defining a distinct boundary between economics and sociology or psychology. Economics takes preferences as given, and the formation of preferences is regarded as an extra-economic issue. Human behaviour, as viewed by economics, is essentially a question of choice under constraints; indeed, some writers would regard economic theory as a general theory of choice.

One consequence that is worth noting – even though it is somewhat tangential to the main subject of this chapter – is that economics is often at odds with popular feeling. Economic theory leads naturally to some basic propositions about the efficiency of markets, and in the real world markets often operate in a harsh and arbitrary fashion, and make the achievement of other socially desirable objectives such as a more equal distribution of income rather difficult to achieve. As Frey (1986) has shown, the price mechanism itself tends to be viewed with distaste by the population at large: he cites an experiment in which respondents objected to rationing by price in the presence of a shortage, even when they were assured that there would be no distributional consequences.[1] The eulogy of markets in which economics indulges therefore often appears one-sided and ideological, and it is the emotional reaction against this which underpins self-styled 'radical' schools such as the post-Keynesians. It is by no means clear that these unorthodox schools actually reject these propositions about the efficiency of markets, or that their positive theorizing is based on radically different premises, but they certainly wish to place the emphasis on other issues.[2]

730

By establishing these widely accepted axioms economics has prevented itself from becoming bogged down in continuous debate about fundamentals and has been able to establish a formidable body of theory. This has undoubtedly been an enormous bonus. However, it is inevitable that some issues are more susceptible to this kind of treatment than others. Understanding the market for coffee beans has proved a great deal easier than understanding the labour market, in which a continuing social relationship is established between buyer and seller through the production process. On the whole, economics has been rather slow to accept its own limitations and to seek insight from other social sciences. For example, attempts to make good use of sociological theory in labour economics have been exceedingly rare.[3] It may be that economists have rightly judged that there is not much useful sociological theory available, but it seems more probable that they have not seriously looked.

There are many academic disciplines that could have a bearing on economics, or *vice versa*. In commissioning the chapters in this section, we are aware that we have not covered all possible candidates. One notable omission is the absence of a chapter on economics and mathematics, an omission that was forced upon us by the failure of the invited author to produce the goods. This was unfortunate, and as a partial attempt to repair the damage we offer some of our own thoughts on this question below.

One way of interpreting the relationship between economics and other disciplines is to focus on the direction of the traffic in ideas. Some subjects have drawn on economics, whereas others have been used substantially by economics. There may be some for which the traffic has been substantial in both directions. Yet others have found themselves in competition with economics in explaining certain phenomena. In this last category would probably come sociology and history. Is human behaviour culturally determined or does it merely respond to the incentives offered? Whereas sociology emphasizes the former, economics stresses the latter. One case, referred to by Balasubraman-yam and MacBean in Chapter 18, is the question of whether agricultural producers in less developed countries respond to price incentives. Another is the economics of the family, which considers the costs and benefits of children and seeks to explain the relatively high birth rates in less developed countries in terms of the period of compulsory education, the anticipated returns to child labour and the absence of social security provision. The economics of the family represents an attempt to bring economic analysis into a field which would previously have been considered pre-eminently sociological. Or suppose that we were to ask the question: why are cows sacred to Hindus? Economists would be much more convinced by an explanation based on the idea that before cows became sacred the cattle population was suboptimal, than by one which made no reference to economic factors. Examples of this kind can be multiplied; they reflect the predisposition instilled in us by our intellectual

731

training. Since our ultimate aim must be to achieve an integrated understanding of the role of cultural factors and economic incentives in social behaviour, the division of academic training into economics and sociology may prove harmful in so far as it sets up debates in which positions become too easily polarized because the relative value of two forms of human capital is at stake.

In the case of economic history, there is an obvious contrast between the traditional historical approach, based on meticulous examination of sources, and the economist's desire to test hypotheses on whatever numerical data are available, often with little regard to their limitations and inaccuracies. As Crafts discusses in Chapter 41, the advent of the so-called new economic history has raised these issues in a particularly acute fashion.

Perhaps the clearest case of economics exporting its mode of analysis to another discipline is that of political science, as McLean shows in Chapter 38. Political parties in a democracy are considered as selling a particular package to voters, adjusting the content in order to be elected, whilst voters make choices much as they would in a supermarket. It is the analogy between this situation and the consumer goods market that renders this approach fruitful.

In other areas economics has been influenced by ideas from other disciplines. Philosophical notions of justice and fairness have an obvious application in welfare economics and public sector economics, although Sen (1987) has argued powerfully that welfare economics would have been considerably enriched if it had maintained more contact with ethics (he also argues, incidentally, that ethics could have benefited from incorporating some of the technical achievements of welfare economics). Since economics focuses so much on the choice process, it is natural that at some stage it should ask how exactly people do make choices. This is one of the topics discussed by Loomes in Chapter 29. In the experiments he describes, which essentially concern choice under uncertainty, economics is approaching its frontier with experimental psychology, which deals with the workings of the human mind.[4] In an interesting article, Durbin (1988) speculated that the evolution of humanity stimulated the development of mathematical reasoning. His argument was that, in the hunter-gatherer societies in which we evolved, it was advantageous to be able to reason logically in order to manipulate the external world. Durbin did not discuss probabilistic reasoning, but the experiments that have been carried out by psychologists and economists strongly suggest that humanity is not very good at it. Following Durbin's line of argument, the explanation which immediately suggests itself is that understanding the laws of probability offered few evolutionary advantages in the hunter-gatherer state. It is not the place to speculate at length on the reasons for this, but one possibility is that the element of exact repetition of all external circumstances required to *identify* the probability of a particular event from a series of observations was absent.

36.2 ECONOMICS AND MATHEMATICS

One discipline which has seemed to be of ever increasing importance to economics is mathematics. Both Marx and Schumpeter are reported to have worked at their mathematics into their old age, in the conviction of its significance to economics. Some of Klamer's (1984) conversations with the New Classical macroeconomists are illuminating in this respect. Speaking of a joint paper on investment with Prescott, Lucas says:

> We thought it was a pretty straightforward applied problem, but then we got in way over our heads technically. We didn't want to quit, so we read tons of difficult mathematical economics and mathematics, even though none of us had any prior familiarity with it. It was a lot of fun; we both learned a lot.
>
> (Klamer 1984: 32–3)

Townsend comments as follows:

> There is always a temptation to settle on a fixed capital stock in terms of mathematical tools. That is a mistake. First of all, you have to keep moving forward. Better techniques are needed for that. A second reason for the importance of developing mathematical tools is that somehow you begin to think about a problem differently. I have often been surprised that after you have learned something of interest in mathematics, you discover there is a neat way to use it.
>
> (Klamer 1984: 82)

Why do these writers appear to attach such importance to mathematical knowledge? Clearly, it is because they wish to set up and manipulate mathematical models. Grubel and Boland (1986) have conclusively shown that the mathematical content of articles in leading economic journals grew considerably from 1951 to 1978. This suggests the hypothesis that high mathematical content increases the chance that a paper submitted to such a journal will be accepted for publication, but it does not explain why that should be so.

The attractions of mathematics clearly lie in its capacity for precision. A statement such as 'if X increases, then Y increases' is capable of an infinite variety of different mathematical formulations, whilst there is a further infinite variety of formulations which allow Y to increase as X increases only over part of the range of X, and to remain constant or fall over the rest. Moreover, any statement that tries to relate Y to a number of variables $X_1, X_2, \ldots, X_k$ quickly becomes very cumbersome when expressed in words, but can still be expressed very neatly and precisely in mathematics, which also readily permits the manipulation of a number of such expressions in order to derive solutions of interest. Thus the idea of expressing economic relationships in mathematical form is extremely appealing. We know from unpublished papers that in his youth Alfred Marshall tried to express the doctrines of Ricardo and Mill in the form of equations, and of course Samuelson made a considerable impact with the publication of his *Foundations of Economic Analysis*, which sought to express basic microeconomic theory in mathematical form.

These writers readily perceived as yet unexploited opportunities for the use of mathematics in economics. Today, the ability to write down and solve a formal model is virtually (though not invariably) a precondition of publication in the best journals, and this requires a facility with mathematics which would have alarmed previous generations of economists. It is not surprising, therefore, that economists tend to have mixed feelings about the role of mathematics in economics. There is survey evidence to suggest that the majority of economists believe that the proportion of journal space devoted to mathematical articles is excessive, and that mathematical specialists can publish and obtain jobs more easily than non-mathematical specialists (Grubel and Boland 1986; Greenaway 1990). All this implies a general view that mathematics is more important than it should be. This view almost certainly stems from the belief that contributions to economic knowledge should come from *economic* intuition and insight, and that mathematics is essentially a piece of technology designed to facilitate the presentation of such insights in elegant and precise form. Since the level of mathematical knowledge of economists is very diverse, there is a widespread suspicion that good mathematics generates publication opportunites even when the economic analysis contains no particular novelties, and this is resented. It is most unlikely, however, that the resentment which is being revealed by these surveys will have a significant impact on the trend of the mathematical content of journals, because the precise identification of assumptions and consequences which mathematics offers is too attractive to be lightly sacrificed.

A quite different issue is the nature of the relationship between progress in mathematics and its application to economic problems. Some of the examples which we gave earlier, and in particular the quotation from Townsend, suggest that advances in mathematical economics come from the application of already known mathematical techniques that were developed without reference to economic problems. This may be largely true for pure economic theory, but the fact that there is a whole branch of statistics which is called 'Econometrics' suggests strongly that it is the statistical problems thrown up by economic data that have often provided the stimulus for new theoretical developments. It is the econometric rather than the statistical literature that has dominated the discussion of the incorporation of distributed lags, limited dependent variables and expectational variables into regression models, to name but a few topics. In applied statistics, journals such as *Econometrica* and *Biometrika* are as important as the statistical journals for those working with economic or biological data. Even where a new development has been initiated by statisticians, as in the case of unit root tests, the idea has often been so swiftly taken up by econometricians that it almost seems to have been invented by them. Statistical time series analysts may have been the first to identify the distinctive properties

734

of estimators in the presence of a unit root, but it was econometricians who explored the link between unit roots and cointegrated variables, and between the latter and error-correction specifications, whilst it is the enthusiastic application of unit root tests to economic data which has provided the spur to further theoretical research in the area, such as the development of testing procedures for general autoregressive moving-average models and the investigation of the small-sample properties of these estimators.

The surveys quoted above did not distinguish between mathematics as used in theoretical papers, on the one hand, and theoretical and applied econometrics, on the other. This is a pity, because there is a clear distinction here which the surveys might have revealed. Econometrics grew out of the attempt to apply statistical theory to economic data in order to test the validity of economic hypotheses. As a discipline, it has been moulded by the special characteristics of economic data, which tend to differ from those encountered in the physical and (perhaps to a lesser extent) biological sciences. To a larger degree, it has been forced to develop its own body of theory, and theoretical progress in econometrics is often prompted by the need to find solutions to urgent practical problems. As we have suggested earlier, however, this is probably not the case with the mathematics that is used in theoretical models. Here, economics tends to contribute little or nothing to the theory, and merely provides a playground for newly discovered mathematical techniques. One example of this is the failure of economics to make good use of game theory in the 1950s, after the contribution of von Neumann and Morgenstern (1947) had stimulated considerable interest in it, because game theory itself had not developed in directions that were particularly useful to economics (see Montet's discussion of this in Chapter 17). It was only after the necessary theoretical advances had been made by game theorists that economics was able to reap substantial benefits from their work.

36.3 THE CHAPTERS IN PART IV

In Chapter 37, Boulding discusses 'Economics and social systems'. He declares his main theme in the title of his opening section: 'All social sciences study the world social system'. Boulding defines this system as comprising the totality of human beings and all their activities, including the social sciences themselves. In turn, the world social system is part of the global ecosystem. Easier travel and more advanced communications, says Boulding, are continually making the world social system more tight-knit. Within this frame of reference, Boulding presents a wide-ranging perspective on the mutual contributions and interactions between economics, other social sciences and more general aspects of the world social system.

Considering the role of economic studies in the context of social systems,

Boulding points out that the main province of economics is the study of exchange (or, rather, exchangeables), with price theory being a central concern of this study. As price relationships change, so shifts will occur in the structure of occupational distribution, immediately illustrating the intimate relationship between economic systems and the wider social system.

Another familiar economic concept, the distinction between flows and stocks, has its counterpart in the demographic variables of births/deaths and populations. Throughout his exposition, Boulding stresses the importance of the interface between economics and demography.

Accounting, continues Boulding, has the task of compiling a 'position statement', or balance sheet, for enterprises. In much the same way, economics may seek to present a position statement relating to the individual, the family or the economy, and it faces similar problems of valuing the diverse components of the balance sheet. The economic concept of 'maximizing behaviour' can be viewed as a process of maintaining homeostasis in the position statement.

As regards the contributions that macroeconomic thinking can make to other social sciences, Boulding cites the realization that the total system can behave in a different way from the sum of its parts. This mode of thinking, he says, has not been well explored in many other areas of social science, although he detects some similarity between the analysis of macroeconomic systems and that of ecosystems.

Turning to consider some of the relative weaknesses of economic science, Boulding criticizes the methodological approach that has attempted to develop the theory of economics along similar lines to the theory of celestial mechanics. In economics and other social sciences, he points out, parameters are not stable, and information must be surprising if it is to be information at all. He also draws attention to the naive taxonomy of microeconomic and growth theory, which portrays land, labour, capital and entrepreneurship as the only ingredients of the productive process. Adam Smith, says Boulding, was well aware that other and less tangible factors enter the equation.

Finally, Boulding reviews the potential and actual cross-fertilizations between economics and other specific social sciences: demography, politics, sociology, psychology, geography, anthropology and biology. He concludes with the hope that a more unified social science may be emerging as part of a more unified world culture.

In Chapter 38 McLean reviews the interface between economics and politics. In Adam Smith's time, says McLean, these two areas of study were viewed as inseparable. He suggests that present-day economists might well gain from re-examining the interplay between the two, so as to create once again a truly coherent social science.

McLean discusses three main areas of interest on the interface between economics and politics: first, public choice theory, as formulated by Buchanan and Tullock; second, the problems of collective action; third, the theory of social choice.

The study of public choice seeks to apply economic postulates, such as that of utility maximization, not only to persons engaged in overtly economic activities but to all actors, including politicians. Theorists in this area are working towards a formulation in which votes and money are analytically equivalent. Real-world outcomes, suggests McLean, will be determined by the interplay of 'vote power' and 'producer-group power'.

Workers in this field, he goes on, have often assumed that politicians are mainly motivated by a wish to be re-elected, just as rent-seeking is viewed as a prime motivation for entrepreneurial pressure groups. Yet, says McLean, reality may not be quite so straightforward: there seem to be at least some politicians who base their actions on genuinely altruistic motives.

Discussing some applications of public choice theory, McLean considers various consequences of introducing the postulate of rationality into a political framework. Here, he reports a range of still controversial questions. Is the rational voter best seen as maximizing her expected utility or as voting retrospectively? How does the rational political party locate a 'median' platform when public opinion varies along more than one dimension? And in discussions of the utility-maximizing activities of the rational bureaucrat, the prior question arises: how are we to define a bureaucrat?

McLean goes on to review the theory of collective action. He refers to the widespread romantic concept that social action can be such as to maximize the good of all while also being in the best interests of each individual, and points out that no way has yet been found of proving the connection between the two sides of this equation. He outlines the theory of 'assurance games', 'chicken games' and the 'prisoners' dilemma' as these have been applied on the political–economic interface.

Turning to his third main topic, social choice, McLean discusses various approaches to voting theory. As long ago as the eighteenth century, theorists showed that the 'first past the post' system of voting was flawed in any electoral situation where there were more than two candidates. What these early thinkers did not succeed in doing, says McLean, was to devise a practically workable voting system that would give more equitable results, and to this day the problems of doing so have still not been conclusively settled.

In a concluding section, McLean outlines the ways in which these concepts at the economic–political interface may prove helpful in throwing light on current policy issues: for example, consumerism, the politics of regulation, electoral reform and conservation of the environment.

Studies at the interface between economics and law, writes Bowles in Chapter 39, have been growing apace during the last twenty-five years or so. In the course of these recent developments, he suggests, economic analysis has had a greater influence on the study of law than vice versa. This contrasts with the approach of the early writers on political economy, who attached great importance to an understanding of legal systems as a framework for their economic studies.

Bowles chooses four aspects of current work in law and economics for discussion in his chapter. They are negligence rules and civil liability, contract, legal procedure and the resolution of legal disputes, and questions of regulation.

Considering the first of these topics, Bowles cites the work of Coase on the problem of social cost. Coase showed that a set of legally enforceable rights could be a more effective means of promoting efficient resource use than the economists' more traditional prescription, in which government was called in to counter market failure. Bowles reviews more recent advances in this mode of analysis, initially as it applies to accident law. The focus of interest here has been the development of an economic analysis of liability rules. In a situation where potential damage can be protected against – at a cost – by either the party who may inflict the damage or the party who may suffer it, what liability rule will bring about welfare maximization? This style of analysis, says Bowles, has a wide range of potential applications to current problems: for example, issues of environmental damage or product liability.

Contracts, Bowles points out, help underpin and assure future economic activity, and hence facilitate the operation of markets. They can be viewed as one way of reducing the risk costs of allocating resources through time. Bowles examines the thesis that the courts, *de facto*, enforce the law of contract in such a way as to maximize economic efficiency.

Bowles turns next to the topic of legal disputes and the procedures by which they are settled. He sets forth a model in which the expected costs of plaintiff and defendant are balanced against the probabilities that either will succeed in the case. This analysis, as he shows, can be extended to model the rationale of a decision to settle out of court. In either case the solution will be influenced by institutional rules concerning the division of legal costs and the procedure for the remuneration of lawyers.

The question of regulation, more than most topics at the interface of law and economics, is a long-established matter of interest to economists, since it figures in discussions of competition policy. Bowles explains that in this area, as in the study of civil liability, current theorists are directing their attention away from questions of market failure and towards a broader economic theory of regulation. He illustrates the use of this analysis by reference to the regulation of 'insider trading' on stock markets.

In Chapter 40, Van Raaij writes of the relationship between economics and psychology. He points out that theory development in economics began when the study of psychology was still in its infancy. For this reason, the behavioural assumptions of economics were originally formulated without the benefit of psychological research. In principle, Van Raaij goes on, the empirical testing of economic theory over the years should have resulted in the progressive refinement of its starting assumptions to bring them closer to behavioural reality. However, in practice, the 'testing' carried on by economists has usually been more concerned with econometric prediction than with assessing the behavioural hypotheses on which economic theory is founded. Therefore, urges Van Raaij, it is important now for economics to take account of the findings of psychological research, which can, as he puts it, 'enrich the explanations of economic behaviour by a better understanding'.

Van Raaij calls for the development of an integrated economic-psychological theory of behaviour. Traditionally, he points out, economics has usually modelled behaviour in terms of direct connections between changes in economic variables and the subsequent response of economic actors (for example, a change in price results in a change in purchases). Psychology, however, can give insight into some important intermediating factors, for example perception, evaluation, and the availability and use of information.

Turning next to a comparison of theory development as between economics and psychology, Van Raaij observes that the hypothetico-deductive testing of theory in psychology typically uses a shorter sequence of deductive reasoning than is usual in economics; as a corollary of this, psychology's high-level hypotheses are, generally speaking, less remote from observable reality than are those of economics. Van Raaij describes a programme of psychologically oriented economic research that enjoyed a brief existence in the interwar years, but was subsequently overtaken by the 'hard' econometric approach.

Psychology, says Van Raaij, shows a greater internal diversity in theoretical schools of thought than does economics. He reviews the main characteristics of these schools and suggests the actual and potential contributions that each can make to economics.

Expanding upon the detail of these contributions, Van Raaij cites the psychological finding that the individual acts not in response to reality but in response to his or her perception and evaluation of that reality. (One economic illustration of this, he suggests, is the role of investors' and entrepreneur's 'sentiment' in the causation of economic fluctuations.) By incorporating such psychological observations more consistently into their theory, economists would be in a position to counter the familiar changes of oversimplification levelled at more traditional concepts such as rationality and perfect information. Further, in applied work there would be less need to use proxies, since more variables would become directly observable – tastes, for example. Van Raaij suggests that psychological research can also help economists check some of their more complex theoretical formulations: for example, the stability and transitivity of preferences, or the nature and real-world incidence of risk aversion and risk seeking.

Van Raaij closes his chapter by listing some of the main areas of current activity in economic–psychological research.

In his discussion of 'Economics and history' in Chapter 41, Crafts stresses the potential benefits of a two-way interchange of ideas between the two disciplines. As it is, he suggests, economics and econometrics have had considerable influence on the current practice of history, but so far there has been little traffic in the opposite direction. Analysing the possible reasons for this, Crafts cites both the process of professionalization in economics and the lack of interest among historians in questions of policy prescription.

Crafts goes on to pose the question: 'Is economic history simply the applied economics of the past?' He supplies his own answer: economic history is, and should be, more than this. The evidence of the past, he asserts, is useful in many ways other than simply to provide estimates of the coefficients of economic models. Historians typically use a more diverse range of data than do economists, and economists might benefit from following their example. At the same time, historians have sometimes harboured outdated notions of economic theory, and could benefit by keeping abreast of current developments in that field. Crafts suggests that interdisciplinary work might provide a useful way ahead.

Next, Crafts describes in some detail a selection of recent advances in the 'new economic history'. Some of these have entailed unearthing new information from primary sources, in the historian's traditional manner. Other research has used revisions of computational methods to throw new light on existing information: for example, time series of national income accounting figures. By these means, economic historians have gained new perspectives on such topics as the United Kingdom's relative growth and employment record from the Industrial Revolution until the present day. Still other studies have reached their insights by reinterpreting existing historical data within a framework of contemporary economic theory; for example, game theory has been used to cast new light on the success and failure of the Gold Standard. Once again, says Crafts, successful work is likely to depend on the two-way interchange of ideas and skills between the two disciplines.

He concedes that not all such work has produced fully convincing results. The 'new economic history' has its potential pitfalls. Among these problems, Crafts cites the misinterpretation of source materials, errors in econometric technique and the use of inappropriate prior assumptions, particularly when these are overly rigid or insensitive to historical context. As one means of meeting this last problem, Crafts recommends that economic analysts of historical data should set out to convince historians as well as other economists.

As long as researchers keep these pitfalls in mind, says Crafts, there is still plenty of opportunity for further advance at the interface between economics and history. He outlines several avenues which he sees as particularly promising; one such, he suggests, is the further application of economic theories of strategic behaviour to the analysis of historical data. Such research programmes, Crafts concludes, will help us tap into the 'wealth of relevant experience in our economic past which bears on present policy issues'.

NOTES

1 The political reaction to petrol price increases announced in the wake of the cut-back in world oil supplies caused by the Iraqi invasion of Kuwait is a good illustration of this point.
2 It is difficult to think of an experiment that would test the true attitudes of radical economists. If all orthodox economists were wiped off the face of the earth, it is quite likely that post-Keynesians would find themselves filling the vacuum that was left as exponents of the virtues of markets. Moreover, radical schools of thought often attract people who are critical of mainstream economics for different reasons, such as their dislike of the extreme assumptions involved in mathematical models.
3 One notable exception is the work of George Akerlof; see Akerlof (1982) or Akerlof and Yellen (1990).
4 The work that is going on in experimental economics is extremely interesting, but the publication in the 1985 *American Economic Review* of an article about how *rats* make choices under uncertainty may be taking things a bit too far!

REFERENCES

Akerlof, G. A. (1982) 'Labor contracts as partial gift exchange', *Quarterly Journal of Economics* 47: 543–70.
Akerlof, G. A. and Yellen, J. L. (1990) 'The fair wage-effort hypothesis and unemployment', *Quarterly Journal of Economics* 55: 255–83.
Durbin, J. (1988) 'Is a philosophical consensus for statistics attainable?', *Journal of Econometrics* 37: 51–61.
Frey, B. S. (1986) 'Economists favour the price mechanism – who else does?', *Kyklos* 37: 537–63.
Greenaway, D. (1990) 'On the efficient use of mathematics in economics: results of an attitude survey of British economists', *European Economic Review* 34: 1339–51.
Grubel, H. G. and Boland, L. (1986) 'On the efficient use of mathematics in economics: some theory, facts and results of an opinion survey', *Kyklos* 39: 419–42.
Klamer, A. (1984) *The New Classical Macroeconomics: Conversations with the New Classical Economists and Their Opponents*, Brighton: Harvester Wheatsheaf.
von Neumann, J. and Morgenstern, O. (1947) *Theory of Games and Economic Behaviour*, 2nd edn, Princeton, NJ: Princeton University Press.
Sen, A. K. (1987) *On Ethics and Economics*, Oxford: Basil Blackwell.

ECONOMICS AND SOCIAL SYSTEMS

KENNETH E. BOULDING

37.1 ALL THE SOCIAL SCIENCES STUDY THE WORLD SOCIAL SYSTEM

All the social sciences are really studying different aspects of the same social system, which is the totality of human beings, plus the changes which they have made in their environments, stretching back into the past and out into the future, as they have spread out over the world and now even to the solar system. This social system includes all human bodies and minds, their knowledge, their images of the world, their character, their behaviour, their artefacts (buildings, furniture, clothes, works of art, commodities of all kinds), their documents (writings, financial instruments, laws), their relationships and organizations (families, tribes, nations, corporations, religious bodies, foundations) and so on. Each of the social sciences looks at this vast spectacle in time and space from somewhat different vantage points, but all of them are looking at parts of what is essentially a single system in three dimensions of space and one of time. The social sciences are part of the very system which they study, and indeed change the system as they study it. Something like the Heisenberg principle indeed dominates the social sciences. When we give people a questionnaire, we change their opinions. When we make a prediction, we change the future, depending on how much the prediction is believed. When we learn about other cultures, we transform our own culture, as well as the cultures that we are studying. We are looking at a system in constant flux, that even changes because we are looking at it.

The social system which is the subject of the social sciences is in turn a subset of a larger system which includes biological structures, genetic patterns and histories, the whole ecosystem of the earth and its physical environment. Social systems indeed are profoundly affected by what happens in other parts of the total system of the earth – climatic changes, earthquakes, rising sea levels, plagues and diseases, genetic mutations, the extinction of biological species and so on. Before the last 500 years or so, the earth consisted of a number of isolated ecological and social systems which were not in contact. The collapse of the Mayan Empire in about AD 900 did not affect the Emperor Leo the Wise in Byzantium at all; his wisdom did not extend over that geographical distance. In the last 500 years, however, with the spectacular development of the ability of humans, and their baggage, to travel all over the world, and with the rise of science and science-based technology, the world has become increasingly a single system in communications, in travel, in trade and in violence and threat systems. Events which used to be confined to local areas now reverberate around the whole world. The collapse of local isolation means that it is all the more important that there should be widespread understanding of the nature of the total social system among human beings. In a world of isolated localities, something can go drastically wrong in one of them without affecting the others. As the world increasingly becomes a total system, then if anything goes wrong, everything goes wrong, and the world becomes much more precarious.

Social thought goes back a long way in human history, certainly as far back as Herodotus[1] and Thucydides[2] in Greece and Sun Tzu[3] in China. However, social science, as an academic subculture or set of subcultures, is a fairly late offshoot of the culture of modern science which originated in Europe, not much earlier than Copernicus in the sixteenth century, although it had roots in Islam, India and China. It is always hard to put a date of birth on a subculture, for every human activity seems to have precursors. Economics as a subculture, however, can be dated pretty much to the Physiocrats and Adam Smith in the mid-eighteenth century. Indeed, economics has some claims to be one of the oldest of the social sciences. Modern economics can certainly be dated from Adam Smith's *The Wealth of Nations* (1776), modern chemistry from Dalton (about 1808), geology from Lyell (about 1830) and modern biology from Darwin's *Origin of Species* (1859). Wilhelm Wundt has some claims to be the founder of modern psychology in the 1860s and 1870s. Sociology is hard to pin down. The term was invented by Comte in the mid-nineteenth century. Political science is even harder to pin down. Political philosophy certainly goes back to the ancient Greeks, and modern political thought to Hobbes and Locke in the seventeenth century. The American Political Science Association was founded in 1903, and the International Studies Association in 1959.

37.2 ECONOMICS STUDIES THE ECONOMY AS PART OF THE SOCIAL SYSTEM

In this chapter we are particularly concerned with the contributions of economics to the social sciences and the understanding of social systems. We must start, however, by looking at economics itself. One is tempted to define economics as the study of how society is organized through exchange and related phenomena. Among these related phenomena are the identification, discovery or production of things to be exchanged, which are most human artefacts. They may include such abstract artefacts as titles to land, human beings themselves under slavery, money and financial instruments, and so on. We might modify the definition slightly and say that economics is concerned primarily with exchangeables, whether they are actually exchanged or not. I myself have argued for the study of the 'grants economy', which is the study of one-way transfers, especially of potential exchangeables (Boulding 1981). This edges towards the phenomenon of reciprocity, which perhaps is more in the domain of sociologists than of economists. Economists usually think of exchange as contractual. A says to B, 'I will give you so much of X if you will give me so much of Y', where it is pretty clear what is exchanged. Reciprocity, as in a marriage, involves subtle non-specified exchanges and each party's image of what has been gained or given up may be different. Both spouses, for instance, may feel that each is giving up a great deal to the other and not receiving very much in return, which would be a bad sign for a marriage. Even in economic exchange, the parties value the exchangeables differently. If A buys a car from B for $10,000, A clearly values the car more than the $10,000 and B values the $10,000 more than the car; otherwise the exchange would not take place. Each will have a fairly similar image of the $10,000 and of the car, although with a complex commodity like a car, these images may differ somewhat. They may also be wrong. A may find after purchasing the car that it turns out to be what we call a 'lemon', i.e. not as good as A thought.

Presumably the earliest form of exchange was the barter of goods for goods. Once society expands beyond the tribe, however, something like money always seems to appear, first in terms of a medium of exchange – a commodity which is very widely accepted in exchange. This may be cattle (which is where the word 'pecuniary' comes from) or even large stones, as on the island of Yap. There is a strong tendency, however, for metals to become a medium of exchange. They are widely desired and fairly easy to transport, handle and measure. It is not surprising that the scarcer and therefore more precious metals like gold and silver become mediums of exchange. Coinage follows and the medium of exchange becomes a measure of value, like the dollar or the mark. This leads to abstract money like bank deposits. Once there is a measure of value we have prices, which is the ratio of exchange of a commodity for monetary units.

One of the great concerns of economics from Adam Smith on has been what determines the set of relative prices of all commodities. Indeed, price theory is the central core of economics. It goes back to Adam Smith in *The Wealth of Nations*, Book 1, Chapter 7 (Smith 1937: 55–63). There are really

744

two theories, with different time frames. Market price theory supposes that there are a number of traders, each of whom possesses certain stocks of commodities and of money. When exchange takes place, these stocks are redistributed among the owners, so that the total number of exchangeables of various kinds remains constant. It is assumed that there is some equilibrium set of market prices at which all people in the market are willing to hold the aggregate of what there is to be held. If people feel that they are holding too much money and not enough goods, there will be a net attempt on the part of the traders to buy goods, but sellers will not sell unless prices are raised. If traders on the whole feel that they are holding too little money, more will want to sell than will want to buy and prices will fall. If the price of any particular commodity, such as wheat, is 'too high', people will be unwilling to hold as much as there is there to be held, and there will be more offers to sell than to buy and the price will fall. Similarly, if the price of wheat is 'too low', it will rise. The equilibrium structure, of course, changes constantly as people's preferences for holding all the different forms of assets change. These preferences may depend a good deal on expectations of the future, which can easily give rise to fluctuations. If people think that prices are going to rise, they will want to hold more at existing prices than there is to be held, and prices will rise. This may confirm this opinion and prices will go on rising. However, they cannot rise indefinitely without becoming 'high', at which point people think that prices are going to fall and they will fall, until they are 'low', at which point they will begin to rise again. Fluctuations in organized markets of all kinds, whether financial markets or commodity markets, tend to follow this pattern.

Over a longer time period, another pattern is perceptible, which also goes back to Adam Smith, who called it 'natural' price structure, and Alfred Marshall (1961), who called it 'normal' price structure. This rests on the proposition that there is a set function relating the set of all relative prices to the set of the relative profitability or desirability of both labour and capital in the occupations which produce the commodites involved. For any given level of productive technology, we can postulate a normal set of relative prices where the corresponding rewards of all the relevant occupations are such that there is no incentive to move from one to another. If the relative market price of wheat, say, is 'too high', i.e. above the normal price for a suitable length of time, the production of wheat will be perceived as abnormally profitable, resources will move from the production of alternative commodities into it, production will rise, consumption may fall, stocks will rise and that will bring down the market price. Production of the alternative commodities will fall, their stocks will fall and their prices will rise. Similarly, if the price of wheat is 'too low', i.e. below the normal price for any period, wheat production will be perceived as relatively undesirable, resources will move out of it into other commodities, production will decline, consumption may increase, stocks will decline and the market price will rise. There is a close connection between the relative price structure and what might be called the structure of occupational distribution. It is fundamental to all social systems. Of course, it can be modified by the grants economy through taxation and subsidies, but it can never be neglected. Many failures of economic planning, especially in the more centrally planned economies, can be attributed to the neglect of this fundamental connection. It is a relationship that cannot be neglected in any social system, even where we have reciprocity rather than exchange.

Another important contribution of economics to the understanding of society is the distinction which it makes between capital and income. Capital is a flashlight photograph at a moment of time, which is a stock. Income is a flow or a succession of events, i.e. something rather like a movie in space–time. This might be described as a demographic approach to the description of society, as the basic theory goes back to the study of populations of all kinds. A population of anything is a stock, i.e. something like capital, whether this be of human beings, automobiles, money or ideas. A population is increased by 'births', i.e. the production of new items, and diminished by 'deaths', i.e. the consumption or destruction of existing items. The growth in population is equal to the births minus the deaths in a given period of time. The birth rate and the death rate are essentially rates of growth of the same dimensions as the rate of interest. The rate of interest or the rate of profit is indeed exactly equivalent to the birth rate of the population of dollar values in the relevant stock. The rate at which interest or profit is paid out of the stock is equivalent to the death rate. In an equilibrium population, the birth and death rates are equal and the population will be stable. If the birth rate exceeds the death rate, the population will grow, and if the death rate exceeds the birth rate, the population will decline, whether of human beings, money values or teapots.

37.3 CONTRIBUTIONS OF DEMOGRAPHY AND ACCOUNTING TO ECONOMICS

The great truism of demography – that the increase in anything is equal to the additions minus the subtractions – can be expanded to include immigration and emigration, in which case the truism can be rewritten as follows: the increase in anything is equal to births plus immigration minus deaths minus emigration. Again, this holds for commodities as well as for humans. Births are production; deaths are consumption. For a given region or subset of the population, immigration of commodities will be imports and emigration will be exports. Another very fundamental demographic identity is that, in an equilibrium population, the average length of life is the reciprocal of the birth rate, which is equal to the death rate. We can visualize this easily if we think

746

of a population, of automobiles, say, in which 1 million are added each year and 1 million are withdrawn at the age of, say, twelve years. The population will be stable at 12 million. There will be 1 million in each age group for twelve years. The birth and death rates will be 1 million divided by 12 million or one-twelfth or 8.33 per cent per annum. Among the various schools of economics, the Austrian economists perhaps recognized this principle most successfully. Of course, it has to be modified where the population is not in equilibrium, particularly where it is increasing, but the average length of life of a capital good is what basically determines the ratio of income, i.e. annual births, to capital, the total stock. This principle applies to all the populations of society – all categories of persons, organizations and even ideas.

Economics is fairly closely related to accounting, although the relation between the two disciplines has not been as close as one might wish (Boulding 1962a: 44–55). The central problem of accounting is the evaluation of a heterogeneous list of items which constitute the balance sheet of an organization or person. The list of items, called a position statement, is an important piece of social information. It identifies items in the total stock of society which are in some sense the property of, and in a wider sense relevant to, a particular person, organization or group. The problem of accounting is how to achieve a 'bottom line', i.e. a number that will represent the total value of such a heterogeneous aggregation. The relative price structure, beloved of economists, is an important guide to such an overall evaluation. We cannot add twenty apples to thirty oranges, but if apples are 20 cents each and oranges are 25 cents each, then the twenty apples are worth $4.00 and the thirty oranges are worth $7.50, and the total is $11.50. Both economists and accountants tend to assume some sort of relative price structure as at least an approximation to what might be called 'social values'. Of course, market prices are not available for many items in the total position statements of society, and even economists recognize that market prices may not correspond to what might be called 'social prices' because of the possibilities of imperfect knowledge, irrational behaviour and valuations which transcend the market, like loyalty, alienation, pride, shame and so on. But any kind of overall evaluation of a person, an ethical system, a wilderness area or a war involves some kind of position statement and some judgement about the relative values of different items in the statement itself. There is no need to be ashamed of first approximations if we recognize them for what they are.

37.4 'MAXIMIZING BEHAVIOUR' AS A CONTRIBUTION OF ECONOMICS TO PSYCHOLOGY

Another contribution of economics to the general study of the social system is described as the theory of maximizing behaviour, which again follows from what might be called a 'near-tautology' – that everybody does what they think is best at the time. The assumption here is that behaviour involves choice, which involves an image of a set of possible futures which we believe are under our control. It involves an evaluation, or at least a rank ordering, of these possible futures from best to worst. And economists have a prejudice in thinking that we choose what we think at the time is the best possible future. If we consider two futures which are fairly close to each other, which in a sense represent two possible future position statements X and Y, then if X contains a little more of A and a little less of B than Y does, the economists argue that if we evaluate 'a little more of A' at a higher value than 'a little less of B', we will choose X. This, of course, leads into marginal analysis, which tends to become a set of mathematical variations on the basic assumption of choosing the best at the time.

Economists apply marginal analysis particularly to decisions about exchange, which involves giving up one item in the position statement and acquiring more of another. This leads into the 'equimarginal principle', which states in effect that our preferred position statement, or balance sheet, is that in which an increase in any one item through exchange or production is not worth the decrease in other items which it would involve. This leads into a theory of economic behaviour, of which the first approximation might be described as the homeostasis of the balance sheet or position statement. The balance that we want to maintain may be in a certain range of possible proportions of different items. There will be some boundary at which we will take action. The householder who looks in the cupboard and finds that the stock of tea is below what is really wanted and the stock of money in the purse is somewhat above what is wanted goes out and buys tea, which diminishes the money stock and increases the tea stock.

All items in the balance sheet diminish by consumption and by depreciation and wearing out and constantly have to be replaced. We are able to replace them because of production – because our activity produces 'births' in our capital stock item – whether this is an increase in the money stock as a result of earning wages (we usually earn wages by producing something for somebody else) or direct increases in stock through household production. Businesses and other organizations similarly have a balance sheet that they want to maintain. When a firm sells a final product, it diminishes its inventory and increases its money stock. When it spends the money stock on wages, materials and other items, it increases its inventory again.

Looking at the longer run, of course, we then recognize that the position statement that is maintained may itself change as we become richer or poorer or older, as we become more or less thrifty, as accidents and catastrophes afflict us, as we experience both good and bad luck, and so on. This is a scheme which has applications to all aspects of society. Organizations, whether families, churches, national states, armed forces or universities, have an image of themselves as a 'position statement' which they seek to maintain in the face of constant attrition. A university takes in a freshman class when the seniors graduate, a nation increases its armed forces when it feels less secure, a church may modify its doctrines or practices when it perceives itself as losing followers and so on. There are sometimes radical changes in the basic image which is maintained. Aggressive nations, as Sweden and Japan used to be, may be converted to having peace-loving neutral national images. Businesses change their product, sometimes dramatically, when the existing structure is perceived to be unprofitable. The family is the least in equilibrium of all institutions. Its image of itself changes constantly as children are born, grow up, marry and leave home, and as everybody ages and eventually dies.

37.5 ECONOMICS CONTRIBUTES TO 'MACRO THEORY'

Another contribution of economics to the study of total social systems is the perception, which economics perhaps has more than any other social science, that total systems behave differently from their parts. This is the essence of what is called 'macroeconomics' – a principle seen even in exchange itself. A single exchanger visualizes a large given environment of exchange opportunities which does not change much when an exchange takes place. I go shopping and spend money for goods, which I bring home, feeling that these purchases have not affected my overall environment of exchange opportunities. However, when we look at exchange as a total system, as suggested earlier, we see it as a redistribution of assets among owners, in which the relative price structure constantly changes and in which the relative price structure in the market may also affect the future quantities of exchangeables which are there to be shifted around among owners. The relationship of the total system of exchange to its environment is different from the relationship between an individual exchanger and the environment.

A few propositions may clinch the point. An individual has no problem in changing his asset structure, for instance, by spending less money than is taken in in a given period, thus increasing his money stock. For a total society, however, spending alone will not increase the money stock. Every dollar that one person gives up another person receives. The money stock can only be increased by expanding it – by creating new 'dollars'. If the money stock in a closed system is constant, then the sum of all individual balances of money payments must be equal to zero. If one person has a positive balance of payments, thus increasing his money stock, others must diminish theirs. Another proposition, somewhat related to the demographic model, is that if people spend more rapidly then a given money stock will support a larger total volume of payments. This leads to the famous Fisher identity $MV = PT$, where

M is the total money stock and V is its velocity of circulation. MV is then the total rate of money payments in purchases, T is what is bought with the money and P is the average price. This reflects the identity that in exchange equal values are exchanged.

Macroeconomic theory, although it tends to look at the system in terms of aggregates such as national income, rests basically on the perception of the economy as a total system. This system has strong resemblances to a total ecological system of many interacting populations of different species. The Walrasian general equilibrium of the price structure (Walras 1954) is a formalization of this, although its dynamic implications are still imperfectly understood. It is clear, however, that the total effects of a given change, transaction or event can often be very different from its immediate effects. A may affect B, B affect C, C affect D and so on through many alphabets, until some Z affects A. I have sometimes called these 'echo effects', as one event reverberates all through the system. These echo effects apply to such things as the incidence of taxation, the impact of tariffs and taxes and so on.

37.6 WEAKNESSES OF ECONOMICS: METHODOLOGY AND TAXONOMY; FACTORS OF PRODUCTION

With all its virtues as an image of the large total system, economic theory, especially in the last few decades, has run into some serious weaknesses and limitations and has become highly technical and rather sterile. Part of the problem here is a failure to examine critically the methodologies which are appropriate to the kinds of systems that are being investigated. Here the success of celestial mechanics has had a disastrous effect on economics and indeed on all the social sciences as they have made attempts to emulate its quantitative rigour, which has not, however, led to predictive power. The predictive power of celestial mechanics rests on the fact that its parameters are remarkably stable. The gravitational constant remains beautifully constant. In systems which involve information as an essential element, as social systems do, parameters are always subject to unpredictable change. There is indeed a non-existence theorem about accurate prediction in such systems, simply because information has to be surprising or it is not information. In understanding systems of this kind, therefore, much looser methodologies are required. However, the social sciences have been very backward in developing these appropriate methodologies. Oddly enough, the physical sciences have now moved further away from what might be called the Newtonian model than the social sciences have, with their identification of the Heisenberg principle and the recognition that the course or the history of the universe is dominated by the exact time at which improbable events happen. Indeed, I have accused econometrics of trying to find the celestial mechanics of a non-existent universe and failing to recognize the existence of 'regions of time' over which parameters are fairly stable but where the parameters change on passing from one region to the next, as occurred, for instance, in the American economy in 1929 and again in 1933, 1941, 1945 and so on (Boulding 1985).

Another problem with all the social sciences, from which economics is by no means exempt, is an absence of critical analysis of the taxonomies which are usually invoked. Taxonomy, i.e. how to identify those subsets of the system that have enough homogeneity to be significant, is a critical problem in any complex system. A good example of the failure of taxonomy was alchemy. It did not get very far until it was recognized that earth, air, fire and water were hopelessly heterogeneous aggregates and that the elements were hydrogen, oxygen and so on. Taxonomies in the social sciences are almost as naive as those of alchemy.

I have argued, I must confess without much effect on the profession, that the economist's taxonomy of the factors of production is somewhat alchemical. The traditional theory is a kind of cookbook theory: we mix together land, labour and capital, and maybe a little entrepreneurship, and out come potatoes or even automobiles. I have argued by contrast that production, whether of the horse or the automobile, begins with a genetic factor which can be described as 'knowhow'. In the case of the horse, of course, this is genes in the fertilized egg. In the case of the automobile, the genetic factors are not contained in the phenotype (the automobile itself), but are scattered around in various brains, libraries, plans, computers and so on, but are still sufficiently organized to direct the process of production. This process involves capturing energy in many different forms to transport, identify and transform many diverse materials into the structure of the phenotype, whether this is the horse or the automobile. Energy in different forms and materials in different forms are limiting factors, as are space and time. The absence or even inadequacy of any one limiting factor can prevent the process coming to fruition, for with limiting factors it is the *most* limiting that is of the greatest significance. The substitution of these different factors is, of course, important. Different forms of energy or materials can be substituted for one another; energy in some form can economize materials, and materials can economize energy. We may make an automobile today out of steel; in the future we may perhaps make it out of plastic. The genes producing an automobile may partly reside in an engineering department, partly in middle management, partly in the assembly line worker and so on. This is a much more complicated process than simply mixing land, labour and capital.

The relative price structure in terms of money wages, the prices of all commodities and capital goods, and the prices of securities of different kinds, as reflected in people's images of this complex structure and of its future, will have an influence on what mixes of different kinds of energy, materials, and

751

even space and time will be significant as limiting factors in the process of production. However, the relationship is extremely complex, much more so than the traditional production function, especially the Cobb–Douglas type including only labour and capital. This very intricate structure cannot be reduced to something like the average wage or the average rate of return on capital and financial instruments. Thus, the relative wages of skilled labour of different kinds and unskilled labour will have an effect on what kind of labour is used. The relative prices of potentially substitutable materials have an effect in determining what materials are used. The relative prices of possible substitutes for energy, whether this is biological energy (muscles) or electrical or other kinds of energy, will certainly have an effect on what actual production processes replace others. A possible general principle emerges – that the factors perceived as 'cheap' will displace factors perceived as 'dear' – but this principle throws a very modest amount of light on the problem.

An interesting question is: what pushes resources into producing change in the genetic factors or knowhow? It may well be that the extraordinary technological stability of the palaeolithic cultures was related to the fact that the sheer process of transmitting the culture from one generation to the next absorbed so much of the available resources that there was nothing left over for change in the knowhow factors. A crucial element here is whether there is a culture of learning which permits change in the knowhow factors. Some societies devote all their educational resources to ensuring that the children replicate the parents, in which case there will not be much change. Unless the culture is tolerant of change and of novelty and learning, it will tend just to reproduce itself generation after generation.

Curiously enough, Adam Smith had a much clearer understanding of the overwhelming importance of human knowledge and knowhow in the productive process than do modern economists. He saw that productivity increased because the division of labour encouraged a learning process, increasing skill and dexterity (Smith 1937: Book 1, ch. 1, pp. 3–12). He also perceived the great importance of the work of what he called 'philosophers', i.e. scientists, in developing new processes and new means of production. This has been forgotten or noted only casually by twentieth-century economists, who have been obsessed by things like the capital-to-output ratio in the theory of development. Economic development is a process that goes on almost entirely in human minds. It is essentially a learning process, although the acquisition of the appropriate human artefacts is part of what we have to learn how to do.

37.7 WEAKNESSES OF ECONOMICS: OBSESSION WITH INCOME AND CONSUMPTION

Another weakness of economics is that it has been obsessed by income almost to the exclusion of capital stocks. This is almost as if demographers were interested only in birth and death rates, with no interest in the population itself. To some extent this unfortunate failure goes right back to Adam Smith, who emphasized consumption as a measure of riches, whereas in fact wealth, the stocks and goods with which we are surrounded, is a much better measure. Consumption is literally the death of goods. This may happen slowly by depreciation, or very rapidly by eating food or setting off fireworks. I obtain no satisfaction, however, from the fact that my clothes are wearing out. What I obtain satisfaction from is wearing them. It is the utilization and enjoyment of goods that is the major source of economic satisfaction. Consumption is not completely irrelevant: I enjoy eating as well as being well fed. I like a certain variety in my housing, furniture, clothing and so on, so that a complete economic satisfaction function would include certain aspects of consumption as well as the capital stock. But, for the most part, economies of consumption are desirable and enable us to have a larger capital stock than would otherwise be available.

This emphasis on consumption has led economists to underemphasize what might be called the 'economics of contemplation'. We neglect the fact that we obtain satisfaction from contemplating, for instance, wilderness areas, pleasant surroundings, agreeable architecture and so on, even though we may not even want to visit them. We certainly do not want to consume them. The exchange relationship out of which relative prices are derived, by which we evaluate things, does not involve consumption, but a rearrangement of existing assets. It is perhaps the emphasis on consumption that has led economics to overdo individualism. While it is true that all evaluations are made by individual human beings, they are also made in a context which involves contemplating the whole of society and those parts of it of which we are particularly conscious in our own environment. This has led to a neglect by economists of grants economics – such things as social valuations, benevolence and malevolence, and so on, which are very important in all aspects of society.

37.8 THE CONTRIBUTIONS OF DIFFERENT SOCIAL SCIENCES TO EACH OTHER

We might ask ourselves: what are the contributions which economics and the other social sciences could make to each other, especially in the development of social science as a unified body of knowledge? We might begin with demography. Demographers, in particular, tend to be confined to human

753

populations. Economics should inspire them to extend their studies to populations of all kinds, which, of course, would lead into a kind of general ecological theory of the world, and also to evolutionary theory.

Political science tends to be somewhat obsessed with the study of threat systems. Economics can point to the importance of exchange and reciprocity in political relations, and the great importance of productivity in creating exchange or even threat opportunities. Political science has also not moved as far as economics in developing a macrotheory of the world political system as a whole. It has not realized adequately the ecological nature of political systems and has tended to concentrate on political behaviour in a fixed environment, without realizing that no environments are ever fixed and that the behaviour of one political body affects the environments of all. A little general equilibrium and evolutionary theory would certainly do political science no harm. While economists will, or at least should, recognize that cost–benefit analysis has limits, nevertheless, it also has its value in areas that are regarded as being outside economics. Thus, there is some value in trying to establish a 'bottom line' of total valuation of such things as national defence organizations, foreign policies, social services and so on. The 'bottom line' of the US Department of Defense might easily turn out to be negative, no matter how we calculate it, especially if we include externalities. It is one of the virtues of economics that it always thinks of values in terms of alternatives. Political science has a certain tendency to think in terms of absolute values. One of the great economic institutions is bankruptcy, an orderly way of removing an organization that should be removed. It has no good equivalent in political structures, although democratic elections may sometimes be the equivalent of the bankruptcy of an existing administration.

The main contribution of sociology to economics may well be to give it an opportunity of expanding exchange theory to include such things as reciprocity. Sociology also deals with integrative structures – such things as legitimacy, loyalty and so on – which provide the environment for exchange and reciprocity. It may indeed be that sociology has more to contribute to economics than economics has to sociology. Economists tend to neglect the sociological complexity of exchange transactions, particularly, for instance, those involving the hiring of people. They also neglect what might be called the 'sociology of the market' and of market information. 'Who knows whom' may be a very important structure which economists neglect.

The relation between economics and psychology is remarkably distant. We might also say that economics has created its own psychology, without much reference to what psychologists are doing, in the development of the theory of maximizing behaviour, indifference curves, opportunity functions and so on. Economists think of human behaviour primarily in terms of choice, which involves images of the future which are derived from the total experience of the past. They are therefore not very friendly to behaviourism – the view that behaviour is determined by some immediate stimulus. Experimental psychology may be all right for rats and pigeons, but it does not do much for economics. Furthermore, because economic man enjoys perfect mental health, his behaviour is always rational, he approaches rather than avoids and he maximizes utility rather than minimizing disutility; therefore he does not need psychoanalysis. This approach, which might be called anti-clinical, may be a little naive on the part of economists, but one wonders if it is not closer to human behaviour in what Marshall called the 'ordinary business of life' than the rather rarefied fantasies of the psychoanalysts. However, economists are very weak on learning theory, particularly when it comes to the process of learning images of the future and valuations. Economists simply tend to assume that human valuations are given, whereas in fact they are largely learned, often by processes that are mysterious. As a result, economists tend to neglect such things as fashion, conversion, identity formation, the transmission of ideas, knowledge and so on, perhaps with the excuse that these subjects should be the providence of sociology and psychology, although they are much neglected there also.

Economists have contributed a good deal to the study of history through the development of economic history – a somewhat neglected and undervalued area in modern economics departments. After all, the economy comprises a very large proportion of total human activity which is fundamentally peaceful – ploughing, sowing, reaping, making things, buying and selling, investing and so on. Professional historians tend to concentrate far too much on war, which is a minor human activity, comprising certainly no more than 10 per cent of the total in terms of time spent, and on kings and rulers, much of whose activity is not very relevant to what goes on in the ordinary business of life. If economists could persuade historians that their business is to study and describe the totality of human life, this might be a great benefit.

Geography is one discipline which touches all the others, for every discipline has spatial aspects. Economics has made some important contributions in terms of location theory, which economists themselves regard, perhaps unwisely, as a very minor aspect of the economy. The development of 'regional science' by Walter Isard (1975), himself an economist, has potential benefits for all the social sciences.

Anthropology has tended to confine itself to societies at low levels of economic development, although these low levels can often be very sophisticated in terms of knowledge of the immediate environment. On the whole one would guess that economics has not made much contribution to anthropology, nor anthropology to economics. This is unfortunate; it leads both economics and anthropology to neglect the study of subcultures like banking and finance, which might well be studied with the skills of the anthropologist.

Curiously enough, classical economics, particularly in Adam Smith, and

755

even up to Jevons, had a strong biological component in terms of the concept of the food chain, which modern economists somehow just ignore. Classical economics starts with the growing of food. If the food producer grows more food than is necessary for life and reproduction, the surplus food can be fed to miners and blacksmiths who will produce ploughs which will increase food production. The greater surplus can then be fed to builders who will build barns, and fed to draft animals that will pull the ploughs so that still more food – greater surpluses – will be produced which eventually can be fed to builders who build cities and armies who build empires. This is a vision that modern economics seems to have lost.

In the last generation or so economics seems to have developed something that might be called 'economics imperialism' – attempts on the part of economists to take over other social sciences. Examples of this would be the work of Gary Becker of Chicago on family economics (Becker 1981) and of James Buchanan on what might almost be called 'economic politics' (Buchanan *et al.* 1978). Even my own work, such as *Conflict and Defense* (Boulding 1962b), essentially applies economic theory to political and military conflicts. If this movement is reciprocal, so that economists are willing to learn from the disciplines that they are trying to invade, there may be some value in it. If it is really imperialistic, however, with the economists looking at the other social sciences simply as areas to be conquered, it can have unfortunate consequences. There are perhaps some signs of reciprocity. There is a small school of humanistic economics in the United States (Lutz and Lux 1979) which attempts to draw upon the other social sciences, although its influence has not been very great so far.

37.9 THE GEOGRAPHY OF ECONOMICS

The geography of economics as a subculture is an interesting and somewhat puzzling problem. There is no doubt that in the eighteenth and nineteenth centuries, and even in the early twentieth century, economics was primarily a western European subculture: the Physiocrats and Cournot and Walras in France, the classical economists in England, the Austrian School, Karl Marx, Pareto, the German Historical School and so on, culminating perhaps in Keynes. In the twentieth century economics moved largely into the United States, beginning perhaps with Irving Fisher, as the list of Nobel Prizewinners suggests.[4] Part of this phenomenon is simply the geographical expansion of higher education. The sheer quantity of higher education in the United States considerably exceeds that in western Europe. Indeed, the United States can be considered as an expansion of European culture, and academically Europe and the United States certainly represent a common culture. Europe, of course, was much more devastated than the United States by the two World Wars.

The triumph of Marxism in eastern Europe restricted economics to a very narrow ideology. Furthermore, in the forty or fifty years since Keynes economics has been a period of 'normal science', working out old models rather than creating new ideas, with the possible exception of game theory which could be looked at as an expansion of the theory of economic behaviour.[5]

The future is hard to predict. However, it does not seem unreasonable to hope for a more unified social science emerging out of a more unified world culture, with greater contributions coming from outside what might be called the Euro-American culture. On the other hand, the very structure of academic life involves the danger of the development of smaller non-interacting subcultures, what have been called 'coteries of co-citation' – groups of people who quote each other and nobody else. The principle that the division of labour is only productive if there is trade holds for intellectual life as well as for commodities. Perhaps one of the hopes of the intellectual world is the development of specialized activity in intellectual trade, of which this book is a good example.

NOTES

1 Herodotus, *History*, approximately 443–425 BC.
2 Thucydides, *History of The Peloponnesian War*, approximately 431–404 BC.
3 Sun Tzu, *The Art of War*, translated by S. B. Griffith, Clarendon Press, Oxford, 1963.
4 In the first ten years of the Nobel Prize in Economics (1969–78), fifteen prizes were awarded (in some years two prizes were given): seven went to residents of the United States and eight to residents of Europe. In the second ten years (1979–88), eleven prizes were given: nine to residents of the United States and two to Europeans. Altogether sixteen have gone to the United States and ten to Europe. Of the ten European recipients, three were from the United Kingdom, two from Sweden and one each from Austria, France, the Netherlands, Norway and the USSR. Of the recipients resident in the United States, six were born outside the United States.
5 See von Neumann and Morgenstern (1964). Morgenstern was an economist and von Neumann was basically a physicist.

REFERENCES

Becker, G. S. (1981) *A Treatise on the Family*, Cambridge, MA: Harvard University Press.
Boulding, K. E. (1962a) 'Economics and accounting: the uncongenial twins', in W. T. Baxter and S. Davidson (eds) *Studies in Accounting Theory*, London: Sweet & Maxwell. Reprinted in Boulding, K. E. *Collected Papers*, ed. F. R. Glahe, vol. 2, pp. 219–32, Boulder, CO: Colorado Associated University Press, 1971.
—— (1962b) *Conflict and Defense: A General Theory*, New York: Harper. Reprinted, Lanham, MD: University Press of America, 1988.
—— (1981) *A Preface to Grants Economics: The Economy of Love and Fear*, New York: Praeger.
—— (1985) 'Regions of time', *Papers of the Regional Science Association* 57: 19–32.
Buchanan, J. M., Rowley, C. K., Breton, A., Wiseman, J., Frey, B. and Peacock, A.

T. (1978) *The Economics of Politics*, London: Institute of Economic Affairs, IEA Readings 18.

Isard, W. (1975) *Introduction to Regional Science*, Englewood Cliffs, NJ: Prentice-Hall.

Lutz, M. A. and Lux, K. (1979) *The Challenge of Humanistic Economics*, Menlo Park, CA: Benjamin/Cummings.

Marshall, A. (1961) *Principles of Economics*, 9th edn, London: Macmillan (originally published 1890).

von Neumann, J. and Morgenstern, O. (1964) *The Theory of Games and Economic Behaviour*, 3rd edn, Princeton, NJ: Princeton University Press (originally published 1944).

Smith, A. (1937) *The Wealth of Nations*, New York: Random House (originally published 1776).

Walras, L. (1954) *Elements of Pure Economics*, 4th edn, transl. M. Jaffe, Homewood, IL: Irwin (originally published 1874). Reprinted, Fairfield NJ: Augustus M. Kelley, 1977.

38

ECONOMICS AND
POLITICS

IAIN McLEAN

38.1 INTRODUCTION

In modern times, economists have made important contributions to political
science but the converse has not been true. This is a sad decline from the
eighteenth and nineteenth centuries. Smith, Malthus, Ricardo and Marx all
saw that politics and economics are inseparable. Much recent work on the
boundaries of politics and economics amounts to a rediscovery of Smith (or
Marx, or Condorcet).

Economists who explore politics sometimes apologize for trespassing (Schelling 1984). Most of them show little interest in the field next door. However,
this can lead to naivety about political actors. When economists learn to treat
the polity with the same sophistication as the economy, social science may
regain its eighteenth-century coherence.

In this chapter we deal with three boundary areas. The first was originally
associated with the Virginia School of J. M. Buchanan and Gordon Tullock
but has now spread geographically and ideologically far and wide. The Virginia
School maintains that it is inconsistent to treat economic actors as rational
utility maximizers while treating political actors – a subset of the same set
of people – as something else. It proceeds to apply standard neoclassical
microeconomic assumptions to political actors, with revealing and controversial
consequences.

The Virginia School methodology shades into the second approach, which
involves collective action problems. The economics of externalities, market
failure and the provision of public goods is inseparable from the politics of
the co-operative and individualistic outcomes of prisoners' dilemmas and other
collective action problems.

The third approach is distinct. It is the theory of social choice, which has
become a cuckoo in the nests of economics journal editors. They have (often
vainly) tried to expel it to make room for proper economics. I share their

759

intuition that social choice is not properly part of economics at all. However, in this century it has been developed almost entirely by economists; its subject matter is politics, and so this seems to be the right chapter for it.

38.2 BUCHANAN, TULLOCK AND THE ORIGINS OF PUBLIC CHOICE

> People of the same trade seldom meet together, even for merriment and diversion, but the conversation ends in a conspiracy against the public, or in some contrivance to raise prices.

Adam Smith's insight is too often forgotten. The public choice school reminds us that politicians, bureaucrats, lobbyists, voters and peasants do not cease to be *homines economici* (*feminae economicae*) when they act in these other roles.
    James Buchanan, recalling the beginnings of public choice, wrote:

> The 1957 mind-set of the academy's members was dirigiste or anti-libertarian socialist. Among economists, market failure was all the rage, and a demonstration that markets could fail by comparison with a totally imaginary idealized construction was widely held to be evidence that political–governmental intervention was justified.

> (Buchanan 1986: 14)

(For a distinguished target see Samuelson 1954.)
    Meanwhile, Gordon Tullock's service in the US State Department had convinced him that 'regardless of role, the bureaucrat responds to the rewards and punishments that he confronts' (Buchanan 1987: 11). Their thirty-year collaboration has begotten the public choice school, centred around the journal entitled *Public Choice* (originally *Papers in Non-market Decision-making*), together with contributions to social contract theory (Buchanan and Tullock 1962; Buchanan 1975, 1986), bureaucracy (Tullock 1965; Niskanen 1971) and the theory of political coalitions (Tullock 1988: chs 1, 6) and rent-seeking (Rowley 1987: chs 13–15; Rowley *et al.* 1987). Others applied Virginia methodology (but not necessarily Virginia ideology) in illuminating ways to the study of lobbying (Olson 1965, 1982; Moe 1980; Hardin 1982). This area, at least, of political science has been changed irreversibly by public choice.
    Buchanan and his associates deplore Keynes. They argue that Keynes gave governments a spurious intellectual justification for fiscal and monetary manipulation, while naively believing that they would not manipulate the economy to maximize their probability of re-election. According to Harrod (1951: 192–3; cf. Buchanan and Wagner 1977: 7, 72, 78), Keynes assumed 'that the government of Britain was and would continue to be in the hands of an intellectual aristocracy using the method of persuasion'. Harrod called this 'the view from Harvey Road' (Keynes's house in Cambridge), and the Virginia

School have used the label with derision. The government of Britain, as of any other democracy, is actually in the hands of politicians who wish to be re-elected. Thus, public choice writers assume that politicians will print money, feather-bed interest groups, especially suppliers of capital and labour, and generally overspend on current account at the expense of capital (posterity has no votes) (for example, Pirie 1988: ch. 6).

Two refinements to this argument concern rent-seeking and log-rolling. Tullock has long argued that it is more tempting for interest groups to seek an economic rent than a normal profit – most obviously when a producer group persuades the government to grant it the monopoly right to produce some good or service. Of course, there is nothing new in either this fact or economists' observations of it; Smith, Turgot and Condorcet had a great deal to say about it. Tullock added that it may be self-defeating. Interest groups must spend real resources in order to persuade the government to grant them the sought-after monopoly. However, if the monopoly does not already exist, there is scope for rival interests to bid for it, and it is rational for them to bid, in aggregate, anything up to the value of the transfer from consumers to producers. As the quantity of monopoly available is fixed, it follows for Tullock that the value of this transfer to producer groups is wiped out.

Hence the public choice school has always cast a beady eye on the politics of lobbying, past and present. One prominent, and rather surprising, theme is that log-rolling is not the evil that it has traditionally been made out to be. Log-rolling is the process in which one legislator supports another's pet project in return for reciprocal support for his own. For decades it has been a much developed feature of bargaining in the US Congress, and it certainly happens elsewhere even though the institutional framework is nowhere else as friendly. It leads to a chronic oversupply of divisible public spending (dams, army depots) and sometimes to self-defeating protectionism, such as the tariffs of 1824 and 1930. (First, one producer group demands tariff protection as a means of securing an economic rent. However, log-rolling results in every other organized producer group acquiring protection as well, so that every group is worse off than in a free-trade equilibrium (for example, Pincus 1975).) But, according to Tullock, a log-roll is a voluntary trade; the parties would not undertake the trade unless each felt that it made him better off; hence it is a move towards the Pareto frontier.

Therefore Tullock is also sceptical about social choice. He is equally unim-pressed by the claim that majority rule is special and by the opposed claim that Arrow's theorem and its sequels (see Section 38.5) undermine democracy. Rather, he wishes to equate votes with money as closely as possible; thus it is efficient that they should be traded as freely as possible, for instance by log-rolling. Among other things, this enables voters to express the intensity of their feelings – a notorious problem for orthodox majoritarian democratic methods.

This leads Buchanan and Tullock to their distinctive views about a constitutional contract. In content, it should put some things out of reach of meddling by election-fighting politicians: they should have no control over the money supply, and the constitution should mandate a balanced budget. In form, it must be unanimously approved by those who are to be subject to it, otherwise they are not free. This harks back to classical seventeenth- and eighteenth-century social contract theory, but its true inspirer was Knut Wicksell, 'the first scholar to recognize that a rule of unanimity for reaching collective decisions provides the institutional analogue to two-person trade in strictly private or partitionable goods' (Buchanan 1975: 38). Unanimity is a precondition for a constitutional contract to be a move towards the Pareto frontier.

However, this reasoning leaves them vulnerable to a well-known criticism of Hobbes, Locke and Rousseau. How would unanimous agreement to a social contract ever arise? A unanimity rule means a veto for each and every voter. Therefore, in the Virginia perspective, it is an opportunity for each and every voter to extract a monopoly rent. It is hard to see how a constitutional contract could be written, even assuming that every voter was a convinced Virginian (Barry 1965: 242–85, 312–27).

Consider two constitutional events: the Philadelphia Convention of 1787, which drafted the US Constitution, and the Balanced Budget and Emergency Deficit Control Act 1985 (the Gramm–Rudman–Hollings Act). The first produced the nearest that the world has yet seen to a Buchanan–Tullock constitutional contract. James Madison, its mastermind, is deservedly one of their heroes. But it was far from unanimous. The delegates decided that the consent of nine states out of the then thirteen would be enough to ratify it, and that if at least nine did, the others could not hold out. They proved correct: even the most obdurate hold-out, Rhode Island, signed the Constitution in 1790. In order to persuade as many as nine states to sign, the framers of the Constitution had to include a wide variety of compromises and rules introduced because they were thought expedient rather than desirable. Each state has two US Senators regardless of population (a sop to small states) and each slave, although unenfranchised, counted as three-fifths of a person for the purpose of determining states' entitlements to seats in the House of Representatives (a sop to the South).

A further difficulty (cf. Buchanan and Vanberg 1989) is how to account for the behaviour of James Madison and others like him. Madison spent months preparing for the Convention, reading about Greece and Rome and thinking about an ideal state; he spent four utterly exhausting months at the Convention, recording what went on and trying to produce a draft that would win the required majority; he spent months afterwards writing the *Federalist Papers*, a classic of political theory intended to persuade the New York delegates to ratify. If this is self-seeking conduct, it is a very odd sort of self-seeking. Nor does Tullock's rule ('Everyone is altruistic, five per cent of the time') help much. Buchanan and Vanberg can only say that Madison wished to maximize his 'posthumous deference', but to go far down that road would void their theories of any predictive value. It is better to analyse the actions of the Framers without assuming that politicians are always maximizers of the probability of re-election (Riker 1984, 1986a: chs 4 and 8, 1986b).

The Gramm–Rudman–Hollings Act mandates Congress to pass a balanced budget. This is a rule long advocated by the Virginia School, but it was passed as an ordinary law, not a constitutional amendment, and in circumstances which make it unlikely that it will ever be binding. At the end of a Congress which had been heavily criticized for doing nothing about the budget crisis, it was 'swept through Congress with gale force', and without the usual interest group bargaining, because Congress needed to be seen to be doing something about the crisis. Even some of its sponsors called it 'neither wise nor workable'; Senator Rudman called it 'a bad idea whose time has come'. It provided for automatic cuts in the federal budget (exempting a number of programmes, such as veterans' pensions and Medicaid) on receipt of a joint report from the executive and legislative budget offices that a deficit was likely. It anticipated that this last provision might be held to be unconstitutional (as violating the separation of powers), and included a provision for accelerating its own judicial review. President Reagan, initially a warm supporter, reportedly cooled rapidly on discovering that Gramm–Rudman would mandate huge cuts in defence spending, and his speech purportedly recommending it to Congress 'virtually invited an early court test of the legislation'. This reached the Supreme Court in July 1986, where the disputed clause was held to be unconstitutional. The legislation contains a fallback clause in which the automatic reduction is to be triggered on a joint resolution of the President and both houses. No such resolution has yet been passed, nor has the deficit been significantly reduced. (Source and quotations, *Congressional Quarterly Almanac* 1985: 459–68, 1986: 579–80.)

The behaviour of Reagan and those who voted for the Bill is well explained in Virginia terms. They wanted to be seen to be doing something about the budget crisis without cutting their favourite programmes. Therefore they passed an act containing a provision inviting its self-destruction. Thus it seems that a constitutional contract may be (fairly close to) unanimous and enforceable, or it may contain the rules that the Virginia School would like to see, but not both. This illustrates the tension between the analytical and normative sides of Buchanan and Tullock's work. The same tension appears between the observation that producer group lobbying, particularly for economic rents, is self-destructive and the normative view that log-rolling is

763

praiseworthy because it is Pareto efficient. What is Pareto efficient from the perspective of legislators may not be so from the perspective of their subjects.

For all that, the Virginia School remains important. We examine next some more general applications in political science.

38.3 SOME APPLICATIONS

The first application was Downs's (1957) model of the rational voter and the rational politician. According to Downs, each voter calculates a 'party differential', which is the difference between the utility income he expects from his favourite party's victory and that which he expects from his less favoured party's victory. His expected utility of voting for his favourite party is his party differential multiplied by the subjective probability that his vote is the crucial one. (Downs generally assumes a two-party system.) Assuming that the electorate can be ranged along some single ideological dimension, the rational party will position itself at the ideology of the median voter, and in equilibrium both parties in a two-party system will coincide at this position.

Both halves of this model have been much discussed. Downs raised an obvious problem with the 'rational' voter: in any plausible view, the subjective probability that one's own vote is decisive is vanishingly small, and therefore it drags the expected utility of voting down to fractions of a penny. As the cost, including opportunity cost, of voting is a few pence, and as information is more expensive, it seems that the rational voter would never vote. Rational choice writers have suggested some unsatisfactory escape routes. Downs suggested that voters might nevertheless vote to save democracy from collapse, but this was to commit 'a common fallacy in social thought which most of the book turns on his avoiding' (Barry 1970: 20), namely that what was in the interests of all was *ipso facto* in the interests of each. Another popular line has been to say that people vote for the incidental benefits (meeting their friends at the polls and so on). This desperate move is instantly destroyed by asking whether, when given the choice of voting in person or by post, anyone ever chooses to vote in person.

Without doubt, a rationally *self*-interested citizen would almost never vote. However, Downs's analysis is a constructive failure because it explains why apparently trivial changes in voting conditions (wet weather versus dry, Sunday versus Thursday, registration at the voter's initiative or at the state's) can generate enormous changes in turnout. It also paves the way for an account based on rational altruism, of which the most persuasive is that of Margolis (1982). Margolis distinguishes between goods and participation altruism. Goods-altruistic actions are those which (I expect) will make others better off, whether done by me or by others; participation-altruistic acts are those where I derive pleasure from the act of doing (what I believe to be) good to others.

People vote because they are participation-altruists, and also because, being goods-altruists, they incorporate their perceptions of other people's utility incomes into their party differentials.

Another important modification is due to Fiorina (1981), who argues that voters heavily discount the promises that politicians make and judge them rather by their performance in office in the past. Hence voting is retrospective rather than prospective. This illuminates the efforts of office-holders to give immediate gratification to voters just before elections and to do painful things just after elections. The neatest illustration of this old truth has been provided by Tufte:

> Normally, ... transfers [from the US Federal administration to US citizens] reach their yearly maximum in December – at least in odd-numbered years.... *But in four of the last seven election years, governmental transfer payments have reached their yearly peak in October or November.* ... if the election in a particular year is 'late' – that is, if the first Tuesday in November falls on the sixth or the seventh – then a November heaping of transfers will still get there in time.... This sequencing suggests a cynical prediction: octokyphosis will occur when the election is early, novemkyphosis will occur if there is a late election date.... such is the case for the four elections in which heaping occurred.
>
> (Tufte 1978: 39–43, original emphasis)

The other half of Downs's model deals with the rational party. If there is just one issue dimension, politicians who wish to be (re-)elected will converge on the ideological position of the median voter. Where politics is truly unidimensional, Downs's hypothesis is robust. Every so often, a politician condemns the consensus of the existing parties and seeks a 'choice, not an echo' (the campaign slogan of Barry Goldwater in 1964). Goldwater, George McGovern and Michael Foot each led their parties to catastrophic defeat after breaking away from the consensus. Margaret Thatcher is often cited as a counterexample. However, on a number of issues, including race relations, trade union reform and nationalistic foreign policy, Thatcherism has moved towards, not away from, the median voter. On many other issues, Thatcherism is admittedly unpopular; it is safe to predict, however, that the Conservative manifesto for the General Election of 1992 will fail to mention the 1988 White Paper on the reform of the National Health Service, the privatization of water or the community charge (the so-called 'poll tax'). The robustness of the Downsian median is also shown by the strenuous efforts of Neil Kinnock to lead the Labour Party to it.

When politics is multi-dimensional, however, the hypothesis gets into trouble. Downs saw it coming, and candidly confessed that he made his model unidimensional in order to avoid 'Arrow problems' of cycling majorities (Downs 1957: 60–4) (see Section 38.5). Generalizing the median voter hypothesis into multi-dimensional issue space may sound easy. Suppose that one issue dimension is 'left–right' judged by voters' attitudes to the distribution of income and wealth, another is 'liberal–conservative' judged by issues such as free speech and the death penalty, and a third concerns the regional distribution of resources. (For empirical evidence that British public opinion is so structured, see Heath *et al.* (1985: 64–8, 81–2).) Then issue space is three dimensional, and the parties aspiring to win should seek out the median-in-all-directions (cf. Enelow and Hinich 1984: especially 54–61). However, whenever issue space contains two or more dimensions, the median-in-all-directions may not exist; when it contains three or more, it almost certainly does not exist in a polity of any size. Possible platforms are in a cycle such that any one loses a majority vote to at least one other. This is explored further in Section 38.5.

Economic explanation of the rational lobbyist has been more successful than that of the rational voter. Olson (1965) attacked the then dominant 'pluralism'. This was both descriptive and normative. It postulated that, in a democracy, the number and intensity of interest groups was a direct function of the number of voters who had the interest in common and of the intensity with which it affected them. Therefore it concluded, contrary to earlier condemnations, that the interplay of interest group bargaining was consistent with democracy. However, Olson pointed out that not all interests generate interest groups. Every interest group is lobbying for something which, if achieved, is a public good from the perspective of its (potential) members. A rise in unemployment benefit is a rise in benefit for every unemployed person. It cannot practicably be restricted to members of the Raise Unemployment Benefits Campaign. As the object of lobbying is a public good, its beneficiaries will be tempted to free-ride on the lobby. Lobbies know this, and so they offer selective benefits to their members and/or selective harms to their non-members. (Trade unions negotiate members' discounts for tyres and carpets, and try to enforce closed shops at work. Trade associations may circulate blacklists of 'troublemaking' employees around their membership, and set themselves up as arbiters of standards in their trade.) But selective benefits and harms can be offered only if the organization already exists; therefore many lobbies for interests will never come into existence at all.

Olson divided interest groups into 'privileged', 'intermediate' and 'latent'. Broadly, the first two could overcome their internal free-riding problem either because the individual benefits of the lobby to some member(s) were so high that they would be willing to carry free-riders or because strategic interaction and credible threats among the potential members would ensure that enough of them joined the lobby to make it effective. Thus an interest group would come into existence if its potential members were few in number, or stood to make substantial gains, or both. Other interests remained latent, and would not generate their own interest groups. Lobbies for the unemployed and for consumers are notoriously weaker than those for the employed and for producers.

Olson (1982) concentrated on producer group lobbies. He noted a tendency for them to form 'distributive coalitions' to lobby for things which were public goods from the perspective of their members and potential members but inefficient from the point of view of society as a whole. Examples are tariffs, subsidies to loss-making industries and regulatory privileges. In spirit, this is very close to Tullock's analysis of rent-seeking (see Section 38.2) and to 'regulatory capture' (Wilson 1980). Olson predicted that the older and more stable a nation's history of democracy, and hence the more mature its pattern of distributive coalitions, the more its economic growth would be frustrated; he contrasted the slow growth of Western Europe and the northeastern United States with the faster growth of the capitalist economies of South Asia and of the southern and western states of the United States (Mueller 1983).

The details of Olson's argument are disputed; the outline is robust. It upsets traditional alignments in an amusing way. Market-oriented conservatives (notably Pirie 1988) have seized on it to justify the supposed success of the Thatcher and Reagan administrations in breaking up interest group coalitions. (One suspects that they have miners rather than barristers in mind.) Social democratic parties are hurrying (in a Downsian way?) to present themselves as the friends of the consumer rather than the producer. But the intellectual tradition which benefits most from Olson is Marxism. Classical Marxism predicted that under capitalism the interests of capital would prevail over those of labour, but failed to give a coherent reason. Olson, although certainly no Marxist, provides one. In every industry, suppliers of capital are fewer than suppliers of labour, and the benefits from a successful lobby to each capitalist exceed those to each labourer. Therefore organizations of capital, such as trade associations, are more likely to be 'privileged' or 'intermediate' than those of labour, such as trade unions. On many issues, the distributive coalitions of capital and of labour are on the same side. It comes as no surprise to find that capital and labour in the US airline industry opposed its 1978 deregulation with equal fervour (Behrman 1980: 94). But where they are on opposite sides, Olson's arguments imply that capital will normally prevail over labour.

Downs's and Olson's approaches should be brought together. Downs implies that vote power determines political outcomes; Olson implies that producer group power does. The truth, of course, is that sometimes one does and sometimes the other. In normal times producer group power probably outweighs voter power, but the balance is most likely to be upset as an election approaches and/or as a consumer issue suddenly becomes salient. One of the most interesting issues for study is the politics of the environment. Around 1970 and again in 1988–9, the normal events of producer group bargaining have been upset by an unexpected surge of voters' environmentalism. Exactly why remains a mystery (but see Ingram 1978).

'It is not from the benevolence of the bureaucrat that we expect our research grant or our welfare check, but out of regard to his own, not the public interest': Tullock's characteristic reworking of Adam Smith (quoted by Jackson 1982: 121) inspired numerous writers, in particular Niskanen (1971), to make a public choice analysis of bureaucracy. Niskanen argued that:

> Among the several arguments that may enter the bureaucrat's utility function are . . . salary, perquisites . . . , public reputation, power, patronage, output of the bureau, ease of making changes, and ease of managing the bureau. All of these variables except the last two, I contend, are a positive monotonic function of the total *budget* of the bureau. . . .
>
> (Niskanen 1971: 38; original emphasis)

Simplifying further by ignoring the qualification 'except the last two', and by assuming linear demand and supply curves for bureau services, Niskanen infers that a budget-maximizing bureau will produce exactly twice the free-market equilibrium output of bureau goods.

There is much of value in this model (Jackson 1982, 1985), but it is too ideological. First, it misinterprets Max Weber. When Weber wrote about bureaucracy, he did not intend to describe only public sector organizations, but any organizations not 'traditional' or 'charismatic' and not directly con-strained by the market. Weber's picture of bureaucracy applies as much, or as little, to the staff of General Motors as of the Department of Defense, as no industrial economist seriously maintains that large corporations are under free-market discipline. Therefore the existence of bureaucratic oversupply cannot of itself be used as an indictment of the public sector. Second, the Niskanen model ignores some arguments in some bureaucrats' utility functions. Some civil servants actually want to save public money (cf. Chapman 1979; Pliatzky 1982). Third, Niskanen, like Olson, has to be confronted with Downs. Pro-ducer group power may be countered by vote power. Sometimes, however rarely, one must expect the producers of bureau services to be voted down by the more numerous payers for them.

38.4 THE POLITICAL ECONOMY OF COLLECTIVE ACTION

Almost everything discussed in this chapter so far has involved dilemmas of collective action. These are now familiar to most social scientists (although UK political science lags in this area). Economists, I suppose, most often encounter collective action problems in discussions of market failure and externalities, and of bargaining games, especially in oligopoly. They exist all over politics, notably in political economy.

Dilemmas of collective action are non-zero-sum games. Some are pure co-ordination games which become trivial when common knowledge exists. Others are tougher in that more information does not necessarily rescue the parties from suboptimal outcomes. A useful three-way classification is into assurance games, chicken games and prisoners' dilemmas (PDs).

Assurance games are those in which co-ordination achieves an individual and social optimum without requiring threats or sanctions:

> Those people who get their thrills from driving at 70 mph the wrong way up the fast lane of a motorway . . . if they are not deterred by the threats posed by the oncoming traffic, . . . would not be deterred by the threat of prosecution for driving on the wrong side of the road.
>
> (Laver 1983: 55)

Thus, government is redundant. Many social conventions can be explained as the outcome of co-ordinated solutions to assurance games. It does not matter whether everybody leaves his fork on the plate when it is taken away for a second helping, or holds is in mid-air; it does matter that there should be a convention. If there is a 'prominent' solution to some dilemma such as 'Where and when should we meet tomorrow?', then it pays all parties to converge on that option, and once they have done so they are in (Nash) equilibrium for repeated plays of the same game. A prominent solution is one that occurs spontaneously to all or most of a set of people asked to solve a co-ordination problem. Schelling (1960), the inventor of the concept, asked a class of Yale students where in New York they would meet one another. They plumped for the information booth at Grand Central Station, which is where the trains from Yale arrive.

If most collective action dilemmas were assurance games, politicians and political scientists would be unnecessary. But chicken and PD games are commoner in political economy. Two-person PD games can be characterized as follows. If both players co-operate, they each receive R (reward). If one co-operates and the other defects, the defector receives T (temptation) and the co-operator receives S (sucker's pay-off). If both defect, each receives P (punishment). $T > R > P > S$, and $2R > T + S$. As is well known, the Nash equilibrium outcome is P, P, even though both parties know that each would be better off at R, R. In other words, once the parties have arrived at the situation where both defect, it does not pay either unilaterally to do anything else – they seem to be locked in. If they play the game just once, each reasons 'If the other player co-operates, I will receive T if I defect and R if I co-operate. $T > R$, and so I should defect. If the other player defects, I will receive P if I defect and S if I co-operate. $P > S$, and so again I should defect. Therefore I should defect whatever I expect the other to do.' In two-person chicken, when both defect, each receives S, and when one co-operates and the other defects, the co-operator receives P and the defector receives T

	Column	
	Co-operate	Defect
Co-operate	R, R	S, T
Defect	T, S	P, P

Row

(a)

	Column	
	Co-operate	Defect
Co-operate	R, R	P, T
Defect	T, P	S, S

Row

(b) $T > R > P > S$ $2R > T + S$

Figure 38.1 (a) Two-person prisoners' dilemma; (b) two-person chicken. In each box, the payoff to Row comes before the comma, and the payoff to Column comes after.

(see Figure 38.1). Here, the two outcomes where one defects and the other co-operates are equilibria, but if the parties are not at an equilibrium then co-ordination will not necessarily get them to one, nor will promises to go to a particular outcome: the latter merely lead to precommitment games, which set up an infinite regress of chicken games (see further McLean 1987: ch. 7).

Many standard political dilemmas have the PD ordering. There is some form of sociable behaviour which we all know would be better for each of us than individualism. However, for each player, the option 'I free-ride, everybody else co-operates' is better than 'Everybody co-operates', which is better than 'Nobody co-operates', which is better than 'I co-operate, everybody else free-rides'. This covers pollution, arms races, voluntary incomes policies and voluntary contributions to any public good. Note especially that many of the products of governments are public goods, and so is the existence of a government of any particular complexion. From the fact that a political party intends to govern in the interests of some set of citizens, it cannot be inferred that it is in the interest of any one of those citizens to vote for, still less to work for, the party.

Contributors' dilemmas are not always strict n-person PDs. Sometimes they have a flavour of chicken, as when there is some level of contribution by the others such that it does pay me to contribute. The game 'Vote or free-ride on the other supporters of my party' is an example (see Taylor and Ward 1982; McLean 1987: ch. 7). However, they share a problem nicely stated by Hollis (1987):

On tablets of stone in some Englightenment heaven there is an equation resolving

770

the central problem of political theory. The left-hand side is the work of a formula for identifying the good of all. The right-hand side is the sum or conjunction of the good of each. The equation itself states that the two components, although arrived at differently, coincide. . . . Sadly, however, thinkers on earth have never been shown how to formulate each half so as to bring them out demonstrably coextensive.

The fallacy that what is in the interest of all is in the interest of each is found in classical Marxism ('Proletarians should become revolutionaries because the revolution will benefit all the proletariat'), in classical economic liberalism ('It is in the interest of employees to ensure that their firm maximizes its profits'), in romantic communitarianism ('In the pre-capitalist village, peasants rationally co-operated for the good of the village') and even in popular biology ('Unselfish animals, such as bees and gazelles, sacrifice themselves for the good of their species').

However, co-operation patently exists; how then to explain it? There is room here for only two samples from a rich and growing literature. One strategy is to deny that the observed facts imply altruism. Popkin's (1979) study of the rational Vietnamese peasant tackles the third formulation of the fallacy with verve. Peasants in pre-capitalist villages typically spread their holdings into scattered strips to spread the risk from flood, disease and infertility. Romantic communitarians attribute this to rational co-operation. However, spread-out holdings typically reduce the village's output by 10–20 per cent compared with consolidated holdings. A true moral community would consolidate holdings and insure its members against chance losses. Therefore Popkin explains this feature (and many others) of the pre-capitalist village as the individualistic suboptimal outcome of a collective action dilemma. Co-operative outcomes in Vietnam were typically secured when a body with an ulterior motive (such as the Society of Jesus or the Communist Party) acted as co-ordinator and obtained for the villagers some of the surplus they could secure by moving from the competitive to the co-operative equilibrium. Some remained available for the priests or the party (Popkin 1979: *passim*, especially 27, 39, 41, 46–50, 67–8, 236).

Another strategy is to explain co-operation as a supergame equilibrium. If we play a PD once only, general defection is uniquely rational. However, if the same game is iterated among the same players (a supergame), then threats, promises and/or co-ordinated strategies for the game of playing the supergame may take players to the co-operative equilibrium. In a nicely designed two-stage computer tournament, Axelrod (1984) found that the most successful strategy submitted was one of the simplest: Tit-for-Tat, defined as 'Co-operate in the first round; thereafter in each round do what your opponent did in the immediately previous round'. The strategies submitted each had to play a specified two-person PD a number of times against each other, against themselves and against a random player. Tit-for-Tat did better than any strategy which cheated because, although it rarely secured T (temptation), it received enough R (reward) pay-offs to compensate. If the pay-offs can be given numerical values, then the discount rate below which it is better to co-operate than to defect can be calculated (Axelford 1984: Appendix B; cf. Maynard Smith 1982: Appendix K; McLean 1986).

Axelrod uses these results to explain the evolution of co-operation in human and animal groups. His extended example is the 'live and let live' convention which arose between British and German troops in the front line on the Western Front during the First World War. Axelrod has been criticized for inferring too much from a simple PD supergame. However, the current sophisticated work on generalizing from PD to more complex games of threats and imperfect information, and from Nash equilibrium to more general concepts of perfect equilibrium, has not been applied to politics.

38.5 SOCIAL CHOICE AND VOTING

An adequate review of social choice would be a book in itself. Here we shall discuss only aspects on the boundary of economics and politics.

With a prehistory that has so far been traced back to 1283 (McLean and London 1990), the theory of voting first flourished in France from 1770 to around 1800. Borda (1784) appealed to, without defining, the concept of the Condorcet winner. A Condorcet winner is an option which can beat every other in an exhaustive set of pairwise comparisons. He proved that the plurality (first past the post) voting rule is defective when there are more than two options. He gave an example for three candidates in which the plurality rule selected the Condorcet loser. He went on to propose the rank-order count method: each voter gives a score of a to his least-liked option, $a + b$ ($b > 0$) to his next-least-liked options $a + 2b$ to the next and so on. The option with the highest aggregate score wins. Most commonly $a = 0$ and $b = 1$. The Marquis de Condorcet (1785) proved that this method did not necessarily select the Condorcet winner. He also discovered majority rule cycles, also known as the Condorcet effect or (incorrectly) as Condorcet's paradox. With more than two voters, more than two options and simple majority voting, it is always possible that option A beats B, which beats C, which (beats D, which . . .) beats A. He proposed an election procedure for selecting the Condorcet winner, and for breaking the cycle of winners if one was found to exist. However, it was impracticable to count without computers (even now it would require substantial computing power for any number of candidates above four), and he also proposed a practical procedure which was implemented in Geneva, where Lhuilier (1794) proved that it, too, could reject a Condorcet winner.

772

By around 1820, these discoveries had been entirely lost, partly because of the extreme difficulty of Condorcet's *Essai* of 1785. They were rediscovered by Lewis Carroll in the 1870s, who did not read Borda or Condorcet, but who also was not understood (see Black 1958). The third independent discovery was by two economists, Arrow (1951) and Black (1958). Because of the circumstances of the third discovery, social choice has for the most part been regarded as a branch of economics.

Arrow's general (im)possibility theorem proves that no social welfare function (i.e. procedure which derives a social ordering from a set of individual orderings) can simultaneously observe the following (for an explanation of the terms see, for example, Plott (1976), Sen (1982: 329–35)):

collective rationality;
universal domain;
the weak Pareto principle;
independence from irrelevant alternatives;
non-dictatorship.

An architect of a choice procedure would certainly want it to observe at least the first three of Arrow's conditions, arguably the independence condition as well, and then a lot more besides. However, any procedure which observed the first four conditions could produce a dictator; i.e. a voter whose ordering became the society's ordering irrespective of the orderings of everybody else.

Much of the enormous literature on Arrow has been devoted to relaxing one of the first four conditions in order to suggest defensible non-dictatorial choice procedures. Black (1958) in effect relaxed universal domain. He proved that, if opinion was single-peaked (meaning, roughly, that a dimension existed such that nobody's least-liked option was in the middle), the option most liked by the median voter would always be the Condorcet winner. Black thus corroborated Downs's model from a different starting point.

Most of Arrow's critics (for example, Dummett 1984) have attacked the independence axiom as unreasonable. Borda's rank-order count violates independence because the ordering of candidates can change according to whether somebody who was not a feasible candidate (say Jesus, or Abraham Lincoln, or somebody who died between nomination day and polling day) is ranked with them or not. Dummett argues that such infeasible alternatives are relevant to the ranking of the feasible ones because they supply information about the subjective distances between the candidates in the voters' minds. Defenders of Arrow (and Condorcet) retort that this is an illegitimate way of importing cardinality into choice procedures which in general must be ordinal. The matter is too complex to dispose of here, but it shows that issues first disputed by Borda and Condorcet have not yet been settled.

Two corollaries of Arrow have deep implications for politics. The first, proved by Gibbard (1973) and Satterthwaite (1975), is that all determinate choice procedures are either dictatorial or manipulable. 'Manipulable' means that at least one voter can advance the chances of some option(s) that he favours by misrepresenting his preference ordering. The Gibbard–Satterthwaite theorem puts an end to one of the cherished aims of electoral reformers – to design a non-manipulable electoral system. But like medieval alchemists, some of them carry on undaunted. The second corollary was proved, by different routes, by McKelvey (1979) and Schofield (1984: ch. 7). It is that as the number of dimensions increases, so, rapidly, does the probability that the possible outcomes are in a global cycle. Indeed, if the number of dimensions is as low as three and the number of voters is reasonably large, the probability of a global cycle is very close to unity. There are, as already stated, at least three dimensions in current UK politics: left–right, liberal–conservative and north–south. All possible political platforms must include a stance in each of these three dimensions. However, because there is almost certainly no median-in-all-directions (no core, in game-theoretical terms), every one of the uncountable millions of policy platforms that could be devised by politicians seeking (re-)election would lose a majority vote to at least one other.

These findings of social choice theory imply much more for politics than they do for economics. They bear both on the realities of the design of electoral systems and on the more cosmic issue of the validity of democracy. In many countries, including the United Kingdom, discussion of electoral systems has been unintelligent and even dishonest. There is no serious argument in favour of first past the post when there are more than two candidates, yet it is still defended with vigour by those whose vested interests it serves. Equally, proponents of electoral reform typically opt for particular systems just because they expect them to favour their party. But concepts like 'Condorcet winner' are coming to be understood and electoral reform is being discussed in a less self-serving way.

There is no consensus on the 'best' electoral system; indeed, there probably is no general answer. For elections to a single post, or the choice of a single course of action, a direct search for the Condorcet winner is now computationally feasible. If there is a cycle, I favour breaking it by Condorcet's method if that can be established and programmed (cf. Michaud 1985), or, failing that, by running a Borda count among the options in the winning cycle. Such a procedure would be simple for voters, who need merely rank the options in order of preference. For parliamentary elections, where it is widely agreed that legislators should in some sense be a microcosm of those they represent, I favour proportional representation in multi-member seats, either by single transferable vote or by modification of the additional member system (see further Hill 1988; McLean 1988; Young 1988).

The proofs by McKelvey and Schofield of the prevalence of global cycling have been used by Riker (1982, 1986a) both destructively and constructively. They demolish any justification of democracy based on its being 'the will of the people', as that concept is undetermined in any complex society. But then they throw up the question: why is there so much stability in politics? If outcomes are in a global cycle and if politics is competitive, one might expect that every outcome would be immediately toppled by a new majority coalition. Instead, the same platform of policies is observed to win election after election, sometimes for several decades. (Three examples of long-run hegemony are the US Democrats from 1828 to 1860, the Japanese Liberal Democratic Party (LDP) since 1945 and the British Conservative Party since 1922.) Riker and others have introduced two main new concepts: structure-induced equilibrium and heresthetics. The three political parties mentioned were able to enjoy their dominance for so long because of a divided opposition and a plurality voting rule. (It is more complicated than that, of course, but that will do to begin with.) The plurality voting rule continues to exist because those in power benefit from it. Those seeking power must adapt their strategies in the light of their knowledge that it is the rule of the game. Thus, although *ex hypothesi* the platforms of the LDP and the Conservative Party can be beaten, they are stable because the rules of the game make it difficult for a winning coalition to be constructed against them. This is a simple example of structure-induced equilibrium.

Heresthetics is the art and science of political manipulation. It takes several forms. One is the ability to introduce new issues so as to build the winning coalition which will upset the structure-induced equilibrium. Riker (1982) argues that abolitionism and the formation of the Republican Party in the 1850s were successful pieces of heresthetics. They broke up the Democratic coalition. (As it happened, they also led to a civil war.) A second form is agenda control. Different electoral procedures produce different results from the same set of preferences. A committee chairman who knows this and who knows voters' preferences can arrange the agenda in such a way as to secure his favoured result, although it is harder to do so if the voters are equally sophisticated. The most advanced form of heresthetics is to write the voting rules themselves. Hence Riker's fascination with US history from the Constitutional Convention in 1787 to Thomas Jefferson's *Manual of Parliamentary Procedure* (1797–1801). Jefferson's *Manual* begot all other handbooks for chairmen, notably *Robert's Rules of Order*, and itself remains the rulebook of the House of Representatives. All Anglo-Saxon legislatures rely on binary voting procedures, which queue the options so that only one yes/no proposition is before the house at a time. This does not eliminate cycles, but it conceals them. The order in which propositions are queued will (if voters are naive) or may (if they are sophistciated) determine the outcome. Jefferson was a friend of Condorcet, and may have understood Condorcet's work on voting. It is an intriguing possibility that the voting rules he devised represent the deepest heresthetic manoeuvre yet known. Like Madison, Jefferson deserves posthumous deference. The Virginia School assertion that that explains his actions is hard to swallow. But then it is equally hard to swallow for James Buchanan and Gordon Tullock.

38.6 CONCLUDING COMMENTS

What then is the current state of play on the boundary of economics and politics? Let us try to review it, both outside and inside the academic community.

In the early 1990s every UK party, including the Green Party, presents itself as the friend of the consumer. Labour and the Conservatives are both shaking off some of their traditional associations with suppliers of the factors of production. The idea that the central political cleavage is between producers and consumers, rather than between capital and labour, is quite new, but parties in the United Kingdom and other democracies are adapting to it rather quickly.

The politics of regulation has come to the fore since 1979. When the Thatcher administration's privatization programme started, few people seemed to realize that privatization entailed regulation. This is particularly, but not only, true for privatized monopolies and oligopolies (gas, telecommunications, water and electricity). A completely new structure for regulating financial institutions has also been devised since 1979. Americans have a century of experience of the politics of regulation; Europeans have much to learn. They are learning that regulation brings rent-seeking and regulatory capture in its train.

Finally, social choice theory is slowly and painfully making its way into the hermetic world of electoral reform. Finding the right electoral system for a given task is a practical as much as an academic problem.

In academic circles, public choice theory is coming to dominate American political science. It is less ideological than in its early days, and it is seen as a powerful technique for generating testable hypotheses about the behaviour of political actors. Up to now, more energy seems to have gone into designing hypotheses than testing them, but I sense that this is changing for the better. On the whole, the hypotheses emanating from public choice theory about why voters, bureaucrats, lobbyists and politicians do what they do seem to be more successful than those derived from pluralism, Marxism or casual anecdotalism. They are most successful in explaining the pattern of lobbying, and less successful in accounting for voters (keener to vote than they should be) and politicians (more ideological than they should be).

The signs are that the environment will be one of the hottest political issues in the capitalist democracies of the 1990s. It is particularly amenable to study using public choice theory because environmental bads such as the greenhouse effect and ozone depletion are conspicuous cases of market failure. Therefore environmental goods are provided, and bads mitigated, by governments. But these activities are themselves public goods, and governments provide what they do under both lobby pressure and vote pressure. Public choice theory is good at predicting the shape which each of these will take, although it is not yet good at integrating them.

Trade and taxation policy is the classic area in which people of the same trade meet together for merriment and diversion, and their conversation ends in a conspiracy against the public, or in some contrivance to raise prices. One expects trade associations to be the most effective producer group lobbyists. Compared with trade unions and even more so with consumer lobbies, they have more concentrated resources and a more tractable internal free-rider problem. Thus, there is reason to expect normal politics to be a producer group conspiracy against consumers. But politics is not always normal politics, even in the arena of trade and taxation. To some extent at least, the European Community plan to free internal trade by 1992 is designed to benefit consumers against producers. However, it would be rash to predict that producer interests will be defeated. Here again there is an interaction between lobby power and vote power which is not yet fully understood.

At the time of writing economic theorists are very busy with sophisticated applications of non-zero-sum game theory which go far beyond the Axelrod model of rational co-operation discussed in this chapter. This work has yet to bear fruit. If and when theorists and empiricists re-establish contact, it may illuminate collective action all the way from social conventions to international relations.

Likewise with social choice: theory still outstrips applications. However, there are welcome moves to apply social choice in two areas. One is the design of electoral systems; now that computers can overcome some of the earlier barriers to a good electoral system, I predict that Condorcet systems will come back into fashion after nearly 200 years of neglect. The other is democratic theory, where it is forcing a radical re-evaluation of classical claims. The theorist most affected is Rousseau, who believed that a good society should follow its general will. But social choice theory has shown that the general will is generally undetermined.

There are even stirrings in the other direction, as some economists take politics into account. In place of the fallacy that politicians are wise and benevolent, and/or the opposite fallacy that politics is an irrational movement of animal spirits, political economists try to substitute a realistic account of political actors' motivations. This is particularly helpful in discussing labour markets and trade policy.

Economics used to be called political economy. In a few staunchly traditional universities, it still is. If students of politics and economics would once again learn how to be political economists, both subjects would gain. They might even have more to contribute to the sum of useful knowledge.

REFERENCES

Arrow, K. J. (1951) *Social Choice and Individual Values*, New York: Wiley.

Axelrod, R. (1984) *The Evolution of Cooperation*, New York: Basic Books.

Barry, B. (1965) *Political Argument*, London: Routledge.

—— (1970) *Sociologists, Economists, and Democracy*, London: Collier-Macmillan.

Behrman, B. (1980) 'Civil Aeronautics Board', in J. Q. Wilson (ed.) *The Politics of Regulation*, pp. 75–120, New York: Basic Books.

Black, D. (1958) *The Theory of Committees and Elections*, Cambridge: Cambridge University Press.

de Borda, J.-C. (1784) 'Mémoire sur les élections au scrutin', *Mémoires de l'Académie Royale des Sciences année 1781*, pp. 657–65. Translated in Sommerlad, F. and McLean, I. (eds) *The Political Theory of Condorcet*, Working paper 1/89, Social Studies Faculty Centre, Oxford University, 1989.

Buchanan, J. M. (1975) *The Limits of Liberty*, Chicago, IL: University of Chicago Press.

—— (1986) *Liberty, Market and State: Political Economy in the 1980s*, Brighton: Harvester Wheatsheaf.

—— (1987) 'The qualities of a natural economist', in C. K. Rowley (ed.) *Democracy and Public Choice: Essays in Honor of Gordon Tullock*, pp. 9–19, Oxford: Basil Blackwell.

Buchanan, J. M. and Tullock, G. (1962) *The Calculus of Consent*, Ann Arbor, MI: University of Michigan Press.

Buchanan, J. M. and Vanberg, V. (1989) 'A theory of leadership and deference in constitutional construction', *Public Choice* 61: 15–27.

Buchanan, J. M. and Wagner, R. E. (1977) *Democracy in Deficit: The Political Legacy of Lord Keynes*, New York: Academic Press.

de Condorcet, M. J. A. N. (1785) *Essai sur l'Application de l'Analyse à la Probabilité des Décisions Rondues à la Pluralité des Voix*, Paris: Imprimerie Royale.

Chapman, L. (1979) *Your Disobedient Servant*, 2nd edn, Harmondsworth: Penguin.

Downs, A. (1957) *An Economic Theory of Democracy*, New York: Harper & Row.

Dummett, M. (1984) *Voting Procedures*, Oxford: Clarendon Press.

Enelow, J. M. and Hinich, M. J. (1984) *The Spatial Theory of Voting: An Introduction*, Cambridge: Cambridge University Press.

Fiorina, M. (1981) *Retrospective Voting in American National Elections*, New Haven, CT: Yale University Press.

Gibbard, A. (1973) 'Manipulation of voting schemes: a general result', *Econometrica* 41: 587–601.

Hardin, R. (1982) *Collective Action*, Baltimore, MD: Johns Hopkins University Press.

Harrod, R. 1951) *The Life of John Maynard Keynes*, London: Macmillan.

Heath, A., Jowell, R. and Curtice, J. (1985) *How Britain Votes*, Oxford: Pergamon.

Hill, I. D. (1988) 'Some aspects of elections: to fill one seat or many', *Journal of the Royal Statistical Society, Series A* 151: 243–75.

Hollis, M. (1987) 'The art of the impossible', Paper presented at the Conference on Public Choice and Political Democracy, Norwich, March 1987.

Ingram, H. (1978) 'The political rationality of innovation: the Clean Air Act Amendments of 1970', in A. F. Friedlaender (ed.) *Approaches to Controlling Air Pollution*, pp. 13–65, Cambridge, MA: MIT Press.

Jackson, P. M. (1982) *The Political Economy of Bureaucracy*, Deddington: Philip Allan.

—— (1985) 'Economy, democracy, and bureaucracy', in R. C. O. Matthews (ed.) *Economy and Democracy*, pp. 168–203, London: Macmillan.

Laver, M. (1983) *Invitation to Politics*, Oxford: Martin Robertson.

Lhuilier, S. (1794) *Examen du Mode d'Election proposé à la Convention Nationale de France en février 1793, et adopté à Genève; présenté au Comité Legislatif par Simon Lhuilier et imprimé par ordre du Comité*, Geneva. Translated in part in Sommerlad, F. and McLean, I. (eds) *The Political Theory of Condorcet*, Working paper 1/89, Social Studies Faculty Centre, Oxford University, 1989.

Margolis, H. (1982) *Selfishness, Altruism, and Rationality: A Theory of Social Choice*, Cambridge: Cambridge University Press.

Maynard Smith, J. (1982) *Evolution and the Theory of Games*, Cambridge: Cambridge University Press.

McKelvey, R. D. (1979) 'General conditions for global intransitivities in formal voting models', *Econometrica* 47: 1085–111.

McLean, I. (1986) 'Some recent work in public choice', *British Journal of Political Science* 16: 377–94.

—— (1987) *Public Choice*, Oxford: Basil Blackwell.

—— (1988) 'Ships that pass in the night: electoral reform and social choice theory', *Political Quarterly* 59: 63–71.

McLean, I. and London, J. (1990) 'The Borda and Condorcet principles: three medieval applications', *Social Choice and Welfare* 7: 99–108.

Michaud, P. (1985) 'Hommage à Condorcet: version intégrale pour le bicentenaire de l'*Essai* de Condorcet', Etude F.094, Centre Scientifique IBM, Paris.

Moe, T. (1980) *The Organization of Interests*, Chicago, IL: University of Chicago Press.

Mueller, D. (ed.) (1983) *The Political Economy of Growth*, New Haven, CT: Yale University Press.

Niskanen, W. A. (1971) *Bureaucracy and Representative Government*, Chicago, IL: Aldine.

Olson, M. (1965) *The Logic of Collective Action*, Cambridge, MA: Harvard University Press.

—— (1982) *The Rise and Decline of Nations*, New Haven, CT: Yale University Press.

Pincus, J. J. (1975) 'Pressure groups and the pattern of tariffs', *Journal of Political Economy* 83: 757–78.

Pirie, M. (1988) *Micropolitics: The Creation of Successful Policy*, Aldershot: Wildwood House.

Pliatzky, L. (1982) *Getting and Spending*, Oxford: Basil Blackwell.

Plott, C. R. (1976) 'Axiomatic social choice theory', *American Journal of Political Science* 20: 511–96.

Popkin, S. L. (1979) *The Rational Peasant: The Political Economy of the Rural Society in Vietnam*, Berkeley, CA: University of California Press.

Riker, W. H. (1982) *Liberalism against Populism*, San Francisco, CA; W. H. Freeman.

—— (1984) 'The heresthetics of constitution-making: the Presidency in 1787, with comments on determinism and rational choice', *American Political Science Review* 78: 1–16.

—— (1986a) *The Art of Political Manipulation*, New Haven, CT: Yale University Press.

—— (1986b) 'The first power index', *Social Choice and Welfare* 3: 293–6.

Rowley, C. K. (ed.) (1987) *Democracy and Public Choice: Essays in Honor of Gordon Tullock*, Oxford: Basil Blackwell.

Rowley, C. K, Tollison, R. D. and Tullock, G. (1987) *The Political Economy of Rent-seeking*, Dordrecht: Kluwer.

Samuelson, P. A. (1954) 'The pure theory of public expenditure', *Review of Economics and Statistics* 33: 387–9.

Satterthwaite, M. (1975) 'Strategy-proofness and Arrow's conditions: existence and correspondence theorems for voting procedures and social welfare functions', *Journal of Economic Theory* 10: 187–217.

Schelling, T. C. (1960) *The Strategy of Conflict*, Cambridge, MA: Harvard University Press.

—— (1984) *Choice and Consequence: Perspectives of an Errant Economist*, Cambridge, MA: Harvard University Press.

Schofield, N. (1984) *Social Choice and Democracy*, Berlin: Springer-Verlag.

Sen, A. K. (1982) *Choice, Welfare and Measurement*, Oxford: Basil Blackwell.

Taylor, M. and Ward, H. (1982) 'Chickens, whales, and lumpy goods: alternative models of public-goods provision', *Political Studies* 30: 350–70.

Tufte, E. (1978) *Political Control of the Economy*, Princeton, NJ: Princeton University Press.

Tullock,. G. (1965) *The Politics of Bureaucracy*, Washington, DC: Public Affairs Press.

—— (1988) *Wealth, Poverty and Politics*, Oxford: Basil Blackwell.

Wilson, J. Q. (ed.) (1980) *The Politics of Regulation*, New York: Basic Books.

Young, H. P. (1988) 'Condorcet's theory of voting', *American Political Science Review* 82: 1231–44.

39

ECONOMICS AND LAW

ROGER BOWLES

39.1 INTRODUCTION

The area of study referred to as 'law and economics' has grown rapidly over the past twenty-five years or so. Distinctive features of this development have been an extension of economic models into new areas such as crime and punishment and civil liability, and a thorough overhaul of the way in which economists think about the role of contractual exchange and the control of externalities. In the United States, at least, economics has become very influential in the analysis of law and in law school curricula. The impact of the increased interest in law and legal institutions on the teaching of economics and the development of economic models has been less obvious and less easy to gauge. Textbook analysis of economic organization, particularly of areas such as competition policy and the control of monopoly, has developed steadily through the twentieth century, and so there is a tradition of legal institutions being taken seriously. Some authors stress the difference between these long-standing interests and the recent development of the property rights and civil liability literature by distinguishing the 'old' law and economics from the new.

There is a certain irony in this distinction if one goes further back in the history of economic thought, because the pioneers of political economy took legal institutions rather more seriously than their successors. It was the evolution of the neoclassical model and the striving after positivist modes of analysis which had the effect of reducing interest in government institutions because they posed normative issues and fitted only with some difficulty into the market model.

The early political economists, in contrast, had regarded the legal system in rather the same way as taxation, namely as an inescapable and important influence of government on the economy. Thus, for example, when John Stuart Mill considers the influence of government in Book V of his *Principles of Political Economy* (Mill 1909) he devotes several chapters to particular sorts of taxes, then a chapter to national debt followed by three chapters concerned with a variety of legal institutions. Some of these chapters concern themselves with issues which now sound rather old-fashioned, such as the law and custom of primogeniture, whilst others, such as the discussion of partnerships as a means of organizing firms, laws against the 'combination of workmen' and the regulation of usury, have obvious contemporary counterparts.

It is probably only fair to point out that the application of economic analysis to law, like other areas of application of economics to policy matters, excites a degree of controversy. The publication of the first edition of Richard Posner's standard text *Economic Analysis of Law* in 1972 provoked a good deal of comment, a considerable part of which was critical of what many reviewers took to be a confusion of positive and normative analysis. In the preface to later editions Posner is unrepentant and argues that his book stresses the difference between the two. But it remains the case that there are many who find Posner's emphasis on efficiency as an explanation of legal institutions a very ambitious, and at the same time rather narrow, view of the cathedral.

In an effort to convey the flavour of the subject this brief survey of law and economics is organized around a review of four topic areas within which significant developments have taken place over the past two decades. This inevitably results in significant omissions, such as a treatment of models of crime and punishment, but has the advantage of making space for a slightly more extended review of the topics we do examine.

39.2 NEGLIGENCE RULES AND CIVIL LIABILITY

The development of law and economics as a recognizable subdiscipline of economics was given major impetus by Coase's (1960) paper on the problem of social cost. The traditional approach to externalities had been to treat them as a market failure and to find some non-market device for their elimination. Thus, for example, taxation had long been regarded, following Pigou (1932), as one means of dealing with divergences between social and private costs, as in the case of seeking to control the emission of smoke from a factory chimney. Coase demonstrated that the creation of a set of legally enforceable rights could be a much more powerful and effective way of encouraging allocationally efficient resource use than the alternatives normally considered. In the absence of transactions cost he was able to show that, irrespective of how the rights were allocated initially, resources would find their way into the socially most valued use. The legal system was able to create, in effect, a means by which trade between parties could be used to resolve conflicts over resource use. In his example of straying cattle eating the crops growing on neighbouring land, he was able to show that an efficient pattern of land use and fencing would emerge from a property rights approach irrespective of whether one assigned the liability to pay for the cost of damaged crops to the herder or the crop-grower.

Since the early work of Coase there have been two major advances, the first associated with the book by Calabresi (1970) and the second with the paper by Brown (1973). Calabresi developed a relatively sophisticated framework within which accident law could be analysed. His book is written in an informal way, entirely accessible to lawyers, and yet it had a very marked impact on the work by economists in this area. His particular contribution lay in articulating a broader framework than that used by Coase, paying attention to the possibility that in accidents involving two parties one side might be in a position to prevent accidents more cheaply than the other. He brought the question of compensation of victims more clearly into the picture, putting emphasis on differences in the arrangements for allocating risks among agents. As a result, the choice between different liability rules could be seen to involve a more elaborate set of trade-offs than those articulated in Coase's relatively simple model.

The work of Brown (1973) involved developing a formal economic analysis of liability rules which served as the basis for a great deal of subsequent work by well-known theorists (for example Diamond 1974; Diamond and Mirrlees 1975; Green 1976; Polinsky 1980; and more recently Shavell 1987). Many of these models have a similar underlying structure. To give a flavour, we consider a model of bilateral accidents which follows the Appendix to Chapter 2 of the recent survey by Shavell (1987).

There is some activity in which there are two groups of participants, and there is some probability that members of one group will be injured by members of the other group when engaging in the activity. The context could be road accidents, or it might involve a manufacturer selling potentially dangerous products. Both groups are in a position to take precautions, and the probability of an accident and/or its severity will decline as more is spent on accident prevention. Prevention activities are costly, and their intensity can be characterized in financial terms. The level of care exercised by a potential injurer (for example, a motorist) is denoted x, with $x > 0$, whilst the level of care exercised by a potential victim (for example, a pedestrian) is denoted y, with $y > 0$. Expected accident losses l depend on the degree of care exercised by both parties. We assume that $l(x, y)$ is decreasing in both x and y, and that l is non-negative, continuously differentiable and a strictly convex function of x and y. Thus, as both parties exercise greater care the probability of an accident and/or its severity diminishes so as to ensure that expected accident losses decline. The unit cost of care to the injurer is g and to the victim is h.

The total social cost Z of accidents plus accident prevention is given by

$$Z = gx + hy + l(x, y) \qquad (39.1)$$

In order to minimize this loss function we need to satisfy first-order conditions as follows:

$$g = -l_x \tag{39.2a}$$

$$h = -l_y \tag{39.2b}$$

where l_i denotes the partial derivative of l with respect to i.

We denote by (x^*, y^*) the welfare-maximizing values, which will correspond to an optimum. The interpretation of the optimality conditions is straight-forward, namely for each party to exercise care up to but not beyond the point at which the marginal cost of additional care is equal to the benefits in terms of reduced (expected) accident costs. The question is whether, or under what conditions, a particular liability rule will produce these required levels of care. The liability rules most often investigated are as follows.

1 Negligence rule: the injurer is liable to compensate the victim for his loss if and only if it can be established by the victim that the injurer failed to exercise due care, i.e. that $x < x^*$.
2 Negligence rule with contributory negligence: the injurer is liable to compensate the victim if the injurer fails to exercise due care ($x < x^*$), but the fraction of loss for which he is liable is reduced if the victim also failed to exercise due care ($y < y^*$).
3 Strict liability rule: the injurer is laible to compensate the victim irrespective of the degree of care exercised by the injurer (or the victim).

Clearly, the liability rule which is chosen will influence the degree of care exercised by both parties. The capacity of a liability rule to produce a social optimum will turn on its capacity to ensure that each party faces an appropriate incentive structure. The analysis requires the use of reaction functions relating each party's choice of level of care to the choice made by the members of the other group. Generally speaking, each side will reduce its own degree of care as the other side is assumed to be exercising a greater degree of care. If these reaction functions are plotted on a diagram which has as axes the degree of care being exercised by each group, the liability rule can be shown to be optimal provided that the reaction functions intersect at the point (x^*, y^*). To put the condition another way, we require that the Cournot–Nash equilibrium associated with a liability rule matches the social optimum which is the solution of equation (39.1) above.

Inevitably, this basic model has been subject to a great variety of refinements. Various authors have investigated the consequences of allowing (a) the parties to have different attitudes towards risk, (b) the costs of accidents to follow a probability distribution, (c) the introduction of insurance, (d) courts to make errors in judging (*ex post*) the degree of care exercised and (e) administrative

784

costs. The results are somewhat equivocal: the choice of liability rule is sensitive to the assumptions made.

From a policy perspective, this literature is of considerable significance. A large number of activities and transactions are subject to control via liability rules, and naturally there continues to be debate not only about the relative merits of alternative liability rule regimes but also about the merits of liability rules as a means of regulating activities by comparison with other means of control. Further, the high legal costs of running a negligence system in relation to the volume of damages paid to successful plaintiffs are often criticized by pressure groups and other commentators. However, it is probably fair to say that defences by economists of the efficiency characteristics of negligence have been an important counter to protagonists of strict liability rules (or whatever) who claim these alternatives to be more 'pro-victim'. For an application of the economic approach to the medical malpractice field, see Danzon (1985).

In the environmental area in particular there continues to be controversy as to how best to control emissions of harmful substances. In many cases the damage done is widely dispersed across the population and is often difficult to attribute to a particular firm or polluter. Civil actions for damages, following a liability rule approach, can be rather ineffective because the individual victim may well judge the costs of bringing an action to be prohibitively high in relation to the private benefit in terms of prospective damage awards. Procedural devices have been created in some countries to try to minimize the impact of these weaknesses of liability rules. Elsewhere, the emphasis has been on finding alternatives to liability rules in the form, for example, of creating and selling rights to pollute.

In the area of product liability there have been important legal developments in both the United States and Europe which have tended to strengthen the capacity of the injured consumer to seek compensation from the producer. Priest, commenting on the traditional suspicion in the US for direct regulation of business, argues that, 'after the tort law revolution of the mid-1960's, courts employ civil damage judgments to establish fine-tuned incentives to control the accident rate by internalizing injury costs to every product manufacturer and every service provider' (Priest 1989: 1). Of course, consumers do pay for these increased rights in the form of higher product prices. The question is whether the hefty legal and other costs of running such systems are offset by the increased care and attention being given to safety.

39.3 CONTRACT

Contracts underpin a good deal of economic activity: workers have a contract of employment with their employer outlining the rights and obligations of the two parties; consumers enter contracts to buy goods and services and contracts governing the terms on which they borrow money. Contract law provides an enforcement mechanism which enables agents to enter with confidence these arrangements which typically involve promises of future action. Such a mechanism, one might argue, is essential for preventing problems of moral hazard and reneging, which would otherwise threaten the smooth operation of markets.

Many wealth-increasing activities require there to be a means of underwriting promises. Suppose, for example, that I employ a builder to construct a house for me. For obvious reasons, I will not agree to pay until after construction is complete. But equally, the builder may be unwilling to go ahead on such a basis for fear of my failing to pay once the work is done. Giving the builder the possibility of legal action for breach of contract may be a relatively effective and cheap way of providing him with the necessary assurance. Of course, it may not be the only way. There may be a means of creating appropriate guarantees through financial or insurance markets, although many of these alternatives will in any event rely on legal enforceability if they are to be credible. The lower the costs of underwriting promises, the more effectively will markets be able to allocate resources between activities involving immediate exchanges and activities where the exchange process is spread over a longer period.

However, this 'nightwatchman' approach to contract law falls a long way short of providing a complete explanation of the use made of it in business. Our description of it thus far rather implies that a contract entails a complete listing of contingencies with an express agreement as to how each risk is allocated between the parties, as in an Arrow–Debreu kind of world. In practice, the law of contract is very often used in precisely the opposite way, as empirical studies by Macaulay (1963) and Beale and Dugdale (1975) have illustrated vividly, for it provides a mechanism for resolving conflicts where a contingency has not been expressly anticipated. Businessmen, knowing that it is very time-consuming and costly to reach agreement about how all conceivable risks are to be handled, can reduce costs by entering a legally enforceable agreement which will fill any gaps they have left. The gap-filling is done by reference to well-established principles and precedents, so that even when an unanticipated problem arises the legal advisers to the parties should be able to predict fairly reliably how a court would decide the case. This means that the parties can discount quite heavily the high costs of going to trial in the event of an unforseen problem.

A considerable amount of contemporary work on the economic analysis of contract concerns itself with the question of the criteria applied by judges, legislators and others in formulating the basic principles of contract law. The argument that courts have evolved rules which are consistent with the achievement of economic efficiency is particularly associated with Richard Posner. This view, which many lawyers find difficult to accept, is based on the assertion that the courts have been constrained to adopt practices which are consistent with efficiency for fear of 'losing custom' to alternative institutions. For further discussion of this, see Posner (1977: ch. 19). To give a flavour of the approach we consider briefly the question of the foreseeability of damage.

Posner (1977: 94) considers a variant of the facts of the famous English case of *Hadley v Baxendale*. A photographer buys a roll of film, the purchase price of which includes an element to cover the cost of processing the film. He then travels to the Himalayas and incurs many expenses in shooting film intended for sale to a magazine. But the manufacturer loses the film when it is sent in for processing. The question is whether the photographer should be allowed to recover the price of the film, amounting perhaps to £5, or the full losses he has incurred, which may well run into thousands of pounds. The latter arrangement would give the photographer little incentive to avoid similar losses in future, since he will be largely indifferent between receiving compensation and the occurrence of the loss. It may well have little effect on the manufacturer either, since such events are very rare. But allowing the photographer to recover no more than the price of the film gives him incentives to take elementary cheap precautions such as shooting a spare roll of film which he sends for processing by a different manufacturer or drawing the attention of the manufacturer to the importance of exercising a particularly high degree of care with the roll of film in question.

A second line of approach, albeit one which embraces the findings thus far outlined, has been developed by Oliver Williamson. The antecedents of the approach can be traced back to the paper on the nature of the firm by Coase (1937). In this paper Coase recognized that many transactions could be organized in different ways, and that many forms of economic organization could be thought of as responses to the (high) costs of organizing transactions. Williamson (1975), in his work *Markets and Hierarchies*, added further substance to this idea. The very existence of firms, according to this view, can be thought of as a means of internalizing transactions within a single firm in preference to trading across a market interface because it is a cheaper means of organizing economic activity. Some of the recent work on contract has exploited the idea that contract law is just one of an array of devices which can be used in the search for the cheapest and most effective means of organizing economic activity.

In some of the recent economic literature Williamson and others (see for example Macneil 1978) have developed analytical models of governance structures. These models seek to treat simple one-off deals as a special case of a broader category of transactions which includes continuing long-term relationships between traders. The simplest sorts of transactions involving simultaneous exchange of money for goods pose few difficulties for the parties to the trade or for the analyst. Exchanges of promises – for example, 'I will give you £x provided that you come and drive me to the airport tomorrow morning' – involve greater uncertainty and greater expenditure on effort on the part of both sides to ensure that the promises materialze. But much more complex than either of these is the kind of agreement under which one firm agrees to supply goods to another as and when required. One firm may install equipment which has value only as long as the other party delivers as agreed, even though there may be a large number of contingencies which might force one or other party to withdraw from the agreement. In these sorts of circumstances there may well be a contract between the firms, albeit a contract drawn in relatively imprecise terms, for example allowing for the price to be renegotiated from time to time.

Williamson (1979, 1981) identifies three critical dimensions for describing transactions, namely (a) uncertainty, (b) the frequency with which transactions recur and (c) the degree to which durable transaction-specific investments are required to realize least-cost supply. He also identifies three principal forms of organization, namely (a) markets, (b) internal organization and (c) an inter-mediate form of bilateral exchange referred to as 'obligational market contract-ing'. He is then able to allocate transactions to the most effective means of organizing them. That is, costs of transacting depend on the nature of the transaction, and the profit-maximizing agent will make choices so as to minim-ize these costs.

39.4 LEGAL PROCEDURE AND THE RESOLUTION OF LEGAL DISPUTES

An area which has been attracting increasing interest in the sphere of law and economics is the question of how legal disputes are resolved. In a recent survey of this literature Cooter and Rubinfeld (1989) distinguish four stages in a legal dispute and assign to each the kind of economic model normally developed. Stage 1 is concerned with the initial harm suffered by an agent, for example in a car accident; stage 2 with the assertion of a legal claim; stage 3 with efforts by the parties to resolve their dispute informally; and stage 4 with the trail which concludes the process when efforts to reach an informal solution have failed. As is usual with sequential problems of any kind, decision-makers, following Bellman's principle of optimality, need to have a view of the entire process and of the possible outcomes from the beginning. After all, it is only worthwhile formulating a claim if the expected benefits exceed the costs of formulation. Equally, the negotiations at stage 3 will take place in the shadow of guesses about what would be the outcome of a trial and how the costs of the trial would be split between the parties. The paper by Cooter et al. (1982) is an earlier example of the notion that the bargaining behaviour of parties to a dispute will reflect procedural rules and will take place 'in the shadow' of the law even when it is done informally.

In order to give a flavour of the analysis, consider a case where one person P is seeking to recover a loss of A at the expense of another person D. Person P (plaintiff) will incur (fixed) non-recoverable costs B in formulating a claim. Should the other party contest the claim, the plaintiff will then devote a further x units of legal resources at a cost per unit of c in bringing the case to trial. The defendant devotes y resource units to defence of the claim. For simplicity, we make the assumption that the defendant faces the same price per unit of legal resources as the plaintiff, namely c. The decision of the court, if the matter goes to trial, can be characterized by a probability q that the plaintiff will successfully recover the amount he is claiming. This probability q depends in some, possibly quite complex, way on the legal resource levels x and y employed by the two parties. But, *ceteris paribus*, we would expect q to increase with x for a given y and correspondingly to increase with y for a given x.

When deciding whether to make a claim, the injured party compares the likely costs and returns. Filing the claim will cost B, but offer a probability q of recovering an amount A. However, that is not quite the whole story because legal costs, which are well known to be high in relation to awards, have to be taken into account. It is at this point that procedural rules need to be taken seriously, since they will govern the assignment of trial costs between the parties. The two most widely analysed rules are the 'American Rule', under which each party pays his/her own costs, and the 'English Rule', under which the loser pays the costs of both sides (see, for example, Bowles 1987; Katz 1987; Miller 1988).

The decision to file a claim under the English Rule, on the unlikely but convenient assumption that the plaintiff is risk neutral, requires the following condition to be met:

$$B < q(x^*, y^*)A - [1 - q(x^*, y^*)]c(x^* + y^*) \qquad (39.3)$$

The values x^* and y^* are Nash equilibrium values for legal resource inputs. The first term on the right-hand side of the inequality refers to the expected returns in the event of winning the case at trial, whilst the second terms refers to the costs in the event of losing. It is clear from his expression that the decision to go to trial is going to be risky, with what one might term 'full compensation' for the loss in the event of winning and a large costs bill of $c(x^* + y^*)$ in the event of losing.

Under the American Rule the decision to file a claim requires that the following condition be met:

$$B < q(x^{**}, y^{**})(A - cx^{**}) - [1 - q(x^{**}, y^{**})]cx^{**} \qquad (39.4)$$

Under this arrangement the plaintiff does not recover his or her own loss in full if we assume that A is an accurate measure of the loss incurred. However, there is an advantage over the English Rule to the extent that there is less variance in wealth levels under the two outcomes. On our assumption of risk neturality this is of little consequence, but if the plaintiff is risk averse it may be of considerable significance (Phillips et al. 1975). We have denoted legal inputs under the American Rule with a double rather than a single asterisk to signify that the Nash equilibrium solutions for x and y may differ from those appropriate under the English Rule because the different cost assignment rules are likely to influence the decision about legal inputs.

Once a claim has been filed there is generally first a period of bargaining during which the parties seek to reach an out-of-court settlement before the matter is finally brought to court for resolution at trial. Since trial costs are extremely high the parties have a powerful incentive to avoid a trial. But, of course, the threat of refusing to settle and taking the case to court becomes a very potent force precisely because of this fact, and as a result many claims are finally resolved 'at the door of the court' just as a trial is about to begin. From an analytical point of view this kind of bilateral monopoly position represents something of a challenge. It is possible, first, to identify a 'settlement range' which defines a range of values within which rational parties could be expected to reach a resolution. As bargaining proceeds and information about the relative strengths of their positions is disclosed, the parties should be able to make an increasingly well-informed guess as to the likely outcome of a trial. Fenn and Vlachonikolis (1990) present empirical evidence which, they suggest, is consistent with parties using a succession of offers as a means of conveying private information to one another.

In the extreme case of unanimity between the parties, where both sides assign the same subjective probability $q(x, y)$ to the plaintiff's winning in the event of a trial, there should be no problem in reaching a settlement. We denote this probability as q_0. Then, under the English Rule, the plaintiff will assign an expected value V to the claim, where

$$V = q_0 A - (1 - q_0)(cx + cy) \tag{39.5}$$

The costs of filing the claim have disappeared from the story because they are now sunk costs. We can treat the value V as the lower bound of the settlement range S. Meanwhile, the defendant calculates the expected cost to himself of going to trial, as

$$W = q_0(A + cx + cy) \tag{39.6}$$

This expression for W sets a maximum bound on the amount that the defendant would pay to settle the case out of court. A simple comparison of V and W indicates that V exceeds W by an amount $cx + cy$, which is the parties' joint spending on legal resources at trial. In practice, of course, the defendant is in

790

a position to dictate terms and will seek to replicate the plaintiff's calculations and to settle the claim for an amount V.

However, the parties may differ in their views as to the likely outcome of a trial. They may miscalculate how much the other side is prepared to spend on the case and may make erroneous guesses about the structure of the relationship between legal input levels and the outcome of a trial. If these disparities are sufficiently large, the settlement range may shrink to zero, so that the most that the defendant is prepared to offer in settlement falls at or below the lowest amount that the palintiff is prepared to accept.

There are many further refinements which can be added to the model. Under the English Rule, in particular, the defendant, who may well be a repeat player like an insurance company, may be less risk averse than the plaintiff, who may often be a one-shot individual player and may stand to gain from establishing a reputation as a very tough opponent. As a result, the defendant may be prepared to offer substantially less than his estimate of the expected cost of going to trial (Phillips *et al.* 1975).

Amongst other lines of development possible here is the introduction of the principal–agent problem as it affects the relationship between the parties and their lawyers. In the United States, it is possible for some prospective plaintiffs to enter contingency fee arrangements with lawyers, who will handle their case in return for a fraction of any final award rather than presenting a bill based on hours spent working on the matter. This clearly changes the incentive structure facing the lawyer. Under a fee for service contract the laywer derives no particular benefit from economizing on the time he devotes to the case. Under a contingency fee contract, in contrast, the lawyer has to decide upon his intensity of effort in the light of the probable returns. If the contingency fee arrangement provides for the lawyer to receive a fraction c of the award A, and the probability q of successful recovery depends in the usual way on the level of inputs x into the case, then the lawyer will seek to maximize profits Z by choosing x such that

$$\max Z = Acq(x) - wx \qquad (39.7)$$

where w is a measure of the opportunity cost of the lawyer's time, for example the hourly rate he could earn from some other line of (risk-free) legal business. The relevant first-order condition follows trivially as

$$w = Acq_x \qquad (39.8)$$

In effect, the lawyer's client has to compare this level of effort with the level of effort (and expected recovery) under a fee for service contract. Under the latter contract the lawyer could expect a well-informed client to agree that the optimal expenditure of effort would occur where the expected return from the last hour of effort (in terms of higher expected award) is equal to the marginal cost of the lawyer's time, which we again assume is measured by an opportunity cost w. Thus we would have a choice of x satisfying

$$\max Z = Aq(x) - wx \qquad (39.9)$$

with the corresponding first-order condition given by

$$Aq_x = w \qquad (39.10)$$

This quite clearly entails a higher value of x than the value found in (39.8) under the contingent fee contract since, by assumption, c is strictly less than unity under the contingent fee. The choice between the contracts will clearly depend on matters such as the degree of risk aversion on the part of the client and the fraction of the award payable to the lawyer under the contingency fee contract.

39.5 REGULATION

Unlike areas of law such as tort and contract, which have come under careful scrutiny by economists only rather recently, regulation has been the subject of interest on the part of economists for a long time, and discussion of competition policy has featured in most microeconomic texts, even at the introductory level (see, for example, Begg *et al.* 1987). Traditional welfare economics had long known about the social costs of monopoly power, and government action to prevent or reduce its abuse was generally viewed in a fairly benign way.

Scholars of the 'new law and economics', particularly the more radical libertarian of them, took a much more critical view, however. They rejected the 'public interest' approach under which government is viewed as seeking to increase social welfare by intervening to prevent 'market failure' in areas of control of externalities, monopoly power or whatever. In its place they sought to develop an 'economic theory' of regulation (see, for example, Stigler 1971; Posner 1974, 1977). The essence of this argument was that a great deal of regulatory work is intrinsically difficult and costly, also that regulation very often benefits certain producer groups even if it is intended to protect consumers. Viewed in this way, regulation looks less inviting: as well as 'market failure' we have to consider the possibility of 'government failure', since the regulatory devices may themselves have perverse effects.

The regulation of insider trading on securities markets provides a useful illustration of how analysts can conclude that regulation designed to protect investors might have a quite different effect in practice. Haddock and Macey (1986) explore the harsh US rules prohibiting insider trading and argue that shareholders in some corporations would benefit if insider trading were permitted, as indeed it is in some European countries at present. They begin by distinguishing three groups involved in stock market trading, namely (a) true insiders (directors, employees and advisers to a corporation), (b) quasi-insiders (stock market professionals with very rapid access to stock market transactions) and (c) outsiders (ordinary shareholders with no special access to insiders or the market floor).

In an efficient stock market, where stock prices constantly adjust so as to reflect the market view as to the profitability of the corporations whose stocks are being traded, market professionals in particular devote large amounts of resources to efforts to 'stay ahead of the game', for only by anticipating price movements is it possible to earn profits in excess of those available elsewhere. Since prices will not move instantaneously to a new equilibrium level in response to new information, market professionals will find it potentially profitable to monitor transactions closely and to execute deals very quickly in the hope of sharing in the windfall gains associated with the arrival of the new information.

Returning to the role of insiders, it is clear that they will on occasion have access to new information before it becomes public. If they are prohibited from making stock market transactions which enable them to capitalize their informational advantage, then the principal beneficiaries will be the market professionals who can move most swiftly as and when the news breaks, as it surely will sooner or later. The ordinary shareholders are affected little either way; by the time that they read about the news in their paper or even on their stock price service it will be too late to take advantage of the price movement. The regulation of insider trading will thus principally affect the distribution of gains as between insiders and market professionals.

As far as the efficiency consequences of this distribution are concerned, the argument formulated by Manne (1966) was that permitting insider trading has the effect of accelerating the incorporation of new information into stock prices. This improves the market's capacity to allocate investment funds efficiently. The other effect it has is to increase the potential earnings of insiders from dealing in a firm's shares, and this would presumably be reflected in smaller salaries for those in a position to take advantage of the permission.

In reaching a decision about insider-trading rules, and thus about this distribution of gains, the government can either follow a 'public interest' approach and weigh up the gains and losses to the various groups of partici- pants, or it can respond to pressure from interest groups. Stock market pro- fessionals are relatively small in number, and the gains that they stand to make from prohibition of insider trading are relatively large, with the result that they will have a stronger interest in pressing for the adoption of a restrictive approach and will find it worthwhile lobbying harder than the more disparate group of ordinary shareholders. This kind of argument is of course more familiar from the public choice literature, where the analysis of voting rules and of rent-seeking behaviour is pursued; for a survey see Mueller (1976) and for a recent analysis of the role of minorities in voting and lobbying see Bowles and Jones (1990).

39.6 CONCLUDING REMARKS

In this brief survey we have concentrated on just four topic areas. Nevertheless, it is possible to make a number of observations about the development of law and economics on the strength of this sample. First, although there are some areas of enquiry which could be identified as belonging to a distinctive sub-branch of economics called 'law and economics', in many cases the results find ready application within the mainstream of microeconomics. The treatment of issues involving externalities, for example, has improved markedly as economists have sought to absorb the role that various legal alternatives such as liability rules and public regulation can play. Understanding of the role of corporations has likewise become more sophisticated as economists have come to take more seriously the question of how best different kinds of transactions between agents are to be handled. At the same time as those interested in law and economics have made contributions to mainstream economics, there are some areas of enquiry which remain of only relatively specialist interest. Work in the area of crime and punishment, pioneered by Becker (1968) and extended by others (see, for example, Allingham and Sandmo 1972) to areas such as tax evasion, is really just an application (albeit a useful one) of the theory of behaviour under uncertainty. Likewise, research into the resolution of legal disputes has involved applying results and models from the theory of bargaining to a particular context.

Law and economics has established itself as a distinctive area of study for both economists and lawyers. However, even if it were to lose its identity as a separate area of study, it has been responsible for many developments over the past decades which will occupy a significant place in other, more firmly established, branches of economics including welfare economics, public finance and economic (and industrial) organization.

REFERENCES

Allingham, M. G. and Sandmo, A. (1972) 'Income tax evasion: a theoretical analysis', *Journal of Public Economics* 1: 323–38.

Beale, H. and Dugdale, A. (1975) 'Contracts between businessmen: planning and the use of contractual remedies', *British Journal of Law and Society* 2: 45–60.

Becker, G. S. (1968) 'Crime and punishment: an economic approach', *Journal of Political Economy* 76 (1): 169–217.

Begg, D., Fischer, S. and Dornbusch, R. (1987) *Economics*, 2nd edn, London: McGraw-Hill.

Bowles, R. A. (1987) 'Settlement range and cost allocation rules: a comment on Avery

Katz's "Measuring the demand for litigation: is the English Rule really cheaper" ', *Journal of Law, Economics and Organization* 3 (2).

Bowles, R. A. and Jones, P. R. (1990) 'Medical indemnity insurance in the UK: a public choice approach', *Geneva Papers on Risk and Insurance* 14 (54).

Brown, J. P. (1973) 'Toward an economic theory of liability', *Journal of Legal Studies* 2 (2): 323–49.

Calabresi, G. (1970) *The Costs of Accidents: A Legal and Economic Analysis*, New Haven, CT: Yale University Press.

Carr-Hill, R. A. and Stern, N. (1979) *Crime, the Police and Criminal Statistics*, London: Academic Press.

Coase, R. (1937) 'The nature of the firm', *Economica (NS)* 4: 336–405. Reprinted in G. J. Stigler and K. Boulding (eds) *Readings in Price Theory*, Homewood, IL: Irwin.

—— (1960) 'The problem of social cost', *Journal of Law and Economics* 3 (1): 1–44.

Cooter, R. and Rubinfeld, D. (1989) 'Economic analysis of legal disputes and their resolution', *Journal of Economic Literature* 27: 1067–97.

Cooter, R., Marks, S. and Mnookin, R. (1982) 'Bargaining in the shadow of the law', *Journal of Legal Studies* 11: 225–51.

Danzon, P. (1985) *Medical Malpractice*, Cambridge, MA: Harvard University Press.

Diamond, P. A. (1974) 'Accident law and resource allocation', *Bell Journal of Economics* 5 (2): 366–405.

Diamond, P. and Mirrlees, J. A. (1975) 'On the assignment of liability: the uniform case', *Bell Journal of Economics* 6 (2): 487–516.

Fenn, P. and Vlachonikolis, I. (1990) 'Bargaining behaviour by defendant insurers: an economic model', *The Geneva Papers on Risk and Insurance* 14 (54).

Green, J. (1976) 'On the optimal structure of liability laws', *Bell Journal of Economics* 7 (2): 553–74.

Haddock, D. and Macey, J. (1986) 'Controlling insider trading in Europe and America: the economics of the politics', in J. M. Graf von der Schulenburg and G. Skogh (eds) *Law and Economics and the Economics of Legal Regulation*, Dordrecht: Kluwer.

Katz, A. (1987) 'Measuring the demand for litigation: is the English Rule really cheaper?', *Journal of Law, Economics and Organization* 3: 143–76.

Macaulay, S. (1963) 'Non-contractual relations in business: a preliminary study', *American Sociological Review* 25: 55–69.

Macneil, I. R. (1978) 'Contracts: adjustment of long-term economic relations under classical, neoclassical and relational contract law', *Northwestern University Law Review* 72 (2): 854–965.

Manne, H. (1966) *Insider Trading and the Stock Market*, New York: Free Press.

Mill, J. S. (1909) *Principles of Political Economy*, ed. W. J. Ashley, People's Edition, London: Longmans Green (originally published 1892).

Miller, G. (1988) 'An economic analysis of Rule 68', *Journal of Legal Studies* 15: 93–125.

Mueller, D. C. (1976) 'Public choice: a survey', *Journal of Economic Literature* 14: 396–433.

Phillips, J., Hawkins, K. and Flemming, J. (1975) 'Compensation for personal injuries', *Economic Journal* 85: 129–34.

Pigou, A. C. (1932) *The Economics of Welfare*, 4th edn, p. 183, London: Macmillan.

Polinsky, M. (1980) 'Strict liability vs. negligence in a market setting', *American Economic Review* 70: 363–70.

Posner, R. A. (1972) *Economic Analysis of Law*, 1st edn, Boston, MA: Little Brown.

—— (1974) 'Theories of economic regulation', *Bell Journal of Economics and Management Science* 5 (2): 335–58.

—— (1977) *Economic Analysis of Law*, 2nd edn, Boston, MA: Little Brown.

Priest, G. (1989) 'Strict products liability: the original intent', Working paper 100, Program in Civil Liability, Yale Law School.

Shavell, S. (1987) *Economic Analysis of Accident Law*, Cambridge, MA: Harvard University Press.

Stigler, G. (1971) 'The theory of economic regulation', *Bell Journal of Economics and Management Science* 2 (1): 3–21.

Williamson, O. E. (1975) *Markets and Hierarchies*, New York: Free Press.

—— (1979) 'Transaction cost economics: the governance of contractual relations', *Journal of Law and Economics* 22 (2): 233–61.

—— (1981) 'Contract analysis: the transaction cost approach', in P. Burrows and C. G. Veljanovski (eds) *The Economic Approach to Law*, London: Butterworths.

40

ECONOMICS AND PSYCHOLOGY

W. FRED VAN RAAIJ

40.1 INTRODUCTION

The development of microeconomics theory started in the nineteenth century, at a time when psychology as a science was still in its infancy. Economists of that period could not employ the present results of psychological research when they were developing the basic assumptions about human behaviour adopted in economic theory. Note that many economic theories do not explain or predict individual economic behaviour, but predict the 'behaviour' of markets and institutions.

Such assumptions are needed in the first stage of theory development, and so it is not surprising that first-stage economic theory was psychologically unrealistic. In later stages, after empirical testing of the hypotheses, the simple theory should be developed in a direction that explains more empirical observations and explains them better. However, this is not necessarily the case in economic theory. Rather, the development of economic theory was in the direction of more sophisticated econometric analysis based on simple assumptions of human behaviour.

However, some results of psychological research have been employed, such as considering goods as bundles of characteristics (Lancaster 1966), the theory of time allocation (Becker 1981) or the introduction of cognitive dissonance into economic theory (Akerlof and Dickens 1982). These introductions of psychological theory have been limited and lag decades behind their introduction in psychology.

Psychology is of crucial importance for economics. The results of research on human behaviour should be taken into account because people react to the economic conditions as they perceive them, and this perception, evaluation and consequent decision-making may be biased. Humans are not perfect decision-makers or utility maximizers. Economic psychology provides evidence about the behaviour of consumers, business people, taxpayers, politicians and investors that is instrumental, in both the development of economic theory and the provision of a richer description of economic behaviour. More generally, economic psychology offers in interdisciplinary framework, in which methods and theories from the disciplines of economics and psychology can be used to explain the economic behaviour of individuals and groups. Economic psychology is an interdisciplinary development from psychology, mainly cognitive and social psychology (Furnham and Lewis 1986; MacFadyen and MacFadyen 1986; Lea *et al.* 1987; Van Raaij *et al.* 1988). The development from economics is called behavioural or psychological economics (Katona 1975; Scitovsky 1976, 1986; Gilad and Kaish 1986a, b; Earl 1988).

The purpose of this chapter is to demonstrate that the contribution of psychology to economics is to enrich the explanations of economic behaviour by a better understanding.

40.2 ECONOMIC BEHAVIOUR

Economics and psychology have in common that that they try to describe, to explain and possibly to predict economic behaviour at the individual or the aggregate level. Economics is mainly concerned with the prediction of economic behaviour at the aggregate level, and with direct relations between inputs and effect, for example between prices and purchases. However, this does not mean that economists should not be interested in psychological variables, for example perception and evaluation, that intervene between input and effect.

Economic behaviour is human decision and choice behaviour with regard to the alternative use of scarce resources (money, time, effort, space, material resources and energy) to satisfy needs. It can be assumed that these scarce resources will be used in such a way as to generate a satisfactory level of utility. The scarcity of means is expressed in the constraints posed by financial, time, effort and other budgets. Some substitution between these budgets is possible.

For instance, we could increase the financial budget by spending parts of our time and effort budgets: paid work. The choice among alternative uses of resources is often a matter of cost–benefit trade-offs, in which the concept should be enlarged to include 'behavioural' costs as well (Verhallen and Pieters 1984). The behavioural costs are the effort, delay and psychological costs of behaviour and behavioural change. However, norms and values, as well as costs and benefits, play a role in the allocation of resources (Etzioni 1988a, b).

Economic theories of this type have proved to be effective. They have been applied not only to the study of consumer and entrepreneur behaviour, but even to the study of partner choice, altruism, cheating and fertility, i.e. the number of children (Becker 1981). The economic model is imperialistic in the sense that it is now also applied to traditionally non-economic phenomena.

Economic theories have developed beyond the traditional microeconomic model of complete information, complete mobility and perfect competition, already criticized by Katona (1953). We refer to the economic theories of political economy (Buchanan and Tullock 1962; Olson 1965) and the 'new' theory of demand and household economics (Lancaster 1966; Becker 1981). In these approaches, preferences and constraints are distinguished, with preferences considered to be stable over time. Changes in economic behaviour can thus be explained by changes in the constraints. Frey and Foppa (1986) describe this new 'economic man' as a problem-solving utility-maximizer with expectations and evaluations.

The utility function usually consists of quantities of commodities and a number of 'importance' parameters. In Antonides (1989), the concepts of utility and attitude are quite similar. Further, preferences are not fixed and stable, but will generally be shaped and changed by the supply of goods and services. Marginal substitution, utility maximization and concave preference functions are approximations of reality, not always able to explain the complexity of economic behaviour.

In order to remove these objections, an integrated economic–psychological behavioural theory should be developed. According to this theory, the actor (person, manager) performs a more or less elaborate decision process in which, frequently, not all relevant information can be acquired and/or processed. Information about future developments is often not available, or is only available with broad margins of uncertainty. Business people do not know the plans of their competitors in time. Advertisers provide only positive information about their products. Complete information, or sometimes even a necessary level of information, is unattainable or unavailable in a market owing to the opposing objectives of the market parties. Sometimes it is even dysfunctional to collect complete information, for example in emergency situations.

The psychological model of economic behaviour supports the notion that actors under conditions of high involvement try to behave rationally, but often do not succeed, owing to constraints of information availability and of processing. Simon (1963), being a professor of psychology with a Nobel Prize in economics, introduced the concept of bounded rationality.

If not all information is available at the same time, a simplification of the decision process, called 'satisficing', is the best which can be obtained. This is another concept introduced by Simon (1963). It is simply impossible to find the single 'best' alternative, as utility maximization suggests. Satisficing is seeking to attain an aspiration level. When the performance falls below this level, search behaviour is induced and the aspiration level is adjusted downwards, until goals reach attainable levels.

Economic motivation is often not to maximize short-term utility; in many cases it is motivated by survival, to continue the household or the business, to muddle through (Lindblom 1959) or to avoid failure.

Economic behaviour is almost always motivated behaviour. It is guided by preferences, expectations, values and norms. It has a certain level of activation or involvement, and a certain direction. People try to reach a goal or to avoid negative consequences. Economic psychology, as a study of economic behaviour, tries to explain behaviour by learning and decision processes, motivation, personality factors, perception, preferences and a number of other factors basic to behaviour. These processes may be explicit and extensive in the case of high-involvement decisions on expenditure, credit or saving. In other cases, these processes are routine and implicit, such as in the case of low-involvement decisions about convenience products.

Learning processes may either precede or follow an economic decision (for example, purchase of a durable good). Learning processes before the decision pertain to the selection of and choice among alternatives. Learning processes after the decision relate to justification and dissonance reduction. Not only the choice alternatives as such, but also situational factors, such as constraints on freedom and the perceived presence of other people, play a part in the decision process.

40.3 ECONOMIC AND PSYCHOLOGICAL THEORY

The development of theory in economics and in psychology differs to some extent. A deductive approach dominates in economics. Hypotheses (conclusions) are derived from a theory and tested with empirical data, or a sequence of logical deductions (from initial assumptions) is developed and the final conclusion is empirically tested. Rejection of a hypothesis is a signal that the theory or the sequence of reasoning should be revised.

One difficulty of the deductive approach is the attribution of a rejection to a specific cause. If a hypothesis is rejected, this might be due to a poor definition or operationalization of the concept under study. It might be a problem of the validity or reliability of the measurement as well. A third cause is an inappropriate test procedure (for example, too small a sample). A fourth reason might be an invalid or incomplete theory. It is impossible to ascertain with one test which cause or combination of causes is correct.

Many economic phenomena are stochastic, which means that we should not adhere to a Popperian approach in which one rejection may be enough to falsify a theory. Clarkson (1963) states that predictive validity is not enough as a criterion for a microeconomic theory. Assumptions should also be realistic, i.e. be in accordance with the results of psychological research. Friedman (1953) accepts 'unreal assumptions' as long as the predictions are correct (predictive validity). My opinion is that heuristic assumptions might be useful in a first stage of theory development, but should be replaced by more realistic descriptions of human behaviour at a later stage (descriptive validity).

Psychological research is dominated by a hypothetico-deductive approach, especially in experimental psychology and motivation theories such as Maslow's (1970) hierarchy of needs. From a theory, hypotheses are derived and tested against empirical data. Depending on the results of the tests, the theory will be adjusted. Through these short theoretical-empirical cycles, theory formation in psychology remains closer to the empirical world and has less stringent assumptions than in economics. In economics a longer string of reasoning or theory development is often used to test a hypothesis. The cycles are thus longer and predictive validity is often the only criterion.

An integration of economics and psychology can be found in this hypo-thetico-deductive approach. A theory of economic behaviour can be built in a sequence of stating hypotheses (theory formation) and consequent empirical testing.

The development of psychological theory in new areas is often inductive. 'Relevant' factors are measured and correlated with the (dependent) variable under study. In an empiricist manner, these relevant variables are related to the dependent variable. This type of theory formation is thus more of an *a posteriori* process. The theory should be test with a second (validation) sample.

Not only theory building, but also the data-collection methods are different. Economists often use secondary data, for example data collected by statistical bureaux. Psychologists often have to collect their own data in surveys, inter-views and experiments. Psychology and economics have to offer each other experience with different methods of data collection.

40.4 HISTORICAL PERSPECTIVE

During the last hundred years, several attempts have been made to integrate psychological findings into economic theory. Coats (1976, 1988) provides an interesting review of these attempts. Psychological research during the nine-teenth century was not yet sufficiently well developed to provide a base for microeconomics. Veblen (1919) was one of the foremost proponents of a total reconstruction of economic theory. The static passive model of man should be replaced by a dynamic active adaptive model of preferences. He proposed a less calculative model of man. In a defence to exclude psychological influences, economics was restricted to a science of exchanges ('catallactics'), in which only prices, budgets and exchange values were considered without reference to underlying motives or meanings.

The alternative psychology-based programme of the period 1920–30 had a number of economic–psychological recommendations, such as the following.

Adopt 'realistic' fundamental assumptions, consistent with psychological findings. Concentrate on the development of middle-level empirically grounded theories. Undertake systematic empirical studies. Replace static by dynamic theories. Broaden the scope of economic theory to take account of the social forces influencing economic behaviour. Go beyond prices and exchange values. A more extensive account of this programme is given by Van Raaij (1985b). However, in the 1940s and 1950s the 'hard' econometric approach triumphed over the 'soft' behavioural one. Physics, rather than the 'soft' social sciences became the ideal model of science for economists (Cross 1988).

Now, in the 1990s, psychology, particularly cognitive psychology, is sufficiently well developed to contribute to a reconstruction of economic theory. More than twenty-five years ago, Simon stated that: 'Economics has been moving steadily into newer areas where the power of the "classical" model has never been demonstrated and where adequacy must be considered anew. . . . In these new areas the economist and the psychologist have numerous common interests in cognitive theory that they have not shared previously' (Simon 1963: 709, 711).

40.5 SCHOOLS IN PSYCHOLOGY

Psychology is less of a unitary science than economics. We should be aware that there are a number of 'schools' in psychology. Some of the major schools are described below, with an indication of their relevance to economics and economic psychology.

The *behaviouristic school* starts from observable behaviour determined by external and internal stimuli. Learning takes place if responses are connected with stimuli by association, by repetition or by reinforcement. Mental constructs, such as 'attitude', are excluded or avoided as much as possible. Alhadeff (1982) developed a psychological foundation of economic theory based on Skinner's psychological theory of instrumental learning (reinforcement). Scitovsky (1976) based his approach on Berlyne's notion of psychological arousal and optimal level of stimulation. This is often called the *physiological school*.

A third school is Lewin's (1935) *field theory*. Behaviour is a function of several forces (valences) in a behavioural field. Lewin (1935) influenced Katona (1975) in his approach to economic psychology. The study of consumer 'sentiment' (evaluations and expectations) is a central topic in Katona's research. Consumer sentiment, as a climate of opinion, is an important factor explaining consumer spending, borrowing and saving at the aggregate level.

The *psycho-analytical school* (Freud) attributes an important role to subconscious motives and desires. Dichter's (1964) approach is an example of a psycho-analytical theory of consumer behaviour. Early youth experiences and repressed sexual desires tend to influence later behaviour, although people may not be aware of or be unwilling to admit these effects. The psycho-analytical approach is difficult to integrate with economic theory, although some examples are present such as Albanese's (1987) and Thaler and Sheffrin's (1981) 'planner versus doer'.

A fifth school is *cognitive psychology*, in which learning and choice processes and the role of memory are the central themes. Bettman (1979) provides an overview of this approach to the study of consumer behaviour. In the 1970s, in particular the cognitive approach was popular (Hansen 1972). The cognitive approach is the easiest to integrate with economic theory. Decision processes can be modelled to select the best option or, in economic words, to maximize utility.

In recent approaches affect (emotion) is taken into account, normally in a cognitive model. Affect influences decision processes and plays a role as a factor in the processes of perception and evaluation (Pieters and Van Raaij 1988; Van Raaij 1989). Norms and values often have an affective connotation (Etzioni 1988a, b).

40.6 ECONOMIC PSYCHOLOGY

Whereas microeconomics and behaviourism assume a direct relationship between stimuli and responses, Katona (1975) introduced the intervening factor of the organism with its perceptions and preferences. Stimuli must be perceived and evaluated before they elicit responses or have an effect on responses. Individuals differ in their perception and evaluation of reality (field theory) and act according to their perceived/evaluated reality and not to the stimuli as such. Economic perceptions and evaluations are not random deviations from a 'correct' value, but show systematic changes, reinforcing or influencing the business cycle. The prediction of economic resonses will thus be improved by adding information on consumer or entrepreneur evaluations and expectations. For this purpose Katona (1975) developed an 'index of consumer sentiment' as an indicator of consumer optimism or pessimism. Optimism and pessimism affect consumer spending, saving and borrowing.

Katona's index is not the only intervening variable, however. To a greater extent than Katona, it is necessary to distinguish perception, evaluation and expectation as intervening variables between stimulus and response. Also, evaluation takes place after the response, particularly as to whether the expectations (for example, with regard to a durable good or a service) were met. This may lead to (dis)satisfaction and complaints. Van Raaij (1981) developed a 'meta-model' in which psychological variables intervene between the economic variables.

The economic environment of personal finances and market conditions is

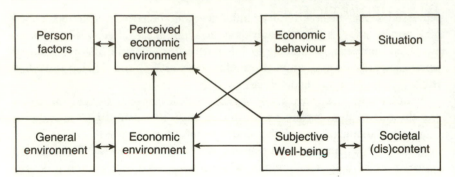

Figure 40.1 A model of economic-psychological relationships.
Source: Van Raaij 1981

affected by the general environment of recession or upswing. The economic environment as perceived by the economic actors (for example, consumers, entrepreneurs) is influenced by person-specific factors, for example personality. The perceived economic environment and situational factors affect economic behaviour. Subjective well-being has impacts on the economic environment and this closes the cycle of Figure 40.1. Thus psychological variables intervene between the economic environment and economic behaviour, and between economic behaviour and the economic environment.

Not only intervening variables are studied in economic psychology. A variable in an economic model may be only an approximation of the real determinant of the phenomenon to be explained. In some models, for instance, 'tastes' are not measured directly, but are approximated by the sociological variable 'status level' (Leibenstein 1974, 1976; Bagozzi and Van Loo 1978). In a psychological model, tastes are operationalized and measured in a more direct way. This might improve the realism of the theory. Another example is that in a 'rational' economic model it is assumed that individuals select the 'best' alternative. In a psychological model, the economic assumption could be replaced by direct measurement of a psychological process of decision-making.

A third contribution of economic psychology is to enlarge the set of explanatory variables by adding psychological variables to the set of economic variables. To explain household finances, we could add managerial skills and internal control to economic variables such as net income and contractual obligations.

Economic psychology adds new variables to increase explained variance, provides a better operationalization of the variables, suggests intervening variables for a better understanding of the relationships or provides a new and better frame of interpretation of the problems studied.

40.7 THEORETICAL INTEGRATION OF ECONOMICS AND PSYCHOLOGY

Consumer preferences are 'given' in many economic models. According to many economists, it is not a concern of economics how preferences are formed and changed by advertising, social contacts or personal experience. Moreover, the general structure of preferences goes unexamined, although this structure may be very important in understanding economic behaviour. For example, preferences may have a hierarchical ordering; alternatives within a preference class are substitutable, but alternatives from different preference classes are not direct substitutes. The hierarchical ordering assumes priorities, in the sense that if primary preferences are fulfilled higher-order preferences or wishes become manifest. Neoclassical economics emphasizes marginal substitution, although this is only possible for divisible goods within a certain preference class.

Psychologists are interested not only in outcomes but also in the processes that lead to these outcomes. These are mainly decision processes. To expedite a decision process, economic actors use simplifying strategies such as lexicographic, conjunctive or disjunctive rules. Using these rules, instead of a linear compensatory rule, it is not certain that the 'best' alternative will be selected. A 'satisfying' alternative, i.e. an alternative that meets reasonable criteria, will often be chosen. Consumers and other economic actors often trade off a possible better decision against the extra effort needed.

Preferences are not necessarily stable. Advertising and public relations are industries that try to change or reinforce preferences. Also preferences are influenced by instrumental conditioning (Alhadeff 1982). Preference formation and change is a topic of research in the context of the individual welfare function of income (Kapteyn and Wansbeek 1982). Preferences are largely adaptive to circumstances. Many wage-earners are less satisfied with an income increase afterwards than they expected before the increase. New reference groups may come into the picture. Finally, preferences may be dependent on the constraints, and this dependence destroys the traditional model of the political economist. People may adapt to a constraint and try to live with it. Some cognitive distortion often accompanies this adaptation to constraints. People feel happy not being rich, because 'wealth does not bring happiness'.

Individuals have some degree of freedom to determine their preferences and constraints. By selective perception, interpretation and retention individuals tend to select the information that supports their *a priori* preferences. Obvious examples are savings or credit contracts, in which people restrict their freedom for a certain period of time in order to reach a desired goal. In a model of this sort, Thaler and Shefrin (1981) developed an economic theory of self-control. Katona (1975) found that many households have a savings account and credit (borrowing) at the same time. The credit contract restricts freedom and forces a regular repayment, which would probably not occur without a contract. At the same time, the savings account serves as a financial buffer.

Earl (1983) gives an example of price-setting by business. According to the neoclassical model of perfect competition, business people are forced to a certain price level by market conditions of supply and demand. The neoclassical model also states that demand is price responsive. In reality, however, many markets are oligopolistic, and a main function of price-setting is to discourage competition. A high price is an invitation to competitors to enter the market, but a low price might be insufficient to recover the development costs of the new product. As long as competitors do not bring a better product or a lower price, the original (high) price will be maintained. This means that the prices of products do not decrease through economies of scale, but through the entrance of competitors or a lower demand.

Finally, there are many behavioural exceptions to the theory of expected utility, in which utility maximization is central. Kahneman and Tversky (1979, 1982) proposed prospect theory to explain a number of exceptions. People tend to evaluate new stimuli from earlier reference points, for example the status quo, or an expected profit or salary increase. They also suggest from their empirical demonstrations that people are risk-avoiders in games with a chance of profit, and risk-seekers in games with a chance of loss. An attributional explanation of risk-seeking and risk-avoiding with losses and gains respectively is given by Van Raaij (1985a). In contrast with the theoretical economist's usual model of profit or utility maximization, one influential alternative from an economic psychology point of view is provided by Simon's (1963) concept of 'satisficing' or bounded rationality in which it is assumed people are satisfied with or only able to reach a reasonable profit and not necessarily a maximum profit or utility.

40.8 SELECTED APPLICATIONS IN ECONOMIC–PSYCHOLOGICAL RESEARCH

Economic behaviour manifests itself in many forms. As it is impossible to describe all topics of economic-psychological research, discussions here will be limited to ten topics (for more topics see MacFadyen and MacFadyen (1986), Lea et al. (1987) and Van Raaij et al. (1988)). In some applications psychological variables contribute to a better understanding of economic behaviour. Some examples are given below.

1 The study of consumer behaviour, especially as applied to marketing, is the most developed. Here, the economic–psychological approach has added

a lot to the microeconomic theory of consumer behaviour. Price and income elasticities are used in conjunction with a host of psychological and sociological factors. Consumer information processing and social influence are dominant approaches. From a marketing perspective, buyer behaviour is central. From an environmental and home economics perspective, usage and disposition behaviour are central.

2 Household production is a neglected topic in economics. Official statistics do not account for household work, which is an important area of production, particularly during recessions. Household production is related to the informal economy. The Becker (1981) model has been amplified by adding psychological factors.

3 Advertising research, mainly as part of marketing, is concerned with the impact of advertising on attitudes, cognition and behaviour. Economics could only explain relationships between advertising budgets and market shares. The psychological approach provides a better insight into how advertising works. The interaction between affective and cognitive factors is a recent research interest (Van Raaij 1989).

4 The study of entrepreneurial behaviour has some similarities with consumer behaviour, particularly the buying and investment behaviour of business people (Sheth 1977). In addition to the economic approach, Simon (1955), for instance, investigated organizational decision-making using the concepts of 'satisficing' and aspiration level.

5 Investor behaviour, risk perception and risk-taking received more attention (McInish 1982). Investors often take risky decisions under conditions of uncertainty. Only a few investigators have tried to introduce psychological factors here (Slovic 1972). Rumours and the recommendations of experts for instance, may have self-fulfilling characteristics.

In other applications psychology contributes to a better understanding of economic aggregates. Examples are as follows.

6 Taxation and its avoidance and evasion is a continuing research interest of economic psychologists (Lewis 1982). Do taxpayers perceive a fiscal connection between their payments and public spending? To what degree do taxpayers consider the tax system as equitable and fair? Which norms and values with regard to the tax system prevail? Which factors influence individual taxpaying behaviour (Kinsey 1986)? Based on economic utility theory, economists would recommend an increase of penalty in the case of tax evasion. Psychologists would recommend improving the fairness and fiscal connection of the tax system.

7 The perception of inflation and the effects of inflation on spending and saving, including money illusion, are topics of economic–psychological research. High levels of inflation often cause advance-buying behaviour or

807

a flight into hard currency, while savers are disadvantaged (Katona 1975). Psychological research contributes here to a better understanding of perception and behaviour.

8 Katona (1975) investigated the effects of consumer sentiment (evaluations and expectation) on spending, saving and borrowing. In periods of recession with lower incomes, people tend to save more and spend less. This is contrary to Keynes' absolute income hypothesis. The explanation is that in periods of recession people are uncertain about the future and want to create a financial buffer.

In a third group of applications a better insight into the psychological effects of economic policy measures and situations will be obtained.

9 Unemployment has become a major problem in many societies. Economic psychologists investigate the experience of unemployment, job search and the spending behaviour of the unemployed. Contrary to economic predictions, for instance, unemployed people tend to be less active than employed workers in the informal economy.

10 Consumer satisfaction after the purchase is a relative concept, focusing on the discrepancy between expectations and actual performance of the product or service (Schouten and Van Raaij 1990). Together with the study of consumer complaints and consumerism it has become more or less a separate field of research related to consumer policy. Andreasen (1977) provides a review of research on consumer satisfaction and its implications for government and business.

40.9 CONCLUSIONS

Economic man and psychological man are in fact close relatives, both descended from their ancestors Jeremy Bentham and Adam Smith. It seems that in the course of history this kinship has been forgotten, and each has gone his own way.

Psychology as a science developed later than economics. Thus it is not surprising that for a long time the economic approach of assumed utility maximization dominated in theories of economic behaviour. The situation has now changed. The explanatory power of models of economic behaviour could be increased by adding and integrating psychological variables, especially those from cognitive and social psychology, into models of economic behaviour (Frey 1983). The study of consumer behaviour, in which psychological variables play an increasingly important role, is indicative of this.

The integration of economics and psychology should be sought in the extension of research on preferences and constraints. Frey (1983) calls this enriched preferences and constraints. The formation and change of preferences, as influenced by socialization, reference groups and mass communication, could be studied using psychological theories, although economics has its influence as well (Kapteyn and Wansbeek 1982). Economic theories have more to say about constraints, such as budgets of income, time and space and institutional constraints. Psychology could contribute to the study of the perception of constraints and self-imposed constraints.

Sometimes, economic behaviour is largely determined by constraints, for example in cases of poverty. However, many people in Western societies have some discretion in their spending and saving. They try to use their scarce resources as well as possible, but do not always succeed owing to psychological constraints on information acquisition and processing.

Economic psychology not only contributes to a number of applied areas of economics, but is also of fundamental importance to economic theory development. It is hoped that we shall witness after the econometric revolution in economics of the 1940s, a 'behavioural' revolution in the 1990s. Such a development will be supported by economic psychology with enthusiasm.

REFERENCES

Akerlof, G. A. and Dickens W. T. (1982) 'The economic consequences of cognitive dissonance', *American Economic Review* 72: 307–19.

Albanese, P. J. (1987) 'The nature of preferences: an exploration of the relationship between economics and psychology', *Journal of Economic Psychology* 8: 3–18.

Alhadeff, D. A. (1982) *Microeconomic and Human Behavior*, Berkeley, CA: University of California Press.

Andreasen, A. R. (1977) 'A taxonomy of consumer satisfaction/dissatisfaction measures', *Journal of Consumer Affairs* 11: 11–24.

Antonides, G. (1989) 'An attempt at integration of economic and psychological theories of consumption', *Journal of Economic Psychology* 10: 77–99.

Bagozzi, R. P. and Van Loo, M. F. (1978) 'Fertility as consumption: theories from the behavioral sciences', *Journal of Consumer Research* 4: 199–228.

Becker, G. S. (1981) *A Treatise on the Family*, Cambridge, MA: Harvard University Press.

Bettman, J. R. (1979) *An Information-Processing Theory of Consumer Choice*, Reading, MA: Addison-Wesley.

Buchanan, J. M. and Tullock, G. (1962) *The Calculus of Consent. Logical Foundations of Constitutional Democracy*, Ann Arbor, MI: University of Michigan Press.

Clarkson, G. P. E. (1963) *The Theory of Consumer Demand: A Critical Appraisal*, Englewood Cliffs, NJ: Prentice-Hall.

Coats, A. W. (1976) 'Economics and psychology: the death and resurrection of a research programme', in S. J. Latsis (ed.) *Methods and Appraisal in Economics*, pp. 43–64, Cambridge: Cambridge University Press.

—— (1988) 'Economics and psychology: a resurrection story', in P. E. Earl (ed.) *Psychological Economics*, pp. 211–25, Dordrecht: Kluwer.

Cross, R. (1988) 'On psyching up economics', in P. E. Earl (ed.) *Psychological Economics* pp. 55–65, Dordrecht: Kluwer.

Dichter, E. (1964) *Handbook of Consumer Motivations*, New York: McGraw-Hill.

Earl, P. E. (1983) *The Economic Imagination. Towards a Behavioral Analysis of Choice*, Armonk, NY: M. E. Sharpe.

—— (ed.) (1988) *Psychological Economics*, Dordrecht: Kluwer.

Etzioni, A. (1988a) 'Normative-affective factors: toward a new decision-making model', *Journal of Economic Psychology* 9: 125–50.

—— (1988b) *The Moral Dimension: Toward a New Economics*, New York: Free Press.

Frey, B. S. (1983) 'The economic model of behaviour: shortcomings and fruitful developments', Working paper, University of Zurich.

—— and Foppa, K. (1986) 'Human behaviour: possibilities explain action', *Journal of Economic Psychology* 7: 137–60.

Friedman, M. (1953) 'The methodology of positive economics', in *Essays in Positive Economics*, pp. 3–43, Chicago, IL: University of Chicago Press.

Furnham, A. and Lewis, A. (1986) *The Economic Mind. The Social Psychology of Economic Behaviour*, Brighton: Harvester Wheatsheaf.

Gilad, B. and Kaish, S. (eds) (1986a) *Handbook of Behavioral Economics* vol. A, *Behavioral Microeconomics*, Greenwich, CT: JAI Press.

—— and —— (eds) (1986b) *Handbook of Behavioral Economics*, vol. B, *Behavioral Macreconomics*, Greenwich, CT: JAI Press.

Hansen, F. (1972) *Consumer Choice Behavior. A Cognitive Theory*, New York: Free Press.

Kahneman, D. and Tversky, A. (1979) 'Prospect theory: an analysis of decision under risk', *Econometrica* 47: 263–91.

—— and —— (1982) 'The psychology of preferences', *Scientific American* 246: 136–42.

Kapteyn, A. and Wansbeek, T. (1982) 'Empirical evidence on preference formation', *Journal of Economic Psychology* 2: 137–54.

Katona, G. (1953) 'Rational behavior and economic behavior', *Psychological Review* 60: 307–18.

—— (1975) *Psychological Economics*, New York: Elsevier.

Kinsey, K. A. (1986) 'Theories and models of tax cheating', *Criminal Justice Abstracts* 18: 403–25.

Lancaster, K. J. (1966) 'A new approach to consumer theory', *Journal of Political Economy* 74: 132–57.

Lea, S. E. G., Tarpy, R. M. and Webley, P. (1987) *The Individual in the Economy. A Textbook of Economic Psychology*, Cambridge: Cambridge University Press.

Leibenstein, H. (1974) 'The economic theory of fertility: promising path or blind alley?', *Journal of Economic Literature* 12: 457–79.

—— (1976) *Beyond Economic Man: A New Foundation for Microeconomics*, Cambridge, MA: Harvard University Press.

Lewin, K. (1935) *A Dynamic Theory of Personality*, New York: McGraw-Hill.

Lewis, A. (1982) *The Psychology of Taxation*, Oxford: Martin Robertson.

Lindblom, C. E. (1959) 'The science of muddling through', *Public Administration Review* 19: 79–88.

MacFadyen, A. J. and MacFadyen, H. W. (eds) (1986) *Economic Psychology: Intersections in Theory and Application*, Amsterdam: North-Holland.

Maslow, A. (1970) *Motivation and Personality*, 2nd edn, New York: Harper.

810

McInish, T. H. (1982) 'Individual investors and risk-taking', *Journal of Economic Psychology* 2: 125–36.

Olson, M. (1965) *The Logic of Collective Action: Public Goods and the Theory of Groups*, Cambridge, MA: Harvard University Press.

Pieters, R. G. M. and Van Raaij, W. F. (1988) 'Functions and management of affect: applications to economic behavior', *Journal of Economic Psychology* 9: 251–82.

Schouten, V. and Van Raaij, W. F. (1990) 'Consumer problems and satisfaction in a retail setting', *Journal of Consumer Satisfaction. Dissatisfaction and Complaining Behavior* 3: 56–60.

Scitovsky, T. (1976) *The Joyless Economy. An Inquiry into Human Satisfaction and Consumer Dissatisfaction*, New York: Oxford University Press.

—— (1986) *Human Desire and Economic Satisfaction*, Brighton: Harvester Wheatsheaf.

Sheth, J. N. (1977) 'Recent developments in organizational buying behavior', in A. G. Woodside, J. N. Sheth and P. D. Bennett (eds) *Consumer and Industrial Buying Behavior*, pp. 17–34, New York: North-Holland.

Simon, H. A. (1955) 'A behavioral model of rational choice', *Quarterly Journal of Economics* 69: 99–118.

—— (1963) 'Economics and psychology', in S. Koch (ed.) *Psychology: A Study of a Science*, pp. 685–723, New York: McGraw-Hill.

Slovic, P. (1972) 'Psychological study of human judgment: implications for investment decision making', *Journal of Finance* 27: 779–99.

Thaler, R. H. and Shefrin, H. M. (1981) 'An economic theory of self-control', *Journal of Political Economy* 89: 392–406.

Van Raaij, W. F. (1981) 'Economic psychology', *Journal of Economic Psychology* 1: 1–24.

—— (1985a) 'Attribution of causality to economic actions and events', *Kyklos* 38: 3–19.

—— (1985b) 'The psychological foundation of economics the history of consumer theory', in C. T. Tan and J. N. Sheth (eds) *Historical Perspective in Consumer Research: National and International Perspectives*, pp. 8–13, Singapore: National University.

—— (1989) 'How consumers react to advertising', *International Journal of Advertising* 8: 261–73.

Van Raaij, W. F., Van Veldhoven, G. M. and Wärneryd, K.-E. (eds) (1988) *Handbook of Economic Psychology*, Dordrecht: Kluwer.

Veblen, T. (1919) *The Place of Science in Modern Civilisation*, New York: Huebsch.

Verhallen, T. M. M. and Pieters, R. G. M. (1984) 'Attitude theory and behavioral costs', *Journal of Economic Psychology* 5: 223–49.

ECONOMICS AND HISTORY

N. F. R. CRAFTS

41.1 INTRODUCTION

In considering the relationships between economics and history it is important to look not just at the use of economics and econometrics in history but also at the place of history in the training and consciousness of economists. While the potential for successfully employing the research tools of applied economics has been increasingly exploited in the recent past, especially by American economic historians, the opportunity to benefit from historical knowledge has been virtually completely excluded as the professionalization of economists' training has grown.

Since at least the beginning of the twentieth century historical study of economic events has been recognized as a separate discipline within history. The best-known early methodological statement, made by Clapham (the first Professor of Economic History at Cambridge), stressed the uniquely quantitative nature of the subject:

> Every economic historian should, however, have acquired what might be called the statistical sense, the habit of asking in relation to any institution, policy, group or movement the questions: how large? how long? how often? how representative?
>
> (Clapham, 1931: 328)

In practice this was to involve the use of descriptive rather than inferential statistics.

Only since the Second World War has there been any substantial use of formal economic analysis in economic history, however, and the notion of 'new economic history' or 'cliometrics' is only about thirty years old. In its early years cliometrics was probably distinctive primarily for the use of price theory rather than econometrics (McCloskey 1978), but in the more recent past quite sophisticated quantification has blossomed together with a rather more eclectic use of economic theory (Crafts 1987). As demonstrated in Section 41.3, the outcome has frequently been to produce much better measurement of the economic past and major reinterpretations of key issues in historiography.

In contrast the scope for enriching empirical economics by absorbing the lessons of history has barely been tapped. This is to an extent a corollary of the requirement for ever higher standards of technical sophistication among newly qualified Ph.D.s in economics. At least as important, however, have been the failures, in general, of economic historians effectively to communicate their knowledge to economists or to mount research programmes driven by the desire to answer questions of interest in terms of a menu of current policy isses rather than those motivated by historiography. From a British point of view this seems particularly unfortunate in the context of the major reinterpretation of the past implicit in the Thatcherite economic reforms of the 1980s.

41.2 IS ECONOMIC HISTORY SIMPLY THE APPLIED ECONOMETRICS OF THE PAST?

A common response among economists to the question whether economic history is simply the applied econometrics of the past is 'basically yes', partly because economists are trained to think in terms of propositions deduced from supposedly very widely applicable axioms and partly because historical data are seen as a useful testing ground for economic hypotheses and as a means of estimating key coefficients in economic relationships.

It is apparent even (or perhaps especially) to economists who would take this view that in practice there are significant differences in research strategies and priorities between cliometricians and economists who use applied econometric techniques. I shall argue that to some extent this is both inevitable and desirable but that nevertheless the present divergence of behaviour should be reduced on both sides.

The chief features distinguishing work in economic history from that in applied economics are as follows:

1 more awareness of and attention to data problems;
2 a much stronger emphasis on primary source materials and case studies;
3 a greater interest in institutional arrangements;
4 a longer lag before the most advanced economics and/or econometrics is diffused;
5 the career need to impress a different peer group.

In general, economic historians have less good data, at least in the form of consistent time series or purpose-built data bases to work with, than do economists working on contemporary problems. Accordingly, economic historians as a whole have to devote substantial efforts to constructing statistical information and thus to learning much about the limitations of data. For

813

instance, it is only relatively recently that research has made available reasonably adequate series for national income (Feinstein 1972) and monetary aggregates (Capie and Webber 1985) for Britain in the years 1870–1914 and even now the national income series are the subject of considerable debate (Greasley 1986).

In other respects historians are more fortunate than economists in the scope of the evidence. Primary source materials exist for the past (and in some cases are very rich), whereas for reasons of confidentiality they are not available for the present. This makes possible the better-informed study of decision-making by firms and governments, gives a larger role to case studies of particular episodes and ensures that archival work and skills will always play a large part in economic history. A further implication is that economic historians do not live by regressions alone, but rather that empirical evaluation of hypotheses can comprise a relatively wide array of evidence, some of which economists are rather too prone to ignore.

Taking a long historical view inevitably brings detailed acquaintance with the workings of a variety of institutions in practice and an emphasis on the importance of the context in the assessment of policy options rather than insistence, for example, on the universal superiority of a particular macro-economic standpoint. Thus historical study emphasizes the strikingly diverse potential for the use of bank rate in 1913, 1925 or 1931 and the very different implications of devaluation in 1949 and 1967 (Cairncross and Eichengreen 1983). From an econometric point of view this implies a rather more thoughtful reaction to the existence of structural breaks, i.e. significant differences between regressions estimated for different periods. On occasions this may be an important finding rather than merely a failed diagnostic test.

Although the technical standards of economic history have improved greatly at the level of the papers accepted for the best quality journals such as *Explorations in Economic History* or *Journal of Economic History*, the average contribution to the literature is still characterized by substantial innocence of developments of the last fifteen or twenty years. Too much economic history is still written on the implicit basis of a crude unreconstructed Keynesianism, in ignorance of any of the insights of the new industrial economics and using (if any) the econometrics of Johnston (1972).

In sum, research in economic history does and should subsume more than the application of econometric techniques and in so doing could provide an important counterbalance to an empirical economics which is rather vulnerable to criticism of its over-reliance on a particular type of evidence and prior assumptions. On the other hand, weaknesses in the training of economic historians and/or the paucity of collaborative research involving both economists and historians make for a substantial amount of low-quality work viewed from the perspective of best-practice economics.

To appreciate fully the distinctions between applied econometrics or economics in general and cliometrics or economic history in particular, it is necessary to complement the above account with an explicit recognition of the impact of the existence of different criteria for professional advancement. In a problem-driven subject (Mathias 1971: 371) economic historians have naturally looked for success in publication by responding to an existing historiography and by adding to the stock of data. Moreover, in the United Kingdom at least, to be elected to a Chair they need to publish partly in book form and to persuade historians, brought up without having been inculcated with economists' priors, of the intuitive reasonableness of their findings and their basis in historical scholarship. Economists have tended to perceive that publication in the best journals involves technical excellence in playing whatever is the latest game in town using a narrow set of pre-existing data without regard for the need to communicate to a wider audience. Both the reward structures and the standards of proof required are different, and these are reflected in the strengths and weaknesses of the historical literature compared with that of applied economics.

The existence of these different peer-group pressures has had substantial costs. It is responsible to an important extent for the divergence in research interests and practices between economics and economic history. It is also reflected in failures fully to exploit the potential of economics in history and vice versa. It is certainly possible in future for economic history to make an effective contribution to the education of economists and to policy debates but this will require both an approach prompted more by the question 'what would people in the 1990s like to know about the past?' than by historiographic concerns and a greater ability to communicate the results of historical enquiry and to be persuasive to economists on the basis of an awareness of (but not undue obeisance to) current theory and econometrics. The likelihood is that this will necessitate the development of teams of specialists combining different sorts of expertise.

41.3 SOME IMPORTANT RECENT ADVANCES

In this section I shall attempt to show something of the major advances resulting from the use of economics and quantitative methods in historical applications. The exposition will inevitably be selective, as the literature is by now voluminous; I shall concentrate largely on examples relating to UK economic history as I am better qualified to judge their merits than I am to comment on other areas.

Many important research findings in economic history have taken the form of better measurement of the economic past. Some of the results now available would come as a considerable surprise to the person in the street or even to the professionals of a generation ago. There has been a vigorous undertaking of a role which McCloskey (1976), in his early survey, highlighted as one of the child benefits to economists of the study of history. This has resulted in the existence now of a very rich data base which unfortunately is significantly underexploited by economists too little aware of its potential. Progress has often come from 'routine' examination of historical records, but many of the most exciting findings stem from the use of appropriate economic concepts and statistical methods such that it should be recognized that more and better facts also should be seen as one of the contributions of economics to history.

Much effort has gone into the construction of national income accounts for the past with notable success in the case of the advanced countries. The results enable a much better perspective on relative economic success and failure than was possible until recently. The advances to knowledge have come not only from archival work but also particularly from better (although inescapably still imperfect) handling of the index number problems involved in constructing estimates of real output.

Table 41.1 offers in summary form a taste of the results from historical measurement of national income; the comparisons are made at purchasing power parity exchange rates. The table reflects a number of important and in some cases surprising findings. For example, the United Kingdom's decline is shown to be serious only relative to the United States before the Second World War, while Japan's high domestic price level, long hours of work and low productivity outside exportable manufacturing combine to vitiate the commonplace view of their post-war economic prowess.

Table 41.1 Real gross domestic product per hour worked: comparisons with the United Kingdom in selected years

	UK	USA	France	Germany	Japan
1870	100	97	48	50	17
1890	100	113	49	55	19
1913	100	135	60	65	23
1929	100	158	70	65	30
1938	100	154	82	73	35
1950	100	185	70	54	24
1960	100	188	84	84	33
1973	100	156	105	100	62
1979	100	150	114	113	70
1986	100	133	119	105	68

Source: Maddison 1989: Table 7.3

Perhaps the most obvious example where such work has led to a major reinterpretation in economic history is in the case of the British economy during the Industrial Revolution. The crucial article was that of Harley (1982) who corrected some fundamental flaws in the widely used index numbers of industrial output for the period. Together with a number of other revisions by various authors to previous data series, each of which stemmed from better use of already known sources, this led to the revised picture shown in Table 41.2 where overall growth between 1780 and 1830 is reduced by about a third and total factor productivity growth by almost a half. The revised estimates have substantial implications for the literature on the Industrial Revolution (Crafts 1985).

Table 41.2 Revised growth estimates for the British economy during the Industrial Revolution

	Industrial output (% per year)		Real GDP (% per year)		Total factor productivity (% per year)	
	New	Old	New	Old	New	Old
1780–1801	2.1	3.4	1.3	2.1	n.a.	n.a.
1801–31	3.0	4.4	2.0	3.1	0.7	1.3

Source: Crafts 1985: Tables 2.7, 2.11, 4.2
Note: n.a., not available

One particularly notable outcome of the effort put into better measurement of economic development in the past is that the famous 'grand theories' of growth put forward by Rostow (1960) and Gerschenkron (1962) can now be seen as misconceived generalizations based on misunderstandings of the experience of Britain and Russia (Gregory 1983) respectively. The general tendency in the literature now is to accept that we do not have a typology of Western growth and that countries pursued very different paths to the modern world rather than following the British model (Crafts 1984: O'Brien 1986).

It is also worth noting that quantitative techniques have produced major breakthroughs in measurement even for the pre-Industrial Revolution period. Thanks to the work of Overton (1979) and Allen (1988) in developing methods of estimating crop yields from inventories and to the massive research project of Wrigley and Schofield (1981), which extracted data from parish registers and developed 'back-projection' methods of inference from them, we now have a much deeper insight into the Malthusian economy of the sixteenth to the eighteenth centuries.

Wrigley and Schofield were able to make estimates of population totals and birth and death rates at five-yearly intervals back to 1541. From these they built a revolutionary interpretation of England as an economy where in the long run preventive checks based on changes in nuptiality could stabilize population at income levels well above subsistence and where fertility was highly variable. This account is in striking contrast with the conventional wisdom of the demographic transition literature of the 1950s and 1960s.

Finally, in relation to measurement, it follows from the extent of revisions resulting from careful rescrutiny of earlier estimates that economists must be careful in what they regard as 'stylized facts'. For example, casual reporting of estimates of unemployment made at the time in the United Kingdom since the First World War, as is sometimes done in macroeconomics texts, can be seriously misleading for the purposes of comparing performance in different periods, as shown in Table 41.3.

Table 41.3 Unemployment rates in the United Kingdom 1921–1987

	Raw data (%)	Revised (%)		Raw data (%)	Revised (%)		Raw data (%)	Revised (%)
1921	17.0	8.1	1948	1.4	1.1	1968	2.5	1.9
1922	14.2	6.8	1949	1.4	1.1	1969	2.5	1.9
1923	11.7	5.6	1950	1.4	1.1	1970	2.6	2.0
1924	10.3	4.9	1951	1.3	1.0	1971	3.4	2.6
1925	11.3	5.4	1952	2.2	1.7	1972	3.4	2.6
1926	12.6	6.0	1953	1.8	1.4	1973	2.6	2.0
1927	9.7	4.6	1954	1.4	1.1	1974	2.6	2.0
1928	10.9	5.2	1955	1.2	0.9	1975	4.0	3.1
1929	10.4	5.0	1956	1.3	1.0	1976	5.5	4.2
1930	16.2	7.7	1957	1.6	1.2	1977	5.8	4.4
1931	21.3	10.2	1958	2.2	1.7	1978	5.8	4.4
1932	22.1	10.6	1959	2.4	1.8	1979	5.2	4.0
1933	19.9	9.5	1960	1.7	1.3	1980	6.7	5.1
1934	16.7	8.0	1961	1.6	1.2	1981	10.6	8.1
1935	15.5	7.4	1962	2.1	1.6	1982	12.5	9.6
1936	13.2	6.3	1963	2.6	2.0	1983	13.7	10.5
1937	10.8	5.2	1964	1.7	1.3	1984	10.7	10.7
1938	12.9	6.2	1965	1.4	1.1	1985	10.9	10.9
1946	2.4	1.8	1966	1.4	1.1	1986	11.1	11.1
1947	3.0	2.3	1967	2.4	1.8	1987	10.0	10.0

Sources: Based on Feinstein 1972 and *Economic Trends* 1989. The revised figures are an estimate of earlier unemployment based on today's methods of counting: for 1921–38 it is the National Insurance estimate multiplied by 0.478; for 1946–71 it is the contemporary estimate multiplied by 0.765; for 1971 on see *Department of Employment Gazette* (1988). Correction factors are based on Metcalf *et al.* (1982) and a comparison of original and today's basis figures for 1971–9.

The use of neoclassical economic theory, particularly models based on profit-maximizing behaviour, in historical analysis has proved fruitful. An early decisive set of papers collected by Aitken (1971) demonstrated conclusively that slavery in the American South was profitable (and would not have collapsed in the absence of the Civil War), that slaves were priced as capital goods and that on the whole owners responded rationally to economic incentives. In the case of British economic history the celebrated example is the examination of choices of technique by British companies in the late nineteenth century. This showed that at British relative factor costs the slow diffusion of techniques widely adopted abroad – such as the basic process of steel-making (McCloskey 1973) and of ring spinning in cotton textiles (Sandberg 1974) – was justified. Thus indiscriminate accusations of entrepreneurial failure alleging amateurism, conservatism and plain incompetence which had proliferated in earlier literature could easily be refuted.

However, it should be recognized that profit maximization is a hypothesis with which to interrogate historical data rather than a law-like statement. Thus examples of entrepreneurial failure in late Victorian Britain have been discovered. For example, Berck (1978) showed that steel-makers should have adopted the hard-driving process earlier than they did. Moreover, throughout the period before the Second World War asymmetries of information and the prevalence of family capitalism could protect inefficient management from being driven out by capital-market forces (Hannah 1974: Chandler 1980).

Nevertheless, in general, it has proved extremely valuable to examine sceptically arguments which are analogous to the proposition that the streets were littered with $100 bills which no one bothered to pick up. This is also true in the realm of government policy. Consider, for example, interwar macroeconomic policy where at one time the standard textbook view talked of a seemingly ostrich-like 'Treasury view' promoting the irrational rejection of Keynesian ideas. Recent work on primary sources, together with recognition of the desirability from the Treasury's point of view of (apparently) adhering to rules (for example, the balanced budget) to prevent discretionary fiscal and monetary policy, has led to a much subtler and more sympathetic view (Howson 1975; Peden 1983; Middleton 1985). Arguably, the Treasury succeeded in developing a coherent and reasonably effective employment strategy, given the institutional and political constraints of the time and the need to raise prices relative to wages (Booth 1987).

Similarly, recent research into interwar industrial policy presents a much more sophisticated view of some of the failures of government attempts at rationalization. Examining decision-making through primary source materials, while regarding government ministers and agencies' interactions with industry essentially in terms of a game-theoretical situation, has produced a picture of politicians' perceptions of the pay-offs generally vitiating effective attempts at modernization and productivity enhancement.

For example, Bamberg (1988) demonstrates how severely the Bank of England's freedom of action in setting up the Lancashire Cotton Corporation was circumscribed by its clear desire to decouple the banks from their continuing commitments to the cotton-spinning industry. Similarly, Tolliday (1987: 295–310) points out that, although there were hopes that tariff protection would enable the modernization of the steel industry, fears of unemployment meant that the sanction of removing the tariff if the producers failed to improve efficiency lacked credibility and the outcome was an ossification of inefficiency. Although the analysis in these works is informal, in principle it would be relatively straightforward to recast it in terms of decision trees with emphasis on consequences of the order of moves.

Another intriguing example of the use of game-theoretical ideas in a historical context is Eichengreen's analysis of the success and failure respectively of
the Gold Standard before and after the First World War (Eichengreen 1984,
1987a). Central banks are modelled as oligopolistic rivals. Eichengreen shows
the plausibility of an account in which before, but not after, the First World
War Britain could act to reduce the deflationary pressures of high interest
rates in the system. This stemmed from the extreme responsiveness of gold
flows to bank rate which produced a reaction function for the Bank of England
enabling it uniquely to act as a Stackelberg leader. Thus he not only makes
sense of commonplace observations about the importance of the rise of Wall
Street but also indicates that the success of the Gold Standard before 1914
was predicated on very special historical circumstances.

Before moving on, it should be noted that both the interwar industrial
rationalization and the Gold Standard cases not only exemplify what history
has to gain from the skilful use of economic analysis but also offer important
lessons to economists in terms of the contingency of appropriate policy advice
on the political and institutional context.

The preceding examples all involved situations where major contributions
required serious historical skills beyond the easy reach of the average economist, as suggested in Section 41.2, although they were also critically dependent
on employing economic analysis. Similar cases constitute the vast majority of
the impressive work based on historical applications of economics. Nevertheless, in some cases advances have come from the employment of relatively new
and powerful econometric techniques rather than through analysis based on
optimizing behaviour, and there are examples where exercises in up-to-date
applied econometrics largely independent of historians' skills other than knowledge of data sources and previous secondary literature have made useful points.

Three illustrations will suffice to make the point. McDonald and Snooks
(1986), using a Box–Cox approach to the choice of functional form, were able
to show that, contrary to previous beliefs, valuations for tax purposes in the
Domesday Book were consistently related to ownership of assets rather than
being haphazard. Edelstein (1982), using a Granger causality analysis, established the importance of 'push factors' in the astonishing surge of foreign
investment undertaken by Britain in the twenty years or so before the First
World War. Crafts *et al.* (1989) used structural time series analysis and Kalman
filter estimation to demonstrate the unimportance of any tendency to a climacteric in late Victorian British economic growth.

41.4 SOME LESS SUCCESSFUL EXAMPLES OF NEW ECONOMIC HISTORY

A further perspective on the use of economics in history and on the requirements for convincing research in the area can be obtained by considering two much criticized pieces of work, each of which has some merit but ultimately fails to be persuasive.

The first of these is the computable general equilibrium analysis carried out by Williamson (1985) of inequality of incomes during the British Industrial Revolution. Williamson claimed to have shown that there was a Kuznets curve of rising and then falling inequality and, using his model which predicted key endogenous variables 'reasonably well', he found that this resulted from differing trends in sectoral productivity growth in the context of inelastic factor supplies.

Subsequently, however, Feinstein (1988) has shown that the surge of inequality which Williamson claimed to have found and to have explained is merely an artefact of an inappropriate use of source materials. Also, the *a priori* assumptions used to parameterize the Williamson model are inconsistent with recent research on the offer curves for Britain and the rest of the world (Irwin 1988) and on productivity performance (Crafts 1989a). Moreover, features of British economic history which most economic historians would regard as fairly central to explaining income distribution, such as trade unions, induced biases in technical progress and endogenous fertility and migration, are all assumed away (Crafts 1987).

It will be unfortunate if the Williamson example leads to a disenchantment with computable general equilibrium models or to dismissive reactions to the new economic history on the part of traditional historians, although both of these are real possibilities. Nevertheless, it is important that the key lessons of this episode are taken to heart before other economists rush into historical exercises which angels would fear to undertake. These lessons are as follows.

1 The context of historical sources needs to be understood or the researcher may extract quite erroneous figures.
2 Strong prior assumptions are dangerous if they are allowed completely to dominate the search for evidence and modelling.
3 The specification of calibrated general equilibrium models must be subjected to serious sensitivity analysis.

In other words, it should be remembered that the apparent ability of a model to track historical series may not depend on particular properties which, however, are crucial to the simulation results obtained from it.

The second example in this section is the well-known paper by Benjamin and Kochin which put forward the hypothesis that in interwar Britain the growing generosity of the benefits system raised the natural rate of unemployment and even in non-recession years produced an army of search unemployed consisting of willing volunteers (Benjamin and Kochin 1979: 468). Drawing attention to the possible role of benefits in interwar unemployment was a useful contribution to a literature imbued with a complacent and naive Keynesianism. Nevertheless, Benjamin and Kochin's paper fails to convince.

The econometric results are not very robust, fail to control for other determinants of the natural rate of unemployment, are subject to simultaneity bias and are potentially quite consistent with a Keynesian view of the labour market (Hatton 1983). Historians found the argument to be incomplete, failing to take account of, let alone to refute, the evidence in the contemporary sources that very few unemployed were work-shy and that many had given up searching for work, or to provide a serious explanation for the very uneven incidence of unemployment in the period (Collins 1982). Subsequent analysis of panel data by Eichengreen (1987b) indicates at best a small role for benefits in promoting unemployment among a 'squadron' of non-household heads. Economists' research grounded in a more eclectic mode has also found a minor role for benefits in raising the non-accelerating inflation rate of unemployment (NAIRU) via the wage equation but does not tend to interpret this as voluntary unemployment (Crafts 1989b; Dimsdale *et al.* 1989). Thus, Benjamin and Kochin appear to have overstated their case and not to have pursued their investigation far enough.

Although ostensibly very different from each other, these two instances have an important common element. In both cases the treatment of evidence required the input of further historical skills and was unpersuasive to historians whose training would lead them to be more demanding. In particular, they would want more detail to be encompassed and alternative hypotheses to be taken more seriously. The need to persuade historians is something which applied econometricians do not usually confront, but it is a discipline that is valuable in economic history and deserves to be taken seriously by new entrants from economics. However, the more general lesson is probably that best practice in applied economics should embrace equivalent requirements in testing economists' conventional wisdom.

41.5 SOME DIFFICULTIES AND SOME OPPORTUNITIES

On balance I would argue that, despite some unfortunate counter-examples, the advent of formal economic analysis and the increasing use of modern econometric techniques has already paid handsome dividends in historical work. In Section 41.3 I gave examples to back up this claim and illustrated the chief contributions that economics has made in terms of better measurement of the economic past, better inference from historical data and gaining insights from making an assumption of rational behaviour and examining its implications. None the less it is the case that there are dangers inherent in this approach and also that we are far from fully utilizing the possibilities of symbiosis between history and economics, and in this section I wish to explore these points.

In practice, of course, we pay a price for the use in history of *a priori* assumptions drawn from economics. Practitioners of the new economic history necessarily must be equipped with a substantial amount of economists' training. This gives rise to the fear that 'economic theory learns nothing from economic history, and economic history is as much corrupted as enriched by economic theory' (Solow 1986: 21). That this can be a major problem is already evident from my discussion of Williamson (1985) where it seems apparent that the author's tight priors discouraged him from either conducting a careful audit of his data or subjecting his model to sufficient testing. In that case, however, errors have come to light so quickly that long-lasting damage may be quite slight.

There may be more insidious dangers of the kind against which Solow warned in cases of apparently successful new economic history. Consider again the debate on the alleged failure of the late Victorian economy. As noted earlier, new economic history made a notable impact by examining choices of technique and to a large extent vindicating the decisions made by the entrepreneurs of the time. Add to this a demonstration that any income forgone as a result of capital market misallocation of funds to overseas investment must have been small and a presumption that product markets were competitive, and take as a maintained hypothesis a neoclassical growth model with an exogenous natural rate of growth independent of the savings rate in the long run. Hey presto, we arrive, as McCloskey (1970) did in his famous paper, at the Panglossian proposition that British growth was as fast as circumstances permitted, despite the relative decline in comparison with the United States shown in Table 41.1.

On reflection, however, these conclusions involve a selective and restricted search for evidence and models with no particular claim to generality. Thus, modern versions of the neoclassical growth model allow scope for persistent divergences of growth between economies with different strategies of investment in research and development and/or human capital (Romer 1986; Lucas 1988). Accordingly, it would also be appropriate to examine, although new economic historians chose not to, British performance in these spheres where there is a long-standing literature of complaint from traditional historians. Similarly, given the obvious deficiencies in capital markets of the period, it would have been better not to announce optimistic conclusions without a full examination of industrial performance.

The extreme version of this scenario of the corrupting of economic history by economic theory would be for the subject to become merely a minor branch of applied economics as taught in Chicago and practised with a view to paradigm support in a mode which would be essentially ahistorical. Thankfully, this danger now seems less serious in a richer and more eclectic literature than it did at the time of McCloskey's own survey of the field when he could claim that 'the conclusions have often been variations on the theme "The Market, God Bless It, Works' . . .' (McCloskey 1978: 21). Keeping in mind the discipline of seeking to persuade historians who do not start out with these strong priors will offer further protection against possible annexation of the field in this way.

On a more optimistic note, it is clear that there are substantial opportunities for further development of historical research and for making some impact on the education of economists. In particular, recent developments in economics and econometrics both enhance the potential pay-off of working with historical data and, as they diffuse into economic history, offer the promise of a more subtle and sophisticated approach more akin to current best practice in economics. Moreover, the rejection of the post-war consensus by the Conservatives after 1979 as responsible for Britain's poor post-war economic performance raises important issues – such as why obvious impediments to faster growth proved impossible to remove – on which historical research can be brought to bear and where, in principle, economists should be seeking insights from economic historians.

The upsurge of interest in the analysis of strategic and opportunistic behaviour in both macroeconomics and microeconomics has already had some impact in economic history, as noted earlier. However, there seems to be ample scope for much more use of concepts from this literature such as 'commitment', 'credibility', 'agency problems', 'asymmetric information', 'tit for tat' etc. This would seem to be particularly true of twentieth-century economic history where analysis of government policy, the performance of large firms, industrial relations and problems of the mixed economy loom large. However, it surely also applies to earlier times, for example, in examining the evolution of institutional arrangements to cope with the requirements of an industrializing economy during the eighteenth and nineteenth centuries.

There are important implications of these ideas. They surely suggest something of a further retreat from the new economic history's original love affair with the invisible hand. Case studies of firms and industries assume a much greater significance than in the days of the structure-conduct-performance paradigm in industrial economics. It becomes interesting to analyse the historical sequence of moves by different players, and political economy assumes a central rather than a peripheral role in analysis. Historical studies at the microlevel become by far the most promising way of obtaining empirical evidence relating to the fascinating suggestion by Mancur Olson (1982) that long-established democracies tend to develop sclerotic tendencies as economic growth is impeded by interest groups.

Thus the stage is set for taking institutions seriously and for today's economists to benefit more from historical research than those brought up to work with simple neoclassical models where the past cannot matter. It may also become necessary to think rather more in terms of models which exhibit path dependence as, for example, in David's (1985) excellent exposition of how the world got locked into the QWERTY keyboard.

The need is also apparent for new economic historians to develop 'new business history' and 'new labour history' rather than generally to neglect these types of economic history as has largely been the case hitherto. For example, the internal workings of the firm can be treated seriously, more effort can be put into the analysis of the development of industries over time and less into biographies of particular firms, and bargaining models can be deployed to examine issues of the evolution of job control.

A major opportunity exists in British economic history for the deployment of these kinds of analytical tools, augmented by traditional historical skills, in the context of seeking to understand the reasons for Britain's relatively slow economic growth and relatively poor productivity performance during much of the twentieth century. In so doing there is the chance to escape from the elementary macromodels proposed by Bacon and Eltis (1978) and Kaldor (1966), and to go beyond the growth-accounting exercises of Denison (1967) or Maddison (1987). The most recent economic historian to survey this field concluded that economists, and by implication new economic historians, had no insights in the area and no prospect of explaining the phenomena (Alford 1988). This has largely been true in the past but now surely reflects an out-of-date view of economic analysis and undervalues the potential for economists to learn about growth and productivity from studying history along the lines I have suggested.

Also available to economic historians, but only in the very early stages of adoption, are the developments of the past ten years or so in time series econometrics which offer the possibility of better modelling in important areas, especially in macroeconomic history, than has largely been achieved so far. In particular, more attention to dynamic structures, better diagnostics, more effort given to testing as opposed simply to estimation of models and better ways of measuring trends and/or changes in trends, and employment of tests of cointegration all need to be further diffused into economic history. Important pay-offs have already been achieved – particularly notable is Solomou's (1987) admirable debunking of the recently fashionable belief in Kondratieff cycles – but there is scope for revisiting many topics such as the best estimates of key equations for the interwar macroeconomy surveyed by Broadberry (1986) or the nineteenth-century trade-cycles literature collected in Aldcroft and Fearon (1972).

There are, then, new and more powerful tools with which to make further progress in historical applications of economics whose possibilities are only just beginning to be exploited. It should also be recognized that there is a considerable unrealized potential for economists to gain from economic history. Partly this can come simply from exposure to issues where familiar simple neoclassical models seem inadequate, as suggested above. There is also, however, a wealth of relevant experience in our economic past which bears on present policy issues. This would be appreciated if it were made more accessible to economists by being analysed in appropriate fashion, by the pursuit of research programmes oriented to understanding the lessons (and debunking the myths) of the past for the present and by being reported more frequently in journals read by a wide body of economists such as *Economic Policy* or the *Oxford Review of Economic Policy*.

For instance, analyses of the necessity for a central bank or of the desirability of free banking can be enriched by careful consideration of Britain's nineteenth-century monetary history prior to modern central banking and Scotland's experience with free banking as reported in studies such as those of Collins (1988) and White (1984), or of the 1847 or 1866 financial crises discussed by Dornbusch and Frankel (1984) and Batchelor (1986). By far the largest stock market collapse is that of 1929–1932 in the United States – the lessons of that episode as analysed by historians such as Bernstein (1987) or economists such as Newell and Symons (1988) are very different from those supposed in many reactions to the stock market crash of October 1987. The history of utilities prior to nationalization can be exploited for interesting inputs to discussions of privatization, and useful insights are available from Hannah (1979), Milward and Ward (1987) and others.

The common feature of all these examples is that they represent important experience which cannot be found in present-day circumstances and about which even most specialist economists in the relevant areas are largely uninformed. The failing is on both sides. Economists are brought up to discount economic history as irrelevant or have experienced years ago a dreadful undergraduate course which seemed to them to be taught for its own sake rather than addressing issues in which they would be interested. Historians have not given a high priority to communication of their results to economists, and in the United Kingdom have had career incentives which are not conducive to their maintaining the capabilities effectively to act as consultants to economists. There is scope to do better.

826

REFERENCES

Aitken, H. G. J. (1971) *Did Slavery Pay?*, Boston, MA: Houghton Mifflin.

Aldcroft, D. H. and Fearon, P. (eds) (1972) *British Economic Fluctuations, 1790–1939*, London: Macmillan.

Alford, B. W. E. (1988) *British Economic Performance, 1945–1975*, London: Macmillan.

Allen, R. C. (1988) 'Inferring yields from probate inventories' *Journal of Economic History* 48 (1): 117–25.

Bacon, R. W. and Eltis, W. A. (1978) *Britain's Economic Problem: Too Few Producers*, London: Macmillan.

Bamberg, J. H. (1988) 'The rationalization of the British cotton industry in the interwar years', *Textile History* 19 (1): 83–102.

Batchelor, R. (1986) 'The avoidance of catastrophe: two nineteenth century banking crises', in F. Capie and G. E. Wood (eds) *Financial Crises and the World Banking System*, London: Macmillan.

Benjamin, D. and Kochin, L. (1979) 'Searching for an explanation of unemployment in interwar Britain', *Journal of Political Economy* 87 (3): 441–70.

Berck, P. (1978) 'Hard driving and efficiency: iron production in 1890', *Journal of Economic History* 38 (4): 879–900.

Bernstein, M. A. (1987) *The Great Depression*, Cambridge: Cambridge University Press.

Booth, A. (1987) 'Britain in the 1930s: a managed economy?' *Economic History Review* 40 (4): 499–522.

Cairncross, A. and Eichengreen, B. (1983) *Sterling in Decline*, Oxford: Basil Blackwell.

Capie, F. and Webber, A. (1985) *A Monetary History of the United Kingdom, 1870–1982*, vol. 1, London: Allen & Unwin.

Chandler, A. D. (1980) 'The growth of the transnational industrial firm in the United States and the United Kingdom: a comparative analysis', *Economic History Review* 33(3): 396–410.

Clapham, J. H. (1931) 'Economic history as a discipline', in E. R. A. Seligman and A. Johnson (eds) *Encyclopaedia of the Social Sciences*, vol. 5, pp. 327–30, London: Macmillan.

Collins, M. (1982) 'Unemployment in interwar Britain: still searching for an explanation', *Journal of Political Economy* 90 (3): 369–79.

—— (1988) *Money and Banking in the United Kingdom: A History*, London: Croom Helm.

Crafts, N. F. R. (1984) 'Patterns of development in nineteenth century Europe', *Oxford Economic Papers* 36 (3): 438–58.

—— (1985) *British Economic Growth during the Industrial Revolution*, Oxford: Clarendon Press.

—— (1987) 'Cliometrics, 1971–1986: a survey', *Journal of Applied Econometrics* 2 (2): 171–92.

—— (1989a) 'British industrialization in an international context', *Journal of Interdisciplinary History* 19 (3): 415–28.

—— (1989b) 'Long term unemployment and the wage equation in Britain, 1925–1939', *Economica* 56 (2): 247–54.

Crafts, N. F. R., Leybourne, S. J. and Mills, T. C. (1989) 'The climacteric in late Victorian Britain and France: a reappraisal of the evidence: *Journal of Applied Econometrics* 4 (2): 103–17.

David, P. A. (1985) 'Clio and the economics of QWERTY', *American Economic Review* 75 (2): 332–7.

Denison, E. F. (1967) *Why Growth Rates Differ*, Washington, DC: Brookings Institution.

Dimsdale, N. H., Nickell, S. J. and Horsewood, N. (1989) 'Real wages and unemployment in Britain during the 1930s', *Economic Journal* 99 (2): 271–92.

Dornbusch, R. and Frankel, J. A. (1984) 'The Gold Standard and the Bank of England in the crisis of 1847', in M. Bordo and A. J. Schwartz (eds) *A Retrospective on the Classical Gold Standard*, Chicago, IL: University of Chicago Press.

Edelstein, M. (1982) *Overseas Investment in the Age of High Imperialism*, London: Methuen.

Eichengreen, B. (1984) 'Central bank cooperation under the interwar Gold Standard', *Explorations in Economic History* 21 (1): 64–87.

—— (1987a) 'Conducting the international orchestra: Bank of England leadership under the classical Gold Standard', *Journal of International Money and Finance* 6 (1): 5–29.

—— (1987b) 'Unemployment in interwar Britain: dole or doldrums', *Oxford Economic Papers* 39 (4): 597–623.

Feinstein, C. H. (1972) *National Income, Expenditure and Output of the United Kingdom, 1855–1965*, Cambridge: Cambridge University Press.

—— (1988) 'The rise and fall of the Williamson curve', *Journal of Economic History* 48 (3): 699–729.

Gerschenkron, A. (1962) *Economic Backwardness in Historical Perspective*, Cambridge, MA: Harvard University Press.

Greasley, D. (1986) 'British economic growth: the paradox of the 1880s and the timing of the climacteric', *Explorations in Economic History*, 23 (4): 416–44.

Gregory, P. (1983) *Russian National Income, 1885–1913*, Cambridge: Cambridge University Press.

Hannah, L. (1974) 'Takeover bids in Britain before 1950: an exercise in business prehistory', *Business History* 16 (1): 65–77.

—— (1979) *Electricity Before Nationalization*, London: Macmillan.

Harley, C. K. (1982) 'British industrialization before 1841: evidence of slower growth during the industrial revolution', *Journal of Economic History*, 42 (2): 267–89.

Hatton, T. J. (1983) 'Unemployment benefits and the macroeconomics of the interwar labour market: a further analysis', *Oxford Economic Papers* 35 (3): 486–505.

Howson, S. (1975) *Domestic Monetary Management in Britain 1919–1938*, Cambridge: Cambridge University Press.

Irwin, D. A. (1988) 'Welfare effects of British free trade: debate and evidence from the 1840s', *Journal of Political Economy* 96 (6): 1142–64.

Johnston, J. (1972) *Econometric Methods*, London: McGraw-Hill.

Kaldor, N. (1966) *Causes of the Slow Rate of Growth of the United Kingdom*, Cambridge: Cambridge University Press.

Lucas, R. E. (1988) 'The mechanics of economic development', *Journal of Monetary Economics* 22 (1): 3–42.

McCloskey, D. N. (1970) 'Did Victorian Britain fail?', *Economic History Review* 23 (3): 446–59.

—— (1973) *Economic Maturity and Entrepreneurial Decline: British Iron and Steel, 1870–1913*, Cambridge, MA: Harvard University Press.

—— (1976) 'Does the past have useful economics?', *Journal of Economic Literature* 14 (2): 434–61.

—— (1978) 'The achievements of the cliometrics school', *Journal of Economic History* 38 (1): 13–28.

McDonald, J. and Snooks, G. D. (1986) *Domesday Economy: A New Approach to Anglo-Norman History*, Oxford: Clarendon Press.

Maddison, A. (1987) 'Growth and slowdown in advanced capitalist economies: techniques of quantitative assessment', *Journal of Economic Literature* 24 (3): 649–98.

Maddison, A. (1989) *The World Economy in the Twentieth Century*, Paris: OECD.

Mathias, P. (1971), 'Living with the neighbours: the role of economic history', in N. B. Harte (ed.) *The Study of Economic History*, pp. 369–83, London: Frank Cass.

Metcalf, D., Nickell, S. J. and Floros, N. (1982) 'Still searching for an explanation of unemployment in interwar Britain', *Journal of Political Economy* 90 (3): 386–99.

Middleton, R. (1985) *Towards the Managed Economy*, London: Methuen.

Millward, R. and Ward, T. S. (1987) 'The costs of public and private gas enterprises in late nineteenth century Britain', *Oxford Economic Papers* 39 (4): 719–37.

Newell, A. and Symons, J. S. V. (1988) 'The macroeconomics of the interwar years: international comparisons', in B. Eichengreen and T. J. Hatton (eds) *Interwar Unemployment in International Perspective*, pp. 61–96, London: Kluwer.

O'Brien, P. K. (1986) 'Do we have a typology for the study of European industrialization in the nineteenth century?', *Journal of European Economic History* 15 (3): 291–333.

Olson, M. (1982) *The Rise and Decline of Nations*, New Haven, CT: Yale University Press.

Overton, M. (1979) 'Estimating crop yields from probate inventories: an example from East Anglia, 1585–1735', *Journal of Economic History* 39 (3): 363–78.

Peden, G. (1983) 'Sir Richard Hopkins and the "Keynesian Revolution" in employment policy, 1929–1945', *Economic History Review* 36 (2): 281–96.

Romer, P. M. (1986) 'Increasing returns and long run growth', *Journal of Political Economy* 94 (6): 1002–73.

Rostow, W. W. (1960) *The States of Economic Growth*, Cambridge: Cambridge University Press.

Sandberg, L. G. (1974) *Lancashire in Decline*, Columbus, OH: Ohio State University Press.

Solomou, S. (1987) *Phases of Economic Growth, 1850–1973*, Cambridge: Cambridge University Press.

Solow, R. (1986) 'Economics: is something missing?', in W. N. Parker (ed.) *Economic History and the Modern Economist*, pp. 21–9, Oxford: Basil Blackwell.

Tolliday, S. (1987) *Business, Banking and Politics: The Case of British Steel, 1918–1939*, Cambridge: Cambridge University Press.

White, L. H. (1984) *Free Banking in Britain: Theory, Experience and Debate, 1800–1845*, Cambridge: Cambridge University Press.

Williamson, J. G. (1985) *Did British Capitalism Breed Inequality?*, London: Allen & Unwin.

Wrigley, E. A. and Schofield, R. S. (1981) *The Population History of England, 1541–1871: A Reconstruction*, London: Arnold.

INDEX